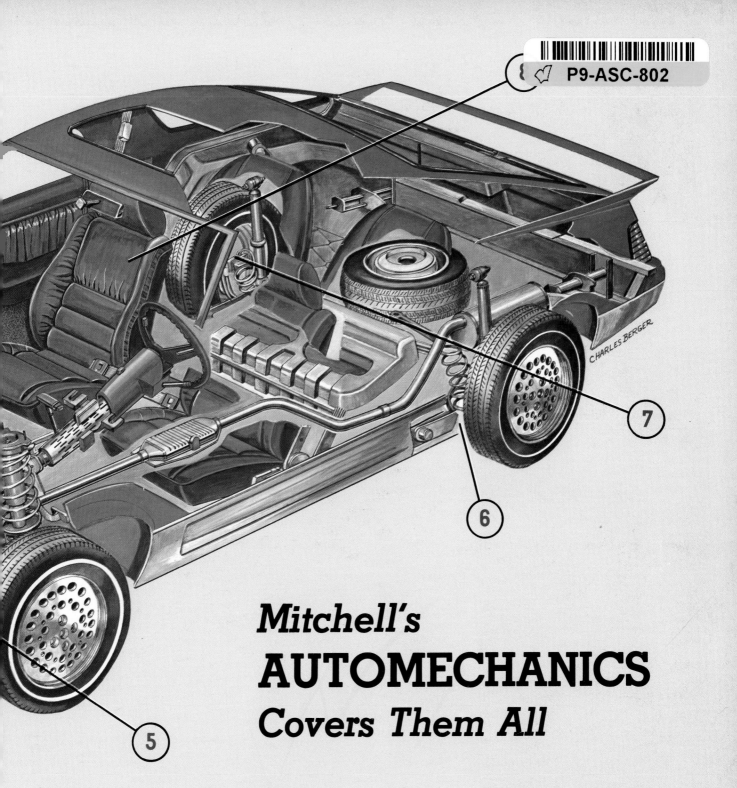

CHARLES BERGER

Mitchell's
AUTOMECHANICS
Covers Them All

MITCHELL
AUTOMECHANICS

MITCHELL AUTOMECHANICS

Mitchell Information Services, Inc.

Prentice-Hall, Englewood Cliffs, New Jersey 07632

Library of Congress Cataloging-in-Publication Data

Main entry under title:
    Mitchell Automechanics.

    Includes index.
    1. Automobiles. 2. Automobiles—Maintenance and
repair. I. Mitchell Information Services.
TL205.M53 1986   629.2'22   85–16861
ISBN 0–13–586124–1

Editorial/production supervision: Lisa Schulz
Interior design: Maureen Eide
Cover design: Celette Limited and Paul Besgans
Manufacturing buyer: Rhett Conklin
Page layout: Diane Koromhas

Printed in the United States of America

10 9 8 7 6 5 4 3 2 1

ISBN 0-13-586124-1 025

Prentice-Hall International (UK) Limited, *London*
Prentice-Hall of Australia Pty. Limited, *Sydney*
Prentice-Hall Canada Inc., *Toronto*
Prentice-Hall Hispanoamericana, S.A., *Mexico*
Prentice-Hall of India Private Limited, *New Delhi*
Prentice-Hall of Japan, Inc., *Tokyo*
Prentice-Hall of Southeast Asia Pte. Ltd., *Singapore*
Editora Prentice-Hall do Brasil, Ltda., *Rio de Janeiro*
Whitehall Books Limited, *Wellington, New Zealand*

Contents

PART FOUR
FUEL, IGNITION, AND EMISSION SYSTEMS 305

21
Fuel Systems: General 307

22
Fuel Systems: Carburetion 319

23
Fuel Systems: Injection 336

24
Computer Engine Control 350

25
Ignition Systems 363

26
Ignition System Service 378

27
Emission Control Systems 387

Preface to the Instructor

Thank you for choosing *Mitchell Automechanics* as your text. It was written in response to considerable input from people like you, with three of your goals in mind. First, you said you wanted the book to be easy to use. We surveyed other texts and successful programs around the country and found that few instructors teach this class in the same order and with the same emphasis. So your text is modular. You can teach in chapter order, or if you wish, mix and match the subjects. Either approach will be successful.

Secondly, you wanted your students to enjoy this text. Along with the subject matter, we have included a color history section and sidebars. These features represent backward and forward glances at our automotive culture. Whether reading about hand cranking or braking by dragging a tree trunk, your students will appreciate the human elements in automotive design and repair. The anecdotes by famous race car drivers are not intended to glorify hot rodding, but allow students a peek into the competitive and fun world of automotive racing and engineering. We think you'll enjoy reading the sidebars, too.

Third among the goals was your belief that a modern automotive text should be timely and accurate. It should reflect current cars as well as older models. So you will find brand-new technology explained in some detail, while older systems (such as point-type ignition) may be mentioned briefly to explain principles of operation. Older designs, ("L-head" engines, for example) may not be mentioned at all.

Let's take a look at the elements of this instructional package:

TEXT FEATURES

1. Inside covers—Front inside cover shows the book's organization graphically, using a car to show how we've divided the text into eight major parts. Rear inside cover illustrates how modern computer systems truly do "copilot" the car.

2. Parts—Eight parts represent the major areas of the car and auto repair methods. Each part includes several chapters which apply to various aspects of same major subject.

   □ Part One—The Automotive Industry
   □ Part Two—Engines
   □ Part Three—Engine Electrical Systems
   □ Part Four—Fuel, Ignition, and Emission Systems
   □ Part Five—Power Train
   □ Part Six—Chassis Systems
   □ Part Seven—Brakes
   □ Part Eight—Chassis Electrical Systems and Accessories

3. Chapters—Chapters each handle a segment of the automobile or one small area of repair. Several types of information are in each chapter:

   □ Objectives—things you can expect your students to know or do after studying the chapter.
   □ Introduction—briefly describes what's covered in the chapter.
   □ Text—explains the subject matter in detail.
   □ Art—illustrates the text, with a second color highlighting important elements
   □ Sidebars—interesting stories related to the chapter's main topic.
   □ Trade Terms—words the student should understand after studying the text. They are shown in color when they first appear.
   □ Review Questions—help you measure how much the students understand and retain. The answers are included in your Instructor's Manual.

4. Color Section—The 16-page color section shows the development of major systems over the past 75 years.

Photographs of both rare and common cars demonstrate that "advanced technology and engineering" are relative terms. The section clearly points out the need for a good education before servicing modern cars.

5. Resource Material—We've included information on the Automotive Service Excellence program. Another handy feature is the metric conversion section.

6. Glossary—All of the trade terms are defined here.

7. Index—Gives page numbers for all the major subjects in the book.

INSTRUCTOR'S MANUAL FEATURES

The Instructor's Manual was written by instructors for instructors. It speeds your preparation and keeps you in touch with the book contents and your students' progress. All the items for each chapter are in ONE place, not scattered around the book. You don't have to search to find what you need—it's all there together.

1. Chapter introductions—Give you a summary of the chapter in 100 words or less. They help you get mentally set for your lecture preparation.

2. Chapter objectives—Repeated here to remind you of the things to expect from your students.

3. Chapter outlines—Useful for lectures and course syllabus preparation.

4. Suggested activities—Help your students learn by doing. Most of these tasks are rated high priority by the ASE. If your students complete them all successfully, they're well on their way to certification.

5. Activity log sheets—Copy them and use them to keep track of your students as they complete activities.

6. Chapter questions and answers—Review questions from the text are reprinted together with the answers for your reference.

7. Overhead transparency masters—Easily copied for use as handouts or projection on a screen. These illustra-tions come from the text and make excellent support for lectures in the classroom. These are bound in a separate book for your convenience.

ACCESS GUIDE FEATURES

This invaluable book will help you direct your students to the proper Mitchell Manual in your reference library or tool room. For example, if the recommended activity calls for a student to repair drum brakes on a domestic car, the Access Guide will refer you to Section 9 BRAKES of your Mitchell Manual for Domestic Cars. It will save you, the tool room manager, and your students valuable time. It also includes additional activity hints which are useful even if you don't have a complete Mitchell library yet.

TECHNICAL NEWSLETTER

This bonus feature is a periodic mailing that provides you with useful service bulletins and shop tips. These items are chosen from the vast number received by Mitchell, and written for the specific use of auto technology instructors.

SUMMARY

You'll stay current with modern technology when you use this text and its support materials. The complete package is supported with a toll-free 800 number for questions and comments. We listened to you when putting the materials together, and we'll continue to refine and improve the product based on your input. We want this to be the best textbook package on the market, and are committed to helping you train the best automotive service technicians of the future.

Preface to the Student

Welcome to the automobile industry, an interesting and rewarding place to work. A variety of jobs are available for technicians, designers, engineers, salespeople, and managers. No matter what your interest, there's a place for you in this industry. In many ways, no area of the field is more challenging than automotive repair.

You are taking this class because you have some interest in learning. We've designed this textbook to help you remain interested while learning. But before we get into the textbook itself, you should know something about Mitchell Information Services, Inc. Popularly known to our customers as "Mitchell," we provide automotive service and repair information to the entire industry.

Our Collision Estimating Guides are used by most body shops and insurance companies to estimate the cost of accident repairs and body work. Our Parts/Labor Estimating Guides help service writers figure the cost of mechanical repairs. The Interchange manual allows recyclers to cross-reference parts from one car to another. Our Service and Repair Manuals ensure that repair jobs are done properly and to factory specifications. We provide this accurate, helpful information in books and microfiche, and are developing other channels such as videodisc or computer terminals.

We have created this automotive text because we want you, as a student, to profit from the same helpful information that you can utilize when you are employed in the automotive industry. Now, just as we discover how to use tools while performing automotive jobs, so we should consider the best ways to use your Automechanics textbook.

Here's a brief description of the items we've included to help you learn:

1. Inside covers—Front inside cover shows you how the book is organized around the car, and divided into eight major parts. Rear inside cover shows how modern computer systems truly do "copilot" the car.

2. Parts—The eight parts represent major areas of the car and the repair industry. Each part includes several chapters which apply to various aspects of the same subject.

3. Chapters—Chapters each handle a segment of the automobile or one small area of repair. Several types of information are in each chapter:

   □ Introduction—briefly describes what's covered in the chapter.
   □ Objectives—things you can expect to know or do after studying the chapter.
   □ Text—explains the subject.
   □ Art—illustrates the subject, with a second color for pointing out details.
   □ Sidebar—an interesting and true story related to the chapter.
   □ Trade Terms—words you should understand after studying the chapter. They are shown in color throughout the text.
   □ Review Questions—help you measure how much you understand and remember.

4. Color section—The 16-page color section shows the development of the car over the past 75 years. A variety of cars and their major systems are illustrated and described. The early designs will surprise you with their technology and creativity.

5. Resource material—We've included information on the Automotive Service Excellence program which can help present your professional knowledge to employers and customers. Another handy feature is the metric conversion section.

6. Glossary—All of the trade terms used throughout the text are defined here.

7. Index—Gives page numbers so you can easily locate all the major subjects in the book.

Acknowledgments

The following individuals and companies have worked together to complete this project:

Mitchell Information Services, Inc.*

Barry A. Norton, *President & Publisher*
Kenneth A. Young, *Vice President & Editor-in-Chief*
Michael Roeder, *Managing Editor, Educational Publishing*
Daniel M. Kelley, *Managing Editor, Repair Manuals*
Eloise S. Stiverson, *Art Director*

* A subsidiary of Cordura Publications, Inc.
  George C. Evanoff, *President*

Creative Design and Development

Eugene Schwartz
Richard Roe

Editorial Production

Slawson Communications, Inc.

Editorial Consultants

Dr. Richard L. Little, *Southern Illinois University/Carbondale*
Dr. Sherry Little, *San Diego State University*
Sue MacLauren

Contributing Editors

Stock Cortez, *Evergreen Community College*
Satch Carlson, *Autoweek*
David Emmanuel

Kent Fisk
Forrest Frame
Jim MacFarland, *Edelbrock Corp.*
Jerry Maillicoat, *Chrysler Performance Center*
Dick Meyers
Roy Mills
Dan Morehouse, *Southwestern Community College*
Spence Murray, *Freelance Automotive Writer*
Gary Nugent, *San Diego Community Skill Center*
Kay O'Cullane, *San Diego Community Skill Center*
Mel Robinson, *San Diego Community Skill Center*
Randy Scites
Leonard Spooner, *Orchard Street Automotive*
Don Taylor
Rich Vogeling
Dan Weems
Bob Welsh
Tom Wilson

Reviewers

ABC Technical and Trade School
Austin Community College, *Austin, TX*
Central Piedmont Community College, *Charlotte, NC*
College of DuPage, *Glen Ellyn, IL*
Indiana Vocational Technical College, *Lafayette, IN*
ITT Bailey Technical School, *Kansas City, MO*
Johnson County Community College
Lakeview Community College, *Lee's Summit, MO*
Monroe Community College, *Rochester, NY*
North Georgia Tech, *Clarksville, GA*
Pinellas Vocational Technical Institute, *Clearwater, FL*
Community Skills Center, *San Diego, CA*

Tarrant County Junior College, *Fort Worth, TX*
Texas State Technical Institute, *Waco, TX*

Art and Information Sources

Mitchell Information Services would like to thank the domestic and import automobile manufacturers and the aftermarket industry for their generous cooperation and assistance. This textbook would not be possible without their help.

AMMCO Tools, Inc.
American Honda Motor Corporation, Inc.
American Isuzu Motors, Inc.
American Motors Corporation
Automatic Transmission Parts, Inc.
Better Engineering
Buick Motor Division, GMC
Cadillac Motor Car Division, GMC
Champion Spark Plug Company
Chevrolet Motor Division, GMC
Chilton Book Company
Chrysler Corporation
Earl Manufacturing Co.
Eaton Corporation
Ford Motor Company
General Motors Corporation
Greenfield Tap & Die
Hayden-Trans Tool
HP Books

Hydra-Matic Division, GMC
Kent-Moore Tool Group
Mack Trucks, Inc.
MATCO Tools, Inc.
Mazda of North America, Inc.
Mitsubishi Motor Sales of America, Inc.
Motor Manuals
National Institute for Automotive Service Excellence
Nissan Motor Corporation in the U.S.A.
Oldsmobile Division, GMC
Peterson Publishing Company
Peugeot Motors of America, Inc.
Pontiac Motor Division, GMC
Repco Corporation Ltd.
Robert Bosch Corporation
Saab-Scania of America, Inc.
Snap-on Tools Corporation
Stanadyne Diesel Systems
Sun Electric Corporation
The L.S. Starrett Company
Toyota Motor Sales, USA, Inc.
TRW Inc.
Volkswagen of America, Inc.
Volvo

Figures 1.10, 1.17, 8.6, 8.32, 16.2 and 42.10 were taken with permission at the San Diego Community College District, Skills Center Automotive Facility, 12th and F Streets, San Diego, CA.

PART ONE

The Automotive Industry

KEY CONCEPTS

- Examining career opportunities
- Learning about tools
- Using test equipment correctly
- Measuring accurately
- Working safely
- Using written tools—manuals
- Maintaining a car carefully
- Viewing the car as a group of systems

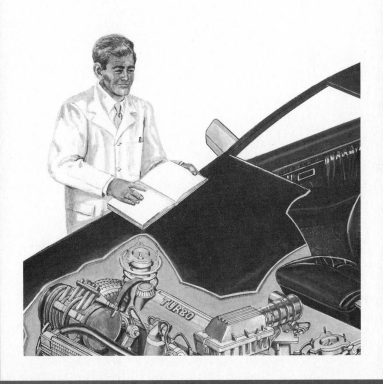

Careers

INTRODUCTION

When most people think about earning a living in the automotive industry, they probably think first about repairing or servicing automobiles. Actually, the automotive industry includes many other job opportunities. The industry is so enormous that within every two families in the United States, one member makes a living in some area of the automotive industry. The automotive industry is the single largest employer in the United States.

This chapter introduces you to some of the many areas of job opportunities in the automotive and transportation fields. It will tell you about the job skills you will need and how you can get these skills. Once you have proven your ability, jobs will not be hard to find.

Keep in mind as you are reading this chapter that it discusses job opportunities for the entire transportation industry. This industry includes cars, trucks, mass transit (buses, trains), motorcycles and other small-engine machines, and even boats and airplanes. Job experience in any of these areas is valuable and can easily be transferred to other types of vehicles.

OBJECTIVES

When you have completed this chapter, you should be able to

■ List four major career areas in the automotive industry
■ Identify typical job opportunities within the major career areas
■ List the general job requirements for these job opportunities
■ Describe how you can acquire the education and training to fulfill job requirements

CAREER AREAS

The four major career areas in the automotive and transportation industry are manufacturing, sales, service and repair, and the aftermarket and specialty equipment industry.

Manufacturing

Manufacturing offers a number of career possibilities at every stage of the process. The best place to begin discussing these opportunities is the beginning, and the beginning for ideas about vehicles is the drawing board.

Design For the engineer, artist, and craftsperson, the *design studio* is at the forefront of the industry. Here, the engineer develops the design of a vehicle, sometimes as many as 10 years before it is produced. The artist draws and paints the engineer's ideas. The craftspeople make scale models in plaster, wood, and clay. Then they make a full-sized model in the same materials. Finally, a working model, called a **prototype,** is built for testing (Figure 1-1). If the new vehicle is given the go-ahead, another department takes over. This department is called **tooling.**

FIGURE 1-1 Testing prototype parts. (Cadillac Motor Division, GMC)

Tooling The tooling department makes all the *jigs* and *fixtures*, devices that hold a part in proper alignment while it is being machined. They also make the special tools and equipment required to form the body, build the frame, and cast the engine parts. They make everything needed for the production department to build the vehicle on the assembly line. If you like machine shop work, this is your area. You'll need to know machining, welding, heavy metalwork, light metalwork, mold making, casting, metallurgy, plastics, fiberglass, and a half dozen other skill areas. Any technical courses you take will help in this field. From tooling, things move out to **production.** Here, you find the assembly line.

Production The vehicle is built on the production line. At one time people assembled the cars (Figure 1-2). Today many dangerous and routine jobs are being done by industrial robots (Figure 1-3). People are still

FIGURE 1-2 Assembly line. (Cadillac Motor Division, GMC)

FIGURE 1-3 Robots on the assembly line. (Cadillac Motor Division, GMC)

needed in the production process, but their jobs are different. Instead of working on the assembly line, technicians are needed to repair and maintain industrial robots. The skills the new technician needs are electronics, computer programming, and hydraulics. Many men and women can work their way from *apprentice* to *assistant foreman*, *foreman*, *supervisor*, and *department head* to *production manager*, making an excellent career for themselves.

CAD/CAM Many manufacturers now use the computer to design their products. This system is called *computer-aided design* (CAD). The CAD system can design a vehicle, do wind tunnel tests on the vehicle without physically testing, and test the vehicle design for structural strength without building a prototype. After the CAD is complete, it is transferred to the *computer-aided manufacturing* (CAM) system. The CAM system can design all of the tooling needed to manufacture the CAD-designed product. The results of the CAM program are then fed into computer-controlled machine tools, such as milling machines, drill presses, and engine lathes, to produce the tooling and, eventually, the vehicle.

CAD/CAM is a new computer area that is rapidly growing (Figure 1-4). Almost all of the car manufacturers now use it. Job opportunities in this field require a drafting and computer background.

Distribution *Distribution*, although a very large part of the industry, generally attracts those with interests other than direct hands-on involvement. Distribution means shipping by truck, rail, and ships to dealers who will sell the product to the customer (Figure 1-5).

FIGURE 1-4 Computer-Aided Design/Computer-Aided Manufacturing. (Cadillac Motor Division, GMC)

FIGURE 1-5 Automotive transport service.

FIGURE 1-6 Dealership.

Sales

Dealerships require large numbers of *salespeople* (Figure 1-6). To be a good salesperson in the transportation area, you must like people, like one-to-one contact, enjoy an office environment, and be prepared to work shifts at night and on weekends (Figure 1-7). Men and women who know and understand the workings of the product they are selling have an advantage over those who don't. Within a dealership there are job opportunities in sales, for both new and used cars, financing, and various levels of management. Sales jobs, for those who really put forth the effort, pay extremely well. The largest number of job opportunities, however, are in the dealership's service and repair area.

Service and Repair

One of the largest areas of employment in the automotive industry is the service and repair area. Many people trained in automechanics have advanced to the supervision level of management.

Dealer Service   New cars have warranties that depend on periodic servicing of the car. Such service in-

FIGURE 1-7   Salesperson showing cars.

cludes oil and filter changes, lubricating, minor and major tune-ups, and a number of other periodic maintenance service tasks (Figure 1-8).

When the car begins to act up and you take it to the dealer, the first person you see is the *service writer* (Figure 1-9). He or she can listen to the customer's description of the problem and direct the vehicle to the right part of the shop.

If it is not clear what the problem is, the car will go to technicians who specialize in performing **diagnostic** tests (Figure 1-10). They will use dynamometers, oscilloscopes, ohmmeters, and many other types of testing equipment to determine what needs repair. Special diagnostic centers using the latest computerized test equipment have been started.

FIGURE 1-8   Shop area of a dealership.

FIGURE 1-9   Service writer.

FIGURE 1-10   Diagnosing repair.

Once the problem is diagnosed, the service writer estimates how much repairs will cost.

Whatever the decision about what work needs to be done, the *shop foreman* will see that the work is performed and generally make sure the shop runs smoothly. The *dispatcher* will distribute the work, make sure it's completed on time, and follow up on the paperwork. Shop foremen are usually very experienced service people. They've had a number of years of experience as mechanics in repair work or in paint and body work, front-end work, or any of the specialized fields of auto repair.

The line mechanics are the men and women who do the actual repairs. They are the *mechanical*, *front-end*, and *transmission specialists*. Other specialty areas include *tune-up*, *electrical*, and *air conditioning* (Figure 1-11). The term *line mechanics* comes from the assembly line mechanic. This term distinguished them from mechanics who worked in other parts of the industry. Today, a line mechanic is one who works in a dealership rather than in an independent service facility.

All of these people are highly skilled in their fields. Imagine the price of today's automobile. If you had that much money invested, you'd expect the people who serviced and repaired such an expensive piece of equipment to really "know their stuff."

Some of the jobs in service and repair have entry-level openings. Because of the legal and technical aspects of these jobs, though, openings go first to those with knowledge of and training in the area. Many of these jobs require certificates of course completion both before and after you begin the job. Some states require

FIGURE 1-11   Line people.

mechanics to be certified before they work on cars. Once employed, you will not only be expected to have considerable skill, but also you will be expected to maintain your skills and meet the challenge of new developments as they come to market.

Supplying the line mechanics with the necessary parts to repair or replace components is another very necessary job that is performed during service and repair (Figure 1-12). People who work behind the parts counter are part of the team that includes the office workers and cashiers who keep track of the paperwork and the money.

Independent Service   All the jobs discussed regarding dealer service have their counterparts in the independent service and repair shops (Figure 1-13). Besides independent garages that do general service and repair, many independent specialty shops provide job opportunities, especially to the inexperienced but not necessarily to the untrained. There are tire stores, parts stores, front-end shops, muffler shops, and a store or shop for every major section of the vehicle (Figure 1-14).

FIGURE 1-12   Supplying parts.

FIGURE 1-13   Independent garage.

FIGURE 1-14   Transmission shop.

AN ENVIABLE CAREER

We met him in the spring of 1966. To many, he represented legend in the automotive community. Somewhat aloof, he had already had an impact upon the car world in ways that remain today. Of Russian origin, he had been involved in the design and manufacture of hemispherical cylinder heads for flathead Ford V8 engines in the 1950s. Some have even said that it was from this design that the Chrysler hemispherical head V8 engine had its beginning. But he would never admit to this.

There were also the years he spent actively on race tracks around the world, including several attempts at the 24-hr LeMans, France road race.

In the early years of the 1950s, he had come to the Chevrolet Division of General Motors and begun a quiet but effective campaign devoted to establishing Chevrolet as a dominant force in the high-performance segment of the original markets and aftermarkets.

Then, in 1953, he wrote an intercorporate memo to his management, detailing what he thought it would take to make Chevy a reckonable force in the aftermarket. His plan was simple. Use the then-upcoming Chevrolet factory sports car to meet, head on, the Ford performance image. He wanted to take factory-developed performance parts and make them available at the dealer level. He also wanted to make a stand by taking two or three of his factory sports cars to the famed beaches of Daytona and setting some speed records just to prove the validity of his concepts.

History records that all of these things happened. The records were set, the performance image was established, and the man who organized the underlying thrust of this success left his mark on the automotive industry.

By name, the "factory sports car" was the Chevrolet Corvette. And by name, the man was Zora Arkus-Duntov.

Jim MacFarland
Edelbrock

Another group of employers you should consider are operators of salvage yards, called parts recyclers (Figure 1-15). They *recycle* parts, and there are jobs in the salvage yards for inexperienced, entry-level people. Here, you'll disassemble the cars as they come in, clean and paint many of the parts, and then place them into the inventory for resale.

Aftermarket and Specialty Equipment

A total industry is involved after the original equipment manufacturers (OEMs) finish their jobs. What better name to give it than the *aftermarket*. The aftermarket includes all the businesses which support the OEM. These businesses include parts, paint, glass, chrome, and sheet metal manufacturers, to name just a few of the many products associated with aftermarket businesses.

CAREERS, EDUCATION, AND TRAINING

At one time, people interested in careers in automotives might have gotten a job in a service station or a small garage and learned by experience. Although doing this today is not totally impossible, it is doubtful that such a person could pick up the necessary skills to enter many areas of the automotive industry. Today's super-sophisticated automobile requires highly technical knowledge. Terms such as *integrated circuits*, *microcomputers*, *closed systems*, *feedback systems*, and other jargon now describe an automobile.

If you are interested in a career in the automotive industry, then you need to know what jobs are available, what skills are required for those jobs, and how you can get those skills.

FIGURE 1-15 Salvage yard.

620.261-010 AUTOMOBILE MECHANIC (auto. ser.) garage mechanic.

Repairs and overhauls automobiles, buses, trucks, and other automotive vehicles: Examines vehicle and discusses with customer or AUTOMOBILE-REPAIR-SERVICE ESTIMATOR (auto. ser.); AUTOMOBILE TESTER (auto. ser.); or BUS INSPECTOR (auto. ser.) nature and extent of damage or malfunction. Plans work procedure, using charts, technical manuals, and experience. Raises vehicle, using hydraulic jack or hoist, to gain access to mechanical units bolted to underside of vehicle. Removes unit, such as engine, transmission, or differential, using wrenches and hoist. Disassembles unit and inspects parts for wear, using micrometers, calipers, and thickness gages. Repairs or replaces parts, such as pistons, rods, gears, valves, and bearings, using mechanic's handtools. Overhauls or replaces carburetors, blowers, generators, distributors, starters, and pumps. Rebuilds parts, such as crankshafts and cylinder blocks, using lathes, shapers, drill presses, and welding equipment. Rewires ignition system, lights, and instrument panel. Relines and adjusts brakes, alines front end, repairs or replaces shock absorbers, and solders leaks in radiator. Mends damaged body and fenders by hammering out or filling in dents and welding broken parts. Replaces and adjusts headlights, and installs and repairs accessories, such as radios, heaters, mirrors, and windshield wipers. May be designated according to specialty as AUTOMOBILE MECHANIC, MOTOR (auto. ser.); BUS MECHANIC (auto. ser.); DIFFERENTIAL REPAIRER (auto. ser.); ENGINE-REPAIR MECHANIC, BUS (auto. ser.); FOREIGN-CAR MECHANIC (auto. ser.); TRUCK MECHANIC (auto. ser.). When working in service station may be designated AUTOMOBILE-SERVICE-STATION MECHANIC (auto. ser.). Additional titles: COMPRESSOR MECHANIC, BUS (auto. ser.); DRIVE-SHAFT-AND-STEERING-POST REPAIRER (auto. ser.); ENGINE-HEAD REPAIRER (auto. ser.); MOTOR ASSEMBLER (auto. ser.).

620.261-012 AUTOMOBILE-MECHANIC APPRENTICE (auto. ser.) automobile-and-truck-mechanic apprentice.

Performs duties as described under APPRENTICE (any ind.).

620.261-014 AUTOMOBILE TESTER (auto. ser.)

Tests and examines automotive vehicles, such as automobiles, buses, and trucks, to determine repairs required: Starts engine of automotive vehicle and listens for sounds indicative of malfunctions. Drives vehicle, noting performance of parts, such as clutch, gears, and brakes. Tests motor timing, cylinder compression, fuel consumption, wheel alinement, and steering, using testing devices. Examines body and fenders of vehicle for scratches and dents. Reports findings to supervisor or customer and recommends repairs required. May examine disassembled engine, differential, or other parts during repair. May be designated according to specialty as MOTOR ANALYST (auto. ser.).

620.261-018 AUTOMOBILE-REPAIR-SERVICE ESTIMATOR (auto. ser.) automobile inspector; collision estimator; manager, service; mechanic, trouble-shooting; sales associate, garage service; service writer.

Inspects and tests automobiles and trucks to determine need for and cost of repairs: Determines need for repairs by road test [AUTOMOBILE TESTER (auto. ser.)], by use of mechanical testing devices [BRAKE REPAIRER (auto. ser.); FRONT-END MECHANIC (auto. ser.)], by questioning customer about vehicle's performance, or by visual inspection of vehicle. Estimates cost of repair and prepares itemized work order, listing costs of parts and labor. May make minor adjustments or repairs, such as brake adjustment, battery cable replacement, or hinge lubrication. May supervise AUTOMOBILE-BODY REPAIRER (auto. ser.); AUTOMOBILE MECHANIC (auto. ser.); PAINTER, AUTOMOTIVE (auto. mfg.; auto. ser.); and other garage workers. May be designated according to specialty as TRUCK-REPAIR-SERVICE ESTIMATOR (auto. ser.).

620.261-026 ELECTRIC-GOLF-CART REPAIRER (amuse. & rec.; auto. ser.) golf-cart mechanic.

Repairs and maintains electric golf carts at golf course or in automotive repair shop, using handtools and electrical testing devices: Determines type of repairs required by reading work orders, talking to cart operator, or test-driving cart. Tests operational performance of motor, using voltmeter, ammeter, and wattmeter. Dismantles motor and repairs or replaces defective parts, such as brushes, armatures, and commutator, using wrenches, pliers, and screwdrivers. Rewires electrical systems, and repairs or replaces electrical accessories, such as horn and headlights. Tests and recharges or replaces batteries. Lubricates moving parts and adjusts brakes and belts. May perform structural repairs to body of cart, seats, and fabric tops. May record parts used and labor time on work order.

620.281-010 AIR-CONDITIONING MECHANIC (auto. ser.) automobile-refrigeration mechanic.

Installs and repairs automotive air-conditioning units: Bolts compressor to engine block and installs driving pulley on front end of crankshaft. Places fan belt on pulleys, adjusts tension, and tightens bolts. Bolts evaporator unit under dashboard or in trunk. Welds or bolts mounting brackets to automobile frame. Drills holes through interior panels, threads hoses through holes and connects hoses to compressor, evaporator, and cool-air outlet. Fills compressor with refrigerant and starts unit. Measures compressor pressure to determine efficiency of compressor, using gage. Listens to operating unit for indications of malfunction. Removes faulty units from vehicles, disassembles them, and replaces worn and broken parts and fluid in unit. Makes electrical connections as required. May specialize in installation of automotive air-conditioning units and be designated AUTOMOTIVE AIR-CONDITIONER INSTALLER (auto. ser.).

620.281-014 AUTOMOTIVE TECHNICIAN, EXHAUST EMISSIONS (gov. ser.) power equipment mechanic.

Conducts and evaluates tests on vehicles to check exhaust emissions: Reviews instructions to determine details of test to be performed. Drives vehicle over dynamometer. Records identifying data. Performs dwell, timing and idle speed tests using gages, evaluates performance and adjusts performance to manufacturer's specifications. Adjusts dynamometer settings to vehicle specifications and connects instrument sensors to exhaust system. Starts and operates vehicle according to test program, compares performance with specifications and records results. Calibrates, cleans and maintains test equipment and recording devices. May diagnose and repair vehicle malfunctions. May install smog-control device on tested vehicle.

620.281-018 AUTOMOTIVE-MAINTENANCE-EQUIPMENT SERVICER (any ind.) automotive-maintenance-equipment repairer; equipment-service engineer; pump-and-tank servicer.

Adjusts and repairs automotive repairing, servicing, and testing equipment, using handtools and power tools: Disassembles defective equipment, such as gasoline pumps, air compressors, and dynamometers. Replaces defective parts, using pipe fitting and welding tools. Reassembles, adjusts, and tests repaired equipment. May be required to register with government agency to adjust meters and gages of fuel and oil pumps serving public. May install new equipment. May specialize in repairing gasoline pumps, lubrication equipment, air compressors, or other type of automotive service equipment.

620.281-026 BRAKE REPAIRER (auto. ser.) brake mechanic; brake-repair mechanic; brakeshoe repairer.

Repairs and overhauls brake systems in automobiles, buses, trucks, and other automotive vehicles: Pushes handle of hydraulic jack or pushes hoist control to raise vehicle axle. Removes wheels, using wrenches, wheel puller, and sledge hammer. Replaces defective brakeshoe units or attaches new linings to brakeshoes. Measures brakedrum to determine amount of wear, using feeler gage. Inserts vacuum gage into power-brake cylinder, starts engine, and reads gage to detect brake-line leaks. Repairs or replaces leaky brake cylinders. Repairs or replaces defective air compressor in airbrake systems. Replaces wheel on axle and adjusts drumshoe clearance, using wrench. Fills master brake cylinder with brake fluid, pumps brake pedal, or uses pressure tank, and opens valves on hydraulic brake system to bleed air from brake lines. Closes valves and refills master brake cylinder. May be designated according to specialty as BRAKE REPAIRER, AIR (auto. ser.); BRAKE REPAIRER, HYDRAULIC (auto. ser.); BRAKE REPAIRER, BUS (auto. ser.).

620.281-030 BUS INSPECTOR (auto. ser.) motor-inspection mechanic.

Examines and adjusts or repairs engines, chassis, electrical systems, and interior furnishings of buses: Starts engine and listens for indications of malfunctions. Tests engine components, such as carburetors, distributors, radiators, and fuel pumps, to determine causes of malfunctions, using timers, gages, and other testing devices. Inspects chassis for defects in parts, such as universal joints, drive shaft, and air-suspension units. Inspects electrical systems and equipment [ELECTRICIAN, AUTOMOTIVE (auto. ser.)] and interior furnishings. May be designated according to specialty as CHASSIS INSPECTOR (auto. ser.); ELECTRICAL INSPECTOR (auto. ser.); ENGINE INSPECTOR (auto. ser.).

620.281-034 CARBURETOR MECHANIC (auto. ser.) carburetor repairer.

Repairs and adjusts motor vehicle carburetors: Disassembles carburetors and gasoline filter units, using handtools. Examines parts for defects and tests needle valves with wire gages and *flowmeter*. Cleans parts in solvents to remove dirt and gum deposits. Repairs or replaces defective parts. Reassembles carburetor and gasoline filter, and installs them in vehicle. Starts engine and turns adjustment screw to regulate flow of air and gasoline through carburetor, using testing equipment. May operate drill press, lathe, and other power tools to retap jets, ream throttle bodies and chokes, and machine seating surfaces of carburetor housings. May install and repair mechanical devices that convert conventional systems to use of other fuels [VEHICLE-FUEL-SYSTEMS CONVERTER (auto. ser.)].

FIGURE 1-16 Resources on jobs.

Job Opportunities and Required Skills

For a complete outline of job opportunities, drop by your local library and look through the *Dictionary of Occupational Titles* (DOT) and its companion volume, the *Occupational Outlook Handbook* (Figure 1-16). These volumes are published yearly by the U.S. Department of Labor, so be sure you look at the most recent publication. The DOT identifies job titles within job clusters (jobs falling into the same general categories). These jobs have numbers assigned to them, and you will need the numbers to look up the information about those jobs in the *Occupational Outlook Handbook*. These reference works describe nearly every job in the industry, the technical requirements for the job, the projected job possibilities, the levels of pay, and where you'd most likely find a job.

Education and Training

Education is a direct way to get many of the skills required of the mechanic (Figure 1-17). Automechanic courses are available in high schools, vocational programs, community colleges, public and private technical schools, and specialized training programs.

For the person interested in the more advanced technical and theoretical skills, colleges offer certificates and degree programs.

On-the-job training (OJT) and work experience (WE) are available with many educational and training programs. Some schools, through cooperative education agreements with local employers, offer students opportunities to work for pay while going to school.

FIGURE 1-17 Educational course.

Such training programs answer the common problem of the beginners in any job field, that of not being able to get a job unless they have experience. Explore such possibilities with your counselors at educational and training institutions in your area.

You can also receive study materials from **Automotive Service Excellence (ASE).** ASE is a national association whose primary concerns are the training and certification of qualified auto mechanics. Their address is Automotive Service Excellence, 1825 K Street NW, Washington D.C. 20006-1249. You will find more information on ASE in Appendix 1.

TRADE TERMS

Automotive Service Excellence (ASE)
CAD/CAM
Diagnostic
Independent Service

Production
Prototype
Tooling

REVIEW QUESTIONS

1. Name the four major career areas in the automotive industry.
2. Where can you find the most comprehensive description of job opportunities?
3. What skills would you say are needed to work in a manufacturing design studio?
4. List six of the job categories in the service department of a major automotive dealership.

5. Salespeople don't need to be mechanics to make money. True or false? Explain.
6. Who is the first person you usually see when you take your car to the dealership for repair?
7. What is a line mechanic?
8. Give an example of an OEM product and an aftermarket product.

2

Tools
of the Trade

INTRODUCTION

This chapter introduces the most common tools of the trade, both hand tools and power tools. A mechanic should have a wide variety of tools to fit the many jobs. You should know the correct name of each tool, the safe procedure for using the tool, and the proper tool for the job. But before we start discussing the right tool for the job, you'll need to know a couple of things about the information you will find here.

THE MEASUREMENT SYSTEMS

Tools used in measurement will be in **United States customary** measurements or a *metric* measurement. For the most part, *United States customary* measurements will be used. These are the measurements with which you are most familiar: ½ inch, ³⁄₁₆ inch, ⅞ inch, and so on. These units of measurement are from the English system of measurement. Years ago the Society of Automotive Engineers (SAE) accepted these measurements, which are fractional units of the foot.

OBJECTIVES

When you have completed this chapter, you should be able to

- Identify and know how to use simple hand tools, power hand tools, and lifting tools
- Name the tools a beginning mechanic needs
- List general safety precautions in using tools
- Explain the difference between standard tools and specialty tools
- Understand how the **metric system** differs from **United States customary** system measurements
- Know the difference between pneumatic and electric power tools

12

The rest of the world uses the **metric system.** The SAE and the U.S. government have been trying, for the last 10 years, to convert to the metric system, but progress is slow. The metric system uses decimal division of the *meter*: 10 mm, 11 mm, 12 mm, and so on. The abbreviation *mm* means millimeter, or one-thousandth of a meter.

The meter is 1/10,000,000 of the distance from the North Pole to the equator, or 39.37 in. The metric system is a decimal system that does not use fractions. Table 2-1 gives the metric system of linear measurement. See Chapter 4 and Appendix 2 for more information about units of measurement, measurement systems, and conversion tables.

TABLE 2-1 The Metric System of Linear Measurement

	SYMBOL	LENGTH (*in.*)
Meter	m	39.37
Decimeter	dm	3.937
Centimeter	cm	0.3937
Millimeter	mm	0.03937
Micrometer	μm	0.003937
Nanometer	nm	0.0003937

In most modern American cars you will find both SAE and metric parts. This is a result of the United States slowly converting to the metric system. Now most mechanics are equipped with both SAE and metric tools.

SAFETY

The second major thing you must be aware of is the safe use of tools. Using common sense again, your using the right tool for the job is the first rule of using tools safely. Obviously, using the tool for the job it was designed to do means you need to know more about a tool than its name. You need to know what it is used for and how to use it safely. Then you need to always work with this knowledge in mind. Chapter 5 discusses more specific safety precautions, but you should always observe some general rules when working with tools.

Keep your tools clean. After using them, wipe them off. Greasy tools can easily slip from your grasp. Always wear *safety glasses* when working with power-driven tools. To protect the rest of your body, wear proper clothing. Long sleeves will prevent burns from hot manifolds. Keep long hair or ties away from radiator fans. Some common sense and a little forethought can save your life, not to mention an eye or finger.

HAND TOOLS

Every mechanic should have a good selection of hand tools. You should have tools in both U.S. customary and metric.

Wrenches

Each mechanic's tool kit should contain a complete set of *wrenches*. The minimum number would be a set ranging from ¼ through 1¼ in. in increments of 1⁄16 in. (Figure 2-1). Wrenches come in a variety of combinations.

In one type, **open-end wrenches** (Figure 2-2), both ends of the wrench are open. One end will be one size different from the other (⅜ and 7⁄16 in., or ½ and 9⁄16 in., and so on). This allows you to have a full set of wrenches at half the investment.

Box wrenches have the same advantage (Figure 2-3). Both ends have either a 6- or 12-point box with a different size at each end (Figure 2-4). Twelve-point box wrenches allow you to work in tighter areas than 6-point wrenches.

FIGURE 2-1 A set of combination wrenches. (Snap-on Tools Corporation)

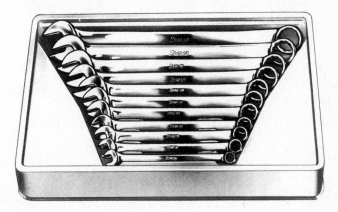

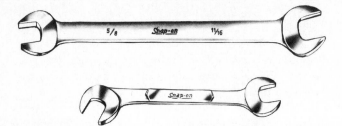

FIGURE 2-2 Open-end wrenches. (Snap-on Tools Corporation)

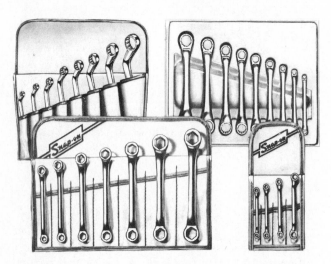

FIGURE 2-3 Box wrench. (Snap-on Tools Corporation)

FIGURE 2-4 Six-point and 12-point box-end wrenches. (Snap-on Tools Corporation)

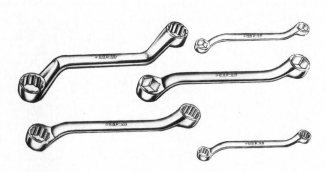

FIGURE 2-5 Combination wrench. (Snap-on Tools Corporation)

A **combination wrench** has an *open end* at one end and a *box* at the other end (Figure 2-5). The box end will have *6 points* or *12 points*. These combination wrenches come in two lengths: standard, for working in tight areas, and long, for working where you need extra leverage. Combination wrenches are usually the same size at both ends.

Consider, now, how to use these wrenches. The box end is generally used for tightening or loosening the first few turns. Its construction makes it less likely to slip off a nut. The open end is usually best suited for turning (running) the nut down or holding a bolt head. As a safety precaution, always pull a wrench toward you. Pushing a wrench invites trouble. You risk slipping and banging your knuckles.

Ratchets and Sockets

The most often used tool in the mechanic's kit is the **ratchet and socket** (Figure 2-6). With a variety of extensions, these are the most versatile of all the tools. The ratchet lets you tighten or loosen a nut or bolt by moving a lever on the head of the ratchet. This lever controls the internal mechanism of the ratchet, allowing force to be applied in only one direction (Figure 2-7).

FIGURE 2-6 Ratchet set. (Snap-on Tools Corporation)

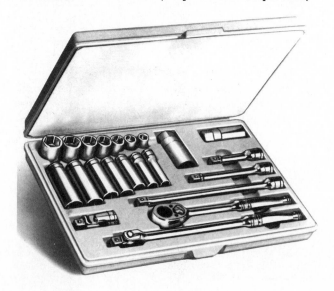

FIGURE 2-7 Ratchet head. (Snap-on Tools Corporation)

A ratchet's size is determined by the length of any one side of the drive. The three standard sizes are ¼, ⅜, and ½ in. Heavy-duty drives of ¾ and 1 in. are available for the big jobs. With corresponding 6-point or 12-point sockets in both *standard lengths* and *deep-well lengths*, you will have a complete set. Deep-well sockets (Figure 2-8) loosen or tighten nuts when the bolt sticks so high above the top of the nut that sockets of that standard length will not reach the nut. Finally, you'll need several extensions. **Extensions** are rods which extend the distance between the socket and ratchet (Figure 2-9). They range from 1 in. to over 36 in. long.

Torque Wrenches

Torque wrenches (Figure 2-10) allow you to measure how tight a nut or bolt is being forced down on the

FIGURE 2-8 Deep-well sockets. (Snap-on Tools Corporation)

FIGURE 2-9 Extensions. (Snap-on Tools Corporation)

FIGURE 2-10 Torque wrenches. (Snap-on Tools Corporation)

surface on which it rests. Many nuts and bolts on a car have a specific torque setting determined by the factory and expressed in *foot-pounds* (SAE) or *Newton-meters* (metric).

A foot-pound is the work or pressure accomplished by a force of 1 lb through a distance of 1 ft (Figure 2-11).

A Newton-meter is the work or pressure accomplished by a force of 1 kg through a distance of 1 m (Figure 2-12).

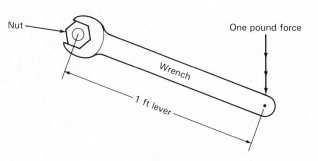

FIGURE 2-11 Foot-pound.

FIGURE 2-12 Newton-meter.

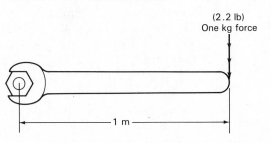

Torque wrenches come with drives that correspond to sockets: $\frac{1}{4}$, $\frac{3}{8}$, or $\frac{1}{2}$ in. There are four types of torque wrenches. The *dial* type (Figure 2-13) has a scale you can read directly. With the *break-over* type (Figure 2-14) you must dial in the desired torque. The torque wrench makes an audible "click" when you have reached the correct force. The third type of torque wrench is the torsion bar (Figure 2-15), and its gauge is a simple pointer that moves across a graduated scale. Digital-readout torque wrenches are now available.

Screwdrivers

Screwdrivers come in many styles. The most used are the *blade* (Figure 2-16) and the **Phillips** (Figure 2-17). A blade style fits into a straight slot in the screw. A Phillips has a cross point, as shown in Figure 2-17. This makes the Phillips just a little more stable than the blade screwdriver.

Both blade and Phillips drivers come in a variety of sizes. As a beginning mechanic, you should have three or four of each style in sizes to include those from 2-in. stubbies to 12–14 in. screwdrivers.

FIGURE 2-13   Torque wrench scale. (Snap-on Tools Corporation)

FIGURE 2-14   Break-over torque wrench. (Snap-on Tools Corporation)

FIGURE 2-15   Torsion bar torque wrench. (AMMCO)

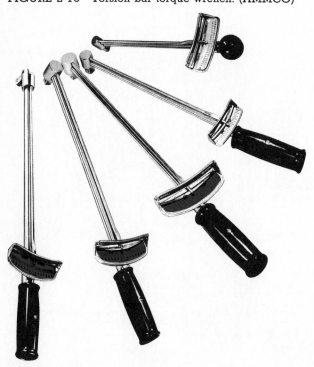

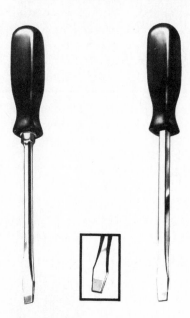

FIGURE 2-16   Blade screwdriver. (Snap-on Tools Corporation)

FIGURE 2-17   Phillips screwdriver. (Snap-on Tools Corporation)

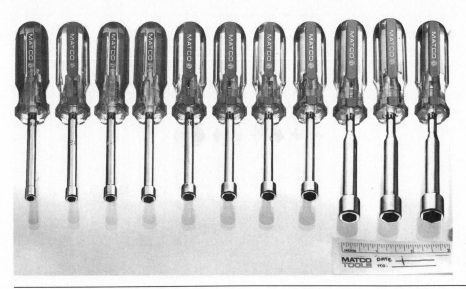

FIGURE 2-18   Nutdriver set. (Matco Tools, A Unit of the Chicago Pneumatic Tool Company)

Nutdrivers

Nutdrivers are a combination of a screwdriver and a socket (Figure 2-18). Use these on small nuts and bolts. The advantages of a nutdriver over the standard socket set are that they are easy and fast to use in tight places.

Pliers

Many more pliers are available to the mechanic today than only the old *slip-joint* style (Figure 2-19). Figure 2-20 shows many different styles including *long nose*,

FIGURE 2-19   Slip-joint pliers. (Snap-on Tools Corporation)

FIGURE 2-20   Types of pliers. (Snap-on Tools Corporation)

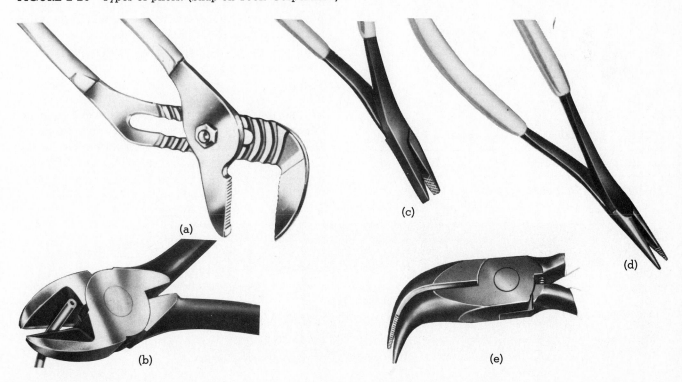

(a)

(b)

(c)

(d)

(e)

duck bill, *adjustable joint* (*water pump pliers*), side cutters, and *offset needlenose*. As a beginning mechanic, select a variety of pliers, including at least one pair of slip-joint pliers, two or three sizes of adjustable pliers, a pair of long-nose pliers, and a pair of side cutters.

There are many special-purpose pliers, for example, vice-grip pliers for holding parts during grinding and pliers used to remove hose clamps.

Hammers and Mallets

The mechanic should have at least three *hammers*: one 8-oz and a 12–16 oz *ball-peen*, plus a small sledgehammer (Figure 2-21). At a minimum, have a plastic and a lead mallet available (Figure 2-22). Hammers are used

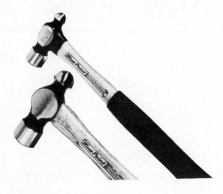

FIGURE 2-21   Hammers. (Snap-on Tools Corporation)

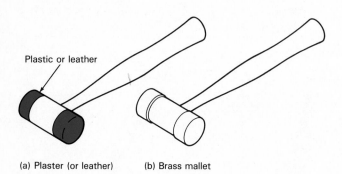

(a) Plaster (or leather)   (b) Brass mallet

FIGURE 2-22   Mallets (soft-face hammers).

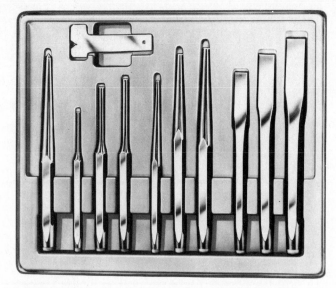

FIGURE 2-23   Punches and chisels. (Snap-on Tools Corporation)

with punches and chisels, and mallets are used for tapping parts apart or aligning parts together. A soft-faced mallet will not harm the part you strike; hammers will.

Punches and Chisels

Punches and *chisels* (Figure 2-23) are necessary parts of a tool kit. A kit should include a variety of different sized punches called *drift punches* or *starter punches*. These punches remove *drift* and *roll pins*. *Tapered punches* can line up bolt holes. *Center punches* can mark the start of a drill hole so that the drill bit will not wander. A group of chisels in a variety of sizes will prove indispensable. These should include *flat chisels*, *cape chisels*, *round-nose cape chisels*, and *diamond point chisels*.

Files

Files are used when you must remove metal by hand. Files most used by the mechanic are either **single cut** or **double cut** (Figure 2-24). Single cut means the cut-

FIGURE 2-24   Cuts of files.

Single cut

Double cut

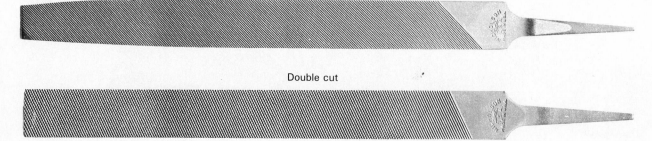

Round	Half Rd.	Flat	Crossing	Knife	Square	Triangle
●	⌒	▬	◆	▶	■	▲

FIGURE 2-25   File shapes.

ting grooves line up diagonally across the face of the file. Double cut means the cutting grooves run diagonally in *both* directions across the face. Double-cut files remove large amounts of metal. They are considered first cut or roughening files. Single-cut files remove small amounts of metal. They are considered finishing files.

File shapes are round, half-round, flat, crossing, knife, square, and triangle (Figure 2-25). Like all other tools, having the right file for the job makes work safer and easier.

Hacksaws

A standard *hacksaw* always comes in handy. Unlike carpenter's saws, hacksaws (Figure 2-26) are specifically designed to cut metal. Buy one that seems sturdy and one that will allow you to rotate the blade 360° in 90° intervals. Hacksaw blades are available with 14, 18, 24, or 32 teeth per inch (TPI). Always have spare blades in your toolbox.

Taps and Dies

Taps and dies cut thread *in* nuts and *on* studs and bolts (Figure 2-27). Very often, a mechanic (even at

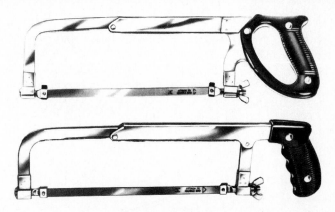

FIGURE 2-26   Hacksaw. (Snap-on Tools Corporation)

the factory) will cross-thread a threaded hole and ruin it. By using the correct tap, you can restore clean, sharp threads to the hole. Dies restore the threads to the bolt or stud. A good mechanic will have two sets of taps and dies: one SAE and one metric.

SPECIAL TOOLS

Car manufacturers and specialty tool companies work closely together to design and manufacture special tools to repair cars. Most car makers refer to these special tools in their service manuals. For example, to repair a Cadillac transaxle, you must have the tools in Figure 2-28. Figure 2-29 shows the special tools required to rebuild a Buick differential.

FIGURE 2-27   Tap and die set. (Snap-on Tools Corporation)

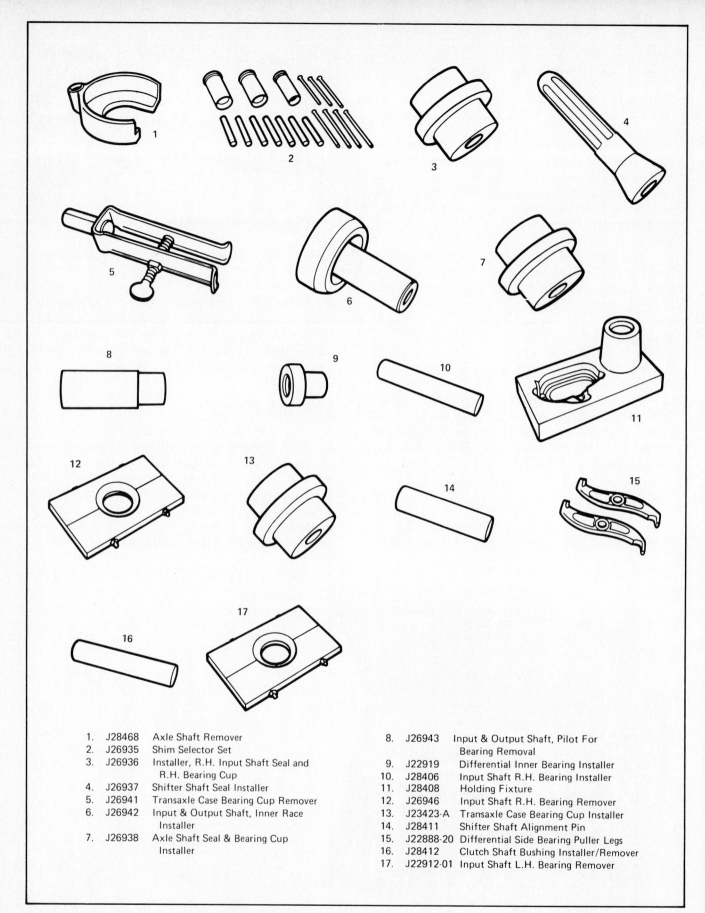

1. J28468   Axle Shaft Remover
2. J26935   Shim Selector Set
3. J26936   Installer, R.H. Input Shaft Seal and
             R.H. Bearing Cup
4. J26937   Shifter Shaft Seal Installer
5. J26941   Transaxle Case Bearing Cup Remover
6. J26942   Input & Output Shaft, Inner Race
             Installer
7. J26938   Axle Shaft Seal & Bearing Cup
             Installer

8. J26943   Input & Output Shaft, Pilot For
             Bearing Removal
9. J22919   Differential Inner Bearing Installer
10. J28406   Input Shaft R.H. Bearing Installer
11. J28408   Holding Fixture
12. J26946   Input Shaft R.H. Bearing Remover
13. J23423-A Transaxle Case Bearing Cup Installer
14. J28411   Shifter Shaft Alignment Pin
15. J22888-20 Differential Side Bearing Puller Legs
16. J28412   Clutch Shaft Bushing Installer/Remover
17. J22912-01 Input Shaft L.H. Bearing Remover

FIGURE 2-28   Special manual transaxle tools. (Cadillac Motor Division, GMC)

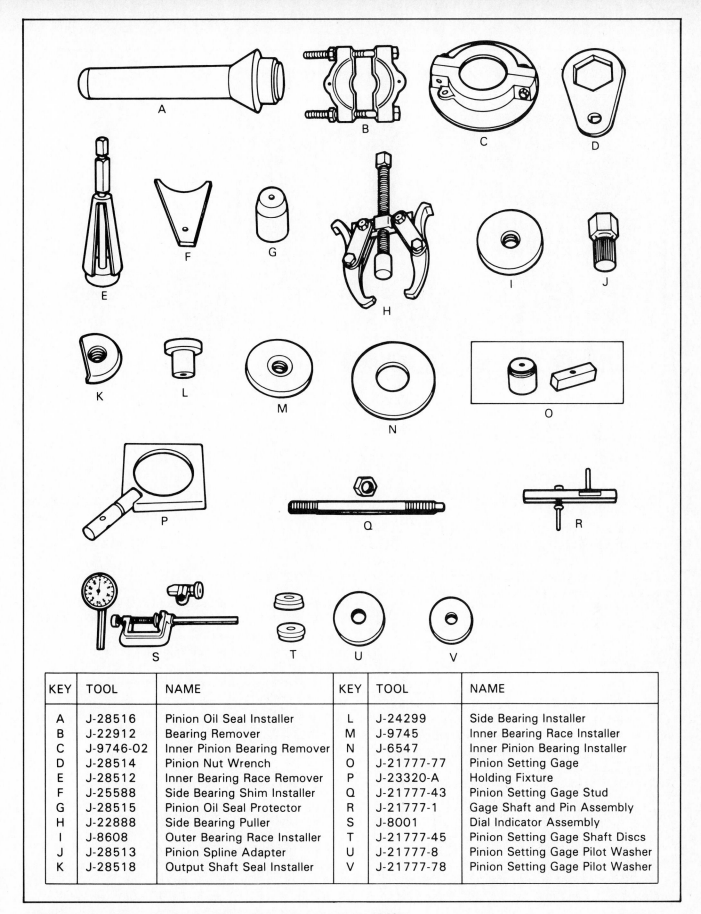

KEY	TOOL	NAME	KEY	TOOL	NAME
A	J-28516	Pinion Oil Seal Installer	L	J-24299	Side Bearing Installer
B	J-22912	Bearing Remover	M	J-9745	Inner Bearing Race Installer
C	J-9746-02	Inner Pinion Bearing Remover	N	J-6547	Inner Pinion Bearing Installer
D	J-28514	Pinion Nut Wrench	O	J-21777-77	Pinion Setting Gage
E	J-28512	Inner Bearing Race Remover	P	J-23320-A	Holding Fixture
F	J-25588	Side Bearing Shim Installer	Q	J-21777-43	Pinion Setting Gage Stud
G	J-28515	Pinion Oil Seal Protector	R	J-21777-1	Gage Shaft and Pin Assembly
H	J-22888	Side Bearing Puller	S	J-8001	Dial Indicator Assembly
I	J-8608	Outer Bearing Race Installer	T	J-21777-45	Pinion Setting Gage Shaft Discs
J	J-28513	Pinion Spline Adapter	U	J-21777-8	Pinion Setting Gage Pilot Washer
K	J-28518	Output Shaft Seal Installer	V	J-21777-78	Pinion Setting Gage Pilot Washer

FIGURE 2-29 Special differential tools. (Buick Motor Division, GMC)

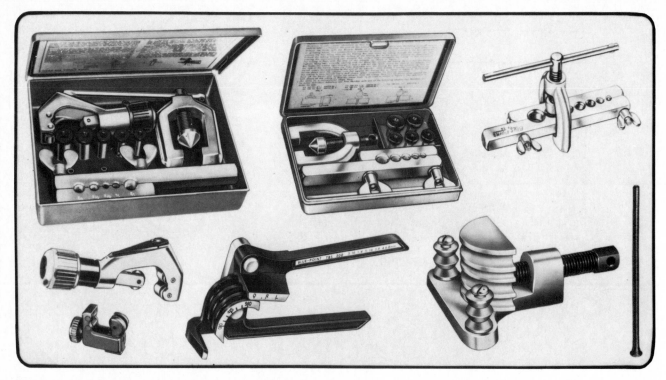

FIGURE 2-30 Tubing cutter, bender, and flaring tool.
(Snap-on Tools Corporation)

Tubing Cutters and Benders

As a mechanic, you will often be called on to make your own fuel lines, brake lines, and other metal lines to carry air or fluid. To do this successfully, you'll need a *tubing cutter*, a *tubing bender*, and a *flaring tool* to make a seal (Figure 2-30). Most shops will have these as part of the shop tools, but if you have your own, you'll know they will work correctly.

POWER TOOLS

Power tools are either pneumatic (air) or electric. You can purchase most power tools as either pneumatic or electric. Pneumatic tools offer the advantages of more torque, less weight, and lower maintenance. They also are more widely used. Their major disadvantage is their original higher cost. Also, you can plug electric tools into most wall sockets, but to use a pneumatic tool, you must have an air compressor and an air storage tank.

Some of the advantages of power tools are that they save time in either assembly or disassembly and allow the mechanic to use much less energy. They are so widely used that there are even power screw-drivers. Although many power tools will become part of your own toolbox, many are found as part of the shop tools.

Impact Wrench

The most important power tool is the **impact wrench** (Figure 2-31). This tool looks like an overgrown pistol. By using compressed air or electricity, it "hammers" or impacts the nut or bolt tight. If you turn the reversing switch, it hammers the nut or bolt loose.

Impact wrenches come in three light-duty sizes—¼, ⅜, and ½ in.—and two heavy duty sizes—¾ and 1 in. Usually the sockets for impact wrenches are constructed of thicker steel to withstand the force of the impact.

Drill Motor

The *drill motor* comes in either electric (Figure 2-32) or pneumatic. The air drill motor works like an electric drill, only it runs on air. It comes in a number of sizes with both forward and reverse. Chuck sizes range from ¼ to ½ in. The chuck is an adjustable clamp that fits on the drill motor and holds the twist drill.

FIGURE 2-31　Impact wrench.
(Snap-on Tools Corporation)

FIGURE 2-32　Drill motor. (Snap-on Tools Corporation)

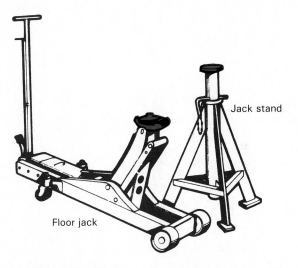

Jack stand

Floor jack

FIGURE 2-33　Hydraulic floor jack and jack stand.

LIFTING TOOLS

Within the shop, you should know about a number of heavy lifting tools.

Jacks

Jacks come in two styles and a variety of sizes. The most common style of shop jack is the *hydraulic floor jack* (Figure 2-33). These jacks are named by the weights they can lift: 1½, 2, and 2½ tons and so on. You operate them by working the handle up and down. A second type of portable floor jack is the pneumatic jack. This jack uses compressed air to lift a car or truck.

Jack Stands

Never work under a car with only a jack supporting it. Always use *safety stands* or **jack stands** (Figure 2-33). Hydraulic seals in the jack can let go and allow the jack to realease.

There are special jacking and supporting places on cars. Always lift and support them in the correct places (Figure 2-34).

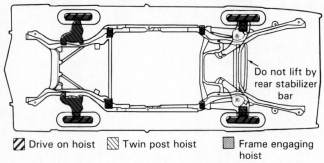

Do not lift by
rear stabilizer
bar

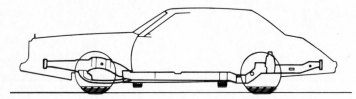

▨ Drive on hoist   ▧ Twin post hoist   ▦ Frame engaging
hoist

Be sure supports do not damage brake lines, fuel lines,
parking brake cable or exhaust system.

FIGURE 2-34   Support points. (Buick Motor Division,
GMC)

Hydraulic Lift

The safest lifting tool is the *hydraulic floor lift*. The hydraulic floor lift raises the car into the air high enough so that you can walk under it (Figure 2-35). Various safety features prevent the hydraulic lift from coming down if a seal does leak or air pressure is lost. Therefore, you can work under the car with an assurance of safety. Figure 2-36 shows typical lift points. Before

lifting the car, always check to see that the floor lift is positioned correctly.

Engine Hoist

The *engine hoist*, as shown in Figure 2-37, allows you to lift an engine from a car. Hydraulic pressure converts power to a mechanical advantage and lifts the engine from the car.

WHERE'D YOU FIND THAT WRENCH?

It's been said that "necessity is the mother of invention." Nowhere is this more true than in the automotive repair business. Specifically, in developing new tools. The right tool saves time, and time is money. The quicker a job can be completed, the sooner the next job can be started.

Let's take an example from auto racing. The famous Woods brothers figured that time could be saved while changing tires if they oiled some lug nuts, threaded them on a string, and held one end of the string in their mouths and tied the other to a shirt button. When

the old wheel was off, they just dropped the free end of the string and the nuts fell into their hands.

These same clear thinkers introduced such items as quick-ratio hydraulic chassis jacks (to save pumping time), quick-flow gasoline cans, larger vent tubes for quicker tank filling, and an endless list of other secrets. The end result was that they won more races.

In the repair shop, creativity can pay off as well. Every large garage has a "specialist" who has figured out the fastest way to do an operation and has the special tools to do it with. In my case, I have a specially-filed piece of sheet metal that sneaks in around the armrest of a Volvo and enables me to pop the door handles right off. It took me 45 minutes to do the first handle—now it takes 45 seconds each time. An-

other guy has an offset ½ in. wrench cut in half and welded to a long screwdriver. He claims it will put fan bolts in faster and safer than any other tool. I can't vouch for the speed, but he has the unscarred knuckles to prove he doesn't put his hand in against the radiator fins.

Most mechanics have some favorite tool that has been brutally torched, bent, cut and pounded into a mess (or so it seems). They've done it because it saves them time and money. Next time you see one of these monstrosities, don't ask where they got it, ask how much money it's made and how much time has been saved.

Leonard Spooner
Orchard St. Automotive
San Diego, CA

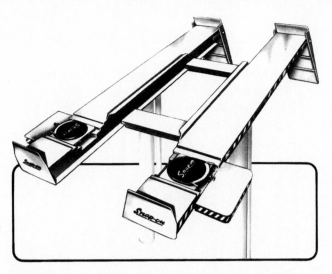

FIGURE 2-35 Hydraulic floor lift. (Snap-on Tools Corporation)

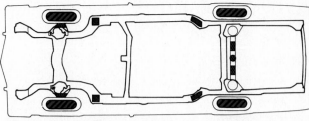

☑Drive on hoist   ▩ Twin post   ▦ Frame engaging
                    suspension hoist   hoist

Be sure supports do not damage brake lines, fuel lines, parking brake cable, or exhaust system.

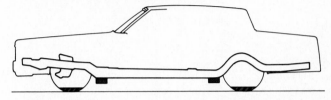

FIGURE 2-36 Typical lift points. (Buick Motor Division, GMC)

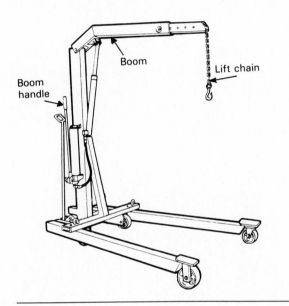

Boom

Lift chain

Boom handle

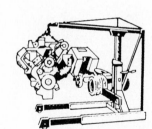

FIGURE 2-37 Hydraulic engine hoist.

TRADE TERMS

Box Wrench
Combination Wrench
Double-cut File
Extentions
Impact Wrench
Jack Stand
Metric System
Nutdriver

Open-end Wrench
Phillips Screwdriver
Ratchet and Socket
Single-cut File
Taps and Dies
Torque Wrench
United States Customary

REVIEW QUESTIONS

1. What does the abbreviation *mm* mean?
2. What is the metric system?
3. When must you wear safety glasses?
4. Name three types of wrenches.
5. Ratchet sizes are determined by the length of any one side of their drives. What three drive sizes are available?

6. Name the four types of torque wrenches.
7. Describe the difference between a blade and a Phillips screwdriver.
8. Name three types of pliers.
9. Name the various types of hammers and mallets used in the auto shop.
10. Identify the types of tools used to cut materials.

3

Test Equipment

INTRODUCTION

Back in the "good ol' days," if something were wrong with your car, a mechanic would "give a listen" and tell you what the problem was and would probably be correct 95% of the time. Many mechanics can still do a pretty good job of telling what's going on just by listening, but even the best must turn to test equipment to diagnose many problems.

This chapter introduces you to some diagnostic test equipment. Become as familiar as possible with test equipment and the theory behind them. Without this knowledge, you'll be handicapped when you want to tune an engine, test a particular circuit, discover why the engine misses under load, or determine the reason for excessive fuel consumption. These are only some of the problems you can diagnose by using diagnostic test equipment.

MULTIMETER

A *multimeter* tests a variety of electrical functions (Figure 3-1). It identifies problems in the electrical system. Measurements often require a different meter setting, or a different meter, and a different way of connecting the meter's test leads or wires.

OBJECTIVES

When you have completed this chapter, you should be able to

- Identify the major kinds of testing equipment used by mechanics
- List the functions that the different kinds of equipment can test and the problems they can diagnose
- Know how to operate these testing tools
- Know what part computers play in testing and in diagnosis

FIGURE 3-2   Digital meter. (Kent Moore Tools)

The measurement made by the meter can be displayed in several ways. The most common type of meter is the dial and needle (or analog) type. Several curved scales and a moving needle indicate measurements. The disadvantage of this type of meter is the difficulty of reading the right scale, especially if the needle is vibrating.

Digital multimeters are becoming more common (Figure 3-2). The measurements are displayed as numbers, like the figures on a calculator. The advantages of these meters are that they are more accurate and you can read them more easily. Some digital meters are specifically designed for ignition service and provide settings marked for specific ignition tests.

Of course each electrical function, such as volts, ohms, and amps (Chapter 19 explains these terms and

how they relate to each other), has a special tester. These special testers usually test only one or two functions (Figure 3-3).

The various types of meters and the properties they measure include the following:

□ **Voltmeters** measure voltage.
□ **Ohmmeters** measure resistance.
□ **Ammeters** measure current.

Each type of meter must be set for the proper measurement and then connected properly. If you make the wrong setting or connections, you might damage the meter or get an incorrect measurement. Be sure to observe the following guidelines when connecting meters.

Normally, hook up voltmeters in parallel with the power on—the positive lead toward the battery positive side. Hook up ohmmeters with the power off, across a component that is disconnected from the cir-

FIGURE 3-1   Multimeters. (Snap-on Tools Corporation)

FIGURE 3-3   Special tester.

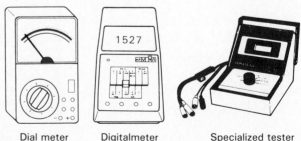

Dial meter   Digitalmeter   Specialized tester

cuit. Always connect ammeters in series with the circuit and before branches split from the circuit. Always connect the ammeter before turning the ignition switch on.

VOLTMETER

Hook up *voltmeters* in parallel where you want to measure voltage. Power must be on, and the circuit must be complete.

Voltage Drop Test

Place the positive (or red) lead of the voltmeter on the side of the circuit coming from the battery positive terminal. Place the negative (black) lead on the other side of the part you are testing. The wire from this side should lead to a ground or other parts. Be sure the meter is on the proper scale before connecting the leads.

In this test, you are measuring how much voltage is used to operate that part in the circuit. If it is the only part, you should read battery voltage. If there are other parts in that circuit, you will read less than battery voltage (Figure 3-4).

Voltmeter Continuity Test

Voltmeters also test to see if a circuit is complete or has a break in it. Disconnect the plug or wire at the part you will be checking. Connect the positive lead of the meter to the disconnected wire coming from the battery positive terminal. Connect the negative lead directly to ground.

If voltage is present, the circuit is complete to the test point. This test is not a voltage test. It is called a continuity test. You will always have battery voltage (or close to it) if the circuit is complete (Figure 3-5).

Voltmeter Starting Circuit Test

To make a starting circuit test, connect the positive voltmeter lead to the positive battery terminal. Connect

---

FIGURE 3-4 Measuring a voltage drop across a part.

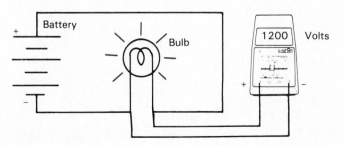

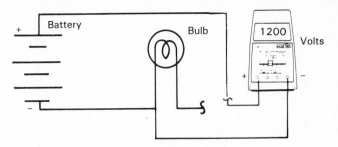

FIGURE 3-5 Voltmeter continuity test.

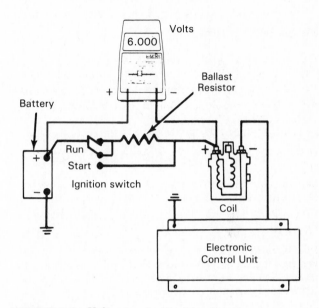

FIGURE 3-6 Voltmeter starting circuit test.

---

the negative voltmeter lead to the positive coil terminal (Figure 3-6). With the ignition switch off, no voltage is supplied to the ignition coil, and no reading will occur on the voltmeter. During starting, the starting controls of the ignition switch bypass the ballast resistor, so its resistance is nearly zero. Because the resistance is nearly zero, the voltage drop across it is also nearly zero. With the ignition switch on and the engine running, the voltmeter reads the voltage drop across the ballast resistor. The meter should read 5–8 V. If any voltmeter reading is not as specified in the service manual, check and repair, if necessary, the battery, battery cables, connections, or starter until readings are as specified.

OHMMETER

Ohmmeters measure the resistance in the circuit. You can either test a single part or the entire circuit, though normally only a part is measured in ignition testing.

Before using an ohmmeter, you must *zero* the meter to get an accurate reading. The meter is zeroed by simply putting the two leads together and adjusting the meter to read 0 Ω.

The first thing to remember when using an ohmmeter is that the power must be off. Second, you must disconnect the part being tested from the circuit on at least one side.

Resistance Test

To measure resistance, disconnect the circuit on either side of the part being tested. Be sure the power is off. Connect one lead of the ohmmeter to one side of the part and the other lead to the other side. Read the resistance on the meter (Figure 3-7).

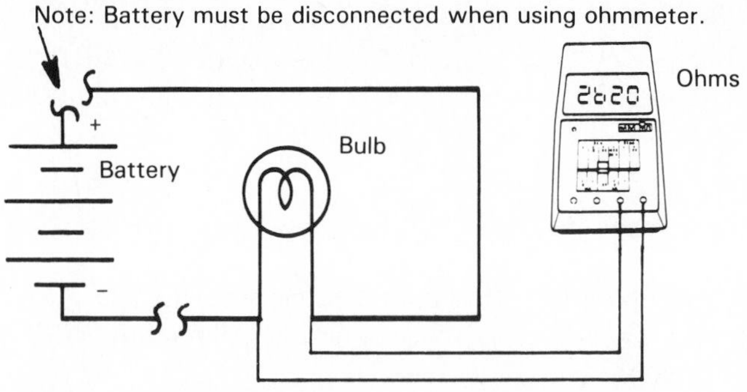

Continuity Test

Like the voltmeter, the ohmmeter can also check continuity. Remove power at the battery by disconnecting

Note: Battery must be disconnected when using ohmmeter.

FIGURE 3-7 Measuring resistance with an ohmmeter.

the positive battery cable. Connect one side of the ohmmeter to the positive battery cable. Connect the other lead to ground. If the circuit is complete, the ohmmeter reading will show low resistance. If there

---

HAVE TEST EQUIPMENT, WILL TRAVEL

Everybody's doing it. The federal government, most car companies, a half-dozen enthusiast magazines, and various other publications offer up whole blizzards of test results, and it's easy to assume that one set of numbers is as good as another. This could hardly be further from the truth, for there is tremendous variation in the scope and precision of automobile testing.

We do our utmost to ensure that our test procedures deliver the most complete and precise performance figures possible. In case you were wondering, here's how we get them.

The foundation of our precision is a highly sophisticated, fifth-wheel system, and the heart of our fifth-wheel equipment is a microprocessor—a compact but extremely powerful computer—that can manipulate time, speed, and distance information in several ways. The fifth wheel itself generates a very precise distance signal in the form of exactly 100 electrical impulses for each foot traveled; the microprocessor measures distance by counting these impulses.

Speed is simply distance per unit of time, so the microprocessor can readily compute speed by comparing the number of distance pulses with a time signal available from an internal, crystal-controlled clock, in which each second is subdivided into one million parts. Successive speed calculations are compared to determine acceleration.

The beauty of computer control is its flexibility. With the flip of a switch, the "black box" on the passenger seat changes the way it manipulates the data to match the test being performed. For acceleration, it holds time and distance counters at zero until the very instant the car begins to move; from that point, the times to the various speeds and distances are recorded. Internal counters can also be manually switched on at any point to measure passing times and distances. During brake testing, a pressure switch on the brake pedal conveys the moment of initiation to the computer.

As these tests proceed, a built-in printer records the results on paper tape. Having this feedback available almost immediately is a tremendous advantage because it allows the tester to experiment with and compare the results of different driving techniques; the goal in every test is to measure the *best* the car can do, whether it's the quickest possible zero-to-sixty time or the shortest possible stopping distance for that particular model. A windshield-mounted display instantaneously provides the tester with additional information (time, speed, distance, acceleration) but no hard copy of the displayed data.

Just like the auto industry, we've gone through several downsizing programs, and now our 60 lb of equipment fits into one 23-by-21-by-11-in. Cycolac shipping case. Since a container can be

no smaller than its largest burden, the fifth wheel itself has been the focus of our downsizing attention. The present unit consists of a 20-in. bicycle tire mounted on a lightened cast-aluminum rim. A fabricated aluminum fork supports the wheel's bearings and the distance-measuring apparatus. This fork, in turn, trails from a steel-and-aluminum telescoping boom, which is bolted to a universal joint welded to a tripod that permits the camber of the wheel to be adjusted. A 10-in. suction cup attaches the entire fifth-wheel assembly to the side of the test car. Although seemingly a precarious mount, the suction cup has withstood the rigors of 180 mph, as dished out by a Le Mans-winning Kremer K3 Porsche. Its convenience of attachment and removal is unsurpassed by any bumper-mount scheme we've seen, and the side-mounting design keeps the wheel within the driver's outside mirror.

All this equipment nestles snugly in our case alongside our weather-measurement apparatus, sound-level testing components, tape measure, stopwatch, and several carefully selected tools, ever ready and waiting to be taken to the Chrysler Proving Grounds in Michigan, Orange County International Raceway in California, or any other flat piece of real estate.

Reprinted from Car and Driver, April 1982 © 1982 CBS Magazine. All rights reserved.

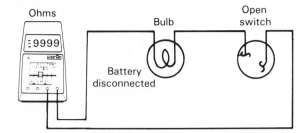

FIGURE 3-8   Ohmmeter continuity test.

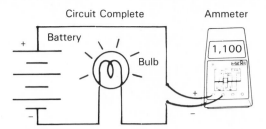

FIGURE 3-9   Measuring current flow with an ammeter.

is a break in the circuit, the ohmmeter will read infinity (Figure 3-8).

AMMETER

Always connect ammeters in series with the circuit you are testing. *Ammeters* measure current flowing through the circuit. If you are measuring a parallel circuit, connect the meter before the branches split, or you will only be measuring the current in the branch where the meter is (Figure 3-9).

To connect an ammeter, turn off power and disconnect the circuit at the proper point. Place the positive ammeter lead to the side of the circuit coming from the battery positive terminal. Place the negative lead on the side going toward ground. Make sure the meter is on the proper setting. Turn on power and measure amps. Be careful: If the meter needle tries to move to the left, quickly disconnect the power. Reverse the leads and retest.

TEST LIGHT

A **test light** has two wires hooked to a filament or bulb. If you touch one wire to one terminal of the battery and the other wire to the other terminal, current will flow through the wires to light the bulb. The test light will also light when you touch one wire to the battery terminal (positive) that is not connected to the engine or other metal parts of the vehicle, and touch the other wire to any metal part that is connected to the battery (Figure 3-10). The term used for all these metal parts hooked to one side of the battery is *ground* (negative).

TACHOMETER

The **tachometer** measures the revolutions per minute (rpm) of an engine crankshaft (Figure 3-11). One revolution is a complete turn of the crankshaft. As the engine idles, it will usually run at about 600–1000 rpm. Most cars have a maximum range of 4000–6000 rpm.

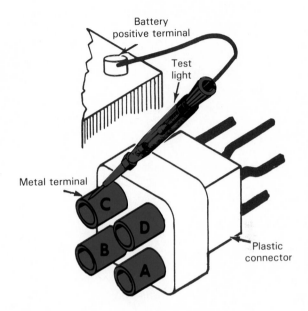

FIGURE 3-10   Test light continuity testing.

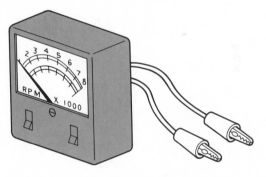

FIGURE 3-11   Tachometer.

Two types of tachometers are used with the automobile engine. One style is mechanical, and one is electronic. Mechanical tachs are not as popular as they once were because they are noisy and expensive and require lubrication.

The electronic tachometer is the most versatile. Tachometers measure rpm in different ways. The standard tachometer for gas engines senses the firing pulses sent to the spark plugs by the distributor. Other tachometers for gas engines have a photoelectric pickup

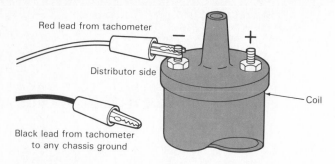

FIGURE 3-12 Tach/dwell meter connections.

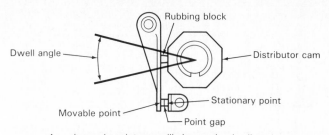

Any change in point gap will change the dwell angle

FIGURE 3-14 Dwell angle.

or a magnetic pickup. Diesel engines use a special pickup on the alternator, photoelectric cell, magnetic pickup, or fuel line sensor to drive the tachometer.

Using a Tachometer

To hook up a standard tachometer on a point-type ignition system, connect the two probes, a red lead and a black lead. Connect the red lead to the negative side, or point side, of the coil. Connect the black lead to any ground (Figure 3-12). Read the rpm from the scale.

TACH/DWELL METER

The tach/dwell meter shows the engine rpm and the dwell, measured in degrees of cam rotation while the points are closed (Figure 3-13). This is called the **dwell**

FIGURE 3-13 Tach/dwell meter. (Snap-on Tools Corporation)

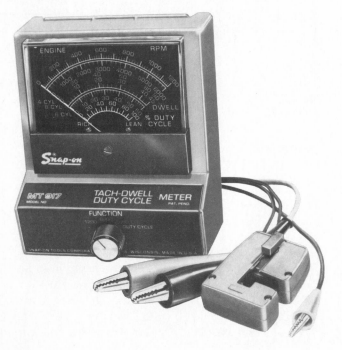

angle. Figure 3-14 shows a set of points and a distributor cam. The rotation of the cam opens and closes the points. How long the points stay closed is determined by how close the rubbing block is to the distributor shaft cam. Factory specifications will tell you what this dwell angle should be.

Using the Tach/Dwell Meter

Because the dwell meter and tachometer are essentially one unit, the dwell meter connects the same way as the tachometer does. Connect the red lead to the negative side of the coil and the black lead to ground (see Figure 3-12). Then read the dwell from the scale. To change the dwell, adjust the point gap closer to or farther away from the stationary point as needed.

Electronic ignition systems do not need to be set with a dwell meter. In these systems solid-state electronic devices are used in place of points. These electronic devices last longer and are more accurate than point ignition systems.

Electronic Ignition Systems

Electronic ignition system checks are done by measuring the input and output signals of the solid-state devices. These signals are expressed in volts, ohms, and amperes.

For example, the Ford Dura-Spark II ignition system has two basic parts that may be tested. They are the electronic control module and the distributor (Figure 3-15).

Electronic Control Module

Each regular Dura-Spark II module has six wires (a two-wire and a four-wire connector). Modules with dual mode timing have nine wires. The red and white wires are the ignition feed wires—the white circuit is for cranking and the red circuit for operation after the engine begins to run. The red wire circuit contains a 1.1-Ω wire resistor. The green wire turns the current to the primary circuit of the ignition coil off and on. The orange and purple wires transmit signals to the

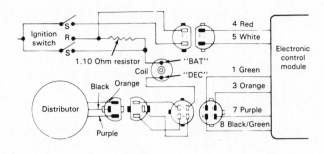

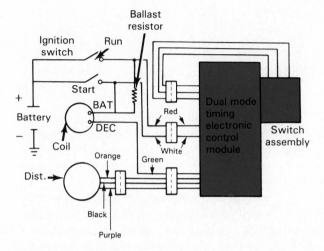

FIGURE 3-15   Ford Dura-Spark II ignition system. (Ford Motor Company)

module from the armature and stator in the distributor. The black wire is used to ground the distributor. The module is on whenever the ignition switch is in the "on" or "start" position.

Distributor

An armature, with the same number of teeth as the engine has cylinders, turns with the distributor shaft. A stator (pickup coil) contains a permanent magnet, causing a magnetic field around the stator. As the teeth of the armature pass the stator, the magnetic field builds and collapses, causing a signal to be sent to the electronic control module. This type of ignition system can be checked to be sure the signals to the control module are okay. All voltages and resistances in the circuit should be measured as well.

The testing procedures for electronic ignition systems are much more complicated than for point ignition systems. Most test procedures use the multimeter and require very exact readouts. Check the procedures specified by the manufacturer for testing any electronic ignition system. They will help you check voltage, pickup coil resistance, and the condition of the wiring.

OSCILLOSCOPE

The **oscilloscope** as shown in Figure 3-16, is probably the most effective and complete diagnostic piece of equipment found in the modern automotive repair shop. With it, you can "see" inside the engine. It displays voltage and time (Figure 3-17), indicating the condition of the alternator, coil, condenser, and all electronic ignition system components. It can also tell cylinder balance, carburetor balance, distributor faults, and resistance or leakage within the spark plugs. The primary use of the scope is to study the primary and secondary ignition circuits (Figures 3-18 and 3-19). Finally, it can do all of the jobs of the meters described thus far.

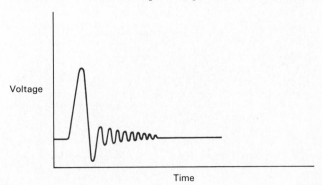

FIGURE 3-16   Oscilloscope. (Snap-on Tools Corporation)

FIGURE 3-17   Oscilloscope voltage and time functions.

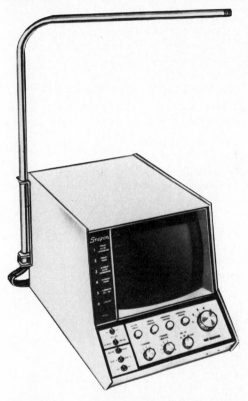

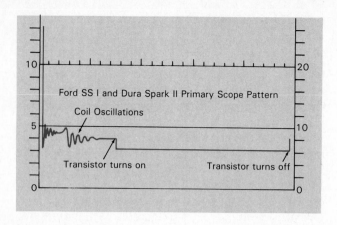

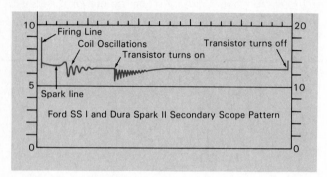

FIGURE 3-18   Typical Dura-Spark ignition patterns. (Courtesy of Sun Electric Corporation)

FIGURE 3-19   GM high-energy ignition oscilloscope patterns. (Courtesy of Sun Electric Corporation)

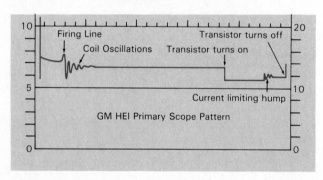

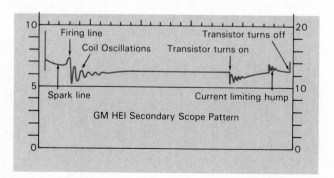

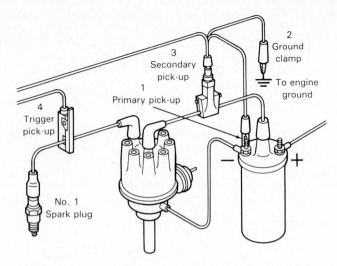

FIGURE 3-20   Oscilloscope hookup.

To fully understand and learn the use of the oscilloscope, you must know the ignition system you are working on and what the patterns mean. The specific information is in repair manuals and the oscilloscope's manufacturer manuals.

The hookup of an oscilloscope uses a variety of clamp-type connectors (Figure 3-20). When the engine is running, the oscilloscope shows patterns that a trained eye can interpret to "see" what's going on with the particular part or parts being diagnosed.

ANALYZERS

State-of-the-art automotive analyzers systems are complete engine and electrical testers. They have built-in oscilloscopes, multimeters, gas analyzers and even a printer that prints out the results of the tests for reference.

TIMING LIGHT

The **timing light** is a strobe light that *freezes* crank pulley rotation (Figure 3-21). If set up correctly, the crank pulley will appear not to rotate. This freezing of rotation is a result of the pulse of light emitted by the timing light happening at the same spot on the crank pulley. Correct ignition timing causes the spark plug to fire when the pistons are a specified number of degrees before top dead center (BTDC).

Using the Timing Light

The timing light hookup for most cars, as shown in Figure 3-22, is simple. The black lead clamps to ground, the red lead clamps to the distributor side of the coil,

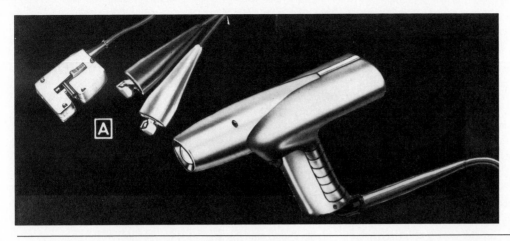

FIGURE 3-21 Timing light.
(Snap-on Tools Corporation)

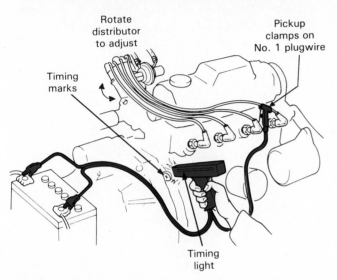

FIGURE 3-22 Timing light hookup. (American Motor Honda Corporation, Inc.)

and the induction pickup snaps on the No. 1 spark plug wire.

The steps in timing most cars are the following:

1. Look up the ignition specifications in a manual.
2. Remove and plug the distributor vacuum hose.
3. Loosen the distributor hold-down bolt.
4. Hook up the timing light.
5. Start the engine.
6. Adjust timing to the specs by tuning the distributor (Figure 3-23).
7. Tighten the distributor hold-down bolt.
8. Check timing once again.
9. Shut off the engine, remove the timing light, and reconnect the distributor vacuum hose.

Many newer cars cannot be adjusted in this manner. Ford cars with EEC systems and GM cars with the 1977 MISAR are adjusted at the crank pulley. Some

FIGURE 3-23 Index marks on the crank pulley and timing cover. (Ford Motor Company)

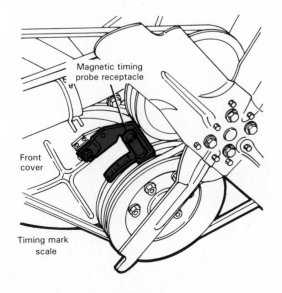

SIX-CYLINDER

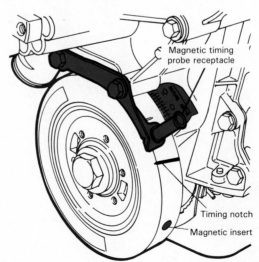

EIGHT-CYLINDER

1984 and newer cars have no distributor and no timing adjustment at all. Be sure to check a shop manual for proper timing procedures.

COMPRESSION GAUGE

The **compression gauge** tests how much pressure in pounds per square inch (psi), or in kilopascals (kPa) in metric, a cylinder will produce. Figure 3-24 shows two types of compression gauges. Hold the cone type in the spark plug hole, or turn the screw type into the spark plug hole.

The compression gauge can do two tests, the dry test and the wet test. The results of doing these two tests will tell the condition of the piston rings, the cylinders, and the valves.

Dry Compression Test

A normal engine will produce a certain amount of pressure in each cylinder. This pressure should be about the same in all cylinders. If this pressure is not about the same, then the engine should be repaired. The steps in doing the dry test are the following:

1. Look in the manual for the compression specifications for the engine.
2. Run the engine until it is warm, then turn the ignition off.
3. Clean around the spark plugs and remove them.
4. Disconnect the coil/distributor lead.
5. Open the throttle all the way.
6. Screw the compression gauge into the No. 1 cylinder.
7. Crank the engine, with the starter, four to six compression pulses (8–12 engine revolutions).

FIGURE 3-24 Compression gauges. (Snap-on Tools Corporation)

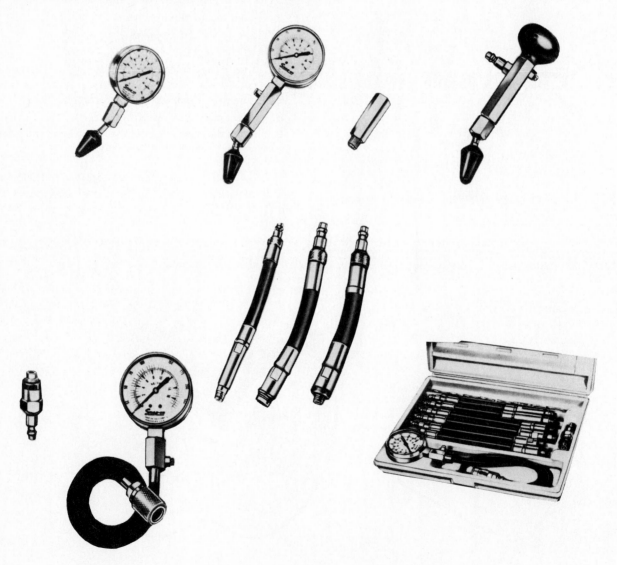

8. Read the pressure on the gauge and write the number down along with the cylinder number, for example, #1—150 psi.

9. Repeat the compression test on all cylinders. If any readings are low, then complete the wet compression test.

Wet Compression Test

The wet compression test is a way to remove the influence of the rings, pistons, and cylinders from the compression test. After completing the dry test, squirt a teaspoon or so of oil into the spark plug holes to seal the piston rings for a short time. Repeat the steps for the dry test. If a cylinder's compression is greater than on the dry test, air is leaking around worn or damaged piston rings. If the reading on the dry test was low and the reading on the compression gauge does not increase after the wet test, then valves, valve lifters, or camshaft lobes are worn or damaged.

Any low reading of cylinder compression indicates worn or damaged parts. *Caution*: Do not perform the wet test on any diesel engine. The higher compression in a diesel may cause engine damage or injury to the mechanic.

VACUUM GAUGE

The **vacuum gauge** (Figure 3-25) measures manifold vacuum. From this measurement you can determine if there are vacuum leaks or exhaust restrictions in the intake manifold and exhaust system, the condition of the valves and valve guides, whether the timing of the valves is accurate, and a host of other possible problems.

Using the Vacuum Gauge

To use the vacuum gauge, hook its hose to either the base of the carburetor or directly into the intake manifold at a convenient vacuum source. Read the measurement on the face of the gauge. Gauge readings can indicate many problems in an engine. Figure 3-26 shows some of the typical problems that the vacuum gauge can help identify.

FIGURE 3-25   Vacuum gauge face.

DYNAMOMETER

The largest piece of test equipment is the **dynamometer.** As shown in Figure 3-27, the car must be driven onto rollers. Running the drive wheels against the rollers tells the relative horsepower of the car. Adjustments can be made to the engine, then it is possible to see the change in relative horsepower and rpm. This is probably the most efficient way to tune an engine. Every adjustment in carburetion emission and timing is immediately seen as a change in relative horsepower.

FIGURE 3-26   Typical vacuum gauge readings.

With motor at idling speed vacuum pointer should hold steady between 15 and 21.

With motor at idling speed dropping back of vacuum pointer indicates sticky valves.

With motor at idling speed floating motion right and left of vacuum pointer indicates carburetor too rich or too lean.

With motor at idling speed low reading of vacuum pointer indicates late timing or intake manifold air leak.

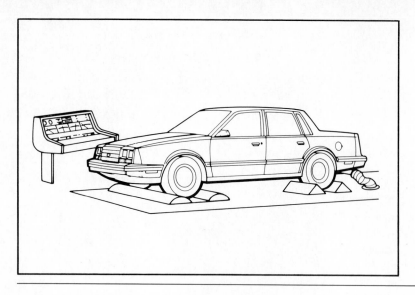

FIGURE 3-27 Dynamometer.

EXHAUST GAS ANALYZER

Since the early 1960s, emissions of exhaust gases (carbon monoxide, hydrocarbons, and oxides of nitrogen) have been limited by law. Today, all cars must be checked to be sure their emissions do not exceed federal and state limits. **Exhaust gas analyzers** have been developed to perform these tests. By inserting a *sniffer*

in the tail pipe of the vehicle, the analyzer can determine emission levels (Figure 3-28). *Three-gas* testers measure hydrocarbons (HC), carbon monoxide (CO), and carbon dioxide (CO_2). Some *four-gas* models can measure unburned oxygen (O_2) as well.

Engines in 1984 cars burn cleaner than a cigarette. Table 3-1 presents the federal allowable HC and CO emissions.

FIGURE 3-28 Emission tester.

TABLE 3-1 Approximate Federal Emission Standards

	MODEL YEAR (ENGINE AT IDLE)					
	1983–79	*1978–75*	*1974–73*	*1972–70*	*1969–68*	*1967*
Hydrocarbon (HC)	50 ppm	50–100 ppm	100–200 ppm	150–250 ppm	200–300 ppm	300–500 ppm
Carbon monoxide (CO)	0.0–0.5%	0.5–1.0%	1.0–1.5%	1.5–2.0%	2.0–2.5%	2.5–3.0%

Note: ppm = parts per million.

COMPUTERS

The future of testing is turning rapidly to computers. Look for increased *on-board* computers, in the form of small integrated circuits, to tell drivers and mechanics what problems are occurring. New cars have access plugs that mechanics can plug into their computers. All tests discussed in this chapter are performed using this one instrument. Previously, oscilloscope patterns had to be read by an expert. Now computers print out descriptions of the problem. Great things are projected for the future.

Ammeter
Compression Gauge
Digital Multimeter
Dwell Angle
Dynamometer
Exhaust Gas Analyzer
Ohmmeter

Oscilloscope
Tachometer
Test Light
Timing Light
Vacuum Gauge
Voltmeter

REVIEW QUESTIONS

1. Explain the functions of a multimeter.
2. Explain the voltage drop test.
3. How do you check for voltage continuity?
4. Can a volt/ohmmeter be used as a continuity tester? How?
5. What kind of vacuum does a vacuum gauge measure?
6. Name four things a vacuum gauge can test for.

7. What does an oscilloscope display?
8. What does a tachometer measure?
9. What is dwell?
10. Name three gases checked during an emissions test.
11. What two tests can be made with a compression gauge?

4

Measuring

INTRODUCTION

Throughout your career as a mechanic you will be making measurements and working with figures. You will need to answer questions like "Do you need two ⅜-in. bolts?" or "How wide should the spark plug gap be?" You will hear statements like "The customer has a 289 cubic in. engine" or "The cylinder walls have an 0.004-in. taper."

You'll be expected to know how to make measurements such as these, how to use the instruments that make them, and how to apply the results. This chapter introduces measuring tools and further discusses systems of linear and temperature measurement. Appendix 2 gives additional information about weight, force, and volume measurement.

MEASUREMENTS

One of the most important areas of study in automechanics is the area of measurement. All of your troubleshooting and repair work will be based on measurements.

OBJECTIVES

When you have completed this chapter, you should be able to

- Identify the major measuring tools used by mechanics
- Explain what these tools measure and how to use them
- Understand what different measurements mean in both United States customary and metric measurement systems

◄ First edge: 100ths.
Front side
◄ Second edge: 64ths.
◄ Fourth edge: 32nds.
Reverse side
◄ Third edge: 16ths.

FIGURE 4-1 Scale reading (hundredths of an inch). (L. S. Starrett Company)

United States Customary

In the United States, the current standard of measurement is the **United States customary** system. Distance is measured by the foot. For example, 12 in. equals a foot, 3 ft. equal a yard, and so on, with all other dimensions broken down into feet or fractions of the foot. (See Appendix 2 for tables of these units of measurement.)

For most of your life you've dealt with fractions of an inch: ¹⁄₆₄, ¹⁄₃₂, ¹⁄₁₆, ¹⁄₈, and ¹⁄₄. Another division of the inch is the *decimal* division. Here, the basis of the inch is tenths. The inch is divided into 10 parts, each a tenth of an inch. They are written as 0.1, 0.2, 0.3, and so on and read as *one tenth*, *two tenths*, and *three tenths*. You would read 2.4 in. as "two and four-tenths inches."

Tenths of an inch are further divided 10 more times into hundredths of an inch. These divisions are written as 0.01, 0.02, 0.03, and so on and are read as *one hundredth*, *two hundredths*, and *three hundredths* (Figure 4-1). The division after hundredths is thousandths and is written as 0.001, 0.002, and so on. The next division is ten-thousandths and is written as 0.0001, 0.0002, and so on.

To review this decimal division, remember that three tenths of an inch is written 0.3, twenty-four hundredths is 0.24, and thirty-four thousandths is 0.034.

Metrics

Most of the rest of the world uses a system called **metric** or the **International System of Units (SI).** In this system, as you learned in Chapter 2, the basic unit of length is the **meter,** a measurement a little over 1 yd (39.37 in.). The meter is also divided into units of 10. The first division (tenths) is called the *decimeter* or dm. You'll seldom use this measurement. The second division, comparable to hundredths, is the **centimeter** or cm. The measurement most frequently used in the automotive industry is the **millimeter** or

mm (Figure 4-2). Appendix 2 has many U.S./metric tables.

You will hear these measurements used to describe things such as engine displacement (750-cc engine means 750 cubic centimeters), wrench sizes (a 14-millimeter wrench is fourteen thousandths of a meter and written 14 mm), or possibly a bolt size (#8 mm, #10 mm).

MEASURING TOOLS

An auto mechanic uses a number of measuring tools. These tools range from a simple rule to a micrometer. Tools needed in the automotive industry are in both U.S. customary and metric.

Rule

A measuring tool used to measure a length of something is called a rule or ruler (Figure 4-3). Rulers are available in U.S. customary, metric, and combined U.S./metric. The small 6- and 12-in. rules are usually marked on one edge in fractions and on the other edge in decimals. Some rules may also be marked in millimeters. Rules do a variety of jobs. Figure 4-4 shows a special steel rule holder holding a small rule to measure a valve seat width.

Feeler Gauge

The **feeler gauge** measures very small openings such as the spark plug gap or breaker point gap. Figure 4-5 shows two types of feeler gauges, the standard and the go-no go gauge. Go-no go gauges have a built-in tolerance to help the mechanic decide if the gap being measured is within specifications.

Feeler gauges also come in a variety of shapes and sizes. Figure 4-6 shows some of the gauges used to check spark plug gap openings. Each of these gauges is stamped from metal of an exact thickness, and their thickness is marked on them in thousandths or millimeters. Their thickness, then, is their measurement. You insert one at a time into a gap (breaker points or spark plug). When you find the gauge that just

Decimal and Metric Equivalents

Fractions	Decimal In.	Metric mm.	Fractions	Decimal In.	Metric mm.
1/64	.015625	.397	33/64	.515625	13.097
1/32	.03125	.794	17/32	.53125	13.494
3/64	.046875	1.191	35/64	.546875	13.891
1/16	.0625	1.588	9/16	.5625	14.288
5/64	.078125	1.984	37/64	.578125	14.684
3/32	.09375	2.381	19/32	.59375	15.081
7/64	.109375	2.778	39/64	.609375	15.478
1/8	.125	3.175	5/8	.625	15.875
9/64	.140625	3.572	41/64	.640625	16.272
5/32	.15625	3.969	21/32	.65625	16.669
11/64	.171875	4.366	43/64	.671875	17.066
3/16	.1875	4.763	11/16	.6875	17.463
13/64	.203125	5.159	45/64	.703125	17.859
7/32	.21875	5.556	23/32	.71875	18.256
15/64	.234375	5.953	47/64	.734375	18.653
1/4	.250	6.35	3/4	.750	19.05
17/64	.265625	6.747	49/64	.765625	19.447
9/32	.28125	7.144	25/32	.78125	19.844
19/64	.296875	7.54	51/64	.796875	20.241
5/16	.3125	7.938	13/16	.8125	20.638
21/64	.328125	8.334	53/64	.828125	21.034
11/32	.34375	8.731	27/32	.84375	21.431
23/64	.359375	9.128	55/64	.859375	21.828
3/8	.375	9.525	7/8	.875	22.225
25/64	.390625	9.922	57/64	.890625	22.622
13/32	.40625	10.319	29/32	.90625	23.019
27/64	.421875	10.716	59/64	.921875	23.416
7/16	.4375	11.113	15/16	.9375	23.813
29/64	.453125	11.509	61/64	.953125	24.209
15/32	.46875	11.906	31/32	.96875	24.606
31/64	.484375	12.303	63/64	.984375	25.003
1/2	.500	12.7	1	1.00	25.4

FIGURE 4-2   Conversion chart.

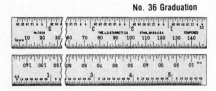

No. 36 Graduation

◄ First edge: 32nds.
Front side
◄ Second edge: ½ mm
◄ Fourth edge: mm
Reverse side
◄ Third edge: 64ths.

FIGURE 4-3   Combination U.S. customary/metric rule. (L. S. Starrett Company)

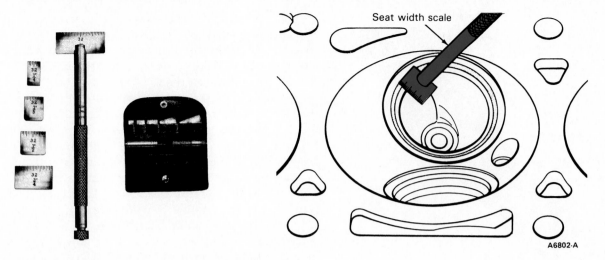

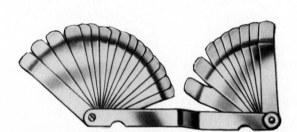

FIGURE 4-4   Using a special rule. (Ford Motor Company)

FIGURE 4-5   Feeler gauges. (Snap-on Tools Corporation)

FIGURE 4-6   Spark plug gap gauges. (Snap-on Tools Corporation)

touches both sides of the gap, you know how wide the gap is by reading the number on the gauge.

Another example of when a mechanic uses feeler gauges is during the valve/tappet clearance check. As Figure 4-7 shows, insert the feeler gauge between the valve and the rocker arm to check the clearance.

Micrometers

Micrometers (commonly called *mikes*) are measuring tools that very accurately measure a given width or depth. Figure 4-8 shows the parts of a micrometer that makes outside measurements.

FIGURE 4-7   Using a feeler gauge to check tappet clearance. (Ford Motor Company)

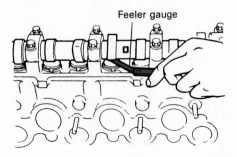

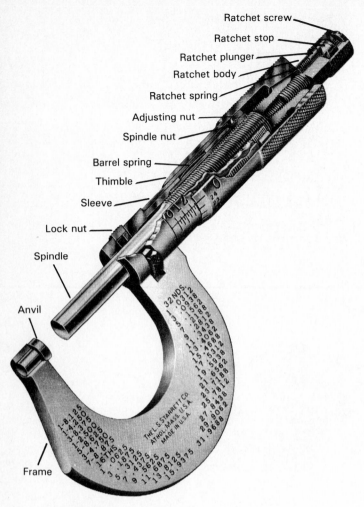

FIGURE 4-8   Outside micrometer. (L. S. Starrett Company)

Using a Micrometer

To use the micrometer, place the object being measured between the *anvil* and *spindle*. Rotate the *thimble*, moving the spindle to clamp the object. Read the width of the object on the *sleeve*.

Figure 4-9A shows how to read a micrometer in thousandths. Along the sleeve are numbers from 0 through 1, 2, 3, and so on. Between each number

FIGURE 4-9A   How to read a micrometer.

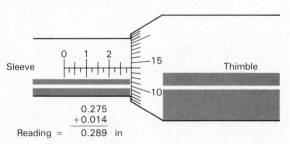

are four divisions. Each division represents 0.025 in. As you turn the thimble on its threaded drive, it either covers or uncovers the numbers and their divisions. Along the thimble are numbers from 0 through 9 with five divisions between them.

To read the scale, begin with the numbers on the sleeve. They read 0.0, 0.025, 0.050, 0.075, 0.100, 0.125, 0.150, and so on, up to 1.000. The sleeve, in Figure 4-9A, reads 0.275. Next, read the numbers on the thimble. These numbers represent units of 0.001, ranging from 0.000 to 0.024. The example in Figure 4-9A shows the thimble at 0.014 in. To get the final reading, add the reading from the sleeve (0.275 in.) to the reading on the thimble (0.014 in.). The reading is 0.289 in. An easy way to remember how to read a mike is to think of the numbers on the sleeve as dollars, the divisions on the sleeve as quarters, and the units on the thimble as pennies. Add them all up and put a decimal point in front of the number instead of a dollar sign.

Read a metric micrometer in a similar way, but instead of thousandths, you use millimeters. The sleeve is divided into millimeters (1.0) with every fifth millimeter marked (Figure 4-9B). The total distance a standard metric micrometer will read is 25 mm.

Outside Micrometer

The standard micrometer is the outside micrometer (Figure 4-8). It can measure anything that will fit between the anvil and spindle. Micrometers come in many different *frame* sizes. The standard sizes are 0–1, 0–2, 0–3 in., and so on in increments of 1 in. up to micrometer frame sizes that can measure very large objects.

FIGURE 4-9B   How to read a metric micrometer. (L. S. Starrett Company)

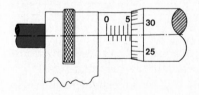

Reading:

Reading 5.78 mm	
5.00	Sleeve
0.50	Sleeve
0.28	Thimble
5.78 mm = reading	

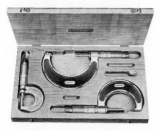

FIGURE 4-10A   0–4 in. micrometer set and storage case. (L. S. Starrett Company)

—Digital readout

FIGURE 4-10B   Digital outside metric micrometer (L. S. Starrett Company)

Remember to always store micrometers in a clean, dry, safe place such as the case shown in Figure 4-10A. Remember also that a micrometer is a delicate measuring tool. Handle it with great care.

The *digital* micrometer is a recent development. This micrometer has the regular micrometer scale, but it also has a digital readout of the numbers (Figure 4-10B).

Inside Micrometer

Inside micrometers (Figure 4-11) come with a micrometer body with a thimble, sleeve, and ratchet. Within the kit are an assortment of spindles of various lengths

FIGURE 4-11   Inside micrometer. (L. S. Starrett Company)

FIGURE 4-12   *Miking* the inside diameter. (L. S. Starrett Company)

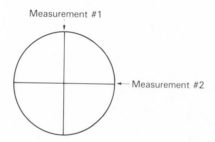

Measurement #1

Measurement #2

FIGURE 4-13   Measuring out-of-roundness.

to use in holes of different sizes. To use this instrument, select a spindle that will just accommodate the inside of a cylinder or a bore when it is threaded to the thimble and sleeve. Extend the thimble until the spindle touches one side of the cylinder and the thimble end touches the other (Figure 4-12). Read the measurement in the same way you read outside micrometers. When you measure a bore, it is good practice to take two or more measurements as a check for out-of-roundness (Figure 4-13).

Depth Micrometers and Depth Gauges

Depth micrometers (Figure 4-14) and **depth gauges** (Figure 4-15), as the names imply, measure the depth of an object. Depth micrometers are more accurate than depth gauges. Both the depth micrometer and the depth gauge can be used to measure the depth of a shoulder or hole (Figure 4-16).

There are also dial depth gauges (Figure 4-17). These dial depth gauges are useful in checking end play and runout on a large number of parts. Figure 4-18 identifies some of the uses of the dial depth gauge.

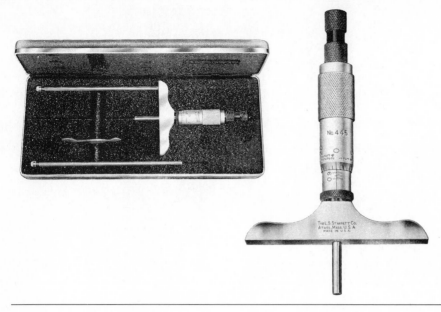

FIGURE 4-14 Depth micrometer. (L. S. Starrett Company)

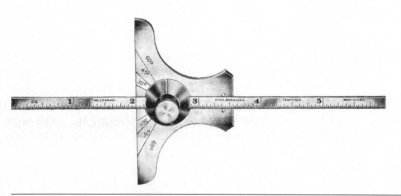

FIGURE 4-15 Combination depth and angle gauge. (L. S. Starrett Company)

FIGURE 4-16 Measuring the depth of a shoulder. (L. S. Starrett Company)

FIGURE 4-17 Dial depth gauges. (L. S. Starrett Company)

End play is how far something moves back and forth on its axis. Runout is a check for out-of-roundness or out-of-flatness.

Bore Gauges

Bore gauges (Figure 4-19) are used like an inside micrometer. Bore gauges measure bore taper, bore out-of-roundness, and scoring. To check for bore taper, insert the gauge and zero the dial indicator. Next slide the gauge down the bore. The taper in the bore will show on the dial indicator. Each engine has a maximum allowable bore taper before it must be rebored.

To check for out-of-roundness, instead of sliding the gauge up and down, turn the gauge in the bore. The dial indicator will show the amount of out-of-roundness either in 0.001 in. or in 0.001 mm. You can

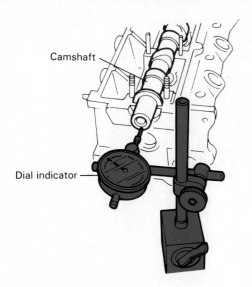

Camshaft

Dial indicator

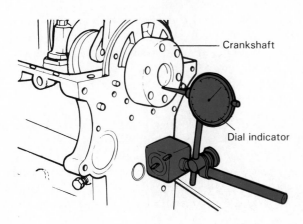

Crankshaft

Dial indicator

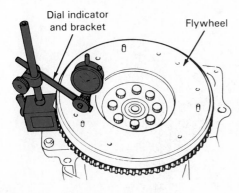

Dial indicator
and bracket

Flywheel

FIGURE 4-18 Checking end play and runout. (Ford Motor Company)

also check for a score or scratch with the bore gauge.

A second type of bore gauge is the out-of-roundness gauge (Figure 4-20). The out-of-roundness gauge is used for checking the roundness of various parts, such as the connecting rod bearings. Remember, always zero the dial indicator after you insert the gauge.

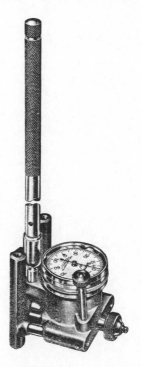

FIGURE 4-19 Bore gauge. (L. S. Starrett Company)

FIGURE 4-20 Out-of-roundness gauge. (L. S. Starrett Company)

Telescoping Gauges

Telescoping gauges (sometimes called snap gauges) are used to determine the size of a hole (Figure 4-21). The gauges do not measure. To use this tool, insert the telescope gauge into a hole and loosen the locking bolt on the end of the handle. A spring inside the gauge forces the plunger to telescope out. Then retighten the bolt on the end of the handle (Figure 4-22). Remove the gauge from the hole and use a micrometer to measure the gauge.

Small-Hole Gauges

Small-hole gauges determine small hole size (Figure 4-23). First you adjust the gauge by turning the knob on the end of the gauge until the gauge makes contact with the part (Figure 4-24). You then remove the gauge and mike it.

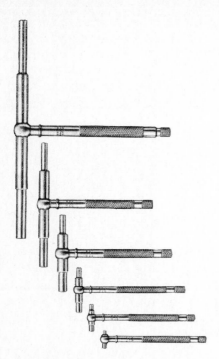

FIGURE 4-21   Telescoping gauges. (L. S. Starrett Company)

FIGURE 4-22   Using a telescope gauge. (L. S. Starrett Company)

FIGURE 4-23   Small-hole gauge. (L. S. Starrett Company)

Expanding guage

FIGURE 4-24   Using a small-hole gauge. (L. S. Starrett Company)

Calipers and Dividers

Use **calipers** to measure inside and outside diameters. Calipers are less accurate than micrometers. The calipers and dividers shown in Figure 4-25 are simple to use. First, take a measurement by adjusting the legs to fit the inside or outside measurement. Then lay the caliper over a rule, and you can read a fairly accurate measurement. Figure 4-26 illustrates how to check valve spring height with dividers.

Vernier Calipers   The *vernier caliper* can make inside, outside, or depth measurements (Figure 4-27). A U.S. customary or metric set of **scales** is built into the tool. These scales are called a vernier scale. A vernier scale is a stationary scale compared to a special movable scale, in this case the vernier bar to the vernier plate.

FIGURE 4-25   Calipers. (L. S. Starrett Company)

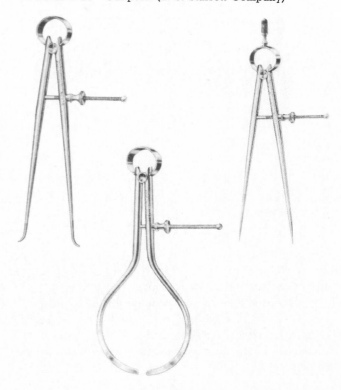

FIGURE 4-26 Checking valve spring height with dividers. (Ford Motor Company)

To read the vernier scale, first count how many inches and tenths (0.100) and twentieths (0.050) are between zero on the plate and zero on the bar. Figure 4-28 shows 1.050. Then match index lines. These will be the only lines that align perfectly on the plate and the bar. Figure 4-28 shows index lines (marked by a star) matching at 5 and 29. Add 1.050 and 0.029 for the reading of 1.079.

To read the metric side of the vernier scale, read the millimeters between zero on the bar and zero on the plate. Figure 4-28 shows 27.0 mm. Then match index lines. Figure 4-30 shows a match marked by a star at 42/48. Add 27.0 and 0.42 for the reading of 27.42 mm.

The Dial Caliper The dial caliper, like the vernier caliper, has a scale wrapped around a dial face (Figure 4-29). The dial indicates, with an arrow, readings in hundredths of thousandths of an inch. Consequently, the dial caliper is much easier to read than the vernier caliper.

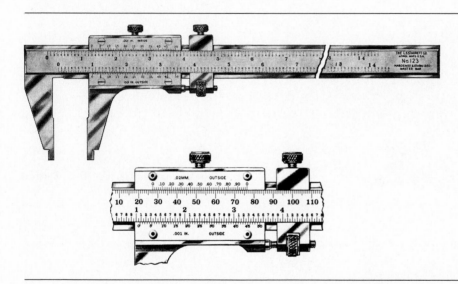

FIGURE 4-27 Vernier calipers. (L. S. Starrett Company)

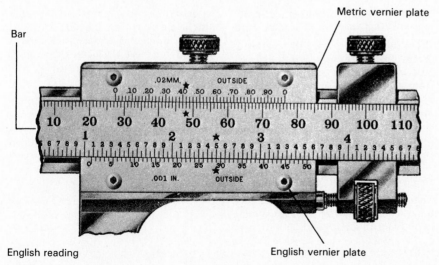

FIGURE 4-28 Reading a vernier scale. (L. S. Starrett Company)

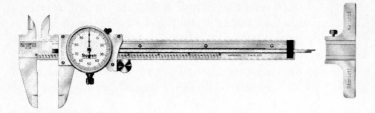

FIGURE 4-29 Dial calipers with depth attachment. (L. S. Starrett Company)

Protractors

FIGURE 4-30   Universal bevel protractor. (L. S. Starrett Company)

Protractors measure angles. Figure 4-30 shows a universal bevel protractor measuring an obtuse angle (any angle over 90°). To use a protractor, remember that a circle is divided into 360 units called *degrees*. Between each degree are 60 further divisions called *minutes*. First, place the base of the protractor along the horizontal or vertical axis of the piece you are measuring. Next adjust the blade to rest against the angle being measured. Read the difference between the axis and the angle as degrees and minutes. Read the measurement in Figure 4-31, 50°, 20', as 50 degrees, 20 minutes.

FIGURE 4-31   Vernier protractor. (L. S. Starrett Company)

IS THAT INCHES OR MILLIMETERS?

More and more auto mechanics in the U.S. are finding themselves working on cars which require metric tools, and which have specifications, capacities and tolerances given in metric terms. Curiously, the legal system of measurement in the U.S. has been the metric system since 1866, although the standard or customary system is more widely used. Although our monetary system is based on factors of ten just as measurements in the metric system are, we find it more comfortable to use the customary system of inches, pounds and quarts. Perhaps growing up with this system makes it easy for us to deal with, but for those who have grown

up with the metric system our customary measurements can be a nightmare.

Take, for instance, the little matter of inches, feet, yards, and miles, as compared to the metric equivalents. To go from centimeter to meter, one multiplies by 100; from meter to kilometer, multiply by 1000. Nothing could be simpler. But try to do the same operation in customary terms. One has to recall that there are 12 inches in a foot, 5280 feet in a mile, or 36 inches in a yard and 1760 yards in a mile.

Then again, there are 16 ounces in a quart . . . or is that 16 ounces in a pound and in a pint, and 32 ounces in

a quart? Not to mention wrench sizes. In the metric system, the next size larger than a number 8 wrench is a number 9. But the next size larger than a ³⁄₁₆ is usually a ¼ inch wrench . . . isn't it?

At any rate, learning one system when you have grown up with another one can be trying, but we've had two systems around for more than a hundred years so it might be a good idea to get used to both of them.

Kay O'Cullane
San Diego Community College
Skill Center

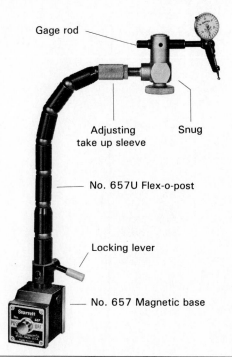

Gage rod

Adjusting take up sleeve

Snug

No. 657U Flex-o-post

Locking lever

No. 657 Magnetic base

FIGURE 4-32   Dial indicators. (L. S. Starrett Company)

Dial Indicators

Dial indicators are multiuse measuring devices that can quickly measure end play runout and variation in size. Figure 4-32 shows a dial indicator on a flexible neck. Suppose you wish to measure runout on a crankshaft. With the engine block upside down and only the crank lying in its bearings, mount the dial indicator on the block. Place the plunger on the center main bearing journal. Rotate the crank until the dial shows the lowest area. Now zero the dial and rotate the crank again. The maximum reading is the amount of runout.

Plastigage

Plastigage is a precision plastic material that comes in stripes. It is used to measure the gap between crank and rod journals and their bearing inserts (Figure 4-33). More information about using plastigage is found in Chapter 17.

THERMOMETERS

Thermometers measure temperature (Figure 4-34). U.S. customary measurements are read in degrees **Fahrenheit** and metric measurements in degrees **Celsius.** In degrees Fahrenheit, freezing occurs at 32°, and water boils (at sea level) at 212°. In Celsius, water freezes at 0° and boils at 100°. Figure 4-35 gives temperature conversions and formulas for making conversions.

Thermometers are used in the automotive industry to measure such temperatures as those of the engine head, coolant, oil, and air conditioning.

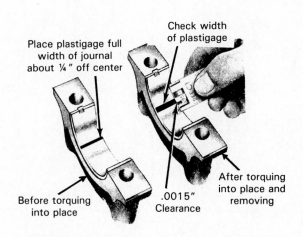

Place plastigage full width of journal about ¼″ off center

Check width of plastigage

Before torquing into place

.0015″ Clearance

After torquing into place and removing

FIGURE 4-33   Using Plastigage. (Ford Motor Company)

FIGURE 4-34   Thermometers.

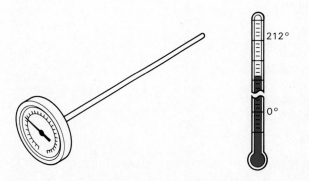

212°

0°

Use this table to convert Fahrenheit degrees (F°) directly to Celsius degrees (C°) and vice versa. Conversions can be made by substituting a known Fahrenheit (F°) or Celsius (C°) temperature figure in either of the following formulas.

$$F° = \frac{C° \times 9}{5} + 32 \qquad\qquad C° = \frac{F° - 32}{9} \times 5$$

F°	C°	F°	C°	F°	C°	F°	C°	F°	C°
− 160	− 107	340	171	840	449	1340	727	1840	1004
− 140	− 96	360	182	860	460	1360	738	1860	1016
− 120	− 84	380	193	880	471	1380	749	1880	1027
− 100	− 73	400	204	900	482	1400	760	1900	1038
− 80	− 62	420	216	920	493	1420	771	1920	1049
− 60	− 51	440	227	940	504	1440	782	1940	1060
− 40	− 40	460	238	960	516	1460	793	1960	1071
− 20	− 29	480	249	980	527	1480	804	1980	1082
0	− 18	500	260	1000	538	1500	816	2000	1093
20	− 7	520	271	1020	549	1520	827	2020	1104
40	4	540	282	1040	560	1540	838	2040	1116
60	16	560	293	1060	571	1560	849	2060	1127
80	27	580	304	1080	582	1580	860	2080	1138
100	38	600	316	1100	593	1600	871	2100	1149
120	49	620	327	1120	604	1620	882	2120	1160
140	60	640	338	1140	616	1640	893	2140	1171
160	71	660	349	1160	627	1660	904	2160	1182
180	82	680	360	1180	638	1680	916	2180	1193
200	93	700	371	1200	649	1700	927	2200	1204
220	104	720	382	1220	660	1720	938	2220	1216
240	116	740	393	1240	671	1740	949	2240	1227
260	127	760	404	1260	682	1760	960	2260	1238
280	138	780	416	1280	693	1780	971	2280	1249
300	149	800	427	1300	704	1800	982	2300	1260
320	160	820	438	1320	716	1820	993	2320	1271

FIGURE 4-35 Temperature conversion.

TRADE TERMS

Bore Gauge
Calipers
Celsius
Centimeter
Decimal
Depth Gauge
Dial Indicator
Fahrenheit
Feeler Gauge
International System of Units (SI)

Meter
Metric
Micrometer
Millimeter
Plastigage
Protractor
Scale
Telescoping Gauge
Thermometer
United States Customary

REVIEW QUESTIONS

1. Write the divisions up to ¼ in. expressed in fractions of 32nds.

2. Convert the following fractions to millimeters: ⅟₆₄, ⅟₃₂, ⅞₄, ¼, and ⅞.

3. Name two types of feeler gauges. How are they different?

4. Name the six major parts of a micrometer.

5. What is the difference between how the vernier and dial calipers provide readouts of their measurements? How does the digital micrometer differ?

6. Name two types of bore gauges.

7. Protractors measure the size of a circle. True or false? Explain.

8. What is the difference between a telescoping gauge and an inside micrometer?

9. What is the U.S. standard of temperature called? Where are freezing and boiling on this scale?

10. What is the metric standard of temperature called? Where are freezing and boiling on this scale?

5

Working Safely

INTRODUCTION

Because of the time you spend at work, you can expect at least half of the accidents in your life to occur there. When you consider the possible dangers in an automobile repair shop, you can add another 25%. So about 75% of the accidents you suffer during your working life will be in the shop. This chapter will reduce your chances of an accident by telling you what to be aware of, how to protect yourself, and how to keep from hurting others.

If you take the following pages of information to heart, you'll prevent many accidents from happening to yourself and your co-workers. If you ignore what you learn here, you can count on being injured. Severe ignorance or disregard of safety practices can lead to death!

Common causes of accidents in the shop are:

1. Fooling around, horseplay, throwing things around the shop
2. Not wearing **safety glasses**
3. Grease and oil on the floor making people slip and fall
4. Worn-out equipment breaking and injuring people
5. The feeling "it can't happen to me"

OBJECTIVES

When you have completed this chapter, you should be able to

- List how to dress safely
- Identify major causes of accidents
- Identify classes of fires and how best to extinguish them
- Describe precautions for handling and storing fuels, solvents, and refrigerants
- List safety precautions in using tools and equipment
- Explain why a clean shop is safer than a cluttered one

54

The intent here is not to scare, only to make you aware of the dangers. So read carefully.

DRESSING FOR SAFETY

Safety in the shop means protecting yourself and your co-workers. Dressing for safety is up to you. Safety is your job.

Eye Safety

The fear of being blinded probably haunts us more than any other fear. This is understandably so. The loss of vision would mean the end of a career.

The best way to protect your eyes is to wear **safety glasses**, goggles, or a face shield. These specially tempered glasses will shatter, but they won't break (Figure 5-1). Always wear safety glasses when working with power tools. This includes such tools as grinders, drills, impact wrenches, and other pneumatic and electric tools. If you normally wear glasses for distance vision or for reading, your optometrist can make your prescription in tempered glass just as regular safety glasses are made. Many mechanics like to wear safety glasses when working under a car. This practice pre-

FIGURE 5-1 Wear safety glasses when using power tools.

vents dirt and grease from falling in their eyes and provides protection.

Rings and Things

Jewelry is nice, but its place is not in the shop. Avoid wearing rings, watches, and necklaces.

When working around the electrical wiring of a car, it is not uncommon to run across wire leads with the insulation worn off and current passing through them. If you should touch one of these bare wires with a ring or watch and the other side of the piece of jewelry touches a ground, you will short out the wire. The result will be to heat the ring or watch (Figure 5-2). If your hand should get jammed in place with current passing through the ring, enough heat would be generated to burn you! Leave your jewelry at home.

Clothing

The easiest way to avoid problems with clothing is to remember not to wear anything that hangs or dangles. Avoid ties. If you wear a smock, keep the belt tightly about you. If you have long hair, tie it up or wear a hat. Anything dangling from your person can be caught in moving pieces of equipment (Figure 5-3).

Keep your clothing clean. If you spill gas or oil on yourself, change that item of clothing immediately. Oil against the skin for long periods of time can produce rashes or other allergic reactions. Infections of any cuts or sores may be caused by gas. Besides, it presents a poor appearance to go around dressed in a greasy uniform or smock.

FIGURE 5-2 Leave jewelry at home.

FIGURE 5-3 Wear proper clothing.

CHEMICAL HAZARDS

Chemicals are used so much in the shop that you sometimes forget they are very dangerous if not handled properly. Remember, liquid chemicals and their fumes are equally dangerous.

Fire

Probably the single greatest safety precaution in a shop is to prevent fires. One cup of gasoline has the same power potential as one stick of dynamite. In a 20-gal gas tank, there are 320 cups of gasoline. If there are three cars in the shop, you're looking at the same potential explosive force (when contained) as nearly a thousand sticks of dynamite!

For a fire to start, three components must be present: oxygen, fuel, and ignition temperature (Figure 5-4). A fire can be put out by removing one or more

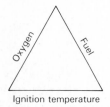

FIGURE 5-4   Fire triangle.

Class	Type of Material	Extinguishing Action
A.	wood, paper textiles	Cooling Quenching
B.	gasoline, oil, grease, paint	Smothering Blanketing
C.	electrical, computers, motors	Nonconducting Smothering

FIGURE 5-5   Classes of fire.

FIGURE 5-6   Extinguishing fires.

Extinguisher Type	Fire Type	Use
Foam	A-B	Spray foam on fire
Carbon dioxide	B-C	Spray base of flames and work towards the center
Multipurpose dry chemical	A-B-C	Spray base of flames with fanning motion
Dry chemical	B-C	Spray base of flames with fanning motion
Soda acid	A	Spray base of flames with slow fanning motion
Halon gas	B-C	Spray base of flames and work toward center

of these parts, and that is basically what fire extinguishers do.

Figure 5-5 describes three classes of fire. Study Figure 5-6 carefully and know how to put out a class A, B, or C fire. It may save your life and the lives of your co-workers. Know where the fire extinguishers are in your shop *before* you need one. The three most used fire extinguishers in an auto shop are the carbon dioxide, the dry chemical, and the halon gas extinguishers. Halon gas extinguishers are more expensive, but they will not damage a car as the others can.

Battery and Electrical

Batteries are dangerous and are due a great deal of respect. A battery is constantly giving off hydrogen gas, especially so when it's being changed. Hydrogen is highly explosive. Keep fire and sparks away from batteries. Never weld around a battery. If you need to weld in the battery area, take the battery out. When hooking up a battery charger, leave the charger *off* until you connect all the leads. This will prevent sparking, thereby preventing a possible explosion.

The acid in a battery is also a danger. It must not come in contact with your skin or eyes. Wash immediately with water if you are splashed with battery acid.

When you are going to work on any part of the electrical system, disconnect the battery ground cable first. This step will prevent shorting a circuit with your wrench or screwdriver. This type of short circuit will melt a complete wiring harness, not to mention the possibilities of starting a fire or melting parts of you. Remember, keep flames and sparks away from the battery and disconnect it if you plan *any* electrical work.

Fuel

Gasoline   Gasoline fumes are heavier than air. When an open container of gasoline is sitting about, the fumes spill out over the sides and onto the floor. These fumes are more flammable than the liquid. They'll explode. This is one of the prime reasons you'll see NO SMOKING signs throughout the shop.

> **CAUTION:** Do not siphon gasoline or diesel with your mouth. They are poisonous and will make you sick or fatally ill.

Store gasoline in approved **safety containers.** These containers have spring-loaded caps which prevent spills if they are knocked over or if you should drop the container while pouring fuel into a car (Figure 5-7). Here's another precaution: Fill gas tanks outdoors.

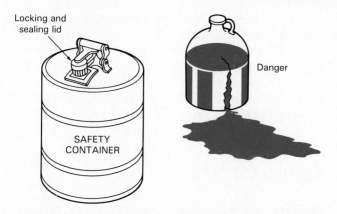

FIGURE 5-7 Store flammable liquids in safety containers.

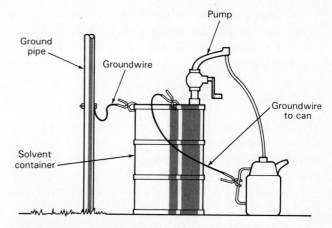

FIGURE 5-8 Outside fuel and solvent storage.

The breeze will prevent a concentration of fumes. The last precaution is never store flammable liquids in glass bottles. The possibility of breakage is too great.

Diesel Diesel fuel is an extremely dirty fuel. Because it is not as highly refined as gasoline, it has many impurities, including active microscopic organisms that can be highly infectious. If diesel fuel gets into an open sore or cut, thoroughly cleanse the area. As with gasoline, do not siphon it with your mouth. Use a pump. The ignition temperature of diesel is much higher than gasoline, making it less volatile; however, it contains more energy per pound than gasoline, so similar precautions should be taken in its storage and handling.

Carbon Monoxide

Carbon monoxide is a colorless, odorless gas produced as a result of combustion. It can kill. Be sure to work in a well-ventilated area if a car is running. Never start an engine with shop doors closed. Always direct or vent exhaust fumes outside. Do not breathe exhaust fumes.

Refrigerant

Air conditioners are charged with a gas called R-12, or freon. It's sold to the industry in small cans like aerosol paint bombs or in large steel bottles like propane tanks. When freon escapes from being under pressure, it cools whatever is around it. It will freeze your eyes, fingers, or any other part of you. Freon is normally an inert or stable gas. However, if it is burned in the atmosphere or drawn into the engine and burned, it will form phosgene gas.

CAUTION: Phosgene gas is poisonous and will make you sick or fatally ill.

Prevent the possibility of puncturing freon cans by storing them in steel cabinets. Keep them away from direct heat. Bring them out of storage only when charging a system. Put the remainder away immediately.

Solvents

Solvents are not as volatile as gasoline, but they are still flammable. Figure 5-8 shows how to store and pump solvents (including gasoline). Note that the 55-gal. drum is grounded and that the can is grounded to the drum. This prevents the possibility of a static discharge. Have you ever walked across a carpet and touched a metal object? If it's cold and dry, you'll get a shock from the small spark that jumps from your finger. This same static spark, if created around a solvent tank or a gasoline tank, could cause an explosion.

A second precaution is to *never use gasoline in place of solvent to wash parts*. Obviously, the flammability of gasoline explains the reason for this precaution.

THE RIGHT TOOL

Here it is again: Use the right tool for the right job. This must become second nature. Wrenches, not pliers, remove nuts (Figure 5-9). Screwdrivers remove screws. They weren't made to pry or scrape gasket material from metal surfaces.

FIGURE 5-9 Use the correct tool for the job.

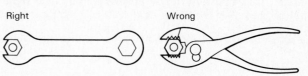

Three things are at work here: If you use the wrong tool, you'll damage the part, the tool, or yourself! Learn what tool to use and how to use it. Remember your lessons.

Tool Use

Be sure that your hands are free of grease, oil, and dirt when using tools. Greasy tools could slip out of your hand into a moving part of an engine or cause you to get hurt.

Remember, if the tool is pointed or sharp, aim it away from yourself. Knives, chisels, and scrapers must all be used in a motion that will keep the point or blade moving away from your body. Pass sharp or pointed tools with the handles first.

Always *pull* on a wrench where possible (Figure 5-10). If you should slip while pushing a wrench, you'll probably lose skin off at least one knuckle, possibly

two. By pulling, if you slip off, the chances of skinning a knuckle are much less.

When using power tools, be sure that equipment, parts, and other people are away from the tool. All electric power tools must be grounded. Always wear eye protection when using power tools. Check all hose connections when using tools powered by compressed air. Never use compressed air to dust off clothing.

EQUIPMENT HAZARDS

Defective and misused equipment is one of the most common hazards in the shop. Defective cords, ungrounded equipment, and unprotected equipment are some of the areas which you must watch.

Lifting Equipment

When placing a floor jack, be sure it's under a frame member (Figure 5-11). In Chapter 2 we discussed the

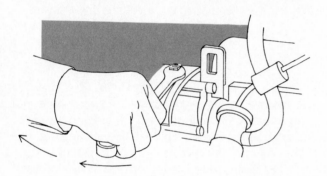

FIGURE 5-10 Always pull wrenches toward yourself.

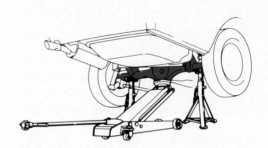

FIGURE 5-11 Place floor jack under substantial part of car.

TERRORIZED BY TRANSMISSIONS

I've always been fascinated with transmissions. They seem to have a grudge against people. No kidding; how else can these stories be explained?

My first interest (and caution) came at the age of 10 when a neighbor tried to remove a Ford transmission. On his back under the car, he pulled it off onto his chest. It knocked the wind out of him. He lay there for several hours, unable to cry for help. Finally his wife came out and found him, bruised but alive.

Then I heard another horror story. A friend had a pit in his barn, which he used in place of a lift. With the car over the pit, he pulled the transmission. Af-

ter repairs were completed, he set the transmission on the edge of the pit. Climbing down into the pit, he then slid the transmission onto his shoulder. Maneuvering himself and the transmission under the car, he happily bolted it into place. When all the bolts were tightened, he dropped the wrench and tried to bend down. No way—his head was trapped between the transmission and frame! With the bolts tight, he just couldn't squeeze out, and he couldn't reach the wrench. No one was close enough to hear his shouts. After some desperation, he remembered leaving an adjustable wrench on the frame of the car. With some struggling he managed to get it and escape.

Terrified by these stories, I kept well clear of transmissions. Finally I was forced to open my Hydramatic to fix the linkage. Confident that instructions would help me avoid disaster, I checked a shop manual. "Drain the oil, and remove the pan." I couldn't find a drain plug, so I figured there wasn't any oil in my transmission's pan. I removed all the bolts, and the pan didn't come loose. Curious, I tapped it with a hammer. Have you ever taken a shower in warm transmission fluid? I have. My advice is to be careful if you have to repair a transmission; they're out to get us!

Leonard Spooner
Orchard St. Automotive
San Diego, CA

proper use of floor and hydraulic jacks; you may want to review this information. When using a block and tackle for lifting an engine, use a lifting plate attached to the intake manifold or use a chain bolted at each end of the block. Have someone guide the engine out of the engine compartment while you lift.

Another piece of equipment you want to take care of when lifting is your back.

Lifting

If you must lift heavy objects, watch the way you lift. First, don't try to show off by lifting heavy objects. You may be able to lift an engine block by yourself, but why run the risk of a back injury? Get someone to help you. Second, when you must lift heavy objects, use your legs to do the lifting (Figure 5-12).

Keep your back straight and your head up. Squat down and grab the object. Keeping your back straight, raise up using only your leg muscles. This technique will prevent using your back muscles and consequently prevent damage to your spine. Back muscles should hold your spine in place, not be used for lifting.

Pulleys and Belts

Be very careful around belts, pulleys, wheels, chains, or any other driving mechanism. Be especially aware of leaning against a belt and pulley when it's not moving. Someone may throw the switch!

When working around an engine's drive belts and pulleys, make certain no rags, shop towels, or loose clothing comes into contact with moving parts. While it may not seem these parts are rotating or traveling at high rates of speed, they are. Hands and fingers can be quickly pulled into a revolving belt or pulley, even at engine idle speeds.

SAFE CONDITIONS

There are two areas of **housekeeping** for which you'll be responsible: your work area and the shop in general. A clean, organized work area will help you be a better mechanic. If your area is clean and organized, chances are your work will be the same.

Housekeeping

Housekeeping within the shop is a safety consideration. A cluttered shop is dangerous. When you jack up a car, set it on safety stands and remove the jack. Don't leave a jack handle sticking out for someone to trip over (Figure 5-13). When it's not in use, shove your creeper back under the car. Don't leave air hoses in walk ways. Keep all exits clear. Think safety as you work. If you see something out of place, pick it up and put it away. If you spill oil or drop grease on the floor, wipe it up. Store oily rags in a special safety container (Figure 5-14).

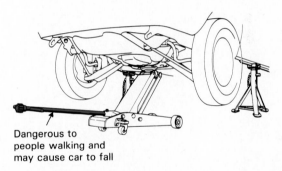

Dangerous to people walking and may cause car to fall

FIGURE 5-13   Don't leave a floor jack handle sticking out.

FIGURE 5-12   Correct lifting procedure.

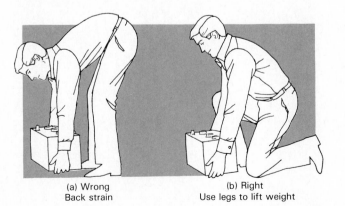

(a) Wrong
Back strain

(b) Right
Use legs to lift weight

FIGURE 5-14   Safety container for oily rags.

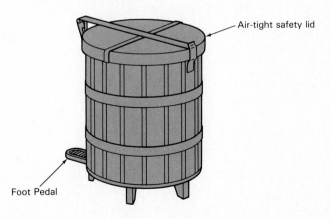

Air-tight safety lid

Foot Pedal

TRADE TERMS

Carbon Monoxide
Housekeeping

Safety Container
Safety Glasses

REVIEW QUESTIONS

1. When should you wear safety glasses?
2. What items of jewelry should not be worn at work?
3. Name three elements that must be present for a fire.
4. Name the flammable gas emitted from a battery.
5. Describe a grounding system for a solvent tank.
6. What is wrong with operating an engine in a shop with the doors closed?
7. Why do you pull on a wrench when tightening or loosening a nut?
8. Why should you keep your tools clean, neat, and organized?
9. How should a sharp or pointed tool be handed to a fellow worker?
10. What is the proper way to lift a heavy box?

6

The Shop Manual

INTRODUCTION

It is virtually impossible for any one person to know everything there is about every single automobile. In what order do you torque the head bolts on a 1981 Chevy six-cylinder engine? What are the point settings on a 1985 Audi? Or does it have an electronic ignition? Details like these are not details that most people carry around in their heads.

For most questions about an automobile, you will find answers in a service manual somewhere. Every well-equipped shop has a large selection of shop manuals, professional manuals, parts books, and all the written materials you'll need to do the job. This chapter tells you about these books and how to use them. Follow along because these books are your road maps. With them, you'll be able to find your way through any automotive problem.

MANUFACTURER'S SERVICE MANUALS

Car manufacturers produce **service manuals** that explain how to service their products (Figure 6-1). These service manuals are sold to dealers, service facilities,

OBJECTIVES

When you have completed this chapter, you should be able to

- List the kinds of manuals that are available to an automotive technician
- Explain what information is in the manuals and how to use them
- Describe newer information and retrieval systems
- Calculate the cost of repairs and parts

egories. As an example, you might find 50 categories divided into such areas as gasoline engines, ignition systems, fuel systems, exhaust system, etc. (Figure 6-2). Under fuel systems you would find such subsections as engines, gasoline—service; engine, 2.3L l-4 (OHC); engine, 3.8L V-6; etc. The subsections are then further divided into more specific areas such as engine removal, engine disassembly, and detailed sections on each part of the engine as it is disassembled and reassembled (Figure 6-3).

These manufacturer's or service manuals will be your first line of information if you work in a dealership. What if, however, you go to work in a general automotive repair shop?

and individual car owners alike. You may have bought one for your own car. From the service manual you should be able to learn almost everything there is to know about your car.

Usually, these manuals are divided into major categories and then into subsections of the various cat-

PROFESSIONAL MANUALS

A number of specialized professional manuals will assist you in troubleshooting and repair work.

FIGURE 6-1   Manufacturer's service manual.

TABLE OF CONTENTS

FIGURE 6-2 Partial service manual table of contents. (Ford Motor Company)

Independent Manuals

Most shops in the United States have sets of manuals. The three most used manuals are *Mitchell Manuals*, *Chilton's Auto Repair Manual*, and *Motor Auto Repair Manual*. Independent auto manuals are written with the group that is going to use them in mind. Writing manuals for a skilled mechanic is different from writing for the nonmechanic or home mechanic. The depth and the speed of technical coverage is usually the key to the level of the manual written. Figure 6-4 shows a page taken from a *Mitchell Manual*. This manual is written for the professional mechanic. Figure 6-5 shows a page taken from the *Motor Auto Repair Manual*. This manual combines over 300 factory manuals into a comprehensive, easy-to-use book. It can be used by the professional mechanic as well as the home mechanic. *Chilton's Auto Repair Manual*, is another widely used manual (Figure 6-6).

Study these three examples. Pay particular attention to the "how to" description of the float level adjustment of each figure. Your choice of manuals should be based on the amount of technical information covered and the depth of that coverage.

Mitchell Manuals are written specifically for the automotive professional (Figure 6-7). Complete sets tell you how to do just about anything you will be doing, be it repair, maintenance, service, or testing on every make, model, and year of every domestic and foreign car and truck. Not every shop will have every manual. Usually, shops subscribe to only those they need.

Each Mitchell Manual contains a number of sections on such areas as tune-up, computerized engine controls, fuel systems, wiring diagrams, accessories and equipment, engines (and their subcategories), suspension, steering, and all the other areas.

All these manuals give step-by-step directions with illustrations. You'll find yourself going to them often. Keep them clean and treat them well.

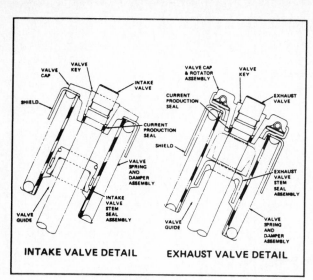

INTAKE VALVE DETAIL   EXHAUST VALVE DETAIL

Fig. 6A3-10--Valve Seals

Exhaust--2, 5, 6, 7
Intake--3, 4, 6, 8

4. Install rocker arm covers as previously outlined.
5. Start engine and adjust carburetor idle speed, if needed.

VALVE STEM OIL SEAL AND/OR VALVE SPRING (6A3-10)

Removal

1. Remove rocker arm cover as previously outlined.
2. Remove spark plug, rocker arm and push rod on the cylinder(s) to be serviced.
3. Install air line adapter Tool J-23590 to spark plug port and apply compressed air to hold the valves in place.
4. Using Tool J-5892 to compress the valve spring, remove the valve locks, valve cap and valve spring and damper (fig. 6A3-11).
5. Remove the valve stem or head oil seal.

Installation

1. Install valve stem seal over valve stem and seat against head.
2. Set the valve spring and damper, oil shedder and valve cap in place. Compress the spring with Tool J-5892 and install oil seal in the lower groove of the stem, making sure the seal is flat and not twisted. A light coat of oil on the seal will help prevent twisting.
3. Install the valve locks and release the compressor tool making sure the locks seat properly in the upper groove of the valve stem. Grease may be used to hold the locks in place while releasing the compressor tool.
4. Using tool J-23994, apply vacuum to the valve cap to make sure no air leaks past the seal.
5. Install spark plug and torque to 22 lb. ft. (30N·m).
6. Install and adjust valve mechanism as previously outlined.

VALVE LIFTERS

Hydraulic valve lifters very seldom require attention. The lifters are extremely simple in design, readjustments are not necessary, and servicing of the lifters requires only that care and cleanliness be exercised in the handling of parts.

Removal

1. Remove intake manifold as previously outlined.
2. Remove valve mechanism as previously outlined.
3. Remove valve lifters. Place valve lifters in a rack so that they may be reinstalled in the same location.

Installation

1. Coat foot of valve lifters with "Molykote" or its equivalent and install valve lifters. Make sure lifter foot is convex.
2. Install intake manifold as previously outlined.
3. Install and adjust valve mechanism as outlined.

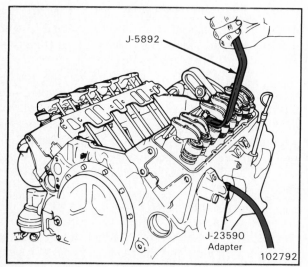

Fig. 6A3-11--Compressing Valve Spring

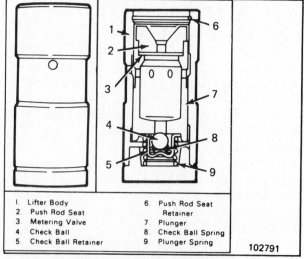

I.	Lifter Body	6.	Push Rod Seat
2.	Push Rod Seat		Retainer
3.	Metering Valve	7.	Plunger
4.	Check Ball	8.	Check Ball Spring
5.	Check Ball Retainer	9.	Plunger Spring

Fig. 6A3-12--Hydraulic Valve Lifter

FIGURE 6-3   Service manual example.

HOLLEY MODEL 5220 2-BARREL

CARBURETOR APPLICATION

CHRYSLER CORP. (HOLLEY) CARBURETOR NO.

Application	Part. No.
2.2L With or Without A/C	
Man. Trans.	R-40067-1
Auto. Trans.	R-40068-1

CARBURETOR IDENTIFICATION

Carburetor identification number may be found stamped on side of float bowl or on a metal tag attached to carburetor.

DESCRIPTION

Carburetor is a 2-stage, 2-venturi type. Primary venturi is smaller than secondary. Secondary stage is mechanically operated by linkage to primary and secondary throttle levers. Primary stage includes curb idle, accelerator pump idle transfer, main metering and power enrichment systems.

Secondary stage includes main metering and power enrichment systems. A single fuel bowl supplies fuel for both stages. Carburetor is equipped with an electric automatic choke which has a 2-stage bi-metal heating element.

TESTING

CHOKE HEATER

1) With ignition off, connect a jumper wire between battery positive terminal and choke heater connection. Remove air cleaner and observe choke plate. Choke plate should fully open within 5 minutes when vehicle is parked inside.

2) Electrical current is supplied to the choke through the oil pressure switch. A minimum oil pressure of 4 psi is required to close the contacts in the oil pressure switch and feed current to the choke.

NOTE: **The choke housing is attached to carburetor with tamper-proof screws. Thermostat setting is not adjustable.**

ADJUSTMENT

NOTE: **For all on-vehicle adjustments not covered in this article, see appropriate TUNE-UP article.**

FLOAT LEVEL

1) Remove air horn and gasket. Turn air horn upside down. Allow weight of float to press down against float needle valve. *See Fig. 1.*

2) Measure float level specified clearance between top of float and air horn gasket surface. Clearance can be checked using a drill or pin gauge.

NOTE: **Do not apply pressure to float needle while checking or changing adjustment.**

Fig. 1: Adjusting Float Level

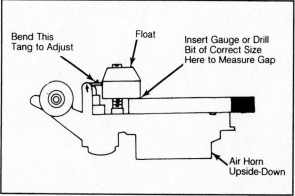

Bend tang to adjust.

3) Make sure float tang still rests on float needle when clearance is checked. To adjust, bend tang that contacts float needle.

FLOAT DROP

1) With air horn and gasket removed, turn right side up. Using a "T" scale, measure specified float drop from air horn gasket surface to bottom of float. *See Fig. 2.*

2) To adjust, bend float tang on float arm that contacts fuel inlet needle seat boss.

Fig. 2: Adjusting Float Drop

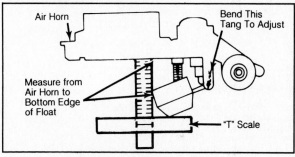

Bend tang to adjust.

CHOKE VACUUM KICK (INITIAL CHOKE VALVE CLEARANCE)

1) Open throttle and close choke. Close throttle to trap fast idle cam in closed choke position. Disconnect vacuum hose at choke vacuum diaphragm. Connect an outside vacuum source and apply 15 in. Hg (minimum) vacuum.

2) Apply slight closing pressure to choke valve without bending linkage. An internal spring within choke system will compress to stop position.

3) Using a drill or pin gauge, measure clearance between upper edge of choke valve and primary air horn wall. Adjust by rotating Allen head screw in center of diaphragm housing. *See Fig. 4.*

FIGURE 6-4   Typical Mitchell manual page.

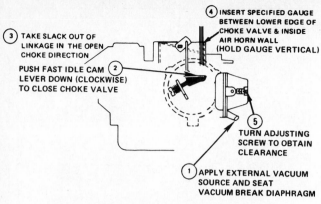

③ TAKE SLACK OUT OF LINKAGE IN THE OPEN CHOKE DIRECTION

PUSH FAST IDLE CAM LEVER DOWN (CLOCKWISE) TO CLOSE CHOKE VALVE

②

④ INSERT SPECIFIED GAUGE BETWEEN LOWER EDGE OF CHOKE VALVE & INSIDE AIR HORN WALL (HOLD GAUGE VERTICAL)

⑤ TURN ADJUSTING SCREW TO OBTAIN CLEARANCE

① APPLY EXTERNAL VACUUM SOURCE AND SEAT VACUUM BREAK DIAPHRAGM

Fig. 6A   Vacuum break adjustment. 1980–82 Units

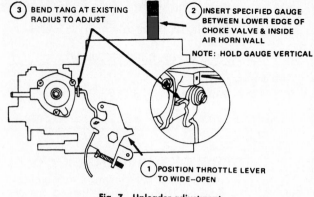

③ BEND TANG AT EXISTING RADIUS TO ADJUST

② INSERT SPECIFIED GAUGE BETWEEN LOWER EDGE OF CHOKE VALVE & INSIDE AIR HORN WALL

NOTE: HOLD GAUGE VERTICAL

① POSITION THROTTLE LEVER TO WIDE–OPEN

Fig. 7   Unloader adjustment

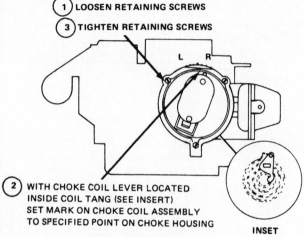

① LOOSEN RETAINING SCREWS

③ TIGHTEN RETAINING SCREWS

L   R

② WITH CHOKE COIL LEVER LOCATED INSIDE COIL TANG (SEE INSERT) SET MARK ON CHOKE COIL ASSEMBLY TO SPECIFIED POINT ON CHOKE HOUSING

INSET

Fig. 8   Choke coil adjustment

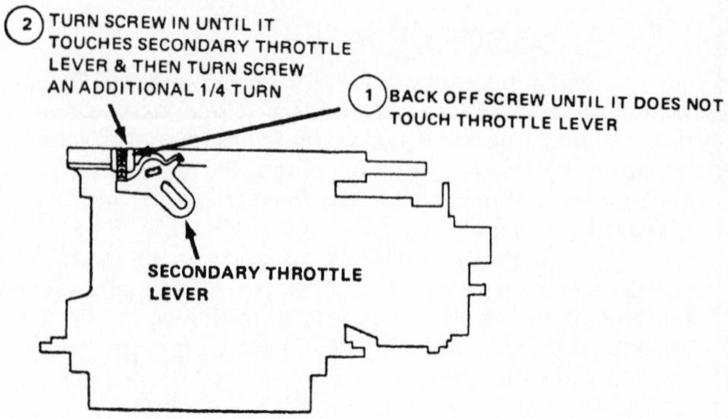

② TURN SCREW IN UNTIL IT TOUCHES SECONDARY THROTTLE LEVER & THEN TURN SCREW AN ADDITIONAL 1/4 TURN

① BACK OFF SCREW UNTIL IT DOES NOT TOUCH THROTTLE LEVER

SECONDARY THROTTLE LEVER

Fig. 9   Secondary throttle stop screw adjustment

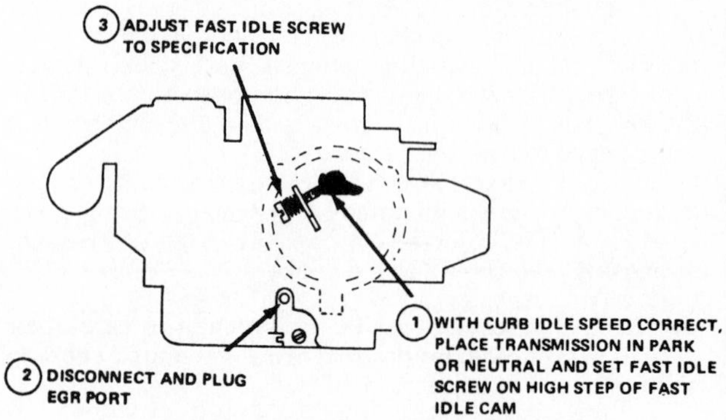

③ ADJUST FAST IDLE SCREW TO SPECIFICATION

① WITH CURB IDLE SPEED CORRECT, PLACE TRANSMISSION IN PARK OR NEUTRAL AND SET FAST IDLE SCREW ON HIGH STEP OF FAST IDLE CAM

② DISCONNECT AND PLUG EGR PORT

Fig. 10   Fast idle speed adjustment

ister and not into the engine when the engine is operating. The vent is used in conjunction with existing internal venting through the air horn.

A hot idle compensator is used to maintain smooth engine idle during periods of excessive high temperature operation by allowing additional air to enter the primary throttle bore.

An electrically heated automatic choke system is used to provide correct air-fuel mixtures for cold start and warm-up operation. The automatic choke system is equipped with a vacuum break controlled by an external vacuum supply and a vacuum delay valve to prevent prolonged fast idle.

ADJUSTMENTS

Float Level Adjustment

Fig. 3—With air horn inverted, insert specified gauge between float and air horn. Bend tang to adjust.

Float Drop Adjustment

Fig. 4—With air horn removed, measure distance between bottom of air horn and top of float. Refer to specifications chart for correct measurement. Bend tang to adjust.

Fast Idle Cam Adjustment

Fig. 5—Set fast idle cam in position so the screw contacts second high step. Insert speci-

fied gauge between lower edge of choke valve and air horn wall. Bend tang to adjust.

Vacuum Break Adjustment

1978–79 Units
Fig. 6—Remove choke coil assembly. Push choke coil lever clockwise to close choke valve. Push vacuum break shaft against stop. Remove slack from linkage in the choke open direction. Insert specified gauge between lower edge of choke valve and air horn wall. Rotate vacuum break adjusting screw to obtain specified clearance. Install and adjust choke coil assembly.

1980–82 Units
Fig. 6A—Apply an external vacuum source to vacuum break to seat diaphragm. Rotate fast idle cam clockwise to close choke valve. Remove slack from linkage in the choke open direction. Insert the specified gauge between choke valve and air horn wall. Turn adjusting screw to obtain clearance.

Unloader Adjustment

Fig. 7—Place throttle lever in wide open position. Insert specified gauge between lower edge of choke valve and air horn wall. Bend tang at existing radius to adjust.

FIGURE 6-5   Typical *Motor Manual* page. (Motors Manuals. Copyright © 1984 The Hearst Corporation.)

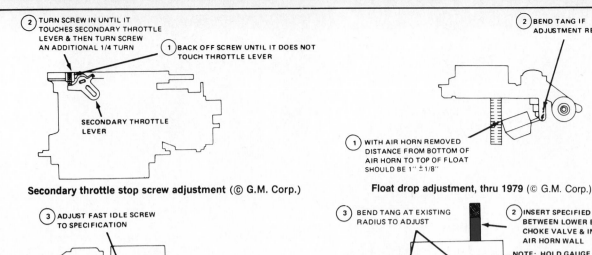

Secondary throttle stop screw adjustment (© G.M. Corp.)

Float drop adjustment, thru 1979 (© G.M. Corp.)

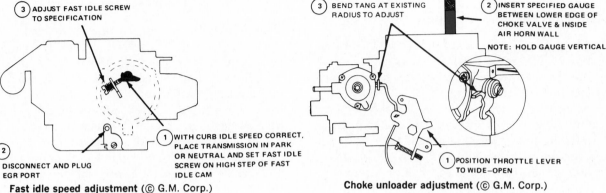

Fast idle speed adjustment (© G.M. Corp.)

Choke unloader adjustment (© G.M. Corp.)

2. Insert the specified gauge between the lower edge of the choke valve and the air horn wall.

3. Bend the tang on the arm to adjust.

Unloader Adjustment

1. Place the throttle in the wide open position.

2. Insert a .350 inch gauge between the lower edge of the choke valve and the air horn wall.

3. Bend the tang on the choke arm to adjust.

Choke Cap Setting

1978-79 ONLY

1. Loosen the retaining screws.

2. Make sure that the choke coil lever is located inside the coil tang.

3. Turn the cap to the specified setting.

4. Tighten the retaining screws.

Fast Idle Adjustment

1. With the curb idle speed correct, place the fast idle screw on the highest cam step and adjust to the specified rpm.

NOTE: The EGR line must be disconnected and plugged.

Float Level Adjustment

1. Remove and invert the air horn.

2. Place the specified gauge between the air horn and the float.

3. If necessary, bend the float arm tang to adjust.

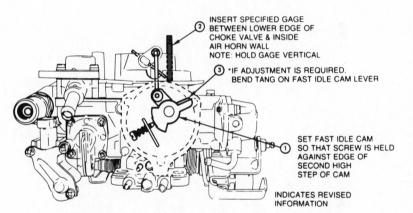

Fast idle cam adjustment—Holley 6510C (© G.M. Corp.)

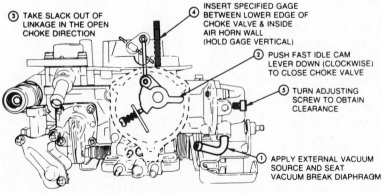

Vacuum break adjustment, 1980 and later—Holley 6510C (© G.M. Corp.)

FIGURE 6-6 Typical *Chilton Manual* page. (Chilton Book Company)

FIGURE 6-7 Set of manuals, tune-up and electrical.

FIGURE 6-8 Mechanical estimating.

Estimating and Parts Manuals

"How long should it take to remove and replace a carburetor?" The estimating (or **flat rate**) guide tells how long the average, well-trained, well-equipped mechanic takes to do tasks (Figure 6-8).

Estimating guides are used by the auto industry to estimate job prices. Removal and replacement (R & R) jobs are listed, with the time it takes, stated in hours and tenths of hours, to do each job (Figure 6-9). Based on these figures, the person in charge of writing estimates can determine what to charge a customer.

He or she multiplies the flat rate by the shop hourly rate, adds the retail price of the parts (Figure 6-10), and comes to a total.

If, as a shop mechanic, you are paid by the job (piecework), the flat rate book will determine how much you get paid. After multiplying the estimated time by the hourly rate of the shop to arrive at a labor charge, you will be paid a percentage of that labor charge. If you can do the job in less than the estimate, you'll make more money than if you take longer. Some shops pay a straight hourly wage.

Self-Propelled Vehicles
A Practical Treatise
on the
Theory, Construction, Operation,
Care and Management
of All Forms of
Automobiles,
1912

PREFACE

Since the publication of the first edition of this book the motor vehicle has passed out of the experimental stage and become a practical reality. That it is now a permanent factor in the world of mechanics, in the domain of travel and recreation, and, latterly also, in commercial life, cannot for a moment be questioned. Already the profession of chauffeur, or automobile driver, has taken rank among skilled callings, affording a new and profitable field of effort. The demand for information of a practical character is insistent. This demand the present revised edition attempts to meet.

The motor vehicle is a singularly complex machine. Its construction and operation involve the consideration of an extensive range of facts in several widely separated departments of mechanical knowledge. The study of its construction and operation is a liberal education in itself. It claims a broad territory.

In order to answer every question that must occur to the practical automobilist, one must produce a whole library of books, rather than a single volume of convenient size. Virtually all such questions may be forestalled, however, by clear explanations of the principles governing the design and construction of the machine, and the most conspicuous situations involved in its operation. It must be said, to the credit of both designer and operator, that questions, perplexities and accidents are far fewer at the present time than several years ago. This is due to the general dissemination of knowledge of a practical character, also to the fact that the public has learned to consider the motor vehicle seriously, and award it the attention it deserves.

To the vast realm of motordom the present volume essays to discharge the function of a general introduction; a convenient guide book to the intricacies that must inevitably be encountered; a summary of the facts and principles that it is necessary to understand. As far as possible, the presentation of subjects has been determined by consideration of the needs of the man behind the wheel.

GROUP 1 - TUNE-UP, IGNITION & EMISSION CONTROL

TUNE-UP & IGNITION

ENGINE - ANALYZE (B)
Includes: Check ignition timing, dwell and emission
control system using analyzer.
1974-83 5

TUNE-UP - MINOR (BREAKER IGNITION) (B)
Includes: Check compression, clean and adjust or
replace spark plugs, points and condenser. Inspect
distributor cap, rotor and ignition wires. Clean or replace
air cleaner. Test crankcase ventilation valve, replace if
necessary. Adjust ignition timing and idle speed.
DOES NOT include distributor R&I.
1974
  Six 1.6
  V8 .... 1.9
1977-79 (Four) 1.5

* COMBINATIONS *
Refer to Combinations following Tune-Up - Minor
(Electronic Ignition).

TUNE-UP - MINOR (ELECTRONIC IGNITION) (B)
Includes: Check compression. Clean or replace spark
plugs and air cleaner. Inspect distributor cap, rotor and
ignition cables. Adjust ignition timing and carburetor idle
speed.
DOES NOT include distributor R&I.
1975-83
  Four 1.1
  Six 1.2
  V8 .... 1.5

* COMBINATIONS *
*Electronic Ignition System - Test (.5) 5
*Distributor Assembly - R&I (.4) 4
*Control, Electronic Ignition - R&R (.3) 3
*Sensor, Electronic Ignition - R&R (.4) 4
*Trigger, Electronic Ignition - R&R (.4) 4
*Cap, Distributor - R&R (.3) 3
*Coil, Ignition - R&R (.3) 3
*Cable Set, Ignition - R&R
  Six (.4) 4
  V8 (.5) 5

COMPRESSION - TEST (C)
1974-83
  Four 8
  Six 9
  V8 .... 1.0

SPARK PLUGS - CLEAN OR REPLACE (C)
1974-83
  Four (.4) 6
  Six (.5) 7
  V8 (.6) 8

POINTS & CONDENSER - R&R (C)
Includes: Adjust ignition timing.
DOES NOT include distributor R&I.
1974 (.3) 4
1977-79 (.4) 6

CONTROL, ELECTRONIC IGNITION - R&R (B)
1975-79 (.3) 5
1980-83
  Four (.5) 7
  Six (.3) 5

SENSOR, ELECTRONIC IGNITION - R&R (B)
1975-83 (.5) 7

TRIGGER, ELECTRONIC IGNITION - R&R (B)
1975-83 (.5) 7

PICK-UP ASSY, ELECTRONIC IGNITION - R&R (B)
1980-83 (Four) (.8) 1.0

DISTRIBUTOR ASSEMBLY - R&R (C)
Includes: Adjust ignition timing.
1974-79 (.5) 7
1980-83
  Four (.6) 8
  Six (.4) 6

DISTRIBUTOR ASSEMBLY - O/H (B)
Includes: Adjust ignition timing.
1974-83 (.9) 1.2

CAP, DISTRIBUTOR - R&R (C)
1974-79 (.3) 5
1980-83
  Four (.5) 7
  Six (.3) 5

VACUUM CONTROL, DISTRIBUTOR - R&R (B)
Includes: Adjust ignition timing.
1974
  Six (.3) 5
  V8 (.4) 6
1975-79 (.4) 6
1980-83
  Four (.7) 9
  Six (.4) 6

COIL, IGNITION - R&R (C)
Includes: Test.
1974-79 (.3) 5
1980-83
  Four (.5) 7
  Six (.3) 5

CABLE SET, IGNITION - R&R (C)
Includes: Test Wires.
NOTE: Deduct .2 if other work is being done in the
engine compartment.
1974-83
  Four,Six (.4) 6
  V8 (.5) 7

* COMBINATIONS *
*To Fabricate from Universal Kit 2

EMISSION CONTROL

EMISSION SYSTEM - CHECK (C)
Includes: Check and adjust idle speed and ignition timing.
1974-83 (.4) 6

AIR INJECTION REACTOR

PUMP, A.I.R. SYSTEM - R&R (C)
1974-79
  Four (.4) 6
  Six,V8 (.6) 8
1980-81
  Four
    w/Air Cond (1.1) 1.3
    w/o Air Cond (.9) 1.1
  Six 8
1982-83
  w/Air Cond (.6) 8
  w/o Air Cond (.4) 6

* COMBINATIONS *
*Valve, Relief - R&R (.2) 2
*Centrifugal Filter - R&R (.2) 2
*Pulley, A.I.R. Pump - R&R (.2) 2

BELT, DRIVE - R&R (D)
1974-83
  w/Air Cond & Pwr Strg 5
  w/o Air Cond & Pwr Strg 3

DIVERTER OR GULP VALVE - R&R (C)
1974-83 (.3) 5

COMBUSTION CONTROL

VACUUM MOTOR, AIR CLEANER - R&R (C)
1974-83 (.4) 6

EVAPORATION CONTROL

CANISTER, EVAPORATION CONTROL - R&R (C)
1974-83 (.3) 5

EXHAUST GAS RECIRCULATION

VALVE, RECIRCULATION (E.G.R.) (C)
1974-83 (.5) 7

POSITIVE CRANKCASE VENT

VALVE, CRANKCASE VENT (P.C.V.) - R&R (C)
1974-83 (.2) 3

GROUP 2 - FUEL & EXHAUST

FUEL

SUPPLY SYSTEM

FUEL PUMP PRESSURE - TEST (B)
Includes: Check capacity.
NOTE: Deduct .2 of other work is being done in the
engine compartment.
All 5

FUEL PUMP - R&R (B)
1974-79
  Four,Six (.5) 7
  V8 (.8) 1.0
1980-83
  Four
    exc Eagle (81-83) (.5) 7
    Eagle (81-83) (1.5) 2.0
  Six (.5) 7

HOSE, FUEL LINE (FLEXIBLE) - R&R (D)
1974-83 (.3) 5

FUEL TANK - R&R (D)
1974-76
  Ambassador,Matador (1.0) 1.3
  Gremlin,Hornet (.9) 1.1
  Pacer (.8) 1.0
1977-78
  AMX,Concord,Matador,Pacer (1.0) 1.3

  Gremlin (.8) 1.0
  Pacer (.9) 1.1
1979-83
  AMX,Spirit (.8) 1.0
  Concord (1.0) 1.3
  Eagle
    exc Kammback,SX4 (1.0) 1.3
    Kammback,SX4 (.8) 1.0
  Pacer (.9) 1.1

* COMBINATIONS *
*Fuel Tank - Clean 7

FUEL LINES - CLEAN (D)
1974-83 5

CARBURETION

CARBURETOR IDLE - ADJUST W/SCOPE (B)
1974-83 5

CARBURETOR &/OR GASKET - R&R (B)
Includes: Adjust idle speed and fuel mixture.
1974-79 .... 1.0
1980-83
  BBD Carb 9
  2SE Carb 1.1

CARBURETOR - O/H (B)
Includes: Install carburetor kit, adjust idle speed and fuel
mixture.
1974-76
  1 Bbl (1.2) 1.8
  2 Bbl (1.5) 2.0
  4 Bbl (1.5) 2.2
1977-79
  1 Bbl (1.1) 1.9
  2 Bbl (1.2) 2.1
1980-83
  BBD Carb (1.2) 1.9
  2SE Carb (1.3) 2.0

FLOAT &/OR NEEDLE & SEAT - R&R (B)
Includes: Adjust float level, idle speed and fuel mixture.
1 Bbl 7
2 & 4 Bbl (.7) 9

ACCELERATOR PUMP - R&R (C)
1 Bbl (.5) 7
2 & 4 Bbl 8

AUTOMATIC CHOKE - O/H (B)
1974-83 6

DASHPOT - R&R (C)
1974-83 (.3) 5

FIGURE 6-9 Typical estimating guide page.

TURBO HYDRA-MATIC
400
(ALUMINUM CASE)
1974-79
CONVERTER, PUMP, CASE & MAIN CONTROL

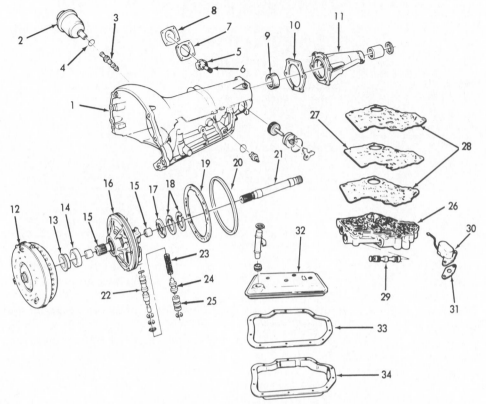

TRANSMISSION ASSEMBLY

1974
Six
  w/Quadra-Trac Transf
    Not Serviced.
  w/o Quadra-Trac Transf 5351792   Disc
V8
  w/Quadra-Trac Transf 5359802 $1205.20
  w/o Quadra-Trac Transf 5351793 $1004.91
1975
Six 5354521 $881.00
V8 .... 5359802 $1205.20
1976
Six
  Cherokee,Truck,Wagoneer 5355260 $1144.60
  CJ Series 5355011 $1144.60
V8
  Cherokee,Wagoneer 5359802 $1205.20
  Truck ① 5358024 $1000.50
  CJ Series 5357054   Disc
1977-78
Six
  Cherokee,Truck,Wagoneer ①
    (77) 5358022 $1000.50
    (78) 5359801 $1205.20
  CJ Series ① 5359799 $1205.20
V8
  Cherokee,Wagoneer 5359802 $1205.20
  Truck ① 5359803 $1205.20
  CJ Series 5358021 $1144.60
1979
Six
  Cherokee,Truck,Wagoneer 5359801 $1205.20
  CJ Series 5359799 $1205.20
V8
  Cherokee,Wagoneer 5359802 $1205.20
  Truck 5359803 $1205.20

  CJ Series 5359800 $1205.20
①Additional components required for replacement - see local supplier.
GASKET & SEAL KIT
  All 8625905 $15.85
RING PACKAGE
  All 8623979 $3.05
SWITCH, Neutral Safety
1974-75 .... 5350284 $17.55
1976-79 .... 5354936 $10.95
1. **CASE, Transmission**
  All 8127307 $444.05
2. **MODULATOR, Vacuum**
1974-75 .... 8625976 $29.25
1976-79
  Trans I.D. #JC,JS 8127273 $25.35
  Trans I.D. #JK,JM,JR 8126090 $29.20
3. **VALVE, Modulator**
  All 8624122 $4.10
4. **SEAL, Modulator Valve**
  All .... 8619568 $.50
5. **GOVERNOR ASSEMBLY**
1974 .... 8627441 $44.80
1975-77
  Trans I.D. #JC 8127303 $55.90
  Trans I.D. #JJ,JL,JM 8627441 $44.80
  Trans I.D. #JK 8126137 $55.90
  Trans I.D. #JR,JS 8623852 $43.95
1978
  Trans I.D. #JC 8127303 $55.90
  Trans I.D. #JK 8126137 $55.90
  Trans I.D. #JM,JR 8627441 $44.80
  Trans I.D. #JS 8623852 $43.95
1979
  Trans I.D. #JC 8127303 $55.90
  Trans I.D. #JK 8126137 $55.90
  Trans I.D. #JM,JR 8627441 $44.80

  Trans I.D. #JS 8623852 $43.95
6. **GEAR, Governor**
  All (Pkg - w/Pin) 8623924 $6.50
7. **GASKET, Governor Cover**
  All .... 8623263 $.55
8. **COVER, Governor**
  All 8623262 $2.00
9. **BUSHING, Case**
  All 8623941 $3.45
10. **GASKET, Extension Housing**
  All .... 8624709 $.60
11. **EXTENSION HOUSING**
1974
  Trans I.D. #JJ,JL 8624113 $112.00
  Trans I.D. #JK,JM,JR 8627466 $107.80
  1975-79 .... 8627466 $107.80
12. **CONVERTER (Exchange)**
1974-78 .... 8624954 $131.90
1979
  Six 8130129 $278.15
  V8 .... 8130128 $278.15
13. **SEAL, Front Pump**
  All 8626916 $5.95
14. **BUSHING, Pump Body**
  All 8623940 $3.00
15. **BUSHING, Stator Shaft**
  All (ea) 8623944 $4.45
16. **PUMP**
  Body 8625954 $116.20
  Cover 8625955 $135.50
17. **WASHER (Selective)**
  All (Cover to Fwd Hsg) 8623300 $1.95
18. **RING, Pump Seal (Each)**
  All 8126228 $1.00
19. **GASKET, Front Pump**
  All 8623978 $2.10

FIGURE 6-10   Flat rate truck parts/estimator.

FIGURE 6-11 A collision estimator at work.

Collision Books

If you're going into paint and body work, your guide will be the **collision estimating guide** (Figure 6-11). Like the mechanical estimating books, the collision guide gives the number of hours it usually takes to perform various body repairs, parts numbers, and retail prices (Figure 6-12). It includes body work and frame and chassis repair plus glass and paint (Figure 6-13).

Parts Books

The total price of a job is determined by the estimated time, multiplied by the shop hourly charge, plus the parts cost. Parts books are used to find the price of the parts (Figure 6-14). Most manufacturers supply a set of books listing all of the body, engine, transmission, and running gear parts. The service writer or shop foreman looks through the parts books and locates the part number. With this part number he or she can check the current retail price list.

With these manuals, estimating guides, and parts books, a shop can determine a fair price which will allow it to pay the mechanics, make a profit, and do the work.

Interchange Manuals

Interchange manuals cross-reference car parts. They will indicate which parts can be interchanged between car years and manufacturers. Interchange manuals will show you what Chevy parts will fit in an Olds and

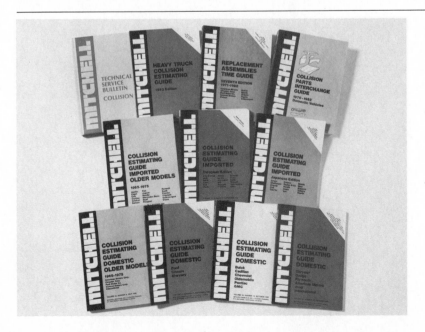

FIGURE 6-12 Collision estimating guides.

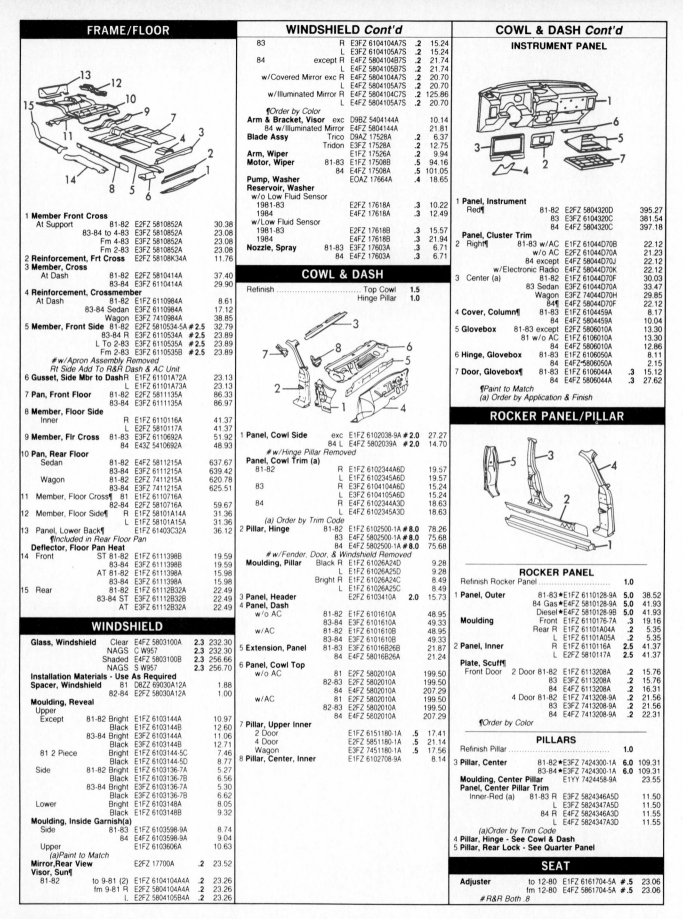

FIGURE 6-13   Estimating collision repair time and cost.

FIGURE 6-14   Parts catalogs.

vice versa (Figure 6-15). Interchange manuals give a breakdown of most makes and models of cars. Such manuals also identify similar parts, parts assemblies, and factory part numbers.

Specialty Manuals

In addition to the professional manuals, there are a number of specialty books available to the mechanic. These include the monthly magazines for hot rod enthusiasts, and those interested in motorcycling, off-road racing or other forms of competitive driving. Many professionals read these magazines to help keep abreast of new developments.

Many parts stores have a number of special automotive manuals. These manuals cover specific subjects, such as computer command control, electronic ignition, fuel ignition, etc. These manuals are helpful in keeping you up-to-date with current technology (Figure 6-16).

FIGURE 6-15   Typical interchange manual pages.

FIGURE 6-16   Specialty books and manuals.

MICROFICHE

As the years go by and more manuals are delivered to the shop, storage space becomes a real problem. Where can all of these books and manuals be placed? To solve this problem, an inexpensive information storage and retrieval system was developed called the **microfiche** (Figure 6-17). Here, book pages are reduced to either 4 by 5 in. or 35-mm film, often with as many as 500 pages to a 4- by 5-in. sheet.

After you insert the film into the microfiche, light is passed through the film and the image is enlarged and projected onto a ground glass screen (Figure 6-

FIGURE 6-18 Using microfiche reader.

18). This allows the user to view the material in a well-lit room. Through various levels of magnification, you can enlarge portions of a page for closer viewing.

A shop may buy a microfiche viewer and manuals that are relevant to that shop's business to go with it (Figure 6-19). In many cases, however, the shop will purchase the equipment alone and then have their collection of manuals put on microfiche film. Either way the microfiche system is an excellent space saver. It

FIGURE 6-17 Microfiche.

FIGURE 6-19 Microfiche cards.

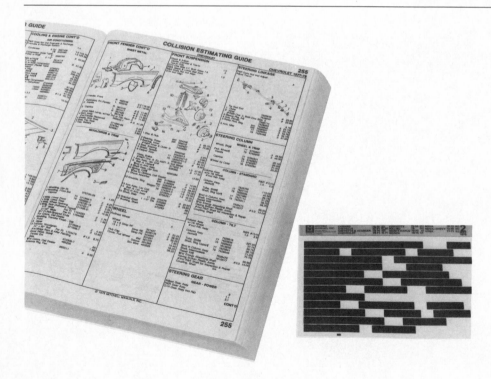

does take time to use though, and can't easily be carried to the car.

COMPUTERIZED MANUALS

The newest information system is the computer (Figure 6-20). As time progresses, more information may be stored on floppy disks rather than in shop manuals. The shop owner will be able to store business records, inventory control, and all mechanic's manuals in one small computer.

In the future, all of this information may be stored along with pertinent data on each customer's engine. This system isn't developed yet, but many people say it won't be long. Many of the high-technology engine analyzers have the necessary engine specifications built into them. Also some cars have an on-board data system.

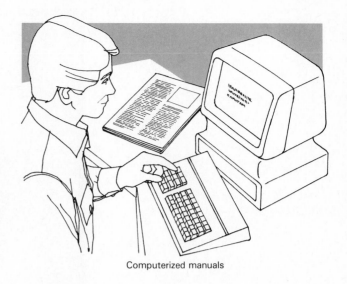

Computerized manuals

FIGURE 6-20 Computerized manuals.

TRADE TERMS

Collision Estimate Guide
Flat Rate
Interchange Manuals

Microfiche
Service Manuals

REVIEW QUESTIONS

1. Service manuals, published by auto manufacturers, cover what information?
2. Name a set of professional auto repair manuals.
3. What is the difference between a specialty manual and a service manual?
4. Name the book which tells how long a job should take.
5. How do you use a parts book?
6. Collision estimating books tell how to estimate collision damage. True or false? Explain.
7. What equipment retrieves information stored on film?
8. Is there a use for the computer in relation to shop manuals? What would the use be?

7

The Car and Its Systems

INTRODUCTION

Just as your body is composed of systems that depend on each other (skeleton, muscles, circulation, nerves), so the automobile is made up of systems. Most of the systems are inter-related. If one breaks down, others stop as well. For example, you know a sore leg can cause you to limp, which could cause your back to hurt the next day. Likewise, a car's wheel alignment could be off, which might lead to erratic steering and brakes that pull to one side.

Since you will be diagnosing the automobile and repairing many different parts of it, you should know all the major systems and how they are related. This knowledge is the foundation for all serious repair work, no matter how specialized. You'll cover the major systems of the automobile in this chapter. We've defined them as the engine, cooling, fuel, emission control, power train, electrical/electronic, suspension, steering and brakes. You'll learn how they work and how they relate to each other. This material is an introduction to the rest of the book, which covers all these systems in detail (Figure 7-1).

OBJECTIVES

When you have completed this chapter, you should be able to

- Describe the major systems of an automobile
- Explain what the function of each system is and how it operates
- Gain a general overview of the systems you will be studying in the rest of the book

76

ENGINES

The **internal combustion** engine powers most vehicles (Figure 7-2). This term distinguishes it from steam turbines, electrical motors, and other means of propulsion. *Internal combustion* means that burning of air and fuel takes place within an enclosed cylinder (Figure 7-3). The resulting expanding gases force the piston down the cylinder. The piston attaches to the crankshaft, which turns as a result of the downward movement of the piston. When the crankshaft turns, the gears in the transmission turn and make the car go forward or backward.

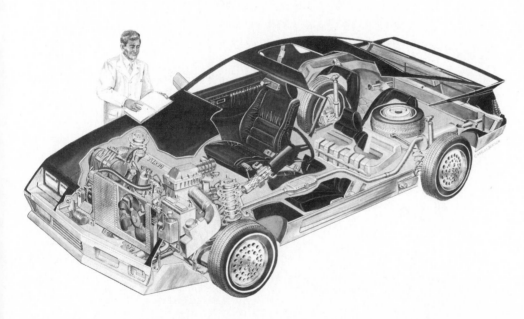

FIGURE 7-1 The car and its systems.

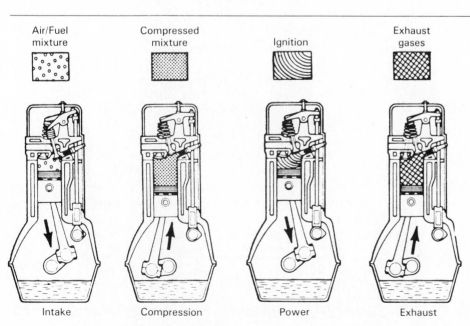

Air/Fuel mixture	Compressed mixture	Ignition	Exhaust gases

Intake	Compression	Power	Exhaust

FIGURE 7-2 Internal combustion engine. (Chrysler Corporation)

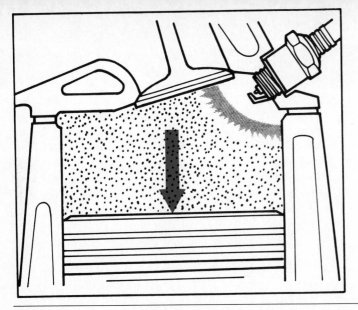

FIGURE 7-3 Expanding gases force the piston down.

ENGINEERS AND BUREAUCRATS DESIGN A CAR

The following solutions to common problems are given by engineers and by bureaucrats. There are different ways of solving problems, not all elegant or effective. Here they are:

ENGINEER'S SOLUTION	PROBLEM	BUREAUCRAT'S SOLUTION
Better suspension, tires, steering, brakes	Car runs off road	Install rail guards, concrete walls on road sides, reduce speed limits
Better suspension, tires, steering, brakes	Car hits building, tree	Bigger bumpers, remove trees, reduce speed limits
Better suspensions and antisway bars or design bending limits in suspension arms	Car flips over	Reinforce roof and pillars or reduce speed limits
Better brakes	Car cannot avoid accident	Bigger engine to get away and reduce speed limits
Use belts and helmets, build "soft" dashboards	Passengers get hurt inside car	Install padding and balloons . . . reduce speed limits
Install "pop-off" windshields	Passengers get hurt going through windshield	Reinforce windshield (causing concussions) and reduce speeds
Take people on tour through a hospital emergency room	People not using seat belts	Install buzzer and flashing lights
Make car sufficiently light that it will bounce away	Passengers hurt: inside collisions	Reinforce doors and pillars, reduce speed limits
Use decent lighting or better road markings	Too many accidents at night	Reduce speed and regulate lighting limits
Better brakes and tires	Car can't stop in emergency	Reduce speed limits
Use decent tires at correct pressure	Tires blow out	Reduce speed or rate tires (under ideal conditions)
Lighter car and clean aerodynamics	Low range, mileage	Bigger gas tank (more danger in collision fire)
Good aerodynamics and intelligent metal work	Noisy car	Install heavy padding and sound deadener, reduce speeds
Design clean burning engines (CVCC)	Engines fumigate neighborhood	Install antipollution hardware (while allowing diesels?)
Higher tariffs, institute quotas, design better cars, or go work for the foreign manufacturers.	"Unfair" competition from foreign cars	Higher tariffs, institute quotas, study the problem, and reduce speed limits.
Move to Emerald City	Cars	Get horse and buggy

John P. Chassin
How Citron FLYG International

Automobiles have changed greatly in the last 90 years. However, both the old and the new still have many systems in common—engines, electrical, fuel and brakes, to name a few. Older cars posed many servicing challenges, as do the new ones. If you understand the technology of 50 years ago, you will appreciate the engineers of those times. They experimented with materials and designs just as today's engineers do. Even though older cars may be *old*, they aren't necessarily *simple* or *crude*. In many cases, they are sophisticated works of art.

This color section shows you some unique cars and some common ones. It has unfamiliar components and some you can identify immediately. Look through these photographs and notice the gradual development of all these systems. You'll see the need for today's mechanic to be well equipped and highly trained.

Photos courtesy of Evans Collection, San Diego, California.

1910 STODDARD-DAYTON
STRAIGHT 4

The 1910 Stoddard-Dayton is noted for its exposed valve train. Two camshafts are placed low in the block, on each side of the crankshaft. Pushrods run up the outside of the two separate cylinder blocks and move rocker arms on top of the cylinder heads. Small springs around each pushrod help keep the pushrods tight. All the pivots and moving parts have to be manually oiled. The engine uses a magneto *and* a distributor for ignition, with 2 plugs per cylinder.

I 1

ENGINES

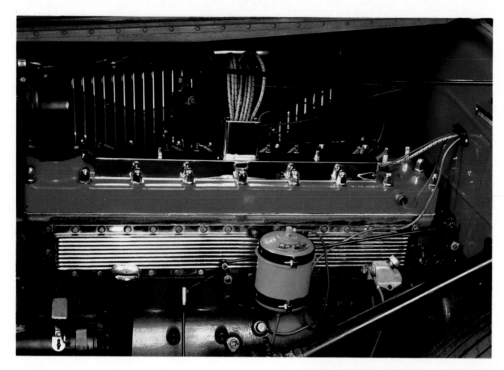

1931 CHRYSLER STRAIGHT 8

The 1931 Chrysler uses a 273 cubic in. straight 8 flathead engine. Low compression models (5.2:1) have a silver cylinder head, while the high compression (6.2:1) engines use a red head. The valve gear is located in the block, behind the side cover. The thermostat (at the top front of the engine) opens and closes louvers in the radiator grille to control coolant temperature.

1962 AUSTIN MINI TRANSVERSE 4

The Mini was the first modern compact with a transversely-mounted 4-cylinder engine. The radiator is at the front of the engine. Air enters through the grille and exits through the left front wheel well. The transmission is located below the engine and shares the engine's oil. This model has two SU carburetors and the optional heater. Several versions of the Mini are still in production.

I 2

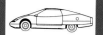

1963 PLYMOUTH VALIANT
SLANT 6

The Slant Six is one of the most reliable engines ever designed. Millions of cars were built with this engine between 1960 and 1983. Since 1983, it has only been used in trucks. The early versions were available in 170 or 225 cubic in. displacement, with either aluminum or cast iron blocks. The "Hyperpack" model came from the factory with a 4-barrel carburetor and was rated at 148 hp.

1980 PORSCHE 911
FLAT 6

The Porsche 911 is the last remaining air-cooled engine sold in the United States. The engine compartment is dominated by the cooling fan and air ducts. The fuel injection unit can be seen in the upper right corner. These engines have a remote oil reservoir, which is why the oil filter seems to screw into the right rear fender. Total oil capacity is 13 liters.

I 3

ENGINES

**1985 CHEVROLET/SUZUKI SPRINT
TRANSVERSE 3**

The Japanese Sprint has the only 3-cylinder automotive engine currently
sold in the United States. Previous 3-cylinder cars sold here include the
Saab 95 and the Bavarian Goliath, both with 2-stroke engines. The 4-
stroke Suzuki displaces 1 liter (61 cubic in.) and produces 48 horsepower.
Total engine weight is less than 150 lbs. The light weight is achieved by
using a hollow crankshaft and camshaft in aluminum block and cylinder
head. The distributor is driven directly off the end of the camshaft.

I 4

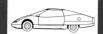

1985 NISSAN MAXIMA
TRANSVERSE OHC V6

The Maxima's overhead cam V6 engine and accessories completely pack the engine compartment. The aluminum 3 liter (181 cubic in.) engine has its cylinders arranged in a 60° V for compactness and light weight. Over 50 electrical relays and motors are squeezed in along with the engine and transaxle. It could take 8 to 10 hours or more to remove and install this engine. Not only the engine compartment is crowded. Every other place in the car is filled with electrical parts, including the underside of the rear package shelf, under both front seats, behind both kick panels, and under the dash.

I 5

1936 CORD

1913 MERCER DASHBOARD

The Mercer dash doubles as a firewall and floorboards. It supports the oil gauge, fuel pressure gauge, magneto switch, speedometer, pedals and foot rail. This right-hand-drive car has an accelerator pedal (off to the right of the dash), a brake pedal, clutch, and a muffler by-pass button (near the foot rail). The acetylene lamps are supplied from a tank on the driver's running board. The magneto has one position and set of plugs for starting, and another for driving. Spark advance and mixture are controlled by levers on the steering wheel. No battery is used on this car.

1936 CORD
DASHBOARD

The Cord has a front-engine, front-wheel-drive layout, with aluminum V8 engine. The dashboard is machine-turned aluminum with a full set of gauges. Large red knobs at each end of the dash open and close the two halves of the windshield (for fresh air). A locking glove box is provided on each side, while lights and heater controls are in the lower center. A large arm off the steering column contains a small chrome gate for the shifter. The little shifter lever is moved to the proper gear, then the clutch is depressed and released. Electric solenoids do the actual gear changing. The car has one fuse for the lights and a circuit breaker for the transmission shifting system.

1958 MERCEDES-BENZ 300 SL
DASHBOARD

The Mercedes-Benz 300 SL Roadster has full instrumentation, with a speedometer, cable-driven tachometer, charging light, oil and water temperature gauges, a mechanical oil pressure gauge, and a fuel gauge. Additional electrical equipment consists of two ignition coils, two horns, two heater blower motors, a trunk light and a backup light. The fuel-injected engine uses a supplementary electric fuel pump, but only for starting. An oil pressure switch turns the pump off once oil pressure builds up. The driver has a manual pump switch to use if the fuel level in the 100 liter tank falls into reserve. The fuse block contains 12 fuses.

ELECTRICAL AND DASHBOARDS

1965 CORVAIR CORSA INSTRUMENT CLUSTER

The sporty Corvair Corsa has a full instrument cluster. The turbocharged, air-cooled engine requires some unusual gauges—vacuum/manifold pressure and cylinder head temperature. The dials also contain a speedometer, tachometer, clock and fuel gauge. "Idiot lights" warn the driver of oil pressure, charging, and cooling problems. The gauges on a Corvair must be specially calibrated. The distance between the engine in the rear of the car and the instrument panel means extra wiring resistance which might throw off the instrument readings if not compensated for by the factory. Another novelty is the speedometer cable which is driven off the left front wheelbearing dust cap rather than from a gear in the transmission.

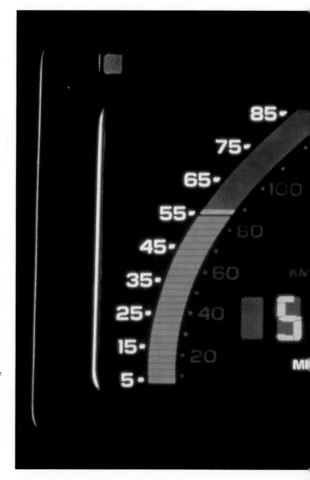

1984 CORVETTE ELECTRONIC INSTRUMENT CLUSTER

The Corvette has a state-of-the-art digital dashboard. Graphic and digital readouts instantly show vehicle speed and engine RPM. The center driver information section shows fuel level with a bar graph. Oil temperature, oil pressure, coolant temperature and volts are digitally displayed. A trip computer calculates average and instant fuel consumption. Another readout provides an estimated trip range based on the current miles-per-gallon average. All these readings are available in customary or metric units. The electrical system uses four circuit breakers and 21 fuses.

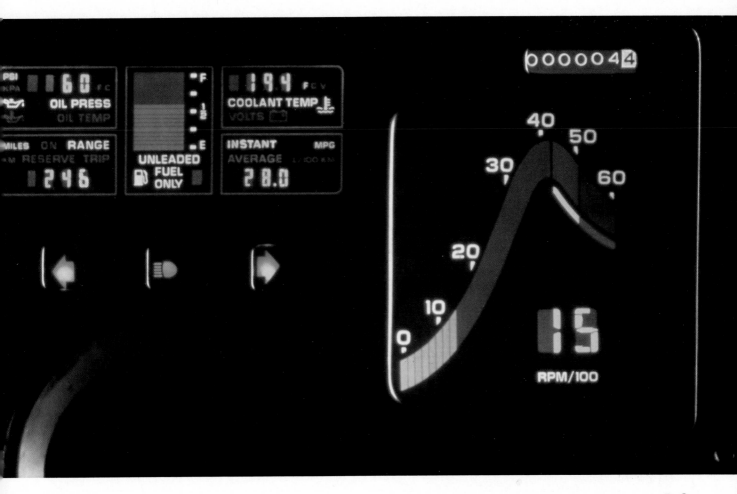

FUEL

1913 MERCER
ZENITH UPDRAFT 1-BARREL

The Mercer has an updraft 1-barrel carburetor which feeds the four cylinders through a brass manifold. Air pressure pushes fuel to the engine, from a tank behind the seat. An air pump and pressure gauge enable the driver to monitor the fuel supply. Brass priming cups are provided for each cylinder. When the car is cold, the driver opens the wing lever, pours in some fuel, and then closes the valve. The car should then start easily.

1928 FORD MODEL A
ZENITH UPDRAFT 1-BARREL

The Model A has a cowl-mounted tank which uses gravity to supply fuel to the carburetor. The filter bowl and fuel line are visible at the top left. The driver can control the mixture using a dash knob linked to the carburetor by the metal rod with the spring wrapped around it. Although many cars of this period had no air cleaners, the Model A shown has a small screen filter.

1955 THUNDERBIRD
HOLLEY CENTRI-QUAD 4-BARREL

This carburetor was used on early 1950's Ford and Mercury V8 engines. Its nickname was "Christmas Tree" carburetor, due to the tapered shape and all the ornaments hanging on it. The float bowl is on top of the throttle body (where cast letters appear). The primary throttle bores are in front of the carburetor, while the secondaries are behind and below the float bowl assembly. A special oil-bath air cleaner sits on top of the carburetor.

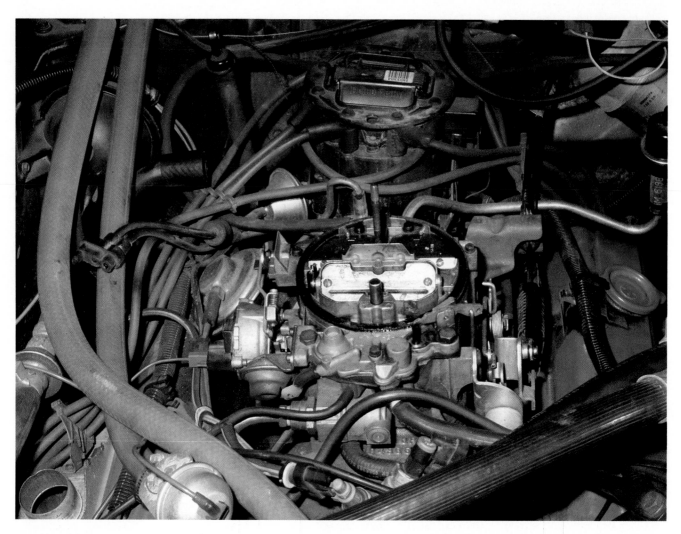

**1980 CHEVROLET
ROCHESTER QUADRAJET 4-BARREL**

The Quadrajet is used on millions of General Motors V8 engines. It has very small primary bores and large secondaries, for good economy and performance. This carburetor has over 100 parts and a list price ranging from $400-900. Notice the tangle of hoses, wiring and pipes. Later feedback models have even more wiring, including a mixture control solenoid in the carburetor itself. An overhaul can take even a skilled professional as long as 3-4 hours.

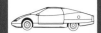

1985 FORD
CENTRAL FUEL INJECTION

The electronic throttle body injection system uses two injectors, spraying into two throttle bores. The tops of the injectors are visible, with wiring connectors on them. The brass cylinder on top of the throttle body is the fuel pressure regulator. An idle speed control motor in the foreground eliminates the need for regular idle adjustments. An overhaul of this unit means changing the injectors and possibly the fuel regulators—a very simple job. Color coding is used on cables, wires and hoses to make assembly easier.

1985 CORVETTE
TUNED PORT INDUCTION FUEL INJECTION

The Corvette uses ram-tuned pipes to pack air into the combustion chambers. The air cleaner is located in front of the radiator support. Clean air flows through a hot-wire airflow meter, through a flexible duct, past the throttle blades, and into the chamber above the tuned pipes. The pipes visible from the left side of the car curve underneath and feed the right bank. The system increases horsepower, torque and mileage compared to the dual throttle bodies used in previous years.

I 13

BRAKES

1931 CHRYSLER IMPERIAL

**1906 PACKARD
REAR ROD BRAKES**

The Packard brakes are on the rear wheels only and operate by adjustable rods and links. They are an externally-contracting design, where the brake friction material is wrapped around the outside of the drum and snugged tight around it. It is easy to see when the material is worn out, but also easy for it to get wet or dirty. The brass container with a small lever in the center is filled with grease. Before each trip, the driver should walk behind the car and give the lever a twist, pumping grease to the wheel bearings.

1946 FORD
REAR HYDRAULIC DRUM BRAKE

This cutaway view of a hydraulic drum brake shows the wheel cylinder (with internal spring between the pistons), the brake shoes, the axle seal and the connecting links. Although production brakes were not chromed or as clean as this one, they were better protected than the external brakes on the Packard and other early designs.

1969 JAVELIN
FRONT 4-PISTON DISC BRAKE

This brake is one of the largest and heaviest ever used on an American passenger car. With a cast-iron, 4-piston design, it has great strength but is complex and expensive to rebuild. It is necessary to use feeler gauges and shims to align the caliper whenever it is removed. Each caliper has six rubber seals and four return springs.

BRAKES

1984 SUBARU
FRONT SLIDING CALIPER DISC BRAKE

This car uses a single-piston, sliding caliper, ventilated disc with integral parking brake and front wheel drive. The parking brake cable is above the axle shaft and below the hydraulic line. It pulls a lever which forces the piston against the disc. This design is light and efficient. All moving parts are well protected from the elements by rubber boots and seals, even the caliper slide pins.

1985 BMW 733i
REAR ANTI-SKID DISC BRAKES

This single-piston, sliding-caliper rear brake unit includes a wheel rotation speed sensor. The sensor counts the notches rotating with the axle shaft, and informs an electronic control unit of the wheel's speed. All four wheels are compared. If any wheel turns too slowly (locks up), the hydraulic pressure unit releases that wheel's brake pressure. The system is effective but expensive—prices for the controller and the hydraulic unit alone add up to about $3000, enough to buy a decent used car.

The driving force of the piston is multiplied by the number of pistons in the engine. Most automobile engines have from four to eight cylinders and pistons, which can be arranged in line, in opposed pairs or in a V (Figure 7-4).

COOLING SYSTEMS

The heat developed by combustion may be removed by either liquid or air cooling. The cooling system keeps the engine at an effective operating temperature.

FIGURE 7-4 Types of engines.

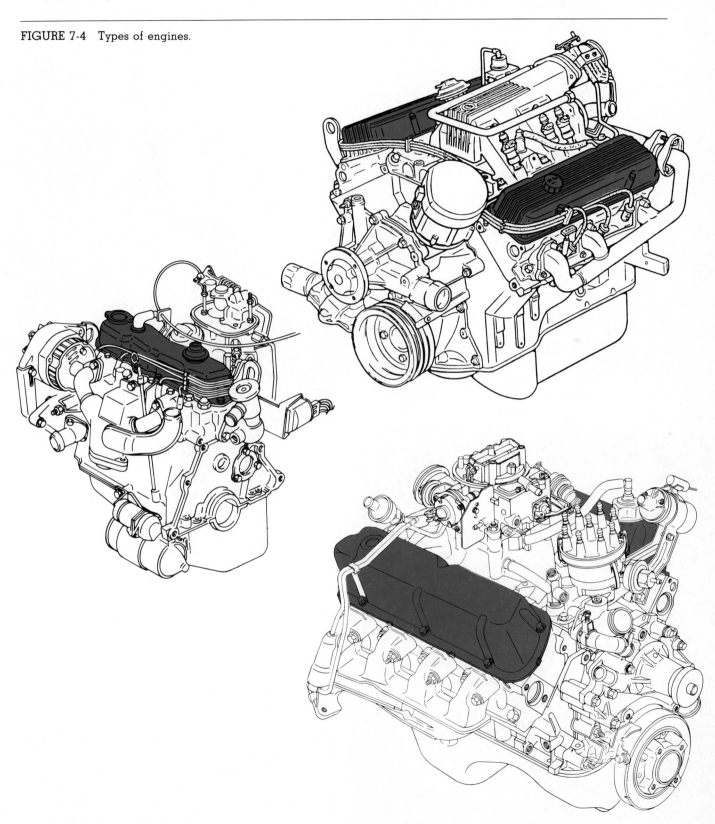

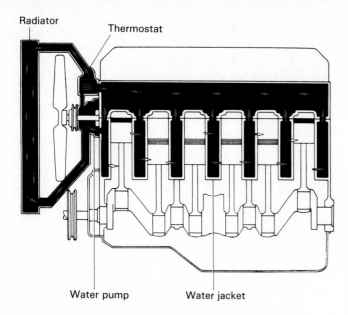

FIGURE 7-5 Water flow in cooling system.

Water-Cooled Engines

All of the burning fuel in the combustion chamber creates extremely high temperatures in the engine. To keep these temperatures in a manageable range, **coolant** is used in the cooling system to cool the block. *Coolant* is a mixture of water, special lubricants, and special antifreezing chemicals. Coolant is circulated through the engine block by a water pump (Figure 7-5). Coolant is drawn from the bottom of the radiator and circulated around the cylinder walls and through the heads, drawing the heat off. This hot coolant is then pulled into the radiator where the action of air passing rapidly across the cooling tubes removes the heat. The cool coolant then starts the cycle all over again.

Air-Cooled Engines

Some engines, such as the Volkswagen Beetle's, are not cooled by water. Figure 7-6 shows an air-cooled

FIGURE 7-6 Air-cooled engine cylinder.
(Volkswagen of America, Inc.)

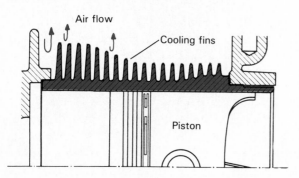

cylinder. The fins on the sides and top carry heat away from the cylinder walls. As cool air passes over the fins, the heat is removed from the cylinders. A fan is always used to aid in the circulation of cooling air.

FUEL SYSTEMS

The functions of the fuel system are storage, delivery of fuel to the engine, and effective mixing of fuel and air.

Fuel Tank

Fuel is stored in the **fuel tank.** On front-engine automobiles it is mounted in the rear. Rear-engine automobiles usually have fuel tanks mounted in the front. The fuel tank is mounted away from the engine. This allows for better distribution of weight and reduces the chance of fire. Figure 7-7 shows the parts of the fuel tank.

Fuel Pump

The **fuel pump** draws fuel from the fuel tank to the carburetor or **fuel injection** system (Figure 7-8). The two types of fuel pumps are mechanical and electrical.

Carburetors

Carburetors or fuel injection systems supply fuel and air to the combustion chamber. The carburetor was the standard of the industry until the early 1960s when fuel injection began to appear on many automobiles.

The carburetor, sensing low intake manifold pressure (vacuum), meters fuel into the venturi and atomizes the gasoline (Figure 7-9). Atomizing is breaking a liquid into small droplets and mixing them with air. The atomized fuel is drawn into the combustion chamber. The **choke** regulates the amount of air coming

FIGURE 7-7 Fuel tank. (Chrysler Corporation)

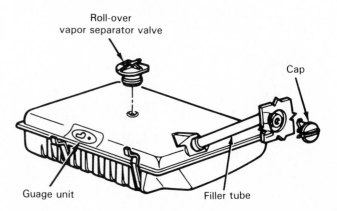

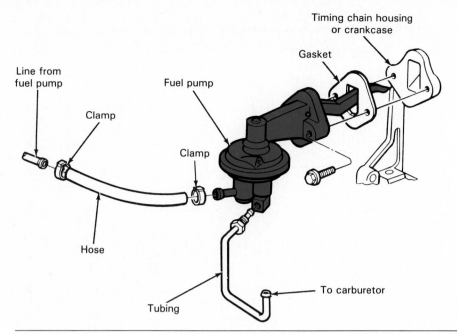

FIGURE 7-8 Mechanical fuel pump.
(Chrysler Corporation)

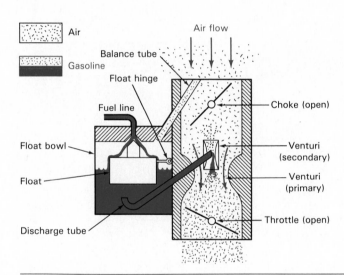

FIGURE 7-9 Elementary carburetion.

in during cold starts. The **throttle** adjusts the amount of air entering the cylinder at all other times. The carburetor senses the airflow and adds gasoline to the airflow to form a fuel and air mixture in the combustion chamber.

Fuel Injection

Fuel injection is more efficient than carburetion. With carburetion the cylinders farthest from the carburetor get less fuel than the cylinders directly beneath the carburetor. *Fuel injection* supplies a metered amount of atomized fuel to the intake manifold.

The different types of fuel injection systems are the single-point and the multipoint injector systems. The single-point system (Figure 7-10) resembles a car-

buretor. It differs from the carburetor in that the fuel is atomized and injected into the intake manifold under pressure. The fuel-injected spray is much like the spray from an aerosol paint can (Figure 7-11).

Multipoint fuel injection systems are used on both gas and diesel engines. Multipoint injection has a fuel injector in the intake manifold at each cylinder. Figure 7-12 illustrates a typical diesel multipoint fuel injection system. Two major parts of this system are the air induction control system (Figure 7-13) and the gas induction system (Figure 7-14).

Fuel injection systems are not just a way to put gas into the cylinders. They are part of the total control of the engine. The engine controls that reduce air pollution are the fuel system, the ignition system, and the on-board computer system (Figure 7-15).

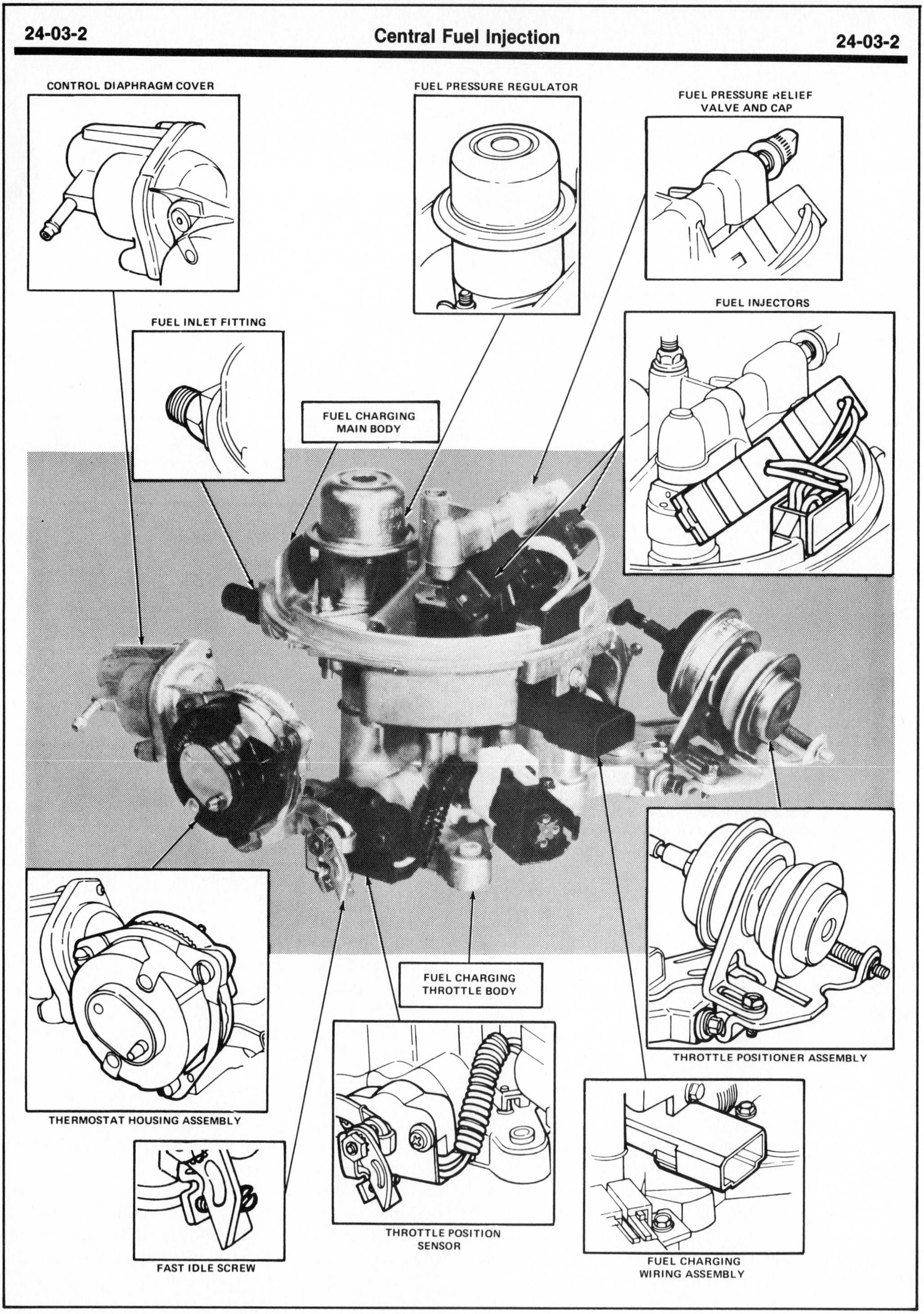

CONTROL DIAPHRAGM COVER

FUEL PRESSURE REGULATOR

FUEL PRESSURE RELIEF VALVE AND CAP

FUEL INJECTORS

FUEL INLET FITTING

FUEL CHARGING MAIN BODY

THERMOSTAT HOUSING ASSEMBLY

FUEL CHARGING THROTTLE BODY

THROTTLE POSITIONER ASSEMBLY

FAST IDLE SCREW

THROTTLE POSITION SENSOR

FUEL CHARGING WIRING ASSEMBLY

FIGURE 7-10   Single-point fuel injection. (Ford Motor Company)

Incorrect spray pattern   Correct spray pattern

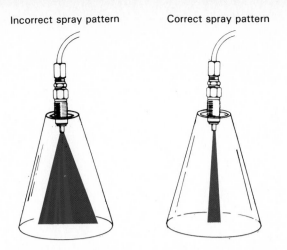

FIGURE 7-11 Injector spray. (Mazda North America, Inc.)

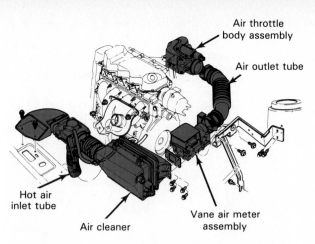

FIGURE 7-13 Air induction control system.

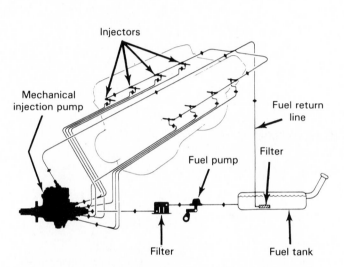

FIGURE 7-12 Multipoint diesel fuel injection system. (Oldsmobile Motor Division, GMC)

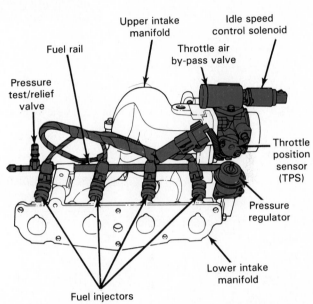

FIGURE 7-14 Gas induction control system. (Ford Motor Company)

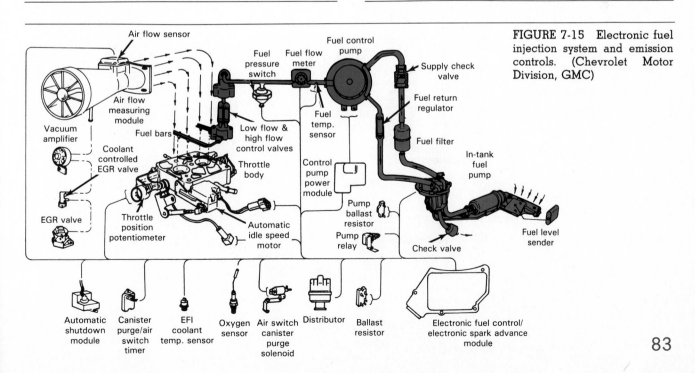

FIGURE 7-15 Electronic fuel injection system and emission controls. (Chevrolet Motor Division, GMC)

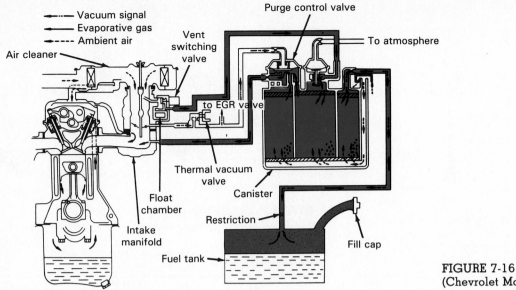

FIGURE 7-16 Emission control systems.
(Chevrolet Motor Division, GMC)

FIGURE 7-17 EGR and PCV in the emission control system. (Nissan Motor Corporation)

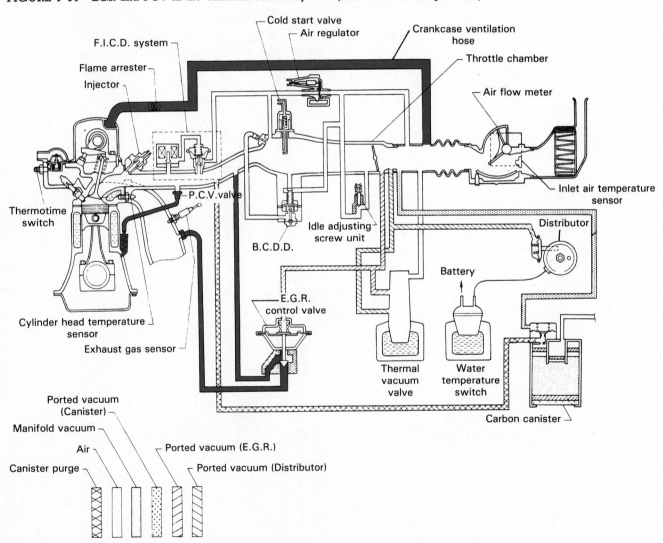

EMISSIONS CONTROL SYSTEMS

Burning petroleum-based fuels produces various gases. These gases or emissions produce pollution that can cause significant health problems. To control pollution, many changes have been made to the fuel and exhaust systems. Carburetion has been adjusted to present the leanest mixture possible (reduced fuel to air ratio), chokes were redesigned to open rapidly, preheaters were added to heat the intake air, and the total fuel control system was redesigned (Figure 7-16).

To further increase complete combustion to reduce unburned hydrocarbons, the operating temperature of the engine was increased. By restricting the flow of coolant and distributor vacuum advance, the combustion was further controlled. The lean mixture and higher temperatures reduced hydrocarbons (HC) and carbon monoxide (CO) but increased nitrous oxide (NO) emissions.

The exhaust gas recirculation (EGR) system produces the greatest decrease in nitrous oxide emissions. This system cools and recirculates some of the exhaust back through the intake manifold and into the combustion chamber (Figure 7-17).

Positive crankcase ventilation (PCV) is a system that draws crankcase vapors into the engine intake system. These vapors are then burned in the combustion chamber instead of being discharged into the atmosphere.

Catalytic converters were introduced in 1975. These chemical reaction systems pass the exhaust gases through catalytic pellets in the canister to reduce hydrocarbons, carbon monoxide, and nitrous oxides (Figure 7-18).

About 20% of total emissions are reduced by the PCV, 20% by fuel evaporation controls, and 60% by all other emission devices combined.

ELECTRICAL/ELECTRONIC SYSTEMS

There are five basic electrical/electronic systems within the automobile. These are the ignition system, starting system, charging system, lighting system, and accessory system.

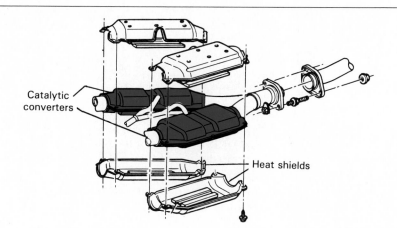

Catalytic converters

Heat shields

FIGURE 7-18 Catalytic converters. (Ford Motor Company)

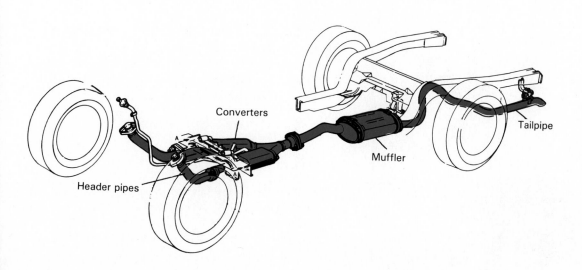

Converters

Tailpipe

Muffler

Header pipes

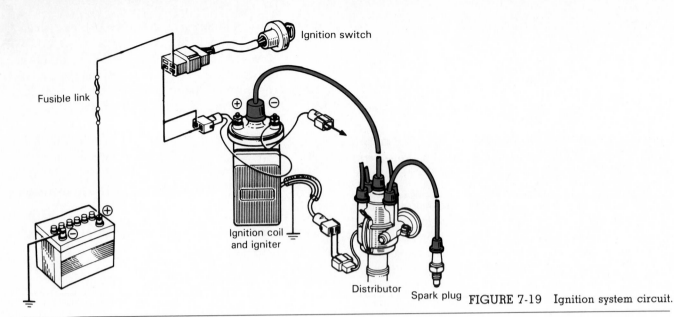

FIGURE 7-19 Ignition system circuit.

Ignition System

The ignition system provides the spark at the spark plug to ignite the compressed fuel and air mixture at the proper time (Figure 7-19). Twelve volts of electricity are applied from the battery to the coil. The coil boosts that 12 V to about 40,000 V, providing enough power to jump the gap in the spark plug. The charge is sent from the coil to the distributor where it is then "distributed" to each of the cylinders at the correct time.

Starting System

The starter cranks the engine over. It turns the flywheel to provide the force to start the pistons moving up and down to start the engine. To activate the starting system, voltage from the battery passes to the solenoid

FIGURE 7-20 Starting system circuit.

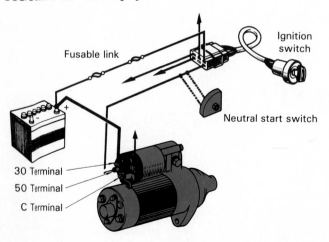

by turning the key (Figure 7-20). It then passes from the solenoid to the starter motor. The solenoid prevents the full current draw from the battery from passing through the ignition switch. If this much current (up to 400 A) were to pass through the ignition switch, it would melt.

Charging System

To keep the battery charged, an **alternator** is turned by the engine. The alternator produces electricity which is passed back to the battery through an alternator regulator (Figure 7-21). The regulator prevents the battery from becoming overcharged because the alternator will often produce more electricity than the battery needs.

Lighting System

The battery also provides electricity to the light system (Figure 7-22). By turning a switch, the headlight, parking lights, and taillight come on. When you put the car in reverse, the backup lights come on. Other lights in the system include the brake light and courtesy lights.

Accessories

The battery also supplies electrical power to all electrical accessories. Most accessories are for driving convenience and comfort. Most cars have a radio plus many other accessories. Figure 7-23 identifies just a few of the many accessories available.

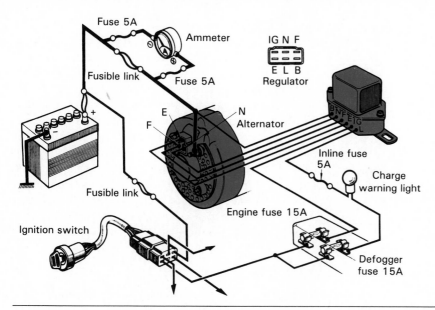

FIGURE 7-21 Charging system circuit.

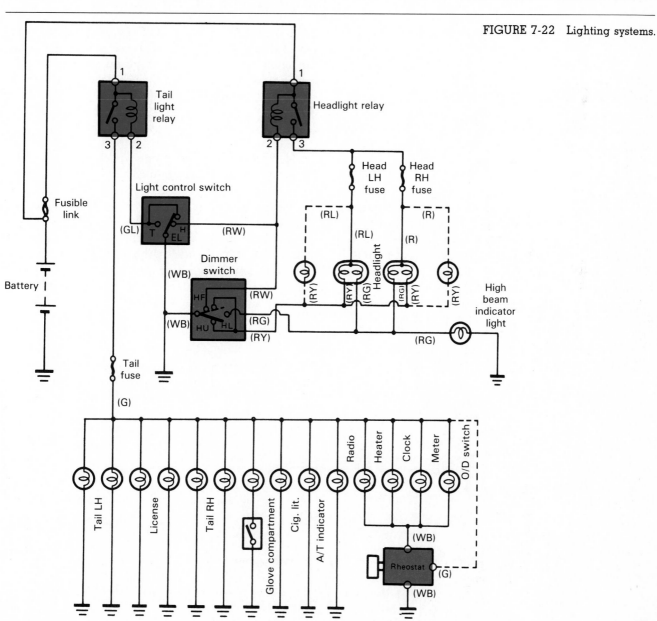

FIGURE 7-22 Lighting systems.

87

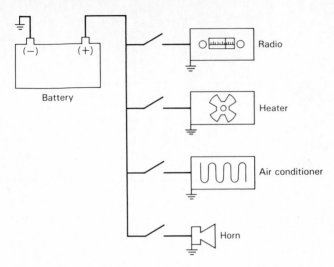

FIGURE 7-23   Electrical accessories.

POWER TRAINS

The **power train** takes rotating power from the engine and transfers it to either the front or rear wheels (Figure 7-24). Each component of the power train is interrelated; if any one part breaks down, the entire system breaks down.

Transmissions

A **transmission** changes the ratio of engine revolutions to wheel revolutions, and multiplies engine torque. Without a transmission, an engine would not be able to overcome the inertia (weight) of the car. A transmission will let the engine develop 2000 rpm while the drive wheels are only turning 200 rpm. This difference in rpm makes it easy to start the car rolling. By the time the car is at highway speeds, the transmission is in high gear, and the engine still is at 2000 rpm. The transmission protects the engine from overload when starting and produces efficient gasoline consumption while at cruising speeds.

Transmissions are either automatic or manual. The automatic transmission works through a series of bands, drums, and clutches brought into contact with one another by hydraulic or electrical controls (Figure 7-25). The manual transmission uses gears in place of drums, bands, and clutches. The gears are shifted manually instead of hydraulically (Figure 7-26). Sometimes the transmission and axles are combined. This system is called a transaxle.

Drive Axles

There are three types of drive trains: front-wheel drive, rear-wheel drive, and four-wheel drive.

Rear-Wheel Drive   Most U.S. cars used to be rear-wheel drive (Figure 7-27). The rear wheels push the car forward. The motive force generated by the engine has to be transmitted from the engine to the transmission and then to the rear of the car. Some rear wheel drive cars have rear engines, although these are less common now than a few years ago.

Front-Wheel Drive   In front-wheel-drive cars, the front wheels are driven in much the same way as the rear wheels are driven in rear-wheel drive. The front wheels are used for pulling the car rather than pushing it as in rear-wheel drive (Figure 7-28). Most front-wheel-drive cars have their engine mounted across rather than in line with the body. Front-wheel-drive cars have fewer parts in their drive trains than do their rear-wheel-drive counterparts, but the parts must be squeezed into one end of the car.

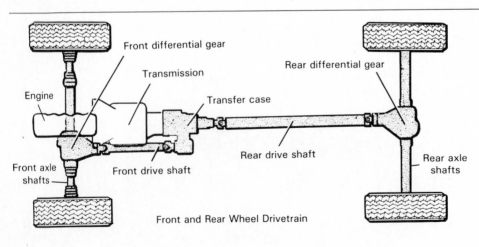

FIGURE 7-24   Power train. (Chrysler Corporation)

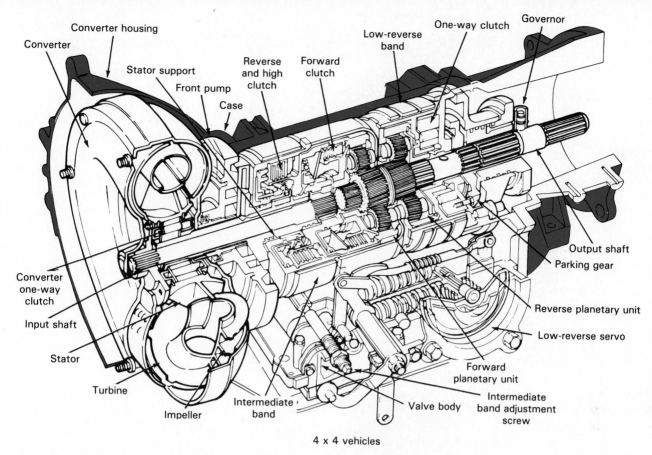

Converter housing

Converter

Stator support

Front pump

Case

Reverse and high clutch

Forward clutch

Low-reverse band

One-way clutch

Governor

Converter one-way clutch

Input shaft

Stator

Turbine

Impeller

Intermediate band

Valve body

Forward planetary unit

Intermediate band adjustment screw

Output shaft

Parking gear

Reverse planetary unit

Low-reverse servo

4 x 4 vehicles

FIGURE 7-25 Automatic transmission.

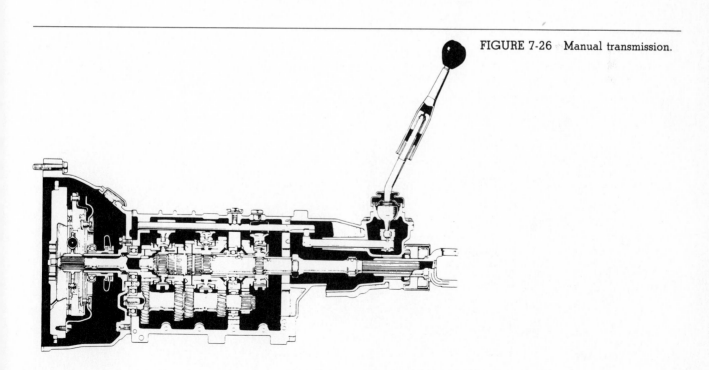

FIGURE 7-26 Manual transmission.

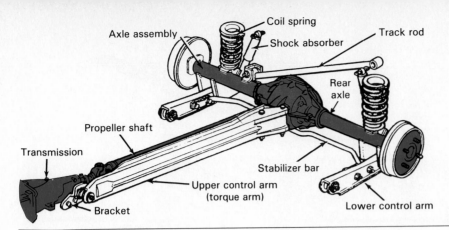

Coil spring
Axle assembly
Shock absorber
Track rod
Rear axle
Propeller shaft
Transmission
Stabilizer bar
Bracket
Upper control arm (torque arm)
Lower control arm

FIGURE 7-27 Rear-wheel drive.

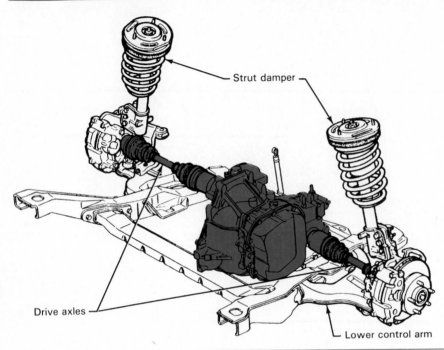

Strut damper

Drive axles

Lower control arm

FIGURE 7-28 Front-wheel drive.

FIGURE 7-29 Typical front suspension, front-wheel drive. (Ford Motor Company)

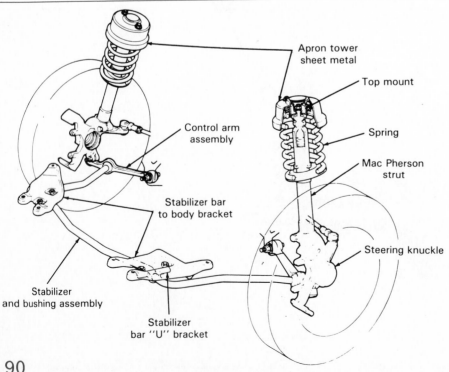

Apron tower sheet metal

Top mount

Control arm assembly

Spring

Mac Pherson strut

Stabilizer bar to body bracket

Steering knuckle

Stabilizer and bushing assembly

Stabilizer bar "U" bracket

Four-Wheel Drive   Most four-wheel-drive vehicles can isolate one pair of wheels so that they are free-wheeling part of the time. The extra weight of the four-wheel drive, the gearing, and the friction still create a drag and may reduce mileage. Four-wheel-drive vehicles, however, have more road control and will go places that front- or rear-wheel-drive vehicles cannot go.

SUSPENSION

Suspension separates the frame and body from both the front and rear wheels and axles (Figures 7-29 and 7-30). This suspension keeps the passenger in the car from bouncing up and down when the car is going over a bumpy road. All four wheels are isolated from the chassis by springs and shock absorbers. The springs allow the wheels to move up and down in relation to the frame. The shock absorbers keep the body from reacting against the spring in an equal and opposite reaction. Without shock absorbers the car would continue bouncing like a ball after hitting a bump. Without springs, the jolt felt by the tire would be passed directly to the passengers.

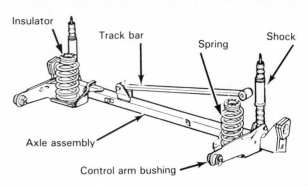

FIGURE 7-30   Typical rear suspension, front-wheel drive.

STEERING AND WHEEL ALIGNMENT

To keep the car going on the road, it must be steered. Steering can be either manual or power assisted. In manual steering, as you move the steering wheel one way or the other, you rotate a shaft in the steering gearbox. A gear converts the steering wheel action to the front wheels (Figure 7-31).

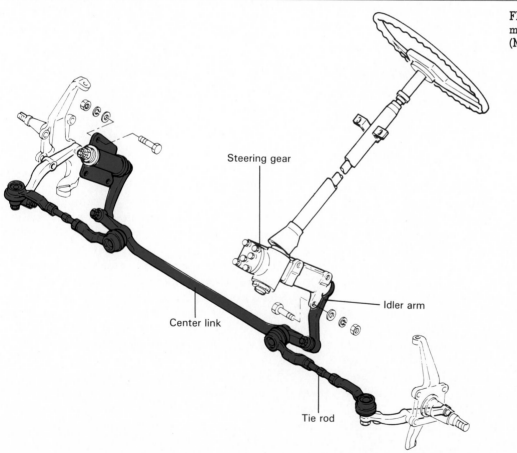

FIGURE 7-31   Typical manual steering system. (Mazda North America, Inc.)

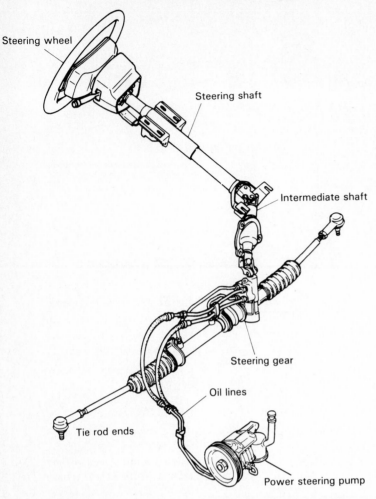

FIGURE 7-32 Power rack and pinion steering system. (Mazda North America, Inc.)

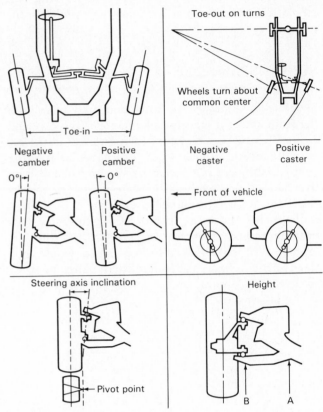

FIGURE 7-33 Definitions of wheel alignment terms. (Chrysler Corporation)

The rack and pinion steering system is used on many imported and small domestic cars (Figure 7-32). The steering shaft has a pinion gear on it. The pinion gear engages the rack, which in turn, through tie rods, moves the wheels right or left. Several other types of steering are also commonly used—worm and roller and recirculating ball.

Steering systems are frequently power assisted. As the steering wheel turns, a power steering pump supplies hydraulic pressure, which moves the connecting rods. In this way the driver need not use muscle power. The hydraulic pressure provides the force.

The steering gear and linkage need periodic adjustment. This is called alignment. Figure 7-33 shows four ways to align wheels and front ends: height, caster, camber, and toe-in. Manufacturers design each of these angles for the best tire wear and drivability. Each of the alignments can be adjusted to conform to factory specifications on most cars.

BRAKES

Brakes stop forward motion of a car through friction. They can be drum brakes, disc brakes, or a combination of the two (Figure 7-34). They can be manually applied or power assisted.

Drum brakes operate by actuating metal shoes to which asbestos composition linings are attached. The friction between lining and drum stops the rotation of the drum. The disc brake works in a similar way. Two linings, one on each side of the disc, squeeze the rotating disc (or rotor) to stop the rotation of the wheel.

To move the brake shoes, hydraulic pressure from the master cylinder passes through steel lines to wheel cylinders. The wheel cylinder pistons push the shoes into the drum or disc. In most cars today, this force is increased by a power booster.

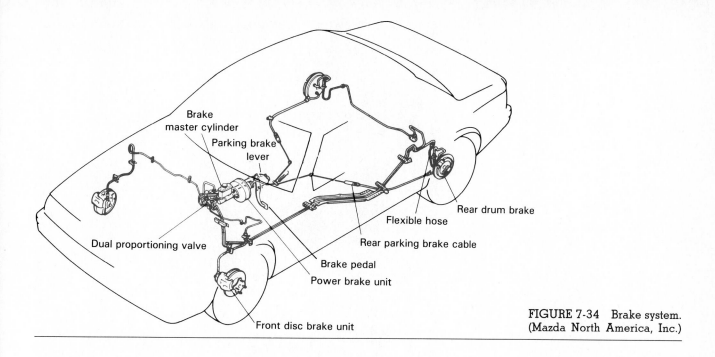

Brake
master cylinder
Parking brake
lever
Dual proportioning valve
Brake pedal
Power brake unit
Front disc brake unit
Rear drum brake
Flexible hose
Rear parking brake cable

FIGURE 7-34 Brake system.
(Mazda North America, Inc.)

TRADE TERMS

Alternator
Brakes
Catalytic Converters
Choke
Coolant
Fuel Injection
Fuel Pump

Fuel Tank
Internal Combustion
Power Train
Suspension
Throttle
Transmission

REVIEW QUESTIONS

1. Name two ways in which you will find the cylinders arranged.
2. Engines are cooled by what?
3. What are the two ways fuel is introduced into an engine?
4. Define the word *atomize*.
5. What do the initials EGR mean?
6. What does a catalytic converter do?
7. Name three electrical systems.

8. What are the major drive axle systems?
9. Name the two types of transmissions.
10. Explain how the frame and body are suspended from both front and rear wheels and axles.
11. Steering is accomplished through a series of pulleys and cables. True or false?
12. What are the four wheel alignment factors?
13. How do brakes stop the motion of a car?

8

Preventive Maintenance

INTRODUCTION

Probably the most important thing car owners can do is to make sure that their cars receive regular and periodic maintenance. A mechanic should assist the car owners with a preventive maintenance plan. Preventive maintenance is as important as servicing a car after parts have failed. This chapter discusses the areas of preventive maintenance, those tasks performed to prevent parts failure. Regardless of how a particular vehicle is used, knowing major service areas and how to monitor them will extend the life of the vehicle.

REASONS FOR PREVENTIVE MAINTENANCE

Reliability

A set regular and scheduled maintenance is important for the reliability, life, and resale of the car. You should encourage your customers to follow the owner's manual for recommendations based on time and miles driven. On new cars a maintenance program is neces-

OBJECTIVES

When you have completed this chapter, you should be able to

- State the reasons for preventive maintenance
- Identify the specific areas of engine transmission, drive transmission, and drive train, electrical, and chassis maintenance
- Explain procedures for servicing these maintenance areas

94

FIGURE 8-1   Maintenance means reliability.

sary to keep the warranty in effect. The thing automotive drivers fear the most, next to having a fatal traffic accident perhaps, is to be left stranded by their car on the road. Brakes failing, a flat tire, an overheated engine, and an alternator not working are just a few things that can happen to spoil a trip or create a real emergency for a driver (Figure 8-1).

Periodic maintenance and checking those areas where problems can occur will significantly reduce the chances of a car breaking down on the road (Figure 8-2). You should encourage customers to set up a regular maintenance schedule for their cars.

FIGURE 8-2   Scheduled maintenance services for a General Motors car. (Cadillac Motor Division, GMC)

SCHEDULED MAINTENANCE SERVICES FOR YOUR GENERAL MOTORS CAR

ITEM NO.	TO BE SERVICED	WHEN TO PERFORM Months or Miles, Whichever Occurs First	7,500 Miles 12 000 km	15,000 Miles 24 000 km	22,500 Miles 35 000 km	30,000 Miles 48 000 km	37,500 Miles 60 000 km	45,000 Miles 72 000 km
Section A — General Maintenance								
A-1	Chassis Lubrication	Lubricate every 12 months or 7,500 miles	•	•	•	•	•	•
A-2	Fluid Levels	Check every 12 months or 7,500 miles	•	•	•	•	•	•
A-3	Engine Oil and Oil Filter*	See Explanation for service intervals						
A-4	Steering, Suspension and Front Drive Axle Boots	Check every 12 months or 7,500 miles	•	•	•	•	•	•
A-5	Brakes Disc Brakes	Check at 7,500 miles, then every 15,000 miles	•		•		•	
	Brake Lines	Check every 12 months or 7,500 miles	•	•	•	•	•	•
	Drum and Parking Brake Systems	Check every 12 months or 15,000 miles		•		•		•
A-6	Tires and Wheels	Check and rotate at 7,500 miles, then every 15,000 miles as shown in Owners Manual	•		•			
A-7	Throttle Linkage	Check every 12 months or 15,000 miles			•		•	
A-8	Cooling System*	Perform maintenance per Explanation every 12 months or 15,000 miles		•		•		•
		Drain, flush & refill every 24 months or 30,000 miles				•		
A-9	Final Drive Axle Output Shaft Seals	Check every 30,000 miles				•		
A-10	Manual Steering Gear					•		
A-11	Transaxle — Manual and Automatic	See Explanation for service intervals						
Section B — Emission Control Maintenance								
B-1	Exhaust System	Check every 12 months or 7,500 miles	•		•	•	•	•
B-2	Carburetor Choke and Hoses	Check at 6 months or 7,500 miles, then at 24 months or 30,000 mile intervals. Also check at 45,000 miles.	•			•		•
B-3	Engine Idle Speed (Canada Only)		•			•		•
B-4	Engine Drive Belts	Check every 12 months or 15,000 miles		•		•		•
B-5	Fuel Cap, Tank and Lines			•		•		•
B-6	Thermo-Controlled Air Cleaner	Check every 30,000 miles				•		
B-7	Spark Plug Wires and Distributor					•		
B-8	Engine Timing	Adjust every 30,000 miles				•		
B-9	Spark Plugs	Replace every 30,000 miles				•		
B-10	PCV Valve					•		
B-11	Air Cleaner and PCV Filter Elements	Replace every 50,000 miles (1)						
B-12	EGR System	Service every 30,000 miles				•		

*Also an Emission Control Service

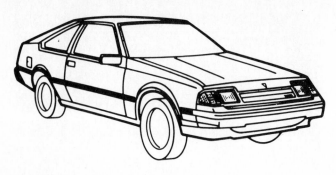

FIGURE 8-3   Maintenance means long life.

Life

Daily care, proper maintenance, and immediate repairs can extend the life of a car longer than its designed life span (Figure 8-3). Any production car, whether it's American or foreign, should be expected to perform properly for about 100,000 mi.

Resale

A well-maintained car has a higher resale value than one that has not been taken care of (Figure 8-4). This

FIGURE 8-4   Maintenance means high resale value.

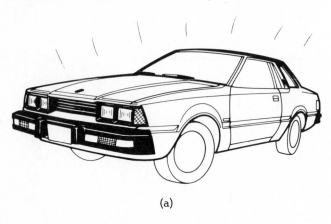

(a)

Maintenance means high resale value

(b)

is simple economics. A good, clean, well-running car with a large number of miles is more valuable than a low-mileage, low-maintained car. If you trade in an abused car, it will have to be sent out for detailing and preparation before the dealer can resell it. This work costs a sizable amount, and the seller of the car must bear the burden of these repairs. The well-maintained car seldom needs this help.

ENGINE MAINTENANCE

Cleanliness

When working on a car, you should point out to the owner that engine maintenance is important in keeping the car in good running condition. Also, with your professional experience, through engine maintenance, you may be able to spot future problems.

A clean engine is easier to work on than a dirty one. A clean engine also runs cooler than a dirty, greasy one (Figure 8-5). It presents a nicer appearance, and problems, such as leaks, are easily spotted. You can keep a new engine clean by periodically washing it with detergent and water. (Be careful to keep water out of the distributor, carburetor, and electronic components.) If the engine is excessively dirty, use a water-soluble grease emulsifier to clean it.

To apply these commercial cleaners, start the engine, let it warm up, turn the engine off, and spray the cleaner over it with a pump sprayer or apply it with a brush. Allow the cleaner to work for a few minutes. Follow up with a strong spray of water to wash away the emulsified grease and dirt. Really dirty engines will require steam cleaning (Figure 8-6). Be careful when cleaning an engine with strong detergents or steam. The cleaner can harm seals, relays, wiring, and air-conditioning systems.

Oil and Filter

The single most important part of engine maintenance is checking the oil and changing the oil.

Self-service gas stations are a threat in disguise to the car. Many drivers will put gas in the car and never check the oil level in the engine. You should suggest to your customers that it is good practice to check the oil every second or third gas fill-up. Checking the oil only takes a few moments. To check the oil, turn the engine off and raise the hood. Next pull out the oil **dipstick** and wipe the oil on it off. Reinsert the dipstick completely and then remove it again (Figure 8-7). The level of the engine oil will now show on the dipstick. The dipstick has index marks, as shown in Figure 8-8, identifying the minimum and maximum amount of oil required for the engine.

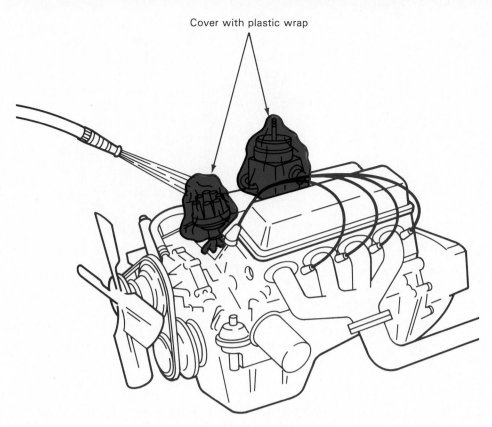

Cover with plastic wrap

FIGURE 8-5   Clean engines are easier to work on.

FIGURE 8-6   Steam cleaner.

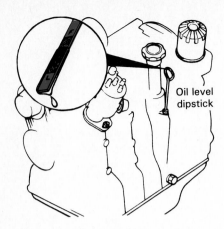

FIGURE 8-7 Checking engine oil level. (Mazda North America, Inc.)

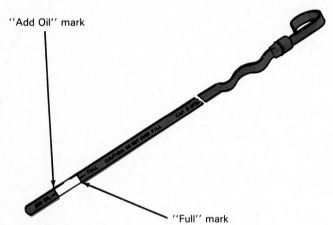

FIGURE 8-8 Dipstick oil level marks. (Chrysler Corporation)

Many manufacturers suggest changing the oil at intervals from 3000 to 12,000 mi. To help the engine to last, change the oil at the manufacturer's specified time. Do not exceed the manufacturer's recommended oil change requirements. One cannot rely totally on the oil filter keeping the oil clean. The oil filter does *not* filter out moisture or acid, two of the most corrosive elements suspended in used oil.

FIGURE 8-9 Cold regions require lighter weight oils. (Chrysler Corporation)

Use a good-quality, manufacturer-recommended oil for your changes. Some engines use multigrade oil such as 20–50 and 10–40. Other car manufacturers recommend single grades, such as 20-, 30-, or 50-weight oils. Colder regions of the country require light-weight oils, and warm regions of the country require heavier weight oils (Figure 8-9).

Oil and Filter Change

Follow these steps to change oil:

1. Warm the engine up to operating temperature. Stop the engine.
2. Remove the oil filler cap (Figure 8-10).

OVERLUBRICATION BETTER THAN NONE?

Excessive lubrication of body parts usually causes more complaints than lack of lubrication. If a soft, dark grease is applied to a door lock bolt or a dovetail wedgeplate on the exposed face of the door, a slight brush across this soft grease may ruin a gown and spoil the entire evening for the owner and others. Too much lubrication applied to exposed parts serves no good purpose. It is not only a waste of material but is a contribution to serious complaints.

Lubricate only where squeaks develop, or where conditions indicate that the addition of lubricant is desirable for easier operation of individual units or points.

1962 Chevy II Shop Manual
Chevrolet Motor Division, GMC

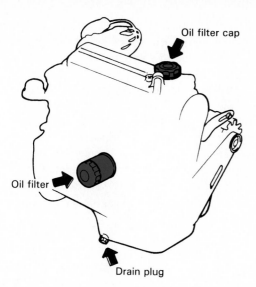

FIGURE 8-10 Oil filter cap. (Mazda North America, Inc.)

3. Raise the car on a hydraulic hoist.
4. Remove the oil drain plug and drain oil into a waste container.
5. Remove the oil filter (Figure 8-11).
6. Allow the oil to continue to drain until it stops dripping.
7. Lightly coat the filter seal with oil and install it.
8. Replace the drain plug.
9. Lower the hoist and add new oil.
10. Replace the oil filler cap.
11. Start the engine and check for leaks.

Some manufacturers recommend that you replace the filter every other oil change. However, a good practice is to replace the oil filter *every* oil change.

FIGURE 8-11 Removing and installing the oil filter. (Mazda North America, Inc.)

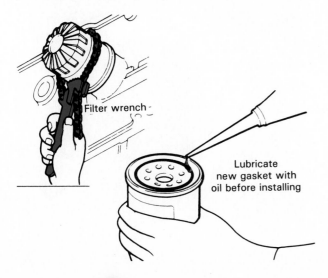

The procedure for changing oil in turbocharged engines is slightly different from procedures for non-turbo cars. After you have changed the oil, remove the center wire on the distributor and crank the engine until either the oil light goes off or the oil gauge indicates oil pressure. Now reconnect the center wire of the distributor. This procedure primes the oil passages to the turbocharger's bearings. If you omit this step, the bearings in the turbocharger may be damaged when the engine is started.

Checking Coolant Level

The cooling system should be checked every two or three gas fill-ups. On most cars you don't have to remove the radiator cap to check the coolant level. The amount of coolant in the recovery/reservoir tank shows the correct amount of coolant in the radiator (Figure 8-12).

The **coolant** is an antifreeze, a lubricant, and a corrosion inhibitor. Adding water periodically dilutes the coolant so that eventually you must replace it. The average amount of time for replacing the coolant is between 1 and 2 years because additives wear out and become corrosive. Be sure to use the recommended coolant. This is especially important on aluminum engines as they will corrode if you use the wrong type.

If there is any evidence of leaks around the hoses, including the heater hoses, replace the hose. Check engine drive belts too for adjustment and wear.

CAUTION:

☐ Do not remove the coolant recovery cap while the coolant is "boiling."
☐ Do not remove the radiator cap while the engine and radiator are hot.
☐ Remember, scalding coolant and steam can be blown out under pressure when either the coolant recovery cap or the radiator cap is removed (Figure 8-13).

FIGURE 8-12 Checking coolant level. (Nissan Motor Corporation)

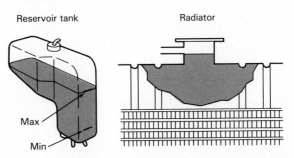

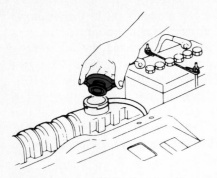

FIGURE 8-13 Be careful of hot radiators (American Isuzu Motors, Inc.)

fuel tank and the carburetor or fuel injection unit. Figure 8-16 shows some of the locations of the filter. The tank filter does not need changing unless someone puts foreign matter in the gas tank.

Diesel fuel filters are generally between the fuel pump and the injection pump (Figure 8-17). Changing a diesel fuel filter is a little more complicated than changing an in-line gas filter. The diesel fuel system must be completely full at all times to operate properly. After inserting a new diesel fuel filter element into the filter, you must refill or **prime** the fuel system. This is done with a small hand pump or by the car's regular fuel pump.

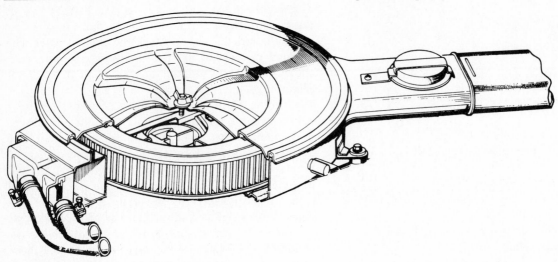

FIGURE 8-14 Air filter. (Mazda North America, Inc.)

Today's cooling system operates at about 195°F (91°C). This is hot! Always treat the cooling system with respect. It can scald or burn you.

Checking Air Filters

The **air cleaner** is usually a paper filter sitting atop the carburetor or fuel injection unit (Figure 8-14). The filter is extremely important because it cleans the air going into the combustion chambers. When it becomes dirty or clogged, less air will pass through. Good engine performance demands lots of clean air. Under normal driving conditions, replace the air filter at 10,000–12,000 miles (Figure 8-15). Newer cars have larger filters that allow 30,000-mile intervals.

Checking Fuel Filters

Replace gasoline in-line filter at about 10,000-mi intervals. The in-line filter can be anywhere between the

FIGURE 8-15 Replacing air filter. (Chrysler Corporation)

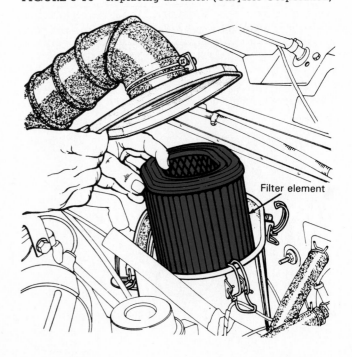

Filter element

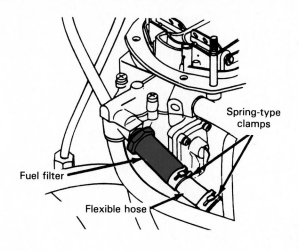

Spring-type
clamps

Fuel filter

Flexible hose

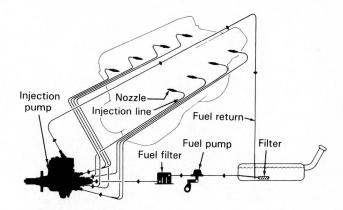

FIGURE 8-17 Diesel fuel filter location. (Pontiac Motor Division, GMC)

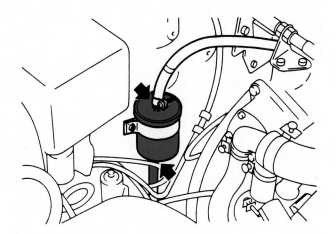

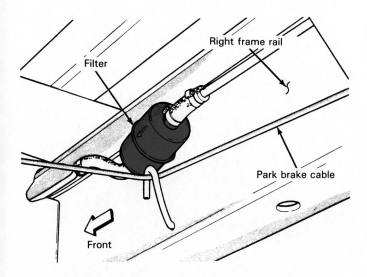

Right frame rail

Filter

Park brake cable

Front

FIGURE 8-16 Fuel filter locations. (Nissan Motor Corporation)

TRANSMISSION DIFFERENTIAL MAINTENANCE

Automatic transmissions use a petroleum-based oil (called automatic transmission fluid or **ATF** for short) to move the internal components of the transmission. Check the ATF periodically. The transmission dipstick location varies with the model of the car.

Checking Fluid Level

The transmission fluid should be checked when it is at normal operating temperature. With the emergency brake set, shift the transmission into Park and start the engine. Then move the selector through all of its positions to warm up the transmission fluid. With the engine in Park, let the engine continue to run.

Remove the dipstick, wipe it off, and stick it back in the tube (Figure 8-18). Remove it again and read the level just like an oil dipstick. If the level is low, add ATF through the dipstick tube or hole until the correct level is read. The marks on the dipstick indicate pints, not quarts as the oil dipstick does. There are several different types of ATF, such as type A or F or Dexron II. Be sure to use the correct type, or transmission shifting will be affected.

To check the oil level on a manual transmission, make sure the car is level and the engine is off. Remove the oil plug. The oil level should be in line with the plug threads. If not, add oil until it reaches the threads. Most older cars use 90-weight oil for the manual transmission, and most new cars use ATF.

Check the differential oil level like the manual transmission. You'll find the oil plug on the differential about halfway up. Most will use 90-weight oil (Figure 8-19).

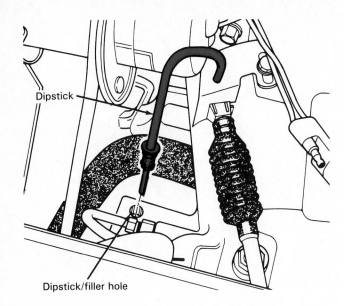

Dipstick

Dipstick/filler hole

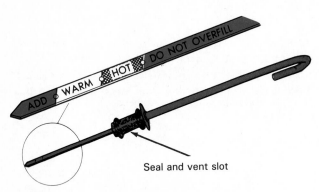

ADD · WARM · HOT · DO NOT OVERFILL

Seal and vent slot

FIGURE 8-18 Checking transmission fluid level. (Chrysler Corporation)

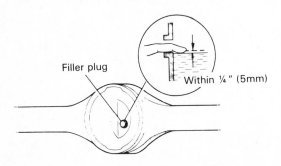

Filler plug

Within ¼" (5mm)

FIGURE 8-19 Checking differential oil level.

ELECTRICAL MAINTENANCE

The battery produces electricity on demand through chemical action. If the engine does not crank over fast enough to start or does not crank over at all, it is normally the result of a battery problem. However, either condition may be caused by other parts of the electrical system.

CAUTION: When servicing a battery, always wear safety glasses. Automotive batteries contain sulfuric acid. If sulfuric acid is splashed in the eyes, flush them with cold water immediately and notify a doctor. If the sulfuric acid comes in contact with skin, clothing, or upholstery, a solution of baking soda and water will neutralize it. The gas that is formed in the battery is explosive. A spark or flame can ignite the gas and cause an explosion.

Checking the Battery

The first step in checking the battery is to look for damage. Check for a cracked case and dirt on the top of the battery and the battery carrier hold-down clamp.

The next check is to remove the battery caps and determine if the electrolyte (acid) is at the correct level. Usually this level is at the bottom of the cap threads. If the level is low, carefully add distilled water until the level is correct.

If the car has a maintenance-free battery, periodically, about every 6 months, check the sight glass (Figure 8-20) if it has one. See Chapter 18 for additional battery service information.

Battery Cables

Check the battery cables each time the hood is opened. Check for corrosion and wear around the insulation (Figure 8-21). Any signs of cracks in the insulation or in the clamp indicates that you should replace the cable.

If corrosion appears, clean away the corrosion with a baking soda and water solution (Figure 8-22).

FIGURE 8-20 Battery test indicator. (Chrysler Corporation)

Sight glass
- Green dot — Battery fully charged
- Black dot — Battery needs recharging
- Yellow dot — Replace battery (Low electrolyte level)

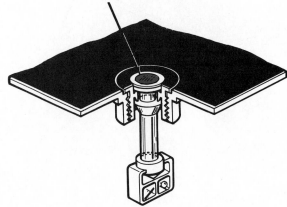

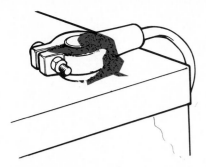

FIGURE 8-21 Battery cable problems.

After cleaning, replace the clamp and apply a thin coat of grease to the terminal.

Circuit Protection

The car's electrical circuits are protected by fuses, fusible links, and circuit breakers. *Fusible links* are special wires smaller than the circuit they protect. They work like in-line fuses. Any excessive load placed on a circuit will melt the fusible link before it melts the wire. Replace these links with new ones (Figure 8-23). Some-

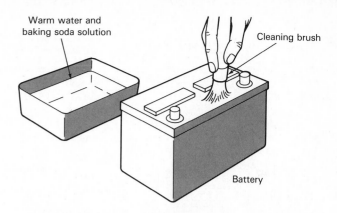

FIGURE 8-22 Cleaning a battery. (Chrysler Corporation)

times it is hard to find where these links are. Use a shop manual to find their locations.

Fuses, like those seen in Figure 8-24, are wires enclosed in glass or plastic. When the load gets too heavy, the wire melts, interrupting the current. Usually a burnt fuse is easy to detect visually. Remove the fuse from the fuse box or panel and inspect it. If it's blown, determine the cause, repair it, and replace the fuse (Figure 8-25). Automotive circuit breakers usually

"YOU CAN'T BE TOO CAREFUL . . ."

For many years, the National Hot Rod Association (NHRA) has held its National Championship drag races in Indianapolis, Indiana. It's a Labor Day event that draws tens of thousands of spectators and hundreds of the sport's best participants.

At the 1977 Nationals, John Lingenfelter became the Super Stock Eliminator for the year. And up to the morning of race day, his performances in qualification trials indicated he was the person to beat.

Following his preliminary win, his car had been subjected to the normal inspection team for legality of engine and chassis.

John's carburetor was removed and taken apart for an internal look. The carburetor passed the tech committee's scrutiny, and John reassembled his engine.

Then came race day. By 7:00 A.M., John was in the staging lines for a test run down the track. Off the starting line and at about half-track, a broken connecting rod shoved a section of cylinder block onto the track, and John was driv-

ing over his own engine oil. It was about 7:30 A.M., and final eliminations were to begin at 1:00 P.M. Furthermore, John had no spare engine. So the number one qualifier was out of the Nationals. Well, almost out.

Helpers appeared from nowhere. Back in the pit area, the engine was out, all usable parts were off and being cleaned, and John was on the telephone making arrangements for helicopter transportation back to his Indiana shop.

The 'copter arrived, John became its passenger, and headed for his home and shop. There he managed to find another cylinder head and performed a quick valve job. He had a spare cylinder block already fitted with seven piston, rod, and ring assemblies and managed to find the eighth and get it installed. All the pieces were loaded into the 'copter, and John was on his way back to Indy. It was about 10:30 A.M.

An hour later, he landed at the raceway. Even the television cameras from Wide World of Sports were on hand to record the final hours of John's dilemma.

Hastily, the engine is assembled. The

work area is roped off, and almost a dozen racers move with almost no conversation. Everyone knows his job and does it. By 12:45 P.M., a scant 15 min before race time, all but the car's hood is in place, and this is accomplished while pushing the car into the staging lanes. In 5 hr and 15 min!

John climbs inside, turns the key, the engine cranks over . . . but fails to start. Repeated push starts are to no avail. His competition is waved to the starting line, on the way for the win while John sits dejectedly in his motionless car. Later it is discovered that when the damaged engine was removed, the fuel line at the carburetor was removed and plugged with a bolt lightly coated with silicone sealer. When the line was reinstalled, the silicone left in the line kept fuel from being pumped into the carburetor.

Jim MacFarland
Edelbrock

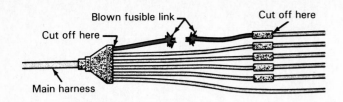

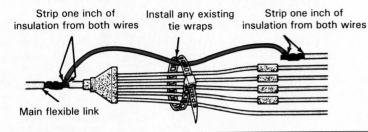

Blown fusible link

Cut off here

Cut off here

Main harness

Strip one inch of insulation from both wires

Install any existing tie wraps

Strip one inch of insulation from both wires

Main flexible link

FIGURE 8-23   Fusible link. (Chrysler Corporation)

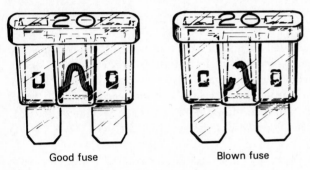

Good fuse

Blown fuse

FIGURE 8-24   Fuse. (Buick Motor Division, GMC)

reset automatically. If the headlights on a car begin to flash off and on, it's the circuit breaker protecting the wiring. The first check you do on a troublesome electrical circuit is to check fuses and circuit breakers (Figure 8-26).

Insulation

All automotive wires are covered with a cloth or plastic insulation. This insulation protects the wire from shorting against another wire or ground. Carefully inspect all of the wiring, especially wire near the exhaust

FIGURE 8-25   Fuses and fuse box. (Oldsmobile Motor Division, GMC)

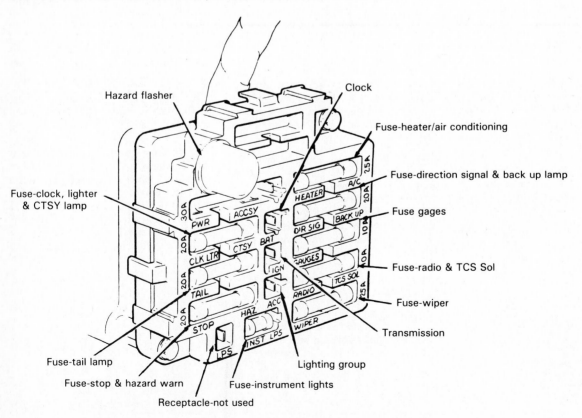

Hazard flasher

Clock

Fuse-heater/air conditioning

Fuse-direction signal & back up lamp

Fuse-clock, lighter & CTSY lamp

Fuse gages

Fuse-radio & TCS Sol

Fuse-wiper

Transmission

Fuse-tail lamp

Lighting group

Fuse-stop & hazard warn

Fuse-instrument lights

Receptacle-not used

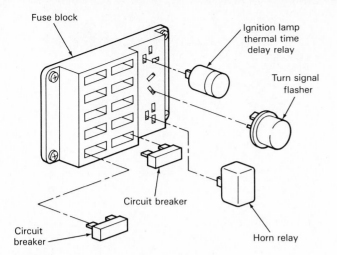

FIGURE 8-26 Fuse block. (Chrysler Corporation)

manifold, for cracking or wear (Figure 8-27). If you find any wear, mend the insulation with electrician's tape or replace the wire.

CHASSIS MAINTENANCE

There are a number of checks that should be made periodically as specified in the owner's manual. You should alert your customers to these service checks.

Brake Fluid

Maintaining the brake fluid level in the master cylinder could save a life. If there is an unseen leak in the brake system, fluid will escape. When all the fluid is gone, so are the brakes. Avoid this possible accident by checking the brake fluid during periodic maintenance. To check the level, remove the spring lock cover retainer that holds the cap to the master cylinder (Figure 8-28). Lift the cap and check the level. If it's excessively low, first check the brake pads. If they are okay, inspect the hydraulic system (lines and hoses). Then add new brake fluid until the level reaches the full line (Figure 8-29). If it's just down slightly, there's no problem. It's normal for the fluid level to drop gradually as the brake pads wear.

Power Steering Fluid

Check the power steering fluid level in the same manner as you check the transmission fluid, only check the power steering level at the power steering pump (Figure 8-30). Start the engine, remove the dipstick, and check the fluid level. If low, add power steering fluid through the dipstick tube.

Windshield Washer Fluid

Check the windshield washer fluid level periodically. If it is low, you will find that windshield washer fluid

---

FIGURE 8-27   Broken electrical insulation. (Chevrolet Motor Division, GMC)

Twisted/shielded cable

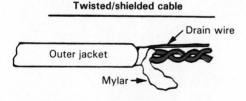

1. Remove outer jacket
2. Unwrap aluminum/mylar tape. Do not remove mylar.

3. Untwist conductors. Strip insulation as necessary.

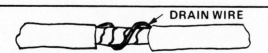

4. Splice wires using splice clips and rosin core solder. Wrap each splice to insulate.
5. Wrap with mylar and drain (uninsulated) wire.

6. Tape over whole bundle to secure as before.

Twist Leads

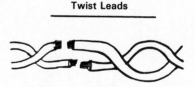

1. Locate damaged wire.
2. Remove insulation as required.

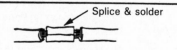

3. Splice two wires together using splice clips and rosin core solder.

4. Cover splice with tape to insulate from other wires.
5. Retwist as before and tape with electrical tape and hold in place.

105

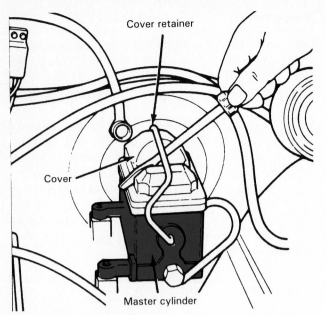

FIGURE 8-28   Removing the cover retainer. (Ford Motor Company)

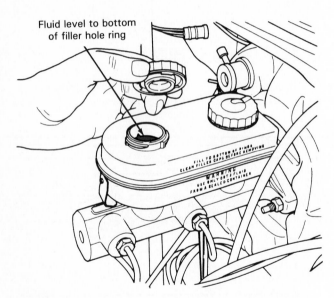

FIGURE 8-29   Filling the master cylinder. (Chrysler Corporation)

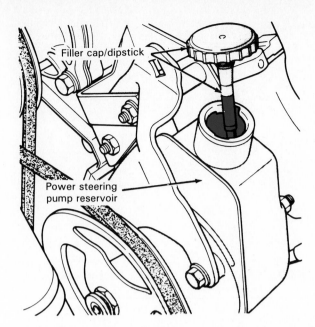

FIGURE 8-30   Checking power steering fluid. (Chrysler Corporation)

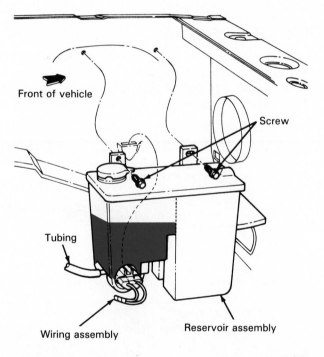

FIGURE 8-31   Windshield washer reservoir. (Ford Motor Company)

works better than plain water. Basically, it's nothing more than a weak ammonia and water solution. Pour a few inches into the windshield washer reservoir and fill the reservoir with water (Figure 8-31). A little isopropyl alcohol keeps the fluid from freezing in winter.

Lubrication

Lubricating the chassis will prolong the life of the suspension system. Raise the car on a hoist and lubricate

all of the parts found in the lubrication chart for the make, model, and year of car you're servicing (Figure 8-32). This may include ball joints, stabilizer, upper and lower control arm bushings, and tie rod ends. Always clean any dirt from the lube fittings before lubing. While you have the car up, check the fluid in the manual transmission and rear end.

FIGURE 8-32   Lubricating the chassis.

FIGURE 8-33   MacPherson strut. (Chrysler Corporation)

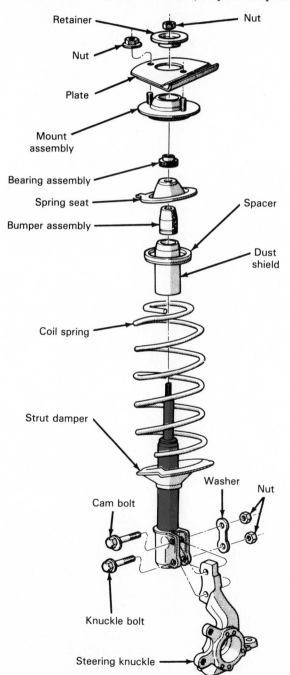

Retainer

Nut

Nut

Plate

Mount assembly

Bearing assembly

Spring seat

Spacer

Bumper assembly

Dust shield

Coil spring

Strut damper

Washer

Nut

Cam bolt

Knuckle bolt

Steering knuckle

Shock Absorbers

Two types of shock absorbers in use today are Mac-Pherson struts and regular shock absorbers (Figures 8-33 and 8-34). MacPherson struts usually have a spring mechanism not found in shock absorbers. Unlike the shock absorber, the steering knuckle and steering arm fasten to the lower end of the MacPherson strut. This strut, like the shock absorber, may be used in both front and rear suspensions.

To determine whether or not a shock absorber or MacPherson strut should be replaced, push down quickly and hard on one corner of the car. The car should spring back quickly and stop. If it continues to bounce up and down, the shock or strut is bad, and you should replace it.

Tires

Check tire wear by visually inspecting tires for wear bars (Figure 8-35). This figure shows a *bar* that appears across the tire. This bar was molded into the tire when it was manufactured. It does not appear in the new tread. It only appears when wear takes off all the tread above it. When these bars *begin* to show, you should replace the tire.

FIGURE 8-34   Shock absorber. (Volvo)

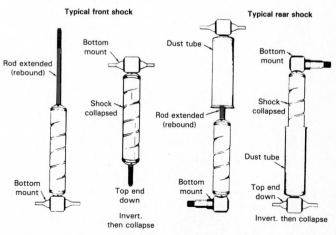

Typical front shock

Typical rear shock

Rod extended (rebound)

Bottom mount

Dust tube

Bottom mount

Shock collapsed

Shock collapsed

Rod extended (rebound)

Bottom mount

Top end down

Bottom mount

Dust tube

Top end down

Invert. then collapse

Invert. then collapse

Position for purging air from shock absorber

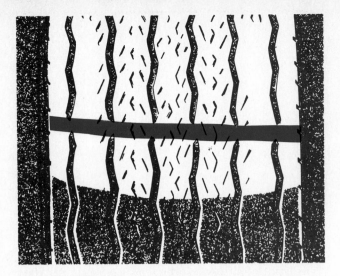

FIGURE 8-35   Tire wear bars. (Chrysler Corporation)

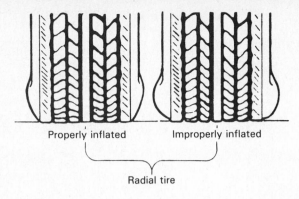

Properly inflated   Improperly inflated

Radial tire

Four important factors govern tire life:

1. Tire pressure
2. Tire rotation
3. Tire balance
4. Front-end alignment

Every tire size has a maximum tire pressure, shown in pounds per square inch (psi) on the side of the tire. The manufacturer's recommended pressure will normally be lower, according to load. Tires will also lose pressure during use. Check tire pressure on a regular basis. Figure 8-36 shows a properly inflated tire and an underinflated radial tire. Be sure to check the spare tire.

Tire rotation is very important to tire life. A set of tires that is rotated every 5000 miles will outlast a set of tires that is not rotated. Check the owner's manual for rotation recommendations. Figure 8-37 shows typical rotation patterns for bias, bias belted, and radial tires.

A balanced tire will run smoothly on the road. Tires that are not balanced will wear faster and transmit vibration to the steering wheel. Figure 8-38 illustrates some of the common causes of tire wear, including balancing, and corrections to make. Wheel balancing is covered in Chapter 37.

Radial Tire Lead

Almost all new cars have radial tires. They are smooth riding, easy rolling, and long-lived. They, however, do have a lead problem. Radial tires sometimes will consistently lead, or steer, to the left or right. This leading is caused by sideways force acting on the front tires. Road crown and crosswinds can multiply the effects of this force. Figure 8-39 shows the procedures for troubleshooting this problem.

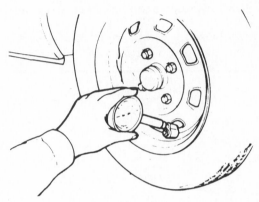

FIGURE 8-36   Tire pressure. (Pontiac Motor Division, GMC)

FIGURE 8-37   Bias and bias belted tires. (Mazda North America, Inc.)

Bias and bias belted tires

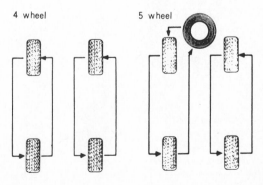

4 wheel   5 wheel

Radial tires

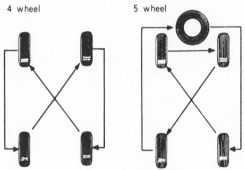

4 wheel   5 wheel

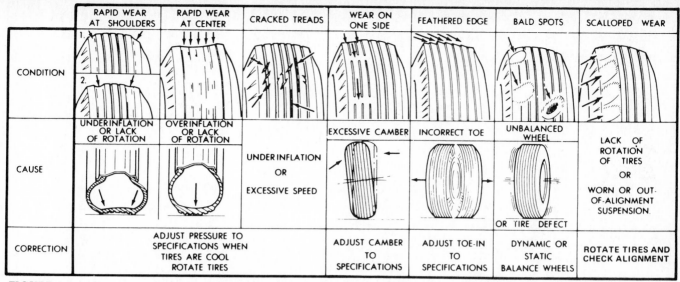

	RAPID WEAR AT SHOULDERS	RAPID WEAR AT CENTER	CRACKED TREADS	WEAR ON ONE SIDE	FEATHERED EDGE	BALD SPOTS	SCALLOPED WEAR
CONDITION	1. 2.						
CAUSE	UNDER INFLATION OR LACK OF ROTATION	OVERINFLATION OR LACK OF ROTATION	UNDER INFLATION OR EXCESSIVE SPEED	EXCESSIVE CAMBER	INCORRECT TOE	UNBALANCED WHEEL OR TIRE DEFECT	LACK OF ROTATION OF TIRES OR WORN OR OUT-OF-ALIGNMENT SUSPENSION.
CORRECTION	ADJUST PRESSURE TO SPECIFICATIONS WHEN TIRES ARE COOL ROTATE TIRES			ADJUST CAMBER TO SPECIFICATIONS	ADJUST TOE-IN TO SPECIFICATIONS	DYNAMIC OR STATIC BALANCE WHEELS	ROTATE TIRES AND CHECK ALIGNMENT

FIGURE 8-38 Tire wear conditions, causes, and corrections. (American Motors Corporation)

LEAD CORRECTION CHART

FIGURE 8-39 Lead correction chart. (Chrysler Corporation)

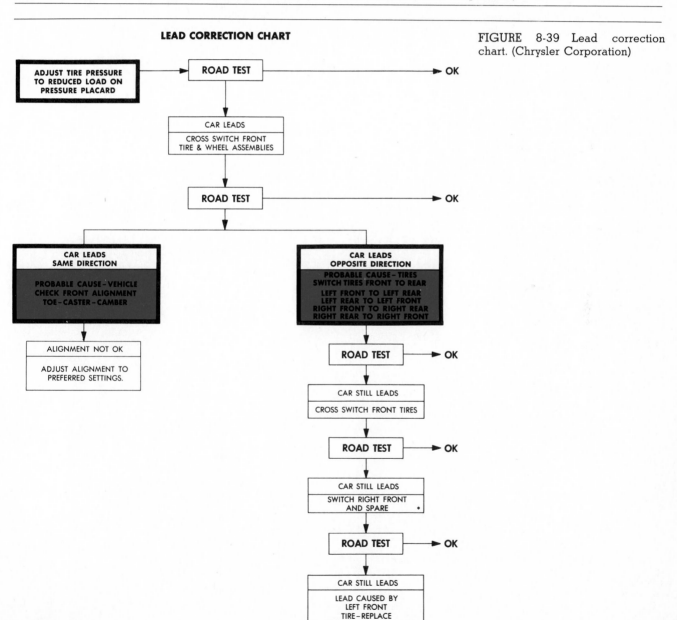

*DO NOT USE LOW MILEAGE SPARE TIRE

RY130A

TRADE TERMS

Air Cleaner
ATF
Coolant

Dipstick
Prime

REVIEW QUESTIONS

1. Name three reasons for preventive maintenance.
2. Name three ways to clean an engine compartment.
3. How often should the oil be changed for maximum engine longevity?
4. How do you check the fluid level in an automatic transmission? In a manual transmission?
5. Cooling system fluid does two things. It lubricates, and it acts as antifreeze. True or false? Why?
6. Name the three things that protect the electrical circuits of a car.
7. What does electrical wire insulation do?
8. What is a MacPherson strut?
9. List the parts you might lubricate in the chassis.
10. What are the four most important things that govern tire life?

PART TWO

Engines

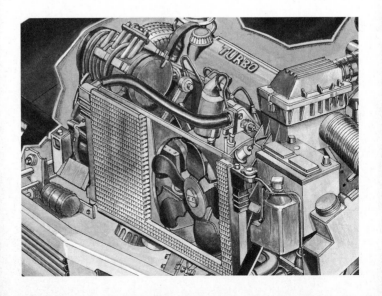

Types of Engines

INTRODUCTION

The modern automobile internal combustion engine converts energy contained in fuel into efficient, inexpensive transportation. This chapter discusses the cylinder block, the typical designs of cylinder arrangement, and how engine performance can be measured and evaluated.

ENGINE TYPES

During the short history of the automobile, hundreds of different engine designs have been invented, built, and tested. Each type of engine layout has certain advantages and drawbacks, but today only a few designs are in wide use. The engine blocks shown in Figure 9-1 are typical of some of these designs. They share common features, since they are all intended to produce usable power by the controlled burning of fuel. For example, all **reciprocating** engines have pistons which move up and down a cylinder bore while valves control the flow of fuel and air through the engine (Figure 9-2).

OBJECTIVES

When you have completed this chapter, you should be able to

- Identify the major types of **engine block** designs and explain why they are designed the way they are
- Identify the components of an engine block and their functions
- Calculate engine displacement
- Locate engine identification codes
- Explain the difference between theoretical and **indicated horsepower**

The simplest engine has a single cylinder. Lawn mowers and mopeds typically have single-cylinder engines because relatively little power is required to cut grass or propel a single person. When more power is needed to move a heavy car or truck, there are at least four ways to obtain it. The first is to make the engine larger by increasing the diameter of its piston and lengthening its **stroke**, the distance the piston travels as it moves up and down the cylinder (Figure 9-3). There are limits to how much the engine's internal dimensions can be increased, however. A single-cylinder engine powerful enough to propel a modern automobile would run very rough. It would be difficult to fit under a hood, and it would be rather inefficient, since the valve system couldn't keep up with its demands for fuel and air. The second way is to increase how fast the engine can run (revolutions per minute or rpm). Another way is to force more air into the cylinders with a supercharger or a turbocharger.

A fourth way to increase an engine's power output is to add more cylinders. By joining several single-cylinder engines on a common crankshaft, the flow of power is much smoother. The individual cylinders remain small enough to be efficient, and they can share a single lubrication and cooling system. Thus a multicylinder engine is really a collection of single-cylinder engines, all housed in a common case called the *engine block.*

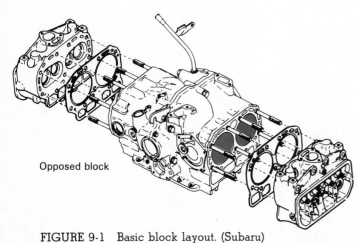

V-type block

Inline block

Opposed block

FIGURE 9-1   Basic block layout. (Subaru)

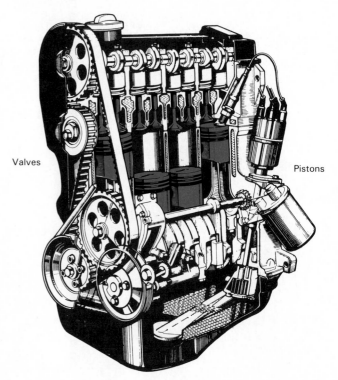

FIGURE 9-2   Four-cylinder in-line engine. (Chrysler Corporation)

Valves

Pistons

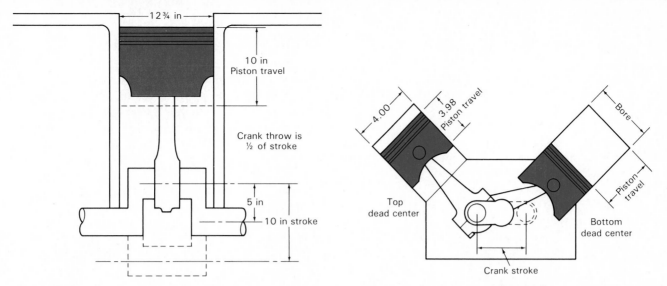

FIGURE 9-3 Comparison of a single-cylinder 400 cubic in. engine and a 400 cubic in. V 8 engine.

In-Line Block

The simplest multicylinder design is an **in-line** engine (Figure 9-2). Cylinders are arranged in a row. The engine block is the main frame of the engine. All the rest of the engine parts attach to the block (Figure 9-4). The block is usually made of cast iron. Cast iron is inexpensive, rigid, and long wearing and has excellent heat dissipation qualities. Although there are still many in-line engines with six cylinders in use, in the

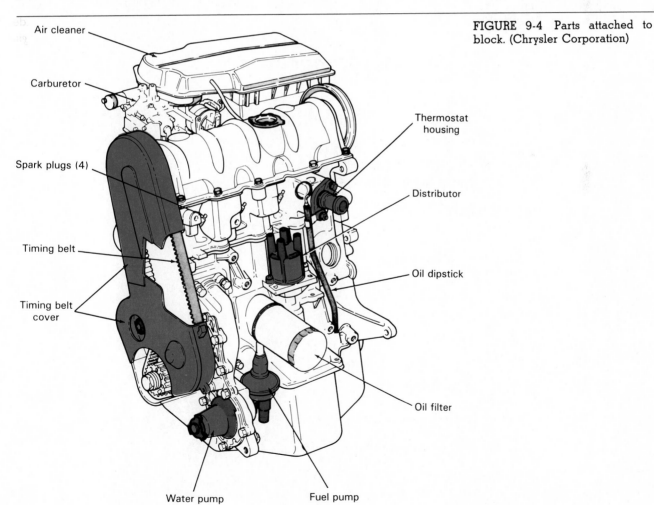

FIGURE 9-4 Parts attached to block. (Chrysler Corporation)

future most in-line engines will have four or fewer cylinders, to keep overall length down for transverse mounting.

Vee Block (V)

The cylinders can also be arranged side by side in a "Vee" (Figure 9-5). Although this arrangement makes the engine wider than an in-line engine, it also allows it to be much shorter than an in-line engine with the same number of cylinders. The best known vee engine is probably the V8, a design which has been popular with American drivers since the days of Henry Ford's flat-head V8. Engine designers have found it easy to change the **displacement** of vee motors by adding or removing pairs of cylinders. V6 engines are becoming more popular as the automakers build lighter, smaller cars (Figure 9-6).

FIGURE 9-5   V block (Ford Motor Company)

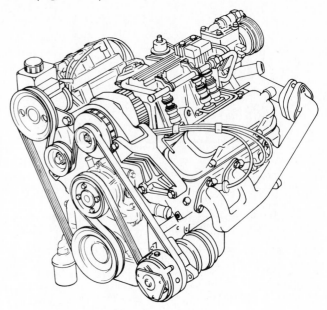

FIGURE 9-6   V 6 engine.

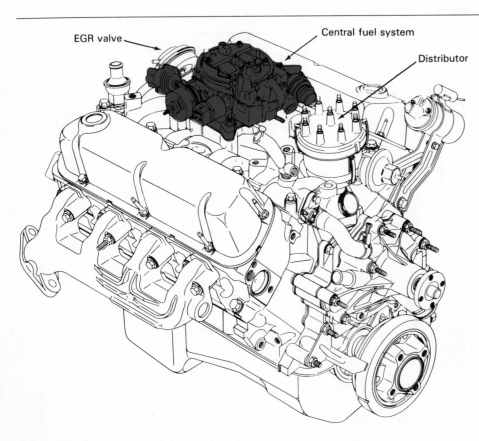

FIGURE 9-7   Central fuel supply.

EGR valve

Central fuel system

Distributor

Both the **vee block** and the in-line block layout offer several advantages. A single fuel supply placed in the center of the engine can supply all the cylinders with a mixture of fuel and air (Figure 9-7). Also, the engines can be mounted transversely (sideways) even in a small front-wheel-drive vehicle.

Opposed Block

If you imagine that you can open up the angle of a vee block until the cylinders are opposite each other, you will have an **opposed block** (Figure 9-8). Opposed blocks are also called *flat* engines or *pancake* engines

because they are short and wide. The Volkswagen, Porsche, and Subaru engines are familiar examples of an opposed engine layout.

Rotary Engines

The **rotary Wankel engine** has a unique way of converting the energy in fuel into usable power. It has no pistons, no connecting rods, and no valves. Instead, the rotary engine has a triangular rotor which revolves inside a chamber shaped like a fat figure 8 (Figure 9-9). As the rotor turns, it opens and closes passageways which are similar to the ports in a two-cycle engine.

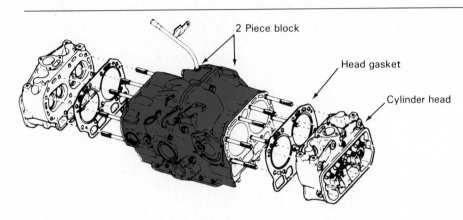

2 Piece block

Head gasket

Cylinder head

FIGURE 9-8 Four-cylinder opposed block. (Subaru)

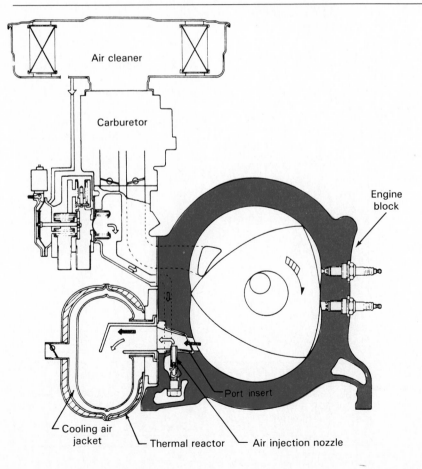

FIGURE 9-9 Rotary engine. (Mazda North America, Inc.)

Air cleaner

Carburetor

Engine block

Port insert

Cooling air jacket

Thermal reactor

Air injection nozzle

A Wankel engine runs very smoothly because there is no up-and-down motion of the pistons to cause vibration. Also, the rotary's cycle provides more power impulses per revolution than a comparable piston engine. The displacement and **horsepower** of a rotary engine can be increased by adding more rotors to the assembly, much like adding more cylinders to a conventional engine. Wankel engines are identified by the number of rotors they contain. For example, a rotary engine with two rotors would be more powerful than an engine having only one rotor of the same type.

ENGINE IDENTIFICATION

Even the most experienced mechanic can have difficulty identifying an engine. Engines which look identical may have important internal differences. Fortunately, there are several ways to tell one engine from another.

The **vehicle identification number (VIN)** provides valuable information (Figure 9-10). Every car has its own vehicle identification number, which is as distinctive as a set of fingerprints. The VIN is a series of letters and numbers which is usually on the dashboard, firewall, or doorjamb. The VIN is a code that states where the car was built, the body style, and the manufacturer. A manufacturer's manual will provide information on deciphering the information contained in a car's VIN. One digit of the VIN usually identifies the engine.

A portion of the VIN, usually the last six digits, is the car's **serial number.** The serial number is used by the car maker to keep track of warranty information, and it is used by police agencies to track stolen vehicles. It is also useful to mechanics because many times a car manufacturer will change the equipment installed on a particular model during its production run. For example, a manual may point out that cars with certain serial numbers require special service procedures.

A serial number is also stamped on many engine blocks. Its location varies among different makes; the manufacturer's manual will tell you where to look for it. The **engine code** generally is found alongside the serial number. A typical engine code might be *DZ* or *MO*. These letters indicate the horsepower rating of the engine, whether it was built for an automatic or manual transmission, and other important details. The engine code will help you determine the correct tune-up specifications for a particular engine.

FIGURE 9-10 Vehicle identification number. (Cadillac Motor Division, GMC)

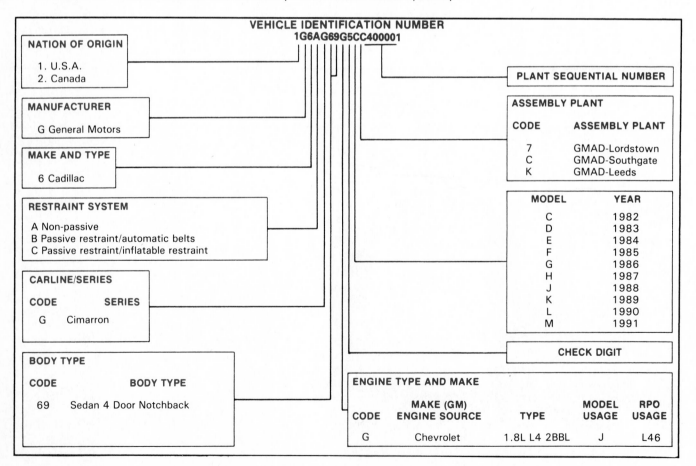

Casting numbers are often mistaken for serial numbers and engine codes. Manufacturers use a casting number to identify major engine parts on the assembly line.

Manufacturing a Block

Most engine blocks and heads are produced by **sand casting** to $\frac{1}{16}$-in. tolerance (Figure 9-11). A pattern is placed in casting sand, and this special sand is packed around the block pattern. The two sand halves are then separated, and the pattern block is removed. Next *cores* are placed in the mold. Cores are made from a special processed sand that is strong enough to hold its shape while being handled. Cores form the internal passages in the engine block. Cylinders, cooling passages, and oil passages are formed by these sand cores. The mold is then clamped together, and the molten cast iron is poured into the mold. After the metal has cooled, high-pressure air and water wash out the core sand from all internal passages. You can see the results of the casting cores in engine **core holes** or *"freeze" holes* and *plugs* (Figure 9-12). They usually are on the sides of the engine block.

The new cast iron block is then aged. Aging a new cast iron block is a process that allows the carbon in the cast iron to dispense evenly throughout the engine block. The result is a relatively lightweight, strong, thin-walled engine block with good abrasive and wear qualities.

The last step in manufacturing an engine block is done with machine tools. The block *deck*, where it

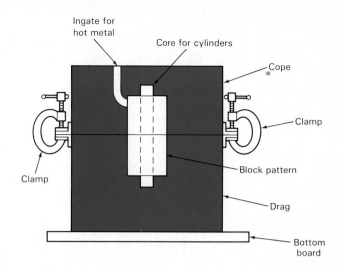

FIGURE 9-11   Sand mold.

mates to the head, is machined flat. The cylinder bores, crankshaft bore, and all other bores are then machined (Figure 9-13). The block is then transferred to a special drill press that drills and taps all of the threaded holes in a few moments. Computers, industrial robots, and automated machine tools now do much of the block machining.

The raised letters and numbers of the casting number are formed when the molten metal is poured into a mold. The serial number and engine codes, in contrast, are stamped on the block much later. Casting numbers are generally not a reliable way to identify an engine, since the same casting number can appear on a variety of different engines (Figure 9-14).

ENDLESS VARIETY?

Engineers have been drawing and building car engines for almost a century. The creativity and variety they've shown is almost endless. For example:

The aircooled Knox had cast-iron cylinders with small holes drilled around the outside. Little iron pegs were driven into the holes, resulting in a funny, porcupine-looking engine. It didn't cool very well either, especially if you were driving with a tailwind. The air helped push you along, but didn't make its way into the engine compartment.

Some early cars used radial aircraft engines, with the cylinders radiating out from the crankshaft like the spokes of a wheel. The main problems with this design were ground clearance and visi-

bility, but the lower cylinder also had the nasty habit of filling up with oil and/or fuel that would seep past the rings. When the engine was cranked, the solidly-filled cylinder would bend rods, crack cylinders and do other damage.

It's hard to fit everything in under the hood of a front wheel drive car, so there are many chances for a designer to play. The early Morgan 3-wheeler had a V-type motorcycle engine in front of the body. The Saab 99 and Citroen DS both located their 4-cylinder engines behind the front axle, with the timing gears toward the dashboard. But Saab had the fan belts driven by the crank pulley, tight against the firewall, while Citroen drove them off the front end of the

camshaft (at the clutch end of the engine).

Audi located its 5-cylinder engine in-line ahead of the front axle. They had to use 2 small radiators, one on each side of the engine, because the long engine fit so tightly behind the front bumper.

Next time you're looking under the hood and think you could figure out a better way, you can bet someone else has already had the same thought. But there's still room for your improvements.

Leonard Spooner
Orchard St. Automotive
San Diego, CA

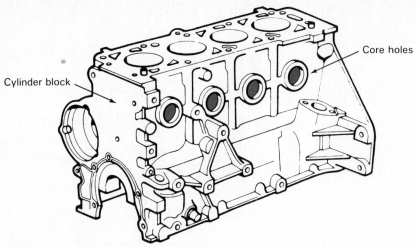

Core holes

Cylinder block

FIGURE 9-12   Core hole. (General Motors Corporation)

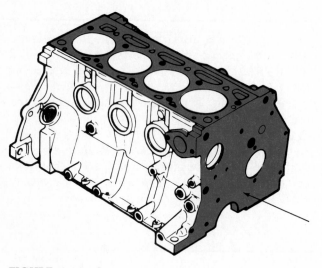

FIGURE 9-13   Some machined surfaces on an engine block.

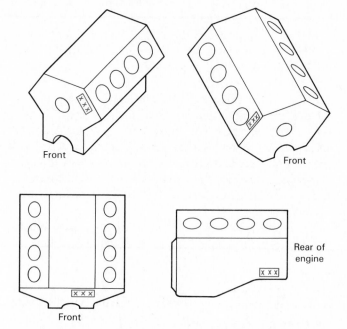

Front

Front

Front

Rear of engine

FIGURE 9-14   Engine identification number locations.

ENGINE MEASUREMENTS

How big is an engine? Well, you could measure the height and width of a motor with a yardstick. But a more useful answer would be to determine the engine's *displacement.*

Displacement

In a piston engine, the displacement is the swept volume of all its cylinders. **Swept volume** is a function of the diameter of the cylinder bores and the stroke of the crankshaft (Figure 9-15). To compute the displacement of an engine, you must know the size of the cylinders, how far the pistons travel in one crankshaft revolution, and how many cylinders there are. The formula for calculating the swept volume of a single cylinder is

$$\pi \times (\tfrac{1}{2} \text{ diameter of bore})^2 \times \text{stroke}$$

If there are eight of these cylinders in an engine, then the total engine displacement is eight times the volume of each single cylinder. Figure 9-16 shows the displacement of an eight-cylinder engine with a bore of 4.00 in. and a stroke of 3.00 in. Displacements are often *rounded off* to an even number, so the size you obtain from these calculations may not match the engine's advertised size.

Compression Ratio

An engine's **compression ratio** indicates how tightly the fuel and air mixture is squeezed into the combustion chamber during the piston's **compression stroke**

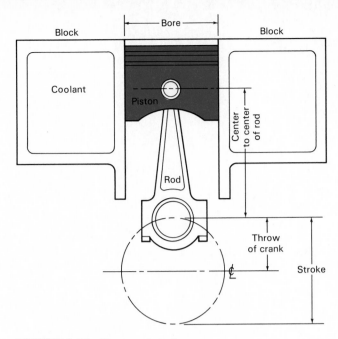

FIGURE 9-15   Bore and stroke.

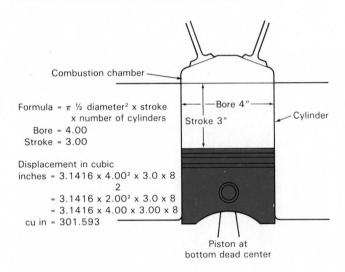

Formula = π ½ diameter² x stroke
                x number of cylinders
    Bore = 4.00
    Stroke = 3.00

Displacement in cubic
inches = 3.1416 x 4.00² x 3.0 x 8
                          2
        = 3.1416 x 2.00² x 3.0 x 8
        = 3.1416 x 4.00 x 3.00 x 8
cu in = 301.593

FIGURE 9-16   Calculating displacement of an
eight-cylinder engine in cubic inches.

(Figure 9-17). Compressing more fuel and air into the combustion chamber improves the engine's performance, but there is a practical limit to how high this compression ratio can be. A gasoline's **octane rating** is a measurement of its resistance to **detonation**. When the fuel and air mixture is compressed in a high-compression engine, it becomes hot. If the gas has a low octane rating, the fuel mixture will self-ignite, causing detonation and engine damage. Currently available gasoline has a relatively low octane rating, which is why most new cars have compression ratios of 9:1 or less. A racing engine which burns only high-octane gas plus additives can have a compression ratio of over 13:1.

The volume of A and B is compressed into volume A to increase pressure and temperature of fuel/air mixture

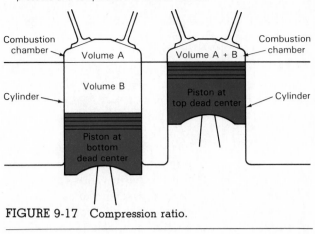

FIGURE 9-17   Compression ratio.

Diesel engines have a much higher compression ratio than gasoline engines. A typical diesel engine has a compression ratio of over 20:1 (Figure 9-18). While detonation is to be avoided in a gasoline engine, it is essential for a diesel engine. A diesel has no spark ignition, so the fuel must always self-ignite. The extremely high compression ratios found in diesels helps superheat the air on the compression stroke. This also increases the stress on all the engine components. That is why diesel engines have stronger blocks, crankshafts, and other components than comparable gasoline-burning engines.

Torque

Measuring the power output of an engine requires running the engine on a special piece of test equipment called a **dynamometer.** The dynamometer records the engine's *torque*—the twisting force it produces. Torque is what makes the transmission gears, drive shaft, and rear wheels go round. In short, torque moves the car.

FIGURE 9-18   Comparison of spark ignition versus diesel fuel injection.

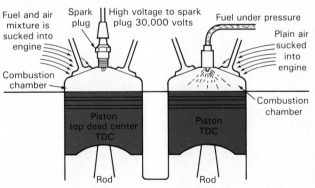

Spark plug to ignite fuel air
mixture of a gas engine (gasoline
9:1 CR)

High temperature and pressure
from compressed air ignites
injection fuel (Diesel, 20:1 CR)

The dynamometer measures the engine's torque by recording the force it exerts against the resistance of a brake (Figure 9-19). A simple equation (torque times rpm divided by 5,252) converts the torque reading to brake horsepower, which is a much more understandable measure of an engine's capabilities. One horsepower is defined as the work required to lift 33,000 lb 1 ft in 1 min (Figure 9-20). Horsepower figures provide a convenient standard for measuring the power output of many different engines.

The torque an automobile engine produces is not constant. It changes with the engine speed, rpm (Figure 9-21). If you measure the torque at various rpm points and plot the readings on a graph, the result is an arching curve. Similarly, if you compute the horsepower ratings and plot them on the same graph, you will get a second curve. The high point of the torque curve (peak torque) and the top of the horsepower curve (peak horsepower) occur at different points in the engine's operating range.

Engine dynamometers are very complex instruments. Because of their high cost, engine dynamometers are rarely used by anyone but large engine manufacturers or rebuilders. Chassis dynamometers (dynos) are more common (Figure 9-22). These machines can be found in many well-equipped shops, where they

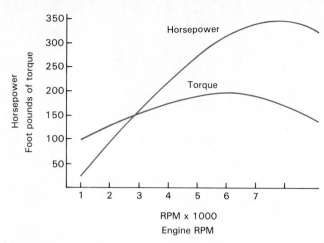

FIGURE 9-21   Comparison of horsepower versus torque.

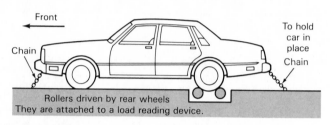

FIGURE 9-22   Car on dyno.

simulate the load on the engine as the car drives down a highway. The car's driving wheels turn on large rollers. A gauge indicates the car's wheel horsepower for the dyno operator. Because of frictional losses in the car's drive train, the readings on a chassis dyno are typically less than the engine's horsepower rating if it were measured on an engine dyno.

ENGINE EFFICIENCY

Earlier in this chapter it was pointed out that an engine is a device that releases the energy contained in a fuel combustion. Unfortunately, much of this energy is either lost or disappears into air before it can be harnessed for useful work. The drag of the pistons and rings, the friction of the bearings, and the power required to turn the oil and water pumps all reduce the engine's power output. As the speed of the engine increases, these losses become greater. It also takes power to compress the fresh fuel/air mixture and to push the exhaust gases out of the cylinders. These pumping losses further reduce the available power. The ratio of the engine's actual brake horsepower to its theoretical horsepower indicates the engine's **mechanical efficiency**. A typical automotive engine has a mechanical efficiency of approximately 80%.

Another measure of engine performance is **ther-**

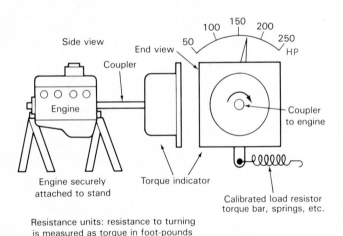

FIGURE 9-19   Engine dynamometer.

FIGURE 9-20   One horsepower.

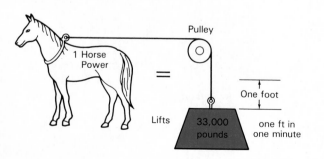

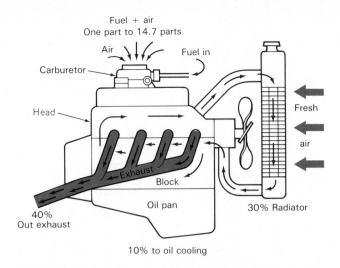

FIGURE 9-23 Approximate thermal losses through cooling systems.

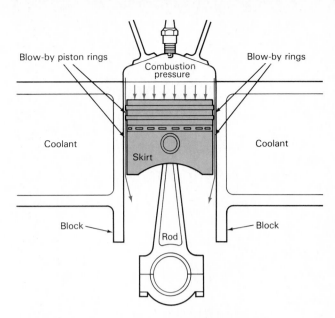

FIGURE 9-24 Blow-by. (Chrysler Corporation)

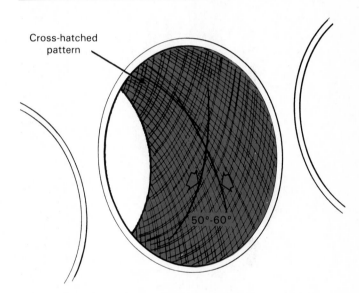

FIGURE 9-25 Cylinder bore crosshatching. (Chrysler Corporation)

mal efficiency. The heat you feel coming out the end of the tail pipe and radiating from the cooling system is lost energy. Without a cooling system, an engine would be more thermally efficient, but it wouldn't last very long (Figure 9-23). An average automobile engine has a thermal efficiency of only 20%. This means that for every 10 gal of gas burned in a typical automobile engine, the energy in 8 gal is simply wasted. The energy in the remaining 2 gal is what moves the car.

CYLINDER BLOCKS

All of the major engine components are installed on or in the engine block, including the cylinder head, crankshaft, and piston assemblies. The cylinder bores in an engine block are machined very precisely. They must be strong enough to contain the pressure of the burning fuel mixture. They must also be as round as possible to provide a good seal for the piston rings. If the cylinders are egg-shaped, then some of the power that would have been used to push the piston down the bore escapes into the crankcase. This is called blow-by (Figure 9-24). Blow-by reduces the efficiency of an engine.

The finish on the cylinder walls also affects the ring seal. The cylinder walls are honed to provide a very smooth finish. Special grinding stones produce small grooves in the cylinder walls which collect oil. These grooves help lubricate the piston rings and piston skirts. The intersecting grooves form a pattern called a crosshatch (Figure 9-25).

For many years, most cylinder blocks were made of cast iron. This material (also called grey iron) is easy to machine. Aluminum pistons wear very well against cast iron cylinder walls. Iron's main disadvan-

tage is its weight. That is why some engine blocks are now being cast from lightweight aluminum. An aluminum block weighs less than a cast iron block.

An aluminum piston skirt rubbing against an aluminum cylinder wall will wear very quickly. Most aluminum cylinder blocks are outfitted with steel or ductile iron cylinder liners (Figure 9-26). These thin metal sleeves are pressed into the block casting to provide a long-lasting cylinder wall finish. A dry sleeve is completely surrounded by aluminum; a wet sleeve is exposed directly to the coolant circulating through the engine block (Figure 9-27). Sleeves are also often used to repair a cast iron block which has a cracked or damaged cylinder wall.

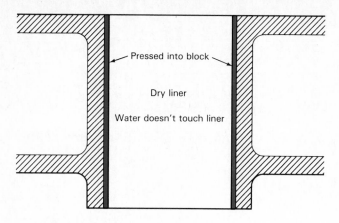

FIGURE 9-26 Block with dry liner.

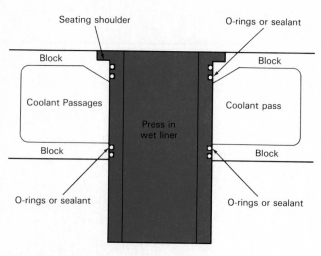

FIGURE 9-27 Block with wet liner.

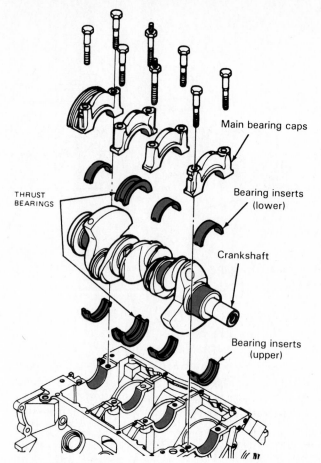

FIGURE 9-28 Crankshaft, main journals, and bearings. (Ford Motor Company)

In the late 1960s, engineers developed a way to run an aluminum block without sleeves. By adding silicon to the aluminum alloy and using a special honing technique, they were able to produce a very hard cylinder wall. These high-silicon aluminum cylinder blocks are used in high-performance cars, such as the Porsche 928 and Mercedes-Benz as well as production automobiles like the Chevrolet Vega. In these engines, the piston skirts are often plated with a thin layer of iron.

Main Journals

An engine block's main journals support the crankshaft. They must be strong enough to resist the downward pressure of the pistons on their power strokes and stiff enough to prevent the crankshaft from flexing. Since cast iron and aluminum are not good bearing materials, the main bearing saddles are machined larger than the crankshaft journals. Precision bearing inserts make up the differences in diameters. Holes in the main journals and bearing inserts supply pressurized oil to the crankshaft journals. The main bearing caps, which are also outfitted with bearing inserts, hold the crankshaft in place (Figure 9-28).

Camshaft Journals

In some automotive engines, the camshaft is in the cylinder block (Figure 9-29). Overhead camshaft engines have their cams in the cylinder heads (Figure 9-30). Circular inserts may be pressed into the block or head to provide a durable bearing surface for the camshaft's journals. Engine blocks with camshaft journals also have tappets, or lifters, that ride on the camshaft. These lifters are housed in a machine lifter bore (Figure 9-31).

Lubrication System

The engine's lubrication system pumps pressurized oil to the bearing surfaces (Figure 9-32). The path is from the oil pan, to the oil pump, and then to the oil gallery for distribution to all bearing surfaces. This circulation

Camshaft

FIGURE 9-29 Camshaft in a block.
(Chrysler Corporation)

FIGURE 9-30 Overhead cam. (Chrysler Corporation)

FIGURE 9-31 Lifter bore. (Ford Motor Company)

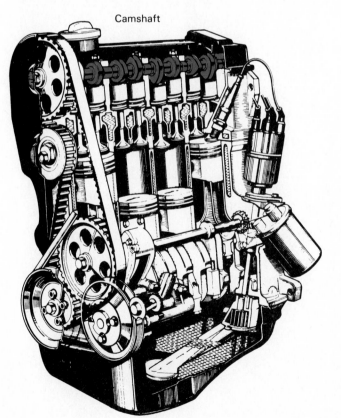

Camshaft

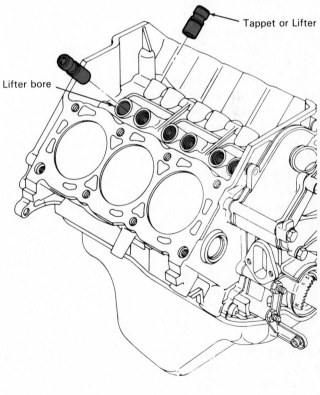

Tappet or Lifter

Lifter bore

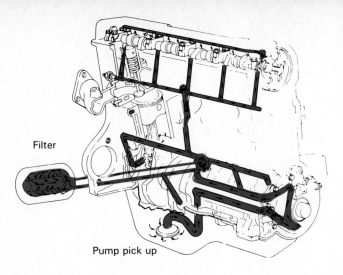

Filter

Pump pick up

FIGURE 9-32   Engine lubrication system.

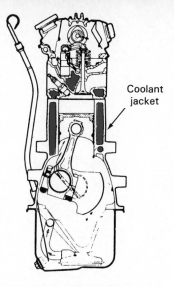

Coolant jacket

FIGURE 9-33   Water jackets.

of oil provides the engine with both lubrication and cooling. The oil is then returned to the oil pan for another cycle.

Cooling Passages

Very little of the heat energy of the burning fuel is converted to useful power because most of the heat is exhausted out the tail pipe or radiated through the lubrication and cooling system. Without a cooling system, the engine would quickly overheat. An automotive engine can be cooled with either water or air. In a water-cooled engine, the coolant (usually a mixture of water and antifreeze) circulates through passages which surround the cylinders and ports (Figure 9-33). As the coolant moves through this **water jacket,** it absorbs heat from the metal surfaces. This heat is then transferred to the radiator, where it is dissipated into the air through the fins in the radiator core.

The water passages in the block must be free of rust and corrosion. This allows the coolant to circulate properly and carry off the excess heat.

Motor and Transmission Mounts

The engine and the transmission are supported in the car by special mounts. Motor and transmission mounts are usually made in three layers of material (Figure 9-34). Mounts are made of two pieces of steel with a rubber pad bonder in between the rubber. The purpose of the rubber pad is to absorb engine and transmission vibration. Figure 9-35 shows a typical three-point motor and transmission installation. Notice how the transmission mount provides rear support for the

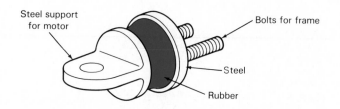

Steel support for motor

Bolts for frame

Steel

Rubber

FIGURE 9-34   Motor mounts.

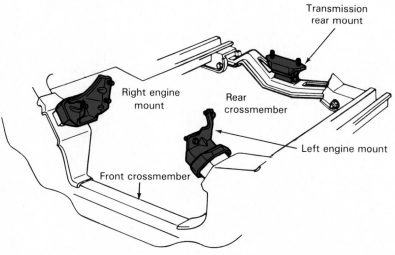

Transmission rear mount

Right engine mount

Rear crossmember

Left engine mount

Front crossmember

FIGURE 9-35   Typical rear-wheel-drive motor and transmission mounts. (Ford Motor Company)

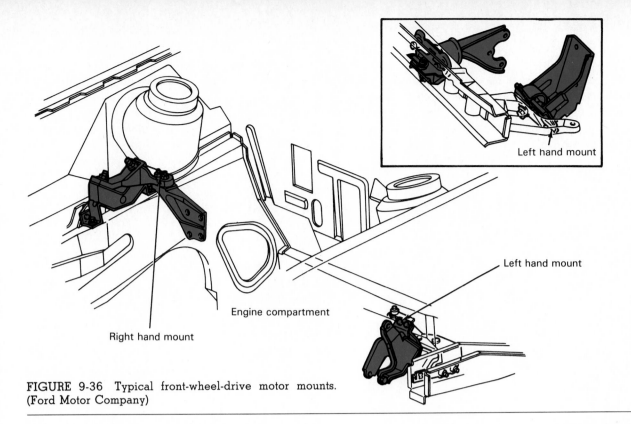

Left hand mount

Left hand mount

Engine compartment

Right hand mount

FIGURE 9-36 Typical front-wheel-drive motor mounts. (Ford Motor Company)

motor. Most engines in front-wheel-drive cars are mounted parallel with the front wheels. Both ends of the engine have motor mounts (Figure 9-36). In addition to these two mounts, there is a transmission mount to help absorb engine and transmission vibration (Fig-

ure 9-37). As engine rpm and torque increase, the engine will try to turn in the opposite direction of the flywheel rotation. Many transverse mounted engines use a torque reaction rod to control this twisting action of the engine (Figure 9-38).

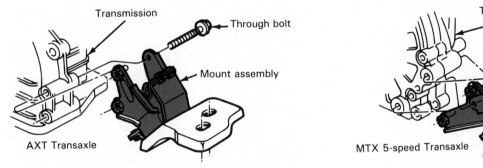

Transmission

Through bolt

Mount assembly

AXT Transaxle

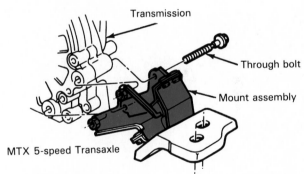

Transmission

Through bolt

Mount assembly

MTX 5-speed Transaxle

FIGURE 9-37 Typical front-wheel-drive transmission mounts. (Ford Motor Company)

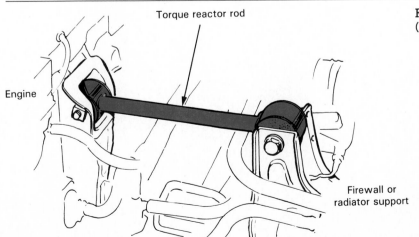

Torque reactor rod

Engine

Firewall or radiator support

FIGURE 9-38 Torque reaction rod. (American Honda Motor Corporation, Inc.)

Inspection

Since the cylinder block is the foundation of the engine, it must be in good condition. An engine which has overheated or been exposed to freezing temperatures without antifreeze protection can crack. These cracks cause coolant leaks. If water enters the lubrication system or oil enters the cooling system, further engine damage will occur. Cracks in a cylinder block can be detected with a special **Magnaflux** inspection process or by pressure testing the water jackets with compressed air and soapy water. If the block is cracked, bubbles will appear when the block is coated with soapy water.

TRADE TERMS

Blow-by
Compression Ratio
Compression Stroke
Core Holes
Detonation
Displacement
Dynamometer
Engine Block
Engine Code
Horsepower
In-line
Indicated Horsepower
Magnaflux

Mechanical Efficiency
Octane Rating
Opposed Block
Reciprocating
Rotary (Wankel) Engine
Sand Casting
Serial Number
Stroke
Swept Volume
Thermal Efficiency
Vee block
Vehicle Identification Number (VIN)
Water Jacket

REVIEW QUESTIONS

1. List the four basic block layouts.
2. Name four ways horsepower can be increased.
3. Calculate the displacement of a 3-in. diameter piston with a stroke of 2.75 in.
4. An engine can be identified by its casting number. True or false? Why?
5. How do you figure brake horsepower?
6. How do you determine an engine's mechanical efficiency?
7. The purpose of water jackets in the block is to help cool the engine. True or false? Why?
8. Lifters ride on what?
9. What supports the engine and transmission in the chassis?
10. How many cubic inches of displacement does a 2.3-liter engine have?

The Crankshaft

INTRODUCTION

The crankshaft (Figure 10-1) runs lengthwise through the engine block and is attached to the pistons by the connecting rods (Figure 10-2). Because the connecting rods attach to journals offset several inches from the crankshaft's center, the force they transmit from the pistons makes the crankshaft rotate. This arrangement converts the reciprocating motion of the pistons to rotary motion at the crankshaft (Figure 10-3).

FIGURE 10-1   Four-cylinder crankshaft. (Mazda North America, Inc.)

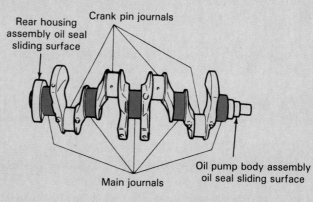

Rear housing assembly oil seal sliding surface

Crank pin journals

Main journals

Oil pump body assembly oil seal sliding surface

129

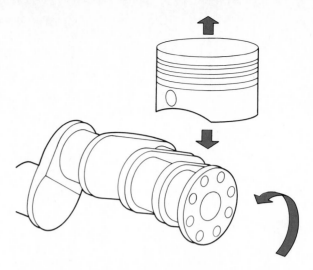

FIGURE 10-3   Reciprocating to rotary motion.

job of the crankshaft is to transfer power to the drive shaft. This power is eventually sent to the wheels, thus propelling the car.

CRANKSHAFT OPERATION

A **harmonic balancer**, or vibration damper, is at the front end of the crankshaft to help control vibration of the crankshaft (Figure 10-4). A **flywheel** or flexplate is at the rear of the crankshaft and provides the connection to the transmission (Figure 10-5). The flywheel or flexplate and torque converter also help to dampen vibration and combustion power pulses.

Main bearings on the crankshaft journals hold the crankshaft in place. In addition, a thrust bearing (usually one of the main bearings) controls the backward or forward motion (end play) of the crankshaft. The bearing does this with special edges which rub against the side of the crankshaft main journal.

Harmonic Balancer

Many forces act on the crankshaft. First, the power impulses from the pistons do not arrive in one continuous stream. Instead, they shove the crankshaft in a series of harsh pushes. The belt, oil pump, and distributor all add loads to the crank. These different loads cause vibrations in the crankshaft. At certain frequencies these vibrations can combine into damaging intensity. The harmonic balancer dampens these vibrations.

The damper smooths vibrations with two rings separated with a layer of rubber (Figure 10-6). The inner ring fits over the front end of the crankshaft, called the *nose*. Vibration makes this part "ring," but the surrounding layer of rubber dampens the vibration as it tries to pass to the outer ring.

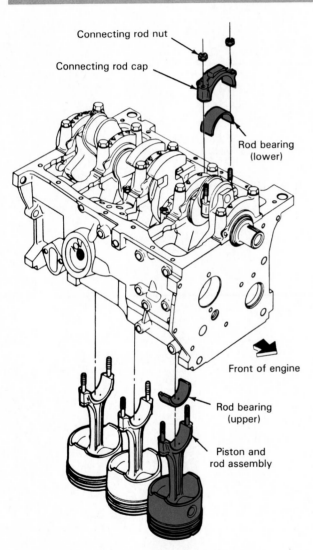

Connecting rod nut

Connecting rod cap

Rod bearing (lower)

Front of engine

Rod bearing (upper)

Piston and rod assembly

FIGURE 10-2   Piston and rod connected to the crankshaft. (Ford Motor Company)

In addition, the crankshaft drives many accessories such as the alternator, oil pump, water pump, distributor, air conditioner, and power steering pump through belts, shafts, and chains. Of course, the main

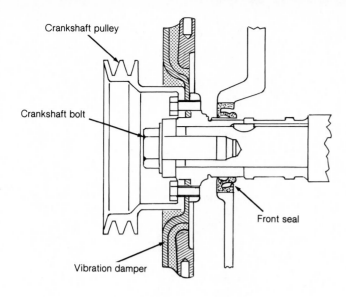

Crankshaft pulley

Crankshaft bolt

Front seal

Vibration damper

FIGURE 10-4   Harmonic balancer (vibration damper).

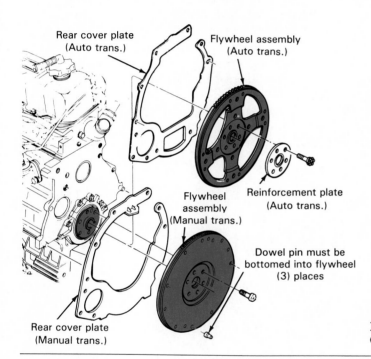

Rear cover plate (Auto trans.)

Flywheel assembly (Auto trans.)

Reinforcement plate (Auto trans.)

Flywheel assembly (Manual trans.)

Dowel pin must be bottomed into flywheel (3) places

Rear cover plate (Manual trans.)

FIGURE 10-5   Crankshaft and flywheel. (Ford Motor Company)

FIGURE 10-6   Harmonic balancer parts. (TRW)

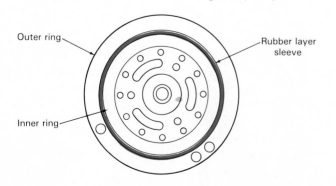

Outer ring

Rubber layer sleeve

Inner ring

Flywheel

The flywheel is attached to the transmission end of the crankshaft and always rotates with it. The flywheel serves several functions.

First, the flywheel has a fair amount of mass, or weight. This mass absorbs the constant twisting and untwisting motion the individual power impulses send through the crankshaft. These pulses are different from those absorbed by the harmonic balancer. The harmonic balancer cancels higher-frequency vibrations. The flywheel stops the crankshaft from twisting out of shape every time a piston is on a power stroke.

The flywheel also provides the inertia to get the car moving from rest. The heavier the car and lower the torque available from the engine, the more flywheel weight needed. Without the flywheel, all but the most powerful engines in the lightest chassis would bog down when starting from rest.

The large outer diameter of the flywheel provides a good housing for the ring gear. The ring gear is engaged by the starter. Its large diameter is necessary to provide the gear multiplication needed to turn the engine over with the small starter motor.

Bearings

Most rotating parts in an engine are supported by bearings to reduce friction and heat. The major characteristics desirable in a bearing are corrosion resistance, conformability, score resistance, and embedability.

Corrosion resistance is a bearing's ability to resist the gases and acids which develop as a result of engine oil breakdown. Oil additives designed to prevent corrosion can absorb only so much heat and pressure. Eventually they break down, and corrosion takes place. This corrosion gradually destroys the surface of a bearing.

Conformability is the bearing's ability to mate successfully with the crankshaft surfaces which ride on it. Bearings literally "conform" to the shaft, thus reducing friction and wear.

Score resistance is related to the bearing's low melting temperature. This characteristic is important when the oil film between the bearing and crankshaft

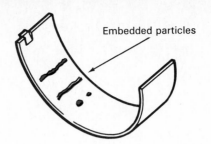

FIGURE 10-7 Bearing containing foreign material.

breaks down. A bearing can then develop hot spots on its surface. These hot spots can stick to the crankshaft and tear out from the bearings. But the low melting temperature allows the bearing material to smooth together. Thus, the hot spots blend into the surrounding bearing material instead of sticking to the crankshaft.

Bearing embedability means that the surface of a bearing must be able to embed or absorb any small particles which could score the crankshaft (Figure 10-7). Figure 10-8 illustrates other reasons for early bearing failure.

FIGURE 10-8 Typical bearing failure. (American Motors Corporation)

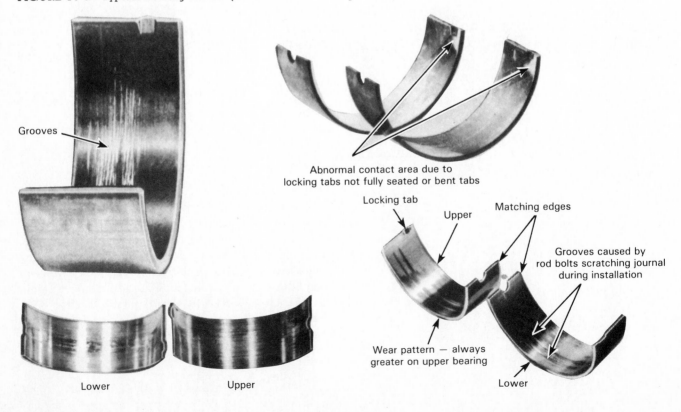

"CAN YOU BUILD ME AN ENGINE?"

In 1915 Bob Burman, America's King of Speed at the time, came to Harry Miller with a new problem and challenge. His four-cylinder Peugeot had scattered its engine. There was no hope of getting a new one from France in time for the big Corona, California, Road Race which was just a few months away. Would Miller study the fragments and build him a new Peugeot engine, from the patterns on up? Miller conferred with Offenhauser, his shop foreman, got an "Oh, yeah, we can do it," and found himself in the engine business. The new engine ran better than the old Peugeot, but it, too, was reduced to rubble when Burman crashed fatally in that very Corona race.

In 1916, Miller designed and built his own four-cylinder engine. It used a barrel-type crankcase which was part of the aluminum casting which included the wet-linered block. The three-main bearing crankshaft was made in two parts and had a single ball-race in the middle and double ones fore and aft. The head was detachable, and a single camshaft, driven by a gear train at the front, actuated four valves per cylinder by means of rocker arms. The Peugeot influence was clear, although the engine bristled with originality. With it, Miller introduced aluminum pistons to America and established himself as a piston manufacturer. Six of these cleanly designed engines were built, and one

served well in a local doctor's aeroplane. Another powered Barney Oldfield's pioneer aerodynamic coupé, the "Golden Submarine," a Miller creation in its entirety. Another went into a race car for the prominent driver Frank Elliott, who said in later years, "It wouldn't pull the hat off your head."

Ronald Baker and
Anthony Harding
*Automobile Design: Great Designers
and Their Work*
Robert Bentley, Inc.

Bearing Construction   Steel, or an alloy of steel and other metals, is used for the bearing backing or shell. A combination of metals is used for the soft bearing surface. This combination is based on the type of bearing desired, its intended use, and cost factors. Such metals as antimony, aluminum, cadmium, copper, lead, and mercury are popularly used in the alloy. Tin and silver are also used, depending on the life expected of the bearing and the engine requirements.

The shell or sleeve is made first, and then the bearing material is applied to the shell (Figure 10-9). Commonly used metals include aluminum, babbitt, and copper-lead, each alloyed with other metals as desired to create the type of bearing required for a specific application.

Small quantities, for example, of tin and copper are added or alloyed to aluminum to create the aluminum-type bearing material. Expensive, but stronger, the aluminum bearing is an excellent choice for high-load use at high speed.

Crush and Spread   In the design of a bearing, two factors are important: One is bearing **crush;** the other

is bearing **spread.** When assembling the engine, the bearing shell is held in the housing by the spread. When the bearing cap is tightened down, the two bearing shells touch and are crushed together by torque on the main bearing cap bolts. This crush helps to form the bearing into a true circle and keeps the bearing in place. It prevents the bearing from rotating with the crankshaft. Bearing spread means the bearing housing is slightly smaller in arc than the bearing shell, approximately 0.004–0.020 in. (0.10–0.50 mm) (Figure 10-10).

Bearing Design and Oiling   The crankshaft main bearing or connecting rod bearing is split into two halves. A bearing cap retains the lower half of this bearing in place; the top half is held in the engine

---

FIGURE 10-10   Bearing crush and spread. (American Isuzu Motors, Inc.)

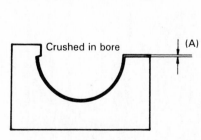

Loose

(A)

Crushed in bore

(A)

FIGURE 10-9   Bearing shell construction.

Copper-lead
sintered metal

Steel base

Zinc plating

block. As for the connecting rod bearings, the top half is installed in the rod itself. The rod cap retains the bottom half. Figure 10-11 shows split bearing halves. Also, the thrust bearing is shown. The thrust bearing takes the front-to-rear loads on the crank. Usually one main bearing has a special lip designed to take thrust loads.

The material used in the bearing must be softer than the part it makes contact with or revolves around. Replacement of a bearing costs far less than replacing the crankshaft itself. Because only a thin oil film actually protects bearing and crankshaft surfaces from physically touching, friction of any kind must be avoided. Each bearing must have a supply of oil around it at all times when the engine is operating.

Not all upper and lower bearings are identical. In some engines, the lower bearing half is made of harder material than the upper bearing half. This provides strength where it is needed on the bottom bearing half and embedability on the upper bearing half.

Normally, the oil holes and grooves in bearings are provided on the bearing side where the load is lightest. Clearances between crankshaft journal and bearing can be 0.0005–0.003 in. (0.013–0.076 mm). This clearance provides the necessary space for an oil film to flow between the bearing and the shaft to prevent friction and wear. Oil pressure, at the same time, must

not be lost because of too large a clearance. When oil is flung off excessively at one bearing, other bearings do not receive enough oil. Ultimately, this condition causes bearing failure.

Crankshaft

All crankshaft designs must incorporate several functions. The crank must be strong enough to withstand the twisting forces placed on it. The bearing surfaces, called journals, must be hard enough not to wear in normal use. Oil passages must be drilled through the one-piece crankshaft to lube the bearing (Figure 10-12). Counterweights are needed to offset the weight of the pistons and rods.

Cast iron is the most common material in crankshaft construction. Stronger, forged steel is more expensive and is reserved for high-performance or heavy-duty applications.

Balance The firing order of an engine is determined by the angle between each crankshaft throw (Figure 10-13). A normal six-cylinder in-line engine will have 120° between each throw. A V8 requires only 90° between throws. These angles are determined by noting where the movement of one piston will cancel the effect of another piston moving in the other direction.

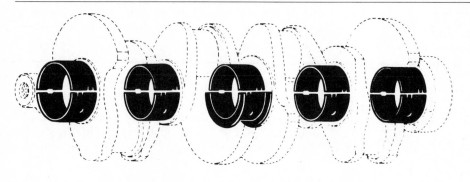

FIGURE 10-11 Crankshaft main bearings, including thrust bearing. (Chevrolet Motor Division, GMC & Isuzu)

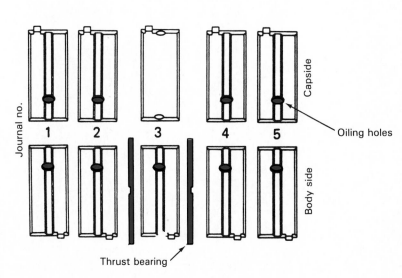

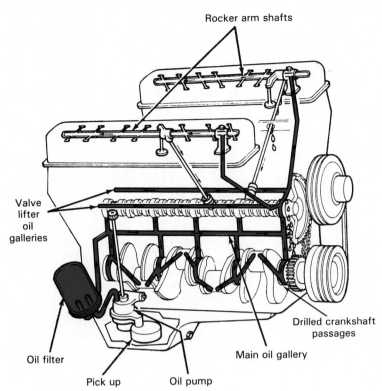

Rocker arm shafts

Valve lifter oil galleries

Oil filter

Pick up

Oil pump

Main oil gallery

Drilled crankshaft passages

FIGURE 10-12 Oil system showing oil passages in crankshaft.

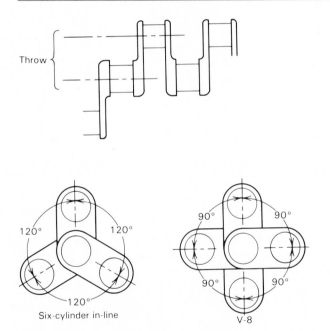

Throw

120° 120° 120°
Six-cylinder in-line

90° 90° 90° 90°
V-8

FIGURE 10-13 Degrees between throws on different engines.

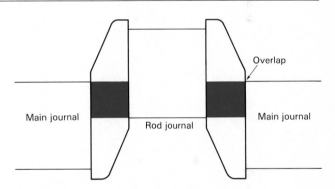

Overlap

Main journal   Rod journal   Main journal

FIGURE 10-14 Overlap between rod and main journals.

This simple canceling puts the crankshaft in **primary balance.**

Other, less severe imbalances exist. These are called **secondary imbalances.** Weights are added to the crankshaft opposite the throws. These weights help with both primary and secondary imbalances.

Strength   Although a crankshaft's strength comes from its material and general design, two factors deserve special mention.

The first factor is journal overlap. If the connecting rod and main bearing journal diameters are superimposed as seen from the front, they overlap. This overlap can also be seen from a side view (Figure 10-14). The overlap strengthens the crankshaft, making it rigid end to end.

The other factor is **fillets.** Fillets are rounded corners found where a journal meets a counterweight (Figure 10-15). These radii evenly distribute stress so it can't concentrate in a sharp, 90° corner.

And while this doesn't really fall under the heading of "strength," the oil holes are drilled in a way that will weaken the crank the least. These oil holes are **chamfered** (beveled) at their ends to reduce stress concentrations (Figure 10-16). The oil passages run

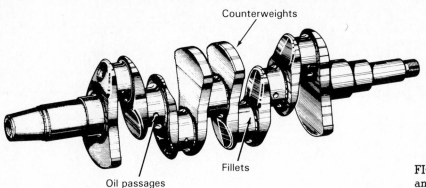

Counterweights

Fillets

Oil passages

FIGURE 10-15   Crankshaft counterweights and fillets. (Peugeot Motors of America)

from the main to the rod journals. They let oil that is pumped under pressure to the main bearings flow to the rod bearings. The oil is eventually lost through crank rotation. Fresh oil is constantly supplied by the oil pump to replace that which is lost.

FIGURE 10-16   Crankshaft oil holes and chamfer. (American Isuzu Motors, Inc.)

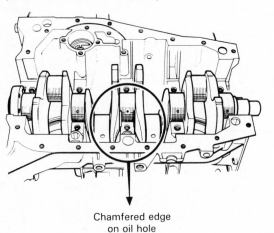

Chamfered edge
on oil hole

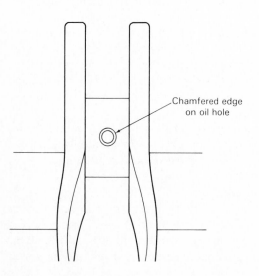

Chamfered edge
on oil hole

Connecting Rods and Bearings

The connecting rod and bearing connect each piston to the crankshaft. The connecting rod transfers to the crankshaft the full force of the piston's downward movement during combustion (Figure 10-17). Both ends of the connecting rod move: The lower (or big) end rotates, and the upper (or smaller) end swings back and forth when the engine is operating. The bearing at the lower end of the connecting rod must have a larger area to allow the crankshaft journal to turn inside it. The speed of the crankshaft produces considerable wear and heat. The upper end of the connecting rod requires a much smaller bearing surface since little movement of the bearing takes place (Figure 10-18).

The weight of a connecting rod must be kept light, but the rod must still remain strong enough to withstand constant motion as the crankshaft and pistons move. Forged connecting rods are used in heavy-duty or high-performance engines. Cast connecting rods are found in most passenger cars. The forged connecting rod is more expensive to produce than the cast version.

The big end of the connecting rod, when assembled and torqued to the crankshaft, must form a circle that is in perfect alignment. Connecting rods and their caps are matched sets. They cannot be interchanged without being remachined (Figure 10-19). After separating, the rod and cap must be returned to the exact original relationship, left to right and front to back. Many bolt heads on the connecting rod bolts have three squared sides and one nonsquared side. The three sides are kept flush against the connecting rod. The fourth, tapered side allows clearance for the cylinder when the crankshaft rotates. Besides their unusual heads, connecting rod bolts are high-strength parts. They are one of the most highly stressed fasteners on the entire car.

Balance   A connecting rod, like the crankshaft, must also be carefully balanced during manufacture. Extra material called a **boss** is placed at special places on the rod to aid in balancing (Figure 10-20). A **spit hole**

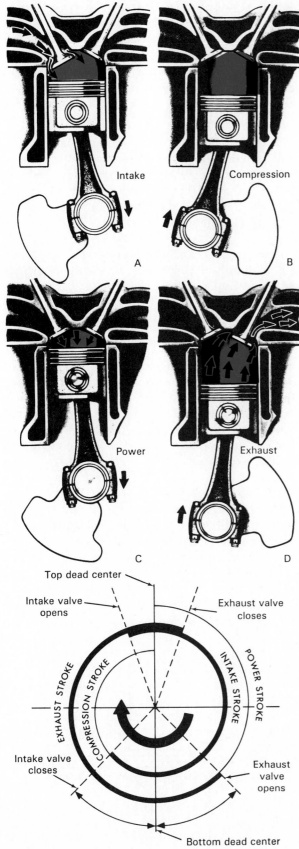

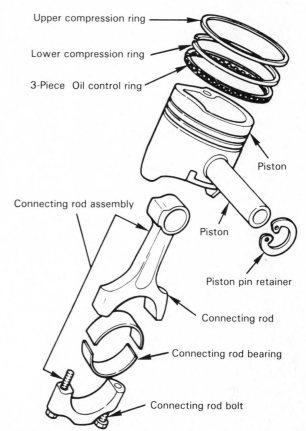

Upper compression ring

Lower compression ring

3-Piece Oil control ring

Piston

Connecting rod assembly

Piston

Connecting rod

Piston pin retainer

Connecting rod

Connecting rod bearing

Connecting rod bolt

FIGURE 10-18   Connecting rod, piston, and rings. (Ford Motor Company)

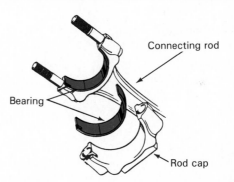

Connecting rod

Bearing

Rod cap

FIGURE 10-19   Connecting rod bearing arrangement. (Buick Motor Division, GMC)

FIGURE 10-20   Location of material (bosses) used to balance rod.

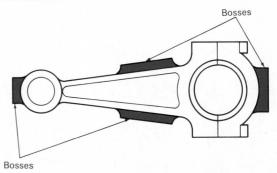

Bosses

Bosses

FIGURE 10-17   Connecting rod movement. (Chevrolet Motor Division, GMC)

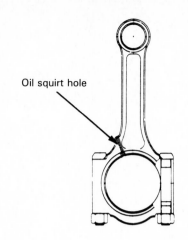

Oil squirt hole

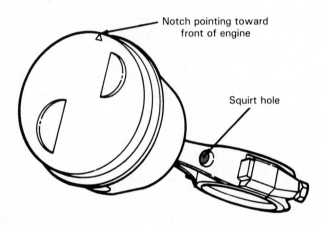

Notch pointing toward
front of engine

Squirt hole

FIGURE 10-21   Location of connecting rod spit holes.
(Chevrolet Motor Division, GMC & Ford Motor Company)

FIGURE 10-22   Piston pin bushing.

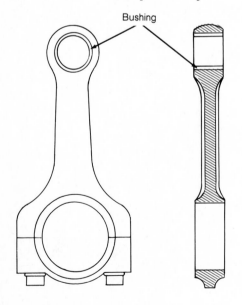

Bushing

or squirt hole on the mating surface of the bearing cap or on the I-beam portion of the rod itself helps to lubricate the cylinder walls, pin, and other portions of the bearings (Figure 10-21).

The small end of the connecting rod also has a bearing insert called a bushing. The bushing provides a bearing surface where the piston is pinned to the rod (Figure 10-22).

Rod Bearing   The material used in a connecting rod bearing is the same as that used in a crankshaft main bearing. The connecting rod bearings have a steel shell with bearing material inside. Each connecting rod bearing must also have the same characteristics of conformability, embedability, score resistance, and corrosion resistance as the crankshaft bearing. Also, like the crankshaft main bearing, the connecting rod bearing must conduct heat and be able to withstand extreme changes in temperature.

PISTONS

Pistons move up and down in the cylinders. They compress the air/fuel mixture and are pressed down the cylinders when the mixture is ignited. Pistons are therefore fitted with a thick top, or **crown** (Figure 10-23) to absorb combustion heat. Rings are fitted around the piston to seal the combustion gases and evenly spread lubricating oil on the cylinder walls. To connect the piston to the connecting rod, a **piston pin** is fitted through the piston. Reinforcing material is added to the piston where the pin passes through.

Two common methods of manufacturing pistons are to cast or forge them. The majority of today's pistons are made of cast aluminum. To help during the break-in of a new engine, a thin coating of tin is often used.

In the high-output or high-performance engine, forged pistons are normal. Forged pistons cost more

FIGURE 10-23   Piston parts.

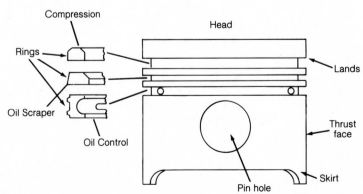

Compression

Head

Rings

Oil Scraper

Oil Control

Lands

Thrust
face

Skirt

Pin hole

than cast pistons, but the forged piston is stronger, because forging more tightly packs the grain structure of the metal. Both methods allow for the many piston crown shapes popular today. Figure 10-24 shows common piston crown shapes.

A piston will **slap**, or tip, inside a cylinder in all engines unless closely matched to its cylinder. Various piston types have evolved as a result of piston slap. Each is designed to prevent excessive rocking against the cylinder wall, holding the gas/air combustion over the piston head. Some pistons have steel struts cast in them (Figure 10-25) to aid in piston expansion control as the piston warms up. This is important, because the piston's temperature will not be uniform throughout engine operating temperature (Figure 10-26). Therefore, growth due to heat expansion must be controlled by piston design to keep the piston round while the engine is running. Without round pistons and cylinders, the pistons may slap. At the same time, a thin film of oil must be allowed to lubricate both the cylinder wall, piston skirt, and rings.

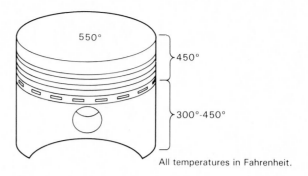

All temperatures in Fahrenheit.

FIGURE 10-26   Piston temperatures.

Piston Designs

The **T-slot piston** reduces engine heat transfer to the piston skirt from the piston head (Figure 10-27). The piston T-slot closes slightly when the piston heats. Another piston type is the **split skirt** piston (Figure 10-28). This type closes slightly when heated. The **cam ground piston** is oval-shaped, and the thrust face has a larger diameter than the expansion face (Figure 10-29). By the time the engine reaches operating temperature, the cam-ground piston has undergone controlled expansion and becomes round. Clearance between the

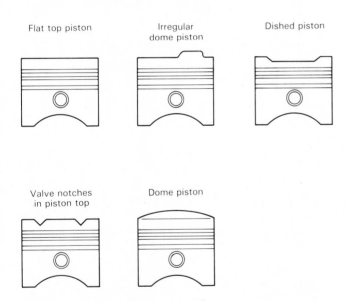

Flat top piston   Irregular dome piston   Dished piston

Valve notches in piston top   Dome piston

FIGURE 10-24   Different types of piston crowns.

FIGURE 10-25   Expansion controls in a piston. (TRW)

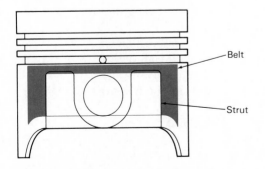

Belt

Strut

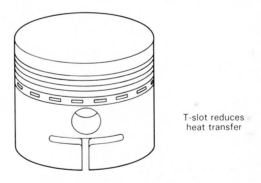

T-slot reduces heat transfer

FIGURE 10-27   T-slot piston.

FIGURE 10-28   Split skirt piston.

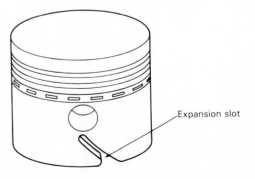

Expansion slot

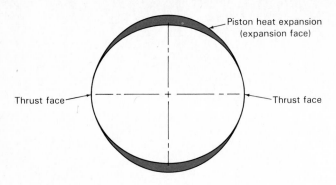

FIGURE 10-29   Cam ground piston expansion.

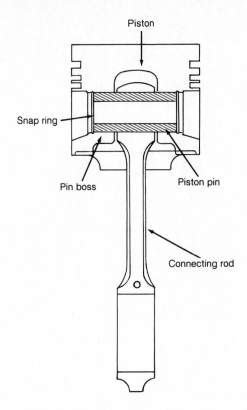

FIGURE 10-31   Piston pin boss location.

piston and the cylinder wall should be 0.0008–0.0040 in. (0.020–0.102 mm). This clearance ensures the piston won't touch the cylinder wall at maximum expansion. Another piston type, the **partial skirt** piston (skipper skirt), is also cam-ground, but part of the skirt is removed to lower the weight and permit the piston to come closer to the crankshaft (Figure 10-30).

Figure 10-31 shows the *piston pin boss*, the part that is strong and thick to support the piston pin. Many times the pin boss incorporates a steel insert. The insert is cast into the piston at the factory.

FIGURE 10-30   Partial (skipper) skirt piston.

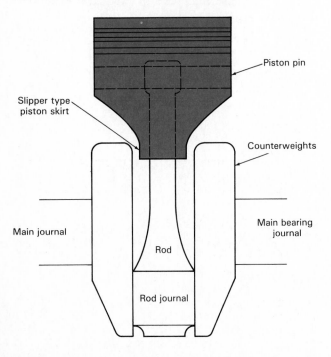

Piston Rings

Piston rings are the *seals* which prevent combustion gases and oil from leaking past the piston (Figure 10-32). They also seal the cylinder to create the vacuum which lets the mixture rush into the cylinder. The rings fit into grooves on the upper sides of the piston, although one ring may be found low on the piston. Figure 10-33 shows a ring being expanded so it can be installed on the piston.

A piston ring is not completely closed, thus causing a gap between the ends. This distance is measured during rebuilds (Figure 10-34). A small gap in each ring allows it to fit over the piston and allows the ring to expand without breaking at engine operating temperature. When the piston and piston ring expand, the ring gap becomes smaller (Figure 10-35). Figure 10-36 shows four types of ring gap joints. The butt gap is the most common.

The two kinds of piston rings used on a piston are the compression rings and the oil control rings. **Compression rings** seal the combustion chamber. **Oil control rings** help lubricate the cylinder walls and control the flow of oil.

Two compression rings and one oil ring are used on most passenger car engines. Figure 10-37 shows several different types of compression rings. Almost all modern compression rings have beveled edges and

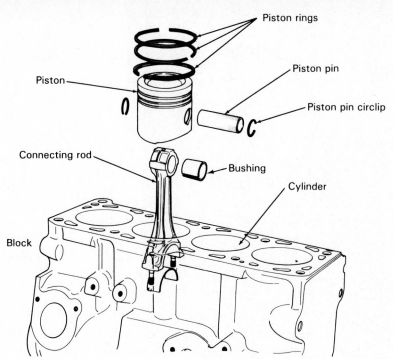

Piston rings

Piston pin

Piston pin circlip

Piston

Connecting rod

Bushing

Cylinder

Block

FIGURE 10-32   Location of piston rings.
(Chrysler Corporation)

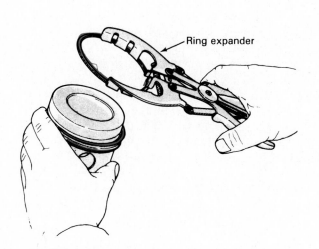

Ring expander

FIGURE 10-33   Removing or installing piston rings.
(Chrysler Corporation)

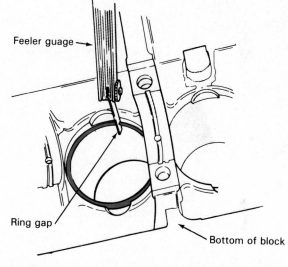

Feeler guage

Ring gap

Bottom of block

FIGURE 10-34   Measuring a ring's end gap. (Chrysler
Corporation)

FIGURE 10-35   Piston ring expansion.

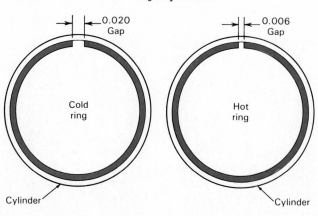

0.020
Gap

0.006
Gap

Cold
ring

Hot
ring

Cylinder

Cylinder

FIGURE 10-36   Piston ring gap joints.

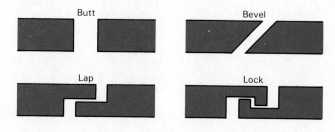

Butt

Bevel

Lap

Lock

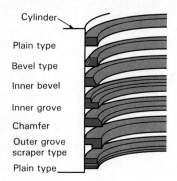

FIGURE 10-37   Types of compression rings.

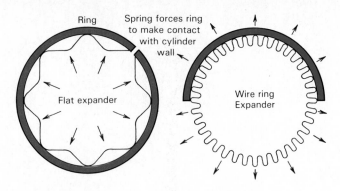

FIGURE 10-40   Types of expander springs.

built-in twist. The twist is not visible to the unaided eye but is there to force opposite edges of the ring against the ring groove. Increased sealing pressure is the result.

Figure 10-38 shows different types of oil control rings designed to scrape excess oil off the cylinder wall. A slot in all oil control rings allows oil to pass through the ring slot to a hole drilled in the ring groove and back to the crankcase (Figure 10-39).

Many oil rings are made up of three parts: two

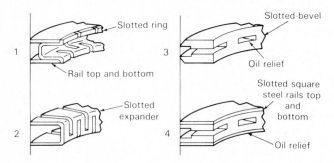

FIGURE 10-38   Types of oil control rings.

FIGURE 10-39   Oil drainage through oil control ring on piston.

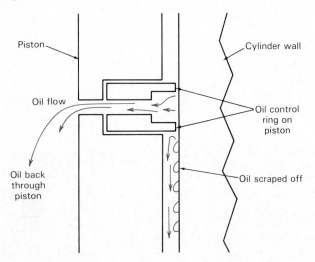

rails that do the scraping and an expander that forces the rails against the cylinder. Figure 10-40 shows two types of expanders.

Piston Ring Material   Not all piston rings are made from the same material. Pistons subjected to dirty conditions or long-wear applications are typically fitted with **chrome rings** (Figure 10-41). A chrome ring has a coating of chromium which is very smooth and hard. Such a surface wears well but does not hold oil well. Because oil is needed between the ring and cylinder wall to completely seal the cylinder, a rough cylinder wall finish is needed with chrome rings. Chrome rings are noted for needing a long break-in time.

Plain cast iron was a popular ring material for many years. Cast iron rings break in quickly because they are much softer than chrome rings. The cylinder wall finish is smoother with iron rings. By coating an iron ring with molybdenum disulfide (Figure 10-42), a longer-lasting, quick-break-in ring is made. The moly coating is porous and holds oil well. Therefore, the ring always has enough oil to seal the cylinder wall. The soft coating allows a fast break-in, and the large amounts of oil reduce ring wear.

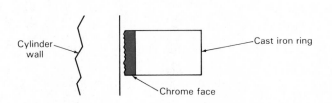

FIGURE 10-41   Chrome-plated piston ring.

FIGURE 10-42   Moly-coated ring.

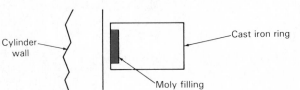

Chrome rings are still used in heavy-duty, dusty conditions. Iron rings are cheap but are usually passed up in favor of **moly rings.**

Piston Pins

Piston pins are simple cylinders of hardened steel (Figure 10-43). The pin passes through one piston pin boss, through the small end of the connecting rod, and then through the other piston pin boss. The pin is the bearing surface for the small end of the connecting rod.

Figure 10-44 shows four ways of securing the piston pin. One of the most common methods is to press the pin into the connecting rod. A very slight clearance is left between the piston and piston pin, but an **interference fit** is used between pin and rod. This is also called a press fit. In an interference fit, the pin is slightly bigger around than the hole in the connecting rod. When pressed together, the rod and pin effectively become one part. This forms a "T" out of the rod, which makes it very strong.

Another method is the use of a **floating pin.** A floating pin has clearance between the piston and the connecting rod. Snap rings are usually fitted to the piston pin bore in the piston. They are installed after the pin, and they keep it from rubbing against the cylinder walls. An alternate method is to do without the snap rings and have **buttons** fitted to the end of the pin. The buttons ride against the cylinder wall. Because they are made of soft aluminum or Teflon, the buttons do no damage.

A few engines have a split connecting rod small end. A bolt passes through the rod's small end. The pin is installed, and the bolt is tightened. This is sometimes called a *cinch bolt* connecting rod.

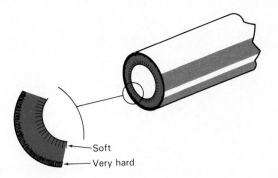

FIGURE 10-43 Hardened piston pin.

Another uncommon attachment method is to pass a bolt through the pin boss and into the pin.

The connecting rod small end can simply be machined to size, or a bronze bushing may be fitted there. If a bushing is used, it is replaceable.

AUXILIARY SHAFTS

A **balance shaft,** or *silent shaft*, is used on some engines to reduce engine vibration. Two shafts with counterbalance weights are rotated at twice the engine speed. One rotates in the same direction as the crankshaft, and one rotates in the opposite direction. The vibrations created by these balance shafts offset crankshaft vibration, resulting in a smoother-running engine. Balance shafts are usually used on larger four-cylinder engines. Balance shafts are driven by the timing belt (Figure 10-45) and require some extra weight. The smoothness justifies the weight penalty in large four-cylinder engines, however.

FIGURE 10-44 Piston pin attachments.

(a) Pin bolt
Rod floats
on pin

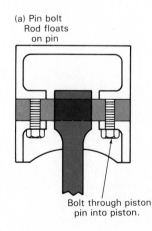

Bolt through piston
pin into piston.

(b) Rod press fit

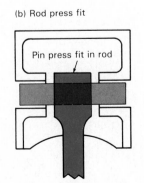

Pin press fit in rod

(c) Free floating pin
retained in piston
by snap rings

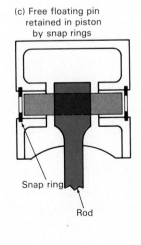

Snap ring

Rod

(d) Rod bolt is
clamped to pin.

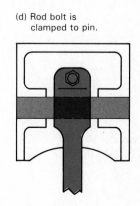

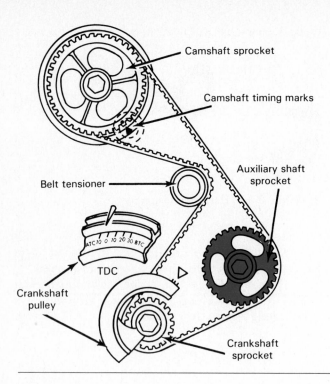

Camshaft sprocket

Camshaft timing marks

Auxiliary shaft sprocket

Belt tensioner

TDC

Crankshaft pulley

Crankshaft sprocket

FIGURE 10-45 Auxiliary shaft drive. (Chrysler Corporation)

TRADE TERMS

Balance Shaft
Boss
Buttons
Cam-ground Piston
Chamfered
Chrome Rings
Compression Rings
Crown
Crush
Fillets
Floating Pin
Flywheel
Harmonic Balancer

Interference Fit
Moly Rings
Oil Control Rings
Partial Skirt
Piston Pin
Primary Balance
Secondary Imbalance
Slap
Spit Hole
Split Skirt
Spread
T-Slot Piston

REVIEW QUESTIONS

1. Name the machined areas of the crank that accept the main and rod bearings.

2. What is the front part of the crankshaft called where the harmonic balancer is mounted?

3. Does the harmonic balancer cancel high-frequency vibrations or very low-frequency power impulses?

4. Are connecting rod caps interchangeable within the same engine?

5. What is embedability?

6. What is the top of a piston called?

7. If you were designing an earthmover engine, what type of piston ring material would you specify?

8. How does oil get to the connecting rod bearings?

9. On what kinds of engines are balance shafts used?

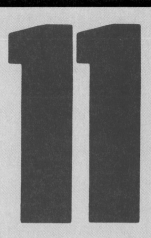

The Cylinder Head

INTRODUCTION

The cylinder head bolts to the top of the block, closing off the top of each cylinder. It can be removed for easy access to the valves and cylinders.

The cylinder head contains intake and exhaust valves for each cylinder, the holes for the spark plugs, intake and exhaust ports, and coolant passages.

Overhead valve engines and overhead camshaft engines require different types of heads. Combustion chambers also come in different types. They include the hemispherical, the wedge, the CVCC, the MCA, the **High Swirl Combustion (HSC),** and **jet-air** types.

A cylinder head has passageways or **ports** in it for intake and exhaust venting. These passageways run from the manifolds to the valves. They must avoid other areas of the cylinder head which are used for push rod openings, cooling passages, valve guides, and head bolts.

Cooling passages help keep the operating temperature of the engine at the proper level. Lubrication of the valve components is through other passageways provided in the head or push rods.

OBJECTIVES

When you have completed this chapter, you should be able to

- Describe the types of cylinder heads and the differences between them
- Understand the function and operation of the **combustion chamber**
- Identify different types of combustion chambers
- Know the function of intake and exhaust ports
- Tell how cylinder head design affects emissions
- Recognize the different passageways in a cylinder head and what they do

inder head must withstand both intense pressure and high temperature. For this reason, metal alloys are also used in the cast iron head to give it greater durability. Although lighter in weight and a better heat conductor, aluminum will warp more quickly if overheated and is actually more expensive.

To provide proper access for spark plugs, head bolts, studs, valve guides, and valve seats, a cylinder head requires special drilling, tapping, and machining. In addition, the various passageways for water, oil, and gas flow must be cast into the head (Figure 11-2). Each passageway requires thorough finishing and inspecting to ensure that proper clearances and sizes are met.

The recessed area in the bottom of a cylinder head helps form the combustion chamber (Figure 11-3).

Gaskets are used throughout the engine to prevent leakage of gases, oil, or coolant. Gaskets must have excellent sealing qualities and be able to withstand extreme temperatures and different kinds of liquids.

This chapter explains the various features of cylinder head design and operation.

TYPES OF CYLINDER HEADS

The engine types most common today on American cars are the in-line 4, the in-line 6, the V6, and the V8. The 3-, 5-, and 12-cylinder engines are found only on imported cars. In-line engines have only one cylinder head, and vee or opposed engines have two cylinder heads. Engine design determines the specific requirements and size for each head, but certain basic features must be present in every cylinder head (Figure 11-1).

Although today many cylinder heads are being made from aluminum, most are still cast iron. The cyl-

The Three-Cylinder Head

The General Motors/Suzuki three-cylinder engine has an aluminum block and head with cast iron cylinder liners. The engine weighs less than 150 lbs. It is an overhead camshaft design, so the camshaft is mounted on the head and not in the block (Figure 11-4). The head has two valves and one spark plug per cylinder. The engine owes its light weight to the aluminum block, aluminum head, and hollow segments in the camshaft and crankshaft. This 1-liter (993-cc) engine develops 48 hp at 5100 rpm and can attain 68 mpg on the highway.

The Four-Cylinder Head

The four-cylinder engine cylinder head is common on today's automobile engine. It generally is used on the

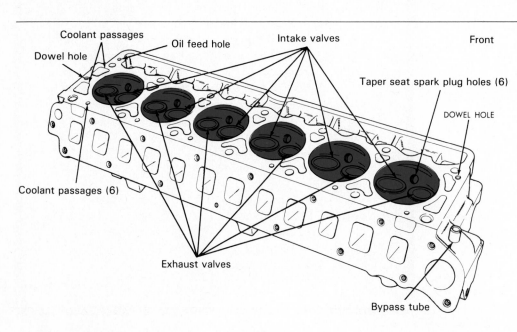

Coolant passages

Dowel hole

Oil feed hole

Intake valves

Front

Taper seat spark plug holes (6)

DOWEL HOLE

Coolant passages (6)

Exhaust valves

Bypass tube

FIGURE 11-1 Cylinder head: six-cylinder engine. (Chrysler Corporation)

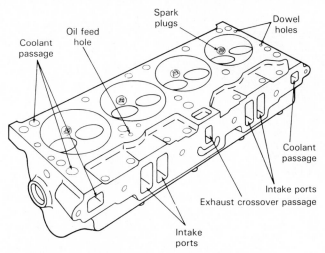

FIGURE 11-2 Cylinder head passages. (Chrysler Corporation)

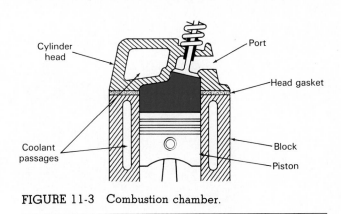

FIGURE 11-3 Combustion chamber.

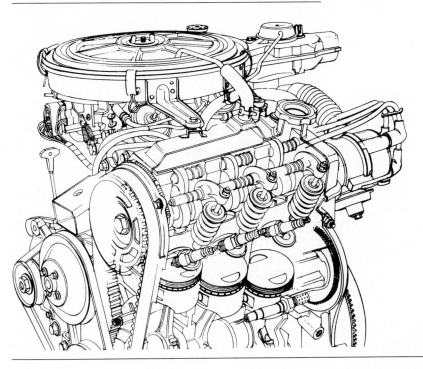

FIGURE 11-4 Three-cylinder engine. (Chevrolet Motor Division, GMC)

FIGURE 11-5 Cylinder head: four-cylinder in-line engine. (American Motors Corporation)

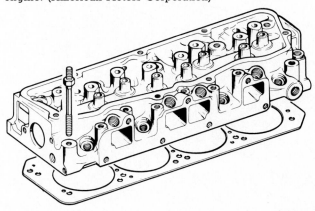

four-cylinder *in-line* engine (Figure 11-5). Other types of engine and head designs are the V4 engine and the opposed four-cylinder engine. Both the V4 and the opposed 4 use two two-cylinder heads, one on each bank of the cylinder. The V4 engine was used on Saabs and the opposed four-cylinder engine is used on Volkswagens, Subarus, and Porsches.

The Five-Cylinder Head

The five-cylinder-head design is found primarily on three automobiles—the Mercedes-Benz, the Audi, and the Volkswagen. The cylinder head is designed for an overhead camshaft engine (Figure 11-6).

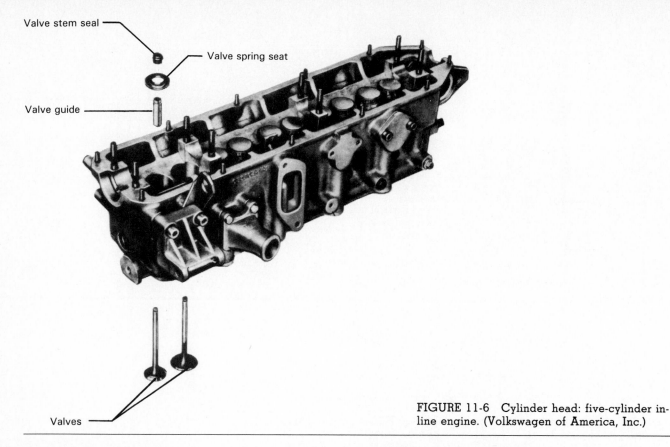

Valve stem seal

Valve spring seat

Valve guide

Valves

FIGURE 11-6   Cylinder head: five-cylinder in-line engine. (Volkswagen of America, Inc.)

The Six-Cylinder Head

Another cylinder head type is for the in-line six-cylinder engine (Figure 11-7). It is identical to the in-line four-cylinder except for the addition of two more cylinders. A V6 design has become more popular today and is found in many American autos (Figure 11-8). The cylinders are arranged in a 90° or 60° V shape. This engine has two three-cylinder heads.

The Eight-Cylinder Head

All modern eight-cylinder engines are V8s, although for many years, straight eights were popular. Two four-cylinder heads (Figure 11-9) are placed at 90° to each other to form a V. Most V8s are overhead valve (OHV) engines; all valves, lifters, push rods, and rocker arms are operated by one camshaft. Also, one crankshaft controls all pistons and connecting rods.

FIGURE 11-7   Cylinder head: six-cylinder in-line engine. (American Motors Corporation)

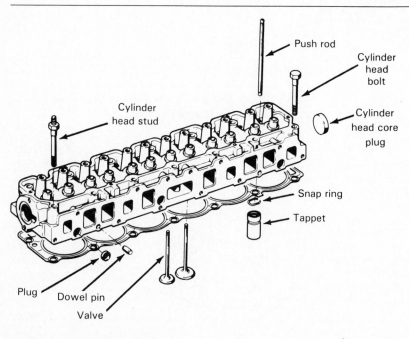

Push rod

Cylinder head bolt

Cylinder head core plug

Cylinder head stud

Snap ring

Tappet

Plug

Dowel pin

Valve

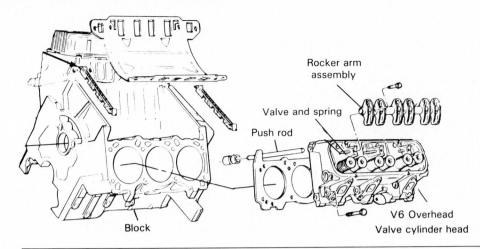

FIGURE 11-8 Cylinder head: V6 engine. (Oldsmobile Motor Division, GMC)

Rocker arm assembly

Valve and spring

Push rod

V6 Overhead Valve cylinder head

Block

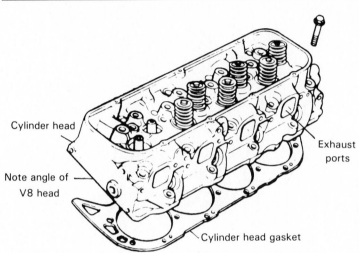

Cylinder head

Note angle of V8 head

Exhaust ports

Cylinder head gasket

FIGURE 11-9 Cylinder head: V8 engine. (Chevrolet Motor Division, GMC)

A HEAD START

As it turned out, we couldn't keep up with the Mustangs. If they weren't faster on the track, at least they spent less time in the pits. For one thing, they could make brake pad changes much faster than we could. Not only did they have a better design to work with, but their crew was more practiced at changing them. Then, at about the halfway point, we cracked another cylinder head. Chevrolet would never admit it, but I'd hate to guess how many hundreds of cracked cylinder heads I've seen on racing engines. I don't know whether it's due to porting or poor coolant flow, but they inevitably crack across the intake valve seat. That's been a problem for as long as I can remember, and it's still a problem today. We changed the head again. That dropped us so far down that we were hard-pressed to finish second in class.

At that point we were even-up with Ford, with one long-distance race each, and we knew our cars were good for the season. Chevrolet was really interested in what we had, so they invited us to bring our Traco engines in to run on their dynos. Traco was getting 410–420 hp, while Chevrolet engineers figured we ought to be getting at least 450 hp. So we hauled our engines to Detroit, set them up on their dyno, and watched then blow the first one apart in warm-up. It's no wonder, either. They fired it up and ran it wide-open throttle without even waiting for the oil temperature to come up. On top of that, both of those engines already had 12 hard hours of racing. The second one survived that ordeal somehow, and sure enough, it showed about 420 hp.

Then they gave us a slide job about

what *they* could do. They pulled our cylinder heads off and snapped on some high-compression heads of their own. They hooked up their doodads that maximize everything like spark advance, and fuel mixture, and so on—and they showed us 460 hp. That was when we began to understand the principle of "seasoning" a short block assembly. You run a newly built engine carefully for as long as possible, so that all the parts get "friendly" with each other; then you pop on a fresh set of heads, and it will give you another 20 hp.

Reprinted by permission of DODD, MEAD & COMPANY, INC. from THE UNFAIR ADVANTAGE by Mark Donohue with Paul Van Valkenburgh. Copyright © 1975 by Mark Donohue.

Overhead Valve (OHV) Cylinder Heads

Modern engines place the valves above the pistons within the cylinder head. This makes sense from many engineering standpoints, and makes valve servicing easier. One of the most important is that the valves can pass the most air when arranged this way, thus increasing engine efficiency. In an OHV design, the cylinder head must accommodate the push rods, rocker arms, and valves (Figure 11-10). The camshaft is in the cylinder block.

Overhead Camshaft (OHC) Cylinder Heads

In the OHC design, the camshaft is mounted either in or right above the cylinder head (Figure 11-11). The

FIGURE 11-10 Overhead valve (OHV) cylinder head. (American Motors Corporation)

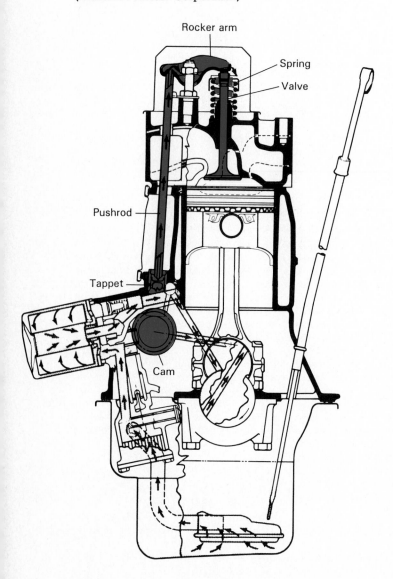

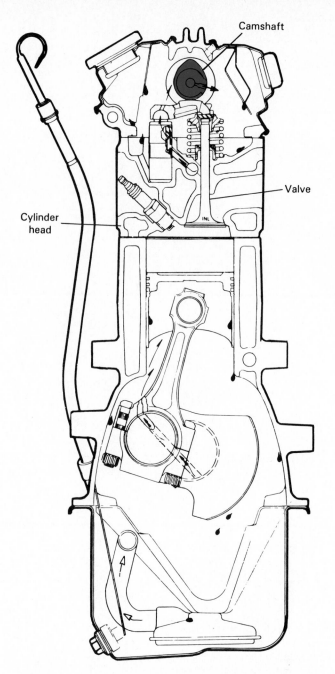

FIGURE 11-11 Overhead camshaft (OHC) cylinder head. (Pontiac Motor Division, GMC)

camshaft can work the valves directly or through rocker arms. There is no need for lifters or push rods in an OHC engine. This means the cylinder head must accommodate the camshaft, valves, and any rocker arms. Because there is less weight and flexing in the valve mechanism, OHC engines can usually rev higher than OVH designs.

When on overhead camshaft is used, the engine is known as a single overhead camshaft (**SOHC**) engine (Figure 11-12).

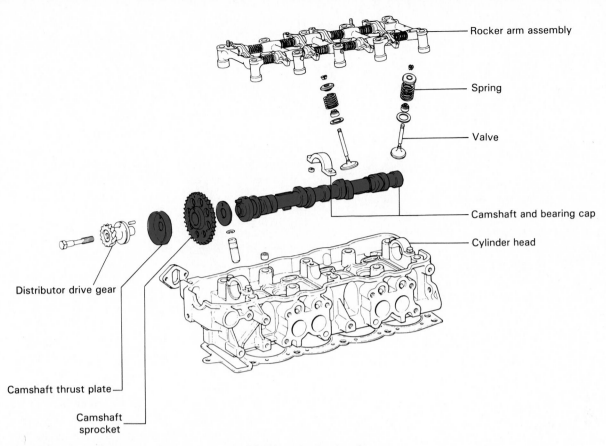

Rocker arm assembly

Spring

Valve

Camshaft and bearing cap

Cylinder head

Distributor drive gear

Camshaft thrust plate

Camshaft sprocket

FIGURE 11-12   Single overhead camshaft (SOHC) cylinder head.

Double Overhead Camshaft (DOHC) Cylinder Head

Two camshafts located in a single cylinder head are known as a double overhead camshaft cylinder head. One camshaft operates the intake valves; the other camshaft operates the exhaust valves. **DOHC** advantages are the following: (1) Valve overlap timing (period when intake and exhaust valves are both open) is easy to change; (2) camshafts are easier to manufacture and are less expensive; and (3) valve locations and angles are easier to arrange (Figure 11-13).

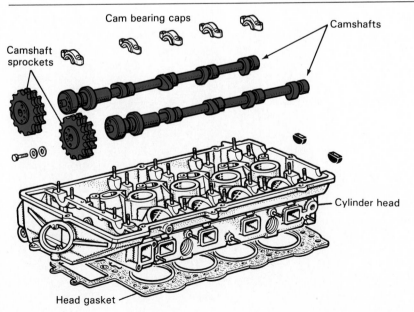

Cam bearing caps

Camshafts

Camshaft sprockets

Cylinder head

Head gasket

FIGURE 11-13   Double overhead camshaft (DOHC) cylinder head.

COMBUSTION CHAMBERS

Combustion takes place in an automobile engine to create the power to operate the automobile. Combustion combines the oxygen in the air with various other elements including carbon or hydrogen. When these elements are compressed together with vapor from the gasoline and then ignited (set on fire) by the spark plug, combustion occurs.

To control and direct this combustion process, an engine must have a *combustion chamber*. The top of the combustion chamber is the cylinder head. The sides and bottom of the combustion chamber are formed by the top of the piston (which is constantly moving up and down) and the cylinder walls themselves. In recent years, six different designs of combustion chambers have been used for efficient combustion, each depending on engine type and displacement.

The Hemispherical Combustion Chamber

The **hemispherical** combustion chamber gets its name from its shape. It is one half (hemi) of a sphere (spherical). The piston is often designed so its top will protrude into the space opened by the cylinder heads.

The most important part of a *hemi* head is the way in which the valves are tilted away from each other (Figure 11-14). In each cylinder, the intake and exhaust valves are tilted so their stems point in the opposite direction. The valve heads are pointed toward the center of the combustion chamber. When the valves open, they open away from the cylinder walls. This leaves the maximum amount of space for gases to flow in and out of the combustion chamber.

Well-controlled combustion is started by the spark plug mounted in the center of the head. This central location gives the shortest path possible to all parts of the combustion chamber. The short path provides quick combustion of the air/fuel mixture, with little time for detonation to get started.

Because of their valve and spark plug placement, hemispherical cylinder heads typically produce more power than other types of combustion chambers. Drawbacks to the hemi head are the amount of machining necessary to form the deep chambers, the more complex valve train, and the piston dome shapes necessary to get the proper compression ratio. The pistons usually need a raised crown to get enough compression. The high crown can inhibit the combustion flame as it travels across the combustion chamber.

The Wedge Combustion Chamber

The **wedge** combustion chamber also gets its name from its shape (Figure 11-15). A wedge chamber has two distinct parts. One part forms a tub. The spark plug and valves (the other part) fit into the tub. The tub slants toward the piston top until it gets quite close to the piston. Then the chamber is flat and is parallel to the piston crown. The name *wedge* comes from the slanted portion of the tub.

The idea behind having part of the cylinder head close to the piston is to squeeze the mixture caught there. This shoots the squeezed mixture into the tub area, mixing the air and fuel more completely (Figure 11-16). This mixing promotes even combustion and reduces the chance of detonation (Figure 11-17). The mixing effect is called **turbulence.**

The majority of combustion takes place in the tub area close to the spark plug. Those gases left in the squeeze or **quench** area are too constricted to detonate, and they burn at a lower temperature than the main air/fuel mass. The lower temperatures in the

FIGURE 11-14 Hemispherical combustion chamber.

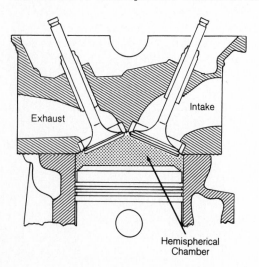

FIGURE 11-15 Wedge combustion chamber.

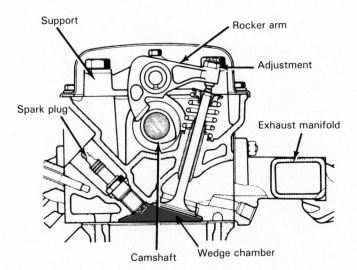

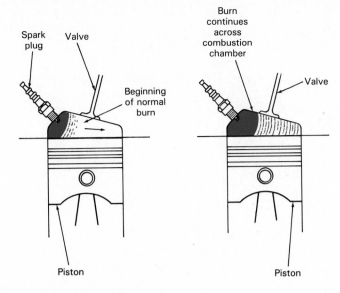

FIGURE 11-16   Normal combustion.

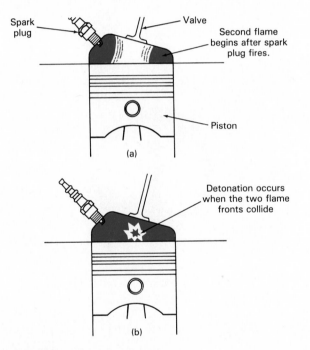

FIGURE 11-17   Detonation.

quench area cause hydrocarbon (HC) and carbon monoxide (CO) emissions. Therefore, modern wedge chambers are designed with a minimum of quench area.

An advantage of wedge chambers is their low cost. Not much machining is required to get the proper shape. Another cost-cutting feature is the valve train. Because the valves must fit into the tub area, they end up in a straight line from one end of the head to the other. This simplifies both valve train complexity and cost and cylinder head machining operations at the factory.

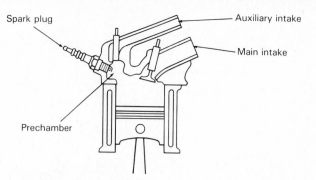

FIGURE 11-18   CVCC combustion chamber. (American Honda Motor Corporation, Inc.)

The CVCC Combustion Chamber

The Controlled Vortex Combustion Chamber (CVCC) is a Honda design and is used on Honda cars only. It uses two chambers, the main combustion chamber and the auxiliary combustion chamber. The usual intake and exhaust valves are found in the main combustion chamber. A third, much smaller, *auxiliary* intake valve opens into the auxiliary chamber (Figure 11-18).

A very rich mixture is admitted into the auxiliary chamber by the small valve. At the same time, a lean mixture is let into the main chamber by the regular intake valve. The bottom of the auxiliary chamber is open to the main chamber through one or more holes. The rich and lean mixtures thus overlap somewhat in the main chamber, near the auxiliary chamber's outlet. Three mixtures are therefore present: the rich one in the auxiliary chamber, the moderate mixture near the auxiliary chamber, and the lean mixture in the rest of the main chamber.

The spark plug fits into the auxiliary chamber and fires the rich mixture. The rich mixture burns quickly, and the combustion flame spreads out of the auxiliary chamber, through the moderate mixture, and finally consumes the lean mixture.

The CVCC is technically a **stratified charge** chamber. This means that the mixture is arranged in layers, called *strata,* as was just explained (overlapping mixtures). This gives excellent combustion control and low emissions. *Charge* is the term for the air/fuel mixture after the intake valve closes.

Low emissions without add-on devices is the CVCC chamber's big advantage. Disadvantages are high machining costs, complication and horsepower restrictions because of the auxiliary valve size limitations.

Mitsubishi Clean Air (MCA)

Another type of three-valve combustion chamber is called the MCA (Mitsubishi clean air) Jet system (Figure 11-19). Instead of using a prechamber, this type

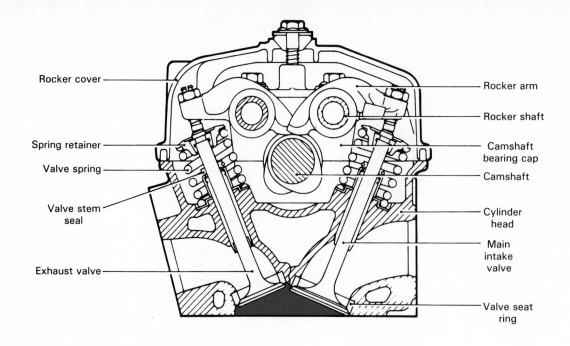

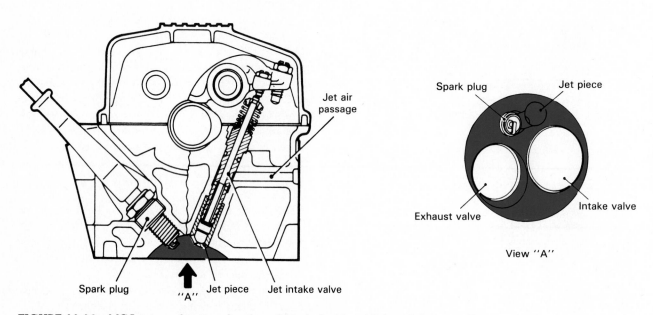

FIGURE 11-19   MCA jet combustion chamber. (Mitsubishi Motor Sales of America, Inc.)

uses a second intake valve. This second valve opens and closes with the regular intake valve. Air for the smaller intake valve comes from above the carburetor throttle plate. When the engine operates at lower rpm, airflow comes into the chamber through the valve. This causes swirling, and the resulting turbulence thoroughly mixes the air/fuel charge. When the engine is running at higher rpm, the carburetor air intake is so located that very little air can flow into this smaller valve and then into the combustion chamber. At higher rpm, the MCA combustion chamber functions much like a normal, two-valve combustion chamber.

High Swirl Combustion (HSC) Chamber

The high swirl combustion chamber is a compact combustion chamber (Figure 11-20). This small combustion chamber uses a flat-top piston and a special masked intake port with a centrally located spark plug. This small highly turbulent chamber design results in a shortened period of combustion and a reduced flame front. The swirling action of the air/fuel mixture provides better mixing of the charge, which helps the charge to burn more completely. The location of the spark plug shortens the distance the flame must travel

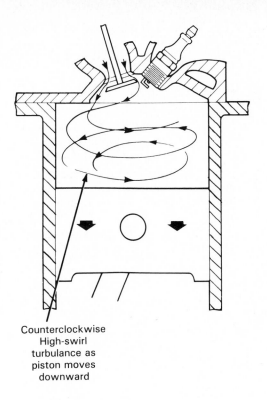

Counterclockwise
High-swirl
turbulance as
piston moves
downward

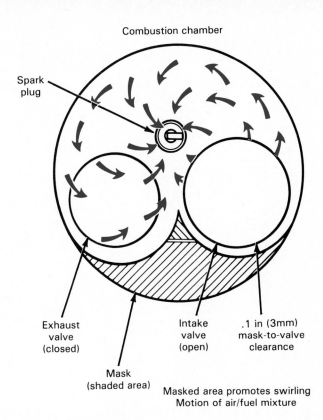

Combustion chamber

Spark
plug

Exhaust
valve
(closed)

Mask
(shaded area)

Intake
valve
(open)

.1 in (3mm)
mask-to-valve
clearance

Masked area promotes swirling
Motion of air/fuel mixture

FIGURE 11-20   High swirl combustion (HSC) chamber. (Ford Motor Company)

to completely burn the mixture. This type of design is becoming more popular as emission and mileage concerns increase (Figure 11-21).

The combination of a compact combustion chamber, swirling action of the air/fuel mixture, and centrally located spark plug result in

1. Increased horsepower output (and reduced knock)
2. Higher thermal efficiency
3. Higher exhaust gas recirculation (EGR) tolerance
4. Lower nitrogen oxide (NO_x) emissions

May Fireball Combustion Chamber

The combustion chamber of the Jaguar XJS-V12 HE is a breakthrough in combustion chamber design. The May combustion chamber is a two-level chamber. The intake valve is in a shallow collecting zone, and the exhaust valve is higher up in the combustion chamber. The cylinder head is mostly flat, and the combustion chamber is above the top of the piston. This design allows for higher compression ratios (10.5:1 to 12:1) on unleaded gas and better power and economy.

PORTS (INTAKE AND EXHAUST)

The main passageways or *ports* in the cylinder head direct the intake and exhaust gases. The intake ports

FIGURE 11-21   Swirl Inlet combustion chamber. (Chevrolet Motor Division, GMC)

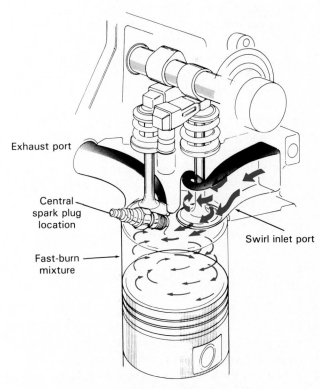

Exhaust port

Central
spark plug
location

Fast-burn
mixture

Swirl inlet port

Swirl inlet combustion chamber

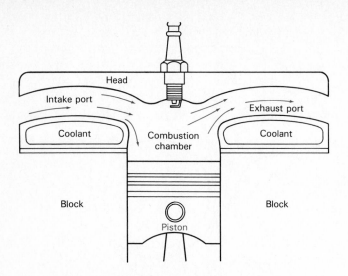

FIGURE 11-22   Crossflow cylinder head.

direct the incoming air or air/fuel mixture from the intake manifold to the intake valves. The exhaust ports direct the exhaust gases from the exhaust valves to the exhaust manifold. On many in-line engine cylinder heads the intake and the exhaust ports are located on the same side of the head. In a smaller engine with limited space, two cylinders may share the same port. These are called **Siamese** ports. When this is done, the single port is made larger to accommodate the extra gas flow.

The cross-sectional area, shape, length, and smoothness of the port determine its efficiency. The fewer bends and restrictions in a port, the better it will flow gas. The ability to flow gas is called **breathing**. You may notice that exhaust ports are smaller than intake ports. Yet both breathe equally. The difference is due to combustion pressure. The expanding combustion gases and upward-moving piston help push the exhaust out, but the intake charge depends on atmospheric pressure for its flow. Thus the exhaust doesn't need as large a port as the intake.

When the intake port is on one side of the head and the exhaust port is on the other, the head is a **crossflow** design (Figure 11-22). Noncrossflow heads have both intake and exhaust ports on the same side of the head. There are advantages to both systems, but the crossflow head generally breathes better.

CYLINDER HEAD COOLING

Passageways, or openings, are provided in a cylinder head to allow coolant to flow around the combustion chamber. This removes excess heat. When the head is originally cast, the casting cores create these openings. Smooth walls in both ports and cooling passage aid flow. The coolant flow between head and block

is controlled by the size of the opening in the head gasket.

VALVE GUIDES

Valve guides are either *replaceable inserts* or machined holes in the cylinder head which support the valve stems (Figure 11-23). When they are machined holes, they are known as integral valve guides (Figure 11-24). When valve guides are replaceable, they are pressed in the cylinder head and can be removed and replaced when worn.

It is important that a tight fit exist between the valve guide and the cylinder head. This tight fit keeps the guide from moving with the valve and permits better heat dissipation. The valve guide must be centered directly over the valve seat to ensure correct valve seating (Figure 11-25).

Aluminum cylinder heads always use replaceable insert valve guides. These guides are generally cast separately and are made of either cast iron or a special bronze alloy.

Cast iron heads use both the replaceable and the integral type of valve guide. The use of integral valve guides transfers heat more efficiently and keeps pro-

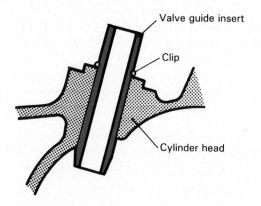

FIGURE 11-23   Valve guide insert. (Mazda North America, Inc.)

FIGURE 11-24   Integral valve guide.

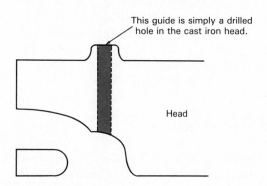

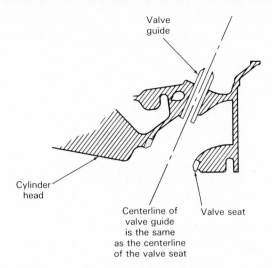

FIGURE 11-25 Valve guide and seat centerline.

duction costs low. The valve stem and valve face remain centered as the valve opens and closes on the valve seat, thus prolonging valve life.

VALVE SEATS

The **valve seat** is where the face of the valve seals. The valve seat can be simply a machined portion of the head or a replaceable insert. Aluminum heads use steel inserts. All modern engines use special hardened valve seats that are able to operate without the lubrication which used to come from lead in gasoline.

The valve seat is ground with three angles. The angles are important to valve sealing and gas flow. The valve face seals against the middle *cut* or angle. That leaves a cut in the combustion chamber and another in the port. The cuts help the gas to make the

FIGURE 11-26 Valve seat angles.

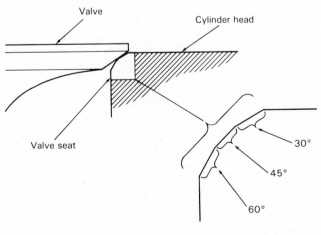

turn into or out of the combustion chamber. Figure 11-26 shows typical valve and valve seat angles.

The 1° difference between the valve and the valve seat is caused by grinding the valve flatter than the seat. This helps in sealing the combustion chamber and ports.

HEAD GASKET

The cylinder head and cylinder block must mate perfectly and not allow leakage of gases, oil, or water. Normal production machining cannot produce a perfect mating. To do so, a head gasket is normally used to seal the surfaces between the head and the block (Figure 11-27).

FIGURE 11-27 Head gasket. (Mazda North America, Inc.)

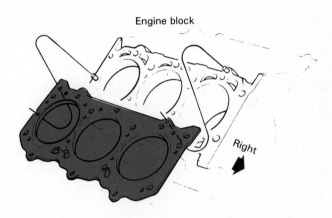

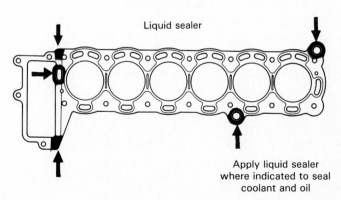

Gasket material must possess certain qualities. First, a gasket must be *resistant*. This means that any change in temperature, pressure, or anticipated conditions under which the gasket will be used must be considered when designing a gasket. Head gaskets must also last the life of the engine.

Gaskets must *conform* to the surface they are used on, including surfaces that may warp slightly or that are rough from machining.

A *resilient* gasket must remain sealed even when a temperature, pressure, or vibration change causes a joint to loosen.

A gasket must be *impermeable*. That is, it must be able to keep all fluids from leaking or seeping out.

Gasket material was originally *cork* because it was impermeable and formed easily. *Fibers* have replaced cork. The fibers are made of asbestos, cellulose, or both. Head gaskets originally used *copper-coated asbestos*. Now *embossed steel* is used in conjunction with a coating of soft aluminum to aid resiliency. Another head gasket type has a *steel core* with a thin coating of asbestos

on both sides. All head gaskets must withstand high engine block and cylinder head pressures and temperatures.

CAUTION: Be careful when working with or when exposed to asbestos. Avoid prolonged contact.

Asbestos or metal, or thin sheets of soft metal, are generally used on today's head gaskets. Holes are cut out of each head gasket to allow for the bolts, valves, cylinders, and water passages in the head and block. The head bolts are tightened down on the head gasket after it is installed. This squeezes the gasket metal which is soft and seals the mating surfaces between the head and the block.

A head gasket will normally be marked "front" or "top" to make sure it is installed correctly. If the gasket is not marked, install it with the trademark facing up. Incorrect installation can block off oil or coolant passages. Be careful.

TRADE TERMS

Breathing
Combustion Chamber
Crossflow
CVCC
DOHC
Hemispherical
High Swirl Combustion
Jet Air
Ports

Quench
Siamese
SOHC
Stratified Charge
Turbulence
Valve Guides
Valve Seats
Wedge

REVIEW QUESTIONS

1. What two materials are used to make cylinder heads?
2. Because of the differences in the valve operating mechanism, which do you think is the more complicated cylinder head: an OHV or OHC head?
3. What does DOHC mean?
4. Name the parts which form the combustion chamber.
5. Why do hemispherical combustion chambers produce more power than most other combustion chambers?
6. Centrally locating the spark plug shortens the flame's path and reduces what?
7. Why do you suppose aluminum cylinder heads always use replaceable valve guides?
8. What four qualities must a gasket have?
9. What three things does the head gasket seal?
10. What is a Siamesed port?

12

The Valve Train

OBJECTIVES

When you have completed this chapter, you should be able to

- Describe all parts of the **valve train**
- Explain the difference between overhead cam and overhead valve engines
- Understand how valves open, close, and seal
- Tell why exhaust valves fail more often than intakes
- Know how the valve lifters and camshaft work together
- Adjust the **valve clearance** on most engines
- Perform a valve job

INTRODUCTION

For an engine to make power, it must breathe in fresh air and fuel and then expel the waste gases of combustion. This is the job of the *valve train*, a collection of mechanical parts which allow the gases in and out of the engine at the proper time (Figure 12-1).

Two basic types of valve trains are in use today: overhead valve (OHV) and overhead camshaft (OHC).

Overhead valve engines have been very popular in domestic cars, especially since the late 1940s (Figure 12-2). Overhead camshaft engines, on the other hand, have been popular with imported car makers since the turn of the century (Figure 12-3). The OHV layout is cheaper to make and is more compact on V engines. Less weight and a higher rpm potential are the advantages of the OHC.

TYPES OF VALVE TRAINS

OHV

Tracing valve movement through a typical OHV layout is a good introduction to valve train parts.

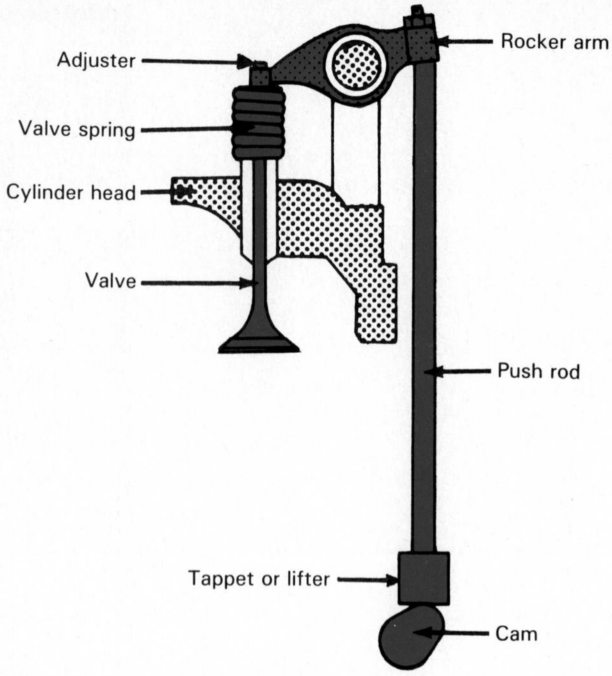

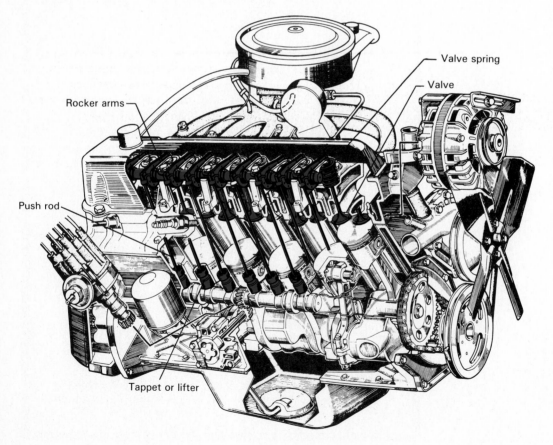

Valve train movement begins at the crankshaft. The crankshaft sprocket is attached to the camshaft sprocket by the timing chain. The sprockets are sized so the camshaft will rotate at one-half crankshaft speed (Figure 12-4). This ratio gives the correct one valve opening per four piston strokes. Another way of saying this is that the valves open once every other crankshaft revolution.

On the camshaft is a series of lobes, eccentric sections which control valve movement. Above the lobes are the lifters. There is one lobe for each valve.

FIGURE 12-2   OHV valve train.

FIGURE 12-1   OHV valve train. (Chrysler Corporation)

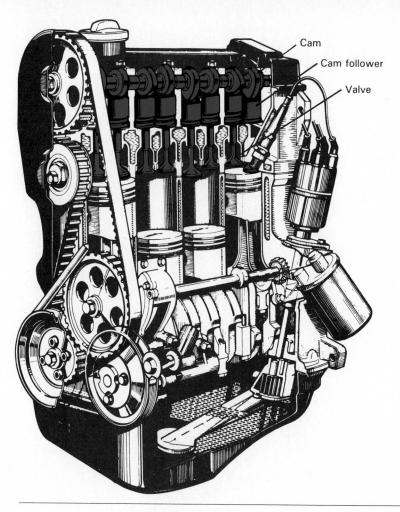

Cam
Cam follower
Valve

FIGURE 12-3 OHC valve train. (Chrysler Corporation)

FIGURE 12-4 Crankshaft/camshaft relationship.

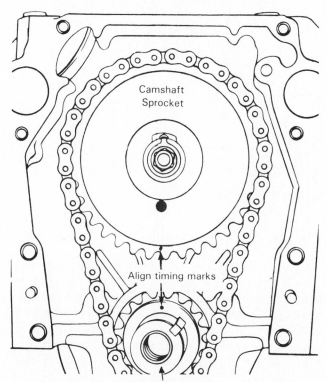

Camshaft
Sprocket

Align timing marks

Camshaft
Sprocket

The lifters fit between the camshaft and the **push rods**, which carry the motion out of the block and to the top of the head. Here the motion is reversed by the rocker arms. The push rod end of the rocker arm moves up while the other end pushes down on the valve, opening it.

When the camshaft lobe has turned past its high point, the valve closes because of valve spring pressure.

OHC

In OHC systems the camshaft is mounted on top of the head. Gears, a chain, or a belt connect the crankshaft and camshaft sprockets (Figure 12-5). In some OHC layouts, the cam lobes work directly on **bucket tappets** (Figure 12-6). A bucket tappet looks like a simple cup turned upside down. The bottom of the cup touches the lobe, and the inside of the cup touches the valve.

Other OHC systems put rocker arms under or over the cam (Figure 12-7). The rocker arms then reach away from the cam to the valves. Rocker arms allow one camshaft to work the widely separated valves of

161

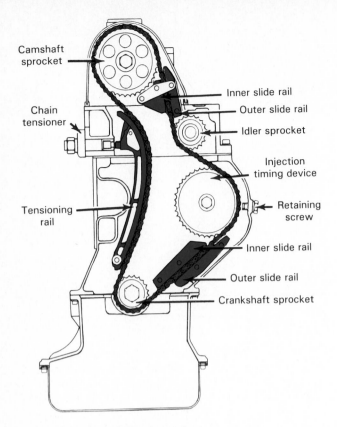

FIGURE 12-5   OHC timing chain.

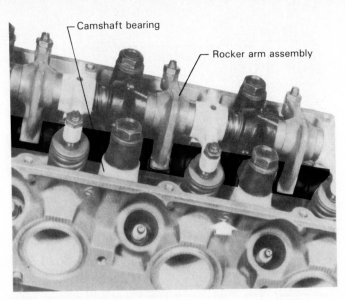

FIGURE 12-7   OHC system with rocker arms under camshaft.

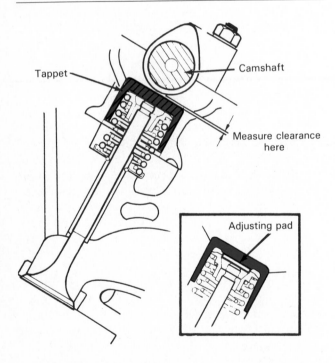

FIGURE 12-6   Bucket tappet.

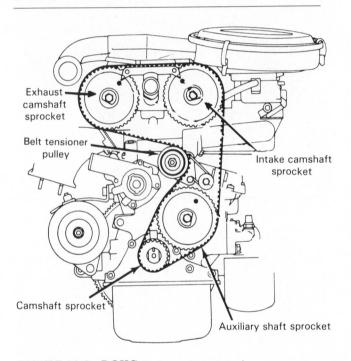

FIGURE 12-8   DOHC timing arrangement.

VALVE TRAIN PARTS

Timing Chain and Sprockets

An OHC or OHV engine used in passenger cars will almost certainly use chains or belts and sprockets to drive the camshaft. Chain drive gives acceptable longevity with very little or no noise. Belts are quieter and lighter. For increased longevity at the expense of slightly more noise, many trucks and competition engines use an all-gear drive (Figure 12-9). With gear

a hemispherical combustion chamber. When rocker arms are not used with widely separated valves, two camshafts are needed. This is called a double overhead camshaft (DOHC) head (Figure 12-8).

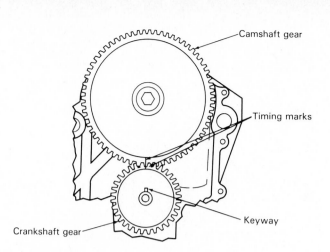

FIGURE 12-9 Timing gears.

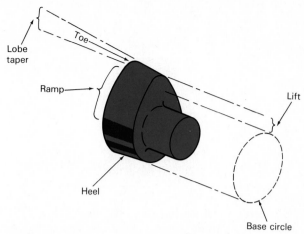

FIGURE 12-11 Camshaft lobe parts.

drive, the crankshaft gear meshes directly with the camshaft gear, or an idler gear is used between the two. Overhead cam V-type engines practically never use gear drives because of the many gears necessary to reach from the crankshaft to the camshafts atop the heads.

Camshaft

The camshaft is the central part of any valve train (Figure 12-10). The shape of the lobes determines when, how fast, how far, and how long the valves open and close. Great care is taken in the design and construction of camshafts, because they are so important to engine performance.

Camshafts are usually cast iron, machined on the lobes and cam-bearing journals. Figure 12-11 shows the parts of each lobe. When the heel rotates under the lifter, the valve is closed. As the ramp turns under the lifter, the valve begins to open. The valve is fully open when the toe contacts the lifter. The valve begins to close as the second ramp turns under the lifter. No valve spring pressure is exerted on the heel of the lobe, and very great spring pressures are "felt" by the toe. Obviously, the greatest camshaft wear is at the toe of the lobes, which is why this area is hardened during manufacturing.

Besides its valve operation function, the camshaft is usually cast with gears to drive the oil pump and distributor. If a mechanical fuel pump is used, it is driven off its own lobe, called the fuel pump eccentric. Figure 12-10 shows a separate fuel pump eccentric.

Camshafts turn in plain bearings, pressure-lubricated by the engine's oil pump. Camshaft bearing wear is very slight because the loads on them are small compared to rod or main bearings. OHV engines use replaceable bearing inserts in the block. OHC engines may have replaceable cam bearings or simply use machined portions of the head or pedestals.

Cam lobes, their lifters, or rocker arms are lubricated by oil draining back to the pan, by splash, or by tubes which drop oil down on the cam.

Lifters

The two types of lifters are *mechanical* and *hydraulic*.

Mechanical lifters are quite simple. They resemble a common water glass (Figure 12-12). Their bottom contacts the cam lobe, and the push rod fits inside the open end. The bottom surface is ground with a large radius (Figure 12-13). Because the radius is so large, around 30 in., you cannot see the roundness on a lifter's bottom very easily. The radius combines with a slight taper ground into the lobe's toe to shift

FIGURE 12-10 Camshaft and related parts.

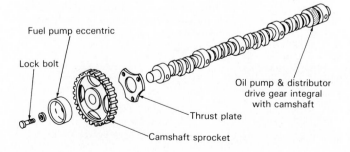

FIGURE 12-12 Mechanical valve lifter.

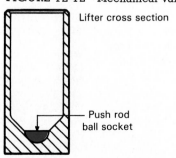

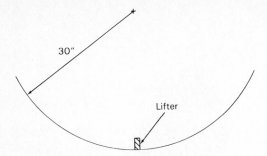

FIGURE 12-13 Radius on lifter bottom.

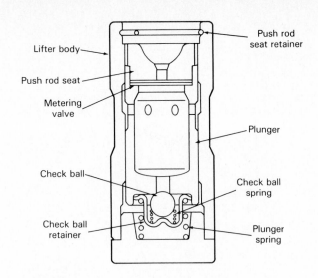

FIGURE 12-14 Hydraulic valve lifter.

the center of pressure between the two parts. This makes the lifter rotate, so it won't wear continuously in one spot. Roller lifters have a roller that contacts the cam lobes. This design reduces friction and wear. Although they are more expensive, the energy savings possible have caused many engines to be converted to roller lifters.

Hydraulic lifters resemble mechanical lifters outside but have several extra parts inside (Figure 12-14). A check valve lets the lifter use oil pressure to take up any slack in the valve train. The check valve is open until the cam lobe begins forcing the lifter up. This pressure closes the check valve, and the lifter then acts like a *solid* or mechanical lifter. When the lobe passes and the valve closes, the check valve opens again. The lifter is "soft" again and ready to cushion the shock of the next valve opening. This process eliminates the need for valve adjustments, because the valve clearance is automatically kept at zero by the lifter. The zero clearance keeps the valve train very quiet.

Push Rods

Most push rods are hollow tubes with hard steel ends. Usually a metal ball pressed into the push rod forms the end. On some engines, a hole is drilled through each ball, and oil is sent through the push rods to lubricate the rocker arm area (Figure 12-15). If the push rods do not carry oil or if no push rods are used, oil is piped to the rockers through passages drilled in the block and heads.

Rocker Arms

Rocker arms may be cast iron, pressed steel, or machined aluminum. Many rocker arms are *shaft-mounted*

MULTIPLE-VALVE TECHNOLOGY

First introduced on the father of modern high-performance engines, a 1912 Peugeot racer. Four-valve technology was, until recently, restricted to very expensive and exotic engines and was only considered practical for high-performance applications. As is generally the case, the systems that prove themselves in the competition arena (i.e., turbocharging, aerodynamic aids, disc brakes, overhead cams) frequently trickle down into production-car usage, and an ever-increasing number of manufacturers are offering four valves per cylinder on their high-line vehicles.

From a manufacturing standpoint, the multiple-valve arrangements must offer significant advantages to offset the in-

creased complexity and manufacturing cost. Primary among these advantages is the increased valve area (and port size) for a given bore size. This is strictly a geometric consideration and is best visualized by considering all the wasted space in a combustion chamber fitted with two valves, even when they are the largest diameter possible in the available space. With two valves, it is also difficult to get a central location for the spark plug.

Central plug location is advantageous because it gives the shortest flame travel and burn time, allowing the engine designer to use higher compression ratios (which improves both power and economy).

One possible cost savings to be realized from the four-valve systems is a reduction in required emissions equipment. Because of the higher volumetric efficiencies, resulting from the increased flow rates of the multiple-valve intake systems, the engineers can decrease valve overlap without sacrificing specific output. The decreased overlap (time that intake and exhaust valves are both open) can reduce exhaust emissions significantly enough to allow a cutback in the onboard emissions equipment.

Multiple Valve Technology
Motor Trend

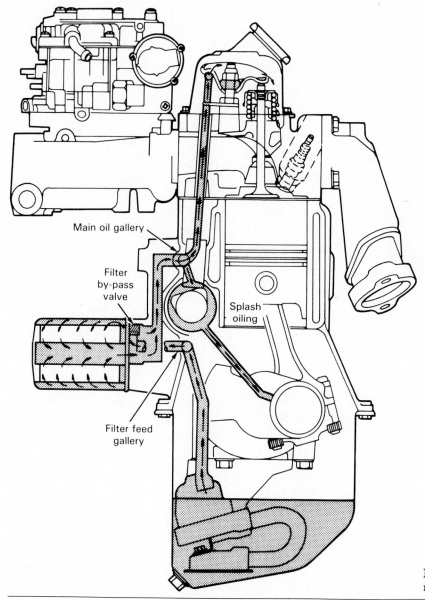

FIGURE 12-15 Rocker arms oiled by push rod. (Cadillac Motor Division, GMC)

(Figure 12-16). That means the rocker arms are in a row with a shaft passed through them. The rockers rotate on the shaft to open the valves. *Pedestal-mounted* rocker arms are very popular also. Instead of a shaft, the rockers are mounted individually on special studs,

FIGURE 12-16 Shaft-mounted rocker arms.

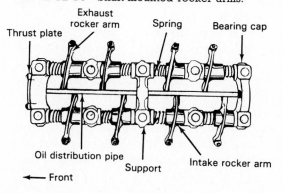

or **pedestals**. Sometimes bolts are used instead of studs, as shown in Figure 12-17. A pivot is placed between the bolt and rocker. Pedestal-mounted rockers work well where the valves are not in a row.

Rocker arm working surfaces—those areas touched by the push rod, camshaft, or valve—are hardened to withstand the high pressures involved. Rockers not used with hydraulic lifters have adjusters. The adjusters allow the manual setting of clearance in the entire valve train. This clearance is called the *valve clearance* or **lash**. It allows for expansion due to engine heat and wear in the valve train.

Some valve adjusters use a screw and locknut (Figure 12-18). Another method of adjustment is the hold-down nut on pedestal-mounted rocker arms. Loosening or tightening the nut adjusts the valve clearance. Because **prevailing torque** nuts are used, no locknut is necessary. A prevailing torque nut is slightly

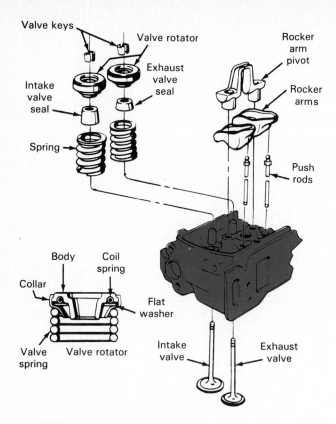

FIGURE 12-17   Pedestal-mounted rocker arms. (Chevrolet Motor Division, GMC)

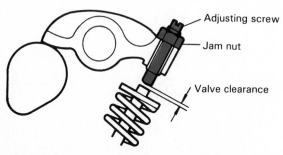

FIGURE 12-18   Valve adjuster. (Mazda North America, Inc.)

smaller than the threads it fits onto. Therefore, you must use a wrench to turn it. This tightness keeps vibration from loosening the nut.

Sometimes on OHC engines the camshaft pushes against a rocker arm located by the valve at one end and a pedestal at the other. Loosening a locknut and threading the pedestal in and out of the head adjusts this type of valve train (Figure 12-19). A variation of this type has a hydraulic lifter in place of the pedestal. Then no adjustment is necessary (Figure 12-20).

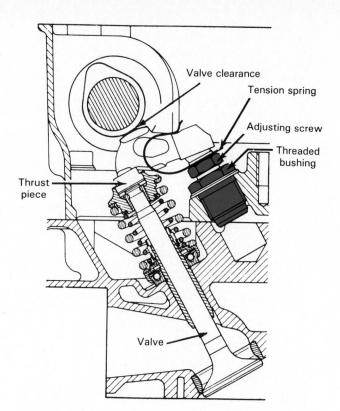

FIGURE 12-19   OHC mechanically adjustable pedestal.

Valves

All modern engines use **poppet valves**. A poppet valve looks like a mushroom with a long stem (Figure 12-21). It seals by being pressed firmly against its seat. In most auto engines, the seat is a replaceable part of the head. Valve seats will be discussed more thoroughly later.

Most engines use two valves per cylinder, one intake and one exhaust. The intake valve is larger than the exhaust valve because the exhaust has combustion pressure pushing it out of the cylinder. The air/fuel mixture has only the pressure differential between atmospheric pressure and cylinder pressure to force it in around the valve.

Some engines use three or four valves per cylinder. If an engine has three valves, two are intake and one is exhaust. If it uses four valves, two are intake and two exhaust.

There is a large difference between the normal operating temperatures of intake and exhaust valves. Because the intake valves pass the cool air/fuel mixture, they don't retain much combustion heat. The exhaust valves, on the other hand, pass nothing but burning hot exhaust gases over both sides of the valve head. The only place an exhaust valve can give off heat is to the valve seat and guide. That heat eventually passes through the head and into the cooling system.

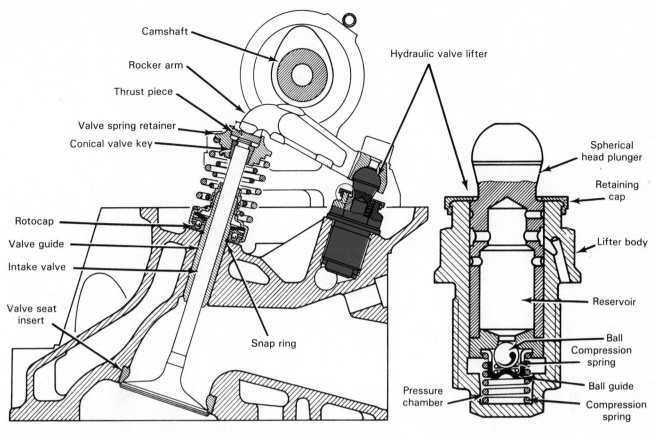

FIGURE 12-20　OHC with hydraulic lifter pedestal.

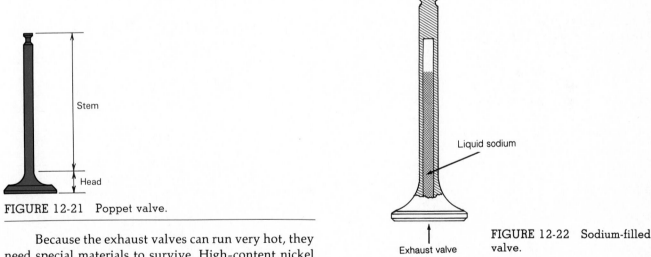

FIGURE 12-21　Poppet valve.

FIGURE 12-22　Sodium-filled valve.

Because the exhaust valves can run very hot, they need special materials to survive. High-content nickel valves are available for extra heat protection. Expensive engines, or those with very high exhaust valve temperatures, may have **sodium-filled valves** (Figure 12-22). A sodium-filled valve has a hollow stem filled with sodium. Sodium melts at 208°F, so it is a liquid at engine operating temperatures. The liquid sodium is tossed back and forth by the opening and closing valve. This action helps cooling by taking heat from the valve head and giving it to the stem end. The stem cools better than the head because of the larger contact area with the valve guide, and most of it is protected from the exhaust gases by the valve guide. Thus, the sodium valve runs cooler than a nonsodium valve.

Sodium is not used in intake valves. They do not need the increased cooling, and sodium valves are

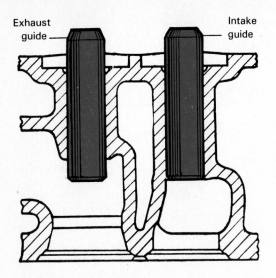

Exhaust guide

Intake guide

FIGURE 12-23   Valve guides.

expensive. Be careful when discarding sodium valves. The sodium in the stem reacts violently if it comes in contact with water.

Valve Guides

Valve guides control the valves as the valves pass through the head. Typically, the guides are separate pieces, pressed into the head (Figure 12-23). Sometimes, though, the guides are just machined portions of the head casting. If a separate guide is used, it is made of softer material than the cylinder head. This softer material increases valve life by not wearing the stem as quickly as the iron cylinder head would.

Valve Stem Seals

Some of the valve guide protrudes on the top side of the head. The **valve stem seal** fits on top of this exposed portion of the guide (Figure 12-24). The seal

FIGURE 12-24   Valve stem seal.

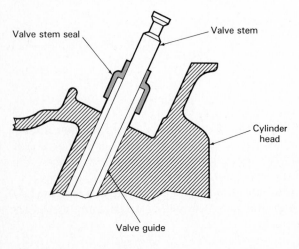

Valve stem seal

Valve stem

Cylinder head

Valve guide

is thus positioned so it can wipe the valve stem as it moves up and down in its guide. The seal keeps too much oil from running down the valve stem and into the port. Oiling past the valve guide is possible on exhaust valves but is more of a problem on intake valves, because of the much greater vacuum in intake ports, sucking the oil down.

Valve Springs

Included with valve springs are valve spring seats, retainers, and **keepers** (Figure 12-25). The spring seat goes between the spring and cylinder head. It keeps the spring from gouging the head. The retainer fits above the valve and around the top of the valve stem. Two keepers, or locks, fit inside the retainer and catch against a ledge in the valve stem. Figure 12-26 shows

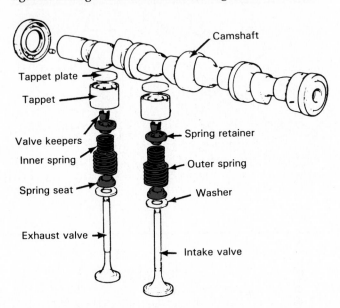

Camshaft

Tappet plate

Tappet

Valve keepers

Inner spring

Spring seat

Exhaust valve

Spring retainer

Outer spring

Washer

Intake valve

FIGURE 12-25   Valve springs.

FIGURE 12-26   Valve spring keeper grooves. (Chrysler Corporation)

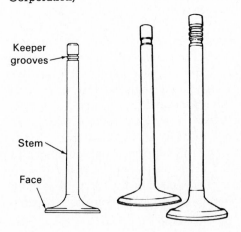

Keeper grooves

Stem

Face

several different keeper ledges and grooves. Because the outsides of the keepers are conical, spring pressure forces the retainer against the keepers, holding the retainers and keepers in place.

A valve spring can be a simple single coil spring or can include a second, inner spring and even a third, innermost spring. Another method is to use a single spring with a *damper* inside it. Dampers are made by winding a length of flat metal. They are used with single springs only.

Single springs are used with lightweight valves and low-revving engines. As either valve weight or engine rpm rises, a stronger spring is needed. To get a progressive spring—one that is more difficult to compress the farther it is compressed—an inner spring is added. For very heavy valves at high rpm, a third spring may be used.

Timing Chain Tensioners

Because OHC valve trains use fairly long timing chains (or belts), some method of removing slack in the chain is needed. Taking up slack is the job of the **tensioner.** The tensioner uses a plastic block to push against the chain. Pressure on the block comes either from a spring or from engine oil pressure. Many tensioners work automatically. Some need a once-only adjustment if they are replaced. Tensioners are also used in some OHV engines, as shown in Figure 12-27.

Timing Belts

Cogged-tooth belts are a relatively recent OHC valve train improvement (Figure 12-28). The advantages of these belts are lower cost, lack of noise, and long life. Their only major disadvantage is that they make the engine slightly longer than if it had a single-row chain.

Tensioners are always used with belts. Usually they consist of a spring-loaded rotating idler pulley.

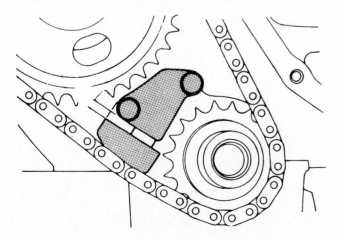

FIGURE 12-27   Timing chain tensioner.

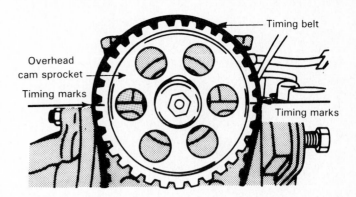

FIGURE 12-28   Timing belt.

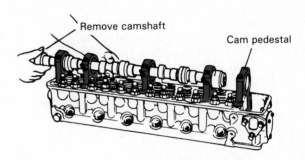

FIGURE 12-29   Camshaft pedestals.

Camshaft Pedestals

OHC installations can place the camshaft right on top of the head with bucket tappets, or with rocker arms above the cam, or with the camshaft raised and the rocker arms under it.

When the camshaft is raised with the rocker arms under it, camshaft *pedestals* hold the cam. Sometimes called **cam towers,** the pedestals function as cam bearings. They are drilled with oil passages to carry lubrication to the camshaft journals. Pedestals may be separate, or they may be an integral part of the cylinder head. Figure 12-29 shows integral pedestals.

Bucket Tappets

Not much needs to be said about bucket tappets except for their adjustments. These single-piece tappets are adjusted with **shims** (Figure 12-30). The shims fit between the tappet and valve. That means you must remove the camshaft for valve adjustments, which is a lot of work. This inconvenience is offset somewhat because shims hold valve adjustment very accurately. The bucket tappets only need adjustment when the valve changes. Variations due to screw and jam nut movement are eliminated.

Some bucket tappets are adjusting shims which fit between the camshaft lobe and tappet. These tappets allow for changing shims without removing the camshaft (Figure 12-31).

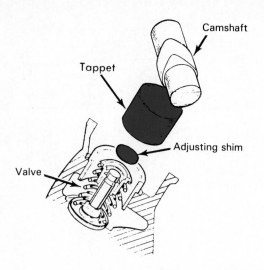

FIGURE 12-30   Bucket tappet and adjusting shim.

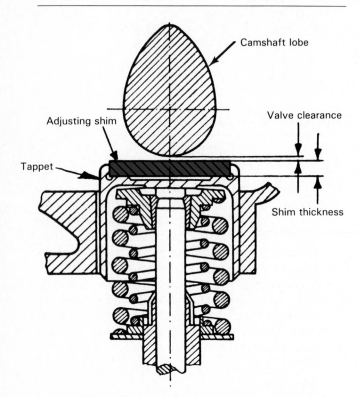

FIGURE 12-31   Adjusting shim between camshaft lobe and tappet.

VALVE TRAIN SERVICE

Adjusting Valves

The most common valve train service is adjusting valves. All valves not used with hydraulic lifters need periodic adjustment. Such adjustments compensate for temperature and wear changes in the valve train.

Temperature changes are due to engine heat. As the engine warms up, the parts in it expand. Because of block and head expansion, the distance from the camshaft to the rocker arms in an OHV engine increases with heat. If you measure between the rocker arm and the valve stem tip with feeler gauges, you'll see an increase of about 0.002 in. as the engine warms up.

This increase is reduced slightly by the growth of the valve, rocker arm, push rod, lifters, and camshaft. When these parts get hot, they tend to close the valve clearance. There is much more growth in the block and heads, however, so the net result is an opening of the valve clearance.

In an OHC engine, valve clearance changes because of heat growth are smaller than those in OHV engines because the distance between camshaft and valves is so much shorter. Only head or head and pedestal expansion changes the valve clearance in OHC layouts. Typical growth is 0.001 in.

Some clearance between the cam lobe heel and lifter is very important. If there isn't some clearance, the valve will not be able to close all the way. When the valve remains partially open, combustion gases will gradually burn the valve away. This is what is meant by a **burned valve.** Once a valve is burned, it cannot seal perfectly. Then combustion gases continue to erode the valve, even if clearance is restored between the lobe's heel and lifter.

Normal wear, millions of openings and closings, heat cycling, and exposure to combustion gases all help erode part of the valve face. With a partially eroded face, the valve sits deeper in its seat (Figure 12-32).

FIGURE 12-32   Valve burning increases the exposed portion of the valve stem.

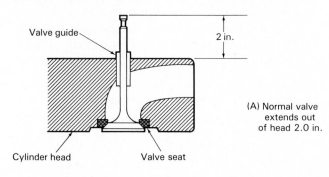

(A) Normal valve extends out of head 2.0 in.

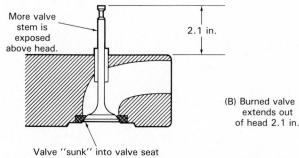

(B) Burned valve extends out of head 2.1 in.

At the valve stem, the distance between the valve stem tip and rocker arm or tappet is then closed. If the designed valve clearance isn't maintained, the valve will eventually take up all the valve train slack. The valve stays open and burns.

Valve Adjustment

To get maximum valve life, the specified valve clearance must be maintained. The valve clearance is the distance which ensures that the valve will not be held open by too close a clearance, nor will the clearance be so wide as to let the valve slam shut.

Check the shop manual to see if the valve clearance specification is for a cold or a hot engine. If a cold engine is called for, the best method is to let the car sit overnight. If this isn't possible, at least let the engine cool until the cylinder head is cool to the touch. If a "hot" engine is specified, warm the engine to operating temperature.

The shop manual will give a valve adjusting sequence. It ensures the valve being adjusted is not on the lobe's toe. A valve can be adjusted only when the lifter is against the lobe's heel. If the adjusting sequence is not available, bring cylinder 1 to **Top Dead Center (TDC)** on its compression stroke. This is close to when the spark plug fires, a time when both the exhaust and intake valves are closed. Adjust both valves on cylinder 1 and then move on to the next cylinder in the firing order. Bring it to TDC on its compression stroke and adjust its valves. Proceed through the firing order until all valves are adjusted.

Measure the valve clearance between the valve stem tip and rocker arm (Figure 12-33) or between the cam lobe and bucket tappet. If a jam nut and screw adjusters are used, loosen the jam nut with a box end

wrench. Then turn the adjusting screw with a screwdriver until there is a slight drag on the feeler gauge. It takes experience to know just how tight a "slight drag" is, so have your instructor adjust a valve. Check your work against that valve's clearance and "drag."

When the drag on the feeler gauge is correct, tighten the jam nut. Tightening the jam nut usually loosens the valve clearance because the jam nut stretches the adjusting screw slightly. Correct the loosened valve clearance by very lightly overtightening the adjusting screw and then tightening the jam nut. Stretch from the tight jam nut will bring the valve clearance to the proper specification. This stretch is why you must always check the valve clearance after tightening the jam nut.

Pedestal-mounted rocker arms are adjusted by loosening and tightening the rocker arm nut. Measure between the valve stem tip and rocker arm, as with any other rocker arm. Turn the nut until the feeler gauge drag is right. The valve is then adjusted.

Bucket tappets require feeler gauge measurements between the lobe heels and tappets. Check all valves, rotating the engine as necessary to keep the tappet being checked on the lobe's heel. Write your findings down. Now subtract the specified valve clearance from each one of your findings. The difference is the shim thickness necessary to bring that valve to specification. Get the adjusting shims from the car manufacturer.

To install the shims, you may have to remove the camshaft. Then you can lift the tappets from their bores in the head, place the shims in the tappet's recess, and replace the tappets. Refit the camshaft and check the adjusted valve clearance.

If the shims fit on top of the tappet, you must rotate the cam lobe out of the way. You will need a special tool to depress the tappet as well. Then you can slip the shim in and release the tappet.

Leakage Testing

The best diagnostic test of valves and how they are sealing is the **leakage test** (Figure 12-34). To do a leakage test, pump compressed air into the cylinder and see how much leaks out. A leakage test quickly rates valve sealing.

A valve leakage tester is needed for this test. The engine should be warmed up, then stopped. Bring the cylinder to be tested to TDC on its compression stroke so that both valves will be closed. Screw an adapter into the spark plug hole and the tester attached to it. Attach a compressed air line to the other end of the tester. Compressed air flows into the cylinder through the tester.

Even in the best cylinder, some air will leak past the rings. The tester shows this leakage in a percentage.

FIGURE 12-33 Adjusting valve clearance. (Chevrolet Motor Division, GMC)

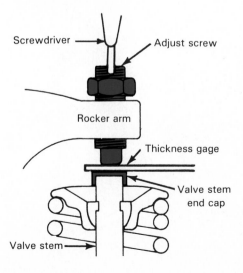

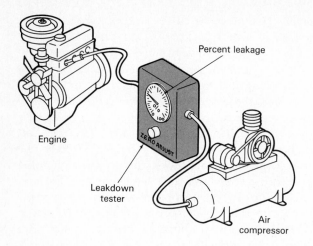

FIGURE 12-34 Leakdown test.

A good cylinder leaks below 10%. If the valves, or rings, are not sealing as they should, the leakage will be higher. Between 10 and 20% indicates a problem but not one which requires immediate attention. If the leakage is above 20%, and especially above 30%, the valves need immediate attention.

If the rings are leaking, you'll hear air escaping by listening at the oil filler or dipstick holes. If an intake valve is leaking, listen for a hiss at the caburetor. Opening the throttle helps. A bad exhaust valve leak can be heard at the exhaust pipe. Bubbles in the radiator or noise from the next spark plug hole indicate a cracked head or blown head gasket.

When it comes to valves, the exhaust is typically at fault. By the time the average driver brings his or her car in for a diagnostic check, the valve will be badly burned. Expect around 30% leakage for a moderately burned valve. Badly burned valves, or those missing a small chunk, will leak close to 98%.

VALVE JOB

When valves are worn to the point where they can't seal, it is time to do a valve job. In a valve job the head is removed and disassembled. The valves, seats, and guides are machined or replaced to new specifications. The head is then reassembled and installed.

On V-type engines both heads are always done at the same time to preserve even combustion pressures on both cylinder banks. Also, valve jobs should not be done on high-mileage engines with poor rings without first restoring correct cylinder wall sealing. If only a valve job is done, the engine will use excessive oil, because the valve job will restore upper combustion chamber sealing. The increased volume will suck more oil past the rings, which will burn during combustion.

Remove Cylinder Head

Start the valve job on a cool or cold engine. Removing a hot cylinder head can warp it. See Chapter 17 for cylinder head removal instructions. If the camshaft needs removing on an OHV engine with the block in the chassis, remove the radiator, ac condenser, and grill. Then follow the procedures in Chapter 17.

Head Disassembly

Removing the valve springs and valves requires a valve spring compressor (Figure 12-35). One end of the compressor fits over the valve head, and the other fits over the valve spring retainer. Levering the compressor brings its two ends together, thus compressing the valve spring. Compress the valve springs only enough to free the keepers. Remove the keepers with a small screwdriver or magnet if your fingers are too large (Figure 12-36).

Without the keepers, the retainer, spring, and spring seat will come off. Remove the old valve stem seals. Finally, push the valve out of the guide. If the valve stem tip is *mushroomed*, pounded wider than stock by the rocker arm, file the wide portion off. Trying to pull a mushroomed tip through the valve guide will ruin the guide.

Valve Springs

All valve springs should be checked for **free height** and **squareness.** Free height is the height of the spring as it sits on the bench. Measure the springs with a steel rule and compare your findings with the shop manual. Squareness is measured with a square, like carpenters use (Figure 12-37). You want to see if the

FIGURE 12-35 Valve spring compressor. (Chrysler Corporation)

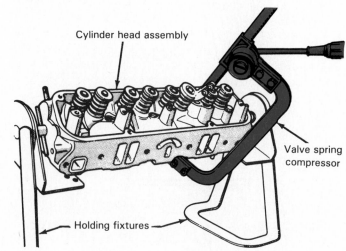

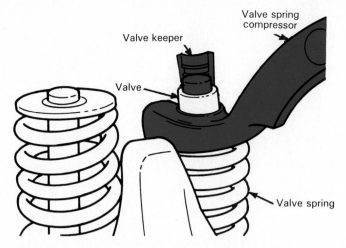

FIGURE 12-36   Removing valve keepers. (Buick Motor Division, GMC)

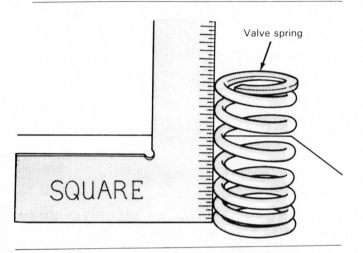

FIGURE 12-37   Checking valve spring squareness. (Chrysler Corporation)

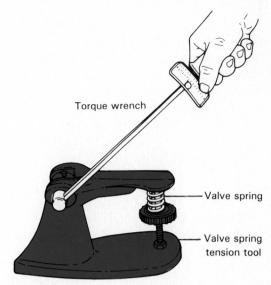

FIGURE 12-38   Valve spring tester. (Chrysler Corporation)

That's when the spring cannot overcome the valve's inertia, and the valve, spring, rocker arm, push rod, and lifter do not follow the cam lobe contour. The valve opens farther and stays open longer than it should. This could let the piston hit the valve, bending the valve or more often the push rod. Severe damage can result from floating valves.

Push Rods

Push rods are easy to check. Find a very flat surface with a corner—a tabletop works well. Lay the push rod over the corner so its ends hang over the table. Roll the push rod and watch its ends. If the push rod is bent, the ends will wobble (Figure 12-39). Replace the push rod.

Inspect the ends of all the push rods which pass the rolling test. When worn, the ends will have small pieces chipped out of them. The ends could be pitted, too. Replace any chipped or pitted push rods.

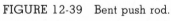

FIGURE 12-39   Bent push rod.

spring leans. By holding the spring in the square's 90° angle, you can see if the spring bends away. Rotate the spring while checking it to make sure you find the side with the maximum lean.

With a **spring tester** (Figure 12-38) many more spring tests are possible. A spring tester works like a bathroom scale. With it, you can compress a spring to a certain height and see how much load it produces. Loads are checked at the spring's *installed* and *open* heights. Installed height is the height of the spring when it is installed in the cylinder head. Open height is shorter. It is the height of the spring when the valve is opened by the camshaft. The load is greater at the open height. Consult the shop manual for height and load specifications.

All of these tests check for fatigue in a spring. Weak, fatigued springs cannot accurately control the valve. At higher rpm weak springs allow **valve float.**

Rocker Arms

Check rocker arms for pitting or wear on their working surfaces. Because rocker arms are hardened, do not attempt to repair them. Replace any worn rocker arms.

You should inspect the mounting hole inside surfaces on the shaft-mounted rocker arms. Sometimes there is a bushing in the rocker which can be replaced if it's worn (Figure 12-40). Otherwise, you must replace the entire rocker arm if worn.

Inspect the rocker arm shaft to check for wear (Figure 12-41). Also thoroughly clean it with solvent. Pay particular attention to any oil passages. They must be clean, or the rocker arms will quickly wear out.

Rocker arm assemblies can be disassembled for inspection. Remove a small bolt, cotter key, or pin from one end of the rocker shaft. This lets all the rocker arms, spacers, spacer springs, and pedestals slide off the shaft. Keep all parts in order! Also note the left/right orientation of parts before disassembly.

The pedestals in a pedestal mount valve train rarely wear. If they show visual wear, replace them.

Lifters

When pulling the lifters out of the block on an OHV engine, be sure to keep them in order. If the lifters are mixed up and installed out of order, they will quickly destroy the camshaft. You will find more information on lifters in Chapter 17.

Checking mechanical lifters is easy. Look at their bottoms for grooves, concave wear, and pitting. The lifters should still be slightly convex in shape. The best way to check their shape is to hold two lifters bottom to bottom. The lifters should rock just a little. Sight between the lifters while you rock them, and you will see the light change. If the lifters do not rock, they are worn and must be changed.

It is okay to use new lifters on an old camshaft, but never use old lifters on a new camshaft. The old

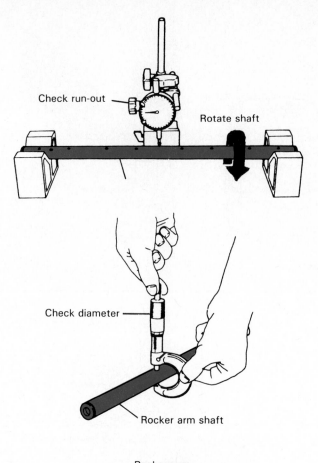

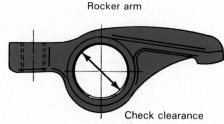

FIGURE 12-41   Rocker arm inspection. (Chevrolet Motor Division, GMC)

lifters will soon ruin it. If the camshaft is changed, the lifters must be changed too.

Hydraulic lifters are checked just like mechanical lifters. But the internal parts also need inspection. Obviously, if the lifter bottom is bad, you do not need to inspect the internal parts. The reverse way of thinking is popular too: If there isn't anything wrong with the lifter bottoms, then the internal parts must be okay, too.

For the most part, mechanics don't disassemble and inspect hydraulic lifters. It takes a lot of time to disassemble, inspect, and then reassemble up to 16 lifters. So, if the lifter bottom looks good and the lifters worked fine before the valve job, most mechanics will leave them alone.

FIGURE 12-40   Replaceable rocker arm bushing.

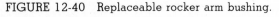

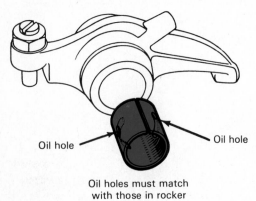

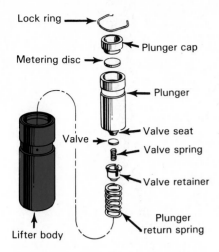

FIGURE 12-42 Disassembled valve lifter.

If an internal inspection is desired, remove a snap ring from the lifter's top and shake out the internal parts (Figure 12-42). Do this only over a clean towel and with only one lifter at a time. Never mix internal lifter parts. Inspect the ball and plunger for wear. Clean out any gunk and reassemble the lifter. If the internal parts are worn, replace the lifter.

Valve Inspection

Check all valves for carbon deposits, burning, cracks, and tip wear.

Carbon deposits are black, crusty clusters around the head/stem intersection. They can be wire-brushed off, or glass-bead blasted.

Burned valves will be black and light brown or white around the valve head. Check the sealing areas on both the valve head and seat. They should be shiny bright. A discolored sealing area indicates improper sealing (Figure 12-43).

After wire-brushing the valves, inspect them for cracks. Cracks are more likely to happen if the valve has been burned.

Tip wear will show either pitting or mushrooming of the valve tip.

Valve Guides

Check wear on the valve stem and guide by inserting the valve into its guide. Position the valve so that the tip of the stem is just flush with the top of the guide. Wiggle the valve head and note how far the valve moves (Figure 12-44). If the stem-to-guide clearance is excessive, the valve head will move a lot. You'll find measurements for this movement in the engine's shop manual.

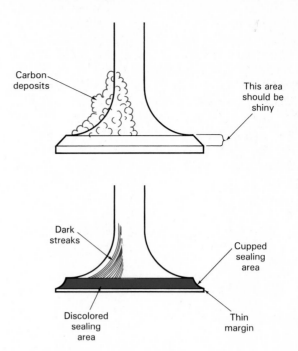

FIGURE 12-43 Valve inspection.

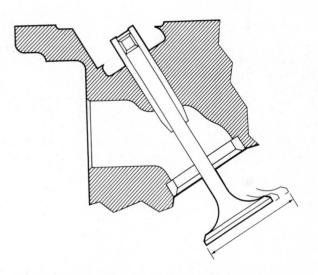

FIGURE 12-44 Checking valve guide wear.

Now remove the valve from the guide and inspect the valve stem. Use a micrometer to measure worn and unworn portions of the stem. If little difference exists between these areas and the valve rocks excessively in its guide, the guide is worn.

Another way to check guide wear is with a **ball gauge** which measures the diameter of small holes. Specifications are given in the shop manual.

If the valve stem is smaller than specifications, replace the valve. If the guide is too large, it can be knurled or replaced or an insert can be installed.

Valve Guide Service

Pass a **knurling** tool through a guide to raise ridges in the guide's ID. These ridges effectively reduce the guide's ID. After knurling, ream the guide (Figure 12-45). Reaming cuts the tops of the ridges to the proper size. After reaming, check the job by wiggling the valve in its guide.

On most engines the guides can be replaced. The old guides are hammered out and the new ones hammered in (Figure 12-46). A shouldered punch and hammer are used to drive the guides. Take care when installing the guides in order to get them at the proper height in the head. Use an old guide for comparison. Also, guides are usually tapered, so they can be driven from one direction only. Guides that are tight in the head may gouge out some of the head material. This is called **galling.** Heating the head before driving guides will help prevent galling. Chill new guides before installing them.

Guide inserts can replace the guide's ID without replacing the entire guide. Ream the old guide oversize and press the insert in. Then ream the insert to fit the valve stem.

Whenever guide work is done, the valve seats must be ground, because servicing the guides moves the valve relative to the seat. If the head was assembled without grinding the seats, the valves will not seat. Because the grinding of seats is done by **piloting** off the guides, valve seat service restores the correct guide/seat relationship.

Valve Grinding

The cure for normal valve wear and light burning is grinding. A special machine grinds the valve sealing face at the correct angle until fresh material shows all the way around (Figure 12-47). After grinding, check the valve against specifications for an adequate *margin*. The margin is the thickness of the valve head. Figure 12-48 gives the angles and dimensions important to valve grinding. If the valve is ground so the margin becomes too thin, then the valve will easily overheat and burn once it is in service again. Too thin a margin means valve replacement.

The same machine used to grind the valve faces is used to grind the valve stem tips (Figure 12-49). Grind the tips until all pitting or mushrooming is gone.

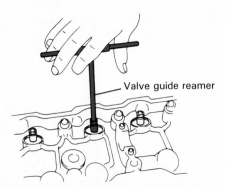

FIGURE 12-45   Reaming valve guides. (Buick Motor Division, GMC)

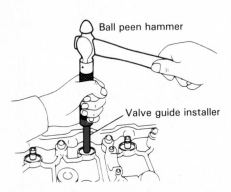

FIGURE 12-46   Changing valve guides.

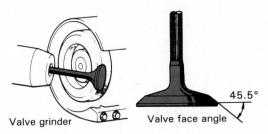

FIGURE 12-47   Valve grinding.

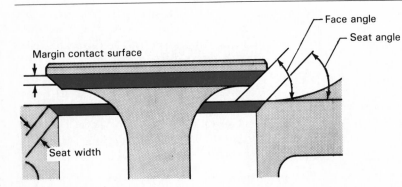

FIGURE 12-48   Valve angles and dimensions. (Chrysler Corporation)

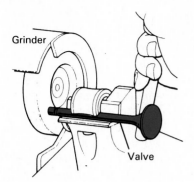

FIGURE 12-49 Grinding valve tips.

There are grinding limits given in the shop manual. If the valve stem tip will not clean up within limits, replace the valve.

Valve Seats

Valve seats are restored by grinding them with special stones (Figure 12-50). Three stones are used. The three stones are **dressed** and shaped at three different angles—30°, 45° and 60° (Figure 12-51). A pilot is placed in the valve guide, and the stone is slipped onto the pilot and then is spun with an electric or air-powered grinder. Machinist bluing is used to easily spot one cut from the other.

The 45° cut is made first. This cut establishes the valve seat. In other words, the 45° cut is the surface which the valve face against seals.

The 30° cut is made next. The shallower angle stone cuts the top of the valve seat. Last, the 60° cut is made. The steeper angle fits past the 45° cut and shapes the port side of the valve seat.

The 30° and 60° cuts shape the valve seat to improve the gas flow over them. They also give the

FIGURE 12-50 Grinding valve seats. (American Honda Motor Corporation, Inc.)

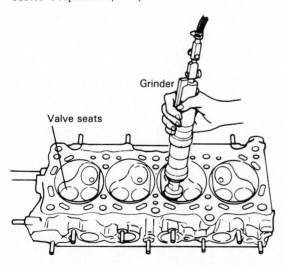

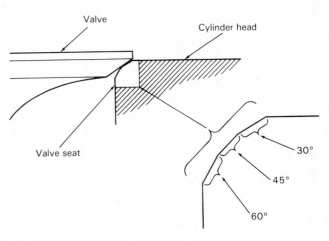

Three valve seat angles

FIGURE 12-51 Valve seat angles.

machinist a way to bring the valve seat (45° cut) to the proper width.

Narrow valve seats give higher sealing pressures because the valve spring pressure is distributed around a small area. Wide valve seats give longer valve life because they give the valve more heat transfer area. Therefore, the specified valve seat widths are a compromise between these two goals: higher sealing pressures and longer valve life. Intake seats are narrower than exhaust seats because the hotter-running exhausts need the extra cooling.

Valve-to-Seat Angle

In the valve seat grinding example just given, 45° was the valve seat angle. Actually, valve seat angles are typically 45°, 45½°, or 46°. The valve seat angle is one degree different from the angle cut into the valve face. This 1° mismatch gives a higher sealing pressure than an exact match would.

Since 1975 and the widespread use of unleaded gasoline, hardened valves and seats have been used. These are commonly called **stellite** valves or seats, after the hardening material. When stellite parts are used, the valve angle and seat angle are the same. No mismatch is used (Figure 12-52).

FIGURE 12-52 Valve face-seat angles.

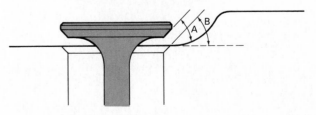

A = Valve face angle
B = Valve seat angle
A = B when hardened face and angle are used

Valve Seat Replacement

If a valve seat is badly burned or has been ground several times, there may not be enough material left to machine. Then you should replace the valve seat. Remove the old seat with a special puller and drive in a new one. If the old seat was loose in the head, install an oversize seat. Then grind the new seat.

Cylinder Head Service

Cylinder head service begins with cleaning. Wire-brush the combustion chambers. While it is not necessary to totally avoid the valve seats or spark plug threads, do not spend lots of time on them. Bead blasting quickly cleans the combustion chambers, ports, EGR passages, and exhaust crossovers. You must remove all bead residue with a thorough hot tanking or solvent cleaning when you are finished, however. Scrape all gasket residue and clean all bolt holes.

Flatness

Measure the head mating surface flatness with feeler gauges and a straightedge (Figure 12-53). The head must be very clean, or the straightedge will sit high and give an inaccurate reading. Slip feeler gauges under the straightedge until you find the one that will just fit. That gauge's thickness is the amount of head warpage. Check your findings against specifications. If warpage is beyond the service limit, the head must be milled flat again.

Heads are milled in a special milling machine. Only enough material is removed to get the head flat again. Milling increases the compression ratio and reduces head thickness. Higher compression ratios may

cause preignition, and reduced head thickness can alter cam timing in OHC engines.

On V-type engines, milling the heads lowers them in relation to the intake manifold. Therefore, once the heads have been milled to a certain depth, the intake manifold must be milled on its bottom and mating surface to match the heads. Always mill both heads the same amount on V-type engines, or the compression ratio will be different on the two banks.

Cylinder Head Assembly

Before assembling, wash all parts in solvent to remove cleaning and machining abrasives.

Install the valves, spring seats, and new valve stem seals. Slip on the valve springs and retainers and use a spring compressor to fit the keepers. Depending on the valve train, install the rocker arms or camshaft next. Valve adjusters should be backed off completely when installing rocker arm assemblies.

A light tap with a plastic hammer to each valve spring assembly will test the installation. If the keepers are not fully seated, they will pop out when hit.

The rest of the installation is the reverse of removal. Specific instructions on head gasket installation are given in Chapter 17.

Hydraulic Valve Lifter Adjustment

After the head is installed, adjust the valves as outlined earlier. When installing hydraulic lifters, a one-time-only adjustment is necessary. For GM and most other hydraulic lifters, rotate the cam so the lifter is against the lobe's heel. Then tighten the rocker arm nut while rotating the push rod between two fingers (Figure 12-54). Resistance in the push rod means that the adjusting

FIGURE 12-53 Measuring the head mating surface flatness with feeler gauges and a straightedge.

FIGURE 12-54 Adjusting GM-style hydraulic valve lifter. (Cadillac Motor Division, GMC)

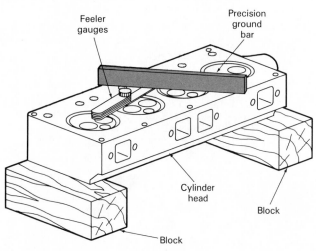

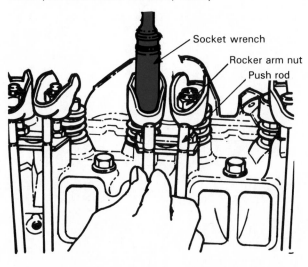

nut has just taken all the slack out of the system. Check the shop manual first and then turn the adjusting nut slowly until you reach the number of turns specified. The lifter will automatically adjust the valve clearance from that point.

Some Ford hydraulic lifters are adjusted after being **bled down.** Bleeding down a hydraulic lifter is done with a special tool which applies pressure to the lifter through the push rod. Check the clearance between valve and rocker arm with feeler gauges. If out of specification, use a longer or shorter push rod.

No break-in period is necessary when only a valve job has been performed. If you installed new piston rings at the same time, break in the engine as described in Chapter 17.

TRADE TERMS

Ball Gauge
Bled Down
Bucket Tappets
Burned Valve
Cam Towers
Dressed
Free Height
Galling
Hydraulic Lifter
Keepers
Knurling
Lash
Leakdown Test
Mechanical Lifter
Pedestals
Piloting

Poppet Valves
Prevailing Torque
Push Rods
Rocker Arms
Shims
Sodium-filled Valves
Spring Tester
Squareness
Stellite
Tensioner
Top Dead Center (TDC)
Valve Clearance
Valve Float
Valve Stem Seal
Valve Train

REVIEW QUESTIONS

1. What are the two types of valve trains? Which style uses push rods? Which style uses bucket tappets?
2. What are the two types of valves? Which one runs hotter?
3. Name two types of valve adjusters.
4. How many revolutions does the camshaft make for each crankshaft revolution?
5. How are push rods checked for straightness?
6. When a valve is fully open, what part of the lobe is the lifter pushed against?
7. Name the three common valve seat grinding angles.
8. Are valve seats ground before or after valve guide service?
9. Is valve guide oil leakage more of a problem with *intake* or *exhaust* guides?

13

Intake and Exhaust Systems

INTRODUCTION

Engines must have a way of taking the air/fuel mixture to the cylinders. They must also have a system of getting rid of the exhaust gases after combustion. These are the jobs of the intake and exhaust manifolds. In this chapter you'll learn about manifold theory and practice. Also, turbosupercharging will be introduced in the exhaust section.

INTAKE SYSTEM

The intake of fuel and air into an engine can be done two ways: by carburetion or with fuel injection.

Carburetion has been used since the invention of the internal combustion engine. A carburetor is used to introduce fuel to the airstream. The resulting mixture is then carried through the intake manifold to the cylinder head. In the head, the intake valve admits the mixture at the proper time.

Carburetors dispense the correct amount of fuel for the amount of air the engine is using. The air/fuel mixture varies. When the engine is warmed up and operating at part power, the mixture is about 14:1.

OBJECTIVES

When you have completed this chapter, you should be able to

- Explain the difference between intake and exhaust manifolds
- Understand the design of a manifold and its effect on engine performance
- Explain the operation of the catalytic coverter
- Understand how a turbocharger works
- Troubleshoot the various components of the intake and exhaust systems

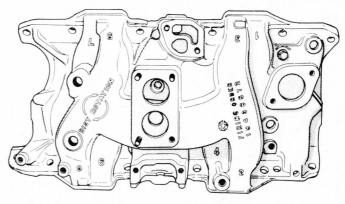

FIGURE 13-2 Intake manifold. (Chrysler Corporation)

That is, 1 part fuel is mixed with every 14 parts of air. For cold starting and maximum power the mixture needs to be richer; a 12:1 mixture may be used (1 part fuel to 12 parts air). Leaner mixtures are used for maximum fuel economy. They can be 17:1 or higher (Figure 13-1).

Carburetors also **throttle** the engine. A throttle restricts the amount of air entering the engine. If there were no throttle, the engine would produce maximum power at all times. You could not let the engine idle. Controlling the car's speed would be impossible, too.

Fuel injection systems, like carburetors, throttle and provide the correct mixture. Because injection systems can easily be electronically controlled, they do a better job of dispensing fuel. What fuel injection and carburetion have in common, however, is intake manifolds.

Intake Manifold

The intake manifold connects the various cylinders of an engine to one source of air (Figure 13-2). If the engine is carbureted, the carburetor is placed at the manifold intake. All air entering the manifold has to pass through the carburetor. The carburetor is the only source of fuel. Therefore, the intake manifold takes the air/fuel mixture from a central source and distributes it to all the cylinders.

FIGURE 13-1 Different air/fuel mixtures.

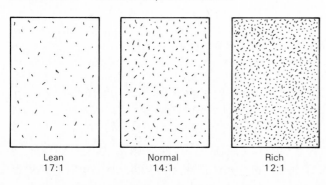

Lean
17:1

Normal
14:1

Rich
12:1

With fuel injection the fuel can be dispensed from one source or several sources. The single-source method is called **throttle body** fuel injection. The throttle body sits right where the carburetor would sit. Throttle bodies contain several throttles and injectors. The injectors are electronically opened valves which spray fuel into the air stream. In **port** fuel injection one throttle is mounted at the intake manifold opening. The fuel is sprayed by injectors mounted in the manifold, near each cylinder. In port injection there is one injector for each cylinder.

Theory of Air/Gas Flow

As you can tell from the description, a carburetor or throttle body requires the intake manifold to carry air and fuel to the cylinders. Port injection, on the other hand, distributes the fuel near the intake port. The intake manifold carries air in a port injection system.

Manifold Design This makes a difference in manifold design. The difference is due to the variation in weight between gasoline and air. Because gasoline is a lot heavier than air, it has more inertia. The more inertia an object has, the more resistance it has to changing its direction of travel. In other words, it is easier to make air change direction than gasoline.

Inside the intake manifold, the air/fuel mixture has to change direction. If the manifold is designed with sharp turns, the fuel will separate from the air (Figure 13-3). Because the individual passages between the carburetor and the ports are shaped differently for

FIGURE 13-3 Effect of sharp bend on air fuel flow.

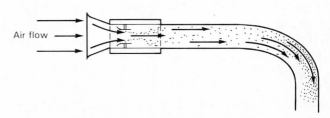

Air flow

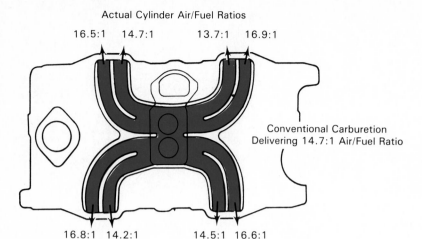

Actual Cylinder Air/Fuel Ratios

16.5:1   14.7:1   13.7:1   16.9:1

Conventional Carburetion
Delivering 14.7:1 Air/Fuel Ratio

16.8:1   14.2:1   14.5:1   16.6:1
Actual Cylinder Air/Fuel Ratios

FIGURE 13-4   Air/fuel ratio differences in a V-type intake manifold.

different cylinders, each cylinder will get a different air/fuel mixture (Figure 13-4). Therefore, the **runners,** as the passages are called, are designed (at least in theory) to be alike as much as possible.

Runner Size   The runners are designed with special attention given to their volume. If small-diameter runners are used, the velocity of the mixture will be high. High velocities keep the air/fuel mixture together. If large runners are used, the mixture velocity will drop. At low velocities the fuel will drop out of the mixture and condense on the runner floors. Uneven cylinder-to-cylinder mixtures result, and the engine runs roughly. Extra fuel has to be added to keep the engine running.

A trade-off is necessary between runners that are too small and too large. If the runners are too small, the engine will not be able to get enough air and fuel. The lack of air and fuel limits horsepower. Such an engine is said to be self-throttled. If ports that are too large are used, the engine will run very poorly at low rpm but will run well at high rpm with lots of horsepower.

Design Features

Intake manifolds are manufactured from aluminum or cast iron. On V-type engines the manifold fits between the cylinder heads (Figure 13-5). On in-line engines the manifold is bolted directly to one side of the head (Figure 13-6). Fittings are provided on the manifold for mounting accessories, such as the distributor on V-type engines. The manifold may also be cast with exhaust gas recirculation (EGR) passages. These passages allow a small amount of exhaust gases into the intake manifold. This is necessary for emission control. EGR is covered thoroughly in Chapter 27.

As noted earlier, the engine's mixture requirements vary. The most extreme variation is when the

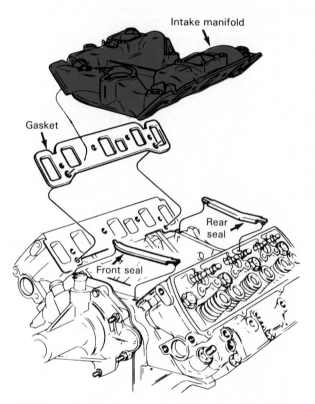

Intake manifold

Gasket

Rear seal

Front seal

FIGURE 13-5   V-type engine intake manifold. (Buick Motor Division, GMC)

engine is cold. A cold engine needs to have a very rich mixture at the carburetor to ensure that enough fuel gets to the cylinders. Keep in mind that during a cold start, vacuum is very weak because of the slow cranking speed. Also, the manifold is cold, so the fuel does not evaporate into the air and form a mixture. Instead, the fuel tends to condense on cold manifold walls and puddle on the manifold floor.

Manifold Heating   To overcome these drawbacks, some form of manifold heating is usually provided.

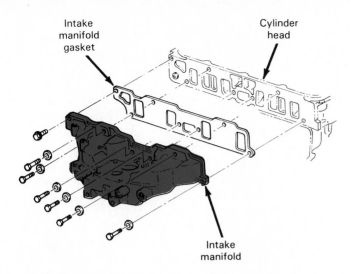

FIGURE 13-6   In line engine intake manifold. (American Motors Corporation)

On V-type engines it is easy to provide an exhaust passage from one cylinder head, through the intake manifold, to the other cylinder head (Figure 13-7). Then the exhaust gases rapidly heat the manifold. As the manifold heats, the puddled fuel evaporates, and the mixture can be leaned. Drivability improves because each cylinder gets an even part of the carburetor's output. This form of heating is called an **exhaust crossover.**

Another way of heating the manifold is to run engine cooling water around it. This method is common on in-line engine manifolds.

Once the manifold is warmed up, excess heating is not desirable. Hot air is less dense than cold air. For any given intake stroke, less air and fuel can be drawn in if the mixture is overheated. Horsepower suffers, and a wider throttle opening is needed for the same power output. The opened throttle hurts fuel economy.

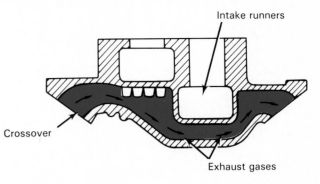

FIGURE 13-7   Exhaust crossover.

To control exhaust heat, a spring-loaded flap is put in the exhaust pipe (Figure 13-8). When the engine is cold, the bimetallic spring keeps the flap shut, forcing exhaust gas through the crossover. When the engine heats up, the bimetallic spring lets the flap open, and the exhaust goes out the exhaust pipe unobstructed. Sometimes the flap, called the **heat control valve,** is vacuum controlled.

Some engines have electrical mixture heating. A fine metal grid is placed between the carburetor and the intake manifold. A thermostat allows electrical current to heat the grid when the engine is cold. This warms the air/fuel mixture.

Manifold heating is not important with port injection because the fuel is injected so close to the cylinder. Also, the injector sprays the fuel in a fine mist. Carburetors dribble out fuel in much larger drops. It takes more time and heat to break big drops down into an air/fuel mixture.

Plenum

Directly under the carburetor or throttle body is the plenum (Figure 13-9). In the plenum air and fuel spread out and turn into a mixture. The plenum also acts as

FIGURE 13-8   Heat control valve.

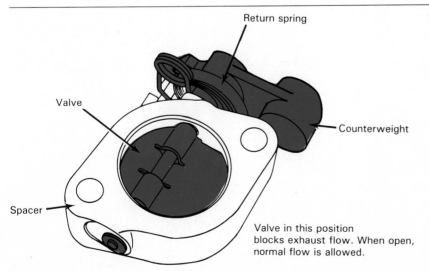

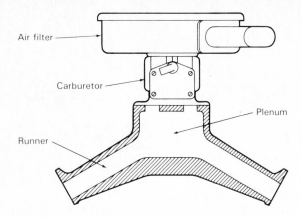

FIGURE 13-9   Plenum in a V-type engine intake manifold.

a reservoir of ready-to-go mixture for sudden throttle openings. The most important function of the plenum is to help equalize the mixture between cylinders. It also aids high-rpm breathing, allowing the use of a smaller carburetor than would otherwise be possible.

Runners and Balance

Runners are designed to get an equal and even distribution of the air/fuel mixture to all cylinders. Sometimes it is necessary to provide uneven runner sizes and shapes because of unequal breathing among the cylinders.

Another design feature of runners has to do with the intake valve opening order. As the valve opens and closes, it causes the mixture in the runners to pulse. When the valve opens, the mixture accelerates rapidly toward that valve. Then the valve shuts and the cycle repeats. This cycle builds "waves" or pulses in the mixture. By shaping the runners to a certain length, these pulses can be used to help ram the mixture into the cylinder.

Reversion

To carry the idea of a "stop-and-go" mixture a step further, it is possible for the mixture to move backwards in the manifold. This happens during periods of low velocity and low vacuum, such as when the throttle is wide open at low rpm. Then when the intake valve opens, a slight pressure in the cylinder can push the mixture backwards for an instant. This phenomenon is typical of high-performance camshafts which leave both the intake and exhaust valves open simultaneously for a long time. Large runners and ports with their poor low-rpm mixture velocities are also to blame. Having a plenum helps with reversion. Without the plenum, reversion can push the mixture right out the top of the carburetor. But the plenum absorbs the momentary backwards push and provides a ready mixture to refill the runner.

In-line Intake Manifold

Manifolds used on in-line four- and six-cylinder engines are usually not as complex as V-type engine manifolds. In-line engines often use a long common plenum with short, individual runners going directly to each cylinder. Because the manifold looks like a log with the runners sprouting from it (Figure 13-10), it is sometimes called a **log** manifold.

Manifold Problems   The major problem with a log manifold is mixture distribution. If a single carburetor is used, the center cylinders get the proper mixture, but those at the ends run too lean. They are too far from the carburetor. By the time the mixture gets to them, a lot of fuel has fallen out of suspension, and other cylinders have consumed most of the mixture anyway. By the time enough fuel is added to make the outer cylinders run correctly, the inner cylinders run too rich (Figure 13-11).

The longer the engine, the worse the mixture dis-

FIGURE 13-10   Runners and plenum in an in line engine intake manifold. (American Motors Corporation)

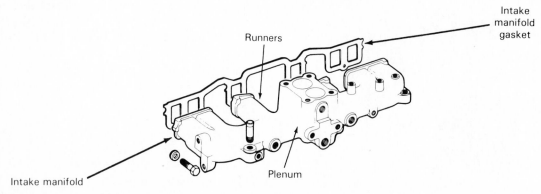

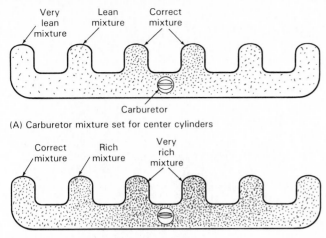

(A) Carburetor mixture set for center cylinders

(B) Carburetor mixture set for end cylinders

FIGURE 13-11 Mixture distribution in a log manifold.

tribution. Four cylinders aren't too bad, six cylinders are difficult, and the mixture distribution for a straight eight is practically impossible to balance.

Mixture Distribution Two methods are used to make the mixture distribution more even: multiple carburetion or fuel injection (Figure 13-12). On an in-line six, three cylinders can be served by one carburetor and the other three by another carburetor. Or port fuel injection can be added, which puts an injector at each cylinder.

Some in-line manifolds also have a heat riser. If the intake and exhaust manifolds are on the same side of the head, the exhaust manifold is run directly under the intake plenum. This provides a constant source of heat for fuel evaporation (Figure 13-13).

FIGURE 13-12 Improving mixture distribution in a log manifold.

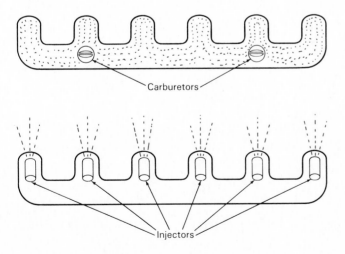

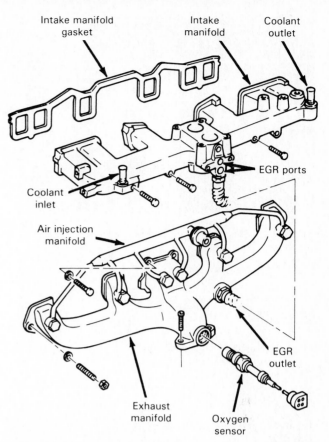

FIGURE 13-13 Manifold assemblies. (American Motors Corporation)

Vee Intake Manifold

Vee-type engine manifolds are more complex than in-line engine manifolds, because the carburetor or throttle body sits in the center and distributes fuel to both sides. Routing the runners is more difficult because they must twist around each other.

Vee manifolds are either open or closed. The closed type is more popular (Figure 13-14). In a closed manifold additional metal is cast around the runners. This extra metal is used to seal the valley between the cylinder heads. Because thick cast iron or aluminum is used, a closed manifold dampens engine noise well. Also, a closed manifold can carry coolant. This makes for a compact engine and keeps the intake manifold at a constant temperature.

An open manifold does not have the extra metal between the runners (Figure 13-15). It is much lighter than the closed intake manifold but requires an extra piece to cover the valley. Usually sheet metal is used as a cover. Sometimes this is nothing more than an extension of the intake manifold gaskets. Because this sheet metal or gasket is thin, it does not dampen noise as well as the closed manifolds.

FIGURE 13-14   Closed vee intake manifold. (Edelbrock)

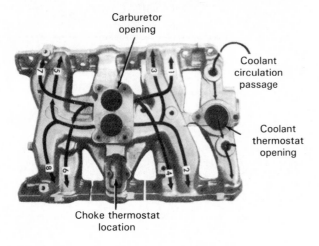

FIGURE 13-15   Open vee intake manifold. (General Motors Corporation)

Single and Multiple Carburetion

Most modern cars use only one carburetor or throttle body. As stated earlier, some in-line engines use multiple carburetors for better fuel distribution. Increased performance is another reason for using multiple carburetors or throttle bodies.

An engine produces horsepower in direct relationship to the air/fuel mixture it can feed to the cylinders. The more air an engine can breathe in, the more power the engine can make. When high performance is desired from an engine, is it often better to use two smaller carburetors than one larger one. It is easier to handle the fuel distribution that way.

Typically a second carburetor is added. More than two carburetors can be used, however. Some engines have as many as one carburetor for each cylinder (Figure 13-16). Such multiple carburetion or throttle body systems have been replaced on many new cars by port fuel injection. Port fuel injection offers superior mixture distribution and fuel economy.

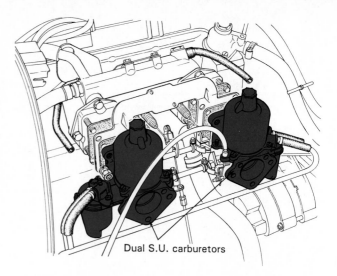

Dual S.U. carburetors

FIGURE 13-16   Multiple carburetion. (Triumph)

Troubleshooting

Troubleshooting the intake manifold is confined to leakage. A manifold can leak air, coolant, and oil.

Air Leaks   Air leaks are also called vacuum leaks. The most common vacuum leak happens when the gasket between the manifold and cylinder head leaks air. Air can then be sucked between the manifold and head into the port. This leans the mixture and can cause severe overheating damage to that cylinder if the leak is large enough. Symptoms of a vacuum leak are felt at idle. The engine will not idle slowly. If the throttle is opened slightly and then closed, the idle speed will drop to the normal level and then rise again. Usually the idle speed increase is around 300–500 rpm.

Use the oil test to find vacuum leaks. Squirt oil around the manifold. If there's a leak you'll see blue smoke come out the exhaust pipe. On turbocharged engines with high manifold pressure, pressure will cause bubbles in the oil puddle. An exhaust gas analyzer probe can also be used to find vacuum leaks.

Gasket Leaks   Coolant and oil leaks are also the result of slipped or torn gaskets. Coolant leaks are rare, but oil leaks are more common. Typically, oil will leak from the valley area of a closed-type intake manifold on a V-type engine. In any case, the manifold must be removed and the gaskets changed to cure the leak.

EXHAUST SYSTEM

Exhaust manifolds carry the hot gases of combustion away from the engine. The exhaust manifold collects these gases and sends them into the exhaust system

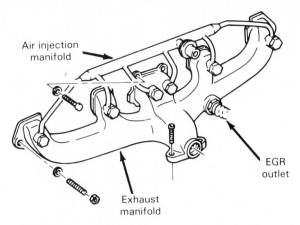

Air injection manifold

EGR outlet

Exhaust manifold

FIGURE 13-17   Cast iron exhaust manifold. (American Motors Corporation)

(Figure 13-17). The exhaust system consists of the exhaust pipe, catalytic converter, muffler, resonator, and tail pipe (Figure 13-18).

Flow Theory

When they are released from the cylinder by the exhaust valve, the combustion gases are very hot (over 1000°F) and are still expanding. The expanding gases have great force, which propels them down the exhaust manifold and through the exhaust system.

Just as the cycling of the intake valve causes pulsing in the intake manifold, there are pulses in the exhaust manifold. For each exhaust valve that opens, a pulse of gases is released. The pulse moves through the **primary pipe** of the manifold and then joins other pulses from the other cylinders in the **collector.** The collector is that part of the manifold where the primary pipes join into one. The collector is larger than the primary pipes because it carries a larger volume of gas.

Design Features

Several design features are important to any exhaust manifold. The exhaust manifold must last under extreme heat, dampen noise, expand and contract many times without cracking, and not overly restrict gas flow.

Most exhaust manifolds are made of cast iron because it is cheap and long lasting and dampens noise. To physically fit the manifolds in the engine compartment and to reduce costs, gas flow is compromised considerably on most cars. Figure 13-19 shows a cast iron manifold design which is less restrictive than most. The manifold is also fitted with a heat riser on most engines. Hot air for the engine intake is taken from the exhaust manifold, too. This is done by wrapping part of the manifold in sheet metal and using the air heated between the manifold and sheet metal.

FIGURE 13-18   Exhaust system. (American Motors Corporation)

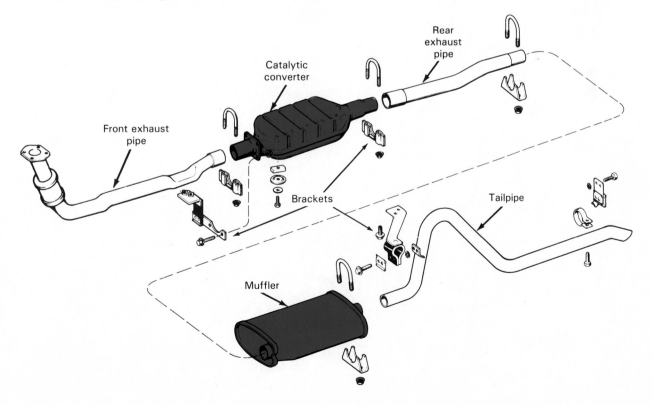

Catalytic converter

Rear exhaust pipe

Front exhaust pipe

Brackets

Tailpipe

Muffler

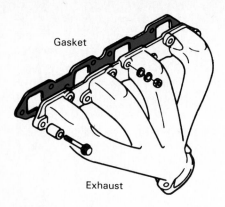

FIGURE 13-19 Exhaust manifold. (Pontiac Motor Division, GMC)

Headers and Tuned Manifolds

By varying the length of the primary pipes, the exhaust manifold can be tuned for a specific rpm range. When the engine is in that rpm range, the exhaust pulses will meet one after another in the collector. The end of one pulse helps pull the beginning of the second pulse out of its primary pipe.

Long primary pipes are used for a low rpm range, whereas shorter pipes help at higher rpm. Obviously, with the wide rpm used in passenger car engines, a tuned exhaust will favor one end of the rpm band over the other. Tuned exhausts, therefore, are normally reserved for very high-performance and racing cars. Physical space is another reason why you'll find tuned exhaust only in high-performance cars. Each primary tube must be the same length. And instead of the 4 or 5 in. common in passenger cars, tuned primary pipes are usually 30 in. or longer. Getting all that pipe into a passenger car engine compartment can lead to very complicated tubing.

Tuned exhaust is made out of lightweight steel

tubing. These pipes are called **headers.** Headers offer increased performance at certain rpm ranges along with less weight, but they cost more and don't last long. The tin pipe rusts through from water in the exhaust in several years, typically. Some high-performance engines have stainless steel header pipes. Although expensive, they improve engine breathing, are light, and last a long time.

Catalytic Converters

Catalytic converters are manufactured from heat-resisting stainless or aluminized steel (Figure 13-20). A monolith (Figure 13-21) or coated pellets (Figure 13-22) serve as the catalyst. Oxidation of carbon monoxide and hydrocarbons takes place as these substances pass the grid or pellets. Air may also be injected into the exhaust gases by an air pump to speed up the oxidation process.

In a dual-way catalytic converter the catalyst converts hydrocarbons into oxygen and water and converts the carbon monoxide into carbon dioxide. The coated pellets are approximately BB size and are coated with platinum or palladium. They allow the gas to pass through. A chemical reaction takes place during the process, changing the exhaust into different, less harmful gases. Another type of catalytic converter operates much the same as the dual-way converter, except that it converts a third emission, oxides of nitrogen (NO_x), out of the exhaust gas. This converter is called a three-way or dual-bed converter. Figure 13-20 shows a three-way converter.

Because leaded gas contaminates a catalytic converter, only unleaded gas can be used in most autos manufactured after 1975. Periodically, the converter (on a monolith type) must be replaced when it becomes contaminated. Only the coated pellets need replacing occasionally on the pellet-type converter.

FIGURE 13-20 Catalytic converter. (Chrysler Corporation)

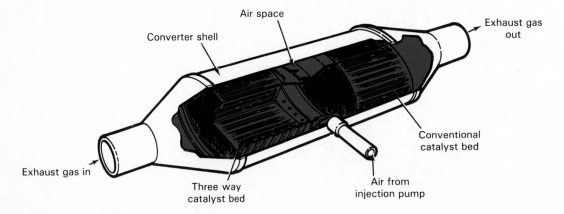

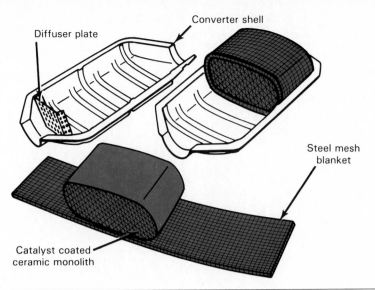

Diffuser plate

Converter shell

Steel mesh blanket

Catalyst coated ceramic monolith

FIGURE 13-21   Monolith-type converter. (Chrysler Corporation)

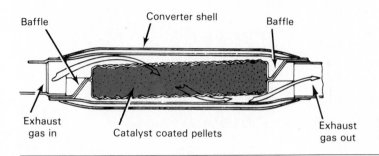

Baffle

Converter shell

Baffle

Exhaust gas in

Catalyst coated pellets

Exhaust gas out

FIGURE 13-22   Pellet-type converter. (Chrysler Corporation)

Mufflers

Mufflers are usually manufactured from aluminized steel. One common type is the glasspack or straight-through type of muffler. Fiberglass is used to surround a pipe with perforations in it. The idea is to dampen noise with a minimum of restriction to the gas. A well-designed baffle muffler will outperform and outlast a glasspack, however.

Baffle   A baffle muffler uses a combination of perforations, chambers (for resonance), and passages enclosed in a housing to reduce noise (Figure 13-23). Most baffle mufflers are very quiet but restrictive. It takes careful designing to get a quiet, minimal-pressure-drop baffle muffler. Using two completely separate exhaust systems on V-type engines helps muffler design. These separate systems form what is called a **dual exhaust.**

Free Flow   In the free-flow system, no muffler is used. Instead, restrictions specifically shaped to reduce noise are designed into the exhaust pipe. While cheap to build, free-flow systems are too loud. They are no longer available from the major auto manufacturers.

Resonator   The resonator is an expander or additional flow controller for exhaust gas. The resonator assists the muffler in baffling and reducing both gas pressure and noise. Essentially a small muffler, the resonator usually is located at or near the end of the tail pipe.

Piping

Exhaust piping is made of mild aluminized or stainless steel. Piping deterioration is caused by road salt, rainwater, and water formed during combustion. Pipes that run hot burn off the water and have longer lives. The exhaust pipe which runs from the manifold to the muffler runs hotter than the tail pipe, which runs from the muffler to the rear of the car. That's why tail pipes frequently rust twice as fast as exhaust pipes.

FIGURE 13-23   Baffle-type muffler.

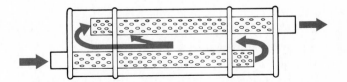

HOT AIR

By late 1919, the little Duesenberg plant at Elizabeth, New Jersey, became a facility where practically every engine of interest to the U.S. Government was brought for testing, and it seems to have been during this period that Fred and Augie first met General Electric's Dr. Moss and were first exposed to centrifugal supercharging. They immediately saw beyond the conservative aeronautical approach, which was merely to maintain the pressure of one atmosphere on the intake system up to a given high altitude. They thought in terms of pouring all the pressure to the engine that its structure would stand. Moss of course was intrigued by the experimental possibilities and offered his help.

The results were slow in coming, as Eddie Miller recalled:

So you enter this new world of the supercharger. You wind it up and nothing happens. You wind more and more and finally you get two or three pounds of pressure and you think that's terrific. Now, if you were just getting by on the compression ratio you had before, it would start knocking and detonating and you'd burn a hole through a piston in nothing flat. It took two or three races when you're having this kind of trouble to figure out what's going on. Finally you do and you lower the compression ratio and boost the pressure, maybe to 4.25-to-one and ten or twelve PSI. You'd almost double the size of the charge by kicking the pressure up to almost an atmosphere, and there was the power at last.

Griffth Borgeson
The Golden Age of the American Racing Car
W. W. Norton & Co.

Troubleshooting

Most exhaust system troubleshooting deals with finding leaks. Leaks are common at the head-to-manifold surface and manifold-to-exhaust-pipe connection (Figure 13-24). Tightening the mounting bolts usually cures exhaust leaks. If the system has been leaking for a long time, the gaskets may have to be changed.

Leaks To find leaks in the remainder of the system, run your hand around the pipes while the engine idles. You'll feel the hot gases blow against your skin where the pipe, muffler, converter, or resonator is leaking. Replace any worn-out exhaust system parts. Welding old components is usually a waste of time because once a part is bad enough to rust through, there isn't much metal left to weld.

You can tell if you have an exhaust leak when you hear an intermittent "whooshing" sound.

Rattles Another exhaust problem is rattling parts. Parts will rattle when the system bangs against the bottom of the car. Readjusting the system on its hangers will stop this rattling. Sometimes an incorrect installation will have to be dismantled to cure a rattle.

Blockage The exhaust system can also become partially or completely blocked. Blockages are commonly caused by catalytic converter failure. Mufflers and exhaust pipes can also be a cause of blockages. Replacement is the cure. Suspect a blockage if engine overheating and poor performance occur.

FIGURE 13-24 Manifold-to-pipe connection. (Buick Motor Division, GMC)

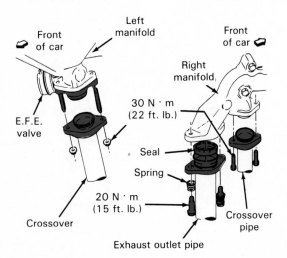

TURBOCHARGERS

One of the most recent and exciting improvements to standard passenger cars is the use of turbochargers. Turbochargers are a form of supercharger. They force air into the combustion chambers instead of letting atmospheric pressure push air in. This forced-air action increases horsepower on any engine. Turbocharging has been used on smaller engines so they can make the same power as larger engines. Turbocharging saves fuel because the smaller engine weighs less but still can produce maximum power only on demand.

A typical turbocharger has a compressor, center housing, wastegate, turbine, and wastegate actuator (Figure 13-25).

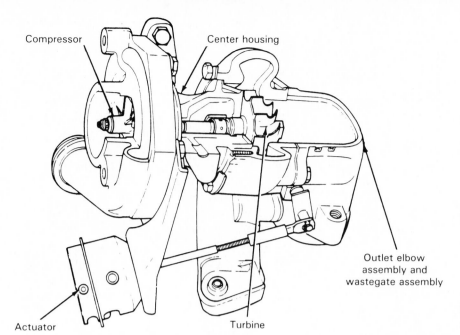

Compressor   Center housing

Outlet elbow
assembly and
wastegate assembly

Actuator   Turbine

FIGURE 13-25   Turbocharger
components. (Ford Motor Company)

Turbocharger Operation

As you can see in Figure 13-26, exhaust gas is routed through the turbine. The gas causes the turbine to spin, just like a model airplane propeller will spin if you blow on it. The turbine wheel is connected by a shaft to the compressor. Thus, if the turbine spins, the compressor must spin also. Intake air is routed through the compressor. The rotating compressor forces the air against the compressor housing, increasing the air's density. This dense air is then routed to the combustion chamber.

The dense air creates more horsepower and more exhaust gases. The increased gases accelerate the turbine as they pass through the exhaust. This further increases the turbine/compressor speed. When the designed speed and inlet air compression are reached, the wastegate opens. Some of the exhaust gas can then

FIGURE 13-26   Turbocharger operation. (Ford Motor Company)

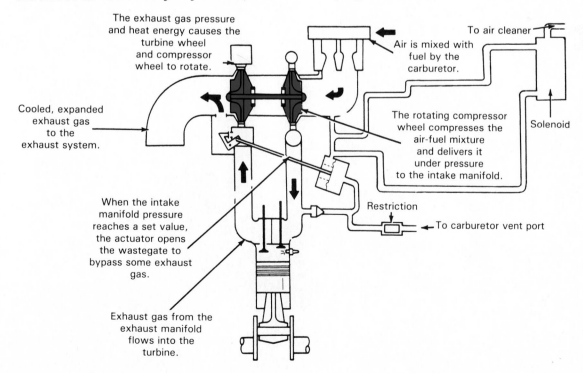

The exhaust gas pressure and heat energy causes the turbine wheel and compressor wheel to rotate.

To air cleaner

Air is mixed with fuel by the carburetor.

Cooled, expanded exhaust gas to the exhaust system.

The rotating compressor wheel compresses the air-fuel mixture and delivers it under pressure to the intake manifold.

Solenoid

When the intake manifold pressure reaches a set value, the actuator opens the wastegate to bypass some exhaust gas.

Restriction

To carburetor vent port

Exhaust gas from the exhaust manifold flows into the turbine.

bypass the turbine and go directly out the exhaust pipe.

Turbocharger Design

A turbo installation poses some design problems for the engineer (Figure 13-27). The turbo unit must be close to the engine to reduce lag—the time between opening the throttle and when the power increases. Also, careful turbo size selection is critical.

The turbo also makes greater demands on the engine. Engine oil is used to lubricate the ball bearings the turbine/compressor shaft spins in. Because this shaft can reach speeds over 140,000 rpm, a continuous supply of clean oil is vital. If the oil supply runs dry or contains dirt or metal from other failed engine parts, the turbo stresses the oil. Oil level, changes, and filtration are very important in a turbocharged engine.

The turbo unit acts like a restriction in the exhaust system. More heat is retained by the cylinder head, exhaust valves, and exhaust manifold. These parts are made of high-quality, temperature-resistant materials on turbo engines. The turbo also dampens exhaust noise. Smaller mufflers can be used with a turbo.

Turbos can be used with throttle body or port injection. Carburetors can also be used, and the turbo can either draw through or blow through the carburetor or throttle body.

Troubleshooting

Turbos are commonly blamed for many problems, but problems usually lie elsewhere. The ignition or fuel system is usually at fault. Before working on the turbo, thoroughly check the ignition and fuel systems. If the turbo does seem to be at fault, most manufacturers don't want you to do much with it. Aside from tightening the clamps that hold the turbine and compressor housings to the center section, they would prefer that you change the entire unit. Because the delicate turbine/compressor blades spin so fast, they are precision balanced. One small nick can lead to bearing failure by throwing the unit out of balance. The bearings must be very clean as well. Opening the turbo in the field risks damage and dirt contamination.

Turbocharged Engine Operation

Probably even more important than knowing how to troubleshoot turbo units is knowing the correct operating procedure.

Always let a turbocharged engine warm up for about a minute before driving off. This warm-up pe-

FIGURE 13-27 Turbocharger installation. (Chrysler Corporation)

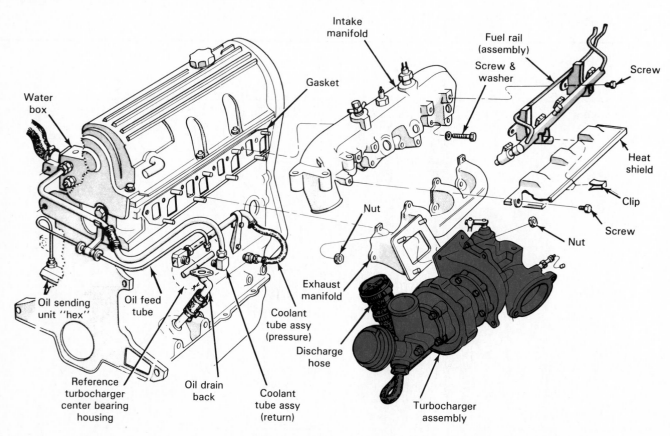

riod lets plenty of oil reach the turbo before it begins spinning at high rpm. When shutting the engine off, let it idle for a few seconds first. Idling lets the turbo slow down before the oil pressure drops. It is not necessary to let the engine idle before a shutdown if the last minute of driving was done at low engine speeds and light throttle applications. At these speeds the turbo is turning slowly anyway. Always follow the recommended oil and filter change intervals exactly. Without clean oil, a turbo will soon fail.

TRADE TERMS

Collector
Dual Exhaust
Exhaust Crossover
Headers
Heat Control Valve
Log

Port
Primary Pipe
Runners
Throttle
Throttle Body

REVIEW QUESTIONS

1. The air/fuel mixture requirements of an engine remain constant under all conditions. True or false?

2. What is the major difference between carburetion/throttle body injection and port injection?

3. What two sources of manifold heat are available on most engines?

4. Do large runners and ports promote *fast* or *slow* mixture velocities?

5. What is the major problem with a log intake manifold?

6. What is a vacuum leak?

7. Name two design features of an exhaust manifold.

8. Why are headers not normally fitted to passenger cars?

9. Very briefly, what does a catalytic converter do?

10. How does a turbocharger increase engine horsepower?

11. How fast can the turbine/compressor unit of a turbocharger spin?

12. Name two reasons why a turbocharger needs a steady supply of clean oil.

14

Engine Lubrication and Cooling

INTRODUCTION

Lubricating an engine is vital to its continued performance and the life of its parts. Besides lubricating the engine, the lubrication system and the cooling system of a vehicle maintain stable combustion temperatures. This chapter discusses typical lubricating and cooling systems, how they operate, and the problems expected in the normal life of such systems. It also describes lubricant types and how they relate to overall engine operation.

LUBRICATION

Purpose of Oil

Oil has three major functions in an engine: lubrication, cooling, and cleansing. Oil forms a thin layer between moving parts and allows them to move more easily. This same layer of oil is constantly being replaced with new cooler oil. This replacement of oil helps to cool the engine. Another function of oil is to collect small pieces of debris, waste products of friction and combustion, and transport this debris into the engine pan.

OBJECTIVES

When you have completed this chapter, you should be able to

- Understand how the lubricating system protects the engine
- Know the major components of the lubricating system
- Explain differences between oil types and grades
- Understand how oil viscosity affects engine lubrication
- Understand how the cooling system keeps the engine operating at the correct temperature

194

The oil pump pickup then draws the oil into the oil filter where these small particles are trapped. The oil filter cleans and cools the oil slightly before sending it back into the engine to start a new cycle. Oil also seals, absorbs shock, and prevents corrosion of internal parts.

Oil Types and Grades

Oil companies spend vast amounts of money to provide the modern motorist with different grades of oil for different driving conditions. Obviously, engine lubrication requirements in frigid Minnesota differ greatly from the hot, dusty Texas panhandle.

Viscosity   Temperature affects oil flow. At low temperatures, oil is very thick and flows sluggishly. As temperature increases, the oil thins out and flows easily. This characteristic, or property, of oil is called **viscosity.** Viscosity describes the oil's resistance to flowing. The Society of Automotive Engineers (SAE) grades oil with a numbering system. A low number indicates oil with a low viscosity (flows easily), and a higher number indicates oil that is more viscous (flows less easily). SAE numbers will sometimes contain a *W*, which refers to winter grade oil of *HD*, which means high detergency. HD oil contains detergents that attract dirt particles the way common laundry detergents do.

Some motor oils have a multiviscosity rating. They have greater stability than single-viscosity oils. For example, SAE 20–50 has the viscosity of both SAE 20 and SAE 50 oil. Multiviscosity oil lets the oil flow easily when the engine is cold and does not thin out when operating or excessive temperatures are reached.

Service Ratings   Additionally, oils have service ratings for different operating conditions. Some service ratings include SA, SB, SC, SE, and SF. An engine used for light loads and short time intervals would use SC oil. Engines exposed to severe loads and long hours of continuous operation would require SE or SF oil.

Oil Additives   Pure mineral oil cannot satisfactorily protect the engine. Motor oils contain chemical additives to help prevent oil oxidation, acid formation, foaming, varnish buildup on cylinder walls, and rust. Oil is a hydrocarbon compound which **oxidizes** or "breaks down" at high temperature. Excessive oxidation causes the oil to lose its lubricating properties and results in engine failure. When gasoline burns, it produces oxides of nitrogen, carbon monoxide, carbon dioxide, and water. These vapors enter the crankcase. The oxides of nitrogen and carbon dioxide combine with water to form acids which not only dilute the oil but also cause metal parts to corrode (Figure 14-1).

Even with protective filters, dirt particles enter the crankcase and contaminate the oil. *Detergents* help clean the oil by keeping the dirt particles in suspension so the oil filter can trap them more efficiently. The churning action of the crankshaft causes the oil to foam. Some engines use a windage tray to help reduce the swirling air in the oil pan area (Figure 14-2). Foaming oil oxidizes faster and does not protect the moving parts very well.

Pour point depressants are also added to lower the cold-temperature viscosity of the oil. (Pour point is the temperature at which a liquid will just barely pour.)

FIGURE 14-1   Corrosion-damaged bearings. (McQuay-Norris)

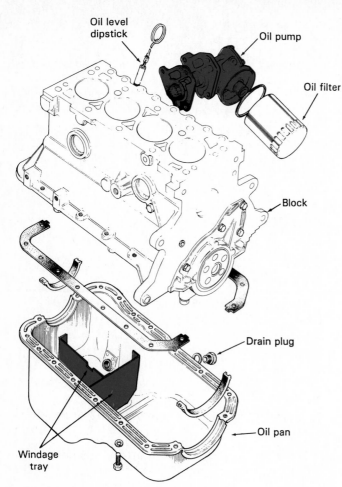

FIGURE 14-2   Oil pump and windage tray. (Ford Motor Company)

The oiling system provides oil to protect all moving metal surfaces in the engine. Without proper **lubrication**, the engine would rapidly overheat, wear out, and fail to operate. Figure 14-3 shows a typical oiling system.

When two metal surfaces rub against each other, the resulting friction causes heat and metal wear. Oil forms a thin film that separates the two metal surfaces and reduces friction (Figure 14-4).

Imagine placing a 500-lb block of metal on the floor and trying to push it around. This would be difficult (if not impossible). However, if you place this heavy metal block on a sturdy cart or wagon, you can move it around much more easily. The cart's wheels and bearings separate the metal block from the floor and greatly reduce the friction. Motor oil separates the moving metal surfaces from each other and reduces friction.

Operation

Because of gravity, oil collects in the bottom of the engine in an **oil pan**, an area below the crankshaft (Figure 14-2). This pan usually holds 3–6 qts of oil, depending on engine size and design. You must consult a service or owner's manual to determine the capacity of a particular engine. The oil pan has a drain plug for draining oil (Figure 14-2).

Oil Pump   The oil must travel against gravity throughout the engine to protect the moving metal

FIGURE 14-3   Typical oiling system. (American Motors Corporation)

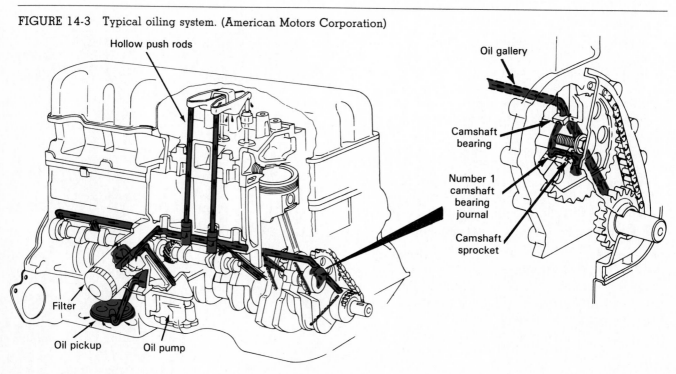

FIGURE 14-4 Oil film separating metal surfaces.

surfaces. The **oil pump** provides this energy or oil pressure. Figure 14-5 shows parts of a typical oil pump. Oil pumps usually have either gears or rotors (Figure 14-6). The oil pump produces oil pressure by rapidly moving the oil through the gears or rotors and into the oil passageways, or *galleries*, into the engine. A shaft normally connects the oil pump to the distributor. A gear on this shaft mates with a gear on the rotating camshaft, driving the oil pump (Figure 14-7).

Oil Pressure   The lubrication must protect the engine during all driving conditions. Loss of oil to bearings for even a few seconds under high-speed, heavy-load conditions may cause damage. Automotive engineers must carefully design the lubrication system to assure reliable lubrication. The oil pump supplies adequate oil pressure at low idle speeds. Oil pump rotation and oil pressure increase with engine speed. A **pressure relief valve** prevents excessive pressure buildup (Figure 14-8). Excessive oil pressure would damage seals and gaskets, which prevent oil loss. The pressure relief valve is "downstream" from the oil pump or housed within the pump itself and transfers some of the oil

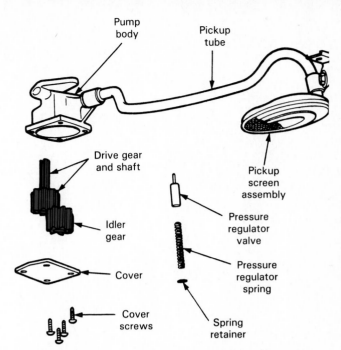

FIGURE 14-5   Oil pump assembly. (Chevrolet Motor Division, GMC)

directly back into the pan area to lower excessive oil pressure.

Oil Passages   The engine block and cylinder heads contain a maze of **galleries** to deliver oil to needed

FIGURE 14-6   Oil pump rotor (left) and gear (right). (Chrysler Corporation)

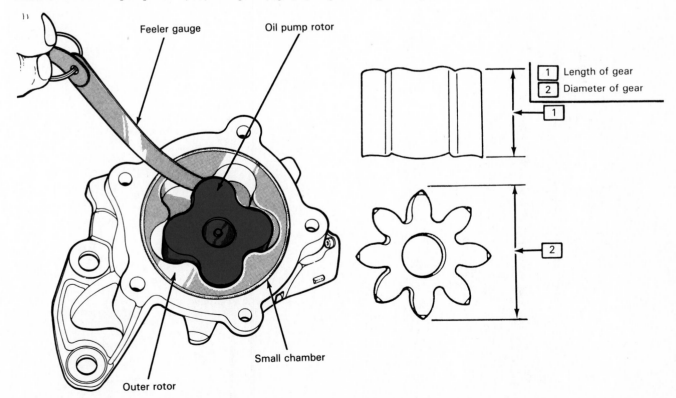

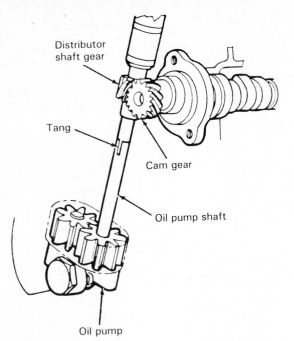

FIGURE 14-7 Typical drive for oil pump. (Chrysler Corporation)

FIGURE 14-8 Oil pressure relief valve. (Chrysler Corporation)

Overhead oiling and return

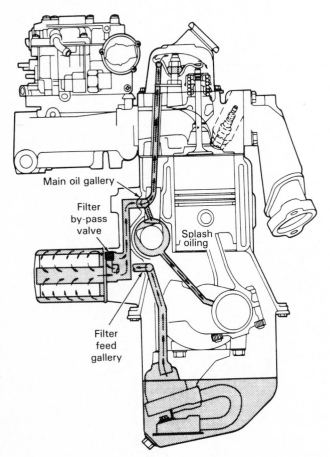

areas. These passageways also connect to holes in the valve lifters and crankshaft, providing lubrication to the tappets and crankshaft bearings (Figure 14-9). Most engines lubricate the cylinder walls by squirting pressure-fed oil out of cross-drilled passageways in the crankshaft, through oil nozzles, or through connecting rod oil holes (Figures 14-10 and 14-11).

Oil Filters Despite design efforts and the carburetor air filter, dirt particles manage to get into the engine and contaminate the oil. Also, small metal particles caused by normal wear enter the oil. These abrasive particles further increase engine wear. An **oil filter** removes most of the larger particles. The oil filter cannot remove liquid contaminates, but it still effectively extends motor oil life. Eventually, the oil filter loses effectiveness, and you must replace it. Figure 14-12 shows the internal parts of a typical oil filter. Replacing the oil and oil filter periodically removes harmful contaminants.

As a protection to the engine the lubrication system includes a filter bypass valve (Figure 14-9). If the filter becomes clogged, the valve will open due to the increased pressure, allowing the oil to bypass the filter and provide lubrication to the engine.

FIGURE 14-9 Oil galleries and filter bypass valve. (Cadillac Motor Division, GMC)

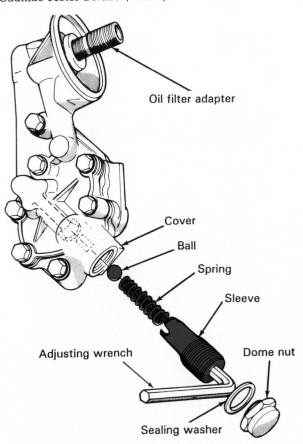

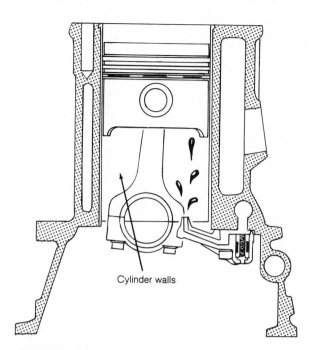

FIGURE 14-10   Lubrication of cylinder walls and cooling piston.

Cylinder walls

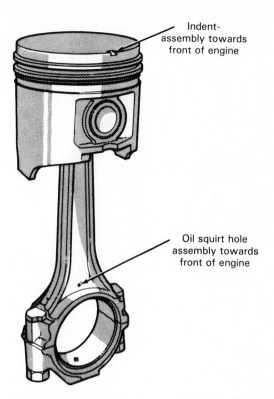

Indent-assembly towards front of engine

Oil squirt hole assembly towards front of engine

FIGURE 14-11   Connecting rod oil hole for cylinder wall lubricating. (Chrysler Corporation)

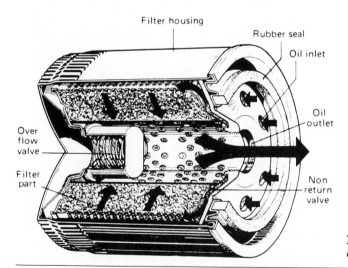

Filter housing

Rubber seal

Oil inlet

Oil outlet

Over flow valve

Filter part

Non return valve

FIGURE 14-12   Oil filter. (Saab-Scania of America, Inc.)

Crankcase Ventilation

Unburned gasoline vapors blow by the piston rings into the crankcase and oil pan area. These vapors combine with water and produce corrosive acids that may damage engine parts. Modern automobile engines use a **positive crankcase ventilation (PCV)** system to remove most of these harmful vapors (Figure 14-13). Venting these vapors directly into the atmosphere contributes to air pollution. To reduce air pollution, the PCV directs these vapors back into the carburetor to be recycled. Clean the PCV system periodically to assure proper operation.

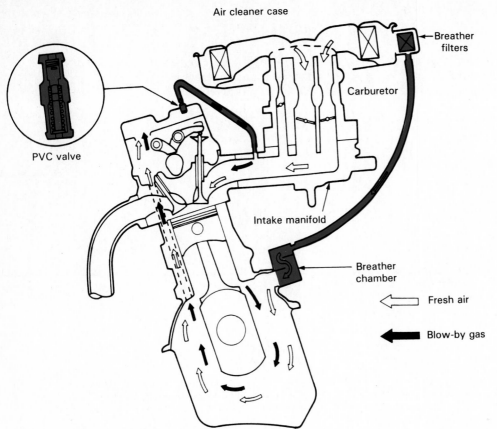

Air cleaner case

Breather filters

Carburetor

PVC valve

Intake manifold

Breather chamber

⇐ Fresh air

⬅ Blow-by gas

FIGURE 14-13 Typical positive crankcase ventilation. (American Honda Motor Co., Inc.)

LUBRICATING SYSTEM SERVICE

Clean motor oil extends engine life. How often should the oil or filter be changed? This is a hard question to answer because operating conditions vary tremendously. Manufacturers recommend an oil change after a certain number of miles or months, but the frequency of replacing the oil filter depends on environment and the condition of the engine. The oil filter is usually changed after every other oil change. However, changing the filter every time the oil is changed will increase engine life. Consult service manuals to determine the manufacturer's recommendations. Keep in mind that individual driving conditions may require different intervals from the manufacturer's recommendations. For example, driving in extremely dusty areas or stop-and-go city traffic reduces the time between oil changes.

Other parts of the lubrication system require little

WIND IT UP!

In the mid-1960s, a group of young Chrysler engineers decided that high-performance engines should go beyond the typical methods of improving horsepower.

They began investigating how a high-performance engine should be provided with lubrication. Recognizing that an engine's oiling system can detract from net horsepower, especially at high levels of operating rpm, this group constructed a set of engine oil pans that enabled a visual "look" into the pan while the vehicle operated.

They could study oil movement within the pan. They analyzed so-called "windage" conditions—how the crankshaft picks up oil and reduces engine rpm. Study showed that under hard acceleration, oil climbed up the backside of the cylinder block, moving toward the front of the engine and along the upper portion of the crankcase. Oil positioned in this area reduced crank rotation and diminished power.

After carefully examining these data, these young Chrysler "mavericks" were able to determine that oil pan baffling could control where the lubrication was needed.

Today, we know of this solution as deep-sump oil pans that prevent excessive oil from attaching itself to the rotating crankshaft. Such creativity enabled Chrysler to assume a commanding position among high-performance sources for drag racing engines and vehicles in the mid- and late-1960 era.

Jim MacFarland
Edelbrock

service. If the oil pump cannot maintain normal oil pressure, it should be removed for repair or replacement. If problems arise with the positive crankcase ventilation (PCV) valve, replacement will be necessary. Refer to Chapter 7 for changing the oil, oil filter, and PCV valve.

THE COOLING SYSTEM

Operation

The **cooling system** removes excess engine heat and keeps the engine operating at its most efficient temperature. Burning gasoline in the cylinders produces a large release of energy. Unfortunately, approximately 60–70% of this energy is wasted as heat. The cooling system is one of a number of systems that remove this excess heat energy. Maximum combustion temperatures can reach 6000°F (3330°C). Engine oil temperatures should not be much over 250°F (121°C), or the lubricating oil will "break down" and lose its ability to protect the metal surfaces.

Because a cold engine runs inefficiently, the cooling system also contains a thermostat that allows coolant to bypass the radiator for faster engine warm up. Figure 14-14 shows a typical cooling system.

Most modern engines are liquid cooled. However, some use air cooling because it is a lighter, less compli-cated way of cooling an engine. Air-cooled engines need a fan, air shrouds, a thermostat, and finned cylinders to help shed the heat. Most also have an oil cooler. The Volkswagen Beetle is the most familiar air-cooled model, although Porsche and Corvair also have air-cooled 6-cylinder engines. The disadvantages of air cooling are the higher noise level, less constant engine temperature, and power loss to the fan.

The liquid cooling system has the following components:

1. Liquid coolant
2. Water jackets
3. Radiator
4. Fan
5. Hoses
6. Thermostat
7. Water pump

Liquid Coolants

Originally, water cooled the engine. Water has the ability to absorb large amounts of heat per unit volume. Early motorists soon discovered that using only water presented two major problems. Water freezes at 32°F (0°C) and expands (increases in volume) when frozen into ice. This expansion causes a pressure buildup and may result in a "cracked" engine block, cylinder head, or radiator.

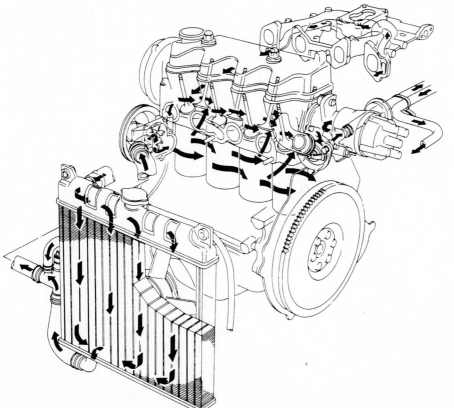

FIGURE 14-14 Typical cooling system. (American Honda Motor Co., Inc.)

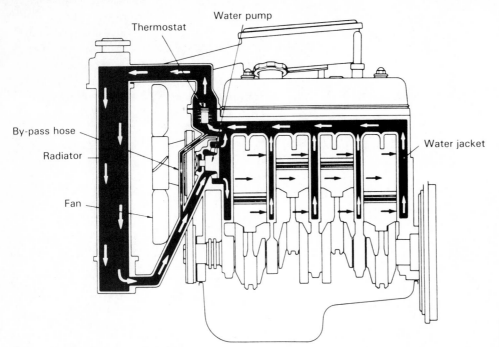

FIGURE 14-15   Engine water jackets.

Modern engines use an **antifreeze** coolant composed of ethylene glycol. **Ethylene glycol** freezes at extremely low temperatures. Manufacturers recommend an ethylene glycol/water mixture of not less than 50% ethylene glycol or more than 70%. This mixture range will protect the engine to temperatures approaching −60°F (−51°C). Antifreeze coolants also contain anticorrosion (antirust) and lubricating additives to help protect the cooling system.

Water Jackets

Automotive engineers design coolant passageways throughout the engine block and heads to efficiently remove excess engine heat. The larger **water jacket** passageways are next to the cylinders for maximum heat transfer to the coolant (Figure 14-15).

Radiator

The radiator transfers engine heat from the coolant to the outside air. Radiator designs allow the maximum surface-to-air exposure for rapid heat exchange. The radiator contains entry and exit tanks and a central core (Figure 14-16).

Vertical Flow   Some radiators use a gravity-feed design in which the hot coolant enters the top tank and flows down through the core to the bottom tank. Most of the heat transfer occurs in the core. The core consists of a series of tubes and metal fins. The metal fins simply increase the surface area exposed to the inrushing air. Radiator cores may be made of brass or aluminum. The tanks can be brass, aluminum, or plastic.

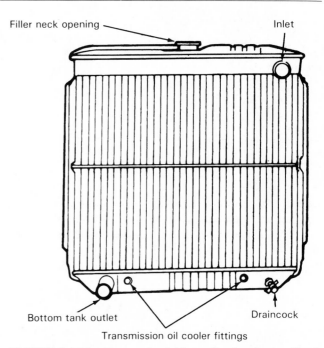

FIGURE 14-16   Gravity feed (down flow) radiator. (Ford Motor Company)

Crossflow   New car crossflow radiators use side-to-side tubes and side tanks instead of vertical flow. The engine size usually determines the radiator style and size (Figure 14-17). If a radiator is plugged or leaking, remove it and take it to a special radiator repair shop.

Coolant Recovery   Newer automobiles contain a **coolant recovery system** (Figure 14-18). A coolant recovery system differs from a normal cooling system in that an overflow bottle connects to the radiator over-

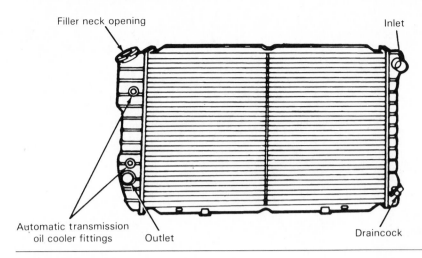

Filler neck opening

Inlet

Automatic transmission oil cooler fittings

Outlet

Draincock

FIGURE 14-17   Crossflow radiator. (Ford Motor Company)

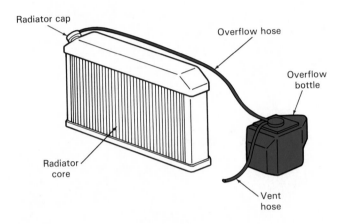

Radiator cap

Overflow hose

Overflow bottle

Radiator core

Vent hose

FIGURE 14-18   Coolant recovery system.

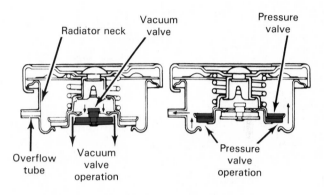

Radiator neck

Vacuum valve

Pressure valve

Overflow tube

Vacuum valve operation

Pressure valve operation

FIGURE 14-19   Radiator cap operation. (Ford Motor Company)

flow hose. The overflow bottle is transparent or translucent so you can check the coolant level without removing the radiator cap. As the coolant temperature rises and the pressure in the system exceeds the pressure relief valve of the radiator cap, excess coolant flows into the overflow bottle. As the engine cools and the coolant contracts, a vacuum forms in the system, drawing the coolant, which is stored in the overflow bottle, back into the radiator. In a properly maintained cooling system, the only coolant losses will be through evaporation. This system also helps to prevent rust by keeping air out of the cooling system.

Radiator Pressure Cap

The cooling system must be a closed system, or the hot coolant will boil away, and the system will require frequent refilling. The radiator **pressure cap** closes the system. The radiator cap has a pressure valve and a vacuum valve (Figure 14-19). The cap has several different functions:

1. It prevents coolant loss when the vehicle is in motion.

2. It prevents impurities (mostly air) from entering the cooling system, keeping corrosion at a minimum.

3. It allows atmospheric pressure to eliminate the vacuum that occurs in the system during cooldown.

4. It raises the coolant boiling point approximately 3°F (1.7°C) per psi of pressure by maintaining a constant cooling system pressure.

Note: Pounds per square inch (psi) in metric are measured in kilopascals (kPa).

Most radiator pressure caps are rated at 15 psi (103 kPa). Check the service manual for your specific engine pressure rating. A 15-psi cap will raise the coolant boiling point to 242°F (134°C). The cap vents excess pressure through the pressure valve to avoid bursting the radiator or hoses. During engine cooldown, the vacuum created inside the radiator could cause the tubes and hoses to collapse from the greater outside atmospheric pressure. The vacuum valve opens, allowing atmospheric pressure to push coolant from the recovery bottle back into the radiator.

A special **pressure-testing tool** tests the radiator cap (Figure 14-20). Test as follows, or follow the tool manufacturer's instructions:

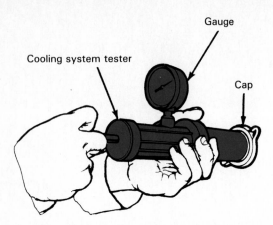

FIGURE 14-20 Testing radiator pressure cap.

> **CAUTION:** Never remove the cap until the system cools. Personal injury may result from the rapid escape of hot coolant.

1. Remove the radiator pressure cap.
2. Visually inspect the radiator cap, dip it in water, and connect it to the tester.
3. Pump the tester to bring the pressure to the upper limit of the cap specification.
4. If the cap fails to hold the pressure, replace the cap.

The **fan** increases the airflow rate through the radiator for faster heat transfer, especially during idling. Some automobiles use a thermostatically controlled electric fan. Many use a drive belt from the crankshaft pulley to drive the water pump and fan. Most automobiles use several drive belts to drive other components (for example, the power steering pump or air conditioner compressor) from the crankshaft pulley. Some of these belts are matched sets. Do not replace only one belt, or the others will be stretched and quickly break unless you replace all belts at the same time.

There are four major fan designs (Figure 14-21):

1. Cross fan
2. Power-flex fan
3. Thermo-clutch fan
4. Electric fan

Cross Fan   The cross fan is the least expensive design, but it has the disadvantages of a fixed pitch angle. Pitch angle is the degree of slope of the blade. A fan with less pitch angle draws less air and produces less drag (fan/air friction) at high road speeds. At low idle speeds, a large airflow volume is needed to cool the engine. However, at high speeds sufficient air usually passes through the radiator. At higher speeds, the

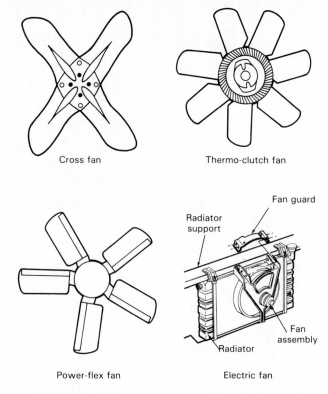

FIGURE 14-21 Fan designs. (Pontiac Motor Division, GMC)

cross-fan fixed pitch angle causes excessive noise, and the increased drag robs the engine of several horse-power. The cross-fan design is a compromise between high and low engine speed requirements, because the rotation speed is fixed to engine speed.

Power-Flex Fan   The **power-flex fan** has flexible blades that draw maximum airflow at low speeds. At high speeds, centrifugal force flattens the flexible blades out. This decreases blade pitch and noise level and saves power. The flex fan requires no adjustment or testing except for keeping the fan belt adjusted to proper tension and making sure that the unit is not damaged.

Thermo-Clutch Fan   The **thermo-clutch fan** has a thermostatically controlled fluid fan and torque control clutch. The thermal control drive is a silicone-filled coupling connecting the fan to the fan pulley. A control valve operates the drive with a temperature-sensitive **bimetal** coil or strip. The control valve maintains the flow of silicone through the clutch. When the temperature of the air discharged from the radiator is low, the fan clutch limits the fan speed. High air temperature causes the bimetal coil to allow a greater flow of silicone to enter the clutch. More silicone increases cooling. A thermo-clutch fan is more expensive than other designs and usually is found on higher-priced automobiles.

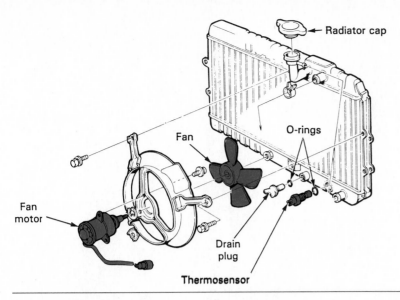

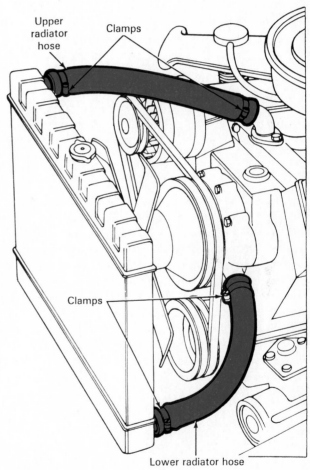

FIGURE 14-22 Electric fan system. (American Honda Motor Co., Inc.)

Electric Fan Any engine-driven fan robs the engine of horsepower, decreasing miles driven per gallon of fuel. The only fan that does not directly rob the engine of horsepower is the electric fan system (Figure 14-22). The electric fan system has a fan, a 12-V motor, and a thermosensor (temperature sensor) that turns the fan on or off. With more and more vehicles using transverse engines, the electric fan has become more popular.

Hoses

Most automobiles have at least five hoses in the coolant system (Figure 14-23). Two small-diameter hoses supply hot coolant from the water pump to the passenger compartment heater core. The heater core is a smaller version of the cooling radiator. A short, small-diameter bypass hose allows the coolant to circulate within the engine while the engine warms up to operating temperature. Two larger-diameter hoses transport the coolant from the water pump to the radiator and back into the engine block.

Eventually, these rubber hoses deteriorate, and you must replace them. The hoses will either develop leaks, resulting in coolant loss, or collapse internally and block the coolant flow, causing overheating. Periodically inspect the hoses visually. Replace individual hoses as necessary. Usually you won't replace the hoses as a set because of cost.

Thermostat

The **thermostat** controls coolant flow in the system and helps maintain correct engine temperature. It is in line between the engine block and a large-diameter inlet hose to the radiator. When the thermostat is closed, only the coolant inside the engine is warmed. As the engine coolant becomes hotter, the thermostat

FIGURE 14-23 Coolant system hoses. (Chrysler Corporation)

begins to open. When the engine is warm, the thermostat will open completely and allow coolant to circulate through the engine and the radiator (Figure 14-24). Without a thermostat, the engine would take much longer to reach operating temperature.

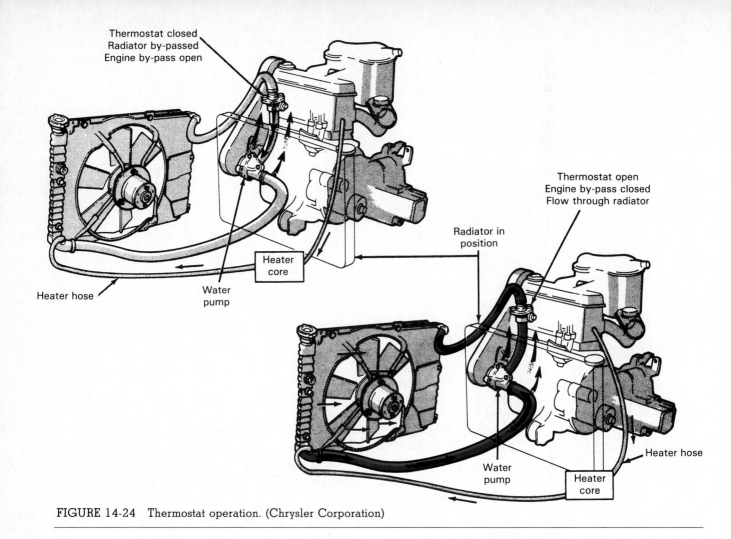

Thermostat closed
Radiator by-passed
Engine by-pass open

Thermostat open
Engine by-pass closed
Flow through radiator

Radiator in position

Heater core

Heater hose

Water pump

Heater hose

Water pump

Heater core

FIGURE 14-24   Thermostat operation. (Chrysler Corporation)

Automotive engineers determine the thermostat temperature requirements. You will have to check your car's service manual to find out the temperature requirements for individual engines. Typical thermostats operate at 160°F (71°C), 180°F (82°C), and 195°F (91°C). Figure 14-25 shows typical thermostats.

To test the thermostat, remove the thermostat from the cold engine block. Visually inspect the thermostat for corrosion and proper sealing. If the thermostat does not pass this inspection, replace it with a new one (Figure 14-26).

FIGURE 14-26   Thermostat installation. (Ford Motor Company)

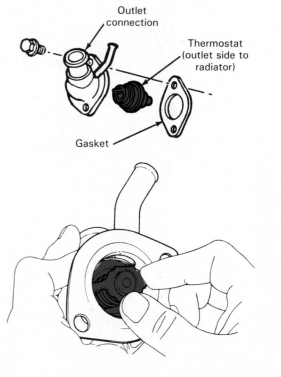

Outlet connection

Thermostat (outlet side to radiator)

Gasket

FIGURE 14-25   Typical thermostats. (Chrysler Corporation)

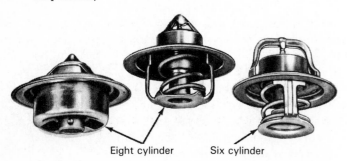

Eight cylinder

Six cylinder

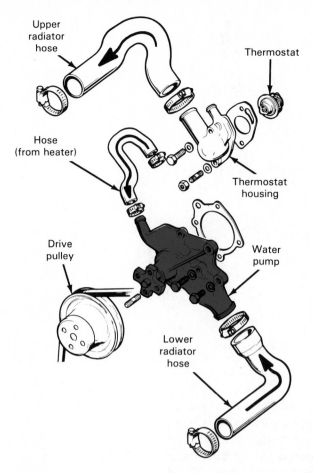

FIGURE 14-27   Typical water pump assembly. (American Motors Corporation)

Water Pump

The **water pump** forces coolant to circulate throughout the engine and into the radiator. The water pump housing mounts near the front of the engine block (Figure 14-27). A drive belt from the crankshaft pulley turns the water pump and fan. The rotating water pump pulley turns an *impeller*, which forces the coolant outward by centrifugal force, circulating several gallons of coolant per minute. It uses a gasket and a bearing seal to prevent coolant from leaking.

Sometimes the bearing or impeller shaft wear excessively and become noisy. Usually when this happens, the seal develops a leak, and you must replace the water pump. Replace the water pump as a unit.

Cooling System Maintenance and Troubleshooting

Follow these maintenance procedures to keep the cooling system working efficiently.

Draining   Remove the radiator cap and open the heater control valve to the maximum heat position. Open the drain petcock valve.

Cleaning   Clean bugs and debris from the radiator air passages by blowing them out with compressed air from the back to the front of the radiator. Remove most rust and *scale* by using a good cleaning compound. (Scale refers to mineral deposits from "hard" water.) Follow the manufacturer's instructions for using the cleaner. If you must remove a good deal of rust and scale, you will have to flush the cooling system.

Flushing   *Reverse* or *back flushing* is a very effective means of removing rust and scale from a cooling system. Reverse flushing means forcing water in the reverse direction of normal coolant flow. For best results, flush the radiator, engine, and heater core separately.

To flush the radiator, connect a **flushing gun** (Figure 14-28) to the water outlet of the radiator and disconnect the water inlet hose. Use a leadaway hose, connected to the radiator inlet, to prevent flooding the engine. Use air in short bursts only because you can easily damage a clogged radiator. Continue flushing until the water runs clear.

To flush the engine, first remove the thermostat and replace the housing. Connect the flushing gun to the water outlet of the engine (Figure 14-29). Disconnect the heater hoses from the engine. Flush using short air bursts until the water runs clean. Flush the heater core as described for the coolant radiator. Make sure the heater valve is set to the maximum heat position before flushing the heater.

Refilling   Be sure the engine is running while refilling the cooling system to prevent air from being trapped in the engine block. Many new car systems require that you remove all of the air from the cooling system. To do this, open the heater valve, loosen a hose at the highest point of the system, and add coolant until the system is full. Check the coolant level in the recovery bottle and add coolant if necessary. After the system is full, continue running the engine until the ther-

FIGURE 14-28   Reverse-flushing radiator. (Mack Trucks)

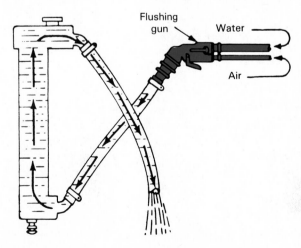

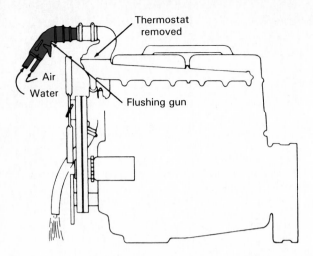

FIGURE 14-29   Reverse-flushing engine. (Mack Trucks)

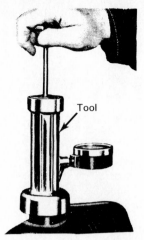

FIGURE 14-30   Pressure testing the cooling system. (Mack Trucks)

FIGURE 14-31   Troubleshooting the cooling system. (Chevrolet Motor Division, GMC)

COOLING TROUBLESHOOTING

Condition	Probable cause	Corrective action
Poor circulation	Restriction in system.	Check hoses for crimps, and clear the system of rust and sludge by flushing radiator.
	Insufficient coolant.	Replenish.
	Inoperative water pump.	Replace.
	Loose fan belt.	Adjust.
	Inoperative thermostat.	Replace.
Corrosion	Excessive impurity in water.	Use soft, clean water. (rain water is satisfactory).
	Infrequent flushing and draining of system.	Cooling system should be drained and flushed thoroughly at least twice a year. Permanent antifreeze (Ethylene glycol base) can be used throughout the seasons of a year.
Overheating	Malfunctioning thermostat, radiator cap and fan coupling.	Replace.
	Radiator fin choked with mud, chaff, etc.	Clean out air passage thoroughly by using air pressure from engine side of radiator.
	Incorrect ignition and valve timing.	Adjust.
	Dirty oil and sludge in engine.	Refill.
	Inoperative water pump.	Replace.
	Loose fan belt.	Adjust.
	Restricted radiator.	Flush radiator.
	Inaccurate temperature gauge.	Replace.
	Impurity in water.	Use soft, clean water.
Overcooling	Malfunctioning thermostat.	Replace.
	Inaccurate temperature gauge.	Replace.
Noise	Squeak at water pump mechanical seal.	Replace pump assembly.
	Damaged or worn water pump bearing.	Replace pump assembly.

mostat opens; then recheck the fill level. Check a shop manual if there is any doubt about the quantity of anti-freeze to use or the proper refill procedure.

Pressure Testing the Cooling System

A pressure-testing tool tests the complete cooling system (Figure 14-30). Follow these steps to test it, or follow the tool manufacturer's instructions:

1. Remove the radiator pressure cap. With the engine stopped, wipe the radiator filler neck clean. Fill the radiator to the correct level with coolant. Attach the cooling system tester to the radiator and pump until the pressure is at the upper level of the radiator rating (check the service manual for ratings). If the pressure drops, inspect for external leaks.

2. If you see no leaks, detach the tester and run the engine until it reaches the normal operating temperature. Reattach the tester and pump until the pressure reaches approximately 7 psi (48 kPa). Race the engine. If the needle on the tester fluctuates, the system has a combustion leak.

> CAUTION: Pressure may build up quickly. Release any pressure above the limit of the pressure cap specifications, or cooling system damage may result.

3. If the needle does not fluctuate, race the engine a few more times and check for water at the tail pipe. Excessive water indicates a faulty head gasket or a cracked block or cylinder head near exhaust ports. Remove the oil dipstick. If water globules appear in the oil, the system has a serious internal leak. Check a repair manual for further instructions about repairing the system.

Troubleshooting the Coolant System

Figure 14-31 describes how to find and fix problems in the cooling system.

TRADE TERMS

Antifreeze
Bimetal
Coolant Recovery System
Cooling System
Ethylene Glycol
Fan
Flushing Gun
Galleries
Lubrication
Oil Filter
Oil Pan
Oil Pump

Oxidizes
Positive Crankcase Ventilation (PCV)
Pour Point
Power-flex Fan
Pressure Cap
Pressure Relief Valve
Pressure-testing Tool
Thermo-clutch Fan
Thermostat
Viscosity
Water Jacket
Water Pump

REVIEW QUESTIONS

1. What is the purpose of the oiling system?
2. Explain why the oiling system must use a pressure relief valve.
3. How are cylinder walls lubricated?
4. Explain the purpose of the oil filter.
5. What does viscosity mean?
6. What is the purpose of the cooling system?
7. What are the major components of the liquid cooling system?

8. The liquid cooling system thermostat is open at low engine temperatures. True or false? Explain your answer.
9. Explain why you add antifreeze to the liquid cooling system.
10. What are some advantages and disadvantages of air cooling?

15

Engine Disassembly

INTRODUCTION

When you disassemble an engine, you can diagnose what you may need to correct when you rebuild it. You can recognize certain wear patterns on parts and find out what is wrong with the engine. This chapter focuses on these topics. It also tells you how to remove an engine from a chassis and how to disassemble certain types of engines.

ENGINE REMOVAL

Safety

Safety is the most important part of engine removal. While you may not think "pulling" an engine is dangerous, it can be. Two aspects of engine removal cause most of the problems: raising the chassis and lifting the engine.

Raising the Car

During engine removal you must raise the chassis and get underneath the car. Obviously, if the car falls, you could be seriously injured or worse. You must always

OBJECTIVES

When you have completed this chapter, you should be able to

- Describe the basic steps in engine removal
- Show the difference between removing an engine from a vehicle with manual transmission and one with an automatic transmission
- Explain the general procedure for engine disassembly
- Understand the difference between disassembling an OHV engine and an OHC engine
- Find clues to an engine's condition during teardown
- Understand the importance of keeping hardware organized
- Explain the safety precautions necessary when removing or disassembling an engine

use jack stands or ramps to support the car. **Floor jacks,** scissor jacks, bumper jacks, and the like are for raising the car only. Only jack stands are for supporting the car. So use a jack to raise the car; then place a jack stand underneath it immediately (Figure 15-1). Be sure that the wheels on the floor are blocked.

Lifting the engine means you run the risk of dropping it. You must be especially careful when first raising the engine off its mounts. It is very easy to get careless and stick a hand under the engine. Don't do it. If the engine needs positioning, do it from the top. If a line or wire is caught on the engine, use a stick to free it. Never put your hand where it could be crushed if the engine should fall.

Special Tools

Removing an engine is a big job. It requires special tools and usually extra help. One of the special tools is the familiar floor jack. You'll need it to support the transmission as well as lift the car. You'll also need jack stands to support the car. Another special tool is the **engine hoist.** Such a hoist uses a hydraulic jack in a special frame. The frame extends over the engine

FIGURE 15-1   Properly raised car.

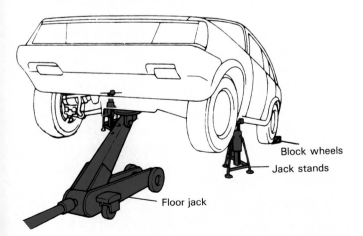

Block wheels
Jack stands
Floor jack

compartment and lifts the engine straight up. Then the hoist is rolled away from the chassis, and the engine is set down.

To connect the engine hoist to the engine, you'll need a chain 3 ft long. You bolt each end of the chain to the engine. The engine hoist hooks onto the center of the chain. An engine sling may also be used. You'll also need fender covers, a drain pan, and normal hand tools.

Hood

A good general rule is to remove anything that gets in your way during engine removal. The first object to remove is the hood. This takes at least two people, one at each side. First scribe a line around the bolts which attach the hood to its hinges. This line will allow rapid aligning at reassembly. Then remove all hood hinge bolts and lift off the hood. Set the hood well out of the way until the engine is out. After engine removal you can refit the hood to its hinges. Removing the hood first protects both engine compartment and hood. For now, set the hood where it won't get scratched or tipped over.

Battery

Disconnect and remove the battery. This step will give you more working room. More importantly, there can't be any sparks from accidental groundings if the battery is out. Clean the battery with water and baking soda. Store it off the concrete floor and cover it with a non-conductive material.

Drain Fluids

Slide the drain pan under the engine and drain the oil. It's a good idea to let the engine drain for a long time. The more oil you get in the pan, the less mess you'll have during engine disassembly.

If the engine is liquid cooled, drain the radiator and block. It helps if you have two drain pans so both oil and coolant can drain at the same time.

You can drain the radiator two ways. The petcock on the lower tank drains the cooling system with little mess. Removing the lower radiator hose drains the system very quickly but also makes quite a mess. Be sure to clean up any fluids on the floor or tools.

Storing Hardware

Use labeled cans or boxes to store hardware. Keep hardware separated by application. For example, all alternator bolts go in one box, carburetor hardware in another, and so on. Don't mix all the mounting hardware in one box, or reassembly will be very difficult.

The same is true of vacuum hoses and electrical wires. Label all hoses and wires with a tape *flag* and felt-tip pen. This step is vitally important on cars with their dozens of vacuum lines. Even if you don't know what a line does, you can mark it. Just assign a number to that disconnection. Write the number on the tape flag. Write the same number on the tape you've placed on the part that the line or hose attaches to. Then later all you have to do is match numbers.

Line Disconnections

Mark and disconnect all lines which connect the engine to the chassis. These are the fuel lines, temperature- and pressure-sending unit wires, throttle and choke cables, alternator, starter and air-conditioning electrical connections, coil high-tension lead, coil lead, and ground strap.

After disconnecting all lines and wires, lay them out of the way. If a wire gets caught on the engine during lift-out, stop and untangle the wire.

Accessories

Remove as many engine accessories as possible. This removal makes the engine lighter and easier to handle. Stubborn attaching hardware is actually easier to break loose when the engine is firmly attached to the chassis.

Some normally removed accessories are the carburetor, alternator, power steering pump, air-conditioning compressor, starter, and alternator.

Most accessories have both a pivot bolt and cinch bolt. The cinch bolt slides in a slot for belt adjustment. The pivot bolt is the one the unit swings on. You must remove both bolts entirely.

Removing the air conditioning compressor deserves special safety attention. If you open one of the high-pressure freon lines—the large, heavily insulated pair—the gas will escape violently. Freon supercools when it expands into the atmosphere. If you are in the way, it will supercool you. The resulting frostbite can cost you your fingers, a hand, or your eyesight. Freon gas is very dangerous.

CAUTION: Freon gas releases phosgene gas when it is burned in an engine. Phosgene is a *deadly nerve gas*. Do *not* have any fire or running engines near freon gas.

The best way to handle freon is to keep it in its lines. When removing the ac compressor, leave the freon lines alone. Just unbolt the compressor from the engine and wire the compressor to the chassis so it cannot slip.

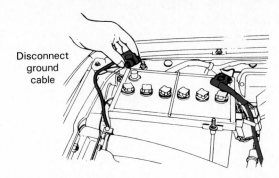

Disconnect ground cable

FIGURE 15-2 Ground cable removed from battery. (Subaru)

Saving Time If a fast engine removal is your goal, you can leave many connections together, like the freon lines. The starter and alternator are good examples. You can unbolt them from the engine and leave the electrical connections alone. Wire the alternator and starter to the chassis. But always remove the ground cable from the battery (Figure 15-2). This step prevents a wrench or a wire from grounding and ruining something. This system is no good if you are going to thoroughly clean the engine compartment.

Radiator

Remove the radiator, even if it looks like it isn't in the way. Radiators are very easily damaged during removal and very expensive to repair. It is better to remove the radiator than risk crushing it. This is a good time to inspect the radiator for leaks, rust damage, or clogged tubes.

Besides the coolant hoses there may be two transmission cooler lines attached to the radiator. If the

FIGURE 15-3 Transmission cooler lines at the radiator. (Cadillac Motor Division, GMC)

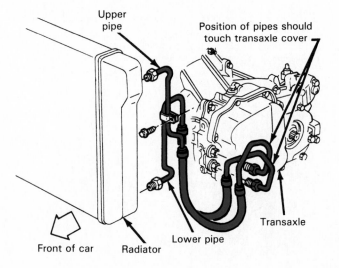

Upper pipe

Position of pipes should touch transaxle cover

Front of car   Radiator   Lower pipe   Transaxle

car has an automatic transmission, inspect the bottom radiator tank. If you find two steel lines, use a tubing wrench to disconnect them (Figure 15-3). Cap the open ends. Follow the lines as they run back to the transmission. Often these lines attach to the engine's oil pan. If so, they will have to be undone.

Bell-housing Bolts

Remove all bellhousing bolts. Look carefully for bolts hidden in casting recesses. Additionally, the lower bell-housing area often has a dust shield. On any car, remove the shield if it bolts to both engine and transmission. On automatic transmission cars, remove the shield in any case.

Exhaust

Disconnect the front exhaust pipe from the exhaust manifold (Figure 15-4). Twist the pipe until you can remove the exhaust seal. Disconnect the air management system pipe.

Flexplate

The dust shield of the automatic transmission must come off to gain access to the flexplate bolts. After removing the shield, inspect the flexplate (Figure 15-5). Look for a bolt which passes through the flexplate and into the torque converter. You may have to rotate the engine so a flexplate bolt shows in the bell housing area open to you. Unscrew the bolt. You may have to hold a nut on the torque converter side. After removing the first bolt, rotate the engine until the next bolt is in view. Remove it and all remaining bolts. Usually there are only three bolts, but there may be more. Place a floor jack under the transmission.

FIGURE 15-4 Disconnecting the front exhaust pipe and the air management pipe. (Cadillac Motor Division, GMC)

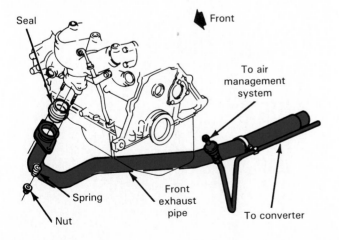

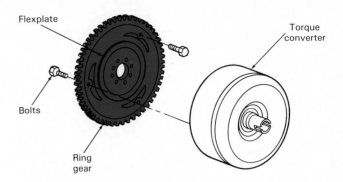

FIGURE 15-5 Flexplate-to-torque-converter attachment. (Chrysler Corporation)

Engine Hoist Attachment

Bolt the chain diagonally across the top of the engine. Use at least ⅜-in. bolts and a grade 5 chain on heavy V8 engines. Smaller, lighter engines can be safely lifted with ¼-in. bolts. Use large-area washers so the chain links cannot slip over the bolt heads.

Now loop the engine hoist's hook onto the chain. Attach the hook slightly forward of the chain's center. This will tilt the engine's front upward slightly. A slight tilt helps the engine disengage the transmission and clear the body.

Engine Mounts

Next disconnect the engine mounts (Figure 15-6). Typical domestic mounts have a horizontally mounted through-bolt. Slip out the bolt after unscrewing its nut. Other designs use bolts and studs passed vertically through rubber cushions. Undo the nuts or bolts. Transversely mounted engines use two mounts plus torque reaction rods (Figure 15-7). These rods attach to the firewall at one end and the engine at the other. It is best to completely remove these rods. There might be a second rod mounted low on the engine.

Engine Lift-out

Take one last look at the engine compartment. Remove any stray tools. Tuck loose wires and hoses out of the way. It may be desirable to remove the distributor and the carburetor to avoid damage. If the car is on stands, lower it to the ground. Once you are sure the engine is free from the chassis, you are ready to lift it out.

Start slowly. As you lift, watch both sides of the engine for hang-ups. It helps if you have a helper on each side of the engine.

At first the engine and transmission will rise as a unit. Keep raising the floor jack under the transmis-

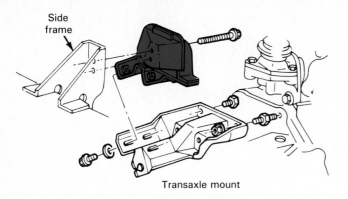

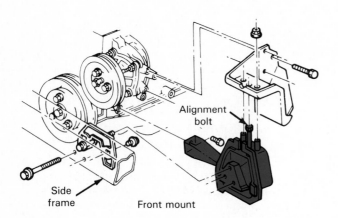

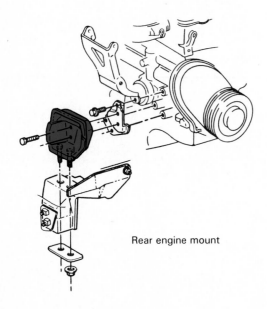

FIGURE 15-6 Motor mounts. (Cadillac Motor Division, GMC)

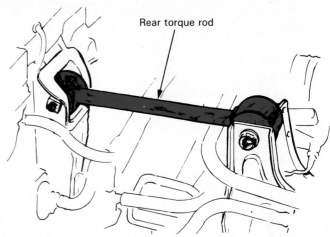

FIGURE 15-7 Torque reaction rods. (American Honda Motor Co., Inc.)

gine has moved forward enough, it is usually several inches up as well. Keep the floor jack raised, or the transmission could be damaged in the resulting fall.

Lift the engine high enough to clear the front sheet metal (Figure 15-8). As soon as the engine will clear the body, pull the engine hoist forward and lower the engine to the floor.

Take a minute to gather up tools and tidy the engine compartment and clean up any oil spills. Reattach the hood. Large parts can be stored in the trunk if they are cleaned off first. Finally, push the chassis to its storage spot. Use the engine hoist to get the engine on the engine stand.

FIGURE 15-8 Engine angled for removal. (American Honda Motor Co., Inc.)

sion. Automatic transmissions separate very easily from the engine.

Manual transmissions, however, require that the engine move forward about 2 in. or so before they separate from the engine because the input shaft must disengage from the pilot bearing. By the time the en-

Engine Stand

The best way to disassemble an engine is on an engine stand (Figure 15-9). A stand holds the engine, leaving you with both hands free. Furthermore, the stand allows you to roll the engine over. This feature makes working on the bottom of the engine much easier.

Mount the engine on its stand while the engine hangs from the engine hoist. Remove the stand's head and bolt it to the block's bell housing area. Then fit the stand's base onto the head. Snug all stand bolts wrench-tight; then lower the engine stand to the ground. Disconnect the hoist.

If no stand is available, set the engine on a bench. Use short wood blocks to steady the engine. As you remove parts from the engine, its weight will shift. Then you will have to change the wooden blocks to keep the engine steady.

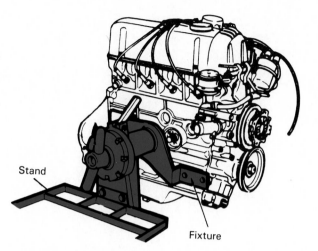

Stand

Fixture

FIGURE 15-9   Engine mounted on a stand. (Nissan Motor Corporation, U.S.A.)

ENGINE DISASSEMBLY

Organization

You can either save time during engine **teardown** or make lots of work for yourself. It depends on how you are organized and how safely you disassemble (*tear down*) the engine. Because disassembly is almost always part of a larger job, the temptation is to disassemble the engine as quickly as possible. Speed, however, is less important than accuracy. *Accuracy in engine disassembly is keeping all parts in order.* Only then can you efficiently repair and reassemble the engine. Figure 15-10 shows the major engine components you will be disassembling.

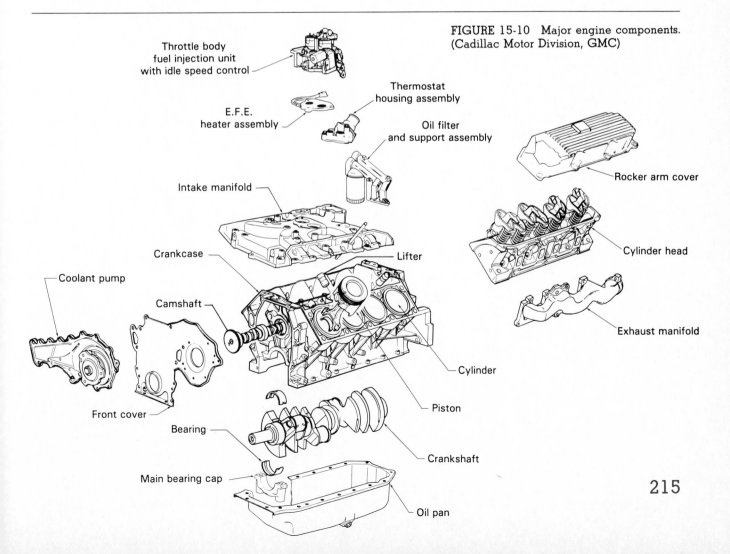

FIGURE 15-10   Major engine components. (Cadillac Motor Division, GMC)

Throttle body fuel injection unit with idle speed control

Thermostat housing assembly

E.F.E. heater assembly

Oil filter and support assembly

Rocker arm cover

Intake manifold

Cylinder head

Crankcase

Lifter

Coolant pump

Camshaft

Exhaust manifold

Cylinder

Front cover

Piston

Bearing

Crankshaft

Main bearing cap

Oil pan

As with engine removal, containers are needed to keep parts separated. Coffee cans, cardboard boxes, metal trays, or bin boxes all work well. Each container must be marked.

Remember to put only one type of bolt in each container. When the engine is apart, you should have one can for head bolts, another for manifold bolts, and so on.

Felt-tip-pen and ball-point-pen markings will fade in several weeks. Rain will fade your numbering even faster. If the chassis sits outside while the engine is apart, keep the engine compartment covered.

Safety

Engine disassembly is not especially dangerous. However, never think you can't get hurt. Beware of falling parts. Always keep the engine securely supported. If it rolls over on your hands, you could be seriously injured. Always *pull* the wrench toward you to loosen a bolt.

Remaining Accessories

Before disassembling the engine, you must remove any remaining accessories. Accessories commonly remaining are the temperature and pressure senders, fuel pump, water pump, clutch, and flywheel. There may be other accessories depending on how complicated the engine is.

If you didn't remove the carburetor or fuel injection and the distributor before taking the engine out of the car, now is the time to remove them. Remove the carburetor's four base nuts and lift the unit off. Some carburetors use long bolts which pass through the top of the carburetor and into the manifold. Handle fuel injection parts carefully to avoid damage.

The distributor may also be on top of the engine. Before removing the distributor, the engine should be turned until the number *one* piston is at top-dead-center (TDC) and the index mark on the crankshaft pulley aligns with the pointer on the timing chain cover (Figure 15-11). Removing the spark plugs makes it easier to turn the crankshaft over to align the index mark and the pointer at TDC. Now mark the distributor housing and the rotor position on the block.

Where the distributor meets the engine there will be a hold-down bolt (Figure 15-12). Remove this bolt and any retaining clip. Then pull the distributor out of the engine and set it aside. If there is a distributor drive shaft, remove it now. Many distributor drives have a threaded hole in their centers. This hole lets you screw a long bolt into the drive shaft. The bolt is then the needed handle to pull the drive out.

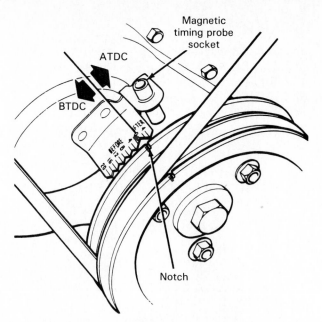

FIGURE 15-11 Harmonic balancer at TDC. (American Motors Corporation)

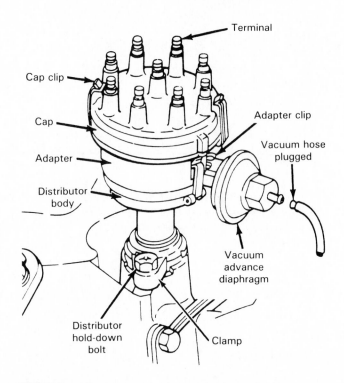

FIGURE 15-12 Distributor attachments. (Ford Motor Company)

Water Pump

At the engine's front you will find the water pump. Leave the pulley attached to the pump unless it must come off for you to get to the bolt. Around the pump are its attaching bolts. Remove all these bolts; then

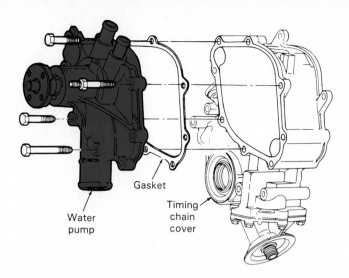

FIGURE 15-13 Removing the water pump. (Ford Motor Company)

gently pry the pump away from the block (Figure 15-13). You will have to pull the pump from the block because the gaskets will be stuck on. This is a good time to inspect the water pump for a leaking seal or a defective bearing.

Clutch Assembly

At the engine's rear there will be either a clutch and flywheel or a flexplate. With a clutch, index the pressure plate relative to the flywheel. Make two small marks on the pressure plate near its outer edge. On the flywheel, make two matching marks (Figure 15-14). These marks allow you to reassemble the clutch and flywheel in the same relationship. This alignment is important if they have been balanced as a unit.

Pressure Plate Now remove the pressure plate bolts. Unscrew them one turn at a time all around the plate. Otherwise the pressure plate springs may bend from the uneven torque. Once the bolts are finger-tight, you can unscrew each one all the way. Pull the pressure plate off the flywheel (Figure 15-15). The clutch disc will fall free, so be ready for it. Keep your fingers off the disc. Grease from your hands can cause the clutch to grab after reassembly. Handle the disc by the edges. Mark the flywheel side for reassembly.

Flywheel The flywheel bolts are next. They may have **lockplates.** Lockplates are metal tabs which bend over the bolt head or nut. They keep the bolts from loosening. Bend back any lockplates with a punch or screwdriver. Now undo the flywheel bolts.

You may have trouble with the flywheel rotating. There are several ways to stop it. The best is to use an air-powered impact gun on the flywheel bolts. The sharp impacts of the air wrench transfer almost all their torque to the bolts. There isn't enough torque left over to turn the engine.

If you don't have an air impacter, put a hand wrench on the front pulley crankshaft nut. You will have to hold the crank from rotating with one hand while pushing on the flywheel bolts with the other. Another way to hold the crank is to slip a large slot screwdriver into the teeth of the ring gear. Brace the screwdriver's shank against a dowel pin. If there is no dowel pin, run a bell housing bolt into its hole and pry against it.

Flexplate Flexplates are much simpler because there is no clutch. Just unbolt the flexplate as you would a flywheel.

Most flexplates and flywheels are pinned by dowels to the crank. If not, mark (index) them to the crank.

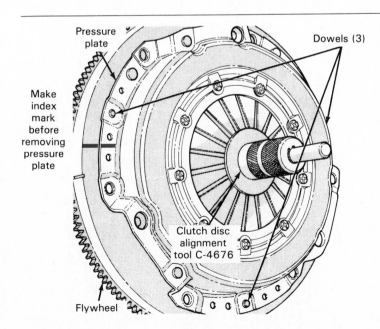

FIGURE 15-14 Marking the pressure plate and flywheel. (Chrysler Corporation)

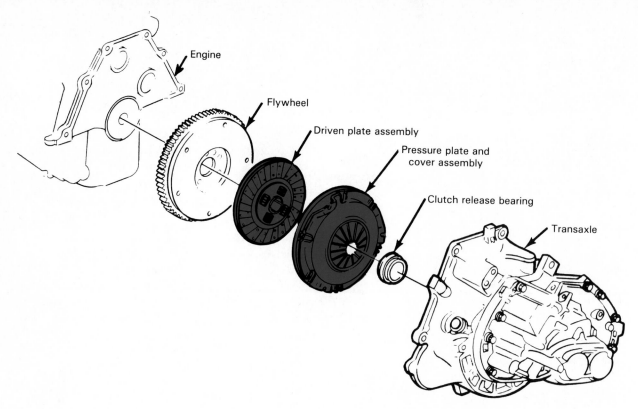

FIGURE 15-15 Remove the clutch and pressure plate. (Chevrolet Motor Division, GMC)

Engine Mounts and Fuel Pump

On the sides of the engine, you will find mounts, sending units, fuel pumps, and the like. Go around the block and systematically remove these parts. Remember to keep the hardware separated.

The fuel pump bolts may feel very tight. If so, rotate the crankshaft 180°. This will move the fuel pump's eccentric on the camshaft, unloading the bolts. When the fuel pump is pulled from the block, it may be followed by a solid rod. This is the pump push rod. On some engines a small plug or plate may need to be removed before the rod will come out of the block.

Manifolds

Before you can remove the head, the manifolds should come off. On in-line engines the manifolds can be on the same side of the head (Figure 15-16). Or they can be on opposite sides (crossflow design).

Typically, manifolds are mounted to the head by studs and nuts. Spray all nuts and studs with penetrating oil before beginning. On crossflow heads, simply unscrew the nuts, remove any washers, and pull the manifold off. If the intake and exhaust manifolds are on the same side, they might be bolted together. Look for bolts running vertically from one manifold

FIGURE 15-16 In-line engine manifolds. (Chevrolet Motor Division, GMC)

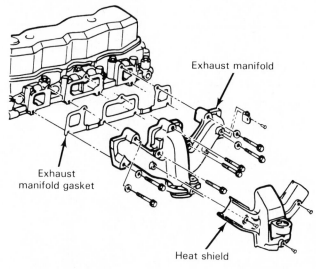

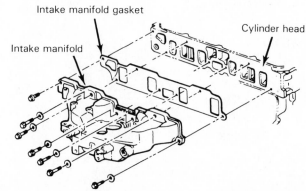

218

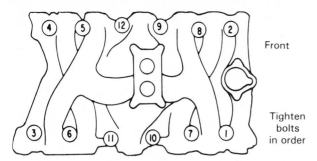

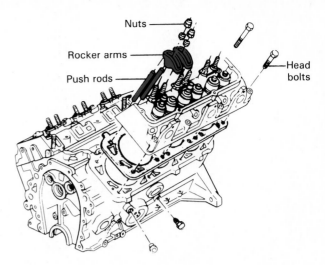

FIGURE 15-17   V-engine intake manifold and bolts. (General Motors Corporation)

FIGURE 15-18   OHV valve train. (Ford Motor Company)

to the next. If you find any, remove them and then remove the head-to-manifold nuts.

On V-engines, the exhaust manifolds are on the outside of the V. The intake manifold sits inside the V. Remove the exhaust manifolds just as though they were on an in-line engine.

V-engine intake manifolds bolt to the heads around their perimeter (Figure 15-17). First check that there is no water hose running between the water pump and the intake manifold. Remove the bypass hose if it is still attached. Then remove all the manifold bolts. You'll probably have to pry the manifold off. Start at a corner. Perhaps you can find a spot where the manifold overhangs the head or block. Use such a spot to pull up on the manifold. It will take some effort to lift the manifold, but excessive force means there is still a bolt installed somewhere. If you aren't careful, you can break the manifold. Never pry directly between the head and manifold.

Heads

Start head removal by unbolting the rocker cover. This cover may attach with perimeter bolts or nuts and studs which pass through the cover's outside edge. Unscrew these bolts or nuts and lift off the cover.

Rocker Arms   Now the valve train is exposed. On overhead valve (OHV) engines the tops of the push rods, rocker arms, and valves are visible (Figure 15-18). Remove the rocker arms. They can be shaft or individually mounted. If shaft mounted, remove the bolts passing through the shaft towers. Then lift the unit shaft, towers, and rockers off the head. Otherwise, remove the nut sitting inside the rocker arm. Then lift each rocker arm, nut, and **ball pivot** off as a unit (Figure 15-19).

Always keep rocker arms and ball pivots together. Just slip the rocker arm and pivot onto a length of wire. When all rocker arms are on the wire, twist the wire ends together. This is important. Mismatched rocker arms and pivots wear very quickly. Unless you keep the pieces together now, you'll have no choice

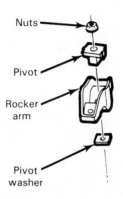

FIGURE 15-19   Individually mounted rocker arm. (Ford Motor Company)

but to install them out of order or replace them with new ones.

Push Rods   With the rockers out of the way, pull out the push rods. Keep them in order by pushing them into a piece of cardboard.

Next, remove the lifters with a puller or a magnet. Use egg cartons or other containers with compartments to keep the lifters in order. Don't skip this step or they'll have to be replaced with new lifters.

Overhead Cam (OHC)

Overhead cam engines may use rocker arms, or the cam may work directly on the lifters (Figure 15-20). If rocker arms are used, they can be shaft or individually mounted. Also, if rockers are used, they can be mounted above or below the cam. You'll have to decide which has to come out first, cam or rockers. Check the manufacture's manual.

Rocker Arms   If the rockers are shaft mounted, they usually require removal first (Figure 15-21). Remember

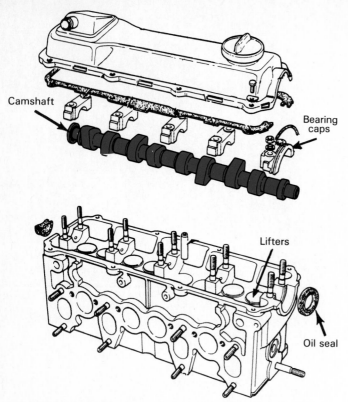

Camshaft

Bearing caps

Lifters

Oil seal

FIGURE 15-20 OHC working directly on lifters. (Chrysler Corporation)

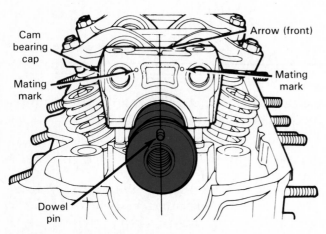

Cam bearing cap

Arrow (front)

Mating mark

Mating mark

Dowel pin

FIGURE 15-21 Shaft-mounted rockers with integral camshaft bearing caps.

always to turn the engine until the marks on the belt, gears, or chain are lined up. If there are no alignment marks on the parts, simply make alignment marks with a dot of paint before removing the chain, belt, or gears. Start by unbolting the cam sprocket from the cam. The chain or belt is now loose. For now, merely drop it into the front cover. If the cam is driven by a belt, first mark its direction of rotation. Use a grease pencil to draw an arrow on the belt's back. Unbolt and remove the rocker assembly just like on an OHV engine.

Removing the rocker arm assembly may also remove the cam's upper bearing halves, or caps. If so, just lift the cam out of the head. Otherwise, slide the cam forward and out.

Camshaft If the cam is mounted above the rocker arms or if there are no rocker arms, you must remove the cam first. Mark the belt; then unbolt the cam sprocket. Drop the belt or chain into the front cover. The cam sits either in the head with cam bearing caps over its journals or up on towers. If caps are used, make sure they are marked; then unbolt and remove them. With towers, find their hold-down hardware, usually nuts on studs near the bottom of each tower. Remove the nuts and lift the cam straight up off the studs.

Now remove the rockers. Individual rockers sit on pedestals. Unclip the securing wire spring and lift off the rocker arm. Keep the rocker arms in order. Later, you must install each rocker on its pedestal.

Remove pedestals by unscrewing them from the head. Make sure you are wrenching on the pedestal's base hex nut, not the valve adjusting nut.

Head Bolts

Only the valve springs and head bolts should be showing in the rocker cover area now. It's time to remove the head bolts. Use a socket and breaker bar. On most engines all head bolts are identical or have obvious differences in length (Figure 15-22). Some engines, however, use bolts with subtle differences in length. Examine the bolts as you remove them. If you find differences, punch the bolts into a marked piece of scrap cardboard. This will keep the bolts in order so you can replace them in their exact holes.

With all bolts out, lift the head off the block. Sometimes a combination of a heavy head and sticky gasket will make this difficult. Try prying the head off. Pry at a corner where the head overhangs the block. Never pry against where the head or block mate. Before

FIGURE 15-22 Typical long and short head bolts. (Buick Motor Division, GMC)

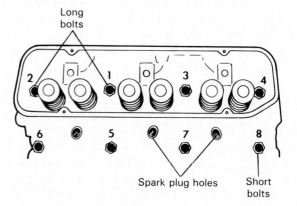

Long bolts

Spark plug holes

Short bolts

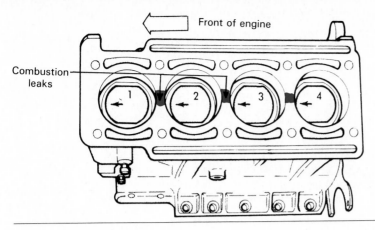

FIGURE 15-23 Combustion leaks between cylinders.
(Buick Motor Division, GMC)

prying, double-check that you have removed all head bolts.

Head Gasket

With the head off you can **read** (inspect) the head-gasket (Figure 15-23). Look at the stainless steel sealing rings around the cylinder openings. They should be a light metal color. If they are burned black, they were leaking at that spot. Both combustion gases and coolant leave a dark trace. These clues will help you decide if the head needs milling.

SHORT BLOCK

The complete block assembly less tire cylinder head is called a short block. If the block is damaged beyond repair, short blocks are available for replacement.

Ridge Reaming

Begin short-block disassembly by inspecting the cylinders. See if you can feel a ridge near the top of the cylinders (Figure 15-24). This ridge was made by the rings wearing the cylinder.

You'll need a **ridge reamer** to remove the ridge

FIGURE 15-24 Cylinder ridge.

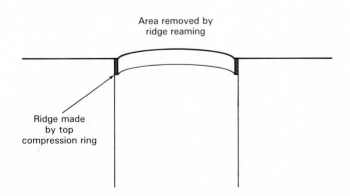

(Figure 15-25). Otherwise the piston ring lands will be damaged during piston removal (Figure 15-26). If the ridge is not removed, the top ring will hit the ridge and break one or more of the piston lands.

Follow the instructions of the manufacturer of the ridge reamer you are using. Remove only enough material to smooth out the ridge. Removing too much will make boring necessary.

FIGURE 15-25 Ridge reamer.

FIGURE 15-26 Piston lands.

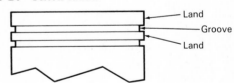

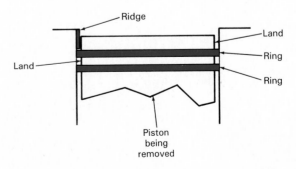

AN "EXPLODED VIEW" OF AN ENGINE

Of the many ways you can disassemble an engine, the following method is generally one to avoid. But it makes a point.

You are inside the building of a well-known engineering firm, long established in high-performance and racing engine building.

As you stand facing out the rear of their building, you can see the freestanding engine dynamometer, complete with all vital oil, fuel, and electrical lines supported above the engine, hanging down and connected to the engine. A series of tests is in progress using a small-block Chevrolet V8 running in an engine rpm range of about 4000–7500. At this point, engine disassembly is only a remote thought because the series of tests is in the beginning stages.

On this particular evening, it is past 10 o'clock. As you would expect, it is dark outside the open, tilt-up door. The only lights are in the room near the dyno area.

Among the parts installed on this particular engine is a stock Chevrolet cast iron flywheel. While intended for high-performance applications, it is a much-used flywheel, long a member of the company's parts bins.

Suddenly, at an engine rpm of about 7500, the cast iron flywheel literally comes apart.

One section of flywheel travels upward from the engine, severing the oil, fuel, and electrical lines in one clean pass, leaving the room in total darkness. This same section of flywheel also jams the throttle in its wide-open position.

So what confronts the occupants of the room is an engine running at wide-open throttle with fuel and oil lines waving around in reckless abandon, spewing fuel and oil in all directions . . . in the dark. In short order, the engine expires in a flash of fire, illuminating the room only briefly, but long enough to cast a shadowed look at what has transpired in the darkness.

It's safe to assume this procedure was never adopted as a workable method for engine disassembly.

Jim MacFarland
Edelbrock

Oil Pan Removal

Roll the engine upside down. Remove the oil pan bolts. A socket, ratchet, and long extension work well for this job. Now carefully pry the pan from the block. The sticky pan gasket will require a strong pry at first. Pry in several areas, not all in the same spot. If you stick to the same spot, you will bend the oil pan. Clean up any oil spills.

Oil Pump Removal

Next, remove the oil pump. Many pumps have only one bolt attaching them to a main bearing cap or the block. Others have two or three. Often one bolt will be hidden inside the pickup screen. If, after removing all visible bolts, the pump will not come off, look under the screen. Gently pop the screen off the pickup. Small screwdrivers make good miniature pry bars. Look for a bolt head inside the pickup and lift the pump off.

The oil pump drive shaft should come out with the pump. If not, make sure you remove it from the block. Again, clean up any oil spills.

Front Cover Removal

Use an impact wrench to remove the front pulley nut. Try pulling the pulley or harmonic dampener off by hand. If it won't come off, use a puller. Use only a puller which attaches to the dampener's center section. If you pull on the outer ring, you can ruin the dampener.

Remove all the front cover bolts (Figure 15-27). Sometimes several pan bolts pass through the pan and into the front cover. You've already removed these.

Inside the front cover are the timing chain (gears or belt) and sprockets (Figure 15-28). There may be a chain tensioner. Other engines use an **oil slinger**, a flat disk with an upturned outer edge. It fits between the timing cover and crank sprocket. It keeps the front seal from receiving too much oil.

On OHC engines, slip off the oil slinger and then the belt. Often a puller is needed. When using a puller here, be sure to install the front pulley bolt. Run it in the crank several threads. Without the bolt, the

---

FIGURE 15-27 Typical OHV front cover components. (Buick Motor Division, GMC)

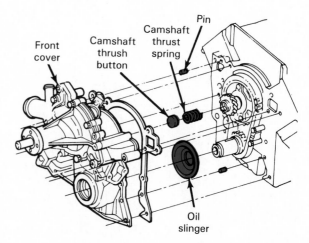

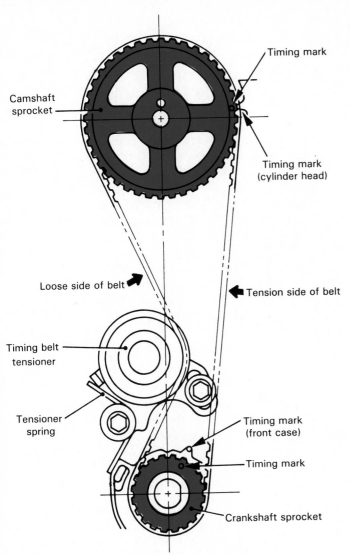

FIGURE 15-28 OHC timing belt and sprockets. (Chrysler Corporation)

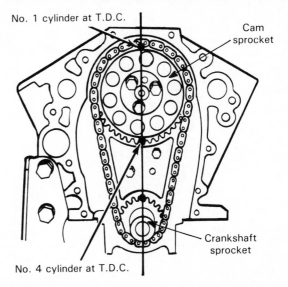

FIGURE 15-29 OHV cam chain alignment. (Buick Motor Division, GMC)

puller's shaft will damage the threads inside the crank.

Next, unbolt the tensioner. It may have a spring attached. Note which end attaches to the block and which to the tensioner. Some tensioners get their push from oil pressure. When you unbolt these, you'll find the plunger is spring loaded. Don't let the plunger pop out onto the floor.

Camshaft Removal

Start with the camshaft on overhead valve (OHV) engines (Figure 15-29). Remove any tensioner. Now unbolt the cam sprocket. There should be a dowel pin locating the sprocket. If not, index the sprocket to the camshaft with a hammer and punch. Before removing the sprocket, check for chain stretch and wear. Pull the sprocket off the cam. This will loosen the chain so it can be removed too.

Under the cam sprocket there may be a retaining plate. Unbolt the plate and set it aside. Now the cam can be pulled from the block. If there is no plate, just pull the cam out.

Pull the cam slowly. Don't bang the lobes against the block or cam bearings. If you are working on a bench, turning the block on end helps. With an engine stand, upside down is best.

To help get the cam started out of the block, run two bolts into the cam. Use the bolts as handles. If the cam still won't budge, look for a fuel pump or distributor drive still attached.

Pistons/Rod Removal

Go back to the crankcase. Rotate the crankcase until some of the rods are sticking straight up. This is bottom-dead-center (BDC) on those cylinders. If the crank is too stiff to move by hand, thread two flywheel bolts into the crank. Then use a pry bar lodged between the bolt shanks to rotate the crank.

Rod Numbering Inspect the rods before removing them. If you find numerals which correspond to the rod's position in the engine, fine (Figure 15-30). Factory-numbered rods are usually numbered on the side away from the camshaft. If not, mark the rods with a numbering set or punch. Stamp one number on the rod and a matching number on the cap. If you are using a punch, make one mark on rod number *one*, two on rod number *two*, and so on.

You may find numbers which don't seem to

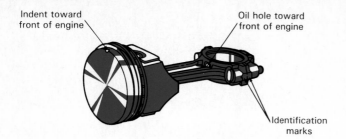

FIGURE 15-30 Connecting rod numbering. (Buick Motor Division, GMC)

match the rod's position in the engine. They don't. These numbers are for bearing sizes. They have nothing to do with where the rod goes in the engine. All Honda engines, very early Mercedes engines, and others use this system. If you don't understand the numbering system you find, make your own.

Rod Caps   Now unbolt the rod cap and pull it from the rod. Grasp the cap tightly and rock it slightly while pulling up. Very slight taps with a plastic or brass hammer are okay. Such blows will often help get a stubborn cap moving. Don't rely on hammer blows to remove the cap, though. A steady, slight rocking motion does the trick.

With the cap off, place a short length of fuel hose over the rod studs (Figure 15-31). If the rod uses removable bolts, this step is unnecessary. The hose keeps the studs from nicking the crank journals.

Pistons   Now push the piston and rod assembly out the top of the cylinder. Push with one hand and catch the assembly with the other. If you can't get your hand far enough inside the cylinder, use a hammer handle to extend your reach.

Before setting the piston and rod assembly aside, replace the cap. Run the nuts or bolts in a couple of threads. Replacing the cap keeps it from getting lost and protects it better.

Remove the remaining piston and rod assemblies. Rotate the crankshaft as necessary to get at the rod nuts.

FIGURE 15-31 Rod with journal-protecting hose.

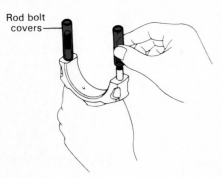

Crankshaft Removal

Main Bearing Caps   Only the main bearing caps remain holding the crankshaft. Check the caps for numbers. Stamp them if necessary. If caps do not have arrows indicating the front of the engine, mark to prevent reversing caps on reassembly. Then, with the engine still upside down, unbolt the main bearing caps. Like rod bearing caps, they can be difficult to remove. Start by tapping each one with a soft hammer (Figure 15-32). Try to wiggle it out of the block. If you aren't getting anywhere, try the wrench method. Place two open-end wrenches into the cap bolt holes. Now you have a handle, which gives you some leverage. Grasp the two wrenches in one hand and wiggle the cap side to side.

Some main bearing caps sit deeply in the block. This style of cap will need a front-to-rear motion to work it loose. Don't get overanxious with main bearing caps. It takes a little work to get them free. Use patience, not force.

Set the removed caps aside. Store their bolts in the main cap holes.

Crankshaft   The crank is now ready to lift out. Grasp the crank at each end and lift it straight up. If you do not lift it straight up, the crank will hang up in the block. Have a surface ready to set the crank on. Use a flat, stable spot. You don't want the crank rolled or knocked to the ground. Don't rest parts or tools against the crank. Hard objects like these can damage the journals.

Core Plugs

In the block and sometimes in the head, you will find core plugs. Although these plugs may look fine from the outside, you should remove them. Core plugs rust

FIGURE 15-32 Loosening main bearing caps.

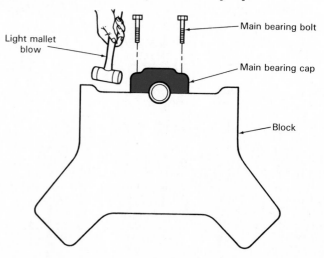

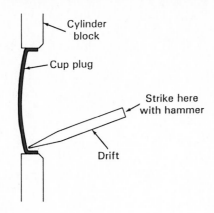

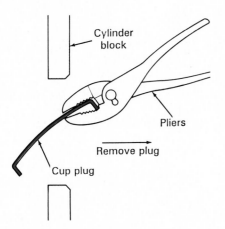

FIGURE 15-33 Core plug removal. (Chrysler Corporation)

from the inside. Therefore, only after a core plug is leaking will it look bad. Because core plugs are inexpensive, it is normal to replace them without hesitation during engine rebuilds.

Place a punch against one edge of the plug and hammer that edge in (Figure 15-33). The other edge will turn out of the block. Grasp this outturned edge with pliers and pry it from the block. Remove the remaining plugs. It is a good idea to save the plugs for comparison when selecting new ones.

Oil Passages

If an engine is very dirty, open the oil passages for cleaning. You will find socket or hex-headed plugs at the ends of each oil gallery. Remove these plugs.

Hex-headed plugs are easy. Simply put an Allen wrench on the hex and turn the plug out. Socket-headed plugs are a different story. First, clean *all* the dirt and grease out of the socket. You can then get a full grip on the hex. Next, use a socket drive Allen wrench. You have a lot more leverage through a ratchet and socket combination than through a standard Allen wrench.

If the socket still won't budge, use a hand impact driver. Several wallops will break the plug loose. Most plugs have pipe threads and are difficult to remove. Don't hesitate to use the impacter. It is better than rounding the hex with a lot of slow pulling. Clean up the work area of any oil or other fluids.

ALTERNATIVE DESIGNS

While the in-line and the V-engine are the most common, you will find other designs, especially in imported cars.

Horizontally Opposed

Certain Porsche, Volkswagen, and Subaru engines are good examples of horizontally opposed engines that you may have to tear down (Figure 15-34). There are several basic differences in removing and tearing down these engines. First, in Porsches and Volkswagens, you must drop the engine out from the bottom of the car. So the car must be raised high enough to clear the engine when it sits on the ground. The engine is separated from the transmission and lowered with a floor jack.

Strip all accessories, including the fan and air shrouding. Don't underestimate the importance of **air shrouds.** Proper cooling depends on correctly installed and sealed shrouds. It is vitally important for correct engine operation. As you disassemble the shrouds, or baffles, make a drawing so you know how all the pieces go back together. Remove the carburetor, fuel pump, and the like.

Remove the heads. They mount on long studs which extend out of the **case.** After pulling the heads, the **barrels**, or individual cylinders, will slip off the

FIGURE 15-34 Horizontally opposed engine. (Subaru)

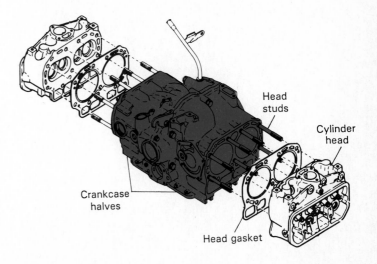

pistons. Remove the pistons from the rods by pushing the piston pins out of the pistons.

Split the case into its two halves. The crank and cam are now loose. You can now remove the rods from the crank.

You can leave the flywheel, clutch, and front pulley on the crank throughout the rebuild. If you want to remove them, which is recommended, do so before beginning disassembly.

Diesels

Diesel engines are no different from other piston engines when it comes to removal and teardown. However, some of the procedures are different.

Steel, high-pressure fuel lines with nutted connections run between the injection pump and the head.

Remove each line, remembering to cap every disconnection. Diesels use a mechanical injection system which must remain very clean. Leaving the fuel connections open is asking for expensive trouble. Also, treat the injection pump with respect. It is a precision part. Don't drop it, and keep it as clean as possible. Mark the pump relative to its mounting pad before removal. This mark speeds installation.

Diesel throttle linkages can be complicated. Disturb the linkage as little as possible. Ball and socket connections can be popped apart. Don't unthread the linkage's turnbuckle adjusters.

Diesels typically use lots of head bolts or studs. Make sure you've got them all out before trying to lift the head.

Finally, diesel oil is particularly black, smelly stuff. It will *permanently* stain anything it contacts. So wear old clothes around diesels.

TRADE TERMS

Air Shrouds
Ball Pivot
Barrels
Case
Engine Hoist
Floor Jack

Lockplates
Oil Slinger
Read
Ridge Reamer
Teardown

REVIEW QUESTIONS

1. What is the only safe tool you can use to support a raised car?
2. What is the first electrical disconnection you should make in engine removal? Why?
3. Can you disconnect an engine faster from an automatic transmission than a manual transmission?
4. After the engine is removed from the engine compartment, what should be used to support it?
5. How can you keep the engine from rotating while unbolting the front pulley or flywheel?
6. When draining an engine, why is it important to keep the work area clean?
7. Why is it important to mark the various parts when disassembling an engine?
8. What tool is used to remove the ridge from a cylinder?
9. Valve lifters must always be kept in order. True or false?
10. What indicates a leaking head gasket?

16

Inspection and Repair

INTRODUCTION

Measuring and machining engine parts are the most important parts of a rebuild. Unless you perform these steps accurately, the rest of your rebuild efforts will be wasted. Even the best disassembled, cleaned, and reassembled engine will not run well if wrong ring end gaps or oil clearances are machined into it.

This chapter tells how to inspect engine parts. It does not deal with accessories like the carburetor, clutch, flywheel, starter motor, alternator, and so on. These components are discussed in separate chapters.

CLEANING METHODS

All parts don't have the same cleaning requirements, so several ways of cleaning parts exist. Physical methods include bead blasting and manual removal. There are more chemical methods. You can solvent-blast, solvent-tank, hot-tank, cold-tank, and steam-clean parts.

227

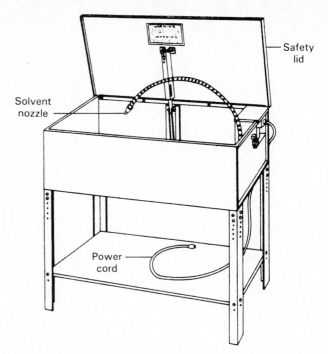

FIGURE 16-1   Solvent tank.

Physical Methods

Manual removal, as you might have guessed, is simply scraping off the heaviest deposits of dirt and grease. It is usually followed by some other cleaning. Bead blasting is done in a **bead blaster.** In the blaster, glass beads under high pressure are blown against the part by compressed air. Dirt is blown away by the multiple impacts of thousands of glass beads. If the part is oil-soaked, it is better to clean it chemically. Otherwise the glass will stick in the grease. The other disadvantage of the glass beading, as it is sometimes called, is that the powdery residue collects in bolt holes. Then it must be blasted out with compressed air. This isn't to say bead blasting isn't popular. It is widely used because it is quick and effective.

Chemical Methods

Of the chemical cleaners, the solvent tank is probably the most familiar (Figure 16-1). It is good for washing off most oily grit. Solvent blasting shoots solvent through a siphon gun with compressed air. It works very well when cleaning oily parts with complicated shapes. An all-around favorite in the machine shop is the **hot tank** (Figure 16-2). A large steel tank is filled with caustic solvents. They are much stronger than normal solvent. Additionally, the tank is heated. Parts are lowered into the tank on a tray so they won't splash the dangerous chemicals. Always wear eye protection and gloves when inserting or removing parts. A few minutes in the tank and parts come out clean to the bare metal. Paint, gasket sealers, and rubber are no match for a hot tank; neither are aluminum and other soft metals. Cam, rod, and main bearings will all dissolve in a hot tank, so they are always removed before tanking. Besides destroying the part, the dissolved bearing dilutes the expensive hot tank solution.

FIGURE 16-2   Hot tank cleaner.

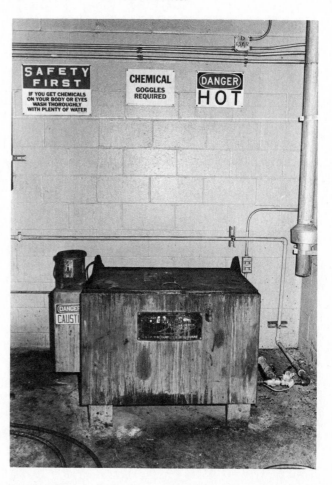

A variation of the hot tank is the **jet tank.** The idea is the same, except the parts are placed on a turntable while hot solvents or hot water are sprayed at high pressure. Jet tanks have become very popular because they work quickly.

To clean aluminum heads, carburetors, and other soft metal parts, a **cold tank** is used. You might know this as carburetor cleaner. A less caustic solvent fills the cold tank. No heat is used, hence the name, and parts are usually left submerged for hours.

After all these chemical baths the parts are washed with high-pressure water. Sometimes they are steam-cleaned—which is boiling hot water sprayed at high pressure. Sometimes a cleaner is added to the steam. When steam cleaning, always wear gloves and eye protection.

INSPECTION METHODS

Visual

The most common inspection method is *visual*. Combined with experience, a good visual inspection is often enough to determine if a part is worth keeping. A good visual inspection means keeping your mind open as well as your eyes. Concentrate on what you see; let your eyes tell you what has happened to the part. Use sunlight, a drop light, a magnifying glass, mirrors, and whatever else it takes to inspect the part completely. A good time to inspect a part is during cleaning. This is why many good mechanics won't let anyone else clean parts they wish to inspect.

Magnafluxing

On ferrous parts, magnafluxing will expose surface cracks. After cleaning, the area to be tested is sprinkled with metal powder. A strong magnet is then placed against the part. With a little tapping, the powder will align itself with the lines of magnetic force. If a surface crack exists, it will interrupt the magnetic lines, and the powder will cluster around the crack. After testing, the powder is returned to its container for reuse.

Dye Penetrant

Nonferrous parts, usually aluminum, can be tested for surface cracks with dye penetrant. The tested area is cleaned; then dye is sprayed on. The dye is tinted a bright color so it will show up. After several moments the dye is wiped off, and developer is sprayed on. If there is a crack, the dye trapped in the crack's recesses will stand out against the white developer.

Ultrasonic Testing

One shortcoming of both magnafluxing and dye penetrant testing is their inability to "see" past the surface of a part. Ultrasonic testing solves the problem by inspecting a part with sound waves. This procedure is not part of normal machine shop procedures, but it is available if an expensive part is suspected of internal cracking. Ultrasonic testers are considered to be a one-sided micrometer. They can check the thickness of metal from one side.

ACCESSORY INSPECTION AND REPAIR

During disassembly and after the parts have been cleaned, all parts should be inspected. After an inspection, judgment will be needed to determine if the part should be replaced or repaired.

Intake and Exhaust Manifold

Clean the intake and exhaust manifolds as necessary with solvent. Bead-blast the intake manifold. If it is a V-type manifold, make sure the exhaust crossover is clear. Exhaust manifolds usually don't need much cleaning because they run so hot they burn off any dirt that gets on them. Check all exhaust studs and bolts though. Exhaust heat and gases cause the threads on fasteners to corrode. If the threads are worn or corroded, replace the fasteners. Inspect the manifolds for cracks and water corrosion. Scrape off all gaskets.

Because they are nonmoving parts, manifolds rarely need more than cleaning. If cracked, welding or replacement is necessary.

If there is a sheet-metal oil shield under the V-type intake manifold, remove it so you can clean the baked-on oil and dirt underneath (Figure 16-3).

Sheet-Metal Parts

Typical sheet-metal parts are the oil pan, front cover, bell-housing dust cover, rocker covers, and side covers. Bead-blast or hot-tank them as necessary. Don't forget the oil separator in the rocker cover. Remove it and swish it out with solvent.

Visually inspect for cracks. Then check all mating surfaces. To seal, these surfaces must be flat. Pressure from the mounting bolts deforms mating surfaces until they look like a washboard. Flatten them again with

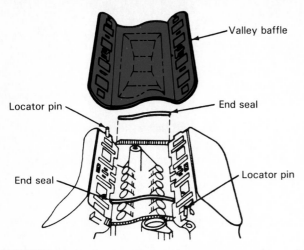

FIGURE 16-3 Removing oil shield from under V-type intake manifold for cleaning. (Ford Motor Company)

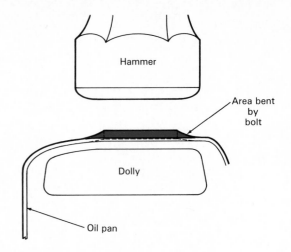

FIGURE 16-4 Flattening pan rails.

a hammer and dolly (Figure 16-4). Support the backside of the surface with a metal dolly. To reach into tight pan rails, you'll need a flat-nose drift punch. Tap the other side with a hammer until flat. The larger your dolly—the drift, anvil, or other metal surface—the faster it will go.

The front cover holds an oil seal for the crankshaft. Change this seal by knocking it out with a hammer and tapping in a new one. Support the cover with two pieces of wood, so the seal has room to push out. Select a socket which is almost the seal's outside diameter (OD) but still smaller than the hole in the timing cover. Set the socket against the seal and then tap it until the seal falls out. Flip the front cover over, clean the seal mating area, and then install the new seal. Begin by coating the seal's OD with nonhardening sealer; some seals will have a sealer from the manufacturer. Set the seal in the timing cover and then tap it in with a seal driver. Use light taps; you must not deform the seal, or it will leak. The hardest part is starting the seal. If it turns sideways at first, don't drive it any farther. Reposition it and try again until you get it to go in straight. Once the seal bottoms,

you'll hear a difference. The cover will "bonk" and not "ring."

BLOCK INSPECTION AND REPAIR

Begin cast iron block overhaul by hot-tanking it. Remove any cam bearings (Figure 16-5) and core plugs first. It is a good idea to note the locations of oil holes before removal. If the block is aluminum, solvent-blast or cold-tank it.

Visually inspect the block for cracks, old welded repairs, and such. If the block passes visual inspection, go over it with a smooth file, making sure there are no burrs or high spots on any mating surfaces. These areas would include the mating surface, main bearing registers, and all accessory mounting pads.

Cylinder Bores

In-depth block inspection begins with the cylinder bores because they wear out first. Several things can be wrong with the cylinders. They can have **taper**, and be **out-of-round.** The bores could have shifted,

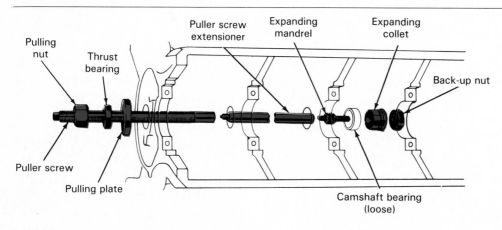

FIGURE 16-5 Screw-type camshaft bearing tool. (Ford Motor Company)

and there could be core shift (Figures 16-6 and 16-7).

Taper   Taper refers to the shape a cylinder wears into (Figure 16-6). Remember the ridge at the top of the cylinder? Well, toward the bottom of the cylinder where the rings do not rub, the cylinder is still its original diameter, and there is no ridge, because bore wear comes from the rings, and the rings push against the cylinder walls due to combustion pressures. These pressures are greatest near the top of the cylinder and less toward the bottom. One reason is because there is more heat and less lubrication near the top. Taper, then, is the normal wear pattern for a cylinder.

The amount of taper determines how worn the cylinder is. Measure taper directly with a bore gauge (Figure 16-8). First, measure the cylinder at its bottom. Then measure right under the ridge, in the area of maximum wear. Take several measurements, varying the gauge's position to make sure you get the maximum dimension. Now subtract the smallest measurement from the largest. The difference is **bore taper.**

Look in the shop manual to determine maximum allowable taper.

Out-of-Round   Because of connecting rod geometry and temperature differences in the cylinder wall, the

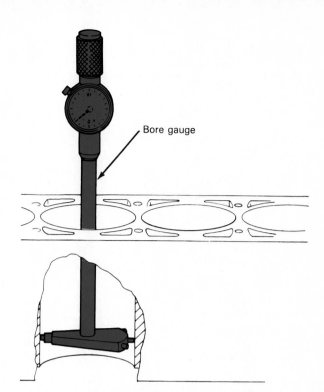

FIGURE 16-8   Measuring taper with a bore gauge. (American Motors Corporation)

cylinder can wear out-of-round. This just means the bore wears into an egg shape. If this is the case, there will be a ridge that is deeper where the egg shape is most pronounced.

Measure out-of-round with an inside micrometer. Take measurements just under the ridge, in several directions, but all at the same level. The difference between the smallest and largest diameters is out-of-round. Consult the shop manual for maximum allowable out-of-round.

The need to bore a cylinder is based heavily on taper. Therefore, you might not find a listing for out-of-round in the shop manual. If so, take any out-of-round into consideration when deciding on how much to bore. What out-of-round really does is move the center of the cylinder. To get the cylinder round again, you'll have to bore the cylinder at least to maximum out-of-round. More metal is removed from one side of the cylinder than the other, restoring the cylinder's center to its original position.

Core Shift   If the cylinders are badly worn or have been bored before, core shift could be a problem. Core shift is a manufacturing flaw. If a core which forms the cylinder is slightly out of alignment when the block is cast, you might bore into the water jacket before you notice. The only way to find out the core has shifted is cutting through it or testing with an ultrasonic tester. There isn't anything to do about it, except to get another block. Luckily, core shift is rare.

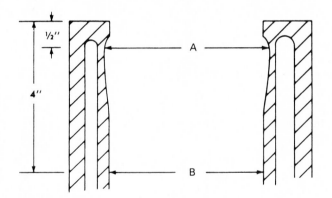

FIGURE 16-6   Normal cylinder wear taper pattern. (Chevrolet Motor Division, GMC)

FIGURE 16-7   Cylinder wear to out-of-round shape.

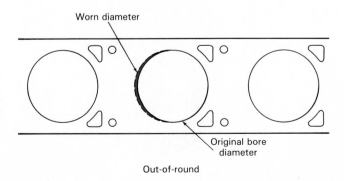

Worn diameter

Original bore diameter

Out-of-round

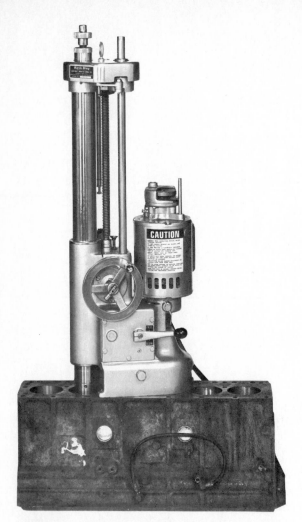

FIGURE 16-9 Boring a block. (Owatonna Tool Company)

FIGURE 16-10 Honing a cylinder with a precision hone. (American Honda Motor Co., Inc.)

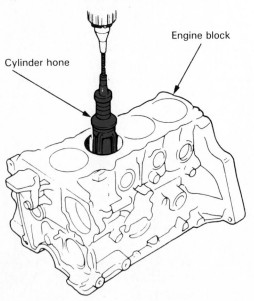

Cylinder hone

Engine block

BORING

To restore a cylinder, bore it to the proper **overize.** The **boring bar** uses a hard steel bit to cut metal from the cylinder wall (Figure 16-9). The final few thousandths of an inch are left uncut. They are removed by **honing** (Figure 16-10).

Oversize refers to bore diameters larger than stock. Typically, oversizes are 0.010, 0.020, 0.030, and 0.040 in. Larger engines may be bored to 0.030 and 0.060 in. Sometimes slight oversizes are used, 0.001 and 0.002 in., when a cylinder needs a little honing. Practically speaking, oversizes are governed by what size pistons are available. The same size oversize piston must be used to match the cylinder. Thus, if a block could clean up with 0.010 in. cut from the cylinders but pistons are only available in 0.030 in. sizes, you'll have to bore to the larger size.

The boring bar is the machine which cuts the cylinders. It leaves a truly round hole with a very smooth finish.

Honing

Honing gives the cylinder walls the proper finish. A perfectly smooth cylinder wall is not desired. Instead, a slightly rough finish is used. It holds oil to lubricate and seal the rings. Different ring types have different oiling requirements. Chrome rings are very smooth and need lots of oil on the cylinder wall. Therefore, they are finished with a rough, 280-grit hone. Moly rings have an oil-carrying surface and don't need much oil on the cylinder wall. They use a 400-grit hone.

Very important to a good hone job is the **crosshatch** (Figure 16-11). As the hone moves up and down

FIGURE 16-11 Bore crosshatch marks. (Chrysler Corporation)

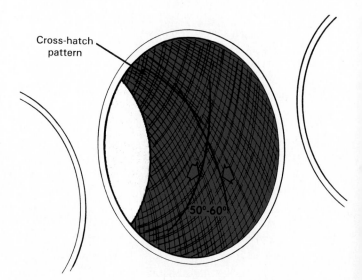

Cross-hatch pattern

50°-60°

in the cylinder, it scratches the cylinder with continuous lines. Because the hone is moving up and down, the lines intersect at angles. The proper angle for all grits is 60°. You can vary the angle by varying the up-and-down speed of the hone.

Shaft Bores

Like cylinders, the crankshaft, camshaft, and balancing shaft bores wear out-of-round and taper. Additionally, there is **bore alignment** to consider.

None of the shaft bores wear anywhere near as fast as the cylinder bores. Camshaft and balancing shaft bores wear even less than the crankshaft bores. This is due to the lack of side loads.

Measure out-of-round and taper with an inside micrometer. If you don't have a micrometer that small, use a snap gauge (telescoping gauge) and outside micrometer.

Out-of-Round   Remove all bearing inserts and torque the main bearing caps to specification. With cam and balancing shafts, merely remove the bearings. Measure out-of-round by measuring the diameter in several places and finding the largest diameter. The differences between largest and smallest diameters is the out-of-round. Remember to keep the micrometer in the same plane during all measurments.

Taper   Taper is found by measuring the bearing bore from front to rear. The difference between large and small dimensions is taper. Check your findings against the specifications in the shop manual.

Alignment   Next check the alignment of the shaft bores in relation to each other. If one of the bores is worn, its center will not be in alignment with the other bores. Measure align bore with a precision straightedge laid in the bearing bore. If a thin feeler gauge can slip under the straightedge, that bore is out of alignment. Or a special dial indicator can be used. Align specs are given in the shop manual.

The solution for out-of-round and taper is align boring and align honing. Use align boring, with cutting or boring bits, for heavy wear problems. Use align honing, with abrasive stones, if wear is not great. The main bearing caps are ground on their mating surface. Then the trimmed caps are bolted to the block, making grossly out-of-round main bearing bores. The block is fitted into an align hone machine, and a special hone is passed through all of the main bearing bores at once. Each bore is honed in exact alignment with the others until all are perfectly round.

No service procedures exist for cam and balancing shaft bores because they rarely need service. Replacement is the only cure. Only on OHC heads will cam bore alignment be a problem. If the head is badly warped, the cam bores may pull out of align. Although the warp can be milled from the head's mating surface, the cam bores cannot be align-honed. The head must be replaced.

Decks

The head mating surface on a block is called the **deck.** It must be flat to seal with the head. Most often any warpage is found in the head, but in extreme cases the deck can be warped.

Warpage   To check for warpage, you'll need a precision straightedge and feeler gauges. Clean the deck of any burrs, carbon deposits, gasket material, and so on. Then lay the straightedge across the deck and try to pass a thin feeler gauge between the deck and straightedge (Figure 16-12). Where the feeler gauge slips under the straightedge is where the deck is "low." Find the thickest feeler gauge which will pass under the straightedge. This is the amount of warpage. Look in the shop manual for the maximum allowable warpage.

FIGURE 16-12   Checking a deck for flatness with a precision straightedge. (American Honda Motor Co., Inc.)

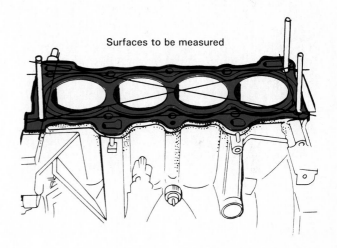

Surfaces to be measured

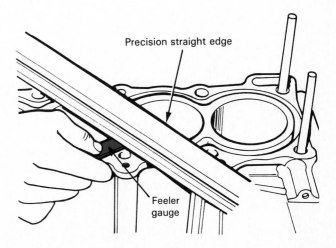

Precision straight edge

Feeler gauge

FIGURE 16-13 Surface grinding the deck of a V8 block. (Repco Corporation Ltd.)

Milling If a deck is warped, it can be cut in a special mill. If one deck of a V-type engine is cut, the other deck must be cut. If the decks, or heads, on a V-type engine are cut a lot, the intake manifold may need cutting because its mating angle with the heads will have changed. How much you can cut from the decks and manifold can sometimes be found in manuals, but usually it's a number derived from trial and error and past experience (Figure 16-13).

Threads

Final block work involves chasing threads. Chasing means running a tap through a bolt hole and blowing out the residue with compressed air (Figure 16-14). Make sure the tap is the correct one for the threads you are chasing.

The tap may bind as it cleans. Whenever the tap begins to bind, back it out one turn and then resume

FIGURE 16-14 Chasing threads. (Greenfield Tap & Die)

cleaning. Backing the tap allows dirt to collect in the flutes and get out of the threads. To get at the threads in the very bottom of a hole, you'll need a bottoming tap.

After chasing the threads, move the tap and blow out the hole with compressed air. Use a rag draped over the hole to capture flying debris. Wear eye protection, and caution any bystanders.

Cleaning

After all machine work is complete, the block must be cleaned to remove any machining residue. If a jet or hot tank is available, use it. If not, wash the block with water and detergent. Scrub the cylinder walls and bearing bores. Gun cleaning brushes are excellent for cleaning oil passages.

After cleaning, thoroughly rinse the block and blow it dry with compressed air. Wipe the cylinders with paper towels. If any dirt comes off, rewash the block. Use paper towels instead of linty cloth rags. The lint can clog oil passages, while paper towels dissolve in oil, so their lint poses no problem.

When dry, spray the block with oil and then cover it with a plastic bag. This keeps dust from sticking to the oiled metal.

CRANKSHAFT

Like other engine parts, clean the crankshaft before inspecting it. A solvent blast should be fine if the engine was clean. Burned-on oil deposits are better dissolved by placing it in a hot tank. In either case, clean the crank's oil passages. Gun cleaning brushes or pipe cleaners handle this job well.

Crankshaft Wear

Normal crankshaft wear comes in three varieties: out-of-round, taper, and undersize. Out-of-round is the egg shape a journal can take on when viewed on end.

Taper is the slope worn into the sides of a journal when viewed from the side (Figure 16-15). Undersize is an even wearing down of the journal's circumference.

Out-of-Round All three types of wear are found with an outside micrometer or a dial gauge. Out-of-round is found by measuring around the journal in the same plane. Subtract the smaller diameter from the larger to find out-of-round.

Taper Taper can be found by measuring the journal at one end. Move over 1 in. and remeasure (Figure 16-16). Subtract the smaller measurement from the larger. The difference is the taper. It is expressed as X in./in.

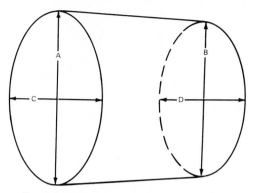

A vs B = vertical taper
C vs D = horizontal taper
A vs C and B vs D = out of round

Check for out-of-round at each end of journal

FIGURE 16-15 Crankshaft taper and out-of-round measurements. (Ford Motor Company)

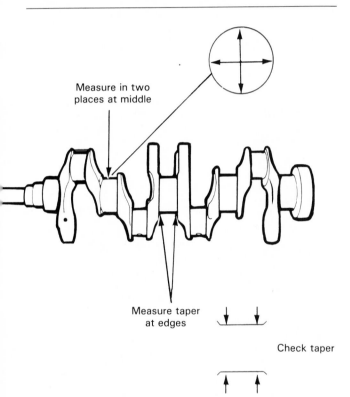

Measure in two places at middle

Measure taper at edges

Check taper

FIGURE 16-16 Measuring taper and out-of-round. (American Honda Motor Co., Inc.)

Undersize Undersize will be found when checking for out-of-round and taper. If the journal is smaller than listed yet there is no out-of-round or taper, the journal is undersize.

Scoring Another form of normal wear will be the general light scratching of the journals. This is called **scoring** and results from dirty oil etching the crank. Abnormal wear results when a large piece of dirt or

metal goes through the oil system and deeply scores the crank.

Grinding Grinding a crankshaft is the remedy for all these problems: out-of-round, taper, undersize, and scoring. A special grinding wheel is used to remove part of the journal. All journals are ground until they are evenly undersize in increments of 0.010 in. Thus, a crank could be ground 0.010, 0.020, 0.030, or 0.040 in. Generally the larger the crank, the more metal you can safely remove. No more than necessary is removed, however, as removing metal weakens the crank.

The rod journals must all be ground even if there is only one bad journal. All mains are ground if one or more is bad. The rods are ground independently of the mains and vice versa. The rods could be ground 0.020 and the mains 0.010 in. or any combination necessary.

Hardening A few crankshafts have a special hardened surface. After grinding, this surface must be replaced by chemical treatment. This is a job for specialists, but you should be aware that Tuftrided, nitrited or cold-quenched surfaces must be renewed after grinding.

Polishing Also after grinding the journals are *polished*. Polishing is like honing the cylinders—it provides the proper oil-carrying finish. A 320-grit cloth is wrapped around a journal and worked shoeshine fashion. Machine shops have a special tool which polishes the crank while it rotates in a lathe. It, too, uses a belt of 320-grit cloth.

If a crankshaft does not need grinding, it should be polished to restore the proper finish.

Welding Abnormal crankshaft wear occurs when the bearings are oil starved (Figure 16-17). Then large amounts of metal are scored away. The journals are beyond grinding limits. They must be built up with welding and then ground to a standard diameter. For most production car work, welding and grinding are more expensive than replacement. Thus this procedure is saved for high-performance and expensive heavy-duty crankshafts.

Thrust Wear One area you should check, but not expect to find appreciable wear, is the crank's thrust area. This is the area rubbed by the thrust bearings. Under abnormal conditions this area can be wiped away so even new thrust bearings won't bring crankshaft end play within specs. This problem is solved by welding or replacement. Usually thrust wear is confined to the bearings, so replacing them will restore end play to within limits.

Harmonic Balancer There isn't much to do to a harmonic balancer, but there are a couple of things you

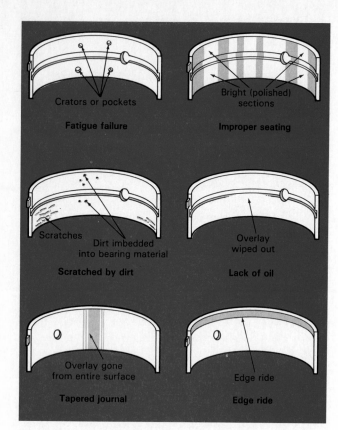

FIGURE 16-17   Bearing wear. (Ford Motor Company)

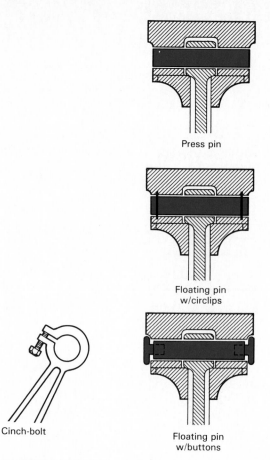

FIGURE 16-18   Pin attachments.

should not do. Because the balancer has a rubber ring holding the outer metal band to the inner, you cannot subject the balancer to anything which harms rubber. Otherwise the balancer may fail later while running on the engine. Don't hot-tank or heat a balancer. If you must tap a balancer with a hammer, do so on the inner metal section only.

As for service, solvent-clean the balancer and check for cracks.

PISTONS AND RODS

The first decision to make about the piston and rod assembly is whether or not to remove the piston from the rod. If you know the cylinders are being bored, remove the pistons. New ones are required to match the oversize bores, so throw away the old pistons. If the bores are being reused, perhaps the pistons can be too. Leave them on the rods for now. Also inspect for loose, worn piston pins and bushings. If, after inspecting them, you find the pistons need replacement, remove them and install new ones.

Piston Removal

Several methods are used to retain the piston and its pin to the connecting rod (Figure 16-18). **Press pins**

fit loosely in the piston but have an interference fit in the rod. The pin must be pressed on and off the rod. **Floating pins** fit loosely in both piston and rod. They are retained with **buttons** or circlips at each end of the pin. A pin button is a rounded piece of soft material. Aluminum or Teflon are common, which rides directly against the cylinder wall. A **cinch pin** is used in a rod equipped with a bolt passed through the rod's small end. The small end is split on these rods so it can expand and contract with the bolt's tension. The pin is passed through the piston and rod, and then the bolt is tightened, pinching the pin in place. These are seldom used in modern engines.

Press Pins   To separate a press pin, you must have a press (Figure 16-19). Support the piston with a piston pin fixture (mandrel) which allows the pin to pass by as it exits the piston. Then press the pin out while supporting the rod. Otherwise it might fall and be damaged. Never hammer on a press pin. You will only destroy the pin, piston, and rod.

Floating Pins   Floating pins will just slip apart if they have buttons. With circlips you must first remove the clips and then slide the pin out. Unbolting the cinch bolt will allow the pin to slide out in that type of installation.

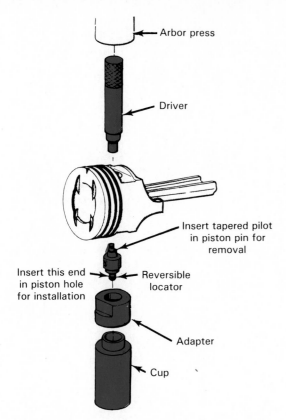

FIGURE 16-20 Ring expander. (American Honda Motor Co., Inc.)

FIGURE 16-19 Pressing piston pins. (Ford Motor Company)

Ring Removal

Remove the rings for piston inspection. Use a ring expander to remove the old rings (Figure 16-20). The ring expander assures against scratching the piston. If you do not have a ring expander, grasp the end of the ring in your thumbs and spread it wide enough to pass over the piston. Take care not to scratch the piston with the ring's ends.

Piston Cleaning

Crown Now remove all carbon from the piston. Use a wire wheel on the crown, but be careful not to let it touch the piston's sides. Using a wire wheel on the piston's sides will round off the ring lands and result in poor ring sealing. Really stubborn carbon on the crown should be chipped away and then wire-wheeled.

Grooves Use a ring groove cleaner to clean the ring grooves (Figure 16-21). Go lightly but get all the carbon out. Also clean the oil slots or holes.

Inspection As you clean the grooves, visually inspect the pistons for damage (Figure 16-22). If the crown shows lots of small indentations like it has been sandblasted, it has been overheated. The pock marks are caused when the piston crown begins melting. Typi-

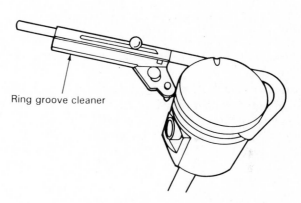

FIGURE 16-21 Ring groove cleaner. (Ford Motor Company)

cally, this damage results from preignition or detonation. If there is no other damage, the piston can be reused. But keep in mind that that piston has been severely heated.

Inspect the skirts for **scuffing** and scoring, usually caused by overheating or lack of lubrication. Scuffing describes the abrasion damage a piston suffers after rubbing against the cylinder wall. Scoring is like scuffing, except there are several large gouges, not many little ones. Some wear is normal but should be confined to a small patch on the lower skirts. If a skirt is cracked, the piston must be replaced. Also, skirt wear should be even side to side. If it isn't, the connecting rod is bent.

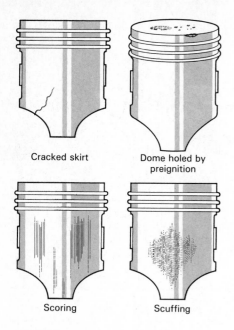

Cracked skirt

Dome holed by preignition

Scoring

Scuffing

FIGURE 16-22 Piston wear.

Piston Measurements

Measure the piston's skirts with an outside micrometer (Figure 16-23). The skirts should be approximately 0.0005 in. (0.0127 mm) wider at their bottoms than at their tops. If they aren't, the skirt has collapsed. A piston skirt collapses when it has been overheated. Extreme heat causes the piston skirt to expand against the cylinder wall. If the piston gets hot enough, the skirts will expand until it is reshaped by the cylinder.

FIGURE 16-23 Measuring piston skirt. (American Honda Motor Co., Inc.)

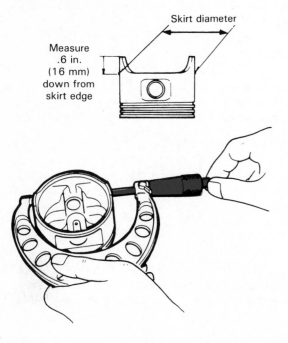

Skirt diameter

Measure .6 in. (16 mm) down from skirt edge

Ultimately the skirts will crack. Even before they crack, though, the collapsed skirt has permanently lost its shape.

Collapsed pistons have poor oil control, make noise, and accelerate cylinder wall wear.

Ring Groove Wear

Typically, the upper compression ring groove wears faster than the lower compression ring or oil ring grooves. Visually inspect the ring grooves for wavy edges. If no damage is visible, measure to be certain (Figure 16-24).

Slip a new compression ring into the ring groove. Then find the feeler gauge or a go-no go gauge which just fits between the ring and the ring land. This is the ring's side clearance. Rotate the piston so you can measure the entire ring groove. If the feeler gauge binds anywhere in the groove, you know that part of the groove is tighter than the rest. Either the groove is not worn at that point or has been compressed. Compare your measurement with the engine's specifications. If you don't know the specification, use 0.005 in. (0.137 mm).

Proper side clearance is very important to effective ring sealing. If the ring grooves are damaged, replace the piston. If the upper groove is worn, a special lathe can cut the groove wider. Inserts are then fitted between ring and groove to take up the gap.

Pin Bore

Inspect the piston's pin bore after removing the piston from its connecting rod. Shiny wear spots in the pin bore mark the high-wear points. Use a snap gauge and outside micrometer to measure the pin bore diameter. Compare your findings against the engine's specifications. Usually a pin bore will wear into an egg shape if it wears at all. If specifications are exceeded, replace

FIGURE 16-24 Measuring ring side clearance. (Mazda of North America, Inc.)

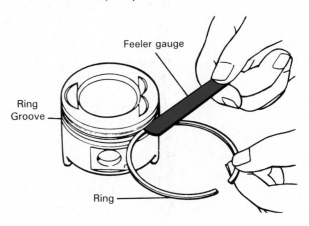

Feeler gauge

Ring Groove

Ring

the piston or use an oversized piston pin and hone the piston rod for the oversized pin.

Replacement pistons usually come with new pins. This assures the proper dimensions between pin and piston. If new pins do not come with the piston, order them separately.

Piston-to-Cylinder Clearance

Feeler Gauges One way to measure piston-to-cylinder wall clearance is with feeler gauges (Figure 16-25). Insert the piston to be tested into its cylinder. It is easiest to insert the piston upside down and hold onto the pin or connecting rod. The piston pin must be parallel to the crankshaft. Now find the feeler gauge which fits between the cylinder and piston skirt, 90° from the pin. The feeler gauge's thickness is the piston-to-cylinder wall clearance.

Micrometers A better way to measure piston fit is with inside and outside micrometers or a bore gauge. First measure the piston at several places and write down the size. Then measure the inside diameter of the cylinder at several places. By subtracting the piston size from the bore size you can find the clearance (Figure 16-26).

Knurling If the clearance exceeds the service limit,

FIGURE 16-26 Measuring piston-to-cylinder clearance with bore gauge and micrometer. (General Motors Corporation)

bore the cylinders and install oversize pistons. If the clearance is very close, pistons can be **knurled** to close the gap. This process embosses a pattern into the side of the piston, raising ridges which increase the piston diameter. Knurling is a short-term solution and should be used only when new pistons cannot be installed.

Connecting Rods

Connecting rod service covers four areas of rod construction: small end, beam on shank, big end, and bolts.

Small End Small end service consists of measuring the pin bore for out-of-round. For press-fit pin and rod combinations, no measuring is needed unless motion is detected while rocking the rod against the pin.

Floating rods are measured with a snap gauge and micrometer. Also mike the pin's outside diameter. Sometimes replacing the pin will reduce clearance to under the service limit.

Restoring the small end inside diameter (ID) is done several ways. Some rods must be replaced. Others have a bushing which can be replaced, or nonbushed rods can be bored oversize and a bushing pressed in.

FIGURE 16-25 Measuring piston-to-cylinder clearance with a feeler gauge. (General Motors Corporation)

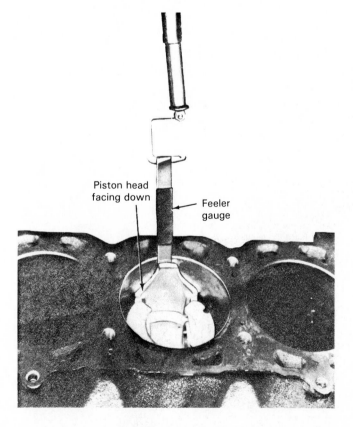

Piston head facing down

Feeler gauge

Beam There isn't much you can do with the rod's beam, or shank. Inspect it for cracks or magnaflux it in heavy-duty applications. Replace any cracked rods.

Big End Most rod service happens at the big end. Out-of-round is the major problem (Figure 16-27). Measure for it with an inside mike, snap gauges, or a dial bore gauge.

Restoring big end roundness is done by **reconditioning** or **sizing.** Reconditioning is done on a special machine using a precision hone. A dial-indicating fixture shows how much honing is required. First the rod cap's mating surface is ground in a special fixture. Then the cap is torqued onto the rod and honed. By

FIGURE 16-27 Big end out of round on connecting rod. (Repco Corporation Ltd.)

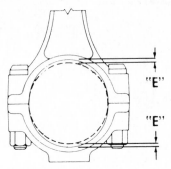

(a) Connecting bore (broken line) has expanded due to heavy stress during service.

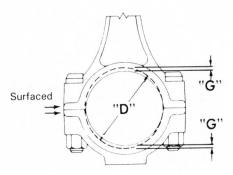

(b) After surfacing of the connecting rod and cap flange surfaces, the con rod bore shows an undersize in ther vertical dimension.

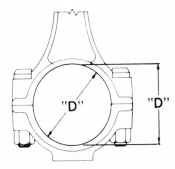

(c) After honing, the bore is again round and guarantees trouble free seating of the bearing shells.

grinding the cap, the big end is made very out-of-round. The hone then restores the big end's inside diameter to the original diameter and roundness. Grinding some material off the cap to start with ensures the hone will cut into fresh material around the entire circumference.

Bolts Rod bolts stretch as they fatigue. In critical applications bolt length is specified so it can be measured with a micrometer. Most of the time rod bolts are merely visually inspected and returned to service. Under these conditions, let rod big end condition guide you. If the big ends were badly out-of-round, then the bolts have probably taken a beating. Replace them. Also, some engines are known rod bolt breakers. Typically they are small-displacement, high-rpm power plants. The rpm is what strains the connecting rods in general and the bolts in particular. These bolts get changed without question.

Use new rod bolt nuts with new bolts. New nuts are also called for when the originals have been rounded off by impact guns or repeated wrenching.

Piston and Rod Assembly

After servicing, the rods and pistons are assembled. Use the shop manual to orient the pistons correctly with the rods (Figure 16-28). A mark on the piston crown needs to be aligned with the rod. Aftermarket pistons will have directions packaged with the pistons.

Depending on the piston pin style, you have your choices of assembly procedure. Floating pins are oil-lubed and assembled. Slip the buttons or circlips in place.

Press-fit pins can be assembled two ways. First, they can be moly-lubed and pressed together, the reverse of disassembly. Or the small end of the rod can be heated, which allows the pin to slide into place by hand. This last technique provides superior assem-

FIGURE 16-28 Typical piston/rod relationship.

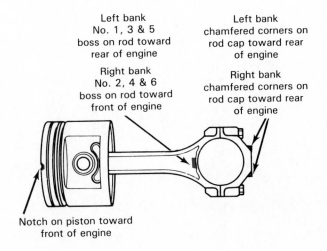

Left bank
No. 1, 3 & 5
boss on rod toward
rear of engine

Left bank
chamfered corners on
rod cap toward rear
of engine

Right bank
No. 2, 4 & 6
boss on rod toward
front of engine

Right bank
chamfered corners on
rod cap toward rear
of engine

Notch on piston toward
front of engine

blies but requires experience and skill. Done "manu-ally," the rods are heated with a torch. Electric rod heaters are common in machine shops, however, and they take lots of the guesswork out of this job.

Rod Alignment

After the rod and piston assembly is fully serviced and assembled, the rod is checked for alignment. Normal service can bend or twist the connecting rod. These unwanted bends can be safely bent out as long as the rod is not heated during bending.

Two fixtures are used for checking rod alignment. One supports the big end at one end and the piston at the other. A vernier-like scale is mounted next to the piston's support. If the rod is not straight, the scale's markings will not line up. The other tool uses a vertical plate, ground flat (Figure 16-29). The piston assembly is placed upright in the fixture and passed by the plate. By watching for light to pass by the piston's holder, the mechanic can see any misalignment.

Out-of-line rods are straightened with a large pry bar. It takes experience to know how much force to apply, but the rod can be safely bent until the rod is aligned.

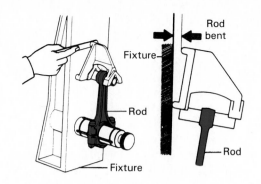

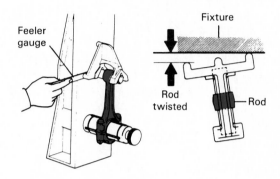

FIGURE 16-29 Aligning a rod with a special rod-aligning fixture.

"JUST GIVE IT A SPIN, OKAY?"

A high-performance engineering company (Edelbrock) once owned and maintained a flat-bottom racing hull fitted with one of the now defunct Chrysler 392 c.i.d. V8 hemispherical combustion chamber engines.

It was 1966, near the end of the season, and the boat was tied for second place in the national standings. No races could be skipped unless the engine required major surgery. To prevent a complete disassembly of the engine, once the engine was removed from the boat, it was mounted onto an engine stand and turned upside down, and the oil pan was removed.

Next, with the oil pan removed, each connecting rod cap was carefully un-torqued and removed and the crank-shaft rod journal and bearing halves inspected for signs of wear before parts were replaced. It was believed, and successfully so, that this method could detect early bearing or crank surface

failure. It also eliminated a complete disassembly of the engine.

On this particular Saturday night, following a long day of racing and towing back to the facility, two employees were alone in the shop. Picture the engine's exhaust system; single, upturned pipes, fondly named "zoomies," that represented the most popular design of the times. To keep stray material from dropping into these otherwise open pipes, soft rubber balls were stuffed into the open ends of the pipes. Since such a bearing checking procedure is tedious and it was late at night, these two employees soon became exhausted. Keep in mind that other than having removed the oil pan, the remainder of the engine was intact.

The procedure was to rotate the engine by hand, using a socket on the crank snout. As each rod was checked and its cap retorqued, the engine was hand-rotated to the next rod in sequence.

Nearing the end of the job, they rotated the engine with a quick motion of the wrench, causing the rubber ball for that particular cylinder to "pop" out of the pipe with a startling bang. Much amused, the mechanic repeated the act again for the next rod.

With only one rod remaining, his final tug on the wrench spun the crank a little more quickly . . . and to the amazement of them both, the engine *started*! In their haste neither of them had thought to put a ground wire on the magneto. And while the engine only ran for about 3 sec, it was sufficient time for two mechanics to become very alert, placing themselves several dozen feet from the gasping hemi. You may assume reassembly of the engine was performed more carefully.

Jim MacFarland
Edelbrock

CAMSHAFT

Often camshaft wear can be detected during a visual inspection. Start with the lobes, then any gears, and finish with the journals.

Lobes

The lobes are the camshaft's working surfaces (Figure 16-30). They are subject to very high pressures from the valve springs and can wear very quickly. Often the lobes will not wear out in thousands of miles. Then one will completely wear out in 1000 mi. Therefore, when you encounter cam lobe wear, it is usually severe.

Hold the camshaft so light reflects off the lobes. The light should reflect evenly, without sharp separations. Run a finger over the lobe. Again, no sharp separations should be felt. The entire lobe should be one smooth radius. If the cam fails these tests, replace it.

Gears

Inspect the distributor, oil pump, or cam drive gears. If the gears are worn, replace the cam. Normal gear wear is confined to the center of each gear tooth. If the shiny wear marks extend to the end of the tooth, the gear is worn.

Journals

Journal inspection is saved for last because cam journals rarely wear out. They are not subjected to any side loads. Watch for scoring. If there seems to be lots of wear, mike the journals for undersize, taper, and out-of-round. Replacing the cam bearings should restore any lost oil pressure at the cam journals. However, if the cam is worn past specifications, replace it.

FIGURE 16-30   Camshaft lobe. (Ford Motor Company)

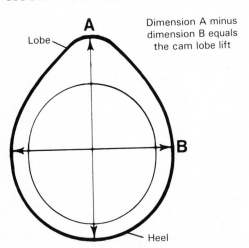

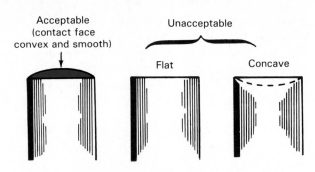

FIGURE 16-31   Lifter surface. (Ford Motor Company)

If the camshaft passes the visual exams, mike the lobes. It is difficult to measure the lobe lift accurately. Instead, look for differences among the lobes. If one is worn, it should be clearly smaller than its neighbors. Also, check the lifters that ridge on the camshaft lobes for wear (Figure 16-31). If new lifters are required, install a new camshaft. If a new camshaft is required, install new lifters.

TIMING CHAINS, BELTS, AND SPROCKETS

Timing chains are tested during engine teardown. This is done by pushing against the chain and measuring the amount of deflection from a straightedge (Figure 16-32). Loose chains are replaced.

Belts do not lose tension like chains. However, check their teeth for rounded corners. Oil soaking and cracked backings are also cause for replacement. If a belt is reused, it must be installed with the same direction of rotation.

FIGURE 16-32   Measuring timing chain deflection. (Pontiac Motor Division, GMC)

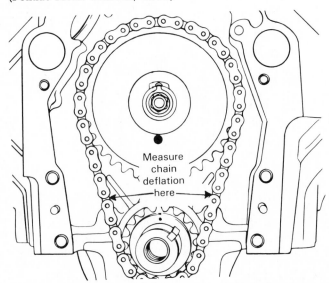

Inspect the timing sprocket teeth for wear. Nylon-covered sprockets used with chains are almost always worn out. The nylon dries from engine heat and breaks off. Then pieces of nylon find their way through the engine. Replace nylon-covered sprockets with all-steel sprockets.

Sprocket teeth have deep, scooped-out-looking areas between them when worn. Extremely worn gears will appear to lean to one side. Replacement is the cure.

Also check the sprocket's backside for thrust wear. This is more of a problem on all-gear timing systems.

If guide rails are used, they should have at least half of their original thickness to be reused. Guide rails often last through several timing chains, so you should not have to replace them the first time around.

Clean and inspect the timing chain tensioner. If it is an oil pressure type, make sure the bore is not worn. Spring-powered tensioners with rollers should not need replacement. Be careful not to submerge the roller in solvent when cleaning. This could dry out the sealed bearing and cause a rumbling noise later. If the tensioner is noisy or will not rotate freely, replace it.

OIL PUMP

Completely disassemble the oil pump for cleaning and inspection (Figure 16-33). Most oil pumps are removed from the sump as units and are disassembled by removing several bolts. The pump then separates into the body and cover. The gears rotate inside the body. Some new engines use an oil pump located in the front cover. This pump has no separate cover other than the front cover. Merely pull the gears out of their housing after removing the front cover.

Light scoring of the gears is normal. You should not be able to catch a fingernail on the scratches. Large scores, $\frac{1}{32}$ in. or more, indicate the passage of large debris. Replace the pump in that case.

End Clearance

Clean the pump and gears with fresh solvent. Replace the gears in the pump body. Then lay the cover or a straightedge across the body. Find the feeler gauge which just slips between the straightedge and gears. This is the pump's end clearance (Figure 16-34). Check your measurement against specifications. If the clearance is too great, reduce it by **lapping.** Place a piece of 220-grit wet or dry paper on a solid, flat surface. A thick piece of glass or marble works well. Flood the paper with water and then lap the pump body against the paper. This will cut the body's height, reducing end clearance. Check your progress often. When checking, be sure to remove all lapping grit, or your measurements will be wide. You'll lap too much off. If you overdo it, lap the gears to increase end clearance.

Side Clearance

Also measure the side clearance (Figure 16-35). This is the distance between the two gears' points. Use a wire gauge, as feeler gauges take up too much room. If wire gauges are unavailable, use feeler gauges, but add 0.002 in. (0.051 mm) to your finding. If clearance is excessive, replace the pump. Figure 16-36 shows additional measurements you must do if you are working on an all-gear oil pump.

The pressure relief valve also needs checking. Open the valve by pulling the cotter key or pin. Re-

FIGURE 16-34 Oil pump end clearance measurements. (Ford Motor Company)

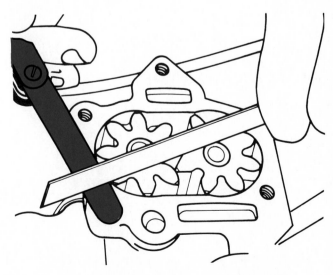

FIGURE 16-33 Oil pump assembly. (General Motors Corporation)

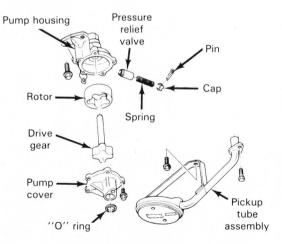

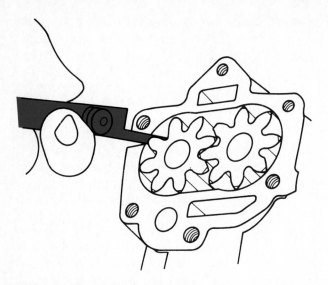

FIGURE 16-35 Oil pump side clearance measurements. (Ford Motor Company)

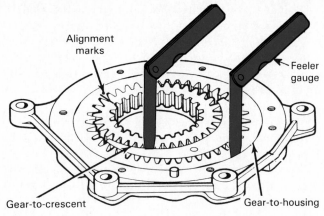

Alignment marks

Feeler gauge

Gear-to-crescent   Gear-to-housing

FIGURE 16-36 Measuring all-gear oil pump. (General Motors Corporation)

move the spring and valve and clean all parts. Look for scoring or indentations on the valve's angled edge. If the valve seat is visible, check it for scoring. If these parts are scored or worn, replace them. Check the spring for free length.

If the oil pump has lots of small parts which need replacing, get a new pump. It will give better and longer service than many new parts in an old pump body.

TRADE TERMS

Bead Blaster
Bore Alignment
Bore Taper
Boring Bar
Buttons
Cinch Pin
Cold Tank
Cross-hatch
Deck
Floating Pins
Honing
Hot Tank

Jet Tank
Knurled
Lapping
Out-of-Round
Oversize
Press Pins
Reconditioning
Scoring
Scuffing
Sizing
Taper

REVIEW QUESTIONS

1. Why aren't aluminum parts cleaned in a hot tank?
2. What types of cracks do magnafluxing and dye penetrants find?
3. Where is the area of greatest bore wear?
4. Why does the bore wear the most there?
5. Name the three types of crankshaft wear.
6. Which end of the connecting rod typically wears the most? What type of wear is normal?
7. Which piston ring groove normally wears the most?

17

Engine Assembly

INTRODUCTION

More than any other part of auto repair, engine assembly requires cleanliness and attention to detail. Lab studies show that it takes no more than two tablespoons of dirt to ruin an engine. That is for grit ingested through the air filter. Imagine how much less dirt it takes to wear out a power plant when the dirt is built right into the engine.

Engine assembly must be done under clean conditions. Besides cleaning the parts, the shop area must be clean, and the mechanic must be clean. Dirty benches, tools, rags, and hands all leave grit in an engine.

Whenever an engine under assembly is not being worked on, it should be covered with a plastic bag. This will keep out general dust as well as flying debris from nearby shop operations. Parts ready for assembly should be stored in clean, covered containers. Store large parts, such as heads and manifolds, in plastic bags.

Paying attention to detail is also an engine assembly requirement. There are no substitutes for time and patience. This doesn't mean reassembling an engine has to take endless weeks, but all the necessary steps must be taken.

OBJECTIVES

When you have completed this chapter, you should be able to

- Explain the importance of engine cleanliness
- Identify the different types of sealants
- Show how to measure for correct oil clearances
- List the basic steps in engine assembly
- Know the basic differences between assembling an OHV engine and an OHC engine
- Describe the proper break-in procedure

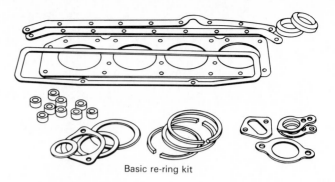

Basic re-ring kit

FIGURE 17-1 Gasket set.

LUBRICANTS, GASKETS, AND SEALERS

Lubricants, gaskets, and sealers are often overlooked in providing engine assembly information. These items provide the various parts and components with the protection and sealing power necessary.

Lubricants

If an engine is assembled without any lubricants, it will suffer extreme damage when it is first started, because it takes time for oil to reach all parts of the engine. So you must lubricate all parts during assembly. Besides providing start-up lubrication, oiling an engine during assembly will stop rust and corrosion from forming while the engine is in storage.

Engine oil is the natural choice for an assembly lubricant. Unless stated otherwise, lube all parts with SAE 30-weight engine oil. Some parts have special lubrication requirements, however. Oil quickly drains off a part unless it is physically retained. Therefore, you will need to use thicker, stickier lubricants on many parts. Also, any part of the valve train loaded by the valve springs is under extreme pressure. These parts might run dry until enough oil flows to them from the pump. To prevent this, special lubricants containing molybdenum disulfide are used when assembling lifters, push rods, etc. Thick enough so it won't drain off, **moly** provides excellent start-up protection.

Gaskets, Sealers, and Locking Compounds

Gaskets and sealers fill the minute voids between parts, keeping out dirt or sealing in liquids and gases.

Gaskets and Seals Gaskets are materials used to seal two or more nonmoving surfaces. There are head, oil pan, and water pump gaskets and others. Figure 17-1 shows a set of gaskets. Gaskets are made from many

materials depending on their use. Cork, asbestos, and synthetic materials are just a few of the materials used. Some gaskets are sandwiches of more than one material. They may be coated with an aluminum alloy, which provides a better sealing.

Seals are typically used between a moving and non-moving part. There are many different types and designs of seals, but two, the lip seal and the O-ring seal, are the most common types. Figure 17-2 shows a cross section of ring seals.

Sealers There is a variety of sealers for different applications. Two broad categories are nonhardening and hardening.

Nonhardening sealer is the standard gasket cement today. Compared to a hardening sealer, nonhardening resists vibration, expands and contracts with the engine, and allows more flexibility in engine assembly. Nonhardening sealers are also easier to clean during engine disassembly.

A special type of sealer is **room temperature vulcanizing (RTV)**. This special rubber compound sets up after exposure to the atmosphere. This lets you squeeze it almost anywhere, bolt the parts together, and let the rubber vulcanize. Soon a rubber gasket has formed, sealing gasoline, water, oil, and other normal engine fluids. Old RTV peels right off for easy cleanup. Because it is so versatile, RTV has become the number one gasket sealer.

FIGURE 17-2 Cross section of ring seals.

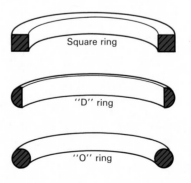

Square ring

"D" ring

"O" ring

There are some disadvantages with RTV, though. Squeezed from between parts it forms a flash which breaks off. Outside the engine this poses no problem. Inside, however, these rubber pieces can circulate with the oil and clog tight passages. Also, RTV is fairly slippery until it sets up; sometimes you need something tackier or with holding power to hold a gasket during assembly.

Locking Compounds Some heavy-duty threaded connections may call for a locking compound. These chemicals act like lockwashers, and extra effort is required to remove fasteners treated with them. These are available in strengths ranging from "wrench removal" to "permanently joined."

ENGINE ASSEMBLY

Core Plugs

Start engine assembly by installing all core plugs. Coat the core plug's mating area and bore with nonhardening sealer. Set the core plug in position and then hammer it in place. Although you can use a socket which fits the core plug's outside diameter (OD), it is better to use the core plug replacer tools (Figure 17-3). This will distribute the hammer blows and help drive the plug straight in.

Some engines have core plugs which have no lips and are used in holes with a cast-in ledge. These plugs are bowed, so from on edge they are saucer-shaped. Place the plug in its bore, butted against the bore's shoulder. The core plug's bow must face the outside of the engine. Now take a flat-nosed punch and smack the center of the plug. This pops the plug's center toward the block and forces the plug's edges against the block.

Don't forget to install any core plugs in the head. Also, there may be an oil plug at the rear of the cam bores.

Overhead Valve (OHV) Camshaft

Install the camshaft for the overhead valve (OHV) now. First, install the camshaft bearings, if necessary. Deburr the bearing's edges first. Then align any oil holes with those in the block. Make sure the bearings are in the proper order. Some applications use gradually smaller bearings from front to rear. Start with the rear bearing and drive it home with a cam bearing installer. This is a special mandrel with a long handle. This handle extends outside the block so you can hammer on it, driving the bearing in. Check that the oil holes line up before and after installation.

Thoroughly oil the camshaft bearings and journals. Then generously lube the cam lobes with a moly

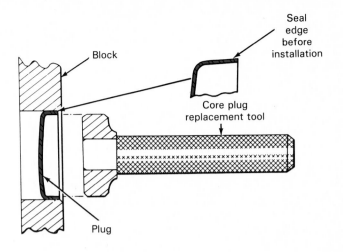

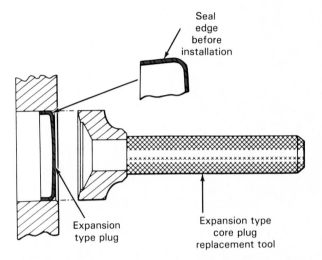

FIGURE 17-3 Core plugs and installation tools. (Ford Motor Company)

compound. Take time to smear the lube evenly around each lobe, making sure no part is left dry.

Slide the camshaft into the block. Hold the camshaft with both hands while guiding it into the block. One hand should be inside the block, feeding the camshaft through its bearings; the other hand should support the shaft outside the block. Try your best not to nick the cam lobes against the block. If there is a cam retainer in the timing chain area, install it now so the cam won't slide out as you move the engine around.

Rear Crankshaft Seal

Three types of rear crank seal are used. First, there is the rope, or split-lip, seal. Most common is the neoprene seal, a rubber, two-part seal. Then there is the single-piece rubber seal. It is a complete circle and is installed after the crankshaft and main bearings. The other two seals are installed now, before the crankshaft.

Rope Seal First, apply RTV to the main bearing cap and block as Figure 17-4 directs. Slide one part of the rope seal into the block and the other into the rear main bearing cap. Work each half into its groove as tightly as possible. A special tool may be available for this. If not, use a large socket. Once fully seated, trim the ends of the seal flush with the block or cap. Use a very sharp knife to trim the seal. Cut away any loose fibers which could get caught between block and cap, upsetting the rear main bearing's oil clearance.

After installing the seal, you may find it difficult to rotate the crank. If so, use the front pulley or thread two flywheel bolts into the crank and use a rod as a lever between the two bolts to move the crank.

Neoprene Seal Neoprene seals come preformed and are as easy to install as an insert bearing (Figure 17-

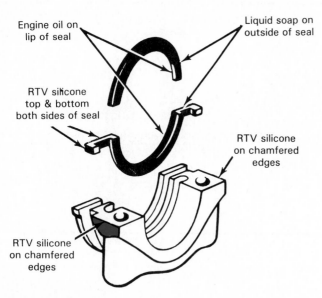

FIGURE 17-4 Applying RTV to main bearing cap and block. (Ford Motor Company)

FIGURE 17-5 Installing single-piece rubber seal. (Ford Motor Company)

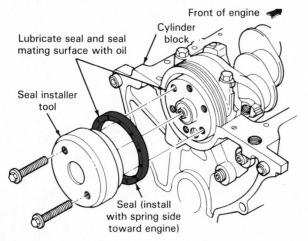

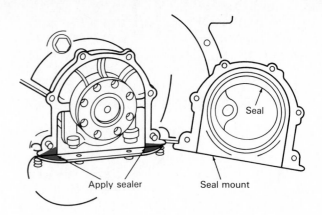

FIGURE 17-6 Rear main oil seal installation.

5). Like a bearing, install the seal in a dry bore (Figure 17-6). The sealing lip must face toward the inside of the engine. Then oil the working surface wiped by the crank.

Crankshaft Bearings

Wipe all the bearing bores with a dry paper towel. Then lay the bearing shells into the bores. Line up the tang with the cutout in the block or cap, place a thumb on each end of the bearing, and push it into its bore. Thoroughly oil each bearing. Also squirt oil down the oil passages in the block. This helps fill them, reducing priming time at engine start-up.

Some bearings have different upper and lower halves. The upper halves typically have an oil hole and groove, while the lower halves are plain. Don't install the two backwards, or you'll ruin both the crankshaft and connecting rods because oil won't reach the bearings.

Crankshaft

Double-check that the crank is clean by wiping it down with a paper towel. Then grasp it by the shaft and flywheel flange. Being careful to lower the crank straight down, set the shaft in its bearings (Figure 17-7). Oil the journals while slowly rotating the crank. Squirt oil into the crank's oil passages to help priming.

Now install the main bearing caps. Pay attention to the cap's number and direction. If in doubt about cap direction, the bearing tangs should butt against each other.

If the engine has separate thrust washers, install them before the main bearing caps. Also, apply sealer to the rear seal's ends before joining cap and block. Before tightening the main bearing caps, align the thrust bearings (Figure 17-8). Do this by lightly snugging the main bearing caps. Then pry the crankshaft to first one end of the block and then the other. The

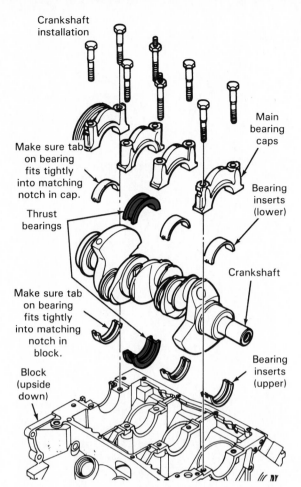

Crankshaft installation

Make sure tab on bearing fits tightly into matching notch in cap.

Thrust bearings

Make sure tab on bearing fits tightly into matching notch in block.

Block (upside down)

Main bearing caps

Bearing inserts (lower)

Crankshaft

Bearing inserts (upper)

FIGURE 17-7 Crankshaft and main bearings. (Ford Motor Company)

crank will move several thousandths of an inch and then contact the thrust bearings. Because the thrust bearings are not clamped down by their cap, the crank

will push them into alignment. Check for excessive turning effort; this indicates binding. Now you can tighten the main bearing caps.

Tighten the main bearings in several steps. If the specification is 50 ft-lb, for example, start at 20 ft-lb. Tighten all caps to 20 ft-lb, rotate the crankshaft making certain it turns without binding, and then tighten it 30, 40, 45, and finally 50 ft-lb. Right before bolting on the oil pan, retighten the mains. This will tighten any bolts that loosened from **normalizing,** the relaxing of the block after the stress of tightening.

Plastigaging

The oil clearance should always be checked on at least one main and rod bearing. Better yet, check all bearings if borderline parts are used. This final check will catch any problems with the crank, bearing bores, or bearings. The best way to do this is with **Plastigage,** a precision wax.

Several thicknesses of Plastigage are available. The green variety ranges from 0.001 to 0.003 in. and covers 90% of the engines you will repair.

Begin the measurement before attaching the bearing's cap. Wipe any oil from the crankshaft journal. Oil melts the Plastigage and will give a faulty reading. Snip off a length of Plastigage and lay it across the journal (Figure 17-9). Install and torque the dry bearing and cap. Don't accidentally rotate the crank, or you'll smear the Plastigage. Now remove the cap and compare the squished width of Plastigage against the scale on the Plastigage package.

The wider the Plastigage is squished, the less the oil clearance. The narrower the wax, the greater the oil clearance. If the Plastigage is untouched, the oil clearance is extra wide.

FIGURE 17-8 Thrust bearing alignment. (Ford Motor Company)

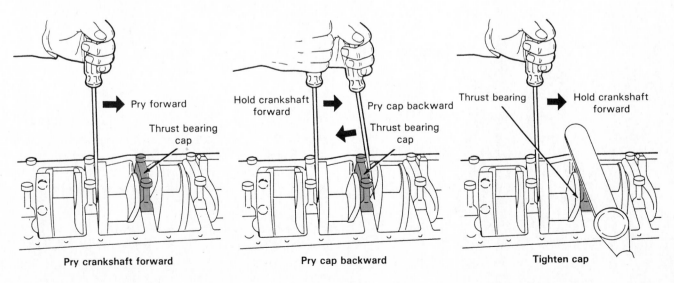

Pry forward

Thrust bearing cap

Pry crankshaft forward

Hold crankshaft forward

Pry cap backward

Thrust bearing cap

Pry cap backward

Thrust bearing

Hold crankshaft forward

Tighten cap

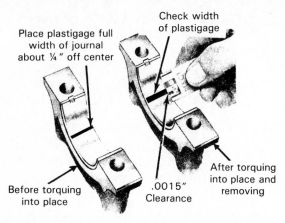

FIGURE 17-9 Using Plastigage to check bearing clearance. (Ford Motor Company)

If the oil clearance is not to specifications (specs), find out why and correct it. If the clearance is okay, wipe off the wax residue, oil the bearings, and install the bearing cap.

Piston Rings

Set the rod and piston assembly in a vise to install rings. Before installing piston rings, check the piston ring gap with a feeler gauge to see that it matches the specs (Figure 17-10). Start with the lowest ring on the piston and finish with the topmost ring. The lowest ring is the oil ring. Most oil rings are multipiece and can be assembled without tools. Follow the ring manufacturer's directions, taking care not to scratch the piston with the ring ends.

Compression rings are best installed with a ring expander. This greatly reduces the chances of breaking a ring because of twisting or overexpanding. It also saves the piston from scratching.

FIGURE 17-10 Piston ring gap check. (Ford Motor Company)

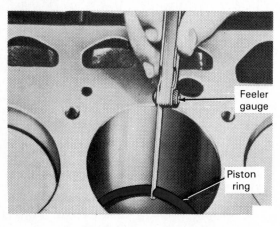

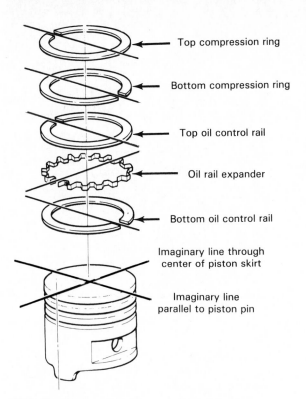

FIGURE 17-11 Piston ring gap positions.

Check that the installed rings are right side up and then arrange the end gaps as shown in the engine's shop manual (Figure 17-11). If no end gap arrangement is given, turn the gaps so none are directly over the piston pin or centered on the thrust faces. Furthermore, the gaps should not be in a straight line. That gives combustion gases a direct route into the crankcase.

Rod Bearings

Remove the cap from the rod and wipe both bearing surfaces dry. Install the bearing halves like the main bearings: dry backside, tangs aligned, oiled front side. Leave the caps off the rods. Install the journal protectors (rubber hoses) over the rod bolts (Figure 17-12).

Piston and Rod Installation

Position the crankshaft so the throw for the rod being installed is with the crankpin at bottom-dead-center (BDC). The notch or marking on the piston head usually faces forward. Oil the rod journal and cylinder wall. Wipe the oil around with your freshly cleaned hands. Be sure that there is no dirt on your hands; the oil will wash some of it off, and it will get inside the engine.

Ring Compressor Fill a clean can with 2 in. of fresh oil. Dunk the piston in the oil and then pull it out

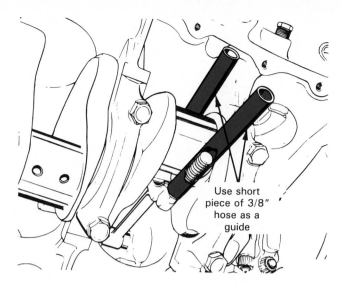

FIGURE 17-12 Journal protectors. (Pontiac Motor Division, GMC)

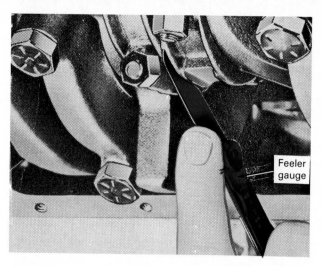

FIGURE 17-14 Connecting rod side clearance check. (Ford Motor Company)

and let the excess oil drain off. Fully compress the rings with a ring compressor (Figure 17-13). Correctly align the assembly with the block and then lower it until the ring compressor butts against the block. As gently as possible, tap the piston into the cylinder with a hammer handle. Don't relax pressure on the ring compressor, or a ring may pop out between the compressor and the block deck. If this happens, you'll feel more resistance through the hammer handle. Also, the sound will become more solid. If this happens, *stop*. Inspect the rings and reposition the ring compressor if necessary. If you continue to hammer the piston, the ring will break before entering the cylinder. You won't know it until later when you see the scored cylinder wall.

While hammering the piston in, guide the rod

FIGURE 17-13 Piston installation. (Ford Motor Company)

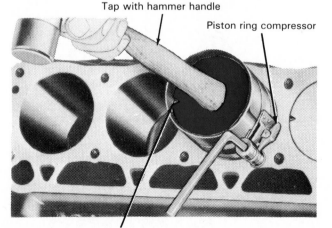

Tap with hammer handle

Piston ring compressor

Notch to front of engine

onto its journal with your other hand. Guide the rod as soon as possible. This will keep it from fouling the crank counterweights if the piston assembly is slightly out of alignment.

Tap the piston until the rod fully seats against the crankshaft. Check the rod bearing to tolerances with Plastigage and then oil and tighten the rod bearing cap bolts.

Install the remaining piston and rod assemblies. Two pistons can often be installed before having to turn the crank. For example, on a four-cylinder engine, install numbers 1 and 4, rotate the crank, and install 2 and 3.

After you finish installing the pistons and rods, check the side clearance of the connecting rod with a feeler gauge (Figure 17-14).

Oil Pump

After installing all pistons and rods, bolt in the oil pump. If the oil pump attaches in the crankcase, bolt it in now (Figure 17-15). Be sure to check the position of the oil pump pickup.

Pump priming happens much faster if the gears are packed with petroleum jelly, or at least fill the pump with oil. If the engine is upside down, pour oil down the pickup. Otherwise, the pump will merely suck air, and the engine will run dry.

Use nonhardening sealer between the pump and block, not RTV. RTV might leave flash inside the oil passage.

On overhead cam (OHC) engines the pan can probably be bolted on now. It depends on whether some of the pan and its gasket fit over the front cover. If the pan is separate, bolt it on now.

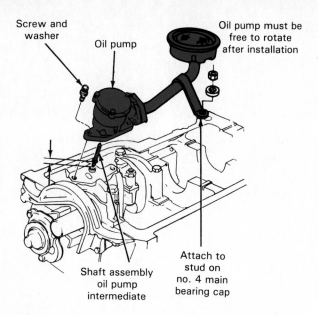

FIGURE 17-15 Oil pump installation. (Ford Motor Company)

Timing Gear

At the front of the engine, fit the timing gear. On overhead valve (OHV) engines, fit the Woodruff key and then the crankshaft timing sprocket to the crank snout (Figure 17-16). Rotate the crankshaft to the position shown in the shop manual. Use the camshaft timing sprocket to rotate the cam to its proper position. Remove the cam sprocket and drape the timing chain over it and then over the crank sprocket. Make sure

FIGURE 17-16 OHV timing chain and sprockets. (Ford Motor Company)

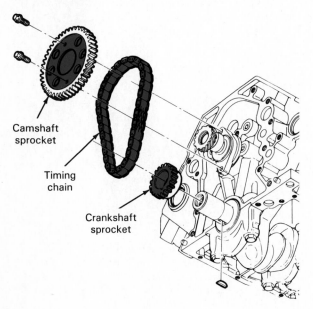

the timing marks are lined up between the crank and cam sprockets; then bolt the cam sprocket to the camshaft (Figure 17-17). Double-check the timing mark alignment.

If there is a chain tensioner, mount it now (Figure 17-18).

Timing Cover Install a new seal in the timing cover. Knock out the old seal with a large socket, or pry it out. Tap the new one in with a seal driver and hammer (Figure 17-19). Nonhardening sealer around the seal's OD will aid installation and stop leaks. Slip on the oil slinger, if used. The curve faces forward.

Run a bead of RTV sealant around the timing chain cover, fit the gasket, and bolt it to the block. Don't tighten the bolts yet. Install the harmonic damper and torque it. Most shop manuals call for a special

FIGURE 17-17 Timing chain and gear alignment. (General Motors Corporation)

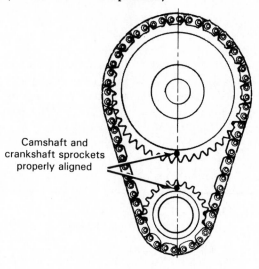

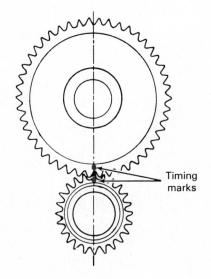

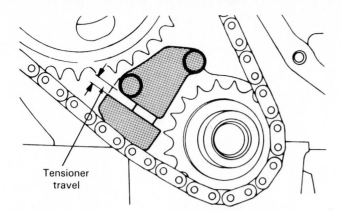

FIGURE 17-18 Timing chain tensioner.

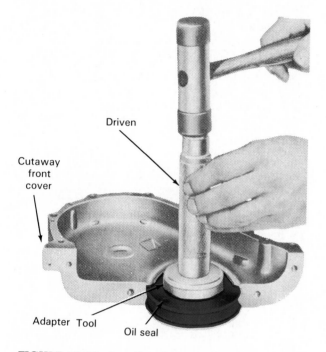

FIGURE 17-19 Installing front cover oil seal. (Ford Motor Company)

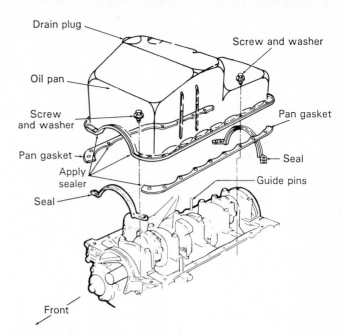

FIGURE 17-20 Oil pan installation. (Ford Motor Company)

puller to pull the harmonic damper in place. If you have one, use it. If not, lightly hammer the damper until you can use its bolts to draw it on the rest of the way. With the damper installed, tighten the front cover. This procedure allows the front cover to "float" so the front seal will center itself on the harmonic damper.

Oil Pan

Next install the oil pan (Figure 17-20). Use RTV sealant on both the pan rails and block rails. Lay the gaskets on the block, set on the pan, and bolt it up. Tighten the pan bolts gradually in a crisscross pattern. This allows the pan gasket to squeeze into shape.

Overhead Cam (OHC) Timing Gear

Install overhead cam timing gear assembly as you do on an overhead valve engine. Install the crank sprocket, timing chain, tensioner, and guide rails. Depending on the design, the front cover may or may not go on now. If it does, don't forget the oil slinger, and follow the same instructions for the harmonic damper and front cover. It may be necessary to hold the timing chain with some support so it won't fall into the timing cover or to wire the timing chain to a bolt hole (Figure 17-21).

Overhead cam timing gear alignment marks differ greatly from engine to engine. You must have the engine shop manual to correctly align the timing marks.

FIGURE 17-21 Holding timing chain with a support.

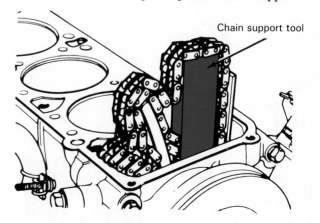

Obviously, if the crank sprocket needs to be seen for timing, leave the front cover off for now.

Head and Head Gasket

Assemble the heads as outlined in Chapter 12. Remove the head gasket from its package and inspect it for flatness, cuts, and manufacturing flaws. Do not bend or tear the gasket. Read the manufacturer's directions. Some gaskets require sealer; others go on dry.

Before placing the head gasket on the block, wipe your hand across the block's deck. It should be perfectly clean. Ensure that any necessary dowel pins are in place and then lay the head gasket on the deck. If the gasket is not marked UP and FRONT, place the manufacturer's name facing up.

Now wipe the head's mating surface with your hand. It, too, should be spotless. Now carefully lay the head on the block, taking care to set it down as straight as possible (Figure 17-22). You don't want to tear the gasket by dragging the head sideways across the block.

Head Bolts Drop in the head bolts and washers, if used. Oil is the preferred lubricant, unless the bolts

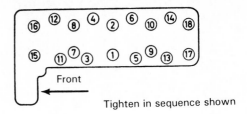

Tighten in sequence shown

FIGURE 17-23 Cylinder head tightening sequence.

extend into the water jacket. Use nonhardening sealer or **anti-seize compound** on the threads in that case. Don't forget any brackets which might use head bolts for attachment. Run all the bolts down snug with a ratchet and then finish with a torque wrench. As with the main bearing bolts, tighten head bolts one step at a time. This allows the head and gasket to normalize. About 20 min. after final tightening of the head bolts, go over them again to see if any have loosened up. Always use the tightening pattern given in the shop manual (Figure 17-23).

On V-type engines, install the other head using the same procedure.

Overhead Valve (OHV) Valve Train

Overhead valve (OHV) engines are ready for lifters. First, if you are using old lifters, they must go on the same lobe they came off of. If they are not in order, get new lifters. If the cam has been replaced, new lifters are a must. New lifters can be used on the old cam, though.

Lifters Mechanical lifters should be moly-lubed on their bottoms and sides and then put in place. Hydraulic lifters get moly too, but they also need priming. On the lifter's sides is a small hole. Hold an oil can up against this hole and gently squeeze oil into the lifter until it bleeds out the lifter's top. Now install the lifters.

Push Rods Next are the push rods. Dab each end into moly lube and then slide them onto the lifters. Rocker arms, either pedestal or shaft mounted, can now be installed (Figure 17-24).

Rocker Assembly Pedestal-mounted rockers need adjustment. First, to adjust a lifter, it must be against the cam's base circle. You should be able to see the camshaft. If not, watch the lifter body while rotating the engine. You'll see when the lifter is "off the cam." After positioning the camshaft, tighten the rocker arm nut. Different engines use different methods from this point on. Some require a specific torque on the rocker's nut. Others tighten the nut until the push rod gets tight and then add one more turn. Consult the shop manual for the engine you are assembling.

FIGURE 17-22 OHC cylinder head installation. (Ford Motor Company)

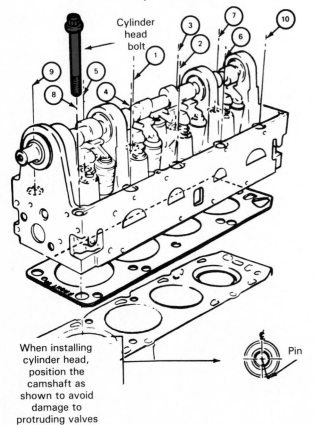

Tighten the cylinder head bolts in the sequence shown

Cylinder head bolt

When installing cylinder head, position the camshaft as shown to avoid damage to protruding valves

Pin

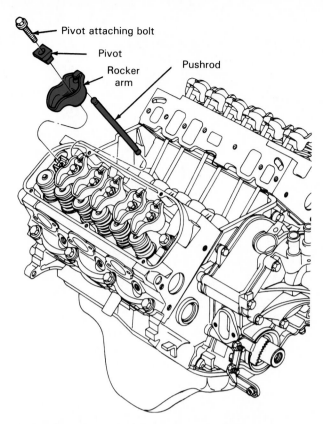

FIGURE 17-24 OHV valve train installation with pedestal-type rockers. (Ford Motor Company)

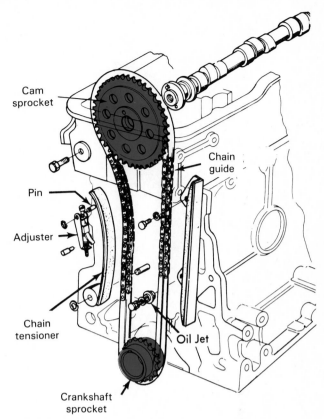

FIGURE 17-25 OHC timing arrangement. (Chrysler Corporation)

Mechanical lifters need adjusting also. Use feeler gauges and the rocker arm's adjuster to reach the clearance specified. These lifters must also be against the cam's base circle when adjusted.

Overhead Cam (OHC) Valve Train

Overhead cam (OHC) valve train installation can be handled several ways depending on its design. Some engines require that the cam be installed first. Others need the rocker arms and then the cam. You'll need a shop manual for cam installation and timing.

Camshaft With the cam-first engines, moly-lube the cam and lay it in its bearing bores. Bolt on the cam bearing caps and then the cam sprocket (Figure 17-25). To attach the sprocket, turn the cam so it is in time with the crank, loop the chain over the cam sprocket, and then bolt it to the cam. Now moly-lube the rocker arms and install and adjust them. If you try to bolt on the rocker arms and adjust them before attaching the cam sprocket, you may have valves hitting pistons as you turn the cam over. Besides, it is much easier to rotate the engine from the front pulley than trying to turn the cam sprocket by hand.

If the cam bearing caps are a part of the rocker arm assembly, be sure to attach the cam sprocket before the rocker arm assembly. This ensures that the cam is in time with the crank, so that when you tighten the rockers down they won't try to push a valve open against a piston which is at top-dead-center (TDC).

Other OHC systems mount the cam in permanent pedestals which are part of the head casting. With these the cam is installed in the pedestals; individually mounted rockers are attached under the cam. Install the cam sprocket first so the pistons and valves don't clash during rocker arm installation (Figure 17-26).

What all these procedures have in common is that the cam must be moly-lubed, the rocker arms moly-lubed, and the valve train installed with the valve adjustment backed off all the way. After all parts are installed, the valves can be adjusted.

> **CAUTION:** Turn the engine over several times by hand to ensure no interference problems with valves and pistons. Waiting to turn over the engine with a starter is a frequent and very expensive error.

When you are finished, rotate the engine to TDC, number 1 cylinder. Besides the timing marks lining up on the front pulley, both valves must be closed on the number 1 cylinder.

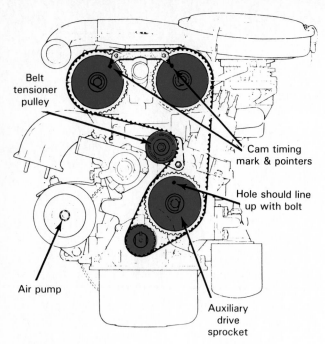

FIGURE 17-26　Double overhead cam (DOHC) belt arrangement.

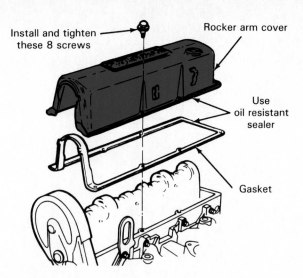

FIGURE 17-27　Rocker cover installation. (Ford Motor Company)

Rocker Covers

Apply RTV to the rocker cover gasket and to the rocker cover. Then install the cover on the head without overtightening the rocker cover hardware (Figure 17-27). Do not put gasket sealer between the gasket and head, or you'll tear the gasket when removing the cover for valve adjustment.

Manifolds

V-type Engines　On V-type engines the intake manifold seals the valley. Therefore, there are gaskets on each head plus each end of the valley. Place all these gaskets. Then, without dislodging the gaskets, install the manifold. It helps if you use a sticky gasket sealer for this job. Put extra gasket sealer on the four corners of the valley. These are typically problem areas with V-type engines.

After the intake manifold, V-type exhaust manifolds are easy. Place the gaskets on dry and then bolt up the manifolds. Sometimes it helps to install a set of plugs and check that a spark plug socket will squeeze between plugs and manifold. Leave the exhaust manifold just snug so you can adjust for maximum clearance and then tighten the manifold.

In-line Engines　In-line engine manifolds are usually attached with dry gaskets (Figure 17-28). With noncrossflow heads it may be necessary to install one manifold before the other. On most noncrossflow

FIGURE 17-28　Crossflow intake manifold. (Ford Motor Company)

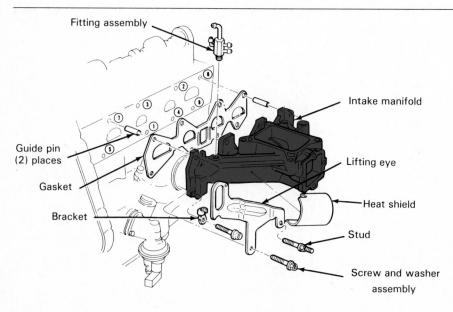

heads the exhaust manifold goes on first. Then the intake is fitted and the bolts tightened. If the exhaust manifold attaches to the intake, leave the bolts loose at the head. Tighten the manifold-to-manifold hardware first and then the manifold-to-head hardware. Don't forget any heat shields which may fit between manifolds.

Engine Accessories

Bolt on the curburetor or injection system, taking care not to overtorque the nuts. Bolt on the engine mounts and dipstick tube. Install a set of new spark plugs. Leave the distributor out for now if the oil pump can be turned through the distributor hole.

Distributor

If the oil pump can be turned while the distributor is in place, go ahead and install the distributor now. Bring the engine to TDC, number 1 cylinder. Make sure both valves are closed at number 1 as well as having the timing marks in alignment. Locate the number 1 cylinder's wire where it attaches to the distributor cap. Now mark the distributor body directly below number 1's wire. This is the place the distributor rotor should end up when the distributor is properly installed. Because the distributor drive gears are not

straight but curved, the rotor will move as the gears engage during installation. So back up the rotor about an inch. Install the distributor while watching the rotor. The rotor should move to cylinder 1's position. If not, remove the distributor and back the rotor up the approximate amount it moved during the first try. Reinstall the distributor.

When the distributor is fully seated and the rotor is at the number 1 position, it is in time. Install the distributor hold-down. Hook the wires to the spark plugs by following the firing order.

Water Pump and Thermostat

Spread sealer on both sides of the water pump's gasket and mount it to the engine (Figure 17-29). Also put sealer on water pump bolts which enter the water jacket. Seal both sides of the thermostat housing gasket and install it. A common and costly mistake is to install the thermostat upside down. Then the thermostat senses the cool water in the radiator and not the warm water in the engine. The thermostat remains closed and the engine overheats, possibly causing engine damage.

Make sure the small cylinder in the center of the thermostat sets in the engine. This is the sensing device. It is often marked with the thermostat's opening temperature.

"BUT THE BOX SAID . . ."

The first amateur race of the 1968 season was in Mexico City.

When practice opened, the blasted motor wouldn't start. Both Jim Travers and Frank Coon of Traco were there with Roger Penske, and the three of them were climbing all over that engine. They tinkered with the fuel injection and the ignition—which was still a point type at the time, because we used such low revs—and they replaced the tiny Varley battery that everybody was using. Finally they got it started, somehow, and I went out and ran half a lap—and the engine locked up. Actually, I could feel it start to freeze, and I shut it off before anything was damaged. So we towed it back to the pits. After cooling down it loosened up a bit, and I took it out again. And it locked up again.

That time we decided we would have to take it out of the car and look into it. We didn't have a spare motor, but Jim and Frank had engineered that one so we reckoned they should be able

to fix it. When we turned it upside down and opened the pan, we discovered that all the bearings were shot. Jim and Frank could replace them easily enough—if they *had* some—so they called George Bolthoff, who worked for them at the time and who had actually assembled the engine. They told him to grab some new bearings and take the next plane to Mexico City. When he finally arrived, he still had to smuggle or bribe the parts past the customs blokes, so Roger got some guy with influence to pay off everybody in sight, and we got the bearings. Meanwhile, I was carrying the bare block around in the bilges of the pits, while everyone else was practicing and qualifying. Finally I went to bed, while they got it back together and back in the car.

I had an opportunity to qualify again in the morning before the race. I carefully warmed up the rebuilt engine and took it out on the track. It went two or three laps and seized again. By that time we'd had enough, and we loaded

it on the truck. Ultimately we found out that the cause of our problems was simply the wrong size bearings. Somehow George had used undersize bearings—they were mismarked or were on the wrong shelf—in both the original build and in our pit rebuild. Because they were only two thousandths off, the crankshaft would rotate, but there wasn't room for oil flow. I don't know why they weren't checking that, but I'll bet it's never happened since. I'll bet that also had something to do with the engine being so hard to start. Anyhow, the week was a total disaster. Roger had arranged everything in his own fantastic way, spending all those dollars to get the equipment there, and flying all those people in, and getting the engine rebuilt, and because of one tiny mistake we never even started the race.

Reprinted by permission of DODD, MEAD & COMPANY, INC. from THE UNFAIR ADVANTAGE by Mark Donohue with Paul Van Valkenburgh. Copyright © 1975 by Mark Donohue.

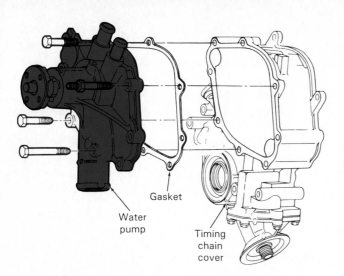

FIGURE 17-29 Installing water pump to front cover. (Ford Motor Company)

Fuel Pump

If a fuel pump push rod is used, moly-lube both ends and slip it in its bore. Place the pump in position and bolt it up. If you have to compress the pump's return spring against the push rod, rotate the engine one revolution. This will turn the camshaft eccentric away from the pump, unloading the return spring.

Oil Filter

Fill a new oil filter with oil and install it. Some filters cannot be filled first because they drain before you can get them on the engine. If the filter can be filled, do so. It will speed priming.

Flexplate or Flywheel

Bolt the flexplate or flywheel to the crankshaft. Watch that you don't install the flexplate backwards. Install the clutch disc and pressure plate using a dummy shaft to align the disc. See Chapters 10 and 28 for complete clutch and flywheel installation.

ENGINE INSTALLATION

The engine is now ready for installation. Reverse the procedure given in engine removal, but pay particular attention to the following.

Engine Placement

Mount the engine on the engine hoist with the flywheel slightly lower than the front of the engine. This helps the engine and transmission to mate. Raise the

transmission with a floor jack so it and the engine can join before the engine is set on its mounts. Use guide pins or headless bolts to help with engine-to-transmission alignment.

If the engine will not join the last couple of inches with a manual transmission, rotate the crankshaft with the front pulley. This will turn the clutch disc so its splines and those on the input shaft will line up. As soon as the engine and transmission are joined, run two bellhousing bolts in to keep them from slipping apart. Don't forget to bolt the torque converter flexplate together.

Keep your hands from under the engine until it is securely attached to its mounts and the transmission.

Engine Connections

Use your numbering system to reconnect the electrical and vacuum lines. Fill the engine with its normal oil and coolant. Getting the cooling system completely full can be difficult. Air traps in the head and behind the thermostat. Some systems have a bleed for such occasions. It looks like a brake bleeder. Open the bleed and add coolant until it spills from the bleed. Close the bleed and top off the system. Or unbolt the thermostat housing to bleed air. Fill until coolant fills up to the thermostat. Close the housing and top off the system.

Charge the battery, and don't forget to install all ground straps.

Fuel System

Install a new fuel filter and see that there is plenty of fresh fuel in the tank. Fuel systems using a low-mounted canister filter or sediment bowl will need priming. Open the canister or bowl and fill it with fuel. Reattach the canister or bowl with a minimum of spillage. If the engine keeps running out of fuel, pressurize the tank very lightly with a compressed air nozzle. This will prime the fuel pump.

Double-check all fuel connections for tightness before trying to start the engine. Have a fire extinguisher handy.

Pre-engine Start-up

Immediately before start-up, prime the engine by rotating the oil pump through the distributor or oil pump drive shaft holes (Figure 17-30). Use a speed handle and hex, screwdriver, or square bit to turn the pump. Check for oil pressure at the instrument and rocker arm area. The engine is primed when oil flows into the rocker arm area. Rotating the crankshaft while priming fills the crank's oil passages and brings oil to all bearings.

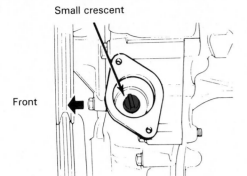

Small crescent

Front

FIGURE 17-30   Oil pump drive used for priming oil system.

If the oil pump drive is not accessible, use an air-powered priming device attached to the oil filter pad or oil press sender switch port. Or crank the engine without the spark plugs until oil flows into the rocker arm area.

After priming, bring the engine to TDC number 1 and install the distributor. Attach the module connector or coil negative wire. Slip on the coil's high-tension lead and connect a timing light. Leave the distributor hold-down loose enough to adjust timing but tight enough to keep the distributor from turning on its own.

Engine Start-up

Start the engine and immediately bring it to a fast idle. Do not rev the engine. The high idle is important for proper oiling, especially for the camshaft, lifters, and rockers.

Check for leaks of any kind. Watch the oil pressure and coolant temperature. If you find any leaks, stop the engine and fix them. If not, run the engine for 10 minutes at fast idle. Then drop the rpm to idle and set the timing. Some engines require a valve adjustment at this point, and most head gaskets need retorquing unless otherwise marked. Do these steps now. If they aren't necessary, disconnect the timing light and road-test the car.

Road Test

In a safe location, accelerate from 25 to 45 mph at full throttle and then completely close the throttle and coast to 25 mph. Be sure your seat (safety) belt is buckled. Repeat this cycle five times. This process seats the rings on both their tops and bottoms.

Return to the garage and recheck for leaks. Change the oil and filter. The oil will have metal particles from the rapidly wearing rings, plus the filter will be about clogged with moly and other assembly lubricants.

The car is ready for service. Instruct the customer to drive the car normally but to avoid both lugging and high rpm for the first 300 mi. Change the oil and filter at 300 mi, getting rid of more metal particles.

The engine should be fully broken in by 300 mi. If the engine still has break-in problems at 500 mi, something is wrong. Diagnose and repair the problem as necessary.

TRADE TERMS

Anti-seize Compound
Moly
Normalizing

Plastigage
Room Temperature Vulcanizing (RTV) Sealant

REVIEW QUESTIONS

1. About how much dirt does it take to ruin an engine?
2. When installing insert bearings, should their backsides be *oiled* or *dry*?
3. What does it mean when you encounter sudden, increased resistance during piston installation?
4. Which side of the head gasket should face up when it is not marked UP or FRONT?
5. What happens if the thermostat is installed upside down?
6. How long is a normal break-in period?
7. What types of materials are used in gaskets?
8. What is Plastigage?
9. Why should you turn an engine by hand after installing the valve train?
10. When installing an engine, why should the flywheel be slightly lower than the front of the engine?

PART THREE
Engine Electrical Systems

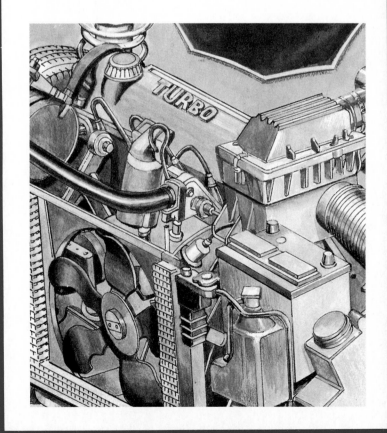

KEY CONCEPTS

- Electricity and how a battery works
- The alternator, regulator and charging system operation
- Starter motors and relays

18

Electricity and the Battery

OBJECTIVES

When you have completed this chapter, you should be able to

- Explain the basic concepts of electricity, how it is used in the automobile, and the special terms used to describe it
- Describe how an automobile battery works and how it is constructed
- Identify what happens when a battery is discharged and recharged
- Explain how electricity operates equipment in an automobile
- Test a battery and know how to service a battery
- Identify electrical wiring circuits and read basic wiring diagrams

INTRODUCTION

Although no one really knows for sure what electricity is, it is possible to describe its characteristics and what it does. This chapter explains the basic concepts of electricity and common electrical terms. It discusses how batteries are built and rated. Battery inspection and testing are also covered. The chapter concludes with a description of electrical wiring and basic testing procedures.

ELECTRICITY

Electricity is one of the basic forces of nature. Understanding the meaning of electricity and its terminology is necessary to service auto electrical components.

Matter

There are several theories about how electricity operates. The most common way to think about electricity is that matter, all matter, is made up of atoms. That includes everything we see, touch, or eat, even our own bodies. Atoms are made of **electrons** in orbit around a nucleus (Figure 18-1). The electrons are nega-

only for wires but also for switch contacts, screw terminals, and circuit boards.

Insulators

Insulators have characteristics quite different from conductors. An insulator provides a very high resistance to the flow of electricity. An insulator's electrons do not move as freely as do a conductor's. Rubber, glass, ceramic, some plastics, oil, and air are good insulators. Under the right conditions, however, almost any insulator can be made to conduct electricity. The plastic distributor cap on an automobile's ignition system may develop conductive paths after several thousand miles of being subjected to the high voltage from the coil.

Resistance

Resistance (R) is the ability of matter to restrict or resist the flow of electricity. The quality of resistance is the opposite of the quality of conductance. A conductor has a very low resistance, while an insulator has a very high resistance. Resistance plays an important role in controlling the work electricity does in the automobile. A ballast resistor or resistance wire, for example, allows full voltage to be applied to the coil when it is bypassed during starting but reduces the battery voltage during engine operation for longer coil, point, and spark plug life.

Resistance is the key element in the lighting of a bulb, or the sensing of the gasoline level in the fuel tank, or the controlling of the variable speeds on the heater fan. So, while resistance is often undesirable, as at the terminals of a battery, for example, resistance is often useful and even necessary.

Resistance is measured in **ohms** and represented by an omega (Ω) or the letter R. For example, 1000 ft of No. 10 wire has a resistance of 1 Ω. Resistance is measured with either an **ohmmeter** (Figure 18-2) or the resistance-measuring function of a **multimeter** (Figure 18-3).

Voltage

Voltage is the difference in potential between two points on a conductor. A way to visualize voltage is to think of it as the pressure causing electron flow, the force that gets work done. If you visualize the flow of water in a pipe as being similar to this electron flow, voltage is the pressure causing the flow, and resistance is blockage or a valve in the way of the flow. Voltage is measured using a **voltmeter** (Figure 18-4) or the voltage-measuring function of a multimeter.

Voltage is measured by the amount of work done. The unit of measurement is the **volt** (E or V), named

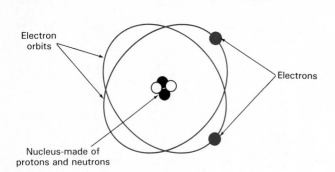

Electron orbits

Electrons

Nucleus-made of protons and neutrons

FIGURE 18-1 Structure of the atom.

tively charged. The nucleus is made up of more particles, but that is another story. More components of the nucleus are being discovered all the time. The electron is what is important to the discussion of electricity, because the electron, or rather its ability to move or flow from atom to atom, is the basis of the energy called electricity.

Conductors

Conductors are a group of materials containing a number of electrons that are free to move about. Most metals, and some liquids and gases, are conductors. The free electrons in conductors normally move about at random. When an electrical field or potential is introduced, for example, by a battery, the electrons flow in the same direction in a more orderly way. This electron flow creates electricity. It's the electrical energy that is used to perform many tasks in an automobile, from starting the engine to wiping the windshield.

One of the very best conductors is gold, but it is too expensive for everyday use. Another good conductor is silver. Although not as expensive as gold, it's still too costly to use except in very special applications. Fortunately, copper is a low-cost, good-quality conductor available for general use. Copper is found throughout the electrical circuits of an automobile not

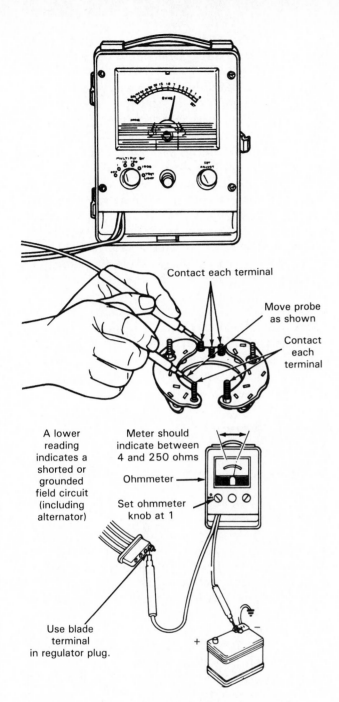

Contact each terminal

Move probe as shown

Contact each terminal

A lower reading indicates a shorted or grounded field circuit (including alternator)

Meter should indicate between 4 and 250 ohms

Ohmmeter

Set ohmmeter knob at 1

Use blade terminal in regulator plug.

FIGURE 18-2 Ohmmeter. (Ford Motor Company)

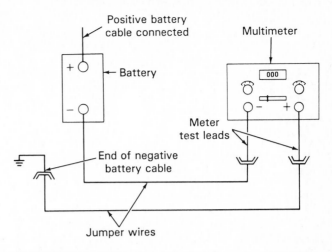

Positive battery cable connected

Battery

Multimeter

Meter test leads

End of negative battery cable

Jumper wires

FIGURE 18-3 Multimeter with digital readout. (Cadillac Motor Division, GMC)

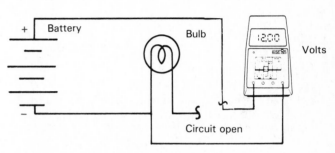

Battery

Bulb

Volts

Circuit open

Circuit complete between test points

FIGURE 18-4 Voltmeter.

after the Italian Count Alessandro Volta, one of the early pioneers in the study of electricity. One volt is equal to the difference in electrical potential between two points on a conductor carrying a current of 1 ampere (A) and dissipating a power of 1 watt (W).

Amperage

Another important characteristic of electricity that determines how much work can be done is called **current** or **amperage**. The flow of electrons in the same direc-

tion in a conductor was described earlier as electricity or electric current. Using the comparison of water flowing in a pipe again, current is the quantity or the amount of the flow. Electrical current or amperage in an automobile is important because it determines how long a starter motor can crank an engine, how long a light bulb will stay lit, and how quickly a battery is recharged after being used. Current is measured in **amperes** (I or A). It is a measure of the quantity or amount of work that can be done. Amperage is measured with an **ammeter** (Figure 18-5) or the current-measuring function of a multimeter.

FIGURE 18-5 Ammeter.

Connect ammeter in series

Battery

Bulb

Ammeter

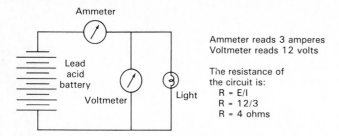

Ammeter reads 3 amperes
Voltmeter reads 12 volts

The resistance of
the circuit is:
R = E/I
R = 12/3
R = 4 ohms

FIGURE 18-6 Application of Ohm's law.

Ohm's Law

The relationship of these three functions—resistance (R) in ohms, voltage (E) in volts (V), and current (I) in amperes (A)—is expressed in a formula known as **Ohm's Law:**

$$E = I \times R$$

That is, the voltage in a circuit is equal to the current (in amperes) multiplied by the resistance (in ohms).

This formula is handy to know, because if you know any two of the values, you can calculate the third by using variations of the basic formula. For example,

$$I = \frac{E}{R}$$

That is, the current (amperage) in a circuit equals the voltage divided by the resistance (in ohms).

$$R = \frac{E}{I}$$

The resistance of a circuit (in ohms) equals the voltage divided by the current (in amperes). Figure 18-6 shows how to use Ohm's law to determine resistance of the circuit.

Another useful formula is one used to find the power of an electrical circuit expressed in watts:

$$P = E \times I$$

Power (P) in watts equals the voltage multiplied by the current (in amperes).

Alternating and Direct Current

Electrons may flow in only one direction, called direct current, or dc. Electrons may also surge back and forth in alternating directions. This is called alternating current, or ac.

Alternating current is the kind used in houses to energize lights and to run refrigerators, television sets, and stereos. Power plants can produce direct current, and, in fact, the first ones developed by Edison and others did. But direct current has one great disadvantage. Because electricity loses some strength when sent over long distances on wires exposed to the elements, it must be renewed or brought back to its operating potential before it can be used. Direct current offers no economical way to restore this lost power.

Alternating current, on the other hand, can be stepped up or down with relatively inexpensive transformers. A power plant sends the electricity at a very high level, on the order of thousands of volts. The line losses that occur are a very small percentage of the total voltage and have a relatively unimportant effect on the voltage reaching the user. A series of power distribution stations reduces the high voltage in stages until the electricity reaches its destination where it is lowered to a level that can be used.

Alternating current has one shortcoming that makes it unsuitable for use in an automobile. It cannot be stored. However, a battery can store direct current rather easily.

THE BATTERY

Theory

A battery is a group of cells connected together to provide a required dc voltage. A cell can be made from a variety of materials, but basically two plates of dissimilar metals immersed in an acid solution are required. You can make a simple cell by placing a copper penny on a dish, covering it with a piece of blotter paper soaked in vinegar, and putting a silver dime on top of the stack. A voltmeter connected to the penny and the dime will register a small voltage. A flashlight battery is a cell made from a zinc outer case and a carbon post in the center with the cell filled with a damp paste made of ammonium chloride and zinc chloride.

A cell generates electricity by converting chemical energy into electrical energy. Chemical processes within the lead/acid automobile battery cause the release of free electrons. When a circuit is completed between the negative and positive poles of the battery, the flow of electrons creates an electrical current (Figure 18-7). Each cell develops an electrical potential of approximately 2 V across its connectors. A 12-V automobile battery is made up of six cells. The automobile battery can be recharged many times and is, therefore, called a storage battery. It supplies the electricity needed to start the engine, or honk the horn, or play the radio.

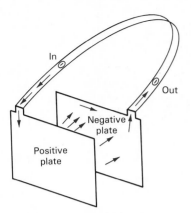

FIGURE 18-7 Electron flow in battery cell.

Discharging

The automobile battery is called a lead/acid battery because it uses plates made of lead peroxide (sometimes called brown lead oxide) and a porous lead called sponge lead (or gray lead) immersed in sulfuric acid (Figure 18-8). The acid is 36% sulfuric acid and 64% water by weight. The sulfuric acid is the **electrolyte,** and its atoms become ionized (broken up into positively and negatively charged atoms) in solution. These ions are free to move through the electrolyte. In addition, the sulfuric acid weakens the bond holding the electrons in place in the plates. This frees the electrons and allows them to move within the plates.

The chemical reactions taking place within the cell cause positive and negative ions to form in the plates. The lead peroxide plate becomes the positive plate, and electrons move from it into the electrolyte. Electrons travel through the electrolyte and enter the sponge lead plate. The sponge lead plate becomes the negative plate. The excess electrons in the negative plate flow out through the connector, through the electrical circuits of the automobile, and return through the positive post of the battery into the positive lead peroxide plate.

This cycle continues until the sulfuric acid is diluted to the point that it no longer has sufficient ions to dislodge electrons from the plates to support the current requirement of the load. The plates, by this time, have also been largely converted to lead sulfate. The battery is now said to be discharged or dead and must be recharged before it can be used again.

Recharging

Recharging reverses the discharging process. A voltage, slightly higher than the battery voltage, is applied to the terminals. This returns the plates to their original condition or as close to it as possible. The strength of the sulfuric acid also is restored.

The state of charge of a lead/acid battery with filler caps can be determined by measuring the **specific gravity** of the electrolyte. The electrolyte of a fully charged lead/acid battery has a specific gravity of 1.27; that is, the sulfuric acid is 1.27 times heavier than water. A completely discharged battery has a specific gravity of 1.07. The specific gravity of plain water is 1.00 and is the standard against which other liquids are compared.

Construction

Plates A lead/acid automobile battery is made of plates connected together in groups and kept apart by separators (Figure 18-9). Two types of plates are used: lead peroxide for the positive plates and sponge lead

FIGURE 18-9 Lead-acid battery construction. (Chrysler Corporation)

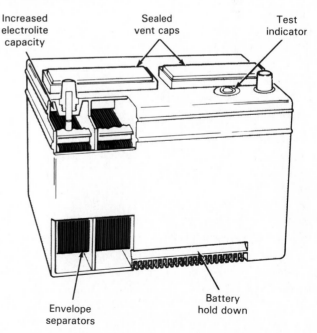

FIGURE 18-8 Electron flow between positive and negative plates in a cell.

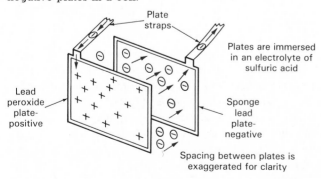

for the negative plates. The separators must be porous to allow the electrolyte to freely circulate. In the past separators have been made of perforated wood, sponge rubber, and fiberglass. Today they are usually made of polyvinyl chloride (PVC) or polyethylene. These elements are placed in cells in the battery case.

Cells Six cells connected together in series provide the 12 V required by most vehicles. If a 6-V battery is needed, 3 cells are used. A 24-V battery for industrial equipment and some marine use can be constructed by using 12 cells in series. The basic construction techniques remain the same.

Vents The standard battery has vent plugs that seal the filler holes in the top of the case. These holes are used for adding distilled water to maintain the electrolyte level and for withdrawing electrolyte with a **hydrometer** to measure the specific gravity of the sulfuric acid (explained later).

A sealed, maintenance-free battery never needs to have water added. Some of the more expensive maintenance-free batteries have a built-in hydrometer for checking the charge condition (Figure 18-10).

Terminals Some batteries have terminal posts on top, as shown in Figure 18-11. Notice that the negative terminal post is smaller in diameter than the positive post to reduce the chance of wrong connections. Other battery styles have screw terminals on the side of the case. This type is known as a side-terminal battery (Figure 18-12).

Life and Warranties

Life An average life for a typical lead/acid automobile battery is 4 years. The life expectancy varies

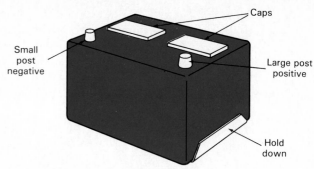

FIGURE 18-11   Battery terminal posts.

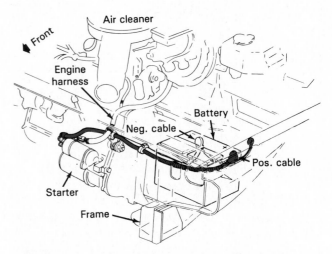

FIGURE 18-12   Side-terminal battery. (Oldsmobile Motor Division, GMC)

greatly, however, depending on battery grade and quality, the condition of the vehicle's electrical system, climate, and maintenance. A standard, original-equipment battery used on a vehicle in a cold climate may be lucky to last 2 years. The same battery used on a vehicle in a hot climate might last 5 years. Some maintenance procedures that will ensure maximum battery life are the following:

☐ Check the electrolyte level regularly.
☐ Use only distilled water.
☐ Keep the vehicle charging system in good condition.
☐ Keep the battery connectors clean.
☐ If the vehicle is only used for short trips, put the battery on an external charger every 2 weeks.

Warranties Warranties can indicate minimum expected life. Generally, the more a battery costs, the longer the warranty period. The manufacturer honors the warranty only when the required forms have been accurately completed and sent in. It is the seller's responsibility to record the sale and file the warranty forms. It is the buyer's responsibility to keep the receipt.

FIGURE 18-10   Maintenance-free battery with hydrometer. (Cadillac Motor Division, GMC)

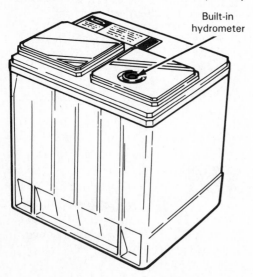

NEGATIVE TO POSITIVE

When early scientists first began experimenting with electricity and developing theories and mathematical formulas to support them, the instruments were very primitive. The earliest way to measure the flow of electrical energy was with a magnetic compass. When placed close to a wire carrying electricity, the compass needle would deflect from its usual north-pointing position. The direction the compass needle pointed was assumed to be the direction the electricity was flowing. The battery pole toward which the compass pointed was called the cathode, or negatively charged pole, and labeled (−). The other battery pole was called the anode, or positively charged pole, and labeled (+). All the theory and mathematical formulas were written with electrical current flow assumed to be from the anode (+) to the cathode (−).

It was not until many decades later that the truth was discovered. Electrons flow from cathode to anode, from negative to positive. But, by then, it was too late—too many books had been written, too many students had been taught, and too many designs had been implemented. The only solution was to teach two theories: the classical current theory and the modern electron theory. When solid-state or semiconductor technology came into being, the problem was magnified. Semiconductor theory is firmly based on electron flow from negatively charged material to positive material. To apply the classical mathematics and avoid having to invent an entirely new set of equations, the hole theory was developed. Instead of thinking of electrons moving from negative to positive, one could envision holes moving from positive to negative. Suddenly, the old classical current theory, and all its mathematics, worked beautifully. But, we're still left with three different theories to explain the same phenomenon. There will also be those who will remain forever convinced that there are two, very real types of electrical flow in a circuit: electrons flowing in one direction and current hurrying along in the opposite direction.

Forrest Frame

Ratings Batteries are graded according to their current capacity: how many amperes they can deliver and for how long. This rating is usually expressed in ampere-hours. Other terms have come into use in an attempt to provide more meaningful information or perhaps larger numbers with which to impress a potential customer. Some of these terms include the following:

1. The cold cranking rate at 0°F is the current in amperes that a battery can provide for 30 sec at a temperature of 0°F while maintaining cell voltages at a minimum of 1.2 V. The average battery would be rated at about 400 A using this method. But at 0° with an average auto electrical system, the low voltage due to the cold battery, and thickened oil, only about 15 sec of starting energy may be available.

2. The cold cranking rate at −20°F: a second cold cranking rating is calculated at −20°F where the voltage of each cell can drop to 1.0 V. A typical rating for an average battery would be about 300 A.

3. Reserve capacity is the length of time that a fully charged battery can deliver 25 A at 80°F. This would typically be 2 h for the average battery and is equivalent to a rating of 50 A-h.

Testing

> **CAUTION:** A lead/acid battery contains strong sulfuric acid that can burn skin and eyes. Wear safety goggles when checking specific gravity.
>
> A charging battery, or one that has been recently charging while the vehicle has been driven, vents hydrogen and oxygen gases, a very explosive mixture. Keep flame and sparks away.

You should make a complete test of the battery at each tune-up. In addition, check the electrolyte level each time the engine oil and other vehicle fluids are checked. To completely test the battery, an instrument known as a carbon pile or battery/starter tester is used (Figure 18-13). This test instrument combines a variable load, a voltmeter, and an ammeter in one handy, portable unit. If such a tester is not available, however, you can reach a fairly accurate judgment by using the procedure outlined in the section on voltage testing.

FIGURE 18-13 Carbon pile battery test (battery capacity).

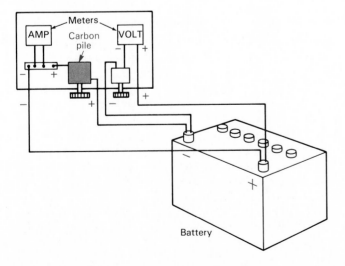

Specific Gravity Test

Hydrometer A quick and accurate method of determining the charge condition of a standard, lead/acid automotive battery (with filler openings in the top) is to measure the specific gravity of the electrolyte with a hydrometer (Figure 18-14). A battery hydrometer is a glass tube with a rubber or neoprene tube at one end and a squeeze bulb at the other. Inside the glass tube is a weighted float with a scale on it. The scale usually has numbers ranging from 1100 to 1300, corresponding to specific gravity values of 1.2–1.3. A second type of hydrometer is available for use on the small batteries that motorcycles use. These smaller batteries may not allow enough electrolyte to be drawn up the tube of the float hydrometer to provide a reading. This second type is called a ball hydrometer. It is smaller, less expensive, and easier to read (Figure 18-15). The float is more accurate and reads directly in specific gravity units.

Testing with Ball Hydrometer The glass tube of this type of hydrometer contains five plastic balls. Test each cell of the battery by placing the rubber tube at one end of the hydrometer into the electrolyte. Gently

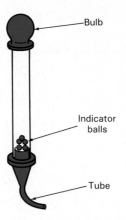

FIGURE 18-15 Ball hydrometer.

squeeze and then release the rubber bulb. Be sure to wear safety goggles, and be sure to squeeze the bulb gently. Vigorous squeezing can splash acid out of the battery into your face.

If all five balls float, the cell is fully charged. If none float, the cell is discharged. You can estimate intermediate levels of charge from the number of balls that float. Remember to test all cells and that each cell should be within one ball reading of the best cell.

Testing with Float Hydrometer As in using the ball hydrometer, place the rubber tube tip in the cell and slowly squeeze and release the bulb to draw sulfuric acid into the tube. Again, be careful. Don't squeeze vigorously, or splashing may result. Wear safety glasses, just in case. Draw enough acid into the tube to allow the float to be freely suspended. The float should neither rest on the bottom nor touch the top of the tube.

Read the number closest to the level of the acid on the float scale (Figure 18-16). The scale is often red, yellow, and green to show the general battery condition. These ranges are too general to be of much use. The values in Table 18-1 can serve as a guide. Obtain the actual ranges for a specific battery from the manufacturer's specifications.

FIGURE 18-14 Specific gravity test with hydrometer. (Chrysler Corporation)

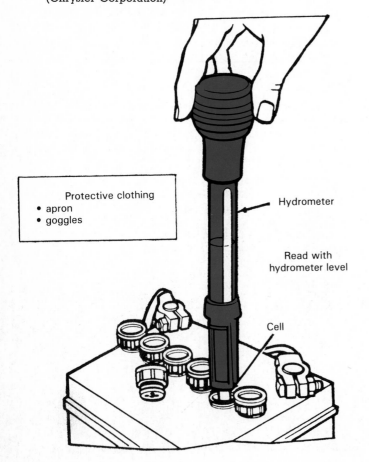

FIGURE 18-16 Reading scale on float hydrometer.

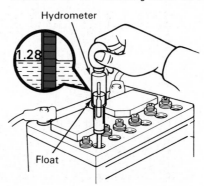

TABLE 18-1 Specific Gravity and Battery Charge

CHARGE	SPECIFIC GRAVITY RANGE AT 80°F
100%	1260–1280
75%	1240–1260
50%	1200–1240
25%	1170–1200
10%	1140–1170

Adjustments These specific gravity ranges are for an electrolyte temperature of 80°F. You must adjust the actual reading to account for temperatures much different from the nominal 80°F. Subtract 4 points from the specific gravity readings for each 10° under 80. Some hydrometers have a built-in thermometer and conversion scale which make the calculations easier (Figure 18-17). More sophisticated devices compensate for temperature. They automatically adjust for the temperature of the electrolyte.

FIGURE 18-17 Hydrometer scale with built-in thermometer. (Chrysler Corporation)

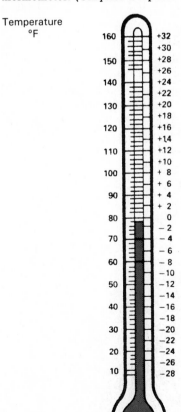

Sealed Batteries

The sealed, maintenance-free batteries cannot be checked in this manner. Some of them have a built-in hydrometer in one of the cells, but this only gives the specific gravity of the electrolyte in that one call. The only way to test these batteries is to assume a charge is needed, recharge them and then proceed with the voltage test.

Voltage Drop Test

Connecting a voltmeter to the battery and measuring the potential across the posts doesn't tell you much. Even a nearly dead battery can have enough residual charge to indicate 12 V on a meter without a load to pull it down. Using a light bulb and observing its brightness is a little better but not much. You need to observe the voltage drop with the battery under load to determine its condition. But before you do that, you need to be sure the battery is fully charged by checking the specific gravity of the electrolyte. With the specific gravity indicating a reasonable level of charge (1225 or more), you can proceed with the voltage drop test.

If you are going to use a carbon pile tester, connect it and proceed as described in Chapter 19 (Figure 18-18). If you do not have a carbon pile tester, the following procedure will work almost as well.

1. Clean the battery posts, connectors, and case as described in the service section of this chapter.

FIGURE 18-18 Carbon pile test hookup. (Cadillac Motor Division, GMC)

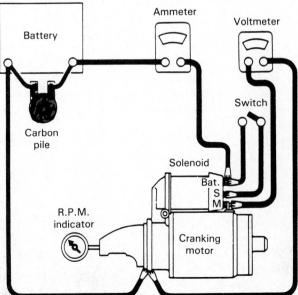

2. Check the specific gravity of the electrolyte. It must be at least 1225. If not, recharge the battery before continuing.

3. Connect a voltmeter (or multimeter set to read dc volts) across the battery. Red lead goes to the positive post, black lead to the negative post.

4. Turn on the vehicle's headlights. After 15 sec, read the voltage on the voltmeter. It should be at least 9.5 V at 80°F or 9.0 V at 30°F.

Please remember that this test is not valid unless the battery is charged, as indicated by a specific gravity reading of 1225 or more.

Service

Cleaning　Keep the outside of the battery clean and dry, or an electrical path may be formed that will lower the efficiency of the battery. The battery may even discharge through this short circuit that is formed by moist dirt and corrosion. First, be sure to wear rubber gloves and safety glasses. The powdery residue that builds up on the battery posts and terminals is corrosive and can burn skin and damage eyes. Also, some sulfuric acid may have overflowed onto the top of the battery if one or more of the cells were overfilled.

Carefully brush off loose corrosion and dirt. Gently hose off the battery and surrounding area. Now mix up a batch of corrosion eater. This is nothing more than baking soda mixed in water. Add about 2 tablespoons of baking soda to 2 cups of water in a jar or can and mix thoroughly. Brush this solution or slowly pour it over the corroded terminals and hold-down brackets. Be very careful not to get any in the cells. The baking soda solution will froth with a great deal of energy as it neutralizes the acid in the corrosion. When the foaming stops, gently hose off the affected areas until all the residue is rinsed away. Repeat the process, if necessary, until all corrosion is gone. Be sure to flush the area under the vehicle, or it will be permanently stained.

Cable Removal　Although you cannot see it, a thin film of corrosion builds up between the battery post and cable clamp. Clean this area by removing the cable clamps from the posts, and using a terminal cleaner (Figure 18-19).

First, remove the cable that is grounded to the engine block and body. Removing this cable first will prevent possible shorts and sparking when disconnecting the other cable. Most vehicles have the negative side of the battery grounded, but some imports may have the positive side grounded. Always check to be sure.

Use a box wrench or battery pliers to loosen the bolts on cable clamps. Regular pliers and open-end wrenches are too thick and may damage the battery

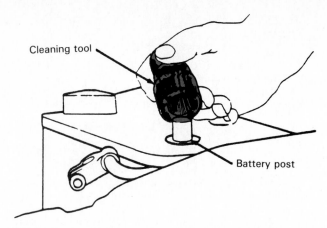

FIGURE 18-19　Battery post cleaners. (Ford Motor Company)

top when turned. Do not pry or twist the cable clamps to remove them because you can break the post loose from the plate connector. In particular, do not pry with a screwdriver; this technique is a sure way to puncture the battery case. Use a battery clamp puller (Figure 18-20).

Terminal Cleaning　Slip the cup of the wire brush battery post cleaner over each post, in turn, and twist several times. Use the cone-shaped brush on the inside surface of the cable clamps and twist (Figure 18-21). Repeat until the contact surfaces are bright. Reinstall the cable clamps, observing polarity. The negative post is smaller than the positive post and takes the smaller clamp. Be sure the clamps are tight to ensure good electrical contact, but don't overtighten. It is easy to distort or break the cable clamps, pull the threads out of the side of the case or strip the threads on the bolt. Coat the posts and clamps with a commercial corrosion inhibitor.

FIGURE 18-20　Battery clamp puller.

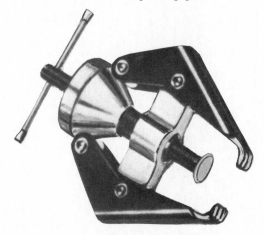

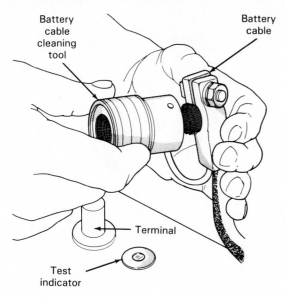

FIGURE 18-21 Cleaning a battery terminal and cable. (Ford Motor Company)

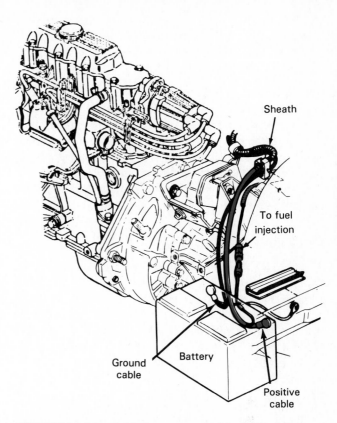

FIGURE 18-22 Cable harness assembly. (Oldsmobile Motor Division, GMC)

WIRING

Usually, the electrical wiring in an automobile completes one half of the circuit to the device being energized. The vehicle's metal engine block, chassis, and body provide the return circuit to the battery. As described in the battery section, one battery terminal is grounded to the engine block, which, in turn, is connected to the vehicle's chassis and body assembly. This ground return system eliminates one half of the wiring that would be required if every device needed two wires, one for +12 V and one for the negative return. Some fiberglass or plastic-bodied vehicles have two wires because the body is nonconducting.

Wire

The various electrical components of an automobile are connected with many different kinds and sizes of wire. Most of the wires are in cable harness assemblies for easy installing at the factory (Figure 18-22). The large number of wires and their burial in the harness sheath, as well as their sometimes hard-to-reach location within the vehicle, can make troubleshooting and signal tracing a difficult and sometimes impossible task. For this reason it is often easier and faster to run a new wire than try to fix a break or short in the original wire. Always remember to disconnect or cut the original wire to isolate it from the circuit when you replace it.

Size The size of the wire for each circuit is based on the maximum amount of current it is expected to carry in normal service. Table 18-2 lists typical wire sizes and uses.

Always replace a wire with one that is the same size or larger than the original. Stranded wire is more flexible than solid wire and will stand up better when subjected to movement. Solid wire is a better conductor, however, so whenever you must use stranded wire, it has to be larger than solid wire to carry the same current.

TABLE 18-2 Typical Wire Size and Use

(*GAUGE*) SIZE	*USE*
10	Alternator, ammeter, panel lights, heater switch
12	Light switch to fuse block or relay
14	Horn switch, radio to fuse block, headlight circuit, cigarette lighter
16	Taillights, gas gauge, heater leads, directional signals, stop lights, starter to relay switch
18	Single light bulbs

Note: Circuits over 10 ft long use the next larger size of wire or a lower gauge number.

Color Coding   Wires are usually color-coded or numbered to make tracing easier. The electrical diagrams for an automobile show the coding of the wire used in each circuit.

Use   Electrical wiring in an automobile is used to supply energy to, and control, all electrical equipment. It provides the path for the electricity to follow. This equipment includes the horn, lights, instruments, windshield wipers, power window motors, power seats, radios and stereos, heater and air-conditioning fans, rear deicers, engine cooling fans, ignition, and starting systems.

Continuity Testing

Tools   The primary method for checking a wire is to test its continuity, that is, to check its ability to transfer electricity from one end to the other. This simple test checks for breaks in the wire that would prevent the circuit from working. Use a multimeter set to a resistance range (Figure 18-23) or a continuity tester made of a battery and bulb (Figure 18-24) or buzzer to check continuity. A length of wire with alligator clips at each end is handy for those tests where the ends of the wire you're checking are separated farther than the test leads can reach. Disconnect the battery before starting continuity testing. The battery voltage could destroy your tester if you should place

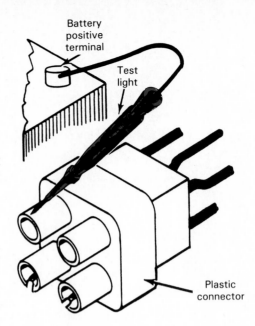

FIGURE 18-24   Test light continuity test.

it across a live circuit. Also the current (amperes) in a battery could melt the wires and burn your hands if you connected your tester across a high-current circuit.

Testing Procedure   Connect your tester to each end of the wire being tested, using the extra length of test lead if required. Check the color code at each end of the wire to be sure you are connected to both ends of the same wire. Be sure any switches located in the circuit between your tester leads are turned on (contacts closed). The tester should show continuity; that is, the bulb should light, the buzzer should sound, or the meter needle should show nearly zero. Move the wire back and forth and wiggle it to see if the indication changes. If the wire tests out okay, don't forget the return path through the body, chassis, or structural member.

Connect the tester to the grounded terminal and touch the second tester lead to a good chassis ground. A bright shiny bolt will usually work. If the tester indicates continuity, you will have to check further. Test all components, such as switches, firewall connectors, and fuses. Replacement may be the only option left if the test does not reveal the problem.

WIRING DIAGRAMS

Automobile service manuals contain wiring diagrams. These diagrams show the interconnection of the various electrical components and the color coding of the

FIGURE 18-23   Ohmmeter continuity test.

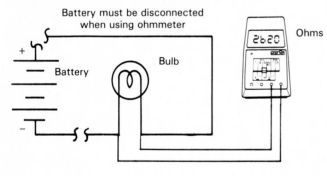

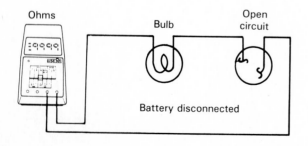

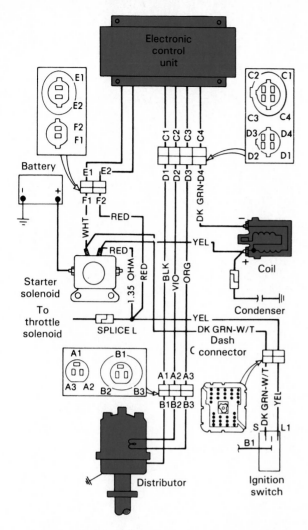

FIGURE 18-25 Typical wiring diagram (schematic).
(Ford Motor Company)

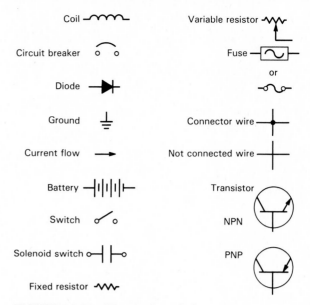

FIGURE 18-26 Electrical symbols.

The diagram may seem complex at first, but if you isolate one circuit and follow it through, you should see how useful it can be. Remember that electrical circuits require a complete path in order to conduct. The wiring diagram shows the insulated side (usually the positive side) of the circuitry. A ground symbol shows the return through the body and chassis of the vehicle (usually the negative side). Notice that the primary connection to the battery is made from a terminal on the starter (actually on the starter solenoid), and from this point power is distributed to the fuse block for distribution to all other accessories. Wires that simply cross each other on the diagram are not connected. A heavy black dot at the juncture indicates a permanent connection.

wire insulation. Figure 18-25 shows a typical wiring diagram. Standard electrical symbols are used, but most parts are labeled so you don't need intimate knowledge of the symbols (Figure 18-26).

TRADE TERMS

Ammeter
Amperage
Amperes
Current
Electrolyte
Electrons
Hydrometer
Multimeter

Ohm's Law
Ohmeter
Ohms
Resistance
Specific Gravity
Voltage
Voltmeter
Volt

REVIEW QUESTIONS

1. Why is direct current used in automobile electrical circuits?

2. Describe the single characteristic that determines whether a material is a conductor or an insulator.

3. What instrument is used to measure current?

4. Use Ohm's law to answer the following problems:
   a. If the current in a circuit is 3 A and the resistance is 2 Ω, what is the voltage?
   b. If the voltage of a circuit measures 11.5 V dc and the current measures 2.3 A, what is the resistance of the circuit?
   c. If the voltage of a circuit measures 12.6 V dc and the resistance measures 2.6 Ω, what is the current in the circuit?

5. What chemical solution is used for the electrolyte in an automobile battery?

6. Why is specific gravity measured?

7. What determines the size of wire to use in an electrical circuit?

8. How many conduction paths are required in a single electrical circuit? Why?

19

The Charging System

INTRODUCTION

Because the automobile can generate its own electricity, it is a self-contained power system requiring only regular refueling and maintenance to keep it operating. You do not have to replace batteries when they run down, as you would if they were the only source of power for starting the engine or driving at night with headlights.

This chapter introduces you to the charging system in the automobile, its basic parts, and how it operates. The charging system has five main parts: the alternator, the regulator, the pulley and belt drive system, the fusible link, and the dash warning light or ammeter (Figure 19-1).

CHARGING

Theory

Two similar devices are used to generate electricity in automobiles: the generator and the **alternator**. Both are driven by a belt, and both rely on the principle that electricity is induced in a coil of wire when it

OBJECTIVES

When you have completed this chapter, you should be able to

- Explain how an automobile's charging system operates
- Describe the difference between a generator and an alternator
- Describe the function of the regulator
- Test alternators on the car and on the bench
- Isolate problems to a specific component in the charging system and repair or replace it

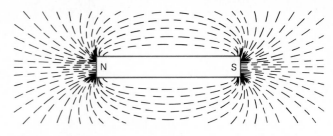

FIGURE 19-2   Bar magnet flux field.

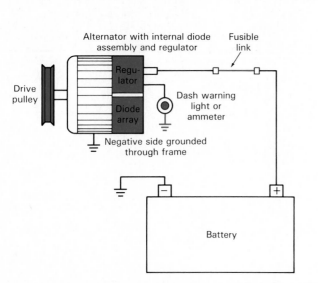

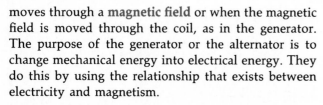

FIGURE 19-1   Basic charging circuit.

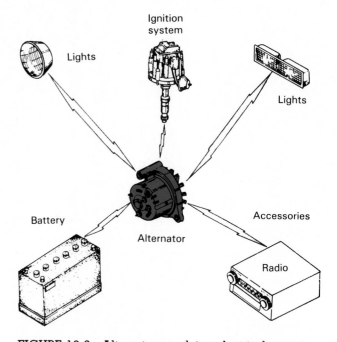

FIGURE 19-3   Alternator supplying electrical power.

moves through a **magnetic field** or when the magnetic field is moved through the coil, as in the generator. The purpose of the generator or the alternator is to change mechanical energy into electrical energy. They do this by using the relationship that exists between electricity and magnetism.

Magnetism   Magnets have lines of flux. These invisible lines of flux can be seen when a magnet attracts iron powder shavings (Figure 19-2). The shavings will arrange themselves into the pattern of the flux lines. When these flux lines are interrupted by an iron core, such as a rotor in an alternator, electricity is produced. The faster this electromagnet turns, the more lines of flux it crossses and the more electricity is produced.

Generators   The dc generator has one serious fault; it produces insufficient current at engine idle speeds. The battery would discharge if the car were left to run at idle for long periods under high electrical load conditions. Such operation is typical of stop-and-go city driving.

Alternators   With the development of solid-state electronics, the ac generator, or alternator, came into widespread use. The alternator produces alternating current which must be changed, or *rectified*, to dc power to supply the electrical energy required. It supplies energy to the engine ignition system, the accessory electrical system, and the battery (Figure 19-3).

ALTERNATORS

Alternators have three main parts: a stator, a rotor, and a diode rectifier assembly. These parts are housed in a case (Figure 19-4).

Stator

The **stator** is a series of copper wire windings on an iron core within which the rotor turns. The stator windings connect to form three circuits. Two stator connections are used: delta and Y (Figure 19-5). The

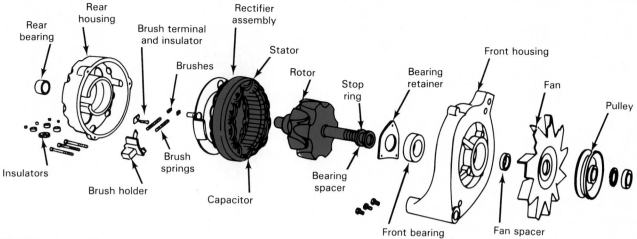

FIGURE 19-4 Alternator construction.

"Y" connected stator

Delta connected stator

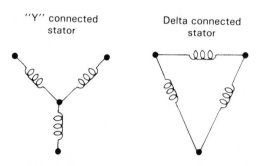

FIGURE 19-5 Y- and delta-connected stators.

Y-type has higher output at lower speeds. The delta has higher output at higher speeds and is usually used for heavy-duty applications.

Rotor

The **rotor** is an electromagnet assembly; that is, it is a magnet only when electricity is applied to it (Figure 19-6). The slip rings mounted on the rotor shaft carry the electrical energy supplied through the brushes to the coil assembly. The coils themselves are inside the metal pole pieces. The rotor is mounted with bearings

FIGURE 19-6 Typical rotor assembly.

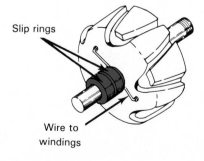

at each end so it can rotate with low friction. The drive end of the rotor has a pulley attached for the belt drive. There is also a fan mounted between the pulley and the case to provide a flow of cooling air through the alternator.

Diodes

Diodes belong to a class of *solid-state* electronic components known as semiconductors (Figure 19-7). Another type of semiconductor is the transistor. Diodes have the valuable characteristic of allowing electrical current to flow through them in only one direction (Figure 19-8). They prevent the battery from discharging to

FIGURE 19-7 Diode.

Positive lead

Right hand threads

Left hand threads

Negative − case

Positive + case

Diode symbol

Current flow

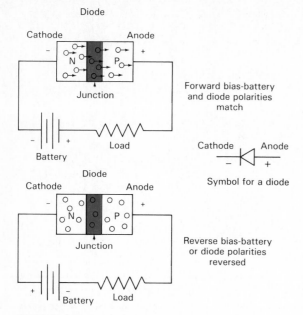

FIGURE 19-8 Diode conduction.

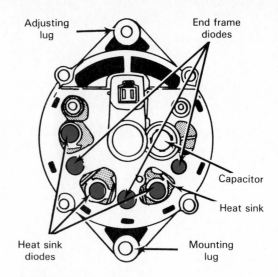

FIGURE 19-10 End view of an alternator showing diode mounting.

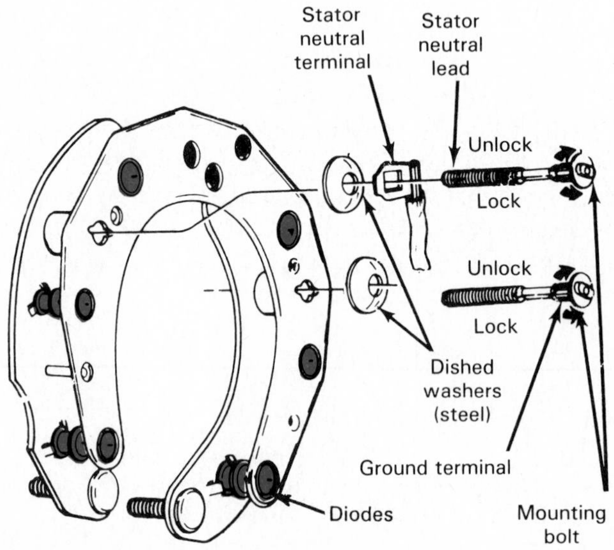

ground through the diodes and stator windings. These semiconductor diodes convert, or rectify, the ac power generated by the alternator into dc power and sometimes are called rectifiers. Full-wave rectifiers allow the negative half cycle and the positive half cycle to be used in the charging system (Figure 19-9).

Mounting The diodes are on a metal plate which serves three functions: (1) mounting, (2) electrical conduction, and (3) heat conduction. The diodes are usually in an assembly at the opposite end of the alternator from the pulley (Figure 19-10). The diodes may be single units mounted individually, or combined in a single package (Figures 19-11 and 19-12).

Diodes are assembled into rectifier bridges for installation in the alternator. Usually there are three positive diodes and three negative diodes. The diodes themselves are the same, but the way they are mounted and wired into the circuit determines whether they function as positive or negative elements.

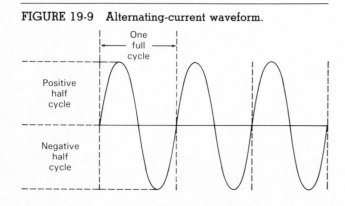

FIGURE 19-11 Stacked rectifier assembly with exposed diodes. (Ford Motor Company)

FIGURE 19-12 Flat rectifier assembly with built-in diodes. (Ford Motor Company)

FIGURE 19-9 Alternating-current waveform.

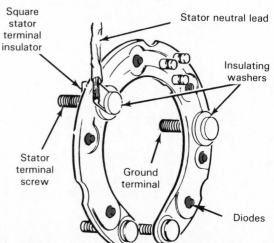

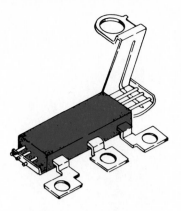

FIGURE 19-13 Diode trio.

A second diode assembly is installed in systems with solid-state regulators that do not have a field relay. The assembly is typically made up of three diodes mounted in a single package and is usually called a diode trio (Figure 19-13).

Rectification

Alternating current is alternatively positive and negative. The number of positive pulses and negative pulses each second is a direct result of the speed at which the alternator rotor rotates. The diodes are arranged in a circuit that converts each pulse into a direct-current voltage (Figure 19-14). Figure 19-15 shows a Y stator diode rectifier wiring diagram.

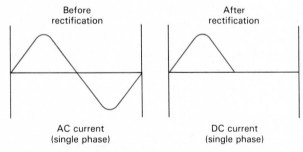

FIGURE 19-14 Single-phase current, ac and dc.

FIGURE 19-15 Diode rectifier wiring diagram.

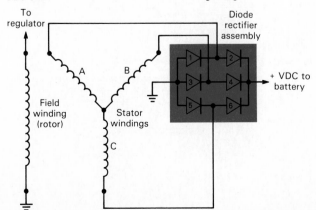

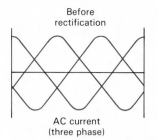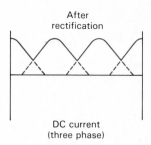

FIGURE 19-16 Three-phase ac and dc current.

As the rotor spins within the stator, its rotating magnetic fields create alternate pulses of positive and negative current in the three stator windings. As a positive cycle is generated in winding A (Figure 19-15), diode 2 rectifies it into a positive pulse of dc voltage. Diodes 3 and 5 serve as the ground return for winding A during this part of the cycle. As the rotation continues, winding B starts to go positive while winding A is passing through the transition from positive to negative. Diode 5 is the sole path to ground at this point.

As winding B becomes fully positive, diode 4 rectifies the ac pulse and adds it to the dc line to the battery. Diodes 1 and 5 provide the return to ground. As rotation continues, winding C outputs a positive pulse to diode 6 which rectifies it and aligns it to the battery. Diodes 1 and 3 provide the ground return.

This sequence is repeated very rapidly with each rotation of the rotor within the stator. Thus, the electrical current is converted from a rapidly changing ac voltage, to a series of dc pulses, to a nearly unbroken, steady dc voltage as the result of the rectifying action of diodes (Figure 19-16).

REGULATORS

Voltage regulation prevents alternator overvoltage from damaging electrical components in the automobile. Abnormally high voltages can burn out bulbs and damage radios and accessories as well as the alternator itself. High engine speed produces an overvoltage condition because the rotor in the alternator is turning faster. A low load demand, such as a combination of a fully charged battery and light accessory use, can allow voltage to climb to higher-than-normal levels. Because all of these conditions are a regular part of automobile operation, the voltage must be controlled somehow. This job is the function of the voltage **regulator** in the automobile charging system.

Theory

All regulators control alternator output voltage by controlling the voltage applied to the rotor through the brushes and slip rings. Controlling the rotor current controls the magnetic field which induces the current flow in the stator. The regulator senses the voltage output of the alternator. In normal operation, the regulator turns the field (rotor) current on and off many times each second.

The regulator is sometimes in a separate box mounted outside the alternator, but it is often inside the alternator. Ford, Chrysler, and early Bosch regulators are mounted externally, and General Motors and late Bosch are mostly internally mounted.

Types of Regulators

Two types of regulators are in common use: electromechanical and **solid state.** The electromechanical regulator is always outside the alternator because of its size and because it needs occasional adjustment.

Mechanical Regulators Early mechanical regulators contained three relays: a field relay, a charge indicator relay, and a voltage regulator. Most modern mechanical regulators have only two: a field relay and a voltage regulator (Figure 19-17). Some Bosch regulators only have a voltage regulator and no field relay (Figure 19-18).

The advantages of external mounting are isolation for ease of in-car troubleshooting and replacement and accessibility for adjustment. The disadvantage of external mounting is the potential for exposure to the dirt, heat, and moisture present in the engine compartment. The same disadvantages exist for internal regulators but to a lesser degree. However, internal regulators do have to withstand more vibration.

Solid-State Regulators The electronic solid-state regulator is a semiconductor circuit sealed in a plastic or metal housing (Figure 19-19). Solid-state regulators can be either internally mounted or externally mounted. Some solid-state external regulators, although smaller

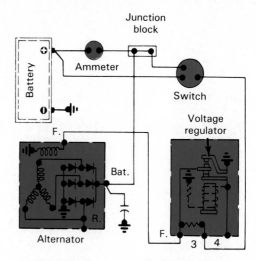

FIGURE 19-18 Voltage regulator without field relay.

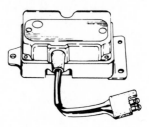

FIGURE 19-19 Nonadjustable solid-state regulator.

than they once were, are still too large to be mounted inside the alternator (Figure 19-20).

Small, solid-state regulators are packaged to fit precisely in a specific model of alternator (Figure 19-21). The regulator field output is often connected directly to the brush holders. Mounting the regulator inside the alternator housing provides more protection and helps keep wiring to a minimum. These both help improve reliability.

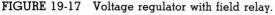

FIGURE 19-17 Voltage regulator with field relay.

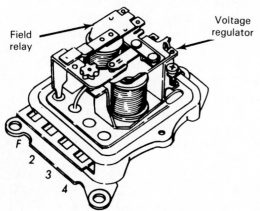

FIGURE 19-20 Adjustable solid-state regulator.

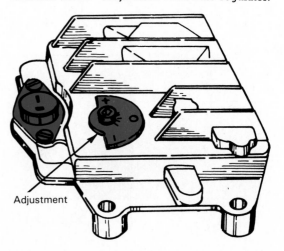

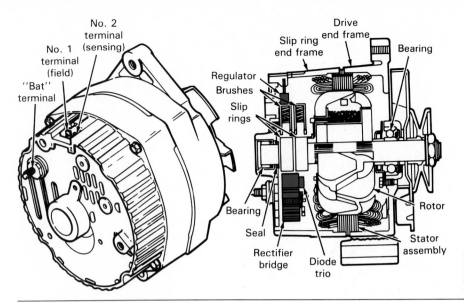

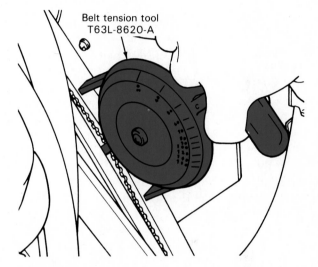

FIGURE 19-21 Alternator with internal regulator. (Cadillac Motor Division, GMC)

PULLEY AND BELT DRIVE SYSTEM

The drive belt and pulley assembly is rotated by the engine and turns the alternator rotor. The drive belt must be in good condition. If it is broken, the rotor will not turn, and electricity will not be generated. The drive belt must have proper tension (Figure 19-22).

If the belt is too tight, the alternator bearing will be under too much pressure and will wear quickly.

FIGURE 19-22 Adjusting the alternator drive belt. (Ford Motor Company)

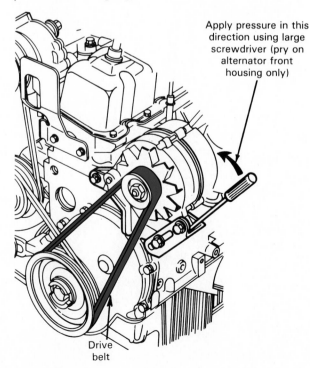

FIGURE 19-23 Belt tension check. (Ford Motor Company)

Too tight a belt can even warp the alternator case. If the belt is too loose, it will slip, and the alternator will not turn at full speed. This also can cause a damaged belt. A loose belt will cause the alternator to produce less than full voltage. A loose belt is a common cause of dead batteries. Figure 19-23 shows a belt tension tool that you should use to tighten the alternator drive belt correctly.

FUSIBLE LINKS

Fusible links are in the circuit to protect the voltage regulator, diodes, and alternator from short circuits that may occur in the electrical system (Figure 19-24). They are safety devices, necessary if one of the fuses protecting an individual circuit fails to blow or if a short

FIGURE 19-24   Typical fusible links.

occurs in a main circuit ahead of the fuse block. Fusible links function like the main fuse or circuit breaker in a household wiring system.

GAUGES AND CHARGING LIGHTS

A dashboard warning light or ammeter gauge warns when the system is not operating properly. Some systems use a voltage gauge. Both gauges and lights provide useful, although slightly different, information. An ammeter gauge shows the exact amount of amperes going into the battery, and the voltage gauge indicates the voltage being generated.

A warning light may attract attention faster, particularly if the driver is not in the habit of scanning the instrument panel regularly. The warning light serves two functions. First, it tells you, when it goes out, that the alternator is charging the battery. Second, the resistance in the warning light bulb itself helps to control the output of the alternator. When the driver turns the ignition key on, 12 V go through the warning light, causing it to glow. After the engine starts and the alternator starts to produce more than 12 V, the alternator cancels the battery voltage, and the light goes off.

IN-CAR TESTS

In-car testing identifies the problem in a replaceable unit or repairable element so the mechanic can correct the problem. Observing the symptoms and logically thinking the problem through can save a lot of time-consuming troubleshooting. Although the tests in this section are primarily for systems with externally mounted voltage regulators, the same principles apply to systems with internally mounted regulators. *The specific test methods will vary, however, so be sure to refer to the manufacturer's service manual or a good commercial service guide.*

Pretest Checks

Check the specific gravity of the battery's electrolyte and recharge the battery, if necessary. Clean and tighten the battery connectors, as required. Check and adjust the drive belt tension.

> **CAUTION:** The hydrogen gas vented by the battery is explosive. A battery explosion will splash acid over a wide area. Always wear eye protection and avoid sparking due to electrical contact or shorting close to the battery. Do not allow fire or flame near the battery.

Charging Circuit Resistance Test

1. Disconnect the ground cable from the battery negative post before making test connections. This will prevent any accidental shorting.

2. Disconnect the lead at the BAT terminal on the alternator. Connect a 0–100 A dc ammeter in series between the BAT terminal and the lead disconnected from it (Figure 19-25).

3. Connect the positive lead of a dc voltmeter to the disconnected BAT lead. Connect the voltmeter's negative lead to the positive terminal of the battery to measure voltage drop during the test.

4. Disconnect the regulator field wire (usually green) from the alternator field terminal (F). Connect a wire from the alternator field terminal (F) to ground.

5. Connect a tachometer for measuring engine speed following the tachometer manufacturer's instructions. Typically two connections are required: the +12 V connection at the coil and a good ground.

6. Reconnect the ground cable to the battery negative post.

7. Connect a carbon pile rheostat (load) across the battery, first making sure it is set to OFF or OPEN to avoid severe sparking and the danger of explosion.

8. Start the engine and immediately reduce the speed to idle. Racing the engine with the field coil grounded can cause excessive voltages to be generated, resulting in damage to electrical components. Adjust engine speed and the carbon pile to maintain a current of 20 A flowing in the circuit.

FIGURE 19-25   Charging circuit resistance test.

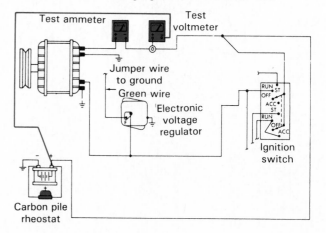

"IT COULD NEVER HAPPEN TO ME . . ."

Batteries can be hazardous to your health . . . and your hair. One of our mechanics got a little preoccupied and forgot to make sure the battery charger was turned off before he attempted to hook it up. When he made the connection, a spark caused the battery to explode, spewing acid over the car and himself. Forgetting about himself for the moment, he hurriedly washed down the car for fear the acid would ruin the paint job. Afterwards, he washed himself off and changed into some spare clothes he kept handy.

The next day, however, he showed up with a considerably shorter haircut. In his haste he had neglected to rinse his hair thoroughly, so when he had combed his hair that afternoon, he found he had some noticeable holes. With some embarrassment, he explained that he decided a shorter hairstyle was preferable to a patchy one.

Kay O'Cullane
San Diego Community Skill Center

9. The voltmeter should indicate a voltage drop of not more than 0.7 V. If the voltage drop is higher, check, clean, and tighten all connections in the charging system.

10. If the voltage drop is still higher, move the voltmeter positive lead from point to point in the circuit. Start at the starter solenoid main battery connection and move down the circuit until you find the connection with the greatest voltage drop.

Current Output Test

1. Except for the voltmeter, all test connections are the same as for the resistance test (Figure 19-26). If you are starting fresh, however, remember to disconnect the battery negative cable before making the test connections.

2. Connect the negative lead of the voltmeter to ground and the positive lead to the BAT terminal on the alternator.

3. Start the engine and immediately reduce the speed to idle. Racing the engine with the test connections can damage components.

4. Adjust the engine speed and the carbon pile for an indication of 1250 rpm on the tachometer and 15 V on the voltmeter.

CAUTION: Do not allow the voltage to exceed 16 V, or component damage may result.

---

5. The current output, as indicated on the ammeter, should be within the specifications for the vehicle under test (typically a minimum of 47 to 50 A).

6. If the output is less than the specified minimum, replace the alternator or remove it for bench testing.

Voltage Output Test

Note: Battery specific gravity should be above 1.200 for a proper regulated voltage check. Charge the battery or use a good test battery before testing the regulator.

1. Connect the positive lead of the voltmeter to the positive post on the battery. Connect the negative lead from the voltmeter to a good vehicle body ground (Figure 19-27).

2. Check the ambient temperature of the voltage regulator. Table 19-1 shows how the temperature affects the voltage output.

3. Start and run the engine at 1250 rpm with all lights and accessories turned off. Check the voltmeter. The regulator is working properly if voltage readings are within specifications.

FIGURE 19-26 Alternator current output test hookup.

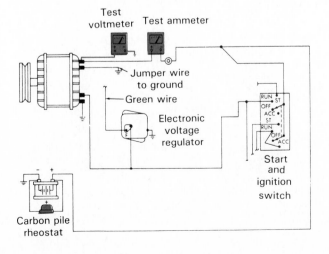

FIGURE 19-27 Voltmeter connection for voltage output test.

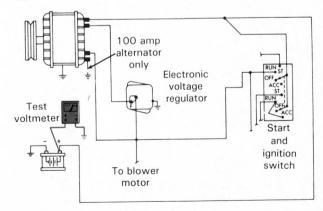

TABLE 19-1 Regulator Ambient Temperature and Voltage Range

AMBIENT TEMPERATURE[a]	VOLTAGE RANGE
−20°F	14.9–15.9
80°F	13.9–14.6
140°F	13.3–13.9

[a]Ambient temperature is measured ¼ in. from the regulator.

4. If the voltage is not within limits or is fluctuating, check that the regulator has a good ground. With the engine off, disconnect the regulator terminals. Turn the ignition on, but do not start the engine. Battery voltage should appear at both the blue and green leads of the connector. If all the tests are satisfactory, replace the regulator and repeat the tests.

BENCH TESTS

Removing the alternator for bench testing separates the unit from the rest of the circuitry and allows you to disassemble it. You can then test and repair individual components in the alternator. The procedures for removing the alternator and disassembling it vary from car to car (Figure 19-28). Two bolts generally hold the alternator in place. Removing the locking bolt and loosening the pivot bolt allows the alternator to rotate, releasing tension on the belt. Slip the belt off the pulley. Disconnect the wiring harness and the battery cable and remove the remaining bolt. To disassemble the alternator, simply remove the screws that bolt to-

FIGURE 19-28 Removing an alternator. (Ford Motor Company)

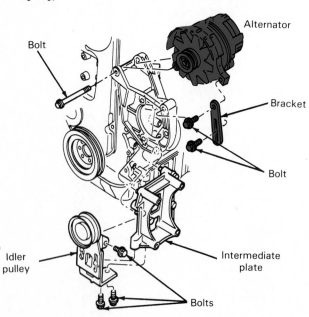

gether the front and rear housings. Carefully separate the individual assemblies for testing. The following tests are for typical models. Use a shop manual whenever you need specific testing procedures.

Field Coil Current Draw Test (Internally Grounded Rotor)

1. Place an insulating pad on the work bench and place the alternator on the pad. Connect a jumper wire between the housing of the alternator and the negative terminal of a fully charged battery.

2. Connect the positive lead of an ammeter to the field terminal of the alternator. Connect the ammeter's negative lead to the positive battery terminal. Connect a voltmeter across the battery's terminals.

3. Rotate the alternator rotor slowly by hand. The ammeter should indicate a current of 4.5–6.5 A, and the voltmeter should indicate 14 V.

4. A low current reading indicates a high resistance in the rotor/field coil circuit. Worn brushes that make uneven contact, corroded slip rings, poor connections, or a problem in the rotor coils themselves can cause high resistance.

5. A high current reading indicates a shorted rotor coil or a grounded rotor.

6. No reading on the ammeter indicates an open rotor winding (coil) or defective brushes.

Diode Test

1. Remove the nuts securing the stator leads and the positive and negative rectifier connectors.

2. Use a 12-V battery and a No. 67 bulb for testing. Connect one test lamp lead to the positive battery post. Connect the other lamp lead to the end of a test probe.

3. Connect a second test probe to the battery negative terminal.

4. Test diode continuity by touching one probe to the heat sink and the other probe to the rectifier pins (Figure 19-29). Now reverse the probes.

FIGURE 19-29 Rectifier testing points.

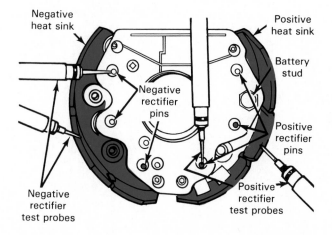

5. If the test lamp lights with the probes in one position but not the other, the diode is good. If the lamp lights with the probes in both positions, the diode is shorted, and you must replace it. If the lamp does not light with the probes in either position, the diode is open, and you must replace it.

6. Test each rectifier in both assemblies. The lamp should light with the probes in the same relative position for each diode in the same rectifier assembly.

Stator Test (Y-Connected Models)

1. Use an ohmmeter or the test lamp to test the stator windings for continuity and shorts to ground.

2. Remove varnish from a small area of the stator frame using sandpaper or a sharp knife. You will use this area for the ground connection.

3. Press one test probe firmly against the cleaned area on the stator frame. Press the other test probe to each of the three winding leads, one at a time (Figure 19-30).

4. If the test lamp lights or the ohmmeter indicates no resistance, the stator winding is grounded, and you must replace stator.

5. Press one test probe to one winding lead and touch the second probe to each of the other two stator coil leads, one at a time. The test lamp should light or the ohmmeter should indicate continuity in each case (Figure 19-31). If not, windings are open, and you will have to replace the stator.

Rotor Test

1. Use an ohmmeter to bench-test the rotor.

2. Touch the ohmmeter leads to the slip rings (one at a time) and to the rotor shaft to check for shorts to ground (Figure 19-32). No continuity should be indicated. If the ohmmeter indicates any continuity, replace the rotor.

3. Touch the ohmmeter leads to the slip rings (Figure 19-33). The ohmmeter should read between 1.5 and 2.1 Ω at room temperature. If the rotor is still warm from recent operation, the readings will be slightly higher.

4. A reading above 3.5 Ω tells you that you must replace the rotor. A reading below 1.5 Ω indicates the field coil is shorted; replace the rotor.

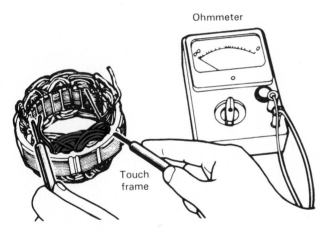

FIGURE 19-30   Stator coil ground test.

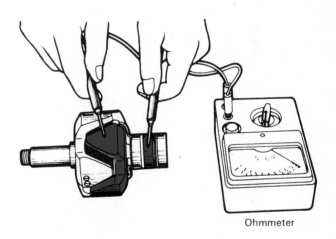

FIGURE 19-32   Rotor coil ground test.

FIGURE 19-31   Stator coil continuity test.

FIGURE 19-33   Rotor coil continuity test.

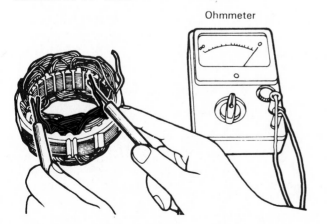

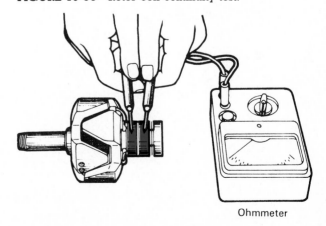

CHARGING SYSTEM DIAGNOSIS

Whenever the charging system is not functioning properly, the first place to start troubleshooting is a manual. Most manuals will have a system diagnosis chart in them (Figure 19-34). From the symptoms, these charts identify the possible sources of faulty operation and the action you must take to repair the charging system.

FIGURE 19-34   Charging system diagnosis. (Ford Motor Company)

CHARGING SYSTEM DIAGNOSIS

CONDITION	POSSIBLE SOURCE	ACTION
• Battery does not stay charged — engine starts OK	• Battery.	• Test battery, replace if necessary.
	• Loose or worn alternator belt.	• Adjust or replace belt.
	• Wiring or cables.	• Service as required.
	• Alternator.	• Test and/or replace components as required.
	• Regulator.	• Test, replace if necessary.
	• Other vehicle electrical systems.	• Check other systems for current draw. Service as required.
• Alternator noisy	• Loose or worn alternator belt.	• Adjust tension or replace belt.
	• Bent pulley flanges.	• Replace pulley.
	• Alternator.	• Service or replace alternator.
• Lights and/or fuses burn out frequently	• Wiring.	• Service as required
	• Alternator/Regulator.	• Test, service, replace if necessary.
	• Battery.	• Test, replace if necessary.
• Charge indicator light flickers after engine starts or comes on while vehicle is being driven	• Loose or worn alternator belt.	• Adjust tension or replace.
	• Alternator.	• Service or replace.
	• Field circuit ground.	• Service or replace defective wiring.
	• Regulator.	• Test, replace if necessary.
	• Lamp circuit wiring and connector.	• Service as required.
• Charge indicator light flickers while vehicle is being driven	• Loose or worn alternator belt.	• Adjust tension or replace belt.
	• Loose or improper wiring connections.	• Service as required.
	• Alternator.	• Service or replace.
	• Regulator.	• Test, replace if necessary.
• Charge indicator gauge shows discharge	• Loose or worn alternator belt.	• Adjust tension or replace belt.
	• Wiring (Battery to alternator for ground or open).	• Service or replace wiring.
	• Field circuit ground.	• Service or replace damaged wiring.
	• Alternator.	• Service or replace.
	• Regulator.	• Test, replace if necessary
	• Charge indicator gauge wiring and connections.	• Service as required
	• Gauge.	• Replace gauge.
	• Other vehicle electrical systems malfunction.	• Service as required.

TRADE TERMS

Alternator
Diodes
Fusible Links
Magnetic Field

Regulator
Rotor
Solid State
Stator

REVIEW QUESTIONS

1. Why does an automobile require a charging system?
2. What are the five main parts of the charging system?
3. What is ac power? dc power?
4. What is the one characteristic of a diode that makes it so useful?
5. Describe rectification.
6. What is the term for an assembly made up of three diodes?
7. What does a voltage regulator do? Why is it necessary?
8. Name two types of voltage regulators in general use.
9. What powers the pulley and drive belt system?
10. What caution should be taken when working around a battery?

20

The Starting System

INTRODUCTION

The modern starter is a reliable and efficient mechanism. It performs its task with little appreciation from most drivers for the complex and difficult series of events that occur when they turn the ignition key. This chapter describes each component of the starting system and the contribution each part makes to the complete system.

STARTING SYSTEM CIRCUIT

The basic starting system circuit consists of wiring, the starter motor and solenoid assembly (Figure 20-1) battery, and starter or ignition switch (Figure 20-2).

Starter Wiring

Two connections are between the vehicle battery positive post and the starting system. One positive cable is relatively small in diameter because it carries the low current required to operate the **solenoid.** This cable

OBJECTIVES

When you have completed this chapter, you should be able to

- Describe the automobile starting system and the function of its components
- Troubleshoot a faulty starting system and isolate the problem
- Repair or replace a malfunctioning component

the battery positive post directly to the contacts in the solenoid.

Solenoid and Starter Switch

When the solenoid is energized, the circuit path to the starter motor is closed. Thus, the starter switch in the ignition switch assembly only has to carry the light current required to energize the solenoid. The high current required when cranking the engine is handled by a direct connection through the high-current contacts in the solenoid and the heavy cable to the battery. The return to the battery negative post is through the vehicle chassis.

The starter switch is normally part of the ignition switch assembly. Its purpose is to supply electric current to energize the solenoid. When energized, the solenoid closes the heavy contacts that provide current to the dc motor assembly.

Motor

Current flows through the field windings in the motor. It then flows through the brushes to the commutator and from there energizes the armature windings. The return circuit is through another set of brushes to the starter case and chassis ground. This series connection of all the electrical components of the starter motor is why the motor is called a series-wound dc motor.

Ballast Resistor

Another element in the circuit of some starter systems is a ballast resistance bypass circuit. A ballast resistor or resistance wire in series with the ignition coil primary lead is used in older ignition systems to protect the ignition points from excessive current when the engine is running. However, the ignition coil must have full current during starting. For this reason the resistance is bypassed in one of two ways during starting. One way is to provide a second path to the coil from the starter/ignition switch through a set of contacts that are closed when the switch is in the START position. Another method frequently used is to provide a second set of contacts in the solenoid to bypass the resistance when the solenoid is energized during starting.

Safety Switch

Cars equipped with automatic transmissions have a safety switch in the starter circuit. This switch, the neutral safety switch, passes electrical energy to the starter only when the automatic shift lever is in PARK or NEUTRAL. Many cars with manual transmissions have a clutch pedal switch. It prevents the engine from starting unless the clutch pedal is depressed.

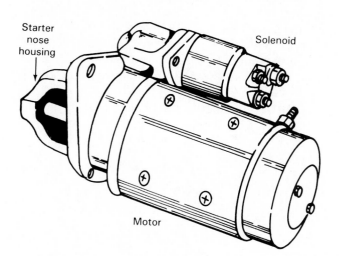

FIGURE 20-1   Typical starter motor.

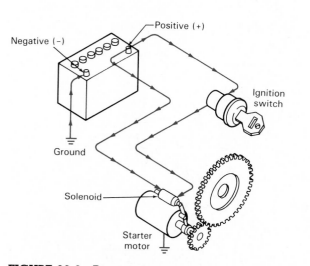

FIGURE 20-2   Basic starting circuit.

runs from the battery to the starter switch and then to the solenoid coil terminal. The second cable is a large-diameter cable that carries the heavy current demand of the starter motor. This heavy cable connects

STARTER MOTOR

A motor operates by following the same principles as the alternator does but in reverse. That is, a motor converts electrical energy into mechanical energy. The automobile is a compact and efficient energy conversion machine. Gasoline, a chemical energy source, is converted to mechanical energy to drive the vehicle. Some of this mechanical energy is used to drive the alternator to produce electricity. The electricity is converted to chemical energy for storage in the battery. This energy is then drawn off to provide electrical power to the starter, which converts it to mechanical energy to crank the engine during starting.

Magnetic Field

The starter motor is an electromechanical device that uses a varying **magnetic field** to create alternating magnetic poles that cause an armature assembly to rotate. The armature rotates because like magnetic poles repel one another, while unlike poles attract each other (Figure 20-3). Two north (N) poles or two south (S) poles will repel each other. A north pole and a south pole will attract each other.

Pole Shoes The pole shoes, north and south, in the starter field frame assembly are a magnet, complete with north and south poles. The field winding is a wire coil wrapped around the pole shoes. Electricity supplied to the field winding creates a strong **electromagnet**. A winding around the armature creates another electromagnet. This electromagnet constantly changes the **polarity** of its poles as the armature rotates

within the field set up by the pole shoes and field windings.

Armature A simple motor can be represented by a loop of wire for the armature and a coil around an iron core for the pole pieces. If a source of electric current is connected to the wire loop, a magnetic field is created (Figure 20-4). The energized loop will have a north and a south pole. An armature in a motor operates in the same way, except instead of a single loop there are several wire windings wrapped in multiple layers over an iron core. The multiple windings increase the strength of the magnetic field and increase the power of the motor.

Figure 20-5 shows a pole shoe and a field coil assembly. When a dc current is supplied to the field coil, the pole shoes are polarized into north and south magnetic poles. If the wire loop is placed inside the pole pieces and both the field coil and loop are energized, the loop will rotate until unlike poles are aligned (Figure 20-6).

The shoe with the north polarity attracts the side of the wire loop that is polarized south and repels

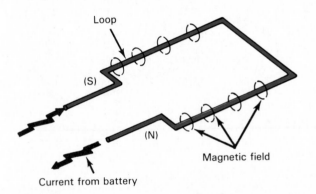

FIGURE 20-4 Wire loop with magnetic field.

FIGURE 20-5 Field winding and pole shoes.

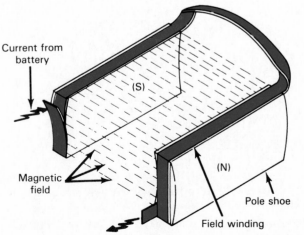

FIGURE 20-3 Like magnetic poles repel each other; unlike poles attract each other.

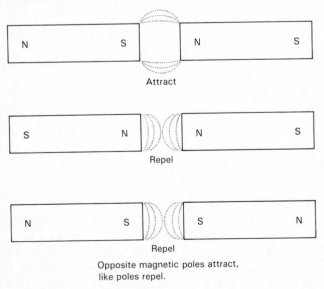

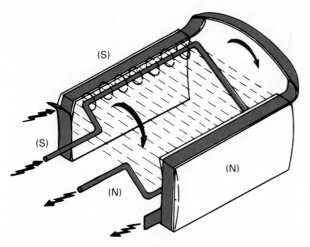

FIGURE 20-6   Wire loop in magnetic field.

the north pole side. The south pole shoe attracts the north pole side of the wire loop. If a means were provided to alternate the plus and minus voltage applied to the wire loop, the magnetic poles would reverse, and what had been attracted would now be repelled. The wire loop would rotate in a more or less continuous fashion as long as the polarities continued to reverse.

Commutator and Brushes

A device called a commutator provides the means to alternate the positive and negative voltage (Figure 20-7).

Stationary brushes make contact with the commutator as it spins, transmitting the dc voltage to the windings. The commutator is made up of separate copper pieces, with two opposing pieces connected to each armature winding. When power is supplied to an armature winding through the brushes and commutator,

one armature segment is repelled from a pole shoe with the same magnetic polarity. At the same time, the other armature segment is attracted to a pole shoe with opposite polarity. As the armature rotates, the first winding loses its path through the commutator to the brushes, and, with no current flowing, its magnetic field collapses. The next winding is now energized, and the cycle is repeated. The switching on and off of current flow to the armature windings, one after the other, provides a smooth, continuous rotation.

Starter motors have from two to six brushes and a corresponding number of armature windings. The greater number of armature windings increases the motor's power. The number of pole shoes and field windings is also increased to provide more power. Starter motors achieve tremendous power for their size by running at an overload condition for short periods of time. This overload style of operation is the reason that starters overheat when energized for long periods while trying to start a balky engine. Hard-to-start engines should be turned over with short periods of cranking followed by long periods of rest.

Starter Construction

Starter motors are a complex arrangement of parts contained in a steel housing (Figure 20-8). There are only three major assemblies: the dc motor, the drive mechanism, and the solenoid/shift lever assembly.

dc Motor

The dc motor typically has four pole shoes and four **series**-wound field coils contained in a housing or field

FIGURE 20-7   Commutator in basic dc electric motor.

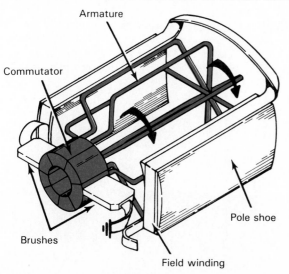

FIGURE 20-8   Basic starting motor.

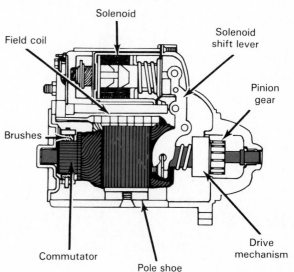

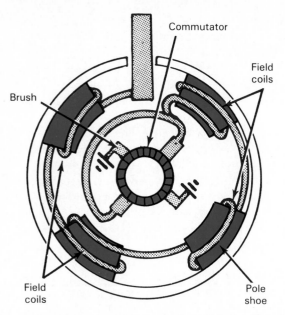

FIGURE 20-9 Typical four-pole and four-coil series wound motor.

frame (Figure 20-9). Many starter motors have a **shunt** winding in addition to the field coils. Such units are called compound or series/shunt starters. The shunt winding is connected in **parallel** with the series windings and serves to prevent an overspeed condition from damaging the starter. Other designs use drive actuating and holding coils which accomplish much the same purpose.

Armature The armature is made up of several laminations forming the pole pieces. Each armature winding is connected to a segment of the commutator (Figure 20-10). The commutator is an assembly of copper segments separated from each other by insulation. Carbon-impregnated brushes slide on the commutator as it rotates and provide the dc voltage to the armature windings. The armature is supported by bearings at each end. The bearings are seated in the end frames.

Brushes The brushes are held in brush holders mounted to the frame. Two opposing brushes are insulated from the case and supply the positive voltage

FIGURE 20-10 Armature construction. (General Motors Corporation)

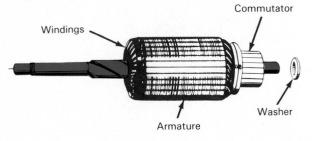

to the armature windings (in the standard negative ground system). The other two brushes are grounded to the frame and provide the negative return. Springs in the brush holders press the brushes firmly against the commutator for good electrical contact. The brushes are connected in series to the field windings. The electrical current flows through the field windings, through the brushes to the armature windings, and then back to the battery.

Starter Drive Mechanisms

There are three categories of starter drives:

1. Direct drive, solenoid actuated
2. Reduction gear, solenoid actuated
3. Positive engagement, relay actuated

Direct Drive, Solenoid Actuated The starter drive mechanism consists of two basic assemblies: the drive assembly and the solenoid (Figure 20-11). The direct-drive assembly uses no gears to step up or reduce the starting torque (Figure 20-12). The armature drives the

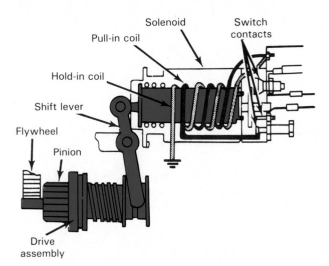

FIGURE 20-11 Solenoid and drive assembly.

FIGURE 20-12 Direct-drive starter.

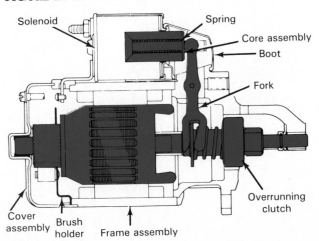

flywheel directly through the pinion gear. When the solenoid is energized and the plunger is drawn into the solenoid, the attached shift lever drives the overrunning clutch and pinion gear assembly forward to engage the flywheel.

Reduction Gear, Solenoid Actuated This type of drive contains a reduction-gear assembly between the armature and the overrunning clutch and pinion gear (Figure 20-13). The reduction gear increases the torque available for cranking the engine, but cranking speed is reduced. The reduction-gear type is usually installed on large engines that require more power to turn them over.

Positive Engagement, Relay Actuated The positive-engagement mechanism acts much like a solenoid, except that the strong magnetic field generated by the field coil is used to pull in the shift lever (Figure 20-14). The heavy current required by the starter motor is supplied by a separate relay (Figure 20-15). The drive mechanism is the direct type. Other than these differences, the starter operates in the same manner as the direct-drive, solenoid-actuated type.

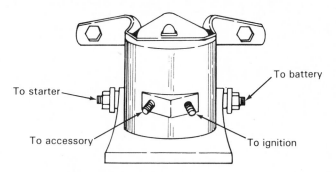

FIGURE 20-15   Typical starter relay.

SOLENOID

The solenoid (Figure 20-16) is an electromagnetic switch controlled by the starter contacts in the ignition switch assembly. The solenoid performs two functions:

1. It closes the heavy-duty contact that provides the high current to the starting motor.
2. It pivots the shift lever to engage the drive assembly (Figure 20-17).

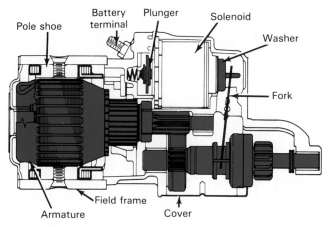

FIGURE 20-13   Reduction-gear drive starter.

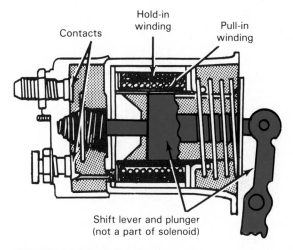

FIGURE 20-16   Solenoid assembly.

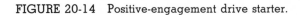

FIGURE 20-14   Positive-engagement drive starter.

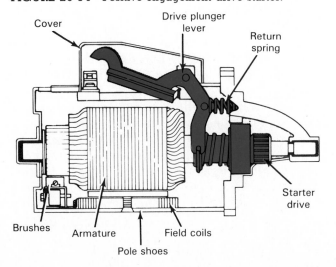

FIGURE 20-17   Starter drive assembly.

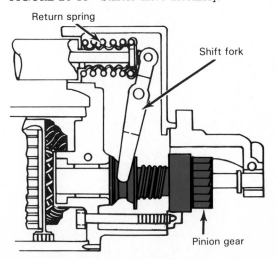

CARS CAN BE CRANKY AT TIMES

The first automobiles were started by hand. A crank was inserted in a special slotted opening in the front of the engine, the choke set, the hand throttle pulled out, the spark advanced using the manual control, the ignition turned on, and the crank spun as rapidly as possible. This process usually had to be repeated several times if the engine was cold. Sometimes the engine would misfire and kick the crank backwards. This often broke the arm of the novice. The following instructions show safety hints from an early driver's handbook.

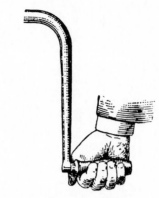

Right way

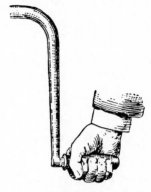

Wrong way

Illustrating right and wrong methods of cranking an engine. As ordinarily practiced, the hand is so placed that the thumb and fingers encircle it. Such a method is decidedly unsafe should the operator press down on the crank and a back fire occur. The correct method is to place the thumb on the same side of the handle that the fingers are placed so that the handle is not entirely encircled, allowing the handle to slip out of the grasp when it is being pressed down, and permitting the fingers to release the handle if it is being pulled up, at the time of back fire.

Windings

There are two windings in the solenoid: a pull-in and a hold-in winding (Figure 20-18). When current from the battery is supplied to the two windings, a strong magnetic field is set up that pulls the plunger into the solenoid. This draws in the top of the shift lever assembly, which causes the lever to pivot on its mounting and engage the drive assembly.

The pull-in winding is made of heavy-gauge wire. One end of the winding is connected to the ignition switch terminal. The other end is connected to the starter motor terminal on the solenoid. The pull-in winding is in series with the starter motor wiring and obtains its ground return through the motor wiring.

The hold-in winding is made up of fine wire and has the same number of turns as the pull-in winding. One end of the hold-in winding is also connected to the ignition switch terminal. The other end, however, is connected directly to ground.

Solenoid Operation

When the ignition switch is turned to the START position, current is applied to both solenoid windings through the switch terminal, usually labeled *S* (Figure 20-19). With both windings energized, the plunger is drawn into the solenoid, closing the contacts supplying current to the motor. This action shunts the pull-in winding but leaves the hold-in winding energized. Current flow through the solenoid windings and the strength of the resulting magnetic field are considerably reduced.

The hold-in winding keeps the solenoid contacts to the starter motor closed. This keeps the starter motor running and maintains engagement of the drive assembly. When the ignition switch is released from the start position, current is removed from the ignition switch terminal and the solenoid windings. This causes the pull-in and hold-in windings to be momentarily

FIGURE 20-18 Solenoid with coil windings.

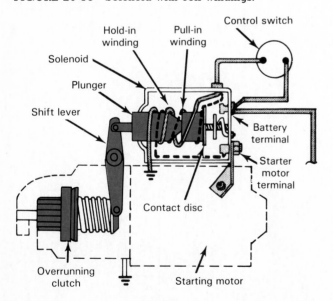

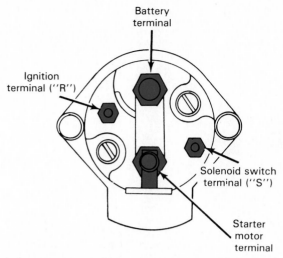

FIGURE 20-19   Solenoid terminals.

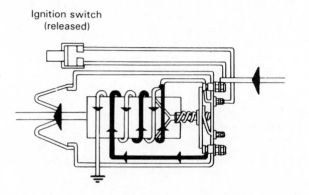

FIGURE 20-20   Solenoid with coil windings engaged.

connected in series, receiving power through the starter motor terminal (Figure 20-20).

With the windings connected in series, the current flow in the pull-in winding is reversed. This in turn causes the magnetic field to reverse polarity. The magnetic field of one coil now opposes that of the other. The result is an immediate collapse of the magnetic field, allowing the return spring to force the plunger back to its original position. The battery-to-starter motor contacts are now open, and the drive assembly is disengaged.

PINION GEAR DRIVES

Overruning Clutch

Most automobiles use an overruning clutch mechanism to separate the pinion gear from the flywheel after the engine starts (Figure 20-21). It is necessary to quickly disengage the pinion gear from the flywheel to prevent damage to the starter. It would be damaged by rapid rotation of the engine, magnified by the starter

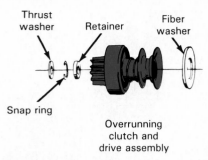

FIGURE 20-21   Overrunning clutch. (Pontiac Motor Division, GMC)

system gearing. The overrunning clutch automatically disengages the pinion gear when the rotational speed reaches a safe limit.

Operation   The clutch has an outer shell attached to the pinion gear. An inner sleeve meshes with the splines on the armature shaft. As the shift lever forces the clutch and pinion gear forward to mesh with the flywheel and the starter motor starts to spin, rollers within the clutch shell lock into notches in the sleeve to provide a rigid assembly. When the engine starts, the pinion and clutch assembly rotate faster than the armature. Centrifugal force moves the rollers back against the spring-loaded plungers into the larger-diameter portion of the notch. Thus unlocked, the clutch shell and pinion can rotate freely, or overrun. When the ignition key is released from the start position, the shift lever return spring pulls the pinion gear back out of mesh with the flywheel (Figure 20-22).

Bendix Drive

In addition to the overruning clutch, other designs have been used to mesh the pinion gear firmly to the fly-

FIGURE 20-22   Shift lever and drive assembly.

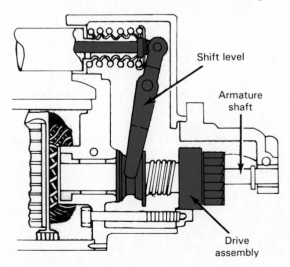

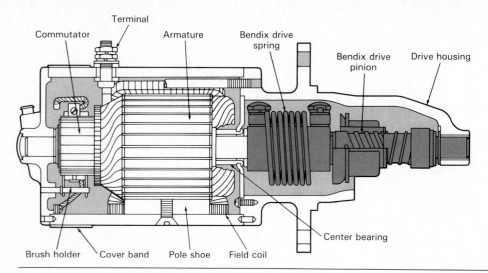

Terminal

Commutator   Armature   Bendix drive
spring

Bendix drive   Drive housing
pinion

Center bearing

Brush holder   Cover band   Pole shoe   Field coil

FIGURE 20-23 Bendix drive.
(General Motors Corporation)

wheel and yet enable quick disengagement upon engine start. The Bendix drive is most common. It is an **inertia** type; that is, it depends on the inertia of the drive assembly itself to produce the meshing of pinion gear to flywheel.

Operation The pinion gear of the Bendix drive has screw threads on its inner surface which mesh with screw threads on the armature shaft (Figure 20-23). As the armature rotates, the stationary pinion gear is screwed out to the end stop on the shaft where it engages the teeth in the flywheel. When the engine starts, the flywheel spins the pinion gear faster than the armature shaft, causing the pinion to back off on the screw threads and disengage from the flywheel.

IN-CAR TESTS

Testing of the starting system to isolate faults begins in the car. Many problems can be repaired without removing the starter from the vehicle, thus saving time and effort. In fact, the problem may not be in the starter but may be caused by a discharged battery or corroded connections.

System Quick Check

1. Test the battery, and, if necessary, recharge it (refer to Chapter 18).

2. Clean and tighten battery connections. Check all starter system connections and clean as necessary. Pay particular attention to the large-diameter cable that runs from the battery to the solenoid and starter motor. This cable supplies the heavy current required for cranking the engine.

3. Check to be sure a ground strap is securely fastened between the engine block and the frame. The connections must be clean and tight. Losses due to corrosion or a loose connection can make the starter inoperative.

4. Try starting the engine. If the starter cranks the engine normally (that is, at a speed usually sufficient to start the engine) but the engine fails to start, then check the ignition and fuel systems. The problem is not in the starter. If the starter does not turn over the engine at all or cranks very slowly, then troubleshoot the starting system using Table 20-1.

TABLE 20-1 Starter Quick Check
(With Headlights On and Charged Battery)

SYMPTOM	INDICATION	PROBABLE CAUSE
No cranking	No lights	Open fusible link
No cranking	Lights bright and no sound from solenoid	Open circuit in solenoid
No cranking	Lights bright and solenoid clicks	Open circuit in starter motor
No cranking	Headlights dim	Jammed drive assembly
Slow cranking	Headlights dim	Pitted contacts in solenoid
		Worn brushes in starter motor
		Pitted commutator
		Shorted commutator
		Engine problem

If the quick check fails to clearly isolate the problem area, then more detailed tests are required.

Cranking Circuit Test

The engine must be as close to normal operating temperature as possible for this test. A cold engine will cause the starter to draw more current and make the results inconclusive.

To prevent the engine from starting during testing, disconnect and ground the high-voltage coil wire in a standard ignition system. On most electronic igni-

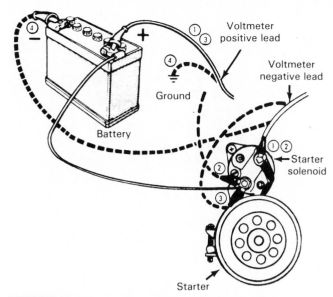

FIGURE 20-24 Cranking circuit test connections.

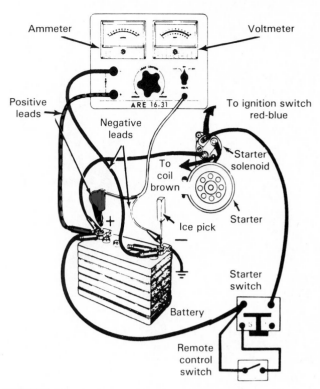

FIGURE 20-25 Starter load test connections.

tion systems, disconnect the wiring harness at the distributor. Use the repair manual for reference before disconnecting. The tester is a standard starter system tester containing a voltmeter, an ammeter, and a carbon pile rheostat.

1. Connect the voltmeter's negative lead to the solenoid starter terminal. Connect the meter's positive lead to the battery positive terminal (Figure 20-24). Select the low-voltage scale, and do not bridge the starter relay except while cranking. Note the voltage reading while cranking the engine. This is the voltage drop while cranking. The maximum allowable voltage drop is 0.5 V.

2. Change the voltmeter's positive lead to the solenoid battery terminal. The voltage drop while cranking should not be more than 0.3 V.

3. Connect the voltmeter's negative lead to the solenoid battery terminal. Connect the meter's positive lead to the battery positive terminal. Crank the engine and observe the voltage drop reading. It should not be more than 0.2 V.

4. Connect the voltmeter's negative lead to the battery negative terminal. Connect the meter's positive lead to the engine block (ground). The voltage drop during cranking should not exceed 0.1 V.

Load Test

Disconnect the ignition to prevent the engine from starting. Make the test connections shown in Figure 20-25.

1. Set the carbon pile rheostat on the tester to the maximum load position (highest resistance). Check that the ammeter reads zero, indicating no current flow.

2. Crank the engine and observe the voltmeter reading.

3. Stop cranking and reduce the carbon pile (rheostat) resistance until the voltmeter indicates exactly the same voltage as when cranking the engine.

4. Note the ammeter reading. This is the current draw under load.

BENCH TESTS

Disconnect both battery cables at the battery to avoid short circuits during starter removal. These can cause burns to the hands or damage to components. Disconnect all wires from the solenoid. Remove the mounting bolts securing the starter to the flywheel housing and carefully work the starter free.

No-Load Test

Secure the starter in a vise, being careful to place pads between the vise jaws and the starter. Tighten the vise just enough to grip the starter securely. Overtightening could warp or crack the starter housing.

1. Connect the starter to a battery and tester as shown in Figure 20-26. Connect a shaft rotation rpm dial indicator to the drive assembly end of the starter motor armature. Connect a remote starter switch between the battery and starter terminals on the solenoid.

2. Adjust the carbon pile to obtain a reading on the voltmeter of 10 V. Do not set for a higher voltage; excessive speed under a no-load condition could damage the starter.

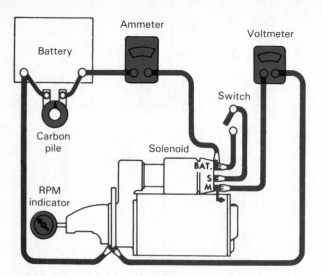

FIGURE 20-26 Starter no-load test connections.

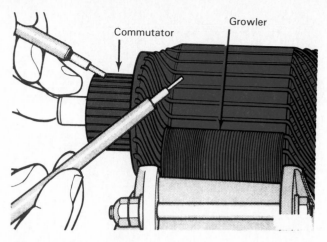

FIGURE 20-27 Testing a starter armature with growler.

3. Close the remote starter switch and record rpm, amperage, and voltage readings. Open the remote starter switch. Compare the readings with the factory specifications for the unit under test. Typical good values are in the range of 50–85 A and 6000–12,000 rpm at 10 V.

4. If current and rpm readings are within specs, the starter is good.

5. If rpm is low and current high, check for tight, dirty, or worn bearings, a shorted or grounded armature, or a shorted field winding.

6. If the starter armature does not rotate and current is high, check for frozen bearings or a short to ground in the field winding.

7. If the armature does not rotate and there is little or no current draw, check for an open field winding, an open armature winding, or a broken brush or spring.

8. Low rpm and current readings indicate high internal resistance. Check for poor connections, defective leads, worn brushes, or a dirty commutator.

9. High rpm, together with high current, indicates a shorted field winding.

Component Tests

Disassemble the starter assembly by removing the two long bolts that hold the drive gear housing, field frame, and end frame together. Some starters require that the solenoid be removed before the starter can be disassembled. Next remove the shift lever mechanism to free the drive assembly and armature. Separate the housing and withdraw the armature, being careful not to damage the brushes.

Armature Test A special tester called a growler is used for checking the armature (Figure 20-27). A growler is a test box containing a cradle for the armature, a meter, a test light, and test probes. The cradle contains a powerful electromagnet powered from the ac power line. Since it is an ac magnet, the magnetic

field alternates at a 60-cycle rate, in response to the frequency of the power supply. The armature is set in the cradle and the electromagnet energized. A thin steel blade, such as a hacksaw blade, is held lengthwise against the armature core as the armature is slowly rotated in the cradle. The blade will vibrate when held against a core containing a shorted windings. This test is necessary because of the construction of the armature. The windings are buried in layers around the core and are connected in series. It is impossible to use a simple continuity test to tell whether all windings are free from shorts to each other or to ground. Replace the armature if there is a short.

Grounded windings are detected using the test light and probes on the tester. Touch one probe to the armature shaft and the other to each commutator bar, one at a time. If the test lamp lights, the armature is grounded and must be replaced.

Field Coil Tests A 12-V test lamp is used when checking for field coil opens or grounds (Figure 20-28).

FIGURE 20-28 Field coil test.

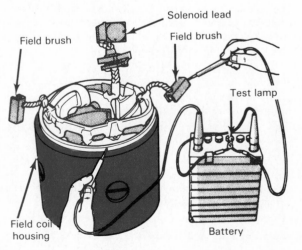

1. *Open coil test*: Touch one test lamp lead to the series field coil terminal and the other to one of the insulated brushes. The lamp should light; if it doesn't, the field coil is open and must be repaired or replaced. Repeat for each insulated brush.

2. *Grounded coil test*: Make certain that brushes, brush holders, and leads are not touching each other or the frame. Touch one test lamp lead to one of the grounded brush holders. Touch the other test lead to either insulated brush. If the lamp lights, one of the field coils is grounded and must be repaired or replaced.

SOLENOID TESTS

Disconnect all leads to the solenoid. Disconnect the solenoid-to-starter motor lead and tape it to the starter motor housing to avoid accidental energizing of the motor during testing.

Pull-in Winding Test

1. Connect a remote starter switch between the positive post of the battery and the ignition switch terminal on the solenoid (Figure 20-29). The terminal is usually marked with an *S*. Check that the ground connection from the solenoid housing to the battery negative post is good.

2. Close the remote starter switch and momentarily jumper the solenoid motor terminal (usually marked with an *M*) to the starter motor housing. The solenoid should engage and remain engaged. If not, the pull-in winding is defective. Do not allow the solenoid to remain energized for long periods; the solenoid windings could overheat and be damaged.

Hold-in Winding Test

This test is performed with the same hookup used above but without the jumper (Figure 20-30).

FIGURE 20-29 Solenoid pull-in winding test.

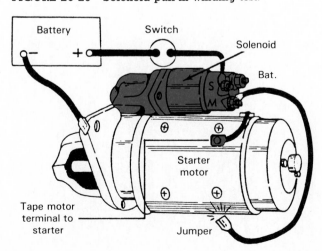

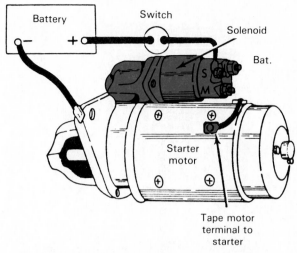

FIGURE 20-30 Solenoid hold-in winding test.

1. Close the remote starter switch, but do not use the jumper. Manually pull out the starter drive assembly. The drive assembly should remain engaged. If it does not, the hold-in winding is defective.

2. Open the remote starter switch. The drive assembly should return without hesitation. If it does not, the return spring is defective.

SERVICE

A visual inspection is the first step in servicing a starter motor. Inspect for loose connections, worn brushes, or a dirty commutator. Make sure that the starter motor is solidly mounted to the engine.

Pinion Clearance Check

After removing the starter from the vehicle and before disassembly, check pinion end play as follows:

1. Clamp the starter in a vise using a shop rag to prevent damage to the housing. Clamp just tight enough to hold the starter securely; do not clamp too tight, or damage may occur.

2. Connect leads from a 12-V battery to terminal *S* on the solenoid and to the starter housing. Connect a jumper from terminal *M* on the solenoid to the starter frame. Hold the pinion forward in the starting position until the battery is disconnected.

3. Push the pinion gear as far back from the stop retainer as possible and measure the clearance between the stop and the end of the pinion gear, using a feeler gauge (Figure 20-31). Clearance should be in the range of 0.01–0.14 in. (0.25–3.6 mm).

4. If pinion gear clearance is not as specified, disassemble the starter and replace worn parts.

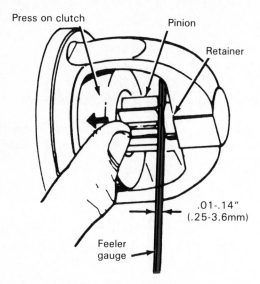

FIGURE 20-31 Checking pinion end play.

Brushes, Springs, and Holders

Replace brushes if they are worn to one half or more of their original length or if they are oil soaked or pitted. Check brush spring tension. If springs are weak or distorted, replace them. Replace deformed or damaged brush holders.

Overrunning Clutch

The pinion gear should turn freely and in one direction only. Check for chipped or broken teeth on the pinion gear. Check the flywheel ring gear if the pinion gear shows excessive wear or chipping. Check for cracks in the gear or clutch housing.

Test the overrunning clutch for slippage by clamping the armature in a vise, being careful to protect the armature from damage by cushioning it with several layers of cloth rag or a shop towel. Use a torque wrench and a socket that fits the pinion gear to apply a force of 50 ft-lb to the clutch assembly. If the clutch slips, replace it.

Armature Bushings

Check armature shaft end bushings for wear by installing an armature in the bushings and observing if any sideplay exists. If you see sideplay, replace the bushings. Lubricate the shaft ends with a silicone-base lubricant before reassembling.

DIESEL STARTING SYSTEMS

Diesel engine starting systems are basically a heavy-duty version of those used in gasoline engines. A more powerful starter motor requires more electrical current. This, in turn, requires a larger battery or, in many cases, two batteries. In addition, the glow plugs used for preliminary heating of the air in the combustion chamber for ignition draw a larger current than do the spark plugs in a conventional engine.

Glow Plugs

A diesel engine is a high compression engine. While operating, the fuel/air mixture is ignited by the heat generated by the compression stroke. However, to make starting easier, **glow plugs** are used to heat the air in the combustion chamber to help ignition during starting (Figure 20-32). One of the functions of the diesel starting system is to provide energy to the glow plugs during cranking and to cut off power to the glow plugs shortly after the starter is de-energized. Contacts in the ignition switch energize the glow plug timer and relay assembly when the switch is turned to the START position. The glow plug relay provides the high current demanded by the plugs through heavy-duty contacts which connect the battery to the glow plugs. When the ignition switch is released from the START position, the timer is de-energized. After the timer times out, power to the glow plugs is cut off.

Fuel Heaters

Diesel engines rely on the high temperature of the compressed air in the cylinder to ignite the diesel oil as it is sprayed into the cylinder. If the fuel is cold enough, as in subzero weather, the heated air in the cylinder could be cooled, and ignition would fail to occur. In addition, wax crystals form in diesel fuel as the temperature drops. The fuel lines then become clogged. To prevent this from happening, heaters pre-

FIGURE 20-32 Glow plugs. (Ford Motor Company)

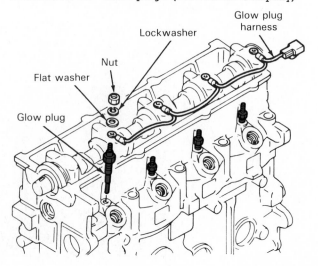

heat the fuel before it enters the injection pump. Fuel heaters also allow the use of less expensive and higher-mileage No. 2 summer diesel fuel in winter, rather than winterized No. 2 or No. 1 fuel. The two types of heating methods are fuel tank warming and recirculating systems and fuel line warmers.

Fuel tank heaters use 12-V immersion heaters and recirculating pumps to maintain temperature within the fuel tank both while the vehicle is operating and when parked. When parked, however, the battery can be discharged rather quickly, making it necessary to use an external power supply.

Fuel line heaters are more popular and are frequently added to diesel engines operated routinely in cold climates. The source of heat can be coolant or electrical heat. Coolant heaters are effective when starting only if a block heater is used during periods of nonoperation. Electrical fuel line heaters quickly warm the fuel as soon as the ignition is turned on. Electrical heaters place an additional load on the electrical system.

TRADE TERMS

Electromagnet
Glow Plug
Inertia
Magnetic Field
Parallel

Polarity
Series
Shunt
Solenoid

REVIEW QUESTIONS

1. What are the four components of the basic charging system?
2. What type of motor is used in the starter?
3. What makes the armature rotate?
4. What is the purpose of the commutator? The brushes?
5. The starter motor gets its tremendous power (relative to size) from being operated in an overload condition. True or false?

6. Name the three major assemblies of the starter.
7. Describe the two functions of the solenoid.
8. Describe the purpose of the overrunning clutch.
9. What are glow plugs used for in diesel starting systems?
10. What are the two types of fuel heating methods used in diesel starting systems?

PART FOUR

Fuel, Ignition, and Emission Systems

KEY CONCEPTS

- Fuel supply systems
- Carburetor theory and operation
- Fuel injection systems and components
- Computer control systems and how they control an engine
- Conventional and computer-controlled ignitions
- Ignition system servicing and testing
- How emission control systems operate

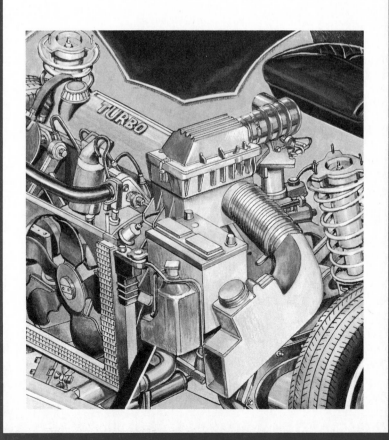

21

Fuel Systems: General

INTRODUCTION

The fuel system of an automobile provides the energy that causes the engine to "drive" the automobile. When engine fuels burn under ideal conditions, hydrogen and carbon combine with oxygen in the atmosphere to produce water and carbon dioxide, releasing tremendous energy. This chapter discusses the fuel and automobile uses, the major parts of the fuel system, and how the system operates. It also tells how to service some of the system's parts.

FUELS AND COMBUSTION

Automobile engine fuels are hydrocarbon compounds manufactured from crude oil (petroleum). Hydrocarbon compounds contain hydrogen and carbon molecules. Petroleum directly from the oil well contains many different hydrocarbon compounds. Each compound has different physical and chemical properties, including volatility. Volatility is the ability of a liquid to change into vapor. The rate of vaporization increases as the temperature increases and as the pressure decreases, with temperature the more important factor.

OBJECTIVES

When you have completed this chapter, you should be able to

- Define fuel volatility
- Explain the four-cycle combustion process
- List the differences between gasoline and diesel engines
- Define gasoline's octane value and diesel's cetane rating
- List and describe the fuel system's major parts
- Check the fuel pump's pressure and fuel flow capacity per minute
- Service the engine's air cleaner

Engine fuels have a high volatility (vaporize easily at low temperatures) and ignite or burn readily. Other petroleum compounds such as lubricating oils and greases have a low volatility and do not burn easily.

Combustion

Automobile engines use a four-stroke combustion cycle. The four strokes are intake, compression, power, and exhaust (Figure 21-1). During the intake cycle or stroke, the camshaft lobe opens the intake valve, and the piston moves downward, drawing the air and fuel mixture into the cylinder. The compression cycle compresses the air and fuel mixture. When gases are compressed (decreased in volume), their temperature rises. This temperature rise is called the heat of compression.

The heat of compression helps further vaporize any fuel droplets for more complete combustion.

In the power cycle, the spark plug ignites the fuel mixture just before the piston reaches top-dead-center (TDC) or maximum compression. The expanding flame should move evenly away from the spark plug. Combustion should be completed just as the piston reaches TDC. The released energy forces the piston downward, turning the crankshaft and providing power to the transmission and drive line. In the exhaust cycle, the exhaust valve opens, and the piston moves upwards to force the burned gases out of the cylinder. However, all the fuel does not burn. The unburned fuel is exhausted from the engine in the form of hydrocarbons. The harmful waste products of combustion, nitrogen oxide and carbon monoxide, are also exhausted from the engine. The entire process repeats several thousand times per minute depending on engine speed.

A four-cycle diesel engine works very much like a gasoline engine. A diesel engine does not use a carburetor but uses an injector to spray the fuel directly into a prechamber near the cylinder. A diesel engine has a much higher compression ratio (18–24:1) than a gasoline engine (7–10:1) and does not use spark plugs to ignite the fuel. Compression ratio refers to the volume of air/fuel mixture during the intake cycle to the air/fuel volume at the end of the compression cycle. A diesel engine's higher compression ratio causes a high enough heat of compression to ignite the diesel fuel. Figure 21-2 compares gasoline and diesel four-cycle engines.

FIGURE 21-1   Four-stroke gasoline engine. (Ford Motor Company)

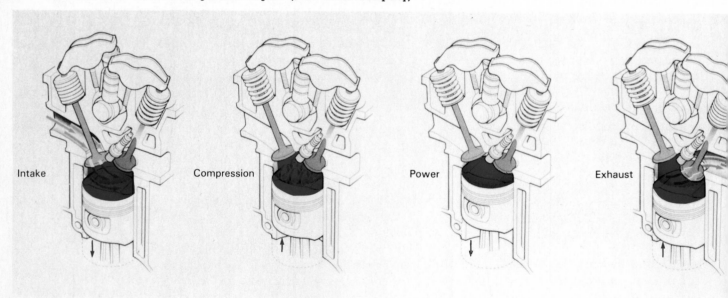

Intake   Compression   Power   Exhaust

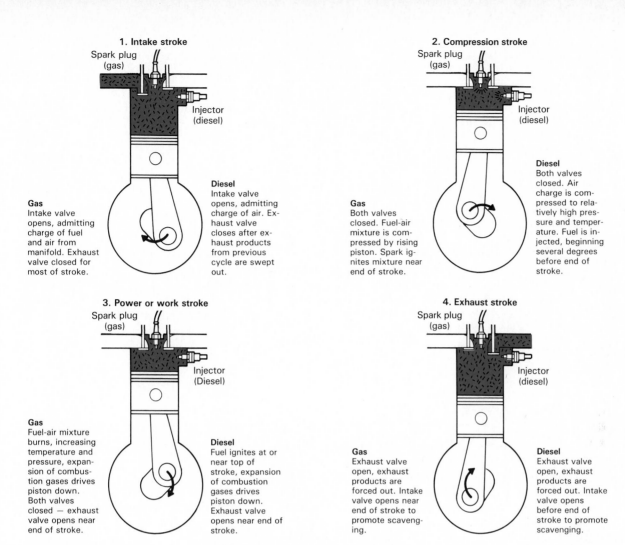

1. Intake stroke

Spark plug (gas)

Injector (diesel)

Gas
Intake valve opens, admitting charge of fuel and air from manifold. Exhaust valve closed for most of stroke.

Diesel
Intake valve opens, admitting charge of air. Exhaust valve closes after exhaust products from previous cycle are swept out.

2. Compression stroke

Spark plug (gas)

Injector (diesel)

Gas
Both valves closed. Fuel-air mixture is compressed by rising piston. Spark ignites mixture near end of stroke.

Diesel
Both valves closed. Air charge is compressed to relatively high pressure and temperature. Fuel is injected, beginning several degrees before end of stroke.

3. Power or work stroke

Spark plug (gas)

Injector (Diesel)

Gas
Fuel-air mixture burns, increasing temperature and pressure, expansion of combustion gases drives piston down. Both valves closed — exhaust valve opens near end of stroke.

Diesel
Fuel ignites at or near top of stroke, expansion of combustion gases drives piston down. Exhaust valve opens near end of stroke.

4. Exhaust stroke

Spark plug (gas)

Injector (diesel)

Gas
Exhaust valve open, exhaust products are forced out. Intake valve opens near end of stroke to promote scavenging.

Diesel
Exhaust valve open, exhaust products are forced out. Intake valve opens before end of stroke to promote scavenging.

FIGURE 21-2 Comparison of gasoline and diesel four-cycle engines.

Abnormal Combustion

The three types of abnormal combustion are pre-ignition, detonation, and incomplete (Figure 21-3).

Pre-Ignition In **pre-ignition**, the fuel does not ignite at the correct time. The spark plug fires too soon before the piston reaches TDC and results in a loss of power because the burning and expanding gases oppose the upward motion of the piston. A faulty or mistimed ignition usually causes this problem, discussed in Chapter 22. Another type of pre-ignition is surface ignition. In surface ignition, a "hot spot" in the cylinder ignites the fuel before the spark plug fires. Fuel or oil deposits on the piston or the intake and exhaust valves may remain hot enough to ignite the fuel before normal spark occurs. These deposits usually dislodge and exhaust with the burned gases. If continued surface ignition occurs, severe engine damage results (for example, a hole in the piston or crankshaft bearing failure). Dieseling or run-on refers to pre-ignition after the driver turns the ignition off. Modern engine design and fuel additives help reduce pre-ignition.

Detonation Fuel with an incorrect octane rating causes **detonation.** In detonation, the heat of compression ignites some of the gases just before the spark occurs. The two flame fronts collide and produce an audible "knock." Fuel manufacturers add antiknock chemicals to reduce this problem. Leaded gasoline usually uses *tetraethyl lead* to reduce detonation; unleaded gasoline may use methanol. Anti-knock additives reduce the rate at which the fuel burns during the power cycle of combustion. Thus, these compounds help prevent explosive burning or detonation. Gasoline with a high octane number knocks less than one with a low number.

Incomplete Combustion Incomplete combustion of fuel causes a power loss, wastes fuel, and more impor-

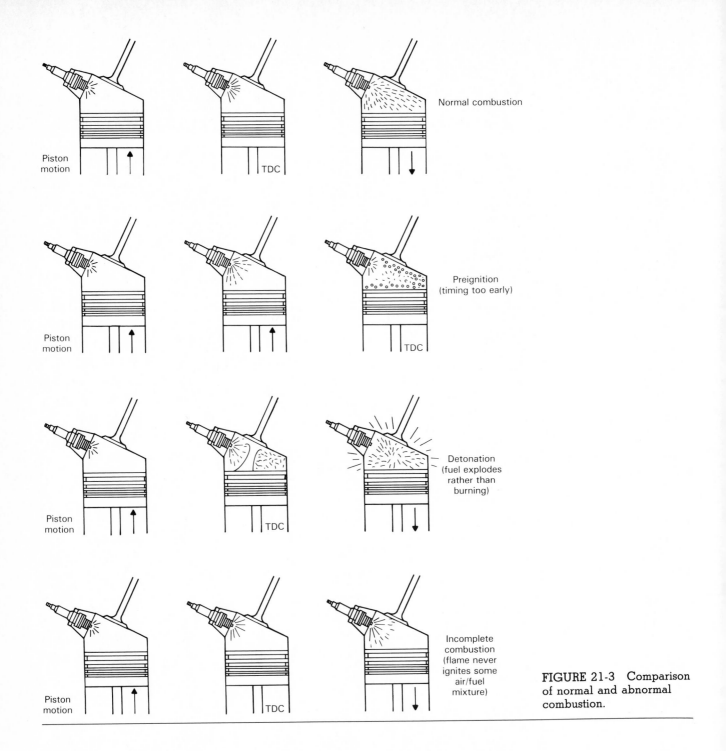

Normal combustion

Preignition
(timing too early)

Detonation
(fuel explodes
rather than
burning)

Incomplete
combustion
(flame never
ignites some
air/fuel
mixture)

FIGURE 21-3 Comparison
of normal and abnormal
combustion.

tant greatly contributes to air pollution. Incomplete combustion has many causes, including engine design, improper air and fuel mixture (misadjusted carburetor or dirty air cleaner), incorrect ignition timing, spark plug voltage that is too low ("fouled" plugs or shorted coil), and poor engine condition. Incomplete combustion results in carbon monoxide (CO) and oxides of nitrogen (NO_x) exhausted into the atmosphere. CO and NO_x greatly contribute to "smog" pollution.

GASOLINE

For use as engine fuel, gasoline must meet rigid requirements. It must vaporize easily and must produce power without *fuel knock.* Do not confuse fuel knock with engine knock. Gasoline must also be free of impurities which would interfere with the engine operation. Liquid impurities such as water produce engine hesitation, "missing," fuel system rust, and a general power loss. Water-contaminated gasoline must be replaced. Solid impurities such as dirt may produce the same problems, but filters help reduce this type of fuel system contamination. Excessive dirt contamination plugs filters and may result in total power loss. If this occurs, replace the gasoline and clean or replace the filters.

Volatility

The volatility of gasoline affects engine starting, length of warm-up period, and engine performance. Gasoline must be a vapor to properly combine with oxygen during combustion. Thus, a gasoline with high volatility is desirable for engine starting because volatility determines how much fuel will be vaporized in the fuel and air mixture. However, if the gasoline is too volatile, it may vaporize in the fuel lines (vapor lock), resulting in a total loss of fuel to the engine (Figure 21-4). Some engines use a vapor return line to the gas tank to reduce vapor lock problems. Generally, the proper fuel and air mixture consists of 1 part fuel to 14.7 parts air, by weight. The fuel system or carburetor mixes the air and fuel. Chapter 22 explains how the carburetor operates.

Octane Numbers

Special antiknock hydrocarbon additives reduce fuel knock or detonation. The antiknock characteristic of a gasoline is measured by its **octane value.** Two of the hydrocarbons added to gasoline are *iso-octane* and *n-heptane.* Iso-octane has high anti-knock qualities, and *n*-heptane has low anti-knock qualities. Petroleum engineers assign number values of 100 for iso-octane and 0 for *n*-heptane.

Octane Testing   The performance of a gasoline of unknown octane value is compared with the performance of mixtures of iso-octane and *n*-heptane in a test engine under specified test conditions.

The proportions of iso-octane and *n*-heptane are varied until a mixture of these two hydrocarbons is found which gives the same degree of knocking as the gasoline with the unknown octane value. The fuel

with the unknown octane value is then given an octane number which represents the percent of iso-octane in the test mixture. For example, gasoline with an 80 octane rating has knocking characteristics which match a test mixture consisting of 80% pure iso-octane and 20% *n*-heptane.

The octane rating has nothing to do with starting qualities, potential energy, or volatility. The higher the octane value of a fuel, the less the fuel will knock. In general, using a higher octane value than engine manufacturer's specifications does not improve engine performance.

Anti-knock additives reduce the rate at which the fuel burns during the power cycle of combustion. Thus, these compounds help prevent explosive burning or detonation.

DIESEL FUEL

Because of the differences in the combustion processes in the fuel systems of diesel and gasoline engines, the fuels for these engines must be refined to meet different requirements (Figure 21-5). In general, diesel engines require a clean fuel which will lubricate; otherwise, the closely fitted parts of the injector will wear rapidly, and the small passages which create the fuel spray within the cylinders will become clogged.

FIGURE 21-5   Cracking tower.

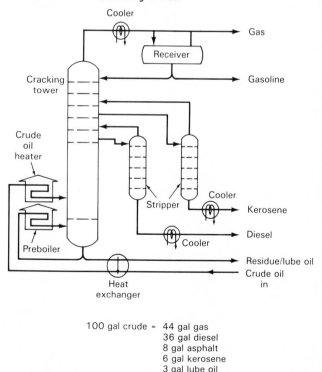

100 gal crude = 44 gal gas
36 gal diesel
8 gal asphalt
6 gal kerosene
3 gal lube oil
3 gal lost

FIGURE 21-4   Vapor lock in a fuel line.

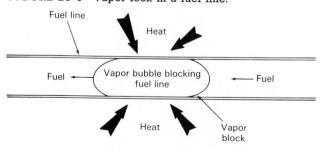

FUEL SYSTEMS

Immediately after World War II, the forerunners of what we know today as sprint cars or outlaw sprinters were the midgets. Born on the dirt tracks of California, these cars were the breeding ground for drivers who would later brave the Brickyard track of the Indy 500. Such men as Tony Bettenhausen, Roger Ward, Bill Vukovich, and many others graduated from the ranks of the midgets. At first, the most popular midget engines were the V8 60 Fords. But soon these gave way to the small Offenhauser four-cylinder engines that quickly dominated this kind of dirt track racing.

But then something happened. A prom-

inent West Coast intake manifold company, that remained a solid believer of the V8 60 Ford, broke from tradition and began a revolutionary series of experiments. To this point in midget racing, alcohol (methanol) was the basic fuel. But with the help of some chemist friends, this company risked the use of another potential engine fuel.

Not only did it work, it worked so well that they had to disguise the exhaust odor so no one else could know what they were using. Additives that produced an orange-peel smell came first. And finally an ingredient that produced the smell of gun powder.

Finally, on a night at the old Gilmore

Stadium in Los Angeles, in a field of midgets with only one V8 60 Ford (all the rest were Offy powered), this manifold company's "strange-fuel" car won the entire event. And then just to prove it wasn't a fluke, the same car won the main event at another southern California track the very next night.

Today, this same fuel is used in certain classes of racing. Pioneered by a manifold company almost 30 years ago, we now know of this chemical as nitromethane.

Jim MacFarland
Edelbrock

Volatility

Diesel fuel's volatility must be high enough to vaporize and burn rapidly when injected into the cylinder. Temperature, pressure, and time affect the self-ignition point of a fuel. In cold weather, diesel fuel will form "wax." This wax will clog the injectors and the pump. Fuel heaters or the blending of diesel fuels prevent this cold weather waxing.

Even though diesel fuel must resist detonation, it must ignite spontaneously at the proper time under the pressure and temperature existing in the cylinder. The ease with which a diesel fuel will ignite and the manner in which it burns determine the ignition quality of the fuel. See Table 21-1. The ignition quality of diesel fuel is determined by its cetane rating or cetane value.

any given fuel is identified by its cetane number—the higher the cetane number, the less the lag between the time the fuel enters the cylinder and the time it begins to burn (Figure 21-6).

Cetane Testing The cetane rating of a diesel fuel is determined in a manner similar to that used to determine the octane value of gasoline. However, the hydrocarbons used for the reference fuel are cetane and alpha-methyl-naphthalene. Cetane has an excellent ignition quality (100), and alpha-methyl-naphthalene has a very poor ignition quality (0). By comparing the performance of a reference fuel with that of a fuel whose ignition quality is unknown, the unknown cetane rating or number can be determined. The cetane number represents the percentage of pure cetane in a reference fuel which will just match the ignition qual-

TABLE 21-1   Diesel Fuel Grades and Flash Point

| Fuel Number | Cetane | Flash Point | Viscosity | |
			Min.	Max.
1D	40	100	1.4	2.5
2D	40	125	2.0	5.8
4D	30	130	5.8	26.4

Note: 2D is the fuel most used.

Cetane Value

The **cetane value** of a fuel is a measure of the ease with which the fuel will ignite. The cetane rating of

FIGURE 21-6   Cetane and octane comparison.

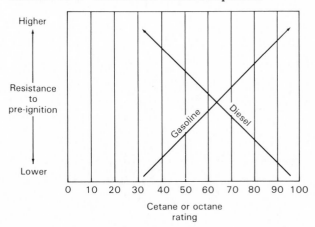

ity of the fuel being tested. The higher the cetane number, the quicker burning the fuel and the better the fuel from the standpoint of ignition and combustion.

PROPANE AND LIQUID PETROLEUM GAS (LPG)

Propane and LPG burn "hotter" and cleaner than gasoline or diesel fuel. Propane and LPG are extremely volatile and must be stored in special tanks to prevent rapid evaporation into the atmosphere. These hydrocarbon compounds release much more energy than gasoline or diesel fuel and contribute much less air pollution. Only a very few automobiles use propane or LPG as fuel, but more may be manufactured in the future because of these desirable qualities.

Propane- or LPG-operated engines only require a modified carburetor and special fuel tank; all other combustion processes are identical to gasoline.

FUEL SUPPLY SYSTEM

The fuel supply system consists of a tank, lines, filter(s), a fuel level gauge, and a pump (Figure 21-7).

Fuel Tank

The tank holds 10–25 gal of fuel depending on the manufacturer's design. Figure 21-8 shows a typical tank. Tanks are usually made of rust-resistant sheet metal or plastic and have an inlet or filler pipe and an outlet. The outlet, with a fitting for the fuel line connection, may be in the bottom or on the side of the tank. The lower end of the outlet pipe is placed about ½ in. from the bottom of the tank so that any sediment collecting in the tank will not be carried to the carburetor. Often manufacturers place a coarse screen filter here. Baffle plates may be inside the tank to reinforce the sides and bottom and to prevent the fuel from surging or splashing. A drain plug is provided in the bottom of some tanks for draining and cleaning.

Newer automobiles use a *closed* ventilation system to prevent the escape of gasoline vapors into the atmosphere that contribute to air pollution. Figure 21-9 shows a typical closed system. The pressure cap (Figure 21-10) seals the tank and prevents the escape of gasoline vapors out of the filler tube. The pressure cap contains vacuum and pressure valves to keep the internal tank pressure equal to the outside pressure. The vacuum valve allows outside air into the tank as the fuel level drops during driving.

FIGURE 21-7 Typical gasoline fuel system. (Ford Motor Company)

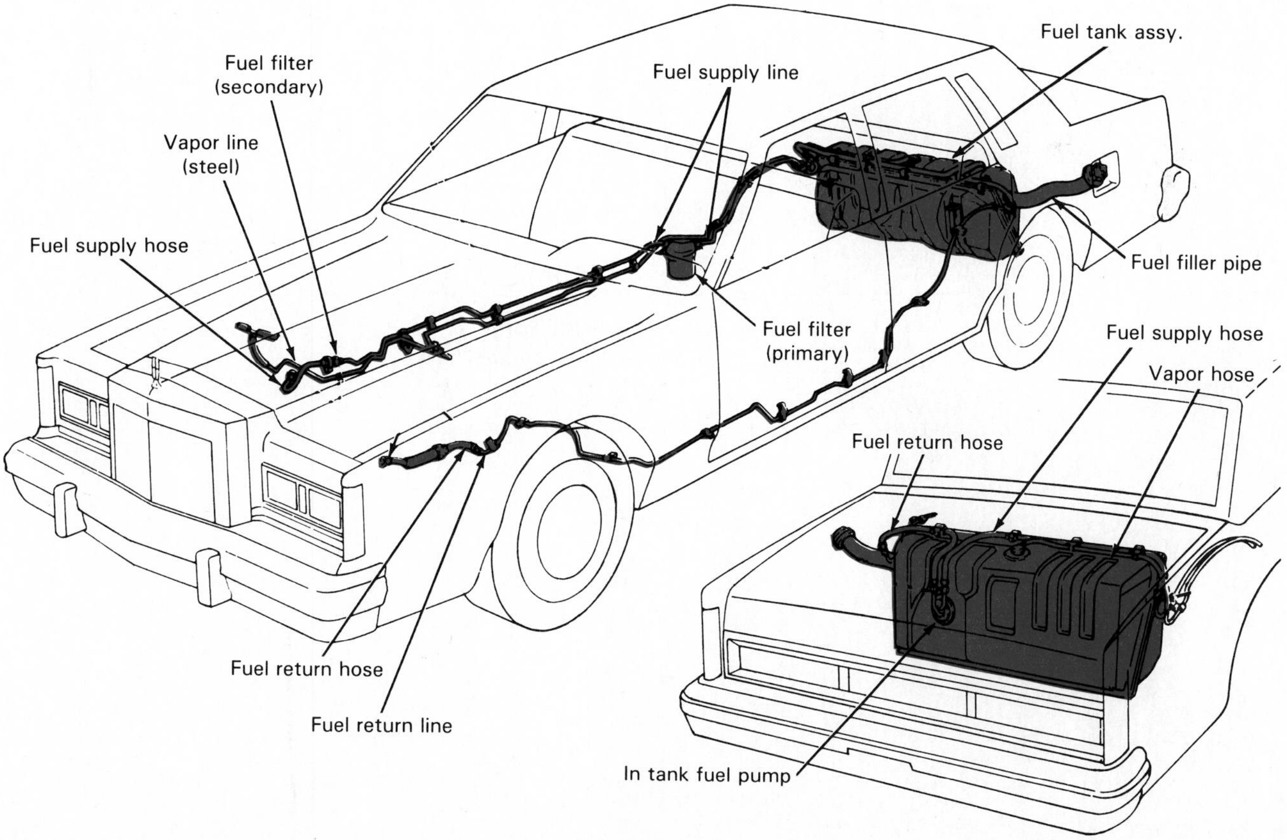

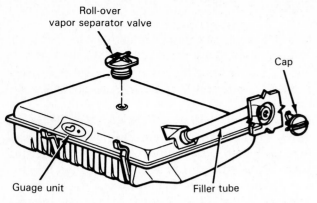

Roll-over
vapor separator valve

Cap

Guage unit

Filler tube

FIGURE 21-8 Fuel tank. (Chrysler Corporation)

The pressure valve prevents excessive pressure buildup, and this pressure is usually vented to a charcoal canister (Figure 21-11). The fuel tank also contains a roll-over/vapor separator valve to prevent fuel leakage if the automobile should roll over in an accident. Automobiles manufactured since 1976 use *unleaded* gasoline and catalytic converters to help reduce emission pollutants. The filler tube has a smaller opening (Figure 21-12) to prevent using leaded gasoline accidentally, which would destroy the catalytic converter.

Fuel Lines

Steel fuel lines connect the tank to the fuel pump and carburetor.

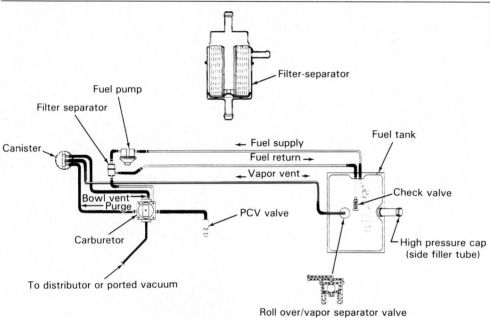

Filter-separator

Fuel pump

Filter separator

Canister

Fuel supply

Fuel return

Vapor vent

Fuel tank

Bowl vent

Purge

Check valve

Carburetor

PCV valve

High pressure cap
(side filler tube)

To distributor or ported vacuum

Roll over/vapor separator valve

FIGURE 21-9 Typical closed fuel supply system. (Chrysler Corporation)

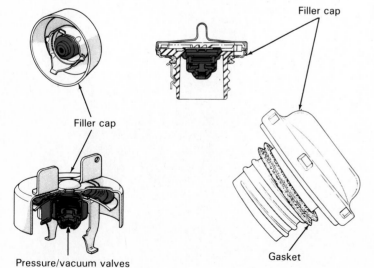

Filler cap

Filler cap

Pressure/vacuum valves

Gasket

FIGURE 21-10 Typical pressure/vacuum filler caps. (Chrysler Corporation)

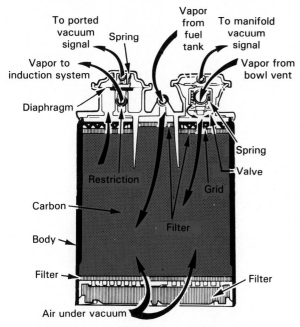

FIGURE 21-11   Vapor canister. (Pontiac Motor Division, GMC)

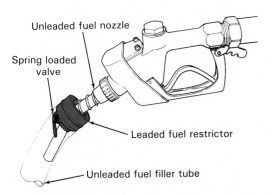

FIGURE 21-12   Unleaded fuel tank filler tube. (Chrysler Corporation)

The fuel lines are usually up against the body or frame for protection against possible damage. Flexible fuel lines are made of special rubber material so that gasoline will not cause them to deteriorate.

> CAUTION: Do not use regular rubber hose for fuel lines.

Fuel Filter

All fuel systems contain at least one filter to remove unwanted dirt particles. Often automobiles use several filters. Possible *fuel filter* locations include the fuel tank, a sediment bowl attached to the fuel pump, or the carburetor inlet line.

Fuel Gauge

The **fuel gauge** (Figure 21-13) monitors the fuel tank level, keeping the driver aware of how much fuel remains. The fuel gauge consists of a fuel level meter in the dashboard and a float and variable resistance rheostat (sensor) in the tank. Figure 21-14 shows a typical fuel tank sensor. A special tool removes the sensor from the tank (Figure 21-15).

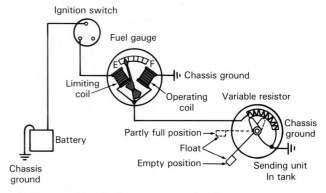

FIGURE 21-13   Coil-type gauge circuit.

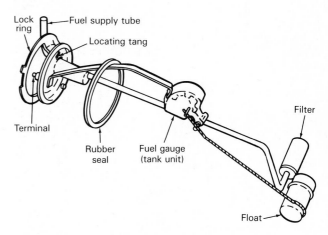

FIGURE 21-14   Typical fuel tank gauge sensor. (Chrysler Corporation)

FIGURE 21-15   Installing or removing fuel tank gauge sensor. (Chrysler Corporation)

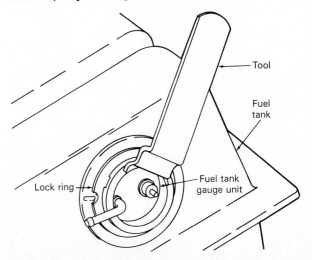

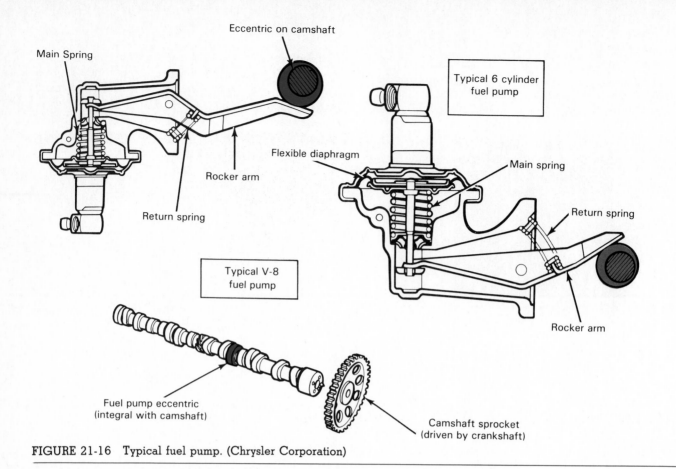

FIGURE 21-16 Typical fuel pump. (Chrysler Corporation)

FIGURE 21-17 Tank electric fuel pump. (Ford Motor Company)

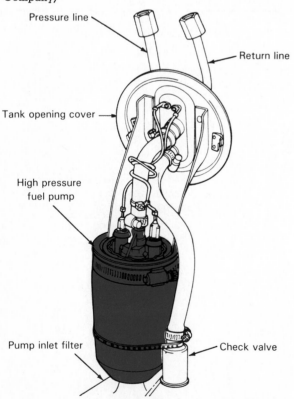

Fuel Pump

The *fuel pump* provides a constant supply of fuel to the fuel system. The fuel pump may be mechanical (Figure 21-16) or electrical. A mechanical pump mounted on the side of the engine uses a camshaft eccentric to "pump" the fuel. The camshaft eccentric pushes the rocker arm against the return spring and moves the diaphragm upwards. The diaphragm's upward motion increases the internal volume and "sucks" fuel out of the tank through the one-way inlet valve. As camshaft rotation releases pressure on the rocker arm, the rocker arm return spring forces the diaphragm down. The downward motion of the diaphragm decreases the volume and forces the fuel out of the pump to the carburetor. An electric fuel pump simply uses a rotating motor and impeller or a vibrating diaphragm to provide fuel to the carburetor. The electric fuel pump may be in the tank, between the tank and the engine compartment, or in the engine compartment (Figure 21-17). Some cars use more than one pump.

FUEL SYSTEM SERVICE

The fuel supply system is fairly reliable and needs no preventive service beyond periodic cleaning or replacement of filters. (Follow the manufacturer's recommendation.)

Tank Repairs

Specialists must repair a ruptured or leaking gas tank. Welding the tank requires extreme caution and special techniques to prevent possible explosion. The most common practice is to replace defective gas tanks. Replace damaged or leaking fuel lines as required.

Fuel Pump Test

A properly operating fuel pump provides a certain volume of fuel per minute at a specified pressure. Check the service manual for a particular engine. To check the volume of fuel, remove the fuel line at the engine and place the fuel line into a measured container (Figure 21-18).

> **CAUTION:** Use proper care to prevent igniting any spilled gasoline.

The carburetor bowl holds enough gasoline to let the engine run for a short time. Start the engine and collect the fuel. With an electric fuel pump, you may have to connect some jumper wires to run the pump. Check the shop manual.

Measure the volume of fuel pumped into the container in 30 secs. Multiply this by 2 to determine the volume per minute. For example, ½ pt in the container times 2 equals 1 pt/min. If the measured volume is

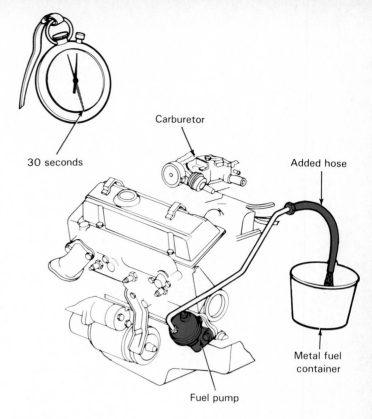

FIGURE 21-18 Measuring volume of fuel from pump. (Chrysler Corporation)

below specifications, the fuel pump may be faulty, or the fuel lines might be plugged. Replace a faulty pump as a unit. Clear plugged lines with short blasts of high-pressure air.

To check fuel pressure, connect a pressure gauge on the outlet side of the fuel pump (Figure 21-19).

FIGURE 21-19 Checking fuel pump pressure. (Chrysler Corporation)

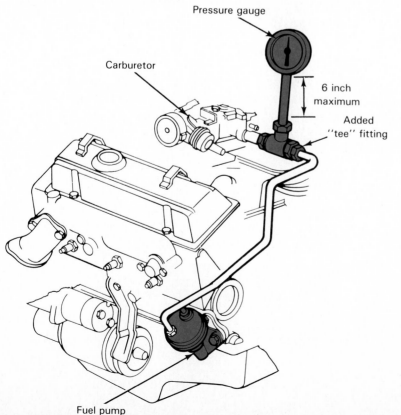

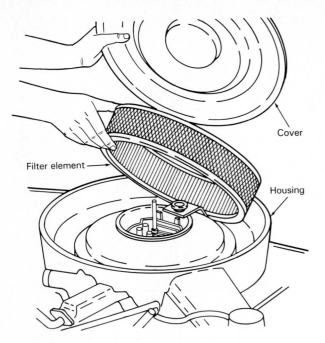

FIGURE 21-20 Air cleaner and cover. (Chrysler Corporation)

Insufficient fuel pressure may not open the carburetor float valve enough to keep the carburetor bowl full. Low fuel pressure indicates a faulty pump.

Air Cleaner

The air cleaner filters dirt or dust particles out of the air that enter the carburetor (Figure 21-20). Unfiltered air would rapidly cause engine damage. Some older air cleaners use an oil-soaked fine wire mesh to trap dust particles, but most air cleaners have paper elements. Automobile manufacturers recommend replacing the paper elements at specific intervals. Check the service manual for these intervals.

TRADE TERMS

Cetane Value
Detonation
Fuel Filter
Fuel Gauge

Fuel Pump
Octane Value
Pre-ignition
Volatility

REVIEW QUESTIONS

1. What does volatility mean?
2. List and explain the four-stroke combustion cycle.
3. Explain the differences between a gasoline engine and a diesel engine.
4. What are the products of hydrocarbon combustion under ideal conditions? Under abnormal conditions?
5. List the three types of abnormal combustion in an engine.
6. Gasoline with a low octane number knocks less than one with a high number. True or false?

7. What gasoline additive decreases knocking or detonation?
8. What happens when leaded gasoline is used in an automobile with a catalytic converter?
9. Name the parts of the fuel supply system.
10. What does the fuel pump do?
11. How does the air cleaner protect the engine?

22

Fuel Systems: Carburetion

OBJECTIVES

When you have completed this chapter, you should be able to

- Describe the carburetor venturi effect
- Explain the basic carburetor circuits and how they work (float, idle, choke, main, accelerator, power valve)
- Describe feedback carburetors and what they require to operate properly
- Describe the differences between downdraft and sidedraft carburetors
- Describe how the number of carburetor throats affect engine performance
- Explain the benefits of and reasons for multiple carburetors
- Describe how you can troubleshoot carburetors and where you can find more detailed information about working on carburetors

INTRODUCTION

First, there is no such thing as "suction" in engines. Engines don't suck air and fuel into the cylinders. In fact, air and fuel flow into an engine because the pressure in the cylinders is lower than atmospheric pressure. As a result, atmospheric pressure forces the air/fuel mixture into the engine like a giant hand pushing on the carburetor.

We are concerned here with **pressure differential.** It's a simple case of finding the path of least resistance. The carburetor is standing in the way of air flowing into an engine. Lower pressure inside the cylinders on the intake stroke (caused by downward motion of the piston) creates the flow.

Basically, a carburetor does two things as air flows through:

1. It breaks liquid fuel into small droplets, a process known as **atomization.**
2. It mixes air and fuel in the proportions required to make the engine run efficiently.

This chapter explains the circuits in the carburetor and how these circuits control engine speed.

maximum horsepower. Air/fuel mixtures are also richer at idle because the air flowing through the induction system is moving slowly, allowing some fuel droplets to fall out of the airstream onto the intake manifold surfaces.

Carburetor Parts

The basic operating parts of the simple carburetor are the air horn, **venturi**, and **throttle plate**, which control the airflows; and the needle valve, float assembly, main metering jet, main well, and discharge nozzle, which provide a constant supply of fuel to the venturi (Figure 22-2).

Whether at idle or wide-open throttle, a carburetor relies primarily on airflow to signal the amount of fuel required by the engine. This signal results from a phenomenon known as the venturi effect.

Venturi Effect

Over 150 years ago, G. B. Venturi, an Italian scientist, discovered that when air flows through an hourglass-shaped tube, velocity is highest and pressure is lowest in the area of smallest diameter (Figure 22-3). Carburetor designers use this principle by positioning the fuel discharge nozzle within the venturi and connecting it through a series of passages to a fuel reservoir. Because fuel in the reservoir is under atmospheric pressure (14.7 psi), lower pressure at the nozzle acts like a vacuum pump and pulls fuel into the airstream (Figure 22-4).

As the air velocity through a venturi increases, the pressure within it decreases, creating a stronger **fuel delivery signal**. The venturi diameter also affects air speed and pressure. With the same airflow volume, reducing only the venturi diameter results in increased velocity and decreased pressure within the venturi (Figure 22-5). This principle is used by the booster venturi. The booster venturi is a very small venturi

CARBURETOR THEORY

Mixture

For gasoline to burn efficiently in an internal combustion engine, it must be in a gaseous or vaporous state and mixed with an appropriate amount of air. Air provides the oxygen essential to combustion. Increasing the amount of fuel or reducing the amount of air brings about a richer **air-fuel mixture.** Conversely, decreasing fuel or increasing air results in a leaner air/fuel ratio. When fuel and air are mixed in ideal proportions that allow a complete chemical reaction during combustion (that is, all the fuel is burned), the mixture is said to be **stoichiometric.**

Before the days of strict exhaust emission and higher gas mileage requirements, the ideal air/fuel ratio for engines operating under a light load, such as when a car cruises down the highway, was thought to be between 14.7 and 14.8 parts of air to 1 part of gasoline. This ratio, expressed as 14.7 : 1 and 14.8 : 1, is measured by weight (Figure 22-1).

With recent technological advances, engines can run satisfactorily with mixtures as lean as 17 : 1 or 18 : 1. However, when the engine is under a heavy load, such as when it accelerates full throttle, it will need a relatively rich mixture, such as 12 : 1–13 : 1, to produce

FIGURE 22-2 Simple carburetor.

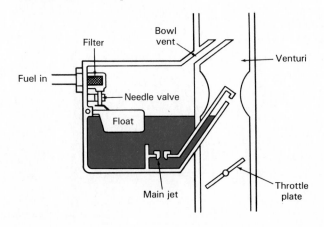

FIGURE 22-1 Air/fuel mixture weight.

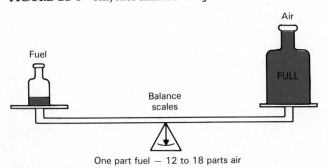

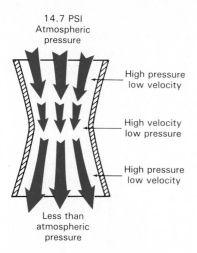

FIGURE 22-3   Venturi effect.

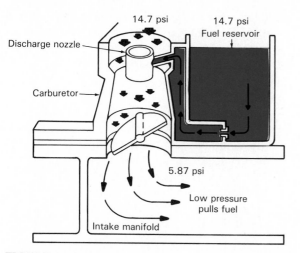

FIGURE 22-4   Pressure differences in a carburetor.

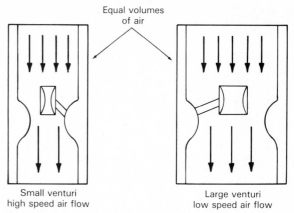

FIGURE 22-5   Venturi airflow.

placed in the center of the main venturi. It supplies a strong vacuum signal at low air-flow velocities.

Variable Venturi

The **variable venturi carburetor** is one method of delivering fuel according to an engine's power needs. The variable venturi valve reduces or enlarges the carburetor's throat depending on the air/fuel requirements of the engine (Figure 22-6). Low engine speeds require less venturi opening than higher engine speeds (rpm).

Venturi size is controlled by the vacuum in the intake manifold, which the carburetor senses. For example, the higher the vacuum, the lower the load, and the less fuel the engine requires. The variable venturi valves restrict the airflow into the throat of the carburetor, lessening the amount of fuel to the engine.

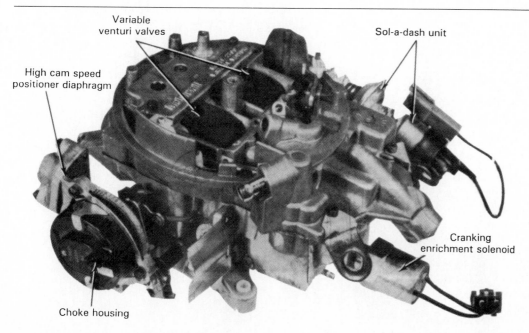

FIGURE 22-6   Variable venturi carburetor. (Ford Motor Company)

CARBURETOR CIRCUITS

Main Metering System

On its journey to the nozzle, fuel passes out of the float bowl through a precisely sized metering orifice called a **jet** and into a main well which leads directly to the nozzle. During the last part of the trip, fuel must travel uphill. If the nozzle were lower than the level of fuel in the reservoir (or float bowl), it would simply act as a drain (Figure 22-7).

The flow of air through the carburetor is controlled by a *throttle plate* positioned at the base of the **barrel** or *bore*. As the plate is opened further and further, airflow increases, the signal becomes stronger, and the fuel flow increases (Figure 22-8). This relationship allows the air/fuel ratio to remain constant at all throttle openings.

To speed up converting liquid gasoline into a vapor, the main metering circuit is so constructed that fuel moving through it is broken up into droplets. Air

is drawn into the main well through a calibrated opening called an *air bleed* and mixes with the fuel to form droplets. In addition to **atomizing** fuel, an air bleed also influences the air/fuel ratio and determines how strong the signal must be before atomized fuel is discharged through the nozzle.

Idle System

With a variety of operating conditions to cope with, a carburetor can't depend completely on pressure levels within the venturi as a means of determining fuel requirements. Sometimes an engine will need fuel, yet there won't be much air flowing through a carburetor. That's where the idle system comes into play.

Manifold Vacuum   If you have ever passed your hand over the top of a carburetor while the engine was idling, you've noticed that airflow is extremely low. And if you brought your palm right up against the carb top, you discovered a "suction" that seemed strong enough to pull the skin right off your hand. The force that grabbed your hand was generated by manifold vacuum.

Manifold vacuum is created by the pistons as they move downward on their intake strokes (Figure 22-9). At idle, manifold vacuum is high because the throttle is practically closed, thus preventing enough air to enter the manifold and fill the vacuum. Because only a trickle of air flows through the carburetor at idle, there is almost no pressure reduction in the venturi. A different circuit is then used, one which can

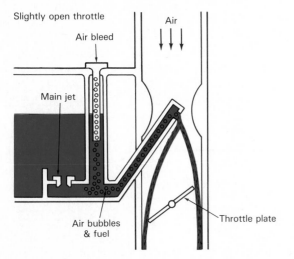

FIGURE 22-7   Venturi vacuum controls the amount of fuel.

FIGURE 22-8   Effect of throttle plate position on airflow.

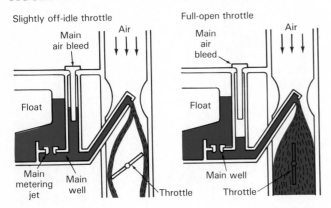

FIGURE 22-9   How a vacuum is made.

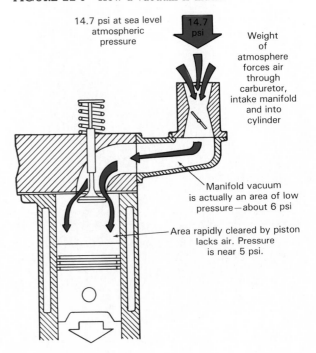

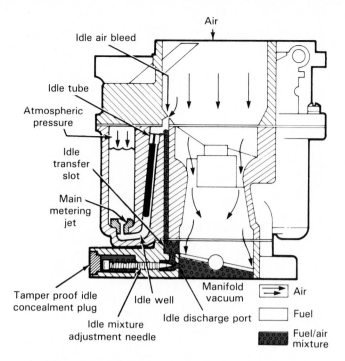

Air

Idle air bleed

Idle tube

Atmospheric pressure

Idle transfer slot

Main metering jet

Tamper proof idle concealment plug

Idle well

Idle mixture adjustment needle

Manifold vacuum

Idle discharge port

→ Air

☐ Fuel

▨ Fuel/air mixture

FIGURE 22-10   Idle circuit. (Ford Motor Company)

operate with a strong vacuum signal. This different circuit is called the idle circuit (Figure 22-10).

Fuel Flow   The idle circuit draws fuel from the main well. Depending on carburetor design, fuel flows either through an idle well or through an idle tube within the main well. It is routed above the reservoir fuel level and metered through an idle restriction. The fuel enters an emulsion well where it is atomized with air admitted through an idle air bleed. Fuel flow continues past a mixture-adjusting needle-tipped screw to the idle discharge port. The discharge port is located below the throttle plate. Manifold vacuum pulls the idle fuel out of the port, where it mixes with the air flowing by the throttle plate. Adjustment of the idle speed screw controls engine speed by altering the throttle plate position to admit more or less air.

Fuel from the idle system can also enter the venturi through a slot or series of ports (depending on the carburetor) located directly above the throttle plate. Called transfer slots or ports, these openings act as air bleeds when the throttle is closed. When the throttle is opened far enough to expose the transfer ports to manifold vacuum, additional fuel begins flowing from the transfer ports. Besides providing the fuel required for off-idle operation, the transfer port also allows a smooth transition from the idle to the main system.

Choke System

You may have noticed that cold temperatures affect engines like humans; the cold weather makes them hard to get going. Why? Gasoline does not vaporize very easily when it and the intake manifold passages are cold. And with the starter spinning the engine over at relatively low speed, vacuum levels are so low that very little fuel is drawn out of the carburetor. Most of it returns to a liquid state as soon as it runs into a cold intake manifold surface.

Choke Plate   Therefore, a choke plate is used to close off the venturi at its opening. Closing off the venturi helps build a vacuum. Even a slow-turning engine generates enough suction to create a vacuum immediately below a closed plate. This vacuum draws fuel out of both the main and the idle systems. With so much fuel reaching the intake manifold, sufficient vaporization occurs to let the engine start. Once the engine is started, vacuum is sufficient to initiate normal fuel flow and a reasonable amount of vaporization. Fuel will still condense on the manifold walls, but a richer-than-normal mixture is supplied until the manifold warms up and the choke plate is fully open.

The choke plate is also linked with the fast-idle cam (Figure 22-11). The fast-idle cam opens the throttle slightly. Opening the throttle raises engine rpm while the choke is operating. The higher rpm ensures the main system is operating by providing adequate air velocity through the venturi.

Most automatic choke systems also have a vacuum-actuated pull-off diaphragm which partially opens the choke when the engine starts and manifold vacuum is developed. This is also called a vacuum break. It keeps the mixture from being too rich. The choke shaft is also partially offset to help air-flow pull the choke open.

Choke Control   Automatic choke operation is typically controlled by a coiled bimetal thermostatic spring. As the spring warms, it expands, allowing the choke plate to open. Several methods are used to heat the choke spring. Air heated by the exhaust can be piped directly to the spring (Figure 22-12), or the spring can be placed in a well in the intake manifold which is heated by the exhaust crossover. Some engines route coolant by the spring, while others electrically heat the spring.

A few chokes are manually operated. A choke cable extends from the choke linkage to the instrument panel. Pulling the cable closes the choke, and pushing it in opens it. Automatic chokes use less fuel and cause less pollution than the typical driver/manual choke combination.

Accelerator Pump

When the accelerator pedal is rapidly pushed to the floor, the throttle is suddenly moved to the wide-open-throttle (WOT) position. Air immediately passes in

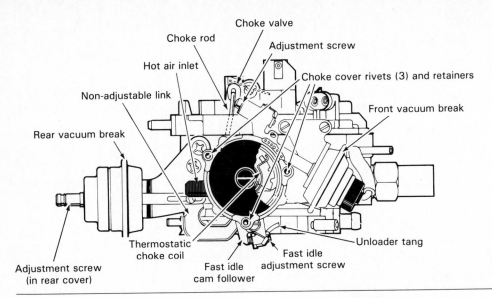

Choke valve
Choke rod
Adjustment screw
Hot air inlet
Choke cover rivets (3) and retainers
Non-adjustable link
Front vacuum break
Rear vacuum break
Thermostatic choke coil
Unloader tang
Fast idle adjustment screw
Adjustment screw (in rear cover)
Fast idle cam follower

FIGURE 22-11 Choke system. (Buick Motor Division, GMC)

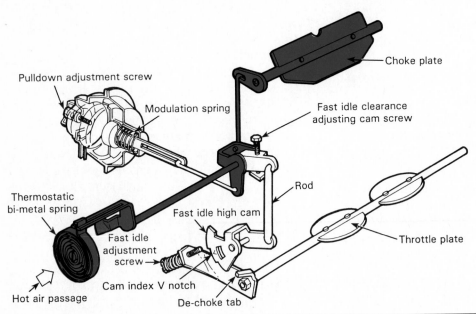

Choke plate
Pulldown adjustment screw
Modulation spring
Fast idle clearance adjusting cam screw
Rod
Thermostatic bi-metal spring
Fast idle high cam
Fast idle adjustment screw
Throttle plate
Cam index V notch
De-choke tab
Hot air passage

FIGURE 22-12 Typical hot air choke system. (Ford Motor Company)

great volume through the carburetor because the throttle restriction is no longer present. But gasoline is heavier than air, so it doesn't move as quickly. Therefore, the air/fuel mixture is very lean.

Eventually the gasoline flow will catch up with the airflow, but until it does, the engine will hesitate, run roughly or die because of the lean mixture.

To overcome this situation, carburetors are equipped with an **accelerator pump** (Figure 22-13). The pump squirts fuel directly into the airstream whenever the throttle is opened suddenly. This discharge, commonly called a pump shot, lasts only a second or so. It is timed to let the fuel in the main circuit reach the flow rate required by the new throttle position.

Pump Parts The pump circuit consists of a piston

(or diaphragm), inlet check valve, fuel-holding chamber, outlet check valve, discharge nozzle (or squirter), and spring-loaded actuating linkage. When the throttle is opened, fuel is pushed out of the chamber through a passage leading to an outlet check valve and the pump jet. Because gasoline isn't compressible and the pump's discharge rate is significantly higher than the nozzle's, the spring on the linkage is partially compressed. Fuel will continue to flow out of the pump jet until the spring expands to its original length. If a spring weren't used, bent or broken linkage would result, and the pump shot duration would be insufficient for some conditions.

When the throttle is closed, the accelerator pump is pulled back to its at-rest position. This movement pulls fuel in through the inlet check valve. The valve is usually located in the float bowl floor.

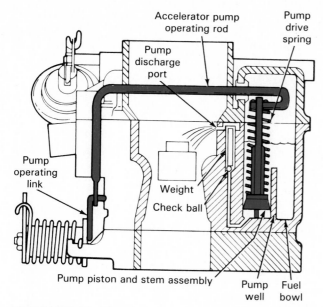

FIGURE 22-13   Accelerator pump system. (Ford Motor Company)

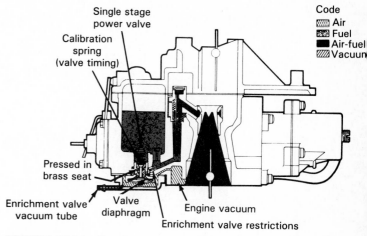

FIGURE 22-14   Enrichment system. (Ford Motor Company)

Power Valves

Propelling a car at normal highway speeds requires only a fraction of an engine's power potential. Therefore, the engine operates under a light load with the throttle barely opened. Under these conditions a relatively lean air/fuel mixture is sufficient and desirable. A lean mixture gives good fuel economy and low exhaust emissions. But when the load is increased, as in rapid acceleration, high-speed operation, or hill climbing, a richer mixture is needed for maximum power.

Enrichment   This mixture enrichment is different from that given by the accelerator pump. The accelerator pump shoots extra fuel into the manifold at a time when there is increased air. Theoretically, the accelerator pump doesn't enrich the mixture; it simply provides the correct air/fuel ratio until the main system can do so. The **power valve,** however, enriches the mixture and does so for prolonged periods.

Heavy loads are present at or near WOT. Under these circumstances, there is little to restrict airflow into the manifold, so vacuum drops significantly. And whenever manifold vacuum drops below a preset level, the power enrichment system is activated to provide the additional fuel required.

In some carburetors the enrichment circuit is controlled by a spring-loaded rubber diaphragm called a *power valve* (Figure 22-14). Others use a spring-loaded piston that alters the position of a tapered or stepped metering rod within the main jet. Another type of power valve consists of a needle-and-seat assembly controlled by a spring-loaded piston. With all three

designs, manifold vacuum is applied against spring pressure. When vacuum drops to the point where it can't overcome the spring's force, the power valve is opened, or the metering rods are repositioned, allowing more fuel to flow into the main well.

Fuel Delivery

Obviously, if the carburetor is to mix fuel with air, it must have a ready supply of fuel at all times. The fuel pump brings the fuel from the tank to the carburetor at a constant rate. Fuel flow into the carburetor is controlled by an inlet system consisting of a float-and-needle-valve assembly (Figure 22-15). The inlet

FIGURE 22-15   Fuel inlet system. (Ford Motor Company)

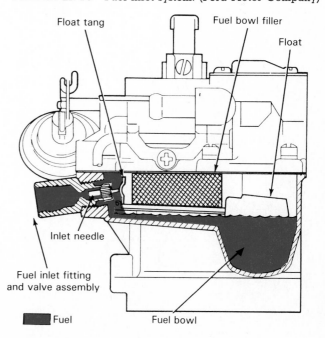

system is designed to maintain a constant fuel level in the float bowl under all operating conditions. The float bowl acts as a reservoir. It provides enough fuel, and it is close to the main system for all engine needs.

As its name implies, a float *floats* on top of fuel in the fuel tank. When the fuel level in the bowl rises, it lifts the float. The float is anchored on one end through a tang-and-hinge pin. The float pivots upward, and the tang moves the inlet needle toward its seat. At a predetermined level, the inlet valve is completely closed, and fuel flow ceases. As fuel is consumed, the level is reduced, allowing the float to drop and the needle to move away from its seat. More fuel is then allowed to enter, raising the level until the flow is shut off again.

Feedback Systems

Traditionally, carburetors have adjusted the air/fuel ratio by monitoring only conditions in the intake system. This method was satisfactory until three-way catalytic converters were installed as a means of controlling exhaust emissions. Proper three-way catalytic action occurs only when the air/fuel ratio is very close to being stoichiometric. **Feedback systems** maintain

exact mixtures by sensing the amount of oxygen in the exhaust gases and feeding the information back to a computer. The computer decides how much to alter the mixture and sends an electrical signal to the carburetor. The carburetor then adjusts the air/fuel mixture (Figure 22-16). This process can happen as quickly as 10 times per second.

Oxygen Sensor Feedback systems rely on an oxygen sensor in the exhaust system to determine the unburned oxygen in the exhaust gases. If the oxygen level is high, the mixture is lean. If the oxygen level is low, the mixture is rich. Computers are used to regulate a mixture-adjusting solenoid valve. Some feedback systems also adjust ignition timing, pollution control equipment, and idle speed.

Open and Closed Loop When the oxygen sensor is sending information and the carburetor is being adjusted, the system is operating in *closed-loop* mode. Sometimes the system works in *open loop*. In the open-loop mode, the oxygen sensor information is ignored, and the carburetor uses preset air/fuel ratios. Typical open-loop modes are cold starting, WOT, and *limp home*. The limp home mode is used when a malfunction occurs, and the feedback system isn't working. The

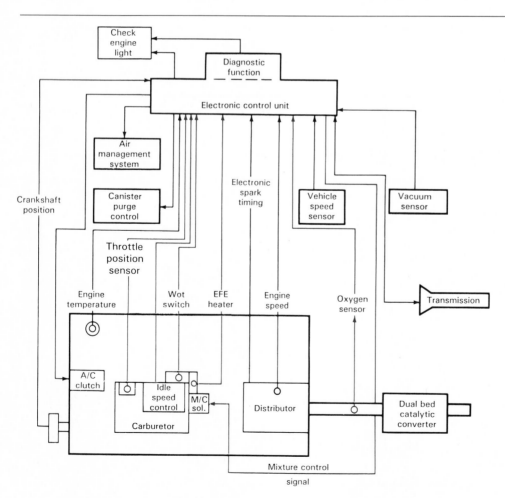

FIGURE 22-16 Computer command control system schematic. (Cadillac Motor Division, GMC)

carburetor then uses an average setting so the car can be driven to a repair shop.

The electronics in a feedback system can also store information about system operation. This information can be recalled and any problems noted and fixed.

CARBURETOR TYPES

Carburetors can be grouped by the general path of air through them and by the number of venturis they have. Modern carburetors are either downdraft or side-draft types when grouped by airflow. When grouped by the number of venturis, one-, two-, and four-venturi carburetors are popular. Updraft carburetors were popular many years ago, but are no longer used on new cars.

Downdraft

In downdraft carburetors, the air enters the tops and exits through their bottoms (Figure 22-17). This arrangement works well on V-type engines and is very popular worldwide. Downdraft carbs can also be used on in-line engines. On in-line engines, the carburetor sits on top of the intake manifold, which is bolted to the side of the head. Downdraft carburetors may have one, two, three or four venturis.

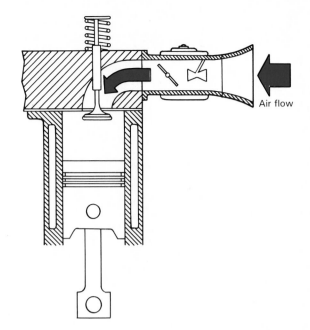

FIGURE 22-18   Side-draft carburetor.

Sidedraft

Sidedraft carburetors are built so their venturis are horizontal. Typically, they are used on in-line engines. The air passes parallel to the ground through the carburetor and intake manifold and then turns down slightly past the intake valve and into the cylinder (Figure 22-18). Sidedraft carburetors may have one, two, or three venturis.

Sidedraft carburetors are common on imported engines, usually high-performance versions. Because of their high-performance nature, most sidedraft carburetors have many adjustment features.

Venturi Number

The theoretical carburetor described in our discussion of carburetor circuits was a single carburetor. Adding more venturis (called barrels) increases the breathing ability of the carburetor. The more power an engine is to produce, the more barrels it will need. Increasing the size of the barrels also improves breathing and power, to a point.

Two-Barrel Carburetors

Single-barrel carburetors were used extensively on in-line engines during the 1940s and 1950s (Figure 22-19). Those engines did not develop a lot of power and did not need more than a single-barrel carburetor. But as engine power levels rose, more carburetion was needed. By adding another barrel, more power was available.

FIGURE 22-17   Downdraft carburetor.

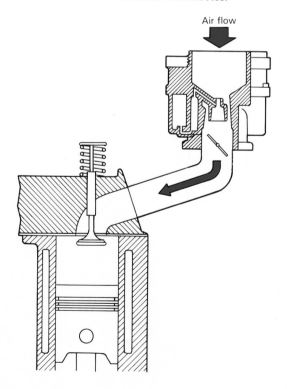

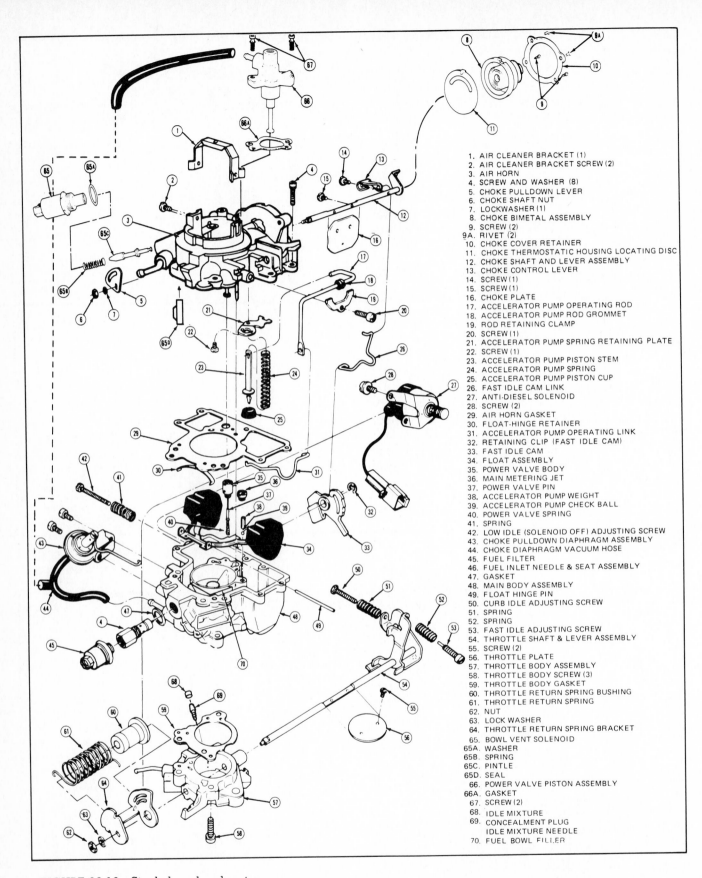

1. AIR CLEANER BRACKET (1)
2. AIR CLEANER BRACKET SCREW (2)
3. AIR HORN
4. SCREW AND WASHER (8)
5. CHOKE PULLDOWN LEVER
6. CHOKE SHAFT NUT
7. LOCKWASHER (1)
8. CHOKE BIMETAL ASSEMBLY
9. SCREW (2)
9A. RIVET (2)
10. CHOKE COVER RETAINER
11. CHOKE THERMOSTATIC HOUSING LOCATING DISC
12. CHOKE SHAFT AND LEVER ASSEMBLY
13. CHOKE CONTROL LEVER
14. SCREW (1)
15. SCREW (1)
16. CHOKE PLATE
17. ACCELERATOR PUMP OPERATING ROD
18. ACCELERATOR PUMP ROD GROMMET
19. ROD RETAINING CLAMP
20. SCREW (1)
21. ACCELERATOR PUMP SPRING RETAINING PLATE
22. SCREW (1)
23. ACCELERATOR PUMP PISTON STEM
24. ACCELERATOR PUMP SPRING
25. ACCELERATOR PUMP PISTON CUP
26. FAST IDLE CAM LINK
27. ANTI-DIESEL SOLENOID
28. SCREW (2)
29. AIR HORN GASKET
30. FLOAT-HINGE RETAINER
31. ACCELERATOR PUMP OPERATING LINK
32. RETAINING CLIP (FAST IDLE CAM)
33. FAST IDLE CAM
34. FLOAT ASSEMBLY
35. POWER VALVE BODY
36. MAIN METERING JET
37. POWER VALVE PIN
38. ACCELERATOR PUMP WEIGHT
39. ACCELERATOR PUMP CHECK BALL
40. POWER VALVE SPRING
41. SPRING
42. LOW IDLE (SOLENOID OFF) ADJUSTING SCREW
43. CHOKE PULLDOWN DIAPHRAGM ASSEMBLY
44. CHOKE DIAPHRAGM VACUUM HOSE
45. FUEL FILTER
46. FUEL INLET NEEDLE & SEAT ASSEMBLY
47. GASKET
48. MAIN BODY ASSEMBLY
49. FLOAT HINGE PIN
50. CURB IDLE ADJUSTING SCREW
51. SPRING
52. SPRING
53. FAST IDLE ADJUSTING SCREW
54. THROTTLE SHAFT & LEVER ASSEMBLY
55. SCREW (2)
56. THROTTLE PLATE
57. THROTTLE BODY ASSEMBLY
58. THROTTLE BODY SCREW (3)
59. THROTTLE BODY GASKET
60. THROTTLE RETURN SPRING BUSHING
61. THROTTLE RETURN SPRING
62. NUT
63. LOCK WASHER
64. THROTTLE RETURN SPRING BRACKET
65. BOWL VENT SOLENOID
65A. WASHER
65B. SPRING
65C. PINTLE
65D. SEAL
66. POWER VALVE PISTON ASSEMBLY
66A. GASKET
67. SCREW (2)
68. IDLE MIXTURE
69. CONCEALMENT PLUG
    IDLE MIXTURE NEEDLE
70. FUEL BOWL FILLER

FIGURE 22-19 Single-barrel carburetor.

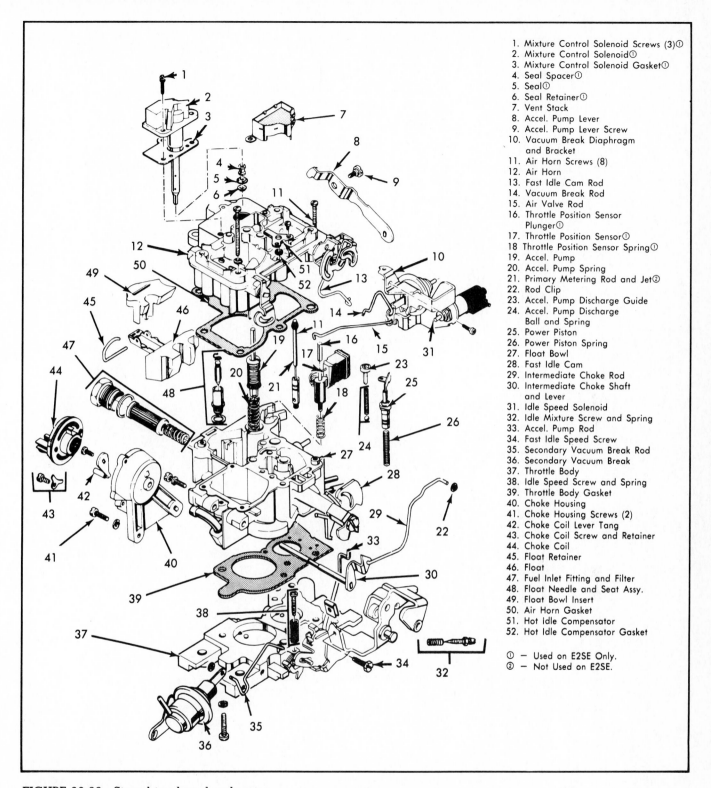

1. Mixture Control Solenoid Screws (3)①
2. Mixture Control Solenoid①
3. Mixture Control Solenoid Gasket①
4. Seal Spacer①
5. Seal①
6. Seal Retainer①
7. Vent Stack
8. Accel. Pump Lever
9. Accel. Pump Lever Screw
10. Vacuum Break Diaphragm
   and Bracket
11. Air Horn Screws (8)
12. Air Horn
13. Fast Idle Cam Rod
14. Vacuum Break Rod
15. Air Valve Rod
16. Throttle Position Sensor
   Plunger①
17. Throttle Position Sensor①
18. Throttle Position Sensor Spring①
19. Accel. Pump
20. Accel. Pump Spring
21. Primary Metering Rod and Jet②
22. Rod Clip
23. Accel. Pump Discharge Guide
24. Accel. Pump Discharge
   Ball and Spring
25. Power Piston
26. Power Piston Spring
27. Float Bowl
28. Fast Idle Cam
29. Intermediate Choke Rod
30. Intermediate Choke Shaft
   and Lever
31. Idle Speed Solenoid
32. Idle Mixture Screw and Spring
33. Accel. Pump Rod
34. Fast Idle Speed Screw
35. Secondary Vacuum Break Rod
36. Secondary Vacuum Break
37. Throttle Body
38. Idle Speed Screw and Spring
39. Throttle Body Gasket
40. Choke Housing
41. Choke Housing Screws (2)
42. Choke Coil Lever Tang
43. Choke Coil Screw and Retainer
44. Choke Coil
45. Float Retainer
46. Float
47. Fuel Inlet Fitting and Filter
48. Float Needle and Seat Assy.
49. Float Bowl Insert
50. Air Horn Gasket
51. Hot Idle Compensator
52. Hot Idle Compensator Gasket

① – Used on E2SE Only.
② – Not Used on E2SE.

FIGURE 22-20   Staged two-barrel carburetor.

A regular two-barrel carburetor is nothing more than two single-barrel carburetors sharing the same housing. Each barrel is the same size, and both have chokes and idle circuits. The full breathing ability of a two-barrel carburetor is rarely needed, however. Most of the time a single-barrel carburetor works bet-ter. The single barrel keeps air velocity high, which improves low-end power and mileage.

Staged Two-Barrel   The next step in carburetor evolution was the staged two-barrel carburetor (Figure 22-20). In a staged two-barrel carburetor the first barrel is called the primary barrel. It has a choke and an idle circuit. The second barrel is called the secondary barrel. It is larger than the primary barrel and has no idle circuit. It may or may not have a choke or accelerator pump.

This arrangement allows starting, idling, slow speed, and most steady throttle cruising to be done on the primary barrel alone. Only when most or all engine power is needed does the secondary barrel operate. The primary barrel's throttle is controlled by the accelerator pedal. The secondary barrel is usually vacuum or mechanically linked to the primary throttle linkage.

Four-Barrel Carburetors

For larger, more powerful engines, more venturi area is needed. Four-barrel carburetors were made by joining two staged two-barrel carburetors together in the same housing. Thus, the typical four-barrel carburetor has two primary and two secondary barrels. Both primaries have choke and idle circuits. Both secondaries do not (Figure 22-21).

With a four-barrel carburetor, even very large engines can run on the smaller primaries most of the time. This helps fuel economy and torque.

Secondary Operation For secondary operation on four-barrel carburetors, three methods are used. One is mechanically operated and uses linkage to open the secondary throttles. This secondary opening method is most often used in high-performance or racing four-barrel carburetors where engine speed or manifold vacuum cannot be relied on for carburetor operation.

The second method senses intake manifold vacuum and opens the secondary throttles as the engine requires additional air and fuel. For example, the greater the air/fuel demand, the lower the *intake manifold* vacuum, and the sooner the secondary side of the carburetor will open.

A TINKER'S EDUCATION

"I want a new car," she said.

"Yeah," I said, "there's nothing quite like a brand-new car; it smells different, it feels dif—"

"That's not what I mean," she said.

"Well, what do you mean?" I said.

"I want a car," she said, "that you haven't had a chance to mess with."

I did not really have this conversation.

Yet.

But I am willing to bet that this conversation has been held with some frequency among the car buffs in our midst. What we seem to be blessed with is a group of people, whom we shall call the Tinkers, who are never satisfied with a car until they have improved it somehow. The Tinker is usually married to one of what we shall call the Copers, who have to endure all the improvements made by the Tinkers.

Try as I might to keep the last vestiges of male chauvinism from tainting my thinking, I must say I believe that the great majority of Tinkers are male, the Copers female, though I have known of isolated instances where these roles are reversed. What I can't understand is why one never seems to find a Tinker married to a Tinker, a Coper to a Coper.

Probably because they'd drive each other crazy.

As it is, the Tinkers drive the Copers at least *half* crazy, but that is not their sole mission in life. A Tinker's sole mission in life is to Cobble Something Together, and he is so pleased with himself for having cobbled that he never quite notices just how frustrating it is for somebody else to have to cope with his cobbling.

In defense of the Tinker, let me tell you of a time when a woman was *grateful* for my Tinkeresque abilities. It was a dark and stormy night (well, not actually, but definitely a cold Alaska night, darker than which there aren't many). Her own car having failed (because, I am sure she irrationally believed, of the work of some Tinker or other), she had borrowed my Lotus. Now she was on the phone.

"Help help," she help-helped. "Your car is broken." And sure enough, the throttle cable had failed, as it was designed to do by dedicated British engineers, at the worst possible moment. Lotus throttle cables are not exactly a hot item at the local Texaco station, but I figured I could braze something together if I could get the car home to my garage.

Now, I ask you: Who else but a Tinker would have had the ingenuity to run a string from the Webers out under the hood and over to the passenger window? And it *worked*, I tell you. Sort of, at least.

We got the Lotus home, though she was laughing so hard she could hardly steer the darn thing and I got a mild case of frostbite to my ears from leaning out the window to pull on the string.

So let us not call the art of the Tinker "messing with" cars. True, in the years since the Lotus adventure I have had a variety of cars, and each of them has received a certain few improvements as I tailored them to my needs; it is true that whenever some Coper needs a car around this place, we have to go through a bit of training in the ways of holding one's foot just so on the accelerator and pinching these two wires together and yanking on the choke cable just after the engine fires once in order to get the darn thing running.

I don't call that *messing*. I call it *Education*.

Satch Carlson
Autoweek, Division of Crain Communications

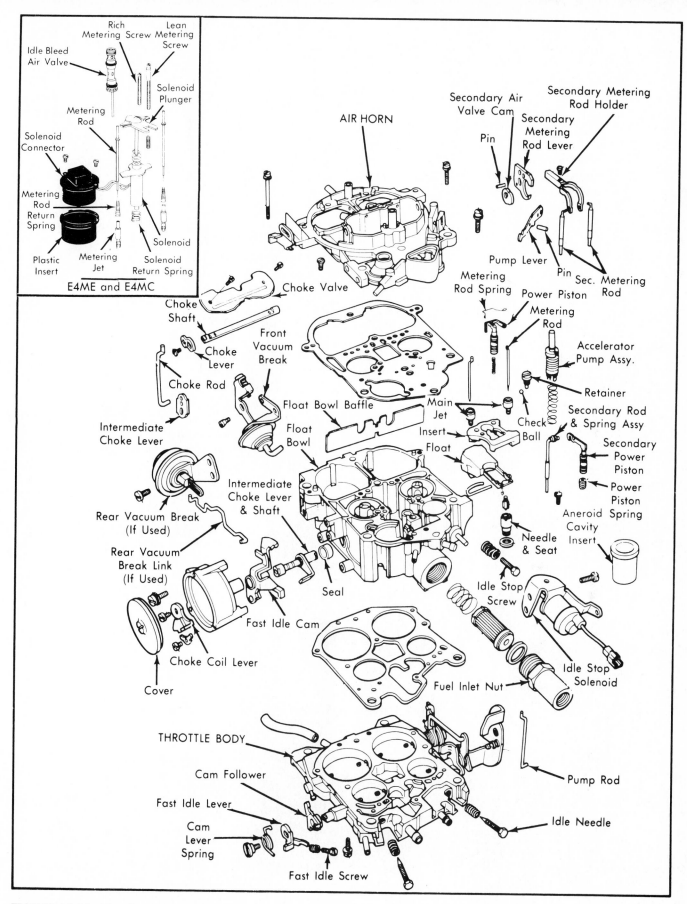

FIGURE 22-21   Four-barrel carburetor.

The third type uses what could be called an *air valve* method of exposing the secondary throttles. Independent of any mechanical linkage or intake manifold vacuum, this method has a preloaded set of blades (like the throttle blades) positioned above the secondaries. These blades open against some amount of weight or spring pressure. As inlet airflow increases, these blades open, exposing the secondary throttle blades which have already opened beneath the air valves. This linkage also lifts the secondary metering jets, letting fuel flow from the secondary jets.

Multiple Carburetion

Another means of increasing overall airflow capacity is to use several carburetors rather than just one. Common multicarb installations contain two four-barrel carburetors or three two-barrel carburetors and are found on V8 engines. In-line engines often use two side-draft two-barrel carburetors (Figure 22-22).

Most V8 systems operate under a primary/secondary arrangement with the secondary carburetors opening only in response to engine demands. Mechanical secondary operation is required on installations where each barrel is connected directly to a single intake port or when the carburetors have no vacuum actuation provisions. This system is more common on in-line and racing engine installations.

CARBURETOR SERVICE

Troubleshooting

Do not service or adjust a carburetor right away when you suspect it of giving poor service. Many times the problem lies elsewhere. Before you can do any meaningful work on the carburetor, examine the ignition system, compression, and valve adjustment. Unless these systems are working correctly, there is no sense in adjusting the carburetor.

After making sure that the rest of the engine is working correctly, turn to the fuel system. Make sure there are no leaking fuel lines, clogged fuel filters, or worn pumps before going to the carburetor. The chart in Figure 22-23 will help diagnose the problem.

Once you have isolated the carburetor as the source of trouble, try outside adjustments. Use the shop manual to ensure that the throttle linkage is correctly adjusted. This linkage adjustment is especially important on multiple-carburetor installations. Remove and inspect the mixture and idle speed adjusting screws. These screws have sharp, pointed tips. If the tips are deformed, they will disrupt that circuit.

Other external checks you should make include tightening the carburetor, mounting nuts, inspecting all vacuum connections, and replacing the fuel inlet filter (Figure 22-24).

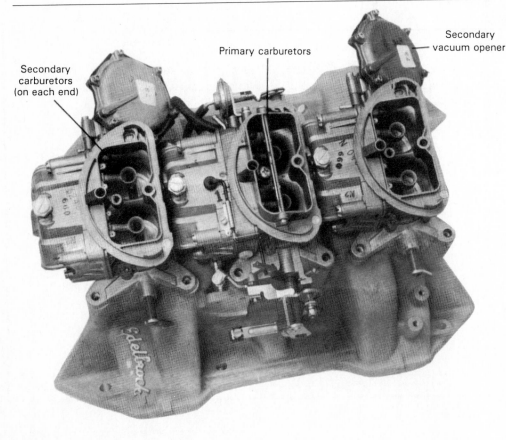

Secondary carburetors (on each end)

Primary carburetors

Secondary vacuum opener

FIGURE 22-22 Three two-barrel carburetors. (Chevrolet Motor Division, GMC)

CONDITION	POSSIBLE CAUSE	CORRECTION
Engine Won't Start	Choke not closing	Check choke operation
	Choke linkage bent	Check linkage
Engine Starts, Then Dies	Choke vacuum kick setting too wide	Check setting and adjust
	Fast idle RPM too low	Reset RPM to specification
	Fast idle cam index incorrect	Reset fast idle cam index
	Vacuum leak	Inspect vacuum system for leaks
	Low fuel pump outlet	Repair or replace pump
	Low carburetor fuel level	Check float setting
Engine Quits Under Load	Choke vacuum kick setting incorrect	Reset vacuum kick setting
	Fast idle cam index incorrect	Reset fast idle cam index
	Incorrect hot fast idle speed RPM	Reset fast idle RPM
Engine Starts, Runs Up, Then Idles Slowly With Black Smoke	Choke vacuum kick set too narrow	Reset vacuum kick
	Fast idle cam index incorrect	Reset fast idle cam index
	Hot fast idle RPM too low	Reset fast idle RPM
HOT STARTING SYMPTOMS		
Engine Won't Start	Engine flooded	Allow fuel to evaporate
COLD ENGINE DRIVEABILITY SYMPTOMS		
Engine Stalls in Gear	Choke vacuum kick setting incorrect	Reset choke vacuum kick
	Fast idle RPM incorrect	Reset fast idle RPM
	Fast idle cam index incorrect	Reset fast idle cam index
Acceleration Sag or Stall	Defective choke control switch	Replace choke control switch
	Choke vacuum kick setting incorrect	Reset choke vacuum kick
	Float level incorrect (too low)	Adjust float level
	Accelerator pump defective	Repair or replace pump
	Secondary throttles not closed	Inspect lockout adjustment
Sag or Stall After Warmup	Defective choke control switch	Replace choke control switch
	Defective accelerator pump (low output)	Replace pump
	Float level incorrect (too low)	Adjust float level
Backfiring & Black Smoke	Plugged heat crossover system	Remove restriction
WARM ENGINE DRIVEABILITY SYMPTOM		
Hesitation With Small Amount of Gas Pedal Movement	Vacuum leak	Inspect vacuum lines
	Accelerator pump weak or inoperable	Replace pump
	Float level setting too low	Reset float level
	Metering rods sticking or binding	Inspect and/or replace rods
	Carburetor idle or transfer system plugged	Inspect system and remove restrictions
	Frozen or binding heated air inlet	Inspect heated air door for binding
Hesitation With Heavy Gas Pedal Movement	Defective accelerator pump	Replace pump
	Metering rod carrier sticking or binding	Remove restriction
	Large vacuum leak	Inspect vacuum system and repair leak
	Float level setting too low	Reset float level
	Defective fuel pump, lines or filter	Inspect pump, lines and filter
	Air door setting incorrect	Adjust air door setting

FIGURE 22-23 Carburetor troubleshooting.

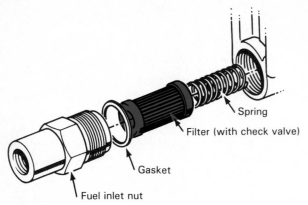

FIGURE 22-24　Fuel inlet filter. (Cadillac Motor Division, GMC)

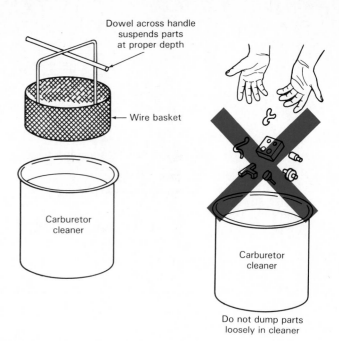

FIGURE 22-25　Carburetor cleaner.

Overhaul

When internal carburetor work is to be done, you will need a carburetor overhaul kit. The kit will include all gaskets and small parts needed to disassemble, clean, and reassemble the carburetor.

Carburetor cleaning is done in a cold, noncaustic solvent called carburetor cleaner. Carburetor cleaner is very dangerous if you splash it on you or breathe its fumes. Always use carburetor cleaner in a well-ventilated place and be careful not to spill it around. Use the wire basket provided to slowly lower the parts into the solution (Figure 22-25).

Removal　When removing the carburetor, mark all disconnections for reinstallation. Block the manifold entrance with a rag to keep dirt and foreign objects out. If you accidentally drop a nut down the intake manifold, make sure you get it out before starting the engine. Otherwise severe engine damage will result.

Because a carburetor doesn't have lots of heavy, fast-moving parts, it doesn't wear out as do internal engine parts. Usually a thorough cleaning and installing a carburetor kit will restore carburetor efficiency.

Disassembly　Disassemble the carburetor over a clean cloth, laying each piece on the rag in the order removed. Use the detailed instructions and exploded drawings of the carburetor in the shop manual. Do not attempt carburetor disassembly without the shop manual.

Cleaning　Clean all metal parts in carburetor cleaner. Carb cleaner will destroy all rubber, paper, or cork gaskets and diaphragms, along with any electrical parts. Make sure these vulnerable parts are removed before cleaning. All gaskets should be replaced, but dipping them in carb cleaner will only gum up the cleaner.

Rinse the cleaned parts with water and then blow-dry with compressed air. Use the compressed air to blast out all the small passages in the carburetor body. Use eye protection when blasting with compressed air.

Reassembly　Reassemble the carburetor, using the new gaskets from the rebuild kit. Check the fit of each gasket before installing. Besides the fit, check the new gasket for the correct number of holes and their position.

Install the carburetor and then crank the engine to fill the float bowl. Check for leaks and then start the engine. If the carburetor leaks, shut the engine off immediately, find the leak, and correct it.

TRADE TERMS

Accelerator Pump
Air-fuel Mixture
Atomization
Atomizing

Barrel
Feedback Systems
Fuel Delivery Signal
Jet

Power Valve
Pressure Differential
Stoichiometric

Throttle Plate
Variable Venturi Carburetor
Venturi

REVIEW QUESTIONS

1. What two basic things does a carburetor do?
2. Identify and explain the basic parts of a simple carburetor.
3. What is the venturi effect?
4. How does vacuum differ at the air horn and at the base of the carburetor?
5. What is the function of the air bleed?
6. Does the idle circuit use a strong or weak vacuum signal?
7. How does the choke help start the engine?

8. What does the accelerator pump do?
9. Does the power valve enrich the mixture?
10. Explain the difference between an open and closed loop.
11. What are the two types of carburetors based on airflow?
12. In a four-barrel carburetor, which two barrels are used the most?
13. When carburetor trouble is suspected, you should start work on the carburetor immediately. True or false?

23

Fuel Systems: Injection

INTRODUCTION

Fuel injection was developed to provide better fuel distribution in the engine as part of a search for more horsepower. Many other advantages have resulted from the use of fuel injection, including better fuel economy and reduced emissions.

Fuel injection delivers fuel to the cylinder under pump pressure, which is much higher than atmospheric pressure. The pump pushes fuel through an injector nozzle, providing a fine fuel spray, or *atomization*. In contrast, the fuel in a carburetor is pushed through the jets by atmospheric pressure.

Generally speaking, all types of fuel injection will provide better *atomization* of fuel than a carburetor. Better atomization improves burning of the air/fuel mixture and reduces emissions. At the same time, power and economy improve. Less fuel needs to be burned, because little ends up on the manifold walls or in an overrich cylinder mixture.

TYPES OF FUEL INJECTION

There are several kinds of fuel injection systems. These include (1) throttle body injection, (2) port fuel injec-

OBJECTIVES

When you have completed this chapter, you should be able to

- explain the advantages and disadvantages of fuel injection (compared to carburetion)
- Describe three different kinds of fuel injection
- List the four parts of an electronic fuel injection system
- Explain the differences between gasoline and diesel fuel injection

tion, and (3) **cylinder injection** (both direct and indirect). Gasoline engines may use a carburetor or throttle body or port injection. Diesel engines use cylinder injection systems. These systems may be operated electrically, mechanically, or electromechanically.

Another possible variation is in fuel flow. Some systems keep the injectors open all the time. These are called **continuous injection** systems. Others provide the fuel in short, timed pulses. No matter what the combination of operation and fuel metering, all injection systems have to measure and/or control the incoming air, determine the engine's need for fuel, and add the right amount at the right time.

Throttle Body Fuel Injection (TBI)

These fuel injection units have a throttle body, much like the bottom half of a carburetor (Figure 23-1). Instead of a float bowl and jets, they have one or two fuel injectors above the throttle plates. Once the fuel is injected from the nozzle, it travels through the manifold into the cylinders.

All the domestic manufacturers have used this type of system. It is relatively inexpensive and can use manifolds developed for engines with carburetors.

FIGURE 23-1 General Motors throttle body injection with two injectors. (Cadillac Motor Division, GMC)

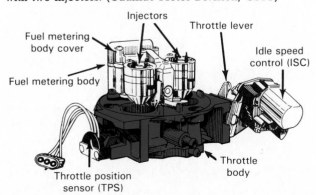

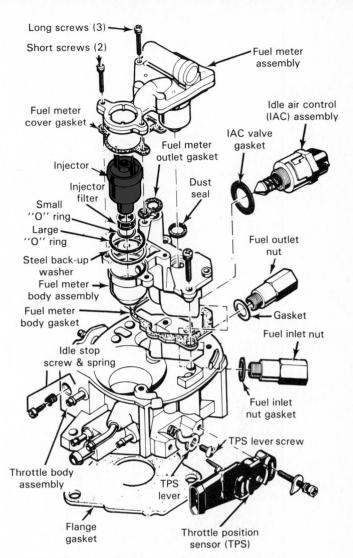

FIGURE 23-2 Exploded view of single throttle body fuel injection unit. (General Motors Corporation)

Fuel pressures are generally between 10 and 40 psi (0.7–2.8 kg/cm²). Most American Motors, Chrysler, Ford, and General Motors models with this injection system have one throttle body unit (Figure 23-2). Some General Motors models have had a dual throttle body system called Cross-Fire-Injection. The second throttle body enabled the engine to consume more fuel and air to produce more power. This system did not outperform a carburetor, so it was quickly discontinued. Some Chrysler Imperial models used a unique fuel injection system that also lasted only a few years.

Port Injection

Port injection systems feature an injector near each cylinder (Figure 23-3). The injector's spray is often aimed directly at the intake valve stem so the fuel will evaporate quickly and mix better with the incoming air. Port injection does not require the fuel and

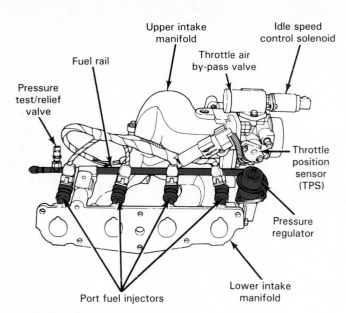

FIGURE 23-3 Ford port injection intake manifold assembly. (Ford Motor Company)

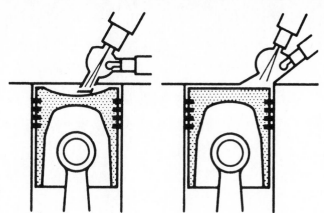

FIGURE 23-4 Diesel cylinder injection designs. (Robert Bosch Corporation)

air to mix in the manifold, so there is no possibility of fuel dropping out at corners or on cold manifold walls.

This system costs more than throttle body injection because it needs more fuel lines, wiring, and injectors. Fuel injection pressures are usually higher, between 40 and 100 psi (2.8–7 kg/cm²). However, the cost may be balanced out by the potential for lower emissions and better economy and power. All major manufacturers have at least one port fuel injection model.

Cylinder Injection

Cylinder injection, as its name implies, injects fuel into the combustion chamber or cylinder. This type of injection is generally limited to diesel engines. Since high combustion pressures tend to force the nozzle closed and prevent fuel from being injected, these systems must use extremely high injection pressures. These pressures range from 800 to 2400 psi (55–170 kg/cm²) on current passenger car diesels.

Timing of the injected fuel is also more critical than that of a gasoline injection system. Since the diesel fuel ignites as soon as it is injected, pump timing is similar to ignition timing on a gasoline engine. The demands for precise timing and high pressures require more expensive fuel lines and precision pumps than gasoline injection systems.

Most light-duty diesels use indirect injection, where fuel is injected into a *prechamber* to the side of the cylinder (Figure 23-4). Direct injection is used on heavy-duty engines but at this time is too noisy and

hard to control for engines that need a wide rpm range. It offers potential for better economy, though, and may soon appear in passenger vehicles.

ELECTRONIC FUEL INJECTION

Throttle Body and Port Injection

Electronic fuel injection systems are those where the amount of fuel delivered is controlled by an electronic "brain" or control unit. All systems have at least four main parts (Figure 23-5): (1) the airflow control system, (2) the sensors, (3) the control unit or computer, and (4) the fuel delivery system. You must understand these parts in order to service or diagnose any system. Both throttle body (Figure 23-6) and port (Figure 23-7) injection systems can be electronically controlled.

Air Induction   The air induction system includes the air cleaner, air intake tubes, throttle plates, and manifold. The throttle plates are used on any gasoline engine and may be part of a throttle body or on the intake manifold. They are controlled by the accelerator pedal. The air induction section of any system is very sensitive to air leaks. Be sure all clamps are tight and the tubing is not damaged or removed.

Sensors   The sensor system is responsible for monitoring engine temperature, load, rpm, and air intake. Some systems include many more sensors. The sensors feed signals to the control unit so it can decide how much fuel to inject for any engine condition.

The most expensive and important sensor is the air intake sensor. This sensor may measure air pressure, volume, mass, or temperature (or a combination of these). The name of the injection system is often determined by the type of air sensor it uses. For example, the Bosch L-Jetronic system uses a moving vane sensor

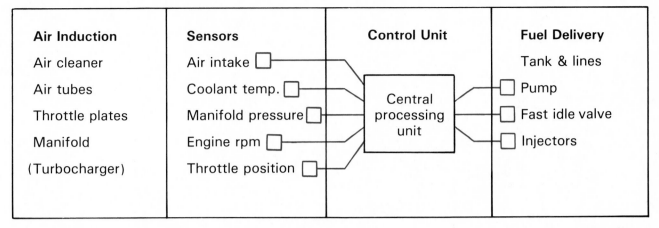

Air Induction	Sensors	Control Unit	Fuel Delivery
Air cleaner	Air intake		Tank & lines
Air tubes	Coolant temp.	Central processing unit	Pump
Throttle plates	Manifold pressure		Fast idle valve
Manifold	Engine rpm		Injectors
(Turbocharger)	Throttle position		

FIGURE 23-5   Four main parts of an electronic fuel injection system.

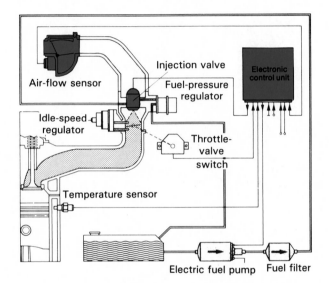

FIGURE 23-6   Throttle body fuel injection system. (Robert Bosch Corporation)

FIGURE 23-7   Port fuel injection system. (Robert Bosch Corporation)

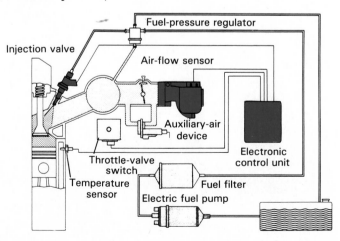

that measures air volume (Figure 23-8). The LH-Jetronic system uses a hot wire that measures air mass. The D-Jetronic uses a manifold pressure sensor. The initials, L, LH, and D refer to German words describing each type of sensor. The critical thing to remember is that they tell the computer *exactly* how much air is entering the engine, so the amount of fuel injected can be precisely controlled.

Control Unit   The control unit receives the sensor signals and acts upon them. It decides how much fuel to inject based on sensor inputs, programming put in at the factory, and "learned" experience. The control unit is connected to the sensors by a network of wiring (Figure 23-9).

FIGURE 23-8   Moving vane airflow meter. (Robert Bosch Corporation)

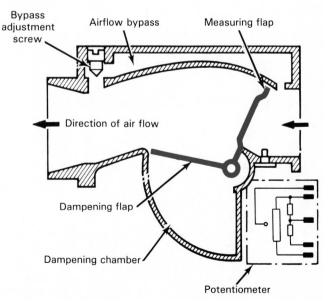

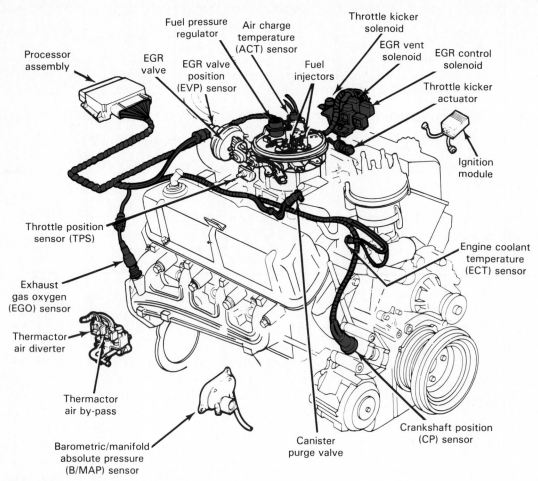

Processor assembly

EGR valve

Fuel pressure regulator

EGR valve position (EVP) sensor

Air charge temperature (ACT) sensor

Fuel injectors

Throttle kicker solenoid

EGR vent solenoid

EGR control solenoid

Throttle kicker actuator

Ignition module

Throttle position sensor (TPS)

Exhaust gas oxygen (EGO) sensor

Thermactor air diverter

Thermactor air by-pass

Barometric/manifold absolute pressure (B/MAP) sensor

Canister purge valve

Engine coolant temperature (ECT) sensor

Crankshaft position (CP) sensor

FIGURE 23-9 Ford fuel injection wiring harness. (Ford Motor Company)

Names for the control unit vary. Each manufacturer has its own terms:

□ Bosch: ECU or electronic control unit
□ Chrysler: computer power/logic module
□ Ford: ECA or electronic control assembly
□ General Motors: ECU or electronic control unit and ECM or electronic control module

Fuel Delivery   The fuel delivery system includes the fuel tank, electric fuel pump, lines, filters, pressure regulators, and of course the injectors themselves. The injectors are opened by an electrical signal from the control unit. Some systems include a fuel flow meter to measure the fuel used.

These four parts (airflow, sensors, computer, and fuel delivery) make up almost any system. Some new models don't use an air sensor, but "guesstimate" the incoming air from other engine sensors. In any electronic system, whether throttle body or port injection, the actual injection is controlled by a computer. An electrical signal opens a small solenoid valve inside

the injector. The open valve allows fuel under pressure to spray into the manifold (Figure 23-10).

Signals to the injector come from the computer and determine when and how much fuel is injected. The injectors may all open at once, or they may open in several groups, as on the early Cadillac EFI. Even when all the injectors are open at once (and some of the intake valves are closed), fuel is in the manifold for a very short time. Buick has a sequential fuel injec-

FIGURE 23-10   Electrical fuel injector nozzle. (General Motors Corporation)

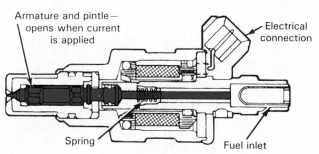

Armature and pintle— opens when current is applied

Electrical connection

Spring

Fuel inlet

tion (SFI) that activates each injector just as its intake valve opens. This system is used for high-performance engines. It is more expensive than an injection system where the injectors pulse together, twice for every engine cycle.

MECHANICAL FUEL INJECTION

Several types of mechanical fuel injection systems are currently produced. Most of them are used for racing only. Some prominent names are Hilborn and Kugelfischer. The designs used for racing are durable and light and flow lots of fuel. But they cannot control fuel carefully enough to meet emission standards. Only one mechanical system is currently used on passenger cars in the United States. It is the Bosch Continuous Injection System (CIS), also referred to as K-Jetronic.

Bosch Continuous Injection System (CIS)

This system is a mechanical system (Figure 23-11). The fuel is continuously sprayed by individual injectors into the intake manifold near each intake valve. It is a port injection system. The air intake and fuel flow are controlled by a fuel distributor with direct mechanical (not electronic) control. The distributor decides how much fuel volume to allow to the injectors. Other controls affect the fuel pressure, which also influences the amount of fuel going through the injectors.

Even though the CIS system is primarily mechanical, there are some electrically operated parts. These include the cold start valve, which enrichens the starting mixture, and the auxiliary air valve, which allows more air in the engine for a *fast idle* when the engine is cold. In some systems, a feedback circuit is used. It varies fuel pressure to fine-tune the air/fuel mixture.

When the throttle plate is open with the engine cranking or running, low pressure occurs inside the intake manifold. Air flows into the manifold, pushing the airflow sensor plate open. The airflow sensor plate has a mechanical arm attached to a control plunger in the mixture control unit. The control plunger moves in proportion to the amount of air drawn through the airflow sensor plate. The movement opens fuel metering slits, one for each injector. The slit opening regulates the fuel to the injectors.

The fuel distributor is part of the mixture control unit. The distributor body has differential pressure valves, one for each injector. These valves consist of two chambers (primary and secondary) separated by a steel diaphragm. The secondary circuit is for fuel distribution. It starts at the fuel distributor unit and ends at the injector.

The primary circuit supplies fuel to the secondary. Fuel pressure in the primary part of the distributor is kept at about 70 psi by the pressure regulator and electric fuel pump. This high pressure is reduced before it goes into the secondary circuit. The pressure control is very important.

It is easy to see that higher fuel pressure forces more fuel through an injector (in a given amount of time) than lower pressure will. The K-Jetronic system can vary air/fuel ratios both by pressure and by the size of the open fuel metering slits. Early systems vary pressure to richen mixture during warm-up. Later *feedback* systems can vary pressure with an electronic regulator and control unit. This lets them control air/fuel ratios for best emission control (Figure 23-12).

Air Induction   Air flows through the air cleaner, into the airflow sensor box, and around the airflow sensor plate. After passing the throttle plate, the air goes into the manifold, through the intake ports, and into the cylinder.

The auxiliary air device is operated by an electrically heated bimetallic switch. It increases engine rpm when the engine is cold by allowing some extra air to bypass the throttle plate. As the engine warms up, the opening closes. Some recent systems have an electronic idle speed control. On these systems, a computer-controlled valve varies the bypass air to keep engine idle speed constant. This system reduces idle speed, fuel consumption, and emissions.

Sensors   The airflow sensor is the pressure-sensing flap. It is carefully sized to the engine it is mounted on. It may operate in a downdraft or updraft position.

The thermo-time switch controls the cold start injector valve and deactivates the valve above a certain temperature limit. The switch is activated through the starter motor operation. Some cars have a hot start relay which pulses the valve for better starting when the engine is hot.

FIGURE 23-11   Bosch mechanical fuel injection (CIS), also called K-Jetronic. (Robert Bosch Corporation)

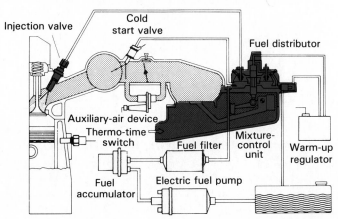

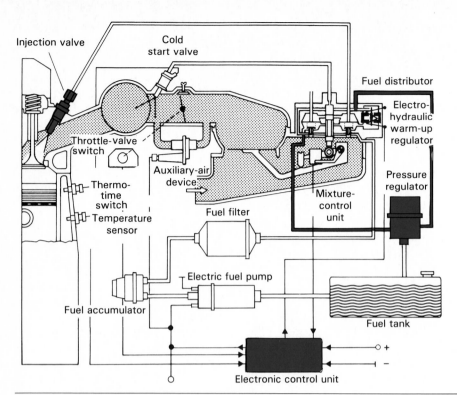

Injection valve

Cold start valve

Fuel distributor

Electro-hydraulic warm-up regulator

Throttle-valve switch

Auxiliary-air device

Pressure regulator

Thermo-time switch

Temperature sensor

Mixture-control unit

Fuel filter

Electric fuel pump

Fuel accumulator

Fuel tank

Electronic control unit

FIGURE 23-12 Bosch feedback mechanical fuel injection, also called KE-Jetronic. (Robert Bosch Corporation)

The warm-up regulator controls the pressure that acts against the top of the control plunger. It reduces the control pressure during starting and during warm-up, which enrichens the fuel mixture. A bimetallic switch turns off the regulator after normal engine temperature is reached.

Electrical Circuits Electrical circuits operate the start valve, electric fuel pump, warm-up regulator, and auxiliary air device. A switch located at the airflow sensor is activated when air flows in the manifold. This tells the fuel pump and other devices when to operate.

Fuel Delivery The fuel goes from the tank through a high-pressure electric fuel pump to a fuel accumulator. The fuel accumulator maintains fuel pressure after the engine is shut off. This fuel pressure helps on restart and prevents vapor bubbles. The fuel flows through an in-line filter and into the mixture control unit. The fuel flows from the fuel distributor to the individual fuel injectors and into the port. Excess fuel goes back from the distributor to the tank.

DIESEL FUEL INJECTION

Diesel systems normally have no throttle plates. There is no fuel in the intake manifold. The intake manifold has the air cleaner mounted above it and flows only air. Engine rpm is controlled by a fuel metering valve and governor. As the accelerator pedal is depressed,

the throttle linkage or cable operates the metering valve that allows increased fuel.

The injection pump supplies fuel under extremely high pressure to the injectors. The high-pressure fuel forces the injector open, resulting in a fine spray of atomized fuel. The high temperature and pressure in the combustion chamber cause the fuel to ignite rapidly. As you can imagine, diesel injection systems must carefully control fuel injection timing as well as quantity. They could be called sequential fuel injection systems.

Current diesel systems have limited electronic controls, which usually help limit emissions. Systems now under development have electronically controlled injectors for more precise timing and better control of noise and smoke. These systems should appear on production models within a few years.

GM Diesel Injection

The General Motors V6 and V8 diesel system uses a Roosa-Master type of camshaft-driven high-pressure fuel pump. The pump is mounted on the top of the engine and operates at camshaft speed. It injects a metered amount of fuel to each cylinder at exactly the proper time to provide correct fuel ignition. The pump has a built-in advance unit to provide for proper fuel timing as engine speed increases.

Fuel drawn from the fuel tank by the fuel pump passes through the fuel filter. Fuel then goes from the

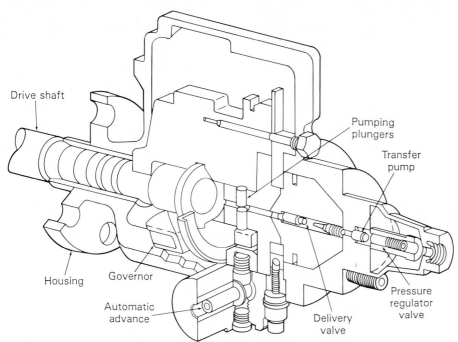

Drive shaft

Pumping plungers

Transfer pump

Housing

Governor

Automatic advance

Delivery valve

Pressure regulator valve

FIGURE 23-13 Diesel fuel injection pump. (General Motors Corporation)

filter to the fuel injection distributor pump (Figure 23-13).

Pump Operation Two pumps are used. A mechanical or electric supply pump brings fuel from the tank to the engine. The injection pump is a high-pressure rotary plunger type with a built-in fuel pressure regulator and transfer pump. Fuel enters the spring-regulating pressure valve. The valve regulates the fuel pressure from the transfer pump to the pumping plunger area.

Charging Cycle The fuel flow during the charging cycle is from the transfer pump through the passage to the pump head barrel (Figure 23-14). The fuel then passes through the metering valve (throttle controlled). After being metered, the fuel goes from the charging ports of the charging ring through the inlet passages to the pumping chambers. The pumping chamber has a cam ring with lobes for each cylinder. Fuel pushes the fuel plungers back against the cam rollers, completing the charging cycle.

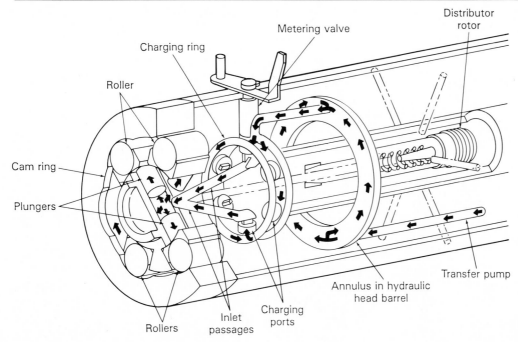

Metering valve

Distributor rotor

FIGURE 23-14 Fuel flow during pump charging cycle. (Stanadyne)

Charging ring

Roller

Cam ring

Plungers

Rollers

Inlet passages

Charging ports

Annulus in hydraulic head barrel

Transfer pump

"ME AND MY BIG MOUTH"

We started into the 1968 Can-Am with a note of mediocrity. The first race was at Elkhart Lake, and the McLaren team showed up with spectacular new cars as we had expected. They were truly gorgeous and much faster than anything we had. All we could hope for was that they weren't as well developed and as finely tuned as we were. That almost happened, too, except for a little slippage of the tongue on my part. We all had the same aluminum 427 Chevrolet engines in our cars, but the McLarens immediately broke some of theirs for unexplainable reasons.

But to go back a little bit. Roger had been trying to help Sun Oil get their transmission fluid approved through GM's standards tests. Along with that we were also evaluating Sunoco racing oil in our Camaro program. It was becoming known, or we were learning on the dynamometer, that mineral-base additives in the oil would cause combustion chamber deposits, the deposits would cause detonation, and the deto-

nation would rapidly destroy a high-compression racing engine. Sun Oil gradually switched away from those additives, and we finally worked out the problem. Then we learned on Traco's dyno that the aluminum engines had an even more critical problem. They had a dip in the torque curve at about 5500 rpm, where they would go lean, detonate, and blow black smoke out the exhaust. This was later avoided by using the staggered inlet stacks, but we minimized it then by using Sun's "ashless" oil.

When McLaren suddenly started losing engines that were otherwise running great, I thought, "What could be more obvious? I'll bet they're failing from detonation." I started feeling cocky, thinking that I knew something about engineering that the great McLaren team didn't. After a while Bruce McLaren came walking up and started joking around, and he very casually said, "Why do you suppose we're breaking these motors?" And I stood

there and listened to myself tell him exactly what I thought the problem was! I guess it was because they always seemed to be one up on us. As one engineer to another, I just couldn't resist giving an engineering answer to show that we had some smarts too.

I don't know if that really was the problem, but I heard they were looking for some Sun Oil oil at the track, and there was a bit of a scene about that, of course, because their sponsor was Gulf Oil. Sure enough, they had no problems, and they came in one-two ahead of me. They never mentioned it again, so I don't know for sure, but that looked like the tipoff. Even at that, I don't think I ever learned to keep my mouth shut. Fate evened us up at the next race, though, when both of them broke, and I won—my only win of the series.

The Discharge Cycle (Injection) Figure 23-15 shows fuel flow during the discharge cycle. The inlet passages on the charging ring now move out of line as the rotor turns. The rollers come up on the rotating cam, which in turn pushes the fuel plungers. As the fuel plungers are pushed by the cam, they cause a very high fuel pressure rise. The fuel goes down the discharge passage. A rotor discharge port opens to one of the discharge head outlets, and fuel flows to the injector. The injector nozzle pops open, and fuel is injected.

The delivery valve in the injection pump rapidly decreases the injection line pressure after the fuel is

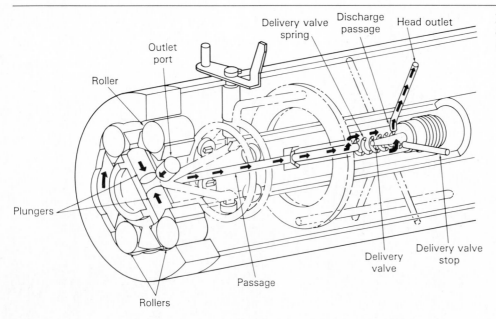

FIGURE 23-15 Fuel flow during pump discharge cycle. (Stanadyne)

injected. This causes the injector nozzle valve to return quickly to its seat to prevent improper atomization of fuel from the injector.

The governor assembly inside the distributor injection pump maintains the desired speed under different engine loads. The idle speed and maximum speed of the diesel engine must be controlled by the governor. The governor senses engine speed (rpm) and regulates the fuel. Most governors have pivoting weights. Centrifugal force moves them outward. The weights are attached to a spring which pulls the linkage in order to advance or retard (increase or decrease) the fuel metering valve opening.

The advance system automatically advances fuel delivery when the engine is operating at higher speeds (rpm). This compensates for piston speed increases due to increased rpm. This gives optimum cylinder pressure for power and economy.

Glow Plugs   **Glow plugs** ignite the air/fuel mixture in the cylinder during cold starting. The glow plugs are on a timer and remain on for about 1 min. Once the engine is running, the cylinders are warmed up quickly, and ignition is provided by cylinder heat (Figure 23-16).

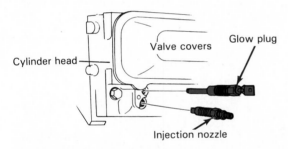

FIGURE 23-16   Diesel glow plug and injection nozzle locations. (Oldsmobile Motor Division, GMC)

FIGURE 23-17   Injector nozzle spray patterns. (Oldsmobile Motor Division, GMC)

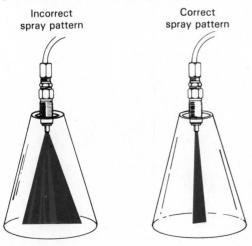

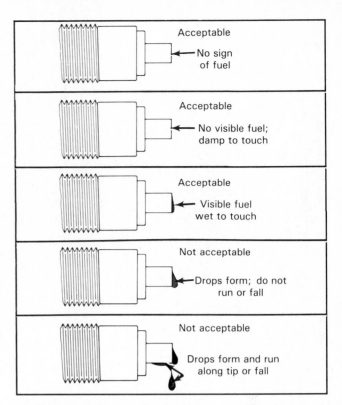

FIGURE 23-18   Injector nozzle seat tightness check. (Oldsmobile Motor Division, GMC)

Fuel Injector Nozzle   The fuel injector nozzle injects fuel directly into the precombustion chamber and is opened by the high pressure provided by the injector pump. The injectors require about 800–1000 psi on V6 models and 1200 psi on V8 models to open and inject the fuel.

The injectors are opened at the proper time and at the correct cylinder by pressure in the fuel lines (from the pump). The injector spray pattern and nozzle seat tightness are very important (Figures 23–17 and 23–18). The fuel lines are all equal in length from the pump to their cylinder injectors in order to guard against variation in the injection timing.

Bosch Diesel Injection

Bosch (and other licensed companies) make two types of injection pumps. One is the in-line pump, used by Mercedes-Benz and others (Figure 23-19). The second is the rotary pump (similar to the General Motors system described above).

The in-line fuel pump is mounted beside the engine and has a separate pumping unit for each engine cylinder. This system has a fuel supply pump that supplies fuel from the tank to the in-line pump. The in-line pump provides the high fuel pressure and meters the proper amount of fuel to each injector in each cylinder. As in other diesel fuel injection systems, there

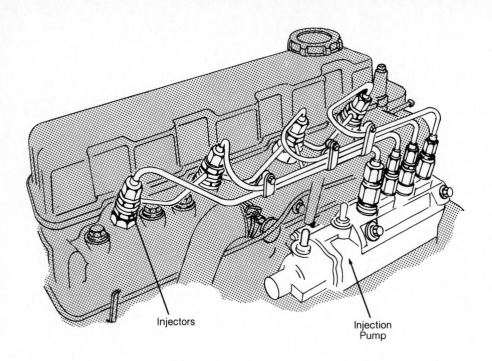

Injectors

Injection
Pump

FIGURE 23-19 In-line diesel
injection pump system.

is no fuel in the intake manifold. Only air is passed through the intake manifold, and no throttle plate is required as engine speed is dependent on the amount of fuel injected into the engine cylinders.

In-Line Fuel Injection Pump Operation The injection pump is driven off the engine crankshaft at one half the engine speed (Figure 23-20). The injection pump has a camshaft with a lobe on it for each engine cylinder. There is a separate pump plunger for each cylinder. Fuel enters a slot above the plunger when it is in the down position. The camshaft pushes the roller tappet upward, driving a plunger control arm into the control sleeve. When the plunger is pushed upward, it forces the fuel out the delivery valve assembly to the injector.

The amount of fuel injected must be controlled. It is controlled by a rack operated by the throttle and governor. The control rack (Figure 23-21) rotates the control sleeve gear, which turns the control plunger. The plunger has fuel ports that line up differently as it is turned by the rack. This allows fuel delivery to be varied from zero to the maximum required. The plunger can uncover a spill port so the fuel returns to the tank and less (or none) is delivered (Figure 23-22).

Injector timing is altered by the flyweight timing device. As the engine speed is increased, centrifugal force causes the flyweight to move out, pushing against the driven cam plate. This rotates the driven flange and hub that are attached to the injector pump camshaft. The camshaft is rotated (advanced), which starts the injection process sooner.

Governor Operation The governor used with the Bosch system may be mechanical or pneumatic. The

FIGURE 23-20 Sectional view of an in-line injection pump. (Robert Bosch Corporation)

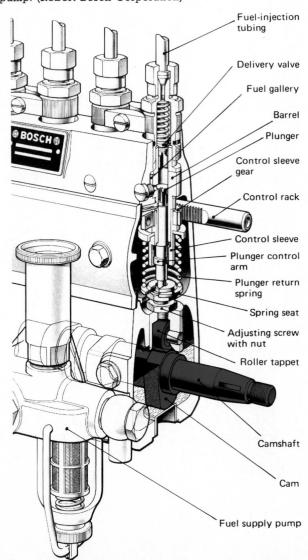

Fuel-injection
tubing

Delivery valve

Fuel gallery

Barrel

Plunger

Control sleeve
gear

Control rack

Control sleeve

Plunger control
arm

Plunger return
spring

Spring seat

Adjusting screw
with nut

Roller tappet

Camshaft

Cam

Fuel supply pump

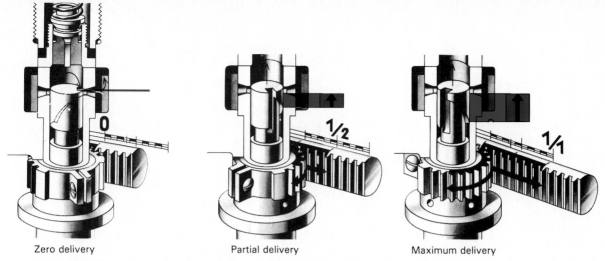

Zero delivery   Partial delivery   Maximum delivery

Rack rotates plunger to vary amount of fuel delivered

FIGURE 23-21   Injection pump control rack. (Robert Bosch Corporation)

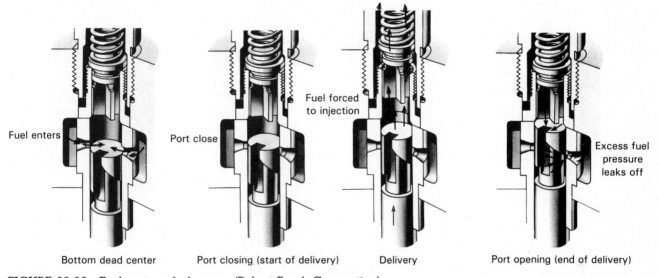

Fuel enters   Port close   Fuel forced to injection   Excess fuel pressure leaks off

Bottom dead center   Port closing (start of delivery)   Delivery   Port opening (end of delivery)

FIGURE 23-22   Fuel ports and plungers. (Robert Bosch Corporation)

FIGURE 23-23   Hole-type injection nozzles. (Robert Bosch Corporation)

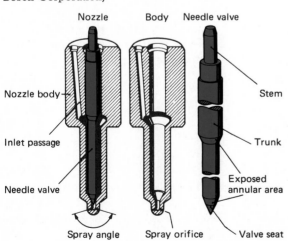

Nozzle   Body   Needle valve

Nozzle body

Inlet passage

Needle valve

Stem

Trunk

Exposed annular area

Spray angle   Spray orifice   Valve seat

mechanical governor is speed sensitive and operates using flyweights. The pneumatic governor is responsive to the airflow in the engine intake manifold. The governor transmits its movement to the control rack. The control rack is moved in the stop or maximum fuel direction so the fuel is automatically regulated.

Glow Plugs   As in other diesel systems, this one uses glow plugs to heat the air/fuel mixture in the cylinder during cold starting. The glow plug system was described in detail earlier in this chapter.

Fuel Injection Nozzle   The injector nozzle has a nozzle body with a needle valve. The needle is forced off the seat by the fuel pump pressure. These are called hole-type injectors and have small spray orifices. Pintle nozzles are used on precombustion and turbulence chamber engines (Figures 23-23 and 23-24).

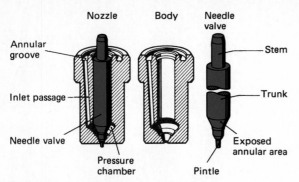

Annular groove

Inlet passage

Needle valve

Nozzle

Body

Needle valve

Stem

Trunk

Pressure chamber

Pintle

Exposed annular area

FIGURE 23-24 Pintle nozzles are used in precombustion and turbulence combustion engines.

SERVICING FUEL INJECTION SYSTEMS

Fuel injection systems don't need much service, but the service they do need they should get regularly. All regular injection service is limited to the fuel supply system, on both diesel and gasoline systems. There is no need to service the computer, injection pump, or injectors under normal conditions.

Fuel Supply

A major injection problem is fuel contamination. Either dirt or water gets into the fuel supply and clogs or damages the system. Dirt can damage injectors if it isn't filtered out. Large amounts of dirt can quickly clog the fuel filter. This can keep the engine from making full power or even running at all. Water corrodes or rusts the many metal parts in the system. If a lot of water is present, the engine will stumble or refuse to run.

Fuel Source While it may not seem like service, the fuel source must always be considered when fuel problems arise. The most common source of bad fuel is the service station's tanks. Water and dirt collect in these tanks if they are not maintained. If fuel problems keep arising, have the customer switch service stations and see if the problems go away.

Fuel Filters Fuel filters must be changed at the recommended intervals. Additional fuel filters may also be necessary. On diesel engines, a water separator is an excellent addition. The water separator swirls the fuel in a cylinder and allows the water to settle to the bottom. Periodic draining of the separator is necessary. A petcock is provided for draining.

Fuel Hazards Whenever working around injection systems, remember the fire hazard. Loosening or removing fuel lines on a running engine may cause high-pressure fuel to squirt over a large area. This can start a very large fire quickly. Also, the high-pressure spray

emitted from a diesel injector will force diesel fuel directly through your skin. Diesel fuel will give you severe headaches, blood poisoning, dizziness, and other problems. See a doctor immediately if you accidentally get sprayed from a diesel injector.

Cleanliness is extra important with injection systems. Keep your hands and work area clean when handling injection components. Otherwise, dirt will clog the small passages in the system.

TROUBLESHOOTING THE INJECTION SYSTEMS

When getting ready to troubleshoot fuel injection systems, you should obtain a detailed repair manual. Although most systems operate in the same way and have the same components, normal pressures and sensor resistances may vary. The biggest mistake you can make when troubleshooting is to start replacing components before checking them. Many mechanics replace part after part before they fix the problem. This wastes time and money.

Inspection

Fuel Supply Common sense can solve many fuel injection problems. If no fuel is getting to the injection system, the engine won't run. The things to check first, in any injection system, are the supply of fuel in the tank, condition of the fuel filters, pump operation, fuel pressure, and fuel flow. Only after these items are checked should the injectors and other fuel injection parts be suspected.

Ignition Many times problems are incorrectly blamed on the ignition system. Make sure the ignition system and all filters are in good shape before digging into the injection system. Valve adjustment and engine compression should also be checked.

Electrical A visual check of the injection system wiring will locate most electrical problems. The most common ones are corroded connections and broken wires. Other frequent breakdown causes are bad ground connections, shorted or open sensors, and physically damaged airflow sensors. Sensor resistances can be checked with an ohmmeter. The ohmmeter can also be used to check the condition of wiring in the fuel injection or glow plug systems.

If the fuel injection system is on a computer-controlled engine, the computer may be able to diagnose some of its own problems. A flashing code light indicates the most likely trouble. By checking the code in a reference manual, the technician can find the most effective troubleshooting procedure. For more information, see Chapter 24.

TRADE TERMS

Continuous Injection
Cylinder Injection
Electronic Fuel Injection

Glow Plugs
Port Fuel Injection
Throttle Body Injection

REVIEW QUESTIONS

1. Name the four major parts of an electronic fuel injection (EFI) system described in this chapter.

2. Fuel pressure in an injection system is usually _____ _____ than the pressure in a carburetion system.

3. Gasoline injection systems inject fuel into the _____ _____, while diesel injection systems inject fuel into the _____.

4. The most important sensor in an electronic fuel injection system is the _____ sensor.

5. Continuous injection systems have no electrical parts. True or false?

6. All diesel fuel injection nozzles are operated electrically. True or false?

7. The main enemy of any fuel injection system is contaminated fuel. True or false?

8. Since fuel is injected under pressure, air leaks in the system won't affect engine operation. True or false?

24

Computer Engine Control

INTRODUCTION

The operation of engine emission controls and ignition systems has progressed from the simple, early designs to the modern, complex systems of today (Figure 24-1). Early designs consisting of little more than PCV, fuel evaporation, and some simple spark controls helped clean up engine exhaust a significant amount. But as emissions regulations became more demanding, many extra devices were needed. This increasing number of components resulted in more complex control problems.

With the invention of the on-board computer, precise engine control was provided. Before the introduction of the computer, some control devices were vacuum controlled, some were electrically controlled, and still others operated in response to changes in engine coolant temperature or engine speed. With several devices responding to different signals, occasional conflicts between the devices could (and did) occur. The result: poor performance at less than peak efficiency.

Computerized systems send engine information signals to the central computer. It is then up to the computer to determine which components to activate to provide the best possible combination of perfor-

OBJECTIVES

When you have completed this chapter, you should be able to

- Explain how a computer-controlled engine works
- Name the major components of a computer control system
- Describe how the computer allows the engine to operate in the case of an electronic failure
- Show why computer controls are necessary
- Describe common precautions and procedures for computer control service

Many of these new programs have included a self-diagnostic ability which allows the computer to detect component malfunctions.

A traditional engine tune-up is performed to help improve engine operating efficiency. In vehicles with computerized engine controls, the computer is constantly tuning the engine. However, the tune-up ability of the different computer systems varies greatly. While some systems monitor air/fuel ratios only, others may control air/fuel, air injection, and EGR operation. On the most sophisticated models, the computer can control fuel injection, air/fuel ratio, ignition dwell and timing, air injection, EGR, canister purge, and more.

DESIGN

The computer itself is a solid-state component consisting of numerous **microchips** and electrical devices. Within the computer, the manufacturer has programmed information that identifies the engine size, vehicle weight, transmission type, axle ratio, firing order, engine operating temperature, spark advance information, basic timing, carburetor settings, and other information for all operating ranges. The computer uses this programmed information to tune the engine to its optimum performance level under any operating condition.

mance, efficiency, and emissions (Figure 24-2). An advantage of the computer system is that the computer "knows" what the effect will be of each component on engine operation. With the addition of the engine control computer and without any extra emissions devices, great improvements can be seen in engine efficiency and emissions levels.

Computers were first added to many engines to coordinate emission controls. Since then, their potential for providing greatly improved engine control has been utilized. This has resulted in the development of computer programs with numerous new engine sensors and switches as well as new types of controls.

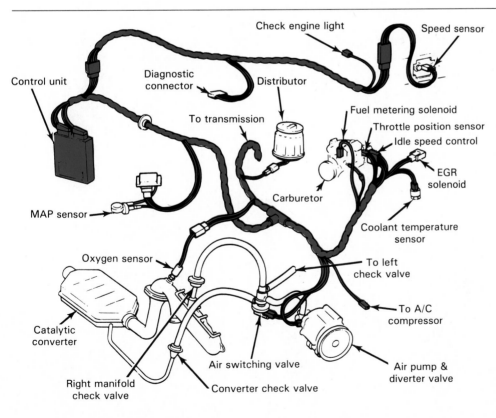

FIGURE 24-1 GM Computer Command Control system. (General Motors Corporation)

Control unit

Check engine light

Speed sensor

Diagnostic connector

Distributor

Fuel metering solenoid

Throttle position sensor

Idle speed control

EGR solenoid

To transmission

MAP sensor

Carburetor

Coolant temperature sensor

Oxygen sensor

To left check valve

To A/C compressor

Catalytic converter

Right manifold check valve

Air switching valve

Converter check valve

Air pump & diverter valve

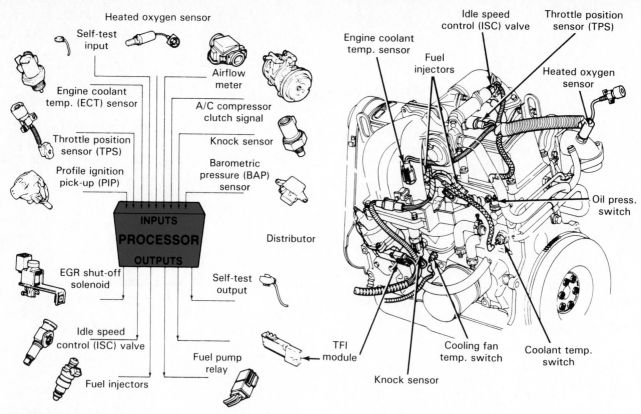

FIGURE 24-2   Ford EEC-IV system inputs, outputs and component locations. (Ford Motor Company)

Control Units

The heart of any computer system is the control unit, or control module (Figure 24-3). These minicomputers are usually sealed in a metal box and are linked to the system by a wiring harness with a multipin connector. The computers on most Ford and Chrysler Corporation vehicles are in the engine compartment, while

General Motors, AMC, and Ford EEC-III and IV computers are located in the passenger compartment (for protection from temperature and vibration).

Some units have a replaceable programming section, referred to as a PROM (GM) or calibration assembly (Ford). These plug into the main computer and "tailor" the programming to fit specific emission requirements or vehicle equipment.

FIGURE 24-3   Several electronic control modules.

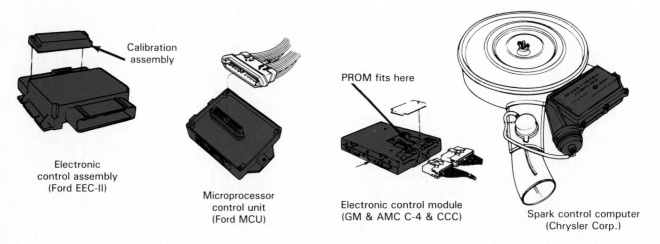

The primary function of the computer is to coordinate the various engine and emissions components with engine operation. Generally speaking, computer control of engine systems is either **open loop** or **closed loop**.

Open Loop During open-loop operation, selected **sensor** signals to the computer are ignored. Instead, preprogrammed values are used to satisfy engine demands. This mode of operation is largely restricted to engine operation at below normal temperatures as well as to special conditions such as full throttle acceleration and high-speed deceleration.

Closed Loop Closed-loop operation is when the computer is controlling engine operation in direct response to sensor input. When the engine temperature has reached normal operating levels and the **oxygen sensor** is at its proper temperature of about 600°F (315°C), the computer begins to accept sensor signals. These signals inform the computer of actual engine conditions so that it can send out appropriate control signals to the engine operating components.

If vehicle operation is faulty in open loop but normal during closed loop, the computer is compensating for the faulty part. The source of the malfunction is located somewhere other than in the computer.

Sensors

The computer receives information from the various engine sensors (Figure 24-4). Most are simple sending units that are either grounded or open (like an oil pressure switch) or provide a varying resistance (like a fuel gauge sending unit). Some engine data come from existing sensors (engine temperature) or a connection to an existing circuit (coil or distributor pickup).

On some systems (Ford EEC and General Motors CCC) the computer sends a reference voltage out to each sensor. Varying resistance in the sensor drops the voltage a certain amount, and the computer uses the return voltage as a signal.

Computer decisions are based on the preprogrammed information put in by the manufacturer and sensor input. The most common sensor inputs include the following:

☐ Air/fuel ratio (from oxygen sensor)
☐ Engine speed (from distributor or crankshaft sensor)
☐ Engine temperature
☐ Engine load or vacuum
☐ Throttle position

Other sensors are used by some systems to pro-

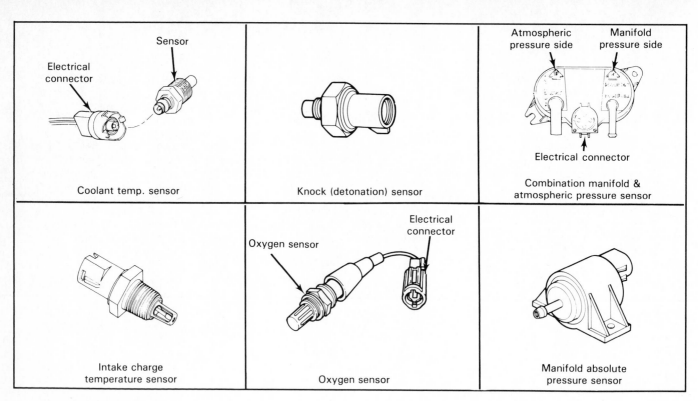

FIGURE 24-4 Sensors.

vide additional information. Some of these are the following:

☐ Intake air temperature
☐ Intake airflow
☐ Barometric/manifold pressure
☐ Vehicle speed
☐ Fuel temperature and pressure
☐ Detonation
☐ Transmission gear position

Two different systems may require the same input but use different sensors to obtain it. For example, one of Ford's MCU systems uses an idle tracking switch to tell the computer when the throttle is against the idle stop. Another MCU system uses a vacuum switch to derive the same information. In spite of this wide variety of sensors, computer decisions are made based on the same kinds of input.

Backup Mode

Should sensor input ever deviate from design specifications, information programmed into the computer is used to provide a dependable backup system. If the sensors fail, the engine develops a malfunction, or the computer decides sensor information is unreliable, it substitutes a known value so that the vehicle can be driven in for repair. In some instances, this override may perform so well that a malfunction in the system will go unnoticed by the owner. This might cause some difficulty for the mechanic if, while vehicle performance has not suffered significantly, the customer must be convinced of the need to replace a faulty engine sensor.

OPERATION

Computerized engine control system operation is based on the information supplied to the computer by the various engine sensors. Computer commands are carried out by **solenoids**, motors, and other control devices (Figure 24-5). Solenoids are used for many functions: vacuum control, *air bleeds,* carburetor fuel flow, etc. Motors are usually used for idle speed control and mixture adjustment.

Feedback Mixture Control

An example of this sensor/computer/control device relationship is **feedback** *air/fuel mixture* control. Nearly all modern emissions control systems use an oxygen sensor to detect the amount of oxygen in exhaust gases. This concentration is directly related to the air/fuel ratio of the intake charge. The oxygen sensor generates

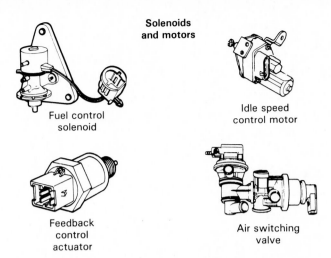

Solenoids and motors

Fuel control solenoid

Idle speed control motor

Feedback control actuator

Air switching valve

FIGURE 24-5 Engine control solenoids and motors.

a small voltage signal which increases with an increase in oxygen. This signal is sent to the control unit, which interprets it as air/fuel ratio. The computer generates a control signal to alter the mixture as needed to achieve the preferred 14.7:1 ratio.

One computer system (Ford four-cylinder MCU) controls mixture ratio by altering vacuum. A vacuum regulator is controlled by computer signal. This regulator in turn generates a vacuum signal for the mixture control diaphragm in the carburetor. In another system (General Motors CCC), the computer controls a mixture solenoid in the carburetor with electrical signals: No vacuum is needed.

Other Computer Controls

Ignition Timing Computers control some functions directly, while others are accomplished by more involved means. For example, some systems are capable of retarding ignition advance when *detonation* ("knocking") is sensed. On one system (Ford six-cylinder MCU), the computer activates a solenoid which cuts off vacuum to the distributor advance diaphragm. On another (General Motors CCC), the computer sends an electrical signal directly to the ignition module, which results in a delayed spark. The method used is different, but the end result is the same.

Most engine sensors and computer controls function in a manner similar to one or the other of these examples. Most of the actual system operation occurs inside the computer. Our primary concern is not how the computer makes its decisions but rather what information is used and how the resulting instructions are carried out.

Turbocharger Boost When a *turbocharger* is used on a computer-controlled engine, some turbocharger

functions are usually controlled by the computer. Typically, the *wastegate* is opened and closed by computer command. This action puts the amount of boost under computer control. If *boost* rises too high or if the engine begins to overheat, the computer can limit boost.

A **detonation sensor** is also used with some computer installations. The detonation sensor is screwed into the *head*, *block*, or *intake manifold*. The sensor is positioned so it can "feel" the characteristic vibrations caused by detonation. If detonation is present, the sensor will pick up the vibrations and send an electrical signal to the computer. The computer will then command the ignition system to retard the timing, or open a turbo wastegate. If detonation still persists, the timing will be retarded further.

GM DIGITAL FUEL INJECTION

One of the more sophisticated computer control systems available is GM's Digital Fuel Injection (DFI). It controls engine functions such as the air/fuel mixture and spark. Additionally, with its Body Control Module (BCM), the DFI controls the heating/cooling system, rear-window defogger, and other chassis functions. Figure 24-6 shows the development of DFI compared to earlier systems.

The following description illustrates how computers can perform all housekeeping functions in a car. The cautions and test procedures mentioned are common to almost all computer systems.

DFI Components

The DFI system consists of the following subassemblies: fuel delivery, air induction, data sensors, **electronic control module** (ECM), body control module (BCM), electronic spark timing (EST), idle speed control (ISC), emission controls, closed-loop fuel control, cruise control, torque converter clutch (TCC), viscous converter clutch (VCC), catalytic converter, and diagnostic system.

Fuel Delivery The fuel delivery system consists of an electric in-tank fuel pump filter, pressure regulator, injectors, and lines. Fuel is supplied to the engine through two injectors located in a throttle body. The ECM controls the amount of fuel metered through injectors based on engine demand.

Air Induction The air induction system consists of a throttle body and intake manifold. Air enters the throttle body and is distributed through the intake manifold. Airflow rate is controlled by throttle valves operated by the accelerator linkage. Idle speed is controlled by idle speed control (ISC).

Evolution of Cadillac Computer-Controlled Functions

	1976	1977	1978	1979	1980	1981	1982	1983/ 1984	1985
Electronic Fuel Injection	X	X	X	X					
Electronic Cruise Control		X	X	X	X	X	X	X	X
Digital Radio Display		X	X	X					
Radio-Electronic Seek & Scan			X	X	X	X	X	X	X
Electronic Spark Selection				X	X				
Digital Fuel Injection					X	X	X	X	X
Modulated Displacement Control						X			
Idle Speed						X	X	X	X
Spark Advance						X	X	X	X
EGR Control						X	X	X	X
Fuel Mixture						X	X	X	X
Air Injection Control						X	X	X	X
Canister Purge						X	X	X	X
On-Board Self-Diagnostics						X	X	X	X
ALDL						X	X	X	X
Fuel Data Center*						X	X	X	X
Electronic Climate Control						X	X	X	X
Torque Converter Clutch Control							X	X	X
Adaptive Learning							X	X	X
Outside Temperature Display							X	X	X
Fuel Used							X	X	X
Fuel Data Panel Mode Lights							X	X	X
EGR Rate Control							X	X	X
Multiple Service Level Indicators								X	X
Functional Enhancements								X	X
Viscous Converter Clutch Control									X
Electronic EFE (Early Fuel Evaporation)									X
Altitude Measurement w/o Barometric Pressure Sensor									X
Electrical System Check									X
HVAC Control									X
Rear Defog Control									X
Outside Temperature									X
Automatic Temperature Control									X
Automatic Blower Control									X
Manual Blower Speed Control (Econ. and Defrost Modes)									X
Continuous A/C Compressor at Idle									X
Variable Speed Cooling Fans									X
Body System On-Board Self-Diagnostics									X
Body System ALDL									X
Standard Digital Fuel Gauge									X
Vacuum Fluorescent Dimming Control									X
English/Metric Conversion									X
Retained Accessory Power									X

FIGURE 24-6 Development of computer system capabilities. (Cadillac Motor Division, GMC)

Each sensor furnishes input to the ECM. Data sensors are interrelated to each other. (See Figure 24-7.) Sensor operation is as follows:

Manifold Air Temperature Sensor (*MAT*) This sensor is mounted on the intake manifold. The MAT sensor measures air/fuel mixture temperature in the intake manifold. Sensor resistance changes as air temperature changes. The ECM receives this change in signal and adjusts the injector pulse accordingly. Low temperature produces high resistance.

Coolant Temperature Sensor (*CTS*) The CTS is located in the intake manifold. This sensor provides information to the ECM which is used for fuel enrichment, ignition timing, EGR operation, canister purge control, air management, early fuel evaporation control, idle speed control, and closed-loop fuel control.

Manifold Absolute Pressure Sensor (*MAP*) The MAP sensor is mounted under the instrument panel, inside the car. A hose from the throttle body to the MAP sensor provides the vacuum signal. The sensor

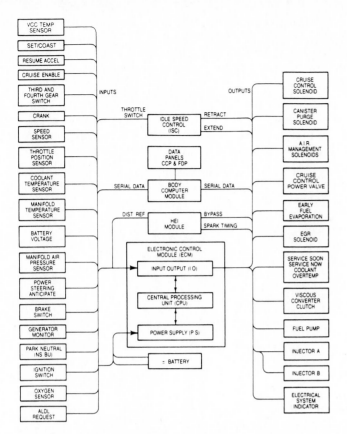

VCC TEMP SENSOR		CRUISE CONTROL SOLENOID
SET/COAST	INPUTS	CANISTER PURGE SOLENOID
RESUME ACCEL	OUTPUTS	
CRUISE ENABLE		A.I.R. MANAGEMENT SOLENOIDS
THIRD AND FOURTH GEAR SWITCH		
CRANK	THROTTLE SWITCH / IDLE SPEED CONTROL (ISC) — RETRACT / EXTEND	CRUISE CONTROL POWER VALVE
SPEED SENSOR		
THROTTLE POSITION SENSOR	DATA PANELS CCP & FDP	EARLY FUEL EVAPORATION
COOLANT TEMPERATURE SENSOR	SERIAL DATA — BODY COMPUTER MODULE — SERIAL DATA	EGR SOLENOID
MANIFOLD TEMPERATURE SENSOR		
BATTERY VOLTAGE	DIST REF — HEI MODULE — BYPASS / SPARK TIMING	SERVICE SOON SERVICE NOW COOLANT OVERTEMP
MANIFOLD AIR PRESSURE SENSOR	ELECTRONIC CONTROL MODULE (ECM)	
POWER STEERING ANTICIPATE	INPUT OUTPUT (I O)	VISCOUS CONVERTER CLUTCH
BRAKE SWITCH	CENTRAL PROCESSING UNIT (CPU)	FUEL PUMP
GENERATOR MONITOR	POWER SUPPLY (P S)	INJECTOR A
PARK NEUTRAL (NS BU)		
IGNITION SWITCH	= BATTERY	INJECTOR B
OXYGEN SENSOR		ELECTRICAL SYSTEM INDICATOR
ALDL REQUEST		

FIGURE 24-7 Cadillac DFI components. (Cadillac Motor Division, GMC)

monitors changes in intake manifold pressure which result from engine load and speed variations. The MAP sensor sends this information to the ECM, which changes the injector pulse width (the time injector is open).

Barometric Pressure Sensor (BARO) The BARO sensor is mounted on the MAP sensor bracket. This sensor measures ambient or barometric pressures and signals the ECM of pressure changes due to altitude and/or weather.

Throttle Position Sensor (TPS) The TPS is mounted on the side of the throttle body and is connected directly to the throttle shaft. This unit senses throttle movement and throttle position and then transmits the appropriate electrical signals to the ECM. The ECM processes these signals to operate the ISC and to supply fuel enrichment.

Vehicle Speed Sensor (VSS) The vehicle speed sensor informs the ECM of vehicle speed. The speed sensor produces a weak signal which is amplified by a buffer amplifier. Both the speed sensor and the buffer amplifier are mounted behind the speedometer cluster. The ECM uses vehicle speed sensor signals to operate the

fuel economy data panel, integral cruise control, and ISC.

Oxygen Sensor (O_2) This sensor produces a very weak voltage that varies with the oxygen content of the exhaust gases. As oxygen in the exhaust gases increases (leaner mixture), the sensor produces a low voltage. As oxygen decreases (richer mixture), voltage increases. Typical voltage variation should be between about 200 and 800 mV. The ECM corrects the air/fuel ratio in response to changes in these voltage signals.

CAUTION: Do not attempt to measure the voltage output of the O_2 sensor. Damage to the sensor may result.

Engine Speed Sensor The engine speed sensor signal comes from a pickup and a seven-terminal HEI module in the distributor. Pulses from the distributor are sent to the ECM where time between the pulses is used to calculate engine speed. The ECM adds spark advance modifications to the signal and sends this signal back to the distributor.

Electronic Control Module The ECM monitors and controls all DFI functions. The ECM consists of input/output devices, a central processing unit (CPU), a power supply, and memories. Digital signals received by the CPU are used to perform all mathematical computations and logic functions necessary to deliver the proper air/fuel mixture. The CPU also calculates spark timing and idle speed information. The CPU commands operation of emission controls, closed-loop fuel control, cruise control, and the diagnostic system. Power for the ECM comes from the battery through the ignition circuit. The three types of memory in the ECM include read only memory (ROM). The ROM is programmed information that can only be read by the ECM. The ROM program cannot be changed. Random access memory (RAM), is the scratch pad for the CPU. Data sensor information, diagnostic codes, and results of calculations are temporarily stored in RAM. Programmable read only memory (PROM) contains calibration information about each engine, transmission, body, and rear axle combination.

Body Control Module The BCM monitors and controls electronic climate controls (ECCs), rear defogger, outside temperature display, cooling fans control, *data center* display information, vacuum fluorescent display timing, self-diagnostics, and retained accessory power system functions.

The BCM consists of input/output devices, the central processing unit (CPU), a power supply, and memories just like the ECM.

Electronic Spark Timing (EST)

The EST system consists of the ECM and a modified HEI distributor with a seven-terminal HEI module. The HEI distributor communicates to the ECM through a four-terminal connector.

Idle Speed Control (ISC)

The ISC is an electrically driven actuator which changes the throttle valve angle (in idle position) according to commands from the ECM. This function is bypassed when the throttle is opened enough to bring TPS off its idle circuit. When the engine is cold, the ECM holds the throttle valve open for a long period of time to provide faster warm-up. The ISC is located on the side of the throttle body.

DFI Emission Controls

The ECM controls the operation of the EGR system, AIR management system, and canister purge control operation. A description of each system follows:

EGR System   When the engine is cold, ported vacuum to EGR is closed with a solenoid valve. When the engine is warm, the solenoid valve is opened, and EGR is allowed.

AIR Management System   Control of this system is similar to that of the EGR system. When the engine in cold, the ECM energizes an air control solenoid, which allows air to flow to the air switching valve. The switching valve is energized by the ECM to direct air to exhaust ports to aid in quickly heating the oxygen sensor to 600°F (316°C). When the engine is warm or in closed-loop operation, the ECM de-energizes the air switching valve, and air is sent directly to the catalytic converter to assist in oxidation of HC and CO. If the air control valve detects a rapid increase in manifold vacuum (deceleration), if certain operating modes exist, or if the ECM detects any failure in the system, air is diverted to the air cleaner or dumped to the atmosphere.

Canister Purge Control Operation   Vacuum to the canister purge control valve is controlled by the ECM with a solenoid valve. When the engine is in open-loop operation, the solenoid valve is energized, and vacuum is blocked to the purge valve. When the system is in closed-loop operation, the solenoid valve is de-energized, and vacuum can be applied to the purge valve to draw collected vapors into the intake manifold.

Closed-Loop Fuel Control

Closed-loop fuel control maintains an air/fuel ratio of 14.7:1. The oxygen sensor monitors oxygen content of exhaust gases, sending information to the ECM. The ECM then corrects the air/fuel mixture by varying the injector "open" time.

Cruise Control

The ECM receives input signals from the cruise control engagement switches, instrument panel switch, brake release switch, drive switch, and speed sensor. The ECM transmits command signals to the vacuum control solenoid valve and power unit solenoid valve to control vehicle speed.

Torque Converter Clutch (TCC) or Viscous Converter Clutch (VCC)

The torque converter clutch is controlled by the ECM via an electrical solenoid mounted in the transmission. At a specific speed, the ECM energizes the solenoid, and the torque converter is mechanically coupled to the engine. Under specific operating conditions (when normal fluid coupling is required) the solenoid is de-energized. The viscous converter clutch is used in some vehicles. It operates more smoothly than the TCC but performs the same job. However, this system is diagnosed using a different flowchart.

DIAGNOSTIC SYSTEM

The ECM of the DFI control system has a built-in diagnostic capability to constantly monitor engine/vehicle performance and operation. The diagnostic system consists of four sets of sequential tests: engine malfunction tests, switch tests, engine data displays, and output cycling tests. A description of each testing sequence follows.

Engine Malfunction Test

This test is constantly performed by the ECM to detect system failures or malfunctions. When a malfunction occurs, the ECM will light the "Service now/soon" or **check engine light.** When a malfunction occurs and the lamp is turned on, a corresponding trouble code is stored in the ECM memory. Malfunctions are recorded as permanent (hard) failures or intermittent failures.

Hard failures cause the "Service now/soon" light to glow and remain on until the malfunction is repaired. If the light comes on and remains on, the cause of malfunction *must* be determined.

Intermittent failures cause the "Service now/soon" light to flicker or go out after the malfunction clears. Intermittent failures may be sensor related. If a sensor fails, the ECM will use a substitute value in its calculations to continue engine operation. In this condition, service is not mandatory, but drivability may suffer. If the sensor malfunction does not happen again within 50 ignition on/off cycles, the trouble code will be erased.

As a lamp and system check, the "Service now/soon" lights should glow when the ignition is turned on and go out 1–4 sec after the engine has started. If these functions do not happen, the ECM has found a fault in the system.

Switch Test

This series of tests checks the operation of the various switches which provide input to the ECM. During this operation, specific switches are cycled, and the ECM analyzes the action to determine if these switches are operating properly.

Engine Data Displays

This is a series of checks which display important engine data information. This information is compared to specifications in the shop manual.

Output Cycling Tests

This series of tests causes the ECM to cycle various output devices on and off. During this test, the operation of engine control solenoids and lamps may be checked by using command signals from the ECM.

TESTING

With the appearance and widespread use of computerized engine controls, many mechanics have become hesitant to diagnose engine malfunctions. Others immediately blame the computer when difficulties arise. Both these views are equally wrong. The addition of the computer has added more electrical components and associated wiring to the engine. However, the engine remains basically the same as it was several years ago, requiring the same three elements for operation that it always has: air, fuel, and spark.

Normal Mechanical Components

Complaints regarding fuel consumption, loss of power, or poor performance should first be diagnosed as they would be on an engine without computerized engine controls. The computer is a sophisticated electronic device which is much more reliable than the various components it monitors and controls. Almost none of the computers that have been returned to the manufacturers in the past few years actually had a problem. Engine

malfunctions should, therefore, be diagnosed as in the past, with the computer system considered as a possible source of the problem only after all other possibilities have been eliminated. So, after all standard components have been checked and approved, the computerized engine control system may be considered as a source of poor performance.

Testing Equipment

Although specific testing procedures for each system will vary, certain aspects will be the same. Some systems need a special testing device. In most instances, its use is mandatory for proper, complete system diagnosis. However, in several cases, other more common tools may be substituted for it. In addition, certain other basic tools are nearly always needed for accurate testing (Figure 24-8). These include the following:

- ☐ High-impedance digital volt/ohmmeter
- ☐ Tach/dwell meter
- ☐ Timing light
- ☐ Vacuum pump with gauge
- ☐ Test light
- ☐ Jumper wires

Self-Diagnosis Systems

The computer is constantly monitoring and adjusting the air/fuel mixture (10 times per second in most applications) in response to signals received from the data sensors. Any careless adjustment of the idle or mixture screw settings could cause the computer to perform its calculations more frequently and result in a loss of power or drivability. To help the computer to maintain proper settings, most fuel delivery system idle and mixture settings are sealed to prevent unnecessary adjustments. Therefore, and because most computerized engine control systems have no serviceable parts, system testing and service is usually restricted to the replacement of faulty components.

Since computerized systems can be quite complicated, most manufacturers provide a self-diagnostic program in the computer which allows it to find and record its own faults.

Trouble Codes   When a computer system is equipped with this self-diagnostic capability, different system malfunctions or failures are stored as numbers. These are called **trouble codes.** When the diagnostic program is activated, these codes are displayed by the flashes of an indicator light. One system, used with Cadillac digital fuel injection, displays the specific code number on a display panel in the vehicle.

No matter how it is indicated, each code represents a specific problem. The codes for each fault may

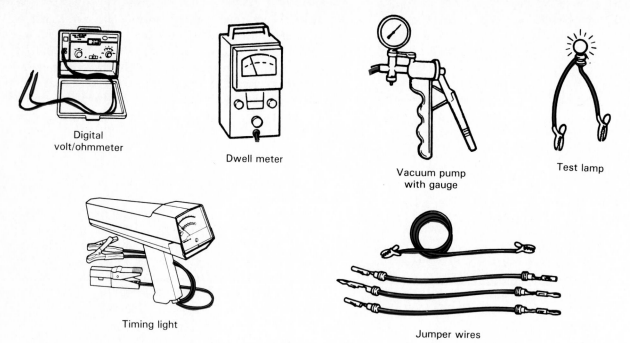

Digital
volt/ohmmeter

Dwell meter

Vacuum pump
with gauge

Test lamp

Timing light

Jumper wires

FIGURE 24-8   Computer system testing equipment.

vary with the different systems, as will the steps to repair these faults. You must have the right information to service computer systems, so check the shop manual.

Diagnosis   Diagnosis begins by activating the computer's diagnostic program and recording the service codes as they are indicated. Once you have the codes, refer to the specific **flowchart** for each code and follow the instructions outlined there (Figure 24-9). These charts make it possible to logically find specific problems and/or failures so that they may be repaired. The proper use of these charts can save you a great deal of time when repairing the system. The most important thing is to have the specific information required to properly interpret the codes provided by the computer. Used properly, these codes can make it possible to diagnose in a matter of minutes what used to take hours and dozens of pages of service information.

Performance Check   As a final check, most manufacturers include an extra chart, sometimes called a *system performance check*. It is very important that this procedure be followed after repairing a system fault. More than one problem may exist in the system. If your diagnosis stops after finding and repairing a single problem, you may have overlooked some other fault. The system performance check is designed to verify proper system operation and will point out additional problems, should they exist.

FIGURE 24-9   Typical self-diagnostic code flowchart. (General Motors Corporation)

TROUBLE CODE 12

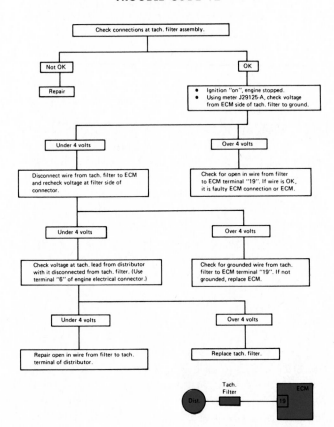

COMPONENT CHECKS

The following inspection procedures may be used to test the basic operation of system components, sensors, and solenoids. However, these are very general procedures and should only be used when specific testing procedures and specifications are not available. System diagnosis using the self-diagnostic capabilities of most modern systems is a simple and accurate method of testing and should always be used if the proper testing tools and information are available.

If all normal systems are found to be operating properly, the computer system may be considered a possible cause of engine difficulties. As stated earlier, the computer itself should only be suspected as a last resort. In keeping with this theme, the component checks presented here are designed simply to verify proper component operation.

Sensors and Solenoids

Check sensors by seeing if they open or close at the right time or if their resistance values are correct. Check solenoids by applying voltage with a jumper wire and watching to see if they operate. Apply voltage only long enough to determine if the solenoid is working. Solenoids should have a measurable resistance; that is, the windings should not be shorted to ground or open.

Oxygen Sensors

You can best check oxygen sensors by observing system operation. Most systems have a mixture ratio test point where you can connect a dwell meter, voltmeter, or special tester. With the engine fully warmed up and at a fast idle, the system should be in closed loop.

Note the readings on your meter or tester and then cause a vacuum leak by pulling off a vacuum hose.

The readings should change and then gradually go back to where they were before. Plug the vacuum leak and then cover part of the air intake to choke the engine and enrich the mixture. The readings should change in the opposite direction and then return to normal again. If so, the oxygen sensor is working properly. If not, the sensor or its wiring may be faulty.

Circuit Wiring

If sensors and solenoids are okay, check the circuit wiring. Disconnect the wiring at both ends of a circuit and measure the resistance of that circuit. If the resistance measured is more than about 5 Ω, the connections need to be cleaned or the wiring repaired. When this has been done, connect the ohmmeter between one end of the circuit and a good ground. If resistance is less than several hundred thousand ohms, the wire is shorted to ground and must be repaired. Wiring diagrams are available for all systems and should be used to check connections and resistance values.

Control Unit

If all sensors, control devices, and wiring are good, the control unit or computer may be suspected. The only positive method of checking computer operation is to substitute a known good unit. If vehicle performance improves, the original computer was in fact at fault, and you should install a new one. It is very important to note that a faulty component anywhere in the system may cause damage to an otherwise good computer. This fact, combined with the high cost of control units, demonstrates the importance of ensuring proper operation of all other components in the system *before* replacing the computer.

TRADE TERMS

CCC
Check Engine Light
Closed Loop
Detonation Sensor
EEC
Electronic Control Module
Feedback
Flow Chart

MAP
Microchips
Open Loop
Oxygen Sensor
Sensor
Solenoid
Trouble Codes

REVIEW QUESTIONS

1. What two systems are commonly controlled by a computer?

2. Two common computer system operating modes are open loop and closed loop. In which of these two modes does the computer ignore the signals from its sensors?

3. Name two typical devices the computer commands which provide the actual movement at the throttle body, distributor, wastegate, and the like.

4. About how often does the computer monitor and adjust the air/fuel mixture?

5. After using the trouble codes to find and repair a problem, what procedure should you follow next?

6. Should engine compression, valve clearance, vacuum connections, and other engine hardware be checked before or after diagnosing the computer?

7. When should you measure the oxygen sensor's voltage output?

25

Ignition Systems

INTRODUCTION

The ignition system is designed to provide a spark to each cylinder, at the right time, to ignite the air/fuel mixture inside. The system is complicated by the need for the spark timing to change with engine load and rpm and the need for a very high voltage (10,000–20,000 V) to fire the spark plugs. Until the late 1960s and early 1970s, most automotive engines used a points-and-condenser ignition system. Since then, however, most automotive engines have switched to an electronic ignition system that eliminates any friction or wearing parts in the distributor.

Point-type ignition systems are still around on many older vehicles, so the theory and operation of points will be discussed here. Keep in mind, though, that electronic ignition is universally used on new engines. Even the distributor has disappeared on some models, to be replaced with a more effective system.

IGNITION SYSTEM COMPONENTS

The ignition system is separated into two circuits: the primary, or low-voltage circuit, and the secondary, or high-voltage circuit.

OBJECTIVES

When you have completed this chapter, you should be able to

- Describe the primary and secondary ignition circuits
- Identify a distributor, condenser, ignition module, and coil
- Explain the differences between point-type and electronic ignition systems
- Describe the vacuum and mechanical advance systems

Maximum voltage during starting ensures a powerful spark.

Secondary Circuit

The secondary circuit includes the secondary portion of the ignition coil, the secondary side of the distributor (cap, rotor, and spark plug wires), and the spark plugs.

Coil

The *ignition* **coil** is designed to change the low primary voltage supplied by the battery into a much higher voltage, one capable of jumping the spark plug gap. It consists of an iron core, primary windings, secondary windings, and an outside container (Figure 25-2).

Windings The primary windings usually consist of several hundred turns of large wire. The secondary winding has several thousand loops of fine wire. The ratio of secondary turns to primary turns determines the step-up in voltage provided by the coil.

Primary windings are attached to primary terminals (Figure 25-3). The secondary winding is attached to the coil tower on one end and to the primary winding on the other end (Figure 25-4). Turning on and cutting off current flow in the primary windings *induces* the much higher voltage in the secondary windings.

Because it is so important to the ignition system, let's take a closer look at **induction.**

Induction When current flows through a wire, a weak magnetic field is formed (Figure 25-5). Wrapping a wire around a soft iron core greatly strengthens this magnetic field. Wrapping the wire into a coil around the iron core allows the lines of magnetic force to cut across the wire. This action produces a current flow in the wire whenever the amount of electricity flowing through the coil changes.

Primary Circuit

Included in the primary circuit are the battery, ignition switch, ballast resistors (if used), the primary circuit of the ignition coil, the primary side of the distributor (breaker points/condenser or electronic pickup), and wires and the vehicle frame necessary to complete the electrical circuits (Figure 25-1).

All ignition systems have to have an electrical power source. This is the familiar 12-V, wet-cell battery. The battery supplies the primary voltage to the ignition system.

Ignition systems also must have an ignition switch. This is an *on-off* device that permits current to flow or prevents it from doing so. Separate circuits are provided for starting and normal engine operation.

Additionally, a ballast resistor or resistor wire is sometimes used in the RUN circuit between the ignition switch and coil. The resistor limits voltage to the coil during normal operation. During the starting process, the ballast resistor is bypassed to furnish full voltage to the ignition coil. Reduced voltage during regular engine operation prolongs the life of the points.

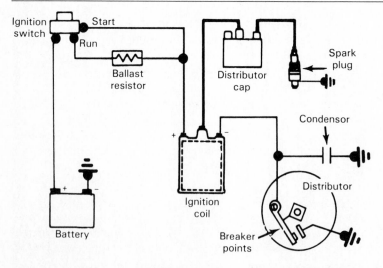

FIGURE 25-1   Point-type ignition system wiring diagram.

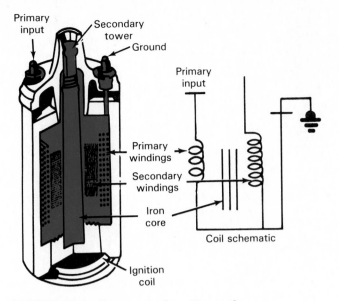

FIGURE 25-2   Conventional ignition coil.

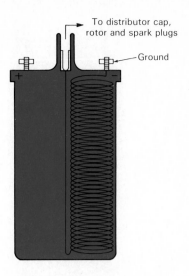

FIGURE 25-4   Coil secondary windings.

FIGURE 25-3   Ignition coil primary windings.

Thus, if you have a simple iron core and coil arrangement and the current flow to it is shut off, there will be zero voltage in the coil. When current flow is restored, there will be the normal amount of voltage in the circuit plus the voltage induced by the rod and coil.

Mutual induction happens when a second coil is added around the first (Figure 25-6). Current flowing through the primary coil induces voltage in the secondary coil. Shutting off the primary coil voltage collapses the magnetic field. Voltage is then induced in the secondary coils. How much voltage is produced depends on how strong the original current is, how many windings are in the two coils, and how quickly the primary current is interrupted (stopped). Automotive coils change 12 V into 20,000 V or more.

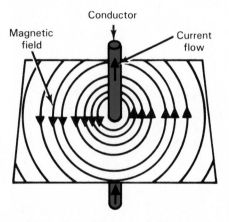

FIGURE 25-5   Magnetic field around a current-carrying conductor.

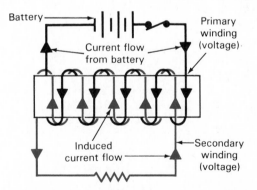

FIGURE 25-6   Voltage induced in secondary coil.

Distributor

The *distributor* contains some components that make up the *primary* circuit. These include a geared or slotted shaft driven by the *camshaft*, a cam with one lobe for

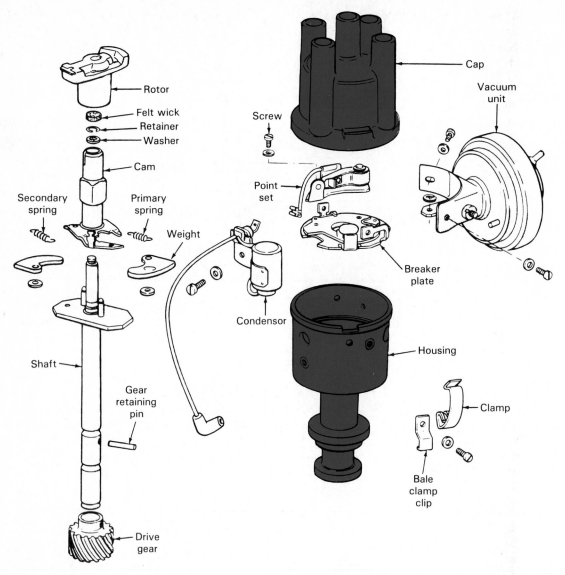

FIGURE 25-7   Conventional distributor. (Volkswagen of America, Inc.)

each cylinder, *breaker points*, a **condenser,** and a mechanical and/or *vacuum advance unit* (Figure 25-7). When the shaft rotates, the cam opens and closes the breaker points (Figure 25-8). The points work as a switch, turning the current flow on and off in the coil **primary circuit.** Figure 25-9 shows a typical distributor component arrangement.

The condenser acts as a storage reservoir for transient voltage (Figure 25-10). You might say it's a shock absorber in the primary circuit. The condenser gives voltage a place to go when the points open, reducing arcing between the points. This greatly increases point life.

The distributor also has a *secondary* side, which includes the *cap*, *rotor*, and secondary wire terminals. Special high-voltage wiring runs from the distributor to the spark plugs. The secondary side distributes electricity to each spark plug at the correct time.

FIGURE 25-8   Cam and points relationship.

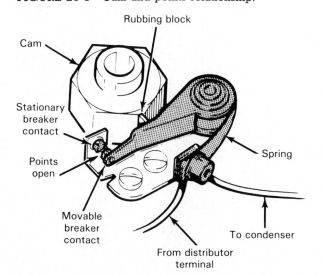

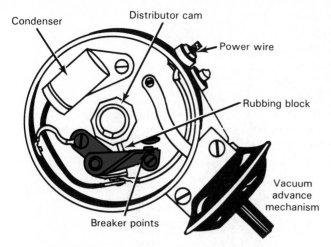

FIGURE 25-9   Typical point-type distributor layout.

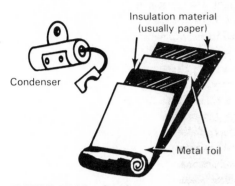

FIGURE 25-10   Condenser construction.

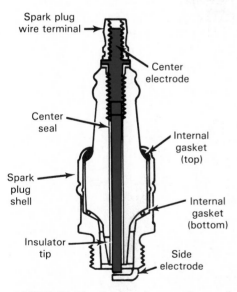

FIGURE 25-11   Sectional view of a spark plug.

Spark Plugs

Spark plugs consist of two **electrodes** (Figure 25-11). The side electrode is grounded to the shell of the plug,

while the center electrode is connected to the secondary wire from the distributor cap. The electrodes are separated by an insulator. Correct spark plug gap—the distance between electrodes—is important for proper spark duration and intensity.

POINT IGNITION OPERATION

Let's see how these components are combined to provide the proper spark at the right time (Figure 25-12). Keep in mind that the primary circuit (low voltage) and the **secondary circuit** (high voltage) are interrelated during operation.

Flow of Electricity

When the ignition switch is turned to the start position, the starter turns the engine over. Turning the engine over opens and closes the points as the distributor cam rotates. Current is free to pass from the battery to the ignition switch when the key is in the "start" or "run" positions.

Points Closed   From the ignition switch if the points are closed, the current goes to the primary windings of the coil, to one side of the points, and then to the second side of the points which are grounded to the distributor housing. The circuit is then completed, and current flows through the coil primary windings. This flow builds a magnetic field in the coil.

Points Open   When the points open, the circuit is broken. The resulting high-voltage surge in the coil secondary circuit forces current through the coil high-tension (high-voltage) wire to the distributor cap. There the rotor, which turns with the distributor shaft, conducts the current to one of the spark plug wire

FIGURE 25-12   Point ignition diagram.

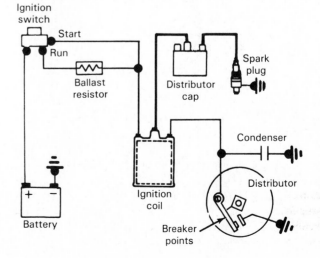

terminals. The current then passes through the spark plug wire and bridges the gap in the plug. Bridging the gap causes a spark, igniting the air/fuel mixture.

When the ignition switch returns to the ON or RUN position, the ignition system continues to work in the manner just described, except when there is a **ballast resistor.** With a ballast *resistor*, less voltage is sent to the coil from the ignition switch. This prolongs point life and protects the coil from too much voltage.

Coil Operation

Primary The coil has two primary terminals: the positive, which receives power from the battery, and the negative, which is connected to one side of the breaker points. The primary terminals are connected internally by a series of continuous wire loops.

Remember, current will flow only when the circuit is complete. That is, current will flow when all switches including the points are closed, the wires are in good condition, and the connections are both tight and clean. Current return to the battery is normally accomplished through wires, the engine block, and the vehicle frame.

The time when current flows through the primary system is called "dwell." In other words, dwell is the amount of time the points are closed.

With the primary circuit complete, current is free to leave the battery and return. As the current flows through the coil primary circuit, a magnetic field builds around the continuous wire loop (Figure 25-13).

Secondary When the points are opened by the distributor cam, current ceases to flow. The magnetic field in the primary coil collapses. This collapse induces a high-voltage current in the finer-wound secondary

windings. These windings are connected to the primary winding and to the coil tower. The coil tower is usually located in the center of most ignition coils.

The coil tower is connected to the center of the distributor cap by a heavier wire—the coil high-tension or high-voltage wire. The high voltage created in the secondary coil then flows in one direction—to the distributor cap, rotor, spark plug wires, and finally to the spark plugs. This voltage surge occurs in the secondary coil circuit each time the magnetic field in the primary circuit collapses, that is, each time the points open.

At the spark plug, the voltage has to jump the gap between electrodes. This voltage produces a spark which ignites the *air/fuel mixture*.

Timing

The spark must be properly timed to occur just as the air/fuel mixture is compressed in the *combustion chamber*. This timing is usually adjusted by rotating the distributor in the block or head. It is further adjusted by the vacuum advance unit and the *centrifugal advance mechanism*.

Timing motion begins at the crankshaft. It turns the camshaft, via the *timing chain* and sprockets, at one-half crankshaft speed. Therefore, the distributor shaft turns at camshaft speed to give each spark plug voltage once every four piston strokes.

Because the distributor cap is attached to the distributor body, rotating the distributor body in its mounting hole changes the relationship between the cap and the point/camshaft arrangement. Turning the distributor body will advance or retard the spark. The spark is advanced when it occurs earlier than normal and is retarded when it happens later than normal.

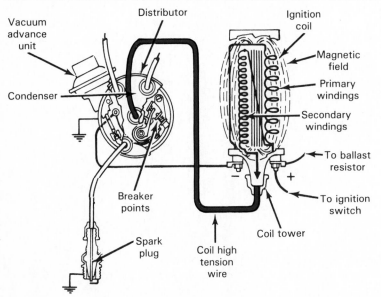

FIGURE 25-13 Magnetic field in ignition system.

Vacuum Advance The vacuum advance unit advances the spark by rotating the plate the points are attached to. The mechanical advance rotates the cam on the distributor shaft. These actions have the same effect as rotating the distributor body—they change the point-to-camshaft relationship.

The vacuum advance uses manifold vacuum to pull the plate toward the vacuum advance unit against spring pressure. Thus, whenever manifold vacuum increases, the spark will be advanced. How far advanced depends on the amount of vacuum available. When high vacuum is available (during low or no-load situations), more **spark advance** occurs.

Mechanical Advance Mechanical advance uses weights swinging outward against spring pressure to rotate the distributor cam (Figure 25-14). The higher the engine rpm, the more advance the mechanical advance will give. More advance is necessary because as engine speed increases, the time available for burning the mixture decreases. The mixture must be ignited earlier at high rpm to compensate for the lack of burning time available (Figures 25-15 and 25-16).

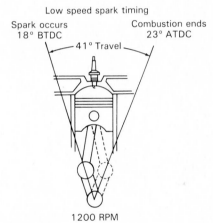

FIGURE 25-15   Low-speed spark timing. (Ford Motor Company)

FIGURE 25-16   High-speed spark timing. (Ford Motor Company)

FIGURE 25-14   Mechanical advance.

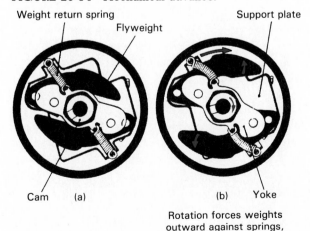

Rotation forces weights outward against springs, rotating cam and advancing timing

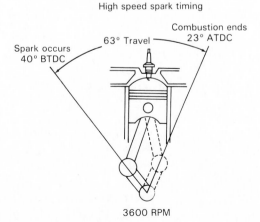

It is possible for both the vacuum and mechanical advance units to work at the same time. Total advance is controlled by weights, spring force, and spring tension in the mechanical advance unit. These limits are designed into the distributor to give the engine the desired performance and emissions.

Disadvantages of Point Ignition

Most objections to point ignition concern the points. The rubbing block, which wears against the cam, gets shorter. This changes the point gap, which leaves less time for a magnetic field to build in the coil. This last idea is called *coil saturation*. The less coil saturation, the weaker the spark. The points can also fail from deposit buildup, burning, and pitting. In any case, regular maintenance is required with points.

Even with these problems, the point system worked well for many years. It was the need to reduce emissions which spurred electronic ignition development. The extremely lean mixtures found in *smog engines* require a spark intensity and spark control that is impossible to achieve with point ignition.

ELECTRONIC IGNITION

The transition from breaker points to fully electronic ignition was not smooth. Three different types of systems were introduced during the change-over period. These systems were the following:

1. Transistorized (transistor assisted);
2. Capacitor discharge; and finally
3. Fully electronic.

Transistorized Ignition

Transistorized ignition was the first step in the development of modern breakerless ignition systems. A **transistor** is an electric switching device (in an ignition system) and is located between the coil and breaker points (Figure 25-17).

The transistor acts as a relay (or the load-carrying switch) so that only a small amount of current passes through the breaker points in comparison with the current that passes through the coil.

The main advantage of transistor ignition is that the larger current passing through the coil primary produces a much higher secondary voltage and thus a hotter spark at the plugs. At the same time, the lower current passing through the breaker points means longer point life. Timing is also more precise with transistor ignition.

Because the points are still technically a part of

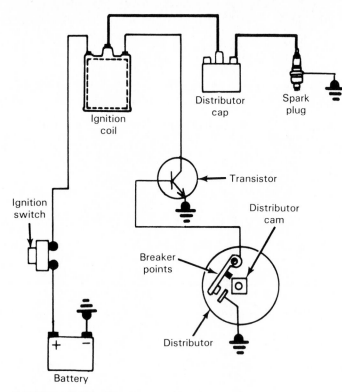

FIGURE 25-17 Transistorized ignition.

transistorized ignition, they will continue to wear and will need to be replaced.

Capacitor-Discharge Ignition

Capacitor-discharge systems were the second major step toward electronic ignition as we know it today. This system uses a capacitor (or condenser) (Figure 25-18).

An energy converter or transformer charges the capacitor with up to 350 V. A signal from a timing circuit travels to a thyristor—an electronic switch between the capacitor and the ignition coil—and prevents the capacitor from discharging until the precise moment the ignition is needed. Most capacitor-discharge systems utilize a magnetic pulse generator instead of breaker points and a pulse transformer instead of a conventional ignition coil.

The advantages of capacitor-discharge systems are the elimination of the points and 30% more voltage at 80% higher speed than with the points. Some capacitor systems do not take full advantage of the design and use points to switch the signal.

Electronic Ignition

Breakerless electronic ignition uses the transistor to switch off the current to the coil primary circuit and

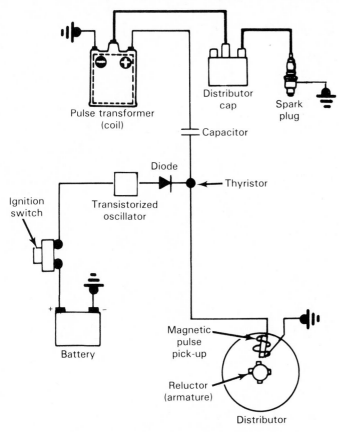

FIGURE 25-18   Capacitor-discharge ignition.

ignitions still have mechanical or vacuum advance units, while others have no mechanically operated or contacting parts (Figure 25-19).

Components   The basic electronic ignition system consists of a *reluctor* that turns with the distributor shaft. The reluctor turns near, but does not contact, the magnetic pole piece of a pickup coil. No electrical current passes between them.

The teeth of the reluctor only interrupt a small magnetic field around the pickup coil. This interruption causes a small varied electrical signal, which is received and interpreted by the electronic control unit. The control unit (by means of the transistor) then cuts off current to the ignition coil primary circuit. A voltage surge occurs in the secondary circuit, firing the spark plugs.

Some electronic systems use Hall effect components instead of the reluctor and pickup coil (Figure 25-20). With Hall effect, a wheel rotating with the distributor shaft interrupts a magnetic field between a small magnet and a sensor. The magnetic field is used to signal between the two pieces. Shutters are placed on the wheel, one for each cylinder. The magnetic field is interrupted with the passing of each shutter, signaling the computer to trigger the coil.

The advantage of Hall effect is the accuracy of the signal. It is extremely precise and allows the computer to make very fine adjustments.

Advantages   There are many advantages to the electronic ignition system. Breaker points are eliminated, replaced by the reluctor and pickup coil. There are no contacting parts and no deterioration in timing. Also, the electronic ignition system operates much

a magnetic pulse generator or **Hall effect** switch instead of breaker points to trigger the transistor.

Other components are used to refine the timing, but the switching is fully electronic. Some electronic

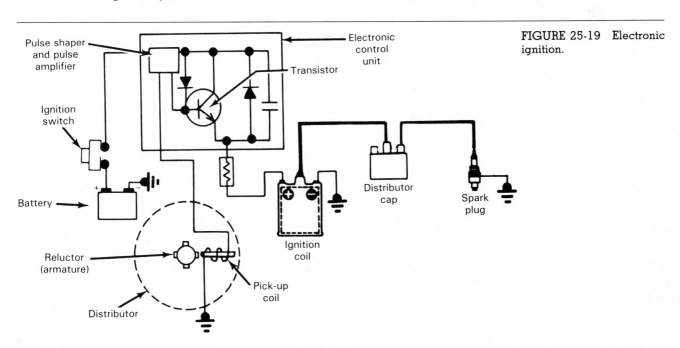

FIGURE 25-19   Electronic ignition.

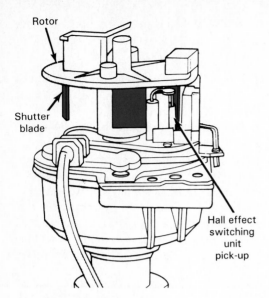

FIGURE 25-20 Hall effect distributor. (Chrysler Corporation)

faster than other previous systems, even taking advantage of constantly changing computer-controlled operations.

Computer-Controlled Ignition

Once electronic ignitions were available, the next logical step was to use electronics and engine sensors to determine the exact instant of ignition based on vehicle operating conditions (Figure 25-21). This exact determination requires the use of minicomputers.

The computer receives information in the form of electrical signals from various engine sensors and determines the optimum instant to fire each spark plug. Using the computer in this way reduces emissions while greatly aiding engine efficiency.

No Pickup One version of Ford's Dura Spark system has no pickup in the distributor. The engine has a crankshaft position sensor which tells the computer each piston's position. This information is used for fuel injection as well as ignition. The computer calculates timing advance or retard and decides when to trigger the coil. The distributor is used only to house the rotor and cap.

No Distributor Computer-controlled coil ignition (C^3I) is used on some General Motors models and has no distributor at all. A crankshaft sensor is used to tell the computer the location of the crankshaft and when the number one cylinder is at top-dead-center. A triple-coil assembly is used, with each coil firing two plugs. The computer triggers the coils at the right time, eliminating any vacuum or mechanical advance, the distributor cap and rotor, and all moving parts. This system promises to reduce even further the need for ignition maintenance (Figure 25-22).

FIGURE 25-21 Computer-controlled ignition/emission system.

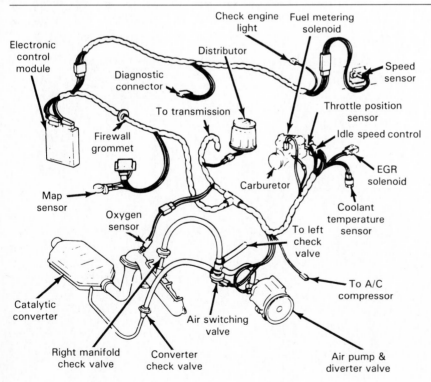

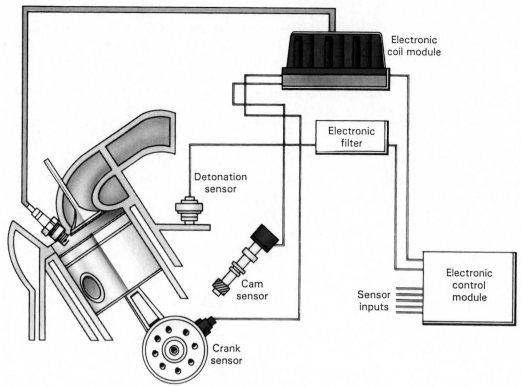

FIGURE 25-22   General Motors computer-controlled coil ignition. (Buick Motor Division, GMC)

ELECTRONIC IGNITION APPLICATIONS

An explanation of electronic ignition systems should include some practical examples. The following systems are widely used and represent typical electronic ignitions on popular vehicles.

Ford Solid State Ignition (SSI) and Dura-Spark I and II Systems

Ford Motor Co. vehicles were first equipped with Ford **Solid State** Ignition (SSI) in 1974. Minor modifications have been made to the system over the years. All SSI systems use an electronic control module, conventional coil, distributor cap, spark plug wiring, and a ballast resistor wire.

The Dura-Spark I system includes an electronic control module, unique coil and primary wiring, high-energy cap, adapter and rotor. It has special plug wires but no ballast resistor wire.

Dura-Spark II uses an electronic control module, high-energy distributor cap, adapter (most models), rotor and wiring, harness-contained ballast resistor wire, and a conventional coil.

Control Modules   Most modules are wired into the ignition system, using two weatherproof connectors—one with four wires and the other with either two or three wires. Care must be taken not to interchange modules between systems. Various replacement modules are used for the SSI system, including one for 1974 Ford models, one for 1975 Ford models, one for 1978–1981 AMC models, and others for later AMC models.

Dura-Spark I, built for California cars, also requires a special module. However, one replacement module serves all Dura-Spark II systems from 1976 to 1983, except for a limited number of Dura-Spark systems with Dual Mode Timing or Dual Mode Crank Retard. Figure 25-23 shows a typical Dura-Spark module design, with the shaded connector being used only on Dual Mode Timing Modules.

Systems can be identified by keyway locations in the four-wire module connectors. Figure 25-24 shows the four different connectors used. The SSI and Dura-Spark II connectors are similar, but the terminals are numbered differently. The distributor cap is larger on Dura-Spark systems to provide better insulation for very high voltage. Secondary wiring also differs.

Operations   The SSI and both Dura-Spark systems function in the same way, except through the ignition primary circuit. These differences are built into the electronic control module.

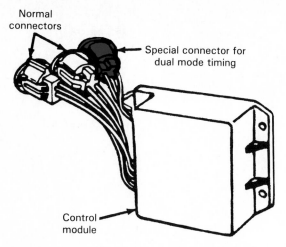

FIGURE 25-23 Typical Ford SSI or Dura-Spark control module. (Ford Motor Company)

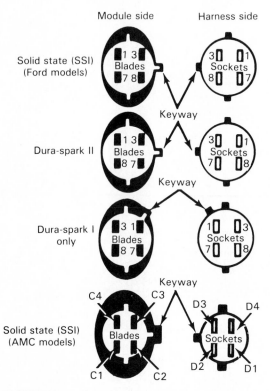

FIGURE 25-24 Ford ignition system identification. (Ford Motor Company)

On Dura-Spark I systems, the module contains a coil current regulator (replacing ballast resistance wire). This regulator will also turn off current to the coil within 1 sec after it senses that the distributor is not rotating. To turn the distributor back on, the ignition switch must be turned to the START position. On SSI and Dura-Spark II systems the ignition primary circuit is on anytime the ignition switch is on.

The distributor contains a *stator* (pickup coil) which produces a magnetic field. The armature (reluctor), turning with the distributor shaft, causes the magnetic field to collapse whenever the armature teeth pass the pickup coil. The module senses the pulse in the magnetic field and turns the coil primary current off and on. This causes a high-voltage surge in the secondary which fires the spark plugs. Figure 25-25 shows various system wiring diagrams.

Ford Thick Film Integrated (TFI) Systems

In the TFI-I and the TFI-IV ignition systems, the small blue plastic TFI ignition module replaces the bulky and much larger Dura-Spark module. The TFI ignition module is mounted on the distributor housing and is retained with two screws. The pickup coil's harness and connector assembly connect directly to the three tabs on top of the TFI ignition module.

Components The TFI ignition system consists of a distributor, TFI ignition module, special E-Core ignition coil, ignition switch, battery, and primary and secondary wiring.

The TFI-I distributor (Figure 25-26) contains the following components: pickup coil assembly with internal teeth, distributor shaft, reluctor with external teeth (mounted on the distributor shaft), TFI ignition module (mounted on the outside of the distributor housing), octane rod (TFI-IV only), centrifugal advance mechanism, vacuum advance mechanism (TFI-I only), rotor, and distributor cap (with male terminals). The TFI-IV distributor is shown in Figure 25-27.

Vehicles equipped with the TFI-I or TFI-IV ignition system also use an E-Core ignition coil. The E-Core ignition coil is unlike any other Ford coil. It is encased in laminated plastic rather than being encased in an oil-filled case, as most other coils are. This ignition coil has a very low primary resistance and is used without a ballast resistor in the electrical system. There are the usual primary connections on this coil.

Operation Each time the teeth on the reluctor pass the teeth on the pickup coil, the magnetic field around the pickup coil builds and collapses. As this occurs, a pulse is generated in the pickup coil and sent to the TFI ignition module.

On TFI-I-equipped engines, the ignition module then turns the ignition coil primary circuit off and on, causing a high-voltage surge in the secondary which fires the spark plugs. Figures 25-28 and 25-29 show the TFI-I and TFI-IV wiring diagrams. The ignition module sends the pulse signal to the engine computer or to the electronic control assembly (ECA) for modifications of the timing signal. Then a modified spark timing signal is returned to the ignition module. This signal tells the ignition module when to turn the igni-

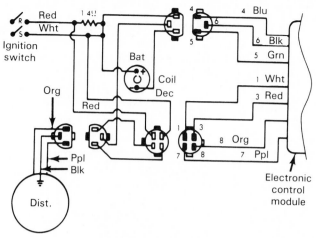

A. Early Solid State Ignition System Wiring Diagram

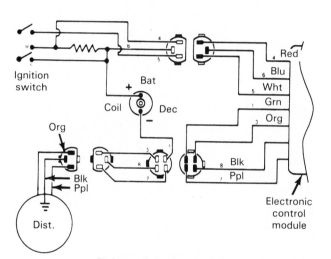

B. Later Solid State Ignition System Wiring Diagram

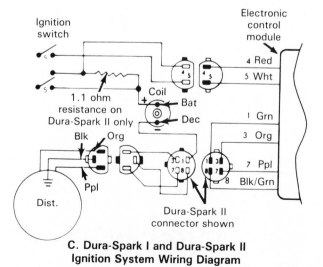

C. Dura-Spark I and Dura-Spark II Ignition System Wiring Diagram

FIGURE 25-25   Ford SSI and Dura-Spark wiring diagrams.

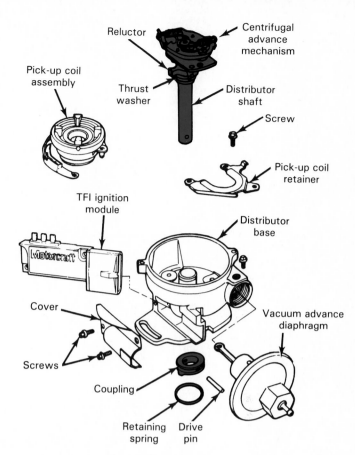

FIGURE 25-26   Ford TFI-I distributor. (Ford Motor Company)

FIGURE 25-27   Ford TFI-IV distributor. (Ford Motor Company)

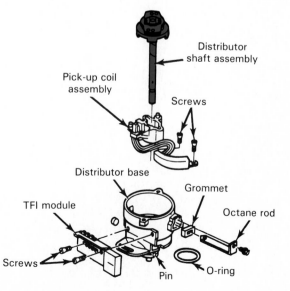

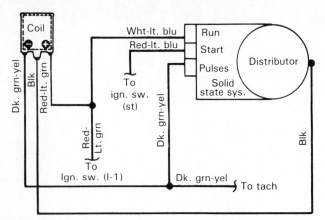

FIGURE 25-28 Ford TFI-I wiring diagram.

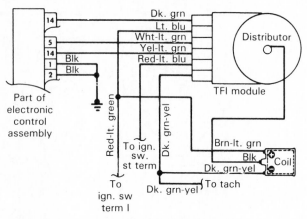

FIGURE 25-29 Ford TFI-IV wiring diagram.

tion coil primary circuit on and off. This causes a high-voltage surge in the secondary which fires the spark plugs.

GM High Energy Ignition (HEI) System

The **HEI** system is used by both GM and AMC and is also the basis for many other GM systems such as EMR, ESS, and EST.

The Delco-Remy High Energy Ignition (HEI) system was introduced as an option on GM V8 engines in 1974. It became standard on all GM engines in 1975. It has been built in two versions, both operating in the same manner.

Components Early in-line four- and six-cylinder engines had a separate, externally mounted ignition coil. Most later engines, except four-cylinder ones, have all ignition components integrated into the distributor housing.

AMC/Jeep began using GM's HEI system in 1980 vehicles equipped with four-cylinder engines. On

AMC/Jeep models, the ignition coil was mounted integrally in 1980–1981 models and externally in 1982–1983.

A special, large distributor housing encloses the vacuum and centrifugal advance mechanisms, electronic module, rotor, distributor shaft, and radio noise suppression capacitor. In addition, the pickup coil, pole piece (with internal teeth), and timing core or trigger wheel (with external teeth) are located in the distributor. The ignition coil is mounted on top of the distributor cap, under a cover, on most models. Figure 25–30 shows the basic HEI system wiring.

All HEI systems use 8 mm spark plug wiring and wide spark plug gaps. An electrical connector on the side of the distributor housing connects the HEI system with the vehicle's ignition and battery wiring.

Operation The pickup assembly has a stationary pole piece (unless moved by vacuum or centrifugal advance units) and a rotating timing core. When the external teeth on the timing core (mounted on the distributor shaft) line up with the internal teeth of the pole piece, a change in current is created in the pickup coil. This signals the electronic module to stop the flow of current through the ignition coil primary circuit.

When current in the primary windings is stopped, a high-voltage surge is created in the coil secondary. This surge is directed to the proper spark plug by the rotor, cap, and spark plug wiring. The system uses special wiring and wide gap spark plugs to take advantage of higher secondary voltages, as compared to a conventional system.

Dwell is determined automatically by the electronic module and cannot be adjusted. Since there are no moving parts that contact, periodic checks for adjustment are not needed.

FIGURE 25-30 General Motors high-energy ignition basic wiring.

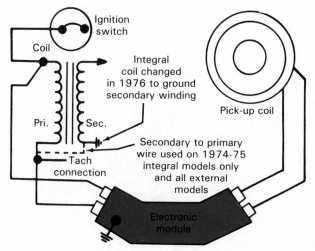

TRADE TERMS

Ballast Resistor
Coil
Condenser
Electrodes
Hall Effect
HEI

Induction
Primary Circuit
Secondary Circuit
Solid State
Spark Advance
Transistor

REVIEW QUESTIONS

1. The distributor rotates at _____ crankshaft speed.

2. Spark plugs have _____ electrode(s).

3. Automotive coils produce about 10,000 V. True or false?

4. Transistorized ignitions never use points. True or false?

5. Advanced timing means the spark is fired earlier than normal in the combustion cycle. True or false?

6. Are there any contacting parts in an electronic ignition?

7. Are the reluctor and pickup coil part of the primary or secondary circuit?

8. What is the most commonly serviced part of the conventional ignition system?

9. Ford TFI ignition systems don't use an electronic control module like other Ford systems. True or false?

10. GM HEI ignition distributors contain the reluctor, pickup, rotor, advance mechanism, coil, and module all in one assembly. True or false?

26

Ignition System Service

INTRODUCTION

Ignition systems are fairly simple collections of electrical and mechanical parts, yet ignition failures are a major cause of no-start or engine performance problems. Because proper ignition performance is critical to engine operation, some regular maintenance is helpful. Electronic ignition systems were designed to reduce or eliminate point-type maintenance needs but have introduced some problems of their own. Instead of burned points or defective condensers, we now have easily damaged high-tension spark plug wires, low voltages traveling in the wiring harness from pickup to module, and mysterious electronic ailments.

This chapter will introduce the normal adjustments and maintenance needed on both point and electronic ignitions and describe the few tools needed.

TIMING ADJUSTMENT

Both point and electronic systems must have initial timing adjustments made occasionally. This is normally done by rotating the distributor and requires a timing light. With simple ignition systems, it was once common practice to advance the distributor until the engine began to "ping" on a test drive. The timing was then backed off slightly, and the adjustment was finished. However, the greater accuracy demanded by today's emission controls means you have to be more exact—to within a degree or two.

Point-System Dwell

On point-type systems, check the dwell (point gap) first. Remove the distributor cap and rotor. Rotate the engine with the starter until the points are fully open, with the point rubbing block on the tip of the distributor cam lobe (Figure 26-1). Measure the gap with a feeler gauge. Loosen the point hold-down screw and move the points if adjustment is necessary. Tighten the screw and recheck the gap. Spread a small amount of cam grease on the distributor cam to minimize rubbing block wear and then reinstall the rotor and cap.

Dwell Meter   Points can also be better set with a dwell meter. *Dwell* is the amount of time the points are closed.

FIGURE 26-1   Points replacement.

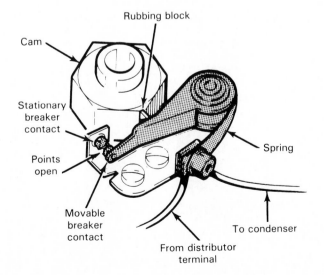

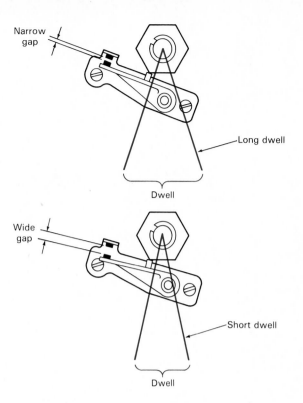

FIGURE 26-2   How point gap affects dwell.

A dwell meter measures this time in degrees of camshaft rotation. Dwell meters are hooked between the coil power lead (the coil negative lead) and ground. Dwell can be read while cranking or while the engine is running. Checking dwell with the engine running is an advantage of a dwell meter. It is more accurate than the feeler-gauge method because dwell changes slightly with engine rpm.

Adjust the dwell just as you adjust the point gap, because dwell and point gap are basically the same thing. Some General Motors distributors have a "window" in the cap to allow dwell to be adjusted with the engine running. Figure 26-2 shows how point gap and dwell are related.

After setting the dwell, set the timing. Dwell adjustments affect the ignition timing, but timing adjustments do not affect dwell. Dwell affects timing because a narrow point gap lengthens the time between point openings, thus retarding the spark. A wide point gap (small dwell) advances the spark because the point openings happen sooner each time.

Timing

To adjust timing, first check a shop manual or engine decal for the correct procedure. Each system has special details that must be checked. On systems with a vacuum advance, the vacuum hose is usually disconnected and plugged. On computer-controlled systems, sometimes a jumper wire must be connected or a special connector unplugged. Perform all the details called for by the manual.

Timing Marks Warm the engine to normal temperature and then stop the engine. Locate the timing marks on the crankshaft puller or flywheel and place a bit of chalk or paint on the timing marks. The timing light is simply a strobe light triggered by the firing of the number one spark plug. Connect the power wires to the battery and clip the pickup lead around the number one spark plug wire (Figure 26-3).

Adjustment Start the engine and let it idle at the recommended speed. Aim the timing light at the mark on the crankshaft puller or flywheel. It will "freeze" the motion of the mark, so you can turn the distributor body until the marks on the pulley and the block pointer line up. Tighten the bolt and recheck the timing. If it is okay, reconnect the vacuum advance hose and remove the timing light.

SECONDARY CIRCUIT

Ignition service is similar for both standard and electronic ignition systems when dealing with the secondary circuit. However, concerning the primary circuit, standard ignition needs the most service. Little servicing is possible in electronic primary ignition circuits, except for testing and parts replacement.

Secondary circuit service covers the distributor rotor, cap wires, spark plugs, and coil. Much of the service is the same for standard and electronic ignitions.

Rotor and Cap

Rotors and caps should be wiped off with a dry cloth whenever they are removed. When the rotor and cap terminals become crusty with burned deposits, they should be replaced. These parts can also get *carbon tracking* (Figure 26-4). Carbon tracking occurs when conductive deposits form inside the cap. The carbon track leads to another spark plug terminal or to ground (the distributor body). This causes the ignition to misfire on that spark plug. Wiping off carbon tracks may help, but with powerful electronic ignitions, replacing the cap may prove the best cure.

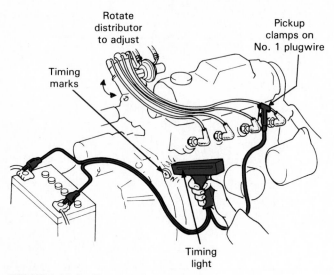

FIGURE 26-3 Timing adjustment.

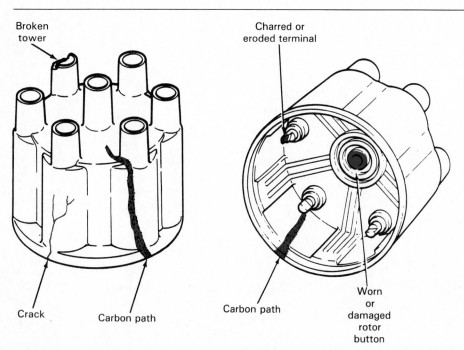

FIGURE 26-4 Carbon tracking. (American Motors Corporation)

Some systems have silicone grease on the distributor cap terminals. The grease reduces corrosion and radio interference. Do not remove this grease when checking, or be sure to replace it when necessary.

Wires

Ignition wires are not wires at all but carbon-coated threads covered with insulation. Bending and other rough handling will break the threads and cause high resistance. Many plug wires are damaged when they are removed from the spark plug. Always twist the boot which fits over the plug before attempting to pull it off. This will break the suction which holds the boot tightly to the plug. Special tools are available for plug boot removal (Figure 26-5).

Resistance Check   When the thread strands break, resistance increases. You can test for this resistance with an ohmmeter. Specifications vary among the different cables used, so check a shop manual before measuring. Resistance specifications may be given in so many ohms per foot of wire or a maximum resistance reading per wire.

Visual Inspection   Be sure to inspect the wires carefully. Small burn marks, especially where two wires cross, indicate the wires are arcing or shorting out. Look for cuts or tears in the insulation or scorch marks from a hot manifold. One way to inspect wires is to check them in the dark. Lift the hood with the engine running and look for small sparks coming from the wires. If the wires have any of these problems, replace them.

Spark Plugs

Spark plugs are tested by removing them from the cylinder head and *reading them*. Reading a plug means to visually examine its center porcelain insulator closely. You will also need to note the plug's condition in general.

Plugs wear out from normal use, heat, oil fouling, carbon fouling, pre-ignition, and mechanical damage.

Wear   Normal plug wear thins the side electrode and rounds the tip of the center electrode. Heat may discolor the porcelain to a light brown, yellow, or green shade. When the ground electrode wears and the porcelain gets a glassy, colored coating, replace the plugs.

Oil fouling is caused by oil being burned in the cylinder. It leaves a shiny, wet coating. Carbon fouling results from too rich a mixture. It leaves a dry, dull black coating. Both types of fouling require plug replacement. Oil and carbon fouling are also excellent clues to mechanical problems (broken rings, worn valve guides, dirty carburetor) (Figure 26-6).

Pre-ignition will actually melt the spark plug with blowtorch-like heat. Mechanical damage comes

FIGURE 26-5   Spark plug boot removal tool. (Chrysler Corporation)

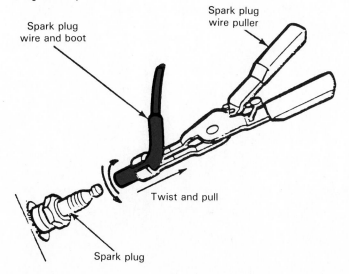

Spark plug wire and boot

Spark plug wire puller

Twist and pull

Spark plug

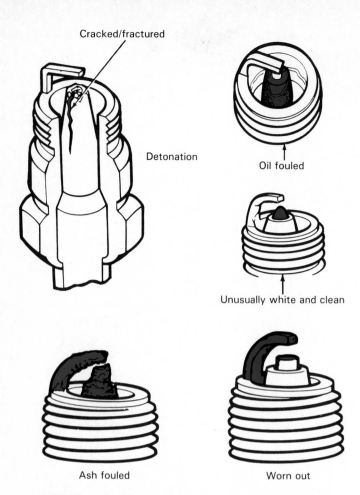

FIGURE 26-6 Plug condition. (Chrysler Corporation)

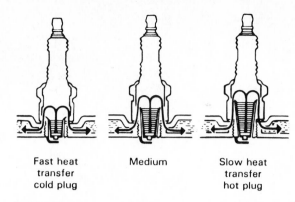

FIGURE 26-7 Spark plug heat range. (Champion Spark Plug Company)

from the piston hitting the plug or loose objects in the combustion chamber. The electrodes may be hammered shut by mechanical damage.

Replacement When replacing plugs, follow the torque specifications published in a shop manual. Use a torque wrench the first few times you change plugs. Once you develop a feel for the proper torque, you won't need the wrench. The correct plug torque is necessary for proper cylinder sealing and plug cooling. Turning a plug too tight can damage both plug and cylinder head threads. Aluminum cylinder heads are especially sensitive.

When replacing spark plugs, you must pay attention to the plug's *heat range* and *reach*.

Heat Range Heat range refers to the normal operating temperature of the spark plug (Figure 26-7). A cold plug conducts heat well. Therefore, the heat it picks up from combustion is rapidly given to the cylinder head and finally to the cooling system. Such a plug resists overheating and is used in high-temperature applications. Racing engines and those used for long-distance, high-speed driving use cold plugs.

Warm (or hot) plugs are used in cold running engines. A warm plug retains heat longer than a cold plug. Heat retention helps the plug burn off excess deposits found in engines that idle for long periods or that are driven slowly in extremely cold weather.

A plug's heat range is coded into the plug number. When buying plugs, look at the catalog to learn the manufacturer's heat range code. Then make sure the plug you are buying has the correct heat range. Running too cold a plug will foul the plug. Running too hot a plug is worse because it can cause pre-ignition and severe engine damage.

Reach This term refers to the physical distance the spark plug threads reach into the head (Figure 26-8). If the plug reach is too short, the electrodes will be shrouded inside the plug hole. Too long a reach puts the electrodes too far inside the cylinder. They may even contact the piston or cause a hot spot and preignition. Plug reach is also coded in the plug's designation number.

FIGURE 26-8 Spark plug reach. (Robert Bosch Corporation)

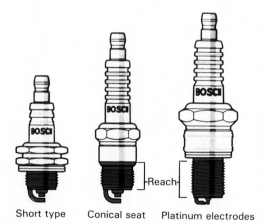

PRIMARY CIRCUIT SERVICE— POINT SYSTEMS

No ignition system can work correctly if it does not have a good ground. Start with the battery. Keep the battery terminals clean and free of corrosion.

Inspection

Inside the distributor, the most common service is changing the points. Points can be burned, pitted, or oil coated. Use a small screwdriver to pry open the points and then inspect the contact surfaces. If they are blackened or pitted, you should replace them. Filing points is a temporary repair but not the best way to ensure trouble-free driving. Besides, the time involved can sometimes exceed the slight cost of a new set of points. The condenser is usually replaced whenever the points are replaced.

Changing Points

To replace the points, remove the distributor cap and set it aside. Pull off the rotor (Figure 26-9). On GM distributors the rotor screws must be removed first. The points can now be removed. Undo the condenser and power leads. Undo the two point retaining screws and remove the point set. Some sets come off in two pieces.

Clean the point plate with a clean rag. Set in the new point set and start the retaining screws. Make

the condenser and power connections. Tighten the retaining screws until the point set can just be adjusted back and forth with a screwdriver. Now adjust the point gap (or dwell) as described earlier.

PRIMARY CIRCUIT—ELECTRONIC

One of the reasons electronic ignitions are so popular is that they have no contacting parts to wear out inside the distributor. However, many electronic ignitions have an adjustable air gap between the pickup and the reluctor. The following adjustment procedure is a general one; check a shop manual for specific details.

Air Gap

Rotate the engine until one of the teeth on the reluctor lines up with the pickup. Use a nonmagnetic set of feeler gauges to check the gap between the tooth and the pickup. Check the specifications and move the pickup to adjust the gap. Tighten the hold-down screw and then recheck the gap. Have someone crank the engine while you watch to make sure there is no contact between the reluctor and any stationary part of the distributor (Figure 26-10).

Check the cap and rotor for any silicone grease and apply fresh grease if necessary. Reinstall the rotor and cap, making sure all the wires are correctly and tightly connected.

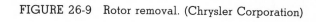

FIGURE 26-9 Rotor removal. (Chrysler Corporation)

A

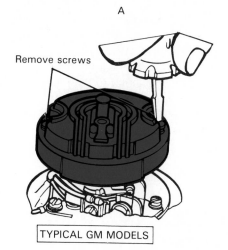

Remove screws

TYPICAL GM MODELS

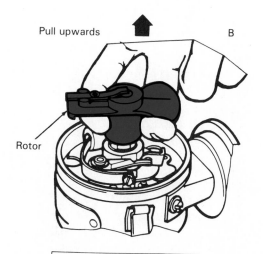

Pull upwards

B

Rotor

TYPICAL FORD/CHRYSLER MODELS

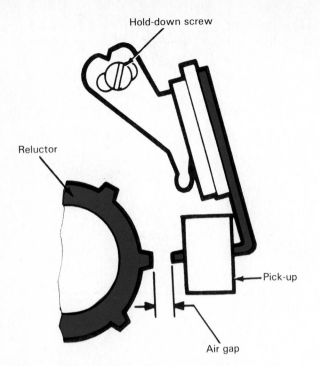

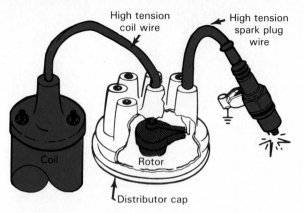

FIGURE 26-11 Secondary ignition circuit test.

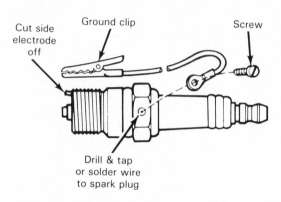

FIGURE 26-12 Spark plug tester.

FIGURE 26-10 Setting air gap. (Chrysler Corporation)

TROUBLESHOOTING

In this section several ignition system checks are outlined. Because so many ignition systems exist, the testing procedures given here are just a sample of what may be required to troubleshoot any one system.

General System Checks

Whenever an ignition problem is suspected in any ignition system, always check the secondary circuit first.

Start with a visual inspection. Check for missing or disconnected wires or spark plug boots. Check the distributor cap, rotor, and ignition coil for carbon tracking and/or cracks.

Spark Test   Remove a spark plug wire from any plug. Attach a spark tester to the wire (Figure 26-11).

A spark tester can be made from an old spark plug with little materials or effort. Figure 26-12 shows a typical spark tester. If you don't have a tester, hold the wire (with insulated pliers) ¼ in. from the engine block.

Now crank the engine and check for a good spark at the spark tester gap. A good spark will be blue-white and will be plainly visible in daylight. Weak sparks are orange or red and may be hard to see in daylight. If a good spark is present, the problem is probably not in the ignition system. Check the fuel system and/or spark timing.

If you did not see a spark, remove the coil wire from the distributor cap. Attach a spark tester to the distributor end of the coil wire (Figure 26-13). Crank the engine and check for a good spark at the spark tester gap. If a spark is present, the problem is probably in the distributor cap, rotor, or spark plug wires.

If you did not see a spark, the problem is in the primary system. With conventional ignitions, the points or a broken wire are most likely at fault. With electronic ignition, make sure the battery connections

FIGURE 26-13 Checking for spark at the coil.

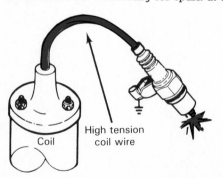

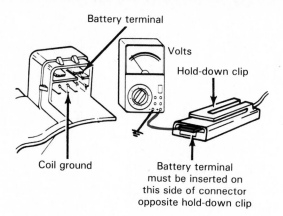

FIGURE 26-14 Battery voltage at the distributor connector voltmeter hookup. (General Motors Corporation)

are good and then troubleshoot the primary system using a shop manual.

Voltage Checks

With any ignition system, there may be a power problem. Using a voltmeter, check to see if battery voltage is present at the coil terminal with the ignition on. On General Motors systems with the coil in the distributor cap, check for battery voltage at the pink distributor wire (Figure 26-14). If 10–13 V are measured at the coil, the power supply is probably okay. If voltage is not present, look for disconnected or broken wires. These account for most ignition problems. If necessary, check the battery, ballast resistor, ignition circuit, and ignition switch.

Coil Checks

In many cases, ignition problems may be in the coil. The following coil resistance checks can be used on all types of ignition systems in which the coil is a separate unit.

Make sure the ignition switch is off. Remove the connectors at the positive and the negative coil terminals. Connect an ohmmeter lead to each primary terminal (Figure 26-15). Set the ohmmeter to the ×1 scale. Check the resistance and compare it to specification.

FIGURE 26-15 Coil primary resistance check.

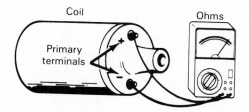

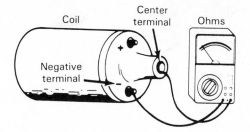

FIGURE 26-16 Coil secondary resistance check.

This tests the coil's primary resistance. Replace the coil if the primary resistance is not to specification.

To check the coil secondary circuit resistance, turn the ignition off and remove the high-voltage wire. This is the heavily insulated wire coming from the coil's center terminal. Set the ohmmeter to the ×1000 scale. Connect one ohmmeter lead to the brass connector in the center terminal and the other lead to the coil negative terminal. Figure 26-16 shows the hookup. If resistance is not to specification, replace the ignition coil.

Conventional Ignition Checks

Conventional ignition troubles are typically found in the points. Always check point gap (or dwell) and point condition. Burning of the points requires replacement. Make sure the points close so their faces are parallel. Bend the stationary arm to align the points, if necessary. Metal transfer from one point to the other requires point replacement as well. Metal transfer is a sign of a poor condenser. If metal transfer is present, change the condenser. Rapid rubbing block wear will close the points (increased dwell) until the engine will not start. Reset or replace the points as needed and be sure to lube the cam.

Electronic Ignition

Electronic ignitions are much more difficult to describe in a general way. For any system, though, the troubleshooting procedure includes several items. The first check is for wiring condition and connector tightness. The order of the following checks may vary but will always include coil voltage, coil resistance, pickup coil resistance or output, and continuity of wiring throughout the ignition circuit. Finally, if all other components seem to be okay, the control **module** will be replaced.

Ignition systems change frequently as new developments in electronics make possible less expensive and more reliable systems. Be sure to use the exact procedures and wiring diagram for the system you need to test.

TRADE TERMS

Module

REVIEW QUESTIONS

1. Ignition timing can be changed by adjusting point gap or dwell. True or false?

2. Dwell is adjustable on most electronic ignition systems. True or false?

3. What is the reason for spreading grease on ignition terminals and connectors?

4. What parts of the spark plug wear out?

5. What two factors do you need to consider when buying new spark plugs?

6. What is the only adjustment needed inside most electronic ignition system distributors?

7. When troubleshooting an ignition system, you should check for spark first at _____ wire and then at _____ wire.

8. An engine is unlikely to start if there is no battery voltage at the _____.

27

Emission Control Systems

INTRODUCTION

Three major by-products of internal combustion engine operation have been identified as hazardous to our health. They are hydrocarbons (HC), carbon monoxide (CO), and oxides of nitrogen (NO_x). Legislation has been passed which limits the amount of these pollutants which can be emitted by cars and light trucks sold in this country (Figure 27-1).

☐ *Carbon monoxide* (*CO*): CO is a molecule consisting of equal parts of carbon and oxygen. It is a colorless, odorless gas which is one of the products of incomplete combustion. It is also very poisonous. By weight, carbon monoxide accounts for aout 47% of air pollution.

☐ *Hydrocarbons* (*HC*): Hydrocarbons consist of carbon and hydrogen atoms in various combinations. They are emitted in an unburned form from any engine using a hydrocarbon fuel which does not operate at 100% efficiency. Hydrocarbons are a major component in the formation of photochemical smog.

☐ *Oxides of nitrogen* (*NO_x*): Oxides of nitrogen consist of nitrogen combined with varying amounts of oxygen. NO_x is produced by heat and pressure during the combustion process. NO_x is also a main component in photochemical smog.

OBJECTIVES

When you have completed this chapter, you should be able to

■ Describe the difference between precombustion and postcombustion emission controls

■ Understand that the different emission controls work together

■ Tell which controls reduce which emissions

■ Describe the relationship between combustion heat and pressure and the formation of the three different pollutants.

■ Service some of the emission control components

Other elements in the exhaust are also cause for concern, including lead and carbon (soot). Lead is being eliminated by no longer using it as a lubricating agent in fuel and because the presence of lead in vehicle exhaust quickly destroys catalytic converter efficiency. Soot is a by-product of incomplete combustion in a diesel engine. At this time, there are no standards for soot emissions. Part of the reason is that a properly adjusted engine emits very little soot; another is that no effective controls yet exist to contain or trap soot.

SYSTEM OPERATION AND TESTING

The emission control systems discussed in this chapter are of two basic types. One type prevents the formation of any pollutants (the preferred method), and the second type "reduces" or controls pollutants after they have been formed. These different controls may be thought of as *precombustion* and *postcombustion* systems.

Precombustion systems are the most popular and logical way to reduce emissions. However, sometimes it is impossible to eliminate the production of emissions. In those cases they must be changed or eliminated after they are formed.

Precombustion improvements can result from a number of methods. These include positive crankcase ventilation (PCV) systems, fuel system evaporative emission controls, exhaust gas recirculation (EGR) systems, ignition timing or spark control, and other engine modifications.

The postcombustion emission control methods are also varied. They include air injection (often called AIR due to an early General Motors system called Air Injection Reactor), and catalytic converters.

Crankcase Ventilation

During normal engine operation, vapor and gases (by-products of combustion) are forced past the piston rings and into the crankcase (Figure 27-2). If these

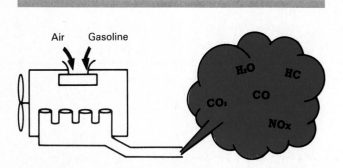

FIGURE 27-1   By-products of imperfect combustion in a modern engine.

Photochemical smog is what results when HC and NO_x are combined in the presence of bright sunlight. *Smog* was the first visible indication of an air pollution problem. A word derived from the combination of "smoke" and "fog," it was first believed to be a mixture of the two. It was not until the middle to late 1950s that air quality studies revealed that this was not the case at all. Instead, smog is a result of the reaction which occurs when HC and NO_x are combined in sunlight. These products form ozone, nitrogen dioxide, and nitrogen nitrate. Nitrogen dioxide is a light brown gas, the brownish haze which appears above highways and around congested city centers.

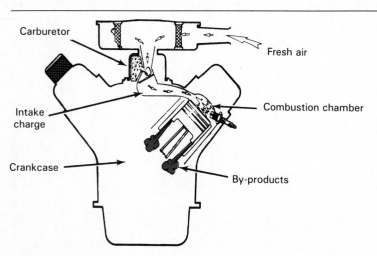

FIGURE 27-2   Combustion by-products enter the crankcase uring engine operation.

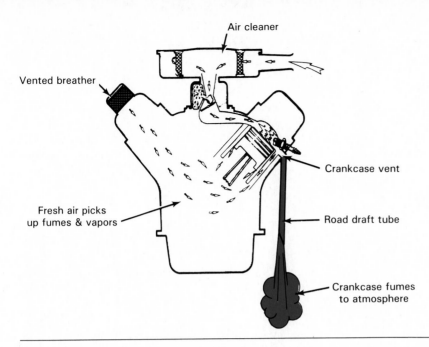

Air cleaner

Vented breather

Fresh air picks
up fumes & vapors

Crankcase vent

Road draft tube

Crankcase fumes
to atmosphere

FIGURE 27-3   Road draft tube.

fumes and vapors are allowed to remain there, engine oil becomes diluted and contaminated, while the formation of engine "sludge" is encouraged. Also, pressure builds up as the engine operates at higher speeds. If this pressure is not relieved, oil is forced out of the crankcase at the rocker covers, oil pan gaskets, and other engine sealing surfaces. To avoid these problems, the crankcase must be ventilated.

Road Draft Tube   The first method of crankcase ventilation was the road draft tube (Figure 27-3). On vehicles using this system, the crankcase must first be fitted with a vent. This vent is usually located in the valve cover, but it may be found at any point on the engine that is open to crankcase vapors and pressure. A tube is attached to this vent and runs down to the bottom of the engine. High-speed airflow past the end of the tube creates a **vacuum** which draws gases out of the crankcase. As these gases are removed, fresh air enters the crankcase through a vented oil filler cap or breather. This fresh air not only replaces vented gases but helps to keep fumes and vapors suspended until they are removed.

This type of system has two drawbacks. First, the system only works at peak efficiency when the vehicle is at speed. Even then, efficiency is not very good, due to unstable airflow and vacuum. At idle, no vacuum is present. This allows fuel vapors to remain in the crankcase, causing sludge formation, diluting the oil, and reducing the ability to properly lubricate the engine.

Positive Ventilation   A positive crankcase ventilation (*PCV*) system routes vented crankcase gases to the intake system where they can be pulled into the cylinders and burned. Actually, a PCV system is quite simple. A breather (air vent) is placed in the valve cover or top of the engine. It allows fresh air into the crankcase and also functions as a separator, condensing out some of the fumes and draining them back into the crankcase. A one-way valve (**PCV valve**) (Figure 27-4) is placed in the valve cover or other crankcase access. It is connected by a tube to engine vacuum at the base of the carburetor or the intake manifold. As engine vacuum builds, the PCV valve opens. Crankcase vapors are drawn in through the valve and burned. This type of a ventilation system is beneficial in a number of ways. First, it routes crankcase vapors into the engine instead of into the atmosphere. Second, vacuum in the intake manifold is stronger, more reliable, and

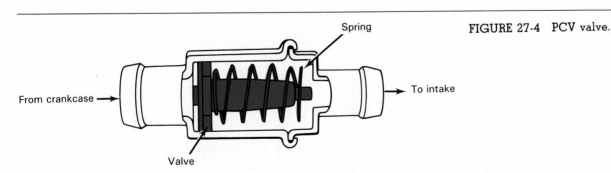

Spring

FIGURE 27-4   PCV valve.

From crankcase

To intake

Valve

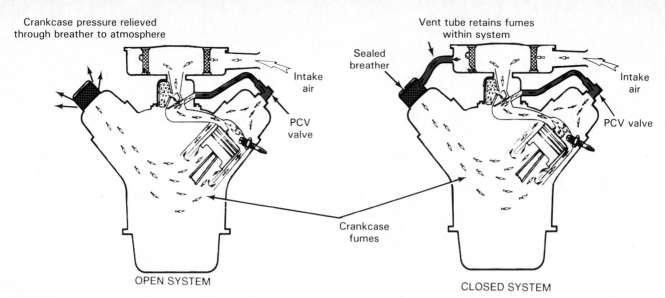

OPEN SYSTEM

CLOSED SYSTEM

FIGURE 27-5   Open and closed PCV system.

much more predictable than that created by a road draft tube. For this reason, some manufacturers began using PCV systems in noncommercial vehicles long before they were required by law. Chevrolet, for instance, installed PCV systems as early as 1955.

PCV Operation   Two distinct types of PCV systems have been used in the industry: the open system and the closed system (Figure 27-5). The difference between the two is the breather which allows air into the crankcase. When this breather is vented to the atmosphere, the system is considered *open*.

Under full throttle conditions, crankcase pressures build up rapidly while vacuum levels drop. Without a vacuum signal, the PCV valve starts closing, forcing this pressure buildup to vent through the breather. This is true of any PCV system, open or closed. The problem with the open system is that, under these conditions, crankcase fumes and vapors are vented to the atmosphere.

A *closed* PCV system solves this problem by sealing the breather and connecting it to the air cleaner.

When crankcase pressures are excessive, fumes and vapors forced out the breather are vented into the air cleaner housing, through the carburetor, and into the cylinders where they are burned. In 1968, federal legislation was passed requiring the use of closed systems on all vehicles. So, as of the 1969 model year, all vehicles sold in the United States were equipped with closed PCV systems.

PCV Valves   The function of all PCV valves is basically the same. They control the flow of crankcase fumes into the intake manifold while, at the same time, preventing gases or flames from traveling in the opposite direction (Figure 27-6).

When an engine is at idle, the vacuum signal to the valve is high. Under such conditions, spring pressure is overcome, and the valve seats in the housing. A small orifice in the valve allows a metered volume of gas to pass into the intake manifold. By altering the strength of the spring used in the valve assembly and the size of the valve orifice, the volume and timing of vapor flow can be tailored to any particular engine

FIGURE 27-6   PCV valve operation.

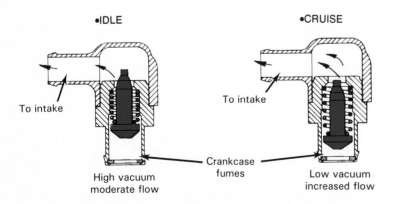
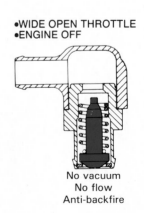

•IDLE

•CRUISE

•WIDE OPEN THROTTLE
•ENGINE OFF

To intake

High vacuum
moderate flow

To intake

Crankcase
fumes

Low vacuum
increased flow

No vacuum
No flow
Anti-backfire

application. These specifications are determined by the manufacturer and vary with valve application. Some engines, in fact, use only an orifice, with no spring-loaded valve.

As engine speed increases and vacuum level drops, the valve is gradually forced off its seat by spring pressure. An increasing volume of crankcase vapor is allowed to enter the intake manifold now that engine operation can handle the extra capacity. This volume can also be controlled by the physical shape of the valve within the housing. At full throttle, when vacuum drops to zero and crankcase pressures build the fastest, vapor flow through the valve is cut off completely. Crankcase fumes (vapors, gases) are forced out through the oil cap or breather, through the air cleaner, and into the cylinders where they are burned.

PCV Testing Procedures   PCV systems should be checked at regular intervals of between 6000 and 12,000 m, depending on the system. More important than mileage, however, is engine operation. The system should be checked whenever stalling, rough idle, or other conditions indicating a ventilation system malfunction occur.

Rpm Drop Test   Attach a tachometer. Bring the engine to normal operating temperature. With the engine at idle, pinch off or block the ventilation tube between the PCV valve and the vacuum source. Engine speed should drop 50 rpm or more. If not, check the valve and system for blockage and clean as necessary.

Vacuum Test

1. With the engine idling at normal operating temperature, disconnect the PCV valve from the rocker cover.

If the valve is not plugged, you will hear a hissing noise as air passes through it. You should feel a strong vacuum when you place a finger over the valve inlet.

2. Reinstall the valve assembly and remove the crankcase breather or oil filler cap. With the engine running at idle, loosely hold a piece of stiff paper over the opening. Within 60 sec, the paper should be sucked against the opening with noticeable force.

3. Stop the engine and remove the valve. You should hear a clicking or rattling noise when you shake the valve. If you don't hear the noise, replace the valve. Also, PCV valves need to be changed at specific intervals. Check the car's service record to see if the PCV valve is due for replacement.

4. If the test results are correct, the system is operating properly. If the system fails any test, replace the indicated component and repeat the tests. If the system still fails any test, clean the system thoroughly.

Evaporative Controls

The function of a fuel evaporative control system is to allow proper fuel system ventillation while preventing fumes from reaching the atmosphere. This means that vapors have to be stored while the engine is off, when most fuel evaporation occurs. Later, when engine operation is resumed, these fumes can be removed from storage and burned. In most systems, storage is provided by an activated **charcoal** (or carbon) **canister.** On a few early systems, charcoal canisters were not used. Instead, fuel fumes were vented into the PCV system and treated as crankcase vapors.

The main components of a fuel evaporative emissions control system are a redesigned fuel filler cap and fuel tank, a vapor separator, and a charcoal canister (Figure 27-7).

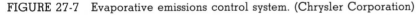

FIGURE 27-7   Evaporative emissions control system. (Chrysler Corporation)

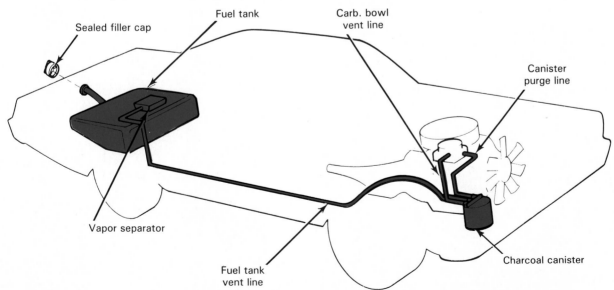

Fuel Filler Cap Directly vented fuel filler caps are obsolete. All fuel filler caps are sealed. Most of them, though sealed, are equipped with pressure/vacuum relief valves. These valves prevent damage to the fuel tank in case of a malfunctioning vent line. If pressure or vacuum in the tank builds to unsafe levels, the relief valve opens. Without these relief valves, excessive pressure or vacuum could distort or collapse the fuel tank if the ventilation system is damaged.

Fuel Tank Design Pre-1970 vehicles release excess fuel vapors through the fuel filler cap and a vent tube or tubes in the fuel tank. The vent tube allows air to enter the tank as the fuel is burned. In addition, it serves as an overflow if high temperatures cause fuel to expand beyond the capacity of the tank.

With the fuel filler cap sealed, all ventilation of the fuel tank is through the vent tube. To eliminate possible overflow, tanks were redesigned. Two methods have been used: the addition of a **thermal expansion tank** inside the main fuel tank and a new tank shape which results in a remaining 10–12% air space in a "full" tank (Figure 27-8).

As an extra safety precaution, most systems now also incorporate a roll-over valve. The valve is located in the vapor vent line. It prevents fuel flow if the vehicle should be turned over in an accident. The average valve will hold pressure to about 3 psi.

Vapor Separator To avoid fuel evaporation into the atmosphere, standard fuel tank vent tubes were redesigned. Most closed ventilation systems use three or four vent lines in the top of the tank so that at least one line is always above the fuel level. This positioning guarantees tank ventilation at any vehicle angle. On early systems, the vapor separator was used to keep liquid fuel in the tank and out of the vent tube to the charcoal canister.

Although various designs of vapor separator have been used (Figure 27-9), basic operation is the same:

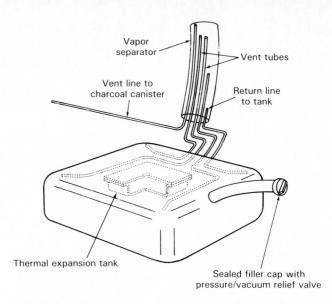

FIGURE 27-8 Fuel tank with vapor separator and thermal expansion tank.

Fuel vapors rise into the separator through vent tubes. Liquid fuel and condensation are drained back to the tank while vapors escape through a vent line to the charcoal canister. This vent line extends to the highest point in the separator and has a small orifice to prevent the transfer of liquid fuel to the canister. The fuel return line, on the other hand, is the shortest in the separator; it allows for fuel drainage back to the tank. The separator itself usually consists of a sealed metal pipe, mounted vertically beside the fuel tank. In other applications, it may be mounted horizontally or inside the fuel tank itself.

In later years, refinements in basic system design have resulted in downsizing and, in most cases, the complete elimination of a vapor separator. Downsized separators include separator valves and separators mounted on the tank. Tank-mounted separators replace the large pipe and numerous tubes of earlier sys-

FIGURE 27-9 Vapor separators.

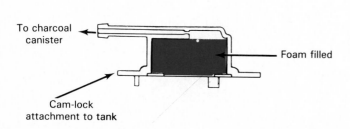

ON-TANK SEPARATOR

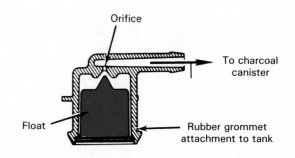

SEPARATOR VALVE

tems with a foam separator element and a single vent line to the charcoal canister.

Where the vapor separator has been completely eliminated, its function is served by fuel tank design and/or liquid check valves. Fuel tank design replaces the separator by allowing extra air space for vapor condensation within the tank, so that only fuel vapors reach the vent tube. Check valves of various designs prevent liquid flow to the canister.

Carburetor Ventilation Carburetor evaporation is contained in one of three ways:

☐ Closed fuel bowl ventilation
☐ Internal venting
☐ Fuel injection

The first method used to contain carburetor evaporative emissions was a simple change in float bowl design. Instead of venting the bowl directly to the atmosphere, a vent hose runs from the float bowl fitting to the charcoal canister where vapors are stored. On systems without charcoal canisters, the carburetor is vented into the PCV system.

More recently, internal bowl vents have been developed to control evaporative emissions. Fuel vapors are retained in the air cleaner assembly. When the engine is started, fumes are drawn into the cylinders and burned. Most carburetors with internal vents have external vents as well. When the external vents are not used, the vent tube is plugged. When the external vents are used, vapors are controlled by a hose to the canister as on other externally vented systems.

Charcoal Canister Most fuel evaporation systems use a charcoal canister to store fuel evaporative vapors. The charcoal canister consists of a fuel-resistant nylon or plastic container filled with **activated charcoal** granules (Figure 27-10) Fuel vapors are "soaked-up" by the charcoal. Venting air through the canister removes the fuel vapors and restores the adsorbant qualities of the charcoal. Some vehicles with large fuel tanks (or dual tanks) use two canisters to ensure that sufficient volume is available for vapors. A basic charcoal canister has a single purge line from the top of the canister to the air cleaner, PCV line, or intake manifold. When the engine starts, manifold vacuum draws fuel vapors out of the canister. This purging action restores the activated charcoal. To gain more control, a *purge valve* is used on some designs. This valve allows the manufacturer to tailor purge timing, as well as the volume of canister fumes purged, to suit a particular application or engine operating condition.

Testing Fuel Bowl Vent Valves The fuel evaporative emissions control system is generally very dependable and does not usually require testing. However, fuel bowl vent valve operation may be easily checked. Use

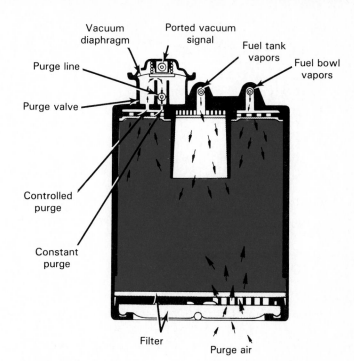

FIGURE 27-10 Charcoal canister with purge valve. (General Motors Corporation)

a shop manual to test charcoal canister purging action if a problem is suspected.

Vacuum-Operated Valves:

1. Disconnect the vacuum line and both bowl vent lines from the valve. Remove the valve. Attach a hand-held vacuum pump to the vacuum connection of the valve but do not apply vacuum.
2. Blow through the valve. With no vacuum applied, air should flow through it. Apply a small vacuum signal to the valve. This should close the valve and block airflow.
3. If the valve is equipped with a temperature override, no air will pass through it, regardless of vacuum, if valve temperature is below closing temperature. Check the shop manual for testing procedures.

Electrically Operated Valves:

1. Disconnect valve wiring at the electrical connector. Disconnect both bowl vent lines from the valve and remove it. Blow through the valve. Air should flow easily through it.
2. Apply 12 V to the electrical lead from the valve. Air should not pass through it as long as power is supplied to the valve. If the valve doesn't respond as indicated, it is faulty and should be replaced.

Exhaust Gas Recirculation

One of the earliest and most effective means developed for the control of NO_x emissions is exhaust gas recirculation, or EGR.

EMISSION CONTROL

It seems there is always some "new" smog law around, and sometimes there are rather heated arguments over the pros and cons of such laws. But the idea that emissions in the form of smoke or smog can be a nuisance subject to regulation appeared in the United States by the middle of the 1800s. Courts of law were awarding monetary damages in private suits for smoke nuisance by that time, and in the 1890s St. Louis adopted an ordinance designed to provide for the measurement and regulation of smoke emissions of its factories. By the early 1900s, many cities had enacted legislation concerning smoke abatement. As the automobile became a more prominent aspect of American life, it was only natural for those laws to be extended to cover automotive smoke as well. Even with such a long history of legislation, however, it always seems there is someone who thinks the emission control regulations are a "get-rich-quick scheme cooked up by mechanics."

Kay O'Cullane
San Diego Community College
Skill Center

Exhaust gas recirculation systems control NO_x emissions by keeping combustion chamber temperatures below that required to produce NO_x. A small amount of exhaust gas is routed into the intake cycle to dilute the intake charge, reducing combustion temperatures. The amount of exhaust gas mixed with the intake charge is controlled by an EGR valve on all current systems.

In addition to its widespread use on gasoline engines, EGR is also the only major emissions control system currently used on diesel engines.

Most EGR systems include an EGR valve, a temperature switch, vacuum lines from the EGR valve to a vacuum source, and an exhaust back pressure sensor. Temperature switches may monitor engine coolant, ambient air, or intake charge temperature. The back pressure sensor is used on later-model systems.

EGR Valves A basic EGR valve consists of a top housing with a spring-loaded diaphragm attached to a valve in the base of the assembly. The complete unit is mounted to the intake manifold (Figure 27-11). Exhaust gases pass through the base when the valve is open and into the intake system. A vacuum tube is attached to the top of the diaphragm housing. This tube supplies vacuum to the chamber above the diaphragm. When the engine is at idle or wide-open throttle (little or no vacuum), the diaphragm spring holds the valve closed. During light acceleration or cruise conditions, the vacuum signal increases, pulls the diaphragm, and opens the valve. This allows exhaust gas flow into the intake system (Figure 27-12).

Temperature Switches Most systems are equipped with a coolant temperature override (CTO) switch (Figure 27-13). The switch is mounted so it can sense coolant temperature. This may be in the intake manifold, cylinder head, thermostat housing, or top radiator tank. It blocks the vacuum signal to the EGR valve until a specified engine temperature is reached. The use of this switch improves cold drivability.

Vacuum Signal EGR valves are vacuum operated. Both carburetor ported vacuum and venturi vacuum are used to control valve operation.

Ported vacuum comes from a port in the carburetor, located just above the throttle blade. When the throttle is closed, there is no vacuum signal at this port. EGR does not occur. As the throttle blade opens, more of the port is exposed to manifold vacuum, which opens the EGR valve. At wide-open throttle, manifold vacuum drops, and EGR ceases (Figure 27-14).

The vacuum signal produced at the carburetor venturi is highly sensitive to changing engine conditions, providing the most accurate source of EGR control. However, the venturi vacuum signal is too weak to operate the EGR valve. Manifold vacuum, on the other hand, provides a strong, consistent signal. Unfortunately, this consistency makes it incompatible with optimum EGR operation.

To combine the advantages of venturi control with the strength of manifold vacuum, a vacuum amplifier is added to the system (Figure 27-15). Manifold vacuum is supplied to the EGR valve via the amplifier. The amplifier allows venturi vacuum to regulate the strength of the manifold signal. This provides the EGR valve with a sufficient vacuum signal without sacrificing the accuracy of venturi control.

FIGURE 27-11   Typical EGR system design.

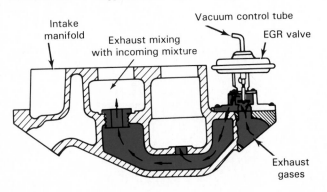

Intake manifold

Exhaust mixing with incoming mixture

Vacuum control tube

EGR valve

Exhaust gases

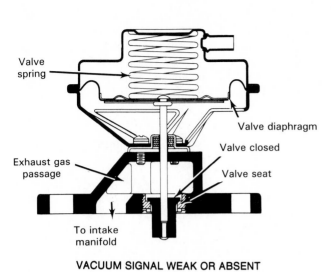

VACUUM SIGNAL WEAK OR ABSENT — Valve spring, Valve diaphragm, Valve closed, Valve seat, Exhaust gas passage, To intake manifold

STRONG VACUUM SIGNAL — Control vacuum, Vacuum chamber, Valve stem, Stem seal, Valve open, Exhaust gas inlet, Exhaust gas

FIGURE 27-12   EGR valve operation.

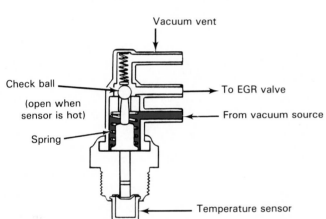

Vacuum vent, Check ball (open when sensor is hot), Spring, To EGR valve, From vacuum source, Temperature sensor

FIGURE 27-13   Coolant temperature override switch.

FIGURE 27-14   Ported EGR.

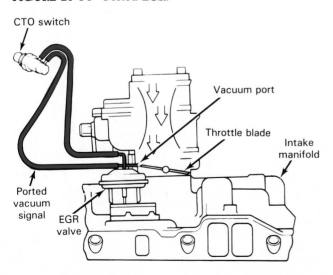

CTO switch, Vacuum port, Throttle blade, Intake manifold, Ported vacuum signal, EGR valve

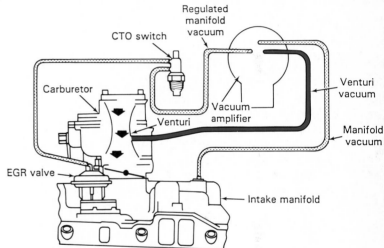

Regulated manifold vacuum, CTO switch, Carburetor, Venturi, Vacuum amplifier, Venturi vacuum, Manifold vacuum, EGR valve, Intake manifold

FIGURE 27-15   Venturi-vacuum-controlled EGR system with vacuum amplifier.

Testing Single-Diaphragm EGR Valves

1. With the engine idling at normal operating temperature, disconnect the vacuum line from the EGR valve and attach a hand vacuum pump to the valve. Apply 10–15 in. Hg of vacuum to the valve. The engine should begin to idle roughly or stall. When the vacuum signal is removed, normal idling should resume.

2. If the engine responds as described, the valve is operating properly. The intake manifold exhaust passages are clear, thus allowing exhaust gas recirculation to occur. If engine idle is not affected, either the valve diaphragm is torn, the valve is not seating tightly or the intake manifold exhaust passages are blocked.

3. With the engine off, watch the valve stem closely as vacuum is applied and released (Figure 27-16). If stem

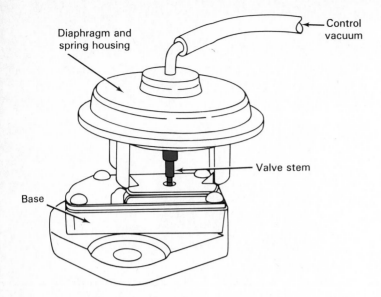

FIGURE 27-16   EGR valve movement.

movement is hard to detect or if the stem is not readily visible, place a gloved finger under the valve to feel diaphragm movement. Be careful, the valve will be hot. If the diaphragm is intact, the stem and diaphragm will move up with the vacuum and back down when vacuum is removed. If not, replace the valve.

4. If the valve operation is correct, remove and clean the valve and the valve seat. Check the intake manifold exhaust passages for blockage and clear as needed.

Testing Exhaust Back Pressure EGR Valves   Testing procedures for an exhaust back pressure EGR valve are basically the same as for standard valves, with the following exceptions: When testing EGR valve function with a vacuum pump, the tail pipe must be partially blocked to create exhaust back pressure. Block the tail pipe briefly with shop towels or rags while applying vacuum to the valve. Wear gloves to prevent burns from the hot pipe. Due to its design, an exhaust back pressure EGR valve cannot be tested with the engine off.

FIGURE 27-17   CTO switch.

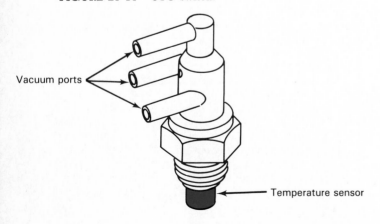

Spark Controls

The best way to reduce any particular emission is to avoid producing it in the first place. NO_x emissions are produced by high cylinder temperatures and pressures. Therefore, one efficient way to reduce NO_x emissions is to reduce combustion temperatures. The two main approaches to this reduction are EGR and control of ignition timing, or spark control. EGR was described in the last section, and spark controls are discussed here.

Vacuum   A carburetor throttle body port has been traditionally used as the distributor vacuum advance source. Vacuum level at this port varies greatly at low vehicle speeds, rising or falling with changes in throttle position. By eliminating or delaying vacuum advance during accleration and at low speeds, more precise control or ignition timing is possible.

Modern spark control systems eliminate or modify vacuum advance during low-speed operation. Two primary designs are used: One blocks the vacuum signal to the distributor using low-speed operation, and the other delays any increase in vacuum signal strength. Either system may be modified by the addition of a coolant temperature override (CTO) switch (Figure 27-17). (CTO switches are discussed in the EGR section as well.) The purpose of this switch is to modify the vacuum control signal to either improve cold drivability or reduce the temperature of an overheated engine.

There are two designs for blocking the vacuum signal during low-speed operation. The difference between the two designs is the method used to determine vehicle speed. One method uses a transmission switch, and the other uses a vehicle speed sensor. Figure 27-18 shows a speed-sensor-equipped system. The heart of either system is the vacuum solenoid valve. This electrically operated valve is located in the vacuum

FIGURE 27-18   Speed-sensor-equipped vacuum delay system.

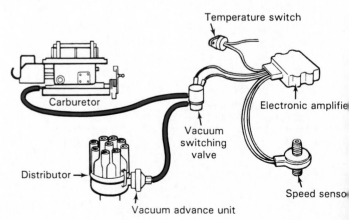

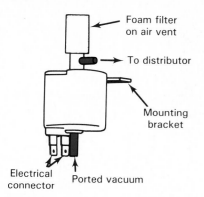
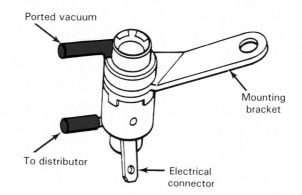

FIGURE 27-19 Vacuum solenoid valves.

line between the carburetor port and the distributor advance mechanism. When activated, it blocks the vacuum signal to the advance unit and bleeds off any vacuum which may be acting on the advance diaphragm.

Vacuum Solenoid Valve During normal vehicle operation, a ported vacuum signal passes through the vacuum solenoid valve (VSV) to the distributor vacuum advance mechanism, resulting in normal vacuum advance. When current is applied to the VSV, the vacuum signal is blocked, and an air bleed into the advance line is opened. Further vacuum advance is prevented while the air bleed vents any vacuum from the advance line. This cancels advance which may already be present. When the electrical signal is removed, normal vacuum control resumes. Figure 27-19 shows two VSVs. In recent years, ported vacuum has been eliminated with the use of ignition computers.

Coolant Temperature Override (CTO) Switch Any design may be modified with the addition of a coolant temperature override (CTO) switch. CTO switches may be activated when cold or hot. The cold CTO switch provides full manifold vacuum to the distributor during cold engine operation. The extra advance improves drivability and gives quicker warm-ups.

The hot CTO switch functions in the same manner as the cold switch, except that full manifold vacuum is supplied when the engine becomes overheated (extended idle, high ambient temperatures). This extra advance increases engine idle speed to aid in engine cooling. The higher idle speed circulates coolant faster and gives more airflow through the radiator. As soon as normal coolant temperature is again obtained, regular operation of the spark control system is resumed.

Vacuum Signal Delay Spark control systems which delay an increase in vacuum signal strength are very simple. They consist of a single valve in the vacuum line between carburetor ported vacuum and the distributor advance unit. Two types of valves are used. One is known as a spark delay valve; the other, used on

Chrysler Corp. vehicles, is the orifice spark advance control (OSAC) valve (Figure 27-20).

Both valves are designed to delay any increase in vacuum strength (vacuum advance) by several seconds. An interesting aspect of these valves is that while vacuum signals which increase in strength are delayed, decreasing signals are immediately relayed to the advance unit. Therefore, vacuum advance is delayed while ignition retard is immediate. The one major difference between the delay valve and the OSAC valve is that some OSAC valves are temperature sensitive. At air temperatures below about 60°F (15°C), the delay function of the valve is bypassed, allowing immediate vacuum advance as signal strength increases. At higher temperatures, normal delay operation is resumed.

Preliminary Checks Many problems with the spark control system can result from simple faults. To save diagnosis time and effort, visually inspect the following areas whenever the spark control system is suspected of malfunction or failure:

Vacuum line connections and hoses: Ensure that all connections are tight and secure. Check that vacuum hoses are in good condition, not dry or cracked.

FIGURE 27-20 Chrysler spark control system with OSAC valve. (Chrysler Corporation)

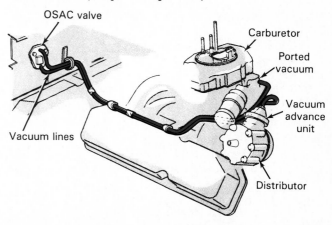

Electrical wiring and connections: Check that all connections are clean and tight. Check wiring for frayed ends, chafing, splitting, or cracking. Ensure that all connectors are clean and secure.

It is especially important that all system components are present and properly installed. A partial spark control system (with one or more components removed or disconnected) will not operate effectively or correctly. Check a shop manual for specifications and complete testing procedures.

Engine Modifications

Engine modifications are defined as an intentional change in engine design. Such a change reduces emissions without the addition of an extra device or system. For example, lowering the compression ratio of an engine lowers combustion temperature, thus lowering NO_x emissions. Since most compression reductions are accomplished through changes to existing components (piston design and combustion chamber volume) without adding anything new to the system, this is considered an engine modification.

Just as air injection, catalytic converters, or computerized engine controls affect engine operation, so different modifications interact. For example, leaning out the air/fuel ratio in the engine can effectively eliminate CO production. But at the same time, too lean a mixture will result in incomplete burning. The quantity of unburned HC in the vehicle exhaust will thus increase (Figure 27-21). Intricate relationships exist between all components of the power train, so there is no such thing as a simple modification. When considering any single engine modification, be aware that all other systems must work with it.

The most important modifications to reduce emissions are those which lower compression pressures and combustion temperatures. One of the earliest and most widespread modifications in use, this continues to be a basic area of concern for emissions control. Pressure and temperature reduction is achieved by reducing compression ratios and modifying camshaft timing. The end results of these changes is a reduction in NO_x emissions.

Compression Ratios Compression ratios are reduced by modifying piston shape and opening up the combustion chambers. Changes in these areas increase combustion chamber volume, thus reducing compression ratios. This directly reduces compression pressure. While redesigning the combustion chambers for greater volume, any sharp edges or angles can also be eliminated. This improves flow and reduces the possibility of hot spots in the chamber which can promote detonation and pre-ignition. Thicker head gaskets are also used to reduce compression.

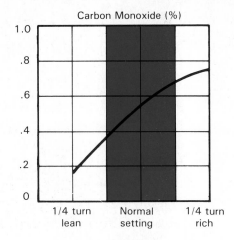

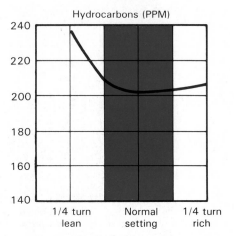

FIGURE 27-21 Effects of the same adjustment on different emissions levels.

Cam Timing Changes in camshaft (or valve) timing can be used to reduce compression pressures as well as to directly reduce combustion temperature. If the intake valve is open until the piston comes up into the compression stroke, some of the intake charge is pushed back out. With less charge to compress, compression pressures are decreased.

As is true of any gas, the more the intake charge is compressed, the hotter it becomes. Therefore, whenever combustion chamber pressures are reduced, combustion temperatures are reduced as well. By lowering compression ratios and changing cam timing to reduce compression pressures, the temperature of combustion is brought down. This reduces both requirements for NO_x production—high temperature and high pressure.

To reduce combustion temperature directly, one additional modification in cam timing has been used. By increasing the length of exhaust/intake valve overlap at the beginning of the intake stroke, some exhaust gas is left in the combustion chamber with the intake charge. This **inert** exhaust gas dilutes the air/fuel mixture in the same manner as an EGR system. Like an

EGR system, this reduces the amount of available fuel in the cylinder. With less fuel to burn, combustion temperatures are lower. This also helps with unburned HC.

Combustion Chamber Design   Computer analysis of combustion chamber design has shown that tremendous improvements in power, economy, and emissions reduction can be achieved by changes made to the chamber. Valve size, location, chamber shape, and volume all affect engine operating efficiency. Although certain designs show marked improvements in fuel economy and emissions control, the cost and complexity of manufacturing must be considered. As emission controls become stricter, the extra production costs may be justified. Improvements in combustion efficiency can be dramatic, as demonstrated by extensive testing (Figure 27-22).

Careful intake and exhaust valve placement enables engineers to create planned turbulence in the combustion chamber (Figure 27-23). The swirling charge promotes better combustion and reduces the effect of the quench areas. Hemispherical chambers are known to produce better results in power output, but valve train complexity has often ruled out their use on domestic vehicles. Wedge-shaped chambers are easier to produce but have some limitations in combustion chamber shape. Prechamber designs are used on diesels and some imported cars (Honda's CVCC and Chrysler Imports' MCA Jet systems). They have been effective in reducing some emissions but require precise control of fuel, extra manifold passages, camshaft changes, and additional valves.

These complicated combustion chamber designs have not always produced results worth the extra cost and complexity. Passenger cars are usually designed with strict cost controls in mind. In a free-spending environment, some racing cars and many motorcycles

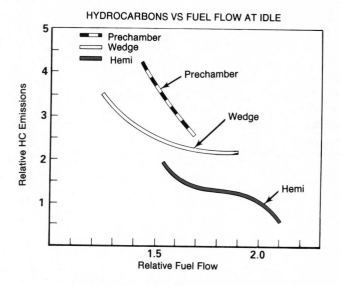

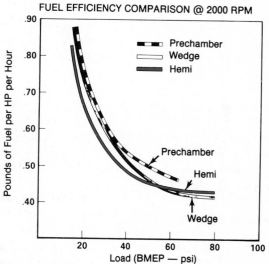

FIGURE 27-22   Emission output due to combustion chamber design. (Ford Motor Company)

FIGURE 27-23   Three combustion chamber designs. (Ford Motor Company)

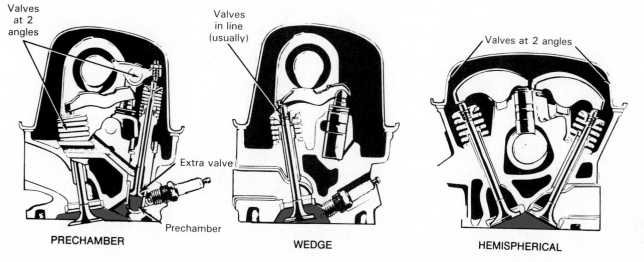

PRECHAMBER   WEDGE   HEMISPHERICAL

use four valves per cylinder. Multiple valves permit better flow and control of intentional turbulence, but complexity costs increase. The cost of the engine modifications has to be weighed against the cost of accomplishing the same emission control with add-on devices. Recently, the benefits of 4-valve cylinder heads have begun to outweigh the cost. More street engines are expected to use 4-valve cylinder heads.

Fringe Benefits   One very important side effect of engine modifications is the improvement in overall engine performance. The simple fact is that nearly anytime the efficiency of an engine is improved (whether for the sake of emissions, fuel economy, or performance), other factors improve as well. An efficient engine runs stronger, uses less fuel, and burns cleaner.

Air Injection

Theory   Combustion requires fuel, oxygen, and heat. Without any one of these three elements, combustion cannot occur. In an internal combustion engine, fuel is supplied by the carburetor, oxygen from the atmosphere, and heat by the ignition system in the form of a spark. Since automobile engines are not 100% efficient, a small amount of unburned fuel remains at the end of the combustion cycle to be expelled with exhaust gases. This left-over fuel is a major source of HC and CO emissions. The amount of excess fuel in the exhaust system is determined by available oxygen. When all of the oxygen is used up, combustion stops. Air injection **(AIR)** systems were developed to provide sufficient oxygen in the exhaust system to complete the burning process and reduce HC and CO emissions.

There are two basic types of AIR systems. One type uses an injection pump to supply air to the exhaust system. The other type, known as a *pulse air* system, is designed to use pressure pulses from the exhaust system to draw fresh air into the exhaust manifold (Figure 27-24).

Pulse Air System   The pulse air system eliminates the need for an air pump. Most systems consist of a single air delivery pipe and a check valve. The check valve performs the same function in this system as it does in the air pump system: It prevents exhaust gases from entering the air injection system.

Exhaust pressure is very high when the exhaust valves open, creating a wave of high pressure in the exhaust system. When the exhaust valves close, continued flow of gases out of the system results in a low-pressure condition or suction. The pulse air system taps into the exhaust system so these pressure pulses pull fresh air into the system. A one-way check valve included in the design allows a flow of fresh air into the exhaust system during periods of low pressure. The valve closes in response to high exhaust pressure peaks, preventing the flow of exhaust gas out through the air tube.

Air Pump System   The air pump system uses a belt-driven pump to collect and pressurize atmospheric air. This air is sent by air pipes and/or hoses so injected air enters the exhaust manifold close to the exhaust valves.

Some air pump systems inject air into the intake manifold exhaust heat crossover passage or into special passages in the cylinder head, eliminating the need for injection manifolds or pipes (Figure 27-25).

FIGURE 27-24   Pulse and air pump air injection systems. (Chrysler Corporation)

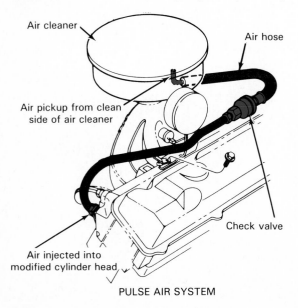

PULSE AIR SYSTEM

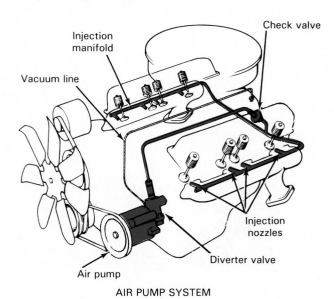

AIR PUMP SYSTEM

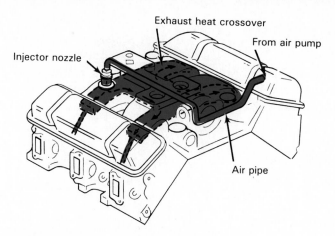

FIGURE 27-25 Air injection into intake manifold exhaust crossover.

Two valves are usually located in the air line between the pump and the exhaust manifold. One is a **diverter valve,** and the other is a one-way check valve (Figure 27-26). The diverter valve prevents backfiring during high-speed deceleration. Closing the throttle quickly at high engine speeds results in a very

FIGURE 27-26 Diverter valve and check valve.

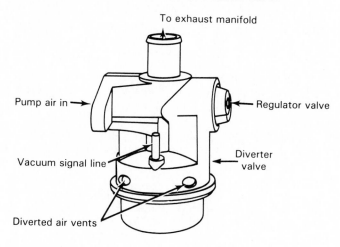

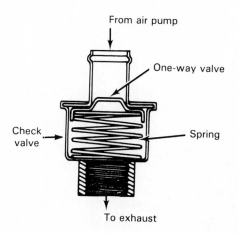

rich air/fuel mixture. Since this mixture cannot be completely burned in the engine, the exhaust gases become too rich. When the air pump injects fresh air into this rich exhaust stream, rapid combustion (backfiring) occurs. The diverter valve prevents these backfires by momentarily diverting air away from the exhaust system.

In the event of air pump failure or if exhaust system pressure should ever be greater than AIR system pressures, exhaust gases could be forced up the air injection pipes and into the injection system. This could cause extensive damage to the system and must be prevented. Check valves are located in the air injection lines to protect the system. A check valve allows air injection to occur while preventing reverse flow into the system.

Air Pump The air pump is a belt-driven, vane-type pump. Air entering the pump is filtered by either an integral filtering device, a small auxiliary air cleaner, or the carburetor air filter.

The integral design consists of a centrifugal filter/fan assembly which is mounted between the pump pulley and the air pump itself. Air is drawn in through the unit while dirt and debris are removed by the centrifugal action of the fan (Figure 27-27).

The air pump itself consists of the pump housing, an inner air cavity, a rotor, and a vane assembly. As the vanes turn in the housing, air is drawn in through the intake port and pushed out through the exhaust port (Figure 27-28).

The volume of air discharged by the pump changes with engine speed, while system pressure is controlled by a pressure relief valve (normally under 5 psi). Pressure is controlled to avoid excessive pres-

FIGURE 27-27 Air pump with centrifugal filter/fan assembly.

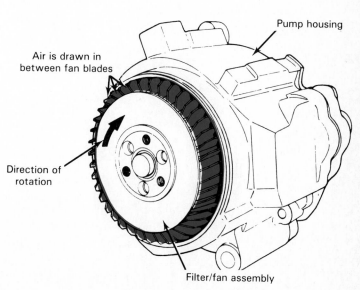

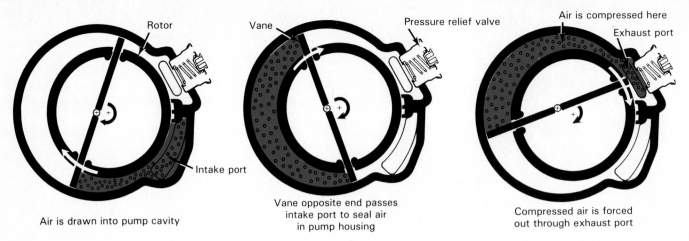

Rotor — Vane — Pressure relief valve — Air is compressed here — Exhaust port

Intake port

Air is drawn into pump cavity

Vane opposite end passes
intake port to seal air
in pump housing

Compressed air is forced
out through exhaust port

FIGURE 27-28   Air pump operation.

sures at high engine speeds and to limit the amount of air injected. This pressure relief function is built into the diverter valve on several systems. On others, a spring-loaded valve is included as part of the air pump housing (Figure 27-29). When pressure in the pump exceeds a preset level, the relief valve spring compresses, and the valve opens. Excess air passes through the valve into the atmosphere.

Preliminary Testing   Before beginning specific tests, ensure that all hoses, injection manifolds, and valves are securely attached and properly routed. With the engine running, apply a soapy water solution to all hose connections and joints to check for air leaks. Repair as needed.

Air Pump Testing   Air pump testing procedures and specifications vary with the manufacturer. To accurately test any air pump, refer to the individual repair manual for details and complete procedures.

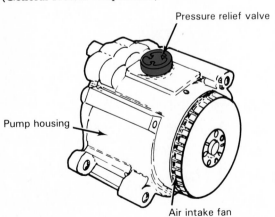

FIGURE 27-29   Air pump with pressure relief valve. (General Motors Corporation)

Pressure relief valve

Pump housing

Air intake fan

Diverter Valve Testing   Standard design:

1. With the engine idling at normal operating temperature, hold a finger over the vent to check for airflow. No air should escape from the vent under these conditions. Figure 27-30 shows a typical diverter valve.

2. Increase engine speed to increase the pump volume. At high engine rpm (varies with manufacturer), you should feel some airflow as the relief valve in the diverter valve assembly operates.

3. Place a finger over the diverter valve vent and reduce engine speed rapidly. You should feel diverted air from this vent for 2 or 3 sec. If the valve operation is not as described, check that the vacuum signal line from the intake manifold is not clogged or restricted. Replace as needed. If the vacuum line is okay but the valve function is still incorrect, replace the diverter valve.

Gulp valve: If the system being tested uses a gulp valve type of diverter valve, use the following testing procedure:

1. With the engine operating at normal temperature, pinch off the air line between the gulp valve and the intake manifold. Engine idle should not change. Release the air line.

2. Disconnect the vacuum control line to the valve. Wait about 5 sec and reconnect the line. The egnine should run rough for about 1–3 sec. If the engine idle does not respond as indicated, replace the valve.

Check Valve Testing

1. Disconnect the air supply pipe from the check valve. With the engine idling at normal operating temperature, carefully check the valve for any leakage at the inlet side. No exhaust gases should escape from the valve. If you detect any leakage, replace the valve.

2. Turn off the engine. If the check valve is on an air pump system, insert a small screwdriver or rod into the valve and push down lightly on the spring-loaded

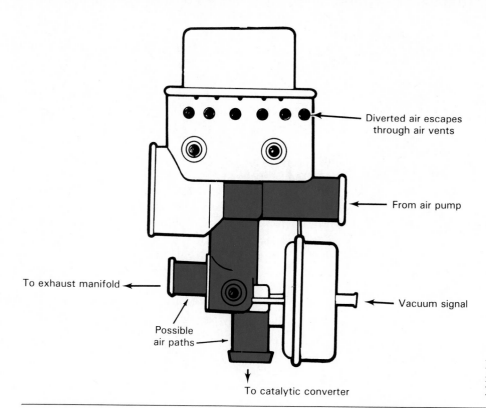

Diverted air escapes through air vents

From air pump

To exhaust manifold

Vacuum signal

Possible air paths

To catalytic converter

FIGURE 27-30 Air vent locations for diverter valve testing. (General Motors Corporation)

valve. The valve should move freely. If the valve sticks or is difficult to move, replace it.

Catalytic Converters

Extensive efforts have been made in the engine to reduce exhaust emissions, but great amounts of the three major pollutants still remain in the exhaust as it leaves the engine. To prevent these pollutants from entering the atmosphere, they must be converted to less harmful elements while still in the exhaust system. Since 1975, the single most important device used to meet this challenge has been the **catalytic** converter.

The catalytic converter is installed in the exhaust system between the exhaust manifold and the muffler so that exhaust gases must pass through it. On some early Ford V-8 systems, a single converter was used. The system was designed so that only half of the exhaust gases was treated by the converter, with the other half bypassing it completely. In 1979 this system was discontinued, due to continued reductions in the allowable amounts of HC and CO in vehicle exhaust (Figure 27-31).

In the converter, platinum and palladium (or platinum alone) are used as **catalysts** to convert HC and CO to carbon dioxide and water. The converter contains aluminum oxide pellets, or a ceramic honeycomb *monolith,* coated with the catalyst.

Systems which reduce NO_x emissions in addition to HC and CO include a converter which uses either

FIGURE 27-31 Catalytic converter installation. (Chrysler Corporation)

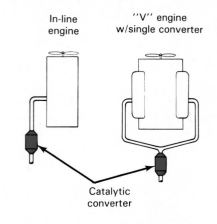

In-line engine

"V" engine w/single converter

Catalytic converter

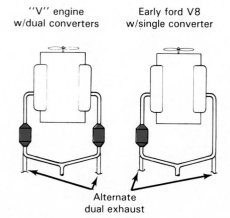

"V" engine w/dual converters

Early ford V8 w/single converter

Alternate dual exhaust

rhodium or rhodium and platinum as a catalyst. Because of its ability to reduce all three emissions, it is known as a three-way catalyst, or TWC.

There are several types of converters in use today. They include conventional, TWC, dual stage (a combination of the first two in one housing), and, on some recent systems, warm-up or minioxidation converters.

Conventional Converter   A conventional converter is so called because it is the most common type of converter in use. It may use pellets or a monolith medium, depending on application. Platinum and palladium (or platinum alone) are used as the catalyst in this type of converter. Those using aluminum oxide pellets have built-in baffles which contain the pellets within the converter and force exhaust gases to pass through the pellet *bed* (Figure 27-32). This ensures that the full capacity of the converter is used and that all exhaust gases are treated.

Converters which utilize a ceramic monolith contain the monolith itself (coated with the catalyst), diffuser plates, and a steel mesh blanket. The monolith

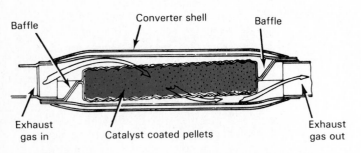

FIGURE 27-32   Exhaust flow through a pellet-type conventional converter. (Chrysler Corporation)

FIGURE 27-33   Monolith converter construction. (Chrysler Corporation)

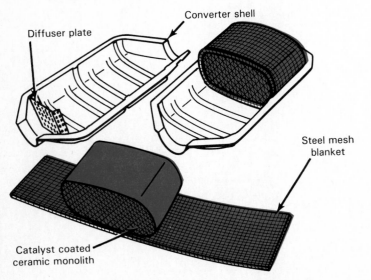

is a honeycomb-like structure with hundreds of small passages through it. It is superior to the pellet design because it causes less exhaust system back pressure, is smaller (resulting in quicker heating time), and is generally more durable and less susceptible to vibration. However, it also requires more catalyst to manufacture (higher cost) and is not repairable. If the catalyst is destroyed, as would happen if leaded gasoline were used often, the entire unit must be replaced. The pellets in a pellet-type converter, on the other hand, can be replaced without replacing the entire assembly. Also, the monolith structure can be damaged by continuous road shock or rapid changes in temperature. The steel mesh blanket is wrapped around the monolith to help protect it from these dangers. It acts as a cushion for the monolith and insulates it from rapid temperature changes.

As exhaust gases enter this type of converter, they encounter a perforated diffuser plate which breaks up and spreads out the flow (Figure 27-33). As the gases pass through the hundreds of passages in the monolith, they are exposed to the catalyst.

TWC Converter   This type of converter is nearly identical to a conventional converter with the exception of the catalyst used. A conventional converter, using platinum and palladium as a catalyst, reduces emissions of HC and CO only. The TWC converter uses rhodium, with or without platinum, as its catalyst. Rhodium helps reduce NO_x emissions as well as HC and CO. This characteristic, that of reducing emissions of all three major pollutants, is why it is referred to as a three-way catalyst.

TWC converters, when used, are usually included in addition to a conventional converter. The TWC converter is added in one of two ways. As a separate converter assembly it is located in the exhaust pipe ahead of the conventional converter. It may also be included as part of a single assembly including the TWC and the conventional converter in a common housing. This assembly is known as a dual-stage converter.

Dual-Stage Converter   The dual-stage converter contains a TWC converter and a conventional converter in a common housing, separated by a small air space. As part of a single-converter assembly, the two catalysts are referred to as catalyst *beds*. Exhaust gases entering the assembly pass through the TWC first, through the air space, and into the conventional catalyst bed. The TWC bed performs the same function as it would as a separate device, reducing all three emissions. As exhaust gases leave this bed, they pass through the air space and into the second, conventional, catalyst bed.

Catalytic converters reduce emissions levels by oxidizing pollutants. This reaction requires specific amounts of free oxygen. In a dual-stage converter, most

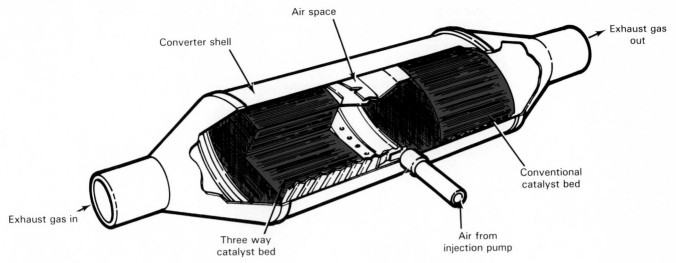

Air space

Converter shell

Exhaust gas out

Exhaust gas in

Three way catalyst bed

Air from injection pump

Conventional catalyst bed

FIGURE 27-34 Dual-stage converter with air injection. (Chrysler Corporation)

of the available oxygen is used up in the first catalyst bed. If oxidation of HC and CO is to continue in the second bed, an additional supply of oxygen is required. Most dual-stage converter systems use the air injection system as the source of this supply. Air is injected into the space between catalyst beds to provide the required oxygen. This injected air also helps to cool the converter assembly (Figure 27-34).

Warm-up Converter   In the past few years, some systems have begun to utilize a small, additional converter, located immediately after the exhaust manifold, known as a *mini converter* or *warm-up* converter. Usually of the monolithic design, the purpose of this unit is twofold. First, it starts oxidation of emissions before they reach the main converter. Second, and more importantly, it provides for some control of exhaust emissions before the large converter has warmed up to operating temperature. Figure 27-35 shows an exhaust system using two warm-up converters.

Before any converter can begin to reduce emis-

sions, exhaust gas temperatures of at least 500°F (260°C) are required to heat the catalyst to necessary operating temperatures of over 1000°F (535°C). Due to its location close to the exhaust manifold and its considerably smaller size, the warm-up converter reaches the required temperatures much more rapidly than the larger, main converter. This reduces the amount of time during which no converter action occurs.

Converter Checks   There are no testing procedures for a catalytic converter. As a standard procedure, the complete exhaust system (including converter, muffler, pipes, and heat shields) should be visually inspected anytime the vehicle is on a hoist for service. Any serious damage to the converter, i.e., gouges, large dents, or tears, means the converter should be replaced. Excessive exhaust system back pressure (as indicated by poor engine performance or overheating) or abnormally high HC and CO levels as detected by a gas analyzer may be an indication of an improperly operating converter.

FIGURE 27-35 Exhaust system with two warm-up converters.

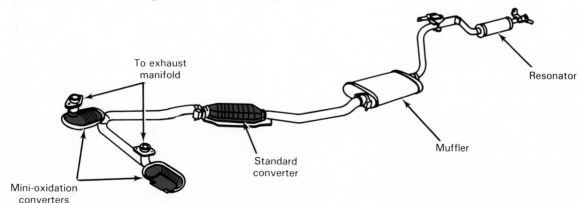

To exhaust manifold

Resonator

Muffler

Standard converter

Mini-oxidation converters

TRADE TERMS

Activated Charcoal
AIR
Canister
Catalyst
Catalytic
Charcoal
CTO Switch

Diverter Valve
Engine Modifications
Inert
PCV Valve
Thermal Expansion Tank
Vacuum

REVIEW QUESTIONS

1. What are the three emissions controlled in auto engines?

2. What two general categories can emission controls fall into?

3. _____ combustion temperatures allow the formation of NO_x.

4. What is the aim of EGR systems?

5. What should happen if you remove a PCV valve and shake it?

6. Why is vacuum spark advance reduced at idle?

7. If you are troubleshooting a spark control system, what should you check first?

8. What is the important side effect of reducing emissions through engine modifications?

9. What is the point of injecting air into the exhaust manifold?

10. A TWC cleans all three emissions. What emissions do conventional converters reduce?

PART FIVE
Power Train

KEY CONCEPTS

- Why and how clutches are used; propeller shaft design and service
- Drive axle and differential operation for both front and rear drive cars
- How synchronizers and shifting work in manual transmissions
- Manual transaxle operation and power flow
- Servicing and adjusting manual transmissions and transaxles
- Hydraulic operation of automatic transmissions and transaxles
- Fluids, filters, and adjustments for automatic transmissions and transaxles
- Common four-wheel-drive designs; how full and part-time transfer cases work

28

Clutches and Propeller Shafts

INTRODUCTION

The manual transmission clutch (Figure 28-1) is a device used to connect and disconnect engine power flow to the transmission at the will of the driver. The driver operates the clutch via a clutch pedal inside the vehicle. This pedal action allows engine power flow to be gradually applied when the vehicle is starting out from rest and interrupts power flow to avoid gear clashing when shifting gears.

When the clutch pedal is depressed, the three major clutch assembly components—flywheel, friction disc, and pressure plate—are disengaged, thus interrupting power flow. As the clutch pedal is released, the pressure plate moves closer to the clutch disc, clamping the disc between the pressure plate and the flywheel. Therefore, if the transmission is in gear, the drive wheels will turn when the clutch disc turns.

Remember this simple rule: The pressure plate and flywheel are bolted to the engine's crankshaft and rotate at engine speed. The clutch disc is *splined* to the transmission input shaft and rotates at transmission speed. Splines resemble a series of keyways cut into a shaft or hole. Parts splined together rotate as a unit, but the parts are free to move somewhat along the shaft's centerline.

OBJECTIVES

When you have completed this chapter, you should be able to

- Describe how the clutch works
- Describe why heat is bad for the clutch
- Tell how to inspect a clutch for wear
- Describe how power is transmitted from the transmission to the final drive
- Show how to change a U-joint

409

ing or throw-out bearing, and the **clutch linkage** (Figure 28-2).

> CAUTION: Like many types of brake-lining material, most friction discs contain asbestos fibers. Always follow safety precautions outlined later in this chapter when handling asbestos.

Bellhousing The *bellhousing* is a large bell-shaped metal casting between the engine and the transmission (Figure 28-3). It houses the clutch assembly and supports the transmission.

Flywheel The *flywheel* is a large-diameter, heavy disc, usually constructed of cast iron. It is bolted to the engine's crankshaft. The flywheel smoothes out, or *damps*, engine vibrations caused by firing pulses. It also acts as a friction surface and *heat sink* for one side of the clutch disc. The teeth around the circumference of the flywheel form a *ring gear*, which, when engaged to the starter motor pinion gear, is used to start the engine (Figure 28-3).

Vehicles with automatic transmission do not have a flywheel. Instead, they use a driveplate or flexplate. These lightweight, stamped steel discs are used only to bolt the torque converter to the engine's crankshaft. They have no clutch friction surface and will not interchange with manual transmission flywheels. They do have a ring gear, for engine starting, though.

Clutch Disc The *clutch (friction) disc* is a steel plate that fits between the flywheel and the pressure plate. It has friction material riveted or bonded to both sides. Figure 28-1 shows a riveted clutch disc. Like brake-lining material, the friction disc lining wears as the clutch is engaged. Some high-performance clutch assemblies use multiple friction discs.

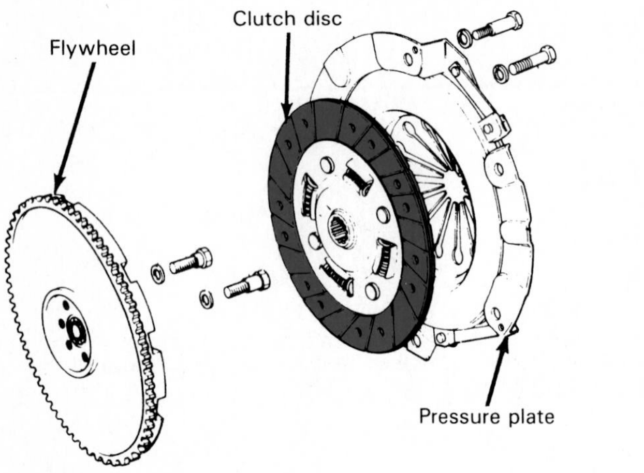

FIGURE 28-1 Clutch assembly.

CLUTCH CONSTRUCTION

The basic elements of the clutch are the **bellhousing** or clutch housing; the **flywheel,** the **friction disc,** the clutch plate or **pressure plate,** the **clutch release bear-**

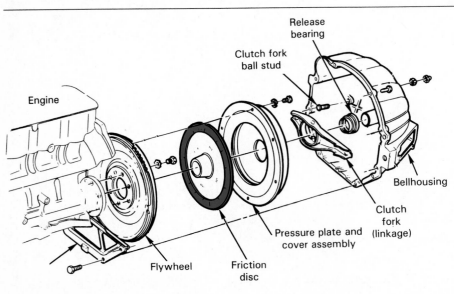

FIGURE 28-2 Complete clutch assembly. (General Motors Corporation)

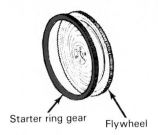

Starter ring gear   Flywheel

FIGURE 28-3 Flywheel with ring gear shown separately. (Volvo)

FIGURE 28-4 Exploded view of a coil spring pressure plate.

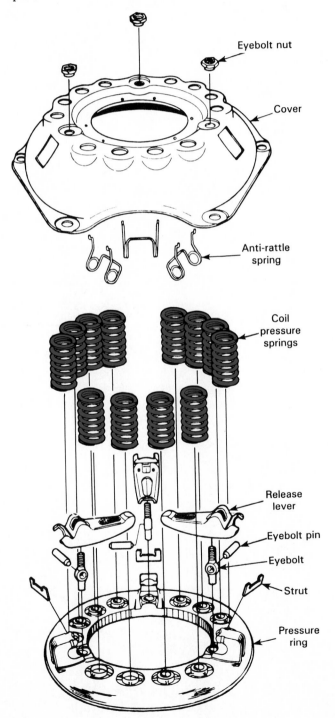

Eyebolt nut

Cover

Anti-rattle spring

Coil pressure springs

Release lever

Eyebolt pin

Eyebolt

Strut

Pressure ring

Pressure Plate The *pressure plate* or clutch plate is a large spring-loaded clamp that rotates at flywheel speed. It consists of a sheet-metal cover, multiple, high-rate coil springs, and levers (Figure 28-4). Or it could have a single, large conical diaphragm or Belleville-type spring, a metal pressure ring to provide a friction surface for the clutch disc (Figure 28-5), and a thrust ring for the release bearing.

FIGURE 28-5 Exploded view of a Belleville-type pressure plate.

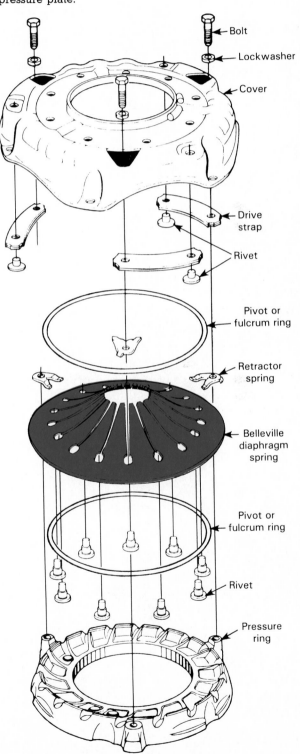

Bolt

Lockwasher

Cover

Drive strap

Rivet

Pivot or fulcrum ring

Retractor spring

Belleville diaphragm spring

Pivot or fulcrum ring

Rivet

Pressure ring

"DON'T WORRY, I'LL FIX IT"

Among the last vestiges of male chauvinism, when society has finally changed and all folks are equal, history will note a peculiar tendency, a sort of atavistic, dark compulsion in the male breast. Against his nature, against his very will, even the most seemingly enlightened man will find himself saying, as he confronts a damsel in distress, "Don't worry, I'll fix it for you."

Sadder words were never spoken.

First of all, there is a governing in these transactions, an immutable truth that says Women You Know Never Have Anything Simple Wrong With Their Cars. The dream that Isabella will show up with horrifying noises under the hood, all eyes and consternation, gnaw-

ing at her luscious lips while you save the day by tightening the fan belt, is only that: a dream.

It isn't that they all drive complicated cars, either: it's just that simple jobs turn ugly when you're trying to impress the princess. Bolts break off. Nuts strip. Wrenches slip, and exhaust pipes retain enough heat to give you third-degree forearms 5 hours into the project.

I changed a clutch for a friend of mine exactly a week after I had changed a similar clutch in a similar car in 3½ hours flat. I hadn't even put the tools away, so I knew it would take me no time at all.

Three days later she had taken to calling

me late at night, wanting to know when she could have her car back. She didn't wake me up, either, because instead of sleeping the sleep of Galahad I was still out in the garage fighting that @#$%£& clutch job and relearning Carlson's First Law of Greasy Parts, which is The Phone Rings At The Worst Time Possible.

Well, I think she still believes I spent 4 days on her clutch for some devious purpose, when actually, my devious purpose evaporated after the first 4 hours, after which all fantasies disappeared in favor of getting the clutch job finished and her car out of my life.

Satch Carlson
*Autoweek, Division of
Crain Communications*

Some pressure plates use centrifugal weights that increase clamping force on the thrust springs with increasing engine speed.

Regardless of design, the pressure plate must provide enough clamping force to transmit full engine torque at the flywheel. The pressure plate moves away from the flywheel when the clutch pedal is depressed, releasing the clamping force. This stops engine torque from reaching the transmission.

Release Bearing   The *clutch release bearing*, or throwout bearing, is a carbon-type or ball-type bearing in the bellhousing, operated by the clutch linkage (Figure 28-6). When the clutch pedal is depressed, the bearing

moves toward the flywheel, depressing the pressure plate thrust pad and moving the pressure plate fingers or levers against pressure plate spring force. This moves the pressure plate away from the clutch disc, thus interrupting power flow. The release bearing must be

---

FIGURE 28-7   Hydraulic clutch linkage. (Volvo)

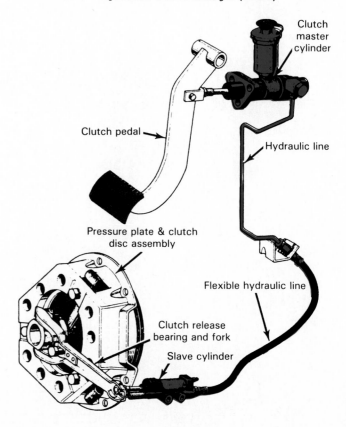

FIGURE 28-6   Clutch release bearing.

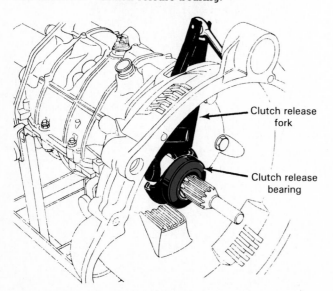

adjusted so it does not touch the release fingers, beveled springs or thrust pad when the pedal is released. Some of the newest release bearings are designed to ride lightly against the pressure plate assembly. Such units are still in the minority, however.

Linkage The *clutch linage* connects the driver-operated clutch pedal to a bellhousing-mounted **release fork** that acts on the release bearing. The linkage may be mechanically or hydraulically operated. Figure 28-7 shows a typical hydraulic system.

CLUTCH LOCATION

Although the exact physical location of the clutch assembly varies with vehicle design, the clutch is usually placed between the engine and the transmission. This is true regardless of engine, transmission, or drive axle location. And, with few exceptions, the clutch assembly and flywheel are bolted to the rear of the engine crankshaft.

Exceptions to the standard clutch location are

FIGURE 28-8 Clutch location.

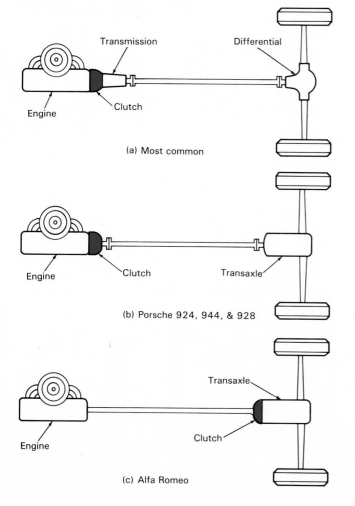

(a) Most common

(b) Porsche 924, 944, & 928

(c) Alfa Romeo

found in the Alfa Romeo Alfetta and GTV6. On these front-engine, rear drive cars, the clutch and remote-mounted flywheel are located in the transaxle housing at the real axle (Figure 28-8). Crankshaft rotation is conveyed via a *transmission shaft*. This tubular steel shaft has flexible Rotoflex couplings at both ends.

SERVICING CLUTCH COMPONENTS

Whenever you replace any clutch component, be sure to check the old part against the replacement part. For example, if the wrong release bearing or disc is installed, you may not discover the mistake until you attempt a road test.

Pressure Plate

In normal use, the pressure plate gives durable service and can last the life of the vehicle. It is not uncommon to reuse a pressure plate when replacing a worn clutch disc.

Damage Conditions that can rapidly damage a pressure plate include insufficient free play, a friction disc worn flush with its attaching rivets, and overheating caused by clutch slippage.

Insufficient free play grooves the release fingers or thrust ring. A disc with a worn-out friction facing allows the rivets to score the pressure ring or flywheel. Overheating the pressure plate can cause bluing (localized hot spots), warpage, heat checks, and cracks in the pressure ring friction surface (Figure 28-9). In most vehicle designs, the transmission must be removed to service the clutch assembly.

When removing a pressure plate, be careful to loosen all pressure-plate-to-flywheel bolts a few turns before removing any of them. This helps prevent warping of the pressure plate.

FIGURE 28-9 Pressure plate inspection.

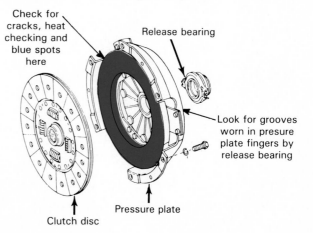

Bolts Special bolts retain the pressure plate to the flywheel. These are manufactured to a specific hardness. Often they have a special shoulder under the bolt head. Threads may not run the full length of the bolt shank.

> **CAUTION:** Never substitute different bolts when installing the pressure plate to the flywheel. Severe damage and personal injury to vehicle occupants and nearby pedestrians could result. The bolts could shear at high rpm or engine load, causing the clutch to explode through the bellhousing.

Be sure the correct pressure-plate-to-flywheel bolts are installed and torqued to specifications. Also, follow a side-to-side torquing sequence, tightening the bolts in several steps.

Alignment On some vehicles, the pressure plate is **doweled** to the flywheel. On others, alignment marks are used to indicate the correct pressure-plate-to-flywheel mounting (Figure 28-10). A doweled pressure plate can be installed in only one way. But failure to align a marked pressure plate and flywheel upon installation may create an out-of-balance condition. This condition may result in drive train vibration at certain speeds.

If no alignment marks are found on a pressure plate you are reusing, *center-punch* the flywheel and pressure plate before removing the pressure plate. This can help prevent an out-of-balance condition when the pressure plate is installed.

FIGURE 28-10   Clutch alignment marks. (Chrysler Corporation)

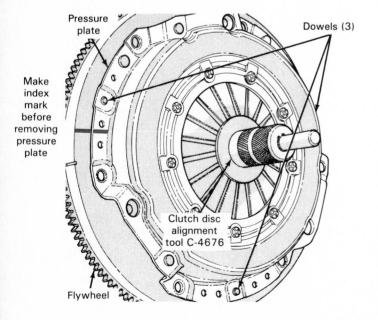

> **CAUTION:** Pressure plates are assembled with very powerful and strong (high rate) thrust springs (Figures 28-4 and 28-5). Do *not* remove any nuts or bolts used to assemble the pressure plate.

You can inspect the pressure plate without disassembling it. If the pressure plate is defective, replace it with a remanufactured or new one. Individual pressure plate parts are not available. Pressure plate disassembly should only be done in a remanufacturing facility with the proper tools, holding fixtures, presses, and test equipment.

Pressure Plate Inspection If the pressure plate provided sufficient clamping force before it was removed, it can likely be reused provided it passes a few visual checks. If the friction-surface area of the pressure ring is free of scoring, bluing, cracks, and heat checks and the release bearing thrust ring isn't scored, check for bent or broken thrust springs. Also look for bent or uneven release levers, or check to see if the pressure ring is not parallel with the clutch cover. Replace the complete pressure plate assembly if any defects are found.

Clutch Disc

The clutch disc, or driven disc, transfers engine torque from the flywheel to the transmission input shaft when engaged. In normal use, the disc is replaced when its friction facing wears thin.

In most modern passenger cars, clutch disc friction material is a woven or molded compound consisting of asbestos, cotton, brass, copper, rubber, and phenolic resin. Proper asbestos handling techniques must be employed when servicing this type of disc. Racing and heavy-duty applications may use sintered metallic or ceramic friction material. Usually, the friction facing is riveted to the disc; sometimes it is bonded. With riveted facings, the disc must be replaced before the friction material is worn flush with the rivets, or rapid pressure plate and flywheel scoring will occur.

Wear Rapid disc wear occurs when the clutch is slipped. This is usually caused by inadequate pressure plate spring force or incorrect clutching and declutching. A driver who "rides" the clutch keeps his or her foot partially on the clutch pedal so full pressure plate clamping force cannot be applied to the disc. This rapidly wears the disc and release bearing. Other conditions that can cause rapid disc wear are insufficient **free play**, binding clutch linkage, high-rpm starts, and clutch overloading. Overloading can occur with increased engine output or increased vehicle weight, such as when towing a trailer.

The clutch disc must remain dry; it must be free of motor oil and other vehicle lubricants. A leaky rear-main oil seal can oil-soak the clutch disc, causing the friction facing to glaze over and slip.

Clutch Disc Inspection   Although the disc must be removed for a complete inspection, you can make a quick check by removing the flywheel inspection cover—a plate under the flywheel. If the inspection cover and bellhousing show signs of metal and friction-material shavings or if the clutch is oil soaked, it must be replaced.

After removing the clutch disc, check the friction lining first. With riveted linings, if the linings are worn close to or flush with the rivet heads, the disc must be replaced. Exposed rivet heads will score the friction surfaces of the pressure plate and flywheel. A scored flywheel can be saved by grinding, but a scored pressure plate must be replaced (Figure 28-11). If the linings are oil soaked, repair the source of the oil leak before installing the new disc. Replace any disc that shows signs of overheating—a bluing of the steel disc backing or glazing of the linings.

If the disc passes these checks, inspect the clutch disc torsion *damper* springs used in most clutch designs. Damper springs dampen, or cushion, the input shaft and drive train from harsh engagement when the clutch is applied. These springs are located between the friction facing and the splines for the input shaft. This area is called the *marcel*, and the springs are sometimes called marcel springs. Try to rotate the damper springs

with your finger. They should rotate, but not easily. If they rotate easily, replace the disc.

Usually, if a clutch disc used for more than 50,000 mi is removed for other vehicle work, it should be replaced, regardless of its condition. The time and labor saved by replacing the disc will benefit the customer.

Asbestos   As previously mentioned, most clutch discs contain asbestos. Asbestos is hazardous to your health because it can cause cancer. Be sure to follow recommended safety procedures when working with asbestos. Do not blow out clutch dust with compressed air. Do not breathe clutch dust. Wash immediately after handling clutch dust, especially before eating.

Clutch Replacement   To service the clutch, either the engine or transmission must be removed. See the engine removal section of Chapter 15 for engine removal. Transmission removal is covered here.

Start by removing the drive shaft as outlined later in this chapter. Disconnect the speedometer cable, shift linkage, and any electrical connections. Place a floor jack with a wooden block on its pad under the transmission. The wood protects the soft aluminum transmission case. Remove all bellhousing and rear transmission mount bolts. Use the floor jack to move the transmission back from the engine until the input shaft clears the pressure plate. Then lower the transmission and set it aside. On cars with front-wheel drive, the axles must also be disconnected.

Once the clutch is exposed, remove it by unbolting the pressure plate bolts. Remove them a half turn at a time to avoid warping the pressure plate. As the pressure plate comes free, the disc will come with it. Don't get greasy fingerprints on it, or they will cause the disc to grab if you reuse it. The flywheel can remain in place unless it must be ground. If it must be removed, **index** it to the crankshaft, remove its bolts, and pull it off the crankshaft. Be careful because the flywheel is heavy.

Before installing the new disc, make sure that the **splines** on the disc fit those on the transmission input shaft. Check this by quickly sliding the new disc onto the input shaft. The disc should slide freely on the shaft. Clean any excess oil or grease from the shaft.

Be sure that the side of the clutch disc marked "flywheel side" faces the flywheel. As a general rule, the disc side with the torsion damper springs protruding the most is the pressure plate side.

The clutch disc must be centered in the pressure plate and flywheel (Figure 28-12). Use an old transmission input shaft for that vehicle or a clutch alignment tool (Figure 28-10) to align the disc splines with the **pilot bushing** or *bearing*. Install the pressure-plate-to-flywheel bolts and tighten in a crisscross pattern. When

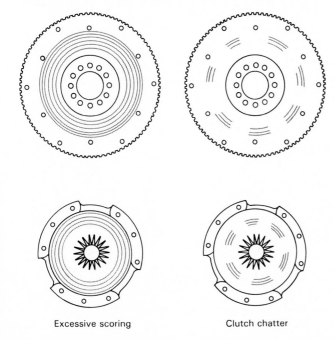

FIGURE 28-11   Scored flywheel and pressure plates.

Excessive scoring   Clutch chatter

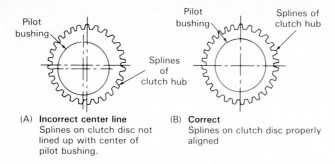

(A) **Incorrect center line**
Splines on clutch disc not lined up with center of pilot bushing.

(B) **Correct**
Splines on clutch disc properly aligned

Front view of clutch disc alignment with the pilot bushing. The pilot bushing is located in the end of the crankshaft.

FIGURE 28-12 Clutch alignment.

all bolts are torqued to specification, remove the tool and check that the clutch disc is centered. If the disc is not centered, the input shaft will hang up in the disc, and the engine and transmission will not mate. Never force the transmission bellhousing to the engine block. When the disc is centered, the bellhousing will slide over the alignment dowels and fit flush against the engine block with minimum force.

Input Shaft Pilot Bushing or Bearing

Most vehicles use a pilot bearing to support and locate the forward end of the transmission input shaft (Figure

FIGURE 28-13 Pilot bearing.

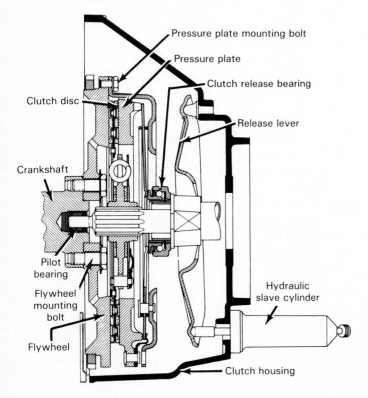

28-13). This can be a ball- or roller-type bearing or an oilite bushing. In most cases, the pilot bearing is installed in a counterbore at the center rear of the engine crankshaft. In some vehicles, the pilot bearing is in the center of the flywheel or driveplate. Some late-model, front-wheel-drive cars, such as the GM X-cars and the Honda Prelude, use no pilot bearings at all.

Replacement Replace a pilot bearing if it is worn, noisy, or otherwise damaged. A seized ball- or roller-type bearing will keep the input shaft from rotating freely.

Remove the ball- or roller-type bearings by inserting a hook end of a slide hammer behind the bearing and pulling it out. Bushings can also be removed by filling the crankshaft counterbore with heavy grease and driving in a tight-fitting dowel; pressure will force the bushing out. Be sure to lubricate the bushing and input shaft tip with heavy grease whenever the clutch is serviced.

Clutch Release Bearing

The release bearing conveys movement of the clutch linkage and release fork to the pressure plate (see Figure 28-6). Its outer race contacts the pressure plate fingers and rotates with the pressure plate when the clutch pedal is depressed, thus moving the pressure ring away from the flywheel and releasing the clutch disc. Its inner race is pressed into a collar, which slides back and forth over the input shaft inside the bellhousing.

Modern release bearing construction is either a sealed ball or roller bearing or a low-friction carbon design. Of the two, the sealed bearing type is more durable. In normal use, the release bearing lasts at least as long as the friction disc. Usages that can cause premature bearing failure include repeated driving through deep water, holding the clutch pedal depressed more often than necessary, and insufficient clutch pedal free play. *Free play* is the distance between the outer race of the release bearing and the fingers or thrust ring of the pressure plate. See the adjustment section later on in this chapter.

The clutch release bearing is lubricated and sealed at the factory. No further release bearing lubrication is required. A very light coating of grease on the bearing collar will help prevent binding. Don't let grease get on the friction surfaces of the disc, pressure plate, or flywheel.

Clutch Linkage

Clutches are operated either mechanically or hydraulically. Mechanical clutch linkage conveys the driver's clutch pedal movement to the release bearing via shafts, levers, and bell cranks (Figure 28-14) or by a single Belden cable (Figure 28-15). Hydraulic clutch linkage, like a brake system, consists of a master cylinder, hydraulic tubing, and an output, or slave, cylinder (Figure 28-16).

Mechanical Linkage The shaft-and-lever mechanical clutch linkage has many parts and pivot points. In older vehicles, the pivot points were equipped with grease fittings; more modern systems pivot on low-

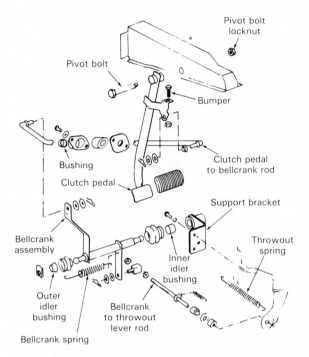

FIGURE 28-14 Mechanical clutch linkage. (American Motors Corporation)

FIGURE 28-15 Belden cable clutch linkage.

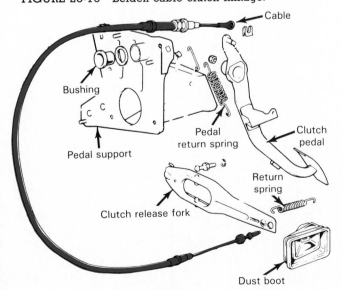

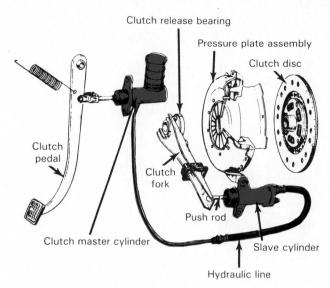

FIGURE 28-16 Hydraulic clutch linkage parts.

friction plastic grommets and bushings. As the pivot points wear, extra play in the linkage makes precise clutch pedal free play adjustment difficult to perform.

Cable Linkage Belden cable mechanical clutch linkage is simple, lightweight, and low cost. A simple cable connects the clutch pedal pivot to the release fork. Drawbacks include gradual cable stretch and cable breakage during temperature extremes. On many late-model vehicles, the cable is self-adjusting. At the pedal pivot, the cable is wrapped around and attached to a toothed wheel. A slight preload is applied to the release bearing by a ratcheting, spring-loaded pawl which engages the wheel. When the clutch is released, the pawl takes any slack out of the cable by engaging the next wheel tooth (Figure 28-17).

FIGURE 28-17 Self-adjusting clutch linkage. (General Motors Corporation)

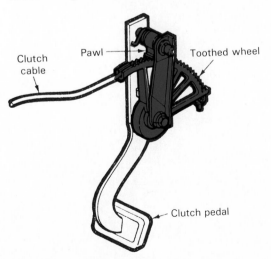

Hydraulic Linkage   Hydraulic clutch linkage is used in vehicles where mechanical linkage would be difficult to route. It is also used to gain mechanical advantage in racing and heavy-duty applications where high pressure plate spring force is required. Movement of the clutch pedal creates hydraulic force in the master cylinder. This force acts on the bellhousing-mounted slave cylinder, moving the slave cylinder push rod against the release fork and bearing. Hydraulic clutch components are serviced like hydraulic brake components. Common service problems include fluid leaks, worn-out piston seals, air in the system, and corrosion buildup. See Chapters 38 and 39 for hydraulic component service. Clutch master cylinders are treated like brake master cylinders. Slave cylinders are the same as wheel cylinders. Brake fluid is used in both systems.

Clutch Free Play   Clutch free play, or free travel, adjustment is probably the most misunderstood aspect of clutch service. The adjustment establishes the distance between the release bearing and the pressure plate fingers or thrust ring (Figure 28-18). It is measured inside the vehicle, at the clutch pedal.

Insufficient free play can cause the release bearing to constantly ride against the fingers or thrust ring of the pressure plate. This action accelerates release bearing and pressure plate wear and causes clutch slippage due to the pressure plate friction ring being partially unloaded. Excessive free play may prevent the clutch from disengaging, even with the pedal fully depressed, causing gear clash and difficult shifting. This is usually most obvious in reverse gear. On most transmissions, reverse gear is a sliding gear, without synchromesh engagement.

In normal use, free play decreases as the clutch disc wears, causing the pressure plate fingers or thrust ring to move closer to the release bearing. On high-mileage vehicles, worn-out rod-and-lever-type mechanical linkage can make accurate free play adjustment difficult due to deflections and worn bushings. Such wear would make free play measured at the pedal seem greater than actual free play at the release bearing.

Adjustment   Refer to a shop manual's clutch section for specific vehicle adjustments. However, as a general rule, you should be able to depress the clutch pedal ½–1 in. before the clutch release bearing contacts the pressure plate. This can be felt as a sudden increase in resistance to depressing the pedal. The simplest way to measure free play is with a ruler against the floor pan.

With mechanical linkage, adjustment is made by turning a nut on a threaded rod or cable end at the release fork, alongside the transmission (Figure 28-19). Although basically self-adjusting, hydraulic linkage sometimes needs adjustment after clutch service or repair. On hydraulic systems, adjustment is made by turning a nut on a threaded push rod where the slave cylinder contacts the release fork. On both types of systems, there is usually a locknut against the adjustment nut or fork to help maintain the adjustment.

Some late-model vehicles have self-adjusting, cable-type mechanical linkage (Figure 28-17). The cable is fixed length; there is no adjustment provision at the release fork. The self-adjusting mechanism consists of a toothed wheel, or **quadrant,** and a spring-loaded pawl. The quadrant is spring-loaded with just enough tension to the cable to keep light pressure against the release bearing. When the clutch disc wears a sufficient amount, the quadrant rotates enough so the spring-loaded pawl engages the next tooth when the clutch is applied, thus maintaining free play within specifica-

FIGURE 28-18   Measuring free play. (Ford Motor Company)

FIGURE 28-19   Adjusting clutch free play.

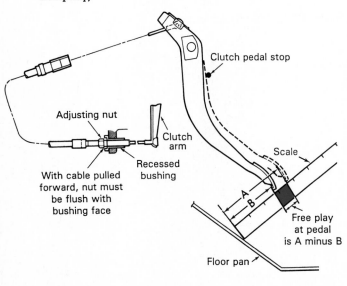

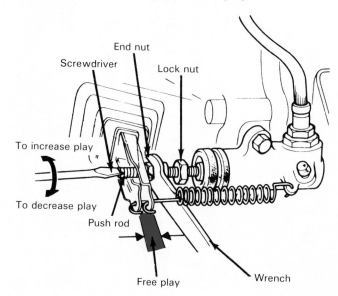

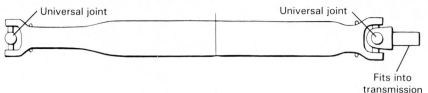

Universal joint   Universal joint

Fits into
transmission   **FIGURE 28-20** Propeller shaft.

tions. No regular service is required; however, check the quadrant and cable for binding if gear clash occurs.

> CAUTION: Never yank on the cable. This could-overload it and damage the stop on the quadrant.

PROPELLER SHAFT

The **propeller shaft,** or drive shaft, transmits transmission output shaft rotation and full engine torque, as multiplied by the transmission, to the drive axle of the vehicle (Figure 28-20). Four-wheel-drive vehicles use two drive shafts, one to drive the front wheels and another to drive the rear wheels.

Front-wheel-drive vehicles, four-wheel-drive vehicles with independent front suspension, and front- and rear-engine, rear-drive vehicles with independent rear suspension use a pair of short drive shafts called halfshafts or axle shafts. Halfshafts transmit rotation

and torque from the drive axle to each drive wheel (Figure 28-21). Halfshafts are discussed in the next chapter.

Most propeller shafts use **universal joints** to transmit rotation at varying angles. There will be more on universal joints later in this chapter.

Types of Propeller Shafts

One- and Two-Piece Shafts Most common is the one-piece, tubular steel propeller shaft with universal joints at each end, shown in Figure 28-20. Tubular steel is light in weight yet strong. Next is the two-piece, tubular steel propeller shaft, used on many long-wheelbase vehicles. It has a third universal joint between the two shaft sections and a center bearing to support the middle of the shaft assembly. Either type of shaft may be exposed or enclosed in a frame tunnel.

Torque Tube A third tube of propeller shaft is called a **torque tube.** Although its use is largely confined to pre-1948 Fords, pre-1955 Chevrolets, pre-1961

FIGURE 28-21 FWD halfshafts. (General Motors Corporation)

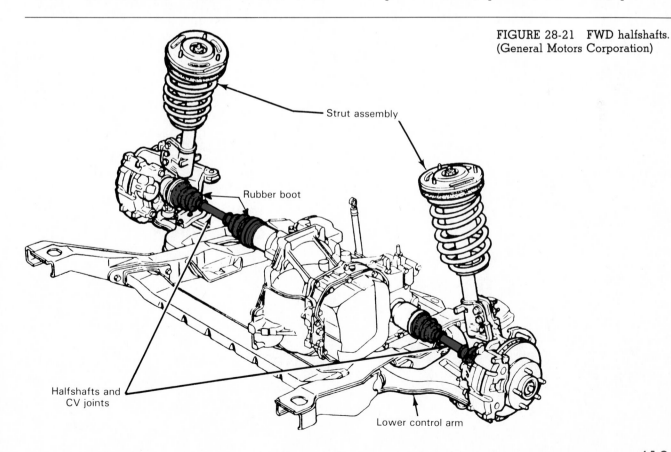

Strut assembly

Rubber boot

Halfshafts and
CV joints

Lower control arm

Buicks, and pre-1963 Ramblers, the torque tube does have some application today.

The torque tube consists of a tubular steel or small-diameter solid drive shaft fully enclosed in a large steel tube. In vehicles with a solid rear axle, the outer tube is rigidly bolted to the differential housing and acts as an axle-locating member, helping to control rear axle torque windup. The forward end of the outer torque tube and the rotating inner shaft pivot via a universal-joint or ball-socket arrangement.

In vehicles with independent rear suspension and a rear-mounted transaxle, such as the Porsche 924/944/928 models, the torque tube is rigidly connected at both ends; the rotating inner drive shaft uses *no* universal joints because transaxle location never changes relative to engine location.

The Chevrolet Chevette uses a two-piece propeller shaft that is half conventional, half torque tube. The forward section is a conventional tubular shaft with universal joints at each end. The rear section is a torque tube, rigidly mounted to the differential (Figure 28-22).

Flexible Shaft   The fourth type of propeller shaft is the flexible type. As used in the 1961–1963 Pontiac Tempest models, this shaft is a flexible steel *rope* not unlike a large-diameter version of a speedometer cable. It uses no universal joints between the engine and the rear-mounted transaxle.

In addition to allowing for angle changes, a propeller shaft mounted between a rigid transmission and a solid rear-axle assembly must be able to change its effective length. Because the drive-axle assembly moves up and down with the rear suspension and the transmission does not, the relative distance between the two changes (Figure 28-23). This can be accommodated by using a *slip yoke* in the propeller shaft or by using a ball-and-trunnion type of universal joint at one end of the propeller shaft.

Figure 28-24 shows a slip yoke design built into the front propeller shaft section. The slip yoke can be located at the center of two-piece designs or at either end but usually is found at the front, behind the universal joint flange.

Ball-and-trunnion U-joint operation follows in the universal joints section.

Universal Joints

As mentioned earlier, universal joints, or U-joints, allow the propeller shaft to transmit rotation at varying angles. On designs using U-joints, forged steel **yokes** or **companion flanges** for the joints are welded onto each end of the propeller shaft.

Cross-and-Yoke   Most common is the cross-and-yoke U-joint (Figure 28-25). A four-bearing cross, or spider, links the two propeller shaft yokes at right angles to each other. Between the cross and yokes are needle bearings and press-fit outer races. The needle bearings are lubricated with chassis grease. On some cross-and-yoke designs, one yoke attaches to the cross bearings with U-bolts. On others, all four cross bearings are press-fit into their yokes.

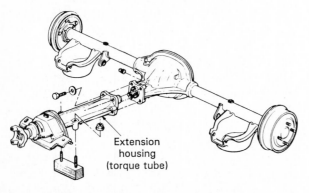

FIGURE 28-22   Chevette drive shaft. (Chevrolet Motor Division, GMC)

Extension housing (torque tube)

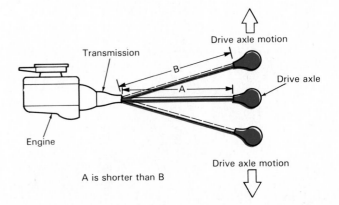

Transmission

Drive axle motion

Drive axle

Engine

B

A

Drive axle motion

A is shorter than B

FIGURE 28-23   Drive axle motion and driveshaft length.

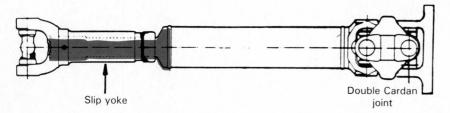

Slip yoke

Double Cardan joint

FIGURE 28-24   Drive shaft with slip yoke.

FIGURE 28-25   Cross-and-yoke U-joint.

Ball-and-Trunnion   Another type of U-joint used on older Chrysler Corporation vehicles and some Jeeps is the ball-and-trunnion type. A pin is fitted at one end of the propeller shaft. On the pin are two spherical bushings on needle bearings. The bushings slide into longitudinal grooves in the U-joint housing, bolted to a *companion flange* (Figure 28-26).

CV Joints   Propeller shafts that operate at large angles require **constant velocity,** or CV, joints. CV joints are designed to maintain a constant shaft speed, regardless of operating angle. CV joints used in most large, rear-wheel-drive vehicles with low drive shaft tunnels are **double cardan joints,** essentially two cross-and-yoke U-joints mounted back to back with a linking yoke

FIGURE 28-26   Ball-and-trunnion U-joint.

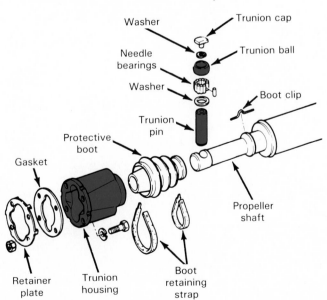

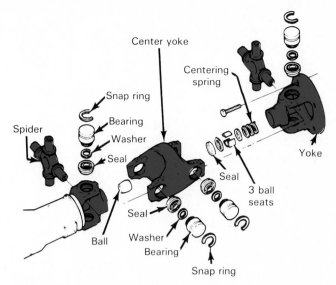

FIGURE 28-27   Double Cardan U-joint. (General Motors Corporation)

and a centering ball (Figure 28-27). The double cardan CV joint splits large propeller shaft angles in two, and the close spacing of the two U-joints tends to have a self-canceling effect on velocity fluctuations.

Rzeppa Joints   The Rzeppa joint is another type of CV joint that allows large propeller shaft angles. Drive is transmitted via steel balls operating in a cage and spherical ball socket. Because use of this joint is confined to front-wheel-drive vehicles, it is covered in that section.

The last type of U-joint is a flexible rubber coupling called a Rotoflex coupling. The coupling bolts between two triangular bolt flanges and is steel reinforced around its OD and through-bolt sleeves. It is found mainly in British and Italian sports cars. Aside from greasing its centering bushing on installation, the Rotoflex coupling needs no routine lubrication.

Testing and Balancing

Except for the Rotoflex coupling, lack of lubrication is the major reason universal joints fail. The needle bearings overheat and are eventually destroyed by friction. Other reasons include overloading the joints by pushing another vehicle or towing a trailer; high-speed propeller shaft direction changes, such as when rocking a stuck vehicle out of a snow bank; or changing the ride height so the joints operate at angles greater than intended.

Universal Joints   Driver complaints with a bad universal joint might include the following:

1. Loud clunk when the vehicle is shifted to drive or reverse.

2. Squeaking noise that occurs three or four times with each drive wheel rotation, depending on the final-drive ratio (i.e., three squeaks for a vehicle with a 3.00:1 ratio). This is most noticeable when the vehicle is driven down a narrow alley between two buildings.

3. Drive-line vibration at highway speeds (beginning at about 40 mph).

Make a quick check for a damaged U-joint by carefully observing it while attempting to rotate a mating propeller shaft section by hand. Any relative movement between a cross and its yoke indicates a defective U-joint.

Shaft Angle The propeller shaft operating angle should be okay if the vehicle has been maintained at factory ride height. Normally, the maximum allowable angle is 3° or 4° from horizontal. CV joints can tolerate 5 to 7 degrees of angle. The propeller shaft angle can be checked with a special protractor/bubble gauge (Figure 28-28). If the shaft angle at the rear axle pinion flange is excessive, it can be corrected by inserting wedge-shaped shims between the rear axle assembly and leaf spring U-bolts or between the rear axle assembly and rear control arms (on coil spring cars). A new rear transmission mount may also help.

Although such an occurrence is rare, propeller shafts can be damaged by contact with rocks or other heavy debris. A dented propeller shaft, or one that has lost its spot-welded balance weight(s), will be out of balance. It too will cause a drive-line vibration at various speeds.

Balance Propeller shaft balance checking is a specialized operation best left to drive shaft specialists. A dented propeller shaft cannot be rebalanced—it must be replaced. Minor propeller shaft balance problems can be isolated by installing a pair of worm drive hose

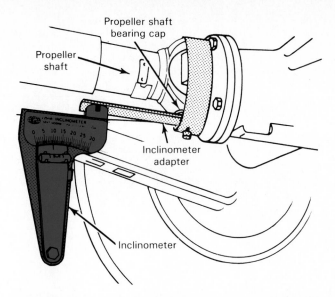

FIGURE 28-28   Checking the driveshaft angle. (Chrysler Corporation)

clamps on the shaft with the heavy end of the clamps opposite the "heavy" side of the shaft (Figure 28-29). As with dynamic wheel balancing, once the "heavy" side of the shaft is known, the hose clamps are installed with their worm screws 45° apart and their central axis 180° opposite the heavy side.

Replacing Universal Joints

CAUTION: Always index all mating flanges of the propeller shaft assembly before disassembly to retain the original factory balance.

FIGURE 28-29   Using hose clamps to balance a drive shaft. (General Motors Corporation)

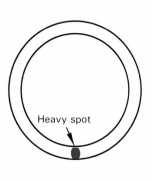

Step 1

Determine point of unbalance

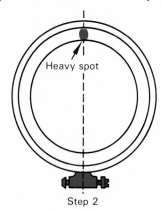

Step 2

Add hose clamps 180° from point of unbalance until they become heavy spot

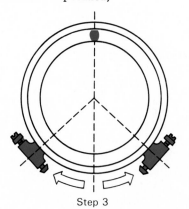

Step 3

Rotate two clamps equally away from each other until best balance is achieved

Removal Unbolt the mating flanges or U-bolts and center support (if applicable) of the propeller shaft and mount the assembly in a vise. With torque tube designs, it may be necessary to unbolt the rear axle assembly in order to gain clearance for propeller shaft removal. The vise should have soft brass or lead jaws to avoid collapsing the tubular steel shafts. If soft jaws are unavailable, try to clamp the shaft at the welded section of the forged steel yoke flange. Never clamp the shaft in the vise on a balance weight. Also, do not clamp the shank portion of a slip yoke into the vise. On vehicles with manual transmission, this will damage the splines of the shaft. It can also damage the smooth area of the yoke that the rear transmission seal rides on, causing a leak.

Disassembly To disassemble the common cross-and-yoke U-joint, remove the retaining clips with snapping-ring pliers (Figures 28-30 and 28-31). Drive each bearing cup out of its yoke with a hammer and brass drift punch, knocking the cross fully one way and removing its cup and bearings and then knocking the cross fully the opposite way. Double-cardan-type CV joints are merely two piggyback cross-and-yoke joints; disas-

semble them in the same manner. Do not hammer so hard the yoke ears bend. This will cause an out-of-balance condition.

An alternate method is to press the joint apart with a vise and sockets. See the assembly section for more on this method. If you do hammer the joint apart, use eye protection.

To disassemble the ball-and-trunnion U-joint, remove its sheet-metal cover, gasket, and spring. Simply slide back its joint body, exposing the two balls, rollers, and thrust washers, and slide those items off the shaft pin. If a new shaft pin is needed, it must be pressed into the shaft and centered and the shaft rebalanced.

Assembly Cross-and-yoke U-joint assembly is made easier by using a vise and a pair of sockets to press in the new cups. Special vises are available which make disassembly and reassembly easier yet. (Figure 28-32). Make sure all needle bearings are lubed and in position against the ID of the cup, or the cup will not fit over the cross. Always use new needle bearings and cup seals. After installing the retaining clips, tap the cross out against the new cups with a hammer and drift punch. This releases the tension and allows the cross to be moved with firm hand pressure. If the U-joint has a grease fitting, fill the joint with grease until the cup seals start to bulge.

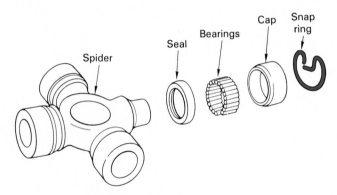

FIGURE 28-30 Snap ring on outside of U-joint. (General Motors Corporation)

FIGURE 28-31 Snap ring on inside of U-joint. (General Motors Corporation)

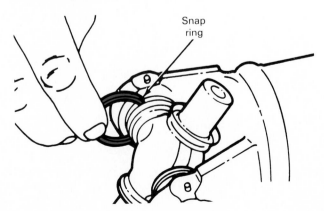

FIGURE 28-32 Using a vise to install a U-joint. (Ford Motor Company)

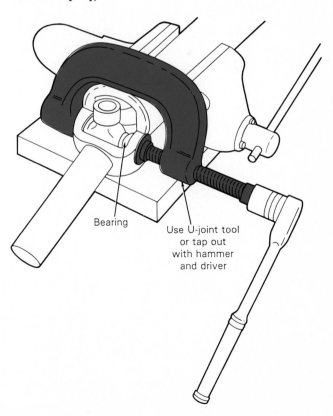

When assembling a ball-and-trunnion U-joint, reassemble balls, rollers, and thrust washers in their original locations, fill the housing with chassis grease, compress the spring, and fit the gasket and sheet-metal cover.

Installation   After installing the propeller shaft, lubricate any slip yoke coupling through its grease fitting. Make sure all companion-flange bolts are torqued to specifications. Road-test the vehicle. A bad U-joint or loose propeller shaft flange is an obvious safety hazard; the propeller shaft could fall out of the vehicle.

TRADE TERMS

Bellhousing
Clutch Linkage
Clutch Release Bearing
Companion Flange
Constant Velocity
Double Cardan Joints
Doweled
Friction Disc
Flywheel
Free Play

Index
Pilot Bushing
Pressure Plate
Propeller Shaft
Quadrant
Release Fork
Splines
Torque Tube
Universal Joints
Yokes

REVIEW QUESTIONS

1. What is the clutch disc material that requires special safety precautions when handling it?

2. The clutch disc is splined to the _____.

3. The pressure plate is bolted to the _____.

4. What are the teeth around the outside of the flywheel used for?

5. If there is no clutch pedal free play, what will happen to the clutch release bearing?

6. Too much free play could damage the clutch. True or false?

7. Too much free play could damage the transmission. True or false?

8. Drive shafts can have a slip yoke on the end or in the shaft itself. True or false?

9. Improper installation is the main reason universal joints fail. True or false?

10. You should not clamp the shank of the slip yoke in a vise. True or false?

29

Drive Axles

INTRODUCTION

Rotational motion and torque are received by the drive axle from the transmission and are then distributed to the drive wheels. Several names are popular for this part of the drive train. You may know it as the differential, final drive, rear axle, drive axle, third member, center section, and even "pumpkin," a popular slang term. No matter what it's called, the drive axle's job is the same: multiply torque, change the direction of the power flow, and allow different speeds between the two drive wheels (Figure 29-1).

To do these jobs, the drive axle uses several gears that are supported by bearings in a housing. Power is transmitted to the drive wheels by the axles. These axles may be covered by a housing, or they may be exposed. Also, they may support all, some, or none of the car's weight.

Rear Drive Axle

For many years the most popular drive axle assembly was mounted at the rear of the car. These assemblies

OBJECTIVES

When you have completed this chapter, you should be able to

- Describe the differential's function
- Describe limited slip differential operation
- Read ring and pinion gear tooth patterns
- Describe the different axle mounting methods
- Remove and replace (R&R) final drive units

Driving wheels
Axle
Axle
Rotation
90° angle change
Front of vehicle
Power flow
Rotation
Drive shaft

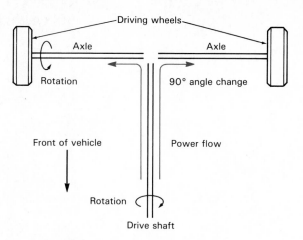

FIGURE 29-1 Power flow direction change in a differential.

use a single housing to mount the differential gears and axles. The entire housing is part of the suspension and helps to locate the rear wheels. These assemblies are called **live axles** (Figure 29-2).

Another type of rear axle is used with independent rear suspension **(IRS)**. With IRS the differential is bolted to the chassis and does not move with the suspension. The axles use U-joints to connect the differential with the drive wheels. Because of the motion

FIGURE 29-2 Live axle. (American Motors Corporation)

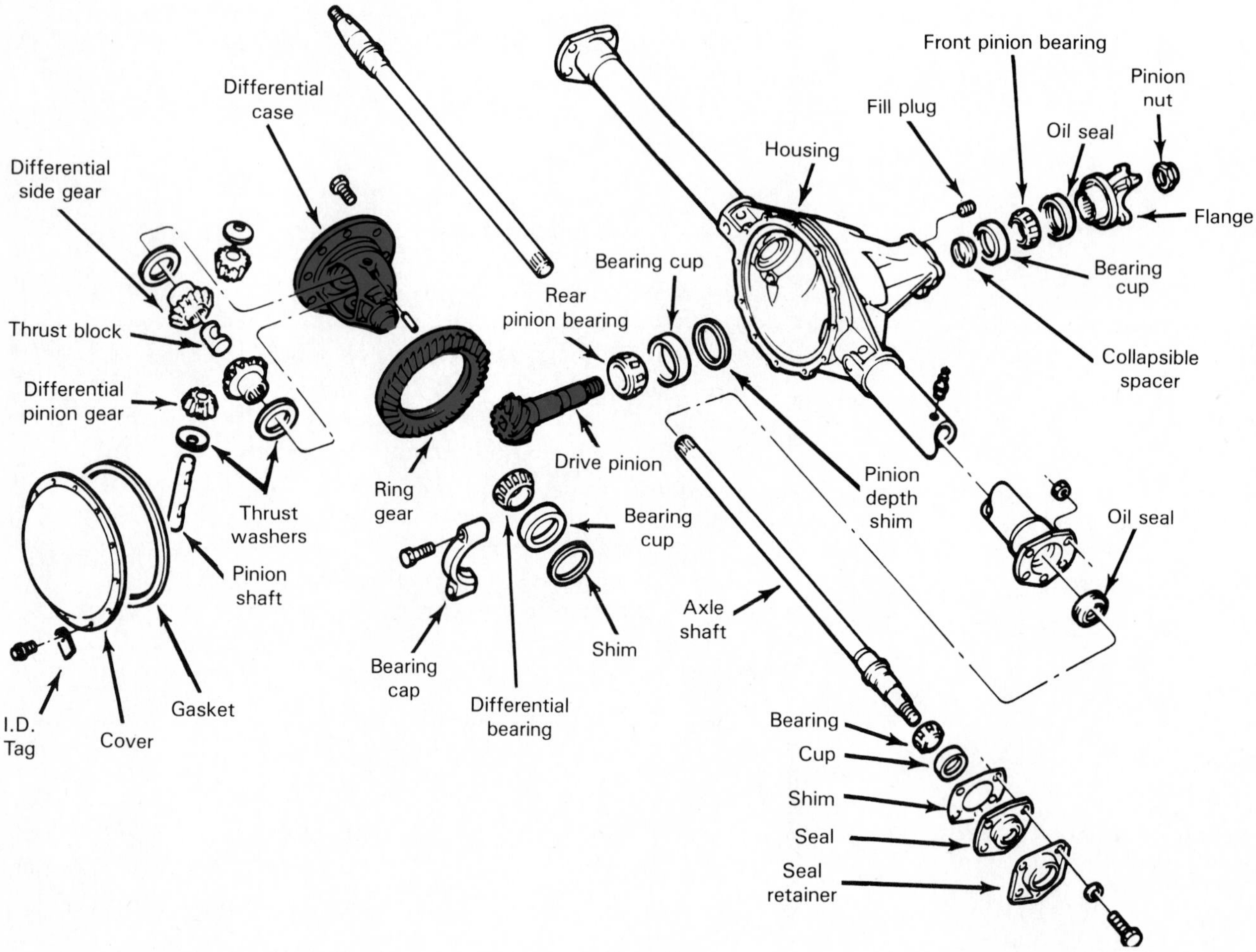

Differential case
Differential side gear
Thrust block
Differential pinion gear
Thrust washers
Pinion shaft
I.D. Tag
Cover
Gasket
Ring gear
Rear pinion bearing
Bearing cup
Drive pinion
Bearing cup
Bearing cap
Differential bearing
Shim
Housing
Fill plug
Front pinion bearing
Pinion nut
Oil seal
Flange
Bearing cup
Collapsible spacer
Pinion depth shim
Axle shaft
Oil seal
Bearing
Cup
Shim
Seal
Seal retainer

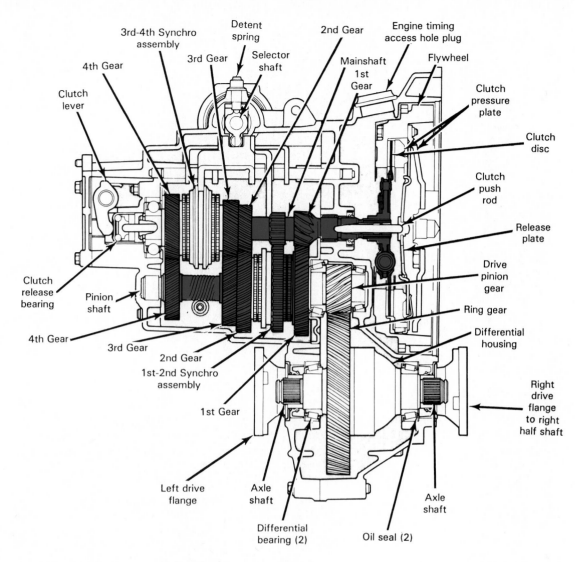

Clutch lever

4th Gear

3rd-4th Synchro assembly

3rd Gear

Detent spring

Selector shaft

2nd Gear

Mainshaft 1st Gear

Engine timing access hole plug

Flywheel

Clutch pressure plate

Clutch disc

Clutch push rod

Release plate

Drive pinion gear

Ring gear

Differential housing

Right drive flange to right half shaft

Clutch release bearing

Pinion shaft

4th Gear

3rd Gear

2nd Gear

1st-2nd Synchro assembly

1st Gear

Left drive flange

Axle shaft

Differential bearing (2)

Oil seal (2)

Axle shaft

FIGURE 29-3   FWD transaxle. (Chrysler Corporation)

between the axles and the differential, there can be no common housing for these parts in such a system.

Front Drive Axles

Drive axles are used at the front on four-wheel-drive and FWD (front-wheel-drive) cars and trucks. In some four-wheel-drive systems a live axle is used with large ball and socket joints to allow the front wheels to steer. In all FWD and some four-wheel-drive systems, a system similar to IRS is used. The differential housing is bolted to the chassis, and the axles pivot on U-joints. In all FWD systems the differential is housed in the transmission case. This particular assembly is known as a **transaxle** (Figure 29-3). Transaxles are covered in detail in Chapter 31.

AXLE HOUSINGS

Housing

Live rear axles use a one-piece housing, sometimes called a *banjo*. The banjo nickname comes from the bulge in the center of the housing. The bulge contains the differential (Figure 29-4). Two tubes extend from each side of the housing. These tubes enclose the axles and provide attachments for the axle bearings. The housing shields all parts from dirt and retains the differential lubricant.

In IRS or FWD systems the housing is in three parts. The center part houses the differential. The outer two parts support the axles by providing attachments for axle bearings. In the rear, these outer sections may

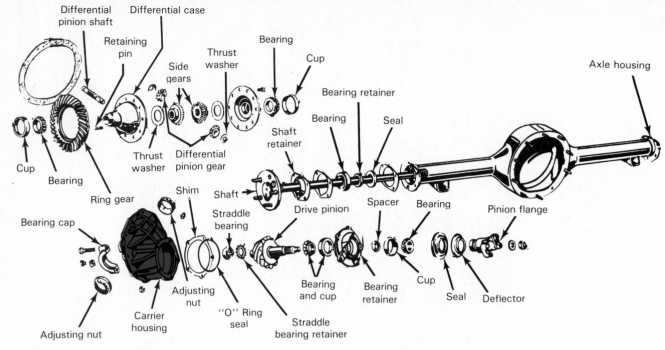

FIGURE 29-4   Axle housing and differential assembly. (Ford Motor Company)

be called the **uprights,** and in the front they are usually called the **steering knuckle.** Both uprights and steering knuckles double as suspension components and feature attachment points for steering gear, brakes, and suspension locating members.

AXLE SHAFTS

Live Axles

Designs   There are three ways of supporting the axles in a live axle design: full floating, three-quarter floating, and semifloating.

These terms refer to the way the axle bearing

FIGURE 29-5   Semifloating and full floating axles.

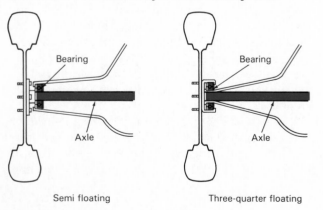

is placed in relation to the axle and housing. In the semifloating and three-quarter floating designs, the axle bearing allows some of the vehicle weight on the axle. In the full floating axle the bearing is on the outside of the axle housing. This places all vehicle weight on the axle housing (Figure 29-5). The axle transmits only torque that comes from the engine. The semifloating and three-quarter floating design axles also transmit torque besides carrying some vehicle load and side thrust from cornering.

Passenger cars use the more inexpensive semifloating and three-quarter floating axle designs. Trucks, especially heavy-duty pickups and larger vehicles, use the full floating design. A truck full floating axle is shown in Figure 29-6.

Independent Suspension

Swing Axle   Swing axles are a form of IRS. In a swing axle car, the differential is bolted to the chassis. The axles are U-jointed only where they meet the differential, not at the wheel end. This makes the wheels move in an arc as they rise and fall with the suspension (Figure 29-7). Swinging in an arc causes large camber changes and raises and lowers the center of the rear of the car. These motions combine to make the car tricky to drive in some situations, which is why swing axles are not found in many new cars. Swing axles were popular from the end of World War II through the 1960s because they were cheap to make and gave a softer ride than a simple live axle. Most newer IRS

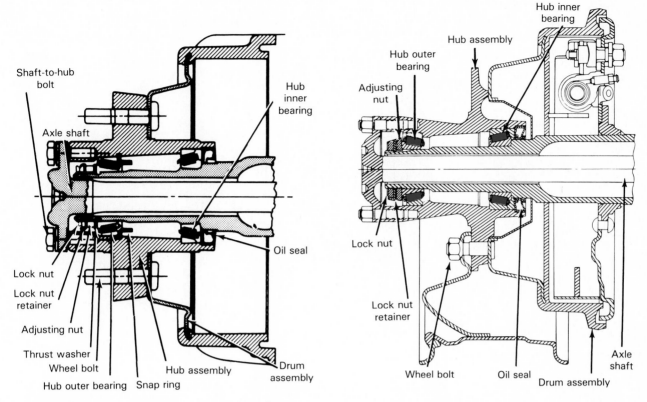

FIGURE 29-6 Full floating axle in a truck application.

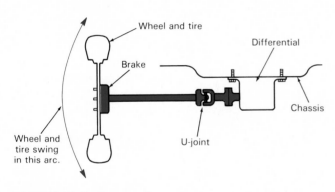

FIGURE 29-7 Swing axle.

systems use linkages and control arms to limit camber changes.

Front Drive Axles Front drive axles used with transaxles are the full floating type (Figure 29-8). Both ends of the axle shaft are splined and fitted with U-joints. The axles support no vehicle weight. As the vehicle goes over bumps, the axles move up and down. This movement changes their length. This is the reason the axles float and use universal joints. The inner CV joints let the axles slide in and out. This arrangement lets the wheels move straight up and down on the suspension. Therefore, the wheels and tires follow the road better for superior traction.

FIGURE 29-8 FWD axle. (General Motors Corporation)

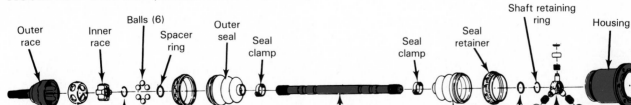

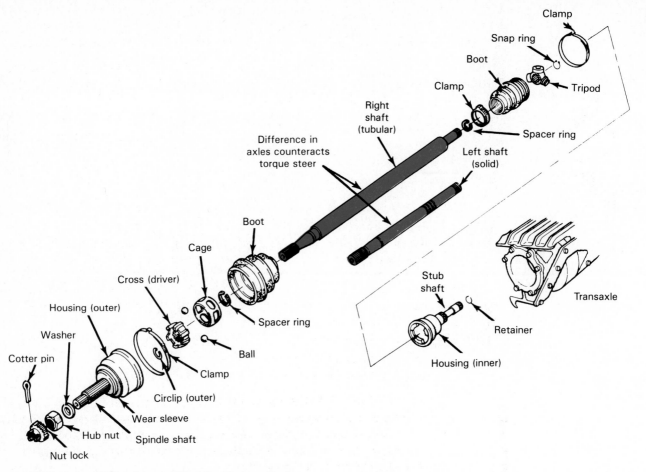

FIGURE 29-9   FWD axle set. (Chrysler Corporation)

Rubber boots protect the U-joints from grit and help seal in lubricating grease. Typically, FWD axles are solid bars of steel. If they are not equal in length, the longer one is usually thicker than the shorter. Or, one axle may be solid and the other tubular. Thus, both axles will flex the same due to engine power. If they flex unequally, the car will pull to one side under power. This is called *torque steering* (Figure 29-9).

DIFFERENTIALS

Operation

If both drive wheels always turned at the same speed, a differential would not be needed. The drive wheels often turn at different speeds, however, so a differential is required.

Different drive wheel speeds occur when one wheel loses traction and spins quickly or when going around a corner (Figure 29-10). Then the outside wheel turns faster than the inner because the outer wheel travels a farther distance in the same amount of time. A mechanism is needed to allow different axle speeds while still transmitting torque.

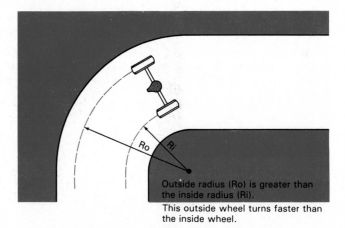

FIGURE 29-10   Speed differential in driven wheels.

Gears   The differential allows different axle speeds. It does this with a series of gears. The first gear is called the pinion or **drive pinion**. It is bolted to the drive shaft or is run directly by the mainshaft in a transaxle. The pinion teeth engage the **ring gear**. The ring gear is mounted upright, 90° to the pinion. Therefore, whenever the drive shaft turns, the pinion and ring gear turn also (Figure 29-11).

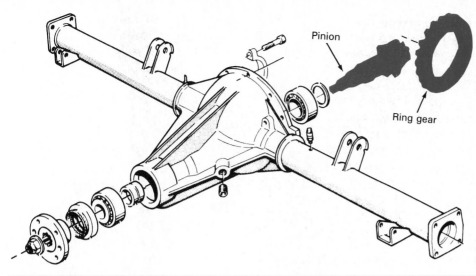

FIGURE 29-11 Drive pinion and ring gear. (Ford Motor Company)

Bolted to the ring gear is the **differential case** (Figure 29-12). The case extends to the side of the ring gear and houses four gears. Two of the gears are mounted so they slip over the ends of the axles. Because they are placed on the side of the differential case, they are called **side gears.** In between the side gears are the **pinion gears.** The pinion gears engage the side gears, thereby making a square of gears inside the differential case. Some differentials use two pinion and two side gears as just described. Others use four pinion gears.

When the vehicle is going straight down the road, the drive pinion rotates the ring gear, which rotates the differential case. The side gears turn in the same plane as the case; therefore, they transfer their motion to the axles. The axles are thus rotated, and the car moves forward.

When the car turns, the outer drive wheel must turn faster. At the same time, the inner wheel must

turn more slowly. The pinion gears make up the difference by rotating relative to the side gears. Their rotation transfers some of the inner axle's velocity to the outer side. Thus, an equal percentage of speed is removed from one axle and given to the other.

Bearings Four bearings are found in all differentials. The first two fit over the drive pinion and support it. The other two support the differential case and are usually mounted just outboard of the side gears. The drive pinion bearing is typically a tapered roller bearing, and the cage bearings are normally ball bearings (Figure 29-13).

Types of Differentials

Integral Versus Removable Carrier Differentials can be placed in one of two groups: integral or removable carrier. An integral carrier differential is constructed so it attaches directly to the rear axle housing (Figure 29-14). A cover fits over the rear of the differential. Differential service is done with the cover removed. The differential must be assembled and disassembled in the axle housing.

A removable carrier differential is arranged so the differential assembly can be removed from the axle housing as a unit (Figure 29-15). The differential can be serviced on the bench and then installed in the axle housing.

Special Traction Differentials A differential like the one just described is called an **open differential.** It is also called a conventional differential. There is no resistance to differential action in it, so it works smoothly and without power loss all the time. However, for some applications an open differential is not desirable.

You have probably been in a car which was stuck

FIGURE 29-12 Differential case. (Chrysler Corporation)

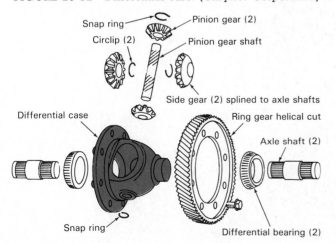

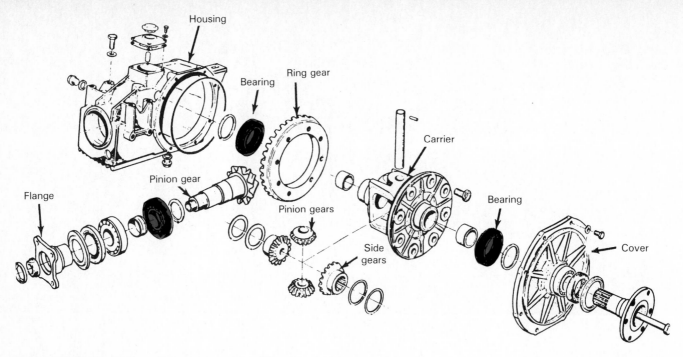

FIGURE 29-13 Differential components and bearings.

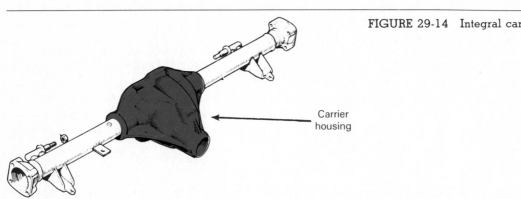

FIGURE 29-14 Integral carrier differential.

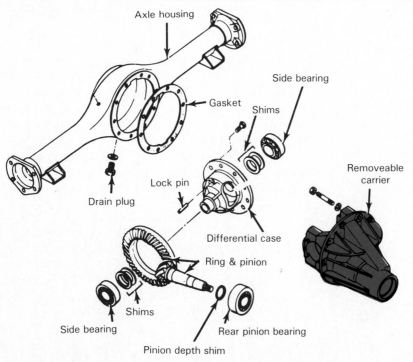

FIGURE 29-15 Removable carrier differential. (General Motors Corporation)

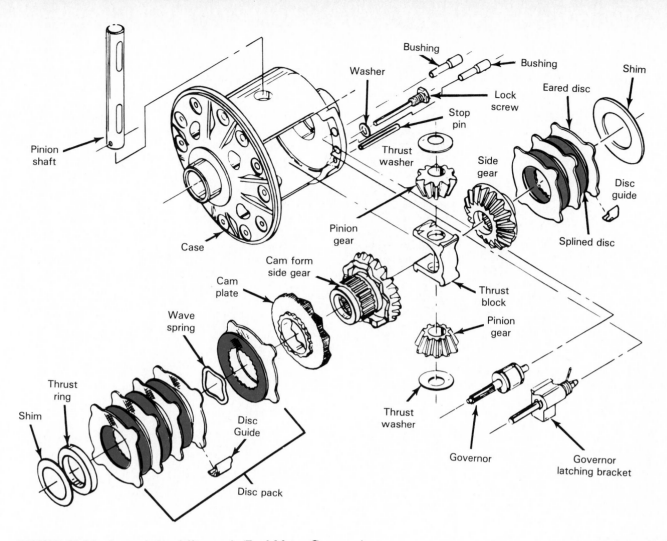

FIGURE 29-16 Limited slip differential. (Ford Motor Company)

in mud or snow. Perhaps you noticed how one drive wheel would spin and the other would remain stationary. This is an excellent example of a differential transferring 100% of torque and rotary motion to the drive wheel with the least resistance. Another word for resistance in this case is traction, and without traction, applying torque to a drive wheel does no good: The wheel just spins.

By adding a series of clutches to the differential case, differential action can be restricted. Then even if one drive wheel has no traction at all, the other wheel that may have some traction will at least get some torque. This is the theory behind the **limited slip differential.**

Limited Slip Differential Limited slip differentials are used on sports cars for increased traction while cornering and on off-road vehicles where the drive wheels are constantly losing traction.

Several friction discs (clutches) stacked together are commonly used to provide a limited slip (Figure 29-16). **Cone clutches** are also used. A cone clutch is simply a cone which fits inside another cone. Pressing the two cones together provides friction between them so they will rotate as one. When cone clutches are used in a limited slip differential, springs are used to preload the cones.

Most limited slip differentials transfer 20% of the available torque to the wheel with traction.

Locked Differential An unusual traction differential is the **locked differential.** Actually, it isn't a differential at all because the pinion and side gears are welded together and then are welded to the case. This locks, or stops, any differential action. Consequently, both drive wheels turn at the same speed all the time.

Locked differentials are used on race cars and some off-road vehicles. Obviously, they provide superior traction while cornering and traveling off the road, but they absorb horsepower, increase tire wear, and hurt fuel mileage. That's because the engine must provide the power to slip the drive wheels when both have traction and are turning.

Some trucks and tractors use differentials which can be locked and unlocked by pressing a button. This gives the advantages of both systems.

"YOU CAN'T WELD AN AXLE SHAFT!"

One major area of improvement in automobiles in the last 50 years has been metal quality. As a result, automobiles have become more reliable, simply because parts don't break in half as frequently. Even though our cars are more complicated, they are built of better alloys and plastics. We no longer have to carry a trunk full of spare parts on every trip. In fact, we don't even plan ahead. For an example, here's a true story about a trip from Michigan to New York.

We were taking my 1930 Durant from Dearborn to Dunkirk, New York in 1974. I'd had the car for 10 or 15 years, and never had any trouble. Because it was so reliable, I was able to convince my friend Oscar to go with me.

We had driven for several hours on the Interstate when the engine suddenly raced higher, while the car slowed down. I knew something had broken—

something serious. We coasted to the side of the road and got out. When I shook the left rear wheel, it almost fell off in my hand. The axle shaft had snapped right off. Oscar began to regret coming along.

I talked him into walking back a couple miles and getting a tow truck, while I wondered what to do. The truck hauled us, with the Durant, to a nearby station. The owner shook his head and said we could use some tools, but said he didn't work on cars that were 40 years old. As soon as we had the car off the ground, the wheel fell off. The axle had snapped in the middle. I told Oscar we'd have to weld it back together.

Once again he started complaining. And rightfully so. You can't weld an axle shaft and expect it to hold. So I sent him off for some cold drinks. When he returned, I explained the plan. We would take the seat out of the Durant

and remove a metal bar that formed part of the seat frame. With a little machine work, it would make a perfect axle. Oscar almost cried, but he helped me remove the seat.

Under the seat was a paper cylinder, and in the cylinder was a brand-new axle shaft. Oscar was so mad he almost hit me. I was laughing so hard I didn't care. Way back when I bought the Durant, I had noticed the axle shaft under the seat. Some previous owner (thinking ahead) had stored it there. We pressed on the bearings, slid the new shaft into place, and were on our way again. I had a good laugh, and Oscar learned a lesson on preparing for a trip in an old car.

Lynn Meeker
Orchard St. Automotive
San Diego, CA

Differential Gearing

Gears The ring and pinion gears are *hypoid* gears. This is a special gear pattern which allows mating the two gears off their centerlines (Figure 29-17). Straight bevel or spiral cut gears can be used, but they require the pinion and ring to meet at their centerlines. Also, these gears are noisy.

Hypoid gear teeth slide against each other when they contact. This produces extremely high pressures between them. Because of the high pressures, only special, hypoid-type lubricant should be used in drive axles.

The reason that mating the gears off their center-

lines is important is vehicle height. By lowering the drive pinion gear on the ring gear, the entire drive shaft can be lowered. This in turn lowers the drive shaft and also the drive shaft tunnel. The results are more passenger room and a lower-riding vehicle.

Gear Ratios Gear ratios express the number of turns one gear makes compared to one turn of its partner. In drive axles the gear ratio is found between the drive pinion and the ring gear.

The ring gear always turns slower than the drive pinion. This lets the ring gear trade speed for torque. Thus, the drive axle multiplies the torque received from the transmission.

On cars with automatic transmissions the torque converter also multiplies engine torque. Therefore, the drive axle doesn't need to multiply the torque much more. A 2.8:1 ring gear to drive pinion ratio is common with automatic transmission.

A 2.8:1 ratio means the drive pinion must turn 2.8 times to rotate the ring gear 1 time. This is commonly referred to as the gear ratio, rear axle ratio, or **final drive ratio.**

With manual transmissions more torque multiplication is needed. Then a 3.5:1 final drive ratio is normal. For faster acceleration some sports cars use 4:1 final drive ratios. Trucks also use final drives with 4:1 or 5:1 ratios. This allows them to pull heavy loads.

Selecting a final drive ratio cannot be done without certain trade-offs. Many factors go into selecting

FIGURE 29-17 Hypoid gears. (General Motors Corporation)

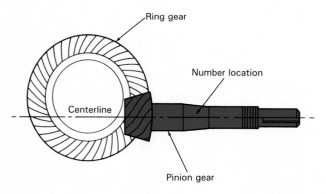

Ring gear

Number location

Centerline

Pinion gear

the final drive ratio. Among them are vehicle weight, engine rpm range, designed vehicle speed, frontal area, fuel economy requirements, engine power output, and transmission type.

Final drives with ratios around 2.5:1 will take longer to accelerate but will give a faster top speed. Such cars are said to be *high geared*. At the other end of the scale, a 4.11:1 ratio will give faster acceleration with a lower top speed. This is *low gearing*. Since the emphasis on fuel economy in the 1970s, most cars have tended toward high gearing.

Determining Final Drive Ratio There are several ways to determine the final drive ratio. If the shop manual is available, it will give a code which can be found on the drive axle (Figure 29-18). You can decode the code into the final drive ratio using a table in the shop manual.

Another way to find the final drive ratio is to compare the number of revolutions of the drive wheels with those of the drive shaft. If both wheels are turned simultaneously, the ratio can be read directly. Note how many times the drive wheels turn for one turn of the drive shaft.

If the final drive is open, count the number of teeth on both the drive pinion and ring gear. Divide the ring gear teeth number by the pinion drive number to get the final drive ratio.

FIGURE 29-18 GM axle ratio codes. (General Motors Corporation)

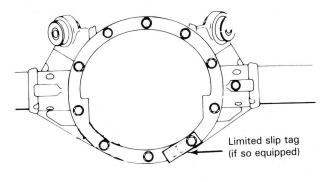
Limited slip tag
(if so equipped)

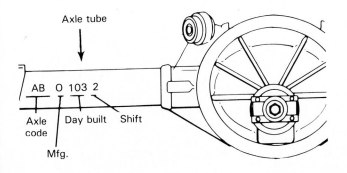
Axle tube
AB O 103 2
Axle code | Day built | Shift
Mfg.

FINAL DRIVE SERVICE

Most all final drive complaints are noise related (Figure 29-19). Road testing is therefore very useful in determining the problem. Common noise sources are the axle, differential bearings, and gear whine. Axle bearings tend to "rumble," whereas differential bearings and gears whine.

Drive pinion and case bearing noise and gear whine between the pinion and ring gear is most noticeable when the vehicle is either coasting (vehicle momentum is driving the engine) or accelerating (engine is driving the vehicle). The noise will change with throttle position. At a constant speed (neither coasting nor accelerating) the noise will usually not be heard. It is not too important to distinguish between case bearing or pinion bearing noise because both bearing sets are serviced using similar procedures. Once these parts are exposed, it is easy to determine which bearing set is causing the noise. Since pinion bearings rotate more than case bearings, the pinion failure rate is a little higher.

It is important to distinguish between axle bearing noise and pinion or carrier bearing noise. Axle bearing failure and noise is a lot more common than pinion or carrier bearing failure. Bad axle bearings make a constant rumbling noise which does not change much with vehicle speed. The rumbling noise may get louder with vehicle speed, but changing throttle position at a given speed won't change axle bearing noise. The noise does change with defective pinion or carrier bearings.

Differential Noise

Because all differential motion is relative when both axles are turning at the same speed, you must listen for differential noise while the vehicle is turning. If this is the only time excessive noise is present, the differential should be inspected for wear or damage. Some noise in limited slip differentials is normal when making turns on paved, high-traction roads. The "clunking" reported by most drivers comes from the clutch pack slipping as it lets the outside wheel speed up. Some manufacturers sell a lubricant additive to quiet the noise.

Lubrication

Final drive fluid types and capacities should be checked in a service manual for the vehicle you are servicing. Some front-wheel final drive units use the same lubricant for the transmission and differential. Other car makers have separate areas and lubricants for the transmission and differential sections.

NOTE — This is a general trouble shooting guide. When using this guide, locate the condition in column one that corresponds to your problem and determine the possible causes in column two. Match the number of the possible cause with the same number in column three, and you will have the suggested correction.

CONDITION	POSSIBLE CAUSE	CORRECTION
▶ Rear wheel noise	1) Wheel loose 2) Faulty, worn wheel bearings	1) Tighten lug nuts 2) Replace bearings
▶ Axle shaft noise	1) Misaligned axle housing 2) Bent or sprung axle 3) Pinion bearing end play 4) Excessive ring gear backlash 5) Incorrect pinion bearing adjustment 6) Loose companion flange nut 7) Incorrect wheel bearing adjustment 8) Scuffed tooth contact surfaces	1) Check alignment and correct 2) Replace axle shaft 3) Check pinion bearing preload 4) Check backlash and adjust 5) Adjust pinion bearings 6) Tighten nut to specification 7) Adjust wheel bearings 8) Adjust or replace gears
▶ Rear axle breakage	1) Incorrect wheel bearing adjustment 2) Misaligned axle housing 3) Vehicle overloaded 4) Clutch grabs	1) Replace axle, adjust bearing 2) Replace shaft and correct alignment 3) Replace axle, reduce vehicle load 4) Replace axle, repair clutch
▶ Differential case breakage	1) Incorrect differential bearing adjustment 2) Excessive ring gear clearance 3) Vehicle overloaded 4) Erratic clutch operation	1) Check gears and bearings for damage, reassemble and adjust bearings 2) Check gears and bearings for damage, reassemble and adjust bearings 3) Check gears and bearings for damage, reduce vehicle load 4) Check gears and bearings for damage, avoid erratic clutch use
▶ Broken differential side gear	1) Excessive housing deflection 2) Worn thrust washers 3) Misaligned axle housing	1) Replace damaged gears, check other gears for damage and check axle housing alignment 2) Replace damaged gears, check other gears for damage and replace worn thrust washers 3) Replace damaged gears, check other gears for damage and check axle housing alignment
▶ Differential gears scored	1) Insufficient lubricant 2) Incorrect lubricant 3) One wheel spins excessively	1) Replace scored gears and fill rear axle to capacity with correct lubricant 2) Replace scored gears, clean housing and fill rear axle to capacity with correct lubricant 3) Replace scored gears and service as necessary
▶ Ring gear and pinion tooth breakage	1) Vehicle overloaded 2) Erratic clutch operation 3) Ice spotted pavement 4) Normal fatigue 5) Incorrect adjustment	1) Replace gears, reduce vehicle load 2) Replace gears and avoid erratic clutch operation 3) Replace gears 4) Replace gears and examine other components for fatigue 5) Replace gears and examine other components for wear. Make sure ring gear backlash is correct

FIGURE 29-19 Drive axle troubleshooting.

Some common transmission/differential lubricant combinations include the following:

1. 90W gear oil in the differential *and* the transmission
2. 90W gear oil in the differential and ATF in the transmission
3. ATF in *both* the transmission and the differential.

Many new models recommend using ATF in a manual transaxle because it is "thinner" (lower viscosity) and improves shifting effort and fuel economy. These cars can use 90W gear oil if desired (to reduce gear noise, for example).

All final drives should be checked for the proper amount of lubricant at the specific intervals. This is done by removing a plug and seeing if lubricant runs out. If it does not, *top off* the housing with fresh lube until it flows from the plug.

Removing Front Final Drives

Front final drives are integral with the transmission case and bellhousing units in most vehicles. This is true for automatic as well as for standard transaxle equipped vehicles. As a result, to service the final drive, you must remove and disassemble the transaxle. Transaxle R&R (remove and replace) procedures differ from vehicle to vehicle and are covered in Chapter 32.

Removing Rear Final Drives

Removable carrier final drives are removed from the axle housing for service. Integral carrier types are serviced in the vehicle unless work is to be done on the rear axle housing itself.

Removable Carrier   General removal procedures for the removable carrier type pictured in Figures 29-15 follow:

1. Raise the vehicle and support it on jack stands. You can raise the vehicle by using a hoist, but once the differential is removed, the vehicle must remain on the hoist until the job is complete. This is not economically feasible. Hoists should be used only for quick service work or diagnostic procedures. Leaving vehicles on the hoist for long periods of time is too expensive.
2. Mark and remove the drive shaft. Cap the transmission extension housing with an old yoke or plug so the transmission fluid will not run out the back of the transmission.
3. Remove the tires, wheels, and brake drums to gain access to the axle shafts. The axle shafts must be removed. Most axles simply slide out, although many need a slide hammer to get them started (Figure 29-20). Others may have a set screw holding them to the hub. Remove the set screw and then pull the axle from the housing.
4. Support the differential housing with a jack and re-

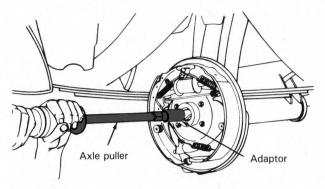

FIGURE 29-20   Removing axle with a slide hammer. (Ford Motor Company)

move all the attaching bolts. Then move the carrier housing forward and down. To install the carrier housing, reverse the removal procedure.

Integral Carrier   Disassembling a removable carrier differential requires detailed instructions. Therefore, use a shop manual to disassemble an integral carrier differential.

As an overview, the axles must be removed first. The differential cover is removed, and the case and ring gear are removed through the back. The drive pinion is removed through the front.

Another difference between integral and removable carrier disassembly is axle retention. Integral carriers may retain the axles at the differential end with C clips. The cover must be removed and the clips pulled before the axles can be removed.

Ring and Pinion Adjustment

Most front final drives use helical cut gears. This eliminates gear tooth contact patterns. All other final drives use hypoid gears that do leave a pattern. These patterns can be examined to see if the differential is correctly adjusted (Figure 29-21).

Anytime the pinion or carrier bearings are replaced or inspected, the bearing preload, pinion gear depth, and the ring and pinion gear tooth patterns must be checked and adjusted. These procedures also apply for ring and pinion gear replacement.

Pinion Depth   The pinion gear depth is adjusted with shims. The shims are placed in the housing, and the rear pinion bearing cup is installed. Some differentials use a different procedure; for specific information, consult the car's shop manual.

There are two ways to determine pinion depth. If you are reusing the old pinion and ring gear, assemble the pinion bearing on the pinion shaft and tighten the pinion nut to approximately 15 ft-lb. Do not install the seal at this time. Using a pinion depth gauge, pictured in Figure 29-22, measure the pinion depth. Com-

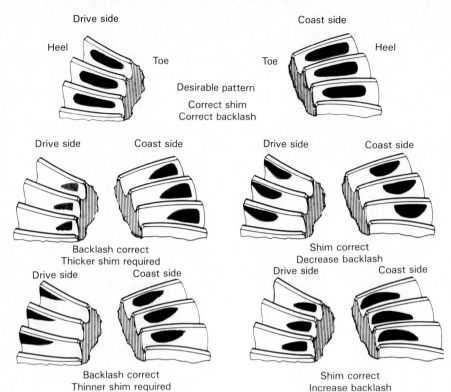

Drive side   Coast side

Heel   Toe   Toe   Heel

Desirable pattern
Correct shim
Correct backlash

Drive side   Coast side   Drive side   Coast side

Backlash correct
Thicker shim required

Shim correct
Decrease backlash

Drive side   Coast side   Drive side   Coast side

Backlash correct
Thinner shim required

Shim correct
Increase backlash

FIGURE 29-21 Hypoid gear patterns.

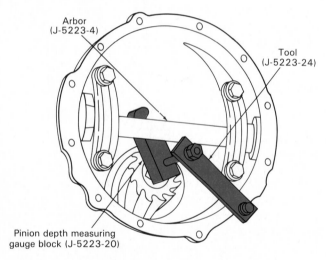

Arbor
(J-5223-4)

Tool
(J-5223-24)

Pinion depth measuring
gauge block (J-5223-20)

FIGURE 29-22 Pinion depth gauge. (General Motors Corporation)

pare the result to the desired pinion depth. If the measurements are equal, further adjustment is not required. If this measurement is not correct, remove or add the necessary shims until the desired measurement is obtained.

The other method is a bit easier. Using the old pinion gear, look at the pinion depth adjustment figure (Figure 29-23). Go to the pinion variance chart for that particular pinion and start at the left under "old pinion marking." Move right until you come to the vertical

column under "new pinion marking" that is the same as the number on the new pinion gear. For our example, we will say the new pinion gear is marked with a −2. In this case we would add 0.004 in. of additional shims.

Pinion Bearing Preload   Pinion bearing preload is set by tightening the pinion nut. This crushes the collapsible pinion spacer until the desired number of inch-pounds are required to turn the shaft. See Figure 29-2 for a picture of the collapsible pinion spacer. Note that while rotating the pinion shaft several revolutions with the pinion seal installed, you are looking for about 17–27 in-lb to rotate the pinion shaft. This is with a new collapsible spacer. Also, the pinion nut has been tightened to approximately 170 ft-lb. Do not overtighten and then loosen the pinion nut to get the desired inch-pounds torque reading; this tightening and loosening will damage the collapsible spacer and will require its replacement. For exact procedures and specifications, use a shop manual for the vehicle you are servicing.

Another method of pinion bearing preloading uses a selective fit washer. It is placed on the pinion shaft between the shaft and the inner bearing race (Figure 29-24). The procedure for selecting the proper washer is similar to the method described above.

Gear Tooth Patterns   Adjusting gear tooth patterns and carrier bearing preload are part of installing the ring gear. After the pinion depth and bearing preload

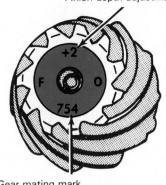

Pinion depth adjustment figure

Gear mating mark
(same as on ring gear)

PINION DEPTH SHIM ADJUSTMENT CHART (INCHES)									
Old Pinion	And here →				New Pinion				
	−1	−3	−2	−1	0	+1	+2	+3	+4
+4	+0.008	+0.007	+0.006	+0.005	+0.004	+0.003	+0.002	+0.001	0
+3	+0.007	+0.006	+0.005	+0.004	+0.003	+0.002	+0.001	0	−0.001
+2	+0.006	+0.005	+0.004	+0.003	+0.002	+0.001	0	−0.001	−0.002
+1	+0.005	+0.004	+0.003	+0.002	+0.001	0	−0.001	−0.002	−0.003
0	+0.004	+0.003	+0.002	+0.001	0	−0.001	−0.002	−0.003	−0.004
−1	+0.003	+0.002	+0.001	0	−0.001	−0.002	−0.003	−0.004	−0.005
−2	+0.002	+0.001	0	−0.001	−0.002	−0.003	−0.004	−0.005	−0.006
−3	+0.001	0	−0.001	−0.002	−0.003	−0.004	−0.005	−0.006	−0.007
−4	0	−0.001	−0.002	−0.003	−0.004	−0.005	−0.006	−0.007	−0.008

Look here ↳

FIGURE 29-23   Pinion variance chart (typical).

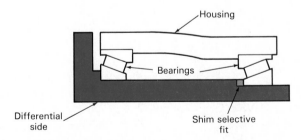

FIGURE 29-24   Pinion preload selective fit washer.

is set, the ring gear is ready to be installed. To check the gear tooth pattern, paint several ring gear teeth with nondrying Prussian blue. Its more common name is *bluing.* Rotate the ring gear so the blued teeth touch the pinion gear. Examine the pattern on the ring gear. It should look like the correct patterns in Figure 29-

21. If it does not, use the pictures shown in Figure 29-21 and correct as necessary by changing the appropriate shims or adjusting the threaded adjusters. The tool in Figure 29-25 is used to gain access to the shims. It's called a spreader tool because it spreads the housing. When using the spreader tool, do not spread the differential case more than 0.010 in. (0.25 mm). Do not leave spreader tension on the case, or damage could result.

Another aspect of setting the gear tooth patterns is ring gear runout and backlash. Both measurements are done with dial indicators and affect tooth patterns. Ring gear runout is any deviation of the ring gear in a motion parallel with the axles. Backlash shows if the ring gear is mounted close enough to the pinion gear, or is too far away. Use a shop manual for these and all other differential operations. The procedures differ widely among differential designs.

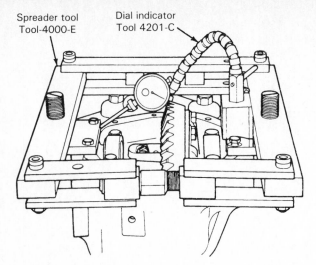

FIGURE 29-25 Spreader tool. (Ford Motor Company)

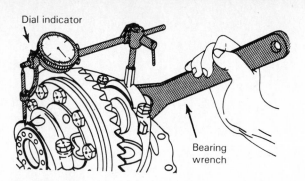

FIGURE 29-26 Adjusting case bearing preload.

When servicing rear final drive units with removable carriers, ring gear and case bearing preload is accomplished by moving the case bearing adjusting nuts (Figure 29-26). No shims are used. Again, use the proper service manual for exact procedures and specifications.

Seals and Bearings

Pinion Seals Pinion seals can be replaced without complete disassembly of the final drive unit. The pinion shaft nut and U-joint yoke are removed, and then the old seal is pried out. If you encounter a leaking pinion shaft seal and the pinion shaft nut is loose, do not attempt to replace the seal without further inspections. Other damage may be found, and replacement of the complete differential unit may be necessary. If seal replacement is to be done, mark the pinion nut so you can tighten it the same amount when you reassemble the shaft with a new seal. Look at Figure 29-2 for a picture of the pinion seal. This seal works on the universal joint yoke.

Rear Wheel Bearing Service Noise is the primary reason rear wheel bearings are replaced. And replacement is the only service normally done to rear wheel bearings, because after the original packing, repacking is not required on most late-model vehicles.

There are three major types of rear wheel bearings used in passenger cars today: ball bearings, roller bearings, and tapered roller bearings.

Axle Shaft Removal Axle removal is required for bearing replacement. Check the shop manual for specific R&R procedures for the vehicle you are working on. As a general rule, you can tell the type of bearing and its removal procedure by taking off the rear wheel and brake drum. Then examine the axle shaft to see if it is held in by a retainer and three or four bolts (Figure 29-27). If it is, you do not have to remove the differential cover to remove the axle. The ball and tapered roller bearing equipped axle shafts are retained in this manner. To remove the axle, remove the four bolts that hold the retainer to the backing plate. Then pull the axle out. Usually the axle shaft will slide out without the aid of a puller, but sometimes a puller is required.

FIGURE 29-27 Externally retained axle. (Ford Motor Company)

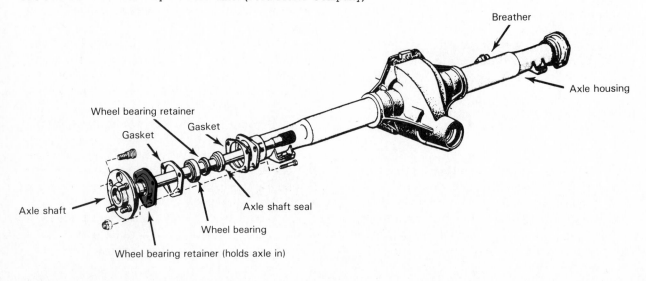

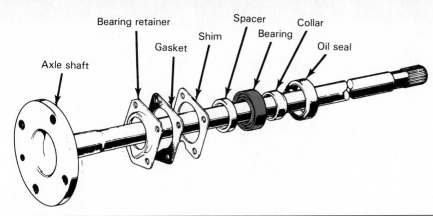

Axle shaft
Bearing retainer
Gasket
Shim
Spacer
Bearing
Collar
Oil seal

FIGURE 29-28 Ball bearing axle bearing.

The roller bearing equipped axle shaft does not have a retainer at the backing plate. Instead, it uses a C washer to retain the axle shaft. This C washer is inside the differential. (See Figure 29-23). The differential cover must be removed to gain access to the C washer. After you have taken off the wheel, brake drum, and differential cover, remove the differential pinion shaft retaining bolt and differential pinion shaft. Push the axle shaft in and remove the C washer and then pull the axle out of the housing.

We'll discuss the axle bearings one at a time, beginning with the ball bearing type (Figure 29-28). This type of bearing is lubricated with grease packed in the bearing at the factory. Final drive oil does not lubricate this bearing. An inner seal rides on the axle shaft, just in front of the retaining ring. It keeps the final drive oil from entering the bearing. The bearing has an outer seal to keep grease out of the brakes.

To replace the axle bearing, first remove the retaining ring (Figure 29-29). Then place the axle shaft in a press and press the bearing off. This is a machine shop operation, and you must follow the proper safety procedures.

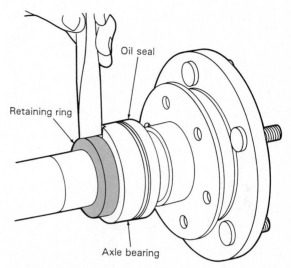

Oil seal
Retaining ring
Axle bearing

FIGURE 29-29 Removing axle bearing retaining ring. (American Motors Corporation)

Roller Bearing Axles Roller bearings use the same lubricating oil used in the final drive unit. Only one seal per axle shaft is then needed (Figure 29-30). To

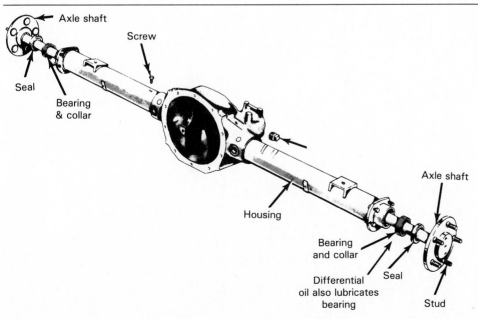

Axle shaft
Screw
Seal
Bearing & collar
Housing
Bearing and collar
Differential oil also lubricates bearing
Seal
Axle shaft
Stud

FIGURE 29-30 Roller bearing supported axle. (Chrysler Corporation)

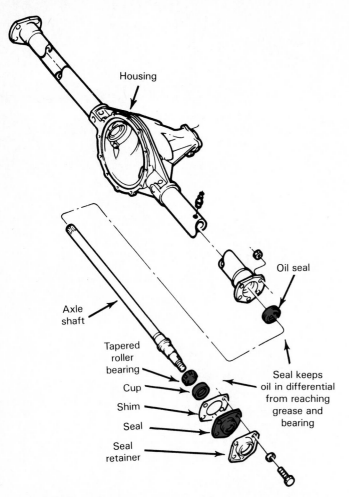

Housing

Oil seal

Axle
shaft

Tapered
roller
bearing

Cup

Shim

Seal

Seal
retainer

Seal keeps
oil in differential
from reaching
grease and
bearing

FIGURE 29-31 Tapered roller bearing supported axle.
(American Motors Corporation)

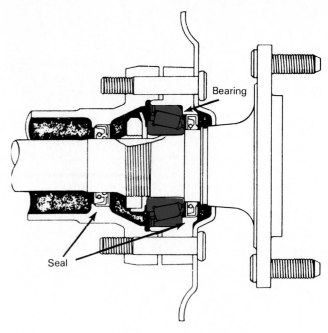

Bearing

Seal

FIGURE 29-32 Tapered roller bearing installation.

replace the bearing, remove the axle and seal and then
pull the bearing out of the final drive housing. Inspect
the axle shaft where it rides on the bearing for pits
or scores. Remember, in this application the axle shaft
is the bearing inner race. If pits or score marks are
present, replace the axle. No press is needed to remove
this type of axle bearing.

Tapered Bearing Axles   Tapered bearings do not use
drive axle oil lubrication (Figure 29-31). An inner oil
seal keeps oil in the final drive housing from getting
into the bearing. An outer seal keeps the grease in
the bearing and does not allow it to reach the backing
plate or brakes (Figure 29-32).

This style of bearing must be pressed on and
off the axle shaft using a press. After you have installed
the new bearing, you must pack it with wheel bearing
grease. After packing the bearing, install the axle in
the housing.

Check axle shaft end play with a dial indicator
and adjust it to the specifications listed in the shop
manual. If the end play is less than the specified
amount, add a thicker bearing shim. If the end play
is greater than the specified amount, use a thinner axle
bearing shim.

TRADE TERMS

Cone Clutches
Differential Case
Drive Pinion
Final Drive Ratio
IRS
Limited Slip Differential
Live Axles
Locked Differential

Open Differential
Pinion Gears
Ring Gear
Side Gears
Steering Knuckle
Transaxle
Uprights

REVIEW QUESTIONS

1. What are the three jobs of all drive axles?

2. In what type of live axle system do the axles carry only torque and side loads?

3. The effective length of axles used in FWD cars must change as the suspension moves. Do you think the axle is longest or shortest when the suspension is fully extended (wheels hanging free)?

4. What percentage of available torque does the differential give to each drive wheel while the vehicle is going straight down the road?

5. When rounding a curve, the (inner, outer) drive wheel must turn faster?

6. What is an open differential?

7. What do hypoid gears allow car designers to do?

8. If a car has a 3.55 final drive ratio, how many times must the drive pinion rotate to make the wheels rotate once?

9. Some FWD transaxles use ATF to lubricate the final drive. True or false?

10. Clutch packs in limited slip differentials are preloaded. True or false?

30

Manual Transmissions

INTRODUCTION

One basic feature of all car engines is that they are all high-speed engines. This means they all run at relatively high rpm, such as 1500–5000 rpm. Internal combustion engines need help getting a car moving because they don't generate enough power at low rpm. Some sort of *torque multiplication* is needed. Multiplying torque is the transmission's job. Cars may have from two to five forward gear ratios, while large trucks may have ten to fifteen gears (Figure 30-1). The number of gears needed depends on engine torque, the load to be moved, and the speed of the vehicle. Large American cars used to have automatic transmissions with only two gears, as did some light Honda models. Now the trend is toward four-speed and five-speed transmissions (both manual and automatic).

TORQUE MULTIPLICATION

The rotational force of wheels, shafts, and gears is called torque. Torque is a twisting form of energy. When you drive a screw or tighten a bolt, you are applying torque to do work. Torque is necessary wher-

OBJECTIVES

When you have completed this chapter, you should be able to

- Explain why transmissions are used
- Show how power flows through a manual transmission
- Explain what a synchronizer is
- Explain what an overdrive unit is and how it works
- Explain how manual transmissions are shifted

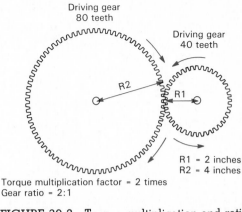

Torque multiplication factor = 2 times
Gear ratio = 2:1

FIGURE 30-2 Torque multiplication and ratio.

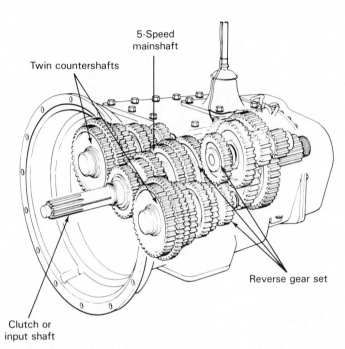

FIGURE 30-1 Multi-speed truck transmission. (Eaton Corporation)

ever circular or rotational work needs to be done. Many objects require torque and the ability to change it. A mechanical clock movement uses gear trains to drive the hour, minute, and second hands at different speeds—all from the same motor. A block and tackle uses pulleys and rope to multiply torque to lift heavy weights. In manual transmissions, gears of different diameters and numbers of teeth are combined to multiply torque.

Units of Torque

The unit of measurement of torque is pound-feet (lb-ft), sometimes called foot-pounds. Smaller amounts of torque are measured in pound-inches (lb-in.), also called inch-pounds. One (1) ft.-lb. is equal to 12 in.-

lbs. In the metric system, the unit is the Newton-meter (N.m.) or kilogram-meter (mkg).

A gear train consisting of a driving gear with a radius of 2 in. and containing 40 teeth and a driven gear with a radius of 4 in. and 80 teeth will have a **torque multiplication** factor of 2× (Figure 30-2). Thus, it will double the amount of torque applied to it.

TRANSMISSION GEARS

Types of Gears

Several different types of gears have been used in transmissions. Early transmissions used **straight cut** spur gears which were easier to machine but were noisy and difficult to shift. Modern manual transmissions use **helical-cut gears.** These gears get their name from being cut in a *helix*—a form of curve. This curve is more difficult to machine but reduces gear noise.

Gear material and design give the gears enough strength to withstand the very high pressures between torque-transmitting gears.

Further changes in gear design are unlikely because the noise and efficiency levels of modern gears are excellent. Most future gear improvements will deal with lighter-weight gears.

Gear Ratios

Gear ratios express the mathematical relationship of one gear to another. Gear ratios can be varied by changing the diameter and number of teeth of the gears.

Figuring Ratios A gear ratio expresses the amount of torque multiplication between two gears. We have already seen an example in which a 2-in-radius 40-tooth gear and a 4-in-radius 80-tooth gear gave a torque multiplication of 2× (Figure 30-2). Expressed as a ratio, with the smaller gear driving the larger gear, this would be 2:1. The ratio is obtained by dividing the diameter or number of teeth of the driven gear by the diameter or teeth of the drive gear. If the smaller driving gear had 10 teeth and the larger gear had 40 teeth, the ratio would be 4:1.

The ratio tells you how many times the smaller, driving gear has to turn to rotate the larger, driven gear once. With a 2:1 ratio, the smaller gear must turn twice to rotate the larger gear once. At 4:1 the smaller gear must rotate four times to turn the larger gear once.

Another aspect of torque multiplication is speed. When torque is multiplied, speed decreases an equal amount. When torque is diminished, speed is increased an equal amount. Therefore, with a 4:1 ratio, the larger gear gets four times the torque and turns only one fourth as fast. With a 2:1 ratio the larger gear gets twice the torque and turns half as fast as the smaller driving gear (Figure 30-3).

Gear Spacing   Another aspect of gear ratios is their spacing. Spacing is the "distance" between gear ratios of the various gears. For example, on a four-speed transmission, first gear may be a 3.63:1 ratio, second gear a 2.37:1 ratio, third gear a 1.41:1 ratio, and fourth gear a 1:1 ratio. From this point, we'll use the common practice of dropping the :1 part of the ratio. Thus, 3.63:1 is written simply as 3.63.

In a **close ratio** transmission for the same car, the ratios could be 2.57 in first, 1.72 in second, 1.26 in third, and 1 in fourth gear. Fourth gear is the same in both transmissions, but the close ratio gearbox moves the three lower gears closer to fourth. This makes the car more difficult to start from a dead stop but gives faster acceleration once the car is rolling. Figure 30-4 charts the **wide ratio** and close ratio examples. Note the large differences between overall gear ratios, especially for first and second gear.

Final Drive Ratio   When considering gear ratios, don't forget that the transmission ratios are further increased by the final drive ratio. Go back to the example of

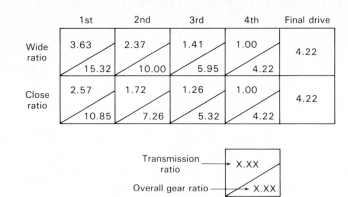

	1st	2nd	3rd	4th	Final drive
Wide ratio	3.63 / 15.32	2.37 / 10.00	1.41 / 5.95	1.00 / 4.22	4.22
Close ratio	2.57 / 10.85	1.72 / 7.26	1.26 / 5.32	1.00 / 4.22	4.22

Transmission ratio → X.XX
Overall gear ratio → X.XX

FIGURE 30-4   Wide versus close ratios.

third gear in close ratio. The 1.26 ratio turns the drive pinion in the final drive once for every 1.26 crankshaft revolutions. The final drive ratio further reduces the speed and increases the torque. Just how much depends, of course, on what the final drive ratio is. Typical final drives are between 2.5 and 4.5:1. The final result is called the **overall gear ratio** and is obtained by multiplying the transmission gear ratio by the final drive ratio.

BASIC CONSTRUCTION

To understand **synchronizer** function, it is necessary to understand the basics of manual transmission construction (Figure 30-5).

Shafts

Torque from the engine reaches the transmission via the clutch. The clutch disc is splined to the clutch **input shaft.** The input shaft enters the transmission case, where it is supported by a large ball bearing. Just inside the transmission case, the input shaft ends. This end of the input shaft is fitted with a gear. A second shaft, called the **mainshaft,** or output shaft, pilots off the input shaft.

This second shaft then runs the length of the transmission case and exits at the rear, where it is supported by a large ball bearing.

Underneath the input shaft gear and the mainshaft is the **countergear.** The countergear is fitted with several gears, all in one piece. One of the countergears is meshed with the gear on the input shaft. Therefore, whenever the input shaft turns, the countergear turns too. The other gears on the countergear mesh with gears slipped onto the mainshaft. These gears are free to rotate on the mainshaft. Only when a gear is selected by the driver is it locked to the mainshaft.

Such a system, in which the gears are constantly meshed together, is called **constant mesh.** Locking the

FIGURE 30-3   Torque and speed distribution in a 2:1 ratio gearset.

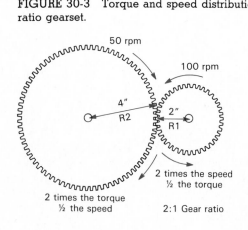

50 rpm

100 rpm

4" R2

2" R1

2 times the speed ½ the torque

2 times the torque ½ the speed

2:1 Gear ratio

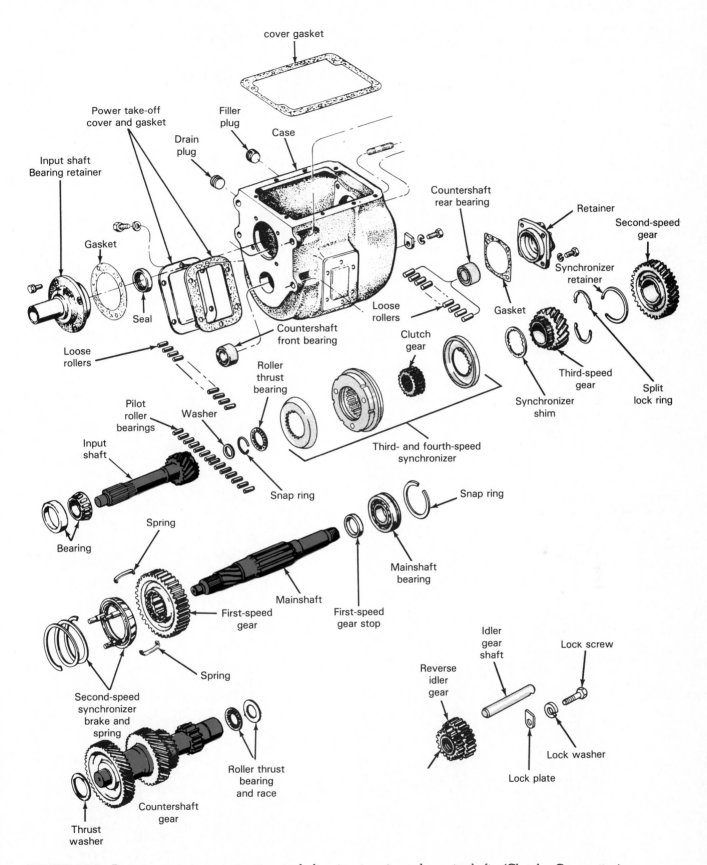

cover gasket

Power take-off
cover and gasket

Filler
plug

Drain
plug

Case

Input shaft
Bearing retainer

Countershaft
rear bearing

Retainer

Second-speed
gear

Gasket

Synchronizer
retainer

Seal

Loose
rollers

Countershaft
front bearing

Loose
rollers

Gasket

Third-speed
gear

Split
lock ring

Loose
rollers

Clutch
gear

Synchronizer
shim

Roller
thrust
bearing

Pilot
roller
bearings

Washer

Third- and fourth-speed
synchronizer

Input
shaft

Snap ring

Snap ring

Spring

Mainshaft
bearing

Bearing

First-speed
gear

Mainshaft

First-speed
gear stop

Spring

Idler
gear
shaft

Lock screw

Reverse
idler
gear

Second-speed
synchronizer
brake and
spring

Roller thrust
bearing
and race

Lock washer

Countershaft
gear

Lock plate

Thrust
washer

FIGURE 30-5 Basic transmission construction, including input, main, and countershafts. (Chrysler Corporation)

gears to the mainshaft is part of the *synchronizer's* job. Because the gears can be locked to the shaft only when both are turning at the same speed, the synchronizer must bring the gears to the shaft's speed.

Synchronizers

Parts Synchronizers consist of a hub, sleeve, blocking ring, and inserts or spring and ball detent devices (Figure 30-6). The hub is internally splined so it will slide on the mainshaft. The hub is also externally splined so the sleeve can slide on it. The inside of the sleeve is splined to mate with the hub, and the outside of the sleeve is grooved to accept the shifting fork. The inserts or spring and ball detent assemblies fit in the hub under the sleeve. In the neutral position, the inserts or balls keep the sleeve lightly locked into position on the hub.

Operation When the gear is selected, the shifting fork forces the sleeve out of the neutral position. This compresses the inserts or balls against their springs. The sleeve moves down the hub toward the gear. The gear, be it first, second, or third, has three areas (Figure 30-7). The first area contains the helical cut gears that transmit torque, the second is a cone area which mates with a matching cone area inside the blocking ring, and the third area is a set of teeth that engage the splines in the sleeve.

As the sleeve is forced toward the gear, it meets the blocking ring, the sleeve's splines, and the blocking ring's teeth mate. The sleeve blocking ring moves closer to the gear until the gear's cone and the blocking ring touch. Friction between the two brings the gear's cone

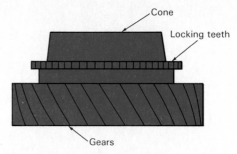

FIGURE 30-7 Gear parts.

to the blocking ring cone's speed. To increase friction between the two cones, grooves are cut into their working surfaces (Figure 30-8). These grooves cut through the lubricating oil so that the two cones actually touch.

The sleeve's splines are almost ready to mate with the gear's locking teeth. In between these teeth, however, is the blocking ring. It keeps the sleeve from mating with the gear. They are not allowed to do this until the two cones are at the same speed, however. This mating is done by keying the blocking rings to the inserts on the hub, so the blocking ring can rotate relative to the hub only slightly. Then, if the splines on the sleeve don't quite match the locking teeth on the gear, the blocking ring stands in the way. Once the cone speeds are fully synchronized, the blocking ring will be lined up with the locking teeth on the gear. The sleeve's splines are then free to slide over the blocking ring and locking teeth. When this happens, the gear and the synchronizer are locked together. Thus, the gear is locked to the mainshaft through the synchronizer sleeve and hub.

Power then flows through the clutch disc to the input shaft. The input shaft transfers the torque to the countergear. The countergear then transfers the power to the gear locked by the synchronizer. Torque flows from the gear through the locking teeth to the sleeve, then to the hub, and finally to the mainshaft.

Synchronizer assemblies like the one just described can serve two gears. By sliding the sleeve in

FIGURE 30-6 Synchronizer assembly. (Chrysler Corporation)

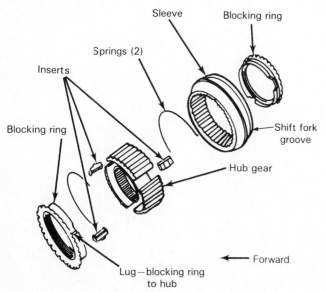

FIGURE 30-8 Blocking ring construction.

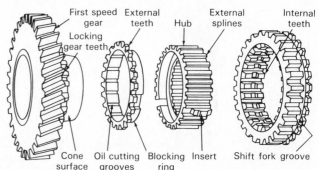

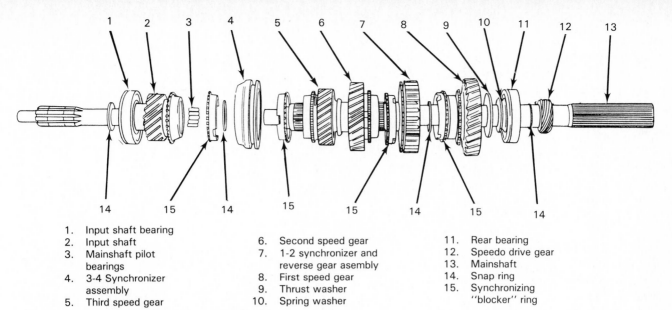

1. Input shaft bearing
2. Input shaft
3. Mainshaft pilot bearings
4. 3-4 Synchronizer assembly
5. Third speed gear
6. Second speed gear
7. 1-2 synchronizer and reverse gear asembly
8. First speed gear
9. Thrust washer
10. Spring washer
11. Rear bearing
12. Speedo drive gear
13. Mainshaft
14. Snap ring
15. Synchronizing "blocker" ring

FIGURE 30-9 First-second and third-fourth synchronizers.

one direction, it can engage one gear; sliding the sleeve the other way engages another gear (Figure 30-9). Reverse gear is similar to the rest, except it has an idler gear between the countershaft and the reverse gear on the mainshaft.

Reverse In some transmissions the reverse gear itself is moved on the mainshaft by the shifting fork (Figure 30-10). No synchronizers are used with this arrangement. That's why shifting into reverse while rolling backward produces gear clash.

FIGURE 30-10 Four-speed transmission with a nonsynchronized, shifted, reverse gear.

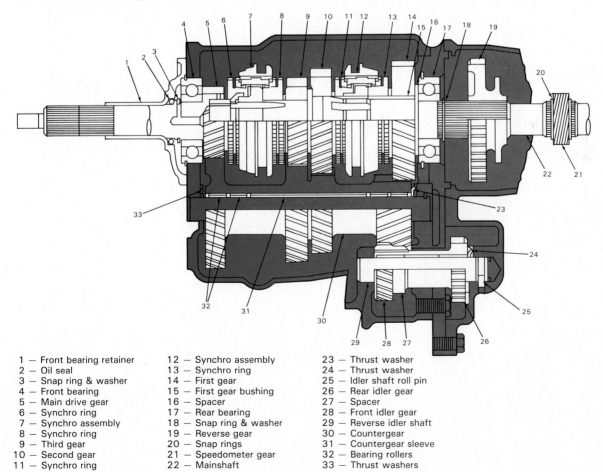

1 — Front bearing retainer
2 — Oil seal
3 — Snap ring & washer
4 — Front bearing
5 — Main drive gear
6 — Synchro ring
7 — Synchro assembly
8 — Synchro ring
9 — Third gear
10 — Second gear
11 — Synchro ring

12 — Synchro assembly
13 — Synchro ring
14 — First gear
15 — First gear bushing
16 — Spacer
17 — Rear bearing
18 — Snap ring & washer
19 — Reverse gear
20 — Snap rings
21 — Speedometer gear
22 — Mainshaft

23 — Thrust washer
24 — Thrust washer
25 — Idler shaft roll pin
26 — Rear idler gear
27 — Spacer
28 — Front idler gear
29 — Reverse idler shaft
30 — Countergear
31 — Countergear sleeve
32 — Bearing rollers
33 — Thrust washers

INDESTRUCTIBLE BRAKES

Our McLaren was the first car I had driven that had truly indestructible brakes. I could push them as hard as I needed to and not have to worry about fade or failure. Simultaneously, the engines were so unreliable, and the gearboxes were so hard to downshift, that it was about the time I started learning not to downshift for braking. We were also learning that early downshifting was upsetting the very carefully set up front-to-rear brake balance, and it would tend to lock up the rears early. I still see some drivers with weak brakes do it the old way—they rush into a corner and downshift about 20 times. But it's really only necessary to downshift once, to the next gear you'll need.

Reprinted by permission of DODD, MEAD & COMPANY, INC. from THE UNFAIR ADVANTAGE by Mark Donohue with Paul Van Valkenburgh. Copyright © 1975 by Mark Donohue.

TRANSMISSION DESIGNS

Three-Speed

Design In a three-speed transmission, one synchronizer assembly shifts first and reverse and another synchronizer shifts second and third (Figure 30-11). Actually there is no third gear. Instead of a separate gear, the input shaft and the mainshaft are coupled together by the synchronizer. This gives a 1:1 gear ratio and is a very popular way of designing the top gear in many gearboxes.

One benefit of coupling the shafts directly is greater efficiency. A direct coupling transmits about 99% of received torque, whereas a gear coupling is about 96% efficient.

FIGURE 30-11 Three-speed transmission mainshaft. (Ford Motor Company)

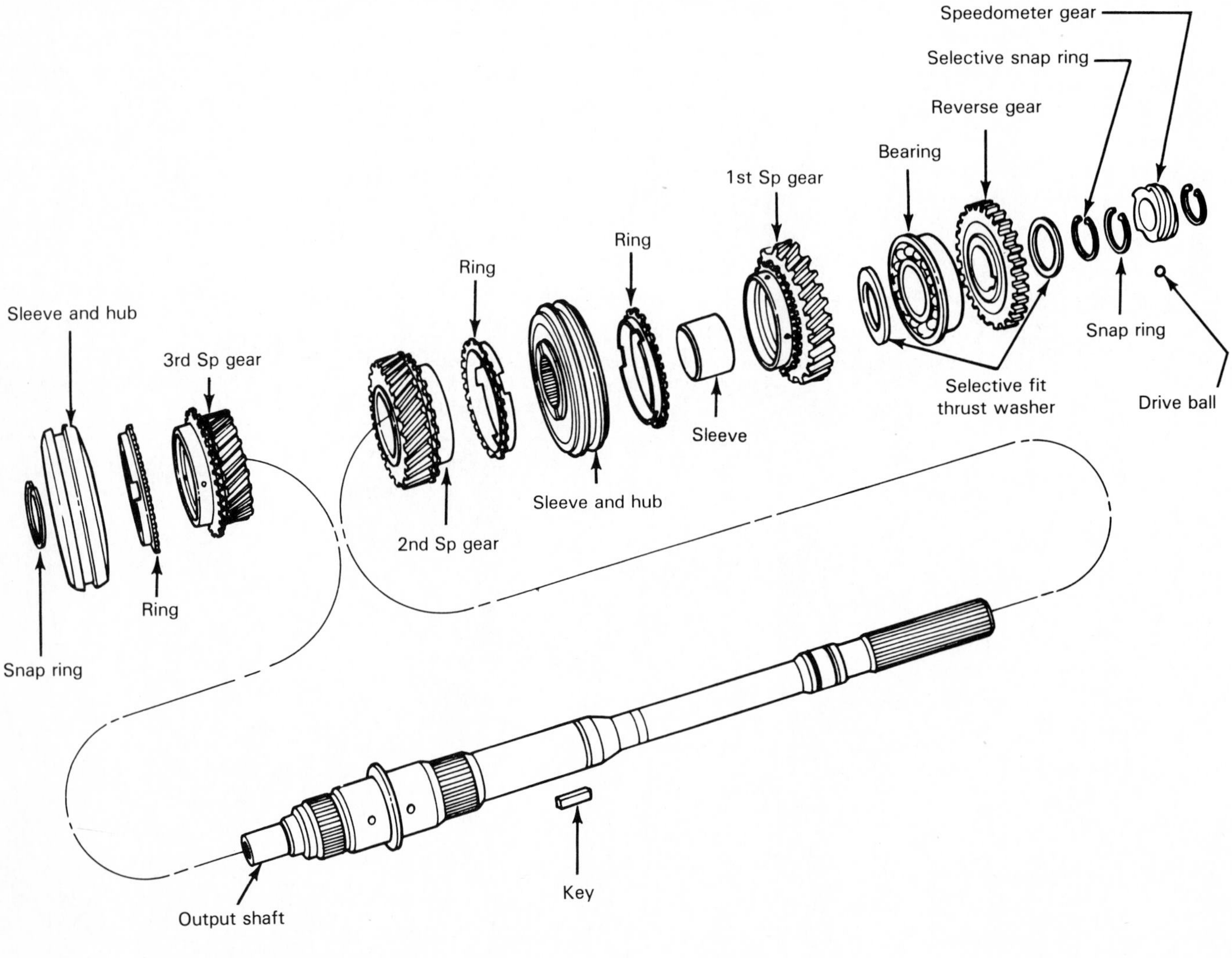

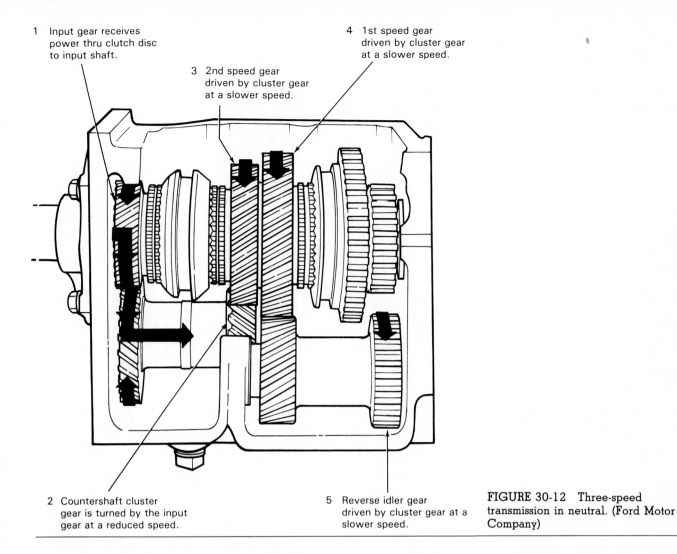

1 Input gear receives power thru clutch disc to input shaft.

3 2nd speed gear driven by cluster gear at a slower speed.

4 1st speed gear driven by cluster gear at a slower speed.

2 Countershaft cluster gear is turned by the input gear at a reduced speed.

5 Reverse idler gear driven by cluster gear at a slower speed.

FIGURE 30-12 Three-speed transmission in neutral. (Ford Motor Company)

Operation When a three-speed transmission is shifted out of neutral (Figure 30-12) into first, the first–reverse synchronizer sleeve slides onto the first gear locking teeth (Figure 30-13). When shifted into second, the first–reverse sleeve slides into its neutral position, and the second–third sleeve slides onto second gear's locking teeth (Figure 30-14). When third is selected, the second–third sleeve moves off second gear, slides

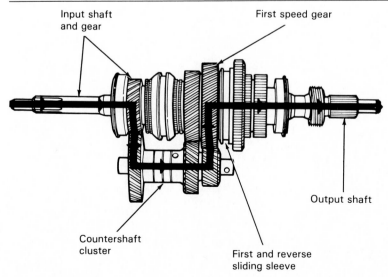

Input shaft and gear

First speed gear

Countershaft cluster

First and reverse sliding sleeve

Output shaft

FIGURE 30-13 Three-speed transmission in first. (Ford Motor Company)

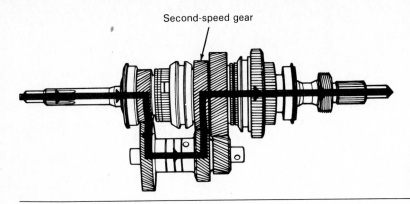

FIGURE 30-14 Three-speed transmission in second. (Ford Motor Company)

through neutral, and engages locking teeth on the input shaft (Figure 30-15).

To engage reverse, the second–third synchronizer is pulled into its neutral position. The clutch is disengaged during the shift, so the input and countergear stop turning. To stop the mainshaft from turning, the vehicle must be brought to a complete stop. Then the first–reverse sleeve can be pushed onto the reverse gear locking teeth (Figure 30-16). All shafts must be stopped because there is no synchronizing action on the reverse gear. There is only the sleeve and locking teeth on the reverse gear—no blocking ring, cones, or inserts.

The reverse gear, by not having these parts, stops the driver from selecting reverse while rolling forward or backward. Doing so would cause severe driveline damage.

Four-Speed

Adding another forward gear to a three-speed transmission turns it into a four-speed transmission. Top, or fourth, gear is a 1:1 ratio like third in a three-speed transmission. The fourth gear is used to provide an extra ratio in the first and second range of the three-speed gearbox.

The fourth gear typically takes the physical location of reverse. A third hub and sleeve assembly is then added to shift the reverse gear, or the fork moves the reverse gear until it meshes with the reverse idler gear.

Figure 30-17 shows the power flow in a four-speed transmission.

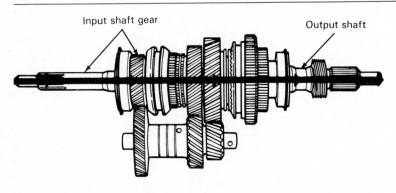

FIGURE 30-15 Three-speed transmission in third. (Ford Motor Company)

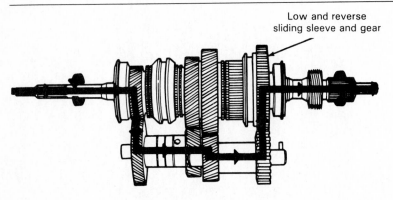

FIGURE 30-16 Three-speed transmission in reverse. (Ford Motor Company)

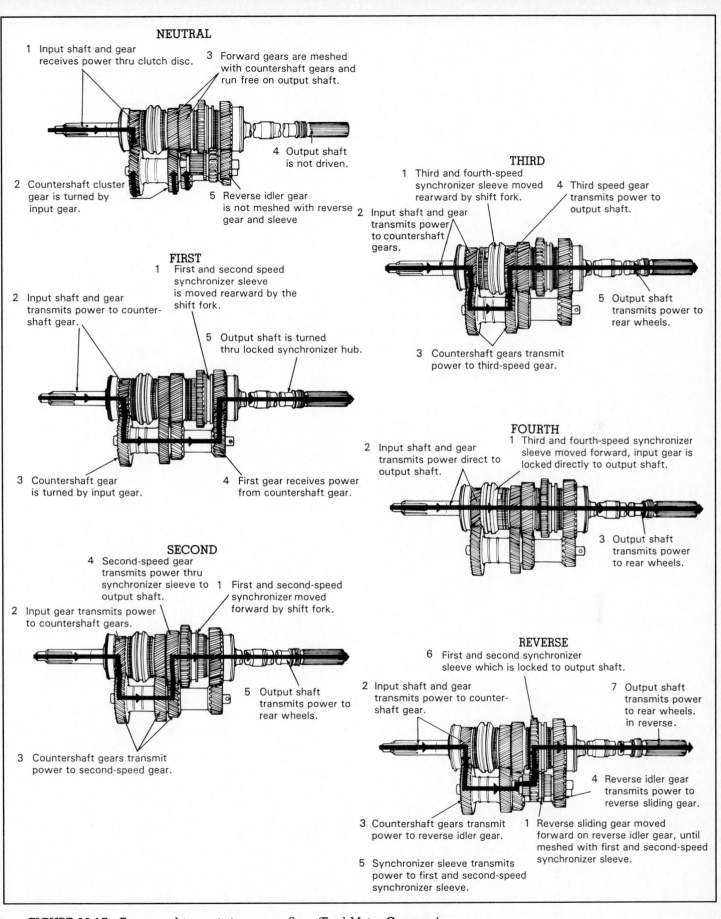

NEUTRAL

1 Input shaft and gear receives power thru clutch disc.

3 Forward gears are meshed with countershaft gears and run free on output shaft.

4 Output shaft is not driven.

2 Countershaft cluster gear is turned by input gear.

5 Reverse idler gear is not meshed with reverse gear and sleeve

FIRST

1 First and second speed synchronizer sleeve is moved rearward by the shift fork.

2 Input shaft and gear transmits power to counter-shaft gear.

5 Output shaft is turned thru locked synchronizer hub.

3 Countershaft gear is turned by input gear.

4 First gear receives power from countershaft gear.

SECOND

4 Second-speed gear transmits power thru synchronizer sleeve to output shaft.

1 First and second-speed synchronizer moved forward by shift fork.

2 Input gear transmits power to countershaft gears.

5 Output shaft transmits power to rear wheels.

3 Countershaft gears transmit power to second-speed gear.

THIRD

1 Third and fourth-speed synchronizer sleeve moved rearward by shift fork.

2 Input shaft and gear transmits power to countershaft gears.

4 Third speed gear transmits power to output shaft.

5 Output shaft transmits power to rear wheels.

3 Countershaft gears transmit power to third-speed gear.

FOURTH

1 Third and fourth-speed synchronizer sleeve moved forward, input gear is locked directly to output shaft.

2 Input shaft and gear transmits power direct to output shaft.

3 Output shaft transmits power to rear wheels.

REVERSE

6 First and second synchronizer sleeve which is locked to output shaft.

2 Input shaft and gear transmits power to counter-shaft gear.

7 Output shaft transmits power to rear wheels. in reverse.

4 Reverse idler gear transmits power to reverse sliding gear.

3 Countershaft gears transmit power to reverse idler gear.

1 Reverse sliding gear moved forward on reverse idler gear, until meshed with first and second-speed synchronizer sleeve.

5 Synchronizer sleeve transmits power to first and second-speed synchronizer sleeve.

FIGURE 30-17 Four-speed transmission power flow. (Ford Motor Company)

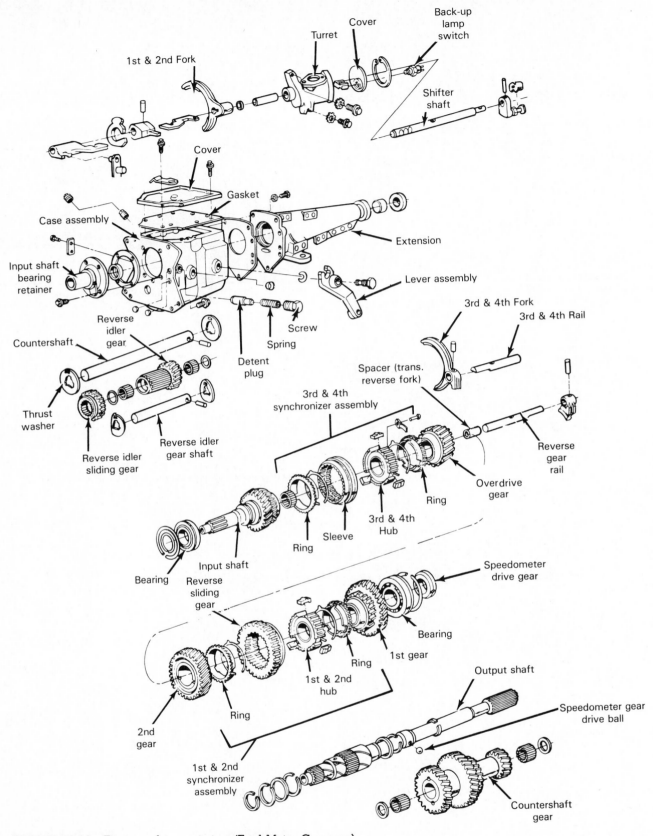

FIGURE 30-18 Five-speed transmission. (Ford Motor Company)

Five-Speed

Just as adding a gear to a three-speed transmission makes it a four-speed transmission, adding another forward gear to a four-speed transmission makes it a five-speed transmission (Figure 30-18). The fifth gear is usually added to the rear of the mainshaft, near the reverse gear. The hub and sleeve shifting assembly used only for reverse in the four-speed transmission becomes the fifth–reverse synchronizer.

The 1:1 ratio of fourth gear is usually retained, and fifth gear is made into an **overdrive.** Overdrive in this case means the gear ratio is less than 1:1. Typical fifth gear overdrive ratios range from 0.70 to 0.90:1. Such gearing greatly reduces engine rpm at freeway speeds and increases fuel mileage and engine life.

Of course, adding gears to the mainshaft, as in a four- or five-speed transmission, means adding corresponding gears to the countershaft. These extra gears add weight and cost, so they are used only when needed.

Keep in mind that not all transmissions are designed exactly as described here. Some four-speed transmissions have overdrive fourth gears, thus they actually have a fourth gear. Some five-speeds have two overdrive gears, and therefore have five gears, not four.

OVERDRIVE UNITS

Overdrive units are separate from the transmission but do basically the same job as an overdrive fifth gear. Overdrive units, called overdrives, were popular before the widespread use of four- and five-speed transmissions. They gave three-speed manual transmissions a freeway cruising gear.

Purpose of Overdrives

The primary purpose of an overdrive is to allow the engine to operate at a lower rpm while vehicle speed is maintained. This gives less engine wear and improved fuel economy. Overdrives were used in high-performance vehicles such as sports cars and large sedans. Trucks also use overdrives to *split* gear ratios. When overdrives are designed for use between gears instead of only as a top gear, gear ratios between the primary transmission gears can be obtained. These split ratios are of great value to a truck with a heavy load climbing a steep grade.

Overdrive Design

Overdrives can be an integral part of a transmission as in a four- or five-speed transmission, or they can be add-on units. The overdrive gear ratio is generally in the range of 0.7:1–0.9:1. The add-on units are usually installed at the rear of the transmission between the transmission's output shaft and the driveline (Figure 30-19). Most add-on overdrives are electrically controlled. A switch, mounted on or near the gearshift lever, is used to actuate the overdrive. An electric solenoid controls the hydraulic system in the overdrive unit to actuate a sliding clutch that forces it to mesh with the overdrive gear.

Hydraulic overdrives are also used. The hydraulic overdrive consists of a planet carrier assembly with three planetary gears, a hydraulically actuated sliding clutch, and an overrunning clutch.

A single planetary gear train is used, consisting of a central sun gear meshing with three planetary pinion gears. These mesh with the internal teeth of an annulus or ring gear. The annulus gear and overdrive mainshaft are a single assembly comprising the rear

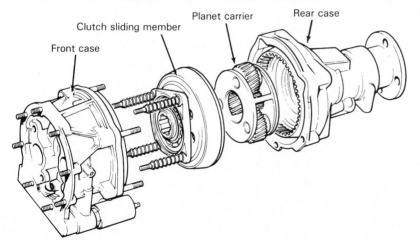

Front case | Clutch sliding member | Planet carrier | Rear case

FIGURE 30-19 Overdrive unit. (Triumph)

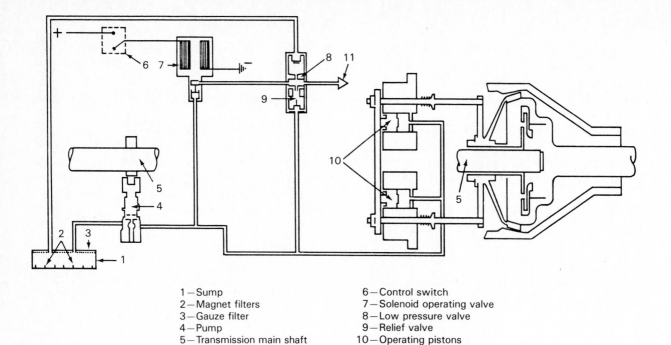

1—Sump	6—Control switch
2—Magnet filters	7—Solenoid operating valve
3—Gauze filter	8—Low pressure valve
4—Pump	9—Relief valve
5—Transmission main shaft	10—Operating pistons
	11—Oil return to sump

FIGURE 30-20 Hydraulic overdrive operation. (Triumph)

case. A flange on the rear case attaches to the drive shaft.

The hydraulic system consists of an electrically operated solenoid valve, mechanical pump, relief valve, and low-pressure valve (Figure 30-20). When the pump is actuated by the solenoid, the pump draws oil from the sump and discharges it to the two operating pistons. The pistons move the sliding clutch, thus engaging the overdrive.

SHIFT MECHANISM

Shift mechanisms control the shifting of gears within the transmission. There are two assemblies involved: the shift control lever and the shift fork assembly. The shift control lever can be either steering column mounted or floor mounted.

Column Mounted

The **column-mount** control lever is typically used with three-speed transmissions. An arrangement of rods and levers connect the column control with the shift fork assembly on the transmission (Figure 30-21). A standard H pattern is generally used, with reverse and second occupying the two top positions and first and third occupying the two bottom positions. Neutral is in the center. A few four-speed transmissions have utilized column-mounted control levers also, but the complex linkage involved tended to be troublesome.

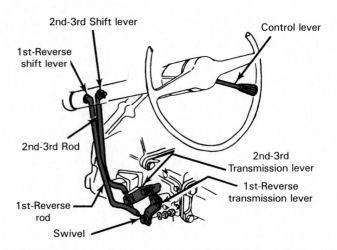

FIGURE 30-21 Column-mounted shifter. (General Motors Corporation)

Floor Mounted

Floor-mount gearshift assemblies are, by far, the most popular. They are used with both four- and five-speed transmissions. Figure 30-22 is an exploded view of a floor shifter. Short levers link the gearshift with the shift linkage (Figure 30-23). The shift linkage on floor-mounted shifters can be outside the transmission as shown, or a set of rods can be built into the transmission. Such internal shift linkages are more expensive to make, but they stay cleaner, need little maintenance, and last longer than external linkages (Figure 30-24).

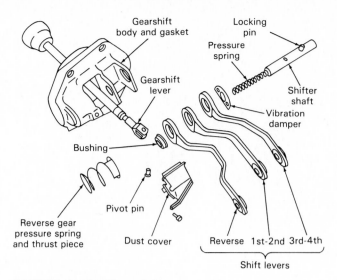

FIGURE 30-22 Floor shifter.

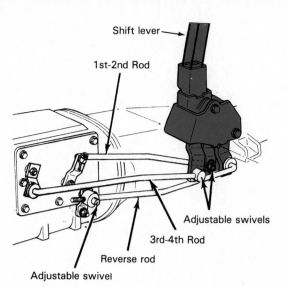

FIGURE 30-23 Floor-mounted shift linkage. (General Motors Corporation)

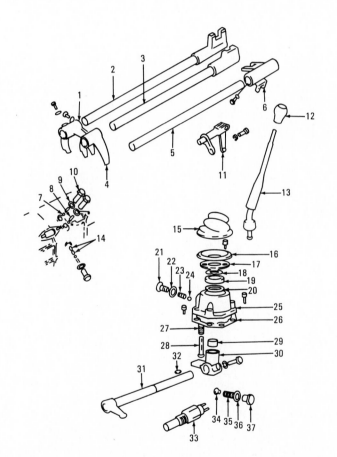

1 — 3rd-4th shift fork
2 — 3rd-4th shift rail
3 — 1st-2nd shift rail
4 — 1st-2nd shift fork
5 — Reverse shift rail
6 — Reverse shift fork
7 — Detent ball
8 — Detent spring
9 — Gasket
10 — Cap plug
11 — Shift lever
12 — Shift knob
13 — Gearshift lever
14 — Interlock pin
15 — Dust boot
16 — Cover plate
17 — Gasket
18 — Washer
19 — Bushing
20 — Shim
21 — Cap plug
22 — Gasket
23 — Detent spring
24 — Detent ball
25 — Change control case
26 — Gasket
27 — Select lock
28 — Select lock spindle
29 — Spring seat
30 — Control end
31 — Control lever
32 — Key
33 — Back-up light switch
34 — Detent
35 — Detent spring
36 — Gasket
37 — Cap plug

FIGURE 30-24 Internal shift linkage.

Shift Fork Assembly

The fork assembly is a combination of lugs, rails, and **forks** that transfer the gearshift movement to the synchronizers and gears within the transmission (Figure 30-25). The rails and forks are mounted inside the transmission case. Shafts, mounted in seals, protrude through the transmission case and connect to the exterior control levers.

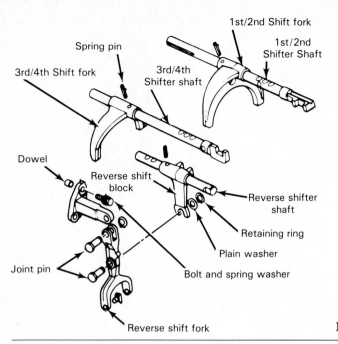

Spring pin
3rd/4th Shift fork
1st/2nd Shift fork
1st/2nd Shifter Shaft
3rd/4th Shifter shaft
Dowel
Reverse shift block
Reverse shifter shaft
Retaining ring
Plain washer
Joint pin
Bolt and spring washer
Reverse shift fork

FIGURE 30-25   Shift forks. (General Motors Corporation)

TRADE TERMS

Close Ratio
Column-mount
Constant Mesh
Countergear
Floor-mount
Forks
Gear Ratios
Helical-cut Gears
Input Shaft

Mainshaft
Overall Gear Ratio
Overdrive
Straight Cut
Synchronizer
Torque
Torque Multiplication
Wide Ratio

REVIEW QUESTIONS

1. Describe why cars need transmissions.
2. What is meant by torque multiplication?
3. How are gear ratios calculated?
4. Modern transmission gears are _____ cut gears.
5. Describe the function of synchronizers in a transmission.
6. What is the primary difference among three-, four-, and five speed transmissions?

7. What does an overdrive do?
8. What is the range of overdrive ratios?
9. What is the difference between an overdrive unit and an overdrive gear in a five-speed transmission?
10. Briefly describe the function of the shift fork mechanism.

31

Manual Transaxles

INTRODUCTION

Manual transaxles are a combination of a manual transmission and a drive axle, complete with differential, and mounted in a single housing. Transaxles are used in these combinations:

☐ Front-engine front-wheel drive,
☐ Rear-engine real-wheel drive,
☐ Front-engine rear-wheel drive,
☐ Front-engine four-wheel drive,
☐ Rear-engine four-wheel drive

The engine is mounted crosswise in modern front-wheel-drive cars to allow the engine, differential, and axles to be directly connected for space saving (Figure 31-1). The advantages of the transaxle include lower weight and, when mounted with the engine, reduction of vibration and alignment problems caused by long drive shafts.

OBJECTIVES

When you have completed this chapter, you should be able to

- Describe a manual transaxle and its components
- Explain how the transmission works
- Explain why differentials are used
- Explain the function of the constant velocity universal joint
- Explain how synchronizers work

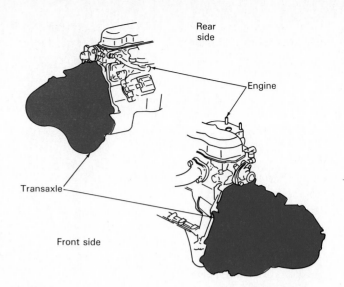

Rear
side

Engine

Transaxle

Front side

FIGURE 31-1 Transaxle installation. (General Motors Corporation)

COMPONENT DESCRIPTION

Clutch

Power is transferred from the engine through the clutch mechanism (Figure 31-2). The clutch is required for manual transmissions, that is, transmissions in which the gears are shifted by hand. The foot-pedal-operated clutch connects and disconnects the engine from the transmission, which is necessary before gears can be shifted. As in standard manual transmissions, the

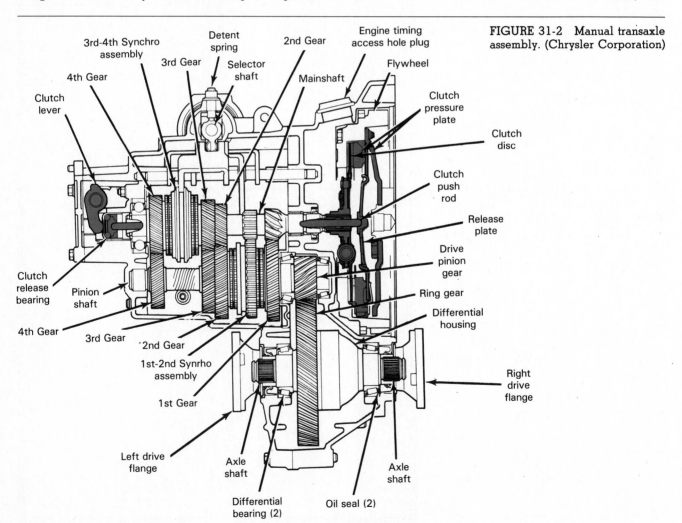

FIGURE 31-2 Manual transaxle assembly. (Chrysler Corporation)

3rd-4th Synchro assembly

Detent spring

2nd Gear

Engine timing access hole plug

4th Gear

3rd Gear

Selector shaft

Flywheel

Clutch lever

Mainshaft

Clutch pressure plate

Clutch disc

Clutch push rod

Release plate

Drive pinion gear

Ring gear

Differential housing

Clutch release bearing

Pinion shaft

4th Gear

3rd Gear

2nd Gear

1st-2nd Synrho assembly

1st Gear

Right drive flange

Left drive flange

Axle shaft

Axle shaft

Differential bearing (2)

Oil seal (2)

clutch uses a friction plate forced against the flywheel by a strong spring assembly. Power is transferred from the engine flywheel to the disc connected to the transmission input shaft.

Operation **Transaxle** clutches differ from regular, in-line transmission clutches only in actuation. Several different methods are used. The usual release arm and bearing method can be used, or it can be replaced by another method that uses less space. One space-saving method is to mount the release arm at one end of the transaxle case. The release arm pushes against a rod that passes through a hollow mainshaft to the release fingers on the pressure plate, as shown in Figure 31-2.

Mechanical, cable, and hydraulic clutch linkage can be used on transaxle clutches.

Transmission

A transmission is required to match the engine torque range with the load requirements, that is, with the amount of work that has to be done. Figure 31-3 shows a four-speed manual transaxle. As noted in Chapter 30, an internal combustion engine is a high-speed, or high-rpm, engine. The gears in the transmission allow the engine to operate at high rpm, while the drive wheels of the automobile operate at a much slower speed. The effect of attempting to couple the engine directly to the drive wheels can be observed by trying to start the vehicle in motion with the transmission in high gear. The engine will stall because its torque is not matched to the load.

Shafts The transmission section of a transaxle is practically identical to those in conventional transmissions. It provides torque multiplication, allows gear shifting, and is synchronized. In some transaxles there is an additional shaft that runs parallel to the main- and countershafts. It offsets the power flow from the mainshaft. This allows a more compact transaxle installation. Power is transferred from one shaft to another by simple helical gears when the shafts are placed parallel. Using a third shaft means that at least one extra bearing is necessary to support the shaft. Because of increased costs and complexity, a third shaft is not used unless an extremely compact installation is required.

FIGURE 31-3 Four-speed manual transaxle assembly. (American Honda Motor Corporation, Inc.)

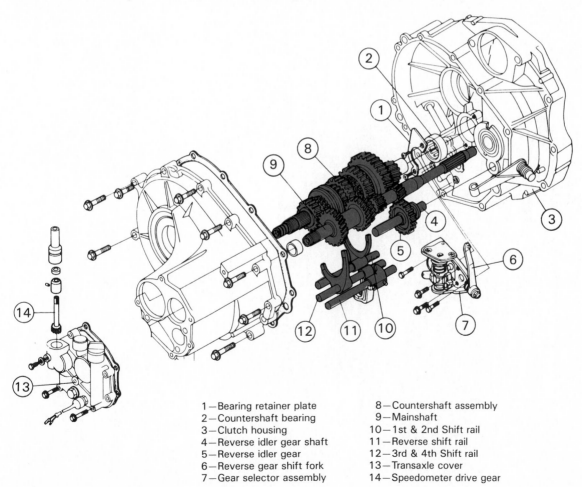

1—Bearing retainer plate
2—Countershaft bearing
3—Clutch housing
4—Reverse idler gear shaft
5—Reverse idler gear
6—Reverse gear shift fork
7—Gear selector assembly

8—Countershaft assembly
9—Mainshaft
10—1st & 2nd Shift rail
11—Reverse shift rail
12—3rd & 4th Shift rail
13—Transaxle cover
14—Speedometer drive gear

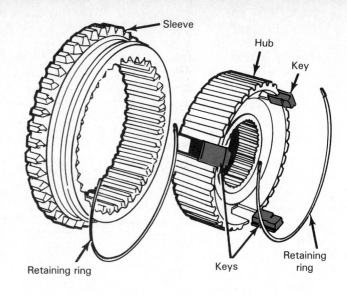

Synchronizers Synchronizers allow for the smooth shifting of gears without a lot of fancy footwork or clashing of gears. The key type of synchronizer is commonly used in transaxles. The synchronizer has three keys assembled into a hub assembly (Figure 31-4). The hub has splines on its inner surface that mesh with corresponding splines on the mainshaft. The outer surface of the hub has splines that mate with teeth on the inner surface of the synchronizing sleeve. The outer surface of the hub has three keys which force the synchronizer (blocking) ring onto the cone of the gear.

Synchronization occurs in three stages. In the first stage, the sleeve is moved toward the gear by the shift lever and engages the hub assembly. In the second stage, the keys press the synchronizer ring onto the cone of the gear. In the third stage, the synchronizer ring completes its friction fit over the gear cone, and the gear is brought up to synchronous speed with the synchronizer assembly. Then the sleeve slides onto the gear's locking teeth. The gear and its synchronizer assembly are now locked to the mainshaft. All forward gears operate in the same manner.

Differential

The final part of the power flow in a transaxle is through the differential (Figure 31-5). The differential

---

FIGURE 31-5 Differential location. (Chrysler Corporation)

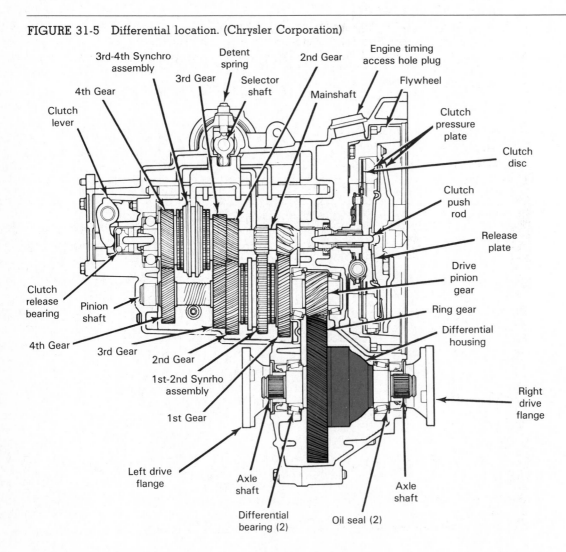

allows the drive wheel on one side to rotate at a speed different from the drive wheel on the opposite side. This is necessary because when turning, the wheel on the outside of the turn must travel a longer distance than the wheel on the inside of the turn. Differentials are covered in detail in Chapter 29.

Power Flow   One major difference between the differential in a rear-drive car and the differential in a transaxle is power flow. In a rear-drive application, the power flow changes 90° between the drive pinion and the ring gear. This change in direction is necessary in a rear-drive automobile but is not needed with a front-drive/transverse engine layout. With the transverse layout, the crankshaft is already rotating in the proper direction. Therefore, the differential need only provide torque multiplication and speed differences between the two drive wheels. Replacing the hypoid cut drive pinion with a spur gear allows the ring gear to be kept in its normal relationship with the drive wheels. A helical cut ring gear is shown in Figure 31-6. A normal differential case, pinion, and side gears are used to provide differential action. Limited slip differentials can be fitted to transaxles.

Some transaxles need the 90° power flow change retained in the differential. These units are used in rear-drive or in longitudinal front-drive applications.

Alfa Romeo and Porsche are good examples of this type of transaxle. When a change in power flow is desired, a normal hypoid drive pinion and ring gear are used.

Drive Axles

Drive axles extend out from each side of the differential to supply power to the drive wheels. The axle is not a single unit but is made up of several pieces fitted together (Figure 31-7). The axle needs to flex up and down with suspension motion. In addition, front-wheel-drive cars must allow the front wheels to turn with the steering. Constant velocity joints are used to provide the required flexibility (Figure 31-8).

CV Joints   As detailed in Chapter 28, constant velocity (CV) joints are similar in function to the universal joints used in the drive shaft of front-engine, rear-drive vehicles. The speed of the driven side of the U-joint may vary with relation to the driving side, depending on the angle of the shaft. The constant velocity joint, however, maintains an equal speed on both sides of the joint, which contributes to less vibration and wear. Some CV joints are made up of two U-joints connected together by a ball and socket assembly. The Rzeppa constant velocity universal joint is

FIGURE 31-6   Spur cut ring gear. (Chrysler Corporation)

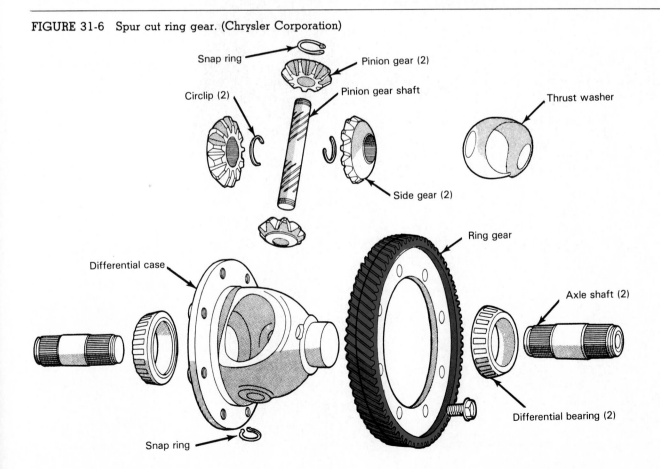

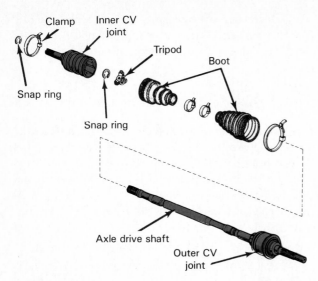

FIGURE 31-7　Drive axle assembly. (General Motors Corporation)

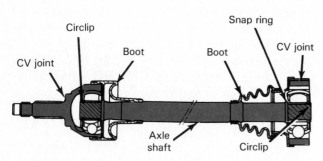

FIGURE 31-8　Cutaway of a drive axle. (General Motors Corporation)

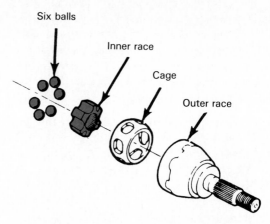

FIGURE 31-9　Rzeppa constant velocity joint. (General Motors Corporation)

commonly used in front-wheel-drive autos (Figure 31-9). This CV joint contains an outer race, a cage with six balls, and an inner race. The balls allow the joint to flex, yet all balls rotate at the same velocity, resulting in a constant velocity transfer of power.

Lubrication

Unlike conventional rear axle assemblies, which use 90-**weight** gear oil almost exclusively, transaxles normally use a wide range of lubricants.

Sometimes the transaxle is open to the engine sump and uses the same 30-weight oil as the engine. Or the engine and the transaxle could be sealed between each other. In the latter case, the transaxle could use its own 30-weight oil, 90-weight gear oil, or even

FRONT WHEEL DRIVE—A NEW IDEA?

Front-wheel drive is as old as the self-propelled vehicle and was a feature of Cugnot's historic steam carriage (only one front wheel) which lumbered over the boulevards of Paris around 1770. Overseas automotive designers Humber, Latil, de Raincey, and others tried and abandoned front drive prior to 1900 due, chiefly, to the universal-joint problems associated with wheels that must be sprung, steered, and driven.

In New York in 1904 J. Walter Christie, who had prospered as a designer and builder of military gun turrets, took out patents on a highly original method of driving an automobile through its front wheels. The chief feature of the design was its mounting of the engine transversely at the front of the vehicle. That

same year Christie built a running prototype and in 1905 founded the Christie Direct Action Motor Car Company for the manufacture of taxis which, in general layout, bore an almost uncanny resemblance to the modern Issigonis-designed BMC Mini.

Between 1904 and 1909 Christie built seven front-drive race cars which were powered by twins, fours, V4s and V8s of his own creation. They were notoriously brutal to handle but won their share of speed contests for years after Christie had given up any commercial hopes for the idea. In 1907 he set a new record for the dirt-track mile at 69.2 mph. On Dec. 18, 1909, on the newly brick-surfaced Indianapolis Speedway he set a record for the flying quarter-

mile at 97.6 mph. Then Barney Oldfield acquired the biggest 140-bhp Christie and barnstormed it from coast to coast for years. In 1915 on the Tacoma boards he averaged 113.9 mph for a mile, and at Indianapolis in 1916 he set a new lap record of 102.6 mph. Ed Winfield saw Barney raise the AAA dirt-track mile record to 77.6 mph at Bakersfield, California, in 1913. The sight, he said, was terrifying. The machine would barely steer, and it bolted around the track in a series of rock-and-dirt spraying leaps which coincided with each power impulse.

Griffith Borgeson
*The Golden Age of the
American Racing Car*
W. W. Norton & Co.

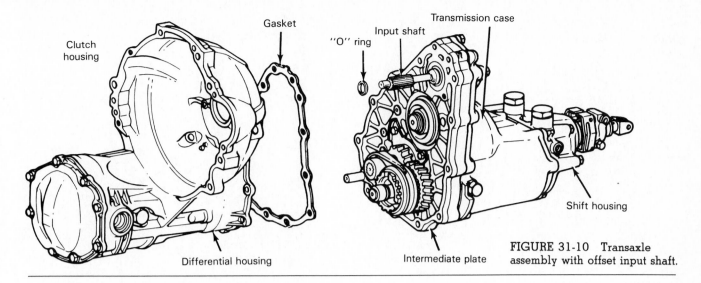

FIGURE 31-10 Transaxle assembly with offset input shaft.

Clutch housing

Gasket

"O" ring

Input shaft

Transmission case

Shift housing

Differential housing

Intermediate plate

ATF (automatic transmission fluid). The current trend is toward 30-weight gear oil and ATF because these thinner lubricants absorb less horsepower and give more mileage.

CONSTRUCTION

The manual transaxle is an integrated assembly of a manual transmission and a final drive or differential (Figure 31-10).

Transmission

The transmission normally contains two main gear shafts mounted in bearings at each end (Figure 31-11). These shafts provide support for the gears and synchronizers and transmit power from gear to gear through the transmission. Some gears are locked to these shafts, and others rotate on the shafts. In the example illustrated, the mainshaft is connected to the clutch assembly via the main drive gear and supports the reverse and forward main gears. It also carries the

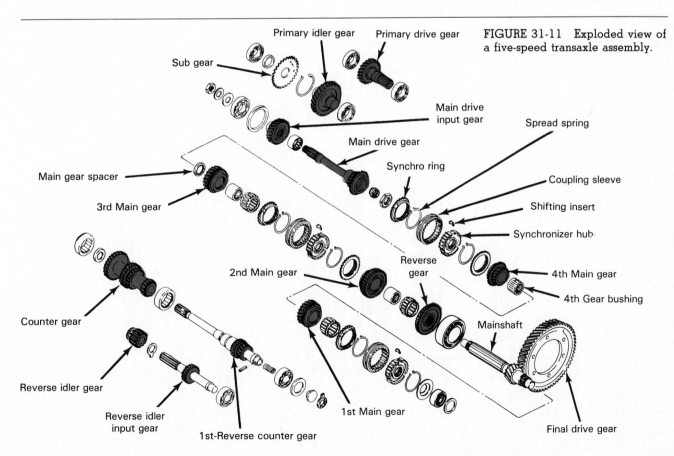

FIGURE 31-11 Exploded view of a five-speed transaxle assembly.

Sub gear

Primary idler gear

Primary drive gear

Main drive input gear

Spread spring

Coupling sleeve

Main gear spacer

Main drive gear

Synchro ring

Shifting insert

Synchronizer hub

3rd Main gear

2nd Main gear

Reverse gear

4th Main gear

4th Gear bushing

Counter gear

Mainshaft

Reverse idler gear

Reverse idler input gear

1st-Reverse counter gear

1st Main gear

Final drive gear

pinion gear that drives the differential ring gear. The transaxle shown also uses an offset input shaft. It is labeled the "primary drive gear" in the illustration.

Final Drive

The final drive assembly or differential is a standard rotating case type of power train (Figure 31-12). The case referred to here is not the outer housing that contains and protects the assembly but the inner case which is driven by the output shaft of the transmission. The case has a ring gear attached to it that meshes with a mating pinion gear on the mainshaft of the transmission. The differential case contains the pinion gear and shaft assembly that rotates around the side gears attached to the end of the drive axles to provide the differential speed function.

Drive Axles

The drive axles used with transaxle systems are actually made up of three pieces attached together in such a way as to allow the wheels to turn and move up and down with the suspension (Figure 31-13). A short

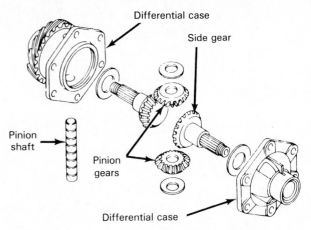

FIGURE 31-12 Differential assembly.

stub shaft extends from the differential to the first or inner CV joint. An axle shaft then extends to the outer CV joint.

A short spindle shaft runs from the outer CV joint to mate with the wheel assembly. The steering knuckle connects to the spindle shaft or stub axle outboard of the outer CV joint. Neoprene boots are installed over each CV joint assembly to keep out mois-

FIGURE 31-13 FWD axle set. (Chrysler Corporation)

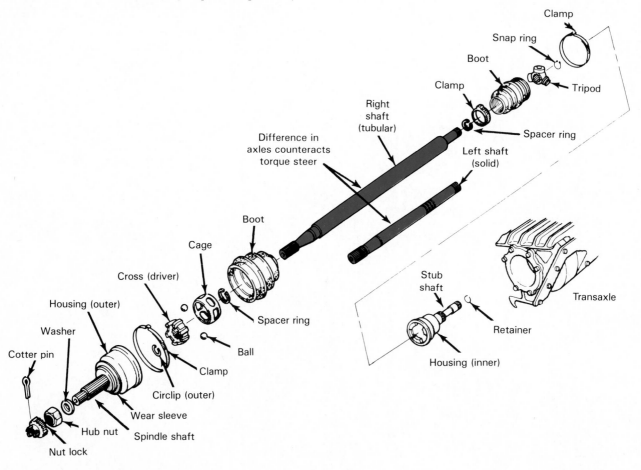

ture and dirt. These boots must be maintained in good condition. If they need replacement, either the axle must be removed and the new boot slipped over its end, or a split boot can be *laced* onto the axle.

Another aspect of front-wheel-drive axles commonly used with transaxles is **torque steer.** Torque steer refers to a self-induced steering condition in response to throttle position. It results from the axles twisting unevenly under engine torque. This is a prob-

lem with axles of uneven length. One cure is to make one axle hollow or to increase its diameter. Then the axle which twisted the most can only twist as far as its mate. Therefore, both axles twist evenly, and no torque steer is felt. Another approach is to make the longer side in two pieces. The inner piece comes out of the transaxle and is supported by a bearing. The outer piece can be the same length as the shorter side axle, so no torque steering problem occurs.

TRADE TERMS

ATF
Torque Steer

Transaxle
Weight

REVIEW QUESTIONS

1. Describe two advantages of transaxles.
2. Why is a clutch necessary in a manual transmission?
3. Why is a transmission required?

4. Describe the function of the differential.
5. What is the function of the synchronizer?
6. What is a CV joint?

32

Manual Transmission Service

INTRODUCTION

Modern manual transmissions are strong, trouble-free units which require a minimum of maintenance. Normal maintenance is limited to linkage adjustments and possibly oil changes. Even these two jobs aren't that necessary anymore. However, manual transmissions and transaxles can have problems. This chapter explains how to deal with them.

IDENTIFICATION

Before any service or repair work can be done on a transmission, the technician must know exactly which transmission he or she is working on. Identification is doubly important with transmissions because they cannot be visually identified precisely. For example, the same case could house wide or close ratio gears. Only positive identification numbers will show the difference.

Transmission identification numbers can be found either stamped in the case or on a metal tab under a bolt head (Figure 32-1). You'll need a shop manual to decipher the identification number. Most often the model, gear ratios, manufacturer, and assembly date are found in the identification number.

OBJECTIVES

When you have completed this chapter, you should be able to

- Diagnose manual transmission problems
- Perform all normal manual transmission service
- Explain manual transmission repair
- Better understand typical customer complaints
- More fully describe manual transmission design

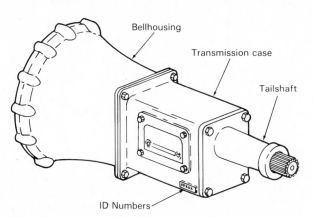

FIGURE 32-1 Transmission identification numbers.

Whenever you work with a transmission with a metal ID tag, make sure the tag is replaced. Then the next technician can tell which gearbox he or she is working with.

TROUBLESHOOTING

Many problems blamed on the transmission are actually the fault of the engine, axle shafts, U-joints, wheel bearings, wheel/tire imbalance, overheating, or other conditions. Unusual sounds, vibrations, and "clunks" must be properly diagnosed before attempting transmission service. This is especially true of transaxles because many components are tightly packed around them.

Complaints based on unusual noises often incorrectly blamed on transmission malfunctions include road noise, tire noise, front-wheel-bearing noise, incorrect drive axle angle due to sagging suspension, engine or exhaust noise, worn drive axle U-joints, loose or deteriorated engine/transaxle mounts, and worn wheel bearings. Make sure none of these is the problem source before working on the transmission.

The chart in Figure 32-2 will help you diagnose and fix most transmission problems.

IN-CAR SERVICE

Because transmissions are so trouble-free, most of the work done to them is in-car. Only when an overhaul or clutch service is needed does the transmission need to be removed from the chassis.

Fluid Changes

Most modern gearboxes have unlimited oil change intervals. That is, unless there is a need for oil removal, like transmission overhaul, the oil doesn't need changing. Older transmissions typically have 20,000-mi oil change intervals, however. Under severe conditions (high heat or dust) the fluid may have to be changed more often. Check the shop manual for details.

Draining To change the transmission oil, raise and safely support the car. Locate the oil drain hole in the bottom of the transmission case (Figure 32-3). Some transaxles share engine oil, so they may not have a separate oil drain hole.

Most drain plugs have square holes that accept a special wrench. In a pinch, most of these plugs will loosen with a ½-in. extension and ratchet assembly. Others use a raised square which can be grasped with an adjustable wrench. After locating the plug, remove it and let the oil drain into a pan. The car must be level to let all the fluid run out. Also, transmission oil can be very thick, so let the transmission drain awhile.

Once the oil has drained out, sweep a small magnet around inside the case by passing it through the drain hole. Most transmission wear is on the brass blocking rings. Because brass is not magnetic, it will not show on the magnet. But worn gear faces and other parts will show. Inspect the oil drainings for gold metallic particles. These shiny particles come from the blocking rings.

Filling Now replace the drain plug. Above the drain plug is another, similar-looking plug. This is the filler plug. To find the proper grade and quantity of oil, consult a shop manual. Fill the gearbox with the proper oil until it just starts to run out the hole. Then replace the plug; the oil change is complete.

Linkage Adjustment

Transmissions with internal linkage need no adjustment, and no provisions for doing so are made. External linkages, both floor and column mount, can be adjusted, however. Linkages are adjusted at the factory and should not need much, if any, adjustment after that. Sometimes, though, worn parts will cause adjustment to be necessary.

The exact linkage adjustment procedure differs with each transmission. You must have a shop manual

CONDITION	POSSIBLE CAUSE	CORRECTION
▶ Improper shift lever operation.	1) Shift rods out of adjustment.	1) Check crossover operation. Gear shift lever should move through neutral gate without drag. Adjust linkage.
	2) Steering column shift tube out of alignment.	2) Check lever position for correct transmission gear selection. Replace steering column shift tube or linkage as necessary.
▶ Transmission shifts gears hard.	1) Clutch pedal free-travel out of adjustment.	1) Adjust clutch pedal free-travel.
	2) Clutch does not release completely.	2) Adjust clutch as required.
	3) Low lubricant level or incorrect type.	3) Add or change lubricant as required.
	4) Shift lever binding or worn.	4) Eliminate binding or replace components as required.
	5) Worn or damaged internal shift mechanism.	5) Check internal transmission shift mechanism by shifting into and out of all gears. Repair or replace as required.
	6) Sliding gears or synchro rings binding.	6) Check for free movement of gears and synchronizers. Repair or replace as required.
	7) Housings and/or shafts out of alignment.	7) With transmission removed, check for binding between input shaft and crankshaft pilot bushing. Check clutch housing alignment. Repair or replace as required.
▶ Transmission jumps out of gear.	1) Shift linkage damaged or out of adjustment.	1) Adjust or repair shift linkage as required.
	2) Engine, transmission or shift lever bolts loose.	2) Tighten bolts as required.
	3) Clutch housing misaligned with crankshaft.	3) Align or replace as required.
	4) Pilot bushing or bearing worn.	4) Replace bushing or bearing.
	5) Damaged internal components in transmission.	5) Repair transmission as required. Check synchro rings and sliding sleeve. Check countershaft gear for wear. Check shift fork system for damage.

FIGURE 32-2 Manual transmission troubleshooting.

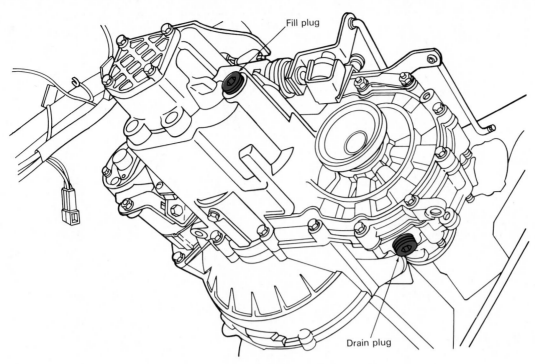

FIGURE 32-3 Transaxle fill and drain plugs. (Chrysler Corporation)

to do the job properly. In some cases, a special measuring tool is needed. Usually when such a tool is required, dimensions are given in the shop manual so you can make one (Figure 32-4).

Rod or Lever Linkage Typical linkage adjustment procedures call for the transmission to be in neutral. This means that both the shifter and the transmission are in neutral. This is normal, but if the linkage is way out of adjustment, it may be necessary to shift the transmission into neutral at the shift levers. Then the shift levers are disconnected from the shifter. Washer and cotter key or spring clip attachments are commonly used at this connection (Figure 32-5). The shift levers have a threaded end secured by a locknut. The locknut is loosened, and the threaded end is rotated until the shift lever end falls exactly in its hole in the shifter mechanism. The locknut is tightened, and the cotter key or spring clip is installed.

Some transaxles use a single tube as the shift linkage. These are adjusted by fitting a spacer at one point and removing all slack. Then the spacer is removed, and the adjustment is tested.

Cable Linkage Cable shifters may or may not be adjustable. In all cases, a cable attachment sequence is given which ensures that the cable is attached in

FIGURE 32-4 Special tool dimensions. (General Motors Corporation)

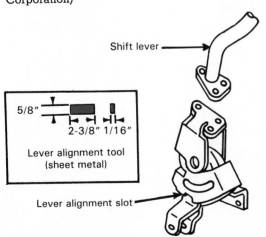

FIGURE 32-5 Shift linkage attachment. (General Motors Corporation)

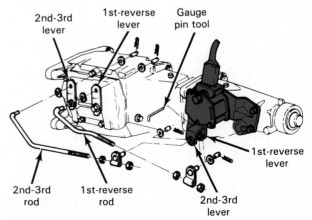

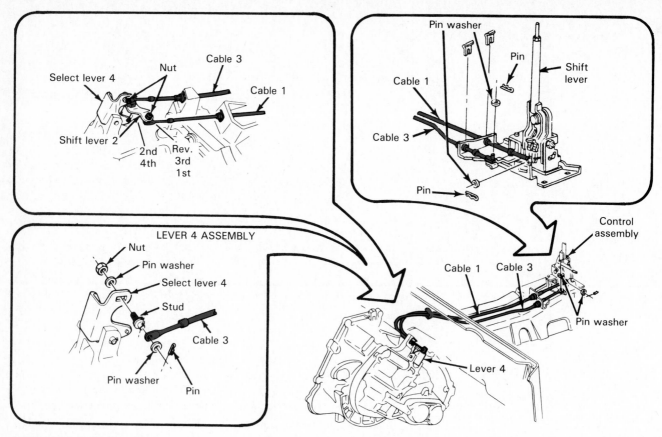

FIGURE 32-6 Cable shifter attachment. (General Motors Corporation)

the proper adjustment range (Figure 32-6). Some shifters are adjustable, and the adjustments differ from shifter to shifter.

Road Test

After any linkage adjustments, road-test the vehicle to ensure correct shifter operation. If the vehicle is cold, expect less precise shifting than if it is fully warmed up. It takes longer to warm a transmission than it does an engine. The best way to warm a transmission is to drive at freeway speeds for at least 10 minutes. Then the transmission will shift gears more easily. This is due to the thinner, warmer oil. The thinner oil lets the synchronizers work more efficiently.

Road tests are also necessary to verify customer complaint or to evaluate a transmission's condition before major work is planned.

Noises During the road test, listen for unusual noises while you are determining if the shifting is acceptable. Gear noise will sound like a whine. In extreme cases it can reach a siren-like pitch. Expect some whine in older cars with unsynchronized first gears. Bad bearings make a "rumble" or "growl."

One of the best ways to test the bearings is to listen to the transmission while the engine idles or

the car is parked. If there is a rumble while the clutch is engaged, you are hearing the transmission input shaft bearing. If the rumble dies when the clutch pedal is depressed, you can be sure the problem is in the transmission. If the rumble starts when the clutch pedal is depressed, the throw-out bearing may be the problem.

Shifting Worn synchronizers will cause gear clash during shifting. If the synchros are mildly worn, they will allow normal shifts but not faster-than-normal shifts. If the synchros are well worn, then gear clash will be evident on all shifts. Many times second gear will wear its synchros first, so pay extra attention to it. Also, thoroughly warming the transmission oil can make shifting easier. If the tested car has just traveled an extended distance, shifting problems may be harder to detect. Try road-testing the vehicle later, after the oil has cooled, if possible.

REMOVAL

Transmission removal is necessary to service the clutch or transmission internals. Before attempting gearbox removal, go over the job procedure in the shop manual and inspect the car. Make sure you have all necessary tools.

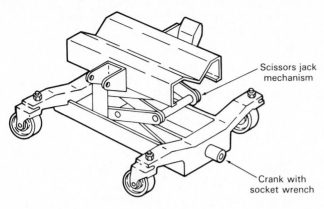

FIGURE 32-7 Transmission jack.

Tools

The vehicle must be raised, either on a hoist or with a jack, and then safely supported. Once the transmission is unbolted from the engine, it must be lowered slowly to the ground. Most transmissions are much too heavy to be lowered without mechanical help. In those cases, a **transmission jack** must be used (Figure 32-7). A transmission jack is a hydraulic jack with a special, large pad on it. The jack sits in a four-caster frame with scissors extension. The jack is extended until it contacts the gearbox. The jack's pad is then bolted to the transmission. This keeps the unwieldy transmission from rolling off the jack.

On a few cars, the engine and transmission must be removed as a unit. This can be done by lifting the assembly with an engine hoist or lowering the assembly underneath the car. Obviously, lifting hoists and jacks are required for this job. The shop manual will tell you if this method is necessary.

Transmission

Disconnecting With the vehicle safely raised, drain the transmission. Mark the propeller shaft and rear universal joint for reassembly and then remove the propeller shaft. Disconnect any electrical leads at the gearbox. There will be at least one for the backup lights plus others for emission controls, trip computers, and other accessories. Remove the speedometer connection from the transmission. If you can remove the speedometer cable, do so. It lets less dirt enter the transmission. Remove the speedometer cable by unthreading its end. Or remove the bolt or pin and carefully pull the entire speedometer drive gear from the transmission.

On column mount shifters, disconnect the shift linkage at the transmission shift levers. Do this by indexing the shift levers to their shafts. This will save readjusting the linkage at reassembly. Then unbolt the

levers' cinch bolt and pull the levers off the splined shafts.

On floor mount shifters, the shifter mechanism may need to be removed to clear the floor during transmission removal (Figure 32-8). Sometimes this is as easy as removing only the shift lever. Other times the entire shifter and linkage must come off.

Removal Install the transmission jack. At this time, double-check that the chassis is high enough to let the transmission clear the vehicle. Many times you can lower the transmission but can't move the transmission out of the **drive shaft tunnel** without raising the car. On some cars, the engine may need a support installed before the transmission is removed. Check the shop manual and engine mounts before disconnecting the transmission or crossmember. With the floor jack in place, disconnect any crossmember. Then remove the bell-housing bolts and slide the transmission to the rear and then down. The transmission must move to the rear to clear the input shaft of the clutch. Lower the jack completely and then slide the transmission/jack out from under the car.

Depending on the chassis, there may be other components in the way. It may be necessary to remove some of the exhaust system before dropping the transmission.

FIGURE 32-8 Removing a floor mount shifter. (Ford Motor Company)

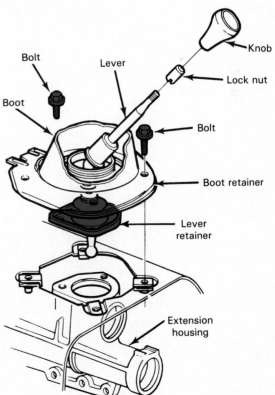

Transaxle

Many of the same precautions that apply to transmission removal also apply to transaxle removal. Make sure the car is high enough and securely supported on jack stands or on a hoist.

Disconnecting Drain the transaxle and remove all electrical connections. Remove the shift linkage. On transaxles, this is normally done by removing one bolt and swinging the shift rod out of the way. Remove starter and exhaust parts as necessary.

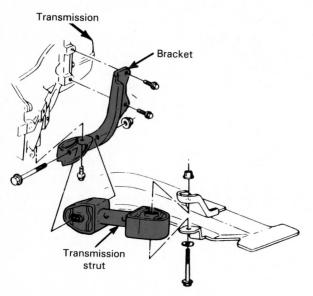

FIGURE 32-9 Transaxle mounts and brackets. (Oldsmobile Motor Division, GMC)

Remove the right and left drive axles. At the least, this requires unbolting the CV joints at the transaxle. Sometimes some of the suspension must be removed at the outer axle ends so the axles can be removed. Do not overextend or bend the CV joints. Do not puncture the dust boots.

Removal Next, examine the transaxle installation and see how many mounts, brackets, and crossmembers can safely be removed before attaching the transmission jack (Figure 32-9). Be sure the transaxle stays firmly bolted to the engine and that the engine is supported in the chassis. Usually, some of the upper brackets and possibly a lower crossmember can be removed before attaching the jack. When you are ready to lower the gearbox, attach the jack, remove the bell-housing bolts, and lower the unit.

The transaxle must be brought away from the engine before it is lowered. This is necessary in order to disengage the input shaft from the clutch disc. Do not let the transaxle hang from its input shaft, or damage to the input shaft bearings and seals could result.

DISASSEMBLY

Remove the bellhousing for increased working room. Four bolts attach it to the transmission case. At the transmission's rear, remove the rear extension housing, sometimes called the **tailshaft** (Figure 32-10). Next, open the side or top cover. This exposes the gears, synchros, and shafts. Removing the cover will also remove the shift forks (Figure 32–11).

FIGURE 32-10 Extension housing. (Chrysler Corporation)

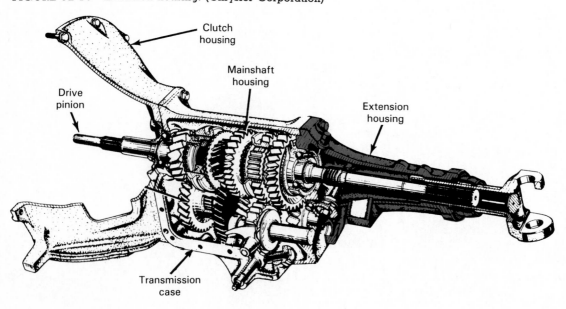

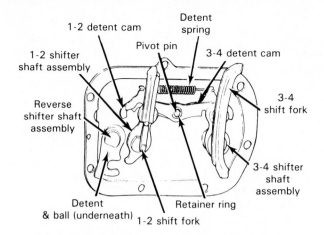

FIGURE 32-11 Inside cover parts. (General Motors Corporation)

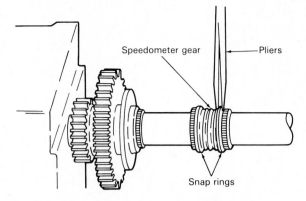

FIGURE 32-12 Removing the speedometer gear. (General Motors Corporation)

As you start to remove the gearbox internals, lay them on a clean rag. Keep them in order to aid reassembly. Also, beware of small springs, balls, and rollers from bearings. These small parts can easily become lost if you are not careful.

Follow detailed instructions in the shop manual. Most transmissions are disassembled by removing the input shaft bearing retainer at the outside front of the case. Remove the input shaft and front bearing. Remove any reverse and speedometer gears from the mainshaft section protruding from the rear of the case

(Figure 32-12). It may be necessary at this point to remove a snap ring retaining the mainshaft rear bearing. Also, the reverse idler shaft should be tapped out and the reverse idler removed (Figure 32-13). Now the mainshaft can be removed from the case. It may be necessary to manually shift the synchros to clear the case. Once the mainshaft is out, drive out the countershaft's shaft and lift out the countershaft.

The case should now be empty. Inspect it for any small parts. Sometimes the rollers from the countershaft bearings fall into the case during countershaft removal.

FIGURE 32-13 Reverse idler gear. (American Motors Corporation)

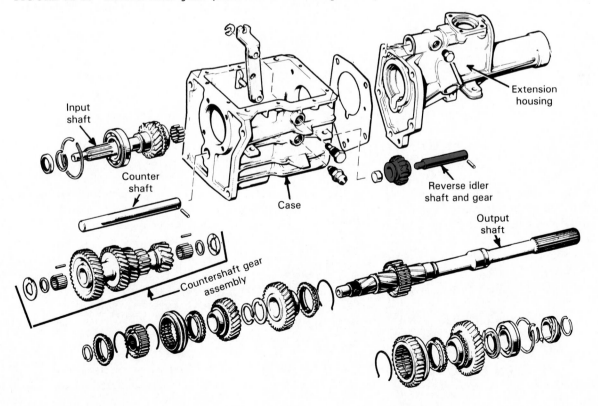

A REAL BASKET CASE

Not long ago, one of the guys was bemoaning a "basket case" transmission job he had been working on. That prompted an old hand to recount his initiation into the ranks of professional automotive mechanics.

It seems that he had spent a lot of time tinkering with his neighborhood's autos, so after high school he enrolled in an automotive trade school. Upon graduation he applied all over town for a position as a mechanic, but the best offer he could come up with was a job as a lot boy at a local dealership.

He had been washing cars and serving as "go-fer" for about a month when the manager asked him if he thought he could handle working on a little manual transmission problem. The "little problem" turned out to be a completely dismantled transmission which was presented to him, quite literally, in a basket. Furthermore, no one around the shop seemed to know from what model car it might have come. His task was simply to reassemble it.

All the mechanics were too busy to give any advice, and none of the manuals were any help because he didn't know what he had. Quite a while later, however, he had managed to get the thing together. The manager inspected his work and then told him he could begin work as a mechanic the following day. That is, as soon as he tore apart the transmission and put it back in the basket, so it would be ready for the next guy.

Kay O'Cullane
*San Diego Community College
Skill Center*

INSPECTION

Cleaning

Clean all parts in solvent. Do this one piece at a time so you don't mix the parts. Inspect all shafts for dings and scoring. Remove dings with a fine file. Dings result from banging the parts around during assembly and reassembly. Scoring results from dirty oil, which indicates lots of metal particles in the oil, or dirt. Dirt comes from loose or missing gaskets and seals.

Case

Inspect the case for cracks. Replace the case if cracked. Also, check for dings in the front and rear faces. File out any dings or high points.

Internal Parts

Inspect all the small parts for wear. There may be specifications to check thrust washers against. Otherwise, replace them if they show wear. In most overhauls, all the small rollers, washers, and spacers are replaced. If not, check each for wear. Scoring is okay on most washers as long as they are the original thickness. Rollers should be mark-free.

All gears should show only centered wear patterns. These patterns should be a polish and should not show substantial wearing of the gear face. Replace the gears if there has been metal removal on the gear teeth. Also check for cracks and chips. Pay particular attention to the locking teeth. They should not be rounded. If they are, replace the gear. The blocking rings are normally replaced as a matter of course. Remember that the blocking rings and locking teeth are the parts responsible for clash-free shifts. Because the blocking rings are relatively inexpensive, they are normally replaced. However, to get like-new shifting action, a new gear and sometimes even an entirely new synchronizer unit are needed.

Inspect the synchro units for smooth operation. Then take them apart and look at the splines, inserts, or spring-and-ball units. Replace any worn parts.

The large front and rear bearings are replaced during most overhauls too. If you wish to check them, clean them in solvent, squirt motor oil in them, and then rotate them by hand. Do not spin them quickly. Rather, rotate them slowly so you can feel any roughness. Replace any rough bearings or those with visually damaged balls and races.

REASSEMBLY

Reassembly must follow the order given in the shop manual. Generally, though, the parts are replaced in reverse of removal. Thus, the countershaft is laid in the case, the components are assembled onto the mainshaft, and the mainshaft is installed in the case. Reverse and speedometer parts are placed on the rear of the mainshaft, and the rear housing is installed on the case. A new oil seal is always used at the rear of the rear housing.

The input shaft and front bearing assembly is installed, and the bearing retainer is bolted over the assembly. The side cover with shift forks is bolted on, and finally the bell/housing is replaced.

Bearings

One special problem of transmission assembly is the many small rollers of the countershaft and input-to-

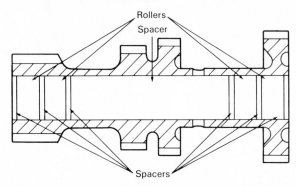

FIGURE 32-14 Cross section of countershaft showing roller and spacer position. (General Motors Corporation)

FIGURE 32-15 Using a dummy shaft. (General Motors Corporation)

mainshaft bearings. These rollers fit loosely inside their housings (Figure 32-14). To hold them in place during assembly, coat the housing, such as the countershaft bore, with thick grease. Petroleum jelly works well for this. Then press the rollers into the grease. The grease will hold the rollers in place.

A **dummy shaft** is needed for countershaft installation. The dummy shaft is just like the countershaft's shaft except a little shorter. It is only long enough to hold the rollers and any thrust washers in place. This allows the countershaft and washers to be lowered into the case. Then the actual shaft is tapped through the holes in the case into the countershaft. The dummy shaft is pushed by the actual shaft out the other end of the case. Figure 32-15 shows the dummy shaft used to remove the countershaft.

INSTALLATION

Installation is the reverse of removal, but keep several points in mind. First, never hang the transmission from its input shaft. This is easy to do when trying to mate

the gearbox with the engine. Use a transmission jack, or at least have a helper hold the transmission while you guide it in place. Most transmissions are doweled to the engine or bellhousing. Use the dowels to locate and support the transmission during installation.

The input shaft should also be lubed before installation. Lightly coat it with grease. This aids installation and lubes the pilot bearing. Don't get too much grease on the shaft, or some of it will fly off and get on the clutch.

Use care when installing the propeller shaft. Rough handling can damage the rear oil seal. On transaxles, care must be used when bolting up the axles. Do not overextend or bend the CV joints. It's a good idea to use new seals where the CV joints meet the transaxle.

Reattach the shift linkage using the match marks made during disassembly. Fill the gearbox with the proper fluid and road-test the installation.

TRADE TERMS

Drive Shaft Tunnel
Dummy Shaft

Tailshaft
Transmission Jack

REVIEW QUESTIONS

1. Where can transmission identification numbers be found?
2. Are all the problems usually blamed on the transmission its fault?

3. Why must transmission oil changes be done while the car is level?
4. Does transmission temperature make any difference in ease of shifting?

5. Which makes the higher-pitched sound, a bad bearing or a gear?

6. Which gear typically seems to wear its synchronizer the fastest?

7. Name a major piece of equipment necessary for transmission removal and installation.

8. How does dirt enter the transmission?

9. What are the two parts responsible for clash-free shifts?

10. How do you test the large front and rear ball bearings?

Automatic Transmissions

INTRODUCTION

The automatic transmission is a convenience that eliminates the driver's need to manually clutch, declutch, and shift between forward gear ranges or into reverse. The automatic transmission adapts engine torque to varying load and road conditions.

Because there is no clutch, all the driver has to do is to select the desired range, and the transmission will shift up or down automatically depending on engine load, road speed, and the position of the throttle.

This chapter explains how the automatic transmission can accomplish these tasks.

HYDRAULIC PRINCIPLES

A mechanism that uses liquids to transmit force is a hydraulic machine. Today's automobile uses a variety of hydraulic systems to assist steering, to brake, and to transmit power to the drive wheels. This chapter deals with only one of these machines, the automatic transmission, but remember that the same principles apply to all hydraulic machines.

Pascal's Law

A young French mathematician and physicist, Blaise Pascal, first studied the science of **hydraulics** in the seventeenth century. He discovered that if a pressure is applied to any part of a confined liquid, the pressure is transferred to any other part of the system with no loss. The shape of the system has no bearing on the pressure. The pressure acts with equal **force** on all surfaces.

Pascal also discovered that liquids cannot be compressed, nor do they expand when pressure is removed. Thus, liquid can transfer motion much the same as a mechanical lever. This motion can be transferred over long distances, and since liquid has no fixed shape, obstacles can easily be avoided.

Mechanical Advantage

In a hydraulic machine, the force applied relates directly to the result you get. A simple system may be constructed using a U-shaped tube with an outlet and inlet piston. As shown in Figure 33-1, each of the pistons has the same surface, and pressure is the same on all parts of the enclosed liquid. If you were to apply

FIGURE 33-1 Simple hydraulic system.

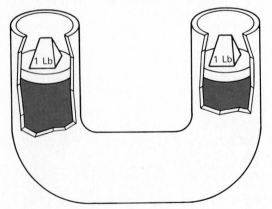

1 lb of pressure on one of the pistons, which has a cross-sectional area of 1 in.^{2}, the other piston would be forced upward in its tube, as Figure 33-2 illustrates. The only way to make the height of the two pistons equal would be to either remove the 1-lb weight or to place weights of equal value on each piston. Remember, when referring to how principles are applied in a hydraulic machine, you are talking about a closed system of lines and cylinders.

Motion Motion may be transmitted some distance in a closed system without change. If you were to connect with a tube two identical cylinders, each having a piston with a surface area of 1 in., when one piston moves, its counterpart in the other cylinder would also move. Figure 33-3 shows that the motion and force would be transmitted from one cylinder to the other. If the piston is forced down 1 in. in cylinder *B*, the piston will rise 1 in. in cylinder *A*.

Surface Area Hydraulic pressure can increase motion or force by using input and output pistons having

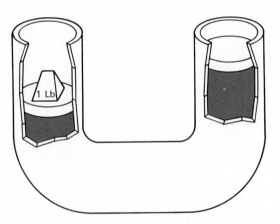

FIGURE 33-2 Liquid transmitting force.

FIGURE 33-3 Motion and force transmitted from one cylinder to another.

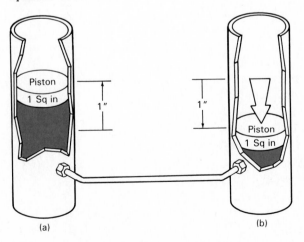

different surface areas. For example, if you were to connect one piston with an area of 1 in.² and another piston with a surface area of 10 square in., and apply a force of 5 lb to the 1-in. piston, liquid in the system would transmit this 5 lb of pressure to every square inch of the system. Because the larger piston has a surface area of 10 square in., the total effect would be to push the larger piston with a force of 50 lb (Figure 33-4).

A formula that will help you figure the forces acting in a hydraulic machine is

$$\frac{F_1}{F_2} = \frac{A_1}{A_2}$$

where F_1 = force, in pounds, applied to the smaller piston
F_2 = force, in pounds, applied to the larger piston
A_1 = area of the small piston in square inches
A_2 = area of the large piston in square inches

At first glance, you might think that you have achieved a mechanical advantage of 5 without any sacrifice. If you take a closer look, you can see that you can't get a 50-lb force from a 5-lb effort without sacrificing distance. The smaller piston (5-lb effort) has to move through a longer distance than the larger piston has to move. Assume the larger piston moved 1 ft. The formula is

$$\text{work input} = \text{work output}$$
$$F_1 \times D_1 = F_2 \times D_2$$

To calculate the distance, enter the known values:

$$5 \times D_1 = 50 \times 1$$
$$D_1 = 10$$

The smaller piston has to move 10 ft in order to move the larger piston 1 ft.

FIGURE 33-4   Determining output force.

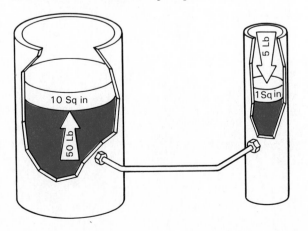

Automatic transmissions use different sizes of pistons at varying amounts of force and pressure to apply various devices and multiply torque.

HYDRAULIC SYSTEM COMPONENTS

Pressure-Regulating Valves

System pressures must be regulated for a hydraulic machine to function properly. This regulation is particularly important in automatic transmissions. Pressures are regulated by using orifices, pressure relief valves, and spool valves.

Orifices

The orifice is the simplest of these regulators. An orifice is a restriction or small opening used to regulate pressures in a line (Figure 33-5). Orifices are also used in transmissions to restrict fluid flow.

When fluid is applied to one side of an orifice, that side will have the higher pressure (Figure 33-6) until the fluid is equal on both sides (Figure 33-7).

To understand how this principle is used in a hydraulic circuit, refer to Figure 33-8. Both of the chambers are the same size and are separated by an orifice designed to restrict flow by 25%. If fluid were allowed to flow, you would have 100% pressure in the first chamber. This pressure would drop 25% upon

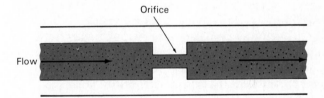

FIGURE 33-5   Orifice.

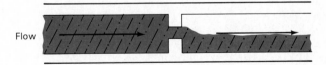

FIGURE 33-6   Orifice creating a pressure drop.

FIGURE 33-7   Pressure equalized.

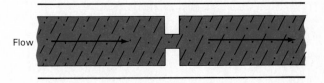

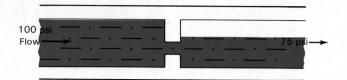

FIGURE 33-8　Orifice restricting flow by 25%.

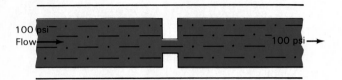

FIGURE 33-9　Full chambers with equal pressure.

leaving the chamber through the orifice. When the second chamber became full, as shown in Figure 33-9, pressure would equalize in both chambers. An orifice regulates by the size of the orifice opening and chamber size. Remember, though, fluid must be flowing for an orifice to be effective.

Pressure Relief Valves

Pressure relief valves prevent excessive pressure from damaging the hydraulic system. For this reason, they are sometimes called pressure-limiting valves. The valve allows fluid to escape through an outlet port when a predetermined pressure is met. The valve also prevents fluid flow until a specific pressure is achieved.

　　The pressure relief valve normally uses a piston and a spring in a chamber that has an inlet and outlet port (Figure 33-10). Fluid enters the inlet port and exerts pressure on the piston. As pressure increases, the fluid pressure overcomes the spring pressure, moving the piston and uncovering the outlet port. The surface area of the piston and spring pressure determine the amount of pressure allowed in the system.

FIGURE 33-10　Pressure relief valve.

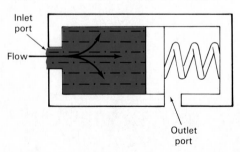

Spool Valves

The third type of pressure-regulating device is the spool valve, so called because it resembles the spools used for sewing thread. Most of the valves used in automatic transmissions are spool valves.

Lands　Figure 33-11 illustrates a simple spool valve. It has two lands, a valley, and four faces. Fluid pressure is exerted on any of the four faces. Different-sized lands move the valve. A larger surface area on one land will cause movement opposite the larger surface area if equal pressure is applied to both areas (Figure 33-12). If one land has twice the surface area of another, the larger land will produce twice the output force.

　　Spool valves may have more than two lands (Figure 33-13). These lands may be different in size. The

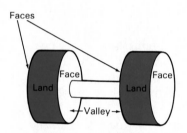

FIGURE 33-11　Simple spool valve.

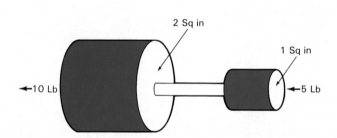

FIGURE 33-12　Land size determining force.

FIGURE 33-13　Multi-land spool.

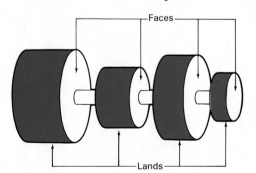

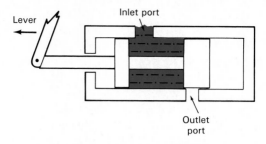

The manually operated switching valve uses a lever to open and close hydraulic circuits.

FIGURE 33-14 Manually-operated switching valve.

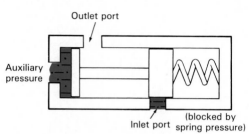

The hydraulically operated switching valve uses auxiliary hydraulic pressure to open circuits. The circuit is closed when the auxiliary isn't high enough to overcome spring pressure.

FIGURE 33-15 Hydraulically-operated switching valve.

FIGURE 33-16 Ball check valves.

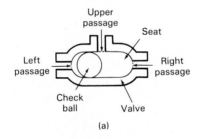

(a)

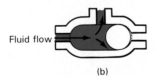

(b)

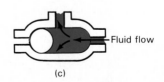

(c)

Two hydraulic circuits can use the same passage. (a) If fluid pressure from the left passage is greater, the right passage is blocked. (b) If fluid pressure from the right passage is greater, the left passage is blocked. (c)

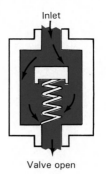

Valve open

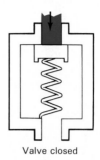

Valve closed

FIGURE 33-17 Poppet check valves.

valve body in an automatic transmission uses spool valves to regulate hydraulic pressures for a variety of driving conditions.

Pressures Spool valves also balance pressures in a hydraulic system. Fluid pressures exerted against one side of the spool valve may be balanced with a spring, a lever, or opposing fluid force. The factors that determine how a spool valve reacts are inlet fluid pressure, inlet port size, the surface area of the spool face upon which hydraulic pressure is acting, opposing spring pressure, and opposing lever action.

Switching Valves

Switching valves in a hydraulic system direct fluid from one passage or circuit to another. They may be operated manually, electrically, or hydraulically. A switching valve directs fluid to one or more circuits. Several examples of switching valves are shown in Figures 33-14 through 33-17.

TRANSMISSION HYDRAULIC PUMPS

Most automotive automatic transmissions use a positive-displacement pump to develop necessary operating pressures. Fluid is drawn into the pump from the transmission's sump or oil pan.

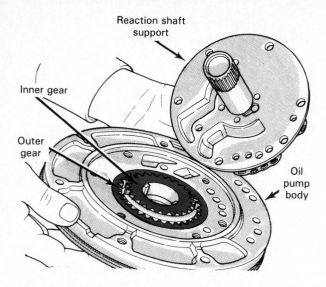

FIGURE 33-18   Gear pump. (Chrysler Corporation)

Positive-displacement pumps are so called because they displace, or deliver, the same amount of fluid during each revolution of the pump. The *volume delivered* per revolution of the pump remains constant regardless of pump speed. *Delivery rate* may be increased by increasing pump speed.

Two types of positive-displacement pumps are used in domestic cars. General Motors, Ford, Borg-Warner, and some Chrysler products use a gear pump (Figure 33-18). Most Chrysler and 1972-and-later American Motors cars use a rotor pump.

Some late-model transmissions use a variable-capacity, vane-type pump. Maximum capacity is used *only* when priming the hydraulic system upon engine start-up and during high-engine-load conditions where high system pressure is required.

Less than maximum capacity is used under other conditions. The GM THM 200-4R transmission uses such a variable-displacement pump.

Some late-model cars use a pump mounted in the front of the transmission case. The pump develops pressure whenever the engine is running. Before the mid- to late 1960s, many cars had a second pump mounted at the rear of the transmission that was driven by the output shaft. The rear-mounted pump developed pressure whenever car speed reached a predetermined value. This feature enabled early automatic transmission cars to be push-started, if necessary.

Gear Pump

A gear pump consists of a two-piece pump body, an inner gear, and an outer gear. When mounted in front of the transmission case, two tabs on the inner gear engage the hub of the torque converter. The torque converter is attached via a flexplate to the engine's crankshaft.

Figure 33-18 shows the working parts of a front-mounted gear pump. The inner gear is driven at engine speed and drives the outer gear. The gears mesh on one side of the pump and are separated by a crescent on the other. A low-pressure area is created where the gears separate. This low-pressure area creates a suction, which draws fluid from the sump. Pressure is created by decreasing the clearance between the drive and driven gears. Fluid is pushed from this high-pressure area into an outlet passage in the pump body.

Rotor Pump

Another type of hydraulic pump used in automatic transmissions is the rotor pump. It, like the gear pump, is named for the internal components used to develop operating pressure. Both pumps operate on the same principle, with the rotor pump using an inner and outer rotor rather than the gears found in the gear pump. The rotor pump doesn't use a separating crescent in its body (Figure 33-19). A low pressure develops as the rotor's clearance widens, and the resulting suction draws fluid from the sump. A high-pressure area is created when the rotor's clearance decreases. This high-pressure area forces fluid from the pump under pressure.

The front-mounted rotor pump is driven at engine speed by the torque converter. It is turning any time the engine is running.

Vane Pump

A third type of hydraulic pump uses sliding vanes and a movable outer slide to vary output per pump revolution, according to transmission needs. On the variable-displacement pump, the effective area of the vanes and the shape of the cavity the fluid is drawn

FIGURE 33-19   Rotor pump.

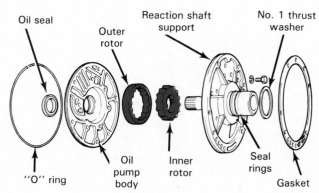

into can be infinitely varied by moving the position of an outer slide (Figure 33-20). In the low-output mode, less horsepower is required to operate the pump, thereby improving fuel economy.

MAINLINE PRESSURE

Mainline pressure is the hydraulic pressure used to operate apply devices. It is the source of all hydraulic pressures in the transmission. The fluid being forced from the hydraulic pump meets several restrictions.

These restrictions increase fluid pressure. If no way to regulate these pressures, the tra. would probably be damaged. The pressure . valve regulates these pressures in automatic tr. sions.

Pressure Regulator Valve

The pressure regulator valve controls the high and lo limits of fluid pressure in an automatic transmission. When used with positive-displacement pumps, the valve provides a variable restriction in the hydraulic

FIGURE 33-20 Variable-displacement, vane-type pump. (General Motors Corporation)

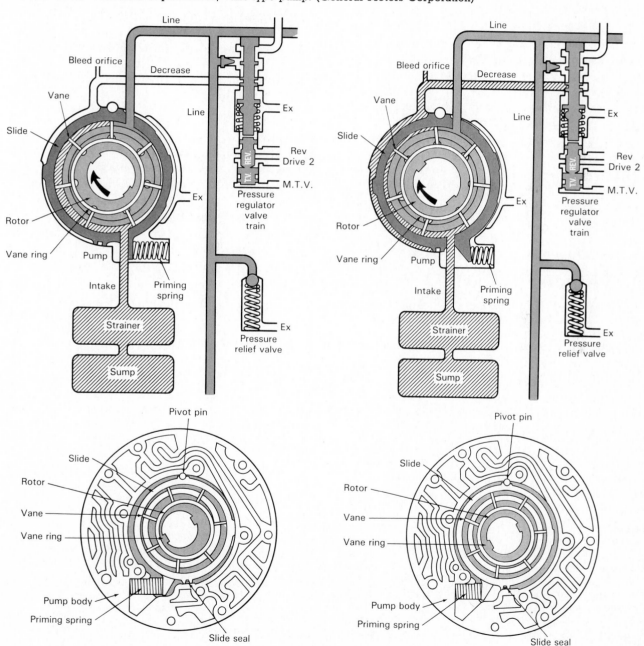

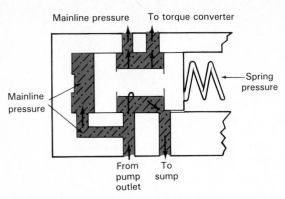

Mainline pressure   To torque converter

Spring pressure

Mainline pressure

Mainline pressure

From pump outlet

To sump

FIGURE 33-21   Pressure regulator valve.

circuit. The size of the opening is changed to keep hydraulic pressures at desired levels. When used with variable-displacement pumps, the valve adjusts the position of an outer slide which determines pump output per revolution.

Figure 33-21 shows an example of a pressure regulator valve used with a positive-displacement pump. The valve has an inlet port, an outlet port to the torque converter, a mainline pressure port, and a port for bleeding excess pressure back to the sump. Fluid from the pump creates pressure that forces the spool valve against the spring. As hydraulic pressure increases, the spring pressure is overcome. The movement of the valve uncovers the port to the torque converter and to the mainline circuit. Fluid pressure will continue to push against the spring, increasing pressure as engine speed increases. A port releases excess pressure into the sump. This port is necessary to protect the transmission from excessively high pressures.

Pressures between the pump and the valve are about the same as at the mainline pressure outlet port. Pressure is almost equal on both sides of the spool valve, creating a balancing effect. Mainline pressure is returned to the sump by this balancing effect.

THROTTLE PRESSURE

Throttle pressure is a function of throttle position and, in some cases, engine load. It's used to control an automatic transmission's upshifts and downshifts. In many cases, it helps regulate mainline pressure. Throttle pressure is developed from mainline pressure and is controlled by the throttle valve.

Vacuum Modulator   The throttle valve may be operated mechanically, via throttle linkage, or controlled by a vacuum diaphragm, called the *vacuum modulator.* The vacuum modulator senses intake manifold vacuum and, therefore, engine load. The following relationships show the conditions which cause a reaction by a modulator-type throttle valve:

CONTINUOUSLY VARIABLE TRANSMISSIONS

The major advantage of a manual transmission is that it offers better fuel economy compared to an automatic. Although much progress has been made in making automatics more efficient with the introduction of four-speed overdrives and lockup converters, they are still not as efficient as manuals, and they are more complicated and expensive to manufacture. What most automakers have been looking for is a transmission that is efficient, convenient, and uncomplicated. And many people believe that the continuously variable transmission (CVT) meets those criteria.

The basic mechanism of a CVT is a belt that runs between variable pulleys: a driving pulley attached to the engine's driveshaft and a driven pulley in the transmission. In concept this arrangement is similar to a 10-speed bicycle, with the belt and pulleys replacing the chain and sprockets. The CVT allows the engine to operate at its maximum efficiency while the transmission does all the work.

Most attempts at CVTs have not been very successful because they used rubber belts that could not stand the wear and tear. Van Doorne Tranmissie has gone a long way toward resolving that problem by developing a metal belt with Borg-Warner. But now the Dayco Corp of Dayton, Ohio has introduced a rubber belt that it claims will, in certain applications, withstand punishment.

The primary advantage of a rubber belt versus metal, according to Dayco, is that it will cost 50% less. This is because rubber is cheaper and doesn't have to be lubricated, and it has a higher coefficient of friction so the pulley system can operate at lower pressures.

Dayco's system is typical of other CVTs: When you accelerate, the engine races up to a predetermined level in accordance to the driver's power demand, and the rest of the car feels as if it's trying to catch up. This is not an annoying feature, and it really lets the driver know that there's something new and different in the powertrain. In fact, the CVT may actually make electric and gas trubine-powered cars more feasible, because these "engines" can be set to operate at their maximum efficiencies.

On Dayco's test car a microprocessor maintains optimum engine output, and to do this the on-board computer monitors engine speed, road speed, throttle position, and vacuum. Interestingly, the computer can be programmed with different performance modes that allow you to obtain maximum fuel economy or ultimate performance at the push of a button.

Road & Track
CBS Publications

□ Engine load high, low manifold vacuum: throttle pressure high

□ Engine load low, high manifold vacuum: throttle pressure low

Remember that there is a direct relationship between engine load and throttle pressure. Whenever there is a high engine load, there is high throttle pressure, and low engine loads will have low throttle pressures.

The vacuum-operated throttle valve is used in the majority of today's automobiles. Most General Motors, Ford Motor Company, and import transmissions use a vacuum modulator to control throttle pressure. Some late-model GM gas and diesel engines, however, use a mechanical modulator.

Throttle Valve All Chrysler Corporation transmissions and some transmissions of other manufacturers use a mechanically operated throttle valve. In the future, the throttle valve may be an electrically operated potentiometer. The Renault Alliance uses such a throttle sensor.

As mentioned, a vacuum-operated throttle valve system uses intake manifold vacuum to control movement of a diaphragm in the vacuum modulator. The diaphragm is connected to the spool-type throttle valve by a push rod (Figure 33-22). Manifold vacuum causes the diaphragm to try to overcome the opposing spring pressure, causing the push rod and spool valve to move.

Mechanically or electrically operated throttle valves work basically the same way as vacuum-operated throttle valves and perform the same function. The only difference is the method used to move the throttle valve. A mechanically operated throttle valve is controlled by a rod or cable attached to the carburetor throttle linkage (Figure 33-23).

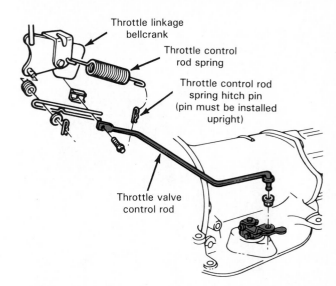

FIGURE 33-23   Throttle control rod. (American Motors Corporation)

GOVERNOR PRESSURE

One other pressure is used in automatic transmissions to time upshifts and downshifts. **Governor pressure** is a function of vehicle output shaft speed, and it opposes throttle pressure at the shift valve(s).

The governor has two flyweights and a spool valve. It may be either gear driven (Figure 33-24) or pinned to the output shaft of the transmission (Figure

FIGURE 33-24   Governor assembly, gear driven. (General Motors Corporation)

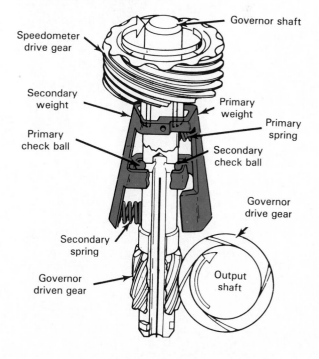

FIGURE 33-22   Vacuum modulator assembly. (General Motors Corporation)

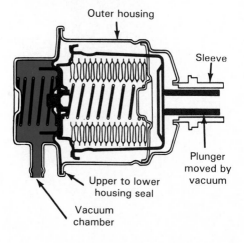

Governor support
and parking gear
Snap rings
Shaft
Governor body

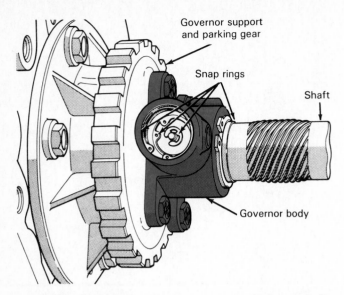

FIGURE 33-25 Governor assembly, pinned output shaft. (Chrysler Corporation)

33-25). As the governor is rotated, both flyweights are thrown outward by centrifugal force. The outward movement of the flyweights causes the governor valve to move farther into its bore. The mainline pressure port is opened, and at the same time the exhaust port is closed. As vehicle speed continues to increase, the inlet port is opened further, causing an increase in governor pressure. At steady vehicle speeds, the valve is balanced, and governor pressure is constant.

OTHER HYDRAULIC CIRCUITS

The transmission pump sends fluid to the torque converter, the transmission cooler, and the lubrication circuits throughout the transmission. Each of these circuits can be studied in a shop manual for specific transmissions.

Valve Body

Most of the valves in an automatic transmission are installed in a casting called a *valve body*. It also contains passages and control circuits for the flow of hydraulic fluid between these valves and to the various clutches and bands (Figure 33-26).

PLANETARY GEARSETS

As with step-type manual transmissions, *planetary gearsets* used in automatic transmissions multiply engine torque by reducing output shaft speed. The gearset

FIGURE 33-26 Valve body assembly.

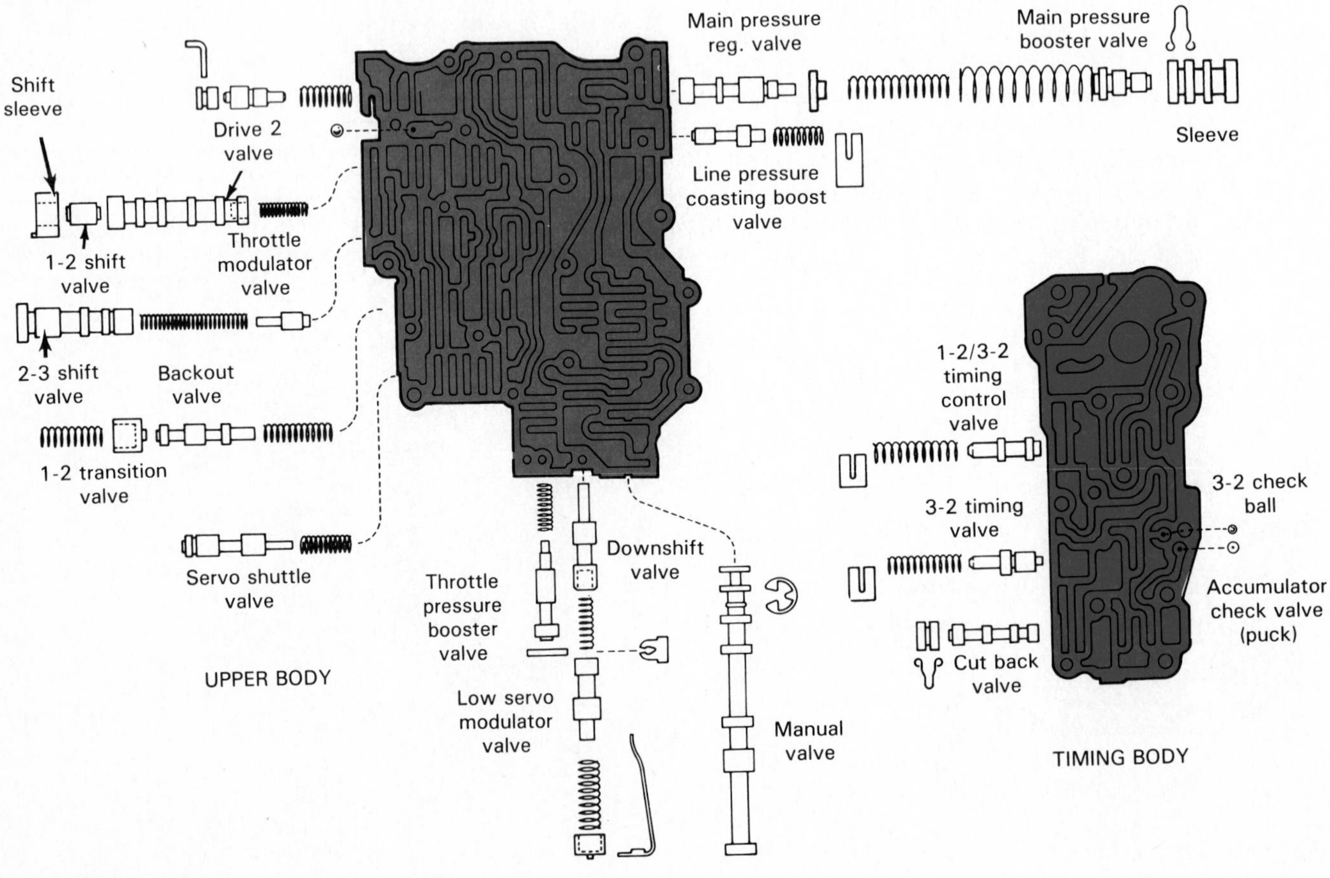

Shift
sleeve
Drive 2
valve
1-2 shift
valve
Throttle
modulator
valve
2-3 shift
valve
Backout
valve
1-2 transition
valve
Servo shuttle
valve
UPPER BODY
Throttle
pressure
booster
valve
Low servo
modulator
valve
Downshift
valve
Manual
valve
Main pressure
reg. valve
Main pressure
booster valve
Sleeve
Line pressure
coasting boost
valve
1-2/3-2
timing
control
valve
3-2 timing
valve
Cut back
valve
3-2 check
ball
Accumulator
check valve
(puck)
TIMING BODY

can also reverse the direction of output shaft rotation and transmit engine torque directly at a 1:1 ratio—all by driving or holding various gearset members. And on overdrive automatic transmissions, an additional planetary gearset gives the capability of increasing output shaft speed over that of engine speed—with a resulting loss of mechanical advantage (torque).

Parts

A simple planetary gearset (Figure 33-27) consists of three members: the *sun gear,* the **planet carrier assembly,** and the **internal gear** or *ring gear.*

The gear at the center of the planetary gearset is the sun gear. The other gears are concentric with it and revolve, like planets, around the sun gear. These revolving gears are referred to as planet gears or *planet pinions.* The planet pinions are held within the gearset by the *planet carrier assembly.* The outer gear of the set is the internal or ring gear. The internal or ring gear has its teeth cut on the inside of the gear and is meshed with the planet pinions. The resulting gearset is compact.

In a planetary gearset, the teeth on each gear are always meshed with the teeth of another gear; therefore, it is very strong. If you were to drive one gear, all the other gears would be affected. To work, one member of the set has to drive while another one is held. The third member becomes the driven or output member. Any member of the gearset may be the drive or **input member.** It may also be the driven or **output member.** The member of the gearset that is held is called the *reaction member.*

FIGURE 33-27   Simple planetary gearset.

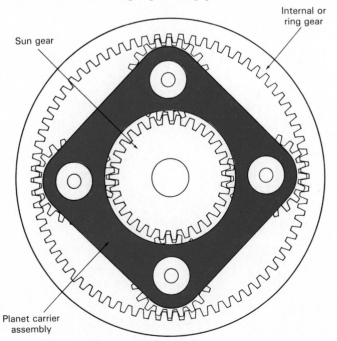

How Planetary Gears Work

As mentioned, planetary gears are used for **gear reduction, overdrive,** reverse, and **direct drive** by holding different members of the gearset. Figures 33-28 through 33-37 show how each of these tasks is accomplished. Check the illustrations carefully to see how so many gear ratios come from this simple assembly.

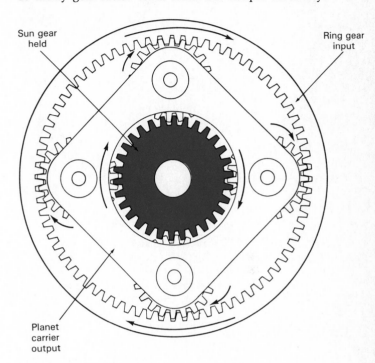

FIGURE 33-28   Gear reduction, sun gear held.

FIGURE 33-29   Gear reduction, ring gear held.

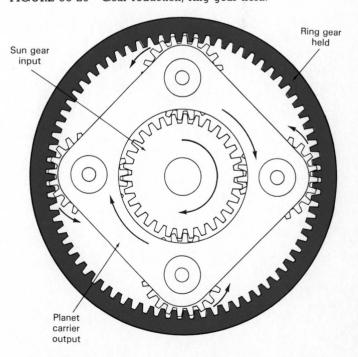

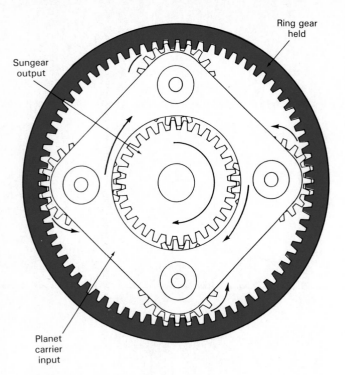

FIGURE 33-30   Overdrive, ring gear held.

FIGURE 33-31   Overdrive, sun gear held.

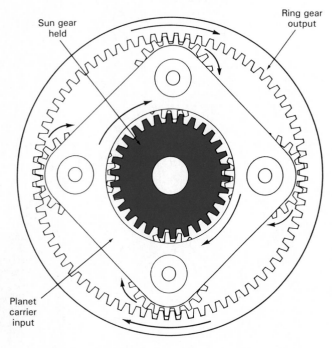

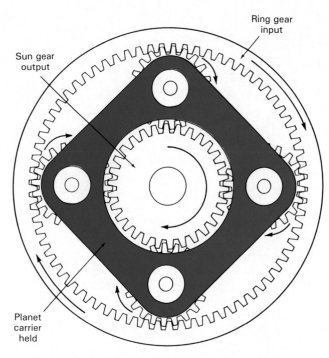

FIGURE 33-32   Reverse, sun gear output.

FIGURE 33-33   Reverse, ring gear output.

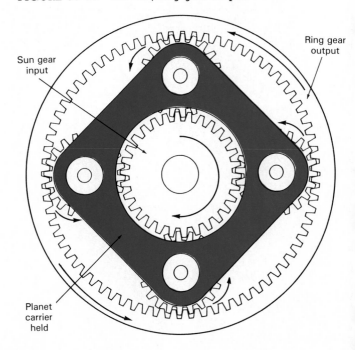

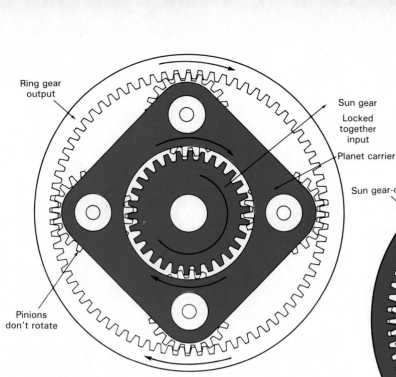

Ring gear
output

Sun gear

Locked
together
input

Planet carrier

Pinions
don't
rotate

FIGURE 33-34   Direct drive, ring gear output.

FIGURE 33-35   Direct drive, planet carrier output.

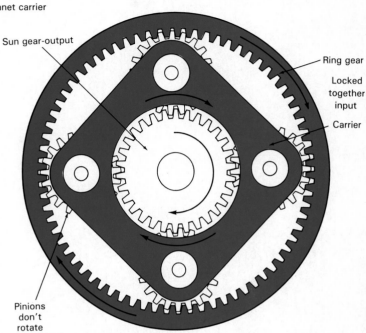

Sun gear-output

Ring gear

Locked
together
input

Carrier

Pinions
don't
rotate

FIGURE 33-36   Direct drive, sun gear output.

FIGURE 33-37   Neutral (no member is held).

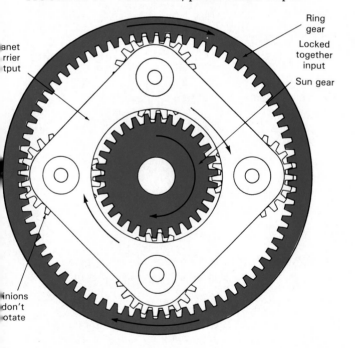

Planet
carrier
output

Ring
gear

Locked
together
input

Sun gear

Pinions
don't
rotate

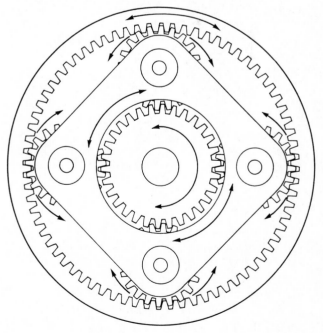

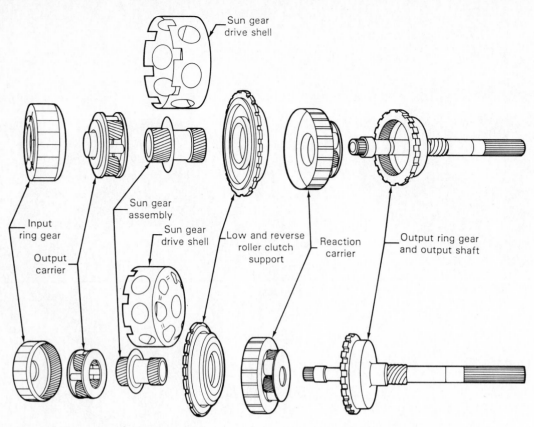

FIGURE 33-38 Compound planetary gearset. (Buick Motor Division, GMC)

Compound Planetary Gearsets

The planetary gearsets described above are simple gearsets. They were used in early automatic transmissions—mostly two-speed units. Most modern three- and four-speed automatic transmissions use a compound planetary gearset. A compound planetary gearset is usually an assembly of two or more simple planetary gearsets that are built together to provide various combinations of gear reduction, overdrive, direct drive, and reverse.

The most common compound planetary gearset is the Simpson gearset. This gearset consists of two ring gears and two planet carrier assemblies sharing a common sun gear (Figure 33-38).

APPLY DEVICES

The mechanical devices that are hydraulically actuated to hold or drive the members of a planetary gearset are **apply devices**. *Servos and clutch pistons* are the apply devices used in automatic transmissions.

Both the servo and clutch piston apply devices develop an output force when hydraulic pressure is applied. The servo applies force to a contracting band, and the clutch piston applies force to a multiple-disc

clutch. The multiple-disc clutch may be used as a holding device, whereas the band is used only as a holding device—similar to an external drum brake.

One other type of clutch is used in many transmissions. It is considered to be an apply device even though it isn't hydraulically applied. This device is a one-way clutch. It prevents a member of the planetary gearset from turning in one direction while allowing it to turn freely in the other direction.

Servos

As mentioned, a servo is a piston and cylinder assembly that applies and releases a band onto a transmission drum. The servo operates when hydraulic pressure is applied to the surface area of its piston. The piston has a large surface area, which multiplies the hydraulic force of the system. The higher force is needed because the pressure necessary to apply the band to its drum is greater than system pressure.

Linkages The servo is connected to a band using one of four operating linkages. Figure 33-39 illustrates the four types of linkages. Pay particular attention to how each uses the linkage to transmit force from the servo to the band and how three of the four have provisions for adjusting the band.

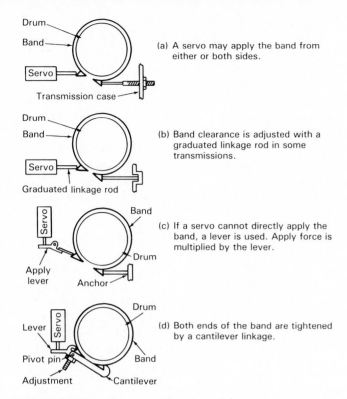

(a) A servo may apply the band from either or both sides.

(b) Band clearance is adjusted with a graduated linkage rod in some transmissions.

(c) If a servo cannot directly apply the band, a lever is used. Apply force is multiplied by the lever.

(d) Both ends of the band are tightened by a cantilever linkage.

FIGURE 33-39 Servo and band applications.

There are several different servo designs currently in use, but all are designed to control the application and release of a transmission band.

The simplest of the servo designs has hydraulic pressure applied against a piston, which in turn moves the linkage toward the band. The band and servo are released by a spring on the opposite side of the piston. The spring causes the piston to return to its original position whenever hydraulic pressure is removed.

A more common design has the servo released by hydraulic pressure on the spring side of the piston. The pressure on the other side of the piston is exhausted, returning the piston to its normal position and releasing the band.

One type of servo uses hydraulic pressure on both sides of the piston and has no opposing spring.

Bands

Transmission bands encircle a drum that is connected to a member of a planetary gearset. When the band is tightened, the gearset member is held. As stated earlier in this chapter, when one member of a planetary gearset is driven and a second member held, the third member develops output motion.

The band is secured on one end by a stationary anchor or by an adjustment screw (Figures 33-40 and 33-41). The opposite end of the band is attached to

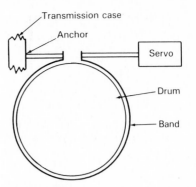

FIGURE 33-40 Stationary anchor used to secure one end of a band.

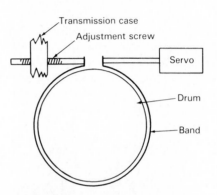

FIGURE 33-41 One end of a band connected to an adjustment screw.

the servo. When pressure is applied to the servo, the band tightens around the drum.

Band Designs   All transmission bands are constructed of steel with a bonded friction lining. Their size and construction vary depending on the work they are required to do. The three most common bands are the light single-wrap band, the heavy single-wrap band, and the double-wrap band (Figure 33-42). The light single-wrap band is used when there isn't much force required to hold the band. The heavy single-wrap band is used in both light- and heavy-duty applications. The double-wrap band is the strongest of the three,

FIGURE 33-42 Transmission bands.

(a) Single-wrap band (light)

(b) Single-wrap band (heavy)

(c) Double-wrap band

gives smoother shifts, and is the most expensive to manufacture.

Adjustments   Transmission bands are designed to slip when they are first engaged. This slippage prevents very harsh engagements and possible transmission damage. Over a period of time, slippage will cause the band's friction to wear. The wear must be compensated for by either manual or automatic adjustments.

Accumulators

Accumulators absorb the shock or surge resulting from sudden pressure changes in an automatic transmission's hydraulic system. By absorbing the shocks and surges, an accumulator helps prevent harsh shifts in an automatic transmission. The cushioning diverts part of the fluid in the circuit to another circuit or chamber.

Accumulators are either piston or valve actuated. The piston type may be either installed inside or outside of the servo (Figure 33-43). Not all servos use accumulators.

Multiple-Disc Clutches

The multiple-disc clutch is another apply device in automatic transmissions. It, unlike the band, may be used as either a holding or driving device.

The multiple-disc clutch consists of a stack of two or more friction clutch discs alternated between two or more steel discs. The friction (drive) discs are splined to the clutch drum or transmission case. The assembly also contains one or more pistons and springs. Pressure plates, seals, return spring retainers, and snap rings make up the rest of the assembly (Figure 33-44).

Operation   The multiple-disc clutch operates as follows: Oil pressure applied to the clutch piston overcomes return spring pressure and moves a pressure plate, clamping the drive and driven discs together. Depending on the function of that particular clutch assembly, it will either drive a planetary gear member or hold one from turning. When hydraulic pressure is released, the clutch return spring(s) move the piston

FIGURE 33-43   Accumulator shown outside the servo and inside the servo.

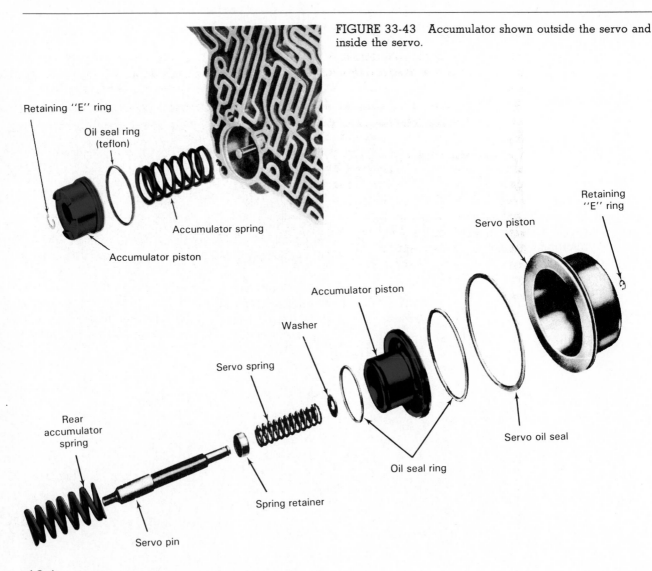

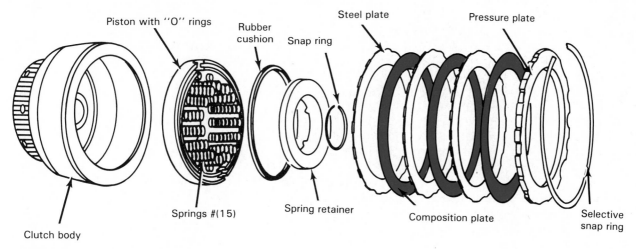

FIGURE 33-44　Clutch assembly.

away from the pressure plate, unclamping the drive and driven discs.

Modern automatic transmissions may have as many as five multiple-disc clutch assemblies—each with different functions. See a shop manual for details on power flow.

One-Way Clutches

As previously mentioned, the one-way clutch is another type of apply device used in automatic transmissions. There are two types of one-way clutches: the roller clutch and the sprag clutch. Either of these can be used only as a holding device. The roller clutch is used more frequently than the sprag clutch.

Roller Clutch　The roller clutch allows whatever unit it is engaged with to rotate in only one direction (Figure 33-45). It has a hub, rollers, and springs surrounded by a cam cut drum. If the drum illustrated in Figure 33-45 rotates counterclockwise, the rollers are wedged into pockets cut into the drum. These pockets lock

the drum and hub together. If the hub is locked to the transmission's case, rotation is prevented in the lockup position. Clockwise rotation of the drum causes the rollers to move outward and away from the pockets, allowing it to rotate freely.

Sprag Clutch　The sprag clutch, commonly called a sprag, performs the same function as the roller clutch. It consists of a hub and a drum separated by figure-eight shapes (sprags) (Figure 33-46). The sprags are asymmetrical, slightly longer on one axis than another. When the hub or drum rotates so that the sprags tilt on their "short" side, there is clearance between the races and the assembly freewheels. But when rotation starts to reverse, the sprags tilt on their "long" side, wedging between the races and preventing rotation.

Both the one-way roller and sprag clutches have several advantages over other apply devices. They are fast acting and do not require hydraulic pressure to operate.

FIGURE 33-46　Sprag clutch.

FIGURE 33-45　One-way roller clutch.

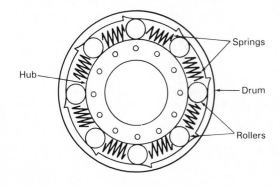

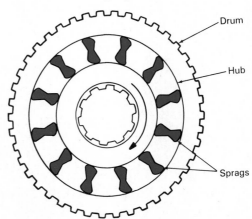

TORQUE CONVERTERS AND FLUID COUPLINGS

For a transmission to be fully automatic, the engine must be coupled or uncoupled from the transmission. A fluid coupling or a torque converter accomplishes this coupling or uncoupling. Both the torque converter and the fluid coupling are used to transfer engine torque to the transmission. The torque converter has the additional capacity to multiply torque to the transmission.

The first fluid coupling in a domestic automobile was used by Chrysler in 1938. This was a semiautomatic setup that still used a manual clutch between the engine and fluid coupling.

Buick was the first to use fluid couplings in their Dynaflow transmission in 1948.

Fluid Couplings

The fluid coupling uses an impeller, the driving member, and a turbine, the driven member (Figure 33-47). Each member has vanes which face each other. The impeller is attached to the engine's flywheel or flexplate. The turbine is attached to the transmission's input shaft. Both members are enclosed in the fluid coupling housing.

Fluid Flow   The transmission's hydraulic pump forces fluid under pressure into the fluid coupling. At the same time, the impeller is being driven at engine speed. The impeller's vanes pick up fluid in the housing and throw it toward the turbine. The expelled fluid moves in one of two paths: rotary or vortex flow.

Rotary flow is the circular movement of fluid in the same direction as the impeller.

Vortex flow is the movement of fluid at a right

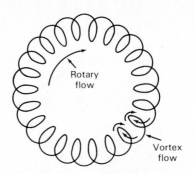

FIGURE 33-48   Rotary and vortex flow paths.

angle to the impeller rotation. Figure 33-48 illustrates rotary and vortex flow paths.

Vanes on the impeller are curved to help direct the fluid. When the fluid leaves the impeller, it is thrown outward and upward into the turbine's vanes. As impeller speed increases, rotary flow and vortex flow become more violent, causing the turbine to turn at a faster speed. Vortex flow remains dominant as long as there is a great speed differential between the engine-driven impeller and transmission-splined turbine. However, as the vehicle reaches cruising speed, turbine speed approaches 90% of impeller speed, and rotary flow prevails.

To keep the oil in the impeller and turbine from working against itself, a split ring is installed in the center of each member. The ring helps curb turbulence by keeping the oil from developing too much force.

The fluid coupling acts to smoothly transfer engine torque to the transmission. However, at low engine speeds, the fluid coupling is an inefficient pump, and performance is sluggish. The lack of low-speed torque was the main reason for developing torque convertors. As mentioned, a torque converter can multiply engine torque for improved low-speed performance.

Torque Converter

The torque converter is constructed in much the same way as the fluid coupling. It has an impeller (drive member) and a turbine (driven member). In some cases there may be more than one impeller or turbine. The vanes on both the impeller and turbine are curved around a doughnut-shaped center section or *torus* to maximize vortex flow (Figure 33-49).

Stator   The stator is the third member in a torque converter. It is a small wheel-like device with airfoil-shaped vanes inserted between the impeller and turbine. Its job is to redirect and accelerate vortex speeds so that the force of the fluid is added to that leaving the impeller. This results in torque multiplication. (Figure 33-50).

FIGURE 33-47   Fluid coupling. (General Motors Corporation)

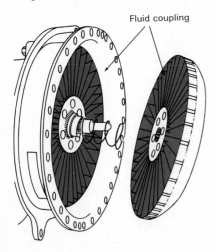

Fluid coupling

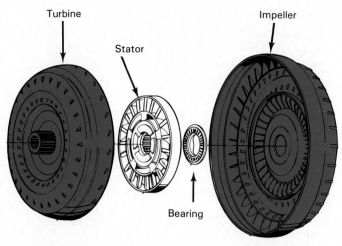

FIGURE 33-49   Torque converter assembly. (General Motors Corporation)

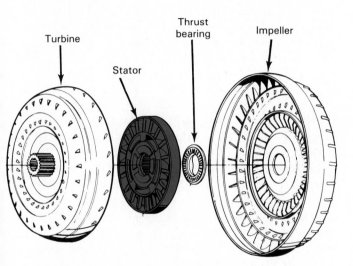

FIGURE 33-50   Stator assembly. (General Motors Corporation)

Fluid Flow   The fluid's flow in a torque converter begins when the impeller starts to spin, throwing fluid into the turbine's curved vanes. The fluid is passed through the turbine's vanes and passed to the stator. The stator is splined to a stationary shaft fixed to the front of the transmission and can turn only in the same direction as the impeller. It is prevented from turning in the other direction by either a sprag or roller one-way clutch. The fluid from the stator is added to the flow from the impeller. This addition accelerates the fluid flow from the impeller and increases the torque transferred to the turbine. As long as there is a relative speed difference between the impeller and the turbine, vortex flow is created, and engine torque can be multiplied. The greater the speed difference between the two members, such as low vehicle speeds

and high engine torque inputs, the greater the torque multiplication.

When turbine speed approaches 90% of impeller speed, fluid flow begins to hit the back of the stator vanes, and the stator unlocks. The one-way clutch overruns, and the impeller, turbine, and stator begin rotating in the same direction at about the same speed. Rotary flow is dominant. This is called the *coupling phase.* At the coupling phase, there is no torque multiplication, and the engine is effectively coupled directly to the transmission.

TORQUE CONVERTER DESIGN VARIATIONS

Variable-Pitch Converter

Torque converter capacity is a function of its size and the **pitch angle** of its stator vanes. A low-capacity torque converter provides high torque multiplication but poor cruising or *coupling* efficiency—it slips more than desired for good fuel economy at highway speeds. A high-capacity torque converter provides less torque multiplication for acceleration but has good coupling efficiency.

In 1956, Buick introduced a *variable*-pitch-stator torque converter in the Dynaflow transmission. The variable-pitch torque converter was designed to solve the problem of how to match high and low torque converter capacity to a specific transmission. General Motors was the last to use this type of converter in some versions of their Turbo-Hydramatic 400 transmissions of the mid-1960s (Figure 33-51).

The ability to adjust the pitch of the stator's vanes accomplishes the following in a variable-pitch torque converter:

1. When the vanes are closed, low converter capacity is achieved (low capacity is used for high-performance

FIGURE 33-51   Variable-pitch torque converter. (General Motors Corporation)

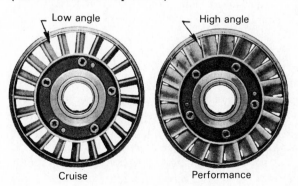

starts and to extend torque multiplication into higher speeds).

2. Opening the stator's vanes causes the converter to achieve a high capacity. A high converter capacity allows torque transfer at lower speeds and also allows a lower coupling speed.

Lockup Converter

For years, automotive engineers wrestled with the torque converter's inherently poor coupling efficiency—90%–95% at best. The slippage created a lot of unwanted heat and hurt fuel economy. The answer was to incorporate a manual clutch inside the converter. When "locked up," the transmission input shaft would rotate at engine crankshaft speed. The idea was first used by Packard and Studebaker in 1949 and 1950. But they dropped it because of the added costs.

In today's quest for fuel economy, lockup converters are back. Most use a single plate clutch that locks to the input shaft. Some, such as the Ford C-5, use a series of centrifugal shoes that provide increasing clamping force as engine speed increases. The control and timing of lockup is done with various road speeds, throttle position, and other sensors. Details of the various lockup torque converters in use today are covered in the shop manual for each transmission.

POWER FLOW

Now that you know the individual components of automatic transmissions, here's how a Turbo-Hydramatic 350 automatic transmission works.

The engine is started, and the front pump pressurizes the transmission operating circuits. The shift lever is placed in *drive,* moving the manual valve and directing mainline pressure through the valve body to the forward clutch. The forward clutch engages, connecting the input shaft to the compound planetary gearset. A compound gear reduction of about 2.5:1 occurs in both gearsets and drives the output shaft. However, the car doesn't move yet because the brakes are applied and the torque convertor impeller is inefficient at idle speed. This allows the converter to slip and keeps the engine from stalling in gear.

Upshifting

As engine speed is increased and the brakes are released, the torque convertor impeller directs high-velocity fluid at the turbine, thus moving the input shaft and the car. Governor pressure increases with vehicle speed and eventually overcomes throttle pressure at the 1–2 shift valve in the valve body. The 1–2 shift valve then moves and directs mainline pressure to the second-gear clutch. The second-gear clutch engages,

locking a second one-way clutch to the transmission case. Because no holding device is applied to the rear portion of the compound planetary gearset, it freewheels. A simple gear reduction of about 1.5:1 now drives the output shaft.

As vehicle speed and governor pressure continue to increase, they overcome throttle pressure at the 2–3 shift valve in the valve body. The 2–3 shift valve directs mainline pressure to the third-gear clutch, engaging it. Applying the third-gear clutch locks all members of the planetary gearset together, resulting in direct drive—input shaft speed equals output shaft speed.

Downshifting

The transmission will automatically downshift as the vehicle slows to a stop because governor pressure drops below throttle pressure. Forced downshifts for passing occur when the accelerator is depressed, raising throttle pressure and detent pressure above governor pressure.

ELECTRIC VALVE BODIES

Some new automatic transmissions, such as those used in some Toyota models and the Renault Alliance, feature electronically controlled valve bodies. In the case of the Renault MB1 transmission, inputs to a control module or "brain" include a throttle position variometer, a vehicle speed potentiometer, and a multifunction switch to determine the drive range selected. At the transmission valve body, outputs are conveyed to solenoid valves, which replace traditional hydraulic spool-type shift valves.

TRANSMISSION SERVICE

Transmission Fluids

For an automatic transmission to perform satisfactorily, it must be properly maintained. The transmission fluid level must be checked regularly, and service recommended by the manufacturer must be done at the prescribed intervals. Before attempting any service other than checking fluid, refer to a good automotive manual.

Automatic transmission fluid (ATF) is a mineral-based oil. It performs four important functions: (1) provides a coupling between the engine and the transmission, (2) removes heat from the transmission and transfers it to the outside air by the transmission's oil cooler, (3) lubricates the transmission's moving parts, and (4) provides pressure to operate clutch pistons and band servos.

Recommended Fluids Manufacturers design their

transmissions with specific friction coefficients and fluids in mind. Their fluid recommendations are as follows:

- *General Motors*: Dexron II in all their automatic transmissions.
- *Ford*: Type F for all early C-4, C-6, and FMX transmissions. The 1977 and later C-6, Jatco 3N71B used in Granadas and Monarchs, and all C-3, AOT, and ATX transmissions require Type CJ or Dexron II fluid, series D. The Ford C-5 transmission requires Type H fluid.
- *Chrysler*: Dexron or Dexron II are recommended for all transmissions.
- *American Motors*: Dexron or Dexron II are recommended for all transmissions.
- *Imported cars*: May require Dexron, Type A, Suffix A, or Type F fluids. See individual transmission manuals for details.

Fluid Levels   Fluids should be checked at time or mileage intervals. Transmissions are designed to operate most efficiently when the fluid level is between the ADD and FULL marks on the dipstick (Figure 33-52). When the fluid is low, it is possible the fluid can become aerated. Aerated fluid can lead to low hydraulic pressure, which would cause delays in clutch and band application. Too much fluid can also cause aeration. If the fluid is too high, it may also be forced from the vent. Aeration can also cause overheating, oxidation, and varnish buildup.

To read the transmission fluid level, the vehicle must be level and the transmission must be at normal operating temperature. Be sure the gear selector is in the gear designated by the manufacturer.

To bring the transmission to operating temperature, the vehicle must be driven for several miles. Just because the engine is at operating temperature doesn't mean that the transmission is too. Attempting to check fluid level on a "cold" transmission will result in mistakenly low dipstick readings.

Always inspect the condition of the fluid when checking its level. Both the color and odor should be analyzed. Most fluid is dyed red, and any change from this color should be a cause of concern (Dexron II will normally change to a reddish brown with age). A pinkish, milky color indicates water contamination. Some aftermarket "racing" fluids are dyed blue, and Ford CJ fluid is gold.

FIGURE 33-52   Checking transmission fluid.

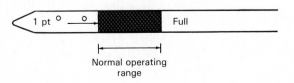

If the fluid smells like burned popcorn or rotten eggs, the transmission has probably been overheated or abused. Don't let fluid condition alone guide your diagnosis, however. If the transmission's operation is good, a fluid and filter change may be all that's required.

Filters

Synthetic fiber, paper, and screen filters are used in automatic transmissions to filter dirt and metal particles. They are located between the pan and oil pump.

Fiber and paper filters should be changed every time you change the transmission's fluid. This change will occur about every 25,000 mi or more often in severe service. General Motors and some other car manufacturers are recommending 100,000 mi fluid change intervals for light service.

Screen filters should be cleaned anytime a transmission is serviced. The filter should be replaced if it is torn or broken or has a varnish buildup on its mesh surface.

Gaskets

The transmission pan gasket is normally the only gasket replaced when servicing (in-car) transmissions. It is usually made of cork or a composition material.

Gaskets used in the rest of the transmission may be made of synthetic materials, plastic, or paper. All gaskets seal two parts together to contain fluid and keep out dirt.

Seals

Seals in automatic transmissions are constructed of three materials: synthetic rubber (**neoprene**), metal (cast iron or aluminum), and Teflon.

Synthetic rubber is used in the O-ring, square cut, and lip seals. Each uses neoprene because of its ability to remain flexible and its resistance to heat and chemical deterioration.

O-ring Seals   An O-ring seal is similar in shape to a doughnut. It works by having its shape distorted. The groove holding the O-ring is not as deep as the thickness of the ring. Figure 33-53 shows how the ring is compressed between the two shapes. This compression creates the desired seal. An O-ring cannot be used where there's either rotational (when either shape illustrated rotates) or axial (when either shape moves parallel to the axis of rotation) movement.

Square-cut Seals   When there is axial movement, a square cut seal is used (Figure 33-54). It, like the O-ring, can't be used where there's rotational force.

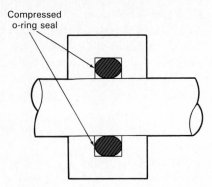

Compressed
o-ring seal

FIGURE 33-53   Compression creates a seal.

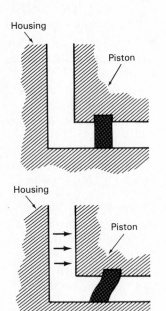

Housing

Piston

Housing

Piston

FIGURE 33-54   Square cut seals.

Lip Seals   Lip seals are installed where both rotational and axial forces exist (Figure 33-55). The lip seal is always installed with its lip facing the source of hydraulic pressure. When system pressure increases, the fluid pressure on the lip increases, expanding it more firmly against the cylinder it seals. Two examples of lip seals are the front pump seal and the output shaft seal. These seals have coil springs incorporated in them to help them retain their shape. They also have metal shells that allow them to be driven into the transmission's case. Lip seals without metal shells are used in some clutch pistons.

Metal Seals   Metal seal rings are used where an absolute seal isn't required and where rotational and axial movement is present. They are used as shaft seals and may act as dams to direct fluid pressure. The types used in transmissions include the butt-end seal and the locking-end seal (Figure 33-56).

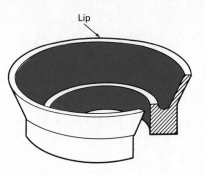

Lip

FIGURE 33-55   Lip seals.

(a) Locking-end seal

(b) Butt-end seal

FIGURE 33-56   Metal seals.

Teflon Seals   Teflon seals do the same job as metal seals. These are usually bevel or scarf cut designs. Some manufacturers recommend replacing them with metal seals when overhauling a transmission.

BEARINGS, BUSHINGS, AND THRUST WASHERS

Bearings

Bearings in transmissions absorb axial and radial play from shaft-mounted drums and gears. Normally, roller thrust bearings separate transmission parts. This type is constructed using needle-type rollers housed in a cage (Figure 33-57). They may be used to control end play in a transmission.

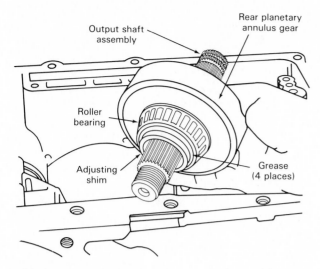

FIGURE 33-57 Roller thrust bearing. (General Motors Corporation)

Bushings

A **bushing** is a metal sleeve that is placed on a shaft to act as a bearing. Bushings can absorb little or no radial play and wear very slowly. Bushings support the rotation of shafts, gears, and drums and can act as internal seals. They must be provided with a constant supply of oil pressure to work properly.

Thrust Washers

Thrust washers control end play and separate components in automatic transmissions (Figure 33-58). They are made of soft steel with a copper facing. The normal practice is to replace all thrust washers when overhauling a transmission. They are made to exact thickness and wear in normal use. If an excessive end play is indicated, you may use a selective-fit thrust washer. These washers come in a variety of thicknesses and control end play.

TRANSMISSION COOLERS

Transmissions generate considerable heat buildup in normal operation. Transmission fluid absorbs this heat and stores it for transfer. The heat buildup occurs mainly in the torque converter, with band and clutch slippage generating additional heat. If this heat were

FIGURE 33-58 Thrust washers. (General Motors Corporation)

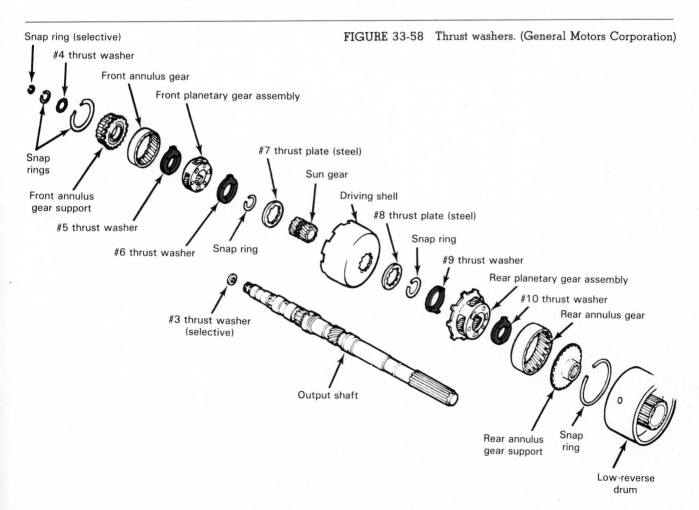

not dissipated, there would be fluid breakdown with its resulting varnish buildup and probably transmission damage.

Cooler Design

In most cars, the transmission cooler transfers the heat from the transmission's fluid to the engine's coolant. The cooler is located at the bottom of a downflow radiator and at the outlet tank of a crossflow radiator. The cooler is connected to the transmission by two lines. Hot fluid is pumped from the torque converter circuit through one line which enters the cooler. The fluid in the cooler transfers its heat to the engine's coolant in the radiator. The fluid, now cooler, returns to the transmission and enters its lubrication circuit. This is a continuous cycle that operates any time the car's engine is running.

Cooler Service

Coolers and cooling lines should be checked if there's any indication of trouble or if the transmission is being serviced or overhauled. The inspection should include checking the transmission's fluid and the engine's coolant for discoloration. Lines should be visually inspected for cracks and leaks along with checking their fittings. If lines are found to be pinched or cracked, they should be replaced. The entire line should be replaced. Replacement lines should be made of *seamless* or *double-wrapped and brazed steel tubing.* Each end of the line must be *double-flared.*

After overhauling a transmission, the cooler and its fluid lines should be flushed to remove metal and friction material particles. To accomplish this job correctly, machine-flush the cooler system. There are several different models of flushing machines. Follow the instructions given for the machine to be used.

If you find that the cooler needs repairs, you must first remove the radiator. If radiator repair facilities aren't readily available, take the radiator to a repair shop specializing in radiator repair. Be sure to state the specific problem when having repairs done. An internal cooler leak will pump ATF into the vehicle's cooling system when the engine is running and allow coolant to seep into the transmission cooler circuit when the engine is off. Antifreeze and water can cause severe internal transmission damage, allowing friction material to separate from bands and clutch parts.

Auxiliary Transmission Coolers

Higher thermostat settings, increased loads, and less fluid capacity in today's vehicles have caused an increase in transmission operating temperatures. Auxiliary coolers are being installed by many shops to lower these temperatures and to extend transmission life. An auxiliary cooler either replaces the radiator cooler or may be installed in addition to the factory system. Both systems have proven to be worthwhile additions.

TRADE TERMS

Accumulators
Apply Devices
Bushing
Direct Drive
Force
Gear Reduction
Governor Pressure
Hydraulics
Input Member

Internal Gear
Mainline Pressure
Neoprene
Orifice
Output Member
Overdrive
Pitch Angle
Planet Carrier Assembly
Planet Pinions

REVIEW QUESTIONS

1. How is hydraulic force multiplied by valves in automatic transmissions?

2. Describe how a positive-displacement pump operates.

3. What does the governor do in an automatic transmission?

4. How do simple and compound planetary gearsets differ in construction?

5. What are the apply devices used in automatic transmissions, and how is each actuated?

6. Why are accumulators used in the transmission's hydraulic system?

7. What is the function of a stator in the torque converter?

8. How can aerated fluid affect transmission operation?

34

Automatic Transmissions/ Transaxles Service

INTRODUCTION

Periodic servicing of automatic transmissions and transaxles prolongs their life and provides dependable service without failure. When problems occur in these modern driveline components, you will need to know how to test and diagnose the problems and how to take apart and put together the assemblies needing repair. This chapter gives you introductory information that you will need for servicing and working on automatic transmissions and transaxles.

TRANSMISSION IDENTIFICATION

Accurate identification is the first step a mechanic must perform when servicing an automatic transmission. The same make and model of an automobile may have several transmission options to fit a variety of engine applications, heavy-duty or severe usage, and owner preference. Without this essential information the mechanic cannot be sure that the correct parts and procedures will be used.

OBJECTIVES

When you have completed this chapter, you should be able to

- Identify common automatic transmissions, using identification tags, serial numbers, bellhousing, and pan shapes
- Describe how and why automatic transmissions require periodic service
- Identify the seals and bushings that can be replaced without removing the transmission
- Describe why testing is essential to properly diagnose transmission problems
- Identify the tools required to safely remove an automatic transmission
- State why it is important to keep components in subassemblies when disassembling a transmission
- State the importance of cleanliness when working on automatic transmissions
- Describe the similarities between automatic transmissions and transaxles

☐ Visual inspection for external leaks

☐ Tightness of engine to transmission attaching bolts

☐ Condition and tightness of the transmission mount

☐ Condition of the transmission cooling lines (tight, bent, or cracked?)

☐ Condition of the universal joints and center support

Attention to these items could prevent major repairs at a later date.

Fluid and Filter Service

The transmission fluid level should be checked every time the engine oil is changed. Always check the fluid when the engine and transmission are at operating temperatures. Put the transmission in park, start the engine, and pull the dipstick. Wipe the oil off the dipstick and reinsert it into its tube. This time when you pull the dipstick, the fluid level will show. Remember, the marks on the dipstick represent pints, not quarts, as on the engine oil dipstick.

Service Intervals The transmission fluid should be changed at intervals specified by the manufacturer. Its filter should be serviced at the same time. The intervals vary, with most manufacturers specifying service after the vehicle has been driven at least 50,000 mi.

This service interval can be considerably shorter, depending on how the vehicle is used. For example, if the vehicle is used in dusty or extremely hot or cold weather, shorter service intervals will be necessary. Using the car for mostly stop-and-go city driving is hard on the transmission, too. Because many, if not most, vehicles fit into one of these categories, shorter intervals between regular vehicle servicing are necessary for almost all vehicles.

The vehicle must be raised to an acceptable working height to service the transmission (preferably on a lift). On the car lift, center the vehicle before raising. On most lifts you must use the extensions to gain clearance off the lift.

Once you have raised the vehicle, visually inspect the transmission linkage and lines. Identify the transmission at this time. Ensure that all the parts you need to complete the service are available before you continue.

Draining Fluid If the parts are available, begin by draining the transmission fluid. You can drain the fluid by using a drain plug on the oil pan or by loosening the oil pan bolts. Transmission fluid in a recently driven vehicle is *hot,* so be careful. If you have to remove the oil pan to drain the fluid, find a large drain pan. Make sure the drain can has a capacity of at least 5 qt. Remove all the bolts holding the oil pan except two, one at either end. By carefully easing both these bolts out, you can avoid splashing transmission fluid.

There are numerous ways to identify specific automatic transmissions. Never assume that just because the vehicle is one model or year, the transmission will be the same. After the vehicle was purchased, a transmission of a different year or model may have been installed. Remember, it's the transmission being serviced, not the car.

Identification Numbers

Most transmissions have either an identification tag or a serial number attached or stamped on the case. Service manuals give information on decoding of serial numbers. Figure 34-1 illustrates how the Chrysler Torqueflite's serial number is decoded.

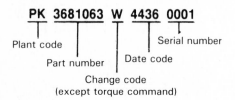

FIGURE 34-1 Transmission identification.

Oil Pan Shape

One of the easiest ways to identify automatic transmissions is by the shape of their oil pans (Figure 34-2). By carefully matching the shape of the oil pan with a pan chart, you can readily identify most transmissions.

The material a transmission is made of, its shape, and the location of its external components also help in identification.

GENERAL SERVICING

When performing transmission service, be sure to check these commonly overlooked areas:

G.M. FILTER & PAN IDENTIFIERS

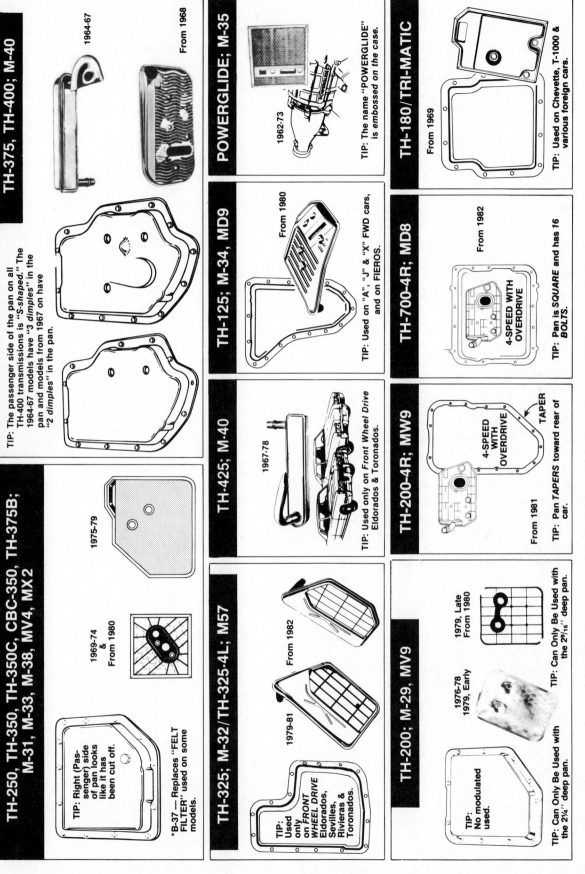

TH-375, TH-400; M-40

1964-67

From 1968

TIP: The passenger side of the pan on all TH-400 transmissions is "S-shaped." The 1964-67 models have "3 dimples" in the pan and models from 1967 on have "2 dimples" in the pan.

TH-250, TH-350, TH-350C, CBC-350, TH-375B; M-31, M-33, M-38, MV4, MX2

1975-79

1969-74 & From 1980

TIP: Right (Passenger) side of pan looks like it has been cut off.

*B-37 — Replaces "FELT FILTER" used on some models.

POWERGLIDE; M-35

1962-73

TIP: The name "POWERGLIDE" is embossed on the case.

TH-125; M-34, MD9

From 1980

TIP: Used on "A", "J" & "X" FWD cars, and on FIEROS.

TH-425; M-40

1967-78

TIP: Used only on Front Wheel Drive Eldorados & Toronados.

TH-325; M-32/TH-325-4L; M57

From 1982

1979-81

TIP: Used only on FRONT WHEEL DRIVE Eldorados, Sevilles, Rivieras & Toronados.

TH-180/TRI-MATIC

From 1969

TIP: Used on Chevette, T-1000 & various foreign cars.

TH-700-4R; MD8

From 1982

4-SPEED WITH OVERDRIVE

TIP: Pan is SQUARE and has 16 BOLTS.

TH-200-4R; MW9

4-SPEED WITH OVERDRIVE

TAPER

From 1981

TIP: Pan TAPERS toward rear of car.

TH-200; M-29, MV9

1979, Late From 1980

1976-78 1979, Early

TIP: Can Only Be Used with the 2¹⁄₁₆" deep pan.

TIP: Can Only Be Used with the 2¼" deep pan.

TIP: No modulated used.

FIGURE 34-2   Oil pan chart. (Reprinted with permission of copyright owner, ATP, Automatic Transmission Parts, Inc.)

505

Once you have removed the pan, clean it with solvent, scrape the old gasket off, and let the pan air-dry. *Do not* use rags to dry transmission parts. The lint on the rags finds its way into the valve body and results in erratic or abnormal operation of the transmission. Clean the gasket mating surface on the case, being careful to keep pieces of the gasket from getting into the cavity of the case. Remove the converter cover and check to see if the converter has a drain plug. If there is a drain plug, remove it and allow the fluid to drain.

If the converter has no drain plug, you must remove the transmission from the vehicle. Then you may drain the converter after removing it from the transmission.

Removing Filter   Next, remove the filter. It is attached to the valve body in one of a variety of ways. Some filters are attached with screws, others with bolts, and some with clamps. Some require a gasket and others don't. If a gasket is called for, don't forget to install it. The same applies to rubber O-rings used in some applications. Not using either of these would result in a loss of oil pressure.

Filters are constructed of either metal or a synthetic material. Service the metal filter screen (if the entire filtering surface isn't visible, replace the filter) by cleaning it in solvent. Let it air-dry after cleaning. Replace any synthetic filters during each service. Install a gasket or O-ring if called for and *torque* the filter to the valve body. This tightening is particularly important because an overtightened filter could distort the valve body and prevent its proper operation. Some Ford filters have a throttle pressure relief valve that is exposed when the filter is removed. Because this valve will fall out when you remove the filter, you must install it before attaching a new filter.

Installing Filter   After you have installed the filter, check the mating surface on the oil pan. If it isn't distorted or bent, install the pan on the case using a new gasket. *Do not* use a gasket cement. If the gasket needs to be held in place, use a little grease. Torque the oil pan bolts down. Reinstall the converter drain plug if removed. If you had to remove the transmission and converter to remove the fluid, reinstall the converter and transmission now. Install the converter cover and tighten its retaining bolts.

Adding Fluid   To refill the transmission with fluid, pour 2 or 3 qt of **automatic transmission fluid** (ATF) into the filler tube. Start the engine, shift the transmission into neutral, and add enough fluid to bring the fluid level up to "add 1 pint" or one mark below "full." Run the engine until it reaches operating temperature and then shift the transmission through all of the gears. Pause at each gear position for a few seconds. This procedure will help the transmission reach operating temperature and ensure an adequate supply of ATF to all the parts inside the transmission. Recheck the fluid level and add ATF until full.

Flushing the Cooler Lines and Torque Converter

After a transmission has become contaminated, you must flush the transmission cooling lines, the lower radiator tank, and the torque converter. You must use a special flushing tool (Figure 34-3) to flush the cooling lines and lower radiator tank. This operation doesn't require you to remove the transmission. Some manufacturers do not recommend flushing converters.

You may flush the torque converter by using another special flushing tool. You will have to remove the transmission to gain access to the torque converter. Many shops find it more practical to buy a rebuilt torque converter rather than to flush an old converter.

FIGURE 34-3   Oil cooler and line flusher. (Trans-Tool Corp.)

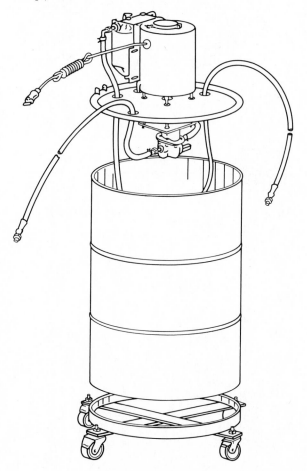

Oil cooler and line flusher

Linkage and Band Adjustment

Once you have serviced the fluid and filter, adjust the shift linkage, kickdown or throttle linkage, and bands.

The shift linkage connects the gearshift lever to the manual valve in the transmission valve body. You must accurately align the shift linkage to keep the manual valve centered in the selected position (Figure 34-4).

The kickdown linkage causes the transmission to downshift when the throttle is opened wide (Figure 34-5). The linkage is adjusted to achieve the downshift below a designated speed.

Bands are adjustable on some transmissions. The adjusting screws are either on the outside of the transmission case (Figure 34-6) or inside its oil pan (Figure 34-7).

You must use a service manual that gives the specifications for the particular transmission you are working on.

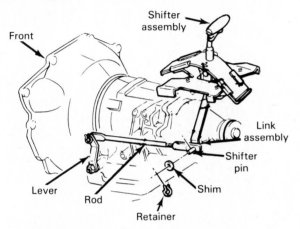

FIGURE 34-4   Shift linkage. (General Motors Corporation)

FIGURE 34-5   Kickdown linkage. (General Motors Corporation)

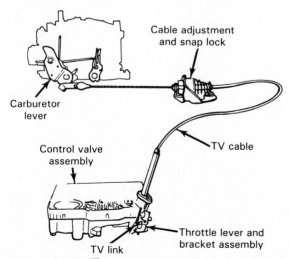

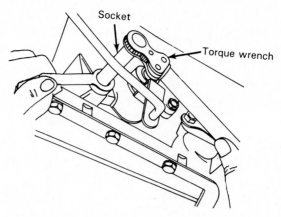

FIGURE 34-6   External band adjustment. (Ford Motor Company)

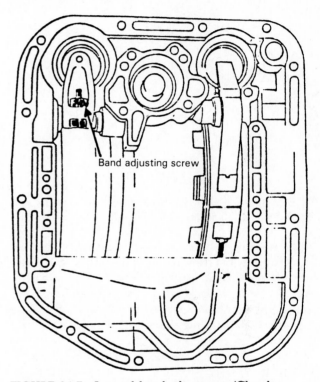

FIGURE 34-7   Internal band adjustment. (Chrysler Corporation)

Seal and Bushing Replacement

You can replace the metal-clad seals at the shift lever and in the extension housing without removing the transmission. The shift lever seal normally requires that the oil pan be removed. The best time to change it would be during a regular service when you have already removed the pan.

The extension housing seal requires that the drive shaft be removed. Once you have removed the drive shaft, it is an easy task to remove and replace the seal.

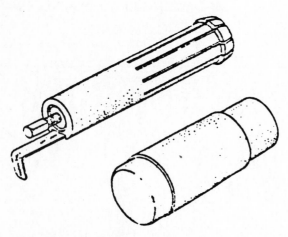

FIGURE 34-8 Extension housing bushing and seal remover and bushing installer. (Trans-Tool Corp.)

The cause for the failure of many extension housing seals is a worn bushing in the extension housing. This bushing may also be removed and replaced without removing the transmission. There are special pullers/installers for the removal and installation of these bushings (Figure 34-8). If one of these tools isn't available, it is possible in some models to remove the extension housing without having to remove the transmission.

DIAGNOSING TRANSMISSION TROUBLES

When diagnosing troubles in an automatic transmission, you should take several steps before attempting any tests or repairs:

- ☐ The first step is always to find out what the specific complaint is.
- ☐ Find out if there were any special circumstances which led to the problem.
- ☐ Check the fluid level and check the fluid for contamination. Contaminated fluid looks brown and smells like it has been burned.
- ☐ Perform a quick visual check to see if any linkage is loose or bent and if all vacuum lines are connected.
- ☐ Know the band and clutch applications for the particular transmission being tested (Figure 34-9).
- ☐ Prepare yourself for testing by consulting a trouble diagnosis chart (Figure 34-10).

After completing the preparations listed above, you are ready to begin testing.

Road Testing

To confirm just what is wrong with the transmission, make a road test. The purpose of the road test is to diagnose transmission operation at various speeds, operating conditions, and gear selections. Take notes as you go through the procedures of the test because there may be several problems that have to be corrected to ensure proper transmission operation.

Pre-Test Checks Make the road test by actually driving the vehicle on the road in a variety of operating conditions or by simulating the same conditions on a chassis dynamometer. *Remember*, check and correct the fluid level and linkage adjustments before you begin the road test. The engine must be operating properly to prevent diagnosing improper transmission operation because of poor engine performance.

While driving the car, check the following operations of the transmission:

- ☐ Shifting at proper mph
- ☐ No slipping while shifting
- ☐ Smooth and crisp shifting
- ☐ *Detenting* (passing gear engaging) at wide-open throttle (WOT)
- ☐ Starting in first gear and shifting up through all gears

Pressure Check During the road test, you must also check hydraulic pressures. Make these checks by attaching an oil pressure gauge to the pressure pickup points on the transmission case. The gauge must have a hose long enough to reach from the transmission

Selector Lever Position	Intermed. Clutch	Intermed. One-Way Clutch	Overdrive Band	Reverse Clutch	Forward Clutch	Planetary One-Way Clutch	Low-Reverse Band	Direct Clutch
O/D — OVERDRIVE								
First Gear					X	X		
Second Gear	X	X			X			
Third Gear	X				X			X
Fourth Gear	X		X					X
3 — OVERDRIVE LOCKOUT								
First Gear					X	X		
Second Gear	X	X			X			
Third Gear	X				X			X
1 — LOW								
First Gear					X	X	X	
Second Gear	X	X	X		X			
R — REVERSE				X			X	
P — PARK							X	
NEUTRAL — All clutches and bands released and/or ineffective.								

FIGURE 34-9 Clutch and band application chart.

CONDITION & POSSIBLE CAUSE	CONDITION & POSSIBLE CAUSE
1-2 Shift at Full Throttle Only • Detent valve sticking. • Vacuum leak. • Case porosity. • Control valve assembly malfunction. Transmission Noisy In "P", "N" and All Driving Ranges • Check transmission after eliminating water pump, generator and power steering as noise source by removing individual belts. • Pump cavitation due to restricted strainer, damaged body or gasket, porosity. • Pump gears damaged or improperly assembled. • Converter or flex plate damaged or mounting bolts loose.	Transmission Noisy During Acceleration • Transmission grounded to underbody. • Motor mounts loose or broken. Transmission Noisy in First, Second and Reverse Gear • Planetary gears or thrust bearings damaged. • Planetary input and output ring gear damaged. Transmission Squeal at Low Vehicle Speed • Speedometer driven gear shafts seal needs lubrication. • Speedometer driven gear shaft seal needs replacement.

FIGURE 34-10 Trouble diagnosis chart.

to the driver's seat. It must also have a capacity of more than the pressures to be checked, 0–300 psi (0–2000 kPa). Some transmissions require the use of a tachometer to check operation at certain rpm ranges.

Some of the problems the road test may reveal are noise, harsh or spongy shifts, improper shift points, and slippage. Use a band and clutch application chart similar to the one shown in Figure 34-9 for the vehicle being tested. The chart shows what device is applied in each gear selection. Armed with this information, diagnose the problem by using the process of elimina-tion. Service manuals have troubleshooting charts, like the one shown in Figure 34-10, which you can use.

Torque Converter Test The torque converter can also be tested on the road test. A slipping one-way clutch in the stator will cause poor acceleration. If the one-way clutch is locked, acceleration will be normal to a certain point, and then the converter will limit vehicle speed and engine rpm. Either of these conditions requires that the converter be replaced because the one-way clutch cannot be repaired.

Stall Test   A final test that you can make on certain transmissions is the stall test. This test checks the ability of the torque converter's one-way clutch and the transmission clutches to hold against engine torque. You should take the following precautions before performing a stall test: The first thing you must do is check the service manual, because many manufacturers do not recommend this test. Set the parking brake and block the front wheels. Make sure no one is standing in front or in back of the vehicle being tested. Limit the test to a few seconds. Follow procedures specified by the manufacturer.

TRANSMISSION OVERHAUL

Transmission Removal

Tools   Should you need to remove the transmission for repair or overhaul, you must have certain tools. You will need a lift or jack and safety stands. A transmission jack (Figure 34-11) is absolutely essential. You will need a clean working area and bench and a set of basic hand tools. Safety is a major concern. Make

FIGURE 34-11   Transmission jack. (Peugeot Motors of America, Inc.)

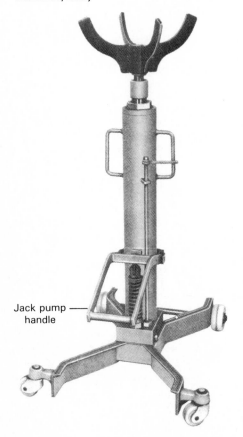

Jack pump handle

sure the car is supported so that you can safely work underneath it.

Transmission removal varies with different cars and transmissions. Each is removed in a different way and presents different problems. Read your service manual before attempting to remove any transmission. This saves time and trouble because the writers of the service manual have attempted to solve the problems that take so much time.

Disconnections   Before raising the vehicle on a lift, always disconnect the battery. Raise the vehicle and drain the transmission fluid. If the pan had to be removed to drain the fluid, reinstall the pan. Remove the selector linkage, throttle linkage, speedometer cable, vacuum, and electrical connections.

Support the transmission on a transmission jack. Remove the drive shaft and frame cross member. Check the condition of the transmission mount at this time and make a note to order one if it is necessary.

Remove the starter if required. Remove the lower splash panel or converter cover from the bellhousing and loosen the bolts attaching the torque converter to the flexplate. Mark the flexplate and torque converter so that they may be installed in the same position. Place a support under the engine to prevent it from dropping when the transmission is removed. Lower the transmission jack and engine support slightly to gain access to the upper bellhousing bolts. Remove the bolts attaching the transmission to the engine, separate the two, and carefully lower the transmission. On some cars, the exhaust, brackets, and other parts may have to be removed in addition to the preceding.

Transaxles

Many new cars have integrated transmissions and differentials. When combined, this unit is called a **transaxle** (Figure 34-12). The advantage of a unit of this type is that it allows the manufacturer to place all the drive units—the engine, transmissions, and differential—at one end of the car. The internal components of both are quite similar to those used on rear-wheel-drive cars.

The drive axle shafts of a transaxle must be separated from the unit before it can be removed from the car. Figure 34-13 shows an example of a drive axle shaft. Note that each end of the drive axle shaft has a **constant velocity (CV) joint.** This type of joint is necessary in a unit like this to keep an even application of power to the drive wheels. Most CV joints can be repaired. Use the particular service manual for the CV joint you are working on. Be careful when handling these units. It is easy to lose one of the many parts when you disassemble it.

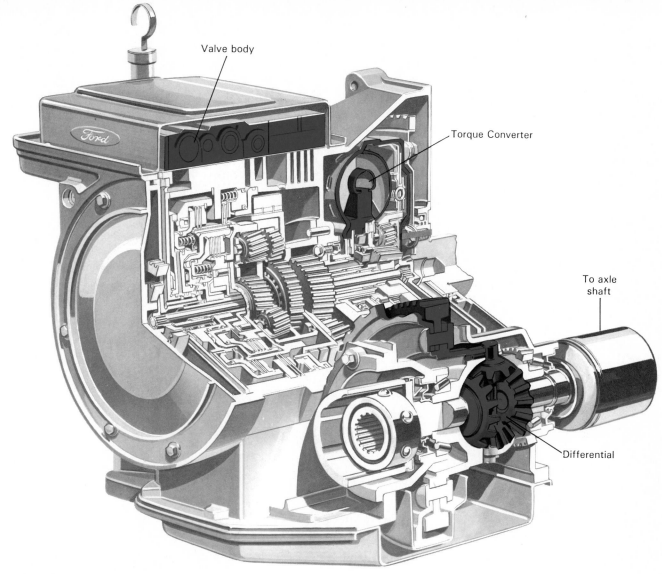

FIGURE 34-12   Transaxle assembly.

FIGURE 34-13   Drive axle shaft.

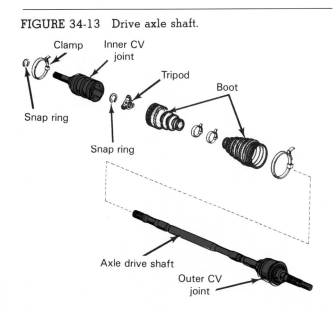

Disassembly

Once you have removed the transmission, thoroughly clean the exterior of the transmission. You don't want dirt getting into the interior of the unit once disassembly starts.

After cleaning the transmission, mount it on a transmission stand or place it on a clean workbench. Check input shaft end play and output shaft end play before disassembling the transmission (Figure 34-14). Mark these figures down. You will use them to select the thrust washer thicknesses when reassembling the transmission.

Subassemblies   Keep the parts separated into subassemblies when disassembling an automatic transmission. Each of the subassemblies will be serviced individually. This keeps the number of parts within reason and makes it less likely to mix up similar components.

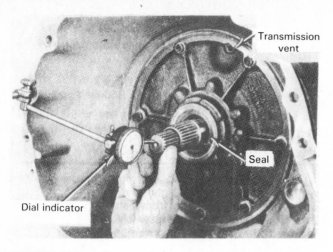

FIGURE 34-14 Using a dial indicator to measure input shaft end play.

Remove the oil pan, filter, and valve body, being careful to keep each unit together (Figure 34-15). Use care when removing the valve body because the check balls may fall out.

Next, remove the servos and accumulators. Remove the modulator with its valve or pin, external governors, and the speedometer drive.

Shift to the rear of the transmission and remove the extension housing. This will expose the speedometer gear, governor, and parking pawl on some transmissions (Figure 34-16). Each of these is removed as a subassembly.

Remove the bolts holding the front oil pump to

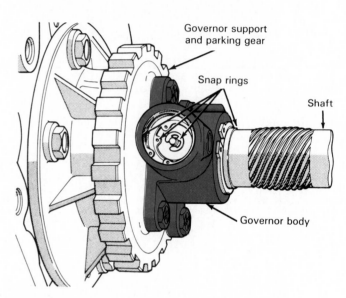

FIGURE 34-16 Transmission parking pawl, governor, and speedometer drive gear. (Chrysler Corporation)

FIGURE 34-15 Transmission oil pan, filter, and valve body. (General Motors Corporation)

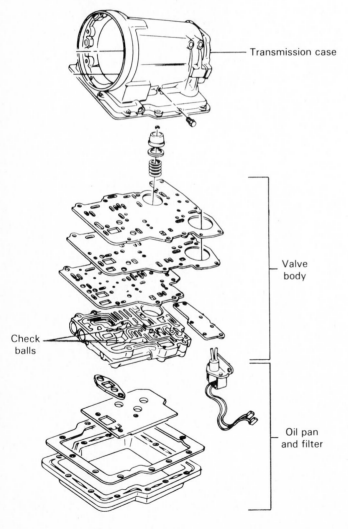

FIGURE 34-17 Using slide hammers to remove oil pump. (General Motors Corporation)

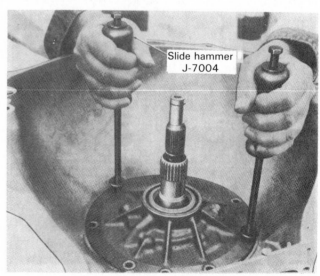

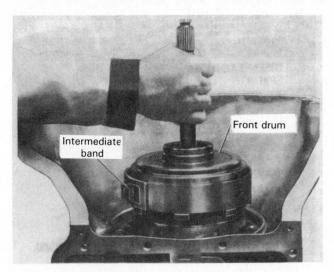

FIGURE 34-18 Removing front drum assembly. (General Motors Corporation)

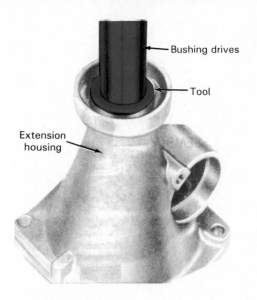

FIGURE 34-19 Installing a new bushing. (General Motors Corporation)

the transmission case. Install two slide hammers and work the pump loose (Figure 34-17). After the pump is withdrawn, remove the front drum assembly (Figure 34-18). Continue removing clutch, drum, and band subassemblies. Keep each in order and note the position of thrust washers and bearings. They must be installed exactly as removed.

Inspection

Disassemble each subassembly and clean in solvent. Do not clean rubber and plastic parts in solvent. Visually inspect each component for signs of excessive wear, scoring, cracks, and overheating. Replace any worn parts at this time along with new rubber and metal seals. Reassemble each subassembly, set it aside, and continue on with the next until all subassemblies are finished. When installing rubber seals, make sure the lip points toward the pressure source. Before installing new clutches, steel plates, and bands, soak them in ATF for 30 min and then install as required.

Oil Pump Disassemble the oil pump. Clean and check it for excessive wear. The maximum gear side clearance allowed on any oil pump is 0.003 in. (0.076 mm). It is advisable to change the pump bushing and front seal before reassembling the oil pump.

Valve Body The valve body should be disassembled and inspected on a clean shop towel. Note the installed position of all check balls to ensure they are reinstalled in the same location. Remove each valve, inspect it for wear or scoring, and place it in its designated place on the towel. When you have removed all the valves, clean the body in solvent. Let these components air-dry or dry them with compressed air. When you have

reinstalled each valve, make sure it moves freely in its bore.

Case Clean the case thoroughly, checking all surfaces such as bores and threaded holes for wear. The case may be cleaned by using solvent, an aluminum hot tank, or a cleaning machine.

Install a new bushing and seal in the extension housing (Figure 34-19).

All subassemblies have now been cleaned, inspected, and reassembled with new seals and gaskets.

Reassembly

Air Check Before beginning to reassemble the transmission, determine if any of the parts can be air-checked individually. Air checking is a bench technique for checking internal assemblies for operation and leaks in an automatic transmission. Air-checking components at this time can save many hours later on. Air-check passages with an air hose to see if they are clear and that there are no leaks. Air checking is accomplished by introducing compressed air into the various lubrication holes. This applies the various clutches and bands to ensure they are working properly. Consult the appropriate shop manual for the specific transmission you are working on (Figure 34-20).

Soak all bands and clutches in clean automatic transmission fluid for at least 30 min before reassembling. Metal components should be coated with automatic transmission fluid. Begin reassembling the subassemblies. They will be installed in reverse order from which they were removed. Any time a component is bolted on, it must be torqued to specifications. Check the input shaft end play and the output shaft end

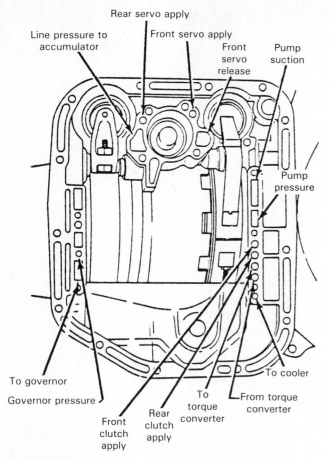

Line pressure to accumulator

Rear servo apply

Front servo apply

Front servo release

Pump suction

Pump pressure

To governor

Governor pressure

Front clutch apply

Rear clutch apply

To torque converter

To cooler

From torque converter

FIGURE 34-20   Air testing locations in transmission. (Chrysler Corporation)

play (a change in thrust washer thickness may be necessary). Check clutch and band application by using air pressure before installing the valve body. Consult a shop manual for the proper procedure and the correct parts for air checking.

Torque Converter   Once you have completely reassembled the transmission, determine if a new torque converter is needed. If the fluid was dirty and gritty when the transmission was pulled or if the road test determined that the torque converter was inoperative, replace the converter. The converter hub should also be checked for wear.

Install the torque converter over the stator support and input shaft. Be sure that it is seated on the oil pump drive lugs.

Installation

Place the transmission and torque converter on a transmission jack, being careful not to displace the converter. Raise the transmission, line up the dowel pins on the rear of the engine block, and begin installing the bellhousing bolts. The torque converter should be about ¼ in. from the flexplate after the bellhousing bolts are tightened. Align the marks that you made during removal on the torque converter and flexplate and tighten the torque converter bolts. Install the cross member, drive shaft, and all other components that were disconnected when you removed the transmission. Adjust the linkage controlling the selector lever position.

Recheck your work and lower the car. Fill it with the proper type of transmission fluid using the same procedures previously given for a fluid change. Examine the car for leaks and perform a road test, using the same guidelines that were given for diagnosing problems.

TRADE TERMS

Automatic Transmission Fluid
Constant Velocity Joint
Transaxle

REVIEW QUESTIONS

1. Why is it so important to correctly identify an automatic transmission before beginning any work?
2. What conditions would require an automatic transmission to be serviced at intervals more frequently than regularly recommended service?
3. Why do many extension housing seals fail?
4. Why should an automatic transmission be road-tested?
5. What should be checked before disassembling an automatic transmission? Why?

Transfer Cases and Four-Wheel Drive

INTRODUCTION

Four-wheel drive is made possible by the interaction of special automotive drive train components that transmit engine power to the four wheels of a vehicle instead of two. The system provides maximum traction over difficult, unpaved ground as well as on wet and slippery roads. With both front wheels pulling and both rear wheels pushing, the four-wheel-drive vehicle is more stable on pavement during bad weather. It can also handle unpaved surfaces that would strand the standard automobile or truck.

Several major components make up the four-wheel-drive system. In addition to the conventional engine, transmission, rear propeller shaft, and rear differential/axle assemblies, other components are (1) the **transfer case**, (2) the **front propeller shaft**, and (3) the **front differential/axle assembly**. We will talk about the more common four-wheel-drive arrangements first. Then we'll explore alternative layouts once you understand the fundamentals.

CONVENTIONAL FOUR-WHEEL DRIVE

A **conventional four-wheel-drive** vehicle contains the following components: a front-mounted, longitudi-

OBJECTIVES

When you have completed this chapter, you should be able to

- Describe how engine power can be delivered to the four wheels on a vehicle
- Explain the advantages of four-wheel drive over conventional two-wheel drive
- State what alternative drive train components are added to conventional drivelines to make four-wheel drive possible
- Describe the variety of drive train layouts, transfer case shift patterns, front axle arrangements, and suspensions
- Describe the individual driveline components in a full-time four-wheel-drive system and a part-time system
- Explain the need for, and operation of, manually locking front-wheel hubs and automatic locking front hubs.

manner, but there is also an auxiliary lever to shift the transfer case for the engagement or disengagement of the four-wheel drive mode (Figure 35-2).

Basic Fundamentals

We must now consider some automotive basics before proceeding. As mentioned elsewhere in this book, the wheels of a vehicle rounding a curve must make slightly different arcs: The outside front wheel rolls the farthest, and the inside rear wheel rolls the least. We have also learned that differential gearing in a rear-drive axle is necessary to provide power to both wheels and to let them rotate at different speeds. Therefore, some means must be found to allow the four driving wheels to receive engine power yet still be able to rotate at different speeds. Failing this, a mechanical disconnect between the axles would have to be used to move the vehicle by the rear wheels only when it is driven on pavement. Undue tire wear, **driveline wrap-up,** and damage to U-joints and gears could result from using the four-wheel-drive vehicle on hard surfaces. Different component manufacturers are trying to solve these problems, as we will see, but the types of front axles in common use will be considered first.

nally placed engine; a torque converter or clutch attached to the flywheel; the transmission (automatic or manual); the transfer case; the rear propeller shaft; and the rear differential/axle assembly, in that order. Also there is the front propeller shaft that runs from a forward power output shaft in the transfer case to the front differential/axle assembly. This shaft includes pivoting hub carriers which permit front-wheel steering (Figure 35-1).

In the conventional layout described above, the transmission is shifted by the driver in the normal

FIGURE 35-1 Conventional four-wheel-drive arrangement. (American Motors Corporation)

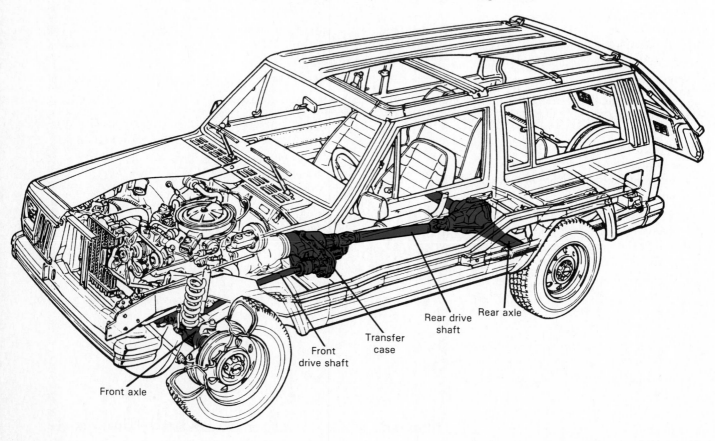

Front axle

Front drive shaft

Transfer case

Rear drive shaft

Rear axle

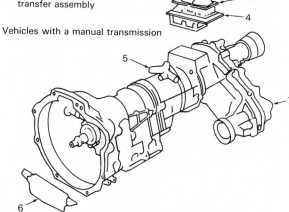

1. Transfer gearshift lever
2. Transmission gearshift lever
3. Dust cover retaining plate
4. Gearshift lever cover
5. Manual transmission and transfer assembly
6. Bellhousing cover
7. Automatic transmission and transfer assembly

Vehicles with a manual transmission

FIGURE 35-2 Shift levers for four-wheel drive with manual transmission. (Chrysler Corporation)

Front-Axle Types

Two types of front-driving axle assemblies are in popular use. The *solid* type is comprised of a single axle housing with an integral differential and third member assembly. It is suspended by fore/aft semielliptical leaf springs or coil springs (Figure 35-3). The second type is the independent front suspension axle assembly. In this assembly, the differential gear case is mounted solidly to the chassis and is suspended by coil springs or torsion bars (Figure 35-4). Each type, of course, must have provision for front-wheel steering.

The Solid Front Axle Since the transfer case is mounted solidly to the transmission and thus to the chassis, the **solid front axle** must somehow be allowed to move on its suspension in answer to surface variations. This is accomplished by adding a front propeller shaft with a sliding, splined U-joint yoke at the rear and by attaching a U-joint to the differential pinion shaft flange at the front. This arrangement is identical to most rear-driven vehicle layouts, but it is turned 180° to extend forward instead of rearward. The assembly is very similar to a conventional rear axle, since the differential and third member assemblies are often

FIGURE 35-3 Solid-type front-drive axle with coil springs. (American Motors Corporation)

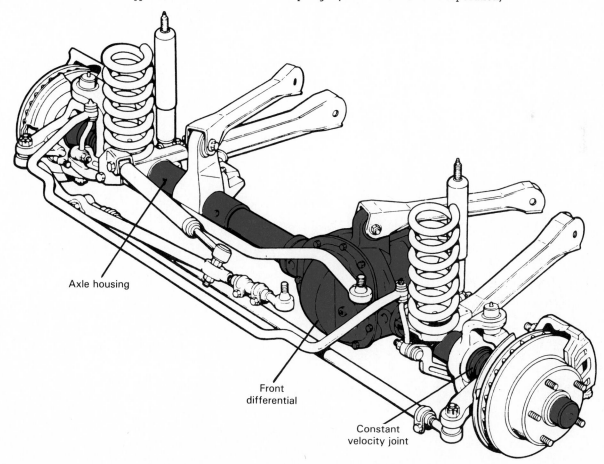

Axle housing

Front differential

Constant velocity joint

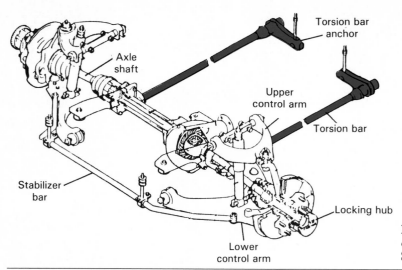

Torsion bar anchor

Axle shaft

Upper control arm

Torsion bar

Stabilizer bar

Locking hub

Lower control arm

FIGURE 35-4 Independent suspension front-drive axle with torsion bars. (Mitsubishi Motor Sales of America, Inc.)

interchangeable with the rear axle. The housing is made narrower, however, to allow for the mounting of a *hub carrier* or *trunnion* which retains a short stub axle. This axle connects to the primary axle with a U-joint (Figure 35-5).

The Independent Front Axle An **independent front axle** has the differential housing connected solidly to the chassis. Power reaches the wheels via the U-jointed *halfshafts*. Because the housing is normally offset in the chassis for engine clearance (usually on the left side

facing forward), the left in-board U-joint is commonly connected to a drive flange that extends from the differential gear case. The right side of the housing uses an extension from the gear case to a drive flange for the right-hand U-joint. In this arrangement, equal-length halfshafts pivot for suspension travel on a plane with the upper and lower control arms in order to produce proper front-wheel steering geometry.

Steering of the independent suspension system is done through a hub carrier and stub axle for each wheel. The carrier and axle are hinged for movement

FIGURE 35-5 Steering layout with solid-type front axle. (Ford Motor Company)

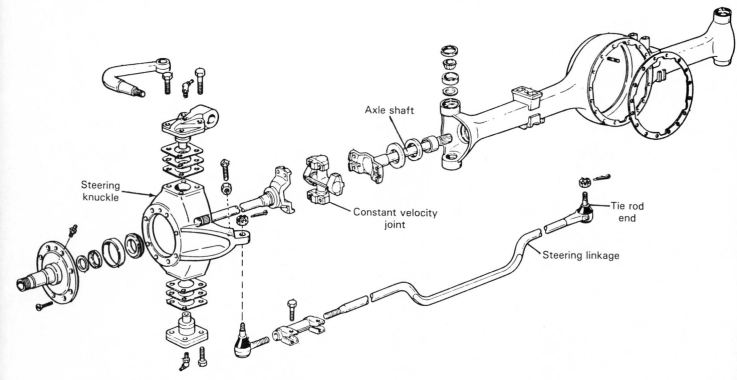

Axle shaft

Steering knuckle

Constant velocity joint

Tie rod end

Steering linkage

with upper and lower control arms. The carriers rotate on upper and lower ball joints for actual steering purposes.

Steering

Steering the four-wheel-drive vehicle is done the same way as steering the conventional vehicle. A tie rod (or jointed links) connects to the steering arms on each hub carrier and is moved by the drag link and Pitman arm (or rack and pinion steering assembly) connected to the steering box. Each axle end includes a U-joint or constant velocity joint that permits power to reach each wheel as it turns through its steering.

Transfer Cases

The **transfer case housing,** usually mounted behind the transmission where engine power is received through its tailshaft, is like a two-speed, selective-gear transmission with a *neutral* position.

Functions The transfer case takes power from the input shaft and, through idler gears or a chain, transfers it to a forward-pointing output shaft. The front propeller shaft sends the power from the output shaft to the front-axle assembly. As the front propeller shaft must pass under or alongside the engine for clearance, the transfer case provides the offset condition as well.

One gearshift position of the transfer case directs power through the input shaft and out the rear output shaft (and rear propeller shaft) without transmitting power down through the front-drive gear train. This is called two-wheel high (Figure 35-6).

The transfer case also allows the selection of several gear ratios: straight through, or 1:1, in which both output shafts revolve at the same rate as the transmission output shaft, or a lower (higher numerically) ratio, commonly 2:1, which doubles torque at the wheels while cutting the road speed in half. Thus, the vehicle can be operated over difficult obstacles and through mud, sand, and snow with the engine running up in its power band but with relatively slow vehicle movement (Figure 35-7). Finally, most transfer cases have a neutral position which disconnects the drive train.

FIGURE 35-6 Transfer case in two-wheel high mode. (American Motors Corporation)

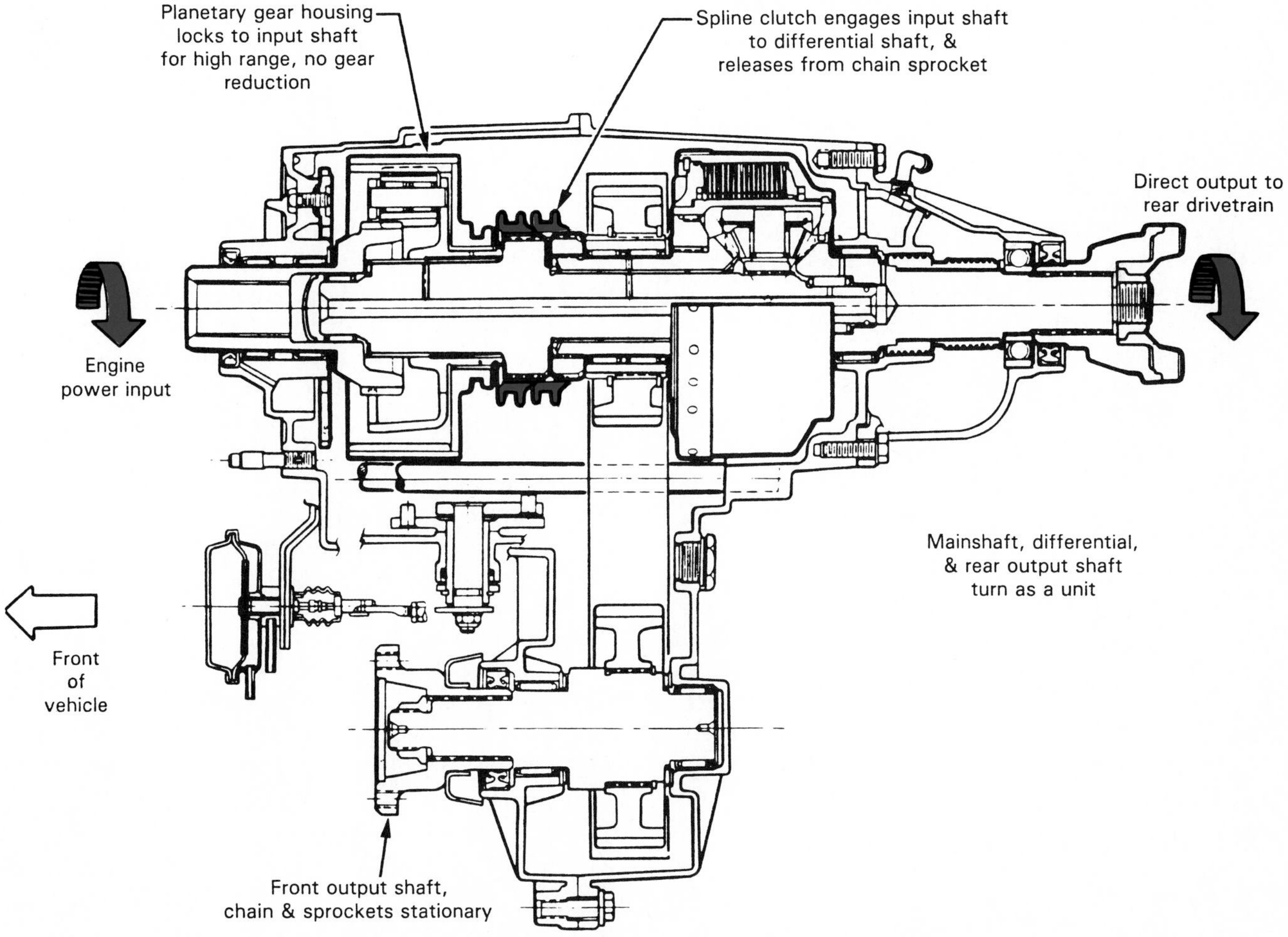

Planetary gear housing locks to input shaft for high range, no gear reduction

Spline clutch engages input shaft to differential shaft, & releases from chain sprocket

Direct output to rear drivetrain

Engine power input

Mainshaft, differential, & rear output shaft turn as a unit

Front of vehicle

Front output shaft, chain & sprockets stationary

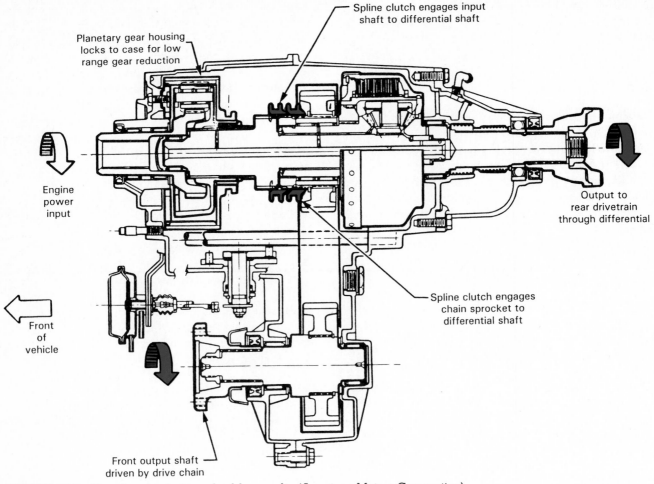

Spline clutch engages input
shaft to differential shaft

Planetary gear housing
locks to case for low
range gear reduction

Engine
power
input

Output to
rear drivetrain
through differential

Spline clutch engages
chain sprocket to
differential shaft

Front
of
vehicle

Front output shaft
driven by drive chain

FIGURE 35-7 Transfer case in four-wheel low mode. (American Motors Corporation)

The transfer case shift pattern is usually imprinted on the shifter knob, though manufacturers use different patterns and designations for the various gear positions. For clarity we will refer to them as **two-wheel high** (rear-wheel drive), **four-wheel high** (four-wheel drive in the 1:1 ratio), and **four-wheel low** (four-wheel drive in the 2:1 ratio).

Front Hubs

The forward motion of a four-wheel-drive vehicle when it is shifted into the two-wheel-drive mode will cause the two nonpowered wheels to revolve. The front axles, the front differential, the front propeller shaft, and some internal transfer case parts will be forced to rotate as well. This rotation is undesirable, as it causes friction and unnecessary wear on machined surfaces.

Manual Locking/Unlocking Hubs

When the transfer case is engaged in the two-wheel high mode, adjustable front-driving hubs can allow the nonpowered front wheels to rotate freely on their axle shafts while the front driveline remains stationary. And because the hubs are adjustable, they can also engage with the axle shafts when the front driveline is in the four-wheel high or low modes. Adjustment is obtained by manually twisting a lever in the center of each hub. This lever moves a spring-loaded, splined sleeve free of the axle for operation in the two-wheel or unlocked position. Moving the hub lever in the opposite direction allows the spring to reengage the sleeve and axle splines when the transfer case returns to the four-wheel-drive mode (Figure 35-8).

Part-Time Four-Wheel Drive A vehicle that can function in either a two-wheel-drive mode or in four-wheel drive at the driver's choice has **part-time four-wheel drive.** A vehicle with part-time four-wheel drive can be operated according to the demands of the road it is driven on. However, because it is awkward to leave the vehicle to lock or unlock the manual front hubs and shift the transfer case into the desired mode before driving on, several approaches have been developed to eliminate manual front hubs.

One recent development in part-time, four-wheel-drive vehicles is a vacuum-operated system that moves a splined collar to connect or disconnect the axle components. These vehicles do not use locking hubs. When the vacuum motor disengages the splined collar, one axle shaft is disconnected from the differential. The shafts continue to turn, but the differential does not, nor does the front propeller shaft. It is a light, simple system that minimizes drive train friction and power loss (Figure 35-9).

Full-Time Four-Wheel Drive **Full-time four-wheel drive** is an alternative to the part-time system and is achieved through complicated mechanics so that the vehicle may remain in the four-wheel-drive mode at all times. It has been noted that damage to driveline parts can occur when using four-wheel-drive vehicles on pavement, since there must be some "give" between the front and rear axles to eliminate tire scrubbing when rounding a curve. The answer to the problem was the introduction of a third differential, usually an integral part of the transfer case (Figure 35-10).

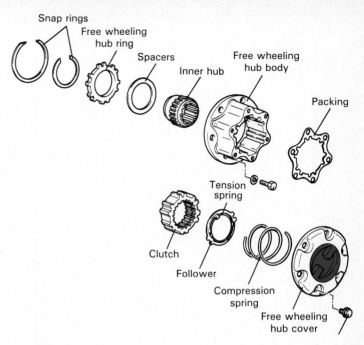

FIGURE 35-8   Manual front hub components and engagement knob. (Mitsubishi Motor Sales of America, Inc.)

FIGURE 35-9   Full-time four-wheel drive compared to part-time four-wheel drive. (American Motors Corporation)

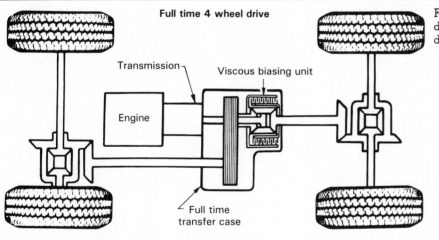

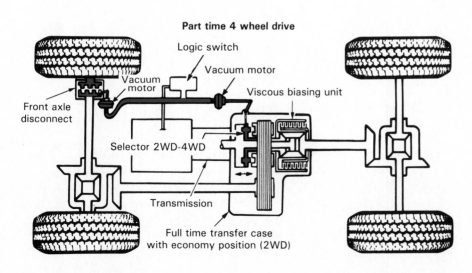

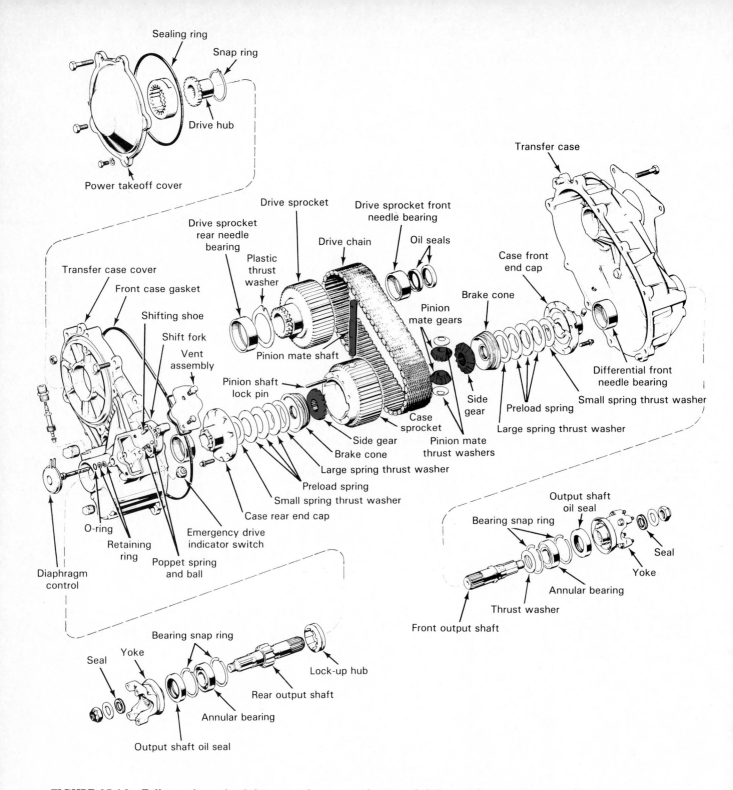

FIGURE 35-10   Full-time four-wheel-drive transfer case with integral differential.

When the full-time four-wheel-drive vehicle is driven on hard surfaces, the axle differentials apply power to each pair of wheels yet allow them to rotate at different speeds when cornering. In the same way, the third (or center) differential allows all wheels to be powered and yet rotate at different speeds. However, just as an axle differential sends engine power to the wheel with the least traction (as on ice or mud) and causes it to spin uselessly, so will the center differential react and send engine power to the *pair* of wheels offering the least resistance.

Therefore, the center differential must be *locked*, or made inoperable, at the driver's option. This is usually achieved through a vacuum control. The driver, when encountering terrain where center differential lockup is required, moves a dash-mounted switch that locks the center differential. A dash light comes on to warn the driver of the lockup driving mode and to remind him or her to reset the center differential when returning to normal pavement.

Because it is easy to operate, the full-time four-wheel drive became popular. The manufacturers either made the system standard equipment on their vehicles, or they offered it as an option. But because the arrangement meant that all driveline parts had to rotate and thus create drag, it resulted in some loss of engine power and increased fuel consumption. When the fuel shortage occurred in the mid-1970s, full-time four-wheel drive was largely abandoned, and a new system was introduced that would allow the driver to disengage his or her front wheels for highway driving yet allow them to be reengaged without having to set the front hubs manually.

Automatic Locking/Unlocking Hubs

As the term implies, **automatic locking/unlocking hubs** can engage and disengage the splined stub axles without being physically manipulated. When the transfer case is put into the four-wheel-drive mode by the driver, rotation of the front axle is "sensed" by a cam within the hub which moves a slide gear or sleeve to engage the hub with the axle (Figure 35-11). The front wheels are thus powered and remain locked to the axles regardless of the direction of motion.

Return to the two-wheel-drive mode is achieved by stopping the vehicle, shifting the transfer case to two-wheel drive, shifting the transmission into reverse, and backing the vehicle a few feet. When this occurs, the hub spring moves the slide gear or sleeve in the opposite direction to unlock the hub from the axle. Each front wheel can now rotate freely, and power is no longer being applied through the front driveline.

On-Road Four-Wheel Drive

While most four-wheel-drive vehicles have either been trucks or special vehicles for off-road purposes, a few four-wheel-drive cars have been designed primarily for on-road use. Manufacturers of these models claim that the benefits of four-wheel drive offset the cost penalties. The most well-known models include the American Motors Eagle, Audi Quattro, Subaru 4WD, and Toyota Tercel 4WD. Their additional traction and handling benefits make them more capable in bad weather or in extreme handling conditions.

Drive Train   Although the drive trains of these vehicles are similar to the basic layout described in this chapter for off-road vehicles, some differences exist. First, their limited ground clearance and light-duty components aren't designed for off-road thrashing. Second, the Audi, Subaru, and Toyota were first designed as front-wheel-drive vehicles. The addition of a transfer case (or rear output off the transmission), rear drive axle, and propeller shaft made them into four-wheel-drive cars. The Eagle added a front axle and propeller shaft.

None of these vehicles have locking hubs. Their manufacturers permit four-wheel-drive operation on hard pavement, having designed in enough differential

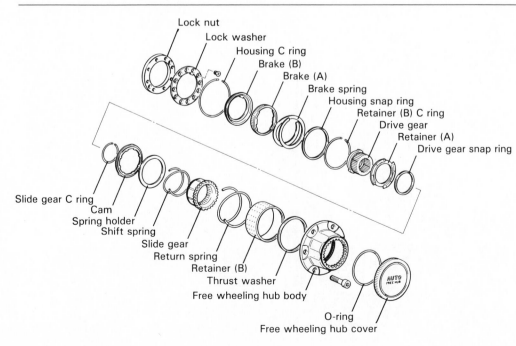

Lock nut
Lock washer
Housing C ring
Brake (B)
Brake (A)
Brake spring
Housing snap ring
Retainer (B) C ring
Drive gear
Retainer (A)
Drive gear snap ring

Slide gear C ring
Cam
Spring holder
Shift spring
Slide gear
Return spring
Retainer (B)
Thrust washer
Free wheeling hub body

O-ring
Free wheeling hub cover

FIGURE 35-11   Automatic front hub components. (Mitsubishi Motor Sales of America, Inc.)

action or slippage to take care of wheel scrubbing and drive train windup. The Audi Quattro has a manual lockup feature on the center differential, while the AMC Eagle uses a viscous fluid clutch to permit slippage. Some new Subaru models even have the futuristic feature of going into four-wheel drive when the wipers are turned on—the theory being that additional traction provides a safer driving experience when it rains.

Single-Speed Transfer Cases

In some light-duty four-wheel-drive applications, especially the systems used in all-wheel drive passenger cars, it is neither practical nor wise to offer a low-range gear ratio. Without the heavier-duty components commonly used on trucks and four-wheel-drive sport utility vehicles, the four-wheel-drive automobile would suffer driveline damage if the power-doubling action of low-range gearing was used.

A **single-speed transfer case** allows the driver to use four-wheel drive or two-wheel drive through a simple gear train, which, in one position, lets the power flow to the rear driveline only. An integral main drive gear in the transfer case (driven by the transmission output shaft) delivers power to the rear driveline at all times and is also meshed with an idler gear on a short auxiliary shaft. The idler gear, in turn, meshes with a front-axle drive gear to rotate the front driveline when in the four-wheel-drive mode. Or the front-axle drive gear is moved out of mesh with the idler gear when the two-wheel-drive mode is wanted.

One manufacturer offers a system in which the transfer case does not have a low-range position, but the transmission includes a low-geared sixth-speed position which can only be engaged when the transfer case is in the four-wheel-drive mode.

The average transfer case does not allow shifting between the two-wheel high and four-wheel high gear positions without bringing the vehicle to a rest. Shifting while in motion and under power can cause gear damage. But one alternative system has a set of planetary gears that are driven by the transmission output shaft. The arrangement lets the shift between two-

FIGURE 35-12 Two-speed transfer case in two-wheel drive mode. (American Motors Corporation)

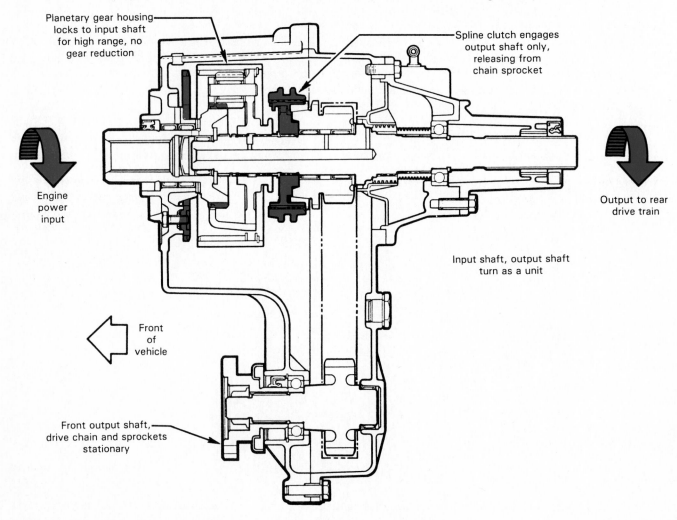

Planetary gear housing locks to input shaft for high range, no gear reduction

Spline clutch engages output shaft only, releasing from chain sprocket

Engine power input

Output to rear drive train

Input shaft, output shaft turn as a unit

Front of vehicle

Front output shaft, drive chain and sprockets stationary

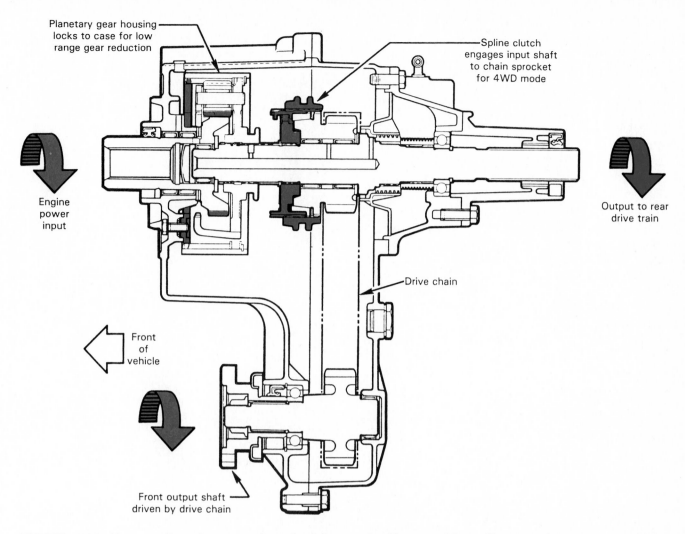

Planetary gear housing
locks to case for low
range gear reduction

Spline clutch
engages input shaft
to chain sprocket
for 4WD mode

Engine
power
input

Output to rear
drive train

Drive chain

Front
of
vehicle

Front output shaft
driven by drive chain

FIGURE 35-13 Two-speed transfer case in four-wheel-drive mode. (American Motors Corporation)

wheel and four-wheel high be made while in motion (Figures 35-12 and 35-13). All systems, however, require that the vehicle be stopped when shifting between high range and low range.

It is obvious that four-wheel-drive vehicles must have identical axle ratios in the front and in the rear. And all tires on the four-wheel-drive vehicle must be of the same diameter and must use equal inflation pressures. If such is not the case, driveline wrap-up and damaging tire scrub would occur when the four-wheel-drive mode was in use. One manufacturer, however, uses different front/rear axle ring and pinion ratios feeling such a combination provides better directional stability and pulling power on soft or slippery terrain.

THE FIRST FOUR-WHEEL-DRIVE VEHICLES

In 1908 Otto Zachow and William Besserdich perfected a unique front-drive axle, using ball and socket hubs, and soon after completed an efficient four-wheel-drive automobile. With local backing in their hometown of Clintonville, Wisconsin, the Four Wheel Drive Auto Company was formed in 1910, and production of passenger cars began the following year. However, by the end of 1912, autos were replaced by a more promising line of trucks. The First World War then created a huge demand for four-wheel-drive military trucks, with thousands being ordered for the British and American forces fighting in Europe. After the war a growing market in the public utility, municipal services, and various off-road applications resulted in the design of an extensive selection of four-wheel-drive truck models.

Workhorses of Yesteryear
Automotive Quarterly Magazine

TRADE TERMS

Automatic Locking/Unlocking Hubs
Conventional Four-wheel Drive
Driveline Wrap-up
Four-wheel High
Four-wheel Low
Front Differential/Axle Assembly
Front Propellor Shaft
Full-time Four-wheel Drive

Independent Front Axle
Part-time Four-wheel Drive
Single-speed Transfer Case
Solid Front Axle
Transfer Case
Transfer Case Housing
Two-Wheel High

REVIEW QUESTIONS

1. What advantages does four-wheel drive have over two-wheel drive?

2. Name the three principal driveline components that are added to a conventional vehicle to make it a four-wheel-drive vehicle.

3. What is driveline wrap-up?

4. What are the two basic types of front-driving axles?

5. Is the steering system of a four-wheel-drive vehicle different from that of a two-wheel-drive vehicle?

6. What are the four major functions of a transfer case?

7. Define full-time four-wheel drive.

8. Define part-time four-wheel drive.

9. What is the purpose of a third differential?

10. Explain why automatic locking hubs are used on some four-wheel-drive systems and manual locking hubs are used on others?

PART SIX

Chassis System

36

Suspensions

INTRODUCTION

The automobile **chassis** is everything from the floor pan down, excluding the engine, transmission, and rear end. This is a rather large part of the automobile. It is, however, like everything else you've studied so far, nothing more than a group of systems. When approached as individual systems, the suspension has traditionally been the least complex in the whole car. However, as electronic controls have become more popular for shocks and suspensions, service knowledge is essential.

The chassis includes a frame, or unibody, a set of springs and shock absorbers to dampen the road bumps, and a steering system. This chapter discusses the various methods used to spring the car and how shock is dampened.

SUSPENSION COMPONENTS

Spring action isolates the passenger from the vibrations of the road. Wheels are connected to springs or torsion bars. The frame and floor pan also flex, acting as further springs. Within the seat are more springs and some foam rubber. All of this keeps the passengers from suffering the bumps and vibrations of the road.

OBJECTIVES

When you have competed this chapter, you should be able to

- Identify coil springs, leaf springs, and torsion bars
- Identify and troubleshoot shock absorbers
- Recognize types of front suspension systems, such as control arm, MacPherson strut, torsion bar, solid axle, and air
- Identify two types of rear suspension
- Explain how electronic level control operates
- Troubleshoot both front and rear suspension systems

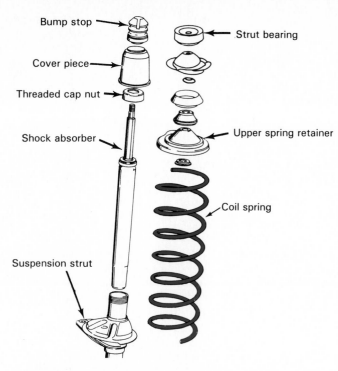

FIGURE 36-1   Coil spring. (Volkswagen of America, Inc.)

If no shock absorber controls the compression or expansion, the spring acts like a bouncing ball. It compresses and expands a number of times after hitting a bump. Adding a **shock absorber** to each wheel reduces this action and reaction to fewer contractions and expansions. They prevent the car from "floating," that is, bouncing up and down after it hits a bump.

There are four basic types of springs used in automotive suspension: (1) coil, (2) leaf, (3) torsion bar, and (4) air springs. Combined with shock absorbers, these springs can virtually eliminate road bumps and vibrations.

Coil Springs

Coil springs (Figure 36-1) have long been the most popular springs used for front suspension, and often they're found in rear suspension units. Coil springs are made from carefully tempered spring steel. In use, one end rests on the frame and the other rests on an axle or suspension member.

Leaf Springs

Leaf springs are used singly or in multiple units (Figure 36-2). Called semi-elliptical because of its geometric shape, the leaf spring is generally used with live axle (the axle that turns with the wheel) rear ends. By using a number of *leaves*, you can increase the spring force. Some heavy-duty trucks may use as many as 10 leaves in one spring assembly. Some vehicles have two-stage springs that allow the vehicle to ride comfortably with both a light or a heavy load (Figure 36-3).

FIGURE 36-2   Multiple-leaf spring. (Ford Motor Company)

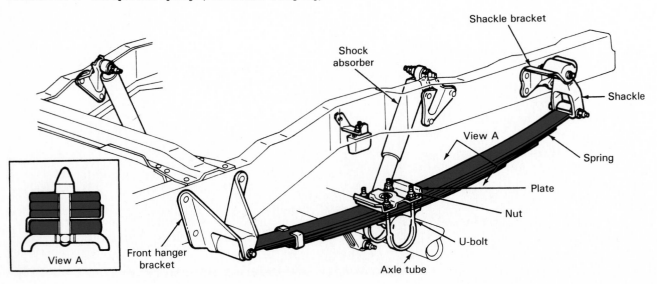

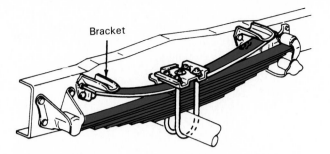

FIGURE 36-3 Two-stage springs. (Ford Motor Company)

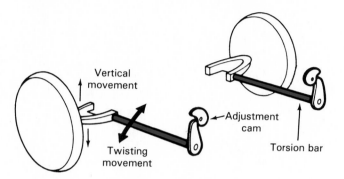

FIGURE 36-4 Torsion bar. (American Motors Corporation)

Torsion Bars

The third type of spring is the **torsion bar** (Figure 36-4). One end of a spring steel rod attaches to the frame of the car. The other end attaches to the suspension member on the wheel. As the wheel moves up and down, the torsion bar twists. Its effort to resist the twist and return to its normal shape gives the spring action necessary to provide a comfortable ride. Torsion bars are used in both front and rear suspension(s) (Figure 36-5).

Air Springs

Air suspension is used on some luxury cars and sports cars. This air spring system replaces the conventional spring system. Either sealed air chambers are used, or an air pump supplies pressure to air bags. This system, shown in Figure 36-6, has excellent cornering, leveling, and riding characteristics. It is also lighter in weight than a conventional suspension. Disadvantages of these systems are high repair costs and complex troubleshooting procedures. A major caution is that you must not jack or lift the car off the ground without first turning the system off.

FIGURE 36-5 Torsion bar suspension. (American Motors Corporation)

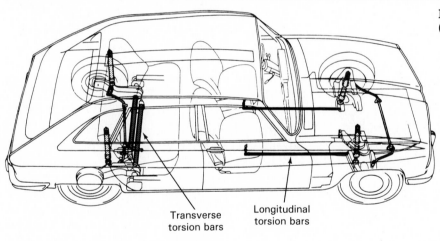

FIGURE 36-6 Air spring suspension system. (Ford Motor Company)

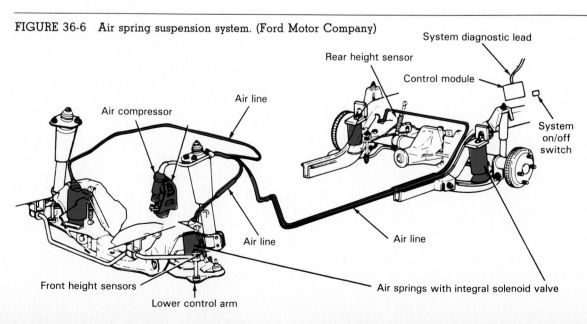

Shock Absorbers

Operation   Although not a spring, shock absorbers (Figure 36-7) are an integral part of the spring action; they, as stated earlier, dampen the action of the spring. The shock absorber is filled with hydraulic fluid or nitrogen gas. A plunger, connected to the top of the shock, is forced down when the spring compresses. Through a series of valves, the hydraulic fluid in front of the plunger is forced into side chambers, slowing the rate of spring compression. As the spring expands, hydraulic fluid at the top of the plunger is forced into the side chambers, slowing the return of the spring (Figure 36-8). It is the alternating up-and-down action of the plunger that provides the required dampening.

A shock absorber is worn out when the plunger or valves allows the hydraulic fluid to pass into the side chambers too quickly.

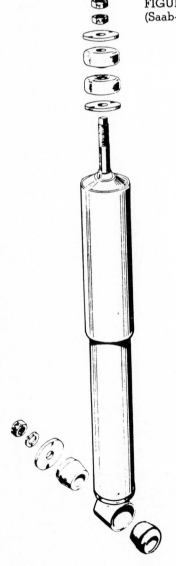

FIGURE 36-7   Shock absorber. (Saab-Scania of America, Inc.)

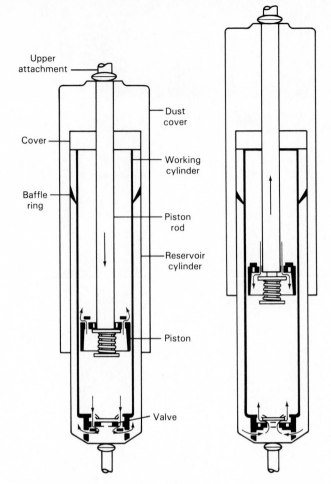

FIGURE 36-8   Cutaway of shock absorber. (Volvo)

Testing   Two quick tests check the operation of shock absorbers. They are a visual check for leaking fluid and the bounce test. The visual check is simply looking for traces of fluid leaking down the side of the shock. Leaks cannot be repaired. Replace the shock absorber. To complete the bounce test, push down on the fender of the car, or the bumper, and watch the car move up and down. A good shock absorber will quickly dampen the up-and-down movement. A worn-out shock will allow the car to move up and down a number of times. If the shock is worn out, replace it. Whenever replacing shocks, replace both front or both rear shocks at the same time.

Stabilizer Bars

Stabilizer bars, or sway bars, as shown in Figure 36-9, are not really springs. However, they function as springs and help in controlling spring action. They also reduce body roll on cornering. At best, they're a kind of torsion bar. They're provided to reduce some of the twisting action of the frame. When the car moves

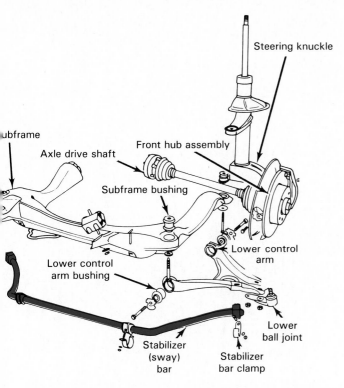

FIGURE 36-9 Stabilizer bar (sway bar). (Volkswagen of America, Inc.)

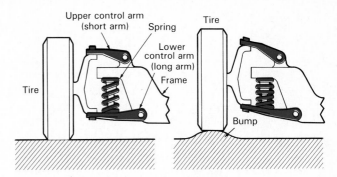

FIGURE 36-10 Action of control arms.

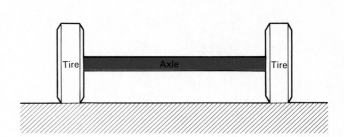

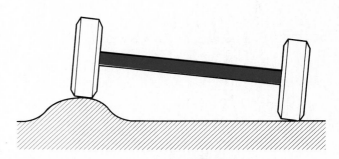

FIGURE 36-11 Action of a solid axle.

down the road with the frame level, the stabilizer bar is at rest. When one side of the frame rises, as in a bump, the opposite side of the frame rises also. This movement is counteracted by the stabilizer. A lifting force on one side causes the stabilizer to twist like a torsion bar, creating a downward force at the opposite side. This helps keep the frame level.

FRONT SUSPENSION

Control Arm

Control arm or independent front suspension allows the two front wheels to move up and down independently of one another. Figure 36-10 shows how the wheel can move up and down and yet not lift the frame. The **solid axle**, as shown in Figure 36-11, behaves in an opposite way. Here, when a tire hits a bump, the axle and frame will lift, tilting the opposite wheel. Solid axles were common in early automobiles and are still in many ¾-ton and larger trucks. Independent front suspension, however, is most common in today's passenger cars (Figure 36-12).

In Figure 36-13, two control arms hold the wheel in a vertical position. The control arm at the top is called the upper or short control arm. The one at the bottom is the lower or long control arm. The spring

and shock absorber connect at the top to the frame and at the bottom to the lower control arm. Each control arm then attaches at the frame and **steering knuckle.** The steering knuckle is separated from the control arms by upper and lower **ball joints.**

This arrangement allows the wheel to move up and down independently of the frame and keeps the tire and wheel vertical. To prevent lateral play, or side-to-side movement, a strut bar attaches to the frame and to the lower control arm. All of these work together to allow the wheel to move up and down, remain vertical, avoid lateral movement, and yet still be steered.

Control arm suspension can be arranged in different ways. As shown in Figure 36-14, the spring and shock absorber can be mounted above the upper control arm. Here, the inner fender well supports the top of the spring. A somewhat different approach is the MacPherson strut.

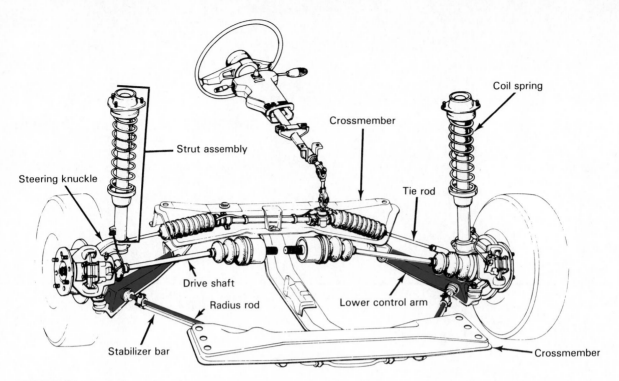

FIGURE 36-12 Independent front suspension. (American Honda Motor Corporation, Inc.)

FIGURE 36-13 Upper and lower control arms.

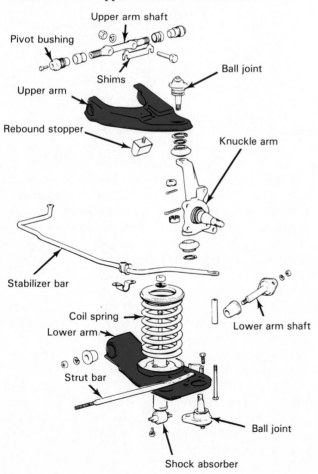

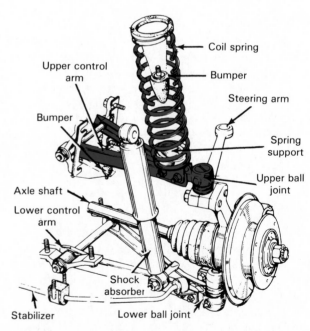

FIGURE 36-14 Coil spring above upper control arm. (Saab-Scania of America, Inc.)

THE MARSH MELLOW SUSPENSION:

Less Bounce Per Ounce of Rubber Springing

Firestone's New Product Market Development group has developed and demonstrated a new type of suspension system that offers a number of advantages for small cars and trucks. The heart of the suspension is a unique rubber spring invented by Firestone engineer Gerry Marsh, and because it provides such a smooth ride, Firestone has named it the Marsh Mellow.

Rubber suspension springs are nothing new. Goodrich introduced one called the Torsilastic in the 1940s, the Morris Minor used them in the 1950s, and Pirelli had a rubberized coil spring in the 1960s. Rubber springs never caught on because of problems with excessive heat buildup and compression set (which means that they did not regain their original height after being compressed). The Marsh Mellow's material properties overcame these problems.

Firestone's rubber spring is a black, rubber cylinder with a hollow center. The core is made of a special rubber with characteristics not unlike those of a child's Super Ball—technically it's a material with low hysteresis, meaning it has low damping properties and doesn't build up heat over rough roads or take a set. The core is wrapped with multiple layers of nylon tire cord layered in bias angles to produce specific ride characteristics—not too unlike bias-ply tire construction.

Surprisingly, temperature has little effect on the spring if a low-damping core is used. Firestone engineers tested the spring at temperatures ranging from $-16°F$ to $+250°F$ and found that a low-damping core material was insensitive to temperature and stroke variations.

Marsh Mellow improves a vehicle's ride because it offers a variable rate that provides an essentially constant ride frequency, which is difficult to obtain with a coil spring. This is especially important in a small car because you can basically achieve the same ride whether the car carries only the driver or is fully loaded. These features are best suited for the rear suspension. The front suspension doesn't see as much load variation as the rear does, but you can still use it in the front because it does give additional resistance to bottoming out.

The Marsh Mellow spring has already been used for several years in the heavy-duty off-highway market, where its variable rate, durability, and packaging flexibility has proved its worth.

Road & Track
CBS Publications

FIGURE 36-15 MacPherson strut.

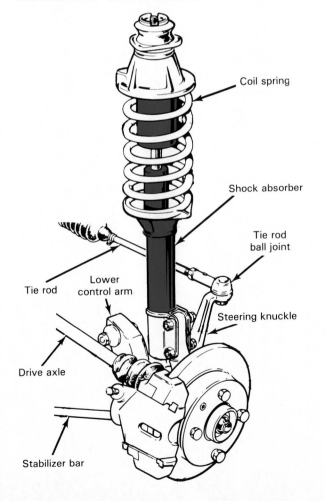

Coil spring

Shock absorber

Tie rod ball joint

Tie rod

Lower control arm

Steering knuckle

Drive axle

Stabilizer bar

MacPherson Strut

Figure 36-15 shows how the **MacPherson strut** is used in front suspension assemblies. This strut is found predominately on imported cars and with increasing frequency on domestic cars. Notice that something is missing—the upper control arm. Everything else is there: spring, shock, stabilizer, and tension rod. With the heavy-duty shock and lighter spring, the upper control arm is no longer needed. This arrangement is much lighter so it saves weight, making it more suitable to today's smaller car. Unfortunately, replacement costs are higher. Instead of replacing an inexpensive shock absorber, the whole strut or an internal cartridge must be replaced. Labor costs are also much higher than they are for replacing shock absorbers.

Torsion Bar

Torsion bar suspension (Figure 36-16) is another type of suspension unit. Notice that there is both an upper and lower control arm. The torsion bar attaches to the lower control arm.

As the lower control arm moves up, the torsion bar twists. The torsion bar tendency to return to its original unstressed position forces the lower control arm back down. This movement creates the springing action. As you can see, a shock absorber still dampens

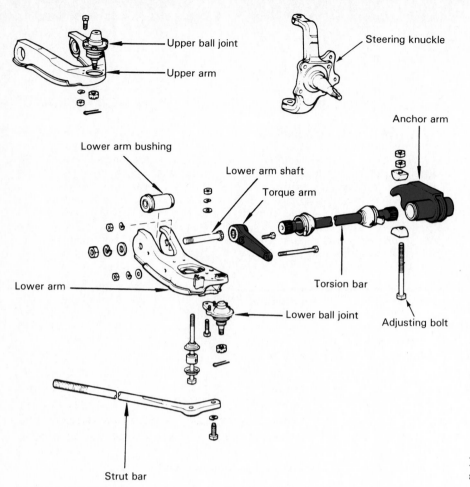

Upper ball joint

Upper arm

Steering knuckle

Anchor arm

Lower arm bushing

Lower arm shaft

Torque arm

Lower arm

Torsion bar

Lower ball joint

Adjusting bolt

Strut bar

FIGURE 36-16   Front torsion bar suspension.

the springing action, a stabilizer prevents chassis roll, and a strut bar controls side movement.

Torsion bars mounted from front to rear are called longitudinal torsion bars. Torsion bars mounted sideways are called transverse torsion bars.

Solid Front Axle

The **solid front axle suspension** (Figure 36-17) is also called a **dead axle** as it does not rotate with the wheel.

The solid front axle is primarily on trucks. Instead of coil springs, it has leaf springs. Generally, two springs run parallel to, and are suspended from, the frame. Two U-bolts fasten the spring to the axle. The wheels are suspended on pivots at each end of the axle.

In the very early years of the automobile, one spring was **transverse-mounted** (parallel to the axles rather than the frame). This arrangement was discarded in favor of the other suspension arrangements discussed in this chapter, but interestingly enough, late-model Corvettes use the single, transverse, leaf spring in their rear suspensions.

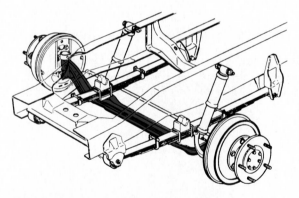

FIGURE 36-17   Solid front axle suspension. (General Motors Corporation)

Ford has developed a solid front axle called the **twin I-beam suspension** that uses the good features of the solid front axle (strength and simplicity) and eliminates the rolling tendency of the single solid front axle (Figure 36-18).

In this suspension system, two solid front axles are mounted with pivot points on opposite sides of

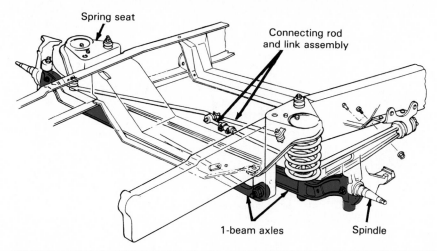

FIGURE 36-18   Twin I-beam front suspension. (Ford Motor Company)

the vehicle. This provides an excellent strength and at the same time returns the independent front suspension to the vehicle. Twin I-beam front-end alignment costs more because the beams must be twisted to align the front end.

REAR SUSPENSION

The type of rear suspension a car has depends on whether it has front-wheel drive or rear-wheel drive. Many vehicles with rear-wheel drive have a live axle suspension. A vehicle with front-wheel drive will often have independent rear suspension.

Rear Leaf Spring Suspension

When a car has rear-wheel drive, the differential and axle housing (called a rear end) must be suspended as a unit. To do this, the general answer has been to use leaf springs (Figure 36-19).

Rear leaf springs work much like front leaf springs. Usually they are mounted parallel to the frame rails, attached in front to a *hanger assembly* that is mounted to the frame. A rubber bushing reduces vibration between the hanger and spring. A spring *shackle* with a rubber bushing holds the rear of the spring to the rear frame hanger. This shackle, usually about 2 in. long, lets the semielliptical spring stretch out straight when it flexes. Without this freedom of movement, the spring could not bend and would soon break. The leaf spring passes under or over the axle housing and is locked in place with two U-bolts.

Transverse Leaf Spring Suspension

Copying the style of suspension found on most buggies and wagons of the preautomobile days, the transverse mounted leaf spring of the old Corvette (Figure 36-20) and some new cars seems like a throwback to days gone by. If that were true, it would sit on top of the differential with one end fastened to each side of the

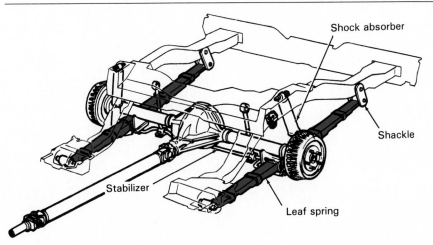

FIGURE 36-19   Rear leaf spring suspension. (Chevrolet Motor Divison, GMC)

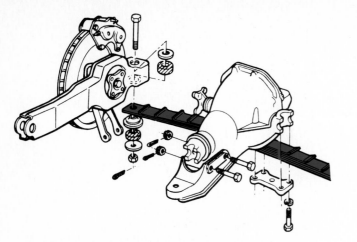

FIGURE 36-20   Transverse leaf spring rear suspension.
(Chevrolet Motor Division, GMC)

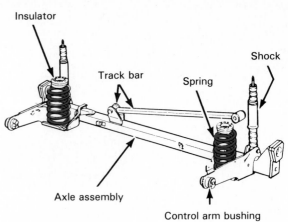

FIGURE 36-21   Front-wheel-drive coil rear suspension.
(Chrysler Corporation)

FIGURE 36-22   Control arm rear
suspension. (General Motors Corporation)

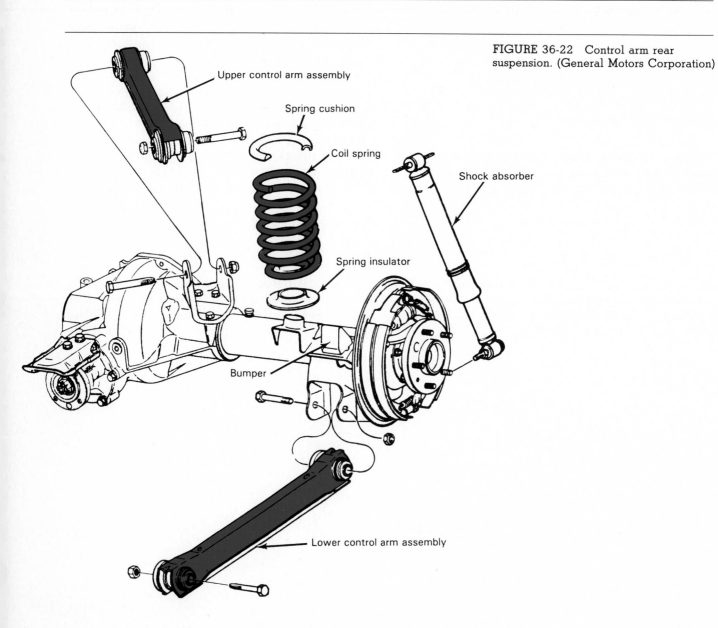

frame. You would certainly have adequate ground clearance—about 3 ft! Instead, the spring mounts under the differential and connects to the control arms that run parallel to the frame. This prevents lateral movement and provides proper ground clearance.

Coil Spring Rear Suspension

Coil spring rear suspensions are used on both front-wheel- and rear-wheel-drive cars.

The front-wheel-drive rear suspension consists of a rear axle assembly, two coil springs, two shock absorbers, and a track bar. The two control arms are welded to the axle housing and are used to mount the axle assembly to the body (Figure 36-21). The two coil springs support the weight of the vehicle in the rear. Each spring is held between a seat in the underbody and a seat welded to the rear axle housing. At the bottom, the shock absorbers are mounted with a bolt and nut to brackets welded to the axle housing. At the top the shock absorbers are mounted to the reinforced body area with a nut. A single-unit hub and bearing assembly is bolted to both ends of the rear axle assembly. On recent models, this hub and bearing assembly is a sealed unit and the bearing cannot be replaced separately.

The rear-wheel-drive rear suspension is a link type with coil springs. Figure 36-22 shows an example of a system that uses two lower control arms and one large upper control arm (torque arm), rigidly mounted to the differential housing at the rear and to the trans-

mission, through rubber bushings, at the front. In addition, a track rod, mounted between axle tube and body, and a stabilizer bar (optional on some models) are used in the rear suspension. The two coil springs and shock absorbers are mounted between the body and rear axle in a conventional manner. Other rear-suspensions use four control arms.

Independent Rear Suspension

Figure 36-23 shows an example of independent rear suspension that uses coil springs. Note that it has all of the same components (except an upper control arm) in the rear suspension as are used in the front suspension. This includes springs, shock absorbers, control arm, tie rod, and stabilizer bar (not shown). Each wheel can move independently of the other.

Another type of suspension is the independent rear torsion bar suspension. Torsion bar rear suspension works much like torsion bar front suspension. The example in Figure 36-24, however, shows a transverse mounted torsion bar instead of the longitudinally mounted torsion bar shown in the front suspension example. Whichever way the manufacturer decides to mount it is of little consequence; it still works the same way.

On both the Audi Quattro and Pontiac Fiero, a front suspension system was moved to the rear of the car. These designs are identical to the front suspension except that the tie rods are connected to the frame instead of the steering gear.

FIGURE 36-23 Independent coil spring suspension. (Ford Motor Company)

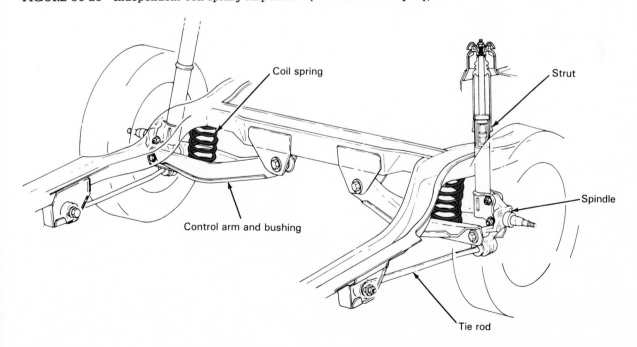

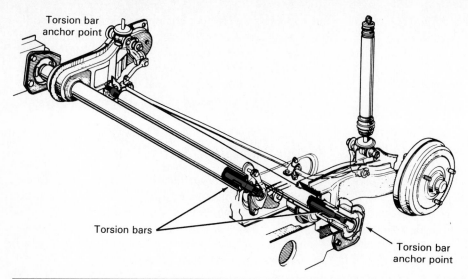

Torsion bar anchor point

Torsion bars

Torsion bar anchor point

FIGURE 36-24   Rear transverse torsion bar suspension. (American Motors Corporation)

Electronic Level Control

Part of the rear suspension on some cars includes **electronic level control.** This control allows the automobile user to load the rear end of the car without changing the angle of the car (Figure 36-25). In other words, the car will not "droop" in the rear. To do this several things must happen.

A height control valve sits at the rear of the car. It is adjusted to sit at any given level. When weight

FIGURE 36-25   Electronic level control system. (American Motors Corporation)

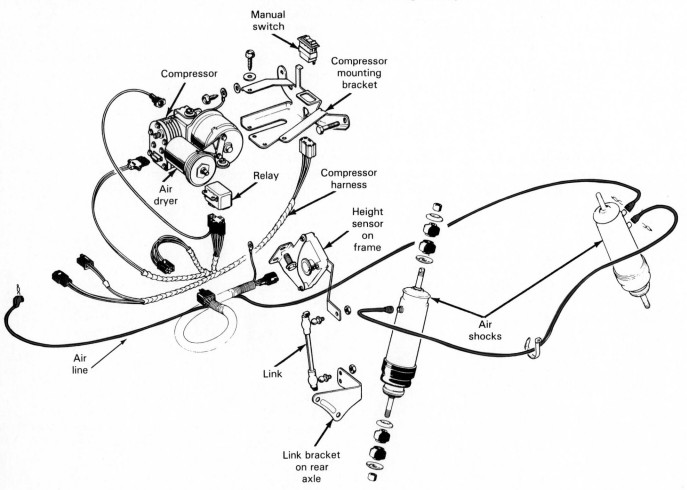

Manual switch

Compressor

Compressor mounting bracket

Air dryer

Relay

Compressor harness

Height sensor on frame

Air line

Link

Air shocks

Link bracket on rear axle

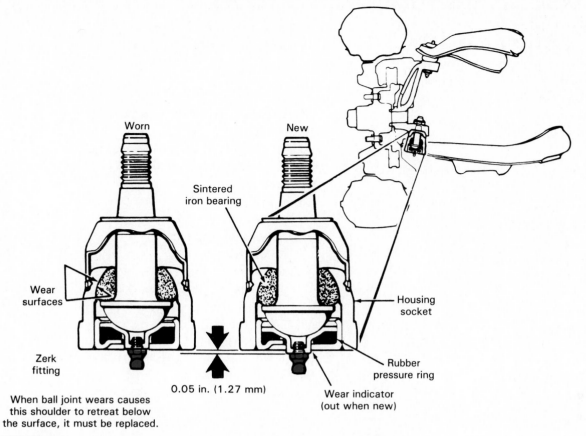

FIGURE 36-26   Zerk fitting on a ball joint. (General Motors Corporation)

is added to the rear of the car, the height control valve moves away from its zero point, opening a valve from the air pressure source.

An electronic compressor supplies air under pressure. When the height control valve senses an increase in the angle of the car, it opens a valve, and compressed air moves to the rear shock absorbers. These lift the height of the rear end back up to level.

When the driver removes the load, an opposite reaction begins. The height control valve is again activated, releasing air from the shock absorbers, lowering the level of the car.

A time delay switch prevents road bumps from activating the height control valve. Most level controls have no storage tank. The compressor is hooked directly to the shocks through a filter/dryer.

SUSPENSION SERVICING AND TROUBLESHOOTING

Servicing the suspension is limited to visual inspections for wear and damage and lubrication at regular inter-

vals. To lubricate, use a heavy grease (such as wheel bearing grease or "axle" grease). With a high-pressure grease gun, lubricate those parts of the suspension which have **zerk** fittings. Figure 36-26 shows where the zerk fittings are and also identifies areas that need to be checked for wear.

When visually inspecting, check shocks and struts to see if they are worn or leaking, check springs to see if they are sagging, and check ball joints and control arm bushings to see if they are worn or loose. Replace any damaged or worn part. Check grommets and all rubber parts to see if they need replacing.

There are many different types of suspension systems. Suspension systems vary among car models and car years. Each model and year of car has special tools and service procedures for replacing worn suspension parts. Before starting any work on a suspension system, look in a shop manual for the procedures to use and the special tools required. Figure 36-27 shows guides for troubleshooting the suspension system. Careful study of these guides will diagnose most of the problems associated with front and rear suspension.

Abnormal Noise, Front End

1. Lubrication - ball joints and tie rod ends.
2. Damaged shock absorbers or mountings.
3. Worn control arm bushings or tie rod ends.
4. Loose stabilizer bar.
5. Loose wheel nuts.
6. Loose suspension bolts.
7. Wheel covers.

Wander Or Poor Steering Stability

1. Mismatched or uneven tires.
2. Lubrication - ball joints and tie rod ends.
3. Faulty shock absorbers or mounting.
4. Loose stabilizer bar.
5. Broken or sagging springs.
6. Rack and pinion adjustment.
7. Front end alignment.

Erratic Steering When Braking

1. Wheel bearings incorrectly adjusted or worn.
2. Broken or sagging springs.
3. Leaking wheel cylinder or caliper
4. Rack and pinion off high point.
5. Warped rotors.

Low Or Uneven Trim Height

1. Broken or sagging springs.
2. Overloaded.
3. Incorrect springs.

Ride Too Soft

1. Faulty Shock Absorbers.

Ride Too Harsh

1. Incorrect shock absorbers.
2. Incorrect springs.

Body Leans Or Sways In Corners

1. Loose stabilizer bar.
2. Faulty shock absorbers or mounting.
3. Broken or sagging springs.
4. Overloaded.

Suspension Bottoms

1. Overloaded.
2. Faulty shocks.
3. Incorrect broken or sagging springs.

"Dog" Tracking

1. Damaged rear suspension arm or worn bushings.
2. Bent rear axle.
3. Frame or underbody alignment.

Steering Wheel Kick-Back (Power)

1. Air in system.
2. Rack pinion attachment loose.
3. Tie rod ends loose.
4. Wheel bearings incorrectly adjusted or worn.

Cupped Tires

1. Front shock absorbers defective.
2. Wheel bearing incorrectly adjusted or worn.
3. Excessive tire or wheel run-out.
4. Worn ball joint.

FIGURE 36-27   Suspension troubleshooting guide.

TRADE TERMS

Ball Joints
Chassis
Coil Springs
Control Arm
Dead Axle

Electronic Level Control
Leaf Springs
MacPherson Strut
Shock Absorbers
Solid Axle

Solid Front Axle Suspension
Stabilizer Bars
Steering Knuckle
Torsion Bar

Torsion Bar Suspension
Transverse-mounted
Twin I-Beam Suspension
Zerk

REVIEW QUESTIONS

1. Name the four major types of springs used in today's automobile suspensions. Describe each type.

2. What does a shock absorber do?

3. How do shock absorbers work?

4. What is a stabilizer bar?

5. Name the types of front suspension discussed in this chapter.

6. Define independent front suspension.

7. What is a MacPherson strut?

8. Where will you find solid front axles?

9. What is I-beam suspension?

10. Are torsion bars found on the front or rear suspension?

11. What is a dead axle?

12. What is a live axle?

13. What type of vehicle usually has a live axle?

14. Can a rear-drive vehicle have independent rear suspension?

15. What are the basic components of an electronic level control?

16. What prevents road conditions from activating the electronic level control?

17. To elevate the rear end of an electronic-level-controlled car, the springs are extended through a series of levers. True or false? Explain.

18. What does suspension service include?

19. A customer complains of hard-to-control steering. Name five things that could be wrong.

37

Steering Systems and Wheel Alignment

INTRODUCTION

In Chapter 36, you saw how the automobile was suspended. This chapter tells how the suspension and steering work together to cause the car to turn, recover from that turn, and go down the road in a straight fashion without wandering from side to side. Steering gears control this function. The various types of steering gears transfer the motion of the steering wheel to the front wheels. At the same time, they prevent excessive road vibration from passing back to the steering wheel.

STEERING GEARS

The two types of steering gears are the **rack and pinion** and the **recirculating ball.** Most small vehicles use the rack and pinion while larger vehicles use the recirculating ball.

Rack and Pinion

Rack and pinion steering is currently the most popular type of steering (Figure 37-1). Figure 37-2 shows how

OBJECTIVES

When you have completed this chapter, you should be able to

- Describe the different types of steering gear systems
- Describe the parts of the steering linkage and **power steering** systems
- Describe the difference among rack and pinion, recirculating ball, and linkage assist steering systems
- Describe power steering pumps
- Identify steering column types
- Explain the fundamentals of front-end alignment.

the steering gear assembly is mounted. Usually, it's mounted to a cross member with two or three bolts. To reduce vibration, rubber insulators, or stand-offs, separate the assembly from direct contact with the cross member.

In operation, the steering shaft connects to the bearing and pinion assembly. As the steering wheel rotates right or left, the **pinion gear** engages the steering rack, pulling it to the right or left (Figure 37-3). As Figure 37-2 shows, the steering rack connects to the **tie rods.** The tie rods then attach to the spindle steering arm, or the struts. The steering arms move the wheels right or left.

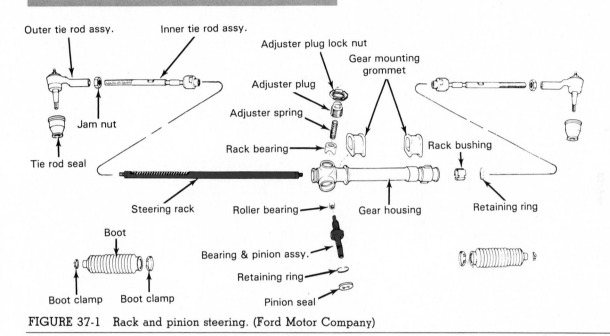

FIGURE 37-1   Rack and pinion steering. (Ford Motor Company)

FIGURE 37-2   Location of rack and pinion steering. (Ford Motor Company)

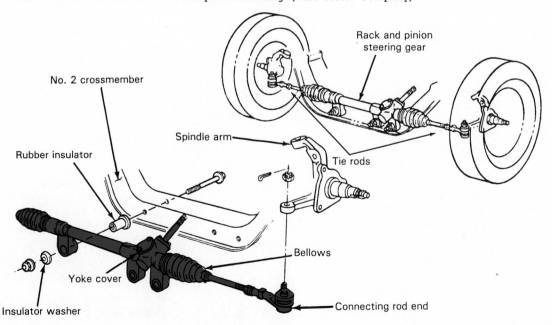

545

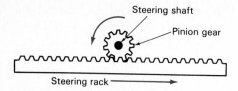

FIGURE 37-3 Rack and pinion.

Recirculating Ball

Figure 37-4 shows the recirculating ball **worm and nut steering gear.** In practice, the name is shortened to recirculating ball. In operation, the steering wheel shaft connects to the worm shaft. When the worm shaft rotates, the recirculating ball worm nut rides back and forth along the threaded screw (Figure 37-5). The worm nut contacts the sector shaft, causing it to turn as the worm nut travels back and forth. The **Pitman arm** connects onto the steering linkage, turning the wheels.

Now, let's go back to the worm nut. Inside the worm nut are separate ball bearings called worm bearings (Figure 37-5). These bearings roll between the worm nut and worm shaft, creating nearly friction-free action. As each bearing reaches the end of its

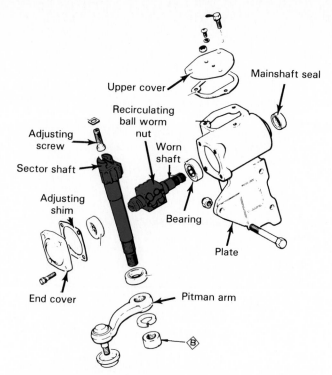

FIGURE 37-4 Recirculating ball bearing worm and nut steering gear. (General Motors Corporation)

FIGURE 37-5 Recirculating ball steering. (General Motors Corporation)

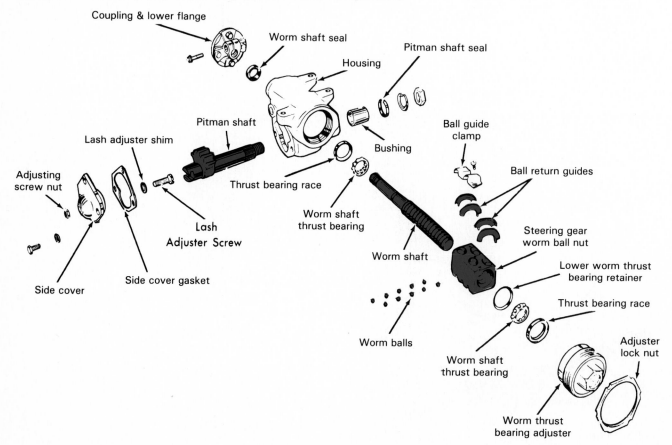

travel, it rotates back to its start through the bearing return guides (Figure 37-5)—hence the name recirculating ball. Before rack and pinion became popular, this was the most used steering gear box.

Worm and Roller

This system, as shown in Figure 37-6, is the simplest of the three systems in design. The steering shaft turns the *worm gear*. It in turn engages the roller, causing the roller shaft to rotate. In both the worm and roller and the recirculating ball systems, the gearbox is mounted to the frame. The amount of play in this gearbox is adjusted by loading tension on the roller with a simple adjuster screw.

STEERING LINKAGE

Steering linkage transfers the side-to-side movement, or front-to-rear movement, of the Pitman arm into left-and-right movement of the wheels. Figure 37-7 shows a typical example of this linkage.

In Figure 37-7 you can see the Pitman arm attached to the center link by a ball socket. The other end of the center link (also called a cross rod) attaches to the **idler arm.** When the Pitman arm moves the

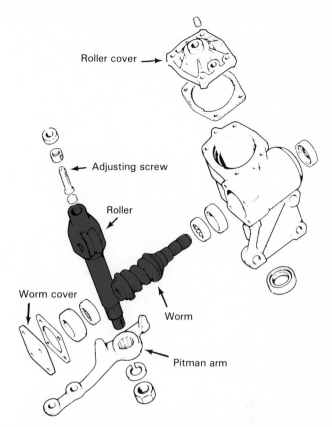

FIGURE 37-6   Worm and roller steering system.

FIGURE 37-7   Typical steering linkage. (Ford Motor Company)

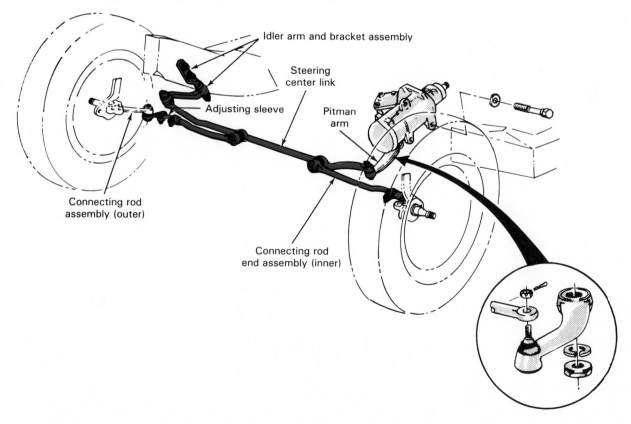

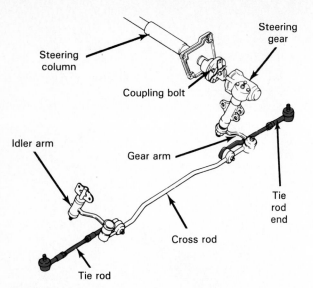

FIGURE 37-8 Tie rods. (Nissan Motor Corporation, U.S.A.)

center link, it activates the tie rod or *connecting rod* assemblies to move the wheels (Figure 37-8).

Servicing the linkage includes greasing the zerk fittings in the tie rod ends. Some newer cars do not have any zerk fittings, while others need no lubrication at all. On cars which need grease but have no fittings, you must remove a bolt in the tie rod end, install a zerk, lubricate with a grease gun, and reinstall the bolt.

Wear in the linkage system is easy to check for. Check to see how much movement is in the system.

If it is loose enough to shake by hand, some of the parts in the linkage system need replacement. Also, if you can move tires in or out by hand, you need to replace parts. Figure 37-9 identifies in color typical parts that are replaced. Remember, any time you replace any part, you must realign the front end.

POWER STEERING

The term *power steering* is a little bit misleading. Actually the term should be power-assisted steering. You, the driver, still do the steering, but you're helped along with hydraulic assistance. The power steering assembly provides about 65% more help than steering manually. Some cars have power steering pumps whose amount of assist varies according to speed or the rate of turning. This gives a quick steering response while allowing the driver to still "feel" the road through the steering wheel.

The power steering system is composed of a pump (usually belt-driven by the engine, although some early models were driven by the crankshaft), a reservoir to hold the hydraulic oil, a control valve, and pressure surfaces. The pressurized hydraulic oil acts on these surfaces to provide the power assist. If these surfaces are contained within the steering gear housing, the unit is called an **integral power steering** (Figure 37-10). If a power cylinder is connected between the frame and steering linkage, the unit is called an **external power steering** (Figure 37-11).

FIGURE 37-9 Typical replacement parts. (American Motors Corporation)

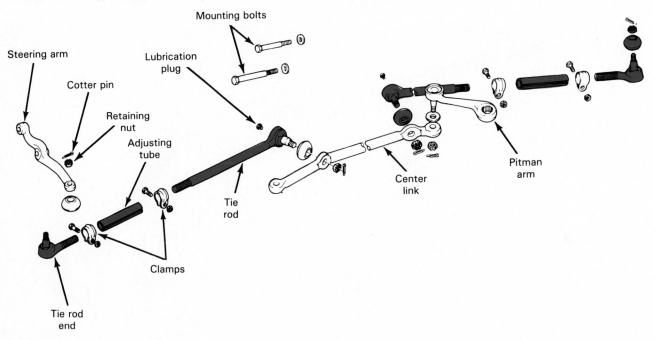

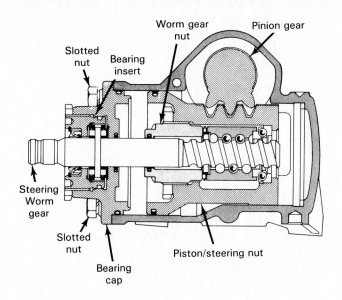

FIGURE 37-10   Integral power steering system.

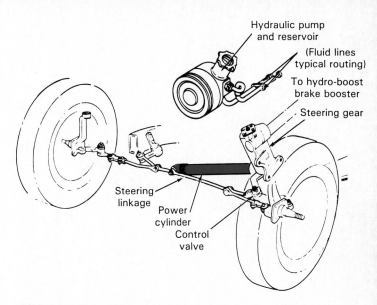

FIGURE 37-11   Linkage power steering system. (Ford Motor Company)

Rack and Pinion Power Steering

In Figure 37-12 is a drawing of an integral-type rack and pinion power steering unit. Notice that the pressure surfaces are the two seals within the cylinder. Power steering fluid under pressure from the pump passes through the control valve and into the cylinder. As you turn the steering wheel right or left, pressure is transferred to either the right or left seal, which moves the rack to the right or left. Figure 37-13 shows typical areas of steering gear leaks.

In Figure 37-14 is a second type of rack and pinion power steering unit. This unit uses an exterior power cylinder rather than a cylinder incorporated as part of the steering unit, as shown in Figure 37-12. Figure 37-15 gives a guide for diagnosing rack and pinion power steering problems.

Recirculating Ball Power Steering

Figure 37-16 will help you understand recirculating ball integral power steering. Like the rack and pinion power steering, recirculating ball power steering uses a pump and control valve to push the hydraulic fluid. Figure 37-16 shows how the hydraulic fluid acts on either the right or left side of the worm bearing nut

FIGURE 37-12   Integral-type rack and pinion power steering unit.

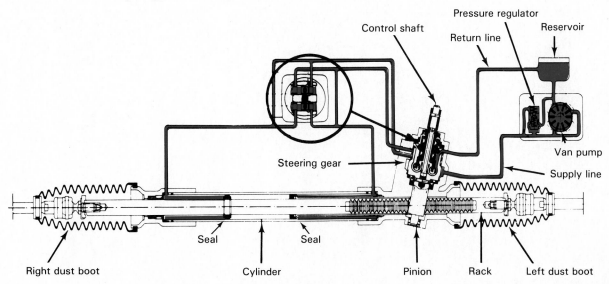

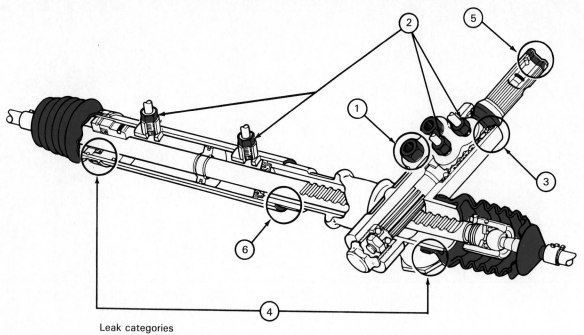

Leak categories
1. Hose fittings
2. Transfer lines
3. Input shaft seal
4. Bellows
5. Input shaft end seal
6. Steel cylinder and housing

FIGURE 37-13   Typical diagnosis for leaking steering gear. (Ford Motor Company)

FIGURE 37-14   Rack and pinion power steering with exterior power cylinder.
(Peugeot Motors of America, Inc.)

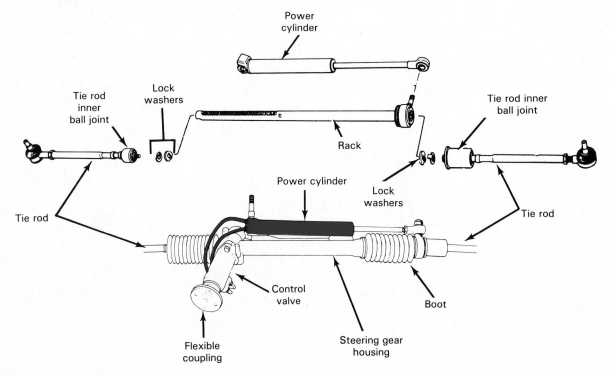

Before any internal service is performed on the rack and pinion power steering, diagnosis of the condition must be performed. Make sure that the tire size is correct, with matched tires (front and rear), all inflated to specifications. The following conditions, possible sources and corrective action will assist in performing the proper service.

Condition	Possible Source	Action
WANDER — vehicle wander is a condition where the car wanders back and forth on the roadway when it is driven straight ahead while the steering wheel is held in a firm position. Evaluation should be conducted on a level road (little road crown).	• Loose tie rod ends. • Inner ball housing loose or worn. • Gear Assembly loose on body bracket. • Excessive yoke clearance. • Loose suspension struts or ball joints. • Loose front hub. • Column intermediate shaft connecting bolts loose. • Column intermediate shaft universal joints loose or worn. • Improper toe setting.	Replace tie rod end assemblies. Replace tie rod end assemblies. Tighten mounting bolts (4) to specification. Adjust yoke clearance. Adjust or replace as required. Check and replace nut if loose or improperly staked — do not reuse nut. Tighten bolts to specification. Replace intermediate shaft. Set toe to specification
FEEDBACK — (rattle, chuckle, knocking noises in the steering gear). Feedback is a condition where roughness is felt in the steering wheel by the driver when the car is driven over rough pavement.	• Column U-joints loose. • Loose tie rod ends. • Loose/worn tie rod ball. • Gear assembly loose on body bracket. • Loose pinion bearing cap. • Loose yoke plug/locknut. • Loose pinion bearing locknut. • Piston disengaged or loose on rack. • Oversized pinion shaft bushing. • Steering gear yoke worn. • Column support bracket loose. • Column intermediate shaft connecting bolts loose. • Loose suspension struts on ball joints. • Loose front hub.	Replace if bad. Replace tie rod end assemblies. Replace tie rod assemblies. Tighten mounting bolts to specification. Tighten to specification. Adjust yoke preload to specification. Tighten locknut to specification. Replace rack assembly. Replace gear housing. Replace yoke assembly. Tighten bolts to specification. Tighten bolts to specification. Adjust or replace as necessary. Check and replace nut if loose or improperly staked—do not reuse nut.

FIGURE 37-15   Power steering diagnosis guide. (Ford Motor Company)

Condition	Possible Source	Action
POOR RETURNABILITY — Sticky Feel — Poor returnability is noticed when the steering fails to return to center following a turn without manual effort from the driver. In addition, when the driver returns the steering to center it may have a sticky or catchy feel.	• Misaligned steering column or column flange rubbing steering wheel and/or flange. • Check rotational torque of U-joints. • Yoke plug too tight. • Tight ball joints. • Tight tie rod end ball joints. • Undersized pinion shaft bushing in the housing. • Binding in valve assembly. • Bent or damaged rack. • Column bearing binding. • Tight suspension struts or ball joints. • Front end lube required. • Improper toe setting. • Contamination in system.	Align column. If binding, replace intermediate shaft. Adjust yoke preload to specification. Replace as required. Replace tie rod end assemblies. Replace gear housing assemblies. Replace input shaft of valve assembly. Replace rack assembly. Replace bearing. Adjust or replace as required. Lube front end. Set toe to specification. Flush Power Steering system.
HEAVY STEERING EFFORTS (Poor or loss of assist) — A heavy effort and poor assist condition is recognized by the driver while turning corners and especially while parking. A road test will verify this condition.	• Leakage/loss of fluid. • Valve plastic ring cut or twisted. • Damaged/worn plastic piston ring. • Loose/missing rubber backup piston O-ring. • Loose rack piston. • Gear assembly oil passages restricted. • Bent/damaged rack assembly. • Valve assembly internal leakage. • Low pump fluid. • Pump external leakage. • Improper drive belt tension. • Improper engine idle speed. • Pully loose or warped. • Pump/flow pressure not to specification. • Hose/cooler line restrictions or leakage.	See external leakage diagnosis for service. Replace ring. Replace ring. Replace/install O-ring. Replace rack assembly. Clear/service as required. Replace rack assembly. Replace valve assembly. Fill as necessary. Service per Pump Diagnosis. Readjust belt tension. Readjust idle. Replace pulley. **See Pump Service Diagnosis.** Clear or replace as required.

FIGURE 37-15 (cont.)

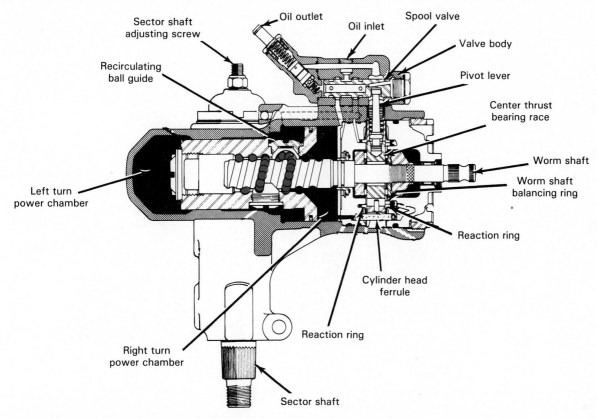

FIGURE 37-16 Recirculating ball integral power steering.

(now called the power piston) to give power assistance to right and left steering action.

POWER STEERING PUMPS

Power steering pumps have a fluid reservoir and are powered by a belt drive from the engine. The pumps pull hydraulic fluid from the reservoir and move it through the control valve and power steering unit. It then returns the hydraulic fluid back to the reservoir. The three types of pumps in the system are the vane, slipper, and roller. These names refer to the parts that actually pull and push the fluid. Figure 37-17 shows a vane pump, the most common type on modern cars. The vanes (Figure 37-18) remain in contact with the thrust plate by pressure of the oil and centrifugal force.

THE ELASTIC STEERING ARM

I have had a long love-hate relationship with Lancia cars, the love persisting sometimes even after something has broken and when their dynamic pleasures are only a memory (those I remember!). Some of the engineering is *so* pleasing to work with. However, there is one dark feature of the design that Lancia fanciers only mention in hushed tones and in carefully screened company. It is the Elastic Steering Arm, a ruse to disguise or absorb side effects of the geometric acrobatics of the Lancia independent front suspension.

Appias have stub-axles that slide on fixed pillars but connect by a single inelastic track-rod ahead of the wheel centers. Any vertical movement of one wheel relative to the other makes the Appia pigeon-toed; the more of one, the more of the other. Thus, when cornering fast with some degree of roll, one leg well compressed and the other leg extended, the regulation toe-in is multiplied. This quirk, added to the low-friction steering pivots, makes all pillar-suspension Lancias super-sensitive to anything not quite right, like out-of-balance wheels and worn steering bushes. The Elastic Steering Arm, splined to the steering box output shaft, is a crude two-piece affair with interposed rubber blocks to catch those shakes and shimmies before they reach the driver's hands. I've had mine welded into one to feel what's going on.

There are a number of Appia features that really date it. The elastic-armed steering box is mounted as near the full frontal accident as can be and easily connected to the driver's chest by a substantial one-piece column.

Ronald Barker
CAR Magazine

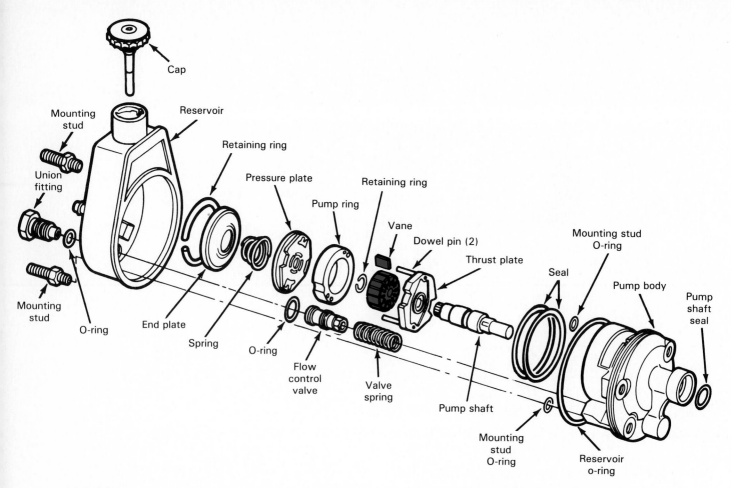

FIGURE 37-17   Exploded view of a vane power steering pump. (American Motors Corporation)

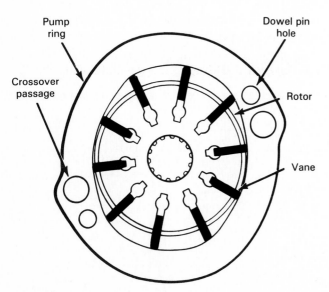

FIGURE 37-18   Power steering pump vane locations. (American Motors Corporation)

Other pumps use slipper vanes, held against the cam by four springs. The roller pump has a rotor with 12 rollers to pump the hydraulic fluid.

STEERING COLUMNS

The **steering column** on today's car is designed to do more than just house the steering shaft. Because it is the closest object to the driver, a number of controls are on it. These include the horn, lights (high and low beams), turn signals, windshield wipers and washers, ignition key, column lock, and a variety of other devices.

Besides its convenience as a location for all of these components, it's also a hazard to the driver in an accident. In a severe collision, the steering column can be pushed back into the driver. Simultaneously, the driver is being forced forward into the steering wheel column. To overcome this hazard, engineers have tried to solve the problem at both ends of the steering column.

At the lower end of the steering column, universal joints (Figure 37-19) allow the lower part of the column to fit around obstacles, and to fold back on itself in a head-on collision. This design feature will help prevent the jamming of the steering column into the driver's chest. To further protect the driver, the steering column has been designed so that it will collapse.

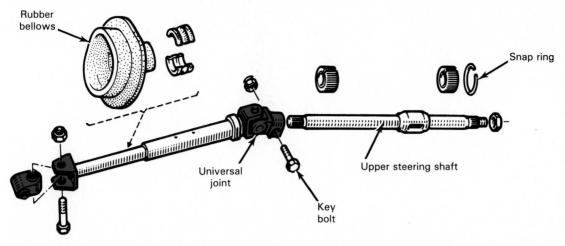

FIGURE 37-19   Steering shaft universal joints. (American Motors Corporation)

Collapsible Steering Columns

There are three common styles of **collapsible steering columns.** Figure 37-20 shows the **tube and ball** column. This type retains a group of steel balls between the inner and outer column. On impact, the inner column is driven forward. This forward movement of the inner column slows down the force of motion and absorbs much of the shock.

The **collapsing mesh** steering column is shown in Figure 37-21. Here, when force is applied to the column, the shock is absorbed by the collapsing of the heavy steel mesh collar surrounding the column.

The third type, the **canister steering column,** works much like the collapsing mesh type. Instead of mesh, this type uses an accordion pleated canister on the steering column. Impact causes the canister to collapse, again protecting the driver from some of the force of the impact.

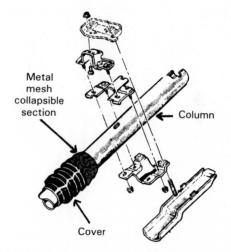

FIGURE 37-21   Collapsing mesh steering column. (Ford Motor Company)

FIGURE 37-20   Tube and ball collapsible steering column. (General Motors Corporation)

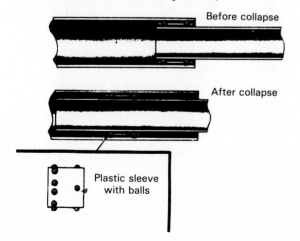

Breakaway Capsule

Another steering column safety device is the **breakaway capsule** shown in Figure 37-22. Although not a

FIGURE 37-22   Breakaway capsules. (General Motors Corporation)

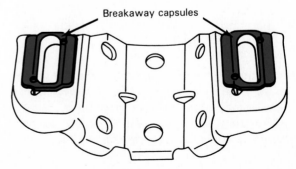

separate collapsing column, it is the breakaway device for the collapsing column. The collapsible steering column is attached to the breakaway capsules in the column mounting bracket. These plastic capsules allow the column to slip forward during impact.

Tilt, Telescope, and Moving Columns

Another feature of many modern steering columns is their ability to adjust to the driver's comfort. As you enter the car, many models allow you to adjust the wheel to whichever angle is the most comfortable for you. This is called a tilting mechanism. If you happen to like the steering wheel close to your body, you can telescope many columns to move 2–3 in. forward or backward.

Likewise, some steering wheels may be pushed aside to allow easier entrance and exit from the car. On these types, you cannot start the car until the wheel has been returned to the driving location and locked in place.

STEERING SERVICE

Power steering pump service is critical. The failure of a pump during cornering or high-speed driving could result in disaster.

Check the fluid level every 6000 mi. Always check it at operating temperatures. Add fluid as needed to bring the level up to the "full" mark on the dipstick.

Be sure to use the correct fluid. Most cars use automatic transmission fluid in the power steering system, but some need special power steering fluid.

Visually inspect the pump belt for wear, cracks, fraying, or weakness. The pump belt should be tight enough to allow only ½-in. deflection. If you can deflect the belt a greater distance, tighten the belt or replace it. Also check the belt; if it is worn or cracked, replace it. If the power accessories are driven by a single, wide belt, check a shop manual for tightening instructions.

Check all connections for hydraulic fluid leaks. While checking for leaks, check the hoses for proper routing and cracks. Hydraulic hoses should be replaced periodically as insurance against rupturing.

WHEEL ALIGNMENT

Proper alignment of both the front and the rear wheels ensures easy steering, long tire life, comfortable ride, and reduced road vibration. To achieve these desirable results, you must make several adjustments. Suspension design determines which adjustments are possible

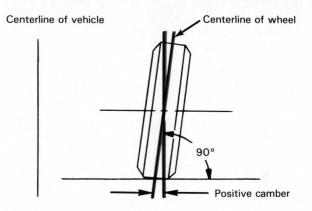

FIGURE 37-23   Camber.

or necessary on each type of front end. Some models may only need one adjustment, while others need several.

Camber

Figure 37-23 demonstrates the condition known as positive **camber**. At the left you can see the vertical centerline of the car. The wheel leans out a few degrees from the vertical centerline of the wheel. If the wheel leans inward from the vertical, it is negative camber.

Positive camber compensates for the weight of the car. When the car begins to move forward, the weight of the vehicle pulls the wheels into a perfect vertical position. If you adjust the alignment with negative camber, the wheel would then be pulled in even more toward the vehicle.

Caster

If you've ever pulled or pushed a shopping cart or a piece of furniture mounted on casters and observed the action of those casters, you have some idea of what **caster** is as it relates to an automotive wheel.

Caster is the tilting of the front steering axis either forward or backward from vertical as viewed from the side of the vehicle (Figure 37-24). When the axis is tilted backward from vertical, caster is said to be positive. Positive caster creates a trailing action on front wheels. When the axis is tilted forward, caster is negative, causing a leading action on front wheels.

Caster and camber are usually adjusted at the same time. The adjusting procedures vary from car to car. Always check a manual for the setting of caster, camber, and toe-in.

Toe-in

Figure 37-25 is an example of **toe-in**. Figure 37-26 shows that you adjust toe-in to point the two front

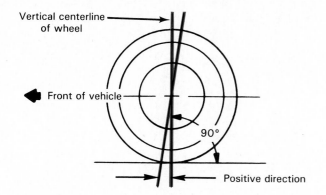

FIGURE 37-24   Positive caster.

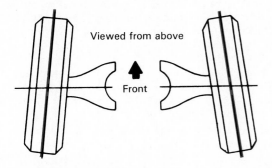

FIGURE 37-25   Toe-in.

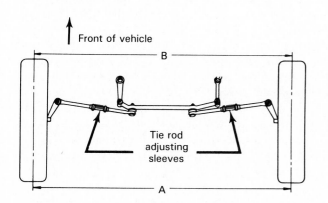

FIGURE 37-26   Adjusting tie rods for toe-in.

wheels inward in a "pigeon toe" configuration. Toe-in helps the car go straight on the road and prevents it from wandering from side to side. It also helps to stabilize steering. Front-wheel-drive cars may call for toe-out specification. Toe-out is the opposite of toe-in.

Steering Axis Inclination

Steering axis inclination is the geometric relationship between the ball joints and the wheel. Notice that the lower ball joint is farther out from the centerline of

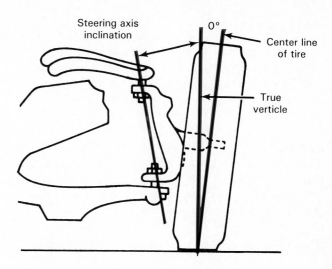

FIGURE 37-27   Steering axis inclination.

the car than the upper ball joint (Figure 37-27). By drawing an imaginary line between the ball joints and measuring the angle this makes with the true vertical centerline of the wheel, you can determine the angle of steering inclination, or, in other words, the angle the ball joints *incline* away from center.

The angle of inclination provides a number of benefits to steering. As usual, and like all the other adjustments, it helps increase tire life. When turning a corner, it increases the rate of recovery. When the car is moving forward, it makes the steering more stable but increases the effort you must put out to move the steering wheel.

Tracking   The greatest effect steering axis inclination has on the car is in **tracking.** Tracking is the tendency a car has to "go where its nose is pointed." This is a result of what happens when the steering knuckle moves.

Because of the angle of inclination, when the steering knuckle turns, it tends to lift the car. The weight of the car then forces the axle (steering knuckle) downward or back into a straight or horizontal angle. This pulls the wheel/tire back into a line with the auto body. The car then continues the same way it was going.

WHEEL ALIGNMENT SERVICE

Tire wear, wander or pull, and hard steering are signs of steering and wheel alignment problems. Before you check for wheel alignment, inspect and correct any brake and front suspension problem and tire inflation and check wheel balance.

Wheel Balance

Both wheels and tires may have heavy and light sections. When the tires are mounted on the wheels, they should be balanced. This is done most accurately by spinning the wheel at high speed (on or off the car) (Figure 37-28). Bubble balancers used to be common, but are not accurate enough for today's wider tires. The balancing machine will indicate where to place the weights and how much weight to use. If excessive weight is needed, the tire should be removed so both tire and wheel can be inspected. Proper wheel balance reduces tire "hop" and vibration.

Prealignment Checks

Before making wheel alignment adjustments, check the following:

1. Wheel bearings must be properly adjusted.
2. Steering linkage and suspension must not have excessive looseness. Check for wear in tie rod ends and ball joints (Figure 37-29).
3. Tires should be approximately equal in tread wear, and runout must not be excessive. Tires and wheels should be in balance and inflated to the manufacturer's specifications.
4. The car must be at curb height with a full fuel tank, no passenger load, the spare tire in place, and no load

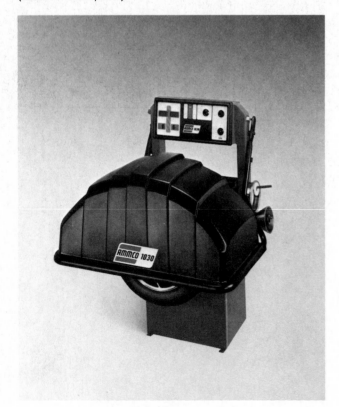

FIGURE 37-28   Electronic wheel balancer.
(Ammco Tools, Inc.)

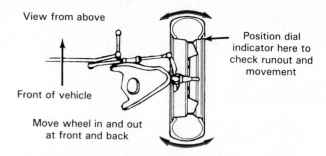

FIGURE 37-29   Checking steering linkage.

in the trunk. If the car is too low or high, wheel alignment measurements will be off.

5. The car must be on level floor and at normal running height. Bounce the front and rear end of the car an equal number of times, always releasing the bumper at the bottom of the down stroke. Allow it to settle to normal running height.
6. If the steering wheel is not centered with the front wheels in the straight-ahead position, correct by shortening one tie rod adjusting sleeve and lengthening the opposite sleeve.
7. Ensure that wheel lug nuts are tightened to the manufacturer's specifications.

Front-Wheel Alignment

Carefully drive the car onto the wheel alignment machine. Remove the hubcaps and set up the machine according to the manufacturer's specifications. Look up the caster, camber, and toe-in requirements for the car. Check these adjustments on the wheel alignment machine. If the caster and camber need to be reset, loosen the retaining nuts, install an adjusting tool, and reset the caster and camber (Figure 37-30). Different makes of cars have different ways of adjusting caster and camber. Refer to a manual for the method of adjustment. Figure 37-31 shows two ways of adjusting caster and camber.

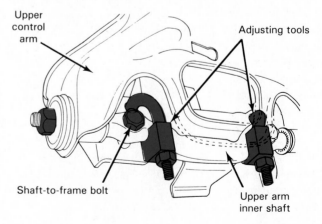

FIGURE 37-30   Resetting caster and camber.
(Ford Motor Company)

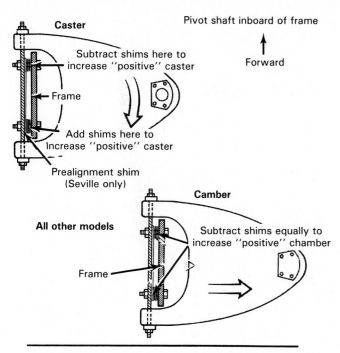

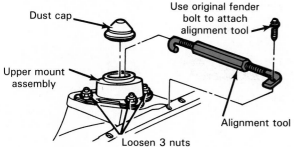

FIGURE 37-31   Caster and camber adjustments. (General Motors Corporation)

Rear-Wheel Alignment

Some cars with independent rear suspension require that you align the rear wheels. Each car manufacturer has a slightly different procedure for aligning the rear

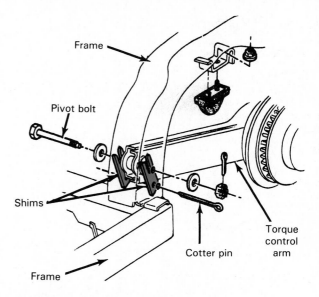

FIGURE 37-32   Rear-wheel alignment. (General Motors Corporation)

wheels. Figure 37-32 shows a Corvette rear-wheel alignment. Before aligning the rear wheels, check the following:

□ The condition of the shock absorbers
□ Tire pressure
□ Tire wear
□ The looseness of the suspension

Follow shop manual instructions to align the rear wheels.

NOTE: When the vehicle is backed onto the alignment machine, toe-in will be read as toe-out, and toe-out will be read as toe-in.

TRADE TERMS

Breakaway Capsule
Camber
Canister Steering Column
Caster
Collapsible Steering Column
Collapsing Mesh
External Power Steering
Idler Arm
Integral Power Steering
Pinion Gear
Pitman Arm

Power Steering
Rack and Pinion
Recirculating Ball
Steering Axis Inclination
Steering Column
Steering Linkage
Tie Rods
Toe-in
Tracking
Tube and Ball
Worm and Nut Steering Gear

REVIEW QUESTIONS

1. Describe a rack and pinion. How is a rack and pinion steering gear mounted?

2. Name the four main parts of a recirculating ball steering gear. Why is it called a recirculating ball steering gear?

3. Describe how a worm and roller steering gear operates?

4. What does an idler arm do? What does a Pitman arm do?

5. What is an integral power steering system?

6. What is a linkage power steering system?

7. Rack and pinion power units can be either integral or linkage powered. True or false? Why?

8. Recirculating ball power units can be either integral or linkage powered. True or false? Why?

9. Name the three types of power steering pumps.

10. How often should you check power steering fluid? Should it be checked hot or cold?

11. What is power steering pump belt deflection?

12. Describe two ways a steering column collapses under impact. Name three types of collapsing steering columns.

13. For driver comfort, steering columns are designed to do three different things. What are they?

14. What four areas of wheel alignment are important to tire wear and steering capabilities?

15. Toe-in produces an angle narrower at the front of the tires than at the rear. True or false?

PART SEVEN

Brakes

Brake Systems

INTRODUCTION

All of us as kids used a variety of vehicles. Bicycles, skateboards, go-carts, motorcycles, and wagons are some of the vehicles we are all familiar with. No matter what vehicle we used, we always needed to slow or stop the vehicle. We needed some form of braking system. These systems varied from well-engineered designs to dragging a foot on the ground.

What all these systems had in common among themselves and with automobile brakes is energy transfer. The braking system stops the car by converting motion (kinetic energy) into heat (heat energy). Dragging a foot against the ground transfers the motion into heat because of friction between the foot and the ground. Some of the heat goes into the ground, some into the air, some into the shoe, and if you leave your foot down long enough, some into you. In a car, the heat is generated by the friction between special braking material and a moving part of the car. Most of the heat passes to the air, and some to the brake and surrounding parts.

OBJECTIVES

When you have completed this chapter, you should be able to

- Name the basic parts of modern braking systems
- Describe the hydraulic function of the brake system
- Tell the difference between disc and drum brakes
- Explain the major differences between the main and parking brake systems
- Explain how brakes transfer energy

end of the line. The other end of the line is one of the four brakes. There, the fluid pushes against another piston, which moves the piston, forcing friction material against the **drum brake** or **disc brake** (Figure 38-1).

HYDRAULIC COMPONENTS

Master Cylinder

At the heart of the system, the master cylinder transfers mechanical energy into hydraulic energy. This transfer has two benefits. First, the fluid quickly and silently transfers brake pedal movement to the brakes themselves. Second, the hydraulic system provides a simple means of multiplying brake energy.

Leverage   Braking energy starts with the force applied by the driver's leg. The mechanical geometry of the brake pedal increases the force. But the big increase happens between the master cylinder and the brakes. The master cylinder piston is usually less than an inch in diameter. It moves about 2 in. The pistons at the brakes are usually $7/8$–$1\frac{1}{8}$ in. in diameter and move less than $1/8$ in. The difference in area and travel acts as a hydraulic lever, increasing braking force. For more information on hydraulic leverage, see Chapter 39.

System Operation

The **brake pedal** is the first part of the system. Connected to the pedal is a rod. The other end of the rod passes into the **power booster** or the **master cylinder.** When you depress the pedal, the rod moves farther into the master cylinder.

Inside the master cylinder the rod moves a piston. The piston slides forward, pushing brake fluid ahead of it. Because liquid cannot be compressed, as soon as you apply pressure to one end of the column of brake fluid, that same pressure is exerted at the other

FIGURE 38-1   Hydraulic brake operation. (Ford Motor Company)

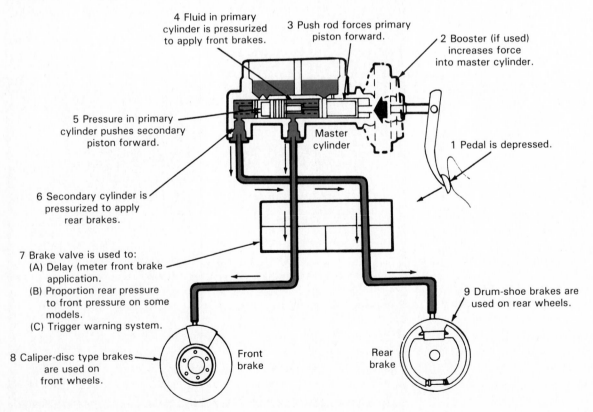

4 Fluid in primary cylinder is pressurized to apply front brakes.

3 Push rod forces primary piston forward.

2 Booster (if used) increases force into master cylinder.

5 Pressure in primary cylinder pushes secondary piston forward.

Master cylinder

1 Pedal is depressed.

6 Secondary cylinder is pressurized to apply rear brakes.

7 Brake valve is used to:
(A) Delay (meter front brake application.
(B) Proportion rear pressure to front pressure on some models.
(C) Trigger warning system.

8 Caliper-disc type brakes are used on front wheels.

Front brake

Rear brake

9 Drum-shoe brakes are used on rear wheels.

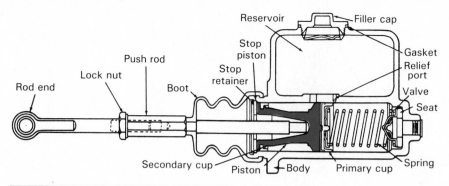

FIGURE 38-2 Single-piston master cylinder. (Chrysler Corporation)

The increase in energy is easily seen in the action of an automobile jack. When you operate the handle up and down, the little work you do is increased 10-fold, lifting an entire car.

Design All master cylinders have a body, either cast iron or aluminum. The piston, usually aluminum, slides inside the body, in the master cylinder bore. The body is drilled and tapped so the **brake lines** can be attached. Extra brake fluid is needed at the master cylinder to compensate for fluid displaced during operation and increased volume due to brake friction material wear. This extra fluid is stored in the master cylinder reservoir. The reservoir is typically mounted right on top of the master cylinder, although it is sometimes mounted well above the master cylinder and connected with a hose.

Single Piston **Single-piston** master cylinders were the norm until 1966 (Figure 38-2). These units use one piston to operate all four brakes. If any part of a single-piston hydraulic braking system fails, the entire system fails.

Dual Piston In 1967 all autos sold in the United States were required to have **dual-piston** master cylinders. One piston operates the front brakes and the other piston the rear brakes (Figure 38-3). Some systems operate three brakes off each piston, duplicating pressure at the front brakes.

Power Boosters

Power boosters increase hydraulic pressure. The booster fits between the brake pedal and master cylinder. It increases, or boosts, the pressure applied on the master cylinder pistons.

Single Diaphragm The common single-diaphragm booster works by atmospheric pressure (Figure 38-4). Vacuum from the intake manifold creates a vacuum on one side of a diaphragm. Atmospheric pressure fills the chamber on the other side, causing a rod to move forward, actuating the master cylinder, and giving more power to the master cylinder than you can produce with your foot alone.

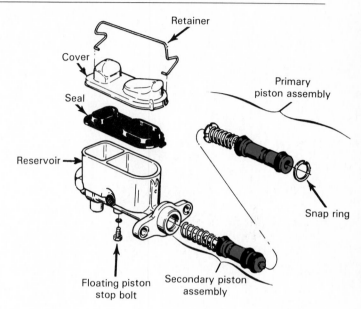

FIGURE 38-3 Dual-piston master cylinder. (Ford Motor Company)

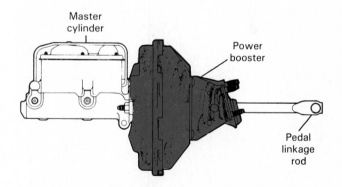

FIGURE 38-4 Single-diaphragm power booster and master cylinder. (American Motors Corporation)

Dual Diaphragm The **dual-diaphragm power booster** (Figure 38-5) is simply an extension of the single-diaphragm booster. The second diaphragm increases the booster's effectiveness and reliability. Dual diaphragm boosters are also called tandem boosters.

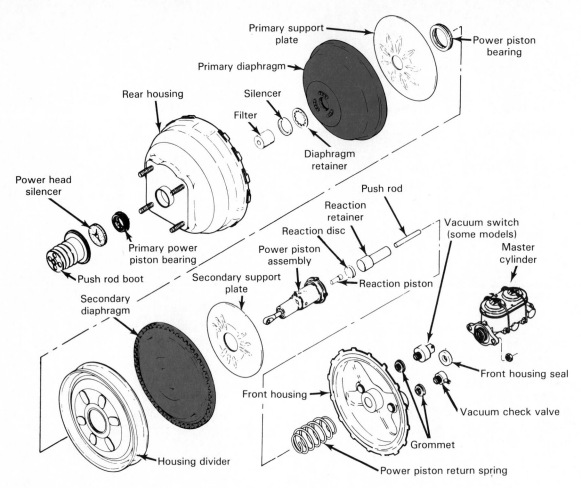

FIGURE 38-5   Dual-diaphragm power booster. (General Motors Corporation)

Hydraulic   **Hydraulic boosters** are completely different from vacuum boosters (Figures 38-6). They take hydraulic pressure from the power steering pump or an electric pump and apply it to the master cylinder (Figure 38-7). Through this hydraulic boost, twice as much pressure can be applied than to a vacuum-assisted booster. Advantages of hydraulic boosters are

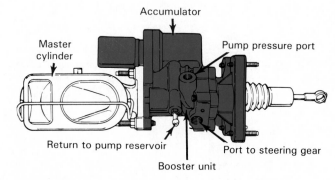

FIGURE 38-7   Hydro-Boost power brake unit. (General Motors Corporation)

twofold: They supply large amounts of assist and the ability to work on engines with little or no vacuum. Diesels on heavy trucks, for example, have no vacuum and must use hydraulic boosters or air brakes.

Fluid and Lines

After the master cylinder has been actuated and the power booster has begun its assist, **hydraulic brake**

FIGURE 38-6   Hydraulic booster fluid circuits. (General Motors Corporation)

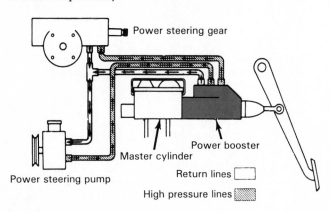

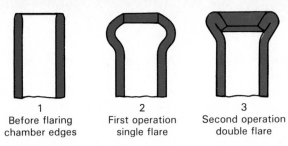

1
Before flaring
chamber edges

2
First operation
single flare

3
Second operation
double flare

FIGURE 38-8   Double-flare steel brake line. (Ford Motor
Company)

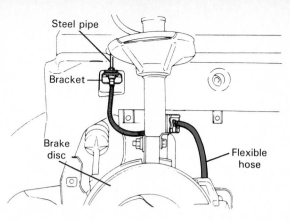

FIGURE 38-9   Flexible brake line. (Mazda North
America, Inc.)

fluid is pushed through the *brake lines* toward the
brakes. *Hydraulic brake fluid is a very special compound and
must never be replaced with anything but other hydraulic brake
fluid.* Anything but DOT (U.S. Department of Transportation) approved hydraulic brake fluid will ruin the
rubber fittings and seals associated with the brake system. It can also be affected by the high temperatures
developed by braking actions. The lines which carry
the brake fluid are special, too.

These lines are made of steel. All steel brake lines
must have a double flare at the ends (Figure 38-8).
Copper or aluminum lines do not have the burst
strength to withstand the high pressures associated
with brake systems.

To allow for movement of the suspension, short
portions of the brake lines are flexible (Figure 38-9).
These portions are made of neoprene, reinforced with
webbing. When they need replacing, ready-made re-
placements are available.

Brake Values

Metering   The **metering valve** is tied into the brake
lines leading to the front brakes. If the front brakes
come on before the rear brakes, directional control becomes difficult. In an emergency, the car could spin.
The metering valve assures you the front brakes will
come on just *after* the rear brakes.

Proportioning   The **proportioning valve** reduces
maximum pressure to the rear brakes during hard braking. When you must make a panic stop, the nose of
the car dips and the rear end comes up. Because more
weight is transferred to the front of the car, the rear
wheels are more likely to *lock-up*. The proportioning
valve, by reducing fluid pressure to the rear brakes,
prevents this type of lockup. When both the metering
and proportioning valves are joined together, the result
is a *combination valve* (Figure 38-10).

Combination   The combination valve not only does
both of these jobs but also has a **brake-warning-light
switch.** This device actuates a red light on the instrument panel to let you know that one or the other of

FIGURE 38-10   Combination metering, proportioning, and brake-warning-light valve.

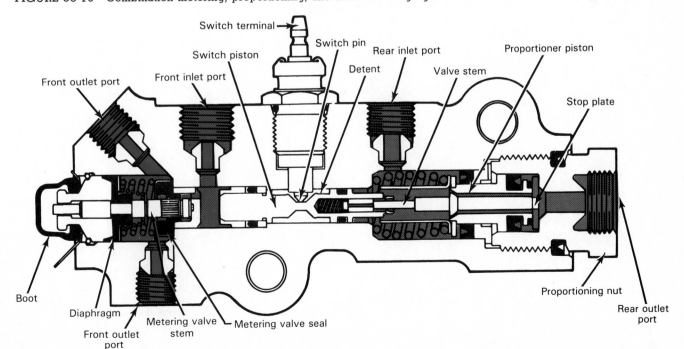

the brake systems has failed. This way, you will not continue to drive with only the front or rear system operating.

BRAKE UNITS

At all four wheels are brake units which stop the car by changing motion into heat. For many years *drum brakes* were used exclusively. They have been almost totally replaced at the front wheels of new cars by *disc brakes*. Drum brakes are still used at the rear wheels of most cars.

Drum Brakes

Brake Shoes **Backing plates** are bolted to the *rear axle housing* or spindle. Attached to the backing plates so they move freely are two **brake shoes.** The shoes are made of a steel frame with a *composition lining riveted* or *bonded* to them (Figure 38-11). This composition material used to be primarily *asbestos*. However, due to the danger of asbestos fibers, most pads are now made of friction material without much asbestos. This friction material prevents the linings from catching on fire due to the tremendous heat generated during braking. Other lining materials are bonded *resin* and *fillers*.

Such asbestos/resin linings are called organic linings. Some heavy-duty linings have powdered iron in them. They are called *metallic* linings. Some linings use a combination of organic and metallic linings. Whenever you work on brakes or with *brake dust*, be very careful. Do not blow dust with compressed air. Wash your hands immediately after contacting brake dust. Do not breathe or ingest brake dust, or you run a high risk of getting cancer.

Wheel Cylinders Rigidly fixed to the backing plate between the brake shoes is the **wheel cylinder** (Figure 38-12). The wheel cylinder resembles a small master cylinder, except it works in reverse and has no reservoir. In the wheel cylinder, hydraulic pressure is converted to mechanical force. There are two pistons which can move freely inside the cylinder bore. Pressure on the fluid at the master cylinder forces the wheel cylinder pistons outward. The pistons are connected to the brake shoes and push them outward as well.

Adjusters At the bottom of the backing plate, the shoes are attached to the **star adjuster** (Figure 38-13). This star adjuster serves as a pivot point and a means of adjusting the brakes to compensate for *lining wear*.

Drums Covering the entire brake—shoes, wheel cylinder, star adjuster, and backing plate—is the *brake drum*. The drum is attached to a suspension hub or

FIGURE 38-11 Brake shoes and drum. (Mazda North America, Inc.)

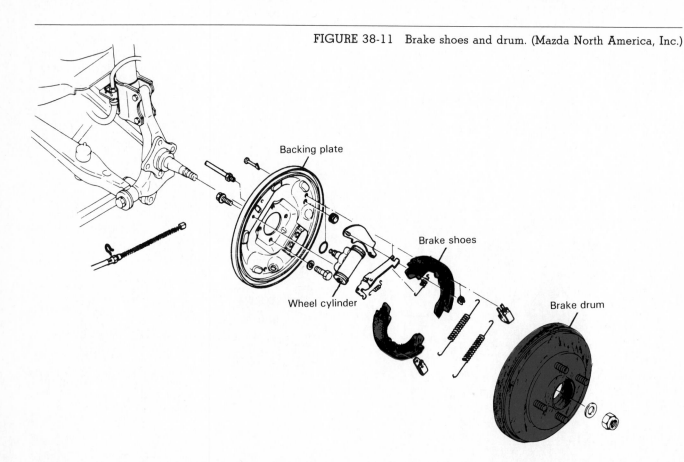

Backing plate

Brake shoes

Wheel cylinder

Brake drum

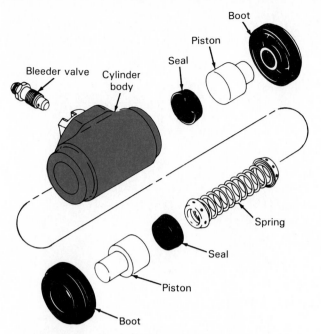

FIGURE 38-12 Wheel cylinder. (Oldsmobile Motor Division, GMC)

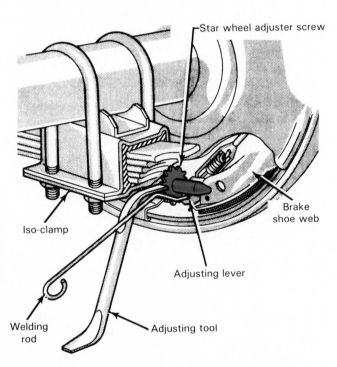

FIGURE 38-13 Star wheel adjuster. (Chrysler Corporation)

axle, so it rotates with the wheel. When the wheel cylinder pistons press the brake shoes outward, they come into contact with the rotating drum. The friction between the lining and drum causes the car to stop.

Springs mounted between the shoes retract the shoes when braking pressure is released.

Because the drum brake is enclosed by the drum and backing plate, cooling is difficult. Heat must pass into the drum and backing plate before it can dissipate into the atmosphere. Many drums are finned to improve this heat transfer.

Disc Brakes

Cooling and light weight are the disc brake's advantages, because there are fewer parts and they sit directly in the air (Figure 38-14).

Parts   Attached to the wheel hub is the *disc*, sometimes called the **rotor** (Figure 38-15). Suspended over the rotor is the *caliper*. Pistons inside the caliper face

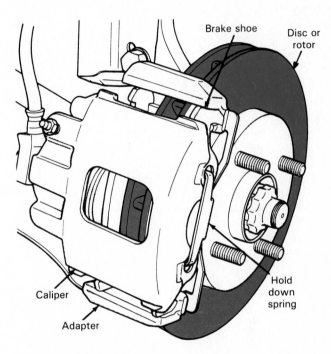

FIGURE 38-14 Disc brake system. (Chrysler Corporation)

FIGURE 38-15 Disc brake rotor. (American Motors Corporation)

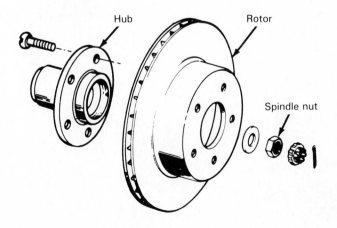

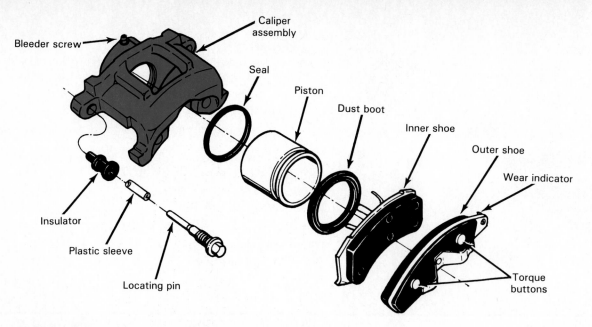

Caliper assembly

Bleeder screw

Seal

Piston

Dust boot

Inner shoe

Outer shoe

Wear indicator

Insulator

Plastic sleeve

Locating pin

Torque buttons

FIGURE 38-16 Single-piston caliper assembly. (Ford Motor Company)

each side of the disc. Between the disc and pistons is the frictional material. Composed of basically the same material as drum brake linings, the material is formed into flat *pads* (Figure 38-16).

Operation Pressure from the master cylinder forces the pads against the disc. Think of squeezing a plate with a C clamp, and you'll understand how a disc brake works. A 10-speed bicycle brake is another example of a disc brake.

Some calipers have only one piston (Figure 38-16). With these, the piston pushes the inside pad against the disc and the travel of the caliper forces the outside pad against the disc at the same time. This is done with a caliper which slides on pins. Other calipers use pistons on both sides of the disc (Figure 38-17).

FIGURE 38-17 Four-piston caliper assembly. (Chevrolet Motor Division, GMC)

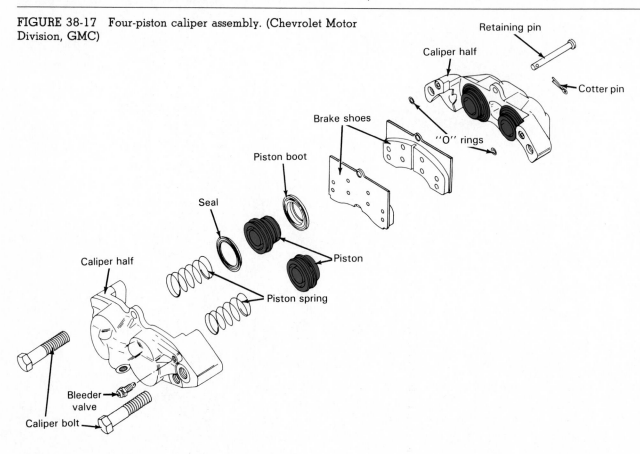

Retaining pin

Caliper half

Cotter pin

Brake shoes

"O" rings

Piston boot

Seal

Piston

Caliper half

Piston spring

Bleeder valve

Caliper bolt

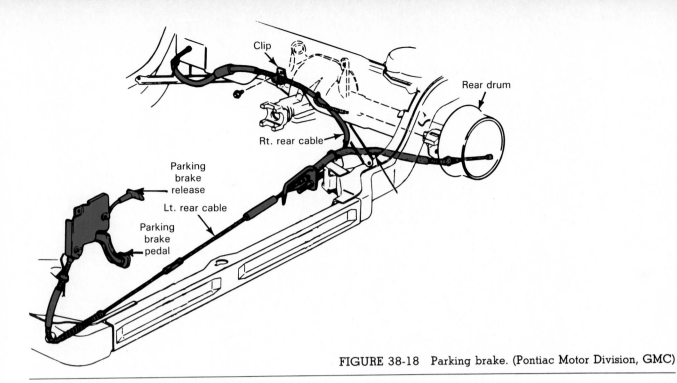

Clip

Rear drum

Rt. rear cable

Parking brake release

Lt. rear cable

Parking brake pedal

FIGURE 38-18   Parking brake. (Pontiac Motor Division, GMC)

When hydraulic pressure is released, the pads and pistons retract slightly as the piston's rubber seal returns to its static shape. Because the pistons and pads don't have far to travel, disc brakes actuate faster than drum brakes where the linings have to travel farther, which is another reason for having a metering valve in a front-disc, rear-drum system.

Parking Brake

There are two types of **parking brake** systems. One operates on drum brakes, and one operates on disc brakes. Both are mechanically applied, bypassing the hydraulic system.

Drum   To mechanically activate drum brakes, a cable extends from the *hand brake lever*, or from the foot lever, to the rear brake (Figure 38-18). The *cable housing* is attached to the backing plate (Figure 38-19), while the cable itself passes through the backing plate and attaches to the parking lever. When you actuate the parking brake, the cable draws the brake shoe into contact with the brake drum, effectively holding it in place. This type of parking brake can also stop the

FIGURE 38-19   Parking brake cable and lever. (Mazda North America, Inc.)

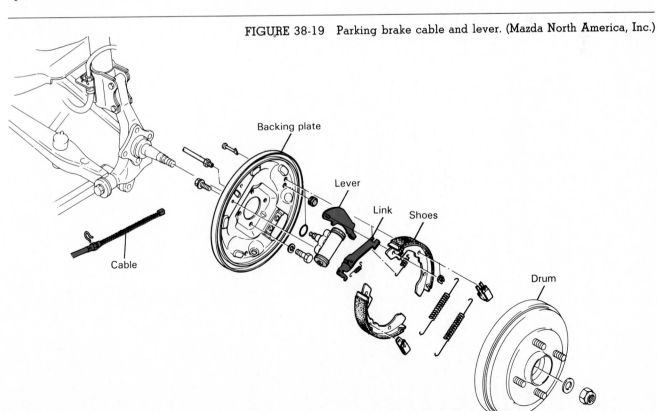

Backing plate

Lever

Link

Shoes

Cable

Drum

BRAKING BY TREE TRUNK

The story of motor car brakes has ironical elements. In the 1930s some manufacturers were still building cars without front wheel brakes. The relative slowness of designers to provide an efficient braking system is even more disconcerting since from the first decade of the century, motor cars were capable of such speeds that instant breaking was essential.

The casual attitude toward braking in the early days is illustrated by the first car crossing of the St. Gotthard Pass, by the French engineer Arrou in a 3½-hp De Dion-Bouton in 1901. The account of the trip records that "the leather-lined brakes were burned out after only a few minutes of the descent" and that, having reduced speed to almost zero to avoid going over the mountain side at every bend, it was necessary "to fasten a tree trunk to the car with a steel cable, which was then dragged behind."

Marco Matteucci
History of the Motor Car
Octopus Books Limited

---

car when moving, although it takes longer than with all four brakes working.

Disc Cars with four-wheel disc brakes often have separate, miniature drum parking brakes. These special drum brakes fit inside the rear disc brake hubs. This system is popular because disc brakes make fairly poor parking brakes, while drum brakes work quite well. The difference is that drum brakes are *self-applying*. This is called *self-energizing*. When the linings touch the rotating drum, they are free to pivot into full contact with it. This forces the lining tighter against the drum, increasing braking once it has begun. Therefore, any forward motion of the car tends to increase the holding power of the drum parking brake. Disc brakes, on the other hand, push against the disc only as hard as the master cylinder forces them.

Many cars with disc brakes use a clamp-type parking brake (Figure 38-20). A normal parking brake cable runs to the brake caliper. The caliper has a piston like other disc brakes, but a screw and lever assembly is also mounted in the caliper. When the parking brake is applied, the cable pulls on the lever, which turns the screw. Depending on the design, either the screw, a cam, or small ball bearings physically force the piston and pad against the disc. This type of system can be used on either the front or rear brakes.

Antiskid Braking

Maximum braking happens right before each tire *locks* (stops turning) and starts to slide. It is very difficult to manually maintain such fine control over braking,

---

FIGURE 38-20   Rear clamp-type parking brake. (Ford Motor Company)

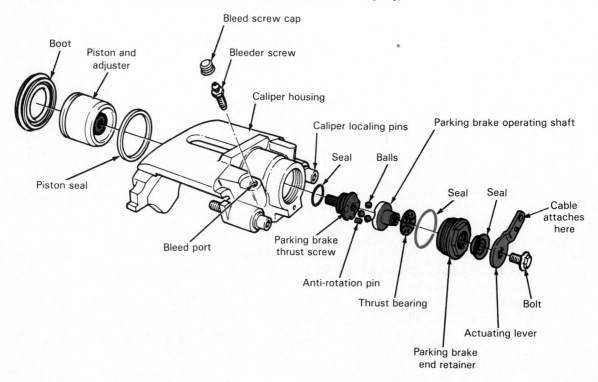

especially when the four tires have a different amount of traction. Traction varies due to sand, snow, ice, bumps, vehicle loading, and weight transfer. Special antiskid braking systems can sense wheel lockup and modulate braking at that wheel many times per second. Such systems use electronics to sense wheel rotation versus the car's speed. A computer then tells a hydraulic modulator to release or restore brake line pressure as needed. High costs restrict antiskid braking systems to being an option on expensive models.

BRAKE SERVICE

System Contaminants

Air and water are common brake fluid contaminants. Air gets in through leaks or when the master cylinder fluid reservoir runs dry. Water forms inside the brake hydraulic system by condensation. Water can also get in the master cylinder reservoir during damp weather because mineral-based brake fluid is **hygroscopic;** that is, it attracts water.

These contaminants pose serious dangers to the brake system. Because air can be compressed, the brake pedal will feel spongy, and braking efficiency will be drastically reduced when air is present. Water boils at normal brake operating temperatures, causing air to form. Water also corrodes brake parts, leading to fluid leaks, lowered braking efficiency, and possible air and water ingestion.

Bleeding

Contaminated brake fluid is removed by flushing. Flushing is simply forcing out all the old fluid while adding new. Any contaminants will be removed with the old fluid. Air is removed from the system by **brake bleeding.**

Pedal Bleeding forces out air bubbles but not necessarily all the brake fluid. There are two ways of bleeding, *pedal* and *pressure*. **Pedal bleeding** begins by topping off the master cylinder reservoir with fresh fluid. Never reuse brake fluid. Do not spill brake fluid, or you'll ruin the paint where the fluid drops. Select the brake farthest from the master cylinder, usually the right rear. Put a box or tubing wrench on the **bleeder** screw or **valve** (Figure 38-21). Now attach a hose to the bleed valve and let the other end hang in a clean jar (Figure 38-22). Fill the jar with fresh brake fluid so the bottom of the hose is submerged. Open the bleed valve and have a helper depress the brake pedal.

Brake fluid will flow into the jar. When clean, air-free fluid flows from the hose, have your helper stop pumping while the pedal is completely depressed. Close the bleeder, remove the hose, and release the

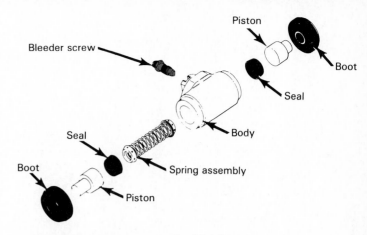

FIGURE 38-21 Wheel cylinder bleeder screw.

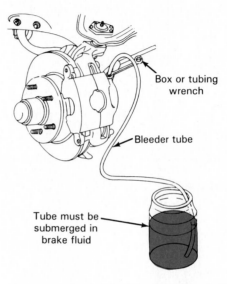

FIGURE 38-22 Bleeding brake fluid. (Buick Motor Division, GMC)

brake pedal. Go to the next closest brake. The usual bleeding order is RR, LR, RF, LF. This order may vary, however. Check a shop manual for specific instructions.

The master cylinder reservoir fluid level must be monitored during bleeding. Otherwise the reservoir will run dry. Air will then be sucked into the system, and you'll have to rebleed.

Master Cylinder The only time it's necessary to bleed a master cylinder is after rebuilding it. Bleeding is done before installing the master cylinder in the chassis. Attach two bleeding tubes from the outlets to the master cylinder reservoir. The tube ends must be submerged in the reservoir. Now push the piston back and forth with a wooden dowel rod until there are no bubbles from the piston action in the master cylinder reservoir (Figure 38-23).

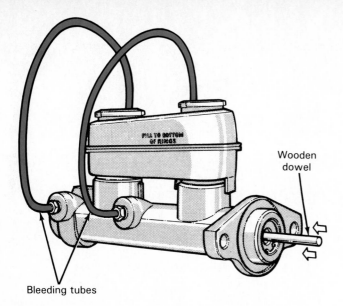

Bleeding tubes

FIGURE 38-23 Bleeding master cylinder. (Chrysler Corporation)

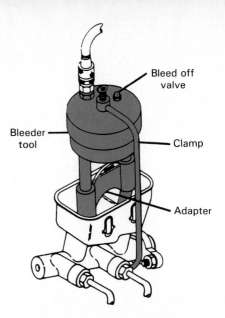

Bleed off valve

Bleeder tool

Clamp

Adapter

FIGURE 38-24 Pressure bleeding assembly. (General Motors Corporation)

Pressure A **pressure bleeding machine** has an airtight connector attaching a hose to the master cylinder (Figure 38-24). By pressurizing the tank to about 35 psi, fluid passes from the tank to the master cylinder. Opening all four bleeding screws (with hoses and con-

tainers attached) bleeds all brakes at one time. This is fast, but the machine is quite expensive. Not every shop will have one. Also, any metering valves must be open. A special tool holds the valve open during the bleeding process.

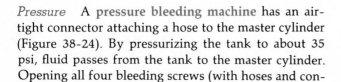

TRADE TERMS

Backing Plates
Bleeder Valve
Brake Bleeding
Brake Lines
Brake Pedal
Brake Shoes
Brake-warning-light Switch
Disc Brake
Drum Brake
Dual-diaphragm Power Booster
Dual-piston
Hydraulic Boosters
Hydraulic Brake Fluid

Hygroscopic
Master Cylinder
Metering Valve
Parking Brake
Pedal Bleeding
Power Booster
Pressure Bleeding Machine
Proportioning Valve
Rotor
Single-piston
Star Adjuster
Wheel Cylinder

REVIEW QUESTIONS

1. Explain the difference between a single- and dual- piston master cylinder.
2. Why are power brake boosters used?
3. What are the two types of power brake boosters?
4. Brake lines are generally made of copper. True or false? Why?
5. Explain why only DOT-certified brake fluid is used in hydraulic brake systems. What can it be replaced with? Why?

6. Explain the differences between the metering valve and the proportioning valve.
7. Describe the action of the wheel cylinder. What is its counterpart in a disc brake?
8. What are the two types of emergency brakes used in the modern automobile? How do each of them work?

Master Cylinders and Power Boosters

INTRODUCTION

This chapter on master cylinders and power boosters introduces you to a new concept and to several functions of that concept. The new concept is the science of hydraulics. This science details the many ideas, functions, and rules of the way liquids behave under pressure, flowing, and at rest.

You'll use these rules to understand how a master cylinder works, how it is assisted by a booster, and how these units are serviced.

BRAKING SYSTEMS

Mechanical Brakes

In the early years of the automobile, even the finest cars were equipped with mechanical brakes.

To actuate a mechanical brake (Figure 39-1), the driver pushed on a pedal which worked as a lever and fulcrum. This energy was transferred by a long rod or cable (Figure 39-2) to the brake pad which was pulled or pushed into the drum. This action slowed and finally stopped the rotation of the wheels.

OBJECTIVES

When you have completed this chapter, you should be able to

■ Explain Pascal's law as it applies to hydraulic systems
■ Describe the working principles of a master cylinder
■ Explain the difference between a single-piston and dual-piston master cylinder
■ Describe a power booster system
■ Describe the different types of power booster systems
■ Describe the disassembly and service of a master cylinder and power booster

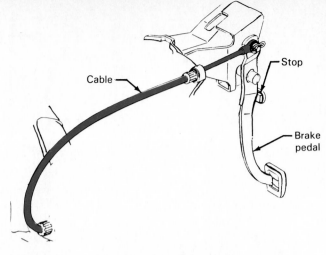

Cable — ·

Stop

Brake pedal

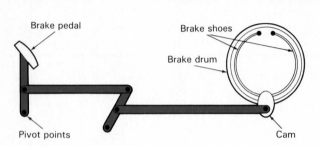

Brake pedal

Brake shoes

Brake drum

Pivot points

Cam

FIGURE 39-1 Mechanical rod brakes.

As cars became heavier and faster, engineers realized they needed a better way to stop their cars. The knowledge of hydraulics had been around for several hundred years and was soon put to work to assist drivers in stopping their cars.

Hydraulics

Before the modern **hydraulic** braking system can be understood, some hydraulic theory must be learned. Hydraulic theory was explained in detail in Chapter 33. To summarize,

Pascal's Law Pascal's law states, "Pressure bearing on a confined liquid is transmitted without a loss of pressure." This statement has a couple of interesting ideas hidden in it. First, it means that pressure is equal in all areas of a container holding pressurized liquid. Second, pressure can be sent from one area to another.

Pressure Transmission Because liquids under pressure transmit pressure without loss, the pressure will be the same everywhere in the container (Figure 39-3). A force is introduced at the main chamber, causing a certain amount of pressure to form. Note how the pressure is the same everywhere in the container. If the force is decreased anywhere, the pressure will drop equally throughout the container.

Pressure Leverage Hydraulic pressure can be used to increase force. The idea is the same as torque multiplication. Remember how torque can be increased be-

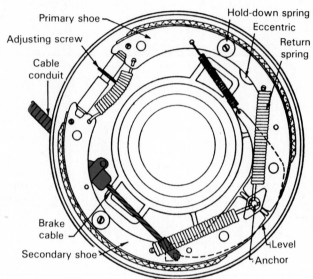

Primary shoe

Hold-down spring
Eccentric

Adjusting screw

Return spring

Cable conduit

Brake cable

Secondary shoe

Level

Anchor

FIGURE 39-2 Mechanical cable brakes.

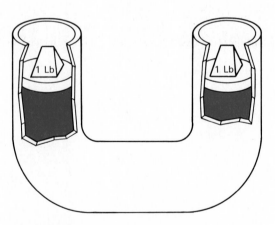

1 Lb

1 Lb

FIGURE 39-3 Equal pressure through a hydraulic system.

tween gears at the expense of speed? The gear with the increased torque turns more slowly in proportion to the gear ratio.

Pressure can be increased in the same way. Figure 39-3 shows a hydraulic system with two **pistons**—a

1 square in. and a 10 square in. piston. Let's say 5 lb of force is exerted on the 1-in. piston. This 5-lb force is now pushing everywhere in the system, including the bottom of the 10 square in. piston. Because 5 lb are pushing against each square inch of the larger piston, there is a total of 50 lb pushing against it.

A practical application of this principle is the garage hoist which can lift a 5000-lb car with 50 psi of compressed air.

Motion transfer If pressure leverage is comparable to torque multiplication, then motion transfer is like speed reduction.

Let's start with two cylinders of equal size. It's obvious that moving piston A will result in piston B moving the same amount. But if the pistons are unequal in size, as in Figure 39-4, piston travel is not equal. In our last example, we saw how the 1 square in. piston used hydraulic leverage to put 50 lb of pressure against the 10 square in. piston. If the 5 lb moved the 1 square in. piston 1 in., the larger piston would only move one tenth as far, because of the larger volume under the 10 square in. piston.

BRAKE SYSTEM HYDRAULICS

All hydraulic systems use the principles just outlined. The modern hydraulic brake system (Figure 39-5) uses

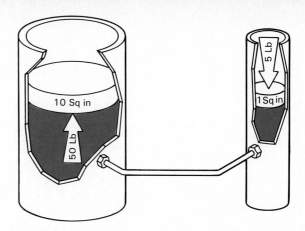

FIGURE 39-4 Using cylinder sizes to multiply pressure.

them to provide a smooth-operating, somewhat self-compensating brake system.

Force is placed on the system by the driver's foot. This moves a piston in the master cylinder, pressurizing the system. This pressure forces the wheel cylinder pistons outward, which operates a mechanical system. The mechanical system provides the friction to stop the car.

Master Cylinder

A standard **master cylinder** (Figure 39-6) can be broken down into three major parts: reservoir, body, and piston.

FIGURE 39-5 Simplified brake system. (American Motors Corporation)

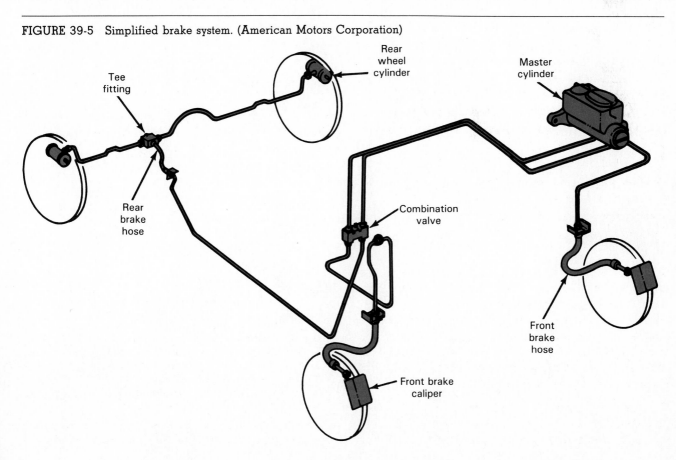

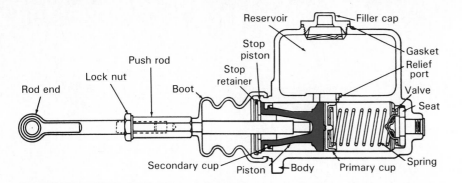

FIGURE 39-6 Master cylinder. (Ford Motor Company)

Reservoir The reservoir holds a reserve of **brake fluid.** This reserve is ready to fill the system as fluid is lost. Under ideal conditions, no fluid is lost. But leaky seals and evaporation can lead to permanent fluid loss. Also, as the friction pads or shoes in the brake system wear, the pistons in the calipers and wheel cylinders move outward. This increases the hydraulic system's capacity. Fluid from the reservoir fills this increased volume.

The reservoir can be made of cast iron, aluminum, or plastic. Plastic is popular because it is lightweight, cheap, and easily formed and doesn't rust or corrode.

Fluid is added to the brake system through a vented cap on top of the reservoir. A vent is necessary to compensate for expansion as the brake fluid heats and cools. Rubber gaskets keep dirt and moisture out of the fluid.

The reservoir can be mounted directly on the master cylinder, or it can be mounted remotely. Remote mountings are used when the master cylinder is not easily accessible. The reservoir is always mounted higher than the master cylinder to form a gravity feed.

Construction Typically the master cylinder is mounted on the firewall (Figure 39-7) with an integral reservoir. The master cylinder body is a solid aluminum or cast iron block with several drilled passages. The main passage is the **cylinder bore.** The piston travels in the bore, pressurizing the fluid. Passages lead from the bore to the brake lines. On some master cylinders, the bore is lined with a stainless steel sleeve for corrosion protection.

Corrosion control is important. If the bore corrodes, the resulting pitting will let fluid pass by the seals. This gives reduced braking ability.

Master cylinder pistons are typically made of aluminum. They have a recess at one end that accepts the rod from the brake pedal. The other end is fitted with a groove for a rubber seal. The seal has a lip that brushes against the cylinder bore. Fluid pressure forces the lip tightly against the bore, making an effective seal.

The piston is retained by a snap ring at the open end of the bore. This open end is covered by a rubber boot to seal out dirt and moisture.

Check Valve

Master cylinders used with drum brakes use a residual **check valve** (Figure 39-8). The valve holds approxi-

FIGURE 39-7 Master cylinder mounting. (Ford Motor Company)

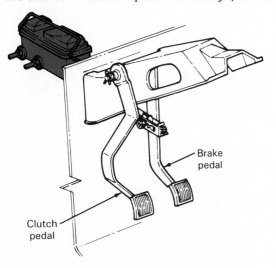

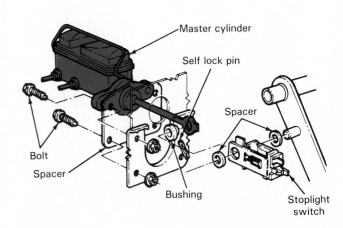

DUAL BRAKING SYSTEMS

A series of tests in New York in 1902 showed that from the braking point of view the car was considerably safer than the carriage. The car could stop in a quarter of the distance required by a carriage with four horses.

Of course, this would now be considered far from a safe braking distance.

In the following years, partly because of the legal requirements operated in some countries, there was general adoption of a dual braking system, one acting on the rear wheels and the other on the transmission.

The first of these continued for some time to depend on external shoes lined with leather or camel skin, but this system was soon replaced by internal shoes and drums. The transmission brake acted on the differential when transmission was by chain or on the transmission shaft itself when these were introduced.

Although the general introduction of four-wheel brakes was slow, the first studies came quite soon. Early experiments took place between 1905 and 1910.

Isotta Fraschini introduced four-wheel brakes in 1909, and they were fitted as standard to most of the Italian company's products by 1914. The credit for a successful system controlled by one action is due to the manager of Argyll, Henry Perrott. In 1913 his brakes were first fitted to racing cars. Slowly, during the 1920s, they were adopted by more and more companies and extended to production cars. Hydraulic actuation gradually came into general use, though the first users met difficulty in guaranteeing their reliable and safe functioning, because of the danger of fracture of the often exposed pipes or because the liquids then used corroded the seals or froze at low temperatures.

Marco Matteucci
History of the Motor Car
Octopus Books Limited

---

mately 10 psi in the brake system while the master cylinder is at rest. This pressure keeps the seals, both in the master and wheel cylinders, pressed against their bores. Thus a tighter seal is formed, keeping air, dirt, and moisture out of the system.

Disc brake systems do not use a residual check valve because the pressure would cause dragging brakes. Dragging brakes are not a problem with drum brakes because 10 psi is not enough to overcome the shoe return springs.

Brake Fluid

Before explaining master cylinder operation, you should understand the fluid used in the master cylinder.

Brake fluid is a nonpetroleum liquid largely unaffected by high or low temperatures. Brake fluid was designed to have a very high boiling point and to work in temperatures well below freezing. It is harmless to the many rubber seals in a brake system, unlike many other common automotive fluids. Never use motor oil, ATF, or hydraulic jack oil in a brake system as these fluids will harm the rubber parts. Also, never use a petroleum-based solvent to clean brake system parts. Use only denatured alcohol because it does not harm rubber parts.

Types of fluid   Commonly used brake fluids are *mineral* based. Other **mineral-based fluids** are turpentine and paint thinner. Like these other mineral-based fluids, brake fluid will damage paint and will absorb water readily. To combat these tendencies, **synthetic**

FIGURE 39-8   Master cylinder and residual check valve in released position. (Buick Motor Division, GMC)

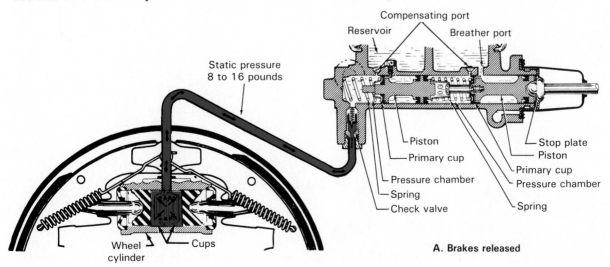

A. Brakes released

brake fluid has been developed using silicone. Silicone brake fluid does not attract moisture, will not damage paint, and has a high boiling point. It is expensive and has been found to break down under extreme heat. Switching synthetic fluid normally requires the flushing of all mineral-based fluid. This can be very difficult.

MASTER CYLINDER OPERATION

In this section, master cylinder operation will be explained from the at-rest, applied, and released positions.

At Rest

Refer back to figure 39-8 which shows the master cylinder and drum brake in the at-rest or *released* position. Note the position of the residual check valve at the master cylinder's outlet and the positions of the compensating and breather ports. Although the drawing shows two compensation ports, for now ignore the port closest to the check valve. Its function will be detailed later.

In the at-rest position, fluid fills both sides of the piston. Fluid enters one side through the compensating port and the other side through the breather port.

Applied Position

When the brake pedal is depressed, the pedal linkage forces the piston to travel down the bore (Figure 39-9). Right away the piston seal passes the compensating port. This seals all fluid in front of the piston. The

only place it can go is through the check valve and toward the brakes.

The back of the piston is kept filled through the breather port. This stops any suction from forming.

The fluid trapped in front of the piston raises the pressure so the check valve will open. Fluid passes through the check valve and goes toward the brakes. Pressure will remain constant in the system as long as the brake pedal is held steady. If the pedal is pushed farther, the pressure will increase, forcing the shoes more tightly against the drums.

Released Position

Releasing brake pedal pressure removes the pressure on the master cylinder piston. A spring in the brake pedal linkage returns the pedal to its at-rest position, ensuring that no pressure remains on the master cylinder piston.

At the brakes, the shoe return springs provide pressure on the wheel cylinders to return to their at-rest positions. But the main return force in the brake system is the great hydraulic pressure trying to escape.

This pressure forces the master cylinder piston back in its bore. As the piston is pushed back, the lips of the seal fold forward, letting fluid fill in front of the piston (Figure 39-10). A series of bleeder holes in the piston ensures that fluid can pass to the back and to the front of the piston. This keeps suction from starting, which would pull air into the master cylinder.

Once the seal passes the compensating port, the remaining hydraulic pressure forces any excess fluid into the reservoir (Figure 39-11). Hydraulic pressure drops rapidly until the shoe return springs cause a greater pressure against the wheel cylinder pistons. This closes the check valve, sealing in approximately 10 psi in the system.

FIGURE 39-9   Master cylinder and residual check valve in applied position. (Buick Motor Division, GMC)

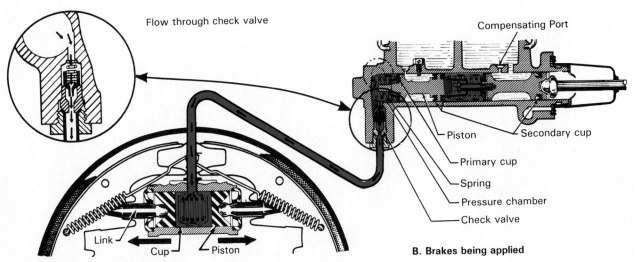

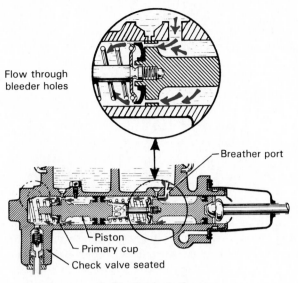

Flow through bleeder holes

Breather port

Piston
Primary cup
Check valve seated

C. Start of fast release

FIGURE 39-10 Master cylinder at fast release. (Buick Motor Division, GMC)

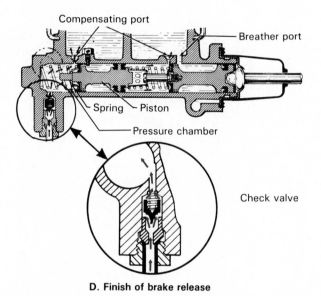

Compensating port

Breather port

Spring   Piston

Pressure chamber

Check valve

D. Finish of brake release

FIGURE 39-11 Master cylinder and residual check valve at release. (Courtesy Buick Motor Division, GMC)

DUAL-PISTON MASTER CYLINDER

The dual-piston master cylinder is a requirement of the dual braking system found on all modern cars. In a dual braking system there are two separate brake circuits. The circuits can be split simply front to rear or diagonally. Then the left front and right rear brakes can be on one circuit and the right front and left rear brakes on the other.

The diagonal system provides better vehicle control when only one of the circuits is working. Both styles will stop the car when only one circuit is working, but it is not safe for normal use. The brake system should receive service immediately to return the other circuit to working condition.

Dual-Piston Master Cylinder Operation

Let's say that pressure is lost in the master cylinder secondary chamber (Figure 39-12). This could happen if one of the flexible brake lines in that circuit broke. Because there would be no resistance in the secondary chamber, the primary piston would travel farther in the master cylinder, and the secondary piston would bottom against its spring.

If the primary circuit fails, the primary piston will travel until it contacts the secondary piston. Then the secondary piston will work like a single master cylinder and will stop the car (Figure 39-13).

In normal operation the primary piston is moved by the brake pedal. As the primary piston's seal passes its compensating port, it seals the primary piston chamber. Pressure is sent to two brakes. Hydraulic pressure

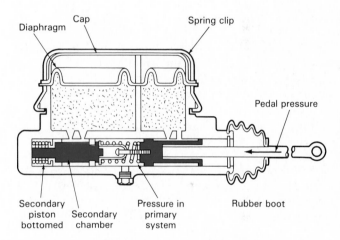

Diaphragm   Cap   Spring clip

Pedal pressure

Secondary piston bottomed   Secondary chamber   Pressure in primary system   Rubber boot

FIGURE 39-12 Secondary chamber pressure loss.

FIGURE 39-13 Primary chamber pressure loss.

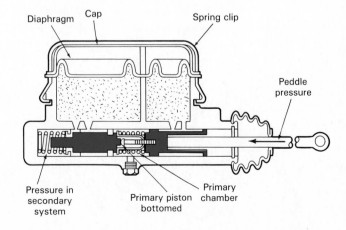

Diaphragm   Cap   Spring clip

Peddle pressure

Pressure in secondary system   Primary piston bottomed   Primary chamber

also pushes against the backside of the secondary piston. It is this pressure, and not any direct mechanical link, that normally pushes the secondary piston down the bore. The secondary piston then seals off its compensating port, and fluid is sent to the other two brakes.

POWER BOOSTERS

Just as the change from mechanical to hydraulic brakes allowed greater braking pressure to be applied at the wheels, so have power boosters.

There are two basic types of boosters, atmospheric and hydraulic; atmospheric types are the most popular. The two types of atmospheric boosters are vacuum suspended and atmospheric suspended. Vacuum suspended boosters have vacuum on both sides of the diaphragm at rest. Atmospheric boosters have atmospheric pressures on both sides. Figure 39-14 shows an atmospheric suspended booster. Some boosters use a single diaphragm, while others use a dual diaphragm.

Power Booster Operation (General)

When the brake pedal is depressed, a vacuum or hydraulic pressure operated device takes over and does the job of pushing the pistons in the master cylinder. Vacuum comes from the intake manifold of the engine. A check valve is used to store vacuum in the booster. Figure 39-15 shows how the system works. The system

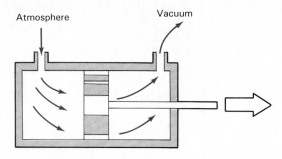

FIGURE 39-15 Atmospheric versus vacuum in booster.

includes a cylinder in which a tight-fitting piston moves. When vacuum is applied to one side of the piston, atmospheric pressure causes the piston to be pushed to the right. This movement pushes the piston rod into the master cylinder.

Single-Diaphragm Booster Operation

The three stages of power booster operation are brake released, brake applied, and holding positions.

Brake Released In the brake released mode, pressure is equal on both sides of the diaphragm. This pressure could be atmospheric or engine vacuum depending on what suspension the booster is. Therefore, when at rest, the diaphragm is centered in its travel.

Brake Applied An atmospheric suspended booster is shown operating in Figure 39-16. When the brake

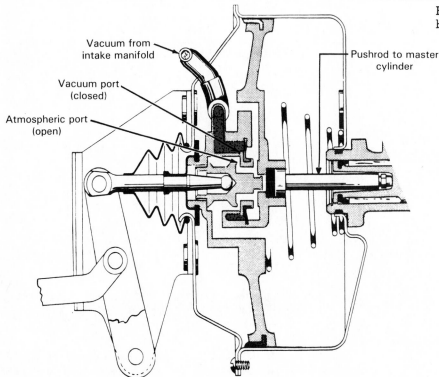

FIGURE 39-14 Atmospheric suspended boosters at rest. (Ford Motor Company)

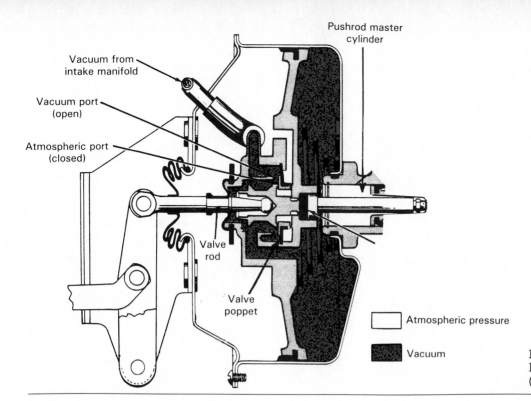

Pushrod master cylinder

Vacuum from intake manifold

Vacuum port (open)

Atmospheric port (closed)

Valve rod

Valve poppet

☐ Atmospheric pressure

▨ Vacuum

FIGURE 39-16 Power booster at applied position. (Ford Motor Company)

pedal is applied, the brake linkage forces the valve rod forward. It in turn forces the valve poppet forward, opening the vacuum port. Engine vacuum is then connected to the forward chamber. The pressure drops on the forward side of the diaphragm and stays the same on the backside. This lets the atmospheric pressure deflect the diaphragm forward. The diaphragm is connected to the master cylinder actuating rod, so the rod is forced forward, operating the master cylin-

der. As long as brake pedal pressure increases, more atmospheric pressure will enter on one side and vacuum on the other. The diaphragm will continue its deflection, and the brakes will be applied increasingly harder.

Holding Position When sufficient braking pressure has been reached, brake pedal pressure stabilizes (Figure 39-17). The diaphragm will continue to deflect until

FIGURE 39-17 Power booster in holding position. (Ford Motor Company)

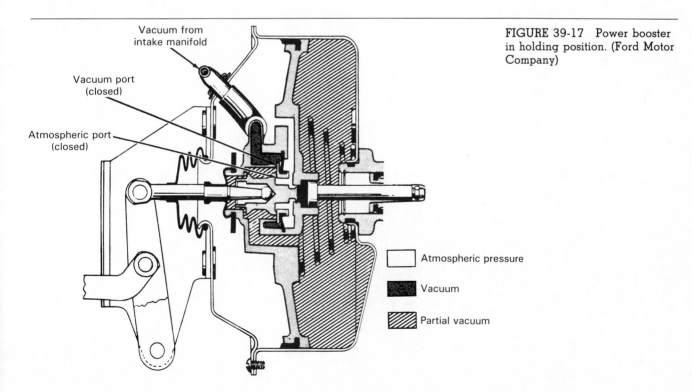

Vacuum from intake manifold

Vacuum port (closed)

Atmospheric port (closed)

☐ Atmospheric pressure

▨ Vacuum

▧ Partial vacuum

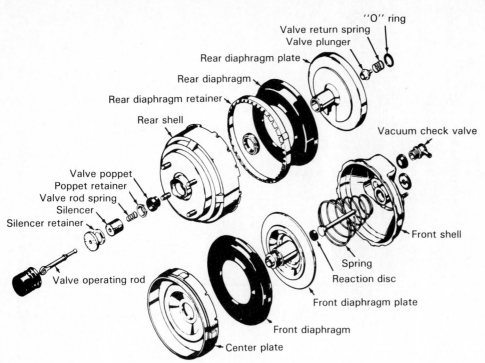

Valve return spring
"O" ring
Valve plunger
Rear diaphragm plate
Rear diaphragm
Rear diaphragm retainer
Rear shell
Vacuum check valve
Valve poppet
Poppet retainer
Valve rod spring
Silencer
Silencer retainer
Front shell
Valve operating rod
Spring
Reaction disc
Front diaphragm plate
Front diaphragm
Center plate

FIGURE 39-18 Bendix tandem diaphragm booster.

both the atmospheric and vacuum ports are closed. This seals the booster, and no more diaphragm movement is possible.

When braking is completed, the booster returns to rest because of hydraulic and spring pressure.

Dual-Diaphragm Booster Operation

A dual-diaphragm booster works just like a single-diaphragm booster, except two diaphragms are deflected at the same time. Two diaphragms are used to increase braking pressure and to provide a safety backup. Figure 39-18 shows a dual-diaphragm booster.

Hydraulic Boosters (Hydro-Boost I and II)

Some cars have a hydraulically powered brake booster (Figure 39-19). It gets its hydraulic pressure from the power steering system. Depressing the brake pedal diverts some steering hydraulic pressure to a hydraulic ram inside the booster (Figure 39-20). This ram actuates the master cylinder. Releasing the pedal prevents power steering pressure from entering the ram. The ram returns to its rest position, venting the remaining power steering return line. The hydraulic flow is governed by a spool valve.

In the case of engine or power steering pump failure, the hydraulic booster keeps a reserve of high-pressure (1400–1600 psi) power steering fluid on tap.

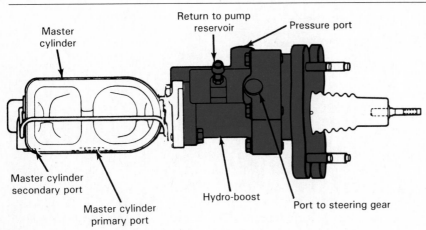

Master cylinder
Return to pump reservoir
Pressure port
Master cylinder secondary port
Master cylinder primary port
Hydro-boost
Port to steering gear

FIGURE 39-19 Hydraulic power booster. (General Motors Corporation)

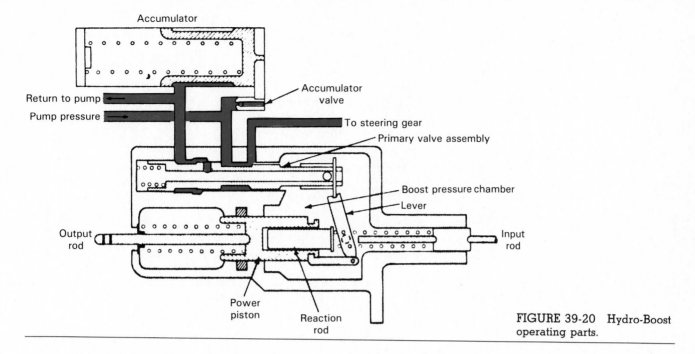

FIGURE 39-20 Hydro-Boost operating parts.

Accumulator

Accumulator valve

Return to pump

Pump pressure

To steering gear

Primary valve assembly

Boost pressure chamber

Lever

Output rod

Input rod

Power piston

Reaction rod

This is the job of the *accumulator*. The accumulator holds enough fluid for a maximum of two brake applications.

Hydraulic boosters are heavier, more expensive, and much more complex than vacuum boosters (Figure 39-21). They do provide twice the assist of a vacuum unit, however. Also, they work on vacuumless diesels and gasoline engines heavily loaded with vacuum accessories.

As for the difference between the Hydro-Boost I and II, the II unit uses the same components in a more compact package.

Electric Boost New hydraulic power brakes are also standard on the many new 1985 models. The system is hydraulically boosted, but boost is provided by an electrically driven pump rather than by the power steering pump. The boost pump comes on only when the accumulator senses that hydraulic fluid pressure has dropped below a set minimum. The new system is more energy efficient, since drain on the battery is less than the drain on the engine under the former system. It is also 20 lb lighter than the previous boost system, lending itself to more efficient underhood packaging.

FIGURE 39-21 Hydro-Boost installation. (Chevrolet Motor Division, GMC)

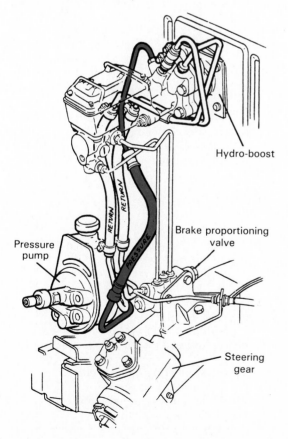

Hydro-boost

Pressure pump

Brake proportioning valve

Steering gear

DIAGNOSING MASTER CYLINDERS AND POWER BOOSTERS

A visual check will, many times, reveal problems in master cylinders. Look for leakage on both sides of the firewall or down the front of the power booster. A master cylinder can also leak *into* a vacuum booster, but you can't see that. The other test is to pump up the brake pedal and hold a firm, constant pressure on it. If the pedal drops slowly to the floor, the master cylinder is bad. A good cylinder will hold a firm pedal indefinitely. Do this with the engine running on boosted master cylinders.

Test all boosters the same way. A simple check of reserve boost is to try the brake pedal several minutes after shutting off the engine. You should get at least one boosted application. If you don't, there is a problem with the vacuum reservoir or accumulator.

Test booster action first by emptying the system of reserve boost. Do this by applying the brakes several times with the engine off. Hold the brake pedal down and start the engine. The pedal should fall slightly. With Hydro-Boost units, the pedal will then rise against your foot. If it doesn't, there is a problem in the booster itself. See Figure 39-22 for diagnosing Hydro-Boost systems.

FIGURE 39-22 Hydro-Boost diagnosis. (Cadillac Motor Division, GMC)

HYDRO-BOOST DIAGNOSIS

Condition	Possible cause	Correction
Excessive brake pedal effort.	1. Loose or broken power steering pump belt. 2. No fluid in power steering reservoir. 3. Leaks in power steering, booster or accumulator hoses. 4. Leaks at tube fittings, power steering, booster or accumulator connections. 5. External leakage at accumulator. 6. Faulty booster piston seal causing leakage at booster flange vent. 7. Faulty booster input rod seal with leakage at input rod end. 8. Faulty booster cover seal with leakage between housing and cover. 9. Faulty booster spool plug seal.	1. Tighten or replace the belt. 2. Fill reservoir and check for external leaks. 3. Replace faulty parts. 4. Tighten fittings or replace tube seats, if faulty. 5. Replace "O" ring and retainer. 6. Repair with new seal kit. 7. Replace booster. 8. Repair with new seal kit. 9. Repair with spool plug seal kit.
Slow brake pedal return.	1. Excessive seal friction in hydraulic booster. 2. Faulty spool action. 3. Broken piston return spring. 4. Restriction in return line from hydraulic booster to pump reservoir. 5. Broken spool return spring.	1. Repair with new seal kit. 2. Flush steering system while pumping brake pedal. 3. Replace spring. 4. Replace line. 5. Replace spring.
Grabby brakes.	1. Broken spool return spring. 2. Faulty spool action caused by contamination in system.	1. Replace spring. 2. Flush steering system while pumping brake pedal.
Booster chatters—pedal vibrates	1. Power steering pump slips. 2. Low fluid level in power steering pump reservoir. 3. Faulty spool operation caused by contamination in system.	1. Tighten belt. 2. Fill reservoir and check for external leaks. 3. Flush steering system while pumping brake pedal.
Accumulator leak down—system does not hold charge	1. Contamination in steering hydro-boost system. 2. Internal leakage in accumulator system.	1. Flush steering system while pumping brake pedal. 2. Repair unit using accumulator rebuild kit and seal kit.

SERVICING THE MASTER CYLINDER

Standard practice within most dealerships and garages today prohibits rebuilding or repairing master cylinders and power brake boosters. Some, but not all, states even have laws against it. These laws limit the responsibility of the repair shop. Almost all shops replace worn master cylinders and boosters with new units.

Master cylinders and some boosters can be rebuilt, however. When a master cylinder fails, it is usually for one of two reasons: pitting of the cylinder wall, which allows fluid to escape past the seals, or the rubber seals themselves becoming worn or broken.

Rebuild Kits You can purchase master cylinder rebuild kits at almost any parts house. These kits include a new piston, spring, and rubber seals (Figure 39-23). You must have the correct shop manual for the master cylinder you are rebuilding. Only the shop manual has the exact procedure and specifications necessary for rebuilding.

SERVICING THE POWER BRAKE BOOSTER

While you can rebuild almost any master cylinder, almost all power boosters are sealed shut. If they fail, you must replace them. The exceptions are GM boosters and Hydro-Boost units.

Special tools are necessary to service GM boosters and Hydro-Boosters. Also, take great care not to mix parts or fluids on Hydro-Boosters because power steering and brake fluid destroy seals they are not designed for.

Do not attempt booster overhauls unless you have the proper shop manual and are supervised by someone familiar with power boosters.

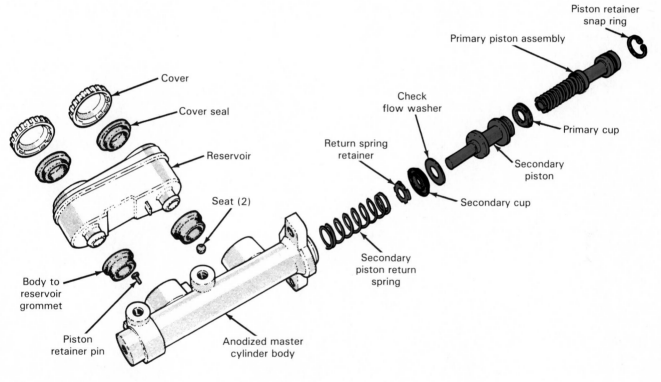

FIGURE 39-23 Parts in master cylinder rebuild kit. (Chrysler Corporation)

TRADE TERMS

Brake Fluid
Check Valve
Cylinder Bore
Hydraulic

Master Cylinder
Mineral-based Fluids
Pistons
Synthetic Brake Fluid

REVIEW QUESTIONS

1. What is Pascal's law?

2. If a 100-lb force is applied to a piston with 1 square in. of area, how much pressure would a piston with an area of 10 square in. exert if both these pistons rested within an airtight column of oil? Assume both cylinders or columns are connected by a pipe.

3. Explain the purpose of a master cylinder.

4. Explain how a master cylinder works in the brake released position and in the brake applied position.

5. Why must a master cylinder have a brake fluid reservoir?

6. The brake fluid reservoir cover must be vented. True or false? Why?

7. Of what use is the master cylinder residual pressure check valve?

8. How does an atmospheric power brake booster work?

9. Explain the action of the power booster in the brake released and brake applied positions.

10. Of what value is the double-piston or dual master cylinder?

40

Drum Brakes

INTRODUCTION

This chapter is on drum brakes. First, you'll learn some safety tips and cover drum brake operation in detail. Then you will have a chance to disassemble one or two different types of drum brakes.

Following this, you will be introduced to the ways in which parts are checked out to determine whether or not you should repair or replace them. Then you'll have a chance to learn how to make those repairs.

After servicing the brakes, you will learn how to reassemble them.

SAFETY

You must take three safety precautions when working on any brake system. First, always use jack stands when working under a car (Figure 40-1). Second, brakes shoes are made of cancer-causing asbestos composition material, so do *not* breathe brake dust. Third, safety glasses must be worn when working around tools or machinery.

OBJECTIVES

When you have completed this chapter, you should be able to

- Explain the difference between primary and secondary brake shoes
- Disassemble a drum brake
- Inspect the parts for wear or damage
- Repair or replace defective parts
- Reassemble and adjust a drum brake
- Explain what servo action is
- Find the legal limit for turning a brake drum

589

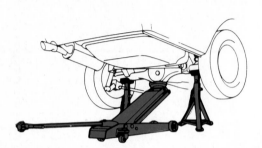

FIGURE 40-1   Jack stand under axle. (Mazda North America, Inc.)

The danger from asbestos is great. Microscopic pieces of asbestos are everywhere in brake dust. The asbestos can get inside you if you breathe or eat the dust. If brake dust is blown into the air with compressed air, it is easy to breathe in lots of asbestos. Asbestos is eaten when it gets on food from your hands.

Obviously, you can avoid these dangers by not blowing out brakes with compressed air and by washing your hands. In fact, you should wash your hands immediately after working on brakes. This will prevent you from rubbing asbestos into your eyes or clothing.

Asbestos is dangerous because it causes cancer. Studies have shown asbestos may remain in your body for decades before causing stomach or lung cancer.

FIGURE 40-2   Cleaning asbestos dust. (Mazda North America, Inc.)

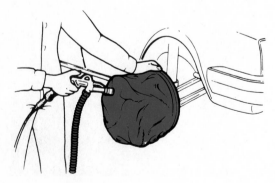

Therefore, do not blow brakes clean. Wash up after any brake work.

Many brake specialists use an unusual vacuum cleaner to remove brake dust (Figure 40-2). It clamps around the backing plate, drawing dust out through a closed system. Other methods use special solvents to wash the dust away. Even water and dish-washing detergent will work. Whatever method is available to you, be sure it does not include blowing asbestos particles into the air.

DRUM BRAKE DESIGN

Components

Of all the drum brake designs possible, the Bendix **dual-servo action brake** type is the most popular (Figure 40-3). It takes advantage of **self-energizing,** or **servo-action,** with both shoes. In a dual-servo brake the wheel cylinder is at the top and works on both shoes. Above the wheel cylinder is an **anchor pin.** This pin is firmly mounted to the backing plate. Both brake shoes locate against it. At the bottom, the shoes are connected by the star adjuster. The star adjuster is not firmly mounted to the backing plate. This lets the shoes move somewhat inside the drum.

A pair of return springs holds the shoes against the anchor at the top. A shoe-to-shoe spring holds the shoes against the adjuster at the bottom. Keeping the shoes from pulling away from the backing plate are two nail and spring assemblies. These are simply small coil springs, retainers, and a rod which pull the shoes lightly against the backing plate.

Operation

While it may seem like there is a lot holding the shoes motionless, they are actually free to move. When the

FIGURE 40-3   Bendix duo-servo brake assembly.

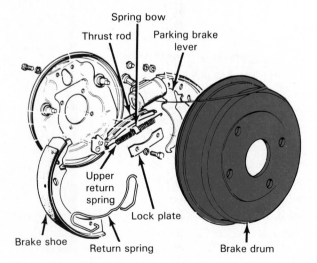

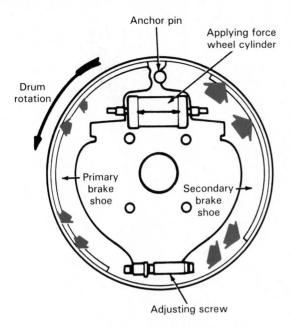

The relative size of the arrows indicates the increase of brake force or pressure.

FIGURE 40-4 Shoe pressure against drum in duo-servo brake. (Ford Motor Company)

brakes are applied, the wheel cylinder forces the shoes against the turning drum. The drum's rotation tries to rotate the shoes. In the Bendix design, the front, or **primary shoe** presses against the adjuster. The adjuster transmits the motion to the rear, or **secondary shoe.** This forces the secondary shoe against the anchor pin above the wheel cylinder. Because the anchor pin stops the shoe from rotating, the secondary shoe tries to pivot around it. This forces the secondary shoe against the brake drum. The forcing of the secondary shoe by the primary shoe is servo action.

As you can see in Figure 40-4, most of the braking is done by the secondary shoe. that's why it has more lining area than the primary shoe.

In the Bendix duo-servo brake, the primary shoe also has some servo action, because the movement of the bottom of the primary shoe forces its top into the drum. Other drum brake designs may have servo action on the secondary shoe only. This is called servo action.

Braking while backing up reverses the servo action. Now the primary shoe is forced against the drum by the secondary shoe. Because there is less lining on the primary shoe, braking is less effective while backing with drum brakes.

Parking Brake

Before getting into drum brake service, let's discuss the parts used in the parking brake and self-adjusters. Up to this point, the drum brake we've looked at could

have been a front brake. But at the rear there are extra parts. Look again at Figure 40-3. The antirattle spring and strut are part of the parking brake. A lever (Figure 40-5) pushes the strut, forcing the shoes outward.

The cable guide, overload spring, and adjuster lever are part of the self-adjuster (Figure 40-6). The self-adjuster works when the brakes are applied while backing up. This forces the secondary shoe away from the anchor pin, tightening the adjusting cable. This moves the adjusting lever which is connected to the star adjuster. If there is enough room between drum and shoes, the adjuster will move. If there isn't the overload spring extends instead.

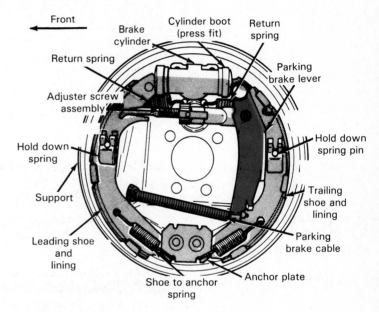

FIGURE 40-5 Parking brake lever. (Chrysler Corporation)

FIGURE 40-6 Self-adjuster. (Chrysler Corporation)

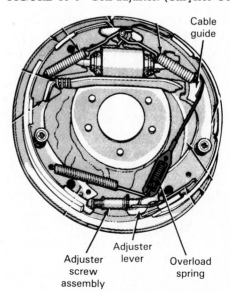

DISASSEMBLY

Preparation

The car must be raised to work on the brakes (Figure 40-1). Use a floor jack to raise the car and jack stands to support it. Never work on a car supported by a jack only. Also, if one end of the car is on the ground, **chock** that end's wheels. If you don't, the car could roll off the jack stands.

Removal

Wheel and Drum   Remove the wheel and tire assembly. This exposes the drum (Figure 40-7). Check for any screws on the drum which might hold it onto the axle flange. Remove any you find and then try pulling the drum off the wheel studs. Penetrating oil around the hub or axle flange helps. Several light hammer raps will, too. If the drum still won't budge, back the adjuster off 10 or more clicks. See the section on brake adjustment at the end of this chapter for this job. Some rear drums are held on by an axle shaft nut. Remove the nut and use a puller to get the drum off. Many drums without axle nuts are drilled and tapped so a bolt can be threaded through the drum until it butts against the axle flange. Two bolts threaded in against the axle flange will remove the most stubborn drum. At the front, removing the wheel bearing retaining nut allows removing the drum and front hub as a unit (Figure 40-8).

Internal Parts   With the drum off, remove the primary and secondary return springs. This is easily done with a brake tool (Figure 40-9). Also remove the parking brake cable (Figure 40-10) from the **parking brake lever.** Use pliers to compress and turn the hold-down pin and spring assembly on the secondary shoe. Hold the rod from behind the backing plate with a finger so you can remove the spring and its retainer (Figure 40-11). Unclip the adjuster lever and linkage from the secondary shoe. Go to the primary shoe and remove its pin and spring hold-down. Slip the anchor plate off the anchor pin.

Pull the shoes out of their slots in the wheel cylinder and lift the shoes, star adjuster, and spring off the backing plate (Figure 40-12). This motion will also free the **parking brake strut.**

Only the wheel cylinder should be left on the backing plate. Disconnect and cap the brake line from the backside of the backing plate. Now remove the bolts or clip holding the wheel cylinder to the backing plate.

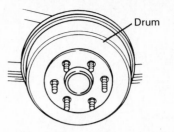

FIGURE 40-7   Brake drum with wheel removed.

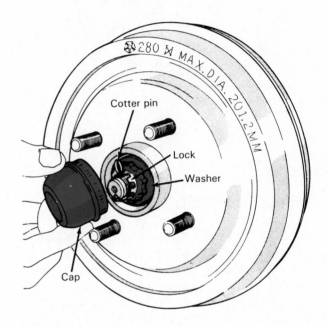

FIGURE 40-8   Hub and brake drum removal. (Chrysler Corporation)

FIGURE 40-9   Removal of brake shoe return spring. (Mitsubishi Motor Sales of America, Inc.)

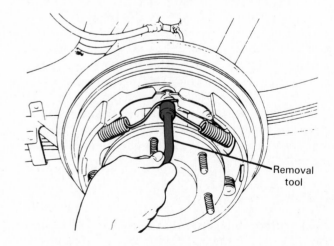

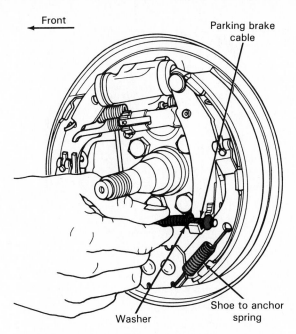

FIGURE 40-10 Removing the parking brake cable. (Chrysler Corporation)

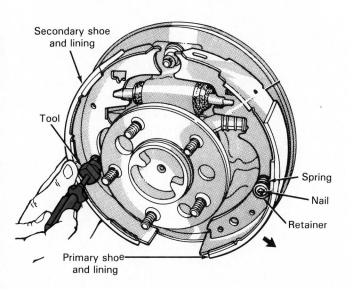

FIGURE 40-11 Spring and nail removal with special tool. (Chrysler Corporation)

INSPECTION

Drums

Drum inspection covers three areas: swept area wear, roundness, and cracks.

Wear The swept area is the part of the drum rubbed by the shoes. Visually check it for **glazing** and scoring.

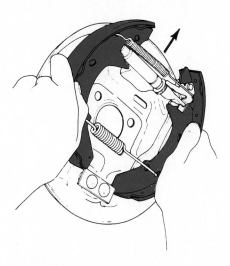

FIGURE 40-12 Removing brake shoes. (Ford Motor Company)

Glazing shows as shiny spots, often called glazed areas. Remove them with an abrasive material such as sandpaper or **emery cloth.** Glazing comes from the resins used in brake shoes. By sanding the glazing, you are removing resin deposits and increasing braking efficiency.

Scoring comes from foreign objects getting between the shoes and drum. Wearing the shoes to their backing exposes rivets or the backing, which will deeply score the drum. Scoring is removed by **turning the drum** on a special lathe.

Roundness Turning the drum will also cure most roundness problems. You can find roundness by measuring the drum's inside diameter in four different places. Use vernier calipers or an inside micrometer to measure the drum's ID (Figure 40-13). If the measurements are equal, the drum is round. If the measurements vary, the drum is out-of-round.

Cracks Cracks are found visually or by magnafluxing. Replace any cracked drum. Do not attempt to weld

FIGURE 40-13 Measuring ID with vernier calipers.

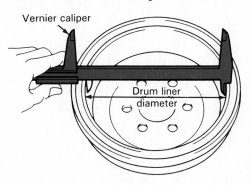

the crack, or the heat from the welder will weaken the drum.

There is a limit to how far a drum can be safely and *legally* turned. This limit is cast right into the drum at the factory (Figure 40-14). Never turn a drum past its limit. It will be unsafe, and you could be liable for any damages caused by a failed drum. If scoring or roundness cannot be cured by turning a drum to its limit, replace the drum. If you find a drum already past its limit on the car, replace it.

Shoes

A visual inspection of the shoes is all that is necessary to tell you whether or not they can still be used. If there is less than $\frac{1}{32}$ in. of lining remaining above the rivets, replace the shoes. On bonded linings, there should be a minimum of $\frac{3}{32}$–$\frac{1}{8}$ in. of lining remaining.

As with the brake drum, if you can see any cracks or excessive wear areas, replace the shoes (Figure 40-15).

In some cases the brake shoes will have overheated to a point of being dangerous. This will be indicated by **galling, carbonizing,** warping, or excessive wear. If you see any signs of overheating, replace the shoes.

Replace shoes soaked in brake or rear axle fluid, grease, or oil. Such contamination causes grabbing and can cause loss of car control. Besides changing the shoes, investigate and cure the cause of contamination, such as a leaky wheel cylinder or rear axle seal.

Most drum brake service is performed when changing shoes because of wear or contamination. Therefore, there is usually little need to decide if the

FIGURE 40-14   Drum maximum diameter. (Chrysler Corporation)

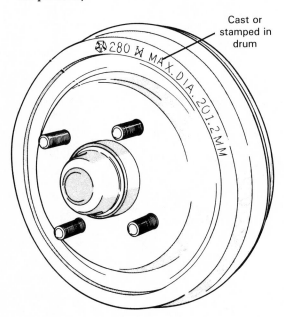

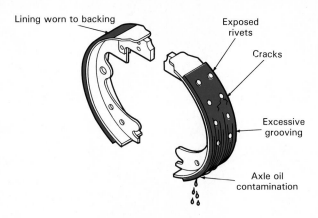

FIGURE 40-15   Brake shoe problems.

shoes should be replaced. If you are faced with the possibility of reusing borderline shoes, don't. Marginal shoes should be replaced because good shoes are both inexpensive and mandatory for good braking.

Wheel Cylinders

Wheel cylinders should be treated like master cylinders. Both contain brake fluid under pressure and can leak depending on bore, piston, and seal condition. Because of the liability and safety aspects of brakes, most shops simply replace wheel cylinders. This doesn't mean wheel cylinders cannot be repaired; they can. But if the cylinder is pitted badly or you think the repaired cylinder will be borderline, replace it.

OVERHAUL

Drums

Always measure drums before turning them to ensure they will not be too thin when finished. The reason for a limit on drum thickness is heat. If the drum is too thin, heat from normal braking will distort the drum. This causes uneven, grabby, increased distance braking. In severe cases, total brake failure could result.

Also, to do any good, all scoring, glazing, and out-of-round must be removed by turning (Figure 40-16). It makes no sense to turn a drum to its limit and leave half the scoring intact. Most drums can be turned 0.060 in. Any scoring deeper than 0.030 in. means drum replacement, because to remove 0.030-in.-deep scores on one side of the drum, you must also cut 0.030 in. from the other side of the drum. The two sides add up to 0.060 in., the maximum allowed.

Wheel Cylinders

If you elect to rebuild a wheel cylinder, start with a rebuild kit. Kits contain new pistons, springs, cups, and dust boots.

FIGURE 40-16   Turning a drum. (Ammco Tools, Inc.)

Disassemble the old wheel cylinder by pulling off the dust boots and pushing out the pistons, springs, and cups. Inspect the cylinder bore for scoring or pitting. Large shiny areas are worn by the piston.

Remove minor pitting and scoring by honing.

Special, small brake hones are sold for this job (Figure 40-17). Lube the honing operation with brake fluid. After honing, clean the cylinder with alcohol or by flooding it with fresh brake fluid. Do not use oil-based solvents or gasoline. They will damage the new seals.

"CAN I HELP?"

Don't help.

I have figured out the basis for the War Between the Sexes. It is not about cars, exactly, since we have finally figured out that female persons are as much car junkies as we of the other persuasion. It is not about love or communication, either, areas that have occupied our attention for lo these many years, time we might have better used in pursuit of the Perfect Whatever. It is about style. It is about cooperation. It is about a basic, fundamental difference between us which, if not understood, can lead to irreparable rifts.

Want to understand the phenomenon? Start working on something awful, like brakes. *Drum* brakes. Something scuzzy and dirty and disgusting, something

that would frustrate even Alan Alda. Get about halfway through the task before you discover that (a) brake jobs require special tools, which (b) even if you own—believe me, you don't—will be out of reach over on the workbench. Or (c) worse, you have put them in a Special Place the last time you went crazy and cleaned up the shop (HOW CAN ANYBODY WORK IN THIS MESS? I'M GOING CRAZY AROUND THIS PLACE!), and now you can't remember where it was.

Anyway, once the scene has been set, you're ready for the Ultimate Test of a relationship: Have Herself walk in just after you slip with the screwdriver you're using as a spring stretcher, mashing your second knuckle for the second time, and have her smile sweetly,

"How's it going? Anything I can do to help?"

I know. I know. The proper, humane response is something on the order of, "Well, gee, it's really a one-man operation, but I'd be pleased if you'd hang around to keep me company. I'm not making too much progress at this point and I'm feeling rather discouraged." I know this is the proper response, as I say, know it in my mind even as I'm really saying, "NO, NO, EVERYTHING IS JUST FINE! I'M JUST HAVING A WONDEFUL TIME WITH THESE !#?/* BRAKES! JUST LEAVE ME ALONE!"

Satch Carlson
Autoweek
Division of Crain Communications

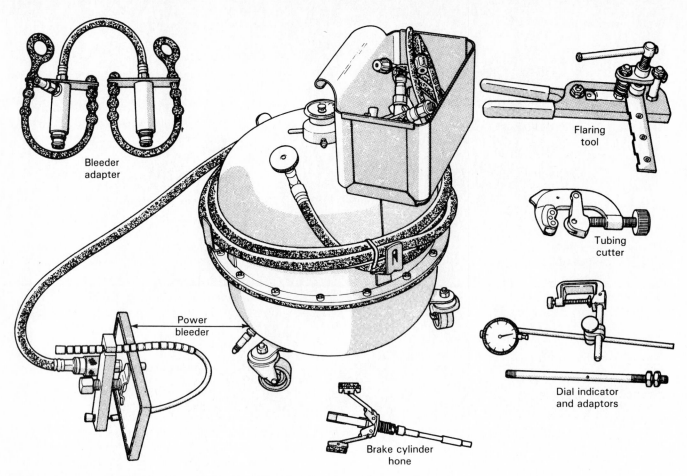

Bleeder
adapter

Flaring
tool

Tubing
cutter

Power
bleeder

Dial indicator
and adaptors

Brake cylinder
hone

FIGURE 40-17 Brake service special tools. (Chrysler Corporation)

If pitting or worn areas still show after honing, replace the wheel cylinder.

Reassemble the wheel cylinder after coating all parts in fresh brake fluid.

Shoes

The only overhaul for shoes is replacement. Relined shoes are available, as well as new shoes. Relining shoes in the shop is no longer done because special remanufacturing shops can do it faster and more cheaply.

DRUM BRAKE ASSEMBLY

Cleanup

Clean all parts you haven't already cleaned and inspected. The backing plate can be unbolted and removed from the chassis for wire brushing and solvent washing. The springs and star adjuster can be solvent-cleaned also. If the brakes have been seriously overheated, replace the springs. Clean and inspect the park-

ing brake levers for wear, especially on their pivots. Replace any worn parts.

Installation

Backing Plate If the backing plate was removed, reinstall it. Bolt on the new or rebuilt wheel cylinder (Figure 40-18). Uncap and thread the brake line into the wheel cylinder. This can be quite a challenge, so take your time. Hold the brake line in one hand while starting the fitting with the other. If the threads are clean, the fitting should thread in by hand. Finish with a tubing wrench. This connection is easy to cross-thread, so think twice before running in a dragging fitting by wrench.

Reinstall the parking brake lever with its cable. Lay the lever to the center of the braking plate.

On the backing plate there are four or more raised areas where the shoes touch. These raised pads are roughly 2, 4, 8, and 10 o'clock. Give each a light dab of **white lithium grease** (Figure 40-19). This grease keeps the shoes from sticking or rattling on the backing plate.

Shoes Lay out the primary and secondary shoes and

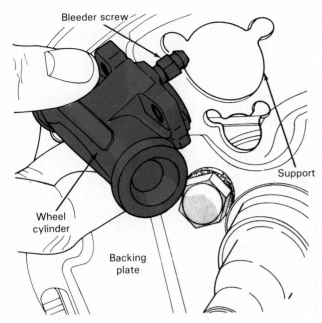

FIGURE 40-18 Installing wheel cylinder. (Chrysler Corporation)

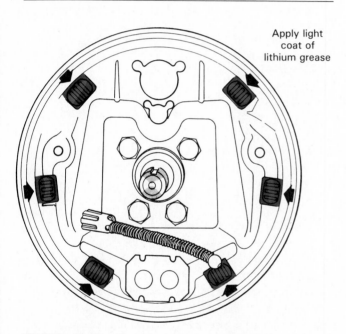

Apply light coat of lithium grease

FIGURE 40-19 Shoe contact areas. (Chrysler Corporation)

attach the star adjuster and **brake shoe return spring.** Typically, the primary shoe has less friction material than the secondary shoe. The primary shoe goes toward the front of the car. Attach the shoes and adjuster to the backing plate as a unit. Use pliers with the jaws spread on the spring and pin hold-downs. Install the parking brake strut and engage the shoes with the wheel cylinder.

Adjuster Now reattach the self-adjuster lever, overload spring, and cable. After looping the cable onto

the anchor pin, attach the primary and secondary return springs.

Test the self-adjuster function by pulling up on its cable. The adjuster should tighten one notch. If you reverse adjusters from one side of the car with the other, the self-adjuster will loosen, not tighten.

The adjuster should have been backed off when installed. This will let the drum slip over the new shoes. If the drum will not pass, back the adjuster off until the drum fits over the shoes. A brake caliper (Figure 40-20) lets you measure the shoes, and then the drum, to see if the drum will fit. Use the caliper if you have it.

Brake Adjustment

A brake adjustment tool (Figure 40-21) is needed for adjusting drum brakes. The tool lets you turn the star adjuster with the brake completely assembled. This

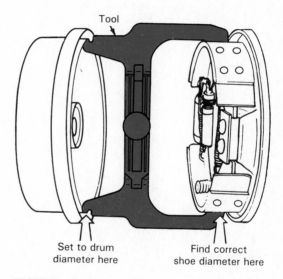

Set to drum diameter here

Find correct shoe diameter here

FIGURE 40-20 Measuring brake adjustment. (Ford Motor Company)

FIGURE 40-21 Adjusting brake shoe clearance.

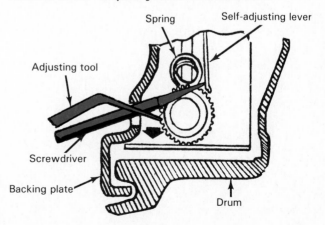

Spring

Self-adjusting lever

Adjusting tool

Screwdriver

Backing plate

Drum

is done by passing the tool through an access hole in the backing plate.

Manual To adjust a brake, raise the car so the wheel and tire assembly can rotate. Be sure to use jack stands and chocks. Locate the access hole and stick a screwdriver and the adjusting tool through it. Push the self-adjusting lever away from the star adjuster. Now engage the star adjuster with the adjusting tool. Lever against the access hole to rotate the star adjuster. Monitor your progress by rotating the wheel and tire. When the shoes begin to touch the drum, you'll hear a soft "swish" as the drum rotates. Continue tightening the adjuster until you cannot turn the wheel by hand. Now back the adjuster off 10 clicks. If your adjuster does not click audibly, back it off 10 star adjusting teeth. The brake is adjusted. This procedure will work on most cars, but check the appropriate shop manual for the exact procedure.

Self-adjusting brakes tighten when the brakes are applied and the car is backing up. Make several firm stops from about 10 mph in reverse to ensure the self-adjusters are operating properly.

If any part of the hydraulic system has been opened, bleed the brakes as described in Chapter 39. And no matter what type of brake work has been performed, always test the brakes while the car is parked *before* test-driving it. Drive the car only after you have a firm brake pedal.

TRADE TERMS

Anchor Pin
Brake Drum Micrometer
Brake Shoe Return Spring
Carbonizing
Chock
Dual-servo-action Brakes
Emery Cloth
Galling
Glazing
Parking Brake Strut

Parking Brake Lever
Primary Shoe
Retaining Springs
Secondary Shoe
Self-energizing
Servo Action
Strut Spring
Turning the Drum
White Lithium Grease

REVIEW QUESTIONS

1. Name three important safety precautions associated with brake work.
2. Identify the three major parts of a drum brake system.
3. Why is asbestos dangerous?
4. What is the difference between servo action and duo-servo action?
5. How can you determine whether or not a brake drum can be turned?
6. What are the critical thicknesses of brake shoe linings (riveted and bonded) beyond which they should be replaced?
7. Today's mechanic must know how to rivet new linings to the steel brake shoe. True or false?
8. What three criteria are used in drum inspection?
9. Define the term *swept area*.
10. What is white lithium grease?
11. When in doubt, use the old brake shoes. True or false? Why?

41

Disc Brakes

INTRODUCTION

Disc brakes were first used on aircraft. By the mid-1950s race cars were using these powerful, lightweight brakes. It was not until the early 1970s that they found their way into American cars. Imported cars had been using them for a decade by then.

Disc brakes on heavy American luxury cars brought new engineering problems. Unlike drum brakes, discs are not self-energizing. Because as much as four or five times the force is needed from the master cylinder with disc brakes, a booster is used on almost all disc brake systems.

Boosters solved the pressure problem but did nothing for the tremendous heat disc brakes generate. Intense disc brake heat caused boiling brake fluid and warped rotors. Higher-boiling-point brake fluid and insulating the brake pad from the brake piston have helped with heat. To prevent disc warpage, the ventilated disc was developed. Vanes between the braking surfaces allow heat to disperse quickly into the air. Air ducts provide even more cooling.

The final problem with disc brakes was overcome when the fixed caliper became a sliding caliper (Figure

OBJECTIVES

When you have completed this chapter, you should be able to

- Tell how disc brakes are superior to drum brakes
- Explain the difference between solid and ventilated discs
- Explain how fixed and sliding calipers differ
- Explain what brake fade is
- Change disc brake pads
- Disassemble and reassemble a disc brake

"float" in relation to the rotor, minor changes in runout and parallelism (which you will learn about later) no longer affect the caliper.

GENERAL OPERATION

Your learned about basic disc brake construction and operation in Chapter 38. Review Chapter 38 if the arrangement of **disc, caliper,** and **brake pads** is not familiar to you.

Heat

Let's examine disc brake advantages more closely. Resistance to fade is the most commonly cited disc brake advantage. Because of its open-air construction, a disc brake is less prone to fade than a drum brake. While

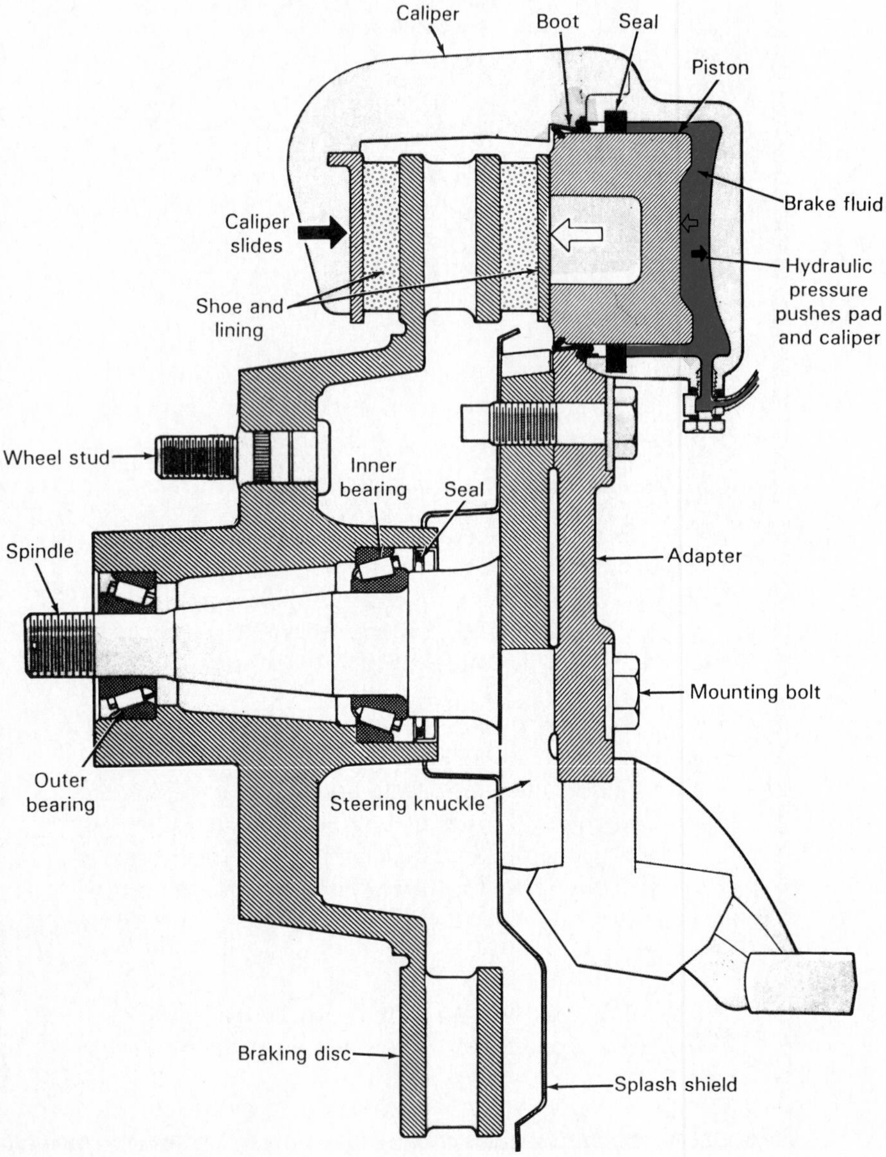

41-1). With a fixed caliper, the slightest mismatch between rotor and caliper can set up a vibration when the brakes are applied. By allowing the caliper to

FIGURE 41-1 Sliding caliper. (Chrysler Corporation)

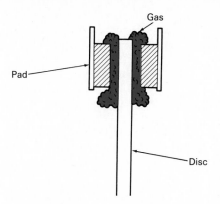

FIGURE 41-2 Gassing pads.

shedding heat is an important part of reducing brake fade, it is only part of the story.

When the friction material in drum or disc brakes gets hot, it gives off a gas. The more heat, the more gas the friction material produces. Under severe use, enough gas can be produced to fill the gap between the shoes and drums or pads and disc. Then the friction material cannot touch the drum or disc because of the gas (Figure 41-2). The brakes are, in effect, riding on air bearings.

Perhaps you've played a game in an amusement park where a puck is knocked back and forth on an air table. These tables pump air through many small holes so the lightweight puck rides on air. If you've ever played *air hockey*, you know just how fast the puck can slide. That's because the air bearing it rides on is extremely efficient.

The same is true of hot, gassing brakes. If you get brakes hot enough, they can fade until you have *no brakes*. That's because of the air bearing.

Disc brakes are doubly good when it comes to gassing and fading. First, they shed heat faster, and, second, they shed gas faster than drum brakes. Both are a result of their open-air design. Therefore, disc brakes don't gas as fast as drum brakes, and when they do, they get rid of it faster.

Weight

Another disc brake advantage is light weight. Less weight means better handling, fuel economy, and performance. Light brakes are especially important because they are usually unsprung weight.

Service

As you'll see later, disc brakes are easier to service than drum brakes. Discs are also much easier to monitor than drums. A glance at a disc brake reveals what condition the pads and disc are in. With drums, the wheel, tire, and drum must be removed for diagnosis.

Adjustment

Another maintenance-related benefit of discs is that they are self-adjusting. Disc brake pistons retract just enough to clear the pads from the disc.

Figure 41-3 shows how the **piston seal** is distorted during braking. When the brakes are released, the seal pulls the piston back into its bore. Because brake fluid pressure can overcome seal friction and slide the piston over the seal but the seal can only retract the piston so much, the piston automatically moves outward as the pad wears.

So, as the pads wear, the pistons must keep creeping out in their bores. Brake fluid from the master cylinder reservoir fills the extra volume behind the piston (Figure 41-4).

FIGURE 41-3 Piston seal distortion. (Chrysler Corporation)

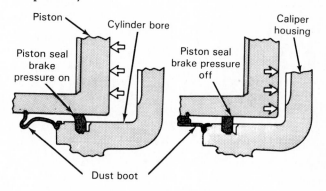

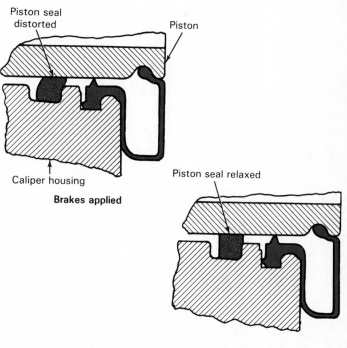

Brakes applied

Brakes released

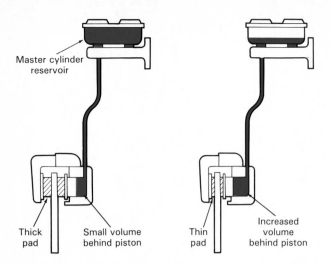

FIGURE 41-4 Worn pads cause lower reservoir level.

Wear

Only one other factor can cause the pads and pistons to retract farther, disc **runout.** If the disc has flat, parallel sides and spins true on the wheel bearings, the pads will never be more than several thousandths of an inch from the disc. Let's say the disc is warped. When the high point of the disc comes around, it will push the pads back. This is called *knockback*. Loose wheel bearings can also cause knockback becuase they let the disc wobble, which pushes the pads and pistons back.

DISC BRAKE PARTS

Caliper

Fixed Early and heavy-duty modern calipers are fixed. This means the caliper is rigidly bolted to the steering knuckle or rear axle (Figure 41-5). The caliper

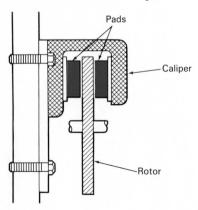

FIGURE 41-5 Fixed caliper.

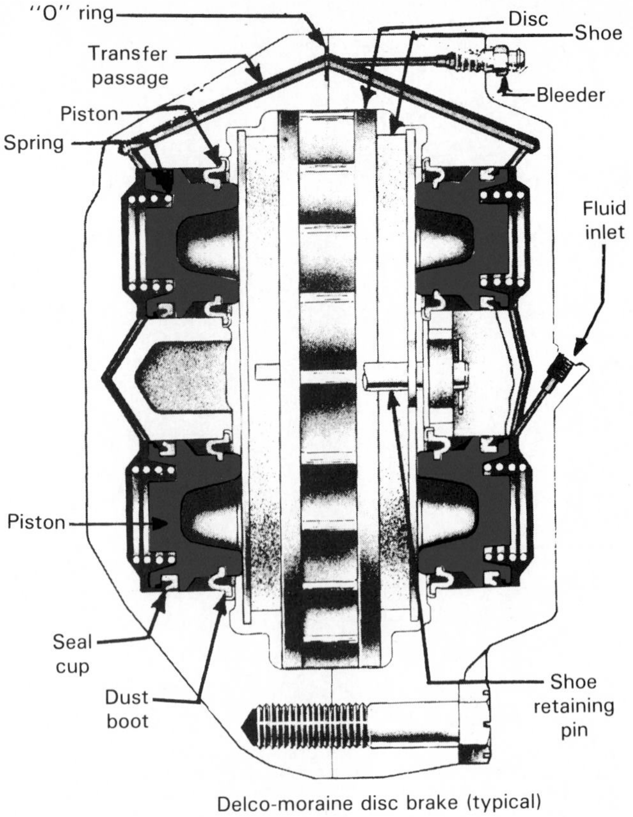

FIGURE 41-6 Four-piston fixed caliper. (General Motors Corporation)

does not move in any direction. All **fixed calipers** have pistons on both sides of the disc (Figure 41-6). There could be two or four pistons in a fixed caliper.

The drawback to this design is vibration from an uneven disc. There are advantages to the fixed caliper, however. It is mechanically simpler than the sliding design and promises even pressure on both sides of the disc under all conditions because it can't bind up. And with four pistons, it is easier to get more piston area for more powerful braking.

Servicing fixed calipers has its pros and cons. Changing pads is usually extremely simple. Two retaining pins are knocked out, and the pads can be pulled out of the caliper. The pistons are retracted so the new, thicker pads will fit, then the new pads are dropped in, the pins replaced, and the brake pumped until firm.

Servicing the pistons, seals, and bores is more difficult. The caliper must be removed and *split*. That is, the two caliper halves must be separated. Then the pistons can be removed, seals changed, and bores honed. The trouble is rejoining the caliper halves. All too often, the caliper will leak at the joint.

Sliding **Sliding calipers** are mounted so they can slide on a pair of pins or bolts (Figure 41-7). When

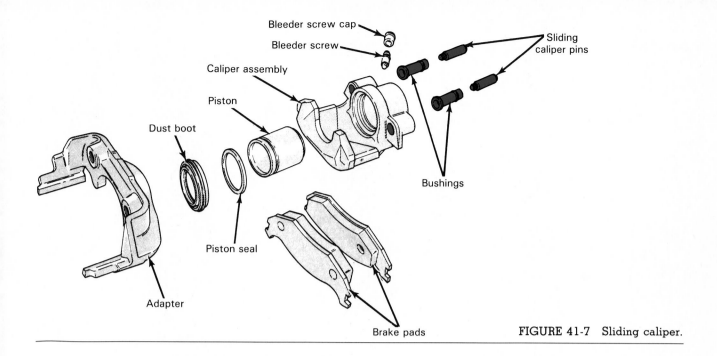

FIGURE 41-7 Sliding caliper.

the brakes are applied, the piston pushes one pad directly into the disc. When the pad touches the disc, it pushes against it. This reverses the applied force. Now the piston side of the caliper slides away from the disc, pulling the other caliper closer to the disc. The pad on the far side soon contacts the disc, and both pads then squeeze the disc.

Advantages of the sliding caliper are less weight and easier servicing of the piston and bore. It is also cheaper to manufacture.

While theoretically there is no limit to the number of pistons a sliding caliper could have, all modern designs have only one.

Disc Rotors

Disc designs are either *solid* or *ventilated*. Solid discs are just that, solid pieces, sometimes forming part of the suspension hub, sometimes not. Ventilated discs could be described as two solid discs about an inch apart. The space between the discs is filled with **vanes** (Figure 41-8). These vanes let air between the discs so they can cool on two sides. Therefore, a ventilated disc cools on four surfaces. Sometimes the vanes are angled for better cooling. Then, the discs are different for each side of the car.

Many times, ventilated discs are on the front wheels, and solid discs are at the rear, because the front wheels do most of the braking and therefore run hotter.

Both solid and ventilated discs can be drilled. Drilling holes through a disc reduces fade by breaking up the air bearing formed by gassing pads. Drilled

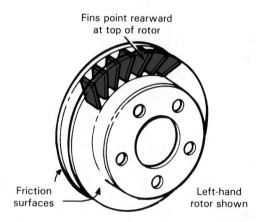

FIGURE 41-8 Ventilated disc.

discs are used only in severe-duty applications, and discs are drilled only by the factory or specialists.

You may see discs with a groove or grooves machined into them. This helps with gassing and provides an exit for water, dirt, and other foreign matter.

Pads

Like the drum brake shoe, the disc brake *pad* has a steel backing and an asbestos composition lining (Figure 41-9). The lining is either bonded or riveted to the backing. Some manufacturers offer pads with different hardness linings for the same brake. A harder lining wears longer, requires higher pedal effort, and is prone to squealing. Softer brake pads wear more quickly, need less pedal effort, and tend not to squeal. Disc brake pads can be grouped as organic or metallic,

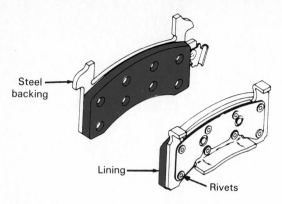

Steel
backing

Lining

Rivets

FIGURE 41-9   Brake pad. (Chevrolet Motor Division, GMC)

like brake shoes. Metallic pads would be very hard pads, which last longer than softer pads.

Squeal   We are all familiar with disc brake squeal. This unpleasant noise comes from the pad rubbing against the piston. With very hard pads, there could be some squeal from the disc and pad. Most brakes have a gasket between pads and pistons to dampen the noise. If softer pads are available, they will sometimes quiet the brakes. Antisqueal chemicals are also available. Keep in mind that all brakes make noise, but most of it is out of human hearing range.

Wear Indicators   Another type of brake noise is made by "talking" pads. These pads have a small metal tab called a wear indicator riveted to their backing and bent around to the lining side (Figure 41-10). When the lining wears out, the tab brushes against the disc, making a screech (Figure 41-11). This alerts the driver that the pads are worn out.

All other pads are checked visually for wear. Technically, a pad is worn out when either the backing or rivets are exposed. Pedal travel and braking efficiency are usually improved by replacing any pads that are worn to the thickness of the pads' backing. Further-

FIGURE 41-10   Wear indicator.

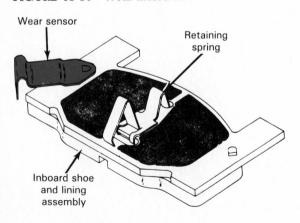

Wear sensor

Retaining
spring

Inboard shoe
and lining
assembly

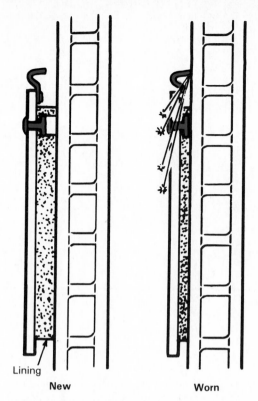

Lining

New   **Worn**

FIGURE 41-11   Brake pad with wear indicator. (Cadillac Motor Division, GMC)

more, many calipers have a spring clip between the pads. When the pads touch the wide, flat steel clip, replace them.

Parking Brakes

There are two styles of parking brakes used with disc brake systems. They are the *caliper style* and the **minidrum.** Either of these may be used with cars having disc brakes. If the car has rear drum brakes and front disc brakes, standard parking brakes are normally used, as described in Chapters 38 and 40.

Caliper   Various methods are used to apply disc brakes for parking. Some manufacturers use a simple lever arrangement; others employ inclined ramps and ball bearings. Figure 41-12 shows the GM design. The back of the piston is threaded so the actuator screw can attach to it. The other end of the actuator screw connects with the lever and parking brake cable. Applying the hand brake pulls the cable, rotating the lever. That threads the actuator screw into the piston, forcing the piston and pads against the disc.

Mini-Drum   The minidrum parking brake is a small, mechanically operated drum brake behind the rear disc. By applying the parking brake, the shoes are forced into the drum, locking the rear wheels and having

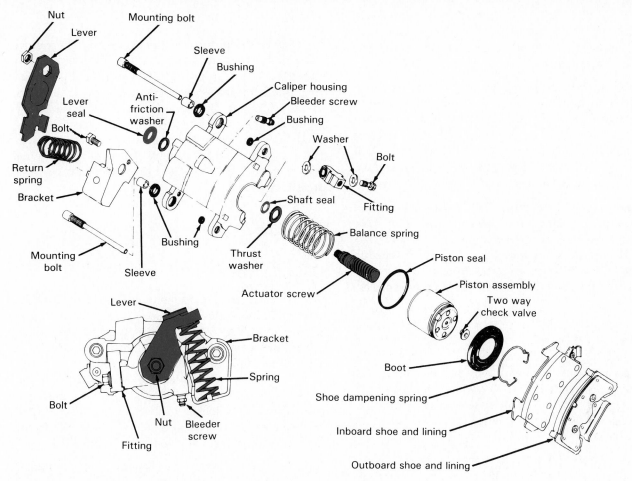

FIGURE 41-12 Caliper-style parking brake. (Buick Motor Division, GMC)

nothing to do with the disc brake. These minidrums are found on Corvette from 1969 on and Volvo, Alfa, and Mercedes-Benz, among others.

INSPECTION

Pads

Most pads are equipped with wear indicators which alert the driver by making a noise when the pad wears to the level of the bar. Other linings require visual inspection. Use the spring clips as a gauge if the brake has one. If there is no clip, you must remove the pads and measure the lining. In most cases, if the lining is less than $\frac{1}{32}$ in. above the rivets, you must replace it. On bonded linings, $\frac{1}{8}$ in. is the minimum (Figure 41–13).

Disc

There are two things that must be checked on the disc besides obvious wear and scoring: *runout* and *paral-*

FIGURE 41-13 Check for lining wear.

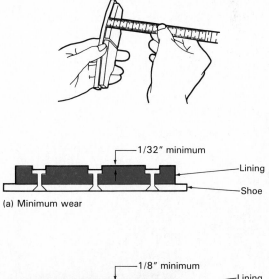

(a) Minimum wear

(b) Minimum wear for bonding linings

lelism. Runout tests the degree to which the **rotor** runs true to the vertical axis of the **hub**. Parallelism measures the degree to which both sides of a rotor are parallel to each other.

Runout   Adjust the wheel bearing to zero free play and zero preload. On front-wheel-drive cars, check that bearing play is within specifications. Mount a dial indicator, set the gauge to zero, and turn the rotor one full revolution (Figure 41–14). There should not be more than 0.005 in. from the zero reading. If there is, the rotor must be resurfaced or replaced.

Parallelism   To determine whether the two outside surfaces of the rotor are parallel to each other, take a micrometer reading around the outside edges of the rotor (Figure 41-15) in four places. The difference in readings should not exceed 0.0005 in. If they exceed this figure, the rotor should be resurfaced or replaced.

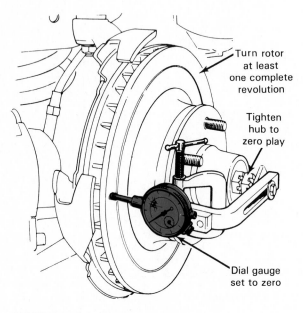

FIGURE 41-14   Measuring runout.

Pistons and Piston Bores

To inspect the pistons and piston bores, the caliper must be removed from the car. After disassembly, you can inspect for rust, pitting, and corrosion. Piston pitting usually means replacement, but some manufacturers allow minor pitting to be removed with emery cloth. Honing the cylinder will remove very light pitting. Some manufacturers allow only emery paper cleanup of the bores. Excessive rust or pitting requires replacement. Some calipers can be saved using stainless steel bore inserts.

SERVICING

Changing Pads

Always start pad replacement at the master cylinder reservoir. Check the fluid level in the reservoir. If it is very low, leave it alone and go on to the brakes. If the fluid level is high, siphon most of the fluid out. Discard the siphoned fluid.

You want the fluid level low in the reservoir because the level is going to rise when you retract the pistons in the calipers. If the fluid level is too high to begin with, the reservoir will overflow. Raise the car, set it on jack stands, and remove the wheels.

Fixed Caliper   If you are working with fixed calipers, knock out the two retaining pins with a hammer and punch. Use slip-joint pliers to squeeze one pad against its piston. This will retract the piston. Before removing this first pad, retract the piston on the other side. Many times, retracting the second piston will force the first piston back out again. If the pad isn't in there to stop it, the first piston will pop right out of its bore. Then you'd have to remove and dismantle the caliper to replace the piston.

With both pistons retracted, remove and replace the pads one at a time. Make sure you get the friction

FIGURE 41-15   Measuring parallelism.

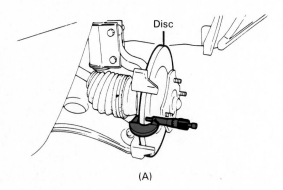

(A)

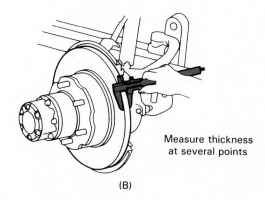

(B)

DISC BRAKE DEVELOPMENT

Disc brakes are now thought of as effective, inexpensive and reliable. That hasn't always been the case. The early systems had more than their share of troubles. For example, the early Dunlop discs. The Dunlop system used fluid seals on the caliper pistons, rather than in the bores (as is now common). The seals worked fine at first, but as the bores got corroded, the seals began to leak. Not only that, the pistons would seize in the bores, making it impossible to install new pads.

The first Audi 100LS models used inboard front disc brakes. The design decreased unsprung weight, but had a number of problems. The calipers were bolted to the transaxle case, behind the engine. Without any airflow to cool the calipers, they overheated and pads wore out rapidly. Some cars would go through front pads in less than 10,000 miles. Another problem was the lack of access. The early models required about 5 hours for rotor replacement, while the later outboard design needed less than 2 hours.

Then there's the Corvette. One for the first American cars with four-wheel disc brakes, it used aluminum calipers with four pistons. They were fairly light and effective, but suffered serious corrosion problems. When a caliper corrodes too far, you have two choices: Replace the caliper, or have it bored out and sleeved. The four pistons bores require lots of work and money to re-sleeve. New calipers just take money. In either case, it could cost over $500 in parts to get the calipers redone, not counting pads or labor.

The agonies suffered by the engineers and owners of these cars have resulted in a generation of disc brakes which are light, efficient, and inexpensive. If you have some of the older ones on your car, be glad you're able to help others by your suffering.

Leonard Spooner
Orchard St. Automotive
San Diego, CA

---

material against the disc and not the piston. Finally, set in the spring clip and install the two retaining pins. Pump up the brake pedal and top off the master cylinder reservoir.

Sliding Caliper Sliding calipers must be removed from the discs to change the pads. First retract the piston by squeezing the caliper with a C clamp (Figure 41-16). Remove the two caliper mounting bolts and hang the caliper with a length of wire. *Never* let a caliper hang by hydraulic brake line.

Now change the pads. There may be a tab which needs bending on the new outboard pad (Figure 41-17). Also change the bushings and sleeves found in the two caliper mounting bolt holes. An anti-squeak compound can be applied at this time, if desired.

Clean the pins the caliper slides on with abrasive

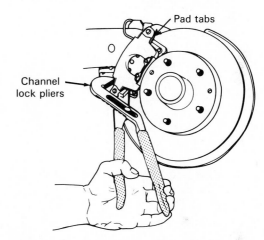

FIGURE 41-17 Bending tab on new pad. (Pontiac Motor Division, GMC)

---

paper. If there is any corrosion, replace the pins so the caliper will slide freely. Install the caliper over the disc, pump the brake pedal until firm, and top off the master cylinder reservoir.

Besides these general instructions, use the right shop manual for the job. Each model brake has its minor variations covered only in the shop manual.

Overhaul

Fixed Caliper Begin fixed caliper overhaul by removing the pads. Unbolt the hydraulic line and caliper mounting bolts. Set the caliper on a bench. After the hydraulic line and caliper are removed, cap the brake line to prevent brake fluid leakage. Split the caliper by removing the caliper through bolts (Figure 41-18).

FIGURE 41-16 Retracting piston with C clamp. (Pontiac Motor Division, GMC)

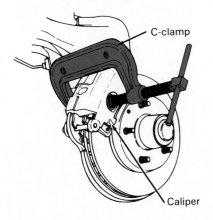

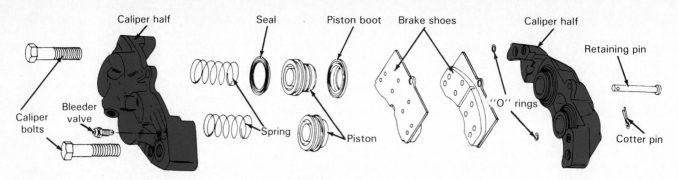

FIGURE 41-18   Split fixed caliper. (Chevrolet Motor Division, GMC)

Discard the O-rings from around the fluid transfer holes. Pry off the *boots* from each piston and then pull the pistons from their bores. Keep them in order so you return them to their original bores. Also remove the piston seals and any spring from the piston bore.

Clean all parts in denatured alcohol and inspect for rust corrosion and pitting. Hone the bores if necessary. Check the piston-to-bore clearance against specifications, typically around 0.006 in. Replace all rubber parts and copper O-rings.

Lubricate all parts in clean brake fluid. Install the new seals, fit any springs, and place the pistons in their bores. Be very careful not to dislodge the seals. A special tool may be available for piston and seal installation and for piston compressing.

Now install the boots between pistons and caliper halves. Silicone sealer may be required here. Another special tool may be required for boot installation. Check that the pistons bottom in their bores and that the piston tops are flush with the caliper body.

After fitting new O-rings, rejoin the caliper halves. Install the caliper on the chassis, fit the pads, and bleed the system.

Sliding Caliper   Remove the caliper from the disc as described for pad changing. Remove the pads and hydraulic line and set the caliper on a bench. Don't forget to cap the brake lines to prevent brake fluid leakage.

Pry the boot off the piston and discard (Figure 41-19). Fold shop rags into the caliper in front of the piston. Now use a very light application of compressed air in the hydraulic passage to pop the piston from its bore (Figure 41-20). Remove and discard the seal.

Clean all parts in denatured alcohol and inspect for rust, corrosion, and pitting. Lightly hone the bore if needed (Figure 41-21). If the bore won't clean up easily, replace the caliper.

Lubricate all parts in new brake fluid. Install the seal and piston (Figure 41-22). Make sure the seal does not come out of its groove during piston installation.

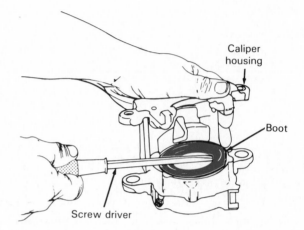

FIGURE 41-19   Prying out boot. (Cadillac Motor Division, GMC)

Caution: Do not place the fingers in front of the piston in an attempt to catch or protect it when applying compressed air. This could result in serious injury.
Notice: Use just enough air to ease the piston out of the bore. If piston is blown out — even with padding provided, it may be damaged.

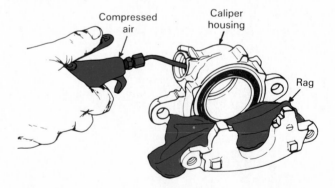

FIGURE 41-20   Removing piston with compressed air. (Cadillac Motor Division, GMC)

Finish by installing a new boot. Special tools may be required for seal and boot installation.

Finish by installing the caliper as you would during a pad change. Bleed the system.

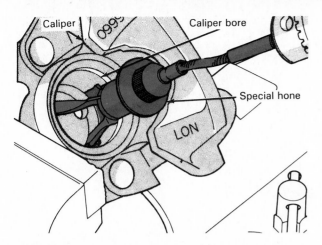

FIGURE 41-21 Honing piston bore. (Chrysler Corporation)

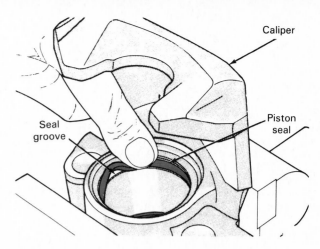

FIGURE 41-22 Installing piston seal. (Chrysler Corporation)

Bore Inserts Normally, no honing of the piston bore should be necessary. Any corrosion should clean up with emery cloth. If you do hone, only make a couple of passes. Any more and the bore will be too large. Then the piston can rock, wearing the seal.

If pitting is bad, caliper replacement is the usual cure. Sometimes it is cheaper to have stainless steel inserts installed in the bore. This is specialized work and is done by only a few shops. Therefore, it is an expensive job but cheaper than replacing some calipers.

Also stainless steel inserts never wear out, so the replacement is permanent.

Disc and Hub Service

The procedure given below is for front discs and hubs cast as one piece. When the disc and hub are separate pieces, you may have to unbolt them from each other (Figure 41-23).

Start by removing the tire and wheel assembly.

FIGURE 41-23 Disc brake components and rotor. (Ford Motor Company)

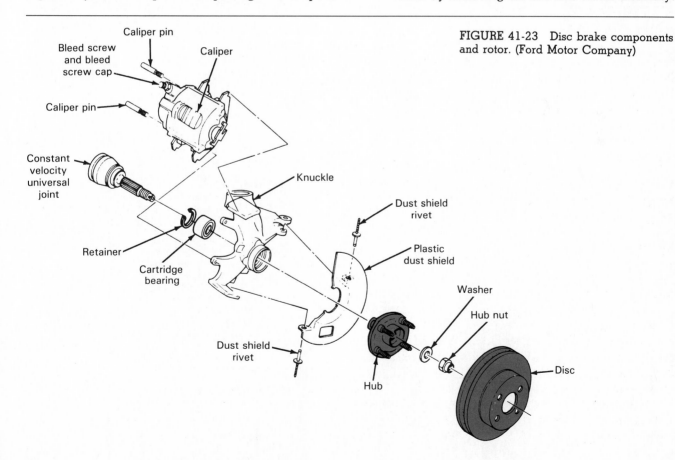

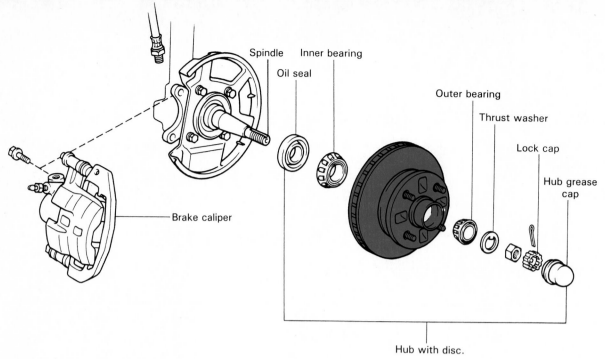

FIGURE 41-24 Integral rotor and hub.

FIGURE 41-25 Troubleshooting chart.

CONDITION	POSSIBLE CAUSE	CORRECTION
▶ Pedal travel decreasing	1) Compensating port plugged 2) Swollen cup in master cylinder 3) Master cylinder piston not returning 4) Weak shoe retracting springs 5) Wheel cylinder pistons sticking	1) Open port with air or wire 2) Replace rubber parts 3) Overhaul master cylinder 4) Replace springs 5) Overhaul wheel cylinders
▶ Dragging Brakes	1) Master cylinder pistons not returning correctly 2) Restricted brake lines or hoses 3) Incorrect parking brake adjustment on rear brakes 4) Parking brake cables frozen 5) Check valve installed in outlet to front disc brakes 6) Incorrect installation of inboard disc pad 7) Power booster output rod too long 8) Brake pedal not returning freely	1) Check master cylinder and repair as necessary 2) Check for soft hoses or damaged lines. Replace with new hoses or brake tubing 3) Check and readjust to correct specifications 4) Repair as necessary 5) Check master cylinder outlet and remove check valve if present 6) Remove and install shoe correctly 7) Replace with correct length 8) Stop light switch not adjusted correctly. Pedal pivot not lubricated. Wiring interference
▶ Brakes grab or uneven braking action	1) All conditions under "Brake Pulls" 2) Malfunction of combination valve 3) Malfunction of power brake unit 4) Binding brake pedal	1) All corrections listed under "Brake Pulls" 2) Replace valve and bleed system 3) Check and repair as necessary 4) Check and repair or lubricate as necessary
▶ Pulsation or roughness felt during normal brake application	1) Uneven pad wear caused by caliper not sliding due to improper clearance or dirt 2) Uneven rotor wear causing a thickness variation between the two braking surfaces 3) Drums out-of-round	1) Remove caliper and repair as necessary 2) Machine rotors to specifications 3) Machine or replace drums
▶ Squeal or squeak with brakes applied	1) Insulator on outboard shoe damaged 2) Incorrect pads or linings	1) Replace insulator 2) Replace with correct linings

Remove the caliper and hang with wire. At the front, pry off the dust cap to expose the wheel bearing adjustment nut. Remove the nut's cotter key and then the nut. Use a small screwdriver to fish out the thrust washer. Pull the disc off the spindle (Figure 41-24). The front wheel bearing will be loose in the hub, so don't let it drop.

On the hub's backside, pry out the grease seal and remove the wheel bearing.

At the rear, there may be rivets to drill out when removing the disc. These rivets are used at the factory only and need not be replaced.

Always use new seals when replacing wheel bearings. Pack the wheel bearings each time they are removed. Do not attempt to fill the void between inner and outer bearings in the hub. Packing each bearing is all that is necessary.

Troubleshooting

The chart in Figure 41-25 will help you find most of the problems and solutions when working with both disc and drum brakes.

TRADE TERMS

Brake Pads
Caliper
Disc
Fixed Caliper
Hub
Mini-drum

Piston Seal
Rotor
Runout
Sliding Caliper
Vanes

REVIEW QUESTIONS

1. Give three reasons why disc brakes are more efficient than drum brakes.
2. Is servoaction employed in disc brakes?
3. Name the two types of parking brakes used with disc brakes.
4. Very briefly describe how they operate.
5. Name the two basic types of calipers.

6. What is runout?
7. What is parallelism?
8. What are the two solutions to excessive pitting in the piston bore of the caliper?
9. Is it necessary to bleed a disc brake system when only the shoes have been replaced? Explain why.

PART EIGHT

Chassis Electrical Systems and Accessories

KEY CONCEPTS

- Basic wiring and common automotive lighting systems
- Operation and diagnosis of gauges and popular power accessories
- Heating and air conditioning principles and service

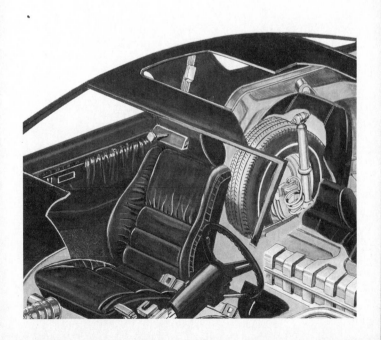

42

Lighting Systems

INTRODUCTION

Electrical systems always seem to worry automotive technicians, probably because they don't fully understand the systems or their problems. In this chapter all the car's light circuits are explained so you can approach lighting problems with an understanding of them. That will keep you from worrying.

ELECTRICAL WIRING

Wiring Diagrams

One glance under the instrument panel of most cars reveals a mass confusion of jumbled wires. But if you look again, you'll notice that some of the wires are color-coded and that some have more than one color. And if you look a third time with the aid of a **schematic** (Figure 42-1), you can start picking out individual wires right away. The point is, while automotive wiring may look hopeless at first, there is a system to it, and once you've learned the system, it's easy.

OBJECTIVES

When you have completed this chapter, you should be able to

- Trace wiring circuits
- Read wiring diagrams
- Explain how circuits are protected
- Tell what a fusible link is
- Explain how car lights are wired and why

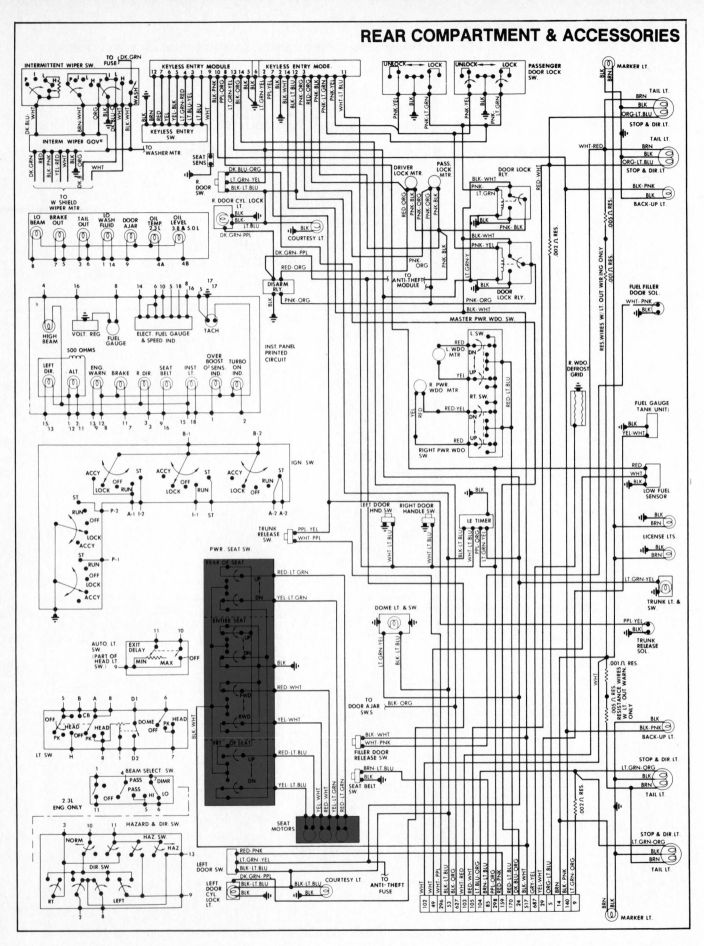

FIGURE 42-1 Instrument panel wiring schematic.

Wire colors are reversed
for each pair of motor leads
on Cougar & Thunderbird

To 12V
and/or
second
seat
switch
& motor
circuit

BLK-WHT

BLK

To
grd.

DN
RED-LT.GRN
UP
YEL-LT.GRN
UP
RWD
RED-WHT
YEL-WHT
FWD
DN
DN
RED-LT.BLU
YEL-LT.BLU
UP

Seat switch

Seat motors

FIGURE 42-2 Power seat wiring diagram.

To make matters a little easier, the manufacturer also supplies schematics for subassemblies. This is shown in Figure 42-2 for the power seat circuit. This circuit is found in the larger schematic of Figure 42-1 but has been isolated so it will be easier to follow.

Sizes

Besides specific colors, wires come in various sizes which are numbered from No. 0 to No. 20 with No. 0 being the largest and No. 20 the smallest. In automotive work you'll usually find wire sizes ranging from No. 10 to No. 18 (4 to 0.75 mm).

The larger the diameter of the wire, the more current it can carry, and the more expensive and heavier it is. Therefore, the manufacturer will use the *smallest* wire possible to carry the load.

Harness

Finally, all these wires are bundled together and wrapped in tape or a plastic sleeve or are protected from abrasion and the elements in some way. This is called a **wiring harness** or *loom*. By fixing a variety

of connectors to these wires (Figure 42-3), the system can be disassembled and reassembled quickly. This allows you to remove the turn signal switch (carrying probably 20 wires) and replace it without removing each wire, one at a time, and remembering where it goes.

CIRCUIT PROTECTORS

Circuits must be protected from overloading. If they aren't, the entire car could burn because of an electrical overload. To guard against this, **fuses, circuit breakers,** and **fusible links** are used.

Fuses

Fuses protect a circuit by melting. When they melt, the circuit is broken, and no more power can pass. This stops any dangerous overheating and protects electric components like motors and relays.

FIGURE 42-3 Typical electrical connectors. (Ford Motor Company)

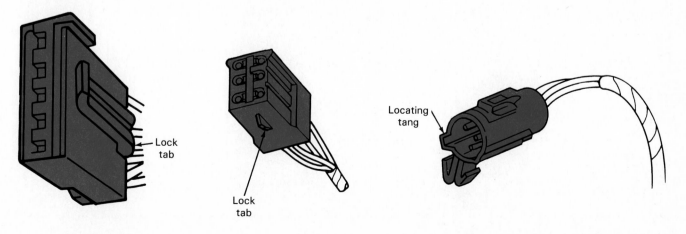

Lock
tab

Lock
tab

Locating
tang

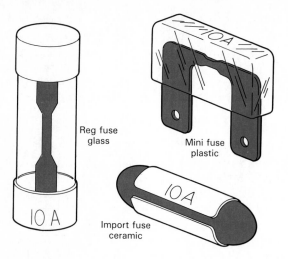

FIGURE 42-4   Fuse.

Cars commonly use a glass-enclosed metal strip (Figure 42-4), a minifuse which encloses the metal strip in plastic, or a ceramic fuse which anchors the metal strip's ends to a ceramic pill. All these fuses work the same way. When the fuse loading exceeds its rating, the metal strip melts. This causes an opening, and current flow stops. Only after replacing the fuse will current flow resume.

Fuses sometimes blow or melt with age, but most of the time a blown fuse points to trouble. Therefore, when replacing a fuse, look for the problem that made it blow in the first place. Never replace a fuse with another of a higher rating.

Fuse Box

Almost all circuits in the car are fuse protected. It's easiest to run all the circuits to one spot and place the fuses there. This is called a **fuse block** or **fuse box** (Figure 42-5).

You can see that each fuse is marked for both its location (radio, horn, taillights) and its size (7.5 A, 10 A, 25 A). *This is the first place you look in the event of an electrical failure or problem*. Mechanics have been known to take 4 hours to replace a wiper motor when it was only a blown fuse!

Many cars use in-line fuse holders. These have to be hunted down because they are scattered around the car. They are frequently used on aftermarket electrical products, such as stereos. Another possibility is multiple fuse blocks. With many electrical circuits it is sometimes easier to have one fuse block under the hood and another in the passenger compartment.

Circuit Breakers

Like a fuse, a circuit breaker disrupts the current flow when things get too hot. Figure 42-5 shows the usual location of circuit breakers, and Figure 42-6 shows how they work.

Operation   The arm is made of two dissimilar pieces of metal. This gives it its name: **bimetal.** The bottom piece will expand when heat is applied at a greater rate than the piece of metal on top. This expansion forces the bottom piece to become larger than the top,

FIGURE 42-5   Fuse block. (General Motors Corporation)

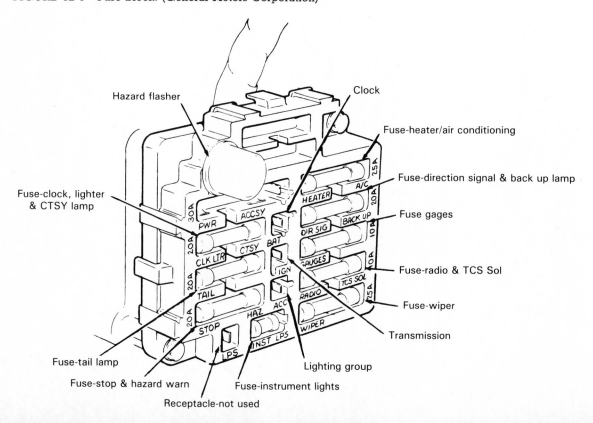

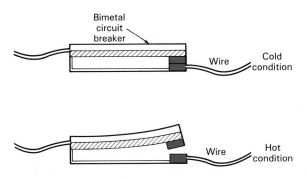

FIGURE 42-6 Bimetal circuit breaker.

bending the arm and breaking the connection. As soon as the arm cools, the bottom strip of metal contracts, allowing both pieces to once again be the same length and closing the circuit.

Use Circuit breakers are used in the headlight and other circuits where a complete power loss would be dangerous. Let's assume the headlight circuit is overloaded. Because it is a self-resetting breaker, it will open and close as it heats and cools. This will make the headlights flash on and off. The flashing provides enough light to safely stop the car. If a fuse were used in this circuit, it would have blown, and there would be no headlights until the fuse was replaced.

Through a variety of means, such as spring-loading the arm or adding a heater coil to it, the arm may be kept suspended from its contact until either it is reset manually or the electrical current is turned off (ignition key or battery cable removed).

Fusible Links

A *fusible link* is shown in Figure 42-7. The link, being four wire sizes *smaller* than the main wire it protects,

FIGURE 42-7 Fusible link. (General Motors Corporation)

To repair damaged fusible link, cut off damaged wire as shown. Strip back insulation, splice wires with splice clip & solder. Tape splice with double layer of electrical tape.

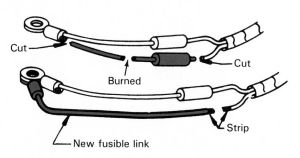

FUSIBLE LINK REPLACEMENT

will melt like a fuse *before* the main wire melts. Fusible links can be used as the only circuit protection, or they can be used in conjunction with fuses and circuit breakers. Once the fusible link has melted, it must be replaced.

Relays

When an accessory requiring a heavy current draw is placed a distance from the switch, a relay is used. The relay allows the use of smaller-gauge wire at the switch because the switch is handling a light electrical load. If the switch handled the full load of the accessory, it would be a very large, cumbersome switch.

Look at the headlight door opening schematic in Figure 42-8. The large electrical current required by the headlight motor is supplied by the dark blue (DK. BLU) wire coming from the fuse circuit. Note how the dark blue wire is protected by a 5-A circuit breaker. The small, lightweight switching wire is light green (LT. GRN). It comes from the headlight switch and goes to the relay. In the relay, the switching circuit can shuttle the heavy supply circuit between the open/close leads of the headlight motor.

If there were no relay, the large current in the dark blue wire would have to pass from the fuse block to the headlight switch and then to the motor. This would increase the weight or wire in the car, and the headlight switch would have to be much larger.

Relays shuttle electricity with the help of an electromagnet. When the switching current reaches the relay, it energizes an electromagnet. The electromagnet closes, like a solenoid. This movement closes a set of

FIGURE 42-8 Headlight door circuit schematic.

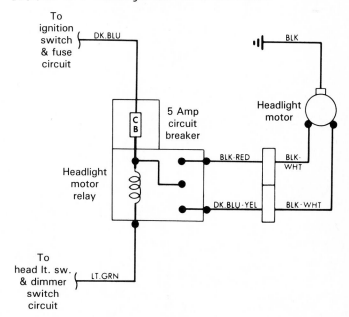

large contacts which are connected to the electromagnet. These contacts look like oversized ignition points. When they connect, the large supply current can flow to the motor.

HEADLIGHTS AND TAILLIGHTS

The *headlights* of the car are probably the most important electrical safety feature of the vehicle. Should they go out at night in an unlit area, almost certain disaster would occur. Special attention, then, should be paid to the headlights to be sure they work properly, switch from high to low beam as they should, and not blind oncoming drivers.

From Switch to Lamps

When you turn on the headlights, a number of things happen. If your car is equipped with two headlamps, each lamp will have a double filament. If the **dimmer switch** is in the low-beam position, only one of the filaments will burn. When the dimmer switch is activated to a high position, the second filament will come on as will the high-beam indicator light in the dash. Headlights have a large current draw, about 10 A. The dimmer switch is usually employed to handle the large supply circuit. Relays are also used.

Simultaneously with turning on the headlights,

the *taillights* and *dash lights* will come on. The taillights, in most cases, are also equipped with two filaments. The second set of filaments is the brake lights. These come on when the brake pedal is pushed, activating a switch which rests against the brake linkage. Another style of brake light switch is connected to the hydraulic system. Hydraulic pressure pushes a disc against the contacts in this switch. A single wire then runs to the brake lights to power them.

Headlight Covers (Doors)

Headlight covers, or *doors*, must be elevated before the lights can serve their purpose. Figure 42-9 is an exploded view of how electrically powered headlight doors operate. Notice that there is a hand wheel on the motor that allows you to elevate the doors in the event of an electrical problem.

Fords and some other models employ a vacuum pump to move the doors. Intake manifold vacuum is stored in a reservoir which, when the light switch is turned off, allows a vacuum-operated pump to close the doors against spring pressure. Should the engine fail while the lights are on, spring pressure keeps the doors from closing.

Electrically operated doors will stay elevated when electricity is lost to the motor because the motor needs electricity to turn the opposite way, closing the doors.

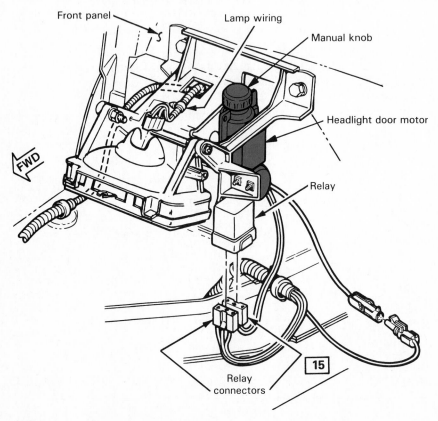

FIGURE 42-9 Electrically operated headlight doors. (Pontiac Motor Division, GMC)

FIGURE 42-10 Mechanical headlight aimer.

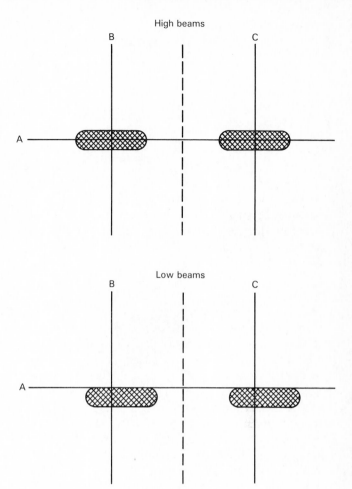

High beams

Low beams

FIGURE 42-11 Headlamp alignment grid.

Headlight Adjustment

Headlight adjustment can be performed mechanically or with the aid of special headlamp aimers (Figure 42-10). These aimers use mirrors with split images, like split-image range finders on some cameras, and spirit levels to determine *exact* adjustment.

Fairly accurate adjusting can be done mechanically (by hand and eye) using the headlamp alignment grid shown in Figure 42-11. Here, tape or string is affixed to a vertical surface 12 ft in front of the car. Line A represents the centerline of the headlamps as measured from the ground to the center of the lamp with the car carrying a full tank of gasoline and the spare tire.

Lines B and C represent the vertical centers of the lights as measured center to center. Of course, the car must be aligned on the centerline. Now, adjust the "hot spot" with the lamps on "high" to the center where A crosses at B and C.

The low beam should fall just below line A and somewhat to the right of B and C. This directs the beam out of the eyes of the oncoming driver. Figure 42-12 shows the *adjusting ring*, *adjusting screws*, and *spring*.

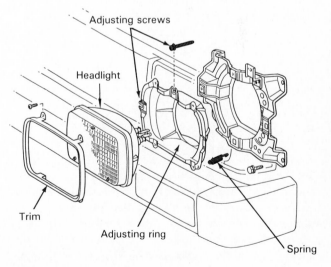

FIGURE 42-12 Headlamp arrangement (with adjusters). (Ford Motor Company)

Figure 42-13 illustrates how to get at the taillights and side marker lamps.

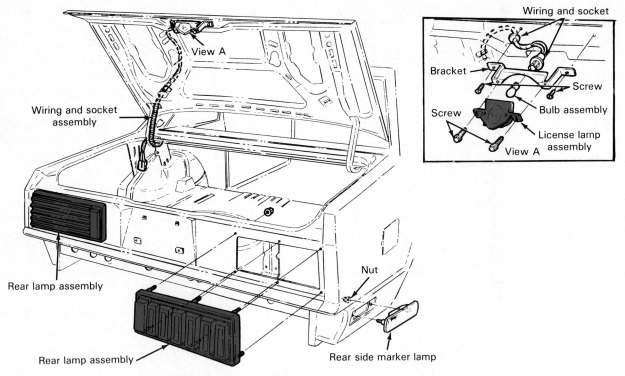

FIGURE 42-13 Accessing Ford-type rear lamp assemblies. (Ford Motor Company)

Troubleshooting

Begin headlight troubleshooting by checking the fuse, fusible links, and circuit breakers. If none of these shows a problem, replace the bulb. Consult the manufacturer's shop manual to determine the correct bulb size. It may have been replaced with an incorrect lamp by the last mechanic or owner. If neither of the operations prove successful, consult a shop manual for the vehicle you're working on.

BACKUP LIGHTS

From Dash to Lamps

Backup lights have been factory-installed on all cars since the early 1970s. Before that time (during the 1950s and into the 1960s) backup lights were a factory option and were not found on all cars. Backup lights are not part of the taillight/brake light assembly, as they are not covered by red lenses. In fact, they're the only legally permissible clear lens on the rear of the car.

The backup light switch is incorporated into a manual transmission's shift linkages. On automatics either the park/neutral switch *or* a transmission-mounted switch is used. When the gearshift is moved into the reverse position, contacts are closed, completing the circuit to the backup lights. To replace the

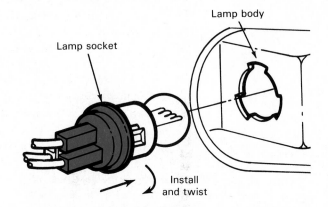

FIGURE 42-14 Installing rear lamps (backup and stop). (Ford Motor Company)

lamps, they may be reached from inside the trunk in most cars.

Figure 42-14 shows the types of sockets which will be found for taillights, brake lights, and backup lights. Pull the socket out of the rear panel, rotate the bulb counterclockwise, and replace it by rotating clockwise. Then return the socket to the back panel.

Troubleshooting

Four problems are common with backup lights. The fuse could blow, the lamp could burn out, the switch could go out of adjustment, or the switch could fail.

Also, there could be a short or open in the wiring. Start with the fuse and work down to the wiring. As with all lighting troubleshooting, make sure you have a good ground. If you spot corrosion inside the lamp socket, clean it out with abrasive paper. And because most lamp sockets ground through their bodies, rotate the lamp holder in its bracket. This can break up corrosion that prevents the socket from grounding.

TURN SIGNALS

From Lever to Lamps

The *turn signal lever circuit* may be called upon to carry a number of things: headlights (high beam and low beam), right turn signal, left turn signal, hazard lights, turn signal indicators, and often the horn. Remember, too, there are front and rear lights included in this arrangement. That's why Figure 42-15 is so complex looking. Figure 42-16 shows the contacts used to carry these separate circuits, while Figure 42-17 shows the wiring schematic.

Referring to Figure 42-16, each of the colored squares represents a metallic contact point for the accessory named. When the turn signal lever aligns with one of these contact points, the contact point on the lever allows the circuit to close. This activates the blinking light, horn, or other accessory.

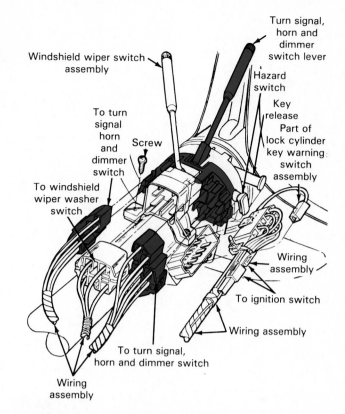

FIGURE 42-15 Turn signal assembly. (Ford Motor Company)

THE ACETYLENE DAYS

The first "horseless carriage" had simple oil lamps when they had any at all. The yellowish flame rising from the wick, immersed in a small container of oil or petrol, provided just about enough light for the driver to avoid the larger holes. "Real" carriages, those with horses, traveled much faster, but this light, conveniently beamed by a parabolic mirror and optical front glass, was good enough even for them. Motorists in those heroic times did not too often commit themselves to night travel, not only because it was ill-advised on the road surface but also because a meeting in the dark with any enemies of their noisy mechanical monsters might well have had unpleasant consequences.

At the turn of the century acetylene lighting began to be used on motor cars

in view of the higher speeds that called for a more vivid and penetrating light. This was in spite of a certain resistance to their use due to a variety of well-known limitations—the danger of explosion, the necessity of frequent inspection of the carbide-water reaction, the short life of the fuel supply. For about 15 years acetylene lighting was the basic system in use on motor cars.

Contrary to popular belief, such systems attained a high level of efficiency. The latest models, produced just before their final disappearance 50 years ago, looked similar to those in use on modern cars.

The problem of dimming had been resolved by means of a hemispherical concave mirror which could be manually rotated through 180° until the flame itself was completely obscured.

In this position, used for cruising in company with other vehicles or in the city, the headlamp sent out only a part of its light, reflected from the parabolic mirror behind. When, however, the dimming mirror was rotated until it was immediately behind the flame, it intensified the light.

This small mirror system, designed by Zeiss, was used for electric headlamps when they were first adopted in spite of the many deficiencies of the batteries of the time. Later it was found more practical to adopt a second, less powerful bulb outside the focus of the parabola.

Marco Matteucci
History of the Motor Car
Octopus Books Limited

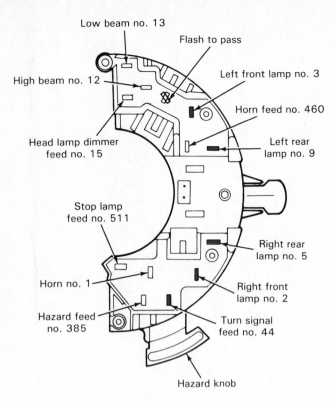

FIGURE 42-16   Turn signal switch. (Ford Motor Company)

The turn signals blink because the electrical signal is passed through a flasher unit. The flasher unit uses a bimetallic connection which opens and closes when heated by the electricity passing through it. The open and close cycling of the flasher unit is similar to a resetting circuit breaker.

Troubleshooting

Troubleshooting begins, as do all the circuit checks, by checking the fuses, circuit breakers, and fusible links. Next, check the lamp bulbs. Turn signal switch operation may be checked by using a jumper wire to bypass switch. If this fails, consult your shop manual or Mitchell Manual to see how each of the circuits may be checked individually with a voltage/ohmmeter.

DOME AND COURTESY LIGHTS

Dome and courtesy lights are an example of lights operated by more than one switch. Power is run from the fuse block to the dome or courtesy lights, but the light is not grounded. Instead, the ground is carried to the door switches. These switches are normally open. Because they are open, the dome light cannot ground and thus doesn't light. When the door is opened, the door switch closes, and the light is grounded. This completes the light circuit, and the dome light comes on.

FIGURE 42-17   Typical turn signal wiring diagram.

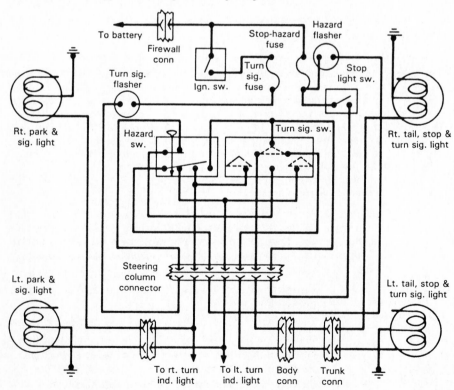

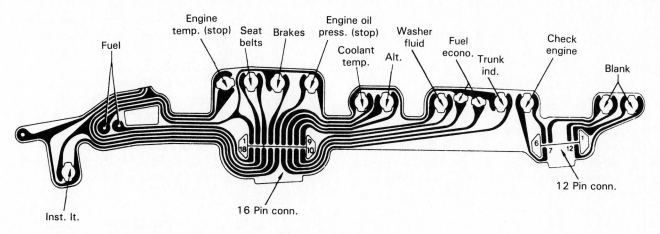

FIGURE 42-18   Printed circuits. (General Motors Corporation)

The driver's side door switch also grounds the key alarm buzzer in the ignition switch circuitry.

Troubleshooting

Dome light circuits rarely give trouble, but if they do, check the fuse and then the bulbs. If they are okay, ground the dome light with a jumper wire or test light. If the light comes on, the switches are at fault. If the bulb still doesn't light, check for power at the fuse and along the wiring until the open in the wiring is found.

HAZARD FLASHERS

The hazard flasher switch connects the four turn signal lights and sometimes the side marker lights to the turn signal flasher unit. On most newer cars the hazard

FIGURE 42-19   Exploded view of instrument panel. (American Motors Corporation)

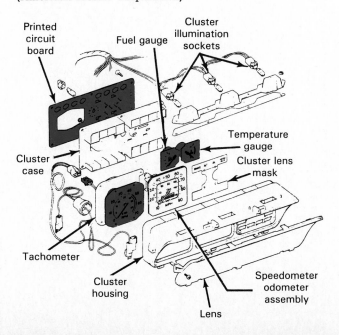

flasher circuit has its own flasher unit. This is necessary to slow the cycling of the flash unit. The more lights that are put on one circuit, the more electricity is drawn through it. The increased electrical load heats the bimetal switch faster, making it cycle faster. After a point, the flash unit cycles too fast for the lights to be effective. Routing the hazard circuitry through its own flash unit distributes the electrical load enough to get the proper flash cycle.

Adding another set of taillights to the system also makes the flash units cycle faster. Trailer lights are, in effect, another set of taillights. To keep directional and hazard flashers slowed down, heavy-duty flash units are available. They use bimetal switches that take longer to heat and can thus handle the increased electrical load.

DASH LIGHTS

Printed Circuits

Into the mid-1960s, most circuitry under the dash was handled by individual wires. Domestic cars used the single-wire system with the metal dash as a common ground. British imports used a two-wire system (a separate ground wire for each component).

A better system which greatly reduces the number of wires and cost is the **printed circuit board.** Figure 42-18 shows two styles of printed circuit board. The light areas are copper foil acting as copper wires. The dark background is plastic insulation which prevents the copper foil strips from shorting out against one another.

Figure 42-19 shows a typical location of a printed circuit board. Notice that such things as the fuel gauge and temperature gauge (and, not shown, the oil pressure gauge and assorted warning lights) are plugged directly into the printed circuit board. Not only is the arrangement less expensive than a wiring system, but you only have to unplug the gauge from the circuit board to change gauges or replace a defective circuit board.

From Switch to Lamps

Printed circuit boards cannot handle heavy current. Therefore, they are only used in the switching side of the circuit. For example, the headlight switching current passes through the circuit board, but the large electrical load still passes through the dimmer switch or a relay. The circuit board easily makes all the necessary connections between the headlight switch and the instrument lights, side marker, front indicator, and tail-lights, however. This saves a lot of wire on connectors and unclutters the back of the instrument panel.

Troubleshooting

After checking all the circuit protectors and finding no problems, consult a shop manual to determine the meter test locations of the printed circuit board. This will allow you to check each circuit individually. If the problem is in the printed circuit board, it may be easily removed and replaced with a new one.

In the case of older cars for which new circuit boards are not available, the copper foil circuit which has been damaged often may be soldered to provide a good repair.

TRADE TERMS

Bimetal
Circuit Breakers
Dimmer Switch
Fuse Block
Fuse Box

Fuses
Fusible Link
Printed Circuit Board
Schematic
Wiring Harness

REVIEW QUESTIONS

1. Name two possible fuse locations.
2. Describe how a fuse protects a circuit.
3. How does a circuit breaker work?
4. What is the difference between a fuse and a fusible link?
5. What do relays do?

6. Name the two power systems for headlight covers.
7. Why must headlights be adjusted?
8. What activates backup lights?
9. Name the items associated with the turn signal switch.
10. Describe a printed circuit board.

43

Electrical and Vacuum Accessories

INTRODUCTION

The gauges of an automobile tell you the condition of the operating systems, while the accessories provide comfort and convenience. As a mechanic, you'll be called upon to repair, replace, and recondition all these at one time or another. Careful attention should be paid to the theory in this section. You can find out how to repair parts by going through shop manuals. They, however, do not go into much theory. Electrical and vacuum accessory theory is explained in this chapter, so you won't need it in shop manuals. We begin the theory section by looking at the way gauges work.

GAUGES

There are four basic types of gauges used in the modern auto: indicator lamps, thermal control gauges, balanced coil gauges and mechanical gauges. Let's look at them one at a time.

Indicator Lamp

Figure 43-1 shows the simplest type of gauge, the indicator lamp. This is generally a warning light. Unfortu-

OBJECTIVES

When you have completed this chapter, you should be able to

- Name the two types of instruments
- Explain how oil pressure is indicated to the driver
- Show how a tachometer works
- Explain how windshield wipers work
- Explain what makes power windows work
- Explain how a cruise control system functions

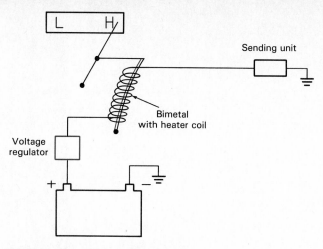

FIGURE 43-2   Thermal gauge.

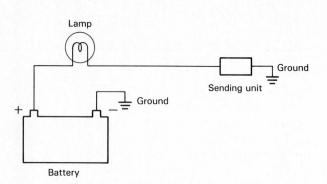

FIGURE 43-1   Indicator lamp.

nately, it has picked up the rather abusive title of "idiot light." This unfortunate nickname is the result of the way it operates. It comes on when pressures or temperatures have reached the critical stage. Usually the radiator is boiling over, or the oil pressure has dropped so low as to no longer be providing lubrication.

The indicator lamp is powered from the battery but has a separate ground wire to the sending unit. The sending unit, which encloses a normally open switch, stops the circuit from being complete. When pressure or temperature closes it, the switch completes the circuit, and the indicator light comes on. Other circuits may use a normally closed switch.

Thermal Controlled Gauge

Figure 43-2 shows a schematic of a thermal controlled gauge. The sending unit is a variable resistor and supplies current to a heater wire wound around the bimetal arm of the gauge. The more electricity which comes from the sending unit, the warmer the heating coil gets. This warmth heats the gauge's arm. As the arm heats, it bends, pulling the arrow across the face of the dial. When the sender lowers the current, the coil cools, and the arm moves toward its zero setting.

To keep voltage variations in the car's electric system from causing erroneous readings, a small volt-

age regulator is placed in the gauge circuit. The regulator keeps voltage a constant 7 V and supplies all thermal gauges in the instrument panel.

Balanced Coil Gauges

One of the most popular gauge designs is the balanced coil (Figure 43-3). By the way the coils are wound and wired, you can see that the *series coil* will maintain a constant current. The *shunt coil*, operating from the variable resistance of the sending unit, develops varying current strengths depending on the flow of electricity from the sending unit.

When no current is passing through the shunt coil, the needle is pulled toward the series coil. As current *increases* in the shunt coil, electromagnetic force pulls the magnet and needle toward the shunt. When current drops, the needle moves back.

Mechanical Gauges

Several automotive gauges work on a mechanical system rather than electrical. This includes most speedometers and tachometers. Refer to Figure 43-4 to see how these mechanical gauges operate.

FIGURE 43-3   Balanced coil gauge.

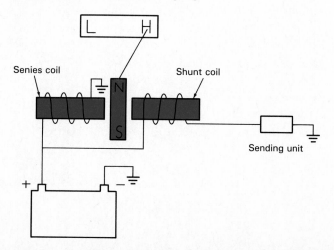

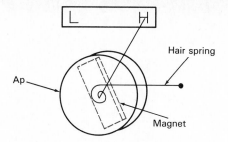

FIGURE 43-4 Mechanical gauge.

As in the case of a speedometer, a drive cable powered by the transmission rotates the magnet. As the magnet turns, the cup tries to rotate with it because of the magnetic force. The needle is attached to the cup. As the cup tries to rotate, the needle swings across the face of the dial. A hair spring forces cup and needle back to zero when the magnet stops rotating.

GAUGE OPERATION

Ammeter Circuit

The **ammeter** indicates the *rate of charge* from the generator or alternator. Electrical needs are gauged by the voltage regulator, which then controls the alternator's output (Figure 43-5). The alternator then produces the electricity. The current, however, passes through the ammeter on its way to the battery. Usually, the ammeter gauge is of the balanced coil design.

Oil Pressure Circuit

Two types of oil pressure indicators are shown in Figure 43-6.

The oil sender, in the case of the lamp circuit, serves as an on or off switch operated by oil pressure. As long as there is pressure on the sender, electrical contacts are kept open, and the bulb remains off as a result.

When oil pressure drops, switch contacts within the sender come together, closing the circuit and causing the lamp to come on.

FIGURE 43-6 Oil pressure circuit.

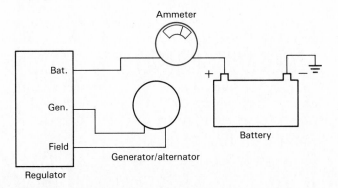

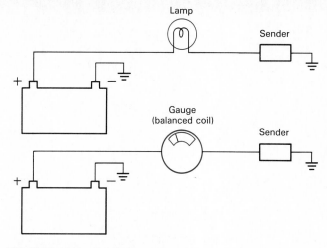

FIGURE 43-5 Ammeter circuit.

The same circuit can have a variable-resistance sender and a meter gauge. As the oil pressure increases within the sender, a variable resistor is activated. This allows a variable amount of current to pass to the gauge, causing the needle to swing. As pressure increases, current increases, and the gauge needle swings right. When pressure is reduced, the variable resistor lowers the current, allowing the needle to swing to the left.

Senders used with gauges are more complex than those used with indicator lights. Indicator light senders are simple on/off switches, while gauge sending units give a variable signal. Therefore, each sender can only be used with its own type of circuit.

Temperature Circuit

Figure 43-7 shows a typical **temperature circuit**. This circuit works much like the oil pressure gauge in Figure 43-6. In this case, the sender is usually located in the head or in one of the upper water jackets of the block. A bimetal arm and variable resistor within the sender increases or decreases current through the temperature gauge. This makes the needle point right or left depending on the current from the sender. A warning light may be used instead of the gauge. Its sender is calibrated to complete the ground circuit when temperatures reach a critical point.

FIGURE 43-7 Temperature circuit.

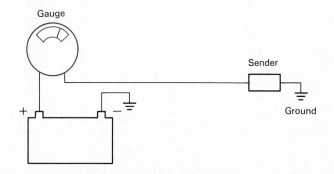

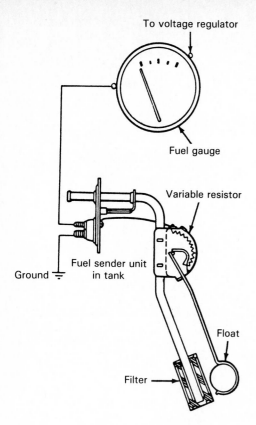

FIGURE 43-8   Fuel-level-indicating system.

Fuel-Level-Indicating System

The fuel-indicating system operates with a float in the gas tank (Figure 43-8). This float is attached to a stationary **variable resistor.** As the float moves up and down with the fuel in the tank, it changes the current flow through the fuel gauge. This causes the needle to move in a corresponding fashion, telling you the level of fuel in the gas tank. Thermal controlled fuel gauges are used because of the natural dampening ability. Without the dampened, or slow, response, the fuel gauge would indicate fuel sloshing in the tank.

FIGURE 43-9   Tachometer circuit. (Ford Motor Company)

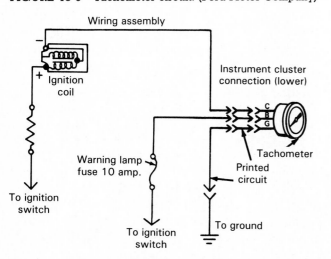

Tachometer Circuit

Today's automobiles sport an **electric tachometer.** This was not always the case. Fashionable sports cars built up to the 1970s were equipped with a **mechanical tachometer.** This was usually connected to the camshaft (generally through the distributor). These gave way to less expensive electric tachometers. Figure 43-9 shows how one of these tachometers is connected. Electrical impulses from the coil are passed to the tachometer. The tach, using a balanced coil gauge, converts these impulses to revolutions per minute for you to read. The faster the engine rotates, the greater the number of impulses from the coil and consequently, the greater the rpm indicated.

Speedometer

Most speedometers are an all-mechanical arrangement. As shown in Figure 43-10, a flexible cable comes from the transmission or left front wheel hub into the speedometer. As the cable rotates within its housing, it activates the mechanical gauge. The gauge is calibrated to indicate the car's speed. No electrical current is drawn in this operation. It's all mechanical.

Many new cars use electric speedometers. A conventional cable runs to the speedometer unit, but instead of depending on gears, the cable's rotation is converted into an electronic signal. This signal then controls an electromagnetic motor connected to the speedometer needle.

Another method is to use a permanent magnet generator. An electrical signal is then sent from the generator sensor to a speed buffer and then to the speedometer. Some GM cars use this system.

Digital Instrumentation

The most advanced forms of gauges are the **digital gauges.** These incorporate a miniature "brain" called a *microprocessor*. **Microprocessors** are not found in regular gauge systems. These are a result of computer technology and are the basis for computer memory.

Used in automotive instrumentation, the microprocessor accepts current from the sensor (oil, water, fuel, or any other) and converts this current into information to be sent to the digital readouts. Figure 43-11 shows a *light-emitting diode* (LED) connected to the microprocessor. The LED is composed of seven miniature lamps. When these lamps are lit in certain sequences, they appear as a number or letter. The microprocessor converts the information from the sender to signals which activate the LEDs, showing as letters or numbers. Another style of display is the *vacuum fluorescent display*. This display electronically arranges particles into numerals.

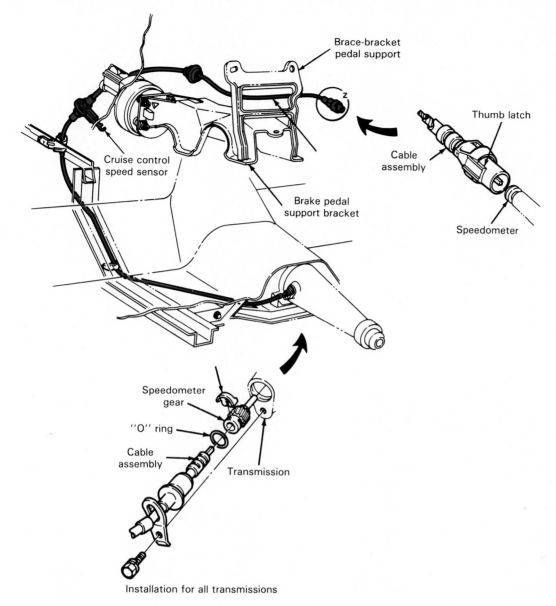

FIGURE 43-10 Speedometer arrangement. (Ford Motor Company)

FIGURE 43-11 Digital instrumentation.

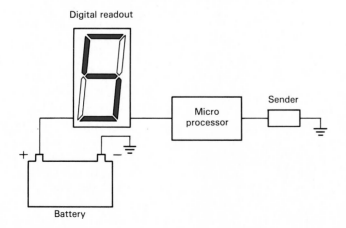

ELECTRICAL EQUIPMENT

Wipers

Two-Speed Motor Windshield wiper circuits vary from manufacturer to manufacturer. In the simpler systems a two-speed motor is used. The wiper switch shuttles power from the low-speed pole to the high-speed pole of the motor. When the wipers are shut off, power is automatically routed through the low-speed pole. This keeps the wipers moving until they reach their park position. In the park position a cam attached to the wiper linkage mechanically opens a relay, grounding the low-speed circuit.

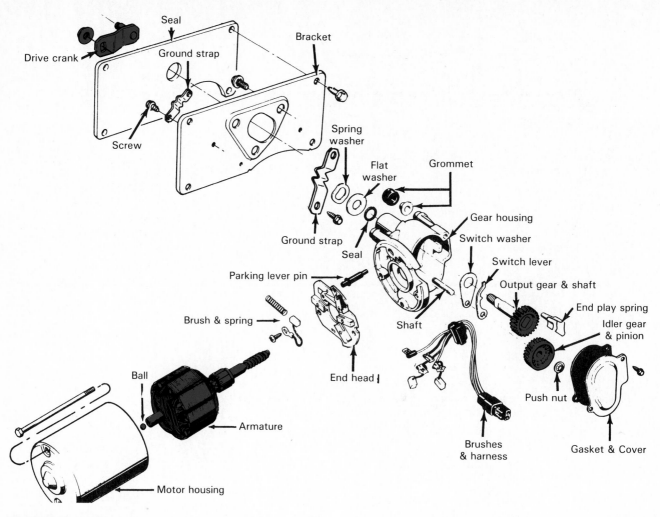

FIGURE 43-12   Wiper motor.

Figure 43-12 shows a two-speed motor used in the system just described.

Single-Speed Motor   Another type of wiper circuit uses a single-speed motor but routes its ground through the wiper switch. Different resistors are used in the ground circuits to give low, medium, and high speeds. The less resistance is put in the ground circuit, the faster the speed.

Intermittent Wipers   With either system, an intermittent circuit can be used. This allows the driver to select the time interval between wiper passes. Typically the passes can be timed from 0 to 15 sec apart. Some systems allow 30 sec between passes. The driver selects the interval by adjusting a knob. The knob controls a variable resistor. The resistor controls the electrical flow to an electronic timing unit. The timing unit then sends the on/off signals to the wiper motor (Figure 43-13).

Washers   Windshield washers are very simple, compared to wipers. When the wash button is pushed,

the ground circuit to the washer pump is completed. The pump operates as long as the button is depressed. The pump can be a diaphragm or turbine-type pump.

Most systems connect the wash button to the wiper motor low-speed circuit, which will cycle the wipers as long as the button is depressed.

Another wash mechanism uses air pressure. The pressure is obtained from the spare tire and fed to an enclosed tank half filled with washer fluid. The air pressure on the enclosed fluid is enough to drive it through the hoses and out the washer nozzle. A check valve between the spare tire and washer reservoir stops airflow below a preset level. This level is the lowest safe spare tire pressure, around 28 psi.

Power Door Locks

Electric   Most power door locks are powered by a solenoid which operates the locking mechanism. A master switch on the driver's door or on the center console operates a relay, which in turn sends current

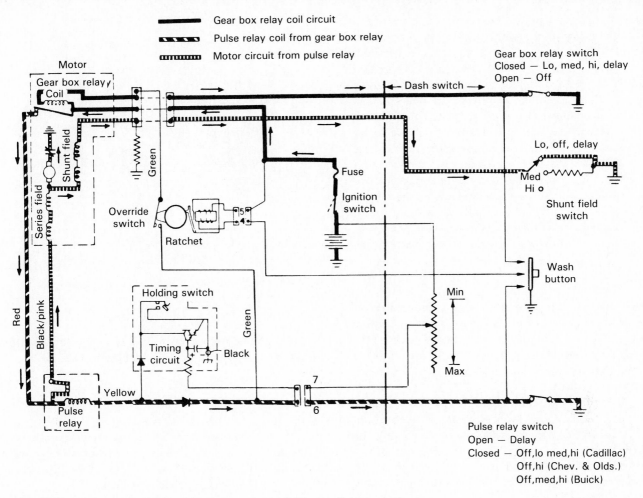

Legend:
━━━━ Gear box relay coil circuit
▬▬▬ Pulse relay coil from gear box relay
▭▭▭ Motor circuit from pulse relay

Gear box relay switch
Closed — Lo, med, hi, delay
Open — Off

Motor

Gear box relay
Coil

Shunt field

Series field

Override switch

Ratchet

Green

Fuse

Ignition switch

Dash switch

Lo, off, delay
Med
Hi

Shunt field switch

Wash button

Holding switch

Timing circuit

Black

Green

Red

Black/pink

Yellow

Pulse relay

Min

Max

7

6

Pulse relay switch
Open — Delay
Closed — Off,lo med,hi (Cadillac)
        Off,hi (Chev. & Olds.)
        Off,med,hi (Buick)

FIGURE 43-13 Wiper/washer schematic. (General Motors Corporation)

to each of the solenoids, locking all four doors. If you look at Figure 43-14, you can see that the locks can also be operated manually. This is a safety precaution, preventing passengers from being trapped in a locked car in the event of electrical failure.

Some automobiles have a timing delay which allows you to lock the doors, exit from the driver's side, and close the door, and the door will then lock.

Vacuum Another type of power door lock is vacuum

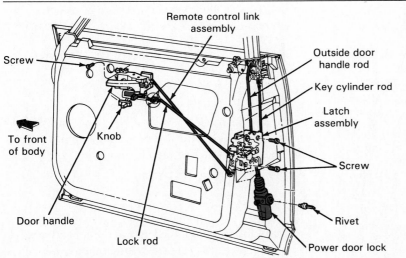

Remote control link assembly

Screw

To front of body

Knob

Door handle

Lock rod

Outside door handle rod

Key cylinder rod

Latch assembly

Screw

Rivet

Power door lock

FIGURE 43-14 Power door locks. (Ford Motor Company)

operated. Vacuum comes from the intake manifold or a vacuum pump on diesel engines. The vacuum is brought to the doors in a vacuum hose. In the door the vacuum operates a vacuum motor. A vacuum motor uses a spring-loaded diaphragm enclosed in a housing. A rod is attached to the diaphragm at one end and the lock mechanism at the other. When the driver's door is locked, vacuum is switched to all the locks. The vacuum pulls the diaphragm against its spring. This pulls the rod and closes the lock. As long as there is vacuum, the door will stay locked. Opening the driver's lock releases the vacuum, and the springs force the diaphragms back and the locks open.

A vacuum reservoir is used to provide one application of the locks when the engine isn't running.

Power Windows

Power windows have been a feature of the luxury car since the early 1950s. At that time, General Motors employed a hydraulic unit, and Ford used electric motors. General Motors soon followed suit with electric motors when hydraulic lines within the doors ruptured with some frequency.

Today's electric-motor-powered window is quite simple. A motor takes the place of the hand crank (Figure 43-15). A switch activates a relay, closing the power circuit to the motor. The activating switch can reverse the current flow, causing the motor to run in one direction or the other. This allows the window to be raised or lowered. A **limiter switch** stops the motor when the window is fully opened or fully closed.

Electric windows are wired through the driver's control panel. This lets the driver open and close all

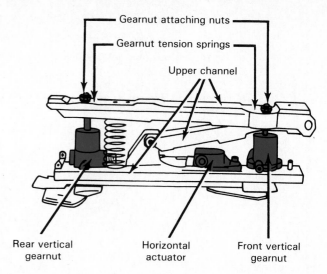

FIGURE 43-16 Six-way power seat mechanism.

windows. This master control panel may also lock all windows so children can't accidentally open the rear windows.

Power Seats

Power seats generally come in two configurations, four-way and six-way. Four-way power seats move forward and backward plus up and down. Six-way seats add a forward and backward tilt.

Figure 43-16 shows a typical six-way power seat application. Generally, two electrical motors are used. One motor provides the entire frame and backward movement. This propels the entire frame along the lower track which is bolted to the floor. The other motor operates the front and rear vertical gearnut. When both operate together, the seat raises and lowers. By operating independently, the front or rear of the seat may be moved, providing the tilt mode.

Cars with computers can store information about seat position. Then the seat can be returned to the preset position with one touch of the memory switch.

Power Mirrors

Power-operated side view mirrors are gaining popularity on modern cars. Here, two motors inside the mirror elevate and lower it or move it left or right. Electric resistance defoggers are also becoming popular on outside mirrors. These are merely miniature versions of electric rear window defoggers.

Trunk Locks

The trunk lock is usually a combination of servo motor and latch. The Cadillac system shown in the schematic

FIGURE 43-15 Power window mechanism. (Ford Motor Company)

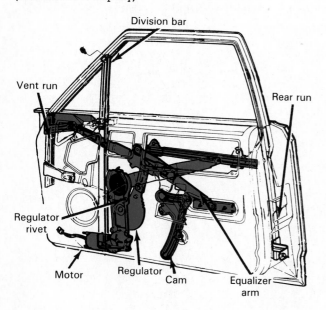

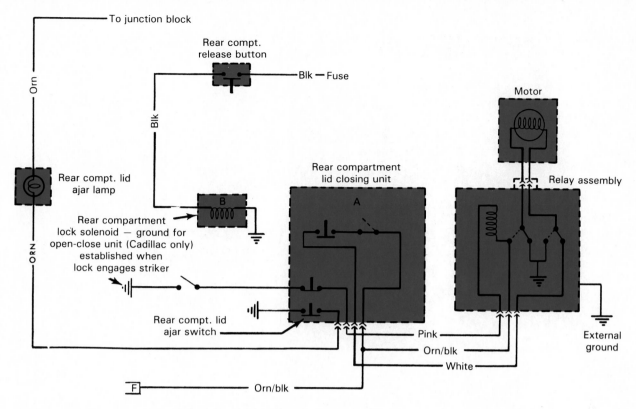

FIGURE 43-17 Trunk lock schematic. (General Motors Corporation)

in Figure 43-17 has the switch located inside the glove box.

When the trunk lid is closed to the first latch, the **lid-closing unit** pulls the trunk lid closed. The **lock solenoid** then secures the lid from accidental opening or tampering.

Most other trunk locks simply use the lock solenoid and delete the lid-closing unit.

Cruise Control

The Chrysler **cruise control**, as shown in Figure 43-18, is *electrically powered* and operates through *manifold vacuum*. Three systems keep the car moving at a predetermined speed; disengage the system when the clutch, brake, or throttle is applied; and allow speed to be resumed after disengagement.

On the Chrysler system shown, the cruise control switch is located on the turn signal lever. To operate the unit, the switch is turned to the "on" position. When the car reaches the desired speed, the "speed set" button is depressed. This will maintain the desired speed and will keep that speed in the memory.

To disengage the system, any contact with the clutch, brake, or accelerator pedal will return control to the driver, as will moving the switch to the "off" position. To resume the speed set in the memory, the slide switch is moved to the "resume" position.

Operation of the unit begins with a speedometer-type cable leading from the transmission to the servo unit. Inside the servo unit the cable's rotation is converted into an electrical impulse by a sending unit. Another cable takes the rotational motion to the speedometer. The control unit uses electronic circuitry to run a vacuum servo unit. The varying vacuum signal opens and closes the servo, which is linked to the throttle at the carburetor.

Warning Devices

Every few years automobile manufacturers add **warning devices** to alert the driver to some existing hazard. The first warning device was the buzzer indicating the key had been left in the ignition switch when the door was opened.

Today, additional warnings in the forms of lights or buzzers have been added to further notify the driver of dangerous conditions. These include seat belts unfastened (lights or buzzer), door ajar light, parking brake light, low fuel warning light, low brake fluid light, brake lining wear light, and, in many cars, a signal warning light to indicate that something is wrong within the engine compartment.

Computerized cars replace many buzzers with voice modules. These modules actually voice the warning "door ajar," for example.

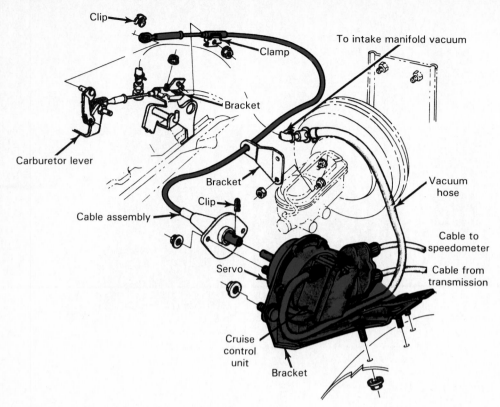

FIGURE 43-18 Cruise control. (Chrysler Corporation)

Headlight Dimmer

The **automatic headlight dimmer** (Figure 43-19) switches the headlamps to low beam when an oncoming car approaches. To accomplish this, a **photoamplifier** (photoelectric cell) senses the oncoming vehicle's headlights. Through a relay, this information is translated to the dimmer switch, lowering the headlight beams. The driver may override the automatic control by touching the floor-mounted dimmer switch. When the switch is released, control returns to the photoamplifier.

Sun and Moon Roofs

Sun and moon roofs are openings in the top of the car. These openings may be fitted with glass or sliding metal covers. Figure 43-20 shows an example of this. To operate, the driver actuates a two-position switch with the ignition switch on. The sun or moon roof will begin to move back into a storage area between the roof and the headliner. The panel will stop moving anytime the switch is released. Operation is by electric motor.

FIGURE 43-19 Automatic headlight dimmer. (General Motors Corporation)

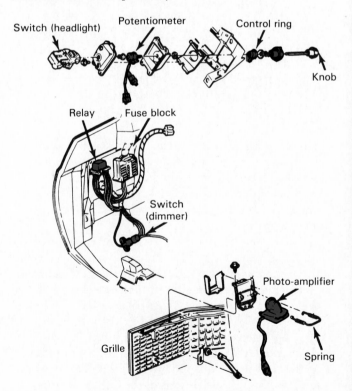

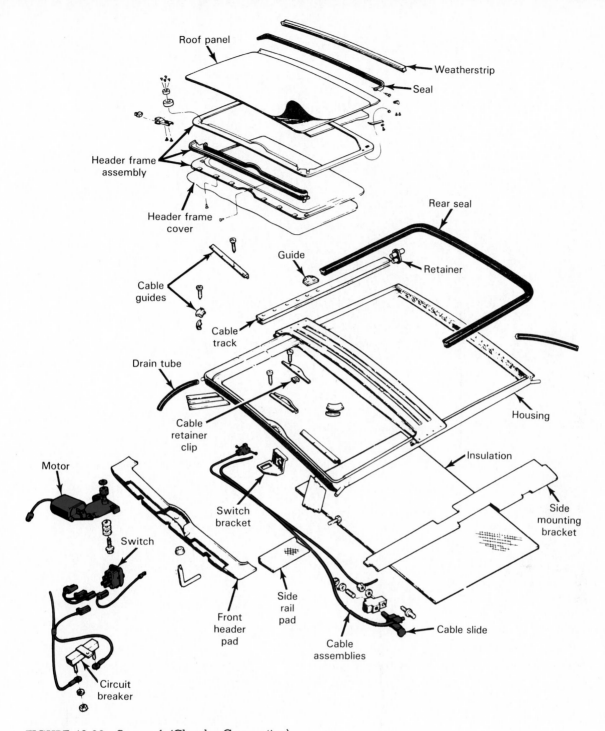

Roof panel

Weatherstrip

Seal

Header frame
assembly

Header frame
cover

Cable
guides

Guide

Rear seal

Retainer

Cable
track

Drain tube

Cable
retainer
clip

Housing

Motor

Insulation

Switch
bracket

Side
mounting
bracket

Switch

Front
header
pad

Side
rail
pad

Cable
assemblies

Cable slide

Circuit
breaker

FIGURE 43-20   Sun roof. (Chrysler Corporation)

Radio and Antennas

When the operator turns the radio on, the **power antenna** (Figure 43-21) raises automatically. When the radio is turned off, the antenna lowers. This is accomplished through a circuit from the battery through a relay to the antenna motor. When the antenna reaches its highest or lowest position, a *limit switch* automatically stops the motor.

The radio is connected to the ignition switch in most cars and will not operate until the ignition switch is turned to "on" or "accessory."

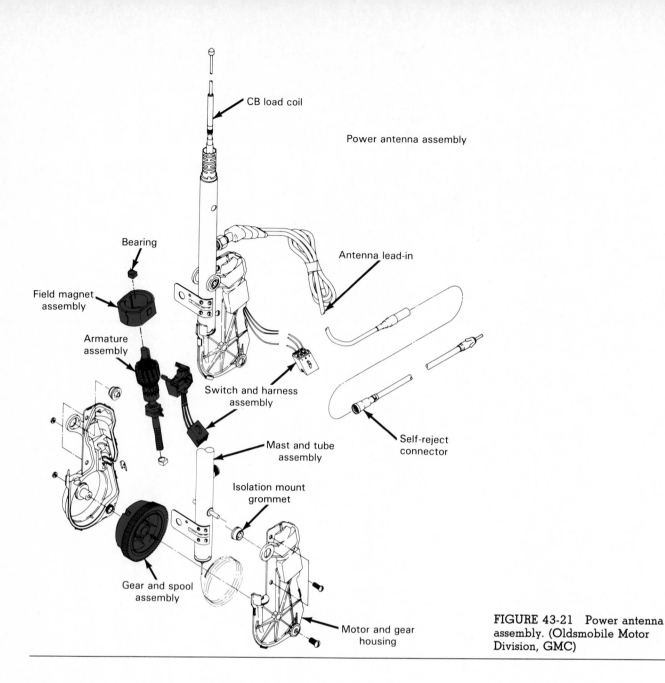

CB load coil

Power antenna assembly

Bearing

Field magnet assembly

Antenna lead-in

Armature assembly

Switch and harness assembly

Self-reject connector

Mast and tube assembly

Isolation mount grommet

Gear and spool assembly

Motor and gear housing

FIGURE 43-21   Power antenna assembly. (Oldsmobile Motor Division, GMC)

THE LUCAS SWITCH

You know what I like about British car people? They know how crazy they are. And they don't even care.

Maybe it all has to do with sportsmanship. The traditional British attitude is one of sportsmanship and perseverance; where's the challenge, where's the sport, in climbing into a car knowing that it will start when you turn the key? Where's the sense of adventure and excitement, the tension inherent in the anticipation of unfolding circumstances: Will it start? Will the fuel pump even click?

At the heart of the contest is, of course, the Lucas electrical system, which has become even more of a symbol of British car ownership than a pool of oil on the garage floor.

The fun part of Lucas electrics is their unpredictability. There is no real challenge, you see, in knowing what's going to fail. When I was growing up, standard equipment in the trunk of every Jaguar was a rock about the size of a softball with which to bash on the SU fuel pump whenever it quit its clickety-clicketing. No particular adventure, just

a ho-hum bashing every week or so; and thus the SU achieved a sort of predictable reliability. Boring.

What we need to keep the blood racing is *true* unpredictability. I know a guy who is building replicas of a certain Lotus, only he is using Japanese components. Horrors! Even though he offers a fake plastic oil pool to toss beneath the car in case your friends come over to see it in the garage, the use of Japanese components negates the true quirky spirit of things mechanical. British.

He has, however, been thinking of retaining at least a semblance of tradition: He wants to put a switch on the dash that reads *Lucas*, which whenever you throw it, it turns something off.

I would suggest going a bit further. In these days of microprocessors, it should be fairly simple to create a sort of mini-computer with about 64K of random capacity. We could program this little gem so that when you threw the *Lucas* switch, absolutely nothing would happen—at least not right away. But according to its own internal random number generation, the computer could put into action a whole sequence of electrical events, *all* completely beyond prediction.

There you would be, driving along in the rain, and presto! The windshield wipers would fail! Pounding on relays and tracing circuits would have absolutely no effect on them, either; but they would start again just as mysteriously, at some future time determined only by the computer, the only predictable factor being the presence of sunshine.

I myself have been playing Lucas roulette for years, being somewhat addicted to Lotuses, in which the Lucas relays are always installed upside-down so they can catch rain water. Never have I seen a manufacturer so dedicated to a multiplicity of wires, all color-coded with various stripes and designs, every wire distinguishable from every other—but with no guarantee whatsoever that a diligent electron could find its way from one end of the wire to the other.

And I, like other British car owners, have come to the odd state of *appreciating* the bizarre behavior of the electrical system, the gearbox, the weatherproofing. There is a sort of Zen acceptance of the Mysterious involved in the ownership of a British car, an understanding of the capricious universe not found in owners of German or Swedish machinery, who think they can control events.

Satch Carlson
Autoweek
Division of Crain Communications

TRADE TERMS

Ammeter
Automatic Headlight Dimmer
Balanced Coil Gauges
Cruise Control
Digital Gauges
Electric Tachometer
Indicator Lamps
Lid-closing Unit
Limiter Switch
Lock Solenoid
Mechanical Tachometer

Microprocessors
Moon Roof
Photo Amplifier
Power Antenna
Speedometer
Sun Roof
Tachometer
Temperature Circuit
Thermal Control Gauges
Variable Resistor
Warning Devices

REVIEW QUESTIONS

1. What part moves in a thermal controlled gauge?
2. In a balanced coil gauge, which coil carries a constant current, and which coil carries a variable current?
3. Why does a mechanical gauge incorporate a hair spring in the gauge dial?
4. Explain how a fuel level sender operates.
5. Name two types of tachometers.
6. What do the initials LED mean?
7. Describe the vertical operation of a power seat.
8. What two power sources operate a cruise control?
9. What is the main controlling device in an automatic headlight dimmer?
10. Are sun roofs electrical, pneumatic, or vacuum operated?

44

Heating and Air Conditioning

INTRODUCTION

Almost all of today's vehicles are equipped with heating systems. More than three quarters of these also have air-conditioning units. Regardless of outside temperature extremes, these systems help maintain temperature, humidity, and proper ventilation for the comfort of the driver and passengers.

When a vehicle is driven in oppressive summer heat, interior temperatures can climb above outside air temperatures. One reason for this is solar radiation, or sunlight. Solar radiation is absorbed by the vehicle's glass and roof panels at a greater rate than it can be dissipated into the outside air. In addition, radiating heat off the hot pavement, the engine, the automatic transmission, and the exhaust system helps interior temperatures to rise. Automotive air-conditioning units lower these temperatures, and humidity as well (Figure 44-1).

Air conditioners can become important safety factors. They can prevent driver fatigue and discomfort and can help reduce driver irritation and hostility. Needless to say, effective heater operation can become a safety issue when driving a vehicle in subzero winter weather.

OBJECTIVES

When you have completed this chapter, you should be able to

- Explain the basic theory of heat transfer as it applies to automotive heating and air-conditioning systems
- Name and describe the functions of heating-system components
- Name and describe the functions of air-conditioning system components
- Explain the differences between expansion-valve receiver/drier systems and expansion-tube accumulator air-conditioning systems
- Describe the components of automatic temperature control systems
- Describe the basic procedures involved in discharging, evacuating, leak-testing, and charging air-conditioning systems
- Explain the importance of manifold gauges in troubleshooting and servicing air-conditioning systems

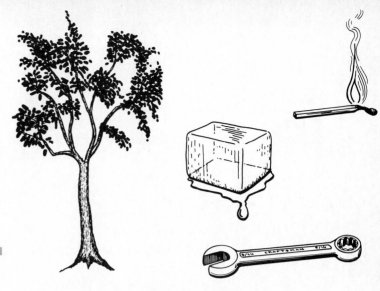

FIGURE 44-2 All objects contain heat.

cause substances to change state, such as the melting of a frozen ice cube into liquid water or the boiling of liquid water into vapor (evaporation).

All substances contain some heat (Figure 44-2), that is, all substances above −459°F. At −459°F, or **absolute zero,** scientists tell us that all molecular activity stops.

Temperature is heat intensity, not heat quantity. What you can measure with a thermometer is called *sensible heat*. Another type of heat, *latent heat*, occurs when a substance changes state. We'll talk more about **change of state** later. Heat quantity is measured in the **British thermal unit** (BTU). A BTU is the heat energy required to raise the temperature of 1 lb of pure water 1°F Fahrenheit (at sea level).

Entropy

The law of entropy states that all substances will eventually be the same temperature. Therefore, there is always movement of heat from a hot object to a cold object (Figure 44-3). (There is no such thing as "cold,"

FIGURE 44-3 Heat moves from warm objects to cooler ones.

70° air temperature

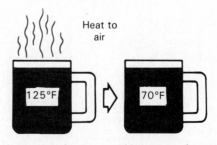

Heat moves from warm objects to cooler one

Heat from sun and outside air

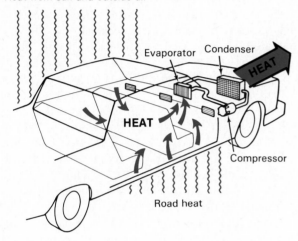

FIGURE 44-1 Heat flow in an air-conditioned car.

Heaters and air conditioners do not generally require servicing at specific mileage intervals. Instead, service is usually generated by a customer complaint: The heater doesn't get hot; the heater fan doesn't work; the air conditioner is not cold enough. These complaints must be fielded by the mechanic or service writer and the unit made to function properly. This chapter will introduce you to these two units (heating and air conditioning), how they work, and what types of service and maintenance must be performed.

> CAUTION: Do not work on an air-conditioning unit without the proper tools and training. Do not attempt to bleed or charge the system until you have been given one-on-one instructions by a professional.

HEAT TRANSFER

What Is Heat?

Heat is a basic form of energy that, among other things, causes substances to rise in temperature. It can also

Heat is absorbed
as water vaporizes

Heat is given off
as water condenses

Heat is given off
as water turns to ice

Evaporation   **Condensation**   **Freezing**

FIGURE 44-4   Evaporation, condensation, and freezing.

just an absence of heat in some objects.) The rate at which this *heat transfer* occurs depends on the temperature differential between the two objects; the rate increases as the temperature differential increases.

Now that we have seen a little about the flow of heat (warm to cold), let's look at another aspect of heat and the effect of heat on other objects—change of state. This term is very important to air conditioning because changes of state of the refrigerant within the air-conditioning system are happening all the time.

Change of State

There are three processes that describe a change of state: **evaporation, condensation,** and freezing (Figure 44-4).

Evaporation   *Evaporation* is the term used when enough heat is added to change a liquid substance to a **vapor** (gas). You are familiar with boiling water and the vapor (steam) that is given off. At the **boiling point** of water (212°F), enough heat is absorbed by the water to change its state. The liquid becomes a vapor. This is called evaporation.

Condensation   Condensation is the term used to describe the reverse of the evaporation process. If you take a vapor and remove enough heat from it, a change of state will occur which causes the vapor to become liquid. The change of vapor to a liquid is called condensation.

Freezing   Freezing is another change of state. Freezing

results when heat is removed from a liquid substance until it becomes a solid. In the case of water, when heat is removed you have ice.

The greatest quantity of heat movement occurs during a change of state. British thermal units are absorbed during evaporation, and they are given off during condensation. This quantity, called latent heat, cannot be read on a thermometer.

When heat is added to a container holding 1 lb of water at 212°F (at sea level), the water will absorb 970 Btu of latent heat without any change in the thermometer reading; however, a change of state from liquid to vapor will occur. The heat that is absorbed is called the **latent heat of evaporation.** The vapor will retain the 970 Btu because they are required to cause the change of state (Figure 44-5).

When heat is removed from 1 lb of water vapor at 212°F (at sea level), the vapor will give off its 970 Btu of heat without causing a drop in the thermometer reading. However, a change of state from vapor to liquid will occur. This heat that is given off is called the **latent heat of condensation** (Figure 44-6).

HEATING

Operation

Here's how the earliest heaters worked. A small radiator and fan were located in the passenger compartment. To operate the heater, a valve allowed hot water from

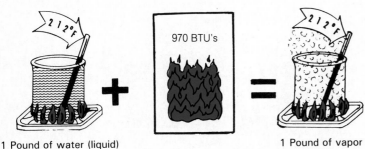

1 Pound of water (liquid)   1 Pound of vapor

FIGURE 44-5   Latent heat of evaporation.

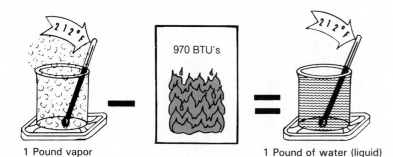

1 Pound vapor   970 BTU's   1 Pound of water (liquid)   **FIGURE 44-6** Latent heat of condensation.

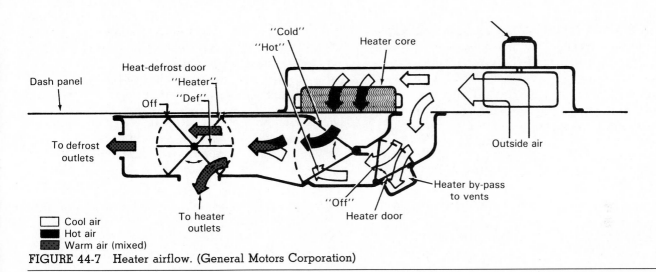

Cool air
Hot air
Warm air (mixed)

FIGURE 44-7 Heater airflow. (General Motors Corporation)

the engine to flow through the radiator while the fan blew air across the coils, thus blowing warm air into the vehicle interior. To turn the heater off, the flow of hot water was stopped, and the fan was turned off.

Air Flow   In today's automobile, the theory is the same, but the application is a bit different (Figure 44-7). Air is drawn from outside or inside the car by a blower motor (or **ram air** as the vehicle moves through the air) and passed to the heater core. The heater core is the small radiator. If the *hot/cold* door is in the hot position, the air will pass over the heater core, which radiates heat into the airstream. If the door is in the cold position, air will bypass the heater core.

After the warm air moves past the *hot* door, it comes to the defroster door. If the defroster door is in the heater position, air will be admitted into the floor area. If it is in the off position, no air can enter the compartment. In the defrost position, the warm air is directed through hoses and vents to the windshield.

Components

Let's now look at the individual components. These consist of a core, a fan, ducting, and controls.

Heater Core   Figure 44-8 shows the heater core in an exploded view of the core housing. The core is simply a small radiator or **heat exchanger.** As hot coolant passes through the core, copper or aluminum fins attached to the core tubes draw heat from the coolant. When air passes across these fins, it is heated and is either exhausted into the interior or is blocked from entering the car.

FIGURE 44-8 Heater core. (Ford Motor Company)

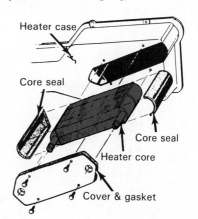

Heater case
Core seal
Core seal
Heater core
Cover & gasket

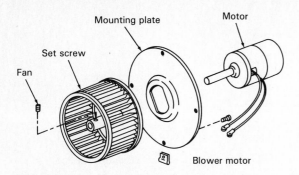

FIGURE 44-9 Blower fan and motor.

Blower Fans Most common is the *squirrel cage* blower fan, shown in Figure 44-9. It's called a squirrel cage fan because it looks like the exercising runner found in small animal cages.

These very efficient fans can pull air through ducting and move it out at a 90° angle. The fan is attached to a simple 12V motor.

Controls The heater controls are found on the instrument panel and may be a combination of electrical, manual, and vacuum operations. Figure 44-10 shows a typical control bezel. The electric fan may have a simple on/off arrangement or a more complex, multispeed configuration. Multiple speeds are accomplished by wiring the fan through one or more resistors that step down voltage to the motor.

The heater/defroster control operates a vent door that directs hot air to the windshield or vehicle interior. On economy cars, this control is usually manually operated through a series of cables and levers. In more expensive luxury cars, the controls may be vacuum operated.

The sliding control shown at the bottom of the bezel in Figure 44-10 is the heat control. Generally, it opens and closes the vent door from the heater core. The wider the door is opened, the more hot air is allowed into the vehicle interior.

Figure 44-11 shows these controls in a typical underdash arrangement.

Rear-Window Defroster/Defogger Some vehicles are equipped with rear-window defrosters or defoggers to remove condensation from the rear window for improved visibility. These are totally separate from the main heater/defroster/air-conditioning system.

FIGURE 44-10 Heater controls. (General Motors Corporation)

HEATER FUNCTIONAL TEST								
CONTROLS					**SYSTEM RESPONSE**			
STEP	MODE LEVER	TEMPERATURE LEVER	FAN SWITCH	BLOWER SPEED	POWER VENT OUTLET	HEATER OUTLET	DEFROSTER OUTLETS	SIDE WINDOW DEFOG OUTLETS
1	VENT	COLD	OFF	OFF	NO AIR FLOW	NO AIR FLOW	NO AIR FLOW	NO AIR FLOW
2	VENT	COLD	OFF TO HI*	OFF TO HIGH	AMBIENT AIR FLOW	NO AIR FLOW	NO AIR FLOW	NO AIR FLOW
3	HEAT	COLD TO HOT	HI	HIGH	NO AIR FLOW	COLD TO HOT AIR FLOW	MINIMUM COLD TO HOT AIR FLOW	MINIMUM AIR FLOW
4	DEFROST	COLD TO HOT	HI	HIGH	NO AIR FLOW	MINIMUM COLD TO HOT AIR FLOW	COLD TO HOT AIR FLOW	AIR FLOW

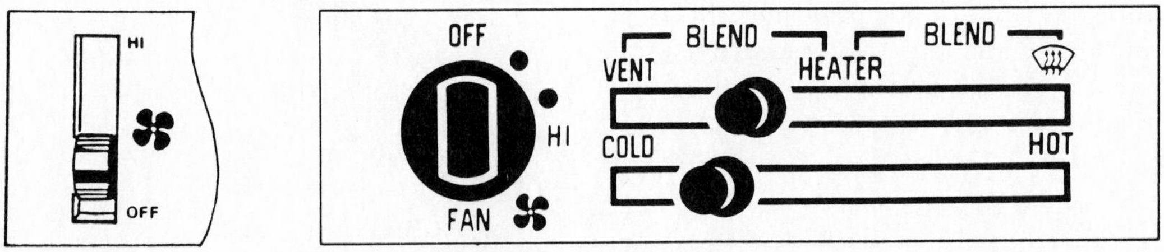

HI / OFF

OFF / HI / FAN

BLEND / VENT / HEATER / BLEND / COLD / HOT

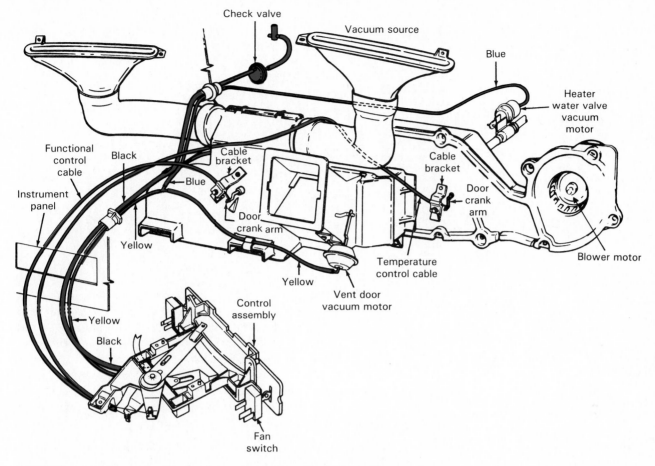

Check valve

Vacuum source

Blue

Heater
water valve
vacuum
motor

Functional
control
cable

Black

Cable
bracket

Blue

Cable
bracket

Door
crank
arm

Instrument
panel

Door
crank arm

Yellow

Yellow

Temperature
control cable

Blower motor

Yellow

Vent door
vacuum motor

Control
assembly

Black

Fan
switch

FIGURE 44-11   Control cables and vacuum system. (Ford Motor Company)

There are two types of rear-window defrosters: The electric-resistance grid type and the blower type. The blower type is nothing more than a small electric fan that directs interior air from the rear-seat area through ducts against the inside of the rear window (Figure 44-12). The resistance type consists of a series of silver oxide grid lines painted inside the rear window. As current passes through the grid, resistance heating takes place, removing condensation from inside the window and melting accumulated ice from outside the window. Figure 44-13 shows how to check voltage in a defective defogger grid.

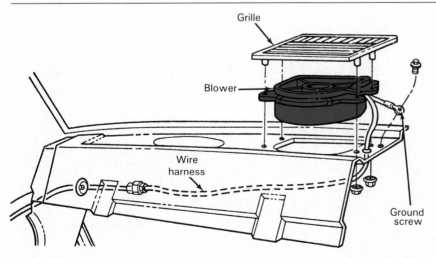

Grille

FIGURE 44-12   Rear-window defogger fan system. (General Motors Corporation)

Blower

Wire
harness

Ground
screw

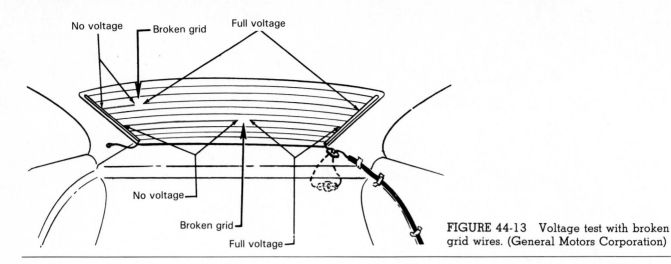

AIR CONDITIONING

Fundamentals

Before we can begin a discussion of **air conditioning**, you must understand the principles of *refrigeration*—or, if you will, what makes "cold."

As you remember from the previous discussion, there is no such thing as cold, only the absence of heat. How, then, is this heat drawn off or removed? Evaporation is the most efficient means of removing heat.

Your body has a natural refrigeration system to keep it cool. You perspire when you begin to get hot. That perspiration evaporates, carrying away body heat with it.

A refrigerator uses the same evaporation process, but water is not efficient enough to cool a refrigerator to the freezing point or below. To remove that much heat, science has developed a product called *freon*. Freon evaporates rapidly and will boil at room temperature.

Imagine a refrigerator with a pan of freon sitting on the shelf. As the freon evaporates, it draws heat out of the inside of the refrigerator. If time, money, and safety were no problem, you could keep replacing freon in the pan in the refrigerator to keep the food cool. This is, however, a very inefficient way to do things.

Instead, let's capture the freon as it evaporates, condense it back into a liquid, and let it evaporate all over again—a closed refrigeration system. Put that system in your car, add a fan, and you'll have air conditioning.

Types of Systems

Automotive air-conditioning systems fall into two major groups: **expansion-valve** types and **expansion-tube** types.

Expansion Valve Figure 44-14 shows a complete expansion-valve-type refrigeration system. The **compressor** which pushes freon gas (the refrigerant) into the **condenser**. Here, the freon converts from a gas into a liquid. The **receiver/drier** picks up the condensed freon and sends it to the **evaporator**. The freon then evaporates by boiling and draws off heat from the surrounding atmosphere (thereby cooling it). The compressor draws off the evaporated gas, pumping it once more into the condenser.

Expansion Tube Figure 44-15 shows a typical expansion-tube refrigeration system compared to an expansion-valve system. Like the expansion-valve system, it uses a compressor, condenser, and evaporator. But the expansion-tube system has no receiver/drier. Instead, an **accumulator** is used. And whereas the receiver/drier is on the high-pressure side of the system, the accumulator is on the low-pressure side.

We have mentioned that an air conditioner has a **high side** and a **low side**. This is true of all air-

FIGURE 44-14 Air-conditioning system.

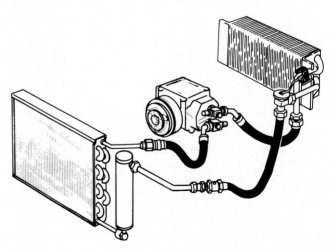

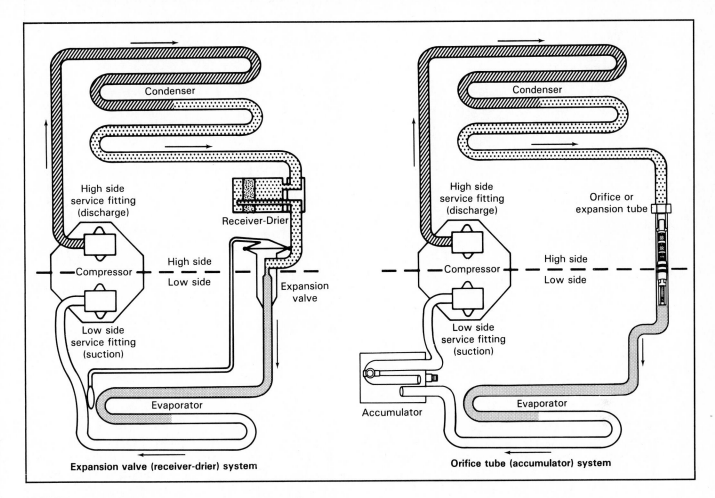

FIGURE 44-15 Expansion-valve and expansion-tube systems.

conditioning systems, and the division of these two "sides" always occurs at the same point.

Parts of a System

High Side   High side simply refers to the side of the system in which high pressure exists. As shown in Figure 44-15, the high side is (following the flow arrows) from the outlet side of the compressor, through the condenser, through the receiver/drier, and to the expansion valve.

It is the compressor's job to create higher pressure (and higher temperature) so the refrigerant will be able to condense and release heat at the condenser. A pressure differential is created at the expansion valve or tube—the dividing point on the front side of the system. The expansion valve will be explained in detail later in this chapter.

Low Side   Low side is the term used for the portion of the air-conditioning system in which low pressure and temperature exist. From the expansion valve or tube, through the evaporator and to the inlet side of the compressor, the refrigerant is in a low-pressure

state. This allows heat to be transferred from inside the car to the "colder" refrigerant, which then carries it away.

Components

Now let's look at the various air-conditioning system components beginning with freon refrigerant.

Refrigerant   All liquids evaporate, some faster than others. Gasoline evaporates faster than water, and lacquer thinner evaporates faster than gasoline. Even more rapidly evaporating liquids are freon, liquid oxygen, and liquid nitrogen. Freon (Figure 44-16) is the refrigerant chosen for automotive air conditioning. It is odorless, nontoxic, nonflammable, nonexplosive, and noncorrosive and possesses an ideal operating range. Below $-22°F$ ($-30°C$) freon exists as a liquid; above $-22°F$ it will boil or vaporize. It is this very low boiling point which tends to absorb heat above $-20°F$. Refrigeration freon is called Freon 12 or **Refrigerant 12.** Its technical name is dichlorodifluoromethane. The industry has shortened this to R-12.

R-12 should be handled with caution. We said

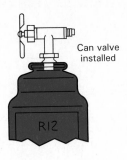

Can valve
installed

FIGURE 44-16 Refrigerant.

earlier that R-12 is both safe and dangerous. Because of its low boiling temperature, it will *boil violently* at normal room temperatures, rapidly freezing anything in its path. Direct contact with escaping R-12 could cause severe frostbite to your hands and could even damage your eyes. For this reason, *always wear goggles* when evacuating, charging, or performing any major service to an air-conditioning system.

Never release R-12 in the presence of an open flame or burn it in a car engine. Deadly *phosgene gas* is formed when R-12 is burned—a poison gas used in World War I.

Pressure/Temperature Relationship of R-12 It is important to know the pressure/temperature relationship of R-12. If the pressure of R-12 is low, the temperature will also be low. If the pressure of R-12 is high, the temperature will also be high. Remembering this is important because pressure is very important in the function of the air-conditioning system. Figure 44-17 charts the pressure/temperature relationship of R-12.

We mentioned that R-12 vaporizes at a low temperature and absorbs great quantities of heat. This is because the R-12 is under very low pressure at this point in the system (in the evaporator). Thus, a low temperature is also obtained. This temperature is much lower than the temperature of the air inside the car; therefore, the heat will travel to the colder R-12. As the heat is absorbed, the R-12 vaporizes and carries the heat through the compressor to the condenser.

At the condenser, the R-12 is at a high temperature and high pressure. The temperature of the R-12 is higher than the outside air at the condenser. The heat again flows from the warmer to the colder object, and thus the heat is released outside the vehicle. By giving off heat, the R-12 condenses back to a liquid, and the cycle starts over again (Figure 44-18).

The two changes of state which we have previously mentioned—evaporation and condensation—take place within every air-conditioning cycle. That is, heat is absorbed from inside the car by the cold, liquid R-12 flowing through the evaporator.

Evaporation takes place, and the heat-laden R-12 vapors move out of the evaporator to the compressor. Here, the pressure and temperature of the R-12 vapors are increased. The vapors are then pumped to the condenser where heat is transferred to the outside air, and condensation takes place (the R-12, while giving off its heat, returns to a liquid) (Figure 44-19).

R-12 will vaporize at a temperature of −21.7°F when at normal (sea level) **atmospheric pressure.** Decrease the pressure (remember the pressure/temperature relationship), and R-12 will readily vaporize to absorb the latent heat of evaporation at temperatures between 11°F (at 15 psi) and 32°F (at 30 psi) in the

FIGURE 44-17 Pressure/temperature relationship of R-12.

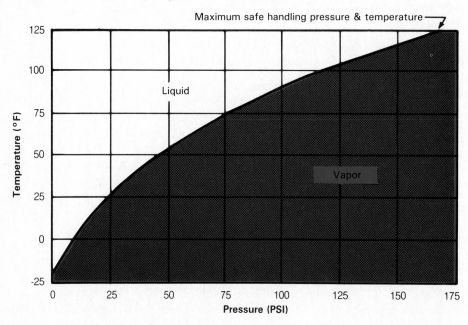

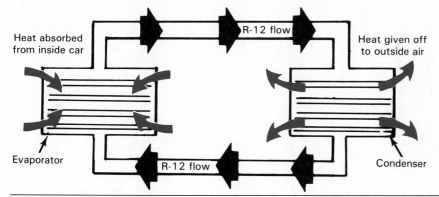

Heat absorbed from inside car

R-12 flow

Heat given off to outside air

Evaporator

R-12 flow

Condenser

FIGURE 44-18   Air conditioner heat exchange.

A - In the evaporator, R-12 liquid absorbs its latent heat of evaporation and becomes a vapor.

B - In the condenser, R-12 vapor gives off its latent heat of condensation and becomes a liquid.

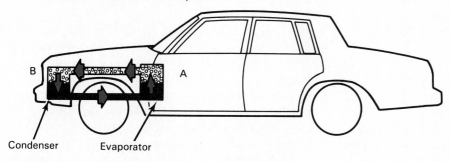

B   A

Condenser   Evaporator

FIGURE 44-19   Latent heat exchanges in the air-conditioning system.

evaporator unit. At higher pressures, R-12 will condense and give off its latent heat of condensation at temperatures between 130°F (at 180 psi) and 150°F (at 230 psi in the condenser).

The latent heat of evaporation of R-12 is 70–71 Btu/lb of refrigerant at normal system operating pressures of 15–30 psi (low side).

Compressor   Compressors are of various makes and types, but they all operate as the "pump" of the system to keep the R-12 circulating and to increase its pressure (Figure 44-20). Other specific functions will be discussed later.

Automotive air-conditioning compressors are belt-driven from the engine crankshaft. They have an electromagnetic clutch which enables the compressor to shut down when compressor operation is not required (Figure 44-21).

The clutch is able to engage or disengage the compressor as required by the air-conditioning control panel setting or by system demands. Some systems use the clutch to cycle compressor operation according to temperature, system pressure sensings, or engine load, while other systems have the compressor running continuously while the system is in the "on" mode.

FIGURE 44-20   Cutaway of a two-cylinder in-line compressor.

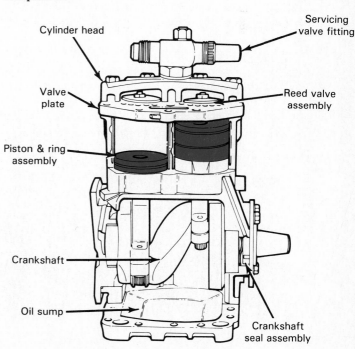

Cylinder head

Servicing valve fitting

Valve plate

Reed valve assembly

Piston & ring assembly

Crankshaft

Oil sump

Crankshaft seal assembly

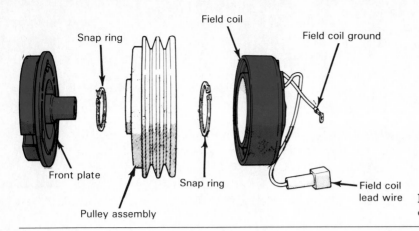

FIGURE 44-21 Typical stationary coil-type clutch assembly.

The compressor, as previously mentioned, acts as the system pump to keep the refrigerant circulating. The **suction side** of the compressor draws in the refrigerant vapor. From there, the R-12 passes to the outlet or **discharge side** of the compressor, where it is compressed (and thus the temperature is raised). The high-pressure, high-temperature, vaporous R-12 is then forced out of the compressor and on into the condenser.

There are two basic types of air-conditioning compressors: the piston type and the rotary type. Piston-type compressors may have their pistons arranged in an inline, **axial**, **radial**, or V design. **Rotary vane compressors** have no pistons.

Piston Compressor Operation The piston compressor is designed to have an intake stroke and a compressor stroke for each cylinder. On the intake stroke, the R-12 from the low side of the system (evaporator) is drawn into the compressor. The intake of R-12 occurs through intake **reed valves.** These one-way valves control the flow of refrigerant vapors into the cylinder (Figure 44-22).

During the upward compression stroke, the vaporous R-12 is compressed. This increases both the pressure and the temperature of the heat-carrying refriger-

ant. The outlet side (discharge) reed valves then open to allow the refrigerant to move to the condenser. The outlet reed valves are the beginning of the high side of the system.

Rotary Vane Compressor Operation Rotary vane compressors consist of a rotor with several vanes and a carefully shaped housing. As the compressor shaft rotates, the vanes and the housing form chambers. The refrigerant is drawn through the suction port into these chambers, which become smaller as the rotor turns. The discharge port is located at the point where the gas is completely compressed (Figure 44-23).

No sealing rings are used in a vane-type compressor. The vanes are sealed against the housing by centrifugal force and lubricating oil. The oil sump is located on the discharge side, so the high pressure tends to force it around the vanes into the low-pressure side. This action ensures continuous lubrication. Because this type of compressor depends on a good oil supply, it is subject to damage if the system charge is lost. A protection device is used to disengage the clutch if this happens.

Condenser The condenser consists of a refrigerant coil mounted in a series of thin cooling fins. This ar-

FIGURE 44-22 Basic piston-type compressor operation.

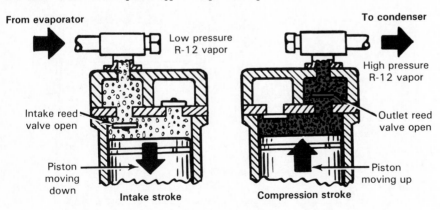

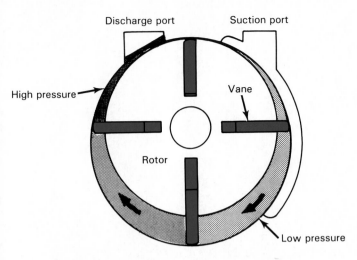

FIGURE 44-23 Sectional view of York rotary vane compressor.

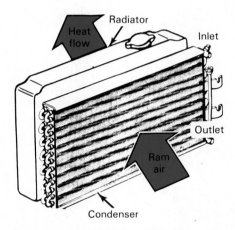

Ram air & heat flow

FIGURE 44-24 Ram air and heat flow in the condenser.

rangement provides maximum surface area for heat transfer within a minimum amount of engine compartment space. The condenser is mounted directly in front of the radiator where it can receive full airflow created by vehicle forward motion and the engine fan (Figure 44-24).

The condenser receives the heat-laden, high-pressure refrigerant vapor from the compressor's discharge hose. This vaporous R-12 enters at the top of the condenser and flows through its coils. Heat follows its natural tendency, flowing from the hot R-12 vapors to the "cooler" ambient air (around the condenser coil).

As the R-12 vapors are cooled and flow down through the condenser, a point is reached where condensation occurs. The vaporous R-12 becomes liquid R-12. At this point of condensation, the largest amount of heat is given by the R-12. The refrigerant in the lower portion of the condenser is a warm, high-pressure liquid. This high-pressure, liquid refrigerant flows from the condenser and on toward the evaporator.

Receiver/Drier The receiver/drier is used on many air-conditioning systems. It receives R-12 flow from the condenser. The receiver/drier is mounted either adjacent to the condenser or somewhere downstream before the expansion valve. It consists of the tank, a filter, a drying agent (**desiccant**), a pickup tube, and (on some applications) a **sight glass** (Figure 44-25). It has several functions.

First, the receiver-drier acts as a storage tank. It receives the liquid R-12 from the condenser and holds this liquid until required by the evaporator. Requirements vary according to operating conditions.

Second, the receiver/drier also acts as a protection agent for the system. The portion of the receiver/drier which contains the drying agent separates any moisture

FIGURE 44-25 Receiver/drier and accumulator location.

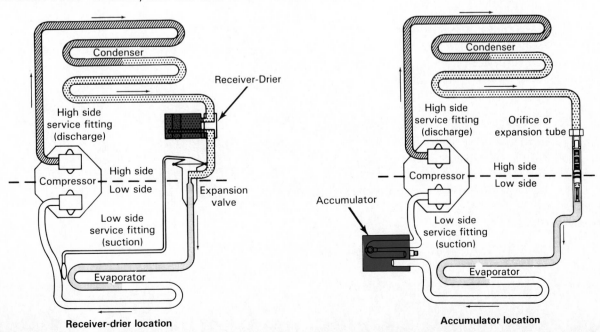

Receiver-drier location

Accumulator location

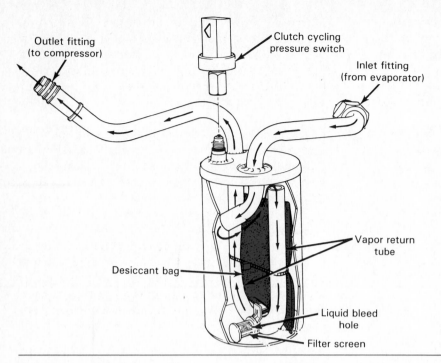

Outlet fitting
(to compressor)

Clutch cycling
pressure switch

Inlet fitting
(from evaporator)

Vapor return
tube

Desiccant bag

Liquid bleed
hole

Filter screen

FIGURE 44-26 Internal view of Ford accumulator assembly.

from the R-12. The drying agent (desiccant) is usually in the form of **silica gel.**

If the receiver/drier is equipped with a sight glass, this component allows the service technician to see bubbles or other contaminants in the system.

Accumulator Note that on General Motors' CCOT **(Cycling Clutch Orifice Tube)** and Ford Motor Company's FFOT (Ford Fixed Orifice Tube) systems, there is no receiver/drier mounted in the high side of the system. Instead, the receiver/drier function is accomplished by a unit called an *accumulator* (Figure 44-26).

This component is mounted in the low side, at the outlet side of the evaporator. The function, however, is basically the same as that of the receiver/drier described above: to accumulate (or store) excess refrigerant and to filter and dry the R-12. The accumulator also contains desiccant (the drying agent) for the latter purpose.

If any liquid passes out of the evaporator, it will be stored by the accumulator. Liquid refrigerant is harmful to the compressor. Moisture is a major enemy of the air-conditioning system, and it is the job of the receiver/drier and accumulator's desiccant to remove any moisture which may enter the system.

If too much moisture enters the system (due to a component malfunction or hose leak), the desiccant will have to be replaced. This replacement may require complete replacement of the receiver/drier or accumulator (desiccant is often nonremovable), or it may involve simply changing the desiccant bag (as in the VIR and VIR-EE systems).

In any case, the receiver/drier and accumulator should be replaced if any contamination is suspected. Moisture which is allowed to mix through the system will combine with the R-12 to form hydrochloric acid harmful to system components. Moisture can also gather on the expansion valve/tube and freeze there. This blocks the flow of R-12 and prevents cooling action at the evaporator.

Evaporator The evaporator, like the condenser, consists of a refrigerant coil mounted in a series of thin cooling fins. The evaporator is usually mounted in a housing under the dash panel or cowl. Warm air from the passenger compartment is blown across the coils and fins (Figure 44-27).

FIGURE 44-27 Evaporator action.

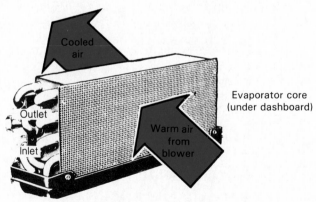

Cooled
air

Evaporator core
(under dashboard)

Outlet

Warm air
from
blower

Inlet

Heat absorbed by evaporator

The evaporator receives refrigerant from the **thermostatic expansion valve** or tube as a low-pressure, cold atomized liquid. As this cold refrigerant passes through the evaporator coils, heat moves from the warm air into the cooler refrigerant. This causes the refrigerant to change from a low-pressure, cold, atomized liquid into a low-pressure, cold, vapor.

The thermostatic expansion valve or tube continually meters the exact amount of refrigerant required to maintain proper heat transfer efficiency. This action also ensures that all the liquid refrigerant will have changed to a vapor by the time it reaches the evaporator outlet. The vaporous R-12 then continues on to the inlet (suction) side of the compressor.

The warm air blown across the evaporator will usually contain some moisture (humidity). The moisture in the air will normally condense on the evaporator coils and be drained off as water. A drain tube in the bottom of the evaporator housing drains the water outside the vehicle.

This dehumidification of the air is an added feature of the air-conditioning system that adds to passenger comfort. It can also be used as a means of controlling fogging of the car windows.

Under certain conditions, however, too much moisture may accumulate on the evaporator coils. An example would be when humidity is extremely high and the maximum cooling mode is selected. The evaporator temperature might become so low that moisture could freeze on the evaporator coils before it can drain off. The ice blocks airflow and stops system cooling action. Many systems include supplemental controls to prevent evaporator freezing.

Refrigerant System Controls

Thermal Expansion Valve/Tube   The refrigerant flow to the evaporator must be controlled to obtain maximum cooling while assuring complete evaporation of the liquid refrigerant within the evaporator. This is accomplished by the thermostatic expansion valve or expansion tube (Figure 44-28). The valve performs the following three functions:

1. *Metering action*: A metered orifice within the valve changes the pressure of the incoming liquid refrigerant from high pressure to a low pressure.
2. *Modulating action*: A thermostatically controlled valve, located within the expansion valve body, fluctuates toward an open or a closed position as required to control the liquid refrigerant passing through the orifice. This supplies the proper amount of refrigerant to the entire evaporator while assuring that all the incoming refrigerant is vaporized.
3. *Controlling action*: The valve must quickly respond to changes in heat load conditions. As increased heat is

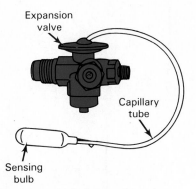

Typical expansion valve

FIGURE 44-28   Typical expansion valve.

sensed, the valve will move toward an open position to increase refrigerant flow. Decreased heat load or increased compressor output volume due to increased engine speed will cause the valve to move toward a closed position, restricting the amount of R-12 entering the evaporator.

Refrigerant from the receiver/drier enters the expansion valve as a liquid under high pressure. As it passes through the metering orifice in the valve, the refrigerant is forced through the small orifice and "sprayed" out the other side. This creates a pressure differential—the pressure and temperature are thus lowered, and the atomized R-12 can flow through the evaporator and become easily vaporized.

Being now at a lower temperature than the interior of the car, the R-12 will absorb heat and carry it away from the passenger compartment.

Expansion Tube   The expansion tube used with General Motors' CCOT system and Ford Motor Company's FFOT system serves the same basic function as the expansion valve but has a different configuration (Figure 44-29).

Both designs create the necessary pressure drop by metering a steady flow of R-12 while the compressor is operating. A cycling clutch switch (either a thermostatic switch or pressure-sensing switch) turns the compressor on and off. The intermittent compressor operation permits control of refrigerant flow and pressure. Like the expansion valve, the expansion tube is mounted on the inlet side of the evaporator.

In-Car Controls   Figure 44-30 shows the interior air-conditioning controls. In most cases, the air-conditioning controls will be coupled with the heater controls as shown in our example of a 1983 Ford.

Moving in a clockwise pattern around the face of the control panel, we come to the *blower switch*. This switch operates at one of four speeds when the *mode*

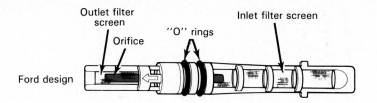

Illustration of orifice tubes used in cycling clutch systems   FIGURE 44-29   Expansion tubes.

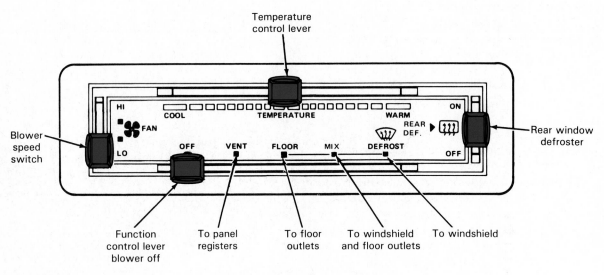

FIGURE 44-30   Air-conditioning/heater control panel. (Ford Motor Company)

FURS, GOGGLES, AND GAUNTLETS

The cars of 1900 were nearly all open—the Renault enclosed driving position had remained unique, an eccentricity viewed with amusement—and this meant that the driver was exposed to all weathers. This was the reason for bearskins, still impressive in today's yellowed photographs, and explains their function: It was the only way to keep warm. This was in spring or autumn (in the depths of winter it was better to give up the idea altogether, in view of the condition of the roads).

The masks, the mufflers, the goggles were all strictly practical accessories often hiding the entire face under the flat, peaked cap worn to fight another terrible enemy, dust.

In the first motoring magazines is found straightforward technical advice ("it is essential to drain the radiator water after each journey, and during pauses it should be kept warm by starting up the engine briefly every twenty minutes or so"), beside invaluable remedies for burns from the exhaust pipe, a process for waterproofing driving clothes, a prescription for "driver's eyesalve" (1 lb cocoa leaf brewed, 1 oz cherry laurel water, ½ oz. sodium borate), a method to prevent steaming of goggles (smear the insides with glycerine), and instructions for cleaning dusty furs at the end of a journey. Fashion advised semiopaque veiling for lady motorists, with a tiny transparent opening over the eyes.

Marco Matteucci
History of the Motor Car
Octopus Books Limited

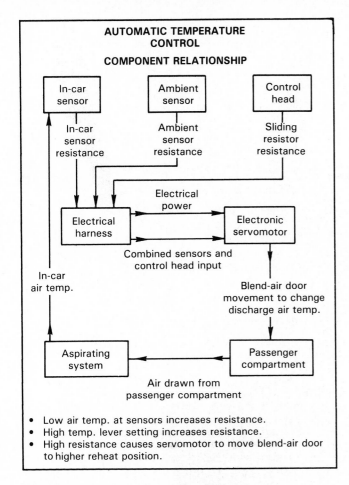

FIGURE 44-31 Air-conditioning system schematic.

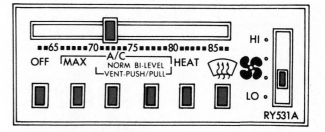

FIGURE 44-32 Automatic temperature control head. (Chrysler Corporation)

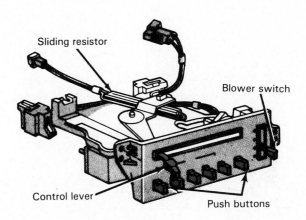

FIGURE 44-33 Internal parts of the automatic temperature control head. (Chrysler Corporation)

lever is *not* in the "off" position. The *temperature control lever* operates a blend door, passing air around or through the heater core. All air is passed through the evaporator. The *mix* switch allows warm or cold air to be vented to the windshield or floor area, while the air conditioner lever controls cold air to the dash panel.

Automatic Temperature Control Some luxury cars are equipped with automatic temperature controls. As the operator, you select the desired interior temperature. The heater and air conditioner then work together to maintain this temperature. Figure 44-31 is a flow diagram showing how this works.

Air is drawn from the passenger compartment by an aspirator (suction) system. This draws driver compartment air over an in-car temperature sensor. The in-car sensor, ambient (outside) sensor, controller, and control head work together to control the electronic servomotor. The servomotor actuates the blend-air door to pass precooled air through, or around, the heater core. This controls and maintains passenger compartment temperature as it was set at the control head.

The control head (Figure 44-32) operates and sets

the temperature you wish to maintain. The sliding control level has a 20° operating range (65°–85°F). The signal is fed to the controller by a sliding resistor at the back of the control lever (Figure 44-33).

When the temperature is set below 65°F, the air conditioner comes on full and cools until you turn it off. Likewise, when the control lever is pushed past 85°F, the heater will operate until you turn it off. This provides rapid cooling and heating when needed to overcome severe **ambient air temperature.**

Some systems are fully electronic. The sliding lever and the resistor are replaced by solid-state parts. System operation remains the same.

TROUBLESHOOTING

Heater System

See Figure 44-34 to search out and discover the problems involved in a malfunctioning automobile heater (the only complaint should be insufficient heat or an inoperative fan or blower). This flowchart will tell you what steps to take and will show you the solutions to the problems you discover.

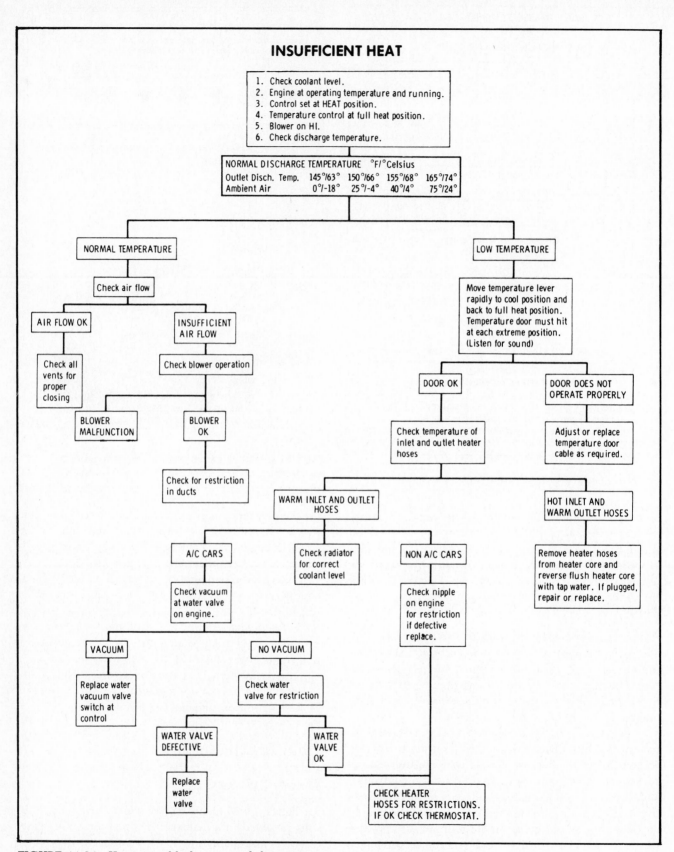

FIGURE 44-34   Heater troubleshooting and diagnosis.

Air Conditioning

Troubleshooting an air conditioner can be a very extensive proposition. You should consult a shop service manual to see what operations to follow prior to trying to discover the source of a problem.

You will also need a **manifold gauge set**, as shown in Figure 44-35. These will allow you to test for proper operating pressures of the freon.

Sight Glass   If a sight glass is used, it will usually be found on the receiver/drier assembly. However, it may be mounted elsewhere in a refrigerant line in the high side of the system, between the condenser and the expansion valve. Most accumulator systems do not use a sight glass. On VIR-type systems, the sight glass is on the VIR housing.

The purpose of the sight glass is to visually check the refrigerant level and condition passing through the system. There are several indicators which help the service technician to diagnose possible problems. These indicators, as viewed through the sight glass, are outlined in the following text and are shown in Figure 44-36.

A clear sight glass indicates the system has the correct charge of refrigerant. It may also indicate that the system has a complete lack of refrigerant, a condi-

FIGURE 44-35   Manifold gauge set.

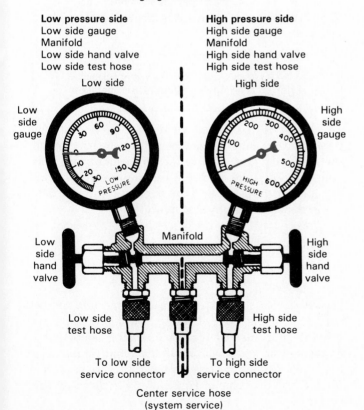

tion accompanied by a lack of any cooling action by the evaporator. Also, the sight glass may be clear, and the system might be overcharged (too much R-12). This must be verified with the test gauge readings.

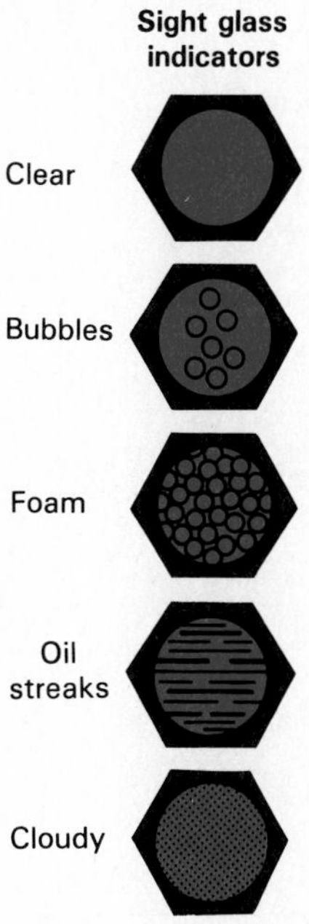

Read the sight glass only when the compressor is running.

A foaming or bubbly sight glass indicates that the system is low on refrigerant and that air has probably entered the system. However, if only occasional bubbles are noticed, during clutch cycling or system start-up, this may be a normal condition.

If oil streaks appear on the sight glass, a lack of refrigerant may be indicated, and the system's compressor oil is circulating through the system.

A cloudy sight glass indicates that the desiccant contained in the receiver/drier (or accumulator) has broken down and is being circulated through the system.

If no sight glass is used, check the system operation with a manifold gauge set or by feeling the temperature of the evaporator inlet and outlet tubes.

Manifold Gauge Set (Test Gauges)   The manifold gauge set is the most important tool used to service air-conditioning systems. The manifold set is used to determine the system's high- and low-side gauge pressures, the correct refrigerant charge, system diagnosis, and operating efficiency. It is designed to read both the high and low sides at the same time, because pressures must be compared to determine system operation. Some vehicles require the use of a third (auxiliary) gauge. All gauges are explained in detail in the following pages and are shown in Figure 44-37.

Low-Side Gauge   **This gauge reads from 0 to 150 psi**

Sight glass indicators

Clear

Bubbles

Foam

Oil streaks

Cloudy

FIGURE 44-36   Sight glass indicators.

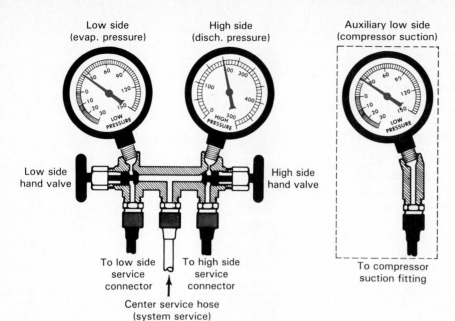

Low side
(evap. pressure)

High side
(disch. pressure)

Auxiliary low side
(compressor suction)

Low side
hand valve

High side
hand valve

To low side
service
connector

To high side
service
connector

Center service hose
(system service)

To compressor
suction fitting

FIGURE 44-37 Servicing with a
manifold gauge set.

(pressure scale) in a clockwise direction and from 0 to 30 in. of Mercury (vacuum scale) in a counterclockwise direction. This low-side gauge is called a **compound gauge** and has a dual purpose—to register both *pressure* and *vacuum*. This gauge may have blue-color identifying features and is used to measure low-side pressure at the **service ports** provided.

High-Side Gauge This gauge reads from 0 to 500 psi in a clockwise direction. The high-scale gauge may have red identifying features and is a pressure gauge only.

Auxiliary Gauge This gauge may be required for testing on Chrysler Corporation vehicles with EPR valves or on Ford Motor Company vehicles with POA valves. This gauge may be either an internal gauge in a three-gauge set or a separate gauge to be used in conjunction with a two-gauge set. The gauge indicator will be within the same range as shown on a low-side gauge. Therefore, the **auxiliary gauge** should be the same type as used for low-side testing.

On Chrysler Corporation systems, this gauge is attached to the additional cylinder head inlet fitting on the compressor. On Ford Motor Company systems, this gauge is attached to the suction fitting.

The manifold is designed to control refrigerant flow. When the manifold test set is connected into the system, pressure is registered on both gauges at all times. During all tests, both the low- and high-side hand valves are in the closed position (turned inward) until the valve is seated. Refrigerant will flow around the valve stem to the respective gauges and register the low-side pressure on the low-side gauge and the system high-side pressure on the high-side

gauge. The hand valves isolate the low and high sides from the central portion of the manifold.

A test hose (normally blue) connected to the fitting directly under the low-side gauge is used to connect the low side of the test manifold into the low side of the system. A similar connection (normally a red hose) is found on the high side.

The center fitting on the manifold is used to connect a service hose to charge or **evacuate** the system. The service hose is normally a neutral color such as yellow or white.

CAUTION: *Do not* open the **high-side service valve** while the air-conditioning system is in operation.

If the high-side service valve is opened at this time, high-pressure refrigerant will be forced through the high-side gauge and to the refrigerant can if it is attached. This high pressure can rupture the can or possibly burst the fitting at the safety can valve, resulting in damage and physical injury.

SERVICE

Heater

Heater service consists of a visual inspection of the unit for leaks and cracked hoses. You should also consult the shop manual for the operating temperature of the heater and check it. If the temperature does not reach the minimum acceptable level, refer to the troubleshooting chart in Figure 44-34 to diagnose the problem.

The most common heater service procedure is replacing heater hoses. In addition to replacing a leaking hose, check for cracked or brittle hoses. When serviceable, heater hose is pliable; you should be able to bend it at a 90° angle without cracking it. First, partially drain the cooling system so the level is below that of the heater and water pump.

Mark the hose connections "inlet" and "outlet" so the new hoses can be installed correctly; otherwise, coolant flow may be backwards. Never pry off a hose, especially at the fragile copper or aluminum heater-core nipples. A cracked nipple here requires heater-core replacement. Remove a stubborn hose by splitting its end lengthwise and then working a screwdriver under the split ends.

Cut the new hoses long enough so there's slack for engine movement. Route the hoses away from the hot exhaust manifold(s) and tie them together with cable ties, if possible. Replace corroded, stripped, or bent heater-hose clamps with new worm drive clamps.

It may also be necessary to replace a leaking control valve or heater core. The control valve regulates the amount of coolant flow to the core. It may be located in line in a heater hose, at the firewall, or under-dash, alongside the core. The heater core is located in the heater housing, either underdash or in the cowl area. Check a shop manual for procedures *before* taking the car apart.

Whenever the heater housing is being removed, first disconnect the battery and drain the radiator. Disconnect the cables from their control levers by loosening the outer cable retainers and levering off the cable pivot spring clips. Before disconnecting any vacuum-control hoses, label them. Check for cracked or brittle vacuum hoses and replace as necessary. Label all electrical leads. If a heater-housing-to-firewall seal was broken when the core was removed, make a new seal with silicone sealer for an air- and watertight installation.

Air Conditioner

Air-conditioning service includes discharging, evacuating, and charging the system. *Do not* attempt to work on an air-conditioning system until you have been checked out and certified by a professional.

If the system must be evacuated (all air and moisture removed from the system), a special vacuum pump must be used.

Finding Refrigerant Leaks   Most air-conditioning service work will consist of checking for and/or locating and repairing leaks. Many leaks are caused simply by vibration and by threaded connections coming loose. Retightening these will solve the leak. Occasionally a hose will rub on a structural part to create a leak. Component deterioration of hoses, seals, etc., may be a cause of leaks. The following types of leak detectors may be used to locate air-conditioning system leaks:

1. *Halide (propane) torch*:   This leak detector uses a propane flame, which draws the leaking refrigerant over a hot copper alloy reactor plate. A dramatic color change in the flame will occur to show the presence of refrigerant (indicating a leak) (Figure 44-38). This test may be illegal in your state. Check local laws before performing it. Do not breathe any fumes from the tester. They contain phosgene gas.

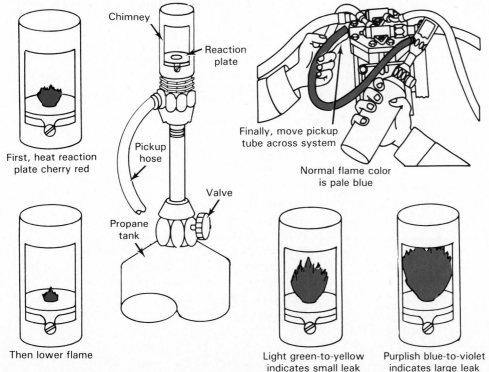

Chimney

Reaction plate

Pickup hose

Valve

Propane tank

First, heat reaction plate cherry red

Then lower flame

Finally, move pickup tube across system

Normal flame color is pale blue

Light green-to-yellow indicates small leak

Purplish blue-to-violet indicates large leak

FIGURE 44-38   Leak testing with a halide (propane) torch.

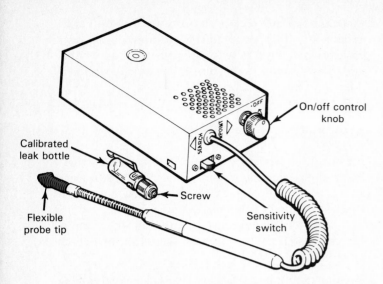

FIGURE 44-39 Electronic leak tester.

2. *Electronic detector:* One of the most commonly used, this instrument will draw in any leaking refrigerant through a test probe and then sound an alarm or create a flashing light if R-12 is found. It is the most sensitive of the leak detectors used (Figure 44-39).

3. *Bubble detector:* This is a soap solution applied externally at suspected leak points. Leaking refrigerant will cause the detector to form bubbles and foam.

Discharging the System Foreign substances can be inadvertently introduced into the air-conditioning system either while service work is being performed or from a defect in the system. A noncondensable is any substance (such as air, moisture, or dirt) that will not readily change state to give off or absorb heat. These substances interfere with refrigerant movement, chemically react to form corrosive acids, and contaminate the refrigerant.

To replace contaminated refrigerant, the system *must* be discharged. It must then be evacuated or pumped down with a vacuum pump to remove all traces of air, moisture, and contaminated refrigerant. Flushing is sometimes required to remove all foreign material from a system.

Evacuating and Charging the System Moisture, in any quantity, is extremely harmful to the air-conditioning system. Moisture reacts with R-12 and forms hydrochloric acid, which will damage the system's internal components. The purpose of the receiver/drier is to trap and retain any moisture which may enter the system. Remember that air contains moisture. Therefore, a leak in the system will allow air and moisture to enter.

Unwanted air and moisture are removed from the system by a vacuum pump. Basically, a vacuum pump controls the pressure inside the system. By lowering the pressure inside the system into a vacuum condition, the boiling point of water (moisture) is also lowered to a point where evaporation will easily occur. This vaporized moisture can then easily be drawn out by the vacuum pump.

A system that has been opened for repairs, or one which is found to be excessively low of refrigerant, *must* be fully evacuated with a vacuum pump to remove all traces of moisture before a new refrigerant charge is added. A 29 in-Hg vacuum held for 30 minutes is adequate.

After all indicated repairs have been made, the compressor oil level has been checked and adjusted as necessary, and the system has been evacuated to remove all air and moisture, the air-conditioning system should be fully charged with refrigerant and then tested.

Because discharging, flushing and charging procedures vary greatly from system to system, be sure to check a shop manual before starting. Do not service an air conditioning system without the proper tools and training.

TRADE TERMS

Absolute Zero
Accumulator
Air Conditioning
Ambient Air Temperature
Atmospheric Pressure
Auxiliary Gauge
Axial
Boiling Point
British Thermal Unit
Change of State
Compound Gauge

Compressor
Condensation
Condenser
Cycling Clutch Orifice Tube
Desiccant
Discharge Side
Evacuate
Evaporation
Evaporator
Expansion Tube
Expansion Valve

Heat Exchanger
High Side
High-Side Service Valve
Latent Heat of Condensation
Latent Heat of Evaporation
Low Side
Manifold Gauge Set
Radial
Ram Air
Receiver-Drier

Reed Valves
Refrigerant
Refrigerant 12
Rotary Valve Compressors
Service Ports
Sight Glass
Silica Gel
Suction Side
Thermostatic Expansion Valve
Vapor

REVIEW QUESTIONS

1. Describe the construction of a heater core.

2. How does a blower fan operate in a heating system?

3. Heater controls are operated by _____ and __ _____.

4. Freon cools by _____.

5. There is no cold, only an absence of heat. True or false? Explain.

6. Name the four major components of an air-conditioning or refrigeration system.

7. Freon boils at temperatures over _____.

8. Which condition does *not* describe freon: odorless, clear in color, low boiling point, toxic, nonflammable, noncorrosive.

9. Describe the operation of an air-conditioning compressor.

10. Where is the compressor located in the system?

11. What does a condenser do?

12. Where is the condenser located in the car?

13. A receiver/drier performs two functions. What are they?

14. The accumulator separates _____ refrigerant from the _____ refrigerant.

15. Where is the evaporator located in the system?

16. The evaporator evaporates water out of the freon. True or false? Explain.

17. What operates the diaphragm in an expansion valve?

18. A _____ allows you to visually check the freon level in some air-conditioning systems.

Automotive Service Excellence

The National Institute for Automotive Service Excellence (ASE) is a non-affiliated, non-profit organization with a program designed to organize and promote the highest standards of automotive service. The ASE offers prestige and recognition to those desiring a career as an automotive technician. These are earned by demonstrating the skills and knowledge needed to pass certain tests. To a shop owner or a service manager, it is impartial and objective assurance that the technicians are competent in one or more specialized fields. ASE certification proves ability to your employer and, in turn, the customers.

The ASE does not license its qualified technicians since actual licensing is considered a mandatory program. ASE certification is a voluntary effort to help technicians help themselves. The program is based on difficult but meaningful tests of technical skill and knowledge. Anyone who passes one or more of the 16 tests offered by the Institute receives his or her certification. It means that you can choose a position in the automotive job market and practice your own specialized abilities. The program offers a way for automotive enthusiasts to position themselves as certified technicians in any or all of the specialty fields offered by the Institute.

The Institute awards its graduate technicians with a shoulder patch for their work uniforms. It is a proud blue seal bearing the initials ASE (Figure A-1). In addition, each certified technician receives a pocket protector and an official card indicating the specific areas of certification. The shop owner may also display a sign indicating employment of ASE-certified technicians which is appealing to the customers.

Technicians certified by the ASE are working today at car dealerships, independent garages, service stations, tire dealerships, and in many other sectors of the automotive industry throughout America. Recent statistics show that over 300,000 technicians have been certified by the ASE since its founding in 1972. Over 174,000 have re-certified themselves at the required five-year intervals to keep their credentials current.

* Courtesy of Automotive Service Excellence.

Anyone passing all eight tests in the automobile arena becomes a Certified Master Automobile Technician, and some 6,000 persons currently hold this valuable credential.

In addition to the eight tests for automobile technicians, the Institute offers six tests for the heavy-duty truck field and one each for body repair and painting/refinishing.

The tests available for automobile technicians include the subjects of: Engine Repair, Automatic Transmission/Transaxle, Manual Drive Train and Axles, Suspensions and Steering, Brakes, Electrical Systems, Heating and Air Conditioning, and Engine Performance.

For heavy-duty truck technicians the tests cover: Gasoline Engines, Diesel Engines, Drive Trains, Brakes, Suspension and Steering, and Electrical Systems. A technician may take any one or all six of the tests toward receiving his or her certification but must only pass five of the six toward receiving a Master Heavy-Duty Truck Technician certificate; either the Diesel Engine or Gasoline Engine test plus the other four.

In May and November, the Institute conducts its tests in over 300 locations and in all 50 States. The tests are changed each time they are given. Community colleges or local high schools are usually used as the test sites. The tests measure both diagnostic and repair skills and are based on written examinations rather

* Courtesy of Automotive Service Excellence.

than hands-on work, which is too complex and costly on a nationwide basis and is less meaningful in the end.

A given test may have as few as 40 or as many as 80 multiple-choice questions, written by automotive experts from all segments of the industry. There is a time limit set for each test and certain other regulations apply while the tests are in session (Figure A-2).

As an example of the contents of a test, there are questions or incomplete statements followed by four suggested answers or completions. The technician must check the *one* that best answers the question or completes the statement. A question might state; *A compression test shows that one cylinder is too low. A leakage test on that cylinder shows that there is too much leakage. During the test, air could be heard coming out of the tailpipe. Which of these could be the cause? A) Broken piston rings. B) A bad head gasket. C) A bad exhaust gasket. or D) An exhaust valve not seating. (The answer is D).*

Once a technician has passed one or more of the Institute's tests, he or she is eligible for ASE certification. To actually receive certification credentials, the technician must be able to show at least two years of work experience in that field. Re-certification every five years helps to assure that the ASE technician has kept up with the fast-paced changes in automotive technology.

The Institute offers an industry-wide self-improvement program. It is non-profit, as noted, and is governed by a 40-member Board of Directors representing not only the automotive industry, but educational fields, consumer groups, and national, state and local governments. Such a diverse group adds to the creditability of the Institute's program and helps assure that ASE tests benefit the automotive industry and its consumers, as well as the individual technician.

The program is a sound one for aspiring automotive technicians. Job opportunities are virtually endless for anyone wearing the ASE logo.

Students wishing to explore the ASE program further, and to learn where and when the next tests will be given, are encouraged to ask for "Bulletin of Information" from: ASE, 1825 K. St., N.W., Washington, D.C. 20006-1249.

APPENDIX TWO

Metric Conversions

Metric conversions are making life more difficult for the mechanic. In addition to doubling the number of tools required, metric-dimensioned nuts and bolts are used alongside English components in many new vehicles. The mechanic has to decide which tool to use, slowing down the job. The tool problem can be solved by trial and error, but some metric conversions aren't so simple.

Converting temperature, lengths or volumes requires a calculator and conversion charts, or else a very nimble mind. Conversion charts are only part of the answer though, because they don't help you "think" metric, or "visualize" what you are converting. The following examples are intended to help you "see" metric sizes:

LENGTH

Meters are the standard unit of length in the metric system. The smaller units are 10ths (decimeter), 100ths (centimeter), and 1000ths (millimeter) of a meter. These common examples might help you to visualize the metric units:

☐ A meter is slightly longer than a yard (about 40 inches).
☐ An aspirin tablet is about one centimeter across. (.4 inches).
☐ A millimeter is about the thickness of a dime.

VOLUME

Cubic meters and centimeters are used to measure volume, just as we normally think of cubic feet and inches. Liquid volume measurements include the liter and milliliter, like the English quarts or ounces.

☐ One teaspoon is about 5 cubic centimeters.
☐ A liter is about one quart.
☐ A liter is about 61 cubic inches.

English-Metric Conversion Chart

CONVERSION FACTORS

Unit	To	Unit	Multiply by	Unit	To	Unit	Multiply by
LENGTH				**WEIGHT**			
Millimeters	Inches		.03937	Grams	Ounces		.03527
Inches	Millimeters		25.4	Ounces	Grams		28.34953
Meters	Feet		3.28084	Kilograms	Pounds		2.20462
Feet	Meters		.3048	Pounds	Kilograms		.45359
Kilometers	Miles		.62137	**WORK**			
Miles	Kilometers		1.60935	Centimeter			
AREA				Kilograms	Inch Pounds		.8676
Square Centimeters	Square Inches		.155	Inch Pounds	Centimeter Kilograms		1.15262
Square Inches	Square Centimeters		6.45159	Meter Kilograms	Foot Pounds		7.23301
VOLUME				Foot Pounds	Newton Meters		1.3558
Cubic Centimeters	Cubic Inches		.06103	**PRESSURE**			
Cubic Inches	Cubic Centimeters		16.38703	Kilograms/			
Liters	Cubic Inches		61.025	Sq. Centimeter	Pounds/Sq. Inch		14.22334
Cubic Inches	Liters		.01639	Pounds/Sq. Inch	Kilograms/Sq. Cen-		
Liters	Quarts		1.05672	Bar	timeters		.07031
Quarts	Liters		.94633	Pounds/Sq. Inch	Pounds/Sq. Inch		14.504
Liters	Pints		2.11344	Atmosphere	Bar		.06895
Pints	Liters		.47317	Pounds/Sq. Inch	Pounds/Sq. Inch		14.696
Liters	Ounces		33.81497	Pounds/Sq. Inch	Atmosphere		.06805
Ounces	Liters		.02957	**TEMPERATURE**	Atmosphere		
				Centigrade Degrees	Fahrenheit Degrees		$(C° \times \frac{9}{5}) + 32$
				Fahrenheit Degrees	Centigrade Degrees		$(F° - 32) \times \frac{5}{9}$

WEIGHT

The metric weight system is based on the gram, with the most common unit being the kilogram (1000 grams). Our comparable units are ounces and pounds:

- ☐ A kilogram is about 2.2 pounds.
- ☐ An ounce is about 28 grams.

TORQUE

Torque is somewhat complicated. The term describes the amount of effort exerted to turn something. A chosen unit of weight or force is applied to a lever of standard length. The resulting leverage is called torque. In our standard system, we use the weight of one pound applied to a lever a foot long—resulting in the unit called a foot-pound. A smaller unit is the inch-pound (the lever is one inch long). Metric units include the meter kilogram (lever one meter long with a kilogram of weight applied) and the Newton-meter (lever one meter long with force of one Newton applied). Some conversions are:

- ☐ A meter kilogram is about 7.2 foot pounds.

- ☐ A Newton-meter is about 1.4 foot pounds.
- ☐ A centimeter kilogram (cmkg) is equal to .9 inch pounds.

PRESSURE

Pressure is another complicated measurement. Pressure is described as a force or weight applied to a given area. Our common unit is pounds per square inch. Metric units can be expressed in several ways. One is the kilogram per square centimeter (kg/cm^2). Another unit of pressure is the Pascal (force of one Newton on an area of one square meter), which equals about 4 ounces on a square yard. Since this is a very small amount of pressure, we usually see the kiloPascal, or kPa (1000 Pascals). Another common automotive term for pressure is the bar (used by German manufacturers), which equals 10 Pascals. Thoroughly confused? Try the examples below:

- ☐ Atmospheric pressure at sea level is about 14.7 psi.
- ☐ Atmospheric pressure at sea level is about 1 bar.
- ☐ Atmospheric pressure at sea level is about 1 kg/cm^2.
- ☐ One pound per square inch is about 7 kPa.

Glossary

Absolute zero: The point at which there is a total absence of heat. Equivalent to −459° F.

Accelerator pump: A small pump which squirts fuel directly into a carburetor barrel. Used to provide extra fuel during sudden throttle openings.

Accumulator: A hydraulic device used in the transmission's hydraulic system to help prevent harsh shifts. Accumulators absorb shock or surge when hydraulic pressure changes suddenly within a system.

Accumulator: Refrigerant storing device, used on many air conditioning systems, that receives vapor and liquid refrigerant from evaporator. Also contains dessicant and acts as a receiver-drier. Located in low side of system.

Activated charcoal: Highly absorbent carbon. It is made by heating granulated charcoal in an air-tight oven, which drives off gases and makes it "hungry" for more.

Aftermarket: Automotive product companies which sell replacement parts and accessories directly to the public.

AIR: Air Injection Reactor. Used to describe the adding of air to the exhaust stream to complete HC combustion.

Air cleaner: A device which filters air entering the engine. Usually made of pleated paper.

Air conditioning: The control of temperature, humidity, and air movement.

Air/Fuel mixture: The amount of air and fuel that is blended for each power stroke of an engine.

Air springs: Rubber sacks filled with pressurized air. Deforming the bag gives the spring action.

Align-bore: Machining process that ensures the straight alignment of any group of bores in an engine. Usually used when referring to the main-bearing bores.

Alternator: A generator which produces alternating current.

Ambient air temperature: Temperature of the outside air surrounding either an air-conditioned vehicle or building.

Ammeter: A meter which measures the amount of electrical current flowing through a circuit in amps.

Amperage: The strength of an electrical current. It is measured in amps.

Amperes: A measurement unit for current flow. One ampere equals 6.28×10^{18} electrons per second.

Anchor pins: Anchoring pins on which the heel of the brake shoe rotates. Seldom used in today's automobile.

Antifreeze: A chemical added to water in the cooling system. It lowers the freezing point of water, raises the boiling point of water, adds water pump lubrication, and prevents engine corrosion.

Anti-seize: Thread compound designed to keep threaded connections from damage due to rust or corrosion.

Apply devices: Devices that hold or drive members of a planetary gearset. They may be hydraulically (clutches and servos) or mechanically (1-way clutches) applied.

ATF: Automatic Transmission Fluid

Atmospheric pressure: Air pressure at a given altitude. Standard atmospheric pressure at sea level is 14.696 psi.

Atomization: The process where fuel droplets are turned into a fine mist. The breaking up of a liquid into a mist.

Automatic headlight dimmer: A photoelectric controlled circuit which automatically places the headlights on the dim circuit in response to oncoming headlights.

Automatic locking/unlocking hubs: Front wheel hubs which can engage or disengage themselves from the axles automatically.

Automotive Service Excellence (ASE): A non-profit organization dedicated to improving and certifying professional mechanics.

Auxiliary gauge: Used to measure compressor inlet pressure on Chrysler Corp. models with EPR valve and to measure evaporator pressure on some STV-equipped Ford models.

Axial compressor: Compressor with pistons which move along its axis or centerline, such as Frigidaire and General Motors 6-cylinder and Sankyo 5-cylinder compressors.

Backing plate: Plates to which drum braking mechanisms are affixed.

Baffling: Sheetmetal work which directs the cooling airflow on air-cooled engines.

Balanced coil gauge: An instrument using one constant voltage coil and one variable voltage coil to move its needle.

Balance shaft: A shaft which is normally at twice crankshaft speed to help cancel vibrations.

Ballast resistor: A resistor used in the ignition system. It limits the voltage available to the primary circuit under normal conditions. During starting it is bypassed to increase ignition system efficiency.

Ball joint: A spherical bearing used on front suspensions. It allows limited motion in two planes.

Ball pivot: A round or half-round hard-steel ball which rocker arms pivot on.

Barrel: Carburetor venturi

Barrels: Individual cylinders in an air-cooled engine. They fit between the case and head.

Bead blaster: Device which uses compressed air to shoot glass beads at a part to clean it.

Bearings: Soft metal inserts which reduce the friction rotating shaft. The bearings are always softer than the shaft so the bearings will wear and not the shaft.

Bellhousing: A housing which fits over the clutch components and connects the engine and transmission.

Bimetal: A construction used for small arms and coils. Two metals with different heat characteristics are formed into the arm or coil. When heated, the arm or coil will bend or tighten because one metal will pull it in that direction. Used in relays, gauges, and circuit breakers.

Blade: The standard or slot-type screwdriver tip.

Bleeder valve: Valve on wheel cylinder, caliper, or master cylinder which allows air and fluid to be drained from the system.

Boiling point: The temperature at which a liquid changes to a vapor.

Boost: Term used to describe the rise in manifold pressure produced by a turbocharger or supercharger.

Boring bar: Machine which cuts cylinder bores oversize.

Box end: Wrench construction where the wrench end is a circle that completely surrounds the nut.

Brake bleeding: Forcing contaminated fluid from the brake hydraulic system.

Brake drum micrometer: Measures the inside diameter of a brake drum.

Brake fluid: A nonpetroleum based liquid for specific use in brake systems.

Brake lines: Lines that carry brake fluid from master cylinder to wheel cylinders.

Brake lining: An asbestos resin and filler composition material. Acts as a friction surface between shoe and drum and between caliper and disc.

Brake pad: The composition pads which contact the disc brake rotor.

Brake pedal: Pedal pushed upon to actuate the master cylinder.

Brake shoes: The drum brake parts which hold the friction material and contact the drums.

Brake warning light switch: Actuates brake warning dash light when front or rear brake system fails.

Breakaway capsule: A steering column mounting which allows the column to break away during a crash.

Breathing: The ability of the engine to admit and exhaust gases.

British thermal unit (BTU): Used to measure heat quantity. One BTU is the amount of heat necessary to raise 1 pound of water 1° F.

Buck: To support the backside of an object which is being hammered.

Bushing: A 1-piece, removable metal sleeve that replaces a bearing.

Button: Soft material fitted to ends of floating pins. Keeps pin from damaging cylinder wall.

CAD: Computer-Aided-Design. A computer system used to design automobiles. It simulates much of the engineering and testing normally done by engineers and field tests.

Caliper: The disc brake part which houses the piston(s) and fits over the disc.

Calipers: A measuring tool with two adjustable legs. The legs are fitted to the measured object, the calipers removed from the object, and the distance found by measuring the calipers against a rule.

CAM: Computer-Aided-Manufacturing. A computer system which designs tooling and programs machine tools in a manufacturing plant.

Camber: The wheel inclination from vertical as seen from the front or rear of the vehicle.

Camshaft: A shaft fitted with lobes. The lobes are connected to the valves by the valve train and force the valves open against valve spring pressure. The camshaft is also typically fitted with a gear for driving the oil pump and distributor. Another lobe may be used for driving the fuel pump.

Canister steering column: A type of collapsible column where a corrugated steel canister folds up during an impact.

Carbonizing: The product left after severe heating of any combustible material.

Carbon monoxide: A colorless, odorless toxic gas produced as a result of incomplete combustion in an engine.

Carburetor cleaner: Form of non-caustic solvent which is commonly used for cleaning carburetors.

Case: Iron or aluminum castings which contain the crankshaft in opposed engines. Can be opened to service the parts inside.

Cast: To mold metal by pouring it hot into a mold.

Catalyst: Something that starts and/or speeds a chemical reaction and enables it to take place.

Catalytic converter: A device which uses platinum, paladium, and rhodium to chemically change exhaust emissions into harmless gases.

CCC: Computer Command Control. A General Motors computer control system.

Celsius: A temperature scale where water freezes at 0° and boils at 100°. Also called Centigrade.

Cetane: The unit of measure of how easily diesel fuel will ignite.

Change of state: Rearrangement of the molecular structure of matter as it changes between any two of the three physical states: solid, liquid, or gas.

Charcoal canister: A container filled with activated charcoal. It collects gasoline vapors from the gas tank or carburetor float bowl.

Charging system: The system which provides all the electrical power necessary to run the car. It can also produce more power than is necessary to recharge the battery.

Chasing: To clean threads with a tap and compressed air.

Chassis: All mechanical systems and assemblies which make up a car, except for the bodywork.

Check engine light: A light on the dashboard of most vehicles with computer control systems. It lights when the vehicle needs service. After the mechanic puts the vehicle into a test mode, the check engine light may flash trouble codes which help indicate what problems exist.

Check valves: Allow air or liquid to pass in one direction only.

Cherry picker: A hydraulic jack in a tall, wheeled frame. Used for removing and installing engines.

Chocks: Any device which can be placed in front or back of a tire to prevent it from rolling.

Cinch pin: Piston pin used with a connecting rod which has a cinch bolt which clamps rod to pin.

Circuit breaker: A bimetallic spring switch which opens and closes from heat when the circuit it is in is overloaded.

Closed loop: Used to describe a computer-controlled system when it is being controlled by sensor inputs rather than by a pre-programmed set of instructions.

Close ratio: A relative term for describing the gear ratios in a transmission. If the gears are numerically close they are said to be close ratio. This design gives faster acceleration at the expense of easy initial acceleration and overall economy.

Clutch (friction) disc: The friction material part of the clutch assembly. It fits between the flywheel and pressure plate.

Clutch linkage: The mechanical or hydraulic mechanism which transfers motion from the driver's leg to the clutch.

Clutch release bearing: The bearing which contacts the pressure plate release fingers. It is designed to rotate with the pressure plate where it touches it and stay stationary with the release arm where it touches it.

Coil: A type of transformer which increases the voltage by induction of the ignition current. Coils raise voltage from 12 volts to 30,000 or higher.

Coil spring: Spring made from a length of round bar, which is wound into a spiral.

Collapsed: Condition describing a piston skirt which has been overheated, deformed, and is no longer in its original shape.

Collapsible steering column: A steering column designed to shorten its length during a crash. This keeps the steering column from entering the passenger compartment.

Collapsing mesh: A collapsible column where a steel mesh folds up during an impact.

Collision guide: A book listing the time and parts needed to repair body damage.

Column mount: Shift linkage which has the shifter mounted on the steering column.

Combination wrench: A wrench fitted with one open end and one box end.

Combustion chamber: The enclosed area where combustion takes place. Formed by the cylinder head, valves, spark plugs, head gasket, cylinder walls, piston, and rings.

Companion flange: The mating part of the transmission or drive axle to the drive shaft. The parts the drive shaft attaches to.

Compound gauge: A gauge, used on the system low side, that will register both pressure and vacuum.

Compression gauge: A tool for measuring the air-tightness of an engine's cylinders.

Compression ratio: The relationship between the volume of the cylinder with the piston at BDC and the volume at TDC.

Compression rings: Rings designed to hold in combustion pressures and provide a seal so the piston will be forced down.

Compression stroke: The upward stroke of the piston as it compresses the air/fuel mixture.

Compressor: Refrigeration pump that circulates the refrigerant and increases the pressure of refrigerant vapor.

Condensation: The act of changing a vapor to a liquid.

Condenser: An electrical storage device. It is used in conventional ignition systems to absorb excess current the moment the points open. Condensers are also used to absorb radio-interfering current and noise.

Condenser: System component that removes heat from the refrigerant, changing it from a hot vapor to a warm liquid. Mounted in the engine compartment, usually in front of the radiator.

Cone clutch: A clutch made from two cones. One fits inside the other. Friction between the cones forces them to rotate together.

Constant mesh: Transmission design where the gears are always meshed.

Constant velocity: U-Joints which maintain constant shaft velocity regardless of shaft angle.

Constant velocity universal joint: Two universal joints coupled closely together to give an output speed identical to the input speed, regardless of the angle of drive.

Continuous injection: A fuel injection system where the injectors spray fuel constantly.

Control arm: A horizontal part which connects the wheel to the chassis. An upper and a lower control arm are used on many suspension designs. One of the arms takes spring and shock absorber loads.

Conventional four-wheel drive: The system most commonly used with a front-mounted engine, a transmission, a transfer case, a front and rear propellor shaft, and two driving axles.

Coolant: The mixture of water and anti-freeze used in water-cooled engines.

Coolant recovery system: A special cap, container, and hoses which keep coolant from escaping from the engine.

Cooling system: The system which removes excess heat from the engine and radiates it to the atmosphere. Water, air and oil are used to carry the heat to the atmosphere.

Cores: Forms which make the internal passages of a block, head, or other cast part. In auto engines, specially treated sand is used for cores.

Core shift: Manufacturing flaw which results in uneven thickness in the cylinder walls.

Countershaft: The shaft which transmits the power flow to the mainshaft. The countershaft carries half the gearsets.

Crossflow: A cylinder head design where the intake charge enters from one side and the exhaust exits from the opposite side.

Crosshatch: A series of lines intersecting at an angle, created by cutting metal. A 60° angle is desired when honing the material used in a cylinder.

Crown: Top of a piston. Also called the dome.

Cruise control: An automatic speed control system. It can keep the speed constant, decelerate to a preset speed and accelerate to a preset speed.

Crush: The distance a bearing is deformed when first installed. Typically about 0.001 inch. Crush results from bearings slightly too long to fit in their bearing bores. When the bearing cap is torqued, the other bearing half crushes its mate. This insures a tight seal between bearing and bore.

Countershaft: The shaft which transmits the power flow to the mainshaft. The countershaft carries half of the gearsets.

CTO switch: Coolant Temperature Override Switch. Used to modify vacuum signals in the Spark and EGR systems in response to coolant temperature.

Current: The movement of negative or positive particles through a conductor.

Cylinder balance test: A diagnostic test which determines how much each cylinder contributes to the total engine output.

Cylinder bore: A hole machine in a metal casting into which a piston usually fits.

Cylinder head: Component which closes the top of the cylinders. It usually contains the valves and provides ports to allow gases to enter and exit the cylinders. Cooling passages, fins, bolt holes, accessory attachments, cam shafts, and valve guides are added as needed to the cylinder head.

Cylinder injection: A type of fuel injection where the injectors shoot into the cylinder. Also called direct injection. This is the only injection possible with diesel engines.

Dead axle: An axle which does not turn with the wheels mounted to it.

Dealership: A private business with an agreement with the auto factory. The dealership agrees to stock, sell, service, and sell parts for the manufacturer's cars.

Decimal: A system which divides units of measure into tenths.

Decimeter: One-tenth of a meter.

Deck: The area on a block where the cylinder heat mounts.

Desiccant: A drying agent used in refrigeration systems to remove excess moisture (silica gel or similar substance).

Design studio: A center where engineers, artists, and model builders design car bodies and interiors. Both full-size and scale models are used.

Detent: An indented or cut-away portion of a part designed to catch and hold another part.

Detenting: Any shifting down in the transmission.

Detonation: A form of abnormal combustion where a second source of ignition ignites part of the mixture after the sparkplug has ignited most of it.

Detonation sensor: A sensor which "listens" for detonation. It sends a signal to the computer which retards the ignition timing when vibrations due to knocking are felt.

Diagnostics: A term used to describe the self-checking program in some computerized engine control systems.

Dial indicator: A measuring tool which displays the movement of its plunger on a dial.

Differential case: A cage which contains the side and pinion gears. It rotates with the ring gear at all times.

Digital gauges: Those using a digital readout, not analog (needle and scale) gauges.

Digital micrometer: A micrometer which senses distance electronically and shows the distance on a digital display.

Digital multimeter: An electrical tester which measures volts, amps, and ohms and shows the results on a digital display.

Dimmer switch: Switch used to direct current to the high- or low-beam headlight circuits.

Diodes: Electrical devices which allow current to flow through in one direction, but not the other.

Dipstick: A metal rod used to measure the fluid level in a car's crankcase or transmission.

Direct drive: The engine, transmission, and drive shaft are all turning at the same speed.

Disc: The flat round braking surface of a disc brake.

Disc brake: A brake using a rotating disc stopped by contracting pads.

Discharge: To bleed some or all of the refrigerant from a system by opening a valve or connection to permit refrigerant to escape slowly.

Discharge side: The portion of refrigerant system under high pressure, extending from compressor outlet to thermostatic expansion valve/tube inlet.

Displacement: The volume of all the engine's cylinders. This includes the area above the piston, when it is at the bottom of its stroke, times the number of cylinders.

Distribution: Moving parts and completed cars from the factory to numerous separate dealers. This includes all aspects of moving parts by air, truck, rail, and ship, plus warehousing.

Distributor: The device which sends the high voltage current to the spark plugs in the proper order.

Diverter valve: A valve that switches air from an air injection manifold to the atmosphere. Also called a gulp valve.

DOHC: Double Overhead Camshaft. A design where two camshafts are located in each cylinder head.

Double-cardan joint: A type of constant velocity joint resembling two normal U-joints.

Double-cut file: A bar of metal with two sets of intersecting ridges cut into its sides.

Dowel: Simple pins fitted to a part. They fit into holes in another part to align the two parts correctly.

Driveline warp-up: A condition where axles, gears, U-joints and related components can bind or fail if the 4WD mode is used on pavement with a part-time four-wheel drive system.

Drive pinion: The gear which takes its power directly from the driveshaft or transmission. It drives the ring gear.

Driveshaft tunnel: The raised portion of the floorpan through which the driveshaft passes.

Drum brake: Brake design which uses a rotating drum stopped by expanding or contracting brake shoes.

Dual diaphragm power booster: Power booster using two diaphragms to increase effectiveness over a single diaphragm booster.

Dual piston: Master cylinder using two pistons. Each piston operates a separate brake circuit.

Dual-piston master cylinder: Master cylinders with two pistons. Although one piston serves the front brakes and other serves the rear, their main function is to act as a safety back-up if a brake line ruptures.

Dual-servo-action brakes: Both brake shoes are self-energizing; that is, they tend to multiply braking force as they are applied.

Dummy shaft: A shaft, shorter than the countershaft, used for countershaft, removal and installation.

Dwell: The amount of time the points stay closed in a distributor. Also called the dwell angle, which refers to degrees of camshaft rotation.

Dye penetrant: Surface crack-finding process, including bright dye and developer.

Dynamometer: A device which measures the power output of an engine. One type of dynamometer measures power at the rear wheels, another style measures it at the crankshaft.

EEC: Electronic Engine Control. Ford's terminology for their computer control systems. There are four versions: I, II, III, and IV.

Electric tachometer: A tachometer which uses electronics to move its needle.

Electrode: The two metal rods in a spark plug. They form a gap which voltage is forced to jump to produce a spark.

Electrolyte: The medium used to generate the chemical activity which causes electron flow through a load connected to a battery. In an automobile battery, the electrolyte is sulfuric acid.

Electromagnet: A magnet produced by placing a coil of wire around a steel or iron bar. When current flows through the coil, the bar becomes magnetized and will remain so as long as the current continues to flow.

Electronic control module: A solid-state box which operates either an ignition or computerized emission control system. It is usually located in the passenger compartment for protection from extreme temperatures and vibration. Known also as ECU (Electronic Control Unit), ECA (Electronic Control Assembly), or MCU (Microprocessor Control Unit).

Electronic control module: The computer in an electronic control system. Used in ignition and fuel electronic management systems.

Electronic fuel injection: Any fuel injection system which uses electronics for control.

Electronic level control: An electronic level sensing system which keeps the car level under all load conditions.

Electrons: Negatively charged particles which move through a conducting material.

Embossed: A manufacturing process which leaves raised sections on the part.

Emery cloth: A cloth impregnated with an emery compound. Used for polishing and removing rust from metal.

Emission control system: A group of devices and adjustments which lower the amount of pollutants exhausted to the atmosphere.

End clearance: Distance between an oil pump's gears and cover.

Engine hoist: A lifting device used to remove and install engines. The lifting force usually comes from a hand-operated hydraulic cylinder.

Engine modification: An alteration in basic engine design to reduce emissions. Usually accomplished without the addition of any new components.

Ethyl glycol: A thick fluid used in engine coolants to keep them from freezing.

Evacuate: To create a vacuum within a system, removing all traces of air and moisture.

Evaporation: A change of state from a liquid to a vapor.

Evaporator: System component in which liquid refrigerant changes to a vapor after removing heat from the air, which is then discharged into the passenger compartment.

Exhaust gas analyzer: A machine which measures different compounds in automobile exhaust gases. Most analyzers measure carbon monoxide, carbon dioxide, and hydrocarbons. Some also measure oxygen.

Exhaust pipe: The pipe connecting the exhaust manifold to the muffler.

Expansion tube: Used on some automotive air conditioning systems. It is a device that meters the flow of liquid refrigerant to the evaporator. It replaces the standard expansion valve, and may be called an orifice tube.

Expansion valve: See "THERMOSTATIC EXPANSION VALVE."

External power steering: When the hydraulic assist is mounted next to the steering linkage and works upon it by a rod.

Fan: A propeller-like device which draws or pushes air through the engine compartment, the radiator, a heater core, or an air-conditioning evaporator.

Fahrenheit: A temperature scale where water freezes at 32° and boils at 212°.

Feedback: A term describing a system which uses input from sensors to control solenoid motors and actuators. The results are measured by the sensors and more corrections are made. See Closed and Open Loop.

Feedback system: A system where the amount of oxygen in the exhaust is measured to determine how lean or rich the mixture should be. The signal is "fed back" to the carburetor and the mixture adjusted.

Feeler gauge: A steel strip of a precision thickness. Feeler gauges are used to determine the gap between parts.

Fillets: The rounded corners where the crankshaft journals meet the counterweights. The rounded edge relieves any stress concentrations.

Final drive ratio: The ratio between the drive pinion and ring gear.

Fixed caliper: A disc brake caliper which has pistons on both sides of the disc. It is rigidly fixed to the suspension.

Fixtures: The separate tie-down points in a jig. Parts are attached directly to the fixtures in a jig.

Flat rate: The amount of time the average, well-trained mechanic needs to perform a certain job.

Flat Rate Manual: A book listing estimated times needed for common automotive jobs.

Floating caliper: A disc brake caliper which has one piston. The caliper is free to move on pins in response to the piston pressing against the disc.

Floating pin: Piston pin which is a slip fit in its rod.

Floor jack: A hydraulic jack in a low-slung, wheeled frame. Used for lifting cars.

Floor mount: Shift linkage which has the shift lever passing through the floor.

Flow chart: Flow charts are logical testing procedures arranged in chart form.

Flushing gun: An adapter which allows water pressure to force cleaning water backwards through the cooling system.

Flywheel: A large, thick disc attached to the crankshaft in most cases. It dampens crankshaft twisting due to the separate power impulses and provides a mounting for the clutch and ring gear.

Foaming: The formation of an oil and refrigerant froth due to a rapid boiling of the refrigerant when pressure is suddenly reduced. Foam in the sight glass indicates a very low refrigerant level.

Foot pounds: The force equal to one pound applied through one foot. The standard unit of measurement for torque.

Force: The amount of push or pull that causes motion. It is usually measured in pounds.

Forge: To mold metal by pressure.

Forks: Semicircle pieces which mate with grooves in the synchronizer sleeves. The forks force the synchronizer toward the selected gear.

Four-stroke: Describes a four-stroke cycle used in most auto engines. The four strokes are intake, compression, power, and exhaust.

Four-wheel high: A transfer case shift position where both front and rear propellor shafts receive power, and rotate at the speed of the transmission output shaft.

Four-wheel low: A transfer case gear position where power is delivered to both driveshafts at about half the transmission output shaft speed, thereby doubling torque relative to road speed.

Free play: Clearance between the release bearing and pressure plate felt as free motion at the clutch pedal.

Freeze holes: Openings in cast parts which allow core sand removal. They have nothing to do with freezing. The holes are filled by freeze plugs or, more correctly, core plugs.

Front differential/axle assembly: Like a conventional rear axle assembly but having steerable wheels.

Front propeller shaft: The drive shaft connecting the transfer case front output shaft with the front axle.

Fuel delivery signal: Vacuum pressure difference that a carburetor senses to supply fuel to an engine.

Fuel filter: A filter which strains the fuel and removes any particulate matter.

Fuel gauge: A device which measures the amount of fuel in the tank.

Fuel pump: An electrical or mechanical unit which forces fuel under pressure from the tank to the engine.

Fuel system: The system which carries fuel from the storage tank and distributes it to the cylinders.

Full-time four-wheel drive: The 4WD arrangement where all four wheels are powered at all times.

Fuse: A replaceable part in an electrical circuit designed to burn into two parts when the circuit is overloaded.

Fuse block: A holder which contains several fuses, usually from several different circuits.

Fuse box: See Fuse Block.

Fusible link: A length of wire smaller than the rest of the circuit it is in. It melts when the circuit is overloaded.

Galleries: Oil passages cast or drilled in an engine block.

Galling: Forcing material out of its regular shape or condition by the act of high pressure rubbing.

Gauge set: Two or more instruments attached to a manifold and used for measuring or testing pressure.

Gear ratio: The mathematical relationship between gears. The ratio expressed denotes the difference in gear diameter, number of teeth, and difference in speed and torque multiplication.

Gear reduction: A condition where the drive gear is rotating faster than the driven gear. The reduction in speed in the driven gear increases its output torque.

Glass beading: See Bead Blaster.

Glazing: The act of one material being forced into another.

Glow plug: A wire loop heated red hot by electricity. It is placed in diesel combustion chambers and provides ignition for the first seconds of a cold start.

Governor pressure: The transmission's hydraulic pressure that is directly related to output shaft speed. It is used to control shift points along with throttle pressure.

Ground: The path electricity uses to return to its starting point in an electrical system; usually the frame or body in a car.

Gussets: Material placed between intersecting planes of a structure to strengthen it.

Half-shaft: A driving shaft U-jointed to permit rotary motion and simultaneous vertical movement of one end.

Hall effect: A primary circuit switching system using inductance to signal the ignition computer.

Hardening: Gasket sealer which dries to a very hard consistency.

Harmonic balancer: A disc consisting of an inner metal ring, a rubber ring, and an outer metal ring. It dampens higher frequency vibrations in the crankshaft. Mounted on the front of the crankshaft.

Heat exchanger: An apparatus in which heat is transferred from one fluid to another on the principle that heat will move to an object with less heat.

Heel: The backside of the lobe. This area is part of the base circle the lobe is designed around, so the valve is shut when the lifter touches the heel.

HEI: High Energy Ignition. The name given to GM's electronic ignition system.

Helical cut: A way of cutting gear teeth on a helix curve. Such gears are practically noiseless.

High side: See "DISCHARGE SIDE."

High side service valve: A device located on the discharge side of the compressor to allow high side pressure to be checked and other service operations performed.

Hoist: A hydraulic floor lift which raises the car high enough to walk under it.

Horsepower: A measure of work done in a certain amount of time. One horsepower is the work of raising 33,000 lbs. one foot in one minute.

Housekeeping: The practice of keeping an area picked up and clean.

Hub: The suspension piece which houses the wheel bearings and rotates with the wheel.

Hydraulic booster: A power booster operated by hydraulic pressure from the power steering pump.

Hydraulic brake fluid: Non-petroleum-based fluid for use in brake systems.

Hydraulic lifter: A lifter with internal passages and a check valve for routing engine oil. It uses engine oil pressure to maintain all valve clearances automatically without forcing a valve open when it should be seated.

Hydraulics: The science of laws governing liquids and their use to transmit force and motion.

Hydrometer: A device used to measure the specific gravity of a liquid. In an automobile, two types of hydrometers are used, one for checking the freezing temperature of the engine coolant, and the second for measuring the charge condition of the battery.

Hygroscopic: Readily absorbing water.

Idler arm: An arm mounted and moving like the pitman arm on the steering box, but on the right side of the car. It allows keeping the tie rod perpendicular to the front wheels.

Ignition system: The system which ignites the air/fuel mixture at the proper time.

Impact wrench: An air pressure or electrically driven socket wrench. Similar in appearance to a drill motor.

Impeller: The turbine in a turbocharger which compresses the incoming mixture.

Independent front axle: An axle assembly with the differential joined rigidly to the chassis and with U-jointed cardan or half-shafts to allow independent front wheel suspension.

Independent service: A repair facility which is not owned or franchised by an automotive manufacturer or chain of shops.

Index: To orient two parts by marking them. During reassembly the parts are arranged so the index marks are next to each other. Used to preserve the orientation between balanced parts.

Indicator lamp: A warning light which calls the driver's attention to a particular system. Also called idiot lights.

Induction: The creation of voltage by movement of a coil of wire through a magnetic field.

Inert: Chemically non-reacting.

Inline: Having all the cylinders in a row.

Inline compressor: Compressor of 2-cylinder design with pistons arranged side-by-side: York or Tecumseh.

Input member: The drive member.

Input pilot bearing: See pilot bushing.

Input shaft: The shaft which connects the clutch to the countershaft.

Intake manifold: The connection between the engine's air intake system and the cylinder head. It supports the carburetor or throttle body and contains the intake runners. Coolant may or may not be routed through the intake manifold.

Integral power steering: When the hydraulic assist is contained in the steering box.

Interchange Manual: Book which lists parts and shows which common parts will fit various automobiles.

Internal gear or ring gear: The outboard member of a planetary gearset that meshes with the planetary pinions. It has gear teeth on its internal side.

IRS: Independent Rear Suspension.

Isopropyl alcohol: An alcohol commonly used to lower the freezing point of water in windshield washer fluid.

Jack: Device using hydraulic or mechanical leverage to raise a car. Used for raising and lowering a car, not supporting it.

Jack stands: Metal supports placed under the car once it has been raised with a jack. Also called safety stands.

Jet tank: A form of hot tank which sprays caustic solvents at a dirty part while it rotates on a turntable.

Jig: A rigid structure designed to hold parts while they are assembled into a unit.

Journal: Machined section of a crankshaft which accepts the main or rod bearings.

Knurl: Cross-hatch pattern rolled into a piston to increase its diameter.

Lapping: Removing material from a part by rubbing with an abrasive.

Latent heat of condensation: The quantity of heat given off when a substance changes from a vapor or a liquid without changing temperature.

Latent heat of evaporation: The quantity of heat required to change a liquid into a vapor without raising the temperature of the vapor above that of the original liquid.

Leaf spring: Spring made from flat or arced bars. Each bar is called a leaf.

Lid closing unit: Electrical motor and controls which close the trunk lid.

Lifter: A part fitted between the camshaft lobes and push-rod.

Lifting equipment: A general term used to describe any device which lifts objects too heavy or bulky for a person.

Limited slip differential: A differential with a clutch which only allows some differential action.

Limiter switch: A switch which cuts power to a motor. Fitted to the driven mechanism so when it reaches a preset position the switch stops the motor. Used in power windows, antennas, and windshield wipers.

Line mechanic: Repair technician who works in the service department of a dealership.

Live axle: Technically, any axle which rotates with the wheel. In common automotive usage, an axle differential assembly contained in one housing.

Lobe: An eccentric shape machined into the camshaft. Lobe shape determines when, how fast, how far, and how long a valve will open and shut.

Locked differential: A differential with the side and pinion gears locked together. This stops differential action.

Lockplates: Metal tabs bent around nuts or bolt heads.

Lock solenoid: Solenoid which engages lock mechanism on doors and trunk lids.

Low side: See "SUCTION SIDE."

MacPherson strut suspension: Suspension design which mounts a coil spring over the shock absorber and uses the assembly to locate the upper part of the suspension. This does away with the upper control arm.

Magnafluxing: Process used for finding surface cracks in ferrous parts. It uses iron filings and a magnet.

Magnetic field: The area affected by lines of magnetic force.

Mainline pressure: The hydraulic that operates apply devices and is the source of all other hydraulic pressures in an automatic transmission. It is developed by pump pressure and regulated by the pressure regulator valve.

Mainshaft: The final shaft through which power flows through the transmission. Also called the output shaft. One-half of the gearsets are free to rotate on the mainshaft until locked to it by the synchronizers.

Manifold: Designed to control refrigerant flow for system test purposes. Used in conjunction with manifold gauges.

Manifold gauge: A calibrated instrument used for measuring system pressures.

Manifold gauge set: A manifold complete with gauges and charging hoses, used for diagnosing and servicing air conditioning systems.

MAP: Manifold Air Pressure Sensor. A sensor that measures air pressure (or vacuum) in the intake manifold. Used on many computer-controlled engines, this helps the computer determine engine load. Sometimes combined with a barometric air pressure sensor and called a B/MAP.

Master cylinder: Converts mechanical force to hydraulic force by action of piston forcing fluid ahead of it. Used with hydraulic brakes and clutches.

Measuring anvil: The fixed end of a micrometer's measuring section.

Mechanical tachometer: A cable-driven tachometer which uses gears to turn its needle.

Meter: The basic unit of measurement in the metric system. It is 39.37 inches long.

Metering valve: Prevents brake application to front brakes until rear brakes come on.

Metric: A system of measurement based on units of 10. It is the official measurement system in most countries around the world.

Microfiche: A system of reducing printed books onto film in greatly reduced size. Microfiche is read on a special machine which enlarges the image and projects it onto a screen.

Micrometer: A precision measuring instrument which uses a threaded screw assembly to find the thickness or spacing of a part.

Micrometer frame: The large stationary base of a micrometer to which all other parts are attached.

Micrometer sleeve: The stationary section of a micrometer spindle. The sleeve is marked with a scale.

Micrometer spindle: The threaded screw assembly in a micrometer.

Micrometer thimble: The knob which rotates the spindle in a micrometer.

Microprocessor: A very small computer.

Millimeter: One-thousandth of a meter.

Mineral based fluid: Brake fluid made from alcohol, glycerine, and other organic, non-petroleum sources.

Mini-drum: A miniature drum-type parking brake used with four-wheel disc brakes.

Module: Short for Ignition Control Module, the ignition computer.

Moly: Short for Molybdenum Disulphide, compound added to grease to form high pressure lubricant.

Moon roof: See sun roof.

Multimeter: An instrument that can be switched to measure several electrical functions; usually volts, amperes, and ohms.

Neoprene: A synthetic rubber.

Neoprene seal: Rubber, two-part oil seal used at the rear main-bearing.

Newton meters: The force equal to one kilogram applied through one meter.

Non-hardening: More modern gasket sealer which never completely hardens.

Normalizing: The relaxing of a structure after stress. Used to refer to the loosening of bolts after torquing.

Nutdriver: A tool which has a handle like a screwdriver and a working end like a socket wrench. Usually purchased in sets.

Octane: Gasoline's resistance to knock.

Octane rating: A number used to represent the antiknock

property of gasoline. Determined by mixing iso-octane and heptane until the mixture knocks equally with the gasoline being tested.

OEM: Original Equipment Manufacturer. The original source of a part or the entire car.

OHC: Overhead Camshaft. A design where the camshaft is placed in the cylinder head, above the combustion chamber.

Ohm: The unit used for measuring a material's resistance to electrical current flow.

Ohmmeter: A meter which tests the resistance in a circuit in Ohms.

Ohm's Law: A set of equations that defines the relationship between voltage, current, and resistance. These equations allow for the third unknown value to be found if any two are known.

OHV: Overhead Valve.

Oil control ring: Ring used to control and evenly spread oil sprayed onto the cylinder wall.

Oil filter: A filter element which strains the oil, removing small particles of metal and dirt.

Oil pan: Encloses the lower portion of the crankcase, and holds the oil when it is not circulating in the engine.

Oil pump: The pump which sucks oil from the pan and pumps it through the engine. It is driven by engine rotation.

Oil slinger: Crankshaft mounted baffle which keeps excess oil from reaching the front seal.

Open differential: A differential which has no resistance to differential action. Not a limited slip or locked differential.

Open end: Wrench construction where the wrench end is shaped like an open C.

Open loop: Used to describe a computer-controlled system when it is operating according to pre-programmed instructions rather than sensor inputs.

Opposed block: A "flat" engine design where the cylinder banks are 180° apart.

Orifice: A small opening in a line or passage used to regulate pressure and flow.

Oscilloscope: An instrument which measures volts and time, then displays lines on a TV-type screen. It is used for diagnosing the ignition, fuel, and other systems.

Out-of-round: Wear of a round hole or shaft. When viewed from on-end, a worn round hole becomes egg-shaped.

Output member: The driven member.

Overall gear ratio: Transmission ratio multiplied by the final drive ratio.

Overdrive: Any transmission gear set which has a 0.99:1 ratio or less. Also used to denote a separate unit fitted with overdrive gears.

Oversize: A reference to a shaft or bore when ground or cut. Does not necessarily mean the shaft is larger than its original diameter, but rather refers to the thicker bearings used with a ground shaft.

Oxygen sensor: A device that measures unburned oxygen in the exhaust gas. It generates a low voltage (under ½ volt) when much oxygen is present, and a higher voltage (up to 1 volt) when little oxygen is present.

The oxygen sensor must be heated to more than 600° F (315° C) to operate. Feedback systems use this sensor to control air/fuel ratios.

Parallel: A circuit with two or more resistance units wired to permit current flow through both units at the same time. The current does not have to pass through one unit to reach the other.

Parking brake: A mechanically actuated brake used to hold the car when parked.

Parking brake lever: The parking brake actuating lever fastened to the trailing brake shoe.

Parking brake strut: A bar between the two brake shoes. When parking lever is actuated, the parking brake strut pushes the leading brake shoe into the drum.

Parts Book: A book which lists parts by number, application, and price.

Part-time four-wheel drive: The 4WD system where the driver can choose to use four- or two-wheel drive.

Pascal's Law: The law of fluid motion.

PCV valve: An integral part of the PCV system. It allows a certain amount of crankcase vapor to enter the intake manifold.

Pedal bleeding: Using the brake pedal to force contaminated fluid from the hydraulic system.

Phillips: The most common form of the cross-shaped screwdriver tip.

Phosgene gas: An extremely poisonous gas, very damaging to the lungs. Created by burning R-12 refrigerant in an engine.

Photo amplifier: Photoelectric cell.

Pilot bushing: A plain bearing in the end of the crankshaft. It supports the front end of the transmission input shaft.

Pinion gears: Gears fitted between the two side gears. They allow the transfer of motion and energy between the two axles.

Piston: Cylindrical plugs which move back and forth within a cylindrical bore.

Piston pin: A cylinder of hard steel used to connect the piston to the connecting rod. Typically hollow to save weight.

Piston seal: The seal fitted to disc brake pistons. It provides the return motion to the piston as well as sealing in brake fluid.

Pitch: Angle of a vane in a torque converter.

Planet carrier assembly: A member of the planetary gearset. The planet pinions are mounted on the planet carrier.

Planet pinions: A member of the planetary gearset.

Plastigage: A plastic material which is crushed between a bearing cap and rod or crankshaft journal. After the bearing cap is removed, the width of the plastic strip indicates the bearing clearance.

Plenum: The opening in the intake manifold where the runners begin. On carbureted engines it is directly below the carburetor.

Points: The number of corners (or flats) in a wrench's box end or in a socket. Normal tools are either six point or twelve point.

Polarity: Direction of flow of electric current or magnetic lines of force through a coil or electromagnet.

Polish: Smoothing a surface with abrasive cloth.

Poppet valve: An elongated mushroom shaped valve which seals against a valve seat. All automotive valves are poppet valves. Other valve types are called Sleeve and Reed, and are used in 2-stroke cycle engines.

Port: The passage leading from the intake manifold runner to the combustion chamber. It is closed at one end by the intake valve.

Port fuel injection: A type of fuel injection where the injectors are placed at the intake ports.

Ports: Passages in the cylinder head which let the air/fuel mixture in and the exhaust gasses out.

Positive Crankcase Ventilation (PCV): A system which uses engine vacuum to draw blow-by vapors out of the engine.

Power antenna: Radio antenna which automatically raises when the radio is turned on and lowers when the radio is turned off.

Power booster: Used to increase pressure to master cylinder.

Power-flex fan: A fan whose blades flatten out as it turns faster. It moves less air, but is quieter and draws less power.

Power stroke: The downward motion of the piston after the sparkplug has ignited the mixture. This is the only stroke which transmits power to the drive wheels.

Power valves: Mechanism which richens the mixture when the engine is making all or most of the power possible.

Pre-ignition: Abnormal combustion when the air/fuel mixture ignites before the sparkplug has fired.

Press pin: Piston pin which must be pressed in and out of its rod.

Pressure bleeding: Pressure bleeding does the same thing pedal bleeding does, but faster. To pressure bleed you need a pressure bleeding machine.

Pressure bleeding machine: Machine to pressurize hydraulic system to remove fluid.

Pressure cap: A special radiator lid which maintains a selected pressure in the cooling system when the engine is hot.

Pressure plate: A heavy steel ring pressed against the friction disc by spring pressure. Commonly used to mean the entire pressure plate, spring, cover, and lever assembly.

Pressure relief valve: A valve located in the oil pump or just before the oil filter which vents excess oil pressure back into the oil pan.

Pressure testing tool: A device for checking cooling systems and radiator pressure caps.

Preventive maintenance: A program of replacing and servicing parts before they fail.

Primary circuit: In the ignition system, all those parts using low voltage, such as points, condenser, reluctor, pickup coil, and so on. It is the switching circuit of the ignition system.

Primary shoe: When the car is moving forward, the shoe facing the front of the car is the leading, or primary shoe.

Printed circuit: A wireless form of circuit. Solder is routed around a non-conducting board in the desired pattern usually connecting several circuits. This saves on wire, is easy to make and service.

Production: The normal process of building automobiles on an assembly line.

Propeller shaft: The shaft which carries torque from the engine/transmission to the drive axle on most cars.

Proportioning valve: Reduces fluid pressure to rear brakes during hard stops. Prevents locking of rear brakes.

Prototype: The first running example of a new car. It is used for testing and is usually modified many times before production.

Protractors: A curved rule marked to measure angles.

Purge: To remove moisture and air from a system or component by flushing with a dry gas refrigerant.

Pushrod: A straight rod used to carry camshaft motion from the valve lifter to the rocker arm. It is used on OHV engines only, where the cam is below the cylinder head.

Quadrant: Part of a ratcheting device with teeth on it. It helps hold the adjustment in one position.

Rack and pinion: A steering mechanism which uses a pinion gear on the end of the steering shaft which engages the rack (bar with a row of teeth cut along one edge) moving it directly right or left.

Radial compressor: Compressor with pistons which radiate out from the center line of the compressor, such as the Frigidaire 4-cylinder.

Ram air: Air forced through the condenser coils by vehicle movement or fan action.

Ramp: Those parts of the camshaft lobe which connect the heel and toe.

Read: To visually inspect a gasket for signs of leakage.

Receiver-drier: A combination container for the storage of liquid refrigerant and a desiccant.

Reciprocating: Back and forth motion, such as up and down strokes of a piston.

Recirculating ball worm and nut: A steering system which uses ball bearing on a worm gear. Force passes from these steering shaft mounted parts to the sector gear on the pitman shaft.

Recondition: To machine a connecting rod's big end back to original diameter.

Recycle: To use parts or supplies again after their normal working life.

Reed valves: Thin leaves of steel located in the valve plate of automotive compressors to act as suction and discharge valves. The suction valve is located on bottom of valve plate; the discharge valve is located on the top.

Refrigerant-12: The refrigerant used in automotive air conditioners. Proper name is Dichlorodifluoromethane.

Registers: Shallow ledges machined into the block to locate the main-bearing caps.

Regulator: An electrical device which controls an alternator's output.

Release fork: A length of material resting against a pivot. One end is pushed by the clutch linkage, the other end moves the release bearing against the pressure plate.

Replaceable insert valve guide: A valve guide design where the guide is separate from the cylinder head and can be replaced.

Resale value: The value of a used piece of equipment.

Resistance: The property of opposing electrical current flow through a material.

Resistor: A device placed in a circuit to limit flow.

Retainer: A disc set on top of the valve spring. The valve stem passes through a hole in the center of the retainer. The valve keepers sit in the center hole.

Ridge reamer: Tool which cuts off deposits at the top portion of a cylinder. Allows piston and rings to be removed from the top of the cylinder without damage.

Ring gear: A reduction gear driven by the drive pinion. The ring gear multiplies torque and changes the direction of power flow.

Rocker arms: An arm which reverses or transfers pushrod or camshaft motion. Some rocker arms used on OHC systems pivot at one end so they do not reverse camshaft motion. A rocker arm may also multiply pushrod or camshaft motion.

Rod-out: To mechanically clean a passage with a rod, as in a radiator.

Rope seal: A fibrous, two-part oil seal used at the rear main bearing.

Rotary vane compressor: Compressor with rotating vanes or rotors which compress and pump refrigerant.

Rotor: That part of the disc brake system which rotates. By stopping the rotation, the car is stopped. Also called the disc.

RTV: Room Temperature Vulcanizing. Rubber gasket sealer which cures at room temperature.

Runner: A passage leading from the carburetor opening through the intake manifold to the cylinder head port. The runner carries air or the air/fuel mixture to the cylinder port.

Run-out: Any variation of a rotating part perpendicular to its plane of rotation.

SAE: Society of Automotive Engineers. A group of engineers which sets automotive engineering standards. The SAE abbreviation is sometimes used to distinguish standard fasteners from metric fasteners.

Safety container: A special explosion-proof can designed for storing gasoline.

Safety glasses: Glasses worn to protect eyes from flying objects. They are usually made from thick, tempered glass.

Sand casting: A method of casting parts using sand molds. When the part is formed the sand mold is destroyed.

Scale: A device used for measuring distance (a ruler) or a device used for measuring weight.

Schematic: A drawing of a system, usually wiring, which uses symbols to represent components. It is used to show the relationship of the various parts.

Scoring: Wear damage from multiple scratches.

Scuffing: Light abrasion damage spread over a large area. Used to describe piston skirt wear.

Secondary circuit: The high voltage part of the ignition system. It includes the secondary windings of the coil, rotor, cap, high voltage wiring, and spark plugs.

Secondary shoe: When the car is moving forward, the shoe facing the rear is the trailing or secondary shoe.

Self-energizing: The increase in friction contact between the toe of the brake shoe caused by the drum rotation tending to pull the shoe into the drum.

Semiconductors: Anything which acts as a non-conductor at some times and a conductor at others.

Sensors: Devices that measure physical conditions (pressure, temperature, movement, etc.) and create a signal which can be interpreted by a control unit or driver.

Serial number: A unique number used to identify a car, engine, or transmission.

Series: An electric circuit in which the parts are connected end-to-end, positive poles to negative poles, so that current flows from part to part in succession.

Service port: A fitting on the service valves and some control devices which allows manifold gauge set charging hoses to be connected.

Service writer: The dealer's representative to the service customers. Service writers listen to the customer's complaints, write estimates, sell service, and give directions to the technicians as required.

Servo-action: Same as self-energizing.

Shock absorber: An enclosed oil, piston, and chamber assembly which dampens spring movements.

Shop manual: The manual written by the factory for use by dealer mechanics. It contains information needed to properly service and repair the car.

Shunt: An alternate or bypass portion of an electrical circuit.

Siamese ports: When two ports for different cylinders are joined to form one port.

Side clearance: Distance between a ring and ring groove, or distance between inner gears and pump body in an oil pump.

Side gears: The gears attached directly to the drive axles.

Sight glass: A window in the liquid line or in top of receiver-drier used to observe the liquid refrigerant flow.

Silica gel: A drying agent (desiccant) used to remove moisture from the refrigerant. Characterized by its ability to retain and absorb large quantities of moisture. Usually located in the receiver-drier.

Single-cut file: A bar of metal with one set of parallel ridges cut into its sides.

Single piston: Master cylinder using only one piston.

Single-piston master cylinders: Have only one piston traveling within the cylinder bore. They have not been sold in new cars since 1967.

Single-speed transfer case: A transfer case without high and low gear positions.

Sizing: See Reconditioning.

Sliding caliper: See Floating caliper.

SOHC: Single Overhead Camshaft. A design where one camshaft is located in each cylinder head.

Solenoid: A wire coil with moveable core. When current is applied to the coil, the core moves. It can be used to control electrical contacts, or vacuum and fuel valves in an emission system.

Solid axle: A rear axle design which places the final drive, axles, bearings and hubs into one housing. Drive and suspension functions are both placed on a solid axle.

Solid front axle: An integral axle assembly with differential and axle housings as a rigid unit. Also, suspension design where the front suspensions are linked by a solid bar or tube. A non-independent suspension.

Solid state: An electrical system that does not use tubes. A transistorized or electronic circuit.

Spark advance: Earlier firing of the spark plug to compensate for faster piston speeds at higher rpm.

Specific gravity: A unit of measure of the viscosity of a liquid. All liquids are compared to water which is assigned the value of 1.00. See Hydrometer.

Speedometer: Instrument which displays the vehicle's speed.

Splines: Splines are individual ridges and grooves cut into a shaft or hole. They permit limited in-and-out movement.

Split lip: A rope seal. Sometimes used to denote any two-part oil seal.

Spring seat: The area where the bottom of the valve spring fits. It can be a machined portion of the cylinder head or a stamped steel washer-like part which fits between spring and head.

Stabilizer bars: Hollow or solid bars connecting the right and left suspension parts. This transfers roll motion to the opposite side, but in the opposite direction. Flatter cornering results.

Star-adjuster: Star-shaped rotor used as an adjustment device in drum brakes.

Starting system: The system which rotates the engine internals so they will begin operation.

Steering axis inclination: The tilt of the steering knuckle from vertical when viewed from the side.

Steering column: The shaft connecting the steering wheel to the steering box or rack.

Steering knuckle: The piece of a front independent suspension which connects the upper and lower control arms. It has a mounting for the wheel bearings. Does the same job as the upright does at the rear.

Steering linkage: All of the rods, arms, and rod ends which connect the front wheels to the steering box or rack.

Stoichiometric (stoi'ke om'e tric): Complete chemical reaction resulting in all the fuel in a combustion chamber being burned.

Straight cut: A way of cutting gear teeth without any turn or twist in the teeth. Such gears are strong, but very noisy.

Strata: The Latin root for layer. The different layers of mixture strength in a stratified charge combustion chamber.

Stratified charge: A combustion chamber design which uses a prechamber and main combustion chamber to form the intake charge into layers of different mixture strength.

Stroke: One complete passage of the piston through its cylinder.

Suction side: The low-pressure portion of the system, extending from the expansion valve to the compressor inlet.

Sun roof: An openable portion of the car's roof. Also called moon roof.

Surface ignition: A condition where the air/fuel mixture is ignited by a hot spot in the combustion chamber.

Swept volume: The amount of volume occupied by a piston as it travels through a cylinder.

Synchronizer: The device which locks gears to the mainshaft after equaling the speed between shaft and gear.

Synthetic brake fluid: Brake fluid made from silicone. It is not compatible with mineral based fluids.

Tachometer: Instrument which displays the engine rpm.

Tailpipe: The pipe leading from the muffler to the atmosphere.

Tailshaft: The rear housing bolted to the transmission case. It covers part of the mainshaft and provides a mounting for the rear oil seal.

Tap and dies: The tools used to cut internal and external threads.

Taper: Wear of a round hole or shaft. The shaft or hole sides are no longer parallel.

Teardown: Engine disassembly.

Temperature circuit: The complete coolant temperature or cylinder head temperature circuit. Includes the sender, wires, and instrument.

Test light: A bulb fitted with two leads. The leads are connected to a circuit. If the bulb lights, current is in the circuit.

Thermal control gauge: An instrument using an electrically heated bimetallic spring to indicate its readings.

Thermal expansion tank: A space inside the gas tank open at the bottom but almost closed at the top. It does not fill when the main tank is filled and allows for fuel expansion.

Thermo-clutch fan: A fan which freewheels when the engine is cool (saving energy) and locks to the water pump shaft when the engine is too warm.

Thermostat: A cooling system which is sensitive to coolant temperature. The hotter the coolant gets, the farther the thermostat opens. This lets more coolant pass through the radiator.

Thermostatic expansion valve: A component regulating rate of refrigerant flow into evaporator as governed by tailpipe temperatures sensed by the remote bulb.

Thermostatic switch: A temperature-sensitive switch used to control system temperature by cycling compressor operation. Both bellows and bimetal switches are used.

Throttle body injection: A type of fuel injection where the injectors are grouped at the opening of the intake manifold. This grouping includes the throttle.

Throttle plate: That piece of the carburetor throat which opens and closes as a result of moving the accelerator pedal. The more pedal pressure, the wider open the throttle plate.

Thrust bearing: A bearing arranged so it takes the front-to-rear motion of a shaft.

Tie rods: Rods connecting the steering knuckle to the steering assembly.

Timing chain: The chain used to carry crankshaft motion to the camshaft. It may also be used to drive various pumps and countershafts.

Timing light: A strobe light, usually connected to the number one cylinder and used to adjust engine timing (when the plugs fire).

Toe: The highest portion of the lobe. The valve is at its maximum opening point when the lifter touches the toe. Also, the portion of the brake shoe which digs into the swept area of the brake drum during rotation.

Toe-in: When the front of the tires point slightly inward when seen from the top. If the front of the tires point out, they are toed-out.

Tooling: Dies and other forms used to shape auto parts at the factory. One piece of tooling makes one part for one car, but can be used many times over.

Torque: A twisting form of energy, measured in ft. lb., N.m or kg-m. When measured through a certain amount of time, torque becomes horsepower.

Torque multiplication: The increasing of torque by reducing the speed of a shaft.

Torque steer: Self-steering caused by unevenly twisting axles. Felt as a pull in the steering wheel under acceleration.

Torque tube: A fixed tube fitted over the driveshaft on some cars. It helps locate the rear axle and takes torque reaction loads from the drive axle so the driveshaft will not sense them.

Torque wrench: A wrench which senses and displays the amount of torque applied to it.

Torsion bar: Spring made from a straight section of round bar. One end of the bar is connected to the suspension and the other is rigidly mounted. Twisting the bar gives the spring action.

Tracking: The ability of the rear wheels to follow the front wheels exactly.

Transaxle: A form of drivetrain combining a clutch, transmission, and final drive into one housing. Also, a transmission final drive axle assembly.

Transfer case: A driveline component with a rear-pointing output shaft for delivering power to the rear axle, and a front-pointing output shaft for delivering power to the front axle.

Transfer case housing or transfer case: A driveline component similar to a selective gear transmission but with front and rear output shafts to transfer power to front and rear axles.

Transistor: A solid state semiconductor switch. It has no moving parts.

Transmission jack: A hydraulic jack used to support the transmission during removal and installation.

Transverse mounted: Mounted at a right angle to the car's direction of travel.

Trouble codes: Numbers generated by the diagnostic (self-test) programs in some engine control computers. These code numbers refer to certain flow charts which help lead to the faulty component.

Tube and ball: A type of collapsible steering column which uses an inner and outer tube connected by balls. An inner shaft slides inside the outer shaft during an accident.

Tuftride, nitride, and cold quench: Chemical treatments which leave a surface hardness of metals. Used on crankshafts.

Turbine: The exhaust driven half of the turbocharger.

Turbocharger: A turbine assembly mounted in the exhaust stream. It uses heat energy in the exhaust to pressurize the air intake of the engine.

Turbulence: A rapid mixing motion of the air/fuel mixture.

Turning the drum: Removing metal from the swept area of the brake drum to true it or remove grooves.

Twin I-beam suspension: A Ford front suspension design which uses two long beams which pivot. It acts much as a solid axle that has been broken in two pieces so it could move.

Two-wheel high: A gear shift position of the transfer case where only the two rear wheels receive engine power.

United States customary: The system of measurement commonly used in the United States based on inches, ounces, pounds, etc.

Universal joints: Mechanical linkage in a drive shaft or axle which allows angular changes while transmitting torque.

Uprights: Rear axle or suspension pieces which house the hubs and bearings and provide attachment and support for the axles, brakes, and suspension.

Vacuum: A condition where air pressure is less than atmospheric.

Vacuum gauge: An instrument which measures the amount of manifold vacuum present. It can be a hand-held diagnostic tool or instrument panel mounted for driver information.

Valley: The area between cylinder banks on a V-type engine.

Valve: That part of the cylinder head where the valves seal.

Valve guide: The machined portion of the cylinder head which touches the valve stem. Most commonly a replaceable insert hammered into the head.

Valve keepers: Small semi-circular metal pieces with a cone-shaped outer surface. They are placed between valve stem and spring retainer to lock the spring, retainer and valve together.

Valve seat: A hardened portion of the cylinder head, or a replaceable insert which the valve seals against.

Valve spring: A small coil spring which tries to keep the valve closed at all times. The camshaft opens the valve against valve spring pressure.

Valve stem: The slender portion of a poppet valve. It provides area for locating the valve and fitting keepers to retain it.

Valve stem seal: A rubber cap fitted to the valve spring side of the valve guide. It stops excess oil from passing between the valve stem and guide and entering the port.

Vane: On a ventilated disc brake, the thin bridge between the two disc surfaces.

Vapor: A gas. Specifically, the gaseous state of refrigerant.

Variable resistor: A resistor which allows different voltages to pass depending on input.

Variable venturi carburetor: A carburetor that regulates air flow by changing the size of the venturi.

Venturi: That area of a carburetor that provides the best flow velocity and lowest pressure. This area usually has the smallest inside diameter of the carburetor throat.

Viscosity: A fluid's resistance to flow. This is affected by temperature. At low temperatures, viscosity is high; at high temperatures, viscosity is low. The lower the viscosity, the "thinner" fluid is and the more easily it will flow. Used to describe oil.

Volatility: A liquid's ability to change into vapor.

Volt: A unit of electrical force or pressure required to push one ampere through a resistance of one ohm.

Voltage: The difference in electrical pressure between two points in a circuit.

Voltmeter: A meter which measures the amount of voltage present. It also measures the voltage across an electric circuit.

"V" type: Compressor with pistons designed in a "V" arrangement, such as the Chrysler 2-cylinder.

Warning devices: Buzzers, lights, and chimes which alert the driver to an unusual condition.

Warped: No longer perfectly round or true.

Wastegate: A pressure relief valve which vents excess exhaust pressure from the turbocharger to the exhaust pipe. It controls boost pressure.

Water jacket: Coolant passages cast into a cylinder block or head.

Water pump: A belt-driven device used to circulate coolant through an engine.

Wear bar: A molded-in section of shallow depth tread in a tire. This section will show as a bar across the tread when the tread is worn to its limit.

Weight: As used with motor oils, a measure of viscosity. Viscosity is a fluid's resistance to flow. The higher an oil's weight, the greater its viscosity.

Wheel cylinders: Convert hydraulic pressure from master cylinder to mechanical force to move brake shoes in drum brakes.

White lithium grease: A special grease with a lithium base (the lightest known metal) which maintains a single viscosity from below zero to over two hundred degrees.

Wide ratio: A relative term for describing the gear ratios in a transmission. If the gears are numerically far apart they are said to be wide ratio. Better initial acceleration and possibly less shifting are wide ratio benefits.

Wiring harness: A group of wires bundled together for convenience. Also called a Wiring Loom, these are sometimes used to refer to all the wiring in the car.

Wrench: A basic hand tool designed to apply torque to nuts and bolts.

Yokes: Y-shaped sections of the drive shaft which help form the U-joints.

Zerk fitting: A very small check valve which allows grease to be injected into a component part, but which keeps the grease from squirting out again.

Index

F

G

H

Hacksaws, 19
Hammers, 18
   ball-peen, 18
   sledgehammer, 18
Hand cranking, 296
Hand tools. *See* specific tool, *e.g.,* Wrenches
Harmonic balancer, 130, 675
Hazard flashers, 625
Head gasket, 157–58
   in engine assembly, 254
   reading, 221
Headers, 188
Headlights, 620–22
   adjustment, 621
   dimmer switch, 620, 636, 672
   headlight covers/doors, 620
   troubleshooting, 622
Heads removal, 219
   ball pivots, 219, 670
   push rods, 219, 678
   rocker arms. *See* Rocker arms
Heat control valve, 183
Heat system, 642–45
   air flow, 643
   blower fans, 644
   controls, 644
   heater core, 643
   operation of, 642–43
   ram air, 643, 678
   rear-window defroster/defogger, 644–45
   servicing, 658–59
   trouble-shooting, 655–56
Heat transfer, 641–42
   absolute zero, 641, 669
   British thermal unit (BTU), 641, 670
   condensation, 642
   evaporation, 642, 673
   freezing, 642
   latent heat, 641, 642
   latent heat of condensation, 642, 675
   latent heat of evaporation, 642, 676
   law of entropy, 641–42
   sensible heat, 641
   solar radiation, 640
Horizontally opposed engine disassembly, 225–26
   air shrouds, 225
   barrels removal, 225–26, 670
   heads removal, 225
   rods removal, 226
Horsepower, 122, 675
Hoses, 205
Hydraulic floor lift, 24, 675
Hydraulic pumps, 483–85
   gear pump, 484
   positive displacement pump, 483
   rotor pump, 484
   vane pump, 484–85
Hydraulic system, 481–84
   orifices, 481–82, 677
   pressure regulating valves, 481–83
   pressure relief valves, 482, 678
   pressures, 483
   speed valves, 482–83

Hydraulics, 479–81, 576–77, 675
   mechanical advantages, 480–81
   Pascal's law, 480, 576, 677

I

Ignition system, 86, 362–67, 675
   ballast resistor, 364, 368, 670
   battery, 364
   coil, 364, 671
   condenser, 366, 671
   distributor, 365–66, 672
   ignition switch, 364
   induction, 364–65, 675
   mutual induction, 365
   primary circuit, 364, 367
   secondary circuit, 364, 367
   spark plugs, 367
   windings, 364
   See also specific type, *e.g.,* Electronic ignitions
Ignition system servicing, 378–85
   air gap, 383
   cap, 380–81
   coil checks, 385
   conventional ignition checks, 385
   point-system dwell, 379
   points changing, 383
   primary circuit (electronic), 383
   primary circuit (point system), 383
   rotor, 380–81
   secondary circuit, 380–82
   spark plugs. *See* Spark plugs servicing
   spark test, 384–85
   timing adjustment, 378–80
   timing marks, 380
   troubleshooting, 384–85
   voltage checks, 385
   wires, 381
Indicator lamp, 627–28, 675
Industrial robots, 4–5
Insulation, 104–5
Intake manifold, 181–85, 675
   air leaks, 186
   design of, 181–82
   exhaust crossover, 183
   gasket leaks, 186
   heating, 182–83
   in-line, 184–85
   inspection of, 229
   log, 184–85
   runners, 182, 184, 679
   troubleshooting, 186
   vee, 185
Intake system, 180–86
Integrated circuits, 9

J

Jack stands, 23, 675
Jacks, 23, 675
   hydraulic floor, 23, 675
   pneumatic, 23
   safety precautions, 58–59

U

Universal joints (U-joints), 420–24, 681
  assembly, 423–24
  ball-and-trunnion, 421
  cross-and-yoke, 420
  CV (constant velocity), 421
  disassembly, 423
  double Cardan, 421, 673
  installation, 424
  removal, 423
  Rotoflex coupling, 421
  Rzeppa, 421
  troubleshooting, 421–22

V

Vacuum gauge, 37, 681
  hooking up, 37
Vacuum solenoid valve (VSV), 397–98
  coolant temperature override (CTO) switch,
    397
  preliminary checks, 397–98
  vacuum signal delay, 397
Valve adjusting sequence, 171
Valve clearance, 165, 171
Valve float, 173
Valve grinding, 176–77
Valve guides, 156–57, 168, 175–76, 681
  servicing, 176
Valve job, 172–78
Valve leakage tester, 171–72
Valve seat angles, 177
Valve seats, 157, 177, 681
  grinding of, 177
  replacing, 178
Valve spring compressor, 172
Valve springs, 168–69, 172–73, 681
Valve stem, 175, 681
  seals, 168, 681
Valve train, 159–72
  OHC (overhead camshaft), 159, 161–62
  OHV (overhead valve), 159–61
  parts, 162–69
  servicing, 170–72
  See also specific part, *e.g.,* Camshaft
Valves, 164–72, 681
  adjustment, 170, 171
  burned, 170–71, 172

exhaust, 166, 167
inspection, 175
intake, 166
leakage test, 171–72
multiple, 164, 166
poppet, 166, 678
sodium-filled, 167–68
Vehicle identification number (VIN), 118
Voltmeter, 28, 29, 682
  continuity test, 29
  hooking up, 28, 29
  starting circuit test, 29
  voltage drop test, 29

W

Water jacket, 126, 202, 682
Water pump, 207, 682
  in engine assembly, 257
  removal, 216–17
Wheel alignment, 92, 556–59
  balancing, 558
  camber, 556, 670
  caster, 556
  front-wheel, 558
  rear-wheel, 559
  servicing, 557–59
  steering axis inclination, 557, 680
  toe-in, 556–57, 681
  tracking, 557, 681
Windshield washer fluid, 105–6
Windshield wipers, 631–32
  intermittent, 632
  single-speed motor, 632
  two-speed motor, 631–32
  washers, 632
Wiring, 273–75
  color coding of, 274
  continuity testing, 274
  diagrams, 274–75, 615–17
  uses of, 274
  wire, 273
  wire size, 273, 617
  wiring harness/loom, 617, 682
Wrenches, 13–14, 682
  box end, 13, 670
  combination, 14, 671
  open-end, 13, 677
  safety precautions, 58
  torque. *See* Torque wrenches

AUTOMOTIVE COMPUTERS

The Hidden Copilot

ENGINE CONTROL

Fuel Injection
Feedback Mixture Control
Idle Speed
Ignition Dwell and Timing
Detonation Sensor
EGR Control
Air Injection Control
Canister Purging
Early Fuel Evaporation
Engine Cooling Fans
A/C Compressor Clutch Control
Turbocharger Boost Control
Electronic Diesel Engine Control
Two-Speed Accessory Drive System
Dual-Circuit Battery

SERVICE AND DIAGNOSIS

Vehicle Service Interval Display
Engine Diagnostics
Body Accessory Diagnostics
Digital Diagnostic Code Displays
Limp-In Capability
Data Link Connectors
Memory and Learning Capability

DRIVETRAIN CONTROL

Economy Shift Indicator Lamp
Electronic Cruise Control
Torque Converter Clutch
Viscous Converter Clutch
Electronic Overdrive
Selectable Transmission Shift Points
Automatic 4WD Shift Control